HOVIUS ON FAMILY LAW

Cases, Notes and Materials

Seventh Edition

by

Berend Hovius
B.A.(Hons.), LL.B., LL.M.
Professor of Law,
The University of Western Ontario

and

Mary-Jo Maur
B.A.(Hons.), LL.B., LL.M.
Assistant Professor (Sessional),
Faculty of Law
Queen's University

CARSWELL®

A cataloguing record for this publication is available from Library and Archives Canada.
ISBN: 978-0-7798-2221-8

Printed in the United States by Thomson Reuters.

 **THOMSON REUTERS**

CARSWELL, A DIVISION OF THOMSON REUTERS CANADA LIMITED

One Corporate Plaza	Customer Relations
2075 Kennedy Road	Toronto 1-416-609-3800
Toronto, Ontario	Elsewhere in Canada/U.S. 1-800-387-5164
M1T 3V4	Fax 1-416-298-5082
	www.carswell.com
	E-mail www.carswell.com/email

This book is dedicated to two giants in the development of Canadian family law,

Professor James G. McLeod (1947-2005)
a friend and colleague of Berend Hovius for over twenty-five years

&

Professor Nicholas Bala, Queen's University, Faculty of Law
Mary-Jo Maur's mentor and friend.

PREFACE

Four years is not a long time. However, in the four years since the sixth edition was published, the Supreme Court of Canada and the provincial courts of appeal have scrutinized several aspects of family law. Ideas about child support, custody, and spousal support, in particular, have been refined. Many of the changes in the law have, of course, resulted from legislative revisions. These, too, are reflected in each of the chapters.

Numerous family law statutes in Ontario are about to be amended through the adoption of the *Family Statute Law Amendment Act, 2008* (Bill 133). At the time of publication, Bill 133 has received Royal Assent but has not yet been proclaimed into force. However, we have introduced and discussed its provisions where appropriate, anticipating that the Bill will soon be proclaimed.

Children's issues have received particular attention in the courts and in the media. In order to focus on these issues more clearly, we have created a new chapter, entitled "The Legal Concept of Parent: Genetic Parentage, Social Parentage, and Adoption". This chapter reinforces a dominant theme in family law over the last forty years or so; namely, the law is evolving to keep pace with changing notions of the family.

We have retained the original format of the book for the most part, with cases and commentary followed by notes and questions relating to each important topic. There are more introductory notes in each section than in previous editions. These supplement the core materials reproduced in the text, as an aid to instructors and students. Reflecting the addition of an experienced family law practitioner as a co-author, this edition also features more notes on the processes, court-based and non-judicial, used to deal with family conflicts.

This book is intended primarily for Ontario law students and so we have focused on Ontario family law legislation and the relevant jurisprudence. However, the law across Canada in most of the key areas of family law has become more and more uniform. The quick and easy availability of decisions from across the country, the strong impact of the general themes in Supreme Court of Canada cases dealing with specific provincial legislation, and the ever expanding body of jurisprudence pursuant to the *Divorce Act* have contributed to the trend towards similar outcomes in family law cases across the country. Only the statutory family property rules remain somewhat immune from this trend. As a result, much of the core material in this book is relevant across the country.

Updating this text has been a daunting task. The pace of change in the law is ever increasing. We are therefore grateful to the authors who have graciously permitted us to reproduce their works. Their generosity has allowed us to present timely and well-written material. A list of the authors, publishers, and institutions who gave permission for the use of materials follows this preface. We also wish to recognize the special contribution made by Denise Marshall of the Children's Aid Society of London & Middlesex to the updating of Chapter 10, *CHILD IN NEED OF PROTECTION*.

Finally, we want to express our appreciation for the support of our families while we undertook this work, and we both appreciate their patience with us as we worked towards completion.

Berend Hovius
Professor of Law
Faculty of Law
The University of Western Ontario

Mary-Jo Maur
Assistant Professor (Sessional)
Faculty of Law
Queen's University

May 2009

ACKNOWLEDGMENTS

Listed below are the authors and sources of published material used in the book. We thank the copyright holders who have generously given their permission for this use.

Ambert, Anne-Marie, *Divorce: Facts, Causes and Consequences* (Ottawa: The Vanier Institute of the Family, 2005).

Austin, Gary, Peter Jaffe and Pamela Hurley, "Incorporating Children's Needs and Views in Alternative Dispute Resolution Approaches" (1992), 8 C.F.L.Q. 69.

Baker, Maureen, "Thinking About Families: Trends and Policies" in Maureen Baker, ed., *Canada's Changing Families: Challenges to Public Policy* (Ottawa: The Vanier Institute of the Family, 1994).

Bala, Nicholas, "Child Welfare Law in Canada: An Introduction" in Nicholas Bala, Michael Kim Zapf, R. James Williams, Robin Vogl, and Joseph P. Hornick, ed., *Canadian Child Welfare Law: Children, Families and the State*, 2nd ed. (Toronto: Thompson Educational Publishing, Inc., 2004) 1.

Bala, Nicholas, "Reforming Ontario's Child and Family Services Act: Is the Pendulum Swinging Back Too Far?" (1999), 17 C.F.L.Q. 121.

Bala, Nicholas, "The Best Interests of the Child in the Post-Modern Era: A Central But Paradoxical Concept" in Harold Niman and Gerald P. Sadvari, ed., *Family Law: "Best Interests of the Child"* (Toronto: Law Society of Upper Canada, 2000) 1.

Bala, Nicholas, "The *Charter of Rights* and Family Law in Canada: A New Era" (2000-2001), 18 C.F.L.Q. 372.

Bala, Nicholas, *Legal Protections for Victims of Spousal Abuse and Their Children: The Role of Health Care Professionals in the Justice System* (Kingston: Queen's University's Faculty of Health Sciences' Program, 2004)

Bala, Nicholas, "Entitlement to Spousal Support: Asking the Tough Questions" in Shaffer, M. ed., *Contemporary Issues in Family Law: Engaging with the Legacy of James G. McLeod* (Toronto, Carswell, 2007).

Bala, Nicholas, "Child Support for Adult Children: When does Economic Childhood End?" (1000 Islands Legal Conference, October, 2008).

Bala, Nicholas, Peter Jaffe, and Claire Crooks, "Spousal Violence and Child-Related Cases: Challenging Cases Requiring Differentiated Responses" (2008), 27 C.F.L.Q. 1.

Castel, J-G and Janet Walker, *Canadian Conflict of Laws*, 6th ed. (Toronto: Butterworths, 2005) c. 17.

Davies, Christine, "Racial and Cultural Matters in Custody Disputes" (1993), 10 R.F.L.Q. 1.

Department of Justice, *Evaluation of the Divorce Act: Phase II: Monitoring and Evaluation* (Ottawa: Department of Justice, Bureau of Review, 1990).

Department of Justice, *The New Child Support Package* (Ottawa: Government of Canada, March 6, 1996).

Giesbrecht, Theodore, "Adoption" in Nicholas Bala, Michael Kim Zapf, R. James Williams, Robin Vogl, and Joseph P. Hornick, ed., *Canadian Child Welfare Law: Children,*

Families and the State, 2nd ed. (Toronto: Thompson Educational Publishing, Inc., 2004) 155.

Hahlo, H.R., *Nullity of Marriage in Canada* (Toronto: Butterworths, 1979).

Hogg, Peter, *Constitutional Law of Canada* (Toronto: Carswell, looseleaf) c. 27.

Hovius, Berend, "Mobility Issues in Custody and Access Cases" in James G. McLeod, ed., *Child Custody Law and Practice* (Toronto: Carswell, looseleaf) c. 7.

Hovius, Berend, "The Matrimonial Home: An Analysis of Part II of the *Family Law Act, 1986*" (1988), 16 R.F.L. (3d) 31.

Hovius, Berend and Timothy G. Youdan, *The Law of Family Property* (Toronto: Carswell, 1991).

Hovius, Berend "Unequal Sharing of Net Family Properties under Ontario's *Family Law Act*" (2008), 27 C.F.L.Q. 147.

Huddart, Carol Mahood and Jeanne Charlotte Ensminger, "Hearing the Voice of Children" (1992), 8 C.F.L.Q. 95.

Law Commission of Ontario, *Division of Pensions upon Marriage Breakdown, Final Report* (Toronto: December 2008).

Law Society of Upper Canada, "Headnote for *Maddock v. Maddock*" [1958] O.R. 810 (C.A.).

Maur, Mary-Jo, "Child Support Below the Guidelines: Why a Bird in the Hand Isn't Always Worth Two in the Bush" (2008), 27 C.F.L.Q. 201.

Maur, Mary-Jo and Nicholas Bala, "Spousal Support in Canada: The Continuing Importance of the Basis for Entitlement" (The National Family Law Institute, July, 2008).

McLeod, James, "Annotation to *Rutherford v. Rutherford*" (1986), 4 R.F.L. (3d) 457.

McLeod, James, "Annotation to *Harden v. Harden*" (1987), 6 R.F.L. (3d) 147.

McLeod, James, "Annotation to *Pelech v. Pelech*" (1987), 7 R.F.L. (3d) 226.

McLeod, James, "Annotation to *Hill v. Hill*" (1988), 10 R.F.L. (3d) 225.

McLeod, James, "Annotation to *Nowell v. Town Estate*" (1997), 30 R.F.L. (4th) 108.

McLeod, James, "Annotation to *Orellana v. Merino*" (1998), 40 R.F.L. (4th) 129.

McLeod, James, "Annotation to *R. (S.) v. R. (M.)*" (1999), 43 R.F.L. (4th) 116.

McLeod, James, "Annotation to *Halpern v. Toronto (City)*" (2003), 36 R.F.L. (5th) 129.

Mnookin, Robert, "Divorce Bargaining: The Limits on Private Ordering" in J.M. Eekelaar and S.N. Katz, eds., *The Resolution of Family Conflict: Comparative Legal Perspectives* (Toronto: Butterworths, 1984) 364, 366–372 and 375–379.

Payne, Julien, "Family Conflict Resolution: Dealing with the Consequences of Marriage Breakdown Through Counseling, Negotiation, Mediation and Arbitration" (Paper presented in the Faculty of Law at the University of Saskatchewan, 1997).

Payne, Julien and Marilyn Payne, *Canadian Family Law* (Quicklaw, 2001).

Rogerson, Carol and D.A. Rollie Thompson, *Spousal Support Advisory Guidelines* (Department of Justice Canada, Ottawa: July, 2008).

Sauvé, Roger, *Profiling Canada's Families III* (Ottawa: The Vanier Institute of the Family, 2004).

Shaffer, "Joint Custody since *Kaplanis* and *Ladisa*: A Review of Recent Ontario Case Law" (2007), 26 C.F.L.Q. 315.

Shields, Ronald W., Judith P. Ryan, and Victoria L. Smith, *Collaborative Family Law: Another Way to Resolve Family Disputes* (Toronto: Carswell, 2003).

Silverman, Hugh "Conflict of Laws: Some Matrimonial Problems" (1979), 2 Fam. L. Rev. 103.

Sinclair, Murray, Nicholas Bala, Heino Lilles, and Cindy Blackstock, "Aboriginal Child Welfare Law" in Nicholas Bala, Michael Kim Zapf, R. James Williams, Robin Vogl, and Joseph P. Hornick, ed., *Canadian Child Welfare Law: Children, Families and the State*, 2nd ed. (Toronto: Thompson Educational Publishing, Inc., 2004) 199.

Sopinka, John, "*The Divorce Act, 1968*: Collusion Confined" (1969), 47 Can. Bar Rev. 31.

Thompson, D.A. Rollie, "Rules and Rulelessness in Family Law: Recent Developments, Judicial and Legislative" (2000-2001), 18 C.F.L.Q. 25.

Wardell, W.J., "*King v. Low*: A Case Comment" (1985), 4 Can. J. Fam. L. 514.

Ziff, Bruce, "Recent Developments in Marriage and Divorce" (1986), 18 Ottawa Law Rev. 121.

TABLE OF CONTENTS

Chapter 3 Divorce

Chapter 4 Family Property

Chapter 5 The Family Home

Chapter 6 Spousal Support

Chapter 7 Custody and Access

Chapter 9 Domestic Contracts

TABLE OF CASES

1

INTRODUCTION

1. Canadian Families

SAUVÉ, *PROFILING CANADA'S FAMILIES III*

(Ottawa: The Vanier Institute of the Family, 2004) xi–xiii and xv-xvi
(Footnotes omitted)

Introduction

What Is a Family?

Most of us can provide a pretty good description of who is part of our own family. Some family members come readily to mind — probably our parents, our brothers and sisters, and our own partners and children if we have any. The larger family may also consist of uncles, aunts, cousins and grandparents. Some of us may also include friends as part of our family and some of us may even include certain organizations that provide support that makes us feel that we are part of a big family. Many of these important people we call family may live in the same household or residence as we do but many may not. And, for various reasons, some of us may exclude people to whom we are closely related.

The basis for including or excluding certain people as part of our family depends a lot on how we view the role of families and how family members interact with one another. Two siblings living in the same household with their parents are likely to think of themselves as a family while the same two siblings living a great distance apart may or may not consider themselves to be part of the same family.

Most Canadians feel their families are very important to them individually. Families are so important, so vital and so varied, that it seems that no one definition can capture their true significance. Individual family members may not even agree among themselves about who is in their specific family.

As such, it seems that even if families are one of the most important elements in our lives, as a society we have a difficult time coming to a clear definition of a family. Who should be included in a family and who should not? What should be the basis of inclusion or exclusion? This is not only a Canadian challenge but also an international one.

According to Roderic Beaujot, in *Earning and Caring in Canadian Families*, "Defining family is so difficult that even some textbooks on the subject do not include a definition." He adds, "In the proceedings of the Cairo International Conference on Population, the chapter on families is one of the weakest, partly because the countries of the world could not agree on the definition of something so close to daily life. Similarly, at the 1995 Beijing Fourth International Conference on Women, the language on families presented some of the most difficult stumbling blocks to consensus."

The range of definitions runs the gamut from very restrictive, based on strict beliefs, to wide open, based on the functions families perform in society. A similar range of opinions is evident with respect to the role of individual members of families. A prime example is the role of the father in the family. In 1983, a survey found that 42% of Canadians felt that "the father must be master in his own house." By 1992 this percentage was down to 26%, and by 2000 it was down to "only" 18%. This is a significant change in a relatively short time span. This growing egalitarian Canadian attitude has not evolved in the same way or even in the same direction among our American neighbours. In the United States, about half of all survey respondents in 2000 still felt that "the father must be master in his own house," which is *up* from a decade earlier. This suggests that the definition of family and how people relate to each other within a family are dependent on national and even provincial geographies.

The Vanier Institute of the Family takes a broad view of families. It defines a family as:

> ... *any combination of two or more persons who are bound together over time by ties of mutual consent, birth and/or adoption or placement and who, together, assume responsibilities for variant combinations of some of the following:*
>
> - *Physical maintenance and care of group members*
> - *Addition of new members through procreation or adoption*
> - *Socialization of children*
> - *Social control of members*
> - *Production, consumption, distribution of goods and services, and*
> - *Affective nurturance — love.*

This definition directs attention toward the work and accomplishments of people who commit themselves to one another over time — to what people do as distinct from where they live and how they are related to each other. It is a definition that acknowledges and respects heterosexual and same-sex couples, lone-parent families, extended patterns of kinship, step-families and blended families, couples with children and those without, the commitments of siblings to one another, and the obligations and affection that unite the young and the old as their lives weave together. People in families provide for and care for one another, they teach and discipline, they are financially, economically, and psychologically dependent upon one another, and they love one another. Within families, we encounter the opportunity and responsibility to act not just as isolated individuals, but as spouses and lovers, mothers and fathers, brothers and sisters, sons and daughters and friends.

Collectors of data are, by necessity, forced to use a more specific definition of family. Statistics Canada is the major collector and distributor of data on individuals and families. It does this through in-depth Censuses conducted every five years and through various sample surveys relating to work, home, leisure and other activities. The way it defines families is closely linked to changing realities and to the needs of policy makers. In addition, Statistics Canada attempts to provide coherent definitions in each of its surveys. This is not always easy to do, given that the users of data are looking for long-term trends and thus want continuity. There is a need to satisfy many users. Thus, definitions tend to change very slowly over time — but they do change.

In the 2001 Census, a Census "family" was defined as follows:

> Refers to a married couple with or without children, or a couple living common-law (can be of opposite or same sex) with or without children, or a lone parent living with one or more children. This excludes persons living in collective households.

While this definition may seem clear, it raises a few questions.

- Same-sex couples are assumed to be a family living in a common-law relationship. Should the option be given to classify them as legally married, if they so choose? [The 2006 Census "family" included married same-sex couples for the first time.]

  - Should other guardianship children, beyond foster children and grandchildren, be included in the census family? In most surveys, a foster child and other guardianship arrangements are considered to be lodgers, while in other surveys no distinction is made among children living in a household.

- Should a child of any age be included as part of the family? Currently, someone over the age of 18 is assumed to be a "relative" living in a family.

- Should units consisting of a grandparent or grandparents and grandchild or grandchildren with no parent present be considered as a family? Currently, these relationships are not always considered a census family. ...

Top 10 Trends for Canadian Families

1. Fewer couples are getting legally married

In 1981, about 65% of both men and women could be expected to legally marry at least once by the time they reached the age of 50. Currently, only 51% of women and 48% of men can expect to be legally married by the age of 50. The number one reason people marry is because they feel that marriage signifies commitment. More couples are now choosing common-law relationships.

2. More couples are breaking up

Based on the latest information, about 38% of all marriages can be expected to end in divorce before their 30th wedding anniversary. This is down from the peak of 41% in the late 1980s following changes to the *Divorce Act* and just a bit higher than the 37% rate in 1981. The main reason couples divorce is because of different values and interests. Common-law couples are more likely to break up than are couples that are legally married.

3. Families are getting smaller

The average family is now comprised of 3.1 persons, down from 3.7 in 1971. Much of this decline is due to fewer children per family, the increase in lone-parent families and the reality that more baby-boomers are now empty-nesters. Even so, children are staying at home longer than in the past. In 1981, about 4 out of 10 youth aged 20–24 lived with their parents; this has now jumped to almost 6 out of 10.

4. Children experience more transitions as parents change their marital status

About 3 out of 10 babies are now born to mothers who are not legally married. This compares to about 2 out of 10 some 15 years earlier. During the late 1990s, of those children aged 6–13 born in couple families, about 22% experienced transitions that related to the marital status of their parents. Among those born in lone-parent families, 84% experienced some transition related to the marital status of a parent. Court orders in divorce cases for parenting arrangements show an increase in the involvement of both parents.

5. Canadians are generally satisfied with life

About 85% of Canadians are either "very satisfied" or "satisfied" with life; only 5% are clearly dissatisfied. Another survey found that 83% of legally-married people claim that their relationships give them "lots or quite a lot of enjoyment with very little strain"; 69% of people who live in a common-law relationship agree with this statement. ...

6. Family violence is under-reported

Fewer than 40% of family abuse incidents are reported to the police. Wives or ex-wives are three times more likely than men to be injured, five times more likely to receive medical attention or be hospitalized, and five times more likely to fear for their lives. The majority of victims do not confide in a formal agency because they fear complications linked to involvement with the justice system, have concerns about losing custody of children and fear reprisals from the violent spouse. In 2002, 67 wives were killed by their husbands or ex-husbands, and 16 husbands were killed by their wives or ex-wives.

7. Multiple-earner families are now the norm

About 84% of couples with children have two or more earners. In 2002, two-earner families with children brought in about $67,200 after transfers and income taxes, which is about $17,300 more than one-earner families. About 72% of couples without children have two earners and 82% of all female lone-parents have at least one earner. All these percentages are at record highs. ...

8. Women still do most of the juggling involved in balancing work and home

About 16% of women who work full-time outside the home do at least another 30 hours of housework per week and about 17% do at least 30 hours of child care per week. About half of women with children who work part-time do so for children and other family reasons. About two out of five women with children who quit their jobs do so for children and other family reasons. All these percentages are much higher than they are for men.

9. Inequality is worsening

The richest 20% of families get 39% of all incomes including transfers and after income taxes, up from 37% in 1980. The share of the total income pie going to the middle 60% of families is down by two percentage points over the same period while the share going to the poorest 20% remains basically unchanged. About 10% of all children now live in poverty and 39% of children in female lone-parent families live in poverty. Some 1.5 million "working poor" work full-time for a full year and earn poverty-level wages. Roughly 778,000 Canadians used a food bank during March 2003. North American Indians living on reserves have average household incomes of about 55% of the average for all Canadian households.

10. The future will have more aging families

In 2016, there will be fewer households aged 35–44, just a few more households aged 15–34 and 45–54, and many more households aged 55 and over. Within a decade, the largest household age group will be seniors and the smallest group will be 15–34 years of age. ...

HOVIUS, "FAMILY FACTS"

Adapted from Statistics Canada, *"2006 Census: Families, marital status, households and dwelling characteristics" The Daily*, Wednesday September 12, 2007; Statistics Canada, *"Divorces" The Daily*, Wednesday, March 2005; and Statistics Canada, *"Marriages" The Daily*, Wednesday, January 17, 2007.

General: In total, the 2006 Census enumerated 8,896,840 "census families" in 2006, up 6.3% from 2001. The 2006 Census used the same definition of "family" as the 2001 Census, but the category of married-couple-families now included some same-sex couples. There were 6,105,910 married-couple families, an increase of only 3.5% from 2001. In contrast, the number of common-law-couple families surged 18.9% to 1,376,865, while the number of lone-parent families increased 7.8% to 1,414,060.

Consequently, married-couple families accounted for 68.6% of all census families in 2006, down from 70.5% five years earlier. The proportion of common-law-couple families rose from 13.8% to 15.5%, while the share of lone-parent families increased slightly from 15.7% to 15.9%. Two decades ago, common-law-couple families accounted for only 7.2% of all census families; while married-couple families represented 80.2%, and lone-parent families, 12.7%.

In Quebec, where the prevalence of common-law-couple families has been one of the defining family patterns for years, the number of common-law-couple families increased 20.3% between 2001 and 2006 to 611,855. Quebec common-law-couple families accounted for 44.4% of the national total. Close to one-quarter (23.4%) of all common-law-couple families in Canada lived in the two census metropolitan areas of Montréal and Québec.

Among lone-parent families, growth between 2001 and 2006 was most rapid for families headed by men. Their number increased 14.6%, more than twice the rate of growth of 6.3% among those headed by women.

The number of same-sex couples surged 32.6% between 2001 and 2006, five times the pace of opposite-sex couples (+5.9%). For the first time, the 2006 census counted same-sex married couples, reflecting the legalization of same-sex marriages for all of Canada as of July 2005. In total, the census enumerated 45,345 same-sex couples, of which 7,465, or 16.5%, were married couples. Half of all same-sex couples in Canada lived in the three largest census metropolitan areas, Montréal, Toronto and Vancouver, in 2006. In 2006, same-sex couples represented 0.6% of all couples in Canada.

Over half (53.7%) of same-sex married spouses were men in 2006. Only about 9.0% of same-sex couples had children aged 24 years and under living in the home in 2006. This was more common for female (16.3%) than for male (2.9%) same-sex couples.

Households: Since 2001, there has been a large increase in one-person households. During this time, the number of one-person households increased 11.8%, more than twice as fast as the 5.3% increase for the total population in private households. The number of households consisting of couples without children aged 24 years and under increased 11.2% from one census to the next. The households with the slowest growth between 2001 and 2006 were those comprised of couples with children under 25; these households edged up only 0.4%.

Over the last two decades, there has been a growing trend for young adults to remain in or return to their parental homes. In 2006, 43.5% of the 4 million young adults aged 20 to 29 lived in the parental home, up from 41.1% in 2001 and 32.1% in the mid-seventies. Among individuals aged 20 to 24, 60.3% were in the parental home in 2006, up from 49.3% in 1986. Among those aged 25 to 29, 26.0% were in the parental home in 2006, up from 15.6% two decades earlier. Among the census metropolitan areas, Toronto had the highest proportion (57.9%) of young adults (20–29) who lived in their parents' home in 2006.

Unmarried People: For the first time, the 2006 Census enumerated more unmarried people aged 15 and over than legally married people. In 2006, more than one-half (51.5%) of the adult population were unmarried, that is, never married, divorced, separated or widowed. This compares with 49.9% five years earlier and 38.6% twenty years earlier.

Marriage: The number of marriages in Canada appears to have reached a plateau following a flurry of activity around the turn of the millennium. A total of 147,391 couples tied the knot in 2003, only 653 more than in 2002 and just 773 more than in 2001, according to vital statistics data from the provinces and the territories, which for the first time include limited information on same-sex marriages. The crude marriage rate in 2003 stayed at its record low of 4.7 marriages for every 1,000 population. This was less than half the rate seen in the 1940s when the rate peaked at 10.9.

The crude marriage rate was highest in Prince Edward Island in 2003, where it was 6.0 marriages for every 1,000 population. The lowest rates in the country were in Quebec with 2.8 marriages for every 1,000 and Nunavut (2.3 per 1,000).

In 2003, Canada's crude marriage rate at 4.7 marriages per 1,000 population was lower than that of the United States, where the rate was 7.5. However, it was practically the same as that of several European countries, notably France, Austria and Germany.

Single people are getting married at an increasingly later age. In 2003, in Canada (excluding Ontario), the average age of persons marrying for the first time (to someone of the opposite sex) was 30.6 years for men and 28.5 years for women. (Note: Ontario is excluded because its 2003 statistics did not distinguish between same-sex and opposite-sex marriages.) In 2002, in Canada (excluding Ontario), it was 30.4 years for men and 28.3 years for women. The data for Canada (including Ontario) from 1973 to 2002 indicate that the average age at first marriage of newlyweds gradually rose. In 1973, the average age at which men (25.2 years) and women (22.8 years) married for the first time was about five years lower than in 2003. This rise in the average age at first marriage is largely due to young couples cohabiting outside of marriage.

Three-quarters (75.2%) of marriages in Canada were performed in a religious ceremony. The vast majority (98.3%) of marriages in Ontario were performed by a member of the clergy, the highest proportion in Canada. The lowest proportions were in British Columbia (41.0%) and the Yukon (26.6%).

Divorce: The number of couples getting a divorce in 2003 edged up 1.0% from a year earlier to 70,828. The total divorce rate by the 30th wedding anniversary increased slightly to 38.3. In other words, using Canada-wide statistics as predictors, there is 38.3% chance that a couple will divorce before their 30th anniversary. This chance decreases significantly if one focuses only on marriages in which neither partner has been married before. The total divorce rate ranged from a low of 17.1 in Newfoundland and Labrador to a high of 49.7 in Quebec.

The divorce rate varies greatly depending on how long couples have been married. It rises rapidly in the first few years of marriage. The peak divorce rate in 2003 occurred after three years of marriage, when 26.2 out of 1,000 marriages ended in divorce. The risk of divorce decreases slowly for each additional year of marriage.

BAKER, "THINKING ABOUT FAMILIES: TRENDS AND POLICIES"

Baker, ed., *Canada's Changing Families: Challenges to Public Policy* (Ottawa: The Vanier Institute of the Family, 1994) 1–4 (Endnotes omitted)

Introduction

Over the past three decades, major changes have occurred in family life, providing new challenges for family members, employers, service providers and policy makers. ...

Families, the State and Society

Social scientists have used the term "state" to refer not only to government departments and their policies, but also to government-funded agencies which implement and enforce these policies. This would encompass the child welfare agencies, social services, the criminal justice system and the public schools. There are many reasons why the state would be interested in people's private lives. Information on marriages, births and deaths needs to be collected in order to plan and provide public services and facilities. Marriages and births are recorded and regulated to ensure that dependents are supported, to help prevent potential birth defects through inbreeding, to assist individuals to preserve private property, to minimize social conflict, and to protect the community. The state monitors childrearing practices and interpersonal relations between family members in order to protect vulnerable members and to maintain social order.

In North America, laws and practices assume that families are responsible for many services which are invaluable to the state. Although adults want children for their own personal reasons, the state needs them to reproduce the taxpayers, consumers and labour force members of the nation. Families help define and enforce at what age a person is allowed to engage in a sexual relationship and with whom, and what degree of closeness is too close for a sexual liaison. The state needs parents to socialize or discipline children to be law-abiding citizens, to fit into educational systems and labour force requirements, to perpetuate the culture, and to establish permanent relationships and reproduce the next generation.

Many critics have argued, however, that state involvement in family life varies for different income and cultural groups, and tends to be more interventionist for visible minorities and for those on social assistance. Furthermore, involvement is not always based on informed policy about how people actually live or why they live this way. Instead, programs and policies are often based on preconceived notions about the preferred structure of families, the role of women in families, the responsibilities of parents toward their children, and the reasons behind the need for social assistance. These ideas permeate our culture but change over time with economic and social trends.

Throughout this century, "the family" has been viewed as the basic unit of economic, physical and emotional support. North American governments have only stepped in to intervene when a child has been neglected or abused or when there are insufficient financial resources. According to current family law both parents are responsible for the care and support of their children, even after divorce, and spouses are expected to assist each other during marriage. Family members are required to register their marriages, births, and deaths; pay their taxes; feed and clothe their children; send their children to school; complete their census forms; and generally be law-abiding and peaceful. As long as these obligations are fulfilled, the state's direct involvement in family life is minimal.

Ideologies Behind Family Policies

Policy makers often bring to their jobs assumptions about the way families live, and these ideas are not always representative of the broad range of lifestyles prevalent in modern society. Also, because their advisors have often come from similar gender, cultural and socioeconomic backgrounds and receive their training in specialized fields such as law or economics, they do not always reflect the thinking of everyday people or even the wider range of the social sciences. ... These factors help to perpetuate the transmission of biases and myths in policy making. Although it was feminist social scientists who first articulated their concerns about these biases, now most researchers and some policy makers are trying to present a more balanced and realistic portrayal of family life.

Regardless of their view of the world, most researchers and social service workers now agree that families are not "havens from the harsh world" as they were once portrayed. The distinction between the so-called "private world of family" and the "public world of work" is now criticized as inaccurate. There is also a recognition that such a distinction has negative consequences in policy-making. For example, this view has allowed governments to assume that domestic services are provided willingly at home for no pay and that workers leave family responsibilities at home when they enter the workplace. Therefore, employees do not need child care services, flexible hours or special leave for family responsibilities.

Until recently, this false dichotomy has also enabled the state and community to turn a blind eye to family violence. In fact, some researchers and activists argue that viewing family life as "private" and outside the realm of government regulation has encouraged social policies which have disadvantaged women and children. ...

Policymakers can no longer assume that what takes place at home is of no relevance to the community or to governments. As a society and as community members, we are becoming more concerned about the physical and emotional safety of women, children and the elderly in their homes. Educators continue to try to counteract some of the more negative influences of their students' family lives. Similarly, there is an understanding of the important connection between domestic responsibilities and employment status, and that parents with dependent children, especially mothers, require assistance in resolving the inevitable conflicts between employment demands and family life.

The field of family policy is not without controversy. An attempt to create a more explicit and cohesive family policy arises from two separate traditions. One tradition is based on the realization that families are changing, with more two-income and lone-parent families, that parents make an important contribution to society in having children and that they increasingly need social support to combine more effectively family life with earning a living. The other tradition assumes that "the family" is deteriorating and attempts must be made to legislate supports to help the traditional nuclear family maintain its position against the intrusion of alternative lifestyles. In both cases, there has been a new emphasis placed on strengthening families. Yet those who applaud new family forms are suspicious of the call for "a family policy" because they fear that it could represent a conservative agenda opposing greater equality for women, gays, and "families of choice." Creating social policies which bring together these two opposing viewpoints and deal adequately with the multidimensional aspects of family life is indeed a challenge. ...

NOTES AND QUESTIONS

1. In *Profiling Canada's Families III* (2004), Roger Sauvé also reports:

- Canadian women, on average, have 1.5 children, well below the "replacement rate" of 2.1. In 2001, 7% of adults aged 20–34 intended to stay childless.

- The percentage of Canadians below the age of 14 dropped from a peak of 35% in 1961 to less than 20% in 2003.

- During the five year period following 1996, 40% of Canadians moved. However, 85% of the moves were within province.

- In 2001, 31% of all births were to non-married women. This percentage was 58% in Quebec.

- Of children born in 1983-84, those least likely (only 14%) to see their parents separate before their tenth birthday are ones whose parents are legally married with no cohabitation before marriage. The highest percentage of children experiencing their parents' separation (over 50%) were those whose parents lived common law and never married.

- 2002 was the first year ever that mothers got sole custody in fewer than half (49%) of custody awards in divorce cases. Joint custody was awarded in 42% of the cases. By comparison, in 1988, mothers received sole custody 85% of the time and fathers received sole custody in almost all the other cases.

- In 2001, 12% of all families were step-families (at least one child in the household from a previous relationship of one of the parents).

- Just over a quarter century ago, a majority of married women aged 25–54 were not in the paid labour force. In 2003, over 80% of women aged 25–64 who were married or living common law were in the workforce. Over 75% of couple families with children under 18 now have two income earners. The average percentage increase as a result of the second earner's presence in the paid labour force is 35%.

- The percentage of children aged 0–17 living in poverty (defined by using Statistics Canada's low-income cut-off) declined to 10% in 2002. It fell to 6% for children living in couple families, but stood at 35% for children in female lone-parent families. People 65 and over were the least likely age group to be living in poverty.

- In 2002, almost 20,000 wives reported to the police that their husbands had used violence against them. Another 9,337 women accused their ex-husbands of violence. Just over 5,000 husbands or ex-husbands accused their wives or ex-wives of violence. In 2001-02, a total of 101,248 women and children were admitted to 483 shelters across Canada.

2. Legal Regulation of the Family

(1) Nature of Family Law

Family law may be defined as that area of the law governing the relationships between members of a family. The focal point of this definition is obviously the concept of family. Until the 1970s, the family in Canadian society could be described as the basic social unit normally consisting of a husband and wife and their children, if any. Traditionally, family law has been concerned with the relationships between husband and wife and parent and child.

The main subjects of family law have, therefore, traditionally been marriage, separation and divorce, property rights of spouses during the marriage and on marriage breakdown, support obligations of spouses to one another, the care and custody of children, support obligations of parents to their children, the intervention of the state in the parent-child relationship through child protection legislation, and the establishment of a parent-child relationship through adoption. The law impinges on family relationships at so many different points, however, that it could be claimed, quite legitimately, that family law also encompasses such diverse topics as the law of succession, income taxation, fatal accidents legislation, juvenile delinquency, and social security schemes such as social welfare and employment insurance. To a large extent, these segments of family law have been allocated to other courses in the typical law school curriculum in order to keep a course on family law within workable limits. A glance at the Table of Contents reveals that these topics are not given separate coverage in this book although they are referred to from time to time.

The traditional definition of family law has to be modified to take into account those laws that now govern non-traditional families. While the majority of cohabiting couples in Canada continue to be married to one another, cohabitation without marriage has become much more common. In a functional sense, these units are clearly families and are frequently indistinguishable from the traditional family except for the fact that there is no marital relationship uniting any of its members. One of the issues confronted by the legislatures and courts in the past few decades is whether this type of familial relationship should be accorded legal recognition. In particular, should the status, rights and responsibilities granted to married spouses be extended to common law partners? If so, should same-sex couples be included in this legal regime? Should marriage be an option for same-sex couples? In one sense, these questions require the legal system to determine what entity qualifies as a "family". Beginning in the seventies, most provincial legislatures gradually extended some of the family law rules, particularly those relating to support, to some common law partners of the opposite sex. The provincial legislatures and Parliament also began to treat certain unmarried cohabitees as spouses for tax purposes and for statutory benefits. However, significant differences in the legal treatment of married and common law couples remained. In the 1990s, this gave rise to litigation based on s. 15 of the *Canadian Charter of Rights and Freedoms*, as did the legislative differentiation between opposite-sex couples and same-sex couples.

These legislative and judicial developments are an important part of family law and will be examined in relation to the subject being covered in a particular chapter of this book. For example, in Chapter 4, *FAMILY PROPERTY*, there is extensive coverage of the law governing property disputes between unmarried couples and of the case law challenging the exclusion of such couples from the legislative matrimonial property regimes in most provinces. The challenge by same-sex couples to the traditional definition of marriage is covered in Chapter 2, *CREATING A VALID MARRIAGE*.

In the following excerpt, Julien and Marilyn Payne examine the changing nature of the Canadian family and of Canadian family law.

PAYNE AND PAYNE, *CANADIAN FAMILY LAW*

(Quicklaw, 2001) (Footnotes omitted)

A. Definitions of "Family"

You might think that a book on Canadian family law would begin with a comprehensive legal definition of "family". But that is not possible. The term "family" does not have a precise legal definition. Law tends to regulate the rights and obligations of individuals, as distinct from groups, such as families, however they may be constituted. Canadian family law might more properly be called the Law of Persons insofar as it concentrates on the rights of individuals whose family relationships have become dysfunctional. In short, Canadian family law deals primarily with the pathology of family breakdown and its legal consequences.

People often perceive "marriage" and "family" as synonymous terms but these words are not interchangeable in law. The term "family" is elusive and defies exact definition. Many, but not all, Canadian families are the products of a marriage. More often than not, the presence of children signifies a family relationship. Children may be born within or outside of marriage. Their parents may or may not live together. The parents may have lived together before or after the birth of the child but may no longer do so by reason of separation or divorce. Some children are adopted. In relatively rare situations, a child's birth may have resulted from surrogate parenting arrangements or the use of new reproductive technologies. Children are usually family members of the household in which they reside, but this is not invariably true. Some children do not live with either of their parents or with aunts, uncles, or grandparents. They may live in foster homes or even with friends or neighbours. A new *de facto* family may co-exist with the family of origin.

Whether family relationships can exist when there is neither marriage nor a parent-child or ancestral relationship has sparked controversy. Are two persons of the opposite sex, who are unmarried but living in a "common law relationship" as "husband and wife," members of the same family for social or legal purposes? Does one's attitude change if we reframe the question by asking whether they are living in a family relationship? What if the two parties are members of the same sex? Can they assert a family relationship for the purpose of claiming rights under a collective agreement? Can a gay or lesbian assert survivorship rights in the pension of a lost lover? ...

Whether the indicia of a family relationship involve marriage, parenthood, a common household, or the sharing of responsibilities, there are many unresolved legal questions concerning the characterization of "families" and the rights and obligations of family members. The definition of "family" for any particular purpose is often crucial to a determination of legal rights and obligations as between members of that family. It may also determine whether certain individuals are included or excluded from various kinds of government benefits.

Although some will look back with nostalgia to the traditional nuclear family of the 1950s, with its breadwinning husband, its homemaking wife, and their two children, that is now a minority group in terms of contemporary family structures in Canada. Today, Canadian families take a wide variety of forms. They include childless marriages, two-parent families, single-parent families in which the mother is the primary caregiver, single-parent families where the father is the primary caregiver, unmarried cohabitants with or without children, and blended or reconstituted families that are the product of sequential cohabitational relationships inside or outside marriage. Family structures may also vary according to ethnic and cultural factors. Customary Inuit adoptions, for example, bear little resemblance to the statute-based systems of adoption that exist in the Canadian provinces and territories.

Traditional notions of the family must clearly be re-examined in the search for rational and equitable social and legal policies. In the final analysis, however, it may be impractical for the law to endorse a monolithic definition of "family" that applies for all legal purposes. As in the past, the extent to which the law will recognize a family relationship may turn on the purpose for which such recognition is sought.

B. Functional Significance of Definitions

Family law in Canada has focused on the traditional nuclear family. Our federal divorce laws are based on monogamous marriage. Scant attention is directed toward the rights and responsibilities of members of the extended family, such as grandparents, aunts, and uncles. Even provincial legislation tends to focus on regulating the economic and parenting consequences of marriage breakdown, although issues of spousal and child support and custody and access can arise independently of the status of marriage. Recent years have witnessed changes in the identification of issues relating to changing family structures in Canada.

The two-income family, the high divorce rate, the increasing incidence of unmarried cohabitation, the changing needs of the labour force, cultural diversity resulting from immigration, the ageing of the Canadian population and many other factors have generated new challenges for Canada. Contemporary policy issues include the following:

i) Is a national child care program feasible or desirable?

ii) Should marriage be re-defined to include cohabitation between persons of the opposite sex or of the same sex? If not, to what extent should Canadian law recognize rights and responsibilities between unmarried cohabitants of the opposite sex or of the same sex?

iii) How should law and society respond to the growing incidence of family violence?

iv) To what extent should Canadians be entitled to regulate the legal consequences of family breakdown by marriage contracts, cohabitation agreements, or separation agreements?

v) Should new human reproductive technologies be outlawed or regulated?

vi) How can the economic interests of women and children be protected in the event of marriage breakdown or divorce?

vii) How can parental ties be preserved notwithstanding separation and divorce?

viii) How will Canada address the problem of an ageing population? What will be its impact on health care, residential care, or family care for the elderly?

ix) How should Canada respond to declining birth rates? Are financial incentives for parenthood, such as those adopted in Quebec, a solution? Does the answer lie in increased immigration?

x) How should Canadian family law be administered? By traditional courts? By Unified Family Courts? By administrative tribunals? By governmental or community agencies? What do innovative processes, such as mediation and arbitration, offer as alternative means of resolving family disputes? Should they be subsidized by the state?

xi) How should Canadian law respond to aboriginal families with their own cultural identity and heritage? Does the answer lie in new substantive laws or in delegating decision-making authority to the aboriginal communities? Do immigrant families require special recognition? ...

. . . . .

D. Family Law in Transition

Forty years ago, family law ... was perceived as a system of law that regulated the formation and dissolution of marriage and the rights and obligations arising therefrom. It focused on the traditional nuclear family, comprising a breadwinning husband, a homemaking wife, and their dependent children. With the phenomenal increase in the divorce rate that followed the federal Divorce Act in 1968, the entry of increasing numbers of married women into the workforce, declining birth rates to a point of zero population growth, and the growing incidence of non-marital cohabitational relationships, family law gradually shifted its focus to include the regulation of non-marital family relationships.

Federal, provincial, and territorial legislation regulating the rights and obligations of family members has been largely piecemeal in its evolution. With the possible exception of the province of Quebec, no coherent family policy has been articulated, particularly in the context of the relationship between the so-called private system of family law, which regulates the personal rights and obligations of spouses, parents, and children as between themselves, and the public system that provides social assistance, tax concessions, pension and medical health schemes, and the like.

So far as family law is concerned, the predominant legislative trend has been toward the assertion of individual rights and obligations, rather than the assertion of any family right. Family law statutes are largely premised on the notion that any form of government intervention is an intrusion upon privacy that can only be justified in the event of a breakdown in the family relationship, a reasonable apprehension of domestic violence, or child abuse and neglect.

Revolutionary changes to family law occurred in Canada with the passage of the first dominion-wide Divorce Act in 1968. ... With the enactment of the Divorce Act in 1968, "no-fault" divorce grounds were introduced in addition to an extended list of "offence" grounds. In addition, formal legal equality of support rights and obligations was established for the first time in Canada between divorcing and divorced men and women. Although the Divorce Act of 1986 amended the law relating to the criteria for divorce, spousal and child support, and custody and access in such a way as to shift the focus of the courts from the grounds of divorce to an almost exclusive emphasis on the economic and parenting consequences of divorce, the truly radical breakthroughs occurred with the Divorce Act of 1968, which paved the way for future federal, provincial, and territorial statutory changes.

Before 1968, the support of divorcing or divorced spouses was regulated by provincial and territorial statutes that imposed a unilateral obligation on a guilty husband to maintain his innocent wife in the event of a breakdown of their marriage ensuing from his commission of adultery, cruelty, or desertion. The same principles applied to spousal support claims brought independently of divorce proceedings. During the 1970s and 1980s, many provinces and territories enacted legislation that eliminated the offence concept as the foundation of spousal support rights and obligations. In addition, following the precedent established by the federal Divorce Act of 1968, the right to spousal support on marriage breakdown in the absence of divorce became no longer confined to wives under provincial and territorial legislation; a financially dependent spouse of either sex might look to his or her marital partner for financial support. The governing consideration was no longer sex-based but turned upon the financial needs of the claimant and the ability of his or her spouse to pay. Each spouse was expected, however, to strive for financial self-sufficiency. Thus, marriage was no longer legally perceived as creating a presumed right to lifelong financial support for a dependent spouse in the event of marriage breakdown.

These changes in the right to divorce and the right to spousal support on divorce or marriage breakdown were accompanied by equally fundamental changes in provincial and territorial statutes governing the division of property on marriage breakdown or divorce. Separated and divorced wives were no longer in the prejudicial position in which Irene Murdoch found herself in 1973 when the Supreme Court of Canada denied her any interest in a ranch registered in her husband's name, because her contributions in the home and in the fields were perceived as non-financial contributions ordinarily expected of a rancher's wife. Although three years later the Supreme Court of Canada abandoned *Murdoch* [*Murdoch v. Murdoch*, [1975] 1 S.C.R. 423, discussed in Chapter 4, *FAMILY PROPERTY* of this casebook] in favour of a more enlightened approach in *Rathwell*, [*Rathwell v. Rathwell*, [1978] 2 S.C.R. 436, discussed in Chapter 4, *FAMILY PROPERTY*] the inequities of the *Murdoch* case triggered provincial and territorial legislation that provided for property sharing on marriage breakdown that was no longer based on ownership or who purchased the property.

Another fundamental change in family law over the past quarter-century has been the evolution of legal rights and obligations between unmarried cohabitants. Following the pattern established in cases like *Rathwell* from Saskatchewan, involving married couples before the implementation of statutory property rights in the 1970s and 1980s, unmarried cohabitants were accorded property rights on the dissolution of their relationships on the basis of the constructive trust and the doctrine of unjust enrichment. Rosie Becker, who did not live to enjoy the fruits of her legal victory in the Supreme Court of Canada in 1980, paved the way for the application of the doctrine of unjust enrichment to unmarried cohabiting couples of the opposite sex, although there is nothing in the Supreme Court of Canada's analysis that precludes the application of similar principles to same sex couples. [The decision in *Pettkus v. Becker* (1980), 19 R.F.L. 834 is examined in Chapter 4, *FAMILY PRO-PERTY*.] Contemporaneously with these judicial developments dealing with property rights, many Canadian provincial statues provided an extended definition of "spouse" to establish spousal support rights and obligations between cohabiting couples of the opposite sex who lived together for a designated period of time or had a child together. A much more recent development in this context has been the extension of similar support rights and obligations as between cohabiting couples of the same sex. This was achieved in 1999 by the Supreme Court of Canada's *M. v. H.* judgment [(1999), 46 R.F.L. (4th) 32, reproduced in Chapter 6, *SPOUSAL SUPPORT*] applying the equality provisions of section 15 of the Canadian Charter of Rights and Freedoms. ...

Major statutory reforms in children's rights have also occurred. Perhaps the most significant change in this regard can more properly be characterized as an aspect of criminal law, rather than family law. In the early 1980s, the *Juvenile Delinquents Act* was superseded by the *Young Offenders Act*. The paternalistic, or perhaps maternalistic, approach under the former statute perceived children before the court as misguided youth who needed help without the protection of due process. Not only did the *Young Offenders Act* implement the principle that juveniles should be held responsible for criminal conduct, it also acknowledged the responsibility of the state to accord legal rights to juveniles in the conduct of legal proceedings. ... [See now the *Youth Criminal Justice Act*, S.C. 2002, c. 1.]

Due process changes respecting children were also promulgated in the late 1970s and early 1980s in the context of child protection legislation. It was as late as 1961 that the phrase "the battered child syndrome" was first coined by Dr. Kempe to acknowledge the incidence of physical child abuse. At that time, no one questioned the practices of residential schools or interprovincial and international transracial adoptions of children from aboriginal communities. Contrast this with the 1990s when child abuse by institutional personnel led to criminal convictions in several Canadian provinces as well as to multiparty civil litigation and multifaceted mediated settlements for victims of abuse. The door has now been opened to address the mistreatment of aboriginal children in residential schools and other institutions but closure has yet to be achieved. Even ten years ago, it was extremely rare for children to sue their parents for damages for emotional, physical, and sexual abuse and recover very substantial compensation. In cases of spousal abuse, few people envisaged domestic violence statutes and specialized domestic violence courts. ...

The above substantive changes in the rights and obligations of family members have been accompanied by the evolution of new procedures for resolving family disputes. It is now mandatory for litigating spouses to file financial and property statements to provide data that will expedite the adjudication of support and property disputes. In contested custody disputes, independent expert assessments may be ordered by the court to determine the needs of the children and the respective abilities of the parents to accommodate those needs. It is only a matter of time before parenting plans become mandatory in contested custody proceedings. Diverse pre-trial processes are now in place to help reduce or eliminate contentious issues. The discretionary jurisdiction of the court over costs is being exercised to promote the consensual resolution of issues. The consolidation of disputed issues in a single court proceeding has been facilitated by statutory changes and by amendments to provincial rules of court. These and other procedural changes have proved their worth, but the legal system has remained adversarial. Separating and divorcing parents are still legally perceived as being in conflict with each other. "Fighting it out" is a legal norm. Significant progress has, nevertheless, been made. In several provinces and territories, including Alberta and Saskatchewan, parenting education for separating and divorced couples is readily available, and voluntary recourse to mediation is encouraged. In some urban centres across Canada, specialized Family Courts have been established with a comprehensive jurisdiction over family law matters and access to support services that may deflect the need for lengthy and costly litigation. There still remains, however, considerable room for improvement in the development of alternative processes to litigation that will aid in the constructive resolution of family conflict.

Before addressing potential future developments in family law, a few words are appropriate concerning the legal profession. ... Today, the responsible family law practitioner is no longer perceived as running a divorce mill where the sole grounds for relief are adultery or perjury. Family law practice has come of age. This is not to say that the family law specialist is held in high regard by the legal profession. Corporate and commercial practitioners and civil litigation lawyers still enjoy prestigious reputations that are not shared by dedicated family law practitioners. It is only in recent years that family law specialists have been appointed to the Superior Courts in Canada. ... Of course, with the development of specialized Family Courts and very extensive family law dockets in courts of general jurisdiction, far more family law specialists have found their way to the Bench over the last ten years. A new type of family law practitioner is slowly emerging in Canada. Following developments that have occurred in California, Minnesota, and elsewhere in the United States, some Canadian family law practitioners have opted into Collaborative Family Law. This approach differs from the traditional practice of family law in that its practitioners focus on settlement to the exclusion of litigation. Written agreements are executed to provide full disclosure and to waive discovery and recourse to litigation for a stipulated period of time. During this period, negotiations are undertaken by the clients and their lawyers in an effort to achieve a settlement. If no settlement is reached, the lawyers withdraw from the case and cannot participate in any subsequent litigation. Opportunities exist for made-to-measure individualized Collaborative Family Law Participation Agreements that can reflect the specific interests of the disputants.

For many years, provincial and federal governments have provided booklets and pamphlets on family law for the general public. More recently, they have created relatively sophisticated web sites to provide information. In particular, the federal Department of Justice currently provides a veritable mine of information on diverse aspects of Canadian family law. Its materials on the Federal Child Support Guidelines are remarkably informative for both lawyer and layperson alike. ... Some farsighted family law practitioners are already providing wide-ranging information on the web, ... but legal practitioners will have to work harder to communicate information to potential clients, if they are to compete with increasing numbers of paralegals, mediators, and facilitators. It will be insufficient to have a web page geared to self-promotion. Potential clients will have to be informed of their basic substantive rights and of the diverse processes available for the resolution of disputes, both within and outside the judicial system. The strategic use of the web, hard copy, disks, and videos will become an integral part of the practice of family dispute resolution. With an increasing number of self-represented litigants, the unbundling of legal services will become widespread within the next few years. "Unbundling" signifies that the lawyer will provide information and input into a client's case, without assuming the responsibility to appear for that client in the courtroom or elsewhere. For the more traditional practitioner, hourly billing may be largely replaced in family law practice by block billings, whereby the lawyer will undertake the carriage of a case through its diverse possible stages, with a maximum global amount being payable at each stage.

The uncontested divorce under the auspices of the judiciary is on its last legs. If the stumbling block of section 96 of the Constitution Act, 1867 can be overcome, administrative divorce will replace the desk order divorces that are currently processed on affidavit evidence without any court appearance. In the meantime, paralegals will assume this task with input from court-based information facilities. Adultery and cruelty will disappear as criteria of marriage breakdown under the *Divorce Act*, leaving no-fault separation as the sole criterion. Collusion, connivance, and condonation will disappear from the statute book as bars to divorce, thereby formalizing their present *de facto* status. Divorces, like marriages, will become subject to an administrative registration system, which will ultimately extend to other domestic partnerships involving unmarried cohabitants of the same sex or of the opposite sex. Current spousal and child support laws will need to be re-addressed with the expanded legal recognition of non-marital domestic partnerships and in light of the ageing Canadian population. The obligation of children to support their elderly parents who are not economically self-sufficient has long existed under provincial legislation in Canada but has been relatively rarely invoked. The present legislation is a sleeping giant awaiting arousal. The clock is ticking but the wake-up alarm is not yet ringing. But it will. In all likelihood, governmental agencies will more actively pursue liable relatives, as the state becomes less capable of absorbing the costs in an ageing population with a substantially reduced workforce.

With respect to parenting disputes, cultural diversity will attract much greater attention than it has in the past. The processing of disputes relating to the treatment of aboriginal children in residential schools underlines the need to more aggressively recognize cultural heritage in resolving parenting disputes on family breakdown. ... Children will become more actively involved in the dispute resolution process in cases where their parenting is at stake.

The voice of the child will be heard more effectively in the formulation of parenting plans. The proprietary legal terminology of "custody" and "access" will disappear; parenting plans involving extended family members will become common; and mediation will be a preferred option to the traditional legal process for the vast majority of parents. The professional training of private mediators and facilitators who engage in family dispute resolution will be regulated so as to preclude anyone from hanging up a shingle after a fast fix at a costly forty-hour training program. Private arbitration will also become an integral part of family dispute resolution across Canada and arbitration may ultimately become court-connected with recourse to a panel of screened arbitrators.

Courts will, nevertheless, continue to play a major role in the resolution of family disputes. New processes for family dispute resolution are complementary to the legal system. They cannot exist without it. Their efficacy lies in the fact that the legal system is there to fall back on when there are no options available or they have proved wanting. But courts themselves face major changes in an age when 20 to 40 per cent of all family litigants, depending on the issue and the province of residence, seek access to the courts without legal representation. As a first step, several provinces are following Ontario's example by seeking to simplify the *Family Law Rules* so as to make them comprehensible to non-lawyers. The next step will be to develop improved information resources to assist self-represented litigants to present relevant data before the court. Videos and computer disks, which inform litigants how to fill in the requisite forms and what financial or other material to provide for the court, will become absolutely vital, if courts are to cope with the increasing number of self-represented litigants. Court lists may need to be divided into cases where the parties are self-represented and those where both sides are independently legally represented. The assignment of judges may be structured according to their willingness and ability to cope with self-represented litigants. Judges will diversify their roles. They will no longer be confined to an adjudicator's role. They will become case managers in the fullest sense from the time when the litigation commences. Mediative techniques and approaches will become the norm. The affidavit war generated by interim motions will become a thing of the past as courts shift to a case management non-adversarial mode of family dispute resolution.

The private certificate system of legal aid in Ontario is destined to disappear. It will initially be replaced by a family law clinic system, such as already exists in Saskatchewan. Within the next twenty years, family legal aid clinics may themselves yield pride of place to community-based family dispute resolution centres, with ready access to a network of lawyers, psychologists, social workers, mediators, business valuators, actuaries, and a host of other paid professionals as well as para-professionals and volunteers.

Multidisciplinary private law practices will emerge in the field of family conflict management and family dispute resolution. ...

Whether past, present, and future changes should be perceived as good or bad for family stability in Canada is a matter of opinion. Some will view changes in family law and family life in Canada over the last thirty years as undermining the institution of marriage. Others will conclude that the changes already encountered and those yet to be experienced merely reflect the family in transition, rather than the family in crisis. In the absence of sophisticated empirical research, strongly held opinions or convictions on the past, present or future state of the Canadian family will remain unsubstantiated and unabated.

In the following paper, Professor Thompson examined the extent to which family law provides for rules and some certainty and predictability. Writing in 2000, he described family law in Canada as largely characterized by "rulelessness", where, at best, the legislation and cases identified "factors" to be taken into account in the exercise of discretion. He acknowledged, however, that there were some "islands of rules" in the areas of family property and child support. His introduction and conclusion are reproduced below.

THOMPSON, "RULES AND RULELESSNESS IN FAMILY LAW: RECENT DEVELOPMENTS, JUDICIAL AND LEGISLATIVE"

(2000-2001), 18 C.F.L.Q. 25 (Footnotes omitted)

We — and I mean all of us, courts and lawyers, parents and spouses — find ourselves at an awkward moment in the evolution of family law. Family law is statute law. But the legislators often appear deer-like, frozen in the bright headlights of divided public opinion and gender politics. Those same "political" disputes are then played out, one case at a time, before trial and appeal courts, and even the Supreme Court of Canada. Constitutional challenges are raised to the differential treatment of family forms by government, whether in the distribution of benefits or the imposition of "family" rights and obligations through legislation. No less "political", however, are difficult questions of property division, spousal support, child custody and child protection.

Buried within each case is the larger question for judges, especially appellate judges: in the absence of clear legislative "rules", should the court enunciate a ruling any broader than this individual case? If not, is it possible to maintain the legitimacy of family law in this state of "rulelessness"?

... My primary theme will be the increasingly uneasy juxtaposition of rules and rulelessness in family law.

... I will start from our most recent massive experiment with "rules", namely the Child Support Guidelines. ... Next along the continuum is pension division [and family property generally]. ... Situated in the middle of the spectrum, but uncertainly so, are spousal support ... and child protection. ... At the other extreme, that of rulelessness, lies child custody. ...

Conclusion: The Homogenization of Canadian Family Law

Thanks to the federal divorce power, the Supreme Court of Canada, and the *Charter*, Canadian family law is becoming homogenized, one law from sea to sea, for better or worse.

The federal divorce power encompasses corollary relief, including custody and access, child support and spousal support. The *Federal Child Support Guidelines* offer a classic example of how the federal government can reform the whole of federal and provincial family law, through its mixture of policy-making resources and spending power. Once "federal" family law has changed, there are strong practical pressures for the provinces to "get into sync", so as not to confuse those parents and spouses who must live under both laws. No doubt the same will hold true once the federal government completes its review of custody and access law. And, sadly, the federal vagueness on spousal support equally infects the interpretation of provincial law, as happened in *Moge* [*Moge v. Moge* (1992), 43 R.F.L. (3d) 345 (S.C.C.), reproduced in Chapter 6, *SPOUSAL SUPPORT*] and more pointedly in *Bracklow* [*Bracklow v. Bracklow* (1999), 44 R.F.L. (4th) 1 (S.C.C.), reproduced in Chapter 6, *SPOUSAL SUPPORT*].

The Supreme Court uses the national impact of the *Divorce Act* as one of its anchors for "national significance" or "public importance" in giving leave for family law cases. A case like *Gordon v. Goertz* then permits the Court to set out relocation law [the law governing mobility of custodial parents, a topic examined in Chapter 7, *CUSTODY AND ACCESS*] for the whole of Canada, a marvel to an American who must cope with 50 state laws and 50 state courts on the same mobility issue. But the Court is not confined to federal statutes.

Thanks to our unitary court structure, the Supreme Court of Canada is also the last court of appeal for the interpretation of provincial statutes, including such areas as child protection, property division, and pensions. No field of family law is exempt from Supreme Court review and hence national direction.

Finally, the *Charter of Rights* is forcing both courts and legislatures to reduce disparities in the treatment of different family forms. Section 15 is a driving force for national homogenization. If all Canadian provinces extend support rights to common law spouses, then why not Alberta? If same-sex couples are read in to Ontario's family legislation, then so too in other provinces. Even section 7 is a homogenizing force. What's shocking about the absence of counsel in New Brunswick child protection cases is that every other Canadian province treats such cases as a priority within their legal aid plans. When the Supreme Court does interpret sections 15 or 7..., then the *Charter* makes it apply across the whole country, as a minimum constitutional content of provincial family laws.

All of these changes leave less and less room for experimentation, for the development of provincial family law "rules", whether legislative or judicial. In any event, the Supreme Court appears to prefer "contextualism" and "standards" and "discretion" in family law, the costs of which fall upon lower courts, counsel and parties. In some areas of law, like child custody and spousal support, the Supreme Court — and courts generally — can fall back upon the "rule-less" legislation. But that's only a partial defence, as the courts can still develop intermediate solutions, something more like presumptions or even tighter and shorter lists of factors.

Decisions like *Bracklow, Gordon v. Goertz*, and *H. (D.) v. M. (H.)* [(1999), 45 R.F.L. (4th) 270 (S.C.C.), discussed in Chapter 7, *CUSTODY AND ACCESS*] make family law appear utterly "rule-less", undermining its very legitimacy in the eyes of the parties and the public. After this recent onslaught of family law decisions, it may be time for the Supreme Court to think about the re-introduction of "rules", or even "law", into family law.

NOTES AND QUESTIONS

1. After writing the article on "rules" and "rulelessness", Professor Thompson teamed up with Professor Rogerson to develop the Spousal Support Advisory Guidelines. The story of this rather unique method of introducing rules into the area of spousal support is told in Chapter 6, *SPOUSAL SUPPORT*.

2. As you examine the various topics that make up "family law", consider where each falls on the spectrum of "rules" to "rulelessness".

(2) Constitutional Framework

(a) Federalism

The distribution of powers over family law and the potential for conflict between laws enacted by the Parliament of Canada and laws enacted by a provincial legislature will be surveyed whenever relevant to the topic covered by a particular chapter in this book. The following excerpt from Professor Hogg's constitutional law text provides a framework for this analysis.

HOGG, *CONSTITUTIONAL LAW OF CANADA*

(Toronto: Carswell) (looseleaf) c. 27 (Footnotes omitted)

The Family

27.1 Distribution of powers

In principle, one would expect the bulk of family law to come within provincial power. Family law has little or no effect on trade or transportation or other aspects of the national economy. It rather concerns the ways in which people choose to live their private lives, and may be expected to reflect values which differ from one part of the country to another.

While most family law is within provincial jurisdiction, the Constitution Act, 1867, by s. 91(26), allocates to the federal Parliament the power to make laws in relation to "marriage and divorce". The national interest in marriage and divorce consists in the desirability of nation-wide recognition of marriages and divorces. If marriage and divorce were provincial responsibilities, and if markedly different rules developed among provinces, there would be no assurance that a marriage or divorce performed or obtained in one province would be recognized by the courts of another province. This has been a problem in the United States where marriage and divorce are state responsibilities. Australia has followed the Canadian pattern of allocating marriage and divorce to the federal Parliament.

The Constitution Act, 1867, by s. 92(12), confers on the provincial Legislatures the power to make laws in relation to "the solemnization of marriage in the province". The boundary between this power and the federal power over "marriage" is discussed later in this chapter. Most provincial power over family law is derived from that expansive phrase in s. 92(13), "property and civil rights in the province", which encompasses property and contract law and other private-law relations, including, for example, matrimonial property, succession, support of spouses and children, adoption, guardianship, custody, legitimacy, affiliation and names.

The various federal and provincial powers are discussed in the following sections of this chapter, including the problem of conflict between differing orders of custody or support made under federal and provincial laws. A final section will briefly examine the constitutional problems of the administration of justice in family law matters.

27.2 Crime and delinquency

Juvenile delinquency and criminal charges arising out of family disputes are within the legislative competence of the federal Parliament under the "criminal law" power (s. 91(27)). The validity of the federal Youth Criminal Justice Act ... Family related offences under the federal Criminal Code, such as corrupting children (s. 172), failing to provide necessaries of life (s. 215), assault (s. 266) and abduction (s. 281), are also clearly valid criminal laws. The Criminal Code also provides a defence to a charge of assault for teachers and parents who apply "reasonable" force "by way of correction" against the children in their charge. These elements of family law that are sustained by the criminal law power will not be further discussed in this chapter.

27.3 Marriage

(a) Formation of marriage

The federal authority in relation to "marriage" — the first branch of s. 91(26) — has to be read side by side with the provincial authority in relation to "solemnization of marriage in the province" (s. 92(12)). In fact, most of the laws concerning marriage have been enacted by the provinces, and the courts have tended to construe the provincial power liberally. The scope of federal power has been left largely undetermined.

The first federal law ever to come before the courts was one which declared that every marriage performed in accordance with the laws of the place where it was performed was to be recognized as a valid marriage everywhere in Canada. In [*Re Questions concerning Marriage*, [1912] A.C. 880, 7 D.L.R. 629 (P.C.), hereinafter cited as] the *Marriage Reference*, the Privy Council through Viscount Haldane held that the law was invalid. According to their lordships, the difficulty with the law was that it assumed that all rules bearing on the validity of a marriage were within the federal power over "marriage". But this would relegate the provincial power over "the solemnization of marriage" to the laying down of merely directory rules, that is, rules which if broken would not impair the validity of the resulting marriage. Their lordships rejected this view, holding that the provincial power extended to the enactment of "conditions as to solemnization which may affect the validity of the contract". Since the provincial power was subtracted from the federal power, it followed that the federal Parliament could not legislate with respect to all questions of validity, and the impugned law was bad.

Following the *Marriage Reference*, it is clear that a province has power to stipulate pre-ceremonial requirements, such as, the issue of a licence or the publication of banns, and to stipulate the qualifications of the person performing the ceremony, even if breach of the stipulations renders the marriage a nullity. These are matters closely associated with the performance of the ceremony — the solemnization. Much less clearly associated with the ceremony is a requirement of parental consent to the marriage of a minor, but in two cases the Supreme Court of Canada has held that a province may enact that parental consent as a condition of a valid marriage. These cases were decided on the dubious ground that parental consent was a "formality" of marriage rather than a matter governing the capacity of the parties. Laws governing the capacity of the parties are outside provincial power, for example, a law prescribing the prohibited degrees of consanguinity and affinity, or a law prescribing the capacity of divorced people to remarry.

While the definition of marriage is a federal responsibility, it remained a matter of common law until the issue of same-sex marriage brought the topic into Parliament's legislative agenda. The common law definition is contained in a dictum of Lord Penzance in *Hyde v. Hyde* (1866), L.R. 1 P.D. 130 at 133 (Eng. P.D.A.): marriage is "the voluntary union of life of one man and one woman, to the exclusion of all others". [The same definition applied in Quebec under a federal statute.] The reference to "one man and one woman" excluded same-sex marriage, and same-sex couples brought challenges to the opposite-sex requirement. Those challenges were successful in the courts of British Columbia, Ontario and Quebec, which held that the opposite-sex requirement was invalid for breach of the equality guarantee in s. 15 of the Chapter. The Government of Canada, which had defended the traditional definition of marriage in those cases, decided not to appeal them to the Supreme Court of Canada. Instead, the Government proposed to introduce a statute changing the definition of marriage, for civil purposes, to "the lawful union of two persons to the exclusion of all others". The reference to "two persons" was intended to legalize same-sex marriage. A draft bill to accomplish this change was not immediately introduced into Parliament, but was referred to the Supreme Court of Canada for an opinion as to its constitutionality.

The answer to the question of constitutionality came in *Same-Sex Marriage, Re* [[2004] 3 S.C.R. 698, 12 R.F.L. (6th) 153 reproduced in Chapter 2, *CREATING A VALID MARRIAGE*]. The Court held that the proposed law would be constitutional. Under s. 91(26), Parliament had jurisdiction over capacity to marry. A law providing that two persons, including two persons of the same sex, were capable of being married was a law in relation to capacity to marry. The Court rejected the argument that marriage was, by its very nature, the union of a man and a woman for the procreation of children. No doubt, that would have been the original understanding in 1867, when marriage and religion were inseparable, and homosexual acts between consenting adults were criminal (as they remained until 1969). But the Court reaffirmed its oft-repeated view that the words of the Constitution are not frozen in their 1867 sense, but must receive a progressive interpretation to address the realities of modern life. In today's pluralistic society, there was no reason to deny that the civil institution of marriage could be expanded, if Parliament so chose, to accommodate same-sex marriage. Following this decision, Parliament did enact the proposed law, making Canada the fourth country (after The Netherlands, Belgium and Spain) to legalize same-sex marriage.

Could Parliament create a relationship short of marriage, perhaps denominated a "civil union" that would provide partners with some or all of the attributes of marriage, while withholding the name of marriage to the relationship? This was not one of the questions put to the Court in the *Same-Sex Marriage Reference*, but the availability of a civil-union alternative for same-sex unions (which had been adopted by some countries) was offered in argument as a reason for excluding same-sex unions from the definition of marriage. (Of course, the institution of a civil union would not need to be confined to same-sex unions.) The Court held that Parliament's power over marriage did not extend to relationships short of marriage. The provinces, under their authority over property and civil rights (s. 92(13)), had the exclusive competence to create legally recognized non-marital relationships. As the Court pointed out, Quebec had already done so [in 2002] by creating a "civil union" between "two persons", which was a formally solemnized and registered relationship with similar attributes to marriage.

Another section of the draft bill that was referred to the Court in the *Same-Sex Marriage Reference* provided that: "Nothing in this Act affects the freedom of religious groups to refuse to perform marriages that are not in accordance with their religious beliefs." Since the new definition of marriage was expressed to be "for civil purposes", this provision could easily have been accepted as a merely interpretative declaration. But the Court held that the provision was *ultra vires* Parliament, because it related to the solemnization of marriage, and was therefore within provincial jurisdiction under s. 92(12). However, the Court hastened to add that the guarantee of freedom of religion in s. 2(a) of the Charter of Rights was "broad enough to protect religious officials from being compelled by the state to perform civil or religious same-sex marriages that are contrary to their religious beliefs".

(b) Consequences of marriage

Does the federal power over "marriage" extend to the consequences of marriage, for example, the obligation to support a dependent spouse or children, custody of children, and the property rights of married people? In fact, until 1968 laws on these topics had only been enacted by the provinces, and the laws had been held to be valid as matters coming within "property and civil rights in the province" (s. 92(13)). In 1968, the federal Parliament provided for alimony, maintenance and custody in the new Divorce Act, but only as corollary relief in divorce proceedings. These provisions of the Divorce Act have been upheld as an exercise of the "divorce" power, and it has not been necessary to consider whether they could have been enacted by the federal Parliament as measures unrelated to divorce. In Australia, the federal marriage power empowers regulation of the relationship between married persons and their children, and it is arguable that the Canadian power is no less broad.

27.4 Divorce

The federal Parliament's power to make laws in relation to "divorce" — the second branch of s. 91(26) — lay almost dormant until 1968 when for the first time a comprehensive, Canada-wide Divorce Act was enacted. Before that time, the law differed from province to province, depending upon the date when English Law had been received in the province, the terms of pre-confederation laws on the topic, and several federal statutes which did not apply in all provinces. In Newfoundland and Quebec, and in Ontario until 1930, there was no judicial procedure to obtain a divorce, and a federal statute was necessary in every case.

The Divorce Act confers jurisdiction on the superior court in each province to grant divorces, establishes a procedure by way of "application" (formerly "petition") for obtaining decrees of divorce, and stipulates the grounds upon which decrees may be granted. The constitutionality of these primary parts of the Act cannot be doubted. The Act also contains provisions for the award of corollary relief to the parties: alimony, maintenance and the custody of children. The provisions for corollary relief cover matters which before 1968 had been the responsibility of the provinces, and they have been constitutionally controversial. In the next two sections of this chapter, we shall see that all constitutional challenges have been unsuccessful.

27.5 Custody and support of children

(a) Custody of children

In the *Adoption Reference* [*Re Adoption Act*, [1938] S.C.R. 398, 71 C.C.C. 110], the Supreme Court of Canada held that it was competent to the province to enact laws providing for the adoption of children and for the maintenance of children and deserted wives. Duff C.J. for the Court explained that the welfare and education of children and the protection of the poor and distressed were matters of provincial responsibility. He did not explain to which head of legislative power this responsibility was to be attributed, but it has subsequently been generally assumed to be "property and civil rights in the province" (s. 92(13)) rather than "matters of a merely local or private nature in the province" (s. 92(16)).

Since the *Adoption Reference* it has never been doubted that adoption, legitimacy, custody, guardianship, child welfare, affiliation, and maintenance of children are within provincial power, and of course every province has enacted statutes on these and related topics. What has not been so clear is the extent of federal power on these topics by virtue of the federal Parliament's power over "marriage and divorce" (s. 91(26)). The possibility of some federal authority was raised but not decided by Duff C.J. in the *Adoption Reference*, and the question was not presented for decision until after the enactment of the federal Divorce Act in 1968.

The question of the validity of the corollary relief provisions of the Divorce Act had to be decided in *Papp v. Papp*, [1970] 1 O.R. 331 (C.A.), a case in which a custody order had been made under the Divorce Act. Laskin J.A., sitting alone as the Ontario Court of Appeal, upheld the custody provisions of the Divorce Act. He pointed out that the provisions applied only to the children of the marriage whose dissolution was sought, and that no corollary relief could be awarded at trial if the petition failed. The provisions were valid, he held, because there was a "rational, functional connection" between them and the admittedly valid provisions of the Act concerning divorce. In his view, the custody of children was "bound up with the direct consequences of marriage and divorce" and was "complementary" to the divorce itself.

Papp v. Papp concerned an "interim" order of custody, that is, an order of custody made after the application for divorce to cover the period up to the trial. But the decision has been consistently followed in subsequent cases challenging other forms of corollary relief. Appellate courts in Manitoba and Alberta have upheld the constitutionality of "permanent" custody orders, that is, orders made on the granting of the divorce. More difficult is the question of the validity of the authority given by the Divorce Act to the court subsequently to vary a custody order made at the time of the divorce. On an application for variation, the divorce is over, and the only issue for decision is the best interests of the child. Is there still a "rational, functional connection" with the divorce? In *Skjonsby v. Skjonsby*, [1975] 4 W.W.R. 319 (Alta. C.A.) the Appellate Division of the Alberta Supreme Court answered yes, upholding the power of variation.

(b) Support of children

The Divorce Act's provisions authorizing the court to order payments of support (formerly called maintenance) in respect of the children of the marriage are as valid as those concerning custody, and for the same reason, namely, their close connection with the divorce. The power to vary support orders, long after the divorce, is also valid. Moreover, the original order for support need not be finally made at the time of granting the divorce. In *Zacks v. Zacks*, [1973] S.C.R. 891, a judge of the Supreme Court of British Columbia, on granting a decree nisi for divorce, ordered that the wife and child of the marriage were entitled to support, but directed a reference to the registrar of the Court to recommend the amount. The decree absolute, finalizing the divorce, was entered before the amount was fixed. The Supreme Court of Canada had no difficulty in deciding that both the language of the Divorce Act and the "divorce" power extended to the fixing of quantum after the grant of the divorce. Of course, in that case the application for support had been made in a timely fashion and the trial judge had declared that the respondent wife was entitled to support. The Supreme Court of Canada therefore did not have to decide, and expressly left open, the question whether a divorce court could entertain an application for support which had been made for the first time after the decree absolute had been granted.

27.6 Support of spouse

The previous section of this chapter dealt with the custody and support of children. This section of the chapter is concerned with payments for the support of a dependent spouse. Such payments used to be called either alimony or maintenance. ...

It is clear that the provinces have the power to provide for support payments by one spouse to the other. This was one of the points decided in the *Adoption Reference*. ...

The federal Divorce Act includes, as part of the corollary relief available in divorce proceedings, provisions ... for the support of a spouse. There is no doubt as to the validity of these provisions. *Zacks v. Zacks*, the decision of the Supreme Court of Canada which has already been discussed in connection with maintenance of children, upheld the validity of an order made under the Divorce Act which was for the support of the wife as well as the child of the marriage. Martland J. for the Court spoke of "alimony, maintenance and the custody of children" as subjects which were all "inseparable from [Parliament's] jurisdiction to pass laws governing the change of status resulting from a dissolution of marriage".

27.7 Division of property

The Divorce Act, by s. 15 [now s. 15.2], authorizes the payment of maintenance for the support of a spouse or children by "lump sum" as well as by periodic sums. The power to order payment by lump sum has been interpreted as not including the power to order the transfer of real estate or other specific assets.

It has been suggested that an order for the transfer of specific property would in any case be outside the constitutional power of the federal Parliament, because it would be within "property and civil rights in the province" (s. 92(13)). It is of course true that laws in relation to property, including matrimonial property, are within the competence of the provinces under their power over property and civil rights. But that is also true of support and custody. The federal Parliament has the power to provide for support and custody as corollary relief in divorce proceedings because of the "rational, functional connection" between laws which provide for the dissolution of a marriage and laws which provide for these forms of corollary relief. It could surely be argued that a similar connection exists between the dissolution of a marriage and the disposition of the matrimonial property. Thus, while the federal Parliament probably could not enact a comprehensive regime of family property, the cases so far decided under the Divorce Act (all of which have sustained federal power) suggest that there would be no constitutional impediment to the expansion of the Divorce Act's corollary relief provisions to permit the court, on the making of a decree for divorce, to order transfers of specific property from one spouse to the other.

All provinces have enacted matrimonial property laws that provide for the division of matrimonial property between the spouses on the dissolution of the marriage. These laws come within "property and civil rights in the province", and are clearly valid. In the absence of a competing federal law, they are not vulnerable to the doctrine of federal paramountcy.
...

27.8 Conflict between orders made under federal and provincial law

(a) General principles

There is provincial legislation providing for support and custody, and the validity of this legislation is not in doubt. Since the introduction in 1968 of the corollary relief provisions of the federal *Divorce Act*, there has been the possibility of conflict between orders made under provincial law and orders made under the *Divorce Act*. In my opinion, the existence of conflict and its consequences should be determined by the relatively well-settled body of constitutional law which resolves conflicts between federal and provincial laws, that is to say, the doctrine of federal paramountcy. Instead, the courts have often disregarded the doctrine of paramountcy and have produced a remarkably inconsistent patchwork of decisions.

Some of the difficulty seems to have been caused by confusion with the rules of conflict of laws (or private international law). In *McKee v. McKee*, [1951] A.C. 352 (P.C.), the Privy Council decided that the Supreme Court of Ontario had jurisdiction to make an order for the custody of a child resident in Ontario, despite the existence of an inconsistent custody order made in another jurisdiction (California). Their lordships pointed out that under Ontario law the welfare of the infant was the paramount consideration in questions of custody, and this consideration should prevail over all others, including the existence of a foreign order.

The rule of *McKee v. McKee* resolves conflicts as to custody between a province and a foreign jurisdiction, or between two provinces. But where the conflict is between federal and provincial law an issue of constitutional law is presented which cannot be resolved by the rules of the conflict of laws. An order for custody or other corollary relief which is made under the Divorce Act by the superior court of a province is not an order of a "foreign" court in other provinces. On the contrary, s. 20 of the Divorce Act provides (and federal legislative power supports the provision) that the order "has legal effect throughout Canada", and s. 20 further provides that the order may be registered in any province as an order of the superior court of that province and may then be enforced "as an order of that court". Surely any order for corollary relief under the Divorce Act must render inoperative any inconsistent order under provincial law by virtue of the doctrine of paramountcy.

The question then arises: when is an order for corollary relief under the Divorce Act inconsistent with an order under provincial law? Under the "express contradiction" test of inconsistency, which has now been accepted by the Supreme Court of Canada, there can be no doubt about custody orders. An order under the Divorce Act granting sole custody of a child to spouse W expressly contradicts an order under provincial law granting sole custody of the same child to spouse H. Assuming that W and H are living apart, a child cannot be in the sole custody of both at the same time. The case of support (whether of spouse or children) is not so clear. An order under the Divorce Act requiring spouse H to pay $500 per month to spouse W does not expressly contradict an order under provincial law requiring spouse H to pay $600 to spouse W. Both orders can be complied with by spouse H paying $1,100 to spouse W! This is absurd because it is obvious that each order was intended to occupy the field, exhaustively defining H's obligation, and by implication excluding any additional obligation. It has been decided that there is an inconsistency between two orders requiring the payment of different amounts of support, and that the provincial order is inoperative. The rest of this chapter will proceed on the realistic assumption that this decision is correct. ...

(b) Variation under provincial law of orders under Divorce Act

The first situation to be examined is where a divorce has been granted by the superior court of a province, and the court has also made an order for corollary relief (custody or support) under the Divorce Act. Is it later open to a court (in the same or another province), acting under provincial law, to make an order for custody or [support] which is inconsistent with the pre-existing Divorce Act order?

In *Emerson v. Emerson*, [1972] 3 O.R. 5 (H.C.), a divorce had been granted by the Supreme Court of New Brunswick, and the Court had awarded the wife maintenance for the support of the child of the marriage. The husband lived in New Brunswick, but the wife and child lived in Ontario. The wife wished to vary the amount of maintenance. The Divorce Act includes a power to vary orders for corollary relief, but at that time the Act provided that the power was exercisable only "by the court that made the order". The wife therefore had to go to New Brunswick to take advantage of this provision. Instead, she applied to the Supreme Court of Ontario for maintenance under the provincial Infants Act. Wright J., invoking an earlier decision of his own, applied the conflict of laws rule of *McKee v. McKee* to hold that the welfare of the child was the primary consideration and that he was free to order maintenance under the provincial law even in the face of an inconsistent order under the federal *Divorce Act*.

Wright J.'s decision in *Emerson v. Emerson* to grant relief in Ontario where the wife and child lived is certainly understandable. The Divorce Act of 1968 was deficient in only allowing orders to be varied in the province where the divorce was granted. (The current Act, enacted in 1986, permits variation by a court in a province where either former spouse is ordinarily resident, whether or not that court granted the divorce and originally ordered corollary relief [ss. 5 and 18]). But the fact remains that the Divorce Act maintenance order, although made in New Brunswick, had legal force in Ontario, and was enforceable in Ontario, by virtue of a valid federal law. Since the Divorce Act of 1968 gave Wright J. no power directly to vary the order made under the Divorce Act, the result of the decision is to produce two inconsistent orders for maintenance, both enforceable in Ontario. This is precisely the situation which the doctrine of paramountcy is designed to resolve, and it dictates that the order made under the federal Act must prevail. Wright J. should have declined jurisdiction, since his order (made under provincial law) would have to be futile.

The authority of *Emerson v. Emerson* has been limited and perhaps destroyed by two decisions of provincial courts of appeal. In *Ramsay v. Ramsay*, [1976] 13 O.R. (2d) 85, 23 R.F.L. 147 (C.A.), the Ontario Court of Appeal held that an Ontario court had no authority to vary an order for maintenance of a spouse made under the Divorce Act in Manitoba. Their lordships added, *obiter*, however, that questions of the custody or welfare of children stood on a different footing: in their view the Divorce Act should not be construed as depriving the provincial courts of the ancient *parens patriae* jurisdiction over children within their territorial jurisdiction. Although their lordships did not refer to *Emerson v. Emerson*, this *dictum* could be read as supporting the outcome of that case since the case did involve the welfare of a child.

In *Re Hall and Hall*, [1976] 4 W.W.R. 634 (B.C. C.A.), the British Columbia Court of Appeal rejected the *obiter dictum* in *Ramsay v. Ramsay* and the decision in *Emerson v. Emerson*. The Court held that a British Columbia court had no jurisdiction to vary an order for the custody of a child made under the Divorce Act in Quebec. The Divorce Act of 1968 gave no such jurisdiction, and an order made under provincial law (whether under statute or the *parens patriae* jurisdiction) would simply be inconsistent with the Divorce Act. It seems to me, with respect, that *Re Hall and Hall* is rightly decided and that the *obiter dictum* in *Ramsay v. Ramsay* and the decision in *Emerson v. Emerson* (as well as cases which have followed it) are inconsistent with the doctrine of federal paramountcy.

The decisions and *dicta* which seem to ignore the doctrine of federal paramountcy reflect a concern that an order for corollary relief under the Divorce Act should not preclude forever the making of an inconsistent order under provincial law. It may be possible to construct a sound constitutional basis to avoid that result. It will be recalled that the validity of the corollary relief provisions of the Divorce Act depends upon their "rational, functional connection" with divorce. It is arguable, therefore, that an order for corollary relief is inherently temporary, expiring naturally as the divorce retreats into the past and its impact on the circumstances of the parties diminishes. On this basis, it would eventually be open to a court to decide that the effects of a divorce had been exhausted, and that an order made under the Divorce Act could be reviewed and replaced by a different order made under provincial law.

(c) *Orders under provincial law where no order under* Divorce Act

The second situation to be examined is where a divorce has been granted by the superior court of a province, but no order for corollary relief (custody or support) has been made. What is the effect of the divorce decree on an order for custody or support made under provincial law? The order under provincial law might have been made before or after the divorce decree.

Wright J.'s decision in *Emerson v. Emerson* would clearly assert the Court's power to act under provincial law. I have already given my reasons for thinking that *Emerson v. Emerson* is wrongly decided. However, it seems to me that the Ontario Court of Appeal in *Richards v. Richards*, [1972] 2 O.R. 596 (C.A.) went too far in the other direction when Gale C.J.O. for the Court asserted that the Divorce Act, by occupying the "field" of corollary relief, had rendered ineffective all provincial laws "in that field". This *dictum* was not necessary for the actual decision in *Richards v. Richards*, and it conflicts with recent decisions of the Supreme Court of Canada which have consistently rejected the covering-the-field test of inconsistency between federal and provincial laws, and have insisted upon a more direct conflict ("express contradiction") to trigger the paramountcy doctrine. On the basis of the express contradiction test, as long as no order has in fact been made under the

Divorce Act, an order made under provincial law would not be deemed inconsistent with the Divorce Act and would therefore be legally effective. Of course, if and when a valid order is made under the Divorce Act, it will render the competing order inoperative.

(d) Variation under Divorce Act of orders under provincial law

The third and final situation to be examined is where an order has been made for support or custody under provincial law before the commencement of divorce proceedings. In subsequent divorce proceedings in the same or another province, can an order for corollary relief be made which is inconsistent with the pre-existing order?

This was the situation in *Gillespie v. Gillespie* (1972), 13 R.F.L. 344 (N.B. C.A.) in which the New Brunswick Appellate Division held that the Supreme Court of New Brunswick had jurisdiction, on the granting of a divorce, to make an order for the custody of a child of the marriage, although the child was in Ontario and was the subject of a custody order made under Ontario's Infants Act. The Court held, correctly in my opinion, that the conflict between the two orders was to be resolved by the doctrine of paramountcy, the order made under the federal Divorce Act prevailing over the order made under the provincial Infants Act. ...

27.9 Jurisdiction of Family Courts

(a) Fragmentation of jurisdiction

In most provinces, matters of family law are adjudicated upon by several different courts. There is now a strong movement to unite the various jurisdictions in a new unified family court. The existing fragmentation of jurisdiction is mainly an accident or series of accidents of history, but part of the explanation, and an impediment to radical reorganization, is the Constitution. Not only does the Constitution divide legislative jurisdiction over family law in the ways already discussed in this chapter, it also imposes restraints on the kinds of courts which can be invested with jurisdiction to determine family disputes.

(b) Federal courts

Section 101 of the Constitution Act, 1867 confers on the federal Parliament the power to establish federal courts. This power has been exercised by the establishment of the Federal Court of Canada, but the Federal Court has not been given any significant jurisdiction in family matters. Section 101 of the Constitution Act, 1867 limits federally established courts to the adjudication of issues governed by federal law. Since much substantive family law is outside federal legislative competence, no federal court could in any event be given an extensive family jurisdiction. Any court exercising comprehensive family jurisdiction would have to be a provincial court.

(c) Provincial courts invested by province

Section 92(14) of the Constitution Act, 1867 confers on the provincial Legislatures the power to make laws in relation to "the administration of justice in the province, including the constitution, maintenance, and organization of provincial courts". Provincial courts established under this provision are not confined to issues governed by provincial law; they may be given jurisdiction to administer federal as well as provincial law. However, s. 96 (and the associated judicature sections) of the Constitution Act, 1867 do impose limits on the power of the provincial Legislatures to invest provincial courts with jurisdiction. It has been decided that s. 96 implicitly stipulates that a province may not vest in an inferior court (that is, a court which is not a superior, district or county court) a jurisdiction analogous to that exercised by a superior, district or county court.

Most of what we now regard as family law has come into existence since confederation, and as the provincial Legislatures have created new bodies of law they have tended to vest adjudicatory power in the inferior courts in the province. In the *Adoption Reference* (1938), the Supreme Court of Canada had to determine the constitutionality of provincial statutes which vested in inferior courts powers to grant adoptions, to award "maintenance" to deserted wives and children, to make affiliation orders and award maintenance for illegitimate children and to make orders for the care of children in need of protection. Duff C.J., for the Court, upheld each of these jurisdictions as "broadly conform[ing] to a type of jurisdiction generally exercisable by courts of summary jurisdiction rather than the jurisdiction exercised by courts within the purview of s. 96". In *Re B.C. Family Relations Act [Ontario (Attorney General) v. Canada (Attorney General)*, [1982] 3 W.W.R. 1 (S.C.C.)], the Supreme Court of Canada held that, since a province could confer on an inferior court jurisdiction over adoption, it could also confer jurisdiction over guardianship and custody, which were "lesser rungs" on the ladder of family relationships. These two decisions of the Supreme Court of Canada establish that most family law can be administered by inferior courts. Of course, the powers upheld in the two cases could also be vested in a s. 96 court if a province wished to follow that route. All that the two cases decide is that there is no fetter on the provincial competence to confer those powers.

There are still some matters of family law that, although within provincial legislative competence, must be vested in a s. 96 court. In *Re B.C. Family Relations Act*, the Court, while upholding the jurisdiction over guardianship and custody (as related above), struck down an attempt to confer on the inferior court jurisdiction over occupancy of (and access to) the family residence. That jurisdiction could be conferred only on a s. 96 court, because of its impact on proprietary rights and its similarity to injunctive relief. This decision shows that a unified family court really has to be established at the level of a superior, district or county court (so that it is a s. 96 court).

(d) Provincial courts invested by Dominion

There is no doubt that jurisdiction to grant a divorce decree, and probably relief ancillary to a divorce decree, may be conferred by the provincial Legislatures only on a s. 96 court. But, because the substantive law of divorce is within federal legislative authority, the federal Parliament also has the power to invest courts with divorce jurisdiction. Moreover, s. 96 and the associated sections of the Constitution Act, 1867 do not apply to federal courts and tribunals. Therefore, the federal Parliament could if it chose confer divorce jurisdiction on a federally established court or tribunal which did not satisfy the rules stipulated by ss. 96 to 100. [In a footnote, Professor Hogg indicates that, as a result of *McEvoy v. New Brunswick (Attorney General)*, [1983] 1 S.C.R. 704, Parliament probably could not confer divorce jurisdiction on a provincially established court or tribunal that did not satisfy ss. 96 to 100.]

The federal Parliament has in fact chosen to confer divorce jurisdiction on the superior court in each province. ...

NOTES AND QUESTIONS

1. In *Kunkel v. Kunkel* (1994), 2 R.F.L. (4th) 1 (Alta. C.A.); additional reasons at (1994), 8 R.F.L. (4th) 225 (Alta. C.A.), the parties divorced in 1985 and the mother was granted custody of their son. The father was ordered to pay child support under the *Divorce Act*. The mother remarried and her new husband adopted the child. A

majority of the Alberta Court of Appeal held that the father's obligation to pay child support ended when the adoption occurred even though there had been no variation of the order. Hetherington J.A. stated (at 9):

> [I]t is an implied term of every order for corollary relief under the *Divorce Act* that it is not final, and that if circumstances change, it may be superseded by an order of any court having jurisdiction, whether under the *Divorce Act*, a provincial statute, or the *parens patriae* jurisdiction of the court. For example, if a court granted an adoption order or a wardship order under provincial legislation, and that order was inconsistent with a prior order under the *Divorce Act*, the adoption order or wardship order would supersede the order for corollary relief.

This approach has not been extended to applications for custody, access or support under provincial legislation when there is already an existing order dealing with these matters under the *Divorce Act*.

2. In *Lewkoski v. Lewkoski* (1998), 40 R.F.L. (4th) 86 (Ont. Gen. Div.), the court confirmed that it had jurisdiction to issue a child support order under the *Divorce Act* even though a final order had been made under provincial legislation. However, the court added that it had a discretion not to exercise this jurisdiction and would do so only because this would be in the child's best interests. See also *Schaff v. Schaff* (1997), 30 R.F.L. (4th) 63 (B.C. C.A.).

(b) The *Charter*

The *Canadian Charter of Rights and Freedoms*, which is Part I of the *Constitution Act, 1982*, became part of the Constitution of Canada in 1982. By virtue of s. 52(1) of the *Constitution Act, 1982* any law that is inconsistent with the *Charter* "is, to the extent of the inconsistency, of no force or effect". Therefore, the *Charter* can be used to challenge a law dealing with family matters on the basis that the law infringes or denies a guaranteed freedom or right. Sections 7 and 15 predictably have been the most commonly used *Charter* provisions in a family law context.

Section 7 specifies: "[e]veryone has the right to life, liberty and security of the person and the right not to be deprived thereof except in accordance with the principles of fundamental justice". It could be argued that "liberty and security of the person" encompasses many aspects of family life and that any law or other government action that affects those aspects must accord with the "principles of fundamental justice".

Section 15(1) provides that "[e]very individual is equal before and under the law and has the right to the equal protection and equal benefit of the law without discrimination and, in particular, without discrimination based on race, national or ethnic origin, colour, religion, sex, age or mental or physical disability". In *Law v. Canada (Minister of Employment & Immigration)*, [1999] 1 S.C.R. 497, the Supreme Court of Canada suggested a framework for determining whether a law or other government action violates s. 15(1) that focuses on three central issues: whether the law or other government action imposes differential treatment between the claimant and others; whether that treatment is based on a personal characteristic listed in s. 15(1) or an analogous ground; and whether the purpose or effect of the challenged law is discriminatory. To determine whether a law is discriminatory, the Court stressed that the purpose of s. 15(1) is to "prevent the violation of human dignity" by eliminating the attribution of "stereotypical characteristics to individuals". To assess whether a law violates human dignity, the Court indicated that four contextual factors should be examined: (1) pre-existing disadvantage, stereotyping or vulnerability of the claimant or the group at issue; (2) extent to which the law takes into account the actual need, capacity or circumstances of the claimant or group; (3) any ameliorative purpose or effect of the law; and (4) the nature and scope of the interest affected.

More recently, in *R. v. Kapp* (2008), 294 D.L.R. (4th) 1 (S.C.C.), McLachlin C.J.C. and Abella J., speaking for the Court on this point, restated the test for the application of s. 15(1):

17 ... *Law* ... established in essence a two-part test for showing discrimination under s. 15(1): (1) Does the law create a distinction based on an enumerated or analogous ground? (2) Does the distinction create a disadvantage by perpetuating prejudice or stereotyping? These were divided, in *Law*, into three steps, but in our view the test is, in substance, the same.

[18] In *Andrews [v. Law Society of British Columbia*, [1989] 1 S.C.R. 143], McIntyre J. viewed discriminatory impact through the lens of two concepts: (1) the perpetuation of prejudice or disadvantage to members of a group on the basis of personal characteristics identified in the enumerated and analogous grounds; and (2) stereotyping on the basis of these grounds that results in a decision that does not correspond to a claimant's or group's actual circumstances and characteristics.

[19] A decade later, in *Law*, this Court suggested that discrimination should be defined in terms of the impact of the law or program on the "human dignity" of members of the claimant group, having regard to four contextual factors: (1) pre-existing disadvantage, if any, of the claimant group; (2) degree of correspondence between the differential treatment and the claimant group's reality; (3) whether the law or program has an ameliorative purpose or effect; and (4) the nature of the interest affected. ...

[20] The achievement of *Law* was its success in unifying what had become, since *Andrews*, a division in this Court's approach to s. 15. *Law* accomplished this by reiterating and confirming *Andrews'* interpretation of s. 15 as a guarantee of substantive, and not just formal, equality. Moreover, *Law* made an important contribution to our understanding of the conceptual underpinnings of substantive equality.

[21] At the same time, several difficulties have arisen from the attempt in *Law* to employ human dignity *as a legal test*. There can be no doubt that human dignity is an essential value underlying the s. 15 equality guarantee. In fact, the protection of all of the rights guaranteed by the *Charter* has as its lodestar the promotion of human dignity. ...

[22] But as critics have pointed out, human dignity is an abstract and subjective notion that, even with the guidance of the four contextual factors, cannot only become confusing and difficult to apply; it has also proven to be an *additional* burden on equality claimants, rather than the philosophical enhancement it was intended to be. Criticism has also accrued for the way *Law* has allowed the formalism of some of the Court's post-*Andrews* jurisprudence to resurface in the form of an artificial comparator analysis focussed on treating likes alike.

[23] The analysis in a particular case, as *Law* itself recognizes, more usefully focuses on the factors that identify impact amounting to discrimination. The four factors cited in *Law* are based on and relate to the identification in *Andrews* of perpetuation of disadvantage and stereotyping as the primary indicators of discrimination. Pre-existing disadvantage and the nature of the interest affected (factors one and four in *Law*) go to perpetuation of disadvantage and prejudice, while the second factor deals with stereotyping. The ameliorative purpose or effect of a law or program (the third factor in *Law*) goes to whether the purpose is remedial within the meaning of s. 15(2). (We would suggest, without deciding here, that the third *Law* factor might also be relevant to the question under s. 15(1) as to whether the effect of the law or program is to perpetuate disadvantage.)

[24] Viewed in this way, *Law* does not impose a new and distinctive test for discrimination, but rather affirms the approach to substantive equality under s. 15 set out in *Andrews* and developed in numerous subsequent decisions. The factors cited in *Law* should not be read literally as if they were legislative dispositions, but as a way of focussing on the central concern of s. 15 identified in *Andrews* — combatting discrimination, defined in terms of perpetuating disadvantage and stereotyping.

[25] The central purpose of combatting discrimination, as discussed, underlies both s. 15(1) and s. 15(2). Under s. 15(1), the focus is on *preventing* governments from making distinctions based on the enumerated or analogous grounds that have the effect of perpetuating group disadvantage and prejudice or impose disadvantage on the basis of stereotyping. Under s. 15(2), the focus is on *enabling* governments to pro-actively combat existing discrimination through affirmative measures.

Even where a claimant can establish that a law or other government action affects a right or freedom guaranteed by the Charter, there will be no violation if the government can convince a court that s. 1 applies. Section 1 stipulates: "The *Canadian Charter of Rights and Freedoms* guarantees the rights and freedoms set out in it subject only to such reasonable limits prescribed by law as can be demonstrably justified in a free and democratic society". The leading case on the application of s. 1 is still *R. v. Oakes*, [1986] 1 S.C.R. 103, 50 C.R. (3d) 1, although the "Oakes Test" has been modified slightly by later cases. There are two broad inquiries. First, is the objective underlying the law or other government action pressing and substantial in a free and democratic society? Second, if so, are the means chosen to achieve this objective reasonable in the sense that they are proportionate? The second inquiry has three elements or branches. Are the means rationally connected to the objective? Is the impairment of the right or freedom reasonably necessary to achieve the objective? Finally, does the objective outweigh the deleterious impact and do the benefits outweigh the deleterious effects? A negative answer to any of these three questions resolves the matter in favour of the challenging party. While, in theory, any limitation on the rights and freedoms protected by the *Charter* can be justified under s. 1, limits on the rights protected by ss. 7 and 15 are rarely upheld.

The potential impact of the *Charter* was dramatically exhibited in *R. v. Morgentaler*, [1988] 1 S.C.R. 30, 62 C.R. (3d) 1, where the Supreme Court of Canada, in a five-to-two decision, struck down s. 251 of the *Criminal Code*, which restricted the circumstances in which an abortion could legally be performed. Canadian courts have also applied the *Charter* to the body of law traditionally referred to as family law, most notably in child protection proceedings and in cases challenging the limitation of familial rights and obligations to married persons or to opposite-sex couples. The leading cases are examined, and often reproduced in part, in later chapters of this book. The following helps to set the background.

BALA, "THE *CHARTER OF RIGHTS* & FAMILY LAW IN CANADA: A NEW ERA"

(2000-2001), 18 C.F.L.Q. 372 (Footnotes omitted)

Introduction

After the *Charter of Rights* came into force in 1982, academic commentators predicted that the Canadian courts would follow American jurisprudence, where there has been a long history of using the Constitution to recognize and protect a broad range familial rights. And soon after the *Charter* came into effect, governments were pressured by litigation, or the threat of litigation, to revise a few family law statutes that obviously discriminated on the basis of gender, in particular against fathers of children born out of wedlock, and to end some of the most blatant types of legal discrimination against children born out of wedlock. A few trial judgments recognized that a child-protection agency exercises a broad set of state powers that can dramatically affect the lives of children and parents, and hence should be subject to *Charter* regulation. However, until recently, decisions from the higher courts dismissed arguments that spousal, parental or other familial relationships were entitled to constitutional recognition and protection, making the *Charter of Rights* essentially an academic curiosity for family law judges and practitioners.

The 1999 Supreme Court of Canada decisions in *M v. H* and *New Brunswick (Minister of Health & Community Services) v. G. (J.)* mark a dramatic change in judicial approach. The Supreme Court has recognized that familial relationships are of fundamental importance and worthy of constitutional recognition and protection. The decision in *M v. H* [[1999] 2 S.C.R. 3, 46 R.F.L. (4th) 32; reproduced in part in Chapter 6, *SPOUSAL SUPPORT*] recognized that denying same-sex partners the statutory rights afforded to unmarried heterosexual partners at the end of a relationship is unjustified discrimination on the basis of sexual orientation. More recently some decisions have invoked section 15 of the *Charter* to extend to unmarried opposite-sex partners the same statutory rights as legally married individuals at the end of long term relationships. The courts are clearly requiring a fundamental rethinking of the legal significance of "spousal" status in Canada. [However, the Supreme Court of Canada held in *Walsh v. Bona* (2002), 32 R.F.L. (5th) 81, that some differential treatment between married couples and unmarried ones is not discriminatory. In particular, the court concluded that a province's matrimonial property regime can be limited to married couples. This decision is reproduced in part in Chapter 4, *FAMILY PROPERTY.*]

In *New Brunswick (Minister of Health & Community Services) v. G. (J.)* [[1999] 3 S.C.R. 13, 50 R.F.L. (4th) 63, reproduced in part in Chapter 10, *CHILD IN NEED OF PROTECTION*], the Supreme Court recognized that child-protection proceedings pose a fundamental threat to the "security of the person" of parents and their children, and hence must be conducted in accordance with "the principles of fundamental justice." This decision dealt with the right of indigent parents to a lawyer paid by the state, but it will affect how courts deal with a range of issues in child protection and adoption proceedings, and has implications for other types of family law proceedings. ...

One important introductory point needs to be made: to successfully invoke the *Charter* in a family law case, it is essential to have a sympathetic factual context, either in terms of the general issues raised or the specific litigant before the court, or preferably both. In some areas of law, most notably in the criminal context, judges are prepared to protect constitutional rights in quite unsympathetic fact situations, allowing those who appear to be guilty of murder to be discharged if there is a serious *Charter* violation. In the family law area, especially when the interests of children are involved, it is clear that judges are only willing to invoke the *Charter* if the specific facts or the general context of this type of case suggests that this is likely "the right thing to do." The courts are only willing to use the *Charter* in the family law cases to promote human dignity or social justice, or to promote the interests of children.

Charter Challenges: Theory and Practice

It is now clear that family law judges and practitioners need to know about the *Charter of Rights* and its implications for litigants. Arguably a lawyer who fails to inform a client of a potential *Charter* challenge that might improve the client's position is professionally negligent. However, for a variety of practical reasons, not all of those with potential *Charter* challenges will want to proceed with them.

Most jurisdictions require the applicant to give the relevant Attorney General or Minister of Justice notice of any case raising a constitutional question, in order to allow the statute in question to be defended by the government, potentially adding another opponent and expense. If the challenge is successful at trial, the government is more likely to appeal than other litigants, and intervenors may seek to join in the appeal, adding further to complexity and expense. Cases that raise *Charter* issues are also more likely to receive publicity, which many litigants would rather avoid.

Although there are some special programs and advocacy groups or clinics that may be of assistance with some *Charter* challenges, a *Charter* challenge can be a major financial burden. There are many cases in which the client, or counsel, must carry the case without special assistance, though even partial success in *Charter* challenges is invariably recognized in an award of costs. In some cases, the *Charter* may be invoked to seek a remedy on a case-specific basis, without directly challenging the validity of legislation, which may make the case less complex and expensive. ...

Protecting Parent-Child Relationships

There are few instances of more dramatic state interference with individual and familial autonomy than in child protection proceedings, in which agents of the state have broad powers to enter premises, apprehend children from their homes, and terminate profoundly important relationships. In the first decade that the *Charter* was in effect there were some trial judges who were prepared to subject this type of state action to constitutional scrutiny, but the appeal courts focused on the fact that this type of proceeding is *intended* to protect children and promote their welfare, and refused to find that constitutional issues are engaged. The Supreme Court of Canada in its 1999 decision in *New Brunswick v. G. (J.)* clearly accepted that child protection proceedings affect vitally important aspects of "security of the person" and under section 7 of the *Charter* must be conducted "in accordance with the principles of fundamental justice." This decision has broader implications for other proceedings that affect the parent-child relationship. ...

A number of American decisions have accepted that apprehending a child by the protection authorities raises constitutional issues. American cases have held that a warrantless search of premises for and apprehension of a child may be justifiable to protect children from the threat of abuse or neglect. This includes the right to a visual inspection of an unclothed young child by a child protection worker to inspect for bruises. However, if without court authorization there is to be this type of intrusive intervention in the lives of parents and children, the child protection worker must have "reasonable grounds" for believing that there is a situation of "urgency" that poses a risk to a child. ...

The Supreme Court of Canada, in its October 2000 decision in *Winnipeg Child & Family Services (Central Area) v. W. (K.L.)* [(2000), 10 R.F.L. (5th) 122, 191 D.L.R. (4th) 1, reproduced in Chapter 10, *CHILD IN NEED OF PROTECTION*], considered a case challenging the constitutional validity of Manitoba child welfare legislation, which permits warrantless apprehensions in non-emergency situations. By a five to two margin, the Court upheld the legislation. Writing for the majority, L'Heureux-Dubé J. concluded that a parent's right to security of the person is infringed by the legislation, but that the law accords with the principles of fundamental justice because procedural fairness is satisfied by requiring a post-apprehension judicial review. When balancing the various interests at stake in the child protection context, she placed pre-eminent importance on society's interest in protecting children from abuse and neglect, emphasizing the difficulty and risk of distinguishing, in her view, between emergency and non-emergency situations in child protection cases. ...

While majority and dissent in *Winnipeg Child & Family Services v. W. (K.L.)* clearly disagreed about how to weigh potential risks and benefits to a child of apprehension and intervention by the child welfare authorities, it is apparent that, in principle, both took similar approaches to determining whether the rules governing intervention are constitutionally justifiable. The entire Supreme Court recognized that state intervention must "accord with the principles of fundamental justice", and that any constraint on the rights of parents and children to enjoy a relationship with each other will be assessed against a standard of whether it serves to promote the interests of children. ...

Conclusion: A New Era for Family Law

Canada is now going through a process of constitutionalizing family law, a couple of decades later than the United States. Interestingly, in some respects, especially in terms of recognizing rights for same-sex partners and unmarried heterosexual partners, the Canadian courts have, in the past couple of years, already gone significantly further than the American courts in using the constitution to promote familial rights.

As in the United States, it is likely that the "core" of divorce litigation and family law ... in Canada will not be directly affected by these constitutional developments. However, it is now clear that family law practitioners, judges, academics and policy makers in Canada will have to consider the *Charter* implications of the issues with which they are dealing. The impact of the *Charter* is likely to be greatest in the child protection and adoption fields, as well as for issues involving those outside of traditional marital relationships.

There has been significant criticism of the judiciary, especially the Supreme Court of Canada, for being too activist, and usurping the role of politicians, especially when dealing with contentious familial issues like abortion, same-sex relationships, and unmarried heterosexual cohabitation. In my view, Canadian politicians have often been reluctant to deal with these contentious issues, and many politicians have been quietly content to let the courts make difficult decisions. Public attitudes towards many of these issues have been changing over time, in part influenced by the decisions of the courts. Public attitudes towards same-sex relationships have been influenced by the rights-based discourse inherent in the judicial process, and there may be more support among members of the Canadian public than among politicians for using the *Charter* to recognize the equality of gay and lesbian relationships. ...

NOTES AND QUESTIONS

1. Perhaps the most revolutionary change initiated by *Charter* litigation involves the recognition of same-sex marriage. This litigation and the legislative changes it has spawned are explored in Chapter 2, *CREATING A VALID MARRIAGE*, where portions of *Halpern v. Toronto (City)* (2003), 36 R.F.L. (5th) 127 (Ont. C.A.) and *Re Same-Sex Marriage* (2004), 12 R.F.L. (6th) 153, 246 D.L.R. (4th) 193 (S.C.C.) are reproduced.

2. In "The Impact of the Charter of Rights and Freedoms on Canadian Family Law" (2000), 17 Can. J. Fam. L. 293, Professor Boyd argues (at 293):

> [T]he Charter has been invoked indirectly to argue that, even in the absence of the required element of government or state action, judges must nevertheless in this situation take into account the fundamental values (such as equality) that are enshrined in the Charter. ... This last aspect is important because many areas of family law involve the exercise of judicial discretion regarding the interpretation of concepts that originated in common law. Indeed, family law is a field that arguably involves more indeterminative normative concepts and standards than many areas of law that are embodied in statutes. For example, judicial interpretation of the "best interests of the child" standard in child custody statutes is known to produce results that vary enormously. The relationship between the Charter and judicial discretion in relation to such concepts has been unclear and the Supreme Court of Canada remains divided on this issue.

3. Harvison-Young notes in "The Changing Family, Rights Discourse and the Supreme Court of Canada" (2001), 80 Can. Bar Rev. 749 at 752 (footnotes omitted):

> The increased profile of family law as an important aspect of the [Supreme] Court's docket cannot be separated from the influence of the *Charter* and the rise of rights discourse in Canada. In this respect, family law serves as a fascinating microcosm of the effect that this constitutional change has had and is having on our law and social fabric. While it would be wrong to understate the impact that the *Charter* has had on family law and its place in the Supreme Court, overstating its impact would also lead one to ignore the fact that significant changes were underway before the *Charter* came into effect. As we review the evolution — and sometimes even revolutionary evolution — of family law over the last number of years we will see that the *Charter* has played a crucial and profound role in directly changing certain aspects of the law. This has been particularly true with respect to the definition of the family, where certain principles, and especially equality, have played an even broader and [more] pervasive role beyond the direct reach of the *Charter* in areas such as spousal support, domestic abuse, and reproductive rights. In fact, the Supreme Court has been cautious about the application of an individualistic rights discourse in family law and, apart from the "family definition" cases, few *Charter* challenges have been ultimately successful.

Later in the article she writes (at 769 and 778):

> By the end of the last decade and the beginning of this new millennium, the notion of the family has changed dramatically and the Supreme Court has led the way in the most important of these changes. ... At the end of the day (so far), and somewhat ironically, the impact of the principles developed pursuant to the *Charter* has been greatest in the non-*Charter* jurisprudence, and almost entirely relat-

ing to section 15 and the principle of equality. The great exception to this has taken place at the end of the decade — the *Charter* cases addressing the very nature and definition of the family itself. ...

... We can draw a few conclusions about the application of rights discourse to family law ... First, neither the law of custody/access nor the laws of child protection has been fundamentally affected by the direct application of the *Charter* in the way that other areas such as criminal law have. In *Young* and *P. (D.)*, the [Supreme] Court was unwilling to apply the *Charter* directly to the best interest [of the child] standard. Though the *Charter* does directly apply to child protection, *B. (R.)* and *K.L.W.* indicate that it is not likely to change the *substance* of the sorts of decisions made concerning the protection of children by child protection agencies and courts. The change brought by the *Charter* is the clear requirement for the state to justify its intervention and the [procedures it uses].

The decisions in *Young v. Young* (1993), 49 R.F.L. (3d) 117 (S.C.C.), and *Droit de la famille — 1150* (1993), 49 R.F.L. (3d) 317 (S.C.C.) are examined in Chapter 7, *CUSTODY AND ACCESS*, while the decisions in *B. (R.) v. Children's Aid Society of Metropolitan Toronto* (1995), 9 R.F.L. (4th) 157 (S.C.C.) and *Winnipeg Child & Family Services (Central Area) v. W. (K.L.)* (2000), 10 R.F.L. (5th) 122 (S.C.C.) are analyzed in Chapter 10, *CHILD IN NEED OF PROTECTION*.

(3) Institutional Framework

A NOTE ON THE COURT STRUCTURE

Historically, matters of family law were adjudicated by several different courts, some with provincially appointed judges and some with federally appointed ones. For years, commentators have noted the problems caused by this fragmented court system and advocated the creation of a Unified Family Court with jurisdiction to hear all family law matters. See Law Reform Commission of Canada, *Family Law Court, Working Paper #1* (Toronto: Ministry of the Attorney General, 1974); Ontario Law Reform Commission, *Report on Family Law, Part V: Family Courts* (Toronto: Ministry of the Attorney General, 1974); and Weisman, "On Unified Family Courts" (1985), 42 R.F.L. (2d) 270.

Because s. 96 of the *Constitution Act, 1867* implicitly prevents a province from conferring upon a provincially appointed judge a jurisdiction analogous to that exercised by a superior, district or county court in 1867, any Unified Family Court must be presided over by a federally appointed judge. Therefore, federal and provincial governments must co-operate in order to create a Unified Family Court.

In Ontario, a Unified Family Court was established in the judicial district of Hamilton-Wentworth in 1977. To deal with the problems created by s. 96 of the *Constitution Act, 1867*, judges of the Unified Family Court were appointed by concurrent action of the provincial and federal governments. A set of rules developed to provide for simplified procedures and for conciliation and mediation. Further, the Unified Family Court worked closely with other social agencies of the province. In *Report of the Ontario Courts Inquiry* (Toronto: Ministry of the Attorney General, 1987), the Honourable T.G. Zuber concluded (at 99):

> The Unified Family Court of Hamilton-Wentworth is working well and has worked for the benefit of the people it serves for the past ten years. It is therefore apparent that the concept of the unified family court is not only good in theory; it is good in practice.

Mr. Justice Zuber recommended that there should be a Unified Family Court for the province of Ontario as part of the provincial court system. He acknowledged (at 102) that this would require a constitutional amendment to permit the province to appoint judges with full power to deal with family law matters. This was not, however, the model that was adopted.

In 1994 the Ontario Legislature amended the *Courts of Justice Act* to create a branch of the Ontario Court (General Division) (now the Superior Court of Justice) known as the Family Court (S.O. 1994, c. 12, s. 8). The Unified Family Court was amalgamated with and continued as part of the Family Court. The Family Court has jurisdiction in the Regional Municipality of Hamilton-Wentworth and in the additional areas named by proclamation of the Lieutenant Governor in Council. In the fall of 1995, Family Courts began to operate in London, Newmarket, Kingston, and Napanee. By 2005, those courts also existed in twelve other centers in the province including Ottawa. As a branch of the Superior Court of Justice, the Family Court is a s. 96 court with federally appointed and federally paid judges. The amendments to the *Courts of Justice Act* provided for the establishment of a "community resources committee" to "develop links between the court and social services resources available in the community, identify needed resources and develop strategies for putting them in place" and also stipulated that an alternative dispute resolution service "may be established, maintained and operated as part of the Family Court".

Under the *Courts of Justice Act*, where a Family Court exists, most issues that arise in the context of what would commonly be labeled a "family dispute" fall within its exclusive jurisdiction. That court deals with, *inter alia*, annulments, divorces, property issues, custody and access disputes, and requests for spousal and child support. It also has exclusive jurisdiction over child protection and adoption issues. It does not, however, have jurisdiction under the federal *Youth and Criminal Justice Act*. That jurisdiction is exercised by the Ontario Court of Justice. See ss. 21.8 and 21.9 of the *Courts of Justice Act* and the Schedule to that Act for a complete picture of the Family Court's jurisdiction.

While Family Courts exist in many Ontario centres, most judicial districts do not have one. In those districts, the fragmented court system continues and jurisdiction over family law matters is distributed between the Superior Court of Justice and the Ontario Court of Justice. The Superior Court of Justice has exclusive jurisdiction to deal with annulments, divorces, property issues, and corollary relief on divorce. The Ontario Court of Justice has exclusive jurisdiction over child protection and adoption issues. Where applications for support and custody and access are brought under provincial legislation, the two courts have concurrent jurisdiction.

Fortunately, since the late 1990s, the same procedural rules generally apply to all family law cases in the Family Court, the Superior Court, and the Ontario Court of Justice. The following note describes the procedure that applies in family law litigation in Ontario.

A NOTE ON PROCEDURE IN FAMILY LAW LITIGATION

Procedure in family law matters in Ontario is governed by a unique set of rules that apply specifically to family law litigation. Knowing a little about the process of a family law case is helpful to students as they study substantive family law.

Pursuant to Rule 1(2) of the *Family Law Rules* ("the FLR"), all family law cases in the Ontario Superior Court of Justice, Family Branch; the Ontario Superior Court of Justice; and the Ontario Court of Justice are governed by one set of rules. The FLR have a stated prime objective in Rule 2(2): "The primary objective of these rules is to enable the court to deal with cases justly." Rule 2 goes on to say that judges must "promote the primary objective by active management of cases", including helping the parties identify the issues, encouraging alternative dispute resolution, helping parties to settle, setting timetables, and controlling the progress of a case. The FLR clearly aim to expedite the process. However, as discussed below, sometimes that objective is undermined by the rules themselves and by a shortage of judicial resources.

Under the FLR, cases are commenced by application if there has never been an order made on the issues before the court. If there has been a previous court order, they are started by a notice of motion to vary. In either case, the next step, after pleadings have been served and filed, is normally a Case Conference, held pursuant to Rule 17.

Case Conferences

A Case Conference is a mandatory meeting between the parties, counsel and (in most cases) a judge. Prior to the Conference, each party must serve and file a brief in the format specified by the Family Law Forms. The briefs do not form part of the court record and are returned to the parties following the conference. This is to encourage parties to consider settlement options in a way that will not bind them later on if the litigation continues. Rule 17(4) of the FLR specifies that the purposes of the Case Conference are to:

a) explore the chances of settling the case;

b) identify the issues that are in dispute and those that are not in dispute;

c) explore ways to resolve the issues that are in dispute;

d) ensure disclosure of the relevant evidence;

e) note admissions that may simplify the case;

f) set the date for the next step in the case;

g) have the parties agree, if possible, to a specific timetable for the steps to be taken in the case before it comes to trial;

h) give directions with respect to any intended motion, including the preparation of a specific timetable for the exchange of material for the motion and ordering the filing of summaries of argument, if appropriate; and

i) organize a settlement conference, or hold one immediately if appropriate.

Rule 17(9) states that Case Conferences may be held before a person who is not a judge, but who has been named by the appropriate senior judge to hold Case Conferences unless one of the parties insists that a judge hear the conference. Most Case Conferences are held in front of judges.

Case Conferences tend to be informal appearances. Some judges hold them in their offices, not in the courtroom. Others hold the conferences in the courtroom, but at a table around which all of the parties, counsel, and the judge are seated. The conversation tends to be direct, and the parties are often encouraged to speak to the judge rather than having counsel speak for them. The thrust of Rule 17 is that the parties are to be encouraged, with the help of the court, to come to an early settlement without protracted litigation.

Rule 17(8) empowers the court to make certain specific orders at a Case Conference:

a) orders relating to disclosure or questioning (discoveries), filing of summaries or argument on a motion, times for events in the case, directions for the next steps to be taken in the case, or the possibility that evidence of a witness at trial be given by affidavit;

b) if notice has been served, a temporary or final order;

c) consent or unopposed orders; and

d) on consent, orders referring any issue for alternative dispute resolution.

In practice, most judges restrict the making of orders at a Case Conference to consent matters. This is because orders are most often made on the basis of evidence, either oral or written. At a Case Conference, the parties have filed briefs, but have not usually provided sworn evidence. As is discussed in several chapters in this book, temporary orders in family law matters often establish a *status quo* which may prejudice the final outcome (see, in particular, Chapter 5, *THE FAMILY HOME* and Chapter 7, *CUSTODY AND ACCESS*).

Judges are well aware of this and customarily want any temporary order to be supported by evidence to ensure a fair outcome to both parties.

A Case Conference is the door through which the litigants must ordinarily pass before they can take any other steps in the case. As a general rule, no substantive motion for temporary (interim) relief can be served or heard until a Case Conference has been held: Rule 14(4). However, Rule 14(4.2) exempts situations of urgency and hardship, as well as entirely procedural motions, and other specified motions (such as contempt and summary judgment). Courts have interpreted "urgency and hardship" very strictly: *Hood v. Hood* (2001), 20 R.F.L. (5th) 78 (Ont. S.C.J.). Support issues, for example, have been held not to be "urgent" within the meaning of the Rule unless the financial consequences are "dire": *Rosen v. Rosen* (2005), [2005] O.J. No. 62, 2005 CarswellOnt 68 (S.C.J.) and *Hyde v. Szabo* (2007), [2007] O.J. No. 4227, 2007 CarswellOnt 7000 (S.C.J.).

Mandatory Case Conferences are controversial in some quarters, mainly because they often delay temporary or interim relief. Once an application is issued, the respondent has 30 days to serve and file an Answer. The court clerk then sets a Case Conference date. In many Ontario jurisdictions, particularly in larger centres, it can take a further 60 to 90 days before the Case Conference is held. After the Case Conference, parties are free to bring a motion; but, if the hearing of the motion is going to take longer than 1 hour, the parties are required (in most jurisdictions) to book a special motion date (a "date for a long motion"), pursuant to the Practice Direction of the Chief Justice of the Ontario Superior Court of August 26, 2005. Regular weekly motion dates are to be used for short matters only, such as removing a lawyer from the record or consent matters. Obtaining a long motion date can take months. In *Oliviera v. Cardozo* (2008), 2008 CarswellOnt 7722 (S.C.J.), Justice Corbett took note of the systemic delay that the combination of the Rules and under-resourced courts can produce:

> The court understands why counsel try to jam "long" motions into a "regular" motions list. It may take two or three months to get a long motions date. But counsel should understand that mischaracterizing their motion may lead to greater delay: the regular motions judge may well adjourn the motion to a long motions date, and as a result the parties will be delayed an extra week or two in their process. Or counsel may persuade the judge to proceed and find the court reserving judgment, as happened in this case. In this case the reserve has been lengthy, far outweighing any delay that might have resulted from proceeding by way of long motion in the first place. If this matter had proceeded by way of long motion, I expect there would not have been a reserve. Why the difference? On a long motions list there is usually one or two motions. The judge usually has at least an hour, and sometimes more, to review each file ahead of time. This review time pays significant dividends during oral argument, since the judge usually has a strong grasp of the issues in dispute, and a preliminary view of where the real issues lie for decision. Counsel can be directed to those issues of concern to the court. Further, all long motions are "briefed" by clerks to assist the presiding judge.

All of this means that, in some parts of the province, no decision may be made about interim support, custody, or access for four to six months after the issuance of pleadings. In the meantime, many couples continue to cohabit in the matrimonial home. In other cases, the delay results in an accumulation of unpaid child and/or spousal support, creating a financial disadvantage for the needy spouse. At least one senior commentator has called for a review of Family Court procedure and for the appointment of more judges to the Family Court in Ontario:

> Most family law cases will settle. However, whether clients settle early or late makes a huge difference in terms of their financial welfare and emotional welfare, not to mention the crisis caused to children where cases are not promptly dealt with. The family courts need to run a front-end loaded system where there is appropriate time for case conferences, settlement conferences and sufficient time set aside to properly dispose of motions. If the system is going to work, then it needs an infusion of more personnel, particularly judges. The hard working judges in these regions simply cannot keep up. (Epstein & Madsen's "This Week in Family Law" FLNWS 2009 - 06).

Motions

After a Case Conference is held, either party is free to bring a motion for temporary relief. A motion is a request to the court for a temporary (formerly known as "interim") order. A temporary order is meant to provide a short-term resolution of the issue until trial.

Motions are heard on the basis of sworn affidavit evidence. Only in rare cases will oral evidence be used on a motion, and then only with the judge's consent: Rule 14(17). Rule 14(2) provides that the moving party must provide all of the evidence for use on the motion in his or her affidavit. The responding party must provide all of his or her evidence in the responding affidavit. The moving party may then provide a supplementary affidavit, responding to any new issue raised by the respondent. The supplementary affidavit may not raise any new issues. This rule prevents parties from filing a series of affidavits for use on a motion.

Temporary orders made on motion are enforceable in the same manner as final orders. All enforcement mechanisms in the Rules can be employed to enforce them.

Motions are most often heard "on notice", meaning that the opposing party has been properly served with the notice of motion and the evidence supporting the motion. In some cases, however, there is no time to serve the other party, because an order is urgently required. In others, there are safety or security reasons why the other party should not be given advance notice of the motion pending before the court. As you read Chapter 5, *THE FAMILY HOME*, and Chapter 7, *CUSTODY AND ACCESS*, you will note that some of the decisions were made on the basis of only one party appearing. Prior to the advent of the FLR, such motions were called "*ex parte*" motions (meaning motions made without the other party). The FLR have eliminated Latin terms, but Latin still appears in older cases or occasionally in decisions made by older judges. The FLR provide for motions to be made without notice in Rule 14(12). Under it, motions may be made without notice if:

a) the nature or circumstances of the motion make notice unnecessary or not reasonably possible;

b) there is an immediate danger of a child's removal from Ontario, and the delay involved in serving a notice of motion would probably have serious consequences;

c) there is an immediate danger to the health or safety of a child or of the party making the motion, and the delay involved in serving a notice of motion would probably have serious consequences; or

d) service of a notice of motion would probably have serious consequences.

Rule 14(14) provides that any order made on motion without notice "shall" require the matter to come back to the court and, if possible, to the same judge for a review within 14 days or on a date chosen by the court so that the opposing party has an opportunity to make his or her case. Rule 14(15) requires the opposing party to be served immediately with the order made without notice and with all documents used on the motion, unless the court orders otherwise. This Rule gives the court a wide discretion to determine what information is to be served on an opposing party on a motion without notice. Parties to any litigation are generally entitled to a copy of all of the information that the court is given so that they can meet the case against them. Where a party's safety is at risk, however, certain information such as the address or location of a party or the children may be removed from the material sent to the responding party: *Barrios v. Barrios* (2007), 43 R.F.L. (6th) 302 (Ont. S.C.J.).

Motions without notice are not uncommon, but judges understandably tend to be cautious in granting relief where only one side is heard. Sometimes the time between the making of the original order without notice and the hearing of the review mandated under Rule 14(14) can stretch out into months. In *N. (A.) v. W. (B.)*, 2005 ONCJ 301 (C.J.), the mother alleged that the father had sexually abused the children and brought a motion without notice for the termination of the father's access. The court granted the order. The father was served with the motion materials and the order, but he had to wait to argue his case while the Children's Aid Society investigated. The Society determined that the allegations were unfounded and the father's access was reinstated. The mother then brought a second motion without notice, again on the ground the father had sexually abused the children. Again, the order was made, and the father had to wait ten months for a full investigation to be completed before he could come back to court and argue his side of the case. The investigation again determined that the allegations were unfounded. The court reinstated the father's access a second time, even though the mother again tried to delay the reinstatement of access by insisting that the court should wait until the Children's Lawyer had completed its own investigation. Justice Wolder held that the court's job on a review under Rule 14(14) was to determine whether facts had been made out on a balance of probabilities and that, while a court should err on the side of caution when sexual abuse of children was an issue, the court was nonetheless required to make findings of fact based on evidence. Because the evidence did not support the allegation of abuse, the mother's request to suspend access was denied.

Questioning and Document Production

Rules 19 and 20 provide for document disclosure and questioning (formerly discoveries), respectively. Rule 19 provides that a party may request documentary disclosure from the other side, in the form of an affidavit listing every document that is relevant to any issue in the case and available to the other party. The FLR provide further that parties must update their list of documents if new documents come to light. Rule 19 has some strict consequences for parties who fail to produce documents as requested, including forcing documentary disclosure free of charge to the other party, striking out the party's pleadings, or dismissing his or her claim altogether. Documentary disclosure is essential to the orderly resolution of family law matters. Many documents such as income tax returns, Canada Revenue Agency Notices of Assessment, bank statements, and an expert's valuation of a pension or of real estate are frequently required as evidence in family law cases. Tardiness in producing these items can increase the expense of litigating and can further add to the already considerable delay inherent in litigation. The Supreme Court of Canada confirmed in *Leskun v. Leskun*, [2006] 1 S.C.R. 920, 34 R.F.L. (6th) 1 that non-disclosure is the "cancer of matrimonial litigation". The language is dramatic, but correct. The FLR are intended to encourage full and prompt disclosure so that matters can move forward expeditiously. Judges recognize that family law litigation costs ordinary people a great deal of money. Quick and fair resolutions benefit individual litigants, their children, and society.

Rule 20 provides for questioning on consent or, on motion, by order. Questioning under this Rule takes place in the same manner as discoveries under the *Rules of Civil Procedure*: out of court, under oath, and before a court reporter who makes a transcript. Such questioning is not common in family law matters. Most family law motions are heard, and many cases proceed to trial, without it.

Questioning can be useful, however, for gathering evidence in cases in which there are complex factual matters. It can take place on consent at any time after the pleadings are issued, but it usually occurs after the Case Conference. The judge at a Case Conference can offer guidance as to whether questioning is really necessary and whether the expense of an out of court examination is justified in the case. Counsel may agree at, or before, the Case Conference that questioning is to take place and they may even agree on the scope of the questioning. The agreement between counsel is often reduced to a consent order, most often made by the court at the Case Conference. If the parties cannot agree on whether questioning should take place, a party can bring a motion for an order for questioning after the Case Conference.

Settlement Conferences

Rule 17 provides for Settlement Conferences as well as Case Conferences. Settlement Conferences are conducted in a similar manner to Case Conferences, but there is one important distinction. Parties are required to make an offer to settle in their Settlement Conference briefs. The offer made in the briefs may be influential after the trial in the consideration of costs.

As with Case Conference briefs, Settlement Conference briefs are returned to the parties following the holding of the conference, so that they are not available in the court record to any future judge adjudicating an issue in the matter. A Settlement Conference judge is not permitted to act as trial judge in the same matter: Rule 17(24).

Trials

Trials involving family law proceed in the same manner as any other civil trial before a judge alone. There are no jury trials in family law matters. The rules of evidence are generally applied as they are in all other civil matters.

Obtaining trial dates is problematic in most jurisdictions in Ontario. Ordinarily, it can take several months from the date of request. When all of the time is added sequentially for the obtaining of conference and motion dates, in most cases, a trial will not occur for well over a year from the date of issuance of the application. In family law cases, this is a very long time to wait for the resolution of important issues such as custody, support, and possession of the matrimonial home and other property issues. This is one of the reasons that temporary orders are so important; they may cover a long period of time.

Prior to the trial, the court may hold a Trial Management Conference pursuant to Rule 17(6). The primary purpose of this conference is to organize the evidence for trial. Evidence can be adduced in written, sworn form at trial if the court so orders and, to shorten the trial, this order is often made at the Trial Management Conference. Parties usually come to a Trial Management Conference knowing what witnesses they will call and how long each witness will take. The court can then determine whether the original trial time estimate was correct and can suggest adjustments so that the trial will fit into the slotted time, or whether extra time is required. Unlike Settlement Conferences, Trial Management Conferences are ordinarily held by the judge presiding at the trial. Accordingly, while Rule 17(6) provides that the court can explore the "chances of settling the case", the parties must be careful not to reveal the terms of any offer made if the trial judge is presiding at the Trial Management Conference (see Rule 18(8)). Many trial judges explore settlement with the parties at a Trial Management Conference, but arrange to have a second judge available to preside over an impromptu settlement conference if it appears that the parties may settle.

Costs

Rules 18 and 24 govern offers to settle and costs. Rule 18(4) mandates that an offer to settle must be signed by both a party and his or her lawyer. Rule 18(14) creates costs consequences for a party who fails to accept an offer to settle that contains provisions as favourable as, or more favourable than, the court's eventual order.

Rule 24 sets out that a party who is successful on a contested aspect of a case (such as a motion or trial, but not including conferences) is entitled to costs. Much of the argument in a costs matter will revolve around which party was "successful". Most family matters are complex and involve competing claims made by both parties. It is not always immediately obvious which party was most successful. Many cases result in "divided success", which usually means that costs are not awarded. The Rule, however, also contains a provision that a successful party who behaved unreasonably may be denied costs or may have costs awarded against him or her. The court is required to consider the party's behaviour from the time the issue arose; the reasonableness of any offers made; and any offer that a party either withdrew or failed to accept (Rule (24(5)).

The utility of the judicial process, featuring the traditional adversarial approach, as a mechanism for dealing with family breakdown is itself being questioned. In the following presentation in 1997 to students in the Faculty of Law at the University of Saskatchewan, Professor Payne examined alternatives to litigation. Professor Payne and Marilyn A. Payne expand on this topic in *Canadian Family Law*, second edition (Irwin Law, 2006).

PAYNE, "FAMILY CONFLICT RESOLUTION: DEALING WITH THE CONSEQUENCES OF MARRIAGE BREAKDOWN THROUGH COUNSELING, NEGOTIATION, MEDIATION AND ARBITRATION"

1. Recent Trends in Family Dispute Resolution

Many lawyers and judges have now joined their critics from other disciplines by acknowledging the limitations of the legal system in resolving disputes between separated and divorced spouses. Statutory provisions, regulations and rules of court governing such matters as mandatory financial disclosure, case management, pre-trials, mediation, independent expert assessments, and formal offers to settle, manifest the realization that litigation must be regarded as a last resort in the resolution of family disputes. There is a desperate need for family law to focus much more on processes for dispute resolution. Sections 9 and 10 of the *Divorce Act* pay lip service to the benefits of counseling, negotiation and mediation as processes for resolving family disputes but do nothing to foster the use of these processes. More far reaching statutory provisions respecting mediation are found in some provincial statutes. Legal aid is sometimes available to meet the costs of mediation. Several provincial law societies have endorsed the practice of family mediation by legal practitioners. These are all signposts for the future.

Although court-connected mediation services are not new to Canada in family dispute resolution, they are likely to play a more substantial role in the future as governments seek to reduce the cost of access to justice. Budgetary restraints will, of course, continue to limit the resources available to promote the consensual resolution of family disputes with the aid of court-connected services. Consequently, there will be a growing demand for private and community services.

2. The Crises of Marriage Breakdown

For most families, marriage breakdown provokes three crises: an emotional crisis; an economic crisis; and a parenting crisis. Both of the spouses and their children suffer severe emotional upheaval when the unity of the family disintegrates. Furthermore, few families encounter separation or divorce without suffering financial setbacks. The emotional and economic crises resulting from marriage breakdown are compounded by the co-parental divorce when there are dependent children. Bonding between children and their absent parent is inevitably threatened by marriage breakdown.

Constructive resolution of these three crises requires the passage of time and appropriate intervention by professionals who are consulted by the family members. The dynamics of marriage breakdown, which are multi-faceted, cannot be addressed in isolation. In the search for appropriate processes to deal with breakdown, divorcing couples must not lose control over their own lives. Judicial decrees and expert assessments that exclude the family members from the decision making are insufficient. Omniscience is not the prerogative of any profession and the family's right to self-determination should not be lightly ignored.

3. The Emotional Divorce

When marriage breakdown occurs, a grieving process is experienced by each of the spouses and their children. This grieving process or "emotional divorce" passes through various stages, including denial, hostility and depression, to the ultimate acceptance of the death of the marriage. Working through the spousal emotional divorce rarely takes less than 2 years. In the meantime, permanent and legally binding decisions are often made to regulate the economic and parenting consequences of the marriage breakdown. Separated spouses, lawyers, and mediators must become more aware of the risk of premature settlements negotiated at a time when one or both of the spouses are undergoing the emotional trauma of marriage breakdown. Indeed, when either spouse is going through severe emotional turmoil, a cooling-off period would be desirable during which time any negotiated settlement should focus on the short term, rather than the long term, needs and concerns of the spouses and their children. Spouses, lawyers and mediators should assess the potential for temporary agreements being only the first stage in the resolution of the economic and parenting consequences of the marriage breakdown.

Although divorce is rarely painless, especially when children are involved, the trauma of marriage breakdown can be eased by therapy, counseling and by access to informational and educational programs. In some urban centres, divorcing parents are required to attend programs that examine the impact of their conduct on the children and offer advice to parents that can reduce harmful conduct, such as using children as weapons or pawns in the spousal conflict, fighting over the children, criticizing the other spouse in the presence of the children, or competing for the children's affection. Time may also be spent in dealing with practical matters such as household budgets, reaching fair child support arrangements and providing guidelines or structures for parenting arrangements. Separate courses are sometimes provided for the children of divorcing parents that are designed to help the children deal with their feelings of loss, guilt, fear and grief.

4. Marriage and Family Counseling

Counseling is readily available to families in crisis who reside in urban centres. Professionals in private practice who have expertise in social work, psychology or psychiatry, offer marriage, family and individual counseling on a fee paying basis. Community agencies may provide counseling services free of charge or assess a fee based on a sliding scale to reflect the ability to pay.

In previous generations, marriage and family counseling focused on reconciliation. A couple contemplating divorce was urged to reconcile. Today, reconciliation is regarded as only one option. Marriage and family counseling is increasingly directed towards helping families understand how they will be affected by separation or divorce and how they can deal with the emotional, economic and parenting consequences of marriage breakdown. Marriage and family counseling is regarded as therapeutic in nature, even if it falls short of providing a sustained program of family therapy. The day-to-day consequences of marriage breakdown are important aspects of family counseling. Family members may be referred to specialized community services, such as safe havens for battered women, alcohol and drug addiction treatment centres, vocational retraining programs, social assistance agencies and housing services. In recent years, community-based Family Service Agencies have provided mediation services to deal with parenting disputes between separated and divorced spouses. They rarely mediate disputes concerning property or spousal support.

5. Negotiation

Less than 4 percent of divorces involve a trial of contested issues in open court. Divorcing spouses normally settle their disputes by negotiation, often with the benefit of legal representation. Couples caught up in the emotional dynamics of marriage breakdown have difficulty communicating with each other. Their emotions cloud their judgment. One or both may not have worked through the emotional divorce. The interplay between the emotional dynamics of marriage breakdown and regulation of the economic consequences of marriage breakdown may be demonstrated by the following examples. A needy spouse who makes no claim for spousal support may be manifesting a hope for reconciliation or a state of depression. A guilty spouse may seek to expiate guilt by asking for too little or by giving too much. A hostile spouse, who is seeking revenge for rejection, may exact too heavy a price, even at the risk of triggering acrimonious negotiations or protracted litigation. These are all inappropriate responses to dealing with the practical consequences of marriage breakdown. The object of any negotiations is to reach a reasonable settlement that both spouses can live with and that reflects the interests of any children.

Equitable and workable settlements in the emotionally charged atmosphere of marriage breakdown or divorce often necessitate the intervention of lawyers or other third parties, such as mediators, who can bring objectivity to the bargaining table.

(a) The Importance of Negotiation

Negotiation is the most effective way of resolving disputes. It leaves the decision-making authority with the disputants. It is also cost-efficient and time-saving when compared to other means of dispute resolution. Good negotiation skills are a prerequisite to the constructive resolution of family disputes.

(b) Negotiation Techniques

There are three basic approaches to negotiation: (i) hard bargaining; (ii) soft bargaining; and (iii) principled negotiation. These approaches are reviewed by Roger Fisher and William Ury in their best selling book, *Getting to Yes*. At the risk of over simplification, the following summary may shed light on their differences.

Hard bargaining reflects a competitive or adversarial approach to negotiation. The hard bargainer takes a position and is difficult to shift from that position. He or she makes concessions reluctantly but demands liberal concessions from the other side. Hard bargaining does not necessarily involve unethical or improper conduct but does imply that the dispute involves a contest of wills which the hard bargainer is seeking to win.

Soft bargaining signifies an excessive degree of compliance and the avoidance of confrontation. Soft bargainers make too many concessions without demanding a fair return. Soft bargainers are particularly vulnerable when negotiating with hard bargainers.

So-called principled negotiators, unlike hard and soft bargainers, strive to avoid positional bargaining. They perceive themselves as joint problem solvers. Fisher and Ury have identified the following five characteristics of principled negotiation:

1. Separate the people from the problem.

2. Focus on interests, not positions.

3. Generate options that will be advantageous to both parties.

4. Insist that the result be based on objective standards.

5. Know the best alternative to a negotiated settlement (BATNA).

In separating the people from the problem in family disputes, the disputants must avoid the blame game. They should attack the problem, not each other.

Fisher and Ury's insistence that negotiations focus on interests, not positions, implies that behind every demand there is a need, desire or concern. Interests may be material, such as money or property, or they may be psychological, such as the need for recognition or security. Focusing on interests can identify complementary and disparate interests of the disputants and provide opportunities for compromise or trade-offs that lead to agreement.

Generating options for mutual gain fosters successful negotiations. For example, it may be better for both the spouses and the children if the parents share responsibility for raising their children rather than leaving the responsibility to one of the parents and relegating the other parent to the status of a passive bystander. Options that are advantageous to both sides increase the prospect of reaching a mutually acceptable solution.

The use of objective standards to evaluate possible solutions promotes reasonable settlements. Objective criteria relied on by family law practitioners include relevant statutory provisions, case law and, most recently, the proposed federal Child Support Guidelines [now enacted and dealt with extensively in Chapter 8, *CHILD SUPPORT*].

Knowing and keeping in mind the best alternative to a negotiated agreement enables disputants to accept reasonable settlements and reject unreasonable proposals.

The idea that principled negotiation will substitute win/win solutions for the win/lose philosophy of adversarial bargaining is not without its critics. It may, nevertheless, prove attractive to separated and divorced spouses who can ill-afford to engage in hostile legal negotiations or protracted litigation.

6. Mediation

(a) Nature of Mediation

The essence of mediation is that the family members are themselves responsible for determining the consequences of their divorce. Self-determination with the aid of an impartial third party is the cornerstone of mediation. The mediator must defuse family conflict to a level where the parties can communicate with each other. They can then look at their options and apply objective standards with a view to negotiating a reasonable settlement. Mediation is not to be confused with family therapy. Divorce mediation is a process that is aimed at facilitating the consensual resolution of the economic and parenting problems that result from marriage breakdown. It is a time-limited process that is intended to produce a formal settlement. Mediators are not marriage counsellors or therapists. They deal with the consequences, not the causes, of marriage breakdown.

(b) Approaches to Mediation

Mediation is not a monolithic process. Systems and processes vary even though the goal of consensual resolution is constant. Mediators may be engaged in private practice. They may be connected with courts. They may work in community agencies.

Many mediators are either social workers or psychologists. There are a few psychiatrists and lawyers who practise mediation. Mediators without legal qualifications usually, but not always, confine their practice to parenting disputes. Some mediators have no direct link with the established professions and are self-made, and in some cases self-proclaimed. Successful mediation presupposes high professional standards because of the control a mediator exercises over the process and because one or both of the clients are frequently disadvantaged by the trauma of marriage breakdown. Mediation may belong to the parties but a successful outcome is dependent on the expertise of the mediator. Family members who look to private mediation as a means of dispute resolution must undertake careful inquiries to ensure that they have recourse to a competent and experienced mediator.

There are two schools of thought respecting the fundamental nature of the mediation process. Some mediators characterize the process as transformational. They contend that it is a process that empowers disputants to foster their personal growth on their way to resolving the particular disputes that brought them into mediation. Others regard the mediation process as being far less ambitious in scope. They believe that mediation focuses on the resolution of practical problems rather than on transforming the disputants who have recourse to the process. The difference between these two schools of thought may be one of degree rather than kind. It is noteworthy, however, that court-connected mediation services often place a heavy emphasis on rights-based, rather than interest-based negotiation, and positive evaluation of these services is usually premised on the settlement rates achieved.

(c) Reasons for Mediation

The most common responses to conflict are "fight or flight." Often neither is the right response. Mediation provides an alternative when spouses or former spouses cannot negotiate directly with each other but wish to avoid the adversarial postures of the legal process. For many couples, mediation offers greater opportunities for them to retain control over their own lives. Mediation can facilitate tailor-made solutions to individual problems. Family members are often intimidated by the formal complexity and adversarial nature of the legal process. Mediation is less threatening than the legal process and its self-determined agreements may prove more durable and adaptable than court-ordered settlements.

Successful mediation is much cheaper than protracted litigation. However, comparing the costs of successful mediation and litigation is misleading. Not all mediation attempts are successful. Furthermore, the vast majority of divorces involve the negotiation of settlements by lawyers. Very few divorces involve a trial. Assisted negotiation through the mediation process is not necessarily cheaper than assisted negotiation through the legal process.

In parenting disputes, mediation can establish a framework for future communication and an ongoing exchange of information and ideas respecting the upbringing of the children.

(d) Circumstances in which Mediation is Inappropriate

Mediation is not appropriate for everyone. In some cases, inequalities of bargaining power between the spouses may render mediation inappropriate. People with a "winner take all" mentality are not good candidates for mediation which requires an attitude of "give and take" and compromise. Some feminist commentators have suggested that mediation is always disadvantageous to women because of an inherent imbalance of power between the sexes. It is questionable whether legal processes, or any other processes, assure any greater protection to women in the absence of domestic violence. Many mediators contend that mediation is inappropriate when either of the parties is physically violent, addicted to alcohol or drugs, or cannot face the reality of the death of the marriage. Spouses falling within the last category may need counseling or therapy as a prelude to participating in a mediation process.

(e) Role of Mediator; Neutrality of Mediator

Unlike the lawyer, whose role is to represent the interests of his or her client, mediators must preserve a neutral stance; they must also be perceived as non-partisan by the disputants. If a mediator is perceived as taking sides, his or her credibility is destroyed and the parties will lose confidence in the process. The term "neutral" does not mean a mediator must be passive. Mediators can take active roles to facilitate settlement and their training and personal value systems will clearly affect their overall approach to the mediation process. Intervention, though quite legitimate for such purposes as restructuring the lines of communication or identifying new avenues for exploration, must stop short of taking the decision making authority away from the parties.

(f) Redressing Power Imbalances

Mediation can be an empowering process insofar as it fosters respect and cooperation but a successful outcome depends on active participation by both spouses and requires a relatively balanced capacity to negotiate. True equality in the balance of power may be impossible to achieve, but the mediator must prevent an abuse of power by either disputant. Mediators can use a variety of techniques to redress an imbalance of power between the parties. For example, if inequality of bargaining power stems from lack of knowledge, information can be provided. Unequal negotiating skills can sometimes be balanced by insightful intervention and restructuring by the mediator or by the allocation of joint assignments to the parties. Intimidating negotiation patterns can be interrupted and reframed in order to provide support to the disadvantaged party. However, where the imbalance of power is considered to be so great that the mediator cannot intervene without endangering his or her neutrality, the mediator should recommend other means of resolving the dispute.

(g) Professional and Community Responses to Mediation

The future of family mediation will largely depend on its use by professional groups and by Canadian families in crisis. There is a public need for broadly based and ongoing sources of information, whether provided through the mass media, the schools, community agencies, or under professional auspices, such as the Church, Medicine and Law. The professions must themselves become educated.

Information is required to dispel the myths of mediation. Members of the legal community, who view their vested interests as being threatened by the emerging process of mediation, have to be reassured that the legal system is not undermined by mediation. Indeed, the legal system and mediation are complementary, rather than competing or contradictory, processes. Both seek to provide a solution to disputes. Each has its place. Neither is self-sufficient.

(h) The Future of Family Mediation

Mediation, whether court-connected or private, has found a growing place in the resolution of family disputes during the last 15 years. At present, divorce mediation in Canada is largely confined to parenting disputes. This is being done primarily by mediators with training in social work, psychology or psychiatry. On rare occasions, support and property disputes on marriage breakdown are mediated. In these cases, the mediator is much more likely to be a lawyer. This division of function, whereby non-lawyers mediate parenting disputes while lawyers mediate the economics of divorce, is a division of convenience that is currently acceptable to most, but not all, mediators. In the long term, comprehensive or "total package" mediation will become commonplace.

A closer association must be established between lawyers and other professionals engaged in advising and assisting families in crisis. Indeed, the time will come when community centres, staffed by lawyers, doctors, psychologists, social workers and other professionals, as well as by volunteers, will provide a comprehensive approach to the resolution of the multi-faceted crises of marriage breakdown. In the meantime, the various professions and federal, provincial and municipal governmental agencies (including Departments as diverse as Communications, Education, Employment, Housing Finance, Revenue Canada, Health and Welfare, and Justice), which are directly or indirectly involved in the systemic management of the human process of marriage breakdown, must recognize their own limitations and foster effective lines of communication in the search for solutions to the human and socio-economic problems associated with marriage breakdown.

7. Arbitration

Mediation of family disputes leaves decision making to the parties. If they cannot resolve the issues, an independent arbiter may be called upon to determine their respective rights and obligations. Traditionally, this function has been discharged by courts.

Private arbitration has displaced litigation as a means of resolving labour disputes. To a much lesser extent, arbitration has also been recognized as an effective means of resolving commercial disputes. The use of binding arbitration instead of litigation to resolve spousal disputes respecting property division, spousal and child support, and child custody and access on marriage breakdown or divorce is rare in Canada.

(a) Advantages of Arbitration

Private arbitration has the following potential advantages over litigation as a family dispute resolution process:

1. The parties are directly involved in the appointment of the arbitrator. An arbitrator can be selected having regard to the nature of the dispute and the arbitrator's qualifications and expertise. In litigation, the parties are not free to select a particular judge. Furthermore, the judge is not usually a specialist in family law and may have no interest in, or even an aversion to, adjudicating spousal or parental disputes.

2. Litigants are often intimidated by the formality and adversarial atmosphere of the court. An arbitration hearing can be as formal or informal as the parties wish.

3. Arbitrators make themselves available to suit the convenience of the disputants.

4. Arbitration can be procedurally less complex and much speedier than contested litigation.

5. Arbitrations are conducted in private. Courtrooms are open to the public and the media.

6. Arbitration is usually cheaper than litigation, even though the disputants pay the arbitrator's fees.

7. The costs of arbitration are more predictable than those of litigation.

Some disadvantages of arbitration may be:

1. Arbitrators, unlike judges, may not be bound by substantive and procedural laws. The absence of "due process" can lead to arbitrary results.

2. Arbitrators may be inclined to split the difference on substantive matters in dispute without sufficient regard to the merits of the case.

3. Some arbitrators are disinclined to order costs in favour of either party.

(b) Court-Annexed Arbitration

Some form of court-annexed arbitration might ultimately be endorsed in Canada as an alternative process for the resolution of family disputes. Court-annexed arbitration has been introduced in several jurisdictions in the United States to cope with the flood of civil litigation. Court-annexed arbitration differs from private arbitration in several ways. Court-annexed arbitration is usually mandatory rather than voluntary and the arbitrator is assigned by the court and not chosen by the disputants. Most importantly, court-annexed arbitration is usually advisory, rather than binding. If the disputants accept the arbitration award, it is entered as a court judgment and is enforceable as such. If the arbitration award is rejected by either party, the issues go to trial and are adjudicated without reference being made to the arbitration award. Most court-annexed programs impose penalties on a disputant if the trial judgment affords no greater relief than that given under the arbitration award.

(c) Evaluation of Arbitration

Arbitration is a rational alternative to litigation for separated and divorced spouses. They should be entitled to opt for binding private arbitration, with or without a right of appeal, instead of being compelled to resort to overcrowded trial courts. A residual discretionary jurisdiction should be vested in the courts, however, to override an arbitration award when the best interests of a child necessitate judicial intervention.

8. Med-Arb

Mediation and arbitration need not be exclusive of one another. "Med-Arb" is a process that utilizes both approaches. Typically, a fixed time will be set aside for mediation, with the understanding that if no consensus is reached, the mediator will then act as an arbitrator who will give a final and binding decision. Knowing that unresolved issues will proceed to arbitration may help parties to reach a consensus in the final stages of the mediation process.

9. Concluding Observations

This paper has focused on counseling, negotiation, mediation, arbitration and med-arb as processes that can be used as alternatives to, or in conjunction with, litigation as means of resolving the emotional, economic and parenting consequences of marriage breakdown. This paper does not canvass or even catalogue all of the processes that can be applied or adapted to family conflict management and dispute resolution. Nor does it recommend the outright rejection of legal processes in favour of other processes. Indeed, separated and divorced spouses will usually find it advantageous to avoid locking themselves into a single process in their attempts to resolve the multi-faceted problems generated by their marriage breakdown. Let me take a few examples of when it is appropriate to utilize more than one process. Negotiations do, and must, continue even after legal proceedings have been instituted. Indeed, the institution of legal proceedings may trigger an early settlement and, even when matters proceed further, eve of trial settlements are common. Divorcing or divorced couples may use different processes to deal with different aspects of their marriage breakdown. Individual or family counseling and therapy may be appropriate as a prelude to mediation. Arbitration may be used to resolve an impasse that has been reached in mediation. Parenting mediation may co-exist with a motion to a court, perhaps on consent, to determine urgent matters relating to interim possession of the family home or the amount of spousal or child support.

Separated and divorced couples must be made aware of the diversity of processes available to foster family conflict management and dispute resolution. Only then can they examine their options in such a way as to reflect their respective interests and those of any children.

A NOTE ON RECENT CHANGES TO FAMILY ARBITRATIONS IN ONTARIO

The origins of the changes to the law governing family arbitrations in Ontario are interesting. Prior to the adoption of the *Family Statute Law Amendment Act, 2006*, S.O. 2006, c. 1, arbitrations involving family disputes took place within the general framework of the *Arbitration Act, 1991*, S.O. 1991, c. 17. The *Arbitration Act, 1991* allows the parties to set many of the rules governing the arbitration, including the substantive law that will apply. In late 2003, a retired Ontario lawyer who wished to ensure that Islamic principles of family and inheritance law could be used to resolve disputes within the Muslim community of Canada announced the establishment of the "Islamic Institute of Civil Justice". He suggested that the Institute would offer a form of "Sharia court" under the *Arbitration Act, 1991*. The announcement and subsequent media reports caused considerable reaction and some anxiety. The critics were especially concerned that women's rights might be at risk in family disputes.

In response, the Government of Ontario appointed Marian Boyd (a former Attorney General) to review the use of arbitration in family and inheritance disputes and the impact that such arbitration had on vulnerable individuals. In her report, *Dispute Resolution in Family Law: Protecting Choice, Promoting Inclusion* (Toronto: December 2004) (available on the website of Ontario's Attorney General at <www.attorneygeneral.jus.gov.on.ca>), Ms. Boyd reviewed the nature and use of arbitration in family disputes in Ontario. She pointed out that the parties could generally choose the rules that the arbitrator was to apply to determine their dispute and that these rules could be based on a religious code. She noted that a Jewish court known as the "Beis Din", in addition to dealing with divorces under religious law, had determined support, property, custody and access issues in a limited number of family disputes in Ontario. In the end, Ms. Boyd recommended that arbitration should continue to be an option to deal with family disputes and that parties should be able to have these disputes determined in accordance with religious law if they so chose. However, these main recommendations were conditional upon a long list of legislative and regulatory reforms. These reforms included the clarification and expansion of the scope of judicial review of family arbitration awards, the development of procedures to ensure that the consent to the arbitration process was fully informed and freely given, the regulation of family arbitrators, and the requirement that such arbitrators receive some training. In particular, the report suggested that the *Family Law Act* should stipulate that the statutory provisions that applied to domestic contracts also applied to arbitration agreements.

The Government of Ontario rejected one of the key recommendations made by Ms. Boyd. It introduced legislation that was eventually enacted as the *Family Statute Law Amendment Act, 2006* and proclaimed into force on April 30, 2007. This Act amended the *Arbitration Act, 1991* and the *Family Law Act* (the "FLA") so that there is now greater regulation of arbitrations of family disputes than of other arbitrations. Perhaps most significantly in light of the context in which the legislation originated, s. 59.2 of the FLA now provides that an award in a "family arbitration" is enforceable only if the arbitration is conducted exclusively in accordance with the law of Ontario or, if the parties so specify, the law of another Canadian jurisdiction. Of course, people in religious communities can still opt out of the legal system by agreeing to arbitrations conducted by religious leaders who apply religiously based law. An award in this type of arbitration will have no legal effect, but the parties may still feel sufficiently obligated to follow it so that legal enforcement is not a concern.

There are also important new procedural safeguards that apply only to a "family arbitration". Agreements to submit family disputes to arbitration constitute domestic contracts (s. 51 of the FLA) and so, to be enforceable, must be in writing, signed and witnessed (s. 55(1) of the FLA). In addition, each party entering into a "family arbitration agreement" must receive independent legal advice (s. 59.6(1)(b) of the FLA). Moreover, a "family arbitration agreement" and an award made under it are unenforceable unless the agreement is entered into after the dispute to be arbitrated has arisen. See s. 59.4 of the FLA. As a result, a term in a marriage contract or a cohabitation agreement providing for arbitration in the event of a breakdown of the relationship is unenforceable. However, the requirement that each party have independent legal advice and the restriction on agreeing to arbitration in advance of a dispute do not apply to "secondary arbitration"; that is, "a family arbitration that is conducted in accordance with a separation agreement, a court order or a family arbitration award that provides for the arbitration of possible future disputes relating to the ongoing management or implementation of the agreement, order or award" (s. 59.7 of the FLA). It follows that spouses can stipulate in a separation agreement that any dispute arising under the agreement will be submitted to arbitration.

Because a family arbitration agreement is a domestic contract, s. 56 of the FLA applies to it. Under s. 56(4), any domestic contract can be set aside where (a) "a party failed to disclose to the other significant assets, or significant debts or other liabilities" or (b) "a party did not understand the nature or consequences of the domestic contract". In "Family Law Mediation and Arbitration" in Shaffer, ed., *Contemporary Issues in Family Law: Engaging with the Legacy of James G. McLeod* (Carswell, 2007), Phil Epstein suggests (at 79):

> Although requiring parties to provide disclosure of significant assets and significant liabilities prior to signing an arbitration agreement seems like a major legislative shift, in reality little will change for most parties, who will likely have already exchanged financial statements for purposes of negotiations or mediation that occurred before the parties decide to proceed to arbitration. In addition, a party will likely find it difficult to argue that a family arbitration should be set aside on the basis that he or she did not understand the nature or consequences of the agreement, in light of the *Family Law Act* requirement that parties have independent legal advice when entering into the agreement. ...

Generally, an enforceable family arbitration award has the same finality as a court order and binds the parties unless it is set aside or varied on appeal. By virtue of s. 50.1 of the amended *Arbitration Act, 1991*, family arbitration awards are enforceable only under the FLA. Under s. 59.5 of the FLA, the award is enforceable "in the same way as a domestic contract" provided, as noted above, the process accorded with the laws of Ontario or another Canadian jurisdiction. In addition, s. 59.6(1) of the FLA stipulates that the award is enforceable only if the following conditions are met:

> (a) the family arbitration agreement under which the award is made is made in writing and complies with any regulations made under the *Arbitration Act, 1991*;
>
> (b) each of the parties to the agreement receives independent legal advice before making the agreement;
>
> (c) the requirements of section 38 of the *Arbitration Act, 1991* are met (formal requirements, writing, reasons, delivery to parties); and
>
> (d) the arbitrator complies with any regulations made under the *Arbitration Act, 1991*.

With regards to paragraph (a) above, s. 2 of *Family Arbitration*, O. Reg. 134/07 (in force as of April 30, 2008), contains standard provisions that must be included in family arbitration agreements, family mediation-arbitration agreements, and secondary agreements. In addition, this regulation requires arbitrators to receive "the training approved by the Attorney General ... as set out on the Ministry's website" (s. 3); to create a record of the arbitration containing listed items (s. 4); and to report to the Attorney General specified, non-identifying information regarding each family arbitration (s. 5). The regulation also stipulates that an arbitrator in a family arbitration must affirm that the parties "were separately screened for power imbalances and domestic violence by someone other than me and I have considered his or her report on the results of the screening and will do so throughout the arbitration".

Where the agreement is for "mediation-arbitration", the mediator-arbitrator can conduct this screening himself or herself.

Disenchantment with the adversarial process as a means of resolving family disputes has caused some lawyers to turn to "collaborate family law". This process is explained in the following brief excerpts from a Canadian book on the subject.

SHIELDS, RYAN, AND SMITH, *COLLOBORATIVE FAMILY LAW: ANOTHER WAY TO RESOLVE FAMILY DISPUTES*

(Toronto: Thomson Canada Ltd., 2003) XIII-XIV, 4, 9-10, and 32-33 (Endnotes and headings omitted)

Collaborative law is a revolutionary new way to practice family law that is spreading like wildfire across North America. It is reframing the experience of separation and divorce for a growing number of families and transforming their lawyers as well.

The traditional process offered to divorcing couples has been the adversarial legal system. Whether or not they eventually wind up in court, negotiations conducted under the implied or overt threat of litigation often inflict personal and financial devastation on families. Despite sincere efforts by lawyers to help, resolution usually comes too late, costs too much, and falls below expectations. The intangible interest of the parties — to preserve relationships with extended family and mutual friends, to co-parent amicably after divorce, to be treated with respect, and to control the process and the outcome — are ignored altogether.

Three decades ago, interest-based mediation was heralded as the answer to the litigation process for families. Indeed, mediation was the first dispute resolution model to recognize the capacity and authority of the parties to determine their own settlements and it continues to be a powerful process option. However, in mediation, the parties work with one neutral facilitator and that approach is not appropriate for everyone. Furthermore, mediated agreements sometimes break down in the hands of lawyers operating in the adversarial paradigm.

In 1990, Stu Webb, a lawyer in Minnesota, spoke out on behalf of divorcing spouses and disillusioned family lawyers. He created an enlightened alternative to the adversarial process that he called Collaborative Law. The concept is simple and profound: tailor the process to the parties, not the other way around, and give lawyers a joint mandate to empower the parties to create their best possible agreement, as they define it.

In the collaborative law process, trained collaborative lawyers represent and support the parties throughout each stage of the process. The parties agree to act in good faith, make full disclosure, put their children first, and consider each other's perspective and interests. Lawyers act as negotiation coaches, information resources, and advocates for the interests of their clients and the integrity of the process. The underpinning of collaborative law is the written agreement between all participants that the collaborative lawyers are retained solely to facilitate the negotiation of a mutually acceptable agreement. If either party decides to go to court, both lawyers are disqualified from further representation.

With the option of drifting to court waived, the creativity and problem-solving skills of all participants are unleashed. Over and over again, collaborative clients confirm the wisdom of Stu Webb's concept by creating customized, *outside-the-box* agreements. Clients take away an improved ability to communicate and co-parent and a process of resolving future issues. They achieve closure of their relationship with dignity, at reasonable cost.

The collaborative process not only benefits clients, it changes the lawyers as well. As we develop the skills and attitude required for effective collaborative practice, we become more self-aware, more skillful communicators and more sensitive to the real needs of our clients. Collaborative Family Law allows us to reconcile our personal and professional values and to discover deep personal satisfaction in our work. Stu Webb is right about something else as well: Collaborative Law is just plain more fun. ...

What do we mean by collaboration? To some, working together means no more than engaging in a process in which the disputing parties voluntarily disclose and exchange all of their information and remain civil and respectful toward one another. They refrain from resorting to destructive behaviour and communication. Their discourse is both informative and pleasant. However, each remains steadfast in his determination to secure the best outcome for himself. That it should likewise be beneficial for the other is incidental to his primary purpose. This view of collaboration might more properly be described as *cooperation*. Does collaboration mean no more?

For those disputing parties who recognize that to commence or continue contentious litigation will be disadvantageous to them both, collaboration promises something else. They recognize that self-destruction is antithetical to the objectives of any dispute resolution process. To avoid that outcome, they collaborate to arrive at some mutually acceptable point between their apparently incompatible positions. They seek a *compromise*. The end result will almost certainly be less for each than what was sought and what might have been realized through litigation. Is this all that we intend through collaboration?

Whether we consider collaboration to be synonymous with either cooperation or compromise, it appears to occupy a place at the opposite end of the conflict resolution continuum from *competition*. When we compete, we seek to win and that goal serves to rationalize any strategy or tactics. A more vigorous exchange between competing forces may be referred to as a *confrontation*, an interaction often associated with provocation. Whatever collaboration is, it is neither competition nor confrontation but [its] opposite. ...

... While collaboration incorporates all of the qualities of cooperation, it contemplates so much more. The primary focus of cooperation appears to lie with the *process* alone while collaboration addresses the *outcome* as well. Throughout this book, we approach our topic from these two perspectives. Compromise and collaboration are alike in that they both involve the satisfaction of the interests of both parties to a dispute. They differ in the degree to which they accomplish their task. Compromisers achieve partial interest satisfaction for each; collaborators maximize their combined interest satisfaction. Collaboration does not require that either participant forego the attainment of his goals. Collaboration is not accommodation; it does not involve sacrifice. Self-interest and other-interest need not be incompatible. The nature of collaboration is their reconciliation.

It is our premise that collaborative negotiation has the potential for creating the best possible agreements for both parties to a dispute in the best possible way. The purpose of this book is to examine why collaboration holds such promise and how to realize its profound potential. ...

What are the common elements of this process that are consistent with our earlier discussion of collaboration and which resolve the dilemmas characteristic of the adversarial approach to family law process and outcome? First, the parties and their lawyers work together. Second, they agree that litigation will not be commenced while the process is ongoing and, to take the negotiations out from under the shadow of litigation, they agree that they should be unable to resolve the dispute, neither of the lawyers will be eligible to represent the parties in any subsequent litigation. Third, the negotiation process they follow is not adversarial. The parties apply the principled negotiation alternative. Fourth, with the facilitative skills of the lawyers to guide them, the parties communicate in a way that promotes the attainment of their mutual goals.

We offer this definition of *collaborative family law*:

> Collaborative family law is a dispute resolution process in which the parties and their lawyers commit themselves to the realization of a negotiated outcome. They agree that litigation will not be commenced while they are negotiating and that, in the event they are unable to negotiate a resolution of their dispute, neither lawyer will be eligible to represent his or her client in any subsequent litigation. In the process itself, the participants communicate to promote the maximum exchange of information, to reveal all concerns of the parties, to generate an array of creative ideas, and, ultimately, to agree upon the terms and conditions of a mutually acceptable settlement that satisfies the interest of both parties.

Those who practice collaborative family law no longer accept the assumptions and principles that underlie the adversarial paradigm. Experienced family litigators know all too well the turmoil and devastation experienced by their clients in contested divorce. We recognize that courts are not appropriate forum for resolving family disputes, which are as much about feelings and relationships as legal issues. An adjudicative process that appears to be less effective today than before is a source of frustration for all lawyers. Many are alarmed by an emergent lack of civility among adversaries in the arena. Others are weary of a process model that leaves them feeling disconnected from their personal values and drained by their clients who are often unhappy despite their best efforts and the results they obtain. For all reasons, lawyers are increasingly seeking another way to resolve family disputes, to restore satisfaction and pride in their work, to be appreciated for their efforts, and to provide a process and outcome of real value to their clients.

To become a practitioner of this approach requires a paradigm shift, a quantum leap for some, from adversarial to collaborative. It requires a radical change in our assumptions about the nature of conflict, the capacity of individuals to resolve their differences, our perception of our role as lawyers and our relationship with our clients, how we measure our success, and how we deliver the services we provide. It requires that we adopt new processes, attitudes, and skills, as we redefine the meaning of advocacy for our clients.

Lawyers who embrace the collaborative process become settlement specialists, leaving matters that must be adjudicated to litigation specialists. Collaborative negotiation is challenging and honourable. It restores integrity and value to the practice of law for those who feel alienated from it. ... Collaborative lawyers rediscover enjoyment and satisfaction as they heed the call of Chief Justice Burger to return to their role as *healers of conflict*.

NOTES AND QUESTIONS

1. An increasing number of litigants in family law cases are unrepresented. Not only does lack of legal representation affect the litigant in obvious ways, but it also has considerable impact on the entire process. For further reading, see the series of articles dealing with the issue of self-representation in the 19th volume of the *Canadian Family Law Quarterly*; Blishen, "Self-Represented Litigants in Family and Civil Law Disputes" (2006), 25 C.F.L.Q. 117; and Cochrane, "A Family Law Practitioner's Guide to Dealing with the Self-Represented Litigant" (2006), 25 C.F.L.Q. 131.

2. In *New Brunswick (Minister of Health & Community Services) v. G. (J.)*, [1999] 3 S.C.R. 46, reproduced in part in Chapter 10, *CHILD IN NEED OF PROTECTION*, the Supreme Court of Canada held that s. 7 of the *Charter* obliged the state to provide state-funded counsel in a child protection hearing. It has been argued that this holding may provide a basis for extending the right to publicly funded counsel to other types of family law proceedings. See Canadian Bar Association, *Making the Case: The Right to Publicly-Funded Legal Representation in Canada* (Ottawa: Canadian Bar Association, 2002).

3. Section 9(2) of the *Divorce Act* requires the lawyer acting in a divorce proceeding to discuss with his or her client "the advisability of negotiating the matters that may be the subject of a support order or a custody order" and inform the client "of the mediation facilities known to him or her that might be able to assist the spouses in negotiating those matters". See also s. 9(3).

Section 31(1) of the Ontario *Children's Law Reform Act* authorizes the court, at the request of the parties, to appoint a person selected by the parties to mediate any aspect of a custody dispute. Mediation conducted pursuant to this section can be either "open" or "closed" at the option of the parties. See ss. 31(4) and (7). In "open" mediation, what goes on and is said during the mediation can be revealed if a settlement is not reached. In "closed" mediation, everything is confidential. The latter type is prevalent.

Do you think that the legislation should go further and impose mandatory mediation of, at least, custody and access disputes? The Special Joint Committee of the House of Commons and the Senate reported in *For the Sake of the Children* (1999), at 32, that Quebec legislation requires divorcing parents to attend at least one information session about the benefits of mediation. If the parents then decide to use mediation, they are entitled to up to six sessions at public expense. The legislation permits opting out of the process, including the information session, in cases of domestic violence. The committee recommended (at 33) that "divorcing parents be encouraged to attend at least one mediation session to help them develop a parenting plan for their children". It added:

> Where there is a proven history of violence by one parent toward the other or toward the children, alternative forms of dispute resolution should be used only when the safety of the person who has been the victim of the violence is assured and where the risk of violence has passed. The resulting parental plan must focus on parental responsibilities for the children and contain measures to ensure safety and security for parents and children.

4. Prompted by advocates for abused women, most mediators recognize the effects of domestic abuse on the power balance between parties. The Ontario Association of Family Mediators' *Policy on Abuse* (available at www.oafm.on.ca) requires mediators to have knowledge about abuse and the training needed to screen spouses for the presence of abuse. It also states that 1) there is a presumption that cases in which there is or has been domestic violence are not suited for mediation, 2) inexperienced mediators or mediators who are not trained to deal with domestic violence should not accept such cases, and 3) that no mediator should act where domestic violence jeopardizes a party's ability to participate effectively. The *Policy* goes on to set specific procedural guidelines for mediation where the mediator decides to proceed even though there may be an allegation of abuse.

It should be noted, however, that mediation is not a regulated profession. Membership in any association is not a prerequisite to holding oneself out as a qualified mediator, nor is there a requirement for any particular training or experience.

5. Even where parties can reach a mediated settlement, independent legal advice may be important. Indeed, good mediators encourage or require the parties to seek such advice prior to mediation so that they can make informed choices during the mediation with knowledge of their legal rights. Furthermore, it is common practice for the parties' lawyers to review a mediated settlement and prepare a formal contract or minutes of settlement.

6. For further information about and commentary on negotiation in the family law context, see Zutter, "Negotiation" (2002-2003), 20 C.F.L.Q. 1. On negotiation generally, see Fisher and Ury, *Getting to Yes: Negotiating an Agreement without Giving In*, 2nd ed. (Toronto: Penguin Books, 1991) and Ury, *Getting Past NO: Negotiating Your Way from Confrontation to Cooperation* (New York: Bantam Books, 1991).

7. Are there any family law disputes that are clearly not suitable for collaborative law processes?

8. For further reading on collaborative family law, see Tesler, *Collaborative Law: Achieving Effective Resolution in Divorce without Litigation* (Chicago: ABA Publications, 2001); Cameron, *Collaborative Practice: Deepening the Dialogue* (Vancouver: The Continuing Legal Education Society of British Columbia, 2004); Spain, "Collaborative Law: A Critical Reflection on Whether a Collaborative Orientation Can Be Ethically Incorporated into the Practice of Law" (2004), 56 Baylor L. Rev. 14; and Keet, Wiegers, and Morrison, "Client Engagement Inside Collaborative Law" (2008), 24 Can. J. Fam. L. 145.

9. Regarding mediation in family disputes, see Noble, *Family Mediation: A Guide for Lawyers* (Toronto: Canada Law Book, 1999); Zutter, "Mediation in the Shadow of Abuse: An Update" (2002-2003), 20 C.F.L.Q. 65; Beck and Sales, *Family Mediation: Facts, Myths and Future Prospects* (Washington, D.C.: American Psychological Association, 2001); and Landau *et al.*, *Family Mediation and Collaborative Practice Handbook*, 4th ed. (Toronto: Butterworths, 2005).

10. As noted above, couples will sometimes choose a person to conduct mediation and also grant him or her the authority to arbitrate the dispute in the event that mediation fails. This arrangement may cause difficulties if one of the parties loses confidence in the person during mediation and attempts to withdraw from the process. See

Duguay v. Thompson-Duguay (2000), 7 R.F.L. (5th) 301 (Ont. S.C.J.) and *Hercus v. Hercus* (2001), 2001 Carswell-Ont 452 (S.C.J.). For a comment on these cases, see Himel, "Mediation/ Arbitration Agreements: The Binding Comes Undone" (2002-2003), 20 C.F.L.Q. 55. However, the Ontario Court of Appeal enforced a "mediation-arbitration agreement" in *Marchese v. Marchese* (2007), 35 R.F.L. (6th) 291 (Ont. C.A.) and such agreements are explicitly recognized in *Family Arbitration*, O. Reg. 134/07 (in force as of April 30, 2008).

11. One unfortunate result of the increased use of arbitration in family disputes is that many significant legal issues are resolved without adding to the body of case law that is available to the legal profession and the public. This is because the awards generally remain private. One suspects that key issues arising from the application of Part I of the *Family Law Act* have been resolved by arbitrators in ways that are only known to a few.

12. For further information on arbitration and on mediation-arbitration, see Epstein, "Family Law Mediation and Arbitration" in Shaffer, ed., *Contemporary Issues in Family Law: Engaging with the Legacy of James G. McLeod* (Carswell, 2007) and Grant, "Alternative Dispute Resolution in Family Law: What's Not to Like?" (2008), 27 C.F.L.Q. 235.

(4) Conflict of Laws

Canadians live in a mobile society. Moreover, many Canadians are immigrants. As a result, courts are often called upon to deal with cases in which there is a relevant foreign element. The body of rules and principles that has developed to resolve these cases is called "conflict of laws". It is hoped that the following extract will help the student understand the nature of conflict of laws and why this subject is important in family law. Although some conflict of laws issues will be referred to at various times in this book, students who wish to practise in the area of family law are urged to take a specific course dealing with conflict of laws.

SILVERMAN, "CONFLICT OF LAWS: SOME MATRIMONIAL PROBLEMS"

(1979), 2 Fam. L. Rev. 103

In the realm of conflict of laws, there are three kinds of problems which the courts have to face. First, a court may have to decide whether to apply the law of its own country or of a foreign country in deciding a case. For example, if a person from Ontario makes a business contract with a person from New York, should it be the law of Ontario or of New York which determines whether the contract has been breached? This is called a *choice of law* problem.

Second, a court may have to decide whether to assume jurisdiction in a certain case. For example, if a husband and wife in New York are fighting about who should have custody of their child, and the husband "kidnaps" the child into Ontario, should he be able to bring an action in Ontario for the custody of the child? This is called a *jurisdiction* problem.

Finally, a court may have to decide whether to recognize the judgment of the court of a foreign country. For example, if a Canadian couple goes to Mexico to get a divorce should a Canadian court recognize the Mexican divorce? This is called a *recognition* problem. One special kind of recognition problem is that of *enforcement*. For example, if a wife obtains a maintenance order against her husband in New York, and then he moves to Ontario, should an Ontario court be able to enforce the maintenance order against him?

Sometimes jurisdiction problems and choice of law problems blend into each other. This is because in some cases the courts feel that they should only assume jurisdiction to hear a case if it is the law of their country which is the proper law to apply. For example, courts may be unwilling to apply the divorce law of other countries, hence they will only assume jurisdiction if the divorce law of their country is the proper law to apply.

As a result, a special body of rules and legal principles has arisen to make some order out of a potentially chaotic situation, and this special body is called Conflict of Laws.

Before a case can be heard in our courts, the first prerequisite is that the court process should be available to the petitioner and that the court has jurisdiction to hear the case, *e.g.* do the parties have status to bring the proceeding in that court, and have all of the prerequisite procedural devices been followed. After that is satisfied, the court has to determine the nature of the case before it, *i.e.* is it one of contract, tort, divorce, or whatever, which is called either classification of the cause of action or characterization of the issue (or question); and then it has to decide which legal system to apply to decide the matter. The foregoing illustration of the stages which a court will follow is really an oversimplification of what may happen, for it should be noted that the questions of jurisdiction and classification are frequently so closely interwoven that they cannot be answered separately and in a step-by-step fashion.

Thus in solving the problems which we have set out above in our various examples, the courts make use of what they call *connecting factors*. For example, in dealing with a choice of law problem in contracts, the court may say that the connecting factor is the place where the contract was made, so that it is the law of that country which should be applied. Or in dealing with a jurisdiction problem in a custody case, the court may decide that the connecting factor is the place where the child ordinarily resides, so that it is the courts of that country which should have jurisdiction. Similarly, in a divorce recognition case, the court may say that the connecting factor is the place where the couple makes their home, so that it will recognize the divorce decree only if it was made by a court of that country. Therefore, one of the most important issues in conflict of laws is determining what connecting factors should be used by the courts in solving conflicts problems.

[For further reading, see Pilcow and Melamed, "A Practitioner's Guide to Conflicts in Family Law" (1988), 3 C.F.L.Q. 227; McLeod, "The Judicial Approach to Matrimonial Property Disputes and the Conflict of Laws" (1993), 9 C.F.L.Q. 203; Welling, "Conflict of Laws Issues Arising from Matrimonial Property Statutes in Canada" (1993), 9 C.F.L.Q. 225; Pitel and Rafferty, *The Conflict of Laws* (Toronto: Irwin Law Inc., forthcoming); and Castel and Walker, *Canadian Conflict of Laws* (Toronto: LexisNexus Canada, looseleaf).]

3. Violence: The Dark Side of Family Life

BALA, "LEGAL PROTECTIONS FOR VICTIMS OF SPOUSE ABUSE AND THEIR CHILDREN: THE ROLE OF HEALTH CARE PROFESSIONALS IN THE JUSTICE SYSTEM"

[Professor Bala originally wrote this paper for the Queen's University's Faculty of Health Sciences' Program on *Assessment and Care of Women in Abusive Relationships* in 2004. The footnotes have been edited and some have been omitted.]

Abstract:

The Canadian legal system no longer views spousal abuse as a "private matter" and responds much more effectively to spousal abuse than in the past. There is also a greater recognition in the legal system that the welfare of children is threatened by spousal abuse, and the interests of children should be considered in any legal response to spousal abuse. While there remain serious problems in how the justice system deals with spousal abuse, the improved social and legal responses in the past decade have contributed to a gradual reduction in levels of spousal abuse in Canada. This paper provides an introduction to the role of the law, the police and courts to the protection of victims of spousal abuse and their children, and considers the relationship of the justice system to other community institutions, such as shelters for abused women. Criminal, family law, and tort issues are discussed. The roles and responsibilities of health care professionals in dealing with spousal abuse in the context of the justice system, and the relationship of the community agencies like shelters to the justice system are also considered.

The Nature & Incidence of Spousal Abuse in Canada

Spousal abuse is an area that is difficult to research because of the tendency of victims and abusers to deny or minimize the extent of the abuse. The most recent Statistics Canada survey on domestic violence is based on telephone surveys of 26,000 Canadians in 1999.[6] According to this survey, 8% of women and 7% of men reported that they were assaulted by an intimate partner in the previous five years; among those who separated, 28% of women and 22% of men reported that they had been assaulted by a prior partner.

In some relationships there is an interactive pattern of abuse with each spouse having a significant role in initiating the violence. Professionals also need to recognize that there are relationships in which the female may even be the more violent partner.[7] Most commonly, however, the male partner is the more abusive partner, and due to their greater strength, men pose a much more serious risk to their partners than women. While 15% of women who reported being assaulted by an intimate partner required medical attention, only 3% of men received medical treatment. Of the women who were assaulted, 38% reported that they feared for their lives because of the violence, while only 7% of the men reported this level of fear.

While spousal abuse occurs in all income and age groups, the incidence is higher in lower income groups, among younger couples and in common-law relationships as opposed to legal marriages.

According to Statistics Canada, over 50% of all homicides perpetrated against women are committed by past or present marital partners, while under 10% of male homicides are perpetrated by a past or present intimate partner. Over 10% of the murders of women by their past or present marital partners involve other victims, such as their children, their parents or current lovers.[8]

These statistics demonstrate that spousal abuse is a very serious problem and that further efforts and reforms are needed to reduce its incidence and human toll. It would seem, however, based on the victimization data, reports to police and spousal homicide data, that spousal abuse has slowly declined over the past quarter of a century. While the decline has multiple causes, better responses by police, social and health services, and the legal system

---

[6] Canadian Centre for Justice Statistics, *Family Violence in Canada: A Statistical Profile 2003* (Ottawa, 2003), available free on the Internet at www.hc-sc.gc.ca/ nc-cn.

[7] See e.g. *R. v. Arsennault*, [1998] B.C.J. 2990 (Prov. Ct.). See also John Archer, "Sex Differences in Aggression Between Heterosexual Partners" (2000), 126 Psychological Bulletin 651–680. Violence is also at least as prevalent in same-sex relationships as in opposite sex relationships, though same-sex victims have greater difficulty in obtaining support from police and health service providers: see Micheal Potoczniak *et al.*, "Legal and Psychological Perspectives on Same-Sex Domestic Violence: A Multisystemic Approach" (2003), 17 J. Fam Psychology 252–259.

[8] "Spousal Violence After Marital Separation" (2001), Jurstat, vol 21, no. 7 (Statistics Canada, Canadian Centre for Justice Statistics); and Statistics Canada, *Homicide in Canada 2001* (2002). See also Joint Committee on Domestic Violence (Chair Judge Lesley Baldwin), *Working Towards a Seamless Community and Justice Response to Domestic Violence* (Ontario Attorney General, 1999). In 2001, roughly three of four victims of spousal homicide were women.

have probably played a role. Demographic changes may also have played a role, with fewer individuals in the younger age groups that are more prone to violence.[9]

Spousal abuse is a complex phenomenon and there are many different patterns of abuse. In about one third of the relationships where a woman reported abuse, there was only one incident of assault in the past five years, though a quarter of female victims reported more than ten assaults. In relationships with multiple incidents of violence, there is often a "cycle of abuse," with an abusive episode followed by a "honeymoon" or contrition phase, and then tension building towards another abusive attack.

From a social and medical perspective, abuse includes physical, sexual, financial and emotional abuse, as well as controlling a partner's relationships, while the law tends to focus on physical and sexual abuse and threats of violence. Domestic abuse can cause serious physical trauma, neurological injury, and death. For many victims of abuse, however, the psychological effects of abuse are more serious than the physical injury. Violence and threats are used to intimidate, humiliate or frighten victims, or to make them feel powerless. An abuser will often insult and verbally abuse his wife, as well as physically assault her. Often the abuser will isolate her from family and friends. Most individuals who are victims of spousal abuse suffer much more than from the physical violence alone. The abuse can result in lowered self-esteem, depression, drug and alcohol abuse, suicidal tendencies and diminished capacity to parent. While emotional abuse of a spouse can occur without physical abuse, physical abuse is almost always accompanied by emotional abuse.

Researchers have suggested classification schemes for different types of situations of spousal violence:[11]

- *Common Couple Violence*: This involves one or both partners resorting to violence during occasional arguments; it is likely to be mutual violence. The acts of violence are of relatively low frequency and intensity, and do not have a pattern of escalation. A distinguishing feature of this type of violence is that the resort to physical violence is not part of a pattern of psychological dominance and control by one partner. This is perhaps the most common situation of violence in couples.

- *Separation-engendered violence*: Violence is notably absent during most of the relationship, but one or more acts of violence occur around the time of separation, perhaps associated with the humiliating discovery of a lover. Because the violence is uncharacteristic of the relationship, it may cast a shadow of fear and distrust over the victim, but there is generally a good prognosis for a positive parent child relationship, and after the incidents at the time of separation, there is likely to be a violence free relationship between the parents. As many as one quarter of separated spouses who reported violence during their relationship may have been in this situation.

- *Intimate Terrorism or episodic battering*: This closely resembles Walker's battered wife scenario. It is a fairly common situation (under 20% of the cases in the Johnston-Campbell study), and the most emotionally damaging and physically dangerous type of spousal abuse. The male is usually the aggressor (at least 80% of this type of case). In these cases the propensity for violence lies within the makeup of the man,

---

[9]   There has also been a decline in the United States; see "Domestic violence declined in United States," *Globe and Mail*, May 18, 2000. While the number of female victims of spousal homicide in Canada rose from 52 in 2000 to 69 in 2001, there is some reason to believe that this was a random fluctuation rather than a dramatic reversal in the trend; see "Spousal homicide increase bucks trend," *National Post*, Sept. 26, 2002.

[11]   The categories set out here combine two overlapping schemes: Michael Johnson & Kathleen Ferraro, "Research on Domestic Violence in the 1990s: Making Distinctions" (2000), 62 J. Marriage and the Family 948–964 and Janet Johnston & Linda Campbell, "Parent Child Relationships in Domestic Violence Families Disputing Custody" (1993), 31(3) Fam. & Con. Cts. Rev. 282–298.

who demonstrates low tolerance for frustration and poor impulse control, at least in the context of the spousal relationship, and is possessive, domineering and jealous about his partner. Physical abuse usually develops early in the relationship and is on-going or intermittent. The potential for violence is high and may escalate after sepa-ration, often with harassment and threats alternated with pleas for return. While chil-dren sometimes have good superficial relationships with these fathers (especially girls who may be treated in a "princess-like" fashion by the father), the children tend to be very afraid of their fathers. These fathers have a low tolerance for stress and tend to be very demanding. Johnson and Campbell recommend that visitation should be supervised or suspended, especially if the threat of violence continues after separation.

- *Mutual Violent Control*: The defining feature of these relationships is the attempt of both partners to use physical violence to maintain control. This situation is rare.

- *Violent Resistance*: In these cases there is one partner, usually the male, who initiates the violence, but the other partner will respond, sometimes using more force than the initial attack. Legally some of these situations may be characterized as self-defence.

- *Psychotic and Paranoid Reactions*: These cases involve often unpredictable attacks by one spouse based on disordered thinking or drug induced state, and leaves the victims feeling traumatized, intimidated and fearful. About 5% of the cases in the Johnston and Campbell study were in this category; some of the children in this situ-ation were badly traumatized while others identified with the psychotic parent and were themselves psychotic like. Visitation between the abusive spouse and children should be supervised or suspended in these situations, at least until the abuser's mental state has stabilized.

Although in many cases, if the spouses separate physical abuse will end, in about a third of relationships in which a woman leaves her abusive partner, violence and intimidation increase after separation as the man fears that his control will end. Women and children may be at the greatest risk after the spouses separate. Statistically women have a much greater risk of being killed by an intimate partner after separation than during cohabitation, with most homicides occurring within a few months of separation.

It has now also been recognized that spousal abuse not only affects the victims directly, but is also harmful for children who witness their mother being abused. Over one third of female victims of spousal abuse report that their children saw or heard the violence, and the actual incidence is likely higher as victims may not always be aware of what their children have observed. Children are more likely to witness spousal violence if it is repeated or more serious. In almost 10% of incidents of physical abuse of women by male intimate partners, the children are subjected to an assault by the time of the incident, and in other cases they may be victims of physical or emotional abuse at other times. Children who live in families where there is a history of spousal violence are more likely to experience a range of social, behavioural and emotional problems than other children. Infants in homes where there is a pattern of spousal abuse are at increased risk of developmental delay or attachment disorder, and babies born to women who are victims of partner abuse during pregnancy have a sub-stantially heightened risk of slow fetal growth, premature delivery and neonatal death.

Domestic violence is different from other acts of violence in that the abuser is breaching a trust, and the victim is particularly vulnerable. However, due to the relationship between the victim and the abuser, and perhaps the abuser and their children, in some cases both partners may want the relationship to continue. The victim may love the abuser and want to continue to reside with him; therefore, the victim may not want to see him punished, espe-cially if she and her children rely on him for economic support. The victim would like the violence to cease, but may want to preserve the relationship. Many women remain in or return to abusive relationships, and some women leave one abusive relationship only to enter a relationship with another abusive man.

In some cases, the woman is ambivalent, wanting to leave her husband after the abusive incident. Then she may be "courted" by him and decide to return to the relationship, only to have the abuse reoccur. Women often stay in abusive relationships because they feel the need for the financial support of their husband, or because of pressure from relatives or friends to stay in the relationship. And the man may threaten that if the woman leaves he will follow her and bring her back, abduct the children, or even kill her. Given the history of violence in the relationship, these may be very credible and intimidating threats.

Professionals also need to be aware that there are cases in which there may be allegations of abuse that are exaggerated or even fabricated, for example if there is a high-conflict divorce with spouses arguing over custody of children or property issues. However, even in divorce cases where there is on-going controversy over various issues, the vast majority of allegations of spousal abuse are true, and the reality is that perpetrators of abuse are much more likely to deny or minimize abuse than "victims" are to fabricate. Indeed, the problem of false recantations by genuine victims due to intimidation, pressure or guilt is more common than fabrication by alleged victims.

It is clear that spousal abuse is a differentiated phenomena, with different patterns, risks, effects and prognosis in different relationships. As psychologist Janet Johnson observes: "All violence is unacceptable, however, not all violence is the same. Domestic violence families need to be considered on an individual basis when helping them to develop post divorce plans."[15] Individual cases must be assessed taking account of the nature and extent of the abuse, its effect on the victim and children, and its likelihood of recurrence.

The Role of Shelters, Health-Care Professionals and Other Agencies

While there is much more awareness of spousal abuse in Canada now than in the past, and there are many more social agencies and resources to deal with this problem, too many victims, especially women and their children, continue to be injured, terrorized and even killed. Victims need greater access to essential services, and those services should be provided in an "integrated" or "seamless" fashion.[16] Increasingly local communities, supported by the provincial government, are establishing domestic violence co-ordinating committees to encourage co-operation between agencies and different professionals. It is also clear that professionals who work with domestic violence cases need more interdisciplinary education and training in order to be able to deal effectively with these cases and work better with one another.

Many women do not leave abusive situations because they have no where else to go, and they fear for their safety and the safety of their children. In most Canadian cities and large towns there is one or more shelters that play a critical role in providing counselling and support, as well as crisis accommodation and security for women and their children who are leaving an abusive relationship and have nowhere else to reside. The shelters usually provide "crisis or transitional accommodation" and support for a period of two to six weeks, but there is an urgent need for long-term accommodation and support. ...

---

15 Janet Johnston, "Domestic Violence and Parent-Child Relationships in Families Disputing Custody" (1995), 9 Aust. J. Fam L. 12–25, at 24.

16 Joint Committee on Domestic Violence (Chair Judge Lesley Baldwin), *Working Towards a Seamless Community and Justice Response to Domestic Violence* (Ontario Attorney General, 1999).

Over half of shelters have programs for children. Abusive husbands may be more likely to abuse their children than other fathers. Even if they are not directly abused, children who have witnessed are often disturbed by that experience. Leaving an established home, even one in which there is abuse, into a shelter is often a disruptive experience for children. Children in shelters often have a range of emotional and behavioural problems, and the individual and group counselling in shelters that is directed at children can have an important role in providing some immediate support for these vulnerable children and their mothers. Shelters receive most of their funding from provincial governments, as well as some from private donations. They are generally operated under the direction of local volunteer boards. Shelter staff may have degrees in social work or psychology, though some do not have formal educational qualifications, and some are abuse survivors. Most shelters have a feminist orientation, and tend to encourage women to leave abusive relationships, at least if the abuse does not end. A smaller number of shelters have religious affiliations or are operated by aboriginal organizations, and have more of a "family orientation" and may be more supportive of an abused woman and her children maintaining a relationship with an abusive man, through encouraging steps to reduce the likelihood of abuse reoccurring. Shelters are often important advocates for abused women, and not infrequently shelter workers are critical of how governments, the police, courts or professionals deal with issues related to abuse.

Women's shelters often have an important role in helping women wishing to leave an abusive relationship. Although it is recognized that only a relatively small percentage of abused women stay at these shelters — usually women with few resources and no family who can take them in — these shelters often play an important counselling, educational and coordinating role. In total, over 70,000 people stayed in shelters across Canada, about 55% of them women and 45% children, but it is clear that if more spaces were available there would be greater use. A few shelters, especially those in aboriginal communities, also accommodate abused men.

In addition to counselling and treatment that may be provided by health care professionals, important counselling and support are provided for female victims by community crisis centres, sexual assault centres and toll free telephone help lines. Counselling services are provided by shelters, but in larger communities there are separate but related agencies that do this type of work. This type of counselling can be crucial for helping an abused woman to leave her partner. Many women have to be counselled many times before having the courage to leave an abusive spouse.

There are also counselling services provided for abusers. Many of the programs operate on a group model, with groups (usually of men) with a history of abuse gathering with one or two group leaders to discuss and confront their problems. One of the realities is that relatively few abusers will voluntarily seek help, and most need to be charged by the police before they recognize that they have a problem. Often counselling will be required as a condition or part of a court sentence imposed on an abusive man. While participation in counselling and other forms of individual and group therapy can reduce the incidence of violence, it is clear that some men do not respond to these programs and continue to abuse their partners. There are also concerns many of the government sponsored programs are less than six months in length, and there is no research to establish the effectiveness of this type of program. Some critics argue that limited government resources should be focussed only on victims and should not be spent on abusers. However, it is important to recognize that an abuser will rarely stop unless he receives counselling, and acknowledges that his behaviour is wrong and unacceptable in our society. There is a large gap between available places and demand for these programs directed at abusers.

Increasingly doctors, nurses and other health care professionals are receiving education in their university and professional training about the identification and treatment of spousal abuse. Health care professionals can have a critical role in working with both victims and abusers. Family doctors are now being encouraged to ask every woman patient if she has been a victim of domestic abuse, as well as to be alert for signs of abuse in trauma cases that women may report as "accidents," though not all physicians adopt this practice.

The Role of the Police in Responding to Spousal Abuse

The police play a critical role in responding to spousal abuse. At one time, police were reluctant to be involved in these cases, and expected a woman who had been abused to launch a "private prosecution." (A private prosecution is criminal prosecution brought by a private citizen — the female victim in these cases — rather than by the police and the Crown prosecutor.) There have been significant efforts to improve training and policies of the police to deal with spousal abuse.

In 1986, the Royal Canadian Mounted Police adopted a wife-assault charging policy and other forces have adopted similar policies. Police officers are no longer expected to ask a woman who has been assaulted by her husband or partner if she "wants" the man charged, but rather the police are expected to charge the man with a criminal offence. Police officers have better training and the police are a key agency for responding to spousal abuse. The police officers are now much more likely to lay charges if they are called to a spousal assault, although some police officers may be still reluctant to lay charges in cases where they cannot see any injuries or where there are no witnesses to a woman's abuse.

The police can have a critical role in coming to a home where abuse is occurring and preventing the escalation of violence. The police are aware that "domestic calls" have the potential to be violent, with a risk to the victim and the police. The police are learning techniques to reduce tensions and the potential for violence. They will often arrest and remove the abuser, and require him to spend the night in jail. Unless he has a serious criminal record, a judge will likely release him until the case can be fully dealt with by the courts, but the judge may make it a condition of his release that he move out of the home. The request for conditions on release requires the police and prosecutor to communicate with the victim about what type of conditions are appropriate, and then persuade the judge to impose these conditions.

The Supreme Court of Canada has recognized the importance of a swift police response to domestic violence in its 1999 decision in *R. v. Godoy*.[21] In this case the police received a telephone call to their emergency (911) telephone line. The phone was hung up before the caller could speak, but the police could locate the place from which the call was made. Four police officers went to the residence where a man partially opened the door. They asked to enter, but the man tried to close the door. The police prevented him from doing so and forced their way into the apartment; as soon as they got inside they heard a woman crying. A police officer entered the bedroom, where he observed the man's common law wife curled up in the fetal position, sobbing with swelling above her left eye; she told the officer that her husband had assaulted her. Based on these observations, the police decided to arrest the man. A scuffle ensued in which the man broke the finger of an officer, and the man was charged with assaulting a police officer with the intent of resisting arrest.

The trial judge dismissed the charge, concluding that the entry by the police into the premises was unauthorized and that therefore all of subsequent actions of the police actions were illegal. This decision was reversed on appeal and a new trial was ordered. The Supreme Court of Canada accepted that there is "unquestionably a recognized privacy right that residents have in the sanctity of the home" but that this must give way to the interest that the police have in protecting "life or safety". A disconnected 911 call gives the police

---

[21] [1998] SCJ 85.

the right to enter premises, and they cannot be denied entry by the person who happens to answer the door. Chief Justice Lamer wrote:

> ... the courts, legislators, police and social service workers have all engaged in a serious and important campaign to educate themselves and the public on the nature and prevalence of domestic violence. One of the hallmarks of this crime is its private nature. Familial abuse occurs within the supposed sanctity of the home. While there is no question that one's privacy at home is a value to be preserved and promoted, privacy cannot trump the safety of all members of the household. If our society is to provide an effective means of dealing with domestic violence, it must have a form of crisis response. The 911 system provides such a response. Given the wealth of experience the police have in such matters, it is unthinkable that they would take the word of the person who answers the door without further investigation .... it takes only a modicum of common sense to realize that if a person is unable to speak to a 911 dispatcher when making a call, he or she may likewise be unable to answer the door when help arrives.

Although official policies call for mandatory charging and prosecution in domestic abuse cases, in practice individual officers still have a discretion about how to deal with cases, and for a variety of reasons charges may not be laid, or they may be discontinued by the Crown prosecutor before a case is resolved in the courts. Research indicates that a rapid police response involving arrest of abusers can bring home to some abusive men the message that their conduct is unacceptable and will reduce the repetition of violence.[22]

However, there are limitations to the effectiveness of the police and the criminal justice system in protecting women. This response is most effective with men who are employed and have respect for the justice system. For some abusive men, especially those with a criminal history, the involvement of the police may heighten the danger to a woman as the man may retaliate against her for having contacted the police. Some women mistrust the police because of their own negative experiences with the police, or because of their own criminal histories. Immigrant women may be especially reluctant to involve the police, fearing social ostracism within their communities or possible deportation, or because of their experiences with the police in their native countries.

Canadian police forces are increasing their training about domestic violence issues, and computerizing records so that they can respond more quickly and effectively in cases where a prior record of domestic violence indicates that there is heightened risk.

Police increasingly work with women's shelters and other agencies, and refer abused women to these agencies. Canadian police forces also increasingly have policies and specially trained officers to deal with domestic violence cases. Some forces have social workers and community volunteers on call to assist police officers who do counselling and support work with victims of crime. Police, working with shelter staff and others, can have a critical role in assessing the risk for an individual woman and helping her to develop a "safety plan." Safety planning may include a "risk" or "lethality" assessment for future danger, a consideration of what type of legal responses are appropriate, and helping the woman organize accommodation, transportation and other aspects of the lives of herself and her children so as to reduce the risk of further assaults, and to have a plan if the abuser appears to pose an immediate threat.[25] Recently some police forces have begun to arrange for some women in high-risk situations to be given a cell phone programmed to call 911 to allow them to have a rapid response if an abusive former partner should appear.

---

[22]   Jaffe, Wolfe, Telford & Austin, "The Impact of Police Charges on Incidents of Wife Abuse" (1986), 1 J. Fam Violence 37. The 1993 Statistics Canada survey indicated that only 26% of women assaulted in intimate relationships reported to the police; reporting to the police was more likely if the violence was more serious, more frequent, or witnessed by children. Of those women who reported, in 45% of cases the violence stopped or decreased, in 40% it remained the same, and in 10% the violence increased.

[25]   See e.g. Baker, Jaffe, Berkowitz & Berkman, *Children Exposed to Violence: A Handbook for Police Trainers* (London, Ont: Centre for Children and Families in the Justice System, 2002).

In the most serious cases of abuse, the police and federal government may place an abused woman and her children in a witness protection program and help her move to another city and assume a new identity in order to escape from a violent man. This, however, is a highly intrusive response and will require the woman and her children to sever ties with her relatives and friends.

Although the police are a prime social agency for responding to spousal abuse, most incidents of violence are not reported to the police. Canadian research suggests that in only about one third of all cases in which a women is assaulted by her spouse are the police called. About two-thirds of the reports to the police were made by victims, and the rest from neighbours or relatives. The police are more likely to be called if the abuse is more persistent or severe. Over half of women who are assaulted by a *former* spouse after separation report their abuse to the police. Most women who do not call the police told researchers that their failure to do so was because they felt that it was a personal matter and did not want to involve the police, though over a third indicated that it was their fear of reprisal that caused them not to report the abuse to the police.

Criminal Prosecutions

A primary legal response to family violence is through the criminal justice system, and there have been significant reforms in the past two decades in how the criminal justice system deals with familial abuse. Since 1983, the *Criminal Code* has made it a crime for a husband to sexually assault his wife. Statutory reforms in 1988 and 1993 have helped children to come to court to testify about their abuse, and about the abuse of their mothers. The police have become much more effective in investigating domestic violence cases, and Crown Prosecutors have become more aggressive about prosecuting these cases.

While the criminal response is important, there are limitations to its use. In Canada, a person charged with a crime has significant legal rights guaranteed under the *Charter of Rights*. Respect for rights is an important aspect of Canadian life and protects accused persons from inappropriate state intervention. Further, there is a strong argument that an abusive man who is held accountable but treated fairly by the police and courts, is more likely to change his attitude and obey a court order than one who perceives that he has been treated unfairly.

Respecting the rights of an accused can, however, be frustrating for victims and may expose them to further danger. A person who is charged with a crime, like assault (which includes both threatening [and] striking a spouse) can only be convicted if the prosecutor proves "beyond a reasonable doubt" that the accused is guilty of the offence. The accused has the right to retain a lawyer, and if he is poor may have a lawyer paid by a government legal aid scheme. The accused has the right to disclosure of the prosecution's evidence before the case is tried, to allow him to prepare for a trial. The accused has the right to call evidence and to cross-examine any witnesses, including the "complainant" (the technical legal term in Canada for victim of the alleged offence), but the accused has the right not to testify if he does not wish to, and his silence is not to be considered evidence of guilt.

The accused is normally entitled to be released pending trial, though in domestic violence cases release is often with conditions such as that he stay away from the family home and surrender any firearms. If the accused has previously been convicted of assault and appears to pose a serious threat, there may be grounds to try to persuade a judge to detain him in custody pending trial, but this does not happen regularly.

It usually takes several months for a domestic violence case to be resolved in the criminal courts. In practice, relatively few cases result in a trial, as the accused often pleads guilty, or the prosecution drops the charges due to the victim recanting and telling the police that the offence did not occur.

While there is an increasing number of successful prosecutions for domestic violence, there are a number of practical difficulties in prosecuting these cases. Many of the difficulties relate to the fact that victims are often intimidated, embarrassed, pressured or feeling guilty about the case, and hence may not appear in court or are reluctant witnesses. In many Canadian courts there are now government paid social workers at the courts who support women and children who are going through the court process. These victim-witness workers provide emotional and practical support to women and children who may testify against abusive partners.

If an accused pleads not guilty to the charges, the prosecution will have to prove "beyond a reasonable doubt" that the abuse occurred. Credibility may be a major issue. It will help the prosecution if there is medical evidence to corroborate that injuries were sustained. Ordinarily in criminal cases, evidence of the "bad character" or the previous criminal conduct of the accused is not admissible to prove that he is guilty of the particular act with which he is charged. However, in spousal and child abuse cases, the courts have begun to display a more realistic approach to admitting evidence that allows the court to "understand the relationship between the parties and the context in which the abuse has occurred." Accordingly the judge may sometimes allow the victim or other witnesses to testify about the entire history of abuse in a relationship to put the charges in context.[28]

In some cases testimony from independent witnesses like health care professionals or neighbours may help corroborate a victim's testimony. There may also be letters or photographs to support her testimony. In some cases, it may be appropriate for children who have witnessed the abuse to be called as witnesses, though there is an understandable reluctance to drag them into what may feel to them like an ongoing dispute between the parents.

The police are increasingly aware that a woman who has called the police may be reluctant to testify against her husband in court. She may have reconciled with her husband by the time a case comes up for trial, or she may have been intimidated by him into "recanting" (or retracting) her allegation, or she may feel pressured by family members or economic circumstances to deny that the abuse occurred. Some police forces are starting to investigate domestic-abuse cases with a view to proving an assault occurred without having to rely on the victim's testimony in court. The gathering of evidence such as photographs of the victim's injuries, tapes of 911 emergency telephone calls,[29] and statements from the victim and other witnesses permit what is called a "victimless prosecution". The idea behind this form of evidence collection is that the victim may feel less pressure from the prosecution going forward, though she will normally be called to testify if the case goes to trial.

The police may take pictures of the injuries that a victim has suffered, and will sometimes audio or videotape statements from the victim and abuser. Canadian courts have now accepted that a taped statement by a woman to the police may be the basis for proving the abuse, even if she takes the witness stand to deny that her husband abused her and say that her injuries were accidental, provided that the judge is satisfied that the earlier statement is true and that she has been pressured into recanting the earlier statement.[30]

---

[28] *R. v. F. (D.S.)*, [1999] O.J. 688 (C.A.).

[29] The tape recording of a 911 call and statements made by a victim that are substantially contemporaneous with the assault will be admissible evidence in court under the *res gestae* exception to the hearsay rule even if she does not testify in court. The courts consider these contemporaneous statements are likely to be reliable and unlikely to be fabricated.

[30] *R. v. Mohamed*, [1997] O.J. 1287 (Prov. Div). Prior to the Supreme Court of Canada's decision in *R. v. B. (K.G.)* (1993), 79 C.C.C. (3d) 257, a prior statement given by a victim to the police that was inconsistent with the witness's testimony at trial could *not* be used as evidence for the truth of its contents, unless the witness adopted the statement as the truth while testifying. The Supreme Court in *B. (K.G.)* held that prior inconsistent statements might be admitted for their truth if they met the dual requirements of necessity and reliability.

Specialized Criminal Courts for Domestic Violence

Increasingly specialized domestic violence courts are being established to deal more effectively with these cases, including specialized courts throughout Ontario.[31] These specialized domestic violence courts typically have resources such as victim-assistance programs to familiarize the victim with the court procedure and to provide support to them throughout the trial process. By having a specific domestic-violence court, prosecutors are more likely to be able to effectively deal with the problem of a recanting victim. A major advantage of this type of specialized court is that the prosecutors, police and support staff have the resources, training, coordination and sensitivity to deal with domestic violence cases. Typically cases are dealt with more quickly than in the regular courts, and there are more guilty pleas from abusers. To ensure fairness to accused persons, judges are not "specialized" but rotate in from the general criminal court.

Many victims, especially those who have not separated from their spouses, do not want their spouse sent to jail. Imprisonment of an abuser can have very serious economic repercussions for a victim and her children, and can be psychologically distressing. Despite the fact that Canadian judges in theory have said that a jail sentence is normally appropriate for an abusive husband, in practice first offenders usually receive a sentence of probation unless it is a very serious assault. The criminal justice system, especially the specialized domestic violence courts try to deal with the underlying causes of abuse. Their goal is to reduce the number of repeat offenders. These innovative programs allow an abusive husband to plead guilty and receive counselling rather than punishment. This option is only available to offenders who have not caused significant harm to their victims, did not use a weapon and have no prior record of spousal abuse.

There are a number of different legal approaches that are used in domestic violence courts. Perhaps the most effective responses involve early police, Crown prosecutor and victim coordination. In some courts if an accused is considered suitable and he is willing, after the initial arrest participation in a Partner Assault Response program may be a condition of release on bail. The case is then adjourned. If he successfully completes the group counselling program (usually 16 weeks), the Crown will usually recommend a conditional discharge, which means he will not have a "criminal conviction" that may affect future employment prospects, though there would still be a criminal record that would appear on police records. At some later point even that limited record of a discharge may be erased if there are no further offences. The hope is that the abuse will stop and the family can remain intact, if this is what both parties want. One aspect of the Partner Assault Response Program is for the staff to contact the victim to ascertain whether the abuse has really stopped. This type of response will not be an appropriate way of dealing with more serious or repeat situations of domestic violence.

The results of these innovative programs generally seem to be positive, though there is a need for further research into their effectiveness. In 1999, the Woman Abuse Council of Toronto released the results of its *Women's Court Watch Project*. This project monitored

---

Although the courts would prefer these past statements to be in the form of a videotape, this will not always be necessary. This ruling makes it possible for prosecutors to ask the judge to receive in evidence statements given by the victim to the police after an attack by her abusive partner if she retracts her allegations in court. This is not uncommon as many victims "recant" due to intimidation, guilt or concern about the economic consequences for themselves or their children of the abuser being convicted. However, if the police fail to tape the victim's statement and caution her about its future use in court ("a *K.G.B.* caution"), an officer's testimony about her statement in the face of her recanting is unlikely to be sufficient to gain a conviction: see *R. v. Chappell*, [2003] O.J. 772 (C.A.).

[31] See the description of domestic violence courts in Statistics Canada, *Family Violence in Canada: A Statistical profile, 2003* (Ottawa, 2003), pp. 52–59.

judges' decisions and outcomes in domestic violence cases and compared the effectiveness of two specialized courts to non-specialized courts. The results indicated that the specialized courts were better able to successfully prosecute domestic violence cases, had lower rates of withdrawal of charges by the Crown, as well as higher rates of guilty verdicts and higher rates of victims attending courts. The success of these courts was attributed to the coordination between the Police, Victim/Witness Assistance Programme, Crown Attorneys, batterers' program, and probation and community agencies.

The effectiveness of the counselling programs at reducing recidivism, however, has yet to be established.

Sentencing in Criminal Court

In the past, sentencing practices have revealed a high level of tolerance for crimes of violence against women. Physical and sexual assaults of women by intimate partners were not treated with the same degree of seriousness as other assaults, and sentences did not reflect adequate concern for these crimes. Judges often failed to appreciate the nature of the crime or its impact on the victim. Often an intimate relationship between the victim and the accused was treated as a mitigating factor in sentencing.

More recently, however, the appeal courts have clearly reflected a change in the legal attitude and response to domestic violence. In its 1989 decision in *R v. Inwood*,[32] the Ontario Court of Appeal imposed a thirty-day jail sentence on a first offender in a domestic violence case and articulated the principle that there is to be a presumption of a jail sentence in domestic violence cases:

> This court has acted on the principle that where there is a serious offence involving violence to the person then general deterrence must be the paramount consideration in sentencing in order to protect the public. In my opinion, this principle is applicable not only to violence between strangers but also to domestic violence. Domestic assaults are not private matters, and spouses are entitled to protection from violence just as strangers are. This does not mean that in every instance of domestic violence a custodial sentence should be imposed, but that it should be normal where significant bodily harm has been inflicted in order to repudiate and denounce such conduct.

... An amendment to the *Criminal Code* in 1997 makes clear that Parliament intends that the facts that an offender abused his spouse or child, or abused a position of trust in relation to the victim are to be treated as "aggravating circumstances" that should increase the sentence above what it would otherwise be.

In practice, however, despite these statements of principle from Parliament and appeal courts, it is still common for abusers to receive probation for a first domestic violence conviction, unless there is serious injury. Often there will be a condition that the abuser attend a counselling program, if one is available, and there may be conditions about not contacting the victim, if this is what she desires. However, in cases where there is significant injury to the victim or there has been a previous conviction, the courts are now likely to impose a jail sentence. The courts are also starting to emphasize the need for jail sentences in cases where an abuser is a repeat offender, or has continued to harass his former spouse while on bail from previous charges.[34] ...

While the courts are taking domestic violence cases more seriously, there is still substantial variation in sentences imposed in cases of spousal assault. Judicial discretion and individual judicial attitudes coupled with incidences where the victim requests that no custodial

---

[32] [1989] O.J. NO. 428 (Ont. CA.). See also *R. v. Brown* (1992), 73 C.C.C. (3d) 242 (Alta. C.A.).

[34] *R. v. Bates*, [2000] O.J. 2558 (Ont. C.A.).

sentences be given may explain why custodial sentences of significant length are generally not imposed in spousal abuse cases.

Peace Bond (or Recognizance)

Under s. 810 of the *Criminal Code*, it is possible for one person to be required by a judge to enter into a "peace bond" (technically called a "recognizance") if another person can establish that she has "reasonable grounds" to believe that the first person will harm her or her children. Although part of the criminal process, this type of proceeding only requires a finding on a "civil standard" of proof for the judge to impose a peace bond. It is not necessary to prove "beyond a reasonable doubt" that an offence has occurred; to obtain a recognizance it is only necessary to establish on "reasonable grounds," based on evidence of past conduct or threats, [or] fear of future violence.

A person who is required to enter into a peace bond by a court is not convicted of a criminal offence. He is, however, ordered by judge "to keep the peace," and usually to abide by other conditions that the court may impose on his behaviour, such as requiring him to refrain from communicating with the victim, stay a certain distance from her residence, or surrender firearms. If he fails to keep the terms of this order, he will forfeit a specified sum of money. More significantly, a person who fails to keep the conditions of his peace bond is committing a criminal offence. A practical advantage of the peace bond (which can be in effect for a maximum of 12 months) is that the person's name is entered on the police computer system and any police officers called by the victim about that person should be alerted to the need for urgency and the recognized potential for danger.

Typically, peace bonds are used in cases where the prosecutor feels that the evidence of abuse is not strong or the victim is unwilling to proceed and the prosecutor decides to "plea bargain" with the accused to drop the charges if he agrees to enter into a peace bond. In some cases in which the police have not laid charges, a victim may decide to seek a peace bond on her own, and in some communities a legal aid clinic may help her do this. The person goes before a justice of the peace, usually at the local criminal court or police station, to make a sworn statement (called an "information") to commence the process of obtaining a peace bond.

Requiring a person to enter a peace bond is most likely to be an effective deterrent against further abuse if the abuser is an individual who wants to preserve his reputation in the community or his relationship either with the victim or his child. The psychological and deterrent effect on an abusive spouse of appearing in court and being told by a judge "keep the peace" and obey other conditions is most likely to be effective if the history of violence is limited and there is no prior criminal record or history of defying court orders. Some victims may feel more comfortable with "preventative justice" than a criminal conviction for the abuser, because of psychological and financial reasons, as well as concern about children.

This type of order may give the victim the sense that she is entitled to protection. However, it is not uncommon for men with a significant history of abuse or offending to violate the terms of a peace bond, and sometimes the police are not aggressive about enforcing the terms of this type of "quasi-criminal" order. Traditionally, peace bonds have not been effectively enforced by the police, and the process of obtaining a peace bond could actually increase a woman's danger by lulling her into a false sense of security. Presently in Canada, relatively few charges are laid by the police for "breaching a recognizance." In some cases, the woman's risk may increase after the man enters into a recognizance as he feels his control is threatened, and the recognizance only provides protection if the police are willing and able to enforce its terms.

Battered Woman's Defence

The acceptance by Canadian courts of the "battered-woman's" defence reflects a changed understanding by judges of the effects of spousal abuse on its victims, especially women, in situations where in a moment of terror or despair, they kill or injure their abusers. In 1990 in *R. v. Lavallee*[39] the Supreme Court of Canada ruled that when a woman is charged with murdering her abusive partner, the court can take account of the "battered-woman syndrome"[40] Her acts might then be considered "self-defence" even though at the time she killed him she faced no immediate threat to her physical safety (for example because he was asleep), if taking account of her mental state as an abused woman, she had a "reasonable apprehension of death or grievous bodily harm." It is not what an "objective observer" would have done in this situation that determines whether she can succeed with this defence. Rather, the question is whether this woman, given her situation and her experience as an abused woman, "reasonably perceived" a threat of serious injury or death if she did not kill him. The jury can hear expert evidence about the mental state of abused women to determine whether this particular victim of battering was acting "reasonably," taking account of all of her circumstances and the context of the abusive relationship.

By allowing expert evidence (from a psychiatrist or psychologist) on the issue of the effect of abuse on the mental state of women, the jury will be able to understand why this particular woman did not simply flee when she perceived her life to be in danger. The *Lavallee* decision was also significant for helping to the dispel misconceptions about why women stay in abusive relationships.

Divorce & Family Law

In Canada, physical or mental cruelty has been a ground for divorce since 1968, but until about a decade ago, relatively few reported family law cases raised spousal abuse issues. Increasingly, however, abuse is a factor that judges consider when dealing with a range of issues that arise in the context of spousal separation. ...

There are concerns that women who have been intimidated by abuse may sometimes feel pressured into accepting unfavourable property settlements, even if they have good lawyers. While in low conflict separation, mediation ... can be an effective way of dealing with many of the issues that arise in the context of separation, [abused] women ... should not be referred to mediation unless there is a high degree of assurance that their interests will be protected. Some mediators have appropriate training and orientation to screen cases for abuse issues, and ensure that a mediated settlement does not jeopardize the safety of a woman or her

---

[39] [1990] 1 S.C.R 852, 55 C.C.C. (3d) 97. In coming to this conclusion, the Supreme Court relied heavily on the work of the American psychologist Lenore Walker. These developments in the courts coincided with the appointment of more women judges, with *Lavallee* written by Bertha Wilson, the first woman appointed to the Supreme Court of Canada. In *R. v. Malott*, [1998] S.C.J. 12, the Supreme Court reaffirmed that merely because a women had been battered, did not mean that she had a defence. Rather, the jury could receive expert evidence to explain why an abused women might stay in an abusive relationship, the effect that being in such a relationship might have on her perception of danger from her abuser, and whether she reasonably believed that her acts were necessary to protect herself from death or grievous bodily harm.

[40] Some critics have argued that being a victim of "battered-woman" syndrome should mitigate a sentence, but should not result in an acquittal. The defence can be used for assault charges or even welfare fraud, if the victim of abuse has been coerced into committing this offence. This defence poses special tactical problems for the Crown after the death of the (alleged) abuser. The fact that most victims of spousal battering do not kill their assailants raises moral and policy questions about whether those who respond most violently should have a full defence. See Alan Dershowitz, *The Abuse Excuse*, (1994, New York, Little Brown).

children, but not all mediators identify and deal with spousal abuse issues in an appropriate way.[41]

Family Separation — Restraining Orders

If there is a significant risk of post-separation harassment or violence and there has not been a criminal sanction imposed, it is often appropriate for a family lawyer to seek a civil "restraining order", such as under s. 46 of Ontario's *Family Law Act*. That section permits a court to make an order "restraining a person from molesting, annoying or harassing" the applicant or a child in her care. The order may be general or may be more detailed and require the abuser to stay a certain distance from the residence or place of work of the applicant, or to refrain from direct or indirect communication. It is common in domestic violence cases for the victim to seek a civil restraining order along with other civil remedies such as custody or support. Judges will generally expect some evidence of recent violence or harassment to obtain such a restraining order, and, for example, a single incident of abuse two years prior may not be a sufficient basis for obtaining such an order.

In Ontario, it is generally necessary for the person seeking a civil restraining order to serve the other party with notice of the court application, and have a hearing in front of a Family Court judge before an order can be made. This process may take days, or quite possibly weeks. In a number of American and Canadian jurisdictions, including Alberta, Saskatchewan, Prince Edward Island and the Yukon, there is special civil legislation that facilitates the obtaining of a civil order on an "urgent basis" with justices of the peace available by phone 24 hours a day; if there is clear evidence of a risk of violence, a short term interim order can be made without the alleged abuser having the right to prior notice that an order is being sought. There is a proposal for similar legislation in Ontario, the *Domestic Violence Prevention Act*.[42] The Ontario government, however, has not yet proclaimed the Act in force, largely because the resources to allow for effective implementation by the courts, legal aid and police are not yet in place.

For some abusers, the mere fact that a court order has been made will be sufficient to actually restrain their behaviour, but for other abusers enforcement of civil orders may be a serious problem. The violation of a civil restraining order is an offence and the police may arrest the person who violates the order. While victims sometimes have difficulties in getting the police to enforce this type of civil order, as police training about domestic violence issues increases, enforcement is improving. Some police forces have policies to monitor the family courts for the making of these civil orders, and ensure that they are entered on police information systems, but counsel for a victim of abuse would be well advised to send the police a copy of any order, and to set out any special concerns.

A civil "restraining order" is similar in effect to a "recognizance" (or peace bond), except that the restraining order is obtained by the victim as part of a civil action in family law proceedings. The recognizance (discussed above) is obtained as part of the criminal process;

---

41   For a discussion of appropriate standards for mediators, see Andrew Schepard, "An Introduction to the Model Standards of Practice for Family and Divorce Mediation" (2001), 35 Fam.L.Q.1 and Deborah Zutter, "Mediation in the Shadow of Abuse — an Update" (2003), 20 Can. Fam. L. Q. 65–95. For a discussion of the problems of mediation in practice, see L.Neilson, *Spousal Abuse, Children and the Legal System: Final Report* (University of New Brunswick, 2001) <*http://www.unb.ca/arts/CFVR/spousal abuse.pdf*>.

42   S.O. 2000, c. 33; not in effect. [This Act would be repealed by *An Act to amend various Acts in relation to certain family law matters and to repeal the Domestic Violence Protection Act, 2000* (Bill 133) (passed but not yet proclaimed). Bill 133 would re-enact s. 46 of the *Family Law Act* so that a restraining order could be made against a person cohabiting with the applicant or who has cohabited with the applicant. In other words, the section's application would not be limited to spouses or former spouses as defined in s. 29 of the Act.]

a Crown prosecutor may only seek a criminal conviction or a recognizance. If there is a concern about police reluctance to enforce a civil order, it may be more useful to obtain a recognizance under the *Criminal Code* s. 810, which only requires that there are "reasonable grounds" to believe that there is a threat to the future safety of the complainant or her children. Some police forces are more willing to enforce a recognizance made pursuant to the *Criminal Code* orders [than] "mere" civil restraining orders.

Ultimately court orders only provide protection if the abusive spouse has a basic respect for the legal system, which is often not the case, or if the abuser has a realistic expectation of a quick police response to any violation. Some abusers pose a high risk to victims and will not be restrained even by the certainty of arrest for continued harassment of the victim, in which case more direct measures must be taken if the victim is to be protected, for example by having her stay in a secure residence if the abuser is not in police custody.

Order for Exclusive Possession of the Home

If a criminal prosecution has been commenced as a result of an incident of domestic abuse, it may be possible for the victim to contact the police or prosecutor to request that the judge in the criminal process deal with the issue of possession of the home. After an accused is arrested, the criminal court judge who is dealing with bail may make it a condition of release that the accused abuser no longer reside in the matrimonial home, and effectively give exclusive possession of the home to the other spouse and children, until the end of the criminal process.

In addition to the possibility of having possession of the home dealt with in the criminal process, all provinces include in their family law legislation provisions that allow one spouse to obtain a civil order for exclusive possession of the matrimonial home, requiring the spouse against whom the order is made to vacate the premises. A woman seeking a civil order for exclusive possession of the home generally must notify her partner of the court application, and have a hearing in front of a Family Court judge. This process may take days, or quite possibly weeks.

Many female victims of domestic violence leave their spouses and seek accommodation in a women's shelter or with relatives. Leaving the home generally has the advantage of obtaining moral and other types of support, as well as accommodation. However, obtaining a court order for exclusive possession of the home — and excluding the abuser — is often the least disruptive alternative for the children, as well as for the abused parent. Canadian courts may grant an abused woman exclusive possession of the family home, ordering the abusive husband to leave, regardless of which spouse owns the property or whether they live in a rented property.

An applicant may appear before a judge on short notice and have an interim exclusive possession order made without a full trial.[43] In theory, an order for exclusive possession can be obtained even without proof of domestic violence, though the fact that a person has been subjected to emotional or physical abuse will be significant in determining whether a court will grant exclusive possession of the home. The best interests of any children are an important factor in any court decision about possession of the home.

In practice it can be difficult to obtain an interim order without clear evidence of abusive conduct. It is generally necessary to have sufficient evidence to persuade a judge that continued cohabitation is no longer appropriate, and the other spouse is at fault and should be

---

[43] See e.g. Ontario *Family Law Act*, R.S.O. 1990, c. F-3, s. 24(3) & (4). Alberta, Saskatchewan (*Victims of Domestic Violence Act*, S.S. 1994, c. V-6.02) and Prince Edward Island (*Victims of Family Violence Act*, S.P.E.I. 1996, C. 47) have legislation that specifies that evidence of spousal abuse may be the basis for a civil order for exclusive possession of the home, and that makes it easier for victims to obtain these orders.

excluded from the home. Some court decisions indicate that the mere fact that there has been an assault at some point in the relationship may not be sufficient to obtain a civil exclusive-possession order; it must be a relatively recent assault with some evidence that violence may reoccur.[44] The better view is that if there has been a recent assault, this creates an environment in which it is psychologically unfair to expect a victim to remain. Even if it is not established that there has been a physical assault, if there is evidence of significant emotional abuse, this should be a basis for obtaining exclusive possession as it may be emotionally harmful to the children to remain in this type of situation.

There may be difficulties in proving abuse or violence, especially at the interim stage, in the face of what will often be the emphatic denials of the other party. Evidence from independent sources, including neighbours or health-care professionals will always be helpful.

With some abusive spouses, an exclusive possession order may not be sufficient protection, and the victim will only be safe if more secure accommodation is found.

Family Separation — Access & Custody Issues

There is growing recognition that spousal abuse should be an important factor when the family courts are dealing with issues relating to the care of children after parental separation. Children have a special role in situations of spousal abuse. In some cases, a husband does not start to become abusive until his wife is pregnant, or serious arguments may develop about the children. Sometimes an abused spouse, usually the mother, may decide to stay in an abusive relationship "for the sake of the children." Research suggests that abused women whose children are witnesses to assaults are more likely to ultimately leave their partners than those women whose abuse "remains between the grown ups."

There is now a substantial and growing body of research on the negative effects on children of growing up in a home where there is inter-parental abuse, even if the children are not direct observers of the abuse.[46] Children who grow up in homes with significant levels of spousal abuse are more likely to experience behavioural and emotional problems. Spousal abuse often has an inter-generational aspect, as boys raised in a family with spousal abuse are more likely to become abusers and girls are more likely to grow up to be victims of spousal abuse.[47]

At least one quarter of those men who physically abuse their partners also physically abuse their children. In some studies as many as three-quarters of abusive husbands also abused their children; at least some of the variation in rates depends on type of population studied, with higher degrees of spousal abuse making abuse of children more likely. Young infants caught in situations of spousal abuse or conflict may be dropped or accidentally injured. Older children may be injured trying to protect an abused mother.

There is also the possibility of abduction by an abusing spouse. Sometimes the abusive spouse will threaten abduction of the children to intimidate or control a partner, and if separation occurs, the abusive parent may abduct the child. The abducting parent may leave the

---

[44] See e.g. *Dolgopol v. Dolgopol* (1994), 10 R.F.L. (4th) 368 (Sask. Q.B.) and *Skrak v. Skrak*, [1993] O.J. 2642 (Gen Div.).

[46] For a review, see Katherine Kitzmann *et al*, "Child Witnesses to Domestic Violence: A 'Meta-Analytic' Review" (2003), 71 J. Consulting & Clinical Psychology 339–352.

[47] See P. Jaffe, D. Wolfe & S. Wilson, *Children of Battered Women* (1990, Newbury Park, Ca., Sage); E. Peled, P. Jaffe & J. Edelson (eds), *Ending the Cycle of Violence: Community Responses to Children of Battered Women* (1995, Newbury Park Ca., Sage); Geffner, Jaffe and Sudermann eds., *Children Exposed to Family Violence: Current Issues in Research, Intervention and Policy Development* (1998, Binghampton N.Y., Haworth Press); and Dauvergne and Johnson, "Children Witnessing Family Violence" Juristat, vol. 21(6) (Statistics Canada, 2001).

country with the child. Although parental abduction is a crime, and Canada has signed treaties to try to deal with the problem, in practice it can be very difficult to locate a parent who
has abducted their child, especially if the parent has gone to another country. Parental abduction is very disruptive to a child, and the abductor invariably lies to the child about what
has happened, sometimes saying that the other parent has died. If there is a possibility of
abduction, this may be grounds for a court order requiring supervised access or denying
access.[49] In the most serious cases, an abusive parent — invariably the father — may kill
both his spouse and his children, or may kill his children and commit suicide; such homicides are likely to occur in the context of marital breakdown or separation.

There is a growing body of research on the negative effects on children of observing or
hearing one parent being abused by another. Children who observe inter-parental abuse are
often terrified by the experience, and may not understand it. Infants growing up in an environment with high levels of spousal violence may suffer from developmental delays or attachment problems. About one half of women who are victims of abuse reported that their
children saw or heard at least one assault; children are more likely to witness domestic violence if the incidents involve injury or occur after separation. Some American studies indicate that most children in homes where there is spousal abuse will witness it. In some cases
witnessing even a single serious incident of abuse can produce post-traumatic stress disorder
in a child.[51] Even if a child does not directly observe spousal abuse, living in a home where
there is spousal abuse can have serious negative effects. ... The worst outcomes for children
are associated with both observing spousal abuse and being directly abused.

There is now a substantial body of research from experts in child development that children from homes where there has been spousal abuse have:

- more behavioural problems and lower social competence; boys tend to externalize
  and have school difficulties or be more aggressive, including the commission of offences for adolescents, while girls tend more towards depression;

- lower self esteem and higher anxiety, as evidenced by sleep disturbance and
  nightmares;

- greater risk of abusing drugs or alcohol; and

- substantially more likely to be involved in abusive situations as adults, boys as abusive partners and girls as abused women.[53]

Fortunately, there is evidence that for most children,[54] there will be substantial improvements in behaviour and emotional state when the child ceases to live with the abusive parent, and that therapy for the child can be helpful. There is a need for more research into
long-term effects on children of spousal abuse, as well as on the effects of different types of
legal arrangements (e.g. no access vs. supervised access vs. open access). There is also a
need to research the effect of different patterns and types of spousal abuse on children, since

---

[49]   See, e.g., *Zahr v. Zahr* (1994), 24 Alta. L.R. (3d) 274 (Q.B.). Although beyond the scope of this paper, it is
submitted the judges should consider spousal abuse as an important factor justifying relocation by a custodial
parent; see *Guthro v. Guthro*, [1997] N.S.J. 91 (C.A.); and Ikem, "You Can Run But Can You Hide: Relocation Rights and Domestic Violence", [1996] Clearinghouse Review 308.

[51]   D.G. Saunders, "Child Custody Decisions in Families Experiencing Woman Abuse" (1994), 39 Social Work
51.

[53]   H.A. Davidson, "Child Abuse and Domestic Violence: Legal Connections and Controversies" (1995), 29 *Fam.
L.Q.* 357–373, at 359; and V. Masliansky, "Child Custody and Visitation Dertminations When Domestic Violence Has Occurred," [1996] Clearinghouse Review 273, at 275.

[54]   P. Mertin, "A Follow Up Study of Children Frm Domestic Violence" (1995) 9 *Aust. J. Fam. L.* 76–85.

most of the research to date has been based on situations where the abusive parent has not had contact and where the women lived in a shelter for a period of time — situations that are likely to involve more severe abuse and lower income families. Some children seem relatively immune to growing up in a violent home, and there is also a need for research into this resilience.

An abused spouse often suffers from lowered self-esteem, depression, drug- or alcohol-abuse or may take out their feelings of powerlessness by mistreating their children. A history of physical aggression in the family is "strongly associated with mother's diminished parenting, in that mothers from violent relationships are less warm and more coercive with their children."[55] While it is clear that children suffer from the diminished parenting capacity of an abused parent, there may be difficulty for judges in deciding how to take account of this in a custody dispute. It may be argued that it is unfair for an abusive parent to be able to "hold against" the abused partner inadequacies that are caused by abuse, though a focus on the "best interests" of the child may weaken this argument. Another response may be for the abused parent to adduce evidence on the positive effects of therapy for victims of spousal abuse, in particular for improving parenting capacity. It may also be important to adduce evidence of the controlling, possessive nature of abusive spouses, and the negative effect that this can have on their parenting capacity.

Recently the courts in Canada have begun to take account of spousal abuse and have tended to deny an abusive man custody of his children, recognizing the negative effects that spousal abuse has on children, and the high likelihood that the man may also directly abuse his children.[56] Proposals have been made to amend the *Divorce Act*[57] to explicitly make a history of violence or threats of violence towards a spouse a factor that judges should take into account in deciding whether it is in the "best interests" of a child to reside with or have contact with a parent. This legislation would certainly be desirable, as it would remind all judges, lawyers and parents of the damaging effects on children of spousal abuse, though already many judges and lawyers are aware of this.

Sometimes an abusive father will be denied the right to visit his children after separation, though some judges appear to accept that even an abusive husband has the right to visit his children, posing a risk to mothers, especially at the time when the father comes to pick up the child for a visit. Judges will be most inclined to terminate access if there is clear evidence that spousal abuse is continuing or escalating after separation, or if there is evidence of direct abuse of the children.[58]

If there has been post-separation abuse, then visitation can pose a serious risk to the mother as well as the children. The exercise of access rights can be used to control a former partner. There are especially great risks for verbal or physical abuse of a parent at the time that care of the child is being changed. In some communities there are programs to supervise visits, or at least supervise the exchange of the children, to minimize the risk to mother and children. Courts are increasingly recognizing that a child's welfare is "inextricably tied" to the "mother's psychological and physical security" and that placing a custodial parent in a situation of risk poses a risk to the child.[59]

---

55 J. Johnston, "High-Conflict Divorce" (1994), 4(1) *The Future of Children* 165–182, at 175.

56 See, e.g., M. Shaffer & N. Bala, "Wife Abuse and Family Law in Canada" (2003), forthcoming in Journal of Emotional Abuse, indicating that in reported cases 1997–2000 involving spousal abuse allegations, there were no cases in which the judge believed the allegations and awarded custody to the abusive father.

57 Bill C-22, 1st Reading, Dec. 10, 2002. [Ontario's *Children's Law Reform Act* was amended in 2006 to require courts to consider violence or abuse in custody and access decisions. See ss. 24(3) and (4).]

58 See, e.g., *Abdo v. Abdo* (1993), 50 R.F.L. (3d) 171 (N.S. C.A.).

59 *Pollastro v. Pollastro* (1999), 45 R.F.L. (4th) 404 (Ont. C.A.).

Children's wishes on access and custody can also be problematic. An abused parent may be viewed as weak and "ineffectual," while the child may view the abuser as "stronger". There can also be a great deal of manipulation and denigration of the abused spouse. Unfortunately, some judges may view the wishes of the child to reside with the abusive father as determinative, but many judges are aware of the danger of placing much weight on the expressed preferences of a child to live with a parent with a history of abuse.[60]

Child Protection

Women who live in relationships where there has been serious spousal abuse, and in particular violence, may find themselves involved in child-protection proceedings commenced by a child-protection agency (the local Children's Aid Society). Some abused women are reluctant to call the police as they are concerned that this may result in the involvement of the child protection authorities and possible loss of custody of their children.

In Alberta, New Brunswick, Nova Scotia, Newfoundland, Saskatchewan and Prince Edward Island, child protection legislation specifically refers to domestic violence as a factor in finding that a child is in need of protection. For example the New Brunswick *Family Services Act* s. 31(1)(f) states that the "security or development of a child may be in danger when ... the child is living in a situation where there is severe domestic violence." The courts in other provinces have also demonstrated a willingness to take account of spousal violence as a factor in child protection proceedings. Spousal violence is rarely the only factor operative in protection proceedings, but rather is often combined with a family environment involving other types of child abuse or neglect. When there is a high degree of spousal abuse, the abusive partner is often abusive towards the children. Victims of spousal abuse not infrequently suffer from depression and alcohol or drug abuse, and their parenting capacity is often compromised, so that neglect concerns may also be present.

In some cases where the father is abusive of his spouse and children, the child protection agency may become involved and allow [the] children to remain in the mother's care only on condition that the father has no contact. In some abusive relationships with a "cycle of violence", the abused mother may support the departure of her partner after an abusive incident, but then allow the man to move back in during his next "contrition phase", again endangering children and provoking the agency to apply to remove the children from the mother's care. In abusive relationships, the agency will want evidence that the mother understands the cycle of abuse and has broken the pattern, for example by seeking counselling, leaving the relationship and moving into a shelter.

In some situations the concerns of the agency are not limited to abuse of the mother by the father, but rather there is a violent relationship involving mutual abuse, often combined with neglect or abuse of children. If there is an ongoing pattern of spousal violence in these mutual abuse cases, the instability of both parents and the lack of protection for the child may make removal of the children more likely.

Tort Law[61]

As lawyers and judges become more aware of domestic violence issues, victims have begun to make tort-based damage claims in the civil courts to seek financial compensation for a range of physical and psychological injuries that occur in a familial context, principally as a result of wife abuse or child abuse. These cases are still not common, but Canadian

---

[60] See e.g. *Mitchell v. Mitchell* (2002), 30 R.F.L. (5th) 365 (Ont. S.C.J.).

[61] See Bala, "Tort Remedies & the Family Law Practitioner" (1999), 16 C.F.L.Q. 423.

courts are receptive to these claims if there has been serious abuse; as judges and lawyers gain awareness of the nature and effects of abuse, damage awards have substantially increased. A tort action can provide financial compensation for a victim of family violence. It may also provide a victim with an important forum for social vindication and for holding an abuser accountable.

It is possible for an abused spouse to join a claim for financial compensation with a claim for matrimonial relief, such as a division of property. ...

In a 1995 Ontario case a man terrorized his estranged wife for four months following their separation, threatening to harm the woman and abduct her daughter; the man stalked the woman and harassed her friends and professional advisors. Medical evidence established that the woman suffered post-traumatic stress disorder, severe depression, insomnia and suicidal tendencies as a result of the abuse. The court awarded her $105,000 in compensation as she suffered psychological injury that impaired her employment. She also required extensive therapy and had expenses to improve her home's security system.[63]

As with other types of family litigation, credibility issues and expert evidence are likely to be central to any tort claim. As soon as litigation is contemplated, counsel should begin to seek out evidence to corroborate a client's position, preferably from such "independent" sources as police reports and medical doctors. Various experts such as doctors and mental health professionals may play a key role in establishing injuries or damages caused by abuse. Evidence in the possession of the parties like photographs, letters or diaries may also be significant for establishing a claim. Victims of abuse should be aware that tort litigation may be a highly intrusive process, with defendants attempting to challenge credibility, for example by seeking access to therapeutic records of a plaintiff.[64] ...

There are special legislative provisions that stipulate that limitation periods for torts allegedly committed against minors, such as assault and battery arising out of child sexual abuse, only commence at the age of majority. The Supreme Court of Canada has recognized that adult survivors of childhood abuse often lack an awareness of the fact that emotional and psychological difficulties experienced as adults may be attributed to earlier childhood abuse, and so may not seek legal redress until they reach their mid 20's or later. The Court has articulated a rule of "reasonable discoverability" for the commencement of the running of a limitation period. Accordingly the limitation period does not begin to run until the plaintiff is reasonably capable of discovering the wrongful nature of the defendant's conduct *and* of understanding the relationship between the earlier abuse and the plaintiff's condition. In practice, for adult survivors of childhood abuse the limitation period may not commence until they are in therapy and appreciate the connection between their psychological condition and earlier abuse. There may be situations in which victims of spousal abuse may be able to make similar arguments to extend limitation periods if they are not aware of the psychological effects of their abuse. Expert evidence from a mental health professional will usually be necessary to establish the right to extend the limitation period.

In a number of Canadian jurisdictions, including Saskatchewan, British Columbia, Nova Scotia, Ontario and Newfoundland, there are special legislative provisions to extend limitation periods where a victim of sexual abuse was dependent upon the alleged perpetrator or

---

63   *MacKay v. Buelow* (1995), 11 R.F.L. (4th) 403 (Ont. Gen. Div.).

64   *A.M. v. Ryan*, [1997] 1 S.C.R. 157 accepted that a claim of privilege might attach to records of the therapist of a plaintiff in a civil abuse suit, but appeared to place significant weight on "ascertaining the truth" in a civil case based on allegations of abuse, suggesting that any therapist-patient privilege claimed by a party is narrow in civil abuse cases.

not aware of the harm they suffered from the abuse.[66] These provisions are most obviously applicable to victims of child sexual abuse, but may also be relevant for some spousal abuse situations.

An initial consideration in deciding whether to commence a civil action is whether any judgment that is obtained is likely to be satisfied by the defendant. This requires some assessment of the assets of the potential defendant. In most situations of intra-familial torts, criminal acts form the basis for civil liability. In these cases, where the defendant lacks resources to satisfy a judgment, an application can be made for a claim under provincial criminal injuries compensation legislation. These applications do not require a criminal conviction; it is only necessary to establish on a civil standard of proof that a crime has occurred. While the amount recoverable in a provincially funded criminal injuries compensation claim is limited (for example in Ontario $25,000 is the maximum lump sum), a person who has been granted government compensation may still pursue a civil tort action against the perpetrator (subject to reimbursing the fund from any judgment enforced).

There are limitation period provisions for making a government compensation application — 1 or 2 years from the date of the alleged offence — but the Board responsible for administering the fund has a discretion to extend the limitation period and is likely to do so if a victim of a domestic crime lacked the social, psychological or financial resources to bring an earlier claim. Again, medical evidence to explain the delay in making a claim may be important. While applications to a compensation fund are generally less adversarial and formal than a full civil trial, the defendant will be notified of the claim and can contest the claim before the Board. This could result in an adversarial tribunal proceeding, in particular in cases where there has not been a criminal charge.

Conclusion

While Canada has made very significant progress in dealing with issues of family violence, many important issues remain to be addressed. Some changes need to be legislated, for example to explicitly require all judges in custody and access disputes to take account of domestic violence factors. In most provinces (including Ontario) legislation dealing with civil restraining orders is also inadequate.

Too often the services to help victims do not have adequate financial resources, and victims continue to face delays in the courts, lack of access to services and insensitivity from professionals. Services need to be provided in a more co-ordinated fashion, which requires better co-operation between agencies and disciplines.

Often women remain intimidated and isolated in abusive relationships, and when they leave too often the courts and police fail to protect them. Problems are especially acute for women in rural areas, poor women, immigrant and aboriginal women, and those with disabilities. Even though there have been a great many improvements in our society's handling of spousal assault issues, more needs to be done.

Unfortunately societal attitudes often lag behind the innovative programs available. Education and awareness are key if the problem of spousal abuse is to be prevented and dealt with effectively.

---

[66] See e.g. Saskatchewan *Limitation Act*, s. 3(3.1) enacted as S.S. 1993, c. 9, s. 2(3); British Columbia *Limitation Act*, R.S.B.C. 1996, c. 266, s. 3(4)(K)(1); Nova Scotia *Limitation of Actions Act*, s. B22(5), enacted as S.N.J. 1993, c. 27, s. 1; and Newfoundland *Limitation Act*, S.N. 1995, c. L-16, s. 8(2).

"BALA, JAFFE, AND CROOKS, SPOUSAL VIOLENCE AND CHILD-RELATED CASES: CHALLENGING CASES REQUIRING DIFFERENTIATED RESPONSES"

(2008), 27 C.F.L.Q. 1 (Footnotes omitted)

1. Introduction — Spousal Violence as a Family Law Issue

Over the past twenty years, the criminal justice system in Canada has come to recognize that spousal violence is not a "private matter," and there have been many changes that have resulted in the police and criminal justice system responding more effectively to spousal violence. The family justice system, however, has been slower to respond, even though spousal violence issues are present in roughly one quarter of all separations and divorces in Canada, and spousal violence is fastest growing category of cases reported to child welfare agencies. Despite the slow pace of change in the family justice system, there is a growing awareness of the harmful effect of spousal violence, not only for direct victims, but also for children who live in families where there is spousal violence. There is also a growing recognition that the types of non-adversarial dispute resolution approaches that are increasingly being used to help separated parents may not be appropriate if there are ongoing spousal abuse issues.

Cases involving spousal violence present complex, challenging issues for judges, lawyers, child welfare workers, assessors, mediators, police officers and other professionals in the family justice system. Some situations involve a high potential for violence, where failure to take an appropriate protective response may place children and adults at grave risk. There are, however, also situations where there may have been violence, but the future risks are minimal and an inappropriately aggressive response can needlessly heighten tension and exacerbate relationships. Justice system professionals must have a sophisticated knowledge of issues related to domestic violence, and an ability to respond in a "differentiated fashion" that recognizes the dynamics and issues of each individual case.

Spousal violence poses many sensitive, complex and contentious issues for society as a whole, as well as those involved in specific cases. These cases are often emotionally charged and it can be difficult for professionals to maintain an appropriate perspective. One dimension of the challenge arises out of the potentially tragic, life threatening dangers that are posed by some cases. Another dimension of challenge relates to the "gender politics" now associated with spousal abuse issues. The rates of male and female violence in intimate relationships are roughly equal, but women are much more likely to be seriously injured or killed, and to fear for their lives. In this paper we argue that the analysis of spousal abuse offered by some feminists — one that emphasizes that women are victims and that gender inequality lies at the root of wife abuse — is important, and provides the best guide to the appropriate handling of some cases, but in many cases, an exclusively gendered analysis is not appropriate. ...

2. The Challenges of Spousal Violence Cases

One of the challenges that arise in family law cases that raise spousal violence and abuse issues, is that these cases often have fault or blame orientation that runs counter to the broad trend in family law towards disregarding marital misconduct and emphasizing non-adversarial dispute resolution, joint custody and other measures to continue to involve both parents in the lives of their children. While the movement away from a fault orientation and towards non-adversarial dispute resolution is generally to be welcomed in family law cases, it is inappropriate for many cases that involve domestic violence issues. This paper offers a differentiated model of how to respond to spouse violence in child-related disputes. Although there may be cases for which some forms of non-adversarial dispute resolution are appropriate despite incidents of spousal violence, if there has been spousal violence, there must be real caution in considering non-adversarial dispute resolution. There are clearly cases involving domestic violence that require judicial suspension or termination of the involvement of parents in the lives of their children. ...

There is a need for all professionals who work in child welfare system or with families experiencing separation to develop knowledge, understanding and sensitivity about issues of spousal abuse. There must be awareness of the different forms, nature and effects of spousal abuse, and an ability to help develop appropriate, differentiated responses, in particular in regard to children. ...

3. The History & Politics of Spousal Violence

... By the mid 1990s, there was a growing awareness among criminal justice system professionals about spousal violence and police were responding to these cases by arresting suspected abusers and laying charges. It is important to recognize that increased public awareness and systemic changes are having an effect on rates of spousal violence in Canada. While there has been an *increase in reports* of spousal abuse to the police and an increase in charges, the actual *incidence of spousal abuse* in Canada (as revealed by victimization surveys and spousal homicide data) has slowly declined over the past quarter century. Although it is difficult to accurately determine the causes of this long term decline, better responses by police, the courts and social services have doubtless played a role. Demographic changes may also have played a role, with fewer individuals in the younger age groups that are prone to violence.

Popular culture (especially television), and the media now regularly report on abuse issues, though there is clearly still a need for more and better public and professional education about spousal abuse. This has helped victims to feel that they can come forward to get assistance, and has led to a larger proportion of victims reporting abuse to the police or other agencies. However, *some* of the public advocacy and *some* of the feminist analysis of spousal abuse may be misleading, and ultimately counter-productive because it exaggerates or distorts the issues. For example, a few years ago some advocates for women warned that Super Bowl Sunday is "the biggest day of the year for violence against women," and the television sponsors of the game responded by broadcasting advertisements warning about wife battering. While public education campaigns about domestic violence, directed primarily at men, are undoubtedly valuable, the "Super Bowl Sunday woman abuse fact" has been exposed as a myth.

Gender based research and advocacy is becoming a "two way street." By the mid 1990's, "fathers' rights" groups began to form in Canada. During the 1998 hearings of the Parliamentary Committee studying reforms to Canada's custody and access laws, some men argued that most allegations of domestic violence and child sexual abuse made in the context of custody or access disputes are false. The hearings became a "gender war zone" with men heckling while women testified about issues of domestic violence. Some fathers' rights advocates charge that "women's shelters have become bunkers in a war against men," but it is clear that some of the men's groups also engage in hyperbolic, distorted advocacy. While false and exaggerated allegations of spousal abuse are a legitimate and important concern, as discussed below, it is clear that there are more cases of false denials of spousal violence by genuine abusers than cases of false allegations by these who are not genuine victims.

There is also now an ongoing and sometimes acrimonious debate in the social science literature about the nature and extent of domestic violence, with some, like Canadian psychologist Donald Dutton, challenging the "Feminist Paradigm" and arguing that male and female perpetrated domestic violence are equally frequent and serious. These critics of the feminist perspective raise important concerns. There is a need to recognize the nature and extent of female perpetrated domestic violence and to recognize that domestic violence often has an interactional or mutual component. Women can be and often are perpetrators of domestic violence, as demonstrated by abuse in lesbian relationships. However, gender remains an important dimension for understanding spousal abuse, especially for the most serious cases that pose the gravest risks of injury or death to women and children.

4. The Nature & Incidence of Spousal Abuse

Professionals need a sophisticated understanding of the incidence and nature of spousal violence and abuse. There is not a single type of behaviour that constitutes spousal abuse, but rather there is a spectrum of behaviour that is abusive, and appropriate responses to abuse must take account of the nature of the abuse, and its effect. The most serious cases of spousal violence typically have a strongly gendered nature, with women most often being the victims of serious abuse by their partners. However, many cases of spousal violence, especially in the context of high conflict separations, involve two violent partners, and there are cases where the female partner is the primary or sole instigator of violence. ...

Some of the most recent Statistics Canada reports on family violence include the results of a telephone survey of 26,000 Canadians in 2004. This study and other research reveals a very broad spectrum of abusive conduct, ranging from a substantial number of cases where there was only one — relatively minor — assault over the course of a relationship, to situations where there was a pattern of serious repeated physical violence and emotional abuse. According to this 2004 study, 7% of women and 6% of men were assaulted by a present or former intimate partner in the previous five years, with 2% of men and women reporting an assault in the past year. For a significant number of victims, 48% of men and 40% of women, there was only a single assault in the previous five years.

Only 36% of the female victims and 17% of male victims reported to the police, with reports more likely if incidents of violence were more frequent, more serious or witnessed by children. The rates of reporting an assault to the police were higher among those victims who separated than those who stayed with their spouses (45% of separated female victims versus only 22% of female victims who remained with their abusive partners).

For less serious forms of spousal violence, based on self-reports by victims to Statistics Canada, rates of perpetration were roughly equal to rates of involved spousal gender. For example 44% of female victims had something thrown at them by a partner, while 49% of male victims reported something was thrown at them, and 57% of male victims were slapped while only 36% of female victims reported being slapped. However, women were much more likely to be victims of serious assaults, with 19% of female victims reporting being choked, and only 5% of males reporting being choked; 13% of female victims received medical attention for injuries resulting from spousal violence, but only 2% of male victims received medical attention. Among female victims, 34% reported that they feared for their lives as a result of an assault by an intimate partner and 21% reported 10 or more assaults, while among male victims only 10% reported that they feared for their lives and 11% reported being victimized by 10 or more assaults.

For many victims of spousal violence, especially female victims, the psychological effects of abuse are very destructive. ...

While spousal abuse occurs in all income and age groups, the incidence of spousal violence is higher:

- among younger couples;
- in common-law relationships as opposed to legal marriages;

- in lower income groups; and

- among Aboriginal Canadians.

Women who were separated or divorced reported [in the 2004 telephone survey] much higher rates of spousal abuse from a former partner than the rates in intact relationships. Among those who *separated*, 21% of women reported that they had been assaulted by a prior partner in the previous five years, while the overall rate for all women was only 7%. In 2004, half of the women who reported experiencing spousal assault by a past partner indicated that the violence occurred after the separation, and in one third of the post-separation assaults the violence began or became more severe after separation. Women who are separated constitute just 4% of adult women, but 26% of women who were victims of spousal homicide.

Thus, while in most cases in which there has been violence during cohabitation, conflict and violence decrease after separation, for a significant minority, the violence and lethality (risk of homicide) increase after separation.

. . . . .

6. The Need for Individualized Assessment

While gender is an important dimension for understanding issues of spousal abuse and violence, it is not the only dimension. This is, for example, illustrated by the fact that partner abuse is a serious problem in same-sex relationships, and that many men who hold traditional patriarchal views of marriage do not abuse their wives. As American psychologist Janet Johnston concludes:

> both men *and* women ... are perpetrating a considerable amount of physical and verbal aggression in ... separating/divorcing families. However ... the consequences of male aggression are ... more serious ... Most men are physically stronger than women and can protect themselves better against female aggression .... aggressive males ... are more likely to dominate, control, and physically injure their partners.

In every case where there is spousal abuse, there is a need to consider the specific nature and context of the abuse. As Johnston points out: "domestic violence is not a unitary syndrome with a single underlying cause but rather a set of behaviours arising from multiple sources, which may follow different patterns for different individuals and families".

In order to assess what is the best response to spousal abuse, it is necessary to consider a range of questions. Who is the primary aggressor? What is the frequency, nature, and intensity of the abuse? Is the abuse perpetrated only by one spouse, or is it mutual? What is the effect of the abuse, since the same acts will affect different individuals in different ways? What is the prognosis for recurrence of abuse, given different possible interventions? And, is there evidence about the effects of the above on the children?

(a) Risk Assessment

One of the issues that police, advocates for women and ultimately judges must consider in deciding how to respond to spousal violence is a consideration of the risk to victims and children, both the recurrence of violence and of an increase in severity of violence. There is a growing body of research about risk of recurrence of spousal violence and a number of different screening tools that are used by police, Crown prosecutors, victim services and shelter workers to undertake risk assessment. All risk assessments involve an assessment of multiple factors; the more factors that are present, the greater the risk of recurrence. Some of the most common risk factors include:

- violence against spouse that is escalating in frequency or severity;
- violence against spouse during pregnancy;
- history of violence against prior partners;
- forced confinement of spouse;
- violence against others;
- violation of restraining orders or other court orders;
- threats of violence, homicide, suicide or abduction of children;
- post-separation staking behavior (surveillance of spouse/children, monitoring of mail etc.)
- abuser is unemployed;
- abuser has alcohol or drug dependency problems;
- abuser is suffering from depression;
- victim expressing fears of repetition of violence;
- abuser is in step-father role in this relationship;
- abuser is under 35 years of age.

There are a number of different risk assessment instruments. Some are quite easy to use, such as the O.D.A.R.A. instrument (Ontario Domestic Assault Risk Assessment) that is commonly used by police forces in Ontario and has 13 questions that are simply answered yes, no or unknown. Some police forces in Canada use the 20 item S.A.R.A. (Spouse Abuse Risk Assessment.) Some instruments that are used by non-police agencies, for example to screen for suitability for mediation are more complex, with more questions and sliding scales of responses (e.g. D.O.V.E. — the Domestic Violence Evaluation instrument).

These instruments are useful, especially for police and service providers. ...

Risk assessment clearly has limitations. For one thing, the scoring on any evaluation is only as good as the information that is available, and in some cases the information about certain aspects of the abuser's history may be unavailable or inaccurate. Further, some items on risk assessment inventories involve some degree of subjectivity and the scoring could be challenged. Most fundamentally, it must be appreciated that assessment of the risk of future violence is not an exact science; individuals with low scores may re-offend, while those with higher scores are not certain to re-offend.

In addition, risk assessment instruments measure the risk of future incidents of spousal violence, not the likely lethality of any future acts of violence. Factors such as access to firearms will affect "lethality assessments" (attempting to predict the likelihood of a serious or fatal attack), that may be part of safety planning by police and other agencies to help protect victims of spousal violence from danger.

7. The Legal Context: Criminal & Civil Responses to Spousal Abuse

. . . . .

(b) Criminal Charges and the Family Court Process

When the police are contacted by a victim (or alleged victim) of spousal violence and come to the home, this will generally afford some immediate protection. Provided the police have reasonable grounds to believe a criminal offence involving an assault or threats has occurred, they will arrest and remove the suspected offender from the home. In some cases the police may arrest both partners if satisfied that this was a situation of mutual violence and not a situation where one spouse was abusive and the other a victim or acting in self-defence. An abusive spouse (or allegedly abusive spouse) will generally only be released after arrest on conditions, such as staying out of the home and not contacting the victim.

If there are criminal charges there may be a possibility of simultaneous family law and criminal proceedings, which adds to the complexity of a case. There is the potential for inconsistent orders being made, with for example the family proceedings allowing for contact between a parent and child, but the criminal proceedings effectively preventing the allegedly abusive parent from making contact or having visits with the children.

If criminal charges are laid, they will tend to "dominate" the resolution of any family law proceedings, at least until the criminal charges are resolved. A common condition of release of the accused on bail pending a criminal trial or of a probation sentence, is a prohibition of contact with the victim and perhaps a restriction on contact with the children. Although it is the role of the Crown prosecutor to suggest and the judge to decide the terms of bail and the sentence, increasingly judges in the criminal courts are making "no contact" orders as conditions of bail release or probationary sentences in domestic violence cases. "No contact" orders can offer victims and their children some protection. These orders supersede any civil custody or access orders under family legislation.

It is preferable if orders that are issued in criminal court are made with an awareness of any existing family court orders or in contemplation of orders that may later be made in family proceedings. In some cases it may be necessary for criminal court orders to be reviewed to take account of subsequent family court orders.

If there is a significant risk of re-offending and safety concerns, it may be appropriate for the criminal court order to specify that there should be "no contact" with either the alleged victim or the children during the time that the criminal proceedings continue, and such a term may later be incorporated as a term of probation or as part of a s. 810 of the *Criminal Code* (recognizance). In many cases, however, there will be more limited concerns, and it may, for example, be appropriate to specify that contact with the other parent may occur only through a named third party and solely for the purpose of arranging visits with the children at specified times. In some cases the criminal court judge will release the accused on bail with a condition that there be no contact with the child unless that contact is permitted by the order of a family court judge. ...

If there are simultaneous criminal and family law proceedings, the person accused of abuse may have different lawyers for each proceeding, though it is obviously desirable for these two lawyers to communicate and coordinate their efforts. Defence counsel in the criminal case will generally be reluctant to allow a person charged with a criminal offence [to] testify in a civil case that deals with the same issues, and will generally want any civil proceedings adjourned until after the criminal case is resolved. If the accused files an affidavit or testifies in the civil case, for example for an interim access application, the Crown prosecutor may use any inconsistencies between that affidavit and testimony in a later criminal trial to impeach the credibility of the accused. Similarly, if the accusing parent testifies in the criminal trial, any inconsistencies between that testimony and evidence in a later family law trial may be used to impeach their credibility in the civil case.

If the accused is convicted of abuse in the criminal trial, the judge in a later family law trial is generally obliged to take the criminal conviction as conclusive evidence that the abuse in question occurred. It is not uncommon, however, in a subsequent family law case for there to be allegations of other abusive incidents that did not result in a criminal conviction, and the family law judge will have to determine, on the civil standard, whether those acts occurred. The fact that an alleged abuser is not charged or is tried and acquitted in criminal court is clearly not binding on a judge in a later civil proceeding. Further, even if there is no judicial finding of abuse in either the criminal or the family law proceeding, there may be other concerns about parenting capacity that lead to a denial of custody.

Some degree of coordination and communication between professionals involved in criminal justice and family proceedings that deal with the same family is desirable, while recognizing that the distinctive nature of the two processes and different professional roles must be respected. Some information clearly cannot be shared between professionals or systems; however, there are cases in which the lack of coordination or sharing of relevant information is due to inadvertence rather than legal constraints. Clearly the primary responsibility for coordination and information sharing rests with counsel, police and victim support services. Judges, however, may also have an important role in questioning counsel about whether appropriate consideration has been given to these issues.

Since the introduction of "mandatory charging" policies for police called to domestic violence incidents, there has been a dramatic increase in the number of criminal prosecutions for spousal violence, and an increased likelihood of simultaneous criminal and family proceedings. Although the mandatory charging policies have clearly increased protection for victims of spousal violence, these policies are also subject to manipulation or misuse and have also resulted in charges being laid against spouses, especially men, involved in high conflict separations, but clearly not guilty of spousal assault. ...

NOTES AND QUESTIONS

1. As is demonstrated by the two articles reproduced above, the presence of domestic violence impacts many family law issues. Consequently, the topic of domestic violence will be raised at various points in these materials. For example, its relevance to court orders for exclusive possession of the matrimonial home is explored in Chapter 5, *THE FAMILY HOME*. That chapter also again briefly examines peace bonds and civil restraining orders. The impact on children of domestic violence will be examined further in Chapter 7, *CUSTODY AND ACCESS* and Chapter 10, *CHILD IN NEED OF PROTECTION*.

2. For further reading, see Ontario Joint Committee on Domestic Violence (Chair Judge Lesley Baldwin), *Working Towards a Seamless Community and Justice Response to Domestic Violence* (Toronto: Ontario Attorney General, 1999); Neilson, "Partner Abuse, Children and Statutory Change: Cautionary Comments on Women's Access to Justice" (2000), 18 Windsor Y.B. Access Just. 115; Geffner, Jaffe, and Sudermann, eds., *Children Exposed to Family Violence: Current Issues in Research, Intervention and Policy Development* (Binghampton, N.Y.: Haworth Press, 2000); Schnall, "Custody and Access and the Impact of Domestic Violence" (2000-2001), 18 C.F.L.Q. 99; Lemon, Jaffe, and Poisson, *Domestic Violence and Child Custody Disputes: Addressing the Essential Clinical and Legal Issues* (Thousand Oaks, Ca.: Sage, 2001); Des Rosiers, *Representing Victims of Sexual and Spousal Abuse* (Toronto: Irwin Law, 2001); Baker, Jaffe, Asbourne and Carter, *Children Exposed to Domestic Violence: An Early Childhood Educator's Handbook* (London, ON: Centre for Children and Families in the Justice System, 2002); Bancroft and Silverman, *The Batterer as Parent: Addressing the Impact of Domestic Violence on Family Dynamics* (Thousand Oaks, Ca.: Sage, 2002); Chewter, "Violence Against Women and Children: Some Legal Issues" (2003), 20 Can. J. Fam. L. 99; Jaffe, Crooks and Possin, "Common Misconceptions in Addressing Domestic Violence in Child Custody Disputes" (2003), 54 Juvenile & Family Court Journal 57; Shaffer, "The Impact of Wife Abuse on Child Custody and Access Decisions" (2004), 22 C.F.L.Q. 85; Johnson, "Domestic Violence: It's Not About Gender — Or Is It?" (2005), 67 J. Marriage & Family 1126; Jaffe, Crooks, and Bala, *Making Appropriate Parenting Arrangements in Family Violence Cases: Applying the Literature to Identify Promising Practices* (Ottawa: Department of Justice Canada, Family, Children and Youth Section Research Report No. 2005-FCY-3E, 2005) (available online at the Department's website); Dutton, *Rethinking Domestic Violence* (Vancouver: UBC Press, 2006); Minaker and Snider, "Husband Abuse: Equality with a Vengeance" (2006), 48 Can. J. Crim. & Crim. Just. 753; Johnston, "A Child-centered Approach to High-Conflict and Domestic-Violence Families: Differential Assessment and Interventions" (2006), 12 J. Fam. Studies 15; Buckingham, "Striking Back: The Tort Action for Spousal Violence" (2007), 23 Can. J. Fam. L. 273; and Jaffe, Johnston, Crooks, and Bala, "Custody Disputes Involving Allegations of Domestic Violence: Towards a Differentiated Approach to Parenting Plans" (2008), 46 Family Court Review 500.

2

CREATING A VALID MARRIAGE

1. Introduction

In this chapter, the legal requirements for a valid marriage will be analyzed. To the extent that the law attaches certain rights and privileges only to the marriage status, the distinction between a valid marriage and an invalid marriage is of obvious importance. It is also significant when the parties wish to end the relationship formally.

In the following excerpt Professor Hahlo outlines the distinction between an annulment and a divorce and examines the significance of the distinction.

HAHLO, *NULLITY OF MARRIAGE IN CANADA*

(Toronto: Butterworths, 1979) 1-2, 4-5 (Footnotes omitted)

A decree of nullity is not a divorce by another name. Divorce presupposes a valid marriage. It is based on a post-nuptial event, and depending on the legal system, the event may be a serious matrimonial offence, such as adultery, cruelty or desertion; irretrievable marriage breakdown; or simply the will of the spouses or even of only one of them to put an end to the marriage. And it dissolves the marriage *ex nunc* — as from the date of the decree. Nullity results from some defect or disability which exists at the time of the marriage ceremony (*ex causa praecedenti*) and prevents an unassailable marriage from coming into existence. Where the ground of annulment is one which renders the marriage void *ab initio*, the decree of nullity declares that there never was a marriage; where the ground of annulment is one which renders the marriage voidable, the decree of nullity annuls it, at common law, with retroactive effect. ...

Although divorce and nullity are, in theory, designed to deal with different situations, in practice they have proved — to some extent — complementary. Actions for annulment thrive when divorce is difficult or impossible to obtain. They wither away when divorce is easy. In the Middle Ages, when *divorce a vinculo* was not admitted, spouses desiring to escape from a hateful marriage looked for, and not rarely succeeded, in discovering an impediment on which an action for annulment could be based.

Today, when almost everywhere in the Western world divorce is easy, nullity actions are, statistically speaking, insignificant, and one or two countries, including Sweden, have done away with them. Where, as in modern Swedish law, a divorce can be obtained on demand, with but a short delay if one party objects and there are young children of the marriage, there is no need for annulment actions. The fact remains that, although the same remedy may provide adequate relief in both situations, the distinction between an initially defective marriage and a valid marriage which has broken up is fundamental and exists even if the legislature chooses to call the judicial remedies by the same name.

In most Western countries nullity actions have been retained, but there is a general trend to approximate the effects of a decree of nullity, at least as regards voidable marriages, to those of a decree of divorce. ...

As Professor Hahlo points out, there has been a tendency to equate the legal consequences of an invalid marriage with those of a valid marriage. See, e.g., the definition of "spouse" in s. 1(1) of Ontario's *Family Law Act*. Persons who have together entered into a marriage that is voidable or void are accorded all the rights and obligations of married persons under the Act, provided that the person claiming a right under the Act acted in good faith. Legal developments have also, to a large extent, assimilated the legal rights and obligations of those who cohabit in a relatively permanent relationship with those of married persons. For example, "spouse" is defined in s. 29 of the Ontario *Family Law Act*, for the purposes of spousal support, to include two persons who have cohabited continuously for at least three years. Note, however, that this extended definition of spouse does not apply to Part I of the Act, dealing with family property.

The law distinguishes between the essential validity of a marriage and the formal validity of a marriage. Essential validity concerns the legal capacity of the parties to marry, while formal validity involves ceremonial or evidentiary requirements. This distinction is important for the purposes of division of powers under the Canadian constitution and for conflict of laws issues.

For constitutional purposes the legal capacity of the parties to marry is a federal matter falling within s. 91(26) of the *Constitution Act, 1867*, while formal validity is a provincial matter falling within s. 92(12). The Parliament of Canada, therefore, has exclusive jurisdiction to pass laws in relation to the essential validity of marriage. On the other hand, the provinces have exclusive legislative power to deal with the formal validity of marriage. Generally, the courts have given an expansive definition to the provincial authority and have specifically held that the provincial legislatures can enact conditions relating to solemnization that affect the validity of marriage. It is now clearly established that provinces have the exclusive power to deal with such ceremonial requirements as the need for a licence, the authority of persons to officiate at marriage ceremonies, the form of the ceremony, and the need for witnesses. However, the Supreme Court of Canada has also held that the provinces can require parental consent as a condition of a marriage involving minors. See *Kerr v. Kerr* (1933), [1934] S.C.R. 72, [1934] 2 D.L.R. 369 and *Alberta (Attorney General) v. Underwood*, [1934] S.C.R. 635, [1934] 4 D.L.R. 167. Professor Hogg notes in *Constitutional Law of Canada* (Toronto: Carswell, 1997) (looseleaf) at s. 26 that these cases were decided on "the dubious ground that parental consent was a 'formality' of marriage rather than a matter governing the capacity of the parties".

The distinction between essential validity and formal validity is also important for conflict of laws problems. The choice of laws rule differs depending on whether the essential validity or formal validity of the marriage is at issue. The formal validity of the marriage is determined by the law of the place where the ceremony occurred. In *Veleta v. Canada (Minister of Citizenship & Immigration)* (2005), 254 D.L.R. (4th) 484 (F.C.); reversed on other grounds (2006), 268 D.L.R. (4th) 513 (F.C.A.) the court refused to recognize a religious marriage that had occurred in Mexico because only civil ceremonies created legal marriages in that country. The traditional view is that a person's capacity to marry is governed by the law of the jurisdiction of the person's pre-marital domicile. However, the Federal Court of Appeal held in *Canada (Minister of Employment & Immigration) v. Narwal* (1990), 26 R.F.L. (3d) 95 (Fed. C.A.), that a marriage will also be valid if each party has the capacity to marry the other according to the law of the jurisdiction of their intended matrimonial home.

The provinces have enacted comprehensive statutes dealing with the formality of marriage. In Ontario, see the *Marriage Act*, R.S.O. 1990, c. M.3 (as amended). By way of contrast, the Parliament of Canada has never legislated comprehensive, specific criteria governing essential validity. In 1930, it passed the *Divorce Act (Ontario), 1930* which conferred jurisdiction on the Supreme Court of Ontario to hear nullity actions and incorporated by reference the law of England relating to the dissolution and annulment of marriage as that law existed on July 15, 1870. Except for specific legislative modifications enacted after 1930, the law of England of July 15, 1870, the common law and the 1857 English *Divorce and Matrimonial Causes Act*, still govern the essential validity of marriage in Ontario. See, now, the *Annulment of Marriages Act (Ontario)*, R.S.C. 1970, c. A-14. Parliament has, however, significantly altered the law governing the prohibited degrees of consanguinity or affinity (see the *Marriage (Prohibited Degrees) Act*, S.C. 1990, c. 46) and redefined marriage to include persons of the same sex (see *Civil Marriage Act*, S.C. 2005, c. 33).

NOTES AND QUESTIONS

1. On the topic of validity of marriage generally, see Hahlo, *Nullity of Marriage in Canada* (Toronto: Butterworths, 1979).

2. Regarding conflict of laws and the validity of marriage, see Lysyk, "Jurisdiction and Recognition of Foreign Decrees in Nullity Suits" (1964), 29 Sask. Bar Rev. 143; MacKinnon, "Nullity Jurisdiction and Problems of Domicile" (1966), 1 Ottawa L. Rev. 216; Maddaugh, "Validity of Marriage and the Conflict of Laws: A Critique of the Present Anglo-American Position" (1973), 23 U.T. L.J. 117; Rafferty, "Recognition of Foreign Nullity Decrees" (1982), 46 Sask. L. Rev. 73; and Davie, "The Breaking-up of Essential Validity of Marriage Choice of Law Rules in English Conflict of Laws" (1994), 23 Anglo-American Law Rev. 32.

3. The possibility that same-sex marriages might be valid in some jurisdictions and not recognized in others has resulted in renewed academic interest in the recognition of foreign marriages. See Adams, "Same-Sex Relationships and Anglo-Canadian Choice of Law: An Argument for Universal Validity", [1996] Canadian Y. B. Int'l L. 103; and Borchers, "Implications of Interjurisdictional Recognition of Non-Traditional Marriages" (1998), 32 Creighton L. Rev. 147.

4. While this chapter focuses only on the legal grounds for annulment, a spouse may also be concerned with the availability of a religious annulment. The grounds for such annulment may differ considerably from those recognized by the civil courts. The Roman Catholic Church has expanded the basis on which an annulment can be obtained from church tribunals. See "Church Adopts Annulment Law", *Globe and Mail* (March 29, 1983); "Church Recognizes Many Grounds for Annulment", *The Montreal Gazette* (July 2, 1983); Riga, "The Catholic View of Marriage in the New Code of Canon Law of 1983 and the Nullity of Marriage in Canon 1095" (1992), 9 J.L. & Relig. 515; and Mendonca, "Consensual Incapacity for Marriage" (1994), The Jurist 477. Of course, an annulment obtained from a church tribunal does not legally end the marriage.

2. Essential Validity of Marriage

(1) The Traditional Opposite Sex Requirement

HALPERN v. TORONTO (CITY)

(2003), 36 R.F.L. (5th) 127, 2003 CarswellOnt 2159 (Ont. C.A.)

Per curiam:

A. Introduction

1 The definition of marriage in Canada, for all of the nation's 136 years, has been based on the classic formulation of Lord Penzance in *Hyde v. Hyde* (1866), L.R. 1 P.D. 130 (Eng. P.D.A.), at 133: "I conceive that marriage, as understood in Christendom, may for this purpose be defined as the voluntary union for life of one man and one woman, to the exclusion of all others." The central question in this appeal is whether the exclusion of same-sex couples from this common law definition of marriage breaches ss. 2(a) or 15(1) of the *Canadian Charter of Rights and Freedoms* ("the *Charter*") in a manner that is not justified in a free and democratic society under s. 1 of the *Charter*.

2 This appeal raises significant constitutional issues that require serious legal analysis. That said, this case is ultimately about the recognition and protection of human dignity and equality in the context of the social structures available to conjugal couples in Canada. ...

5 Marriage is, without dispute, one of the most significant forms of personal relationships. For centuries, marriage has been a basic element of social organization in societies around the world. Through the institution of marriage, individuals can publicly express their love and commitment to each other. Through this institution, society publicly recognizes expressions of love and commitment between individuals, granting them respect and legitimacy as a couple. This public recognition and sanction of marital relationships reflect society's approbation of the personal hopes, desires and aspirations that underlie loving, committed conjugal relationships. This can only enhance an individual's sense of self-worth and dignity.

6 The ability to marry, and to thereby participate in this fundamental societal institution, is something that most Canadians take for granted. Same-sex couples do not; they are denied access to this institution simply on the basis of their sexual orientation.

7 Sexual orientation is an analogous ground that comes under the umbrella of protection in s. 15(1) of the *Charter*: see *Egan v. Canada*, [1995] 2 S.C.R. 513 (S.C.C.), and *M v. H*, [1999] 2 S.C.R. 3 (S.C.C.). ...

8 Historically, same-sex equality litigation has focused on achieving equality in some of the most basic elements of civic life, such as bereavement leave, health care benefits, pensions benefits, spousal support, name changes and adoption. The question at the heart of this appeal is whether excluding same-sex couples from another of the most basic elements of civic life — marriage — infringes human dignity and violates the Canadian Constitution. ...

[The Ontario Court of Appeal first concluded that the traditional definition of marriage was not constitutionally entrenched in s. 91(26) of the *Constitution Act, 1867*. It followed that Parliament could legislate regarding the capacity to marry so as to meet the changing realities of Canadian society and that the common law definition was subject to scrutiny under the *Charter*.

Next, the Court concluded that religious rights and freedoms were not engaged. Marriage was a legal institution as well as a religious and social one and only the legal institution of marriage was under scrutiny.

Determining whether the common law definition of marriage constituted discrimination involved an assessment of the definition in light of the purpose of s. 15(1) of the *Charter*; namely, the prevention of violations of human dignity and the promotion of a society in which all persons were secure in the knowledge that they were equally deserving of concern, respect and consideration. More specifically, those challenging the definition had to demonstrate that 1) the common law rule imposed differential treatment; 2) this differential treatment was based on one or more of the grounds set out in s. 15(1) or a ground analogous thereto; and 3) this differential treatment constituted discrimination in a substantive sense.

The Court found that there was differential treatment because the common law definition of marriage created a formal distinction between opposite-sex couples and same-sex couples. It was irrelevant that the common law adopted rather than invented the requirement that persons had to be of opposite sex. Historically, Parliament and the provincial legislatures had built a myriad of rights and obligations around the institution of marriage and some of these were still only available to married persons. Moreover, the provincial legislatures provided licensing and registration schemes so that marriages could be formally recognized by law. Denying same-sex couples access to these schemes constituted a formal distinction between opposite-sex couples and same-sex couples.

This differential treatment was based on sexual orientation. Sexual orientation was a personal characteristic that was analogous to the grounds listed in s. 15(1).

Finally, the Court's examination of four contextual factors led it to find that the differential treatment constituted substantive discrimination. First, the common law definition of marriage further disadvantaged gay men and lesbians who had been historically disadvantaged. Second, the differential treatment disregarded the needs, capabilities, and circumstances of same-sex couples. It, therefore, perpetuated the mistaken view that their relationships were unworthy of legal recognition as marriages because they were not capable of forming loving and lasting relationships. Third, the common law definition did not serve an ameliorative purpose. Even if it were accepted that the ameliorative purpose underlying the common law rule was the alleviation of the economic disadvantage for opposite-sex couples due to child rearing, the rule would be under-inclusive since same-sex couples also raised children. Under-inclusive ameliorative legislation that excluded members of a historically disadvantaged group rarely escaped the charge of discrimination. Fourth, the common law rule severely affected a fundamental interest. Although legislation now gave same-sex couples many of the same benefits and obligations as opposite-sex couples, the same-sex couples were still not accorded equal treatment. In many instances, benefits and obligations did not arise until the same-sex couple had been cohabiting for a specified period while they attached immediately upon marriage. Additionally, not all benefits and obligations had been extended to cohabiting couples. In any event, excluding same-sex couples from a fundamental societal institution such as marriage perpetuated the view that same-sex relationships were less worthy of recognition than opposite-sex relationships. In so doing, the common law rule offended the dignity of persons in same-sex relationships.

Because the challenged rule that infringed s. 15(1) of the *Charter* was a common law rule, the Court noted that an assessment under s. 1 of the possible justification for the infringement might not be strictly necessary. However, it decided to engage in such an assessment because it provided a familiar structure through which the objectives of the rule could be kept in focus and alternative means of attaining those objectives could be assessed. Further, it considered such an analysis appropriate because marriage was the foundation of a myriad of government benefits and because Parliament had recently confirmed the common law definition of marriage.

The Court concluded that the Attorney General of Canada had not demonstrated any pressing and substantial objective for excluding same-sex couples from the institution of marriage. It was not sufficient to state that marriage had always been understood as a special kind of monogamous opposite-sex union with spiritual, economic and contractual dimensions. Nor could the three more specific purposes of marriage advanced by the Attorney General justify maintaining the institution as exclusively heterosexual. The first suggested purpose of encouraging the union of a man and a woman demeaned the dignity of those involved in same-sex relationships by implicitly indicating that such relationships were of lesser importance. Such a purpose was contrary to the values of a free and democratic society. The second suggested purpose of encouraging procreation and child-rearing was a laudable goal and could be regarded as pressing and substantial. However, this goal did not explain why same-sex couples should be precluded from marrying. Heterosexual married couples would not stop having or raising children if same-sex couples married. Also, an increasing percentage of children were being raised by same-sex couples. A law that restricted marriage to opposite-sex couples on the basis that a fundamental purpose of marriage was the raising of children suggested that same-sex couples were not equally capable of raising children. In the absence of cogent evidence, this was a stereotypical assumption that was unacceptable in a free and democratic society. The third suggested purpose of marriage was the fostering of life-long companionship. Again, this might be a laudable goal. However, encouraging such companionship only between persons of the opposite-sex perpetuated an unacceptable view of same-sex relationships as less worthy.

Even if the Attorney General's suggested objectives were characterized as pressing and substantial, the Court considered the means chosen to achieve them disproportionate. It did not believe that the exclusion of same-sex couples from the institution of marriage was rationally connected to any of the suggested objectives. Moreover, in the Court's view, the common law definition did not impair the equality rights of same-sex couples as minimally as possible because same-sex couples were completely excluded from a fundamental societal institution. Finally, it concluded that the deleterious effects of limiting marriage to opposite-sex couples outweighed the suggested purposes underlying the exclusionary rule.

The Court next turned to the question of remedy.]

. . . . .

(6) Remedy

143 Having found that the common law definition of marriage violates the Couples' equality rights under s. 15(1) of the *Charter* in a manner that is not justified under s. 1 of the *Charter*, we turn to consider the appropriate remedy.

144 The Couples [the eight same-sex couples who wished to marry] and MCCT [the Metropolitan Community Church of Toronto] seek an immediate declaration that the common law definition of marriage is invalid, and an order reformulating the definition to refer to the union of "two persons" to the exclusion of all others. Additionally, the Couples seek an order directing the Clerk of the City of Toronto to issue a marriage licence to each of them, and an order directing the Registrar General of the Province of Ontario to register same-sex marriages. ... The AGC takes the position, in the event that we dismiss its appeal, that the appropriate remedy is to declare the common law definition of marriage unconstitutional, but to suspend the declaration of invalidity for two years.

145 *Schachter v. Canada*, [1992] 2 S.C.R. 679 (S.C.C.), remains the seminal authority regarding constitutional remedies. Lamer C.J.C. identified the court's obligation to fashion a remedy for a constitutional breach and the scope of such remedies, at p. 695:

> Section 52 of the *Constitution Act, 1982* mandates the striking down of any law that is inconsistent with the provisions of the Constitution, but only "to the extent of the inconsistency". Depending upon

the circumstances, a court may simply strike down, it may strike down and temporarily suspend the declaration of invalidity, or it may resort to the techniques of reading down or reading in.

146 Lamer C.J.C. set out three steps to be followed in determining the appropriate remedy for a *Charter* breach. First, the court is to define the extent of the impugned law's inconsistency with the *Charter*. Second, it should select the remedy that best corrects the inconsistency. Third, the court should assess whether the remedy ought to be temporarily suspended.

147 Turning to the first step, we hold that the common law definition of marriage is inconsistent with the *Charter* to the extent that it excludes same-sex couples.

148 With respect to the second step, in our view the remedy that best corrects the inconsistency is to declare invalid the existing definition of marriage to the extent that it refers to "one man and one woman", and to reformulate the definition of marriage as "the voluntary union for life of two persons to the exclusion of all others". This remedy achieves the equality required by s. 15(1) of the *Charter* but ensures that the legal status of marriage is not left in a state of uncertainty.

149 We reject the AGC's submission that the only remedy we should order is a declaration of invalidity, and that this remedy should be suspended to permit Parliament to respond. A declaration of invalidity alone fails to meet the court's obligation to reformulate a common law rule that breaches a *Charter* right. ...

150 In addition to failing to fulfill the court's obligation, a declaration of invalidity, by itself, would not achieve the goals of s. 15(1). It would result in an absence of any legal definition of marriage. This would deny to all persons the benefits of the legal institution of marriage, thereby putting all persons in an equally disadvantaged position, rather than in an equally advantaged position. Moreover, a declaration of invalidity alone leaves same-sex couples open to blame for the blanket denial of the benefits of the legal institution of marriage, a result that does nothing to advance the goal of s. 15(1) of promoting concern, respect and consideration for all persons.

151 We are also of the view that the argument made by the AGC and several of the interveners that we should defer to Parliament once we issue a declaration of invalidity is not apposite in these circumstances. *Schachter* provides that the role of the legislature and legislative objectives is to be considered at the second step of the remedy analysis when a court is deciding whether severance or reading in is an appropriate remedy to cure a legislative provision that breaches the *Charter*. These considerations do not arise where the genesis of the *Charter* breach is found in the common law and there is no legislation to be altered. Any lacunae created by a declaration of invalidity of a common law rule are common law lacunae that should be remedied by the courts, unless to do so would conflict with the principles of fundamental justice.

152 The third step remains to be considered, that is, whether to temporarily suspend the declaration of invalidity. As previously noted, the AGC argues for a suspension in order to permit Parliament an opportunity to respond to the legal gap that such a declaration would create. Again, *Schachter* provides guidance on the resolution of this issue. Lamer C.J.C. emphasized, at p. 716, that "[a] delayed declaration allows a state of affairs which has been found to violate standards embodied in the *Charter* to persist for a time despite the violation." He stated, at pp. 715-16 and 719, that temporarily suspending a declaration of invalidity is warranted only in limited circumstances, such as where striking down the law poses a potential danger to the public, threatens the rule of law, or would have the effect of denying deserving persons of benefits under the impugned law. ...

153 There is no evidence before this court that a declaration of invalidity without a period of suspension will pose any harm to the public, threaten the rule of law, or deny anyone the benefit of legal recognition of their marriage. We observe that there was no evidence before

us that the reformulated definition of marriage will require the volume of legislative reform that followed the release of the Supreme Court of Canada's decision in *M v. H*. In our view, an immediate declaration will simply ensure that opposite-sex couples and same-sex couples immediately receive equal treatment in law in accordance with s. 15(1) of the *Charter*.

154 Accordingly, we would allow the cross-appeal by the Couples on remedy. We would reformulate the common law definition of marriage as "the voluntary union for life of two persons to the exclusion of all others". We decline to order a suspension of the declaration of invalidity or of the reformulated common law definition of marriage. We would also make orders, in the nature of *mandamus*, requiring the Clerk of the City of Toronto to issue marriage licences to the Couples, and requiring the Registrar General of the Province of Ontario to accept for registration the marriage certificates. ...

NOTES AND QUESTIONS

1. As noted earlier in this chapter, in the *Annulment of Marriages Act (Ontario)*, R.S.C. 1970, c. A-14, Parliament adopted the law of England as of July 15, 1870, to govern the capacity to marry in Ontario. Does legislative adoption of common law rules give them a legislative basis? If so, should this have affected the court's analysis in the *Halpern* case? No party appears to have raised the existence of the *Annulment of Marriages Act (Ontario)* in the *Halpern* litigation.

2. The Ontario Divisional Court's reasoning in *Halpern v. Toronto (City)* (2002), 28 R.F.L. (5th) 41 (Ont. Div. Ct.) captured the differing views on the nature and purpose of marriage that underpinned the debate over the recognition of same-sex marriage. In particular, Justice Blair noted that the view one took of the nature of marriage might well be the beginning and the end of the discussion. Historically, marriage had been almost universally conceived as a union between a man and a woman. Undoubtedly, this had much to do with the need for society to provide a setting in which human life could be sustained and perpetuated. The family had long been perceived as the ideal unit in which to raise children. Since procreation, at least until recently, was the product of heterosexual intercourse, the family was classically considered to be founded on the heterosexual union. Thus, although marriage always had many dimensions, historically its ultimate, defining characteristic was as a union between a man and a woman. The justice accepted that, if this understanding of marriage prevailed, it could be argued that the rule limiting marriage to opposite-sex unions did not infringe the *Charter* since same-sex couples were then not excluded from the institution because of their sexual orientation. Rather, they were simply ineligible because they fell outside the definitional boundaries of marriage. They were then incapable of entering the institution rather than precluded from doing so on the basis of a personal characteristic or as a result of stereotypic prejudice. There was, therefore, no discrimination or, in any event, the same analysis would justify the classic definition under s. 1 of the *Charter*.

Justice Blair then went on to state that marriage could and should be viewed from a broader perspective, one that took into account the changes that had occurred in Canadian society. While the production, care and raising of children was still a principal purpose of marriage, he stated that there was much more to marriage than the act of heterosexual intercourse leading to the birth of children. He believed that marriage was more fully characterized by its pivotal child-rearing function and by a long-term conjugal relationship between two individuals that involved mutual care and support, companionship and shared social activities, intellectual and moral and faith-based stimulation, and economic and psychological interdependence. Since same-sex couples lived in long-term, caring, loving and conjugal relationships and were involved in raising children, their relationships were characterized by all the indicia of marriage, save for heterosexual intercourse. If heterosexual procreation were not essential to the nature of the institution, then same-sex couples were not precluded from participating by reason of the institution's innate nature. Rather, they were precluded from doing so simply because of their sexual orientation and this infringed the equality guarantee of s. 15(1). In particular, Justice Blair saw marriage as society's highest acceptance of the worth of a couple's relationship and so he believed that the exclusion of same-sex couples from that institution touched their sense of human dignity to its core.

3. In his annotation ((2003), 36 R.F.L. (5th) 129), to the Ontario Court of Appeal's decision in the *Halpern* case, Professor McLeod, while generally supporting societal acceptance of same-sex relationships, was quite critical of the Ontario Court of Appeal's decision:

> The actual result in *Halpern v. Toronto (City)* is rather anti-climactic, given the prior decisions in British Columbia, Quebec, and Ontario on whether same-sex partners should be allowed to marry.

However, the order disposing of the appeal is not. With respect, the court's order to allow immediate marriage is short-sighted and smacks of judicial muscle-flexing. In the end, the case is an exercise in symbolism. Most of the substantive economic benefits which accrued to married spouses have now been extended to unmarried cohabiting partners, including same-sex partners. Those that have not been dealt with soon will be. All that is left is giving same-sex partners the same social recognition as opposite-sex partners. The critical question is who should make this decision.

... The fundamental question that the Court of Appeal did not even mention is whether courts have any role in changing fundamental social institutions like marriage where it is possible to remove any substantive legal discrimination without restructuring the fundamental social institution. With respect, it is submitted that the courts can and should extend "spousal" rights to same-sex partners who have publically affirmed they intend their relationship to have legal consequences, without rewriting fundamental values in the abstract, in isolation from any legal benefits or detriments.

Halpern was all about social recognition and validation for same-sex relationships. The respondents were not satisfied with having the same legal rights as married spouses. They wanted the same social recognition and acceptance as married spouses in the eyes of the general public. With respect, if there is any distinction between judicial and legislative powers, this would appear to be where the line should be drawn. It is surprising that courts who do not think it is their function to create a cause of action where one parent denies access or turns a child against the other parent, to recognize in an unborn child the same right to protection against its pregnant mother's destructive behaviour as born children in need of protection or to recognize the rights of an unborn child in tort law have no difficulty assuming responsibility to rewrite basic Canadian social values where the only thing that turns on the decision is social recognition and a sense of personal satisfaction. ...

4. The most surprising and controversial aspect of the Ontario Court of Appeal's decision in *Halpern* was the remedy. All the previous decisions in the same-sex marriage litigation had suspended the remedy to give Parliament time to decide exactly how to act. Everyone was also aware that Parliament was actively studying the issue. Indeed, the Parliamentary committee's discussion paper of November 2002 was overshadowed by the appellate court decision.

The suggestion by the Ontario Court of Appeal that a reformulated definition of marriage did not require "the volume of legislative reform that followed the release of the Supreme Court of Canada's decision in *M. v. H.*" proved to be questionable. Shortly after the decision was announced, a lesbian couple who had married within days of the decision discovered that they could not obtain a divorce under the *Divorce Act*. Eventually, a court ruled that this aspect of the *Divorce Act* was unconstitutional and granted a divorce. See *M. (M.) v. H. (J.)* (2004), 247 D.L.R. (4th) 361 (Ont. S.C.J.). Ultimately, the *Civil Marriage Act*, S.C 2005, c. 33, amended s. 2(1) of the *Divorce Act* to redefine spouse as "either of two persons who are married to each other" rather than "either of a man or woman who are married to each other". It also amended several other federal statutes. In February 2005, the Ontario legislature passed the *Spousal Relationships Statute Law Amendment Act, 2005*. It amended numerous provincial statutes in light of the recognition of same-sex marriages.

In the Ontario Divisional Court decision in *Halpern v. Toronto (City)* (2002), 28 R.F.L. (5th) 41 (Ont. Div. Ct.), Justice Blair noted (at paras. 134-135):

Even if opening up marriage to same-sex couples as the Dutch have done is the appropriate alternative, in order to comply with *Charter* dictates, legislatures and not courts are the proper venue for the crafting of that solution, in my opinion. Even the Dutch "marriage" maintains some distinctions between same-sex and opposite-sex marriages: same-sex marriage will have no consequences in relation to the law of filiation based on descent, meaning that a child born into a same-sex marriage will not have an automatic legal filiation link to both spouses; presumptions of paternity do not apply; in the context of a marriage between two men, a child born into the marriage by means of a surrogate mother will have to be recognized by the biological father (or have paternity judicially established), and be adopted by the other "parent" with the consent of the mother; in the context of a marriage between two women, only the biological mother would have a direct filiation link to the child and the other parent would have to adopt; a Dutch same-sex marriage will not likely be recognized abroad.

Undoubtedly, issues similar to these will have to be addressed in Canada, together possibly with other questions arising in connection with the alternative birthing methods necessarily resorted to by same-sex couples. It strikes me that such matters are more effectively dealt with by legislatures rather than by the Court simply "reformulating" the common law definition of marriage by reading out the words "one man and one woman" and reading in the words "two persons".

Incidentally, Ontario's *Spousal Relationships Statute Law Amendment Act, 2005* did not deal with any of the specific issues raised by Justice Blair regarding parentage of children.

5. The same-sex marriage litigation occurred in the context of significant judicial and legislative developments concerning benefits for same-sex couples. In *M v. H* (1999), 46 R.F.L. (4th) 32 (S.C.C.); reconsideration refused (2000), 2000 CarswellOnt 1913 (S.C.C.), the Supreme Court of Canada held that an Ontario statute that extended spousal support obligations to unmarried opposite-sex couples who cohabited for at least three years discriminated on the basis of sexual orientation contrary to the *Canadian Charter of Rights and Freedoms*. See Chapter 6, *SPOUSAL SUPPORT*. In response to the *M v. H* decision, the Ontario legislature passed the *Amendments Because of the Supreme Court of Canada Decision in M. v. H. Act, 1999*, S.O. 1999, c. 6. The Act amended the *Family Law Act* and many other statutes so that they would apply to same-sex couples in the same way as they applied to unmarried, opposite-sex couples. This result was achieved, however, not by redefining the term "spouse" but by having separate provisions indicating that the statutes applied to same-sex, cohabiting partners. The most publicized portions of the *Spousal Relationships Statute Law Amendment Act, 2005* amended the *Marriage Act* and the *Human Rights Code* to stipulate that religious officials are not required to solemnize a marriage or to allow a sacred place to be used to solemnize a marriage where to do so would be contrary to their religious beliefs or those of the religious body to which they belong. However, the Act also amended numerous statutes to remove the references to "same-sex partners" and to include them within the term "spouse" on the same basis as persons in opposite-sex relationships. Most of the other provinces similarly have redefined "spouse" so that same-sex partners can qualify.

The Parliament of Canada has saved the term "spouse" for married persons. It responded in 2000 to the *M v. H* decision by passing the *Modernization of Benefits and Obligations Act*. This Act amended numerous federal statutes so that the benefits, rights and obligations that apply to married persons or spouses now apply in the same way to "common law partners". The term "common law partnership" is defined as "the relationship between two persons who are cohabiting in a conjugal relationship, having done so for a period of at least one year". Section 1.1 of this statute expressly declares: "For greater certainty, the amendments made by this Act do not affect the meaning of the word 'marriage', that is, the lawful union of one man and one woman to the exclusion of all others."

6. A few provinces have created "civil union" or "registered partnership" legislation. Registration by either same-sex or opposite-sex couples effectively means that the partners acquire the same rights and obligations under provincial legislation as married persons. See *Law Reform (2000) Act*, S.N.S. 2000, c. 29; *The Common-Law Partners' Property and Related Amendments Act*, S.M. 2002, c. 48 and *An Act instituting civil unions and establishing new rules of filiation*, S.Q. 2002, c. 6. Alberta's *Adult Interdependent Relationships Act*, S.A. 2002, c. A-4.5, allows registration by "adult interdependent partners" who may be of the same sex. Registration under this Act leads to the acquisition of some of the same rights and responsibilities as married persons (e.g., spousal support). However, other rights and responsibilities (e.g., sharing of property) are not acquired.

Some have suggested that "civil union" or "registered partnership" legislation is the solution to the dispute over same-sex marriage because it accords legal recognition to same-sex unions while preserving the traditional concept of marriage. The Vermont Supreme Court accepted this position in *Baker v. State*, 744 A.2d 864 (U.S. Vt. S.C., 1999). See also the United Kingdom's *Civil Partnership Act 2004*, 2004, c. 33.

Do you think that the Ontario Court of Appeal would have reached the same result in *Halpern* even if Ontario had accorded rights and obligations to registered civil unions involving same-sex couples? This issue was addressed to some extent in the Ontario Divisional Court, where Justice Smith suggested that the court should not prejudge whether a comprehensive domestic partnership regime might be an acceptable way to recognize same-sex relationships. Justice Blair ultimately accepted that position, but indicated (at para. 130) that he had "some concerns about the adequacy of the registered partnership regime to meet the requirements of the *Charter*". Justice LaForme stated specifically (at para. 282) that such an "alternative status" was unacceptable as it only demonstrated "society's tolerance" and not the required "recognized acceptance of equality". The preamble to the federal *Civil Marriage Act* specifically states that

> [W]hereas ... only access to marriage for civil purposes would respect the right of couples of the same sex to equality without discrimination, and civil union, as an institution other than marriage, would not offer them equal access and would violate human dignity, in breach of the *Canadian Charter of Rights and Freedoms*.

Following the Ontario Court of Appeal decision in *Halpern*, the Government of Canada announced that it was not appealing either that decision or the one in *EGALE Canada Inc. v. Canada (Attorney General)* (2003), 38 R.F.L. (5th) 32 (B.C. C.A.); additional reasons at (2003), 42 R.F.L. (5th) 341 (B.C. C.A.). As a result, the British Columbia Court of Appeal, with the consent of the Attorneys General of Canada and British Columbia, lifted the suspension of the remedies so that same-sex couples in British Columbia could marry immediately. See *EGALE Canada Inc. v. Canada (Attorney General)* (2003), 228 D.L.R. (4th) 416 (B.C. C.A.). In Quebec, the Superior Court declared s. 5 of the *Federal Law — Civil Law Harmonization Act, No. 1*, S.C. 2001, c. 4, unconstitutional, but stayed the enforcement of the declaration for two years. Section 5 of this federal statute, which applied only in Quebec, stated: "Marriage requires the free and enlightened consent of a man and a woman to be the spouse of the other". When the Attorney General of Canada discontinued his appeal and agreed to waive the stay of the trial judgment, the Quebec Court of Appeal dismissed the appeal and ended the stay: *Hendricks c. Québec (Procureure générale)* (2004), 238 D.L.R. (4th) 577 (Que. C.A.). Courts in Manitoba, Nova Scotia, Saskatchewan, and the Yukon subsequently also recognized same-sex marriages. See *Vogel v. Canada (Attorney General)* (2004), [2004] M.J. No. 418, 2004 CarswellMan 527 (Q.B.); *Boutilier v. Nova Scotia (Attorney General)* (September 24, 2004), Doc. S.H. No. 227691, [2004] N.S.J. No. 357 (S.C. [In Chambers]); *W. (N.) v. Canada (Attorney General)* (2004), 11 R.F.L. (6th) 162, 246 D.L.R. (4th) 345 (Sask. Q.B.) and *Dunbar v. Yukon Territory* (2004), 8 R.F.L. (6th) 235 (Y.T. S.C.). By the time that the last case was argued, neither the federal nor provincial Attorney General opposed the application for an immediate reformulation of the definition of marriage.

During the litigation over the definition of marriage, the Government of Canada announced that it was referring the matter to the Supreme Court of Canada. An edited version of the court's response follows.

REFERENCE RE SAME-SEX MARRIAGE

(2004), 12 R.F.L. (6th) 153, 246 D.L.R. (4th) 193, 2004 CarswellNat 4422 (S.C.C.)

By The Court:

I. Introduction

1 On July 16, 2003, the Governor in Council issued Order in Council P.C. 2003-1055 asking this Court to hear a reference on the federal government's *Proposal for an Act respecting certain aspects of legal capacity for marriage for civil purposes ("Proposed Act")*. The operative sections of the *Proposed Act* read as follows:

> 1. Marriage, for civil purposes, is the lawful union of two persons to the exclusion of all others.
>
> 2. Nothing in this Act affects the freedom of officials of religious groups to refuse to perform marriages that are not in accordance with their religious beliefs.

It will be noted that section 1 of the *Proposed Act* deals only with civil marriage, not religious marriage.

2 The Order in Council sets out the following questions:

> 1 Is the annexed *Proposal for an Act respecting certain aspects of legal capacity for marriage for civil purposes* within the exclusive legislative authority of the Parliament of Canada? If not, in what particular or particulars, and to what extent?

2 If the answer to question 1 is yes, is section 1 of the proposal, which extends capacity to marry to persons of the same sex, consistent with the *Canadian Charter of Rights and Freedoms*? If not, in what particular or particulars, and to what extent?

3 Does the freedom of religion guaranteed by paragraph 2(a) of the *Canadian Charter of Rights and Freedoms* protect religious officials from being compelled to perform a marriage between two persons of the same sex that is contrary to their religious beliefs?

3 On January 26, 2004, the Governor in Council issued Order in Council P.C. 2004-28 asking a fourth question, namely:

4 Is the opposite-sex requirement for marriage for civil purposes, as established by the common law and set out for Quebec in section 5 of the *Federal Law — Civil Law Harmonization Act, No. 1*, consistent with the *Canadian Charter of Rights and Freedoms*? If not, in what particular or particulars and to what extent?

4 With respect to Question 1, we conclude that s. 1 of the *Proposed Act* is within the exclusive legislative competence of Parliament, while s. 2 is not.

5 With respect to Question 2, we conclude that s. 1 of the *Proposed Act*, which defines marriage as the union of two persons, is consistent with the *Canadian Charter of Rights and Freedoms*.

6 With respect to Question 3, we conclude that the guarantee of freedom of religion in the *Charter* affords religious officials protection against being compelled by the state to perform marriages between two persons of the same sex contrary to their religious beliefs.

7 For reasons to be explained, the Court declines to answer Question 4. ...

A. Question 1: Is the *Proposed Act* Within the Exclusive Legislative Authority of the Parliament of Canada?

. . . . .

a) Determination of Legislative Competence

16 The dominant characteristic of s. 1 of the *Proposed Act* is apparent from its plain text: marriage as a civil institution. In saying that marriage for civil purposes is "the lawful union of two persons to the exclusion of all others", this section stipulates the threshold requirements of that institution: "two persons", regardless of gender, are legally capable of being married. In pith and substance, therefore, the section pertains to the capacity for marriage.

17 Turning to the assignment of this matter to an enumerated head of power, we note that legislative authority in respect of marriage is divided between the federal Parliament and the provincial legislatures. Section 91(26) of the *Constitution Act, 1867* confers on Parliament competence in respect of "Marriage and Divorce" whereas s. 92(12) of that Act confers on the provinces competence in respect of "[t]he Solemnization of Marriage in the Province".

18 As early as 1912, this Court recognized that s. 91(26) confers on Parliament legislative competence in respect of the capacity to marry, whereas s. 92(12) confers authority on the provinces in respect of the performance of marriage once that capacity has been recognized: see *Re Marriage Legislation in Canada* (1912), 46 S.C.R. 132 (S.C.C.).

19 We have already concluded that, in pith and substance, s. 1 of the *Proposed Act* pertains to legal capacity for civil marriage. *Prima facie*, therefore, it falls within a subject matter allocated exclusively to Parliament (s. 91(26)).

[The Court went on to reject the argument that the *Constitution Act, 1867* entrenched the definition of marriage as it stood in 1867. It stressed that the Canadian constitution was a living tree that, by way of progressive interpretation, accommodated and addressed the realities of modern life. Read expansively, the word "marriage" in s. 92(26) of the *Constitution Act, 1867* did not exclude same-sex marriage. Also, while the recognition of same-sex marriage would have an impact on the provincial sphere, the Court found that these effects were incidental rather than in relation to the core of the provincial powers over solemnization of marriage or property and civil rights under ss. 92(12) and 92(13) of the *Constitution Act, 1867*. However, the Court did find that s. 2 of the proposed legislation related to the performance or solemnization of marriage, a matter allocated exclusively to the legislative jurisdiction of the provinces under s. 92(12) of the *Constitution Act, 1867*. Accordingly, the Court held that Parliament did not have authority to enact section 2 of the proposed legislation.]

B. Question 2: Is Section 1 of the *Proposed Act*, Which Extends Capacity to Marry to Persons of the Same Sex, Consistent with the Charter?

40 To determine whether a provision is consistent with the *Charter*, it is first necessary to ascertain whether its purpose or effect is to curtail a *Charter* right: *R. v. Big M Drug Mart Ltd.*, [1985] 1 S.C.R. 295 (S.C.C.), at p. 331. If so, the further question arises of whether the curtailment is justified under s. 1 of the *Charter*.

(1) Purpose of Section 1 of the Proposed Act

41 The purpose of s. 1 of the *Proposed Act* is to extend the right to civil marriage to same-sex couples. The course of events outlined below in relation to Question 4 suggests that the provision is a direct legislative response to the findings of several courts that the opposite-sex requirement for civil marriage violates the equality guarantee enshrined in s. 15(1) of the *Charter*. ...

42 The preamble to the *Proposed Act* is also instructive. The Act's stated purpose is to ensure that civil marriage as a legal institution is consistent with the *Charter*: ...

43 Turning to the substance of the provision itself, we note that s. 1 embodies the government's policy stance in relation to the s. 15(1) equality concerns of same-sex couples. This, combined with the circumstances giving rise to the *Proposed Act* and with the preamble thereto, points unequivocally to a purpose which, far from violating the *Charter*, flows from it.

(2) Effect of Section 1 of the Proposed Act

[The Court concluded that the effects of s. 1 of the proposed legislation did not violate s. 15(1) of the *Charter*. It reasoned that the mere recognition of the equality rights of one group could not, in itself, constitute a violation of the rights of another. It stated that the promotion of *Charter* rights and values enriched Canadian society as a whole and the furtherance of those rights could not undermine the very principles that the *Charter* was meant to foster. The Court also concluded that it had not been shown that impermissible conflicts would arise between the right to same-sex marriage and freedom of religion guaranteed by s. 2(a) of the *Charter*.]

C. Question 3: Does the Freedom of Religion Guaranteed by Section 2(a) of the Charter Protect Religious Officials From Being Compelled to Perform Same-Sex Marriages Contrary to Their Religious Beliefs?

55 The *Proposed Act* is limited in its effect to marriage for civil purposes: see s. 1. It cannot be interpreted as affecting religious marriage or its solemnization. However, Question 3 is formulated broadly and without reference to the *Proposed Act*. We therefore consider this

question as it applies to the performance, by religious officials, of both religious and civil marriages. We also must consider the question to mean "compelled by the *state*" to perform, since s. 2(a) relates only to state action; the protection of freedom of religion against private actions is not within the ambit of this question. We note that it would be for the Provinces, in the exercise of their power over the solemnization of marriage, to legislate in a way that protects the rights of religious officials while providing for solemnization of same-sex marriage. It should also be noted that human rights codes must be interpreted and applied in a manner that respects the broad protection granted to religious freedom under the *Charter*.

56 Against this background, we return to the question. The concern here is that if the *Proposed Act* were adopted, religious officials could be required to perform same-sex marriages contrary to their religious beliefs. Absent state compulsion on religious officials, this conjecture does not engage the *Charter*. If a promulgated statute were to enact compulsion, we conclude that such compulsion would almost certainly run afoul of the *Charter* guarantee of freedom of religion, given the expansive protection afforded to religion by s. 2(a) of the *Charter*. ...

59 The question we are asked to answer is confined to the performance of same-sex marriages by religious officials. However, concerns were raised about the compulsory use of sacred places for the celebration of such marriages and about being compelled to otherwise assist in the celebration of same-sex marriages. The reasoning that leads us to conclude that the guarantee of freedom of religion protects against the compulsory celebration of same-sex marriages, suggests that the same would hold for these concerns.

60 Returning to the question before us, the Court is of the opinion that, absent unique circumstances with respect to which we will not speculate, the guarantee of religious freedom in s. 2(a) of the *Charter* is broad enough to protect religious officials from being compelled by the state to perform civil or religious same-sex marriages that are contrary to their religious beliefs.

D. Question 4: Is the Opposite-Sex Requirement for Marriage for Civil Purposes, As Established by the Common Law and Set Out for Quebec in Section 5 of the *Federal Law — Civil Law Harmonization Act, No. 1*, Consistent with the Charter?

(1) Threshold Issue: Whether the Court Should Answer Question 4

61 The first issue is whether this Court should answer the fourth question, in the unique circumstances of this reference. This issue must be approached on the basis that the answer to Question 4 may be positive or negative; the preliminary analysis of the discretion not to answer a reference question cannot be predicated on a presumed outcome. The reference jurisdiction vested in this Court by s. 53 of the *Supreme Court Act* is broad and has been interpreted liberally: see, e.g., *Secession Reference*, supra. The Court has rarely exercised its discretion not to answer a reference question reflecting its perception of the seriousness of its advisory role.

62 Despite this, the Court may decline to answer reference questions where to do so would be inappropriate, either because the question lacks sufficient legal content (which is not the case here) or because attempting to answer it would for other reasons be problematic.

. . . . .

64 A unique set of circumstances is raised by Question 4, the combined effect of which persuades the Court that it would be unwise and inappropriate to answer the question.

65 The first consideration on the issue of whether this Court should answer the fourth question is the government's stated position that it will proceed by way of legislative enactment,

regardless of what answer we give to this question. In oral argument, counsel reiterated the government's unequivocal intention to introduce legislation in relation to same-sex marriage, regardless of the answer to Question 4. The government has clearly accepted the rulings of lower courts on this question and has adopted their position as its own. The common law definition of marriage in five provinces and one territory no longer imports an opposite-sex requirement. In addition, s. 5 of the *Federal Law — Civil Law Harmonization Act, No. 1*, S.C. 2001, c. 4, no longer imports an opposite-sex requirement. Given the government's stated commitment to this course of action, an opinion on the constitutionality of an opposite-sex requirement for marriage serves no legal purpose. On the other hand, answering this question may have serious deleterious effects, which brings us to our next point.

66 The second consideration is that the parties to previous litigation have now relied upon the finality of the judgments they obtained through the court process. In the circumstances, their vested rights outweigh any benefit accruing from an answer to Question 4. Moreover, other same-sex couples acted on the finality of *EGALE*, *Halpern* and *Hendricks* to marry, relying on the Attorney General of Canada's adoption of the result in those cases.

. . . . .

68 There is no precedent for answering a reference question which mirrors issues already disposed of in lower courts where an appeal was available but not pursued. ...

69 The final consideration is that answering this question has the potential to undermine the government's stated goal of achieving uniformity in respect of civil marriage across Canada. There is no question that uniformity of the law is essential. This is the very reason that Parliament was accorded legislative competence in respect of marriage under s. 91(26) of the *Constitution Act, 1867*. However, as discussed, the government has already chosen to address the question of uniformity by means of the *Proposed Act*, which we have found to be within Parliament's legislative competence and consistent with the *Charter*. Answering the fourth question will not assist further. Given that uniformity is to be addressed legislatively, this rationale for answering Question 4 fails to compel.

70 On the other hand, consideration of the fourth question has the potential to undermine the uniformity that would be achieved by the adoption of the proposed legislation. The uniformity argument succeeds only if the answer to Question 4 is "no". By contrast, a "yes" answer would throw the law into confusion. The decisions of the lower courts in the matters giving rise to this reference are binding in their respective provinces. They would be cast into doubt by an advisory opinion which expressed a contrary view, even though it could not overturn them. The result would be confusion, not uniformity.

71 In sum, a unique combination of factors is at play in Question 4. The government has stated its intention to address the issue of same-sex marriage by introducing legislation regardless of our opinion on this question. The parties to previous litigation have relied upon the finality of their judgments and have acquired rights which in our view are entitled to protection. Finally, an answer to Question 4 would not only fail to ensure uniformity of the law, but might undermine it. These circumstances, weighed against the hypothetical benefit Parliament might derive from an answer, convince the Court that it should exercise its discretion not to answer Question 4.

NOTES AND QUESTIONS

1. The only real surprise in the *Reference re Same-Sex Marriage* was the Supreme Court of Canada's refusal to answer the fourth question. Some commentators have speculated that the court, as a political actor, wished to ensure that the Government of Canada could not avoid responsibility for the recognition of same-sex marriage by claiming that the Supreme Court of Canada required such recognition. If so, the tactic was only partially successful. After the

Civil Marriage Act (Bill C-38) was introduced, most of its supporters did not articulate public policy arguments in favour of the recognition of same-sex marriage. Rather, the focus was on the need to protect minority rights as guaranteed by the *Charter*. Indeed, Young Liberals at the National Liberal Convention in March 2005 wore buttons sporting the slogan "It's the Charter, stupid!"

The Supreme Court's refusal to answer the fourth question was used by Stephen Harper, in opposition at the time, to argue that Parliament could pass legislation affirming the traditional definition of marriage without using a "notwithstanding clause" to override equality rights (as permitted by s. 33 of the *Charter*). He also suggested that a statutory definition of marriage as a union of a man and a woman might survive renewed *Charter* challenges because it would represent a contemporary expression of Parliament's view and that this might encourage the courts to be deferential. Do you think that a statutory definition would have made any difference to the judges who decided *Halpern*?

Why do you think that the Supreme Court of Canada refused to answer the fourth question? As the court itself noted, a negative answer would have ensured uniformity across the country and ended the uncertainty that continued to exist until Parliament passed the *Civil Marriage Act*. It would also have virtually ended the debate over same-sex marriage in Canada because the Parliamentary opponents did not wish to use a "notwithstanding clause" to achieve their goal.

2. Royal Assent was granted to the *Civil Marriage Act* (Bill C-38) on July 20, 2005. Section 2 specifically states: "Marriage, for civil purposes, is the lawful union of two persons to the exclusion of all others", while s. 4 provides: "For greater certainty, a marriage is not void or voidable by reason only that the spouses are of the same sex". Section 8 amends s. 2(1) of the *Divorce Act* to redefine "spouse" as "either of two persons who are married to each other".

The House of Commons revisited the issue of same-sex marriage briefly in the fall of 2006. On a free vote, a majority voted not to re-open the matter.

3. Other jurisdictions with same-sex marriage (in early 2009) include Holland (since 2001), Belgium (2003), Massachusetts (2003), Spain (2005), South Africa (2006), California (2008), Connecticut (2008), and Norway (2009). In the three listed American states, same-sex marriage arrived as a result of constitutional litigation. However, Californian voters approved Proposition 8 in the November 2008 election. That proposition expressly amended the state constitution by adding the following section to Article 1: "Only marriage between a man and a woman is valid or recognized in California." The election result, therefore, threw into doubt the status of the thousands of same-sex marriages that had already occurred in the state. In late May 2009, the California Supreme Court rejected several challenges to the amendment on procedural grounds but concluded that the amendment had no effect on the marriages of same-sex couples performed before the adoption of Proposition 8.

4. In February 2005, the Ontario legislature passed the *Spousal Relationships Statute Law Amendment Act, 2005*. It amended the *Marriage Act* and the *Human Rights Code* to stipulate that a religious official is not required to solemnize a marriage or to allow a sacred place to be used to solemnize a marriage where to do so would be contrary to the religious beliefs of the religious body to which he or she belongs. It also amended s. 24(3) of the *Marriage Act* to alter the form of the ceremony so that it could apply to same-sex couples.

5. Since 2005, same-sex couples from foreign countries have obtained marriage licences from provincial authorities and proceeded to get married in Canada. However, these marriages may not be considered valid in the couple's home jurisdiction. See, e.g., *Wilkinson v. Kitzinger*, [2006] EWHC 2022 where the Family Division of the High Court of Justice refused to issue a declaration that the marriage of two English women in British Columbia was a valid marriage.

6. While some provinces have permitted public officials authorized to perform marriage ceremonies (marriage commissioners or municipal clerks) to decline to officiate at same-sex marriages for religious or conscientious reasons, most have not. For an analysis of this issue, see MacDougall, "Refusing to Officiate at Same-Sex Marriages" (2006), 69 Sask. L. Rev. 351 and Trotter, "The Right to Decline Performance of Same-Sex Civil Marriages — A Response to Professor Bruce MacDougall" (2007), 70 Sask. L. Rev. 365.

(2) Ability to Consummate

While the ability to consummate a marriage as a requirement to a valid marriage has been abolished in some jurisdictions such as Australia, it continues to be a pre-requisite in Canada. Yet, its continuing existence is hard to reconcile with the view that a same-sex marriage is valid. First, the rationale underlying the rule that the parties must be able to consummate their marriage is closely related to the view that a key purpose of marriage is the procreation of children. Second, the definition of the ability to consummate a marriage means that the partners in a same-sex marriage lack the ability to consummate their marriages. In this regard, it should again be noted that s. 4 of the *Civil Marriage Act* states: "For greater certainty, a marriage is not void or voidable by reason only that the spouses are of the same sex". Does this implicitly preclude a finding that a same-sex marriage is voidable because the partners cannot consummate their marriage? If so, should Parliament abolish the rule that a marriage between two persons of the opposite sex is voidable where the spouses lack the ability to consummate their marriage? Consider that, although the annual number of annulments on this ground is small, the cases indicate that some married persons still prefer to seek an annulment on this ground rather than obtain a divorce.

GAJAMUGAN v. GAJAMUGAN

(1979), 10 R.F.L. (2d) 280, 1979 CarswellOnt 289 (Ont. H.C.)

CARRUTHERS J.: — This is an action for annulment. The parties went through a civil form of marriage on 23rd June 1978, followed by a religious ceremony on 24th June 1978. Following the religious ceremony on 24th June, in the evening, the parties retired to a room in a hotel and there slept together for the first time.

The plaintiff's evidence and the defendant's evidence consisted, in part, of an extremely detailed account of their respective memories of what occurred during the evening and night that they first slept together. The effect of the plaintiff's evidence is that he attempted to have sexual intercourse with the defendant but as soon as he touched her face with his hand he had a mental revulsion to the marks on her face. The effect of this reaction, so far as sexual intercourse is concerned, according to the plaintiff, was that his penis, which had become erect, became flaccid. He said that this occurred within a minute. There never was any penetration. Thereafter, the parties slept in the same bed, but, as the plaintiff said, "apart". This abortive attempt at sexual intercourse occurred about 10:30 or 11:00 p.m. on the evening of 24th June 1978. No further attempts were made over the course of that evening. The parties slept together again on the evening of 25th June 1978 and a further attempt was made at sexual intercourse and, according to the plaintiff, "the same thing happened". He was not able to proceed with intercourse. There was no penetration. He said in evidence that when he kissed and touched the defendant's face he "lost his erection". They again slept together, that is, in the same bed, but, as the plaintiff said, "apart". There were no further attempts made at sexual intercourse while the parties were together in Malaysia where they were married.

As planned the plaintiff left Malaysia to return to Canada on 27th June. The defendant was unable to accompany him because of difficulty with her visa. She arrived in Woodstock on 3rd January 1979. On the night of her arrival, the parties again attempted sexual intercourse. The plaintiff said again that he lost his erection because of "the same mind", due to a revulsion because of the marks on the defendant's face. He described it as being a repeat of what had happened on the previous attempts at intercourse. He said it was "in my mind" and it was caused by "touching". That night the plaintiff slept in a separate room. They never slept together again and no further attempts at sexual intercourse have ever been made.

The plaintiff said in evidence that he tried to overcome the problem by simply trying to forget it. He said he could not. The plaintiff denies that he had any problem of impotence, having had a child by his first marriage and, from his description, a reasonably active sexual life during the course of that marriage and on occasions thereafter, prior to his marriage to the defendant. He had no idea before this marriage to the defendant that he would have the problem he now describes as having had on the occasions when he attempted sexual intercourse with the defendant. His first knowledge was in the hotel where they first slept together on the evening of 24th June 1978.

The defendant remained with the plaintiff in his house in Woodstock for nine days after her arrival. He said that during that time he could not look at her face. He could not talk with the defendant and after three days he did not want to come home. He could not eat what she cooked.

He said that on no occasion was his problem due to the consumption of alcohol or a drug. On 12th January 1979 the plaintiff advised the defendant that, "This marriage isn't going to work out". He bought her a ticket to go home. He felt that it was best for her to go home because she had a sister there "to console her". He bought her a one-way ticket on Air France. He took her to the airport in Toronto and left her at security.

The defendant did not return home in January 1979. Apparently she passed out at the airport and eventually she was returned to Woodstock. The incident at the airport followed by five days an incident which occurred at the home in Woodstock when she drank a quantity of liquid bleach upon learning that the plaintiff was sending her back to Malaysia. She indicated that in Malaysia, girls can only marry once. She could not, if she returned to Malaysia, face people and, therefore, wished to remain in Woodstock, married to the plaintiff.

In her evidence she confirmed the evidence of the plaintiff as to the nights upon which they had slept together following their marriage. She denied, however, that the plaintiff had any other difficulty other than being "impatient" and his refusal to "push hard enough" in order to bring about penetration. Specifically she said that at no time was she aware of any problem that the plaintiff was having in maintaining an erection. She said that he never mentioned anything about the marks on her face. At the time of her first attempt to have intercourse with the plaintiff she was a virgin, never having had sexual intercourse previous to that date.

For the purposes of my decision, I am prepared to adopt an overview of the essential ingredients to be proved in an action of nullity because of impotence as outlined in an article by J. David Fine, "Annulment of Marriage for Impotence in the Common Law of Canada" (1973), 8 R.F.L. 129. It reads as follows [p. 129]:

> A good overview of the essential ingredients to be proved in an action for nullity because of impotence was provided by Laidlaw J.A. in the Ontario Court of Appeal in 1944: *Rae v. Rae*, [1944] O.R. 266, [1944] 2 D.L.R. 604; summarized in *Hardick (Fox) v. Fox* (1970), 3 R.F.L. 153 (Ont.); (1) Impotence must exist at the time of the marriage: *Napier v. Napier*, [1915] P.184 at 190; (2) the incapacity pleaded must be such as to render intercourse impractical: *D. v. A.* (1845), 1 Rob. Ecc. 279, 163 E.R. 1039; (3) the incapacity may stem from 'a physical or mental or moral disability': *H. v. P.(H)* (1873), L.R. 3 P. & D. 126; and (4) the impotence must be incurable: *Welde (Aston) v. Welde* (1731), 2 Lee 580, 161 E.R. 446.

I am prepared to accept the evidence of the plaintiff, particularly where it conflicts with that of the defendant. When I consider her evidence in the light of her demeanour and attitude seen while she was in the witness-box, I conclude that what she had to say was influenced by her personal concern of having to return home not married.

I must confess that the decision I have reached in this matter was not reached without anxious consideration. My prime concern stems from the requirement that the disability, mental in this case, must be found to be incurable. No evidence was led specifically to deal with this point. Counsel for the plaintiff asks that the court infer, because the condition existed on two nights in June 1978 and again in January 1979, that it be deemed incurable, particularly when it is such a subjective matter and something about which medical evidence would be of little value in assisting the court to come to a conclusion. I am prepared to accept that position.

There will, therefore, be a declaration that the marriage in question is void. ...

[The court ordered the plaintiff to pay the defendant a lump sum of $3,000, plus $100 per week, as spousal support under the *Family Law Reform Act*.]

AISAICAN v. KAHNAPACE

(1996), 24 R.F.L. (4th) 143, 1996 CarswellSask 558 (Sask. Q.B.)

GUNN J.: — The applicant seeks to annul her marriage to the respondent on the basis that he is impotent and cannot consummate the marriage. The only evidence presented to support the petitioner's claim is her own affidavit in which she says: "... b) The Respondent, Sheldon Troy Kahnapace, was *insofar as the depondent knows*, unable to have sexual intercourse. The depondent and the Respondent did not engage in sexual intercourse whatsoever after the date of the marriage. (c) The Respondent was, two weeks prior to the marriage, shot by persons unknown and as such, is a quadriplegic and is incapable of having intercourse." [emphasis added]

The evidence is clear that the parties did not engage in sexual intercourse following the marriage, but what is not so clear is the incapacity of the respondent to do so. The petitioner's claim is qualified by the phrase "insofar as the deponent knows". Further there is no medical evidence before me to suggest that either the respondent in particular or quadriplegics in general are incapable of having intercourse.

A further question to be addressed would be the knowledge of the applicant at the time of the marriage, assuming the respondent's incapacity is established.

Cowan C.J.T.D. addressed this issue in *R. v. R.* (1976), 28 R.F.L. 283 (N.S. T.D.), at 287 and 288:

> The position of an impotent spouse, who seeks a declaration of nullity on the ground of his own impotence, was exhaustively considered by the Court of Appeal in *Harthan v. Harthan*, [1949] P. 115, [1948] 2 All E.R. 639. In that case, it was decided that, provided that there are no circumstances which bar him or her, e.g. knowledge of the defect at the time of the marriage, an impotent spouse is entitled to petition for a decree of nullity, and the right to do so is not conditional on the repudiation of the marriage by the other spouse. As I understand the decision of Lord Merriman P. in that case, knowledge on the part of the petitioning spouse of his or her impotence is only one reason for denying the remedy of nullity to the impotent spouse.

Arguably, this bar to a decree of nullity should work both ways. Therefore, if the petitioner knew of the respondent's incapacity prior to the marriage and married him despite that knowledge, she too ought to be denied a decree of nullity. In *G. v. M.* (1885), 10 App. Cas. 171 (H.L.), at 186 for example, the court discussed the doctrine of sincerity and held that if an applicant approbated the marriage with knowledge of the circumstances set forth as grounds for the annulment, the decree would not be granted.

> ... [T]here may be conduct on the part of the person seeking this remedy which ought to estop that person from having it; as, for instance, any act from which the inference ought to be drawn that during the antecedent time the party has, with a knowledge of the facts and of the law, approbated the marriage which he or she afterwards seeks to get rid of...

More recently, in *Norman v. Norman* (1979), 9 R.F.L. (2d) 345 at 349 (Ont. U.F.C.), the court held that where the parties have married for companionship and separate because of a quarrel rather than for the lack of sexual contact, it is not open to the applicant, who knowingly entered into a platonic marriage, to complain of the absence of sexual intercourse.

Finally, if the applicant is not entitled to a decree of nullity for the evidentiary reasons previously identified, the mere fact the respondent has not opposed the application is irrelevant. In *W. v. W.* (1987), 5 R.F.L. (3d) 323 (P.E.I. S.C.), at 325, McQuaid J. stated that "[i]f the facts and the law warrant its granting, then she [the petitioner] is entitled to the relief sought; if the facts and the law do not warrant it, the husband's consent alone will not further her cause."

I decline to grant the order [a declaration of nullity] on two grounds:

1.   The evidence adduced to establish the claim is insufficient.

2.   The physical condition of the respondent, if established, pre-dates the marriage. If the petitioner entered into the marriage with knowledge of this condition, she would be barred from successfully prosecuting an action to annul the marriage on that basis.

NOTES AND QUESTIONS

1. In determining whether an inability to consummate exists, the courts have attempted to apply the principle laid down by Dr. Lushington in *D. v. A.* (1845), 1 Rob. Eccl. 279, 163 E.R. 1039 at 298 [Rob. Eccl.]: "Sexual intercourse, in the proper meaning of the term, is ordinary and complete intercourse; it does not mean partial and imperfect intercourse." On the question of what constitutes complete intercourse, see also *H. v. H.*, [1927] 2 W.W.R. 366, 22 Alta. L.R. 565, [1927] 3 D.L.R. 481 (C.A.); *Miller v. Miller*, [1947] O.R. 213, [1947] 3 D.L.R. 354 (C.A.); *Baxter v. Baxter* (1947), [1948] A.C. 274, [1947] 2 All E.R. 886 (U.K. H.L.); and *S. v. S. (Otherwise W.)* (1962), [1963] P. 162, [1962] 2 All E.R. 816 (Eng. C.A.). In the last case, the wife had a malformed vagina too short to admit full penetration but according to medical evidence capable of being enlarged by an operation. The operation would involve removal of the soft tissues where the normal vagina would be in order to create a passage that would be lined by skin from the thigh. The absence of the natural membrane and its special sensory quality and of normal secretions would affect the degree of sexual satisfaction obtained from intercourse by the wife but not materially that of the husband. The passage would end in a cul-de-sac and there could be no conception as the wife had no uterus. The court, on a petition for a decree of nullity by the husband, held that the wife's incapacity was curable and that the decree had to be refused. Would the incapacity have been incurable if the wife had refused the operation? See *Dashevsky v. Dashevsky* (1973), 13 R.F.L. 1 (Ont. H.C.).

2. The Canadian and English cases on the inability to consummate due to psychological repugnance or aversion to the sexual act were reviewed in *W. v. W.* (1987), 5 R.F.L. (3d) 323 (P.E.I. T.D.). McQuaid J. made the following comment on the *Gajamugan* decision (at 331): "With all respect to the learned trial judge, however, I am unable to agree that one might 'infer' incurability in the absence of medical evidence, on the experience of the parties on only three nights." The wife's petition was dismissed in *W. v. W.* because, although she could establish that a psychological condition inhibited her from consummating the marriage with the respondent, she could not prove that this was caused by an "invincible repugnance or aversion to the sexual act with the respondent".

See also *Juretic v. Ruiz* (1999), 49 R.F.L. (4th) 299 (B.C. C.A.) where the wife indicated on two occasions that she did not want her husband to embrace her, but that he could have sex with her as long as "he did not touch her". The husband considered sexual intercourse under these circumstances to be tantamount to rape and he made no further attempt to have sexual relations with his wife. The trial judge's conclusion that the husband had not established an "invincible aversion" was upheld by the appellate court which noted (at 303): "Put another way, it could be said that Mr. Juretic's situation fell short of an 'unconquerable repugnance'".

In *Sangha v. Aujla* (2002), 32 R.F.L. (5th) 445 (B.C. S.C.), an arranged marriage failed. The wife and husband had little contact with one another before the marriage, but the husband's relatives assured the wife's relatives that he did not have a criminal record. After the marriage, the wife told the husband that they should get to know one another before they had sexual relations. The husband respected her wishes. In one of their talks, the husband revealed that he had spent four years in prison in England for robbery. This was too much for the wife and she soon left her husband. The wife applied for a declaration of nullity on the basis of her inability to consummate the marriage. She explained that divorce would significantly diminish her reputation and prospects of marriage in her culture. The husband agreed that the marriage had never been consummated, but he argued that there was no evidence to indicate that the wife lacked the ability to consummate it. Justice McEwan granted the declaration, stating (at para. 16):

> Here, the plaintiff is in the position that a clear precondition or promise on which the marriage was founded did not exist. I think it quite understandable that this, and the fact that in this particular arrangement, the parties remained effectively strangers until they were married, renders consummation a practical impossibility for the plaintiff. I do not think it necessary for the court to describe her normal, predictable reaction to the situation in pathological terms in order to grant the declaration sought. There can be no basis in public policy for promoting marriage to the extent of denying this application.

In *L. (K.H.) v. L. (G.Q.)* (2003), 39 R.F.L. (5th) 326 (B.C. C.A.), a woman, who was a Canadian citizen, married a man shortly after he arrived in Canada as a visitor. About two years later, the woman brought an action to have the marriage annulled. She testified that she had never resided with the man and that he had disappeared for long periods of time, reappearing when he needed her help to stay in Canada. She stated that he had rebuffed all her attempts at intimacy and that he had claimed to be homosexual. The woman's sister testified that she and the woman had never ceased residing in the home that they shared with their mother. The man, however, claimed that he and the woman had cohabited in two locations and had had sexual intercourse approximately 60 times. The trial judge accepted the woman's evidence wherever it conflicted with that of the man. He granted a declaration of nullity on the basis that the man was incapable of consummating the marriage because of an invincible aversion to sexual intercourse with the woman. The appellate court dismissed the man's appeal. It held that there was ample evidence from which the trial judge could draw the inference that the man's refusal to have any physical contact with the woman was due to an invincible aversion to sexual intercourse with her. The manipulation of the woman for immigration purposes explained why the man nevertheless married her.

The court granted a wife an annulment on the basis of her inability to consummate the marriage in *Grewal v. Sohal* (2004), 2004 CarswellBC 2787, 12 R.F.L. (6th) 55 (S.C.). In this case, a woman domiciled in British Columbia married an Indian national, a lawyer, in India. The couple's parents arranged the marriage and the man and woman only met once before the ceremony. During the meeting, the man represented himself as being in good health and free from any addictions to alcohol or other drugs. The woman also believed that the man would come to live permanently with her in Canada once the immigration authorities permitted this. In subsequent annulment proceedings, the wife argued that the marriage was a nullity because the husband fraudulently entered into the marriage solely to enable him to immigrate to Canada and because she was unable to consummate the marriage as a result of the husband's misrepresentations about his health and character. She testified that, on the wedding night, the husband disclosed that he was addicted to drugs and would not have sexual relations with her until he was cured. She also stated that the marriage was not consummated thereafter. The wife's parents indicated that the husband and wife did not sleep in the same room during the husband's first visit to Canada. The wife also testified that the husband brought numerous drugs with him to Canada and admitted his continuing addiction. She produced a letter from an Indian physician indicating that the husband had undergone addiction treatment. Finally, she asserted that the husband had told her after his arrival in Canada that he had married her only for immigration purposes.

The husband insisted that the marriage had been consummated on the wedding night and that the couple had had sexual relations on numerous occasions thereafter. He also denied ever telling his wife that he was addicted to drugs, although he acknowledged that he had become reliant on painkillers to deal with an injury. Finally, he insisted that he loved his wife and had married her fully intending to live with her in Canada.

Justice Davies concluded that the wife's evidence was to be preferred whenever it contradicted the husband's. Accordingly, the Justice held that the wife had established that the husband married her only to obtain lawful entry into Canada and that the marriage was never consummated, initially because of the husband's addiction to painkillers and later because of the wife's reaction to his misrepresentations regarding his health and his motive for entering into the marriage. The Justice also concluded that binding precedent required the court to hold that the husband's desire to marry only for immigration purposes did not render the marriage invalid. However, the Justice then found that the wife developed a psychological incapacity to have sexual relations with her husband when she discovered that he had misrepresented his health and character and that he had married her only to gain entry into Canada. Her reaction was described as "normal and predictable" and the Justice held that there was no need for expert evidence to establish her psychological incapacity to consummate the marriage.

3. Inability to consummate renders a marriage voidable, not void: *Jones v. Jones* (1947), [1948] O.R. 22 (C.A.). Accordingly, the marriage continues to exist until terminated by a declaration of nullity or by divorce.

(3) Outside Prohibited Degrees of Consanguinity and Affinity

In order for two persons to marry, they must not fall within the prohibited degrees of consanguinity (relationship by blood) and affinity (relationship by marriage). In 1990, Parliament enacted the *Marriage (Prohibited Degrees) Act*, S.C. 1990, c. 46, which came into force in 1991. By virtue of s. 4, this legislation contains "all of the prohibitions in law in Canada against marriage by reason of the parties being related". Under this Act, as amended in 2005 to take into account same-sex marriages, two persons are within the prohibited degrees only if "they are related lineally, or as brother or sister or half-brother or half-sister, including by adoption". The background to the 1990 legislation is outlined in the following article.

For a history of Canadian legislation (up to 1997) on prohibited degrees, see Stevenson, "Federal Marriage Legislation in Canada" (1997), 9 J. Church L. Assoc. Can. 149.

ZIFF, "RECENT DEVELOPMENTS IN MARRIAGE AND DIVORCE"

(1986), 18 Ottawa Law Rev. 121 at 135–137 (Footnotes omitted)

In its original form, the Bill provided that a marriage would be void if entered into by two persons related lineally by consanguinity, or as brother or sister by the whole or half-blood. These were intended to be the only marriage prohibitions based on the proximity of relationships. Following deliberations, the Standing Committee on Legal and Constitutional Affairs recommended that the prohibitions be extended to include lineal and sibling relationships arising from adoption.

The traditional policies behind affinal restrictions, put succinctly, are the insulation of the nuclear or extended family from sexual meddling, the promotion of marriage outside of the family and the preservation of perceived societal norms or Judeo-Christian religious beliefs. Restrictions based on consanguinity have been supported on these grounds, but there is, as well, the additional concern that genetic and even eugenic defects are more common in the offspring of close blood relations. The amendments reflect an abandonment of the first cluster of reasons, presumably either because they no longer reflect public policy, or because marriage prohibitions are seen as ineffective vehicles with which to pursue these goals. A reduction in the restrictions based on consanguinity seems in accord with current scientific opinion that the physical dangers are not as significant as once thought, particularly where the blood relationship between the parents is not close.

It is with respect to the relevance of adoption that the major debate under the Bill has festered. The policy issues centred on whether or not adopted children should be treated in exactly the same way as natural children for these purposes. ...

In considering the appropriate policy, one must look beyond the question of whether or not the reasons supporting the remaining marriage prohibitions under the Bill apply to adopted children. Insofar as these reasons relate to matters of eugenics or genetics, clearly they would not be relevant. But the policy underlying adoption law demands attention too. Adoption creates a legal fiction and is designed to facilitate the adopted child's assimilation and integration into the new home. Holding such a child to the prohibitions attached to natural children promotes the integrative process. Admittedly, these concerns are weakened when one remembers that it is only when the adopted child becomes an adult that the practical issue will have to be addressed. In any event, this entire issue will be far less acute under the proposed legislation as the ambit of the prohibitions would be drastically reduced.

(4) No Prior Existing Marriage

A marriage is void if one of the parties is, at the time of the marriage, already a party to a prior existing marriage. Therefore, a declaration of invalidity is not required to end the marriage. However, often a party will seek to have this state of affairs affirmed by a court. Invariably, the issue in such cases is whether the prior marriage was terminated as a result of death or divorce.

MESZAROS v. MESZAROS

[1969] 2 O.R. 336, 5 D.L.R. (3d) 294, 1969 CarswellOnt 102 (H.C.)

PARKER J.: — This is an action for dissolution of marriage based on the ground of cruelty.

The petitioner was married on February 23, 1953, to Theodor Hamaida at the Town of Paris, in the Province of Ontario. She and Mr. Hamaida lived together until about the month of December, 1956, when he deserted her. Shortly before the desertion he advised her that he had a wife in Russia but she was unable to verify this information.

On June 20, 1966, she secured an order under s. 11(1) of the *Marriage Act*, R.S.O. 1950, c. 228, declaring that Theodor Hamaida was dead. The supporting affidavit executed by her at that time was filed as an exhibit in the present action. The petitioner deposed that she had not heard from her husband since the separation, that he had been continually absent for seven years, that to the best of her knowledge and belief no other person or persons had heard from her husband, that she had made inquiries among their friends and relatives to ascertain whether they had heard from or of her husband from the time of the separation up to the time she deposed to and she was informed and verily believed that they had not heard from him nor of him and by reason thereof she had no reason to believe that her husband was living.

On April 23, 1966, the petitioner married the respondent Leslie Meszaros and lived with him until the month of May, 1968, when he forcibly ejected her from the matrimonial home. The evidence indicated that during their cohabitation the petitioner was subjected to considerable mental and physical cruelty. At the conclusion of the evidence I found that the cruelty was sufficient to come within s. 3(d) of the *Divorce Act*, 1967-68 (Can.), c. 24, but reserved judgment to consider the validity of the marriage.

Dealing first with the marriage between the petitioner and the respondent there is a strong presumption that the parties who have lived together and held themselves out as man and wife are validly married: *Beattie v. Beattie*, [1945] O.R. 129, [1945] 1 D.L.R. 574. This is a presumption that can only be overcome by the most cogent evidence but may be rebutted by evidence of a prior marriage. The certificate of the Hamaida marriage having been filed is probably sufficient to rebut this presumption. I think the same initial presumption of validity would apply to the petitioner's marriage to Mr. Hamaida. ...

I doubt that the hearsay evidence that Mr. Hamaida had a wife in Russia is sufficient to rebut this presumption of validity.

If Mr. Hamaida was still alive at the time of the petitioner's second marriage, then her second marriage is a nullity. However, there was no evidence before me to suggest that he was alive at that time. On the contrary, the evidence in her affidavit raises a presumption of death. The rule with respect to presumption of death is set out in *Re Phene's Trusts* (1870), L.R. 5 Ch. 139 [headnote]:

> If a person has not been heard of for seven years, there is a presumption of law that he is dead; but at what time within that period he died is not a matter of presumption, but of evidence, and the *onus* of proving that the death took place at any particular time within the seven years lies upon the person who claims a right to the establishment of which that fact is essential.

If Mr. Hamaida may be presumed to be dead then the petitioner was a widow at the time of her second marriage and this marriage may once again be presumed to be valid. What was the effect of the order under the *Marriage Act*, s. 11(3)? ...

Since marriage and divorce are under Dominion jurisdiction by reason of s. 91(26) of the *B.N.A. Act, 1867*, and solemnization of marriage is reserved to the Provinces under s. 92(12) one must presume that s. 11 of the *Marriage Act* intended to deal only with the formality of securing a licence without regard to the status of the applicant. The order permitted the petitioner to apply for a marriage licence. The second union may therefore be presumed to be valid unless and until it is shown that the person presumed dead was not in fact dead at the time of the solemnization of the second marriage. Until that event occurs the petitioner is entitled to petition for a divorce.

BATE v. BATE

(1978), 1 R.F.L. (2d) 298, 1978 CarswellOnt 218 (Ont. H.C.)

BOLAND J.: — This matter concerns a petition for divorce on the grounds of adultery and three years' separation. The wife is also seeking maintenance and costs. The husband opposes the action on the grounds that the alleged marriage between the petitioner and the respondent on 19th May 1969 in Las Vegas, Nevada, was *void ab initio* by reason of a valid marriage subsisting at the time between the petitioner and her first husband, David Whitfield Simser.

The issue to be determined by this court is whether the parties are presently married under the laws of this jurisdiction. This will depend on whether this court recognizes the 1957 Nevada divorce purporting to dissolve the marriage between the petitioner and her first husband, David Whitfield Simser, as a valid and effective divorce in Ontario.

The petitioner has been married three times. Her first marriage was to David Whitfield Simser on 10th December 1950, in the town of Keswick, Ontario. There were two children of this marriage and the husband has never remarried. This marriage was purportedly dissolved by a decree of divorce granted on 23rd May 1957 in the Eighth Judicial District Court of the state of Nevada. The second marriage was to John Arne Smedstam on 19th August 1958, in the state of Indiana. This marriage was dissolved by a judgment of the Falu South Judicial District Court, Sweden, on 1st February 1963. Her third marriage was to the respondent on 19th May 1969, in Las Vegas Nevada. At the time of the marriage ceremony, both parties were Canadian citizens and were residing in Toronto, Ontario, where they returned shortly after the alleged marriage and where they have continued to reside. There were no children with respect to the second and third marriages. It is the first divorce, granted on 23rd May 1957 in the state of Nevada, which purported to dissolve the marriage between the petitioner and David Whitfield Simser that is under attack in this action. Hence, only that divorce concerns us and will be discussed here.

Submissions were made at trial concerning certain presumptions and raising the question of who has the onus of proof in a case of this type. Before dealing with the issue of recognition of a foreign divorce, I think it advisable to settle this issue. On the authority of *Powell v. Cockburn*, [1977] 2 S.C.R. 218, 22 R.F.L. 155, 68 D.L.R. (3d) 700, 8 N.R. 215, counsel for the petitioner submitted that there are certain presumptions in favour of his client which shift the burden of proof to the respondent. That is, once the petitioner adduces evidence that a marriage ceremony took place between the petitioner and the respondent, which has been done by the filing of the marriage certificate, then there is a presumption of the validity of that marriage. Similarly, once evidence is presented in support of the foreign divorce, which was done by filing the decree of divorce, then there is a presumption of the validity of the foreign divorce decree. The burden then shifts to the respondent to prove his allegations of the invalidity of the marriage and the foreign divorce on the balance of probabilities. The relevant passage from *Powell v. Cockburn, supra*, dealing with this question can be found at p. 161:

> The factums in this case make frequent reference to 'presumptions', each side seeking to throw the burden of adducing evidence upon the other. There would seem to be some confusion as to the legal effect of presumptions. In the case before us, there are three presumptions which may be relevant: (i) the presumption of validity of marriage ... (ii) the presumption of validity of a foreign divorce decree ... and (iii) the presumption in favour of the domicile of origin. Strictly speaking, they do not conflict nor cancel each other out, nor do they give added probative value.
>
> Their only effect is to impose a duty on the party against whom they operate to adduce some evidence: see 9 Wigmore on Evidence, p. 281, s. 2487. They may, as in the present case, impose an alternating duty to produce evidence which shifts from one party to the other, a process which Wigmore describes as 'successive presumptions': p. 292, s. 2493. At the outset the appellant Powell faced a presumption of validity with regard to his marriage to the wife. He satisfied this presumption by leading evidence to show the existence of her prior marriage. With regard to this marriage, too, there was a presumption of validity, but the two presumptions did not conflict. Rather, the wife had to lead evidence to show that the previous marriage had been terminated. This she did by evidence of the foreign divorce. Evidence having been led on each issue the presumptions disappeared. It fell then to the trier of fact to decide the issues upon all of the evidence adduced. In this case if the trier of fact was not satisfied on a balance of probabilities that Powell had proved his case (that the Powell-Cockburn marriage was a nullity), then Powell must fail. The ultimate burden of proof, the risk of non-persuasion of the trier of fact, rested on Powell throughout.

It is clear from the above that the presumptions in question do not provide any probative conclusiveness. Rather, they merely require from the party against whom they operate a rebuttal, the test of which is the adducing of "some evidence". Thus, at the outset, the respondent was faced with the presumption of validity with regard to his marriage to the petitioner. He satisfied this presumption by giving evidence in the form of a marriage certificate to show the existence of her prior marriage to David Whitfield Simser. This first marriage also carried with it a presumption of validity imposing on the petitioner a duty to produce "some evidence" to show that the previous marriage had been terminated. This she did by filing the Nevada decree of divorce. The foreign divorce decree also carried with it a presumption of validity imposing a duty on the respondent to submit some evidence establishing its invalidity. This he did by presenting some evidence concerning the intentions of the petitioner in travelling to Las Vegas, Nevada, in 1957, which will be discussed in more detail. Some evidence having been led on all issues, the presumptions of validity disappeared. It is now up to this court to decide the issues upon all of the evidence adduced. There is no question that the ultimate burden of proof, the risk of non-persuasion, on a balance of probabilities rests with the respondent.

[Justice Boland found that the Las Vegas divorce could not be recognized in Ontario and that the petitioner was still validly married to David Whitfield Simser. This rendered her marriage to the respondent null and void. The divorce petition was dismissed.]

NOTES AND QUESTIONS

1. In the *Meszaros* case, the Court apparently never considered the fact that the petitioner wife remarried some two months before she obtained the presumption of death order. Should this fact have affected the result?

2. What is the effect of an order under Ontario's *Declarations of Death Act, 2002*, S.O. 2002, c. 14, Sched.? See also s. 9 of the Ontario *Marriage Act*.

In *Re Larsen* (1980), 18 R.F.L. (2d) 14 (B.C.S.C.), Mr. Larsen re-appeared some 17 years after Mrs. Larsen obtained an order under the *Survivor and Presumption of Death Act* specifying that he was presumed dead. Mr. Larsen obtained an order revoking the original order even though Mrs. Larsen had remarried twice in the interim.

3. For further reading on the use of presumptions in this area of law, see Bates, "Presumption of Marriage in Canada: Its Past, Present, and Future" (1979), 17 U.W.O.L. Rev. 169.

4. In the United States, a presumption of validity operates in favour of a second marriage to the extent that the party attacking the validity of the marriage must prove a valid prior marriage that has not been dissolved by divorce or ended by death. See Hahlo, *Nullity of Marriage in Canada* (Toronto: Butterworths, 1979) at 14. Is this similar to the position taken in *Meszaros* and *Bate*? How do the various presumptions relate to the ultimate burden of proof?

5. Recall that the 2005 federal *Civil Marriage Act* defines marriage as the "union of two persons to the exclusion of all others". Accordingly, a polygamous or plural union is not accorded the status of marriage in Canada. However, polygamous marriages may be recognized for some purposes. For example, Ontario and Prince Edward Island's property and spousal support regimes extend to a marriage that is actually or potentially polygamous if "it was celebrated in a jurisdiction whose system of law recognizes it as valid": s. 1(1) of Ontario's *Family Law Act*. Generally, see Kaufman, "Polygamous Marriages in Canada" (2005), 21 Can. J. Fam. L. 315 and Kelly, "Bringing International Human Rights Law Home: An Evaluation of Canada's Family Law Treatment of Polygamy" (2007), 65 U.T. Fac. L. Rev. 1.

6. Section 290 of the *Criminal Code* makes it an offence (bigamy) for someone who is married to go through a form of marriage with another person. In addition, s. 293 stipulates that anyone who practices any form of polygamy or enters into any kind of conjugal relationship with more than one person at the same time is guilty of an indictable offence. For many years, members of a fundamentalist Mormon sect in Bountiful, British Columbia, have been practicing polygamy with impunity. In recent times, the authorities' inaction was based on a fear that the courts might hold that the *Code* provisions dealing with polygamy unjustifiably limit freedom of religion. However, in January 2009, charges were laid under s. 293 of the *Code* against two male leaders in the local branch of the Fundamentalist Church of Jesus Christ of Latter Day Saints. The accused have indeed indicated that they will challenge the constitutional validity of the section. Do you think that this challenge is likely to succeed?

A successful challenge to s. 293 would not lead to legal recognition of polygamous marriage. It might, however, pave the way to a *Charter* challenge of the current definition of marriage as a union between only two people. Do you think that such a challenge is likely to succeed?

7. In 2005, the Status of Women Canada commissioned four research reports on polygamy that were eventually published as *Polygamy in Canada: Legal and Social Implications for Women and Children — A Collection of Policy Research* (Ottawa: Status of Women Canada, 2005). None of the four reports recommended allowing polygamous marriages to take place in Canada and all emphasized the harms to women and children associated with polygamy. However, the academics differed on whether s. 293 of the *Criminal Code* could survive a *Charter* challenge and whether it should, in any event, be repealed.

In *Polygyny and Canada's Obligations under International Human Rights Law* (Ottawa: Department of Justice Canada, 2006), available online on the Department's website, Rebecca Cook and Lisa Kelly stress that polygamy is a form of discrimination against women and a violation of international law. The authors suggest ways in which women and children in or leaving polygamous relationships should be protected and assisted.

(5) Consent

(a) Capacity to Understand

BANTON v. BANTON

(1998), 164 D.L.R. (4th) 176, 1998 CarswellOnt 3423 (Ont. Gen. Div.); additional reasons at (1998), 1998 CarswellOnt 4688 (Ont. Gen. Div.)

CULLITY J.: — *Background*: The issues to be tried in this case were defined in an order for directions of Sheard J., dated June 6, 1996. Before I address them, the following bare chronological outline of facts that are, for the most part, not materially in dispute will indicate the background and the context in which the issues arose.

1. George Banton was born in England on June 13, 1906. He emigrated to Canada and for the greater part of his life he lived in Toronto where he was employed by a chemical company for over 60 years. For most of that time he was a sales representative.

2. George Banton married three times. He and his first wife, Kathleen, had five children, Victor, George (George Jr.), Joan, Patricia and Sheila, each of whom is a respondent to this application. There are 18 grandchildren. Kathleen died in 1970. In 1971 George Banton married her sister Lily.

3. In the 1980's Lily became increasingly afflicted with Alzheimer's disease. By the end of that period, George Banton's physical deterioration was also evident. In 1990 he was diagnosed as having cancer of the prostate. He underwent surgery in 1991, 1992 and 1993. After the second operation his family was told that his life expectancy was two or three years. In the third operation, in November 1993, his testicles were removed in an attempt to retard the spread of the disease.

4. George Banton was also severely afflicted with deafness. He had a number of different hearing aids but by the early 1990's, and perhaps even earlier, this problem was so acute that, in order to carry on any serious discussion, he was accustomed to use headphones and a microphone that would be placed between him and the person with whom he was conversing. His mobility also became affected and, by 1994, he required a frame to enable him to move about. He had several falls and was incontinent.

5. By the time of his operation in 1991 it was evident to George Banton's family that he was no longer able to care for Lily and, in July, she was placed in a retirement or nursing establishment ("Meadowcroft") that had facilities for the care of individuals suffering from Alzheimer's disease.

6. On January 30, 1991, George Banton executed a will in which he directed that $25,000 be set aside for the care and maintenance of Lily if and after her own funds were exhausted. Subject to that provision, his estate was to be divided equally among his five children with substitutional gifts to the legitimate children of any children who predeceased him.

7. George Banton continued to live by himself in his house at 22 Coral Cove Crescent, North York, until July 1993 when a decision was made for him to move into a retirement home ("Lifestyles"). ...

8. Lily died in June 1994. By at least the end of the following month — and probably earlier — George Banton had formed a friendship, which quickly developed into a close attachment, with the Applicant, Muna Yassin ("Muna"), a waitress in the restaurant at Lifestyles. Muna was 31 years of age. ...

10. During the last three months of 1994, George Banton's children became increasingly disturbed about his relationship with Muna. At the beginning of November, Joan made an appointment for George Banton with Dr. Janice Lessard, the Director of Geriatrics at Scarborough General Hospital, where his third operation in November had been performed. Dr. Lessard saw him on two occasions. Patricia was present each time, and Joan, also, was there on the second occasion. As a result of these meetings, Dr. Lessard expressed the opinion that George Banton was financially incompetent and issued a Certificate of Incompetence under the *Mental Health Act* on November 14. She notified the Public Guardian and Trustee and, two days later, she

issued a Notice of Continuance of Certificate of Incompetence to Manage One's Own Estate pursuant to the statute. Dr. Lessard was not called as a witness and her opinion is not relied upon by the Respondents for the purpose of these proceedings. I mention it, and it is admissible, only for the purpose of explaining subsequent conduct of the parties and events that occurred in the remaining months of George Banton's life.

11. On hearing that George Banton had been certified under the *Mental Health Act* and after receiving reports from officials at the bank that George Banton, accompanied by Muna, had withdrawn $10,000 from his account and that he had been trying to cash further cheques, George Jr. and Victor, became concerned to protect his assets which at this time consisted of term deposits and bank accounts in excess of $470,000. ...

12. Unknown to any of his children, on December 14, 1994, George Banton and Muna had obtained a licence to marry. ...

14. On Saturday, December 17, 1994, George Banton and Muna were married at her apartment by the Reverend Jack Allen who had a license to perform marriages. No one else was present except the minister's wife, who had to be fetched from Brampton to act as a witness, and another person who had been approached in the foyer of the apartment building for that purpose. George Banton's children were not aware that the marriage was taking place.

15. George Banton stayed at Muna's apartment on the night of December 17 and returned to Lifestyles on the following day. In the meantime, the staff at Lifestyles had become aware of his absence and had contacted the family as he had not signed out or informed anyone that he would be leaving the premises.

16. George Banton's family were concerned and contacted the police. Victor, Joan and Victor's wife were present at Lifestyles on Sunday, December 18, when George Banton and Muna entered the building. Although the details are disputed, it is clear that some sort of argument or altercation occurred. It was alleged by Muna, and denied by Victor and Joan, that Victor pushed his father into a door causing bruises to one of his arms. Victor testified that he put his hand on George's wrist or his arm and guided him through the door into his room.

17. The next day, Monday, December 19, George Banton and Muna attended at the offices of the law firm, Devry, Smith & Frank in Don Mills and met with Wayne Wolfe, a solicitor experienced in drawing wills. Mr. Wolfe was informed that George Banton and Muna were married, and that George Banton wished to make a new will and to give Muna a power of attorney. At that first meeting, Mr. Wolfe asked them for a copy of their marriage certificate. They left and returned with this the next day, Tuesday, December 20, 1994. On that day, Mr. Wolfe was instructed that in George Banton's new will his entire estate would be left to Muna with a gift over to the Salvation Army in the event of her prior death. Mr. Wolfe prepared the will and his secretary, Carol Davis, prepared the power of attorney and these documents were signed by George Banton on Wednesday, December 21, 1994. Mr. Wolfe and Ms. Davis signed as witnesses to each of the documents.

18. In January 1995, the family were informed that George Banton had retained Devry, Smith & Frank to challenge Dr. Lessard's finding of incompetence. On April 10, 1995, an application was made on his behalf to the Consent and Capacity Review Board for this purpose. On May 1, George Banton's solicitors were informed that the application had been dismissed for want of jurisdiction.

19. On April 13, 1995, George Banton left Lifestyles and moved into Muna's apartment.

20. On May 4, George Banton and Muna attended again at the offices of Devry, Smith & Frank where George Banton executed a will and power of attorney identical to those dated December 21, 1994.

21. On May 11, 1995, Dr. Michel Silberfeld of Baycrest Geriatric Centre conducted an assessment of George Banton at the request of his solicitors. Dr. Silberfeld reported on May 17, 1995, that, in his opinion, George Banton had capacity to manage his property and to give a power of attorney.

22. On May 27, 1995, the Public Guardian and Trustee brought an application to be appointed statutory guardian of George Banton's property, and an order was made for an assessment of his capacity. This assessment was made by Dr. Chin Kwan Chung, a newly-appointed designated capacity assessor under the *Substitute Decisions Act*. On June 19, 1995, Dr. Chung provided his opinion that George Banton was incapable of managing property but had capacity to give a power of attorney and capacity for personal care "under the present circumstances and support structure".

23. The application of the Public Guardian and Trustee was opposed by George Banton and he and Muna swore affidavits deposing to his capacity. Muna also brought an application to be appointed his statutory guardian in the event that the Court made a finding of incapacity.

24. On October 27, 1995, George Banton was [admitted] to Sunnybrook Hospital severely ill and confused. He had further surgery.

25. On November 16, 1995, Muna was cross-examined on her affidavit in the guardianship proceedings.

26. On December 22, 1995, George Banton was discharged from Sunnybrook Hospital to the Village Park Nursing Home.

27. On February 5, 1996, George Banton was admitted to Women's College Hospital where he died on February 14, 1996. ...

No expert medical evidence was given with respect to capacity to marry or testamentary capacity and, on the issue of capacity to manage property, the medical experts were not in agreement. They agreed only that George Banton had capacity to give a power of attorney over property. While there is no reason to doubt the appropriateness of having different tests for different capacities, the task of reaching conclusions — even on the balance of probabilities — on the basis of rather fine distinctions when the issues relate to the deteriorating mental state at a particular time of an elderly person now deceased, is not easy. The difficulty is exacerbated where, as here, there are significant discrepancies between the testimony of the applicant and the respondents.

The law with respect to the burden of proof of capacity to marry, testamentary capacity and undue influence is also reasonably settled. In the first case, the burden is on a person attacking the validity of the marriage. ...

It is hardly necessary to say that the principle of freedom of testamentary disposition is in the background to the issues relating to the validity of the wills of December 21, 1994 and May 4, 1995. If George Banton had capacity and was not subject to undue influence at the time of the execution of one of those wills, its validity and effect are not open to challenge on the ground that he thereby disinherited his children. In this jurisdiction, unlike others in Canada and elsewhere, unless the children are dependants, a capable parent, acting voluntarily, is entitled to do this however mean and ungrateful it may seem, or how selfish the motive; hence the focus in this case, as in so many others, on testamentary capacity and undue influence.

[Cullity J. concluded that the wills of 1994 and 1995 were invalid because Banton lacked testamentary capacity and Muna had subjected him to undue influence. The Justice characterized Muna as a strong-willed person out to get the property of a lonely, depressed, terminally-ill, severely disabled and cognitively impaired old man. To determine whether the will of 1991 had been revoked by the deceased's third marriage in accordance with the *Succession Law Reform Act*, it was necessary to enquire into the validity of this marriage.]

The marriage of George Banton and Muna was solemnized at her apartment by the Reverend Jack Allen on December 17, 1994. George and Muna had completed the application for a licence to marry on December 14. Mr Allen had been contacted by Muna through a company in the business of arranging marriage services. No one else had been informed of the pending ceremony and, after arriving at Muna's apartment and finding that there were no witnesses, Mr Allen returned to Brampton to fetch his wife. Muna asked a person she found in the foyer of the apartment building to act as the second witness.

Mr. Allen testified that he was aware of the prohibition in the *Marriage Act* of marriages of persons who are "mentally ill". He stated that he had no concerns at all about George Banton's mental condition. He said he remembered George as being "quite a good conversationalist" and that there was nothing to indicate that he did not understand the purpose and nature of the ceremony. Mr. Allen also saw no signs of depression and nothing to suggest that George was afraid of, or being manipulated or controlled by, Muna. On the contrary, George's mood was convivial, he seemed affectionate towards Muna and, after the marriage was performed, he responded to the invitation to kiss her. Mr. Allen testified that he left immediately after the ceremony and did not participate in any reception or party. He did not see a walking frame or canes and he made no mention of any hearing disability or of hearing aids. His conclusion about George Banton's mental capacity appears to have been formed on the basis of George's general demeanour and his answers to the questions in the service rather than from any questions asked specifically for the purpose.

The formal validity of George Banton's marriage to Muna has not been challenged. It was submitted by Mr. Shaw that it was void on the ground of undue influence and lack of capacity. ...

A marriage can be set aside on the ground of duress or coercion of a degree sufficient to negative consent. Although I am in respectful agreement with Mendes da Costa J. in *S. (A.) v. S. (A.)* (1988), 15 R.F.L. (3d) 443 (Ont. U.F.C.) at pp. 453–6 that fear need not be proven, the evidence does not warrant a conclusion that there was duress in this case with respect to George Banton's participation in the marriage.

In late September and early October 1994 George Banton had tried to resist Muna's attempts to seduce him into marriage but, in November, he capitulated and consented to it. Although I have also found that marriage was part of Muna's carefully planned and tenaciously implemented scheme to obtain control and, ultimately, the ownership of his property, as far as the marriage was concerned he was, at the end, a willing victim. Shortly thereafter he told Victor that he had wanted "one last fling". ...

George Banton wanted to marry Muna and the evidence of Ms. Yolanda Miranda, referred to below, indicates that he never regretted this. She may have misled him as to her motives but he was, as I have said, a willing victim who consented to the marriage. In these circumstances, I do not believe the marriage can be set aside if George Banton had the requisite capacity and, particularly, not by persons other than the parties to the marriage. My finding that there was undue influence sufficient to invalidate his testamentary dispositions does not require a similar conclusion with respect to the marriage from which he obtained benefits of care and companionship.

Consent, in the sense in which I have used the term, is an act of will. In this sense it must be distinguished from capacity to marry. Although a lack of mental capacity may be said to vitiate or negative consent, they are obviously different concepts. A lack of consent does not presuppose, or entail, an absence of mental capacity.

A finding of a lack of testamentary capacity does not necessarily determine whether an individual has the mental capacity to marry; nor is testamentary capacity at the time of marriage required before the marriage will revoke a will: *Re McElroy* (1978), 22 O.R. (2d) 381 (Ont. Surr. Ct.); *Re Park Estate*, [1953] 2 All E.R. 1411 (Eng. C.A.).

It is well established that an individual will not have capacity to marry unless he or she is capable of understanding the nature of the relationship and the obligations and responsibilities it involves. The burden of proof on this question is on those attacking the validity of the marriage and, in my judgment, it has not been discharged in this case. There is virtually nothing in the evidence to suggest that George Banton's mental deterioration had progressed to the extent that he was no longer able to pass this not particularly rigorous test. The medical evidence indicates his acceptance of the marriage and even in the last months of his life when he was at Village Park, he spoke of his wish to return to his wife — albeit along with his then caregiver and companion, Ms. Yolanda Miranda.

The only matter that raises any doubt in my mind with respect to George Banton's understanding of the responsibilities of marriage are the fact that he permitted Muna to return him to Lifestyles the day after the marriage, and that he remained there until the beginning of April 1995 when he moved to Muna's apartment. I do not believe I would be justified in concluding from this that he did not appreciate that the duty to cohabit is inherent in the marriage relationship. I believe it is far more likely that he would have preferred to cohabit with Muna but that this was not part of her plan until the commencement of the guardianship proceedings made it desirable, from her point of view, that he be continuously under her control, and not accessible to his family. We do not know what reason Muna gave him for returning him to Lifestyles on December 18 but, as I have already indicated, I am satisfied that he was, by then, completely under her domination and quite incapable of insisting on his right to cohabit with her.

George Banton had been married twice before his marriage to Muna and I find that, despite his weakened mental condition, he had sufficient memory and understanding to continue to appreciate the nature and the responsibilities of the relationship to satisfy what I have described as the first requirement of the test of mental capacity to marry.

In the Canadian cases to which I have been referred, no other requirement for mental capacity has been considered. ...

While I believe that it may well be the case that a person who is incapable both with respect to personal care and with respect to property may be incapable of contracting marriage, I do not believe that incapacity of the latter kind should, by itself, have this effect. Marriage does, of course, have an effect on property rights and obligations, but to treat the ability to manage property as essential to the relationship would, I believe, be to attribute inordinate weight to the proprietary aspects of marriage and would be unfortunate. Elderly married couples whose property is administered for them under a continuing power of attorney, or by a statutory guardian, may continue to live comfortably together. They may have capacity to make wills and give powers of attorney. I see no reason why this state of affairs should be confined to those who married before incapacity to manage property supervened.

George Banton was found by Dr. Chung to have capacity as far as personal care was concerned. Moreover, despite his physical problems, his weakened mental condition and his loss of memory, he was able to carry on more or less normal discourse on simple everyday matters. Strangers, like Carol Davis and Mr. Allen, who met him briefly did not notice anything abnormal about his mental state. On the basis of a one-hour examination Dr. Silberfeld concluded that he had capacity to manage his property. Obviously he was still capable of presenting a brave face to the world. The more thorough examination by Dr. Chung revealed what those close to him already knew: that his judgment was severely impaired and his contact with reality tenuous. Despite these problems, I have no doubt that, with care and attention and avoidance of stress, he was capable of coping with the more mundane problems of everyday living and I do not see why the right to marry should be withheld from persons in his position.

Accordingly, on the basis of *Browning v. Reane* and in the absence of binding authority to the contrary, I find that, notwithstanding George Banton's incapacity to manage property on December 17, 1994, he had capacity to marry and that his marriage to Muna was valid. In consequence, his will of January 30, 1991, was revoked and, in view of my other findings, he died intestate.

NOTES AND QUESTIONS

1. In *Webb v. Webb* (1968), 3 R.F.L. 129, 3 D.L.R. (3d) 100 (N.S. T.D.), Cowan C.J.T.D. quoted Sir James Hannen P.'s statement in *Durham v. Durham* (1885), 10 P.D. 80 (Eng. P.D.A.) (at 81-82):

> [I]t appears to me that the contract of marriage is a very simple one, which does not require a high degree of intelligence to comprehend. It is an engagement between a man and woman to live to-gether, and love one another as husband and wife, to the exclusion of all others.

Judge Cowan held that the marriage of two residents of a Nova Scotia psychiatric hospital was valid.

2. For a case holding that an elderly, dying man lacked the capacity to consent to a marriage with his caregiver, see *Re Sung Estate* (2004), 9 R.F.L. (6th) 229 (Ont. C.A.). However, the court in *Moyer v. Keleman* (2006), 2006 CarswellOnt 8479 (S.C.J.); affirmed (2007), 2007 CarswellOnt 124 (C.A.) refused to annul a marriage where the wife argued that she had been confused at the time of the marriage due to her untreated depression.

3. In *Davison v. Sweeney* (2005), 255 D.L.R. (4th) 757 (B.C. S.C.), a woman who resided in British Columbia went to Las Vegas for a long weekend. Around midnight on the second day, she met a man who was resident in Alberta. Both had been drinking and within minutes they were discussing marriage. A few hours later, they found a wedding chapel where they were directed to obtain a licence at the local courthouse. They returned with the licence and were married in the presence of two witnesses. The man and woman then parted without consummating the marriage. Two days later, the woman returned to British Columbia and the man to Alberta. The woman applied for a declaration that the marriage was void because she was too intoxicated to consent. Although the man did not file a defence, the court dismissed the application, holding that the woman was not so intoxicated that she was incapable of understanding the nature of marriage. It noted that she took deliberate and time-consuming steps to obtain a marriage licence and then willingly participated in the ceremony. The court concluded that, while the woman's judgement was undoubtedly impaired, the evidence fell short of proving that she was incapable of understanding that she was getting married.

4. Regarding the question of whether a marriage is void or voidable as a result of incapacity to understand, Professor Hahlo suggests in *Nullity of Marriage in Canada* (Toronto: Butterworths, 1979) at 26:

> As the essential ingredient is lacking, a marriage contracted by an insane person should, on principle, be treated as void, and this is also the prevailing judicial opinion in Canada. And certain it is that either party, the sane as well as the insane, is entitled to have the marriage annulled. However, there is much to be said for the view that the marriage becomes unassailable if the parties continue to cohabit as man and wife after the insane partner has recovered his reason.

He therefore categorizes a marriage contracted while one of the parties is insane as "void but capable of ratification by continued cohabitation after recovery".

5. Note ss. 7 and 35(2) of the Ontario *Marriage Act*.

(b) Duress

S. (A.) v. S. (A.)

(1988), 15 R.F.L. (3d) 443, 1988 CarswellOnt 277 (Ont. U.F.C.)

MENDES DA COSTA U.F.C.J.: — In this case, the applicant is A.S. and the respondent is A.S. The applicant seeks the annulment of her marriage to the respondent or, in the alternative, a divorce. The respondent did not file an answer or appear at the hearing. The applicant's testimony was the only evidence adduced to the court.

1. The facts

The applicant was born on 9th April 1969. On 28th February 1986 she went through a form of marriage with the respondent, who had recently arrived in Canada. The marriage was celebrated at the city hall, Hamilton, and the certificate of marriage was filed as Ex. 2. At this date, the applicant was 16 years of age. Her parents had separated, and she was living with her mother and her stepfather. The consent of the mother to the marriage was contained in a certificate of consent filed as Ex. 3. ...

The applicant stated that she was first approached by her mother and her stepfather, who applied pressure to her to marry the respondent. The applicant was told that the respondent wished to marry because he wanted to live in Canada. She testified that her mother and stepfather told her that there was $2,000 involved and that they said that "we can have all this nice stuff that we didn't have before with all this money." The applicant said that she told her mother that she did not want to marry the respondent, that her mother "was talking to my step-father and then there was more pressure." The applicant further testified that she did not want to marry the respondent, that she did not live with him after the ceremony, that the parties never engaged in sexual intercourse, and that the respondent subsequently left Canada. The applicant, in her evidence, stated that a few years ago she had been made a ward of the Children's Aid Society in Alberta because she had been sexually abused by her stepfather, and that she had remained in care until she turned 16 years.

I was impressed with the demeanor of the applicant. In my opinion, she gave her evidence in a forthright fashion and I consider her a credible witness. However, during the submissions of Mr. Rogers, counsel for the applicant, I expressed doubt as to whether the applicant was entitled to the relief of annulment. Mr. Rogers requested an opportunity to file written submissions. He stated that he had canvassed with his client the effects and the meaning of divorce and annulment, and that she had expressed a preference for annulment. Accordingly, the matter was adjourned for the filing of written submissions. In my deliberations, I have had the benefit of the submissions. ...

[The judge concluded that the fact that the respondent entered into the marriage so as to facilitate residence in Canada did not affect the validity of the marriage. He next considered the issue of parental consent. Mr. Rogers submitted that the consent given by the mother was invalid because it was motivated by improper considerations. Mendes da Costa U.F.C.J. concluded (at 453) that the Ontario *Marriage Act* "does not render the quality of consent a justiciable issue, and the court is not empowered to determine whether consent was given too readily, or, indeed, for an improper motive." Further, the judge held that lack of parental consent did not affect the validity of the marriage under the Act.]

4. Duress

It was submitted by Mr. Rogers that the applicant was pressured into marrying the respondent by her mother and stepfather and that, given the surrounding circumstances, she was not able to withstand that pressure. During argument, I questioned this submission.

The applicant made no allegation of the use of physical force, nor did she allege that the use of physical force had been threatened. Moreover, the conduct alleged as duress did not emanate from the respondent. The conduct contended by Mr. Rogers to constitute duress was pressure of a non-physical nature, which was directed at the applicant by the mother and stepfather, who sought to obtain financial benefit from the proposed marriage, be it $500, as stated in para. 8(b) of the application, or $2,000 as related by the applicant during her evidence.

There are relatively few reported cases dealing with annulment of marriage induced by duress, and the applicable principles seem to have emerged in a series of older decisions: *Field's Marriage Annulling Bill* (1848), 2 H.L. Cas. 48, 9 E.R. 1010, where there is a reference to early cases; *Scott v. Sebright* (1886), 12 P.D. 21; *Cooper v. Crane*, [1891] P. 369. In *Scott v. Sebright*, Butt J., at pp. 23-24, in an oft-cited passage, stated:

> The Courts of law have always refused to recognize as binding contracts to which the consent of either party has been obtained by fraud or duress, and the validity of a contract of marriage must be tested and determined in precisely the same manner as that of any other contract. True it is that in contracts of marriage there is an interest involved above and beyond that of the immediate parties. Public policy requires that marriages should not be lightly set aside, and there is in some cases the strongest temptation to the parties more immediately interested to act in collusion in obtaining a dissolution of the marriage tie. These reasons necessitate great care and circumspection on the part of the tribunal, but they in no wise alter the principle or the grounds on which this, like any other contract, may be avoided. It has sometimes been said that in order to avoid a contract entered into through fear, the fear must be such as would impel a person of ordinary courage and resolution to yield to it. I do not think that is an accurate statement of the law. Whenever from natural weakness of intellect or from fear — whether reasonably entertained or not — either party is actually in a state of mental incompetence to resist pressure improperly brought to bear, there is no more consent than in the case of a person of stronger intellect and more robust courage yielding to a more serious danger. The difficulty consists not in any uncertainty of the law on the subject, but in its application to the facts of each individual case.

The principles expounded by Butt J. seem as sound today as they were when they were uttered in 1886. Public policy still requires that marriages "should not be lightly set aside". No doubt, also, there is in some cases the "strongest temptation to the parties more immediately interested to act in collusion". A court is, indeed, required to exercise care and circumspection to ensure that the ground alleged as duress has been established. However, since 1886 there has been a considerable change in the availability of divorce. ... At this point in time there seems no need for parties to turn to the law of nullity simply to obtain relief denied them by divorce law. I believe, therefore, that the courts should approach a proceeding for nullity in a manner no different from that of any other matrimonial cause.

The above passage from *Scott v. Sebright* was referred to in *Thompson v. Thompson*, 4 R.F.L. 376, [1971] 4 W.W.R. 383, 19 D.L.R. (3d) 608 (Sask. Q.B.). In this case, the plaintiff sought the annulment of her marriage to the defendant. The court found that the plaintiff had agreed to marry the defendant as a result of his persistent urging, at a time when her resistance was reduced by her state of depression arising from her rejection by another man. Once the wedding plans were underway, the plaintiff was not able to muster sufficient courage to cancel them, because of the social consequences insofar as her family was concerned. She believed that, if she did cancel the marriage plans, there would be a rift between herself and her family. The plaintiff's mother, the court concluded, had exerted influence on the plaintiff to continue with the plans. The marriage was consummated, albeit reluctantly on the part of the plaintiff. The court held that the plaintiff had not established a case that would fall within the principles enunciated in the authorities and dismissed the action. ...

In *Pascuzzi v. Pascuzzi*, [1955] O.W.N. 853 (H.C.), the plaintiff sought an annulment of her marriage. The claim was unopposed. At the time of the marriage she was 15 years of age and the defendant was 19 years of age. Prior to the marriage, during a visit to Toronto, the parties engaged in sexual intercourse. The plaintiff being a juvenile, complaints were made to the police and both the plaintiff and the defendant were taken into custody, the plaintiff being detained on a charge of juvenile delinquency and the defendant being faced with a criminal charge. According to the evidence, it was intimated to the plaintiff that if she and the defendant were married no criminal charges would be laid. It was necessary to secure the consent of the plaintiff's mother to the marriage and, at first, she refused but finally, after she had been called upon by a solicitor representing the defendant, she gave her consent. The plaintiff was not only reluctant to go through a form of marriage but, on more than one occasion, protested that she would not do so. As stated by Aylen J. at p. 854:

> No doubt with the best intentions in the world, those to whom the plaintiff turned for advice all urged her so strongly to marry the defendant that it became practically an impossibility for a child of her age to continue to refuse, especially as her only home at the time was with the defendant's parents.

The ceremony was performed on 27th February 1954, and the plaintiff left the defendant on or about 31st December 1954. The court considered the delay in the plaintiff leaving the defendant understandable in the circumstances. After a reference to the law of duress, the court held that the marriage between the plaintiff and the defendant should be declared a nullity. ...

A valid marriage is grounded upon the consent of each party. Oppression may vitiate consent and, if there is no consent, there is no valid marriage. Different people may respond to oppression in different ways, and conduct that may overmaster the mind of one person may not have this impact upon the mind of another. It matters not, therefore, whether the will of a person of reasonable fortitude would — or would not — have been overborne; the issue is, rather, the state of mind of the applicant. To constitute duress, it must be established that the applicant's mind was so overcome by oppression that there was an absence of free choice. The point that falls for decision is whether the consent given at the time of the ceremony was a real, understanding and voluntary consent. Oppression can take various forms; it may be generated by fear, or by persuasion or pressure. Essentially, the matter is one of degree, and this raises a question of fact for the court. The determination involves a consideration of all relevant circumstances, including the age of the applicant, the maturity of the applicant, the applicant's emotional state and vulnerability, the lapse of time between the conduct alleged as duress and the marriage ceremony, whether the marriage was consummated, whether the parties resided together as man and wife and the lapse of time between the marriage ceremony and the institution of the annulment proceeding. As long as the oppression affects the mind of the applicant in the fashion stated, physical force is not required and, no more so, is the threat of such force a necessary ingredient. Nor is the source of the conduct material. Where duress is alleged, the onus of proof is upon the party seeking annulment, and it is an onus that is not lightly discharged.

The principles of law relating to duress seem to be relatively clear and certain. However, as pointed out by Butt J. in *Scott v. Sebright*, the difficulty consists in the application of the law to the facts of each individual case. I have given this matter my most anxious consideration and, upon reflection, I am satisfied that the applicant has discharged the onus of proof and is entitled to a declaration of nullity. It appears to have been the view that lack of consent rendered a marriage void. Curiously, however, it seems also to have been considered that a marriage, void for lack of consent, could be subsequently ratified when oppression was withdrawn. I prefer, however, to adopt the view of Taylor J., in the *Kawaluk* case, that consent obtained by duress renders a marriage voidable on the application of the aggrieved party. ...

For reasons I have stated, a decree of annulment is granted.

NOTES AND QUESTIONS

1. In *Re Sung Estate* (2003), 37 R.F.L. (5th) 441 (Ont. S.C.J.); additional reasons at (2003), 2003 CarswellOnt 4002 (Ont. S.C.J.); affirmed (2004), 9 R.F.L. (6th) 229 (Ont. C.A.), Justice Greer held that a vulnerable, dying man had been pressured into marrying his caregiver who wanted his property. The court held, on an application by the man's children after his death, that the marriage was void *ab initio*. Accordingly, a will made by the man prior to the marriage remained valid. In dismissing the caregiver's appeal, the Ontario Court of Appeal focused only on the alternative holding that the man lacked capacity to consent.

2. A claim of duress failed in the recent case of *Moyer v. Keleman* (2006), 2006 CarswellOnt 8479 (S.C.J.); affirmed (2007), 2007 CarswellOnt 124 (C.A.) even though the wife was in a stressed state at the time of the marriage and the groom had convinced her to stop taking her prescription pills for depression.

3. There is, of course, a distinction between a forced marriage and an arranged marriage. In a forced marriage, a person is coerced into marrying someone and the marriage is invalid for lack of consent. In an arranged marriage, third parties, usually relatives of the bride and groom, are involved in the selection of a suitable mate. The bride and groom may freely consent to marry the person selected. However, an arranged marriage may create a context in which the bride or the groom or both of them feel pressured to consent.

In *Parihar v. Bhatti* (1980), 17 R.F.L. (2d) 289 (B.C. S.C.), the bride's family arranged a marriage with some-one she hardly knew. Although she protested several times before the wedding date, she participated in the cere-mony. MacKinnon L.J.S.C. stated (at 291 and 292):

> I accept as a fact that great pressure from her family was brought upon the plaintiff to marry the defendant. The freedom of choice to marry — or not to marry — a person of one's choice, enjoyed by most people in our country, is not shared by all societies. The plaintiff was clearly caught in such a dilemma. Had she wanted to alienate herself completely from her family, probably necessitating leav-ing home, she could have refused to go through with the marriage. ...
>
> There are many situations where families, or others, bring great persuasion upon a person to enter into marriage. However, the cases indicate that the duress sufficient to set aside the marriage must be of such a nature that her powers of volition were so affected that it really was no consent. ...
>
> In my opinion, the evidence here does not satisfy me the marriage ought to be declared null and void. There was no corroboration at all of the plaintiff's allegations of fear. It may be that the alternative to her going through with the marriage would be most unpleasant for her but I do not consider that the facts presented to me justify the relief requested.

Several Commonwealth decisions suggest, however, that the duress threshold may be lowering in the context of arranged marriages. In *Hirani v. Hirani* (1983), 4 F.L.R. 232 (C.A.) a young Hindu woman was faced with the choice of marrying a man chosen by her parents or leaving home on her own. It appears she had no alternative accommodation or means of support. She was held to have married under such duress as to destroy consent. For a discussion of this case, see Bradley, "Duress and Arranged Marriages" (1983), 46 Mod. Law Rev. 499. In *Marriage of S.* (1980), 42 F.L.R. 94 (Austrialia Fam. Ct.) a young Egyptian woman participated in an arranged marriage solely out of love and respect for her parents and to avoid any prejudice to the future marital opportunities of her younger sisters. There were no other tangible or intangible repercussions that would have flowed from a refusal to marry. Watson S.J., emphasizing the need to view the situation from the subjective vantage point of the unwilling bride, held that duress vitiating consent should be broad enough to encompass non-violent but controlling parental coercion. The marriage was annulled. See also *Mahmood v. Mahmood*, [1993] S.L.T. 589 and *Mahmud v. Mahmud*, [1994] S.L.T. 599. For comment on the last two cases, see Lim, "Messages from a Rarely Visited Island: Duress and Lack of Consent in Marriage" (1996), IV Feminist L.S. 195. For a more recent English case, see *P. v. R.*, [2003] 1 F.L.R. 661. For further reading on arranged marriages, see Bradley, "Duress, Family Law and the Coher-ent Legal System" (1994), 57 Mod. Law Rev. 963 and Parkinson, "Taking Multiculturalism Seriously: Marriage Law and the Rights of Minorities" (1994), 16 Sydney L. Rev. 473.

4. The United Kingdom recently enacted the *Forced Marriage (Civil Protection) Act 2007* (U.K., c. 20). It empowers courts to make protection orders to control the conduct of persons who are attempting to coerce someone into marriage. In December 2008, a court issued a series of orders under the Act prohibiting the Bangladeshi parents of a U.K. doctor from removing her from the U.K., harassing or threatening her. The case received international attention because the orders followed the doctor's return to the U.K. after she had been tricked into returning to Bangladesh where her parents held her captive and forced her into a marriage. See "HNS doctor saved from forced marriage gets court orders" at www.guardian.co.uk, Friday 19 December 2008 13-41 GMT.

The U.K. Forced Marriage Unit reports that the majority of the cases it has handled are from the Pakistani, Bangladeshi, and Indian communities, communities with strong commitment to traditional practices such as arranged marriages. See Khanum, *Forced Marriage, Family Cohesion and Community Engagement: National Learning Through a Case Study of Luton* (Watford: Equality in Diversity, 2008).

(c) Limited Purpose Marriages, Fraud, and Mistake

Although there have been a few lower court decisions to the contrary, Canadian courts have generally held that a marriage is valid even if one party enters into it only for immigration purposes. The same result follows if both parties are aware that this is the sole purpose of the marriage. See *Iantsis (Papatheodorou) v. Papatheodorou* (1970), 3 R.F.L. 158 (Ont. C.A.); *Leonotion v. Leonotion* (1977), 4 R.F.L. (2d) 94 (Ont. C.A.); *Laroia v. Laroia* (1986), 54 O.R. (2d) 224 (C.A.); *Ciresi (Ahmad) v. Ahmad* (1982), 31 R.F.L. (2d) 326, [1983] 1 W.W.R. 710 (Alta. Q.B.); *Fernandez (Alarcio) v. Fernandez*, 34 R.F.L. (2d) 249, [1983] 4 W.W.R. 755 (Man. Q.B.); *Singla v. Singla* (1985), 46 R.F.L. (2d) 235, 69 N.S.R. (2d) 60 (T.D.); *S. (A.) v. S. (A.)* (1988), 15 R.F.L. (3d) 443 (Ont. U.F.C.); and *Grewal v. Sohal* (2004), 12 R.F.L. (6th) 55 (B.C. S.C.).

In *Iantsis*, the Ontario Court of Appeal approved (at 162) the English cases that

> [c]onsistently lay down the rule that neither a fraudulent nor an innocent misrepresentation will of itself affect the validity of a marriage unless, of course, the misrepresentation induces an operative mistake, e.g. as to the nature of the ceremony, or deception as to the identity of one of the persons to the marriage, as when A is induced to marry B, believing that she is marrying C.

In *S. (A.) v. S. (A.)*, Mendes da Costa U.F.C.J. stated (at 448):

> The mere fact, therefore, that parties go through a form of marriage for a "limited" or "extraneous" purpose will not, of itself, render the marriage invalid. In this respect, no heed is paid to their mental reservations. Indeed, their motive would seem to support a finding of validity. Where parties seek, by marriage, to confer upon a respondent a right to reside in Canada, it would seem to follow that they do only what they intend: enter into a marriage relationship as the means of achieving the desired result.

However, Justice Davies expressed regret in *Grewal v. Sohal* (at para. 47) that binding precedent took this position.

In contrast to the predominant view of the Canadian courts, the courts of France and Scotland, as well as Judge Learned Hand in *United States v. Rubenstein*, 151 F.2d 195 (1945), have held such marriages to be nullities on the ground of lack of consent. In the *Rubenstein* case, Judge Learned Hand stated (at 918-919):

> It is quite true that a marriage without subsequent consummation will be valid; but if the spouses agree to a marriage only for the sake of representing it as such to the outside world and with the understanding that they will put an end to it as soon as it has served its purpose to deceive, they have never really agreed to be married at all. They must assent to enter into the relation as it is ordinarily understood, and it is not ordinarily understood as merely a pretence, or cover, to deceive others.

Which approach do you prefer?

NOTES AND QUESTIONS

1. A and B go through a marriage ceremony. At the time A thinks B is pregnant with his child. B is, in fact, pregnant by C. Is the marriage valid? See *Moss v. Moss*, [1897] P. 263 (Eng. P.D.A.).

2. In order to win a bet with friends who "dare" them to get married, Bob and Sue obtain a marriage licence and go through a marriage ceremony before someone legally authorized to officiate at weddings. They have no intention of living as husband and wife and, indeed, never do so. Are they validly married? See *Brooks-Bischoffberger v. Brooks-Bischoffberger* (1930), 149 A. 606, 129 Me. 52 (U.S. Me. Sup. Jud. Ct.) and *Parker v. Parker* (1757), 2 Lee 382, 161 E.R. 377.

3. In some jurisdictions, misrepresentation or concealment of certain essential information may cause a marriage to be invalid. For example, California courts annulled marriages in *Aufort v. Aufort* (1935), 9 Cal. App. 2d 310 (Ct. App. 1 Dist.) and *Vileta v. Vileta* (1942), 53 Cal. App. 2d 794 (Ct. App. 2 Dist.) because the wives deliberately concealed their inability to have children. In *Torfehnejad v. Salimi* (2006), 32 R.F.L. (6th) 115 (Ont. S.C.J.); affirmed (2008), 298 D.L.R. (4th) 191 (Ont. C.A.), Justice Greer granted a man an annulment where she concluded that an Iranian woman had never intended to enter into a real marriage but had only intended to go through a marriage ceremony in Iran to obtain permission to enter and remain in Canada as the ostensible wife of a Canadian citizen. The case is poorly reasoned and it is unclear whether the Justice was applying Iranian law or Canadian law. It was likely the former as she made a point of accepting the evidence regarding Iranian law of a paralegal in the Iranian community in Toronto and referred to a leading text describing that law. In dismissing the woman's appeal, the Ontario Court of Appeal simply stated (para. 2): "We agree with the reasons of the trial judge and in particular with her analysis of the law that applied in this particular case based on the evidence that was before her concerning the law of Iran." This reference to the law of Iran suggests that the appellate court was not casting doubt on its earlier statement regarding Canadian law in *Iantsis*.

4. Mistakes as to the nature of the ceremony occasionally occur. See *Sobush v. Sobush*, [1931] 2 W.W.R. 900 (Sask. K.B.) and *Jiwani (Samji) v. Samji* (1979), 11 R.F.L. (2d) 188 (B.C. S.C.).

5. Whether an essential mistake regarding the identity of the party one is marrying or the nature of the ceremony renders a marriage void or only voidable is not settled. Professor Hahlo concludes in *Nullity of Marriage in Canada* (Toronto: Butterworths, 1979) (at 30):

> Seeing that essential mistake nullifies consent, one should think, on principle, that it renders the marriage null and void, not only voidable. However, it would appear that only the mistaken party can attack the validity of the marriage, and that the marriage becomes unassailable if he or she approbates or acquiesces in it after the discovery of the mistake. If this is so, the marriage is voidable rather than void.

6. Even if the "immigration marriage" is valid, the immigrant's desire to enter into or remain in Canada may be frustrated. Under s. 12(1) of the *Immigration and Refugee Protection Act*, S.C. 2001, c. 27, a "foreign national may be selected as a member of the family class on the basis of their relationship as the spouse, common-law partner, child, parent or other prescribed family member of a Canadian citizen or permanent resident". However, s. 4 of the *Immigration and Refugee Protection Regulations*, SOR/ 2002-227 (as amended), then states that no foreign national shall be considered "a spouse, a common-law partner, a conjugal partner or an adopted child of a person if the marriage, common-law partnership, conjugal partnership or adoption is not genuine and was entered into primarily for the purpose of acquiring any status or privilege under the Act".

7. Parties to a "sham marriage" entered into for immigration purposes may have difficulty obtaining a divorce in Canada because some courts conclude that the bar of collusion set out in s. 11(1)(a) of the *Divorce Act* applies where the applicant knew of the motive. Justice D. Lee recently reviewed these cases in *Merchant v. Dossani* (2007), 77 Alta. L.R. (4th) 140 (Q.B). What public purpose is served by leaving these marriages in limbo? If there is a "collusive marriage", does it follow that the attempt to end it is collusive? Keep these questions in mind as you study the concept of collusion in the next chapter.

8. In *Raju v. Kumar* (2006), 26 R.F.L. (6th) 451 (B.C. S.C.), a wife successfully sued her husband for his deceit prior to and shortly after their marriage. In this case, a female Canadian citizen of Fijian origin and a Fijian citizen entered into an arranged marriage in Fiji. The court found that the husband had never intended to live with the wife and that he had lied about his continuing relationship with a Fijian woman. After the husband arrived in Canada, he commenced divorce proceedings and the wife brought an action in tort. Although the court found that

the maxim "caveat emptor" had traditionally applied, it noted that British Columbia had legislatively abolished inter-spousal immunity in civil actions and ruled that there was no compelling public policy reason why the wife should be precluded from suing her husband for his deceit. The wife was compensated for her expenses relating to the wedding, the husband's visa application, an immigration appeal and his landing fee. She was also awarded $10,000 as general damages for hurt feelings, humiliation, inconvenience and postponement of the opportunity to marry another man. In a comment on the case on ECarswell's *This Week in Family Law*, April 25, 2006, Phil Epstein and Lorna Madsen express "very serious concerns about this case" on public policy grounds. They suggest that "there are a host of more commonplace contexts where [liability] could also be found: what, for example, of the husband who conceals his sterility, proclaiming that he wants children? Of the prospective wife who hides her genital herpes until after the marriage? Or of the partner who says 'I love you' but in fact does not?"

(6) Age

The age at which a person has the capacity to marry is a matter within federal legislative competence under s. 91(26) of the *Constitution Act, 1867*. As previously noted, the *Annulment of Marriages Act (Ontario)*, R.S.C. 1970, c. A-14 incorporates by reference the law of England relating to the annulment of marriage, as that law was on July 15, 1870. The law of England governing the age at which a person could validly marry at that time was common law. The British Columbia Supreme Court, in *Legebokoff v. Legebokoff* (1982), 28 R.F.L. (2d) 212 (B.C. S.C.) at 215, held that the following rules applied:

> [T]he marriage of a child of less than seven is void. The marriage of a male older than seven years but younger than 14 years, or a female older than seven but younger than 12 years is voidable at the instance of the infant upon his or her attaining the requisite minimum age. Further, a marriage where either or both parties were under age becomes validated if they continue to cohabit as husband and wife after reaching the age of capacity.

(See also Hahlo, *Nullity of Marriage in Canada* (Toronto: Butterworths, 1979) at 21 and Ontario Law Reform Commission, *Report on Family Law, Part II: Marriage* (Toronto: Ministry of the Attorney General, 1970) at 36–38).

Regarding the minimum age at which a person should have capacity to marry, the Ontario Law Reform Commission concluded (at 38):

> [C]ontinued reliance upon the rules provided by the common law is completely unjustified in a nation which is otherwise as advanced as Canada. A legislative correction of this situation would be recommended were the matter one within provincial jurisdiction. The Commission strongly feels that the ages defining capacity to marry should be revised upward but can go no further than to say that the power to enact the necessary corrective legislation is clearly within the powers assigned to the Parliament of Canada by the British North America Act.

Notwithstanding this constitutional concern, the provinces have attempted to make it difficult for young persons to obtain marriage licences. The effect of these provisions on the validity of a marriage contracted by minors is explored in the next section of the casebook.

It should also be noted that, under the Canadian *Criminal Code*, generally the age of consent for sexual acts is fourteen. See ss. 150–153. There are special rules dealing with consensual sex between persons over the age of twelve who are close to one another in age, but being married to a young victim is not a general defence.

3. Formal Validity of Marriage

As noted in the introduction to this chapter, a province has the power under s. 92(12) of the *Constitution Act, 1867* to legislate regarding the formalities to be followed by those intending to marry. It may make the creation of a valid marriage conditional upon the observance of these formalities.

The provinces have enacted comprehensive legislation concerning marriage. In Ontario, the *Marriage Act* deals with such formalities as the need for a licence or banns, who can officiate, the form of the ceremony, and registration of the marriage. All of these provisions clearly relate to the formal validity of marriage. However, many of the provisions in the Act are directed at the person who issues the licence or publishes the banns or officiates at the marriage. Some of the grounds on which they are obligated to refuse to issue a licence, publish banns, or officiate would appear to relate to the capacity of the individuals to marry. The Act raises several legal issues that are examined in the cases and Notes and Questions that follow:

1.   Are any of the provisions of the *Marriage Act* preconditions to a valid marriage?

2.   What is the effect of s. 31? How is it interpreted and applied?

3.   Can the province, as a constitutional matter, attach the sanction of invalidity to marriages performed in breach of a section of the *Marriage Act* that appears to relate to capacity? Can the province, as a constitutional matter, prevent the issuance of a licence on grounds that relate to capacity?

ALSPECTOR v. ALSPECTOR

[1957] O.R. 454, 9 D.L.R. (2d) 679, 1957 CarswellOnt 39 (C.A.)

[Mr. Alspector, an elderly widower, married Mrs. Noodleman, an elderly widow, in a marriage ceremony performed at the home of a cantor in accordance with all the requirements of the Jewish faith. The parties had neglected to obtain a marriage licence. The evidence indicated that Alspector had been informed by a friend and by the cantor that he should obtain a licence. Alspector believed that they did not need a licence as they intended to live in Israel after the marriage. The couple lived together for some seven years. After Alspector suffered a stroke, his family challenged the validity of the marriage. Alspector brought an action for a declaration that the marriage was valid. Alspector died before trial.

The trial judge took the view that both parties intended to be married in accordance with both Jewish law and Ontario law and that s. 33 of *The Marriage Act* (now s. 31 of the Ontario *Marriage Act*) applied. Alspector's daughter appealed.]

ROACH J.A.: — ... I turn now to a consideration of the provisions in *The Marriage Act* concerning a marriage licence.

It must now be taken as established beyond legal controversy that it is within the legislative competence of a Provincial Legislature to enact conditions as to solemnization of marriage in the Province which may affect the validity of the contract: *Re Marriage Legislation in Canada*, [1912] A.C. 880, 11 E.L.R. 255, 7 D.L.R. 629. In *Kerr v. Kerr*, [1934] S.C.R. 72, [1934] 2 D.L.R. 369, Duff C.J. at p. 75 put it thus:

> The authority of the provinces, therefore, extends not only to prescribing such formalities as properly fall within the matters designated by 'Solemnization of Marriage': they have the power to enforce the rules laid down by penalty, by attaching the consequence of invalidity, and by attaching such consequences absolutely or conditionally.

The issuance of a licence or special permit and the publication of banns as preceremonial requirements, are formalities falling within the matters designated by "Solemnization of Marriage". The legislature has sought to enforce compliance with those requirements by the imposition of a penalty on the official who solemnizes a marriage without one of those three alternative requirements having been complied with. The question is, has the legislature also enacted the consequence of invalidity either absolutely or conditionally for non-compliance therewith? In my opinion it has enacted it conditionally [through s. 4 which stipulated the need for a licence or the publication of banns and s. 33]. ...

In considering s. 33 it becomes necessary, in the circumstances of this case, to determine only the scope and meaning of the words "intended to be in compliance with this Act." It should be held that the legislature did not assume, believe or expect that every couple who should intermarry in the Province would be familiar with *this* Act. It would be the rare case, indeed, in which either of them would know of the existence of *The Marriage Act*. All that they would know is that there would be some law in effect in the Province respecting the solemnization of marriages. The phrase should therefore be interpreted as meaning, — intended to be in compliance with that law. The next question is, — intended by whom? Must it be so intended by both of the parties or if it is so intended by one of the parties is that sufficient?

I cannot conceive a case in which if *both* of the parties acted in good faith *one* of them could be held not to have intended the marriage ceremony to be in compliance with the law of the Province, and therefore, a nullity. If, for example, the groom knew of the non-compliance with some essential requirement to the solemnization and went through the ceremony intending that the result would be a nullity then he would not be acting in good faith. Moreover, if knowing of such non-compliance, he intended the ceremony to be a nullity, the law will not permit him in a subsequent action to plead his own fraud upon the bride in order to have the ceremony declared a nullity. The law would not permit him thus to bastardize the offspring of the union and the fact that there may be none does not alter the policy of the law.

Turning now to the evidence: —

Even if the cantor's evidence be accepted that he told Mr. Alspector that because no licence had been issued the marriage would not be a civil marriage there is no evidence that that opinion was conveyed to the plaintiff. The evidence is confused as to whether or not the plaintiff knew that a licence had not been issued. In a number of places in her evidence she states that she did not know it; in other passages she says that she heard the cantor and Mr. Alspector discussing it as a fact. Even if it should be held that she knew as a fact that a licence had not been issued, I think it fair to conclude on her evidence that she did not know that the absence of a licence in the circumstances of this case could affect the validity of her marriage, and that she intended that the marriage be in compliance with the law of the Province. As for Mr. Alspector, it is not unreasonable to conclude that although he knew that a licence had not been issued he proceeded in good faith believing that a licence was not necessary because of his intention shortly thereafter to go with the plaintiff to reside in Israel.

The appeal should be dismissed with costs.

McKENZIE v. SINGH

[1972] 5 W.W.R. 387, 29 D.L.R. (3d) 380, 1972 CarswellBC 163 (B.C. S.C.)

DRYER J.: — ... In October 1970 the plaintiff, then 18 years of age, as a result of some difference with her mother, left her parents' home and went to live with a woman friend. She was unable to find work and became short of money. A female acquaintance told her that she could arrange for her to be paid $200 if she would marry someone "in name only", i.e., on the understanding that after the ceremony she would never have to see the man she married again and that in three months the marriage would be "wiped out" and there would be no record of it. The plaintiff agreed and on 13th November 1970 the female acquaintance introduced her to a man whom I will hereafter call "the broker". At the same time she met the defendant. The four of them then drove to Abbotsford.

At Abbotsford she and the defendant sat in the car while the broker went into the office of a marriage commissioner, one A.K. Paul, and returned with a form which was apparently intended to take the place of the notice of marriage (Form M3) and the statutory declaration (Form M2) referred to in s. 19 of the *Marriage Act*, R.S.B.C. 1960, c. 232, before its repeal in 1971. The defendant signed that form while in the car and a copy of it as signed is now Ex. 8 in these proceedings. Later the plaintiff, the defendant, the broker and the female acquaintance went into the marriage commissioner's office and the plaintiff and defendant went through a marriage ceremony before him with the two others as witnesses.

The date "November 9th, 1970" on Ex. 8 is therefore false; and it is apparent on the evidence that notice was not given to the marriage commissioner three days before the day of the marriage as required by s. 19 of the *Marriage Act*.

Following the ceremony the broker gave the plaintiff $100 and the four drove back to Vancouver. The plaintiff and defendant then separated and she did not see him again until around 1st December 1970, when she accompanied him to the Immigration Offices and there declared herself to be married to him. She then parted from him again. On this occasion the broker gave her another $100, the balance of her fee. The marriage was never consummated and she has never at any time cohabited with the defendant.

She now asks for a declaration that she is not married to the defendant.

I reject the contention of plaintiff's counsel that the plaintiff went through the ceremony of marriage because of fear and that there was therefore no real consent on her part. She did consent to the marriage and went through with it and the subsequent visit to the Immigration Office in complete disregard of principle simply to obtain money. She is not entitled to sympathetic consideration by the Court. However, the matter not being discretionary or equitable, if no valid marriage was effected, the Court should, on application, so declare: see *Pertreis v. Tondear (Pertreis)* (1790), 1 Hag. Con. 136 at 138, 161 E.R. 502. It is clear that s. 19 (and consequently s. 20) of the Act were not complied with.

In *Gilham v. Steele*, 8 W.W.R. (N.S.) 62, [1953] 2 D.L.R. 89 at 96 (B.C. C.A.), Bird J.A. (as he then was) referred to ...

> the principle expressed by Dr. Lushington in *Catterall v. Sweetman (Catterall)* (1845), 1 Rob. Ecc. 304, 163 E.R. 1047, applied by the Court of Appeal, Saskatchewan, in *Wylie (Patton) v. Patton*, 24 Sask. L.R. 285, [1930] 1 W.W.R. 216, [1930] 1 D.L.R. 747, i.e., that although a statute prohibits a solemnization of marriage without observance of requirements, therein described as prerequisite, failure to observe any such requirement does not render a marriage void, nor is nullity to be implied in consequence unless the statute so provides either expressly or by clear necessary intendment.

Here, as in that case, counsel for the plaintiff does not question the soundness of that principle but submits that "the provisions of ss. 19, 20 and 21 of the *Marriage Act*, by necessary intendment, enact the consequence of invalidity for non-compliance with ss. 19 and 20 if the condition of good faith is not present". In November 1970 the *Marriage Act*, s. 21 read as follows:

> No irregularity in the compliance with sections 19 and 20 invalidates a marriage solemnized in pursuance of these sections if the marriage is entered into in good faith.

Ordinarily, a claim of lack of good faith is made by someone against someone else. Here the plaintiff was herself guilty of lack of good faith. So, of course, was the defendant. However, guilt on the part of the plaintiff cannot convert the marriage ceremony in question in these proceedings into "a marriage ... entered into in good faith".

Section 21 does not say directly that if the marriage is not entered into in good faith it will be invalid if the provisions of ss. 19 and 20 are not complied with, but I think it does so by "clear necessary intendment" since, if the legislature did not so intend, I can see no reason for saying in s. 21 that if the marriage were entered into in good faith it would not be invalid. In contrast, s. 31 reads as follows:

> 31. Nothing in section 29 or 30 contained invalidates any marriage.

Section 29 and 30 relate to the marriage of minors. ...

[The marriage was annulled.]

HASSAN v. HASSAN

(2006), 30 R.F.L. (6th) 104 (Alta. Q.B.)

[The parties participated in a "Nikah" (a marriage ceremony under Islamic law) in Alberta in 1984. The husband was in Saudi Arabia and participated by proxy, while the wife was in Alberta, but not in the room when the ceremony took place. After the ceremony, they attempted to obtain a marriage certificate in Alberta but were unable to do so. Later, they obtained a letter from the High Commission of Pakistan stating when they were married. In 1987, they sought and obtained a "marriage certificate" from the Nikah registrar in Peshawar, Pakistan, where they were then living. Later that year, Ms. Hassan sponsored Mr. Hassan, as her husband, to come to Canada. They lived together until 2000, when they separated. In 2002, the wife commenced an action in Pakistan in which she stated that the parties were married in 1984. In 2003, the husband applied for a share of matrimonial property in Alberta. The wife then took the position that the marriage was a nullity.]

B.E. ROMAINE J.:

Is the marriage between the parties legally valid?

4 In submitting that the marriage is not valid, Ms. Hassan relies upon settled conflict law to the effect that the formal validity of a marriage is determined by the *lex loci celebrationis*. Since the marriage was performed in Alberta and failed to comply with numerous requirements and prerequisites under Alberta law, Ms. Hassan submits that it is not valid, and that Mr. Hassan is not entitled to a division of property.

5 There is no dispute that the parties did not comply with many of the provisions of the *Marriage Act* of Alberta, including the requirement to obtain a licence and the requirement to register the marriage after its solemnization, although the parties attempted to do so and were refused a registration. They are not sure if the Iman who performed the ceremony was registered to do so in Alberta, and they clearly violated the Alberta prohibition against marriage by proxy: section 9(1) of the *Marriage Act*. While the *Marriage Act* provides some relief against noncompliance in section 23(1), that relief does not extend to the failure of the parties themselves, deliberate or otherwise, to comply with the *Act*: *Lin, Re* (1992), 137 A.R. 1 (Q.B.).

[Section 23(1) of Alberta's *Marriage Act* stated that a "marriage is not invalidated by reason only of a contravention of or non-compliance with this Act (a) by the person who solemnized the marriage, or (b) by the person who issued the licence for the marriage. ...]

6 While Ms. Hassan is correct that conflict law supports her submission that there was no valid marriage, this is a troubling conclusion in this case where the parties clearly intended to contract a valid marriage and lived together for many years representing their status as married to various government authorities in Canada and elsewhere where they resided. The parties may have ignored the requirements of the Alberta *Marriage Act* in marrying according to the customs of Islamic law, but they attempted to register the marriage shortly after the fact in Alberta and, when that route was not available to them, took considerable pains to have the marriage recognized by the Pakistani authorities, both while in Canada and when they moved to Pakistan. While no expert opinion evidence was presented that would establish that the marriage would be accepted as valid in Pakistan, the certificate of marriage

issued by the Pakistani embassy and the subsequent registration of the marriage by the Nikah Registrar in Pakistan raise the possibility that the marriage may be considered valid in one country while invalid in another. Ms. Hassan has in fact relied upon the presumptive validity of her marriage in commencing litigation in Pakistan, while now disclaiming its validity in Alberta. The courts should be loath to countenance such international self-serving manipulations.

7 Despite the strong presumption that parties who undergo a ceremony of marriage followed by cohabitation are lawfully married, courts have consistently allowed evidence of defect in the formal requirements of the *lex loci celebrationis* to rebut this presumption, with only narrow exceptions to the general rule. It appears that a marriage that does not comply with the *lex loci celebrationis* in terms of formality may be recognized as a valid common law marriage: "(a) where it is impossible to conform to the local form of marriage, or (b) where the parties have not submitted to the local law.".…

8 The first scenario does not arise in this case. While it may be possible to argue the second, such submissions fail on closer analysis. While Ms. Hassan has deposed that she and Mr. Hassan did not intend that their relationship be governed by Alberta law but by Pakistani law, and while the parties certainly intended to have an Islamic ceremony of marriage, they attempted to register the marriage in Alberta shortly after the ceremony. This situation does not fit within the narrow category of English cases that characterize this exception to the general rule, which largely centre around marriages of military personnel in occupied territories or marriages contracted in prison camps. …

12 I must, therefore, find that the marriage between Ms. Hassan and Mr. Hassan was not legally valid. In consequence, I do not strike Ms. Hassan's Statement of Defence as requested by Mr. Hassan. Mr. Hassan asks for an order allowing him to amend his Statement of Claim to include claims for resulting and constructive trusts arising out of a common law relationship. Counsel for Ms. Hassan submitted that he was not given adequate notice of this application and I, therefore, leave the question open for further argument. I also leave open the issue of estoppel or other equitable relief to the extent it may be applicable at a later stage of the proceedings.

NOTES AND QUESTIONS

1. If the parties go through a marriage ceremony and then cohabit, it is presumed that they complied with the necessary formalities. The person who is claiming that there was a formal defect has the onus of proving it. See *Friedman v. Smookler* (1963), 43 D.L.R. (2d) 210 (Ont. H.C.); *Re Lin* (1992), 44 R.F.L. (3d) 60 (Alta. Q.B.); and *Lehoux v. Woolward* (1994), 2 R.F.L. (4th) 382 (B.C. S.C.).

2. Would the Hassan marriage have been valid if the ceremony had occurred in Ontario? Note s. 31 of the *Marriage Act*. Which defects are cured by s. 31 of the *Marriage Act*? Some formal defects, such as a failure to have two witnesses or a failure to solemnize the marriage in the presence of the parties (see s. 25), may not be covered by s. 31. Does this mean that such defects are of no effect or that they result in invalidity that cannot be cured?

In *Upadyhaha v. Sehgal* (2000), 11 R.F.L. (5th) 210 (Ont. S.C.J.), a priest officiated at a traditional Hindu wedding in the presence of some of the bride's relatives. The bride testified that the groom neglected to get a licence, but that she considered herself to be married after the ceremony. The couple spent the wedding night in a hotel and the groom spent several nights at the bride's house during the months that followed. Justice MacKenzie described (at para. 18) the failure to obtain a marriage licence as an "egregious breach of the *Marriage Act*" and also concluded (at para. 30) that s. 31 did not operate to save the marriage because the parties never "lived together and cohabited as man and wife". In *Ayoub v. Osman* (2006), 2006 CarswellOnt 1808 (S.C.J.); additional reasons at (2006), 2006 CarswellOnt 5456 (S.C.J.) the couple went through a Muslim wedding ceremony at which an Imam officiated but they failed to obtain a marriage licence. The couple then cohabited for almost 12 years and had two children. The court applied s. 31 of the *Marriage Act* to save the marriage, only to grant the husband's application for a divorce.

3. Mr. Hassan's application depended on his status as a spouse under Alberta's *Matrimonial Property Act*, R.S.A. 2000, c. M-8. Section 1 of that Act defines "spouse" to include "a party to a marriage notwithstanding that the marriage is void or voidable", but s. 2 adds: "Nothing in this Act confers a right on a spouse who at the time of marriage knew or had reason to believe that the marriage was void." Mr. Hassan's lawyer and the judge appear to have accepted that s. 2 precluded him from qualifying. Do you agree? Would Mr. Hassan have qualified as a "spouse" under Ontario's *Family Law Act* if it had applied? See the definition of "spouse" in s. 1(1).

In *Reaney v. Reaney* (1990), 28 R.F.L. (3d) 52 (Ont. H.C.), the Ontario High Court held that a man who knew that he was already married when he went through a second wedding ceremony did not enter the marriage in good faith and could not qualify as a "spouse" under Part I of the Act. In *Debora v. Debora* (1999), 43 R.F.L. (4th) 179 (Ont. C.A.), the parties were married in a religious ceremony that did not comply with the *Marriage Act*. The man advised the woman that he wished to continue receiving a widower's pension and, therefore, their marriage should not be registered with the authorities for some time. Seven years later, the couple married in a civil ceremony. The Ontario Court of Appeal held that the woman only became a "spouse" for the purposes of Part I of the *Family Law Act* after the second ceremony. It stated (at 184) that a person who participated in a marriage ceremony knowing that it did not comply with the provincial law could not claim to be acting "in good faith" even if he or she believed that the ceremony created a marriage.

4. A number of cases hold that marriages entered into in conformity with aboriginal custom will be recognized in some circumstances: *Connolly v. Woolrich* (1867), 11 L.C.J. 197, 17 R.J.R.Q. 75, 1 C.N.L.C. 70 (Que. S.C.); *R. v. Nan-E-Quis-A-Ka* (1889), 2 C.N.L.C. 368, 1 Terr. L.R. 211 (Que. S.C.); *R. v. Bone* (1899), 4 Terr. L.R. 173 (N.W.T. S.C.); *R. v. Williams* (1921), 30 B.C.R. 303 (S.C.); and *Re Noah* (1961), 32 D.L.R. (2d) 185, 36 W.W.R. 577 (N.W.T. S.C.). See also *Casimel v. Insurance Corp. of British Columbia* (1993), 106 D.L.R. (4th) 720 (B.C. C.A.) where these cases are examined. For further reading, see Zlotkin, "Judicial Recognition of Aboriginal Customary Law in Canada: Selected Marriage and Adoption Cases" [1984] 4 C.N.L.R. 1.

5. When the federal *Civil Marriage Act* was adopted, there were media reports that the Alberta government was contemplating legislation precluding the issuance of licences to same-sex couples and protecting that provision from *Charter* challenge through a "notwithstanding clause" as permitted by s. 33. Would this have ensured the constitutional validity of the legislation? Consider that in *Christians (Wiltshire) v. Hill* (1981), 22 R.F.L. (2d) 299, the Alberta Court of Queen's Bench held that a province could not withhold a marriage licence where a woman wished to marry her divorced husband's brother since this relationship did not fall within the federally-established prohibited degrees.

6. Examine ss. 5 and 6 of the Ontario *Marriage Act*. The courts have held that the provinces may require parental consent as a formal requirement and may stipulate that a marriage without such consent is void: *Kerr v. Kerr* (1933), [1934] S.C.R. 72 and *Alberta (Attorney General) v. Underwood*, [1934] S.C.R. 635.

What is the status of a marriage entered into in Ontario by a 16-year-old without parental consent or a court order dispensing with the requirement of parental consent? In *S. (A.) v. S. (A.)* (1988), 15 R.F.L. (3d) 443 (Ont. U.F.C.), Mendes da Costa U.F.C.J. concluded (at 452) "that there is nothing in the [*Marriage Act*] that shows an intention on the part of the legislature to make parental consent a condition precedent to the validity of a marriage". Do you agree? Is the curative section (s. 31) applicable where there is a failure to obtain parental consent? If so, how does this affect Justice Mendes da Costa's conclusion?

Section 5(2) of the Ontario *Marriage Act* directs licence issuers to refuse to issue licences to anyone under 16. Has the province overstepped its constitutional powers? Is a marriage entered into in Ontario between two persons aged 15 valid if the parties somehow manage to obtain a licence and persuade an authorized person to officiate? Does this make any difference to the constitutional issue?

The requirements of s. 5 may also be subject to a constitutional challenge on the ground that they discriminate on the basis of age and therefore violate s. 15 of the *Canadian Charter of Rights and Freedoms*. Do you think such a challenge would be successful? In *Moe v. Dinkins*, 533 F. Supp. 623 (S.D.N.Y., 1981) the U.S. District Court of New York held that the requirement of parental consent for a marriage by a minor was constitutional as it was "rationally related to the State's legitimate interest in mature decision-making with respect to marriage by minors and preventing unstable marriages".

7. Section 6 of the Ontario *Marriage Act* allows a court to dispense with the need for parental consent. An application for such an order under previous Ontario legislation was granted in *Re Fox* (1972), [1973] 1 O.R. 146

(Co. Ct.), where the bride was 16 years old and the groom 18 and in *Evans, Re* (2007), 44 R.F.L. (6th) 223 (Ont. C.J. [In Chambers]) where the 17-year-old bride had given birth to a child fathered by the 21-year-old groom.

4. The Effect of Invalidity

(1) The Void/ Voidable Distinction

Reproduced below is a table identifying different defects and their consequences. Since the table appeared in a book that was published in 1979, it lists "identity of sex" as a defect leading to a void or non-marriage. Obviously, this is no longer so in Canada. Also, it should be noted that, with regards to insanity, essential mistake, and non-age, Professor Hahlo takes the view that the marriage might be void but capable of ratification. He explains this apparent contradiction (*Nullity of Marriage in Canada* (Toronto: Butterworths, 1979) at 42-43):

> [I]t is generally recognized by now that the stark differentiation between void and voidable juridical acts is an over-simplification, and that there are cases which fall somewhere between these two categories. A marriage contracted without the required consent may well be one of those cases. If, to take an example, a person goes through a form of marriage, while insane, the essential consent is lacking, with the result that on principle, the marriage ought to be regarded as null and void *ab initio*. But assuming the parties live together for years after the erstwhile lunatic has recovered his mental health, is there a court in the world which would, perhaps decades later, perhaps after the death of one of the spouses, annul the marriage on the ground that at the time of the solemnization of the marriage one of the parties was insane? Either the marriage was voidable only, which goes against the principle that lack of consent renders a juridical act void; or this is one of the cases where a void act, contrary to norm, is capable of ratification.

HAHLO, *NULLITY OF MARRIAGE IN CANADA*

(Toronto: Butterworths, 1979) 43-44

Table Of Impediments and Defects

Impediment or Defect	*Effect on the Marriage*
Identity of Sex	Marriage void (non-marriage)
Prior Existing Marriage	Marriage void
Relationship within the Prohibited Degrees	Marriage void ...
Informal Marriage	Marriage void (non-marriage)
Failure to comply with specific statutory formalities	Marriage valid, except where the applicable *Marriage Act*, expressly or by necessary intendment, decrees nullity

Impediment or Defect	*Effect on the M*
Non-age: either party below the marriageable age of the common law (boys 14 years, girls 12 years)	Marriage void (except, pos ...ere the applicable *Marriage Act* otherwise decrees) but capable of ratification by continued cohabitation after attainment of age
Non-age: marriage contracted by a minor of marriageable age but below the age of marriage majority without the required consent of parent or guardian	Marriage valid unless the applicable *Marriage Act*, expressly or by necessary intendment, decrees nullity
Insanity	Marriage void but capable of ratification by continued cohabitation after recovery
Drunkenness or drug intoxication depriving party of reason and volition	Marriage void but capable of ratification by continued cohabitation after sobering-up
Force, fear, duress	Marriage voidable at instance of coerced party
Mistake as to the nature of the ceremony or the identity of the other party	Arguable whether marriage void or voidable. Better view: voidable at instance of the party in error. If void, capable of ratification by mistaken party.
Mistake as to qualities or attributes of the other party	Marriage valid
Fraud	Marriage valid, unless fraud induced a material mistake, *i.e.*, a mistake as to the nature of the ceremony or the identity of the other party
Formally correct marriage contracted without the intention to establish a true marriage relationship (limited or extraneous purpose marriage, such as an "immigration marriage")	Marriage valid (controversial)
Impotence	Marriage voidable at the instance of either spouse.

(2) The Effects of the Void/ Voidable Distinction

Lord Greene M. R. succinctly expressed the basic distinction between a void and voidable marriage in *De Reneville v. De Reneville* (1947), [1948] P. 100, [1948] 1 All E.R. 56 (Eng. C.A.) at 111 [P.]:

> [A] void marriage is one that will be regarded by every court in any case in which the existence of the marriage is in issue as never having taken place and can be so treated by both parties to it without the necessity of any decree annulling it; a voidable marriage is one that will be regarded by every court as a valid subsisting marriage until a decree annulling it has been pronounced by a court of competent jurisdiction.

A voidable marriage can end through divorce, but no divorce can be granted if the marriage is void. In proceedings to determine the right of a third party, a court may hold that a particular marriage is void whenever the validity of the marriage is relevant to the third party's rights. The validity of a voidable marriage can only be questioned in proceedings brought by one of the parties to the marriage during the subsistence of the marriage. A voidable marriage can, therefore, never be challenged after the marriage is ended by the death of one of the parties.

As noted earlier, legislative provisions can equate parties to a void and voidable marriage. They can also accord the same rights and obligations to parties of a void or voidable marriage as are accorded to parties to a valid marriage. Recall the definition of "spouse" in s. 1(1) of the *Family Law Act*.

3

DIVORCE

1. Introduction

(1) History of Canadian Divorce Law

Prior to 1968, the divorce law varied from province to province. In Newfoundland and Quebec, there was no judicial divorce. Persons domiciled in these provinces had to procure the passage of a private Act of Parliament to dissolve their marriages. In 1967, judicial divorce could be obtained in Alberta, British Columbia, Manitoba, the Northwest Territories, Ontario, Saskatchewan, and the Yukon Territory on the following grounds. A husband could obtain a divorce only by proving his wife's adultery, while a wife could petition on the grounds of adultery, rape, sodomy, bestiality, or bigamy. Unlike the other provinces, New Brunswick, Nova Scotia and Prince Edward Island each enacted a divorce law prior to Confederation. These laws continued in effect until the Parliament of Canada enacted the *Divorce Act* of 1968. In all of these provinces, adultery was a ground for divorce. In New Brunswick and Prince Edward Island, frigidity or impotence was also a ground. Divorce on the basis of cruelty was available only in Nova Scotia.

Section 23 of the *Divorce Act* of 1968 repealed all prior divorce laws. This statute provided, for the first time, a Canada-wide law of divorce and introduced no-fault divorce. Section 4 of the Act provided that where a husband and wife were living separate and apart a petition could be brought on the ground that there had been a permanent breakdown of marriage by reason of one of the circumstances listed in s. 4(1). A petitioner could rely on the permanent marriage breakdown ground only by establishing one of the following circumstances.

Section 4(1)(a) — Imprisonment: The respondent must have been imprisoned for an aggregate period of at least three years during the five year period immediately preceding the petition. If the sentence were a death sentence or for a term of ten years or more, then a petition could be presented to the court after two years of imprisonment.

Section 4(1)(b) — Alcohol or Narcotic Addiction: The Act required that the respondent be "grossly addicted to alcohol or a narcotic", without reasonable expectation of rehabilitation within a foreseeable period.

Section 4(1)(c) — Whereabouts of Spouse Unknown: If, for a period of not less than three years, the petitioner had no knowledge or information as to the whereabouts of the respondent it was considered that the whereabouts of the spouse were unknown.

Section 4(1)(d) — Non-consummation: The marriage must not have been consummated and, for a period of not less than one year, the respondent must have been unable to consummate the marriage by reason of illness or disability or refused to consummate it.

Section 4(1)(e) — Separation and Desertion: The spouses must have been living separate and apart for a period of not less than three years immediately preceding the petition. If the petitioner were the deserting spouse, then he or she had to wait a period of at least five years before a petition could be presented. Desertion involved abandonment of marital obligations without agreement between the spouses.

Section 3 retained the matrimonial offence basis for divorce. The offences under s. 3, which included adultery, sodomy, bestiality, rape, homosexual acts, going through a form of marriage with another, and physical or mental cruelty, were considered to strike at the very root of the pledge that the spouses remain faithful and devoted to each other.

The Law Reform Commission of Canada urged substantial reforms of the divorce law in 1976 (see *Report on Family Law* (Ottawa: Canada Law Reform Commission, 1976)). It proposed that "marriage breakdown", conclusively established whenever a spouse claimed that it had occurred, be the only basis for divorce. There would be a minimum waiting period of six months following the filing by a spouse or both spouses of the "notice of intent to seek dissolution" before a court could dissolve the marriage.

In January 1984 the Liberal government tabled Bill C-10, *An Act to Amend the Divorce Act*, which provided for divorce solely on the basis of one year of separation. Due to the dissolution of Parliament in the summer of 1984, this Bill died on the Order Paper. In May 1985 the Progressive Conservative government introduced Bill C-47, which ultimately received royal assent on February 13, 1986, and came into force as the *Divorce Act, 1985* on June 1, 1986. The excerpts from the Department of Justice study that follow explain the background to and leading features of the 1985 *Divorce Act*.

DEPARTMENT OF JUSTICE, *EVALUATION OF THE DIVORCE ACT: PHASE II: MONITORING AND EVALUATION*

(Ottawa: Department of Justice, Bureau of Review, 1990) 1–9 (Footnotes omitted) (Reproduced with the permission of the Minister of Supply and Services Canada, 1991)

On June 1, 1986, the *Divorce Act* came into force. The Act represents an attempt to modernize the law pertaining to divorce. The stated objectives at the time of Bill C-47 were:

(a) to make the divorce process less adversarial while increasing chances for the reconciliation of the spouses;

(b) to provide a more humane and fairer resolution of the consequences of divorce; [and]

(c) to recognize provincial responsibilities and provide for a process of divorce which will operate with as few complications or duplications as possible.

The *Divorce Act* is, in many ways, a response to a number of criticisms of the 1968 *Divorce Act*. Almost from its inception, that Act was seen as a compromise piece of legislation, one which, even at the time, did not reflect the realities of marriage breakdown. Indeed, as early as 1973, Julien Payne, in preparing his massive background report on unified family courts, could already draw upon an impressive body of literature critical of family law and its administration. And, over the rest of that decade, the Law Reform Commission prepared a number of focused working-papers which documented what were then perceived to be the main problems and inadequacies of existing legislation and procedures in the area of family law in Canada. ...

The general conclusion reached by the Law Reform Commission and echoed by many other critics was that the adversarial approach and the related notion of fault are inappropriate in the context of marriage dissolution. In particular, the adversarial approach was seen not only as inappropriate but as also intensifying and exacerbating pain and suffering and impeding the likelihood of an amicable settlement. Thus, the Commission depicted the adversary system as "one of Canada's great self-inflicted wounds" and as an approach "inherently inconsistent with the harmonious resolution of family disputes". In the Commission's view, it is an approach which should not be available "as an extension of the destructive capacity of spouses who disagree over their personal relationship."

Also under attack was the fault orientation of the existing legislation. Fault, and therefore the notion of a guilty party, was seen as seldom relevant in marriage breakdown since the *grounds* for divorce and the *reasons* for divorce are usually quite far apart. The Commission argued that the fault principle merely reflects the futile effort of the state to attempt, through legislation, to uphold the sanctity of the traditional family by reducing the incidence of marriage breakdown. As the Law Reform Commission concluded, restrictive divorce laws simply force those committed to obtaining a divorce to find or fabricate grounds. Those who can do neither are left in the position of living apart, neither married nor unmarried. For similar reasons, the Commission was equally critical of the present three- or five-year waiting period or any designated waiting period for that matter. Rather, where both spouses are agreed that their marriage has broken down, the waiting period was seen as too long and as creating unnecessary hardships and delays in the process of reorganization.

In the period between the Law Reform Commission's studies and the 1983 proposal for reform of the divorce legislation, many changes had occurred in family law. All provinces and territories had, by then, enacted legislation concerning division of matrimonial property, child custody and child and spousal support. Usually, these reforms replaced the plethora of antiquated and sexist acts pertaining to various aspects of family relations and conflicts with new legislation gender neutral in its language and premised on an assumption of sexual equality in marriage. The "best interests of the child" principle became the sole basis for awarding custody, thereby undermining the earlier notion of paternal rights and the later maternal preference when children are in "their tender years".

It is apparent, too, that through less formal means, many of the problems identified by the Law Reform Commission were being addressed. In terms of attitudes and practices, family law was no longer the same as the Law Reform Commission had depicted it in the 1970's. For example, alternatives to the adversarial approach, such as divorce mediation, seen, in the 1970's as novel and controversial had, by the mid-1980's, become institutionalized in many parts of Canada. And, while there no doubt remain some extremely litigious lawyers in the area of family law, there is reason to believe that most family law practitioners were coming to believe that when custody and access are at issue, a better settlement results from negotiation than from litigation. Moreover, there now seemed to be few family court judges who believed that, in the matter of custody, the adversarial approach will "reveal the truth" of who is the better parent. Many were coming to rely much more — sometimes invariably — on custody assessments or investigations or they were referring the disputing spouses to mediation.

It is evident that the proposed divorce reform was, in many respects, an effort to catch up with the provincial legislation and the changing climate in family law. The proposed divorce reform drew heavily upon the Law Reform Commission reports and, depending on point of view, addressed many of the concerns and recommendations of the Commission. However, in retrospect, these can be seen as concerns of the 1970's. Many of them emerged from or were influenced by the radical critiques of the family and the generally positive conception of divorce as often a constructive rather than a destructive process — a solution rather than a problem. Family and marriage — went this argument — oppresses everyone, but particularly women, and it was not the role of the state to stand in the way of individual fulfilment or to buttress failed marriages.

When new divorce legislation was being proposed in the 1980's, the climate had shifted and new issues and concerns had surfaced. First, in a more conservative era, the traditional nuclear family was under less attack than in the two previous decades. Indeed, new and voluble groups had emerged to oppose legislation and programmes which, in their view, undermine the sanctity of the traditional male breadwinner nuclear family. Second, the rather short-lived period during the early 1970s when divorce was seen as a creative process had given way to a more dismal image as more was learned about the social, psychological and economic consequences of marriage breakdown, particularly for women. The American experience had suggested that family law reform though based on assumptions of sexual equality is actually premised on an "illusion of sexual equality". Many of the innovations and assumptions, initially welcomed by feminists, were being shown to produce unanticipated and negative consequences for women and children in divorce. Third, fathers' rights groups also were beginning to see sexual equality in family law as largely illusory since in terms of support and custody, the courts are alleged by them to be biased in favour of women.

Thus, by the time Bill C-47 reached the Committee stage, many women's groups and religious groups of long-standing existence and newly formed fathers' rights groups were anxious to make their concerns known and to press for amendments to the proposed legislation. The criticism by religious and fundamentalist groups was diffuse and aimed, ultimately, at making divorce more difficult to obtain on the premise that more liberal divorce laws threaten the sanctity of the family. Predictably, the concerns of fathers' rights groups were more focused. Their demand was for a presumption of joint legal custody.

Women's groups represented a far larger constituency than the fathers' rights groups, but were also focused in their concerns. First, much of their effort went to opposing a presumption of joint legal custody. Second, they wished to broaden the grounds for variation of support orders in order to soften the possible impact of time fixed orders. Here, the concern was that the principle of self-sufficiency, if taken too literally, would be unfair to older women who had not worked outside the home during the marriage. This was opposed by various lawyers' groups who wanted legislation which would allow for finality and greater certainty in advice given to their clients. As well, the recently formed association, Family Mediation Canada, wished there to be a provision requiring a mandatory visit to divorce mediation where child custody is being contested. Finally, there were some who urged that the language of "custody" and "access" be abandoned in favour of terms such as "primary caregiver" and "secondary caregiver."

By the time Bill C-47 was ready for passage, four major issues had emerged: a presumption of joint custody; mandatory mediation; factors and objectives of spousal support, especially potential abuse of the objective of self-sufficiency; and variations of support orders. As in 1968, the legislation was again an attempt by the government to find compromises which would meet these sometimes conflicting demands. As we describe in the next section, the various groups were only partially successful in their efforts to include amendments which would address their particular concerns. ...

The *Divorce Act*

Grounds

For those undergoing divorce, an important change, one which affects virtually all divorces, is the adoption of "marriage breakdown" as the sole ground for divorce and, in particular, the reduction of the separation period from three or five years to one year. The previous legislation contained 15 different fault grounds and ways of demonstrating marriage breakdown. Of these, the vast majority of divorcing couples relied on separation (to demonstrate marriage breakdown) and adultery and physical or mental cruelty (as methods of demonstrating fault). Adultery and mental and physical cruelty are retained but they are now viewed, along with one-year separation as methods of demonstrating marriage breakdown. In principle, use of these former fault grounds would allow for "immediate" divorce. In practice, since it is possible to file for divorce before having actually lived separate and apart for one year, it is debatable whether there would be much time advantage in choosing one of these methods over another.

Reconciliation and Mediation

The provision in the 1968 *Divorce Act*, requiring lawyers to inquire as to the possibility of reconciliation and to advise clients of marriage counselling services in the community, is retained in the new legislation. Lawyers are now under the additional legal obligation to advise their clients about the advantages of negotiation and of the divorce mediation services available in their community. There is not, however, any obligation on the part of lawyers actively to refer clients with disputes to mediation though, of course, they are free to do so if they so desire.

As well, the provision that spouses may resume cohabitation for purposes of reconciliation for 90 days during the separation period has been retained. Now, however, it is possible for couples to make several attempts at such cohabitation as long as the total time does not exceed 90 days.

Spousal and Child Support

In making an order for support, the *Divorce Act* specifies that the court shall *not* take into consideration fault or misconduct of the spouse in relation to the marriage. Courts are required to take into account not only the "conditions, means, needs and other circumstances of each spouse" but also "the length of time the spouses cohabited and the functions performed by each spouse during cohabitation". It was made clear, at the time the legislation was announced, that this provision was intended to take into account the plight of older women coming out of a long-term traditional single income family.

Courts are also directed to take into account four objectives of support:

(a)   to recognize any economic advantages or disadvantages to the spouses arising from the marriage or its breakdown;

(b)   to apportion between the spouses any financial consequences arising from the care of any child of the marriage over and above the obligation apportioned between the spouses pursuant to subsection (7);

(c)   to relieve any economic hardship of the spouses arising from the breakdown of the marriage; and

(d)   insofar as practicable, to promote the economic self-sufficiency of each spouse within a reasonable period of time.

Courts are, therefore, empowered to make orders of fixed duration when the goal of self-sufficiency can and should be achieved and, conversely, to make permanent orders when there is no likelihood of self-sufficiency and there is evidence of economic hardship.

Variation of Support Orders

Before a variation [of an order of fixed duration] will be considered, it must be demonstrated that present economic hardship is directly related to the marriage and the changed circumstances would have resulted in a different original order had they existed at the time of the original order. We note, however, that this provision does not include variations downward.

Child Custody and Access

The sole criteria for the making of an order of custody and access is "the best interests of the child of the marriage as determined by reference to the conditions, means, needs and other circumstances of the child". Subject to the criteria of best interests of the child is what is known as the principle of "maximum contact". A child should have as much contact with each parent as is consistent with his or her best interests and, for that purpose, courts shall consider the willingness of any person seeking custody to facilitate such contact.

Two other significant additions were made to the custody section. First, the Act seeks to eliminate the consideration of past conduct by allowing the court to consider only conduct relevant to the ability of that person to act as a parent of a child. Secondly, the legislation recognizes joint custody by permitting courts to grant custody or access to any *one or more persons*. In the marginal note is stated "joint custody or access".

The additional provisions favour non-custodial parents. First, she or he may now make inquiries and is to be given information concerning the health, education and welfare of the child. Second, the court may include a term giving the right to receive a minimum 30 day advance notice of any change in residence and the address of the new residence.

Procedures

The *Divorce Act* introduces the possibility of two new procedures both of which are intended to simplify the divorce process and to make it less adversarial. The first of these, which is built into the Act, is that parties to the divorce may now petition jointly when, presumably, no matters are in dispute. The second is that the necessity, under the previous legislation, of a trial has now been eliminated. Provinces are now permitted to make rules by which, if no matters are to be litigated, divorce may be granted by a judge without an oral hearing.

NOTES AND QUESTIONS

1. In explaining the retention of fault grounds in s. 8(2), The Hon. J.C. Crosbie, Minister of Justice, told the Ontario Branch of the Canadian Bar Association (Feb. 6, 1986, as quoted in Ziff, "Recent Developments in Canadian Law: Marriage and Divorce" (1986), 18 Ottawa L. Rev. 121 at 141):

> Many Canadians for moral or religious reasons feel that it is immoral to withhold a divorce for one year where adultery or cruelty can be shown. Others are concerned about the well-being of an abused spouse. Immediate divorce might remove the spouse from the dangerous situation. Furthermore, adultery and cruelty have long been considered proof of marriage breakdown.

Do you agree that there are good reasons for retaining fault grounds?

2. To some extent the grounds for divorce are symbolic, signaling societal attitudes about the institution of marriage. In *Elgaard v. Elgaard* (1986), 1 R.F.L. (3d) 256 (B.C. S.C.), at 261, Southin J. made the following observation regarding the 1985 *Divorce Act*:

> Social attitudes have so changed since the early 1960s that Parliament ... has embodied in legislation the concept that marriage is a trivial social custom unworthy of judicial attention. When the Act is proclaimed, a marriage will more easily be put asunder than a contract of purchase of realty.

Although divorce is now available virtually on demand, the process still requires a judicial decision even when both spouses wish the marriage to end. Should this process be replaced by a purely administrative one where a state agency simply records the divorce? Why is divorce not simply a private decision in which the state has no role?

3. Under the 1968 *Divorce Act*, an innocent spouse had considerable bargaining power if the other spouse wished an immediate divorce because the latter would have to wait five years before petitioning. Because this bargaining power is lost under a liberal divorce law, Doris Anderson, President of the National Action Committee on the Status of Women, described the Liberal government's reform proposals in 1984 as "bad for women" (*Cal-*

gary Herald (January 21, 1984)). In *The Divorce Revolution: The Unexpected Social and Economic Consequences for Women and Children in America* (New York: Free Press, 1985), Lenore Weitzman also emphasizes the bargaining power of innocent spouses under fault divorce. She concludes, however (at 383): "The solution, at least for California today, is not to reintroduce fault and its penalties, but rather to strengthen the economic provisions of the new laws to assure adequate protection for wives and children." See also Ellman, "The Misguided Movement to Revive Fault Divorce, and Why Reformers Should Look Instead to the American Law Institute" (1997), 11 Int. J. Law & Fam. 216 and Melnick, "Reaffirming No-Fault Divorce: Supplementing Formal Equality with Substantive Change" (2000), 75 Ind. L.J. 711.

4. Statistics Canada reports that of the 71,241 Canadian divorces in 2005, 67,526 were based on living separate and apart. Adultery, physical cruelty, and mental cruelty were listed as the reasons for marriage breakdown in 2,218, 619, and 878 divorces respectively. There was some regional variation in the use of "fault grounds". Quebec accounted for over 75% of the divorces that were based on findings of fault even though its percentage of all Canadian divorces was less than 22. See Statistics Canada, *Table 101-6516 — Divorces, by reason for marital breakdown, Canada, provinces and territories, annual (number)*, CANSIM (database).

5. By the time a divorce proceeding instituted on the basis of either cruelty or adultery is determined by the court, the parties may have been living separate and apart for over a year. The allegations of fault are then irrelevant to the granting of the divorce. The court may decline to determine if the adultery or cruelty is proved and simply use the separate and apart ground. For recent examples, see *Z. (S.) v. R. (D.)* (2006), 2006 CarswellQue 4423 (S.C.) and *Robert v. Robert* (2007), 2007 CarswellOnt 5782 (S.C.J.). Compare these cases with *I. (S.) v. E. (E.)* (2005), 2005 CarswellQue 8765 (S.C.), where the court stated (para. 53):

> Both parties are entitled to it on the basis of living separate and apart for over one year. Moreover, Ms. I. is also entitled to it on the basis of physical cruelty during the parties' 21 years of life together; Mr. E. is not entitled to it on the basis of alleged "mental cruelty" by Ms. I., which allegation is far-fetched and without substance.

In *McPhail v. McPhail* (2001), 15 R.F.L. (5th) 137 (B.C.C.A.), Justice Donald stated, (paras. 10 and 11):

> As it usually takes a year to bring a contested matter to trial a divorce can usually be given on the ground of one-year separation. In those circumstances a cruelty allegation is unnecessary and will only prolong the hostility between the parties. A cruelty finding bears stigma; it should be avoided when no useful purpose is served. ...

> [I]t would have been better if the trial judge [who found that the wife was entitled to a divorce on the basis of the husband's cruelty] had proceeded with the divorce on separation only and declined to hear the cruelty issue.

Do you agree with this approach? Should a spouse be able to obtain a societal recognition of the matrimonial misconduct?

6. Cruelty may be relevant to other issues such as possession of the matrimonial home, spousal support, and custody and access. See Chapter 5, *THE FAMILY HOME*, Chapter 6, *SPOUSAL SUPPORT* and Chapter 7, *CUSTODY AND ACCESS*. Also, spousal abuse may be a basis for a tort action. See, e.g., *Valenti v. Valenti* (1996), 21 R.F.L. (4th) 246 (Ont. Gen. Div.); affirmed (1998), 41 R.F.L. (4th) 289 (Ont. C.A.). See generally, Krause, "On the Danger of Allowing Marital Fault to Re-Emerge in the Guise of Torts" (1998), 73 Notre Dame L. Rev. 1355 and Bala, "Tort Remedies & the Family Law Practitioner" (1998-99), 16 C.F.L.Q. 423.

7. Section 9(1)(a) of the 1968 *Divorce Act* stipulated that a divorce decree could only be granted "after a trial which shall be by a judge, without jury". Now, s. 7 of the *Divorce Act* specifies that the jurisdiction to grant a divorce "shall be exercised only by a judge of the court without a jury". There is no longer a requirement that a formal trial be held. Section 25 of the Act authorizes provincial rule-making bodies to make rules governing divorce practice and procedure including the manner in which the divorce comes before the court. Further, the rule-making bodies may make rules providing for the disposition of a divorce proceeding without an oral hearing. The intent is to permit the provincial rule-making bodies to limit trials to those cases where they are absolutely necessary to deal with contested issues. The vast majority of divorces are now uncontested and granted without a personal appearance in court by either party. These divorces are variously known as "affidavit divorces", "paper divorces", or "desk divorces"

8. Where the divorce is uncontested but collateral issues such as property or support remain in dispute, a court has jurisdiction to grant a divorce prior to the trial of the remaining issues. This is likely to be done where the

granting of a divorce does not prejudice a spouse's right to pursue collateral claims. See *Gibson v. Gibson* (1999), 1 R.F.L. (5th) 60 (Man. C.A.); *Spiring v. Spiring* (2004), 247 D.L.R. (4th) 342 (Man. Q.B.); and *Nicolaides v. Nicolaides* (2008), 48 R.F.L. (6th) 78 (Ont. S.C.J.); additional reasons at (2008), 48 R.F.L. (6th) 91 (Ont. S.C.J.); leave to appeal refused (2008), 57 R.F.L. (6th) 275 (Ont. Div. Ct.).

9. In 1990, Parliament amended the *Divorce Act* to specify that the court can dismiss an application filed under the Act or strike out any other pleadings filed under the Act if the spouse has failed to remove any barriers to the remarriage of the other spouse within the latter's religion. See s. 21.1. An example where this power may be used is where a husband petitioning for divorce unreasonably refuses to request a "get" from a Jewish Rabbinical Court or a wife refuses to consent to the request. The amendment was an attempt to prevent spouses from using the "get" as a bargaining chip, but its general language could affect practices of other religions. See ss. 2(4), (5), (6) and 56(5) of the Ontario *Family Law Act* for similar provincial legislation. For a review of the case law dealing with these provisions, see *Tanny v. Tanny* (2000), 8 R.F.L. (5th) 427 (Ont. S.C.J.). See generally, Syrtash, "Removing Barriers to Religious Remarriage in Ontario: Rights and Remedies" (1986-87) 1 C.F.L.Q. 309 and Syrtash, *Religion and Culture in Canadian Family Law* (Toronto: 1992).

10. A bill to amend the *Divorce Act* (Bill C-22) was introduced into the House of Commons in 2002, but the bill died with the 2004 election call. There are references to Bill C-22 in this book because it raised issues worthy of discussion and a revised version of this bill may be re-introduced. However, the proposed changes to the *Divorce Act* focused mainly on issues relating to children and so the references to Bill C-22 in this chapter are few and brief.

11. Only a spouse or both spouses together can apply for a divorce under the *Divorce Act*. As noted in Chapter 2, *CREATING A VALID MARRIAGE*, same-sex couples who married following the decisions altering the definition of marriage discovered that they could not obtain a divorce under the *Divorce Act* because it defined "spouse" as "either of a man or woman who are married to each other". Eventually, a court ruled that this aspect of the *Divorce Act* was unconstitutional and granted a lesbian couple a divorce. See *M. (M.) v. H. (J.)* (2004), 2004 CarswellOnt 5548 (S.C.J.). The *Civil Marriage Act* of 2005 amended s. 2(1) of the *Divorce Act* to redefine spouse as "either of two persons who are married to each other".

(2) The Social Context of Divorce

AMBERT, *DIVORCE: FACTS, CAUSES AND CONSEQUENCES*

(Ottawa: Vanier Institute of the Family, revised edition, 2005) (References omitted)

Understanding the Numbers

Is it true that "one out of every two marriages breaks up"?

Definitely not. The latest estimates by Statistics Canada (2005) put the risk of divorce by the 30th wedding anniversary at 38% for the country as a whole — ranging from 17% in Newfoundland and 50% in Quebec. This compares with an estimated 44% in the U.S. For instance, in 2003, 16% of the divorces included husbands who had already been divorced at least once and 15% involved wives who had also been divorced before (Statistics Canada, 2005). Although there is some overlap in the sense that some divorces are subsequent divorces for both, these numbers mean that the probability of divorcing for a first marriage is lower because, as we see later, remarriages have a higher divorce risk than first ones.

How do we measure divorce?

The most commonly used method to measure divorce for the purpose of international comparison is the rate for every 1,000 or 100,000 people in the population. In 2002, this rate in Canada was 2.2 per 1,000 people in the population. This method of calculation allows us to say that there are more or fewer divorces in any year per 1,000 or 100,000 population.

Holding the denominator constant allows us to see fluctuations in the annual rates. But there are two main problems with this measure.

First, this measure is sensitive to a population's age distribution. For instance, as seniors become proportionately more numerous, the number of divorces goes down, thus lowering the overall divorce rate even though younger people might still be divorcing at a high rate. The second problem is that, when we calculate divorces per 100,000 population, children are included as well as single persons. All of these people reduce the divorce rate because they can't divorce: they are not even married! A more realistic method is to focus on those who are eligible to divorce, namely legally married couples, which gives us a divorce rate per 1,000 or 100,000 married couples. But, then again, this still includes those who are in a second or subsequent marriage and is not therefore a perfect method for the purpose of studying the rates of divorce for *first* marriages. This approach shows that in:

1981, there were 1,180 divorces per 100,000 married couples, or a rate of 1.2%;

1987, there were 1,585 divorces per 100,000 married couples, or a rate of 1.6%;

1995, there were 1,222 divorces per 100,000 married couples, or a rate of 1.2%.

In other words, both in 1981 and 1995, the risk of divorcing in any of these two years for a married couple was 1.2% compared to 1.6% in 1987, the peak year. Of course, the lifetime risk of divorcing for a couple is higher than the annual 1.2% — as seen earlier, the overall prediction is around 38% if current rates hold. ...

But is this the entire story?

No. Several points need to be emphasized.

1. Predictions are just that: predictions. They are made on the basis of yearly trends. Unfortunately, the "yearly" is often forgotten in heated discussions! Thus, predictions have to be constantly revised to fit new realities.

2. Some of the divorces that take place each year are actually second or third divorces for some people. These redivorces increase the overall number of divorces and artificially inflate the proportions of people who divorce during their lifetime because some people contribute more than their fair share to the divorce rate.

3. Consequently, young people who marry for the first time are worried about these dire predictions. Keep in mind that the divorce rate for *first* marriages is lower — probably closer to 30%. In other words, first marriages have a 70% chance of surviving and even thriving! Furthermore, some couples are at even lower risk of divorcing, as we will see later on.

4. Cohabitation is rising. The end result is that when a cohabiting union breaks up, the dissolution does not appear in divorce statistics. It is said that cohabitations which break up constitute hidden divorces and, therefore, divorce rates do not provide an accurate picture of conjugal dissolution rates (combining cohabitations + marriages that end). However, including all cohabitations under the rubric of conjugal relations may be misleading and so would be equating their break up with divorce. Indeed, many cohabitations last a few months at best and merely constitute a "glorified" dating period. Including cohabitations of two years or more might be more appropriate. This is an issue which requires more thought and research.

5.   Finally, an unknown number of couples separate but never divorce. This type of conjugal dissolution may be as real as a divorce, yet it does not appear in divorce statistics. So, when caveats 4 and 5 are put together, it is certainly true that at least one out of every two unions ends in dissolution. And the percentage may become even higher if young people or younger cohorts continue to enter into cohabitation as a first union. But unions are not necessarily the equivalent of marriages.

Are divorce rates going up or down?

They have gone down substantially during the 1990s. In Table 2, Statistics Canada presents us with the following rates of divorce throughout the years:

TABLE 2			
Years	# of divorces	Rates per 100,000 pop.	Rates per 100,000 Married couples
1921	558	6.4	N/A
1941	2,462	21.4	N/A
1961	6,563	36.0	N/A
1968*	11,343	54.8	N/A
1969	26,093	124.2	N/A
1981	67,671	271.8	1,174.4
1985**	61,980	253.6	1,103.3
1986	78,304	298.8	1,301.6
1987***	96,200	362.3	1,585.5
1990	80,998	295.8	1,311.5
1995	77,636	262.2	1,221.9
1997	67,408	224.8	N/A
2000	70,292	228.4	N/A
2002	70,155	223	N/A
2003	70,828	224	N/A
* Reform of Divorce Laws ** Divorce Act ("no fault") *** Peak year			

Divorce has greatly increased since 1968 when the Divorce Laws entered into effect; in fact, we have experienced a five-fold increase from 1968 to 1995. Divorce rates peaked in 1987 in Canada and in 1981 in the U.S. and have since stabilized at lower levels. However, Table 2 also indicates a slight upward trend since 2000. [There are] large provincial variations: Quebec consistently shows the highest rates with the Maritime provinces the lowest ones along with Saskatchewan and Alberta. Whether rates will go up or down in the future largely depends on demographic factors and on people's lifestyle as well as values. For instance, as more young couples choose to cohabit before marriage and as the "children of divorce" who are at a higher risk of divorcing enter into marriage themselves, there are chances that divorce rates could keep rising — as has been the case for Quebec in particular. Or, if the rates of never-married women bearing children skyrocketed, divorce rates would go down for their cohort as these never-married mothers have far fewer chances of ever marrying — but their children's cohorts would then have higher divorce rates, assuming they married. ... Furthermore, if the proportion of adults between 25 and 45 in the population declines, the rates of divorce will go down because, as indicated below, this is the age range most susceptible to divorce. As you can see, predictions depend on many "ifs."

How many people divorce many times?

There is no readily available information on this for Canada at this time but Statistics Canada estimate that well over 16% of divorces are redivorces for one or both spouses. In the U.S., one third of all divorces occurring each year are redivorces for at least one of the spouses. ...

How many children are involved in divorce cases?

The number of *dependent* children involved in a parental divorce was 36,252 in 1998 — the total number of divorces had been 69,088 — compared to over one million in the U.S. Many couples who divorce either have no children or do not have as many as same-age couples who remain married, in great part because a good proportion of them divorce within the first few years of marriage. Those who have children do not have as many as other couples of their age who remain married.

What about predictions that 40 to 50% of children will experience the divorce of their parents?

Not too realistic! If we consider that only about 38% of all marriages may end in divorce and that, as seen earlier, a proportion of these marriages, perhaps 50%, do not include dependent children, then this prediction is far too high. However, some couples do divorce when their children are adult. Furthermore, many children who live in cohabitational families also experience the dissolution of their parents' union. Celine Le Bourdais and her colleagues (2004) have found that Quebec children whose parents cohabit have a threefold chance of going through a parental separation compared to children in married families; the risk for the remainder of Canadian children was nearly 5 times greater than that of children with married parents. For these children, the results are the same, even though they are not included in the divorce statistics.

Who is responsible for children after divorce?

Both in Canada and the U.S., children are predominantly in the physical custody of their mother, that is, they live with her. Only about 10 to 12% of children live with their father — a percentage which has not changed much over the years. However, joint custody has become more common and now accounts for about 42% of custody cases: it means that both parents have equal decision-making rights and access to the children. Even in these cases, however, most children live with their mother. Mothers prefer sole custody but are favorable to joint custody when they perceive their ex-husbands to be good parents and when the post-marital relationship is not conflictual [*sic*]. ...

Resident fathers compared to resident mothers are more likely to be remarried or have another adult living with them. They also tend to have older children, perhaps because smaller children require too much work. For men, residence with their children results in a better father-child relationship and contributes to fathers' mental health. ... They are less subjected to feelings of lack of control over their paternal situation, as is the case among non-residential fathers. However, resident fathers find their role constraining — they have less freedom and more demands are placed on them — and are less happy as persons than visiting fathers. ... Mother and father custody have somewhat different but equivalent results for children; on average, neither is as good in terms of child outcomes as a stable two-parent situation. ...

How common is remarriage?

Less so than before because of the increasing tendency to cohabit after divorce. Approximately 70% and 58%, respectively, of divorced men and women remarry in Canada, excluding Quebec, and remarriage is more common among immigrants than Canadian-born citizens. In Quebec, remarriage has become a minority phenomenon because of a preference for cohabitation.

How many families with dependent children are stepfamilies?

... In 2001, 12% of families composed of a couple with children were stepfamilies, for a total of 503,100. Of these stepfamilies, 50% included only the mother's child(ren) from a previous union; 10% included exclusively the father's child; 32% were the result of a child having been born to a union in addition to the children born from previous ones, and 8% consisted of both spouses' children from previous unions. ... About 10% of all Canadian children under the age of 12 are living in a stepfamily.

For the entire country, half of stepfamilies are remarriages. In Quebec, nearly 75% of all stepfamilies are common-law unions whereas less than 45% of stepfamilies are common-law in Ontario, the Prairies, and B.C.

Are remarriages as stable as first marriages?

No. Although remarriages are as happy as first marriages, controlling for the number of years married, remarriages after a divorce have a higher rate of dissolution, probably 10% higher. ... But remarriages that endure often outlast a first marriage.

Why are they less stable? First, remarriages are constituted of persons who have already shown that they can divorce once; they may be more accepting of divorce as a solution and more ready to have recourse to it a second time. Second, spouses in remarriages may be less willing to compromise and may become disenchanted more rapidly. Third, the structure itself of remarriages is a more complex one when children are brought in along with ex-spouses and ex-in-laws. Fourth, there are fewer norms that guide these relationships, making it more difficult for the spouses to feel secure within their respective roles. Remarriages without children from previous unions or with children born to the union have a rate of divorce equivalent to that of first marriages. ...

Are cohabitations as stable as marriages?

... *They definitely are not* and this is true in most countries. ... Furthermore, cohabitations tend to dissolve more rapidly than marriages. More than 50% of all these unions end in dissolution within five years. ... However, cohabitations are somewhat more stable in Quebec than in the rest of Canada. For instance, it is estimated, based on 2001 information, that 55% of Quebec women aged 30 to 39 who opted for a cohabitation as a first union will go through a separation compared to 66% among women in the other provinces. ...

Causes and Consequences

What causes divorce?

Cultural factors

Multiple, interlocking factors have contributed to the rapid rise of divorce in Canada and other western countries in the second part of the 20th century. These same factors have contributed to the maintenance of high rates of divorce into the 21st century.

1. Divorce rates were already slowly inching up in the 19th century as the result of secularization trends, the liberalization of norms concerning individual choice, and the lessening of religious influence. The religious aspect is now largely missing in the institution of marriage: this is often referred to as the desacralization of marriage. Marriage has become an individual choice rather than a covenant before God and this change has contributed to the acceptance of its temporal nature.

2. These sociocultural trends later came to influence the liberalization of divorce laws. In turn, easier divorce laws, such as those promulgated in 1968 and 1985, are usually followed by an increase in divorce. Then, such laws signal the normalization of divorce. Hence, divorce lost its stigma and became socially accepted. These cultural and legal factors have made it easier for people to be less attached to marriage as an *institution* and consequently to turn to divorce.

3. The trends toward individualism that began two centuries ago have resulted in an emphasis on rights rather than duties. When individualism is coupled with an ideology of gratification, particularly sexual and psychological, where people are encouraged to be "happy" and "fulfilled," it follows that the spouses' mentality about their marriage is affected. ... Marriage is no longer seen as an institution centered on mutual responsibilities but is now based on the pursuit of happiness, fulfillment, and companionship. More is demanded of marriage in terms of personal gratification. As Simons et al. (1996:219) put it, "If the raison d'être for marriage is mutual love and support, it is difficult for people to justify staying in a relationship where this is no longer present."

4. Along with the trends above, Canadians and Americans have developed a lower threshold of tolerance when their marriage does not meet with their expectations for personal fulfillment. ... All things considered, while more is expected of marriage, couples are also less tolerant about its challenges and less willing to shoulder the sacrifices it may require. At the positive level, however, this also means that women now leave abusive relationships that would have kept them captive 40 years ago.

Demographic factors

1. Youthful marriages are a risk factor to divorce: young people may be in a less good position to marry for the right reason. Furthermore, they are not as mature as older persons to cope with conflict and their personalities have not yet stabilized. Very young people also have low incomes.

2. Low incomes and poverty are risk factors for divorce as is a very rapid upward social mobility where the acquisition of money and status is a prime mover. This may be

because such a pursuit of materialism takes time away from relationships or reflects values which are incompatible with a good conjugal life.

3. At first, this may appear counterintuitive, but cohabitation prior to marriage is a strong risk factor to divorce. ... Le Bourdais et al. (2000) found, in the General Social Survey, that, in the 20- to 30-year-old group, 63% of those women whose first relationship was a cohabitation had separated by 1995 compared to 33% of those who had married first. Of course, the first figure included women who had cohabited and had separated before marrying their partner and others who had gone on to marry this partner and then separate. However, cohabiting couples with their own children have a higher level of stability than other cohabitants. ... Nevertheless, ... their risk for divorce is still much higher than those of married couples with children. In a nutshell, cohabitations have high rates of dissolution and, when they are followed by marriage (to the same partner or to another one), they become a risk factor for divorce — although much less so for couples who are engaged before deciding to cohabit. ...

4. Another demographic factor related to divorce is solo mothering, perhaps in great part because mothers who have children without a partner are more likely to cohabit before marrying — if they marry at all. Furthermore, families with a resident stepfather are less stable than families with a resident stepmother. ...

5. Remarriages are a risk factor for divorce that has become more prevalent — in great part because of the complexities of reconstituted families. ... For instance, in 2000, 33% of all marriages had one or both partners who had been previously divorced and, of these, well over a third included two previously-divorced persons (Statistics Canada, 2003).

6. Men are more likely to divorce when there is a high proportion of unmarried women with them in the labor force and the same occurs for women, who work in domains with a male preponderance. ... These conditions raise married persons, especially men's, chances of meeting a more attractive alternative to their current spouse.

7. Parental divorce correlates with higher divorce rates among their children later on, especially so when the parental marriage had a low level of conflict — such parents are less committed to marriage and may transmit this value to their offspring. ...

8. Low religiosity is related to lower marital happiness and a higher propensity to divorce. ... Furthermore, religious and to some extent racial heterogamy are risk factors for marital instability, perhaps because of a lack of shared values. ...

Reasons for divorcing that people give, such as alcoholism, domestic violence, adultery, "didn't get along," and "no longer loved each other" are actually caused by the socio-demographic factors enumerated above. For instance, without an emphasis on individualism and gratification, people would not divorce because they "fell out of love" or because they did not get along. In countries where marriage is strongly institutionalized within a context of family solidarity, these reasons would be considered frivolous. In a society where divorce is more difficult to obtain and less acceptable, only "strong" reasons, such as abuse and abandonment, are tolerated. Therefore, before people decide to divorce on particular grounds, a social and cultural climate has to exist that offers a legitimate framework for their reasons. Furthermore, personal grounds for divorce such as fighting, alcoholism, violence, tend to be mentioned more by couples with some of the demographic characteristics discussed above, such as youthful marriages, prior cohabitation, and poverty. Thus, cultural and demographic factors related to divorce "push" people out of marriage and into divorce via their own personal reasons.

Consequences of divorce

In this section, I will proceed by presenting the two most salient consequences of divorce: poverty and an increased risk for the development of problems among the children involved. Then, consequences for adults will be discussed. These consequences apply both to Canada, the U.S., and to many other countries.

Divorce causes poverty

Divorce is a direct cause of poverty for a large proportion of women and their children, although a sizeable proportion of divorces are themselves caused by economic hardship. Once separation takes place, the mother and child unit *becomes* even poorer in these cases (Statistics Canada, 1999). Studies [from the 1990s] indicate that, in the first year after divorce, and adjusting for family size, women's household income plummets by about 20 to 40% while men's declines far less. Even three years after divorce, women's income remains far below what they had during marriage and far below their ex-husbands' current income.

Ex-husbands, compared to ex-wives, are less likely to be poor because their income is generally higher, they do not have full care of their children with all the attendant expenses, and their support payments are usually not crippling. Nevertheless, it should be added that in a decade when most families have two breadwinners, men lose far more economically than in the past when they divorce, especially those who are married to a high-earning wife. As support payments become better enforced, these two factors may contribute in the long run to dissuade many men from endangering their marriage.

Another way of looking at this is to consider single-mother families. In 2002, according to the Vanier Institute of the Family (2004), 35% of all female lone-parent families lived in poverty while many more hovered just one precarious step above the level. It should also be noted that the younger the children are at the time of parental divorce or common-law dissolution, the more likely they are to be poor. This is because they have younger parents who earn less. On average, single parents who are poor have an income that is 40% below the poverty line. This is dire poverty. ...

Increased risk of problems for children of divorced parents

In a nutshell, although most children do not experience developmental problems, divorce is certainly a strong risk factor ... and a source of stressors. Divorce is, above all, an emotionally painful transition and ... it can "create lingering feelings of sadness, longing, worry, and regret that coexist with competent psychological and social functioning." Connidis (2003) remarks that relationships are changed after divorce and have to be renegotiated many times over the years, and the effects are felt across several living generations within a family. Although average differences are *not* huge, children whose parents are divorced (and even after they are remarried or repartnered) are *more likely* than children whose parents remain together to:

- suffer from depression, anxiety, and other emotional disorders;
- exhibit behavioral problems including hyperactivity, aggressiveness, fighting, and hostility;
- become young offenders;
- do less well in school and stay less long in school; [and]
- have more relationship problems, in part due to their behavioral problems.

Finally, when they are older, adults whose parents divorced during their childhood and teen years, compared to adults from intact two-parent families, tend to:

- have had a child out of wedlock more often, particularly during adolescence;
- have achieved lower educational levels;
- be more often unemployed and do less well economically; [and]
- have more marital problems and divorce more.

Adults are more likely to report a less happy childhood when their parents separated (Williams, 2001). As well, a study by Boyd and Norris (1995) has found that older children of divorced parents leave home earlier than others. They leave home in even greater numbers when their custodial parents remarry and even more so when both parents remarry. A consequence of this earlier home leaving is that for many it becomes too expensive to continue their education. This, in turn, contributes to lower occupational skills and higher unemployment. Frederick and Boyd (1998) have shown, on the basis of Statistics Canada data, that 80 to 84% of men and women aged 20–44 who lived with their two parents when they were 15 years old completed high school. This compares with figures ranging from 65 to 73% for those whose parents had divorced, including those whose parents had remarried.

There are, however, several cautions that are advised in interpreting the above information

The first is that, among an unknown number of children, *some* of what appear to be negative effects of divorce already existed before parental separation. That is to say, many children and adolescents who are difficult after divorce were also difficult before, either because of their personalities, peer pressure, problems with parents, or interparental conflict and lack of parenting investment. Therefore, when studying children after divorce, it is important to know how they were before the divorce. Even so, researchers who utilize a longitudinal methodology have found that, even when these past characteristics are taken into account, there still were effects specifically attributable to divorce. ...

The second important point is that whatever statistics you read concerning the negative outcomes of children "of divorce," they do *not* apply to the *majority* of these children. What these statistics indicate is that children of divorced parents have a greater *risk* of developing problems than children whose parents remain together. ...

Nevertheless, I do not wish to err in the opposite direction and shrug off the negative effects of divorce. *They are real and costly for children*, parents, and schools, as well as the welfare and health care systems. ... Furthermore, as the concept of distress implies, at the time of their parents' separation, children generally suffer a great deal: most do not want them to divorce; they miss the other parent; when little, they may feel that they are partly to blame for the divorce; some desperately try to get their parents together again; they are sad; some cry a lot while others lash out and develop temporary behavioral problems.

There are six main explanations for children's negative outcomes following a parental divorce

1. As we have seen, *poverty,* or even a *significant reduction in financial resources*, so often follows divorce, and is a root cause of children's problems. ... In the case of divorce, when children are poor or become poor, they experience a great many stressors in their lives. This is because divorce is not a single event but a series of transitions. To begin with, at least 55% of Canadian women and their children move after separation ...; they often have to move into more crowded and dilapidated housing, where there is more noise and pollution. They may be less healthy as a result and

more stressed. The neighborhood may be less safe, have more children who are equally poor, and who do less well in school, and engage more in delinquency.

Moreover, the custodial parent, generally the mother, has difficulty making ends meet and may work long hours. When she returns home, she may be tired and generally has less time to devote to her children. As a result, children of divorced mothers who are poor or who are financially insecure (near poor) may receive less attention, guidance, supervision, encouragement, and affection than other children. These mothers may not be able, for a variety of reasons, to monitor their child's school progress or lack thereof. When the children are out of school, they may be home alone or with peers, all unsupervised, or on the streets so to speak. Unsupervised children are far more likely than others to engage in delinquent acts and premature sex. Thus, if we were to eliminate or even significantly reduce child poverty, the consequences of divorce on children would be far less negative.

2. The above [paragraphs have] already hinted at the second cause of children's problems after divorce: diminished parenting. Divorce creates a series of stressors for parents, particularly for the custodial parents. In turn, as we have seen, these stressors diminish parenting time, skills, expressed affection, and increase parenting instability, harshness, or yet permissiveness. After divorce, many parents experience a dramatic downfall in their ability to care for their children, to provide them with a regular routine, to shelter them from stressors and dangers. Faced with their own problems, many divorced parents too often become their children's pals and abdicate their parental responsibilities. These adolescents then lack guidance and authoritative parenting. Amato and Gilbreth (1999) suggest that children of divorce have better outcomes when *non-residential fathers* are more than "Sunday daddies" and *behave as parents* — that is, when they provide emotional and practical support, make behavioral demands, place limits on what can be done, and administer consistent discipline.

3. Many divorced parents, both as a result of divorce and poverty, are so burdened emotionally that they become, at least temporarily, depressed while others initiate a desperate search for a new mate that makes them far less available to their children and responsive to their needs. All of these factors bring instability and insecurity to the home life and thereby burden children emotionally. Carlson and Corcoran (2001) have found that a decent family income, mothers' sound psychological functioning, and a good home environment, including adequate parenting, reduce or eliminate the potentially negative effects of family structure.

4. Parents who continue quarrelling and verbally abusing each other in front of their children after divorce cause immense distress to their offspring. Continued parental conflict — especially when the children are caught in the middle — may result in depression, hostility, aggressiveness, and other acting-out activities on the part of children. Moreover, parental conflict presents a dysfunctional role model. Children learn that disagreements can be solved only by fighting. This lesson may carry further negative consequences down the road in their own relationships.

    However, divorces that end severe inter-parental conflict have positive consequences for children; in contrast, low-conflict marriages that end in divorce have a strong negative effect on children, perhaps because, from the children's point of view, they are so unexpected and unwelcome. ...

5. Some of the causes of divorce are actually in part causes of the troubled home in which the children lived during their parents' marriage. This would apply mainly to those couples which were conflictual [sic] and were ineffective parents because of

their troubled relationship. Thus, as we have seen earlier, these children had pre-existing problems which divorce may further exacerbate. ...

6. A last cause is one that is rarely mentioned and it has to do with genetics. ... A proportion of people who divorce do so because they are difficult, conflictual [*sic*], or problematic individuals who pass on these predispositions to their children via genetic inheritance. These children are already predisposed to being difficult by temperament, have a home environment which fosters these difficulties, and the divorce situation generally exacerbates their condition.

Are there differences by age and sex to children's adjustment to divorce?

Yes. Girls adapt generally better to divorce although not necessarily to the remarriage of a custodial mother. There is, however, a wide diversity of adaptation levels depending on the child's personality and the family circumstances. The same applies in terms of age. On the one hand, very small children, younger than 4, may not note the absence of a parent they had rarely seen; if the mother who has always been their primary caretaker functions well, they will not be significantly affected. They will also more than likely adapt well to a parental remarriage. On the other hand, children between 4 and 10 may be the most negatively affected because they are not yet mature enough to understand their loss and their changing family circumstances. ... They may even blame themselves for the divorce.

Moreover, when poverty is present, these young children are likely to be even more affected than adolescents, particularly in terms of their intellectual development. New research clearly indicates that poverty during the early childhood years hinders cognitive and verbal development. ...

Even so, older children can also be significantly affected by the six main causes of negative outcomes discussed earlier. For adolescents, a particularly difficult situation arises when the custodial parent loses the opportunity to communicate with and supervise them. Adolescence is already an age when "temptations" towards deviance abound and a youth who is bereft of parental support may succumb to detrimental peer pressures. School work may suffer accordingly. Adolescent girls whose parents have separated, are at higher risk than others of becoming sexually active and pregnant. ... This risk is further elevated when their custodial mother is openly active sexually.

Does parental remarriage help children?

There is not a large body of research on this question in Canada. In the U.S., studies are finding that, while a custodial mother's remarriage helps the family financially, and may be very good for the mother, results are more mixed for children. ... Often remarriage results in additional negative consequences for children, particularly girls who had a close relationship with their mother. These girls may resent the intruder. In my research, some women students have written that they had purposely destroyed their mother's remarriage by becoming horrendous and behaving very badly toward the new husband. For their part, boys are able to escape as they tend, in adolescence, to spend less time at home — which may in itself lead to delinquency. Still on the negative side, girls are more likely to be sexually abused by their stepfathers or mothers' boyfriends than by their own fathers. ... We have already mentioned that older adolescents and young adults tend to leave home earlier once their custodial parent remarries. This may be a result of conflict with the new stepparent, or because the new couple does not make them feel welcome, or because they are subtly or not so subtly "encouraged" to leave.

On the positive side, younger children usually adapt better, especially when they have always known the stepparent. Many children do enjoy or benefit from the presence and affection of a stepparent. Many boys are advantaged by the addition of an authoritative adult male role model in the family. ... Children may also benefit from an extension of their kinship network with the addition of stepgrandparents and stepsiblings. Studies of young adults whose custodial parent's *remarriage had endured* have found that they were strongly attached to their reconstructed family and benefited emotionally from it. It is thus possible that some of the positive effects of a parent's good remarriage do not appear until later on in adulthood.

What are the consequences of divorce for adults?

On the negative side, besides poverty for a proportion of women, there is often a loss of social support, mainly from ex-in-laws and friends whom the couple shared. Elder women and those with little employment experience have a more difficult time. The spouse who is left generally suffers more, at least in the first three years. ... Rates of alcohol abuse go up among divorced men and depression among divorced women as well as a general feeling of being less healthy. ... However, let's keep in mind that remaining in a bad marriage will also produce the same noxious effects.

In my own study (Ambert, 1989) and that of other researchers since, many divorced persons admit that they are not any happier and even are more unhappy than during their marriage. In fact, Waite et al. (2002) have found that even unhappily married people who divorce were not necessarily happier five years later than those who had remained married. Divorce generally involves a period of stress, instability, loneliness, hurt feelings, and often hostility. That period lasts a few months to two years but may persist after five years. Furthermore, as shown by the high rates of divorce in remarriages and dissolution of subsequent cohabitations, *one* divorce often triggers many other unpleasant passages.

On the positive side, divorce is or should be a good thing when there is abuse, alcoholism, and severe conflict. It can also be functional for the spouse of a person who is criminal, severely emotionally disturbed, or is chronically unemployed. But at best one third of all marriages that end fall under these categories or are "bad" marriages from the spouses' perspectives. In fact, nearly one third of all marriages ending in divorce were "average to very good" marriages for both spouses, and another third were good to very good marriages for one of the spouses — in the latter case, generally for the one who does not want to divorce.

For many, especially women, divorce results in the finding of new strengths, the building of supportive relationships, the relief from fear, peace and quiet. For many as well, it means a new love that remains "until death do us apart." There is such a thing as a "successful" divorce. ... But, often, the ex-spouses have to work hard at it when they share children. All things being said, even for adults, divorce is no cure all.

For society as a whole, *the dissolution of average to very good marriages and cohabitations*, is a costly proposition. It is so in moral terms (after all, what can be said in favor of the "virtue" of a society where relationships become part of the throw-away culture?), in terms of consequent problems for children, including juvenile delinquency, welfare costs for those single-parent families that fall into poverty, health costs, as well as a loss of productivity on the part of the affected adults and older children.

Conclusions

The phenomenon of divorce is a far more complex issue than generally believed. Furthermore, statistics pertaining to divorce are difficult to understand and, as a result, are frequently misinterpreted. Overall, over a third of all marriages in Canada end in divorce and the rate is higher for remarriages and especially cohabitations. For the latter, the rate hovers around 60%. Currently, there are no solid predictions of either a sharp decline or a sharp rise in divorce rates in the near future. It is regrettable that we do not have more information regarding the dissolution of cohabitations, especially when they involve children. ...

Divorce and remarriage are *adult* institutions. That is, they were intended to separate couples who could no longer live together and to allow the ex-spouses to repartner. As institutions, divorce and remarriage are not necessarily in the best interest of the children and, as seen above, divorce is not necessarily good for adults either, nor are high rates functional for society.

We have seen that divorce is often accompanied by poverty or a significant reduction in financial resources. This factor contributes to amplifying the negative effects of divorce on the mother-child family unit and on children's life chances. In some European societies, particularly Norway and Sweden, the social safety net compensates greatly so that single-mother families have a (low) rate of poverty similar to that of two-parent families. The negative consequences of divorce for children do not disappear entirely but are less pronounced than they are in Canada and the U.S.

We have also seen that a sizeable proportion of marriages that end in divorce were actually quite "salvageable," and that many of these ex-spouses are no happier after. One cannot but help to wonder if couples who marry should not be more encouraged to face the inevitability of ups and downs in relationships, and I am not referring here to severe conflict, which after all, afflicts only about a third of divorcing couples. After 25 years of studying divorce, I have come to conclude that along with the necessary divorces, too many others are avoidable and even useless; the same remarks probably apply to serious cohabitational unions that dissolve.

It is often said that the family has become an outdated institution: the high rates of divorce, cohabitation, and births to solo mothers are often used to justify this statement. Is this true? No. What is true is that high rates of conjugal dissolution (marriage + cohabitation) *complicate* family life but do not destroy it. As I document elsewhere (Ambert, 2005), families fulfill more functions now than was the case 50 years ago. Thus, families are currently more needed by society than ever. However, when families (which I define as being intergenerational, not just a matter of couples) are fractured because of parental divorce and then reassembled, or not, by repartnering, adults' lives become more complex and often less functional for the care and socialization of children. ...

NOTES AND QUESTIONS

1. The divorce statistics do not include separated married couples who never divorce or unmarried couples whose relationship has ended. In *Custody, Access and Child Support: Findings from the National Longitudinal Survey of Children and Youth* (Canadian Department of Justice, 1999), Marcil Gratton and N. and C. Le Broudrais found that almost half of all children from broken marriages had not seen their parents divorce after three years of separation and after five years after separation this percentage was still 28. This suggests that there may well be a significant number of married couples who separate but never divorce. The authors also found that children whose parents separated came disproportionately from common-law unions. For the 1983-84 cohort (children in the study born in those years), 60% of children whose parents cohabited but never married saw their parents separate before their tenth birthday. About 28% of children whose parents were in a common law relationship at the time of the child's birth and subsequently married experienced their parent's separation before their tenth birthday. Only 13% of children born of married parents who had not cohabited before their marriage saw their parents separate before their tenth birthday.

2. Roger Sauve reported in a study for The Vanier Institute of the Family entitled *The Current State of Canadian Family Finances: 2006 Report* (2007) (available online at the Institute's Web site), that 7.8% of all families had incomes in 2004 below the Statistics Canada low income cut-offs (a frequently used, but controversial, basis for determining relative poverty levels). Families headed by divorced, separated or never-married mothers had a poverty rate of 36%. Although this was by far the highest poverty rate of any family type, it was down from 42.6% in 1990. The improvement was largely due to increased participation of the mothers in the workforce. The rate for

male lone-parent families was 14.2%. Another family type with a high poverty rate of 18.4% in 2004 consisted of a married couple with children in which there was only one earner.

In "A Profile of Recently Divorced or Separated Mothers and Fathers" (2008), 38 Transition (Vanier Institute of the Family), Clarence Lochhead and Jenni Tipper report that recently separated or divorced mothers are more than twice as likely as recently separated or divorced fathers to have personal annual incomes of less than $30,000 (44% compared to 19%). Similarly, a comparison of total household income shows 28% of recently separated or divorced mothers below $30,000, compared to 12% of recently separated or divorced fathers.

3. In *Young v. Young*, 49 R.F.L. (3d) 117, [1993] 4 S.C.R. 3, Justice L'Heureux-Dubé described (at R.F.L. 208-211) several influential studies of the effects of divorce on children:

> I acknowledge at the outset the limits in applying such research to the wider population, as the studies to date have tended to focus on groups within a particular social class or locale. Furthermore, the conclusions of some studies, for example, those by Judith S. Wallerstein and Joan Berlin Kelly, *Surviving the Breakup: How Children and Parents Cope with Divorce* (New York: Basic Books, 1980), have been used to support a number of different propositions concerning the best interests of the child on divorce. (See M. Fineman, *The Illusion of Equality*, [(Chicago: University of Chicago Press: 1991)] at p. 118.) In addition, notions concerning the optimum child-rearing conditions on the breakdown of the marriage are subject to a degree of difference and controversy between professionals working in the field. This is illustrated, for example, in the contrasting conclusions reached by Goldstein, Freud, and Solnit [*Beyond the Best Interests of the Child* (New York: Free Press, 1979)], and those of Wallerstein and Kelly.

> Nonetheless, a number of conclusions about the effects of divorce on children emerge with remarkable consistency in all of the major studies and psychological literature on children after divorce. One of the most important of these is the role of conflict in the welfare of the child. Along with the quality of the relationship with the custodial parent and the ability to maintain contact with the non-custodial parent, there is substantial evidence that continuing conflict is the most important factor affecting the ability of children to readjust to the new family situation after divorce (Weisman, ["On Access After Parental Separation" (1992), 36 R.F.L. (3d) 35,] at pp. 47-48). It appears that, above and beyond the disruption caused by divorce or separation itself, it is the discord and disharmony within the family which are most damaging to children in the aftermath of divorce.

> Two of the major studies on divorce and the effects of conflict on the emotional and psychological well-being of children forcefully make the point that the ability to reduce conflict is crucial to the welfare of children. The study of Wallerstein and Kelly, although limited to white middle class families in California without previous clinical histories who volunteered to participate in the study, is the most comprehensive long-term study on the effects of divorce on children. A ten-year follow-up of the same subjects is reported in Judith S. Wallerstein and Sandra Blakeslee, *Second Chances: Men, Women, and Children a Decade after Divorce* (New York: Ticknor & Fields, 1989). Among the most significant findings of these two reports is that separation or divorce cannot be regarded as a discrete event to be dealt with once and for all, but is most often the beginning in a continuum of disruptive events in the life of the child. The stress resulting from changing family structures and reduced financial support following divorce in many cases continues to be experienced by children long after the divorce is final. While many children do adjust in such situations, the notion that children automatically can and do "get used to" new family situations in a relatively short period of time is not borne out by the results of the study. By all such indicators as success at educational endeavours and the later ability to establish stable personal and professional lives, children of divorce appear in general to be subject to more stresses than their counterparts in intact families. While the authors found considerable evidence that divorce was beneficial to the parents, there was no comparable evidence regarding children. The majority of such children neither experienced relief at the time of the divorce nor felt it had resulted in an improvement in their lives five years later. Moreover, Wallerstein and Blakeslee reported in the later study that problems and conflicts in some children resulting from divorce did not manifest themselves until much later, particularly in the case of girls, who, in the earlier study, had generally appeared to cope better with divorce than boys. Rather, it appears that the long-term effects of divorce cannot always be predicted from the reactions of children at the outset. (See Wallerstein and Blakeslee, at p. 15.)

> At the five-year point, Wallerstein and Kelly concluded that, while no factor could in every case be associated with a good outcome, the extent to which conflict between the parents had been resolved was the single most important factor in the well-being of the child. Following interviews ten years after their initial contact with the subjects, Wallerstein and Blakeslee again identified prolonged hos-

tility between the parents as the single most destructive outcome for the children of divorce. Children subject to fierce legal battles between parents appear to be the most vulnerable group, and ongoing litigation is consistently identified as detrimental to the welfare of children (*Second Chances*, at p. 196). Wallerstein and Kelly also determined, as have other researchers, that children generally fare best when they are able to maintain a continuing relationship with both parents. However, an equally important corollary to this conclusion is often ignored. That is, continued contact may only be in the best interests of the child where parents are not adversarial and where interaction between the child and the access parent is not beset by conflict. Where conflict cannot be resolved or minimized, the detriment of continued contact may outweigh the benefit, as forced co-operation between hostile parents may lead to further litigation and conflict, which itself extends and increases the difficulties faced by children. ...

These findings are largely corroborated in another U.S. study of the impact of divorce on children. Hetherington, Cox, and Cox in "Effects of Divorce on Parents and Children," in Michael E. Lamb, ed., *Nontraditional Families: Parenting and Child Development* (Hillsdale, N.J.: L. Erlbaum & Associates, 1982), in a study of white middle class preschool children in the custody of their mothers, focused on the effects of conflict on children by comparing its effects in both divorced and intact families. The role of conflict in the welfare of children is highly visible in this study, as the authors determined that two years after divorce, children in low conflict divorced families actually fared better than those in high conflict intact families. Other studies which have come to similar conclusions about the role of conflict in the adjustment of the child after divorce include: Edythe S. Ellison, "Issues Concerning Parental Harmony and Children's Psychosocial Adjustment" (1983), 53 Am. J. Orthopsychiatry 73; R.E. Emery, "Interparental Conflict and the Children of Discord and Divorce" (1982), 92 Psych. Bull. 310; M. Rutter, "Protective Factors in Children's Responses to Stress and Disadvantage," in Martha Whalen Kent and Jon E. Rolf, eds., *Primary Prevention of Psychopathology: Social Competence in Children*, Vol. 3, p. 49; J.R. Johnston, M. Kline, and J.M. Tschann, "Ongoing Postdivorce Conflict: Effects on Children of Joint Custody and Frequent Access" (1989), 59 Am. J. Orthopsychiatry 576. Thus, while most research discloses that continued contact with both parents after divorce is normally in the best interests of the child, that finding cannot be separated from a consideration of the degree of conflict to which the child will be subject (Weisman). Ironically, unrestricted access may, in some circumstances, cause the continuation of the very stresses from which the parties sought relief when they divorced, and the desire to maintain the pre-existing roles of each parent may in fact result in no ending at all.

4. In *Growing Up with a Single Parent: What Hurts, What Helps* (Cambridge: Harvard U. Press, 1994), Professors McLanahan and Sandfur set out their conclusion in the first two pages:

We have been studying this question for ten years, and in our opinion the evidence is quite clear: *Children who grow up in a household with only one biological parent are worse off, on average, than children who grow up in a household with both of their biological parents, regardless of their parents' race or educational background, regardless of whether the parents are married when the child is born, and regardless of whether the resident parent remarries.* Compared with teenagers of similar background who grow up with both parents at home, adolescents who have lived apart from one of their parents during some period of childhood are twice as likely to drop out of high school, twice as likely to have a child before twenty, and one and a half times as likely to be "idle" — out of school and out of work — in their late teens and early twenties. [Emphasis in the original.]

At p. 3 they state:

Low income — and the sudden drop in income that is often associated with divorce — is the most important factor in children's lower achievement in single-parent homes, accounting for about half of the disadvantage. Inadequate parental guidance and attention and the lack of ties to community resources account for most of the remaining disadvantage.

They also suggest (at 7) that studies such as Furstenberg, Morgan, and Allison, "Paternal Participation and Children's Well-Being" (1987), 52 American Sociological Review 52 and King, "Nonresident Father Involvement and Child Well-Being: Can Dads Make a Difference?" (1994), 1 Journal of Family Issues 78 have found little evidence that high levels of contact with both biological parents can reduce or eliminate the negative consequences associated with family breakdown.

5. The complexity of the subject of the impact of divorce on children and the increasing sophistication of the research is evident in Kelly, "Current Research on Children's Postdivorce Adjustment: No Simple Answers"

(1993), 31 Family and Conciliation Courts Review 29. The author reports that the research demonstrates that children, especially boys, of divorced parents face significantly more adjustment problems than children in families with two biological parents. However, when assessed years later, these children generally are functioning within normal limits. Ms. Kelly also states (at 34-35):

> Recent studies suggest that the relationship between child adjustment and conflict is neither universal, simple, nor particularly straightforward. ...

> It appears that, rather than discord *per se*, it is the *manner* in which parental conflict is expressed that may affect children's adjustment. ...

> These studies indicate that children can escape the negative consequences of parental conflict when they are not caught in it by their parents or when their parents avoid direct, aggressive expressions of their conflict in front of the child or use compromise styles of conflict resolution. [emphasis in original]

In addition, she reports (at 37) that findings are increasingly mixed or inconclusive regarding the role of the non-custodial parent in children's adjustment after divorce. She concludes as follows (at 45):

> Overall, the evidence suggests that when children begin the divorce experience in good psychological shape, with close or loving relationships with both parents, their adjustment will be maintained by continuing their relationship with both parents on a meaningful basis. There will be gender and age differences within this framework. Parents will maintain their children's positive adjustment by reducing their conflict or working their disputed issues out in a mediative or counseling forum and avoid placing their children in the middle of their struggles.

> When children are compromised by a highly conflicted marriage, compromised parent-child relationship, and a history of adjustment problems, there is no specific formula that will produce better adjustment for these youngsters after separation. Some will need counseling or other support systems and the collective resources of two struggling parents. Others will need relief from an abusive, critical or rejecting parent or from the anxiety and fear of violence between parents, thus enabling these children to benefit from the changes in their lives.

6. Carol Smart, Bren Neale and Amada Wade caution in *The Changing Experience of Childhood: Families and Divorce* (Cambridge: Polity Press, 2001) that policy makers have a tendency to characterize divorce as only harmful and to blame divorce for any negative characteristics detected in children of divorced parents. They label this tendency "harm-ism" and conclude (at 37-38):

> "Harm-ism" insists that the greatest harm to children is their parents' divorce; it pushes out or minimizes considerations of poverty, domestic violence, poor housing, inadequate financial provision and the possibility that an ongoing marriage might be worse than a divorce. It has developed an independent existence and is resistant to any evidence which might modify the harm thesis.

2. Conflict of Laws

(1) Jurisdiction

HINTER v. HINTER

(1996), 23 R.F.L. (4th) 401, 1996 CarswellOnt 2724 (Ont. Gen. Div.)

EPSTEIN J.: — This case involves questions of jurisdiction. The petitioner (wife) has commenced three separate proceedings against the husband. They are as follows:

(a) On 11 December 1995, action No. 95-28131 in Miami, Florida, against the husband for an injunction against domestic violence.

(b) On 28 December 1995, action No. 95-29645 in Miami, Florida, against the husband for support unconnected with divorce, and against R.C. Consulting Corporation and Jody-Jen Investments Limited, restraining the disposition of certain property.

(c) On 22 March 1996, a divorce petition against the husband in Ontario claiming a divorce, relief under the *Family Law Act* ... and corollary relief under the *Divorce Act* ...

The husband disputes the jurisdiction of the Ontario Court and moves for an order dismissing the petition in this action on the basis of this court's lack of jurisdiction, and for an order staying all claims on the grounds of duplication with the Florida proceedings.

The thrust of the husband's jurisdictional argument is that the wife was not ordinarily resident in Ontario for the 12 months prior to when the petition was issued in March of 1996. In fact, she was a resident of Miami, Florida. Secondly, the support claim ought not to proceed in two jurisdictions and the convenient forum for this claim is Florida. ...

The Facts

For the past two and a half years, the husband has been spending most of his time living and working in Amsterdam. He has come to Ontario periodically. When he did so, at least until November 1995, he stayed with the wife in their home in Toronto.

During this period of time, the wife alternated staying in Toronto and in a condominium in Miami, Florida. This condominium is in the name of a company that is owned by both parties. The key issue centres on the wife's connection with Florida. I find the facts relevant to this issue to be as follows:

(a) In mid-1994, the wife began to consider separation seriously;

(b) Some time that year, the wife started an intimate relationship with a man who resides in Florida. In fact, the wife from time to time works with this man in his business;

(c) The wife had at least reduced contact with her family doctor from October 1994 to September 1995;

(d) In November 1995, the wife told the husband that she did not want him in the Florida condominium at Christmas. Apparently, she spent Christmas 1995 in Florida with her new partner;

(e) On December 11, 1995, the wife started her first Florida action, in which she swore that she "lived" in Florida;

(f) On December 28, 1995, in her second Florida action, the wife swore two statements that the Florida condominium was "where she currently resides" and that she "is presently residing apart from the husband, in the state of Florida."

(g) An order has issued on consent out of the Florida court granting the wife exclusive use and occupancy of the matrimonial home;

(h) The wife's 1995 tax return is filed on the basis that she is a resident of Ontario;

(i) The wife is in Florida now. Virtually all of her affidavits in these various proceedings have been sworn there;

(j) Her house in Toronto has been according to her "stripped bare of all its contents"; yet, she has stayed in Florida rather than come here to investigate and deal with the situation;

(k) She has provided no evidence as to when she plans to return to Toronto. All she says is that she plans to "return to Toronto shortly."

It is also of note that in this divorce petition the wife states that both parties have lived in Ontario since 1980. However, she lists her husband's address as "unknown." Further, in this proceeding she has sworn an affidavit that she "is not a permanent resident of Florida." ...

Finally, to address one additional factual issue relevant to jurisdiction, I find that the husband is not ordinarily resident in Ontario. There is no evidence before me to the contrary and, in fact, the wife states in her Notice of Motion that the husband has been working and living in Amsterdam for the past 18 months.

The question is: does the evidence placed before the court by the husband support the dismissal of the petition or the staying of all claims for corollary relief and all claims under the *Family Law Act*, based on the failure of the parties to meet the residency requirement under the *Divorce Act*, and based on *forum conveniens*?

The Law

Section 3(1) of the *Divorce Act* reads as follows:

> A court in a province has jurisdiction to hear and determine a divorce proceeding if either spouse has been ordinarily resident in the province for at least one year immediately preceding the commencement of the proceeding.

Numerous cases have dealt with the proper interpretation to be given to the phrase "ordinarily resident". One of the earliest of these is *Thomson v. Minister of National Revenue*, [1946] S.C.R. 209, which dealt with the meaning of the phrase in question as used in the *Income War Tax Act*, R.S.C. 1927, c. 97. In the course of his reasons, Rand J. stated at page 224:

> The expression "ordinarily resident" carries a restricted signification, and although the first impression seems to be that of preponderance in time, the decisions on the English Act reject that view. It is held to mean residence in the course of the customary mode of life of the person concerned, and it is contrasted with special or occasional or casual residence. The general mode of life is, therefore, relevant to a question of its application.

In a separate concurring judgment, Estey J. stated at page 231:

> A reference to the dictionary and judicial comments upon the meaning of these terms indicates that one is "ordinarily resident" in the place where in the settled routine of his life he regularly, normally or customarily lives. One "sojourns" at a place where he unusually, casually or intermittently visits or stays. In the former the element of permanence; in the latter that of the temporary predominates. The difference cannot be stated in precise and definite terms, but each case must be determined after all of the relevant factors are taken into consideration, but the foregoing indicates in a general way the essential difference. It is not the length of the visit or stay that determines the question.

In *Hardy v. Hardy*, [1969] 2 O.R. 875 (H.C.), the petitioner was born in Ontario and resided there until he joined the army. He returned to his parents' home in Ontario while he was on leave. In arriving at the conclusion that the petitioner was "ordinarily resident" in Ontario, Houlden J. stated the test as follows at page 877:

> Where did the petitioner regularly, normally or customarily live in the year preceding the filing of the petition? Or using the test of Karminski, J., "Where was his real home in that period?"

The Ontario Court of Appeal has also dealt with this issue in *MacPherson v. MacPherson* (1976), 28 R.F.L. 106. In that case, the petitioner was born in Ontario and resided there until her marriage in 1968. The respondent husband was born in Glace Bay, Nova Scotia, where he resided until he came to Ontario in search of employment in 1965. The parties were married in Glace Bay and resided there until 1969, when they moved to Ontario. In 1973, the parties moved back to Glace Bay, where they established a home. Apart from a three-week long visit by the wife to Ontario, the family lived in Glace Bay until 1974, when the wife returned to Ontario. The wife stated that she never intended to establish a permanent residence in Glace Bay, while the husband maintained the opposite.

In concluding that the petitioner had not fulfilled the "ordinarily resident" requirement, Evans J.A. stated at page 112:

> In my opinion, the arrival of a person in a new locality with the intention of making a home in that locality for an indefinite period makes that person ordinarily resident in that community. In the present matter, while the husband and wife expressed opposing views as to their intention with respect to the establishment of a permanent residence in Nova Scotia, I do not believe that that intention alone can determine the issue of ordinary residence. Mrs. MacPherson left Ontario to reside with her husband and family with the intention of residing in Nova Scotia for an indefinite period of time. Her stated intention of returning to live in Ontario does not detract from the fact that she was ordinarily resident in Nova Scotia for that period which continued until she moved and established her residence in Ontario. The fact that Mr. MacPherson returned to Ontario in search of employment, leaving his wife and children in Nova Scotia, does not destroy the intimate community ties which Mrs. MacPherson had established in that province.
>
> In the view which I take of the matter, the petitioner wife has not complied with the jurisdictional requirement that she be ordinarily resident in Ontario for a period of at least one year immediately preceding the presentation of her petition. Accordingly the trial judge had no jurisdiction to grant a judgment nisi.

Interestingly, Evans J.A. referred in his reasons to the following comments of Somervell L.J. in *Macrae v. Macrae*, [1949] P. 397, [1949] 2 All E.R. 34 (C.A.):

> Ordinary residence is a thing which can be changed in a day. A man is ordinarily resident in one place up till a particular day. He then cuts the connection he has with that place — in this case he left his wife; in another case he might have disposed of his house — and makes arrangements to have his home somewhere else. Where there are indications that the place to which he moves is the place which he intends to make his home for, at any rate, an indefinite period, as from that date he is ordinarily resident at that place.

In *Wrixon v. Wrixon* (1982), 30 R.F.L. (2d) 107 (Alta. Q.B.), the petitioner, who had resided in Alberta for more than 20 years, filed a petition for divorce in that province only two months after returning from an 18-month stay in Hawaii. During at least part of her stay in Hawaii, the petitioner was gainfully employed. Her furniture was stored in Alberta for the eighteen-month period. Purvis J. found that, in the circumstances, the petitioner was not ordinarily resident in Alberta "for a period of at least one year immediately preceding the presentation of the petition". ... His Lordship stated at pages 108-109:

> She [the petitioner] testified that her stay in Hawaii was "an extended vacation". While she did not maintain living accommodation in Alberta to be immediately available for occupancy upon her return, she did put her furniture in storage in the province. It appears that while she was in Hawaii, she acquired fixed addresses at several locations, and was gainfully employed for at least part of the time. This is inconsistent with her suggestion that her sojourn of a year and a half in Hawaii was merely an extended vacation. ...
>
> In my view, in the circumstances of this case the period of one year within which the petitioner must have been ordinarily resident in Alberta must be calculated from 1st May 1982. It cannot be said that in the 12 months immediately preceding presentation of the petition, the petitioner in the settled routine of her life regularly, normally or customarily lived in Alberta, which the phrase "ordinarily resident" connotes: *Thomson v. M.N.R.*, [1946] S.C.R. 209 at 232, [1946] C.T.C. 51, [1946] 1 D.L.R. 689.

I am mindful of the fact that an application to stay or dismiss a divorce proceeding should only be granted "in a clear and obvious case": see *Fareed v. Latif* (1991), 31 R.F.L. (3d) 354 (Man. Q.B.). Based on the governing case law as set out above and on the particular circumstances of this case, it is "clear and obvious" that this court does not have jurisdiction to entertain the petitioner's claim for a divorce.

The wife has lived in Florida since she left the matrimonial home in November of 1995. In fact, she has spent a good part of her time in Florida over the last two years. The wife has not fixed any time limit for her stay in Florida. She has failed to provide the court with any date on which she plans to leave Florida and return to Ontario. In my view, when the wife left for Florida in November of 1995, she did so with the intention of making her home there for an indefinite period.

The wife has exclusive possession of the condominium in Florida. She has established a personal relationship with a gentleman there, and has worked in his business. As well, even though the matrimonial home in Toronto "has been stripped of most of the household contents", and the locks have been changed, the wife has not seen fit to return to Toronto to deal with this matter herself, preferring instead to send a friend. The wife, herself, gave two separate sworn statements in December of 1995 in which she referred to herself as a "resident" of Florida.

The overwhelming preponderance of the evidence is that the wife is ordinarily resident in Florida, and has been since early December, 1995. The wife "regularly, normally or customarily lives" in Florida. Consequently, the wife has not been ordinarily resident in Ontario for "at least one year immediately preceding the commencement of the proceeding" on March 22, 1996, as required by section 3(1) of the *Divorce Act*. This court therefore does not have jurisdiction to hear and determine the petition.

[Nevertheless, the Justice denied the husband's request for an order staying the support and property claims brought pursuant to the *Family Law Act*.]

NOTES AND QUESTIONS

1. In *Byrn v. Mackin* (1983), 32 R.F.L. (2d) 207 (Que. S.C.) the petitioner's husband administered a company's business in Montreal, living in apartments leased by the company. The wife and children continued to reside in the matrimonial home in British Columbia. After approximately one year, during which the husband returned frequently to his family in British Columbia, he announced that the marriage was over. He took his personal effects to Montreal and petitioned for divorce in Quebec. The court held that the husband had been ordinarily resident in British Columbia prior to his decision to end the marriage relationship.

2. In *Quigley v. Willmore* (2008), 50 R.F.L. (6th) 1 (N.S. C.A.), the appellate court upheld the dismissal of a wife's divorce application in Nova Scotia. After reviewing the leading cases on the meaning of "ordinary residence", the court stated (para. 22):

> The factors that Justice Wilson relied upon in coming to his conclusion that Ms. Quigley was not ordinarily resident in Nova Scotia for the year prior to her filing her petition are numerous and significant. For example, Ms. Quigley established and moved into a home purchased by the couple on a farm in Texas, registered Ryan for school, transported 10 horses from Nova Scotia to Texas and had the person who looked after them in Nova Scotia move with her to Texas, took steps to begin a riding school, attended courses in mediation and looked into the possibility of working as a lawyer there. Although Ms. Quigley maintained her home in Nova Scotia and intended to return to the province at some point, the totality of the evidence supports Justice Wilson's conclusion.

3. In *Blair v. Chung* (2006), 30 R.F.L. (6th) 111 (Alta. Q.B.), a husband who was in Canada illegally applied for a divorce so that his common law partner could sponsor his immigration application. Justice Veit ruled that, even if illegal residence might in some circumstances qualify as ordinary residence for the purpose of the *Divorce Act*, there were public policy reasons why the husband should not be considered ordinarily resident in Alberta. For a critical comment, see Epstein and Madsen, *This Week in Family Law*, 2006-34, August 29, 2006.

4. Section 5(1) of the 1968 *Divorce Act* referred to a period of ordinary residence of at least one year "immediately preceding the presentation of the petition". The courts held that a petition was presented for the purpose of s. 5(1) when it was filed with the Registrar of the Court. See, e.g., *Stapleton v. Stapleton* (1977), 1 R.F.L. (2d) 190, 80 D.L.R. (3d) 562 (Man. C.A.). Section 3 of the 1985 *Divorce Act* refers to "the commencement of the proceeding" rather than the "presentation of the petition". This change in wording does not alter the previous law. A proceeding should not be considered to have commenced for the purpose of s. 3 until the document that begins the proceeding is filed with the court. Under the *Family Law Rules*, O. Reg. 114/ 99, r. 36, this document is an "application".

5. There may be some situations where a spouse with grounds for divorce is unable to obtain one because no court has jurisdiction. This led to an unsuccessful challenge to s. 3(1) of the *Divorce Act* based on ss. 6 and 7 of the *Canadian Charter of Rights and Freedoms* in *Thurber v. Thurber* (2002), 322 A.R. 242 (Q.B.).

6. If a husband and wife get divorced and no order is made in the divorce proceeding regarding child support, spousal support or custody, either former spouse or both of them together may ask the court to deal with these matters in a corollary relief proceeding under the *Divorce Act*. In such cases, s. 4 sets out the rules governing territorial jurisdiction. The Ontario Court of Appeal held in *Rothgiesser v. Rothgiesser* (2000), 2 R.F.L. (5th) 266 (Ont. C.A.) and *Okmyansky v. Okmyansky* (2007), 38 R.F.L. (6th) 291 (Ont. C.A.) that s. 4 only gives a court jurisdiction to deal with a corollary relief proceeding if there has been a Canadian divorce. See also *Leonard v. Booker* (2007), 286 D.L.R. (4th) 451, 44 R.F.L. (6th) 237 (N.B. C.A.). The Quebec Superior Court disagreed in *M. (O.) v. K. (A.)* (2000), 9 R.F.L. (5th) 111 (Que. S.C.).

7. By virtue of s. 6(1) of the *Divorce Act*, where a divorce proceeding involves an application for a custody or access order that is opposed and the child concerned is most substantially connected with another province, the court having original jurisdiction may transfer the divorce proceeding to a court in that other province. Subsections 6(2) and (3) govern transfers of corollary relief and variation proceedings in similar circumstances. The court to which the proceeding is transferred will then be vested with exclusive jurisdiction: s. 6(4). For a review of the cases on s. 6, see Hovius, "Territorial Jurisdiction and Civil Enforcement Issues in Interprovincial Custody and Access Disputes in Canadian Common Law Provinces" (2002-2003), 20 C.F.L.Q. 155 at 163–169.

8. A husband and wife are ordinarily resident in Ontario until January 2 when the husband leaves to take up a new job in Newfoundland. The wife, who refuses to accompany her husband to Newfoundland, moves to Alberta on the same day. Each has severed all connections with Ontario and intends to live in Newfoundland and Alberta respectively for the foreseeable future. Assuming that each has grounds for divorce, when and where can each commence proceedings? If the husband commences divorce proceedings in Newfoundland on February 2nd of the following year and the wife commences divorce proceedings in Alberta on February 3rd, which court has jurisdiction? If both commence such proceedings on February 2nd, which court has jurisdiction?

(2) Recognition of Foreign Decrees

CASTEL AND WALKER, *CANADIAN CONFLICT OF LAWS*

6th ed. (Toronto: Butterworths, 2005) c. 17

Canadian divorces have legal effect throughout Canada pursuant to section 13 of the 1985 *Divorce Act*. The question of the recognition to be accorded to a foreign decree of divorce has arisen in nullity suits, claims for spousal support, the custody of children, or a share in an estate, efforts to obtain a marriage licence, prosecutions for bigamy, and in many other situations. ...

Section 22(1) applies to foreign decrees granted after June 1, 1986, the date of the coming into force of the Act. Decrees granted before June 1, 1986 continue to be subject to the previous rules as to recognition. The important change involves the adoption of the test of ordinary residence of either spouse in the foreign country for at least one year immediately preceding the commencement of the proceeding for the divorce. In other words, if either spouse was ordinarily resident in the granting country for at least one year immediately preceding the institution of the proceeding, the decree will be recognized in Canada even if the foreign court took jurisdiction on a different ground.

Section 22(2) preserves the statutory ground for recognition of foreign divorces adopted by s. 6(2) of the 1968 *Divorce Act*, namely the independent domicile of the wife in the country where the divorce was granted. Since the existing rules for recognition for foreign divorces in Canada are retained by section 22(3), the old common law rules as to recognition are still available but they have not been relied upon extensively to recognize divorces granted after June 1, 1986. In determining the conditions for recognition of foreign divorces in Canada, the courts of the common law provinces and territories have followed the common law rules developed by English courts. In Canada, the basic common law jurisdictional rule of recognition was the domicile of both spouses in the foreign jurisdiction at the commencement of the proceeding combined with the now obsolete common law rule that upon marriage the wife acquires the husband's domicile. In determining whether the husband's domicile was in the foreign jurisdiction, Canadian courts apply the *lex fori*. Thus, Canadian courts have held that a foreign divorce decree rendered by the court of the husband's domicile will be recognized as valid in Canada[1] provided proper notice was given to the respondent and the divorce was not obtained by fraud. ...

The jurisdictional bases on which foreign divorce decrees are recognized by Canadian courts have been summarized as follows:

(i) where jurisdiction was assumed on the basis of the domicile of the spouses;

(ii) where the foreign divorce, though granted on a non-domiciliary jurisdictional basis, is recognized by the law of the domicile of the parties;

(iii) where the foreign jurisdictional rule corresponds to the Canadian jurisdictional rule in divorce proceedings;

(iv) where the circumstances in the foreign jurisdiction would have conferred jurisdiction on a Canadian court had they occurred in Canada;

(v) where either the petitioner or the respondent had a real and substantial connection with the foreign jurisdiction wherein the divorce was granted; and

(vi) where the foreign divorce is recognized in another jurisdiction with which the petitioner or respondent has a real and substantial connection.[2]

Canadian courts give recognition to a foreign decree of divorce, wherever pronounced, if it would be recognized by the domicile of the spouses at the time it was pronounced[3] or immediately thereafter.[4] The justification for this rule is that if the status of the spouses is changed or it is recognized as having been changed in the country of their domicile, the change of status must be recognized in Canada. However, as a matter of policy, Canadian courts do not recognize the retroactive legislation of a foreign state purporting to validate a divorce even though the spouse who obtained the divorce was domiciled in the state at the time of the original proceeding.[5]

For reasons of comity, Canadian courts have also recognized foreign divorce decrees, where in roughly comparable circumstances they would have exercised jurisdiction by virtue of Canadian domestic law.[6] This rule applies regardless of the basis upon which the foreign court assumed jurisdiction. A divorce should also be recognized when it would be recognized by the courts of the country with which the petitioner had a real and substantial con-

---

[1] Based on *Le Mesurier v. Le Mesurier*, [1895] A.C. 517, 11 T.L.R. 481 (P.C.); *Hill v. Hill* (1981), 10 Sask. R. 276 (Q.B.); *Re Jones* (1974), 6 O.R. (2d) 11, 51 D.L.R. (3d) 655 (H.C.). ...

[2] J.D. Payne, *Payne on Divorce*, 4th ed. (Scarborough: Carswell, 1996) at 111.

[3] Based on *Armitage v. A.G.*, [1906] P. 135, 75 L.J.P. 42, 22 T.L.R. 306 and *Walker v. Walker*, [1950] 2 W.W.R. 411, [1950] 4 D.L.R. 253 (B.C.C.A.).

[4] *Schwebel v. Ungar* (1964), 42 D.L.R. (2d) 622 at 633 (Ont. C.A.); affd. [1965] S.C.R. 148, 48 D.L.R. (2d) 644; for the decision of the High Court see 37 D.L.R. (2d) 467 (Ont.); for a note on this case see Lysyk, (1965), 43 Can. Bar Rev. 363; Hartley (1965), 4 West. Ont. L. Rev. 99; Webb (1965), 14 Int. & Comp. L.Q. 659.

[5] *Ambrose v. Ambrose* (1959), 30 W.W.R. 49, 21 D.L.R. (2d) 722; affd. (1960), 32 W.W.R. 433, 25 D.L.R. (2d) 1 (B.C.C.A.).

[6] Based on *Travers v. Holley*, [1953] P. 246, [1953] 2 All E.R. 794 (C.A.). ...

nection at the relevant time, though she or he had no such connection with the country where it was granted.[7]

In recent years, Canadian courts have been committed to the view that they will recognize foreign decrees of divorce where there existed some real and substantial connection between the petitioner or the respondent and the granting jurisdiction at the time of the commencement of the proceedings.[8] The purpose of the rule is to avoid limping marriages. Whether there exists a real and substantial connection between the granting jurisdiction and either the petitioner or the respondent must be determined by the court upon an analysis of all the relevant facts.[9] Although ordinary residence is a sufficient real and substantial connection at common law, one would anticipate that it might be slightly more difficult to have a foreign decree recognized in Canada on the basis of ordinary residence of less than a year since at common law no particular length of ordinary residence is necessary, whereas the *Divorce Act* requires a period of one year immediately preceding the commencement of the proceeding in the foreign country. However, where a divorce has been granted in a place in which the petitioner had resided for substantial periods of time in the past, the real and substantial connection might be established upon returning for less than a year.[10] ...

NOTES AND QUESTIONS

1. The concept of domicile is an important connecting factor in conflict of laws. Every person has a domicile. At birth, an individual is fixed with a domicile of origin. At common law, a legitimate child took as his or her domicile of origin the domicile of the father at the time of birth, while an illegitimate child's domicile of origin was that of the mother at the time of birth. Section 67 of the *Family Law Act* establishes statutory rules for determining the domicile of a minor (these rules first appeared in slightly different form in s. 68 of the *Family Law Reform Act, 1978*). In light of the abolition of the concept of illegitimacy by s. 1 of the *Children's Law Reform Act*, it would appear that s. 67 is intended to alter both the rules governing a person's domicile of origin and those dealing with a minor's domicile of dependency.

A domicile of choice can be acquired by a person who has capacity to acquire an independent domicile. It is the jurisdiction, other than a person's domicile of origin, in which a person resides with the intention to remain there permanently. A domicile of choice can be changed by an actual change of residence coupled with an intention to remain in the new place of residence. If a person abandons his or her domicile of choice without acquiring a new one, that person's domicile is once again his or her domicile of origin.

At common law, married women, minors and mental incompetents did not have the capacity to acquire an independent domicile. A married woman's domicile was that of her husband. She, therefore, had a domicile of dependency. The common law rule that a married woman had the same domicile as her husband was abolished for purposes of recognition of divorce decrees by the *Divorce Act* of 1968 (see now s. 22(2) of *Divorce Act*). Section 65 of the *Family Law Reform Act, 1978* abolished the remaining vestiges of the concept of unity of legal personality of husband and wife (see now s. 64 of *Family Law Act*). This concept formed the basis for the common law rule that a married woman had the same domicile as her husband.

---

[7] Combining *Indyka v. Indyka*, [1969] 1 A.C. 33 (H.L.), with *Armitage v. A.G.*, [1906] P. 135; *Mather v. Mahoney*, [1968] 3 All E.R. 223; *Messina v. Smith*, [1971] P. 322. ...

[8] *Indyka v. Indyka*, [1969] 1 A.C. 33 (H.L.); *Powell v. Cockburn* (1976), 68 D.L.R. (3d) 700 (S.C.C.); *Re Edward and Edward* (1987), 8 R.F.L. (3d) 370 (Sask. C.A.).

[9] *Kish v. Director of Vital Statistics*, [1973] 2 W.W.R. 678 (Alta S.C.); *Rowland v. Rowland* (1973), 2 O.R. (2d) 161, 13 R.F.L. 311, 42 D.L.R. (3d) 205 at 212 (H.C.J.); *El-Sohemy v. El-Sohemy* (1978), 21 O.R. (2d) 35, 3 R.F.L. (2d) 184, 89 D.L.R. (3d) 145 (H.C.J.); *Bate v. Bate* (1978), 1 R.F.L. (2d) 298 (Ont. H.C.J.); *Clarkson v. Clarkson* (1978), 86 D.L.R. (3d) 694 (Man. Q.B.); *Singh v. Mohammed* (1986), 41 Man. R. (2d) 235 (Q.B.). ...

[10] *Wlodarczyk v. Spriggs* (2000), 2000 Sask. R. 129 (U.F.C.).

For a more complete analysis of the concept of domicile, see Mendes da Costa, "Some Comments on the Conflict of Laws Provisions of the *Divorce Act, 1968*" (1968), 46 Can. Bar Rev. 252 and Castel and Walker, *Canadian Conflict of Laws*, 6th ed. (Toronto: Butterworths, 2005).

2. For some recent cases applying the "real and substantial connection" test to determine whether to recognize a foreign divorce, see *Wlodarzyk v. Spriggs* (2000), 12 R.F.L. (5th) 241 (Sask. Q.B.); *Janes v. Pardo* (2002), 24 R.F.L. (5th) 44 (Nfld. T.D.); *Johangiri-Mavaneh v. Taheri-Zengekani* (2003), 39 R.F.L. (5th) 103 (Ont. S.C.J.); and *El Qaoud v. Orabi* (2005), 12 R.F.L. (6th) 296 (N.S. C.A.).

3. If the foreign divorce has been rendered by a court that had jurisdiction in the eyes of Canadian law, the ground upon which the decree was granted or the law which the foreign court applied is irrelevant. However, recognition may be refused in a limited number of circumstances. These were summarized by Justice D. Martinson in *Pitre v. Ngugen* (2007), 2007 CarswellBC 2229 (S.C.) as follows (para. 15):

> Recognition of a foreign divorce order, therefore, can be refused in fairly limited circumstances. Those include situations where the respondent did not receive notice; where the foreign order is contrary to public policy; where the foreign court did not properly have jurisdiction; or where fraud was present. If fraud is alleged, it must go to jurisdiction and not simply the merits of the case.

In the *El Qaoud* case, *supra*, a husband and wife who were born in Kuwait immigrated with their two children to Canada in early 2002. Later that year, the husband returned to Kuwait and visited Jordan for three days. While in Jordan, he obtained a "Revocable Divorce Document" from the Shariite (Canonical) Council. Thereafter, he soon returned to Canada. The Nova Scotia Court of Appeal held that none of the rules for recognition allowed it to recognize this divorce, but Justice Fichaud added (paras. 17 and 18):

> I would dismiss the appeal for a second and independent reason. ...

> Mr. El Qaoud knew where Ms. Orabi resided. Yet Mr. El Qaoud did not serve Ms. Orabi with notice of the divorce proceeding. This was not a case where the respondent was difficult to locate, avoiding service, or subject to an order for substituted service. The Jordanian tribunal granted the divorce apparently without requiring any proof that Ms. Orabi had been served with notice. In December, 2002, Ms. Orabi received her couriered divorce decree, issued by a tribunal before which there was no role for her participation, in a country to which she had no connection, after a proceeding of which she received no notice. This divorce decree would affect her status and corollary relief. This violates the principles of natural justice. I would deny recognition of the Revocable Divorce Document on that ground.

4. What are the policy issues underlying the law regarding the recognition of foreign divorces? In *Messina v. Smith*, [1971] P. 322, [1971] 2 All E.R. 1046, Omrod J. stated (at (P.) 336):

> All through the history of the recognition rules in this country there can be traced, in different shapes and guises, two fundamental *desiderata*. The first is the need to avoid creating 'limping' or 'unilateral marriages' or 'the scandal which arises when a man and a woman are held to be man and wife in one country and strangers in another'. ... The second is the wish to protect the standards of marriage in this country against the laxer standards believed to obtain in other countries.

As divorce becomes easy to obtain domestically, courts may more readily accept foreign divorces. In *Janes v. Pardo* (2002), 24 R.F.L. (5th) 44 (Nfld. T.D.), Justice LeBlanc suggested (at para. 21): "... [C]onsidering the legal presumption of validity of a foreign divorce even as limited as it may be, modern-day attitudes towards divorce, the laws of most countries permitting divorces on less stringent grounds than in the past and the modern-day mobility of the population, it should only be in rare circumstances that a foreign divorce properly obtained pursuant to the laws of that jurisdiction should not be recognized as being valid."

3. Grounds

Although s. 8(1) of the *Divorce Act* specifies that there is only one ground for divorce; namely, marriage breakdown, there are three, and only three, ways to establish marriage breakdown.

(1) Living Separate and Apart

(a) Definition

Under the *Divorce Act* of 1968, a petitioner could establish permanent breakdown of the marriage by proving that the spouses had lived separate and apart for a period of three years prior to the presentation of the petition. If the petitioner had deserted the respondent, the requisite period was five years. There were numerous cases under the Act explaining the meaning of the concept of living separate and apart. These cases continue to guide the courts in the application of s. 8(2)(a) of the 1985 *Divorce Act*. See, e.g., *Thorogood v. Thorogood* (1987), 11 R.F.L. (3d) 82 (Ont. U.F.C.) and *Ginter v. Ginter* (1988), 15 R.F.L. (3d) 203 (Sask. Q.B.).

RUSHTON v. RUSHTON

(1968), 66 W.W.R. 764, 2 D.L.R. (3d) 25, 1968 CarswellBC 196 (B.C. S.C.)

MCINTYRE J.: — The parties were married in 1936. By 1960 they had come upon difficulties and had begun to live separate lives, although they continued to reside in the same suite in an apartment building. In February 1965, and probably from an earlier date, sexual intercourse ceased entirely. The petitioner lived in one room of the suite, the respondent in another, there was almost no contact between them. The wife performed no domestic services for the husband. She shopped and cooked only for herself. He bought his own food, did his own cooking, his own laundry and received no services from his wife. He paid her a sum monthly for maintenance. While it is true that they lived in the same suite of rooms, they followed separate and individual lives.

The petitioner continued to live in the suite because she and her husband were the joint caretakers of the apartment building in which the suite was situate, and to keep the position it was necessary to be, or to appear to be, husband and wife and to reside in the caretaker's suite.

In August 1968, they became responsible for another apartment building where no such requirement exists. They now maintain separate suites in the same building. ...

I am of the opinion that in the case at bar the parties have been living separate and apart for three years within the meaning of s. 4(1)(e)(i) of the *Divorce Act*. The words "separate and apart" are disjunctive. They mean, in my view, that there must be a withdrawal from the matrimonial obligation with the intent of destroying the matrimonial consortium, as well as physical separation. The two conditions must be met. I hold that they are met here. The mere fact that the parties are under one roof does not mean that they are not living separate and apart within the meaning of the Act. There can be, and I hold that here there has been, a physical separation within the one suite of rooms. To hold otherwise would be to deprive the petitioner here of any remedy under the new *Divorce Act* simply because she is precluded, or was for a period of time precluded, by economic circumstances from acquiring a different suite in which to live. There will be a decree nisi. ...

DUPERE v. DUPERE

(1974), 19 R.F.L. 270, 9 N.B.R. (2d) 554, 1974 CarswellNB 7 (Q.B.); affirmed (1974), 1974 CarswellNB 187 (C.A.)

STEVENSON J.: — ... In any case where the parties continue to live under the same roof the court must carefully consider the evidence in determining whether the spouses have been "living separate and apart" resulting in "a permanent breakdown of their marriage". Particular care is called for where, as here, both spouses seek a divorce on that ground alone.

The parties were married on 27th February 1960. The petitioner was 26 and the respondent 18. She had borne a child, Randle, of which the petitioner was the father, on 13th July 1958. There are two other children of the marriage — Heather, born 30th November 1960, and Jacqueline, born 9th February 1965.

Difficulties between the parties apparently developed in 1965 and they separated in 1966. A written separation agreement (Ex. R-1) was entered into on 12th July 1966. The respondent was to have custody of the children and the petitioner assumed financial obligations which were not clearly defined. The respondent took an apartment. When she was unable to pay the rent she rented a small house without toilet facilities for $30 per month. She and her two daughters resided there. Randle stayed with his maternal grandmother. The petitioner provided some financial support on a rather irregular basis.

In the fall of 1968, the petitioner moved in with the respondent and normal marital relations were resumed for about a month. However in December of that year the parties began to occupy separate bedrooms and both testify there has been no sexual intercourse between them since that time. They subsequently moved twice and had lived together at 72 Pauline Street in East Saint John from March 1970 until a week before the trial when the respondent moved to another address, taking the children with her.

The petitioner says he and the respondent stayed in the same house "for the sake of the kids". While I suspect the respondent may have stayed as a matter of economic necessity the evidence does not justify such a finding. The petitioner has supported the home, has clothed his wife and family and has given the respondent a $20 weekly allowance. The respondent says she was just a maid. It is not a situation where there was no communication between the parties and apparently where the children were concerned there was often mutual discussion and agreement. For instance the parties were able to jointly decide on how much should be spent on the children at Christmas and they "always made a big thing of Christmas". As between the parties discord continued and on only two occasions in the past five years did they go out together. The respondent has been friendly with another man with the knowledge and at least tacit consent of the petitioner.

The situation is not unlike that described by Holland J. in *Cooper v. Cooper* (1972), 10 R.F.L. 184 (Ont.) [at 186]:

> The parties obviously cannot get along and clearly there is considerable bad feeling between them. At the same time there is clearly good feeling towards the children, the children are being well looked after and are receiving all necessary care and attention from their parents, in spite of the fact that the attitude of the parents toward each other must be upsetting for each of them.

I have read most, if not all, of the decisions reported since the advent of the *Divorce Act* dealing with cases where marriage breakdown is alleged on the grounds of separation even though the spouses continue to live under the same roof. ...

I think the following general statements can be extracted as representing the weight of judicial opinion:

(1) Great care must be exercised in considering the evidence and each case determined on its own circumstances.

(2) There can be a physical separation within a single dwelling unit.

(3) A case is not taken out of the statute just because a spouse remains in the same house for reasons of economic necessity.

(4) To meet the statute there must be both (a) physical separation and (b) a withdrawal by one or both spouses from the matrimonial obligation with the intent of destroying the matrimonial consortium.

(5) Cessation of sexual intercourse is not conclusive but is only one factor to be considered in determining the issue.

(6) There may be an atmosphere of severe incompatibility but remain one household and one home — a distinction may be drawn between an unhappy household and a separated one. ...

In *Cooper v. Cooper, supra,* Holland J. pointed out that generally a finding that spouses were living separate and apart was made where the following circumstances were present [p. 187]:

(i) Spouses occupying separate bedrooms.

(ii) Absence of sexual relations.

(iii) Little, if any, communication between spouses.

(iv) Wife providing no domestic services for her husband.

(v) Eating meals separately.

(vi) No social activities together.

It is probably not necessary to establish all six elements in each case and each case must stand or fall on its own merits. I refrain from commenting on the wisdom of incompatible spouses remaining together "for the sake of the children" but I do not think it was the intention of Parliament that a spouse who does so, under circumstances in this case, can at his or her option at any time after such circumstances have continued for three years or more elect to opt out of the marriage and claim a divorce on the ground of permanent marriage breakdown. A mutual opting out in such circumstances would be little more than divorce by consent, something Parliament has not yet provided for.

The evidence does not satisfy me that for three years or more prior to presentation of the petition in this action the parties were living separate and apart within the meaning of the Act or that there was an intention on the part of either spouse to destroy the matrimonial consortium. Accordingly both the petition and the counter-petition will be dismissed.

[This result was affirmed on appeal: (1975), 10 N.B.R. (2d) 148 (C.A.). Limerick J.A., who wrote separate, concurring reasons, stated at 154-155:

I am in accord that husband and wife live separate and apart even though they live under the same roof where the six circumstances exist as set out in the judgment of Holland, J. in *Cooper v. Cooper.*
...

I would however qualify somewhat circumstance (4), where the husband and wife enter into a contract for economic reasons and the husband pays the wife an agreed amount for preparing his meals for him I would consider them living separate and apart if the other five circumstances applied. In such case the service of the wife would not arise out of or be referable to a matrimonial relationship but would be a matter of separate and independent contract. I would add a further condition; viz., they do not share living room and recreational facilities, such as television, together.

The living conditions of the parties in this action do not comply with the above circumstance. I therefore concur with the judgment of my brother Ryan and dismiss the appeal.]

DORCHESTER v. DORCHESTER

3 R.F.L. 396, [1971] 2 W.W.R. 634, 1971 CarswellBC 50 (B.C. S.C.)

MACFARLANE J.: — The bare facts are that the petitioner took his wife to the Riverview Hospital for treatment of a mental illness on February 17, 1967, and she has been since that date a patient. The parties have not cohabited since the admission of the wife to the said hospital.

The date of the presentation of the petition was June 11, 1970.

The following evidence was given by the petitioner in cross-examination by counsel for the Public Trustee:

Q Who took your wife to hospital when she was admitted in February, 1967?
A I did.

Q Why did you take her?
A Or did they take her with the ambulance? I can't remember.

Q Why did you take —
A On the doctor's recommendation.

Q You were living with her up to the time that she was admitted to the hospital, is that correct?
A Yes.

Q Then when did you decide to destroy, or shall we say, forget about the marriage entirely? When did you make up your mind that the marriage was broken up and decided to leave your wife for good?
A Well, it was about the time I came in here and filed for a divorce for the simple reason that my property is tied up. Nobody will listen to me. I can't do anything. Nobody listens to me.

Q You made up your mind about the time you filed your divorce papers?
A Yes.

Q Mr. Dorchester, your petition for divorce is dated June 11th, 1970. In other words according to what you just said you decided to leave your wife for good and forget about the marriage, so to speak, as of June 11th, 1970?
A Yes.

The physical separation of husband and wife is one of the factors which must be taken into consideration in cases of this kind, but there may be physical separation of the parties without there being a finding that the parties are living "separate and apart". For instance, a serviceman may be posted overseas and be away from his wife for over three years without the parties living "separate and apart" within the meaning of the Act.

The evidence in any given case must be examined to determine upon what date the parties were not only living apart but also on what date did the matrimonial relationship cease to exist.

In this case the matrimonial relationship was subsisting when the wife was admitted to the hospital. The only evidence I have from the petitioner with regard to the cessation of the matrimonial relationship was that this occurred just prior to the presentation of his petition on June 11, 1970. On that evidence I am unable to find that the spouses had been living separate and apart for a period of not less than three years immediately preceding the presentation of the petition.

The petition therefore must be dismissed, without costs.

NOTES AND QUESTIONS

1. Which of the factors listed in *Cooper v. Cooper* (1972), 10 R.F.L. 184 (Ont. H.C.) should be given the greatest weight in determining whether spouses residing under the same roof are living separate and apart for the purposes of the *Divorce Act*? Does the seventh circumstance suggested by Limerick J.A. in *Dupere* add anything to the *Cooper* test? To what extent should the court be influenced by the reason why the spouses are still residing under the same roof?

For a recent case in which a court found that the spouses were living separate and apart for the purposes of the *Divorce Act* even though they still lived in the same house, see *Callahan v. Callahan* (2007), 2007 CarswellNS 72 (S.C.).

2. As *Dorchester* illustrates and as is made clear by s. 8(3)(a) of the *Divorce Act*, physical separation alone does not mean that the spouses are living separate and apart for purposes of divorce. Where the parties are physically separated for reasons such as hospitalization and employment, what evidence should a court rely on to determine if and when the period of living separate and apart has begun? For another case, see *Fotheringham v. Fotheringham* (1999), 1 R.F.L. (5th) 50 (Nfld. C.A.).

In *Severo v. Severo* (2007), 44 R.F.L. (6th) 57 (B.C. S.C.), the wife stayed in the family home when the husband moved into a water bottling plant located on the same property. Thereafter, the husband supported the wife financially, occasionally had sexual relations with her, continued to involve her in the financing of his business, and stated that he was married for income tax purposes. After reviewing several cases in which the courts had to determine whether spouses who were no longer residing in the same house were living separate and apart, Justice Melnick concluded that the spouses continued to cohabit for an additional five years after the husband moved into the plant. See also *Campbell v. Campbell* (2007), 49 R.F.L. (6th) 320 (Alta. Q.B.).

3. Under the *Divorce Act* of 1968, the parties had to be living separate and apart for the requisite three or five years prior to the presentation of the petition. Under the 1985 *Divorce Act*, the one-year period of separation need not immediately precede the commencement of the divorce proceeding, merely its determination. The parties must, however, be living separate and apart at the commencement of the proceedings. It is now possible for spouses to separate and for one or both of them to apply for divorce on the ground of separation a day after the separation. May divorce proceedings be resorted to prematurely under this provision?

4. Section 8(1) of the *Divorce Act* contemplates that a divorce judgment may be granted to both spouses. The spouses may jointly apply or petition for divorce where the grounds for divorce are separation for the requisite period and there is no contested claim for other relief. See ss. 8(1) and (2) of the *Divorce Act* and *Family Law Rules*, O. Reg. 114/ 99, r. 36(2).

5. As indicated in the cases reproduced and noted in this section, separation has both a physical and mental element. In *Calvert (Litigation Guardian of) v. Calvert* (1997), 27 R.F.L. (4th) 394 (Ont. Gen. Div.), the court concluded that a wife who was in the early stages of Alzheimer's disease had the capacity to separate. The Ontario Court of Appeal affirmed this conclusion, (1998), 36 R.F.L. (4th) 169 (Ont. C.A.); leave to appeal refused (1998), (sub nom. *Calvert v. Calvert*) 111 O.A.C. 197 (note) (S.C.C.), and also held that it was irrelevant whether the wife still had this capacity when the divorce proceedings began. As the wife had the capacity to separate when the parties first began to live apart and she did not waver from her wish to remain separate and apart as long as she had capacity, the period of separation continued uninterrupted by virtue of s. 8(3)(b)(i) of the *Divorce Act*.

6. There are few cases in which spouses are motivated to dispute the date of separation for the purposes of the *Divorce Act*. *Steinberg v. Fields* (2005), 2005 CarswellOnt 9983 (Ont. S.C.J.) provides a unique example of such a case. The husband applied in January 2005 for a divorce on the basis that he and his wife had been living separate and apart since December 6, 2003, the day that he moved out of the family home. The wife argued that, although they had lived in separate residences since that date, they were not living separate and apart for the purposes of the *Divorce Act* until the husband applied for the divorce. As Justice Herman explained in dealing with the issue of costs (para. 25): "While the subject matter of this hearing was ostensibly the determination of the date of separation, it was really about membership in a club — Ms. Field's desire to continue her membership and Mr. Steinberg's desire to prevent her." The husband wanted a divorce by November 18, 2005, so that his wife would not be eligible for continued membership in a golf and country club without paying an initiation fee of $125,000. Under the by-laws of the club, a female spouse of a member retained her membership after a divorce as long as she had been a member for five years during the marriage. The couple's fifth wedding anniversary fell on November 19, 2005. The wife's attempt to get the husband's application for a divorce dismissed failed because the court found that separation had occurred in 2003. However, the court next refused to grant the divorce before giving the wife thirty days from October 14, 2005 within which to amend her Answer to make a claim for corollary relief. If the wife did not obtain such leave within that time, the husband could move for judgment. It appears that the wife won this battle over the club membership because the earliest that the husband could move for judgment was mid-November. Even if a divorce were then granted, it would not become effective under s. 12(1) of the *Divorce Act* until the thirty-first day after that date.

7. The determination of the date of separation is often most significant because of its impact on property rights. See Chapter 4, *FAMILY PROPERTY*. Also, the Spousal Support Advisory Guidelines take into account the length of cohabitation in determining the amount and duration of spousal support. See Chapter 6, *SPOUSAL SUPPORT*.

(b) Reconciliation and Resumption of Cohabitation

ROGLER v. ROGLER

(1977), 1 R.F.L. (2d) 398, 1977 CarswellOnt 137 (Ont. H.C.)

FANJOY L.J.S.C.: — ... The husband and wife separated in September 1973 and the divorce proceedings commenced on 28th December 1976. In or about the fall of 1974 the petitioner and the respondent had sexual intercourse and the only issue is whether this sexual intercourse interrupted the period of living separate and apart. At the outset I would say that I accept fully the evidence of the petitioner and find her to be a most credible witness. The only evidence before me with respect to these acts of sexual intercourse is her evidence. She stated that her husband would now and again come to her house around 2:00 a.m. in the morning and would leave at approximately 4:00 a.m. They would have sex and her stated reason was that she felt that it was the right thing to do "in the sight of God" since they were married. Other than that, they did not live together. He did not eat at the house; she performed no services for him. His presence in the house was only during these nightly hours "once in a while".

In *Foote v. Foote*, [1971] 1 O.R. 338, 2 R.F.L. 221, 15 D.L.R. (3d) 292, Donnelly J. held that the period of "living separate and apart" was interrupted by an act of sexual intercourse between the petitioner and the respondent and dismissed the petition.

However, the Ontario Court of Appeal in *Deslippe v. Deslippe* (1974), 4 O.R. (2d) 35, 16 R.F.L. 38, 47 D.L.R. (3d) 30, since the decision in *Foote v. Foote* reviewed the law fully and came to a different conclusion on the facts before them. In that case the husband insisted on going with the wife to a party and during the evening the husband became intoxicated and "pushy"; to avoid difficulty with him, the wife stayed with him at her girlfriend's home and had sexual intercourse with him. It was found, as a fact, that the wife did not intend, by this act, to reconcile with her husband. In the case before me I make the same findings with respect to the intention to reconcile.

Following the reasoning set out in the *Deslippe* case I am of the view that the issue of whether the couple were living together must be determined on all the facts. Sexual intercourse is only one of the concomitants of marriage. While more recent trends in society have, to some extent, changed the services normally performed by a wife in marriage, I am still of the view that they generally include the preparation of meals, the washing and ironing of clothes and many other services too numerous to mention. They also, of course, include the many mutual, physical, mental and moral supports, including those with respect to the children.

In the case at bar the only element which existed was that of sexual intercourse which was somewhat in the nature of an "affair", even though the two parties were married. I cannot distinguish in this case between one act of sexual intercourse and a number of acts under the same conditions.

I therefore find that the acts of sexual intercourse did not interrupt the period of "living separate and apart". There will therefore be a *decree nisi* [of divorce].

NOTES AND QUESTIONS

1. In *McGeachy v. McGeachy* (1980), 15 R.F.L. (2d) 274 (Ont. H.C.), the spouses, after separation, had frequent contact with each other and on several occasions took vacations together. On some of these occasions, sexual intercourse occurred. Applying *Deslippe* and *Rogler*, McCart L.J.S.C. held that there had been no resumption of cohabitation or interruption of the period of living separate and apart. See also *Spinney v. Spinney* (1981), 33 Nfld. & P.E.I.R. 61 (P.E.I. C.A.) and *Velisek v. Velisek* (2000), 7 R.F.L. (5th) 192 (B.C. S.C.).

2. Section 9(3)(b) of the *Divorce Act* of 1968 specified that a period during which a husband and wife were living separate and apart was not considered to have been interrupted or terminated "by reason only that there has been a resumption of cohabitation by the spouses during a single period of not more than ninety days with reconciliation as its primary purpose". There was conflicting case law on whether more than one period of cohabitation was permitted. How does s. 8(3)(b) of the 1985 *Divorce Act* deal with this issue?

3. Section 8(3)(b)(ii) is only one of the provisions of the *Divorce Act* designed to encourage attempts at reconciliation. See *RECONCILIATION AND CONCILIATION*, below.

(2) Adultery

(a) Nature of Adultery

Under s. 8(2) of the *Divorce Act*, the breakdown of a marriage is established if the respondent to a divorce application has committed adultery since the celebration of the marriage. The term "adultery" is not defined in the Act and, until the recognition of same-sex marriage, there was usually no need or attempt to define it expressly. This section begins with two older cases that examined in some detail the legal definition of adultery and why it constituted a "matrimonial offence" that could signal the end of a marriage. The third case is a recent decision adopting an expanding meaning of adultery in light of the recognition of same-sex marriage.

ORFORD v. ORFORD

(1921), 49 O.L.R. 15, 58 D.L.R. 251 (H.C.)

[In this case, the wife sought alimony. The husband responded by claiming that the wife had committed adultery. At that time, a wife's adultery was a complete bar to alimony. The wife admitted that she had given birth to a child some two years after the marriage and that the husband was not the father. This, of course, logically led to the conclusion that the wife had had sexual intercourse with another man. However, she denied this, claiming that the child had been conceived as a result of artificial insemination. Justice Orde indicated that he did not believe her story, but went on to discuss the legal issue raised if it were believed.]

MR. JUSTICE ORDE: — ... The plaintiff contends ... that it is not adultery for a woman to become "artificially inseminated" or "artificially impregnated" by means of a man other than her husband and without her husband's knowledge, and to bear a child in consequence thereof;. ...

Mr. White [the wife's lawyer] argues that to constitute adultery there must be actual sexual intercourse in the ordinary natural way, and he cites many definitions of the word "adultery" from legal dictionaries and text-books in support thereof. He lays stress upon the distinction between the act of adultery and the consequences of it, contending that insemination or pregnancy is merely the result of the act of adultery, and that as a matter of law adultery is confined to the act of sexual intercourse in the ordinary acceptance of that term.
...

Mr. White contended that the essential element of adultery rested in the moral turpitude of the act of sexual intercourse as ordinarily understood. With this I cannot agree. The sin or offence of adultery, as affecting the marriage-tie, may, without going farther back, be traced from the Mosaic law down through the canon or ecclesiastical law to present date. ...

In its essence, adultery was always regarded as an invasion of the marital rights of the husband or the wife. When the incontinence was that of the wife, the offence which she had committed rested upon deeper and more vital ground than that she had merely committed an act of moral turpitude, or had even seen fit to give to another man something to which her husband alone was entitled. The marriage-tie had for its primary object the perpetuation of the human race. For example, the Church of England marriage-service, which in this respect may well serve as the voice of the Ecclesiastical Courts of England, gives as the first of "the causes for which matrimony was ordained" that of "the procreation of children."

That no authority can be found declaring, directly or indirectly, that "artificial insemination" would constitute adultery is not to be wondered at. This is probably the first time in history that such a suggestion has been put forward in a court of justice. But can anyone read the Mosaic law against those sins which, whether of adultery or otherwise, in any way affect the sanctity of the reproductive functions of the people of Israel, without being convinced that, had such a thing as "artificial insemination" entered the mind of the lawgiver, it would have been regarded with the utmost horror and detestation as an invasion of the most sacred of the marital rights of husband and wife, and have been the subject of the severest penalties?

In my judgment, the essence of the offence of adultery consists, not in the moral turpitude of the act of sexual intercourse, but in the voluntary surrender to another person of the reproductive powers or faculties of the guilty person; and any submission of those powers to the service or enjoyment of any person other than the husband or the wife comes within the definition of "adultery."

The fact that it has been held that anything short of actual sexual intercourse, no matter how indecent or improper the act may be, does not constitute adultery, really tends to strengthen my view that it is not the moral turpitude that is involved, but the invasion of the reproductive function. So long as nothing takes place which can by any possibility affect that function, there can be no adultery; so that, unless and until there is actual sexual intercourse, there can be no adultery. But to argue, from that, that adultery necessarily begins and ends there is utterly fallacious. Sexual intercourse is adulterous because in the case of the woman it involves the possibility of introducing into the family of the husband a false strain of blood. Any act on the part of the wife which does that would, therefore, be adulterous.

That such a thing could be accomplished in any other than the natural manner probably never entered the heads of those who considered the question before. Assuming the plaintiff's story to be true, what took place here was the introduction into her body by unusual means of the seed of a man other than her husband. If it were necessary to do so, I would hold that that in itself was "sexual intercourse." It is conceivable that such an act performed upon a woman against her will might constitute rape.

Mr. White was driven, as a result of his argument, to contend that it would not be adultery for a woman living with her husband to produce by artificial insemination a child of which some man other than her husband was the father! A monstrous conclusion surely. If such a thing has never before been declared to be adultery, then, on grounds of public policy, the Court should now declare it so. ...

MACLENNAN v. MACLENNAN

[1958] Sess. Cas. 105 (Scotland Ct. Sess.)

LORD WHEATLEY'S OPINION: — The pursuer [the husband] seeks decree of divorce from the defender [the wife] on the ground of her adultery, and *prima facie* his case is essentially simple. The parties were married on 25th August 1952, and it is a matter of agreement that they have not lived together or had marital relations since 31st May 1954. On 10th July 1955 the defender admittedly gave birth to a female child in Brooklyn, New York, and on that historical narrative of events the pursuer asks the Court to find proven facts, circumstances and qualifications from which an inference of the defender's adultery can be drawn. In the uncomplicated days before science began to innovate on the natural processes of procreation, the lapse of time between the last act of marital intercourse and the birth of the child would have led to the inevitable inference that the defender had been guilty of an adulterous act with another man by means of the normal and natural physiological mechanism, as a result of which the child was conceived. The defender, however, has tendered an explanation by way of defence, which is unique in the annals of our law, and which seeks to establish that she conceived the child not as a result of sexual intercourse with another man, as that phrase is commonly understood, but as a result of artificial insemination from a donor. She does not aver, however, that the pursuer was a consenting party to such an artificial process of conception, and the pursuer maintains that he never agreed to the defender adopting it, if in fact it ever took place. The defender submits that artificial insemination by a donor, even without the consent of the husband, is not adultery as the law understands and has interpreted that term, and that proof of conception by such means would rebut the inference which would otherwise be raised from the fourteen months' period of non-access followed by the birth of a child. ...

There are manifestly grave moral, ethical, social, and personal considerations involved in the practice of artificial insemination in its various forms which will no doubt be fully developed elsewhere. It is almost trite to say that a married woman who, without the consent of her husband, has the seed of a male donor injected into her person by mechanical means, in order to procreate a child who would not be a child of the marriage, has committed a grave and heinous breach of the contract of marriage. The question for my determination, however, is not the moral culpability of such an act, but is whether such an act constitutes adultery in its legal meaning. A wife or a husband could commit an act of gross indecency with a member of the opposite sex which would be a complete violation of the marital relationship, but which could not be classified as adultery. It would indeed be easy according to one's personal viewpoint to allow oneself to be influenced by the moral, ethical, social, and personal considerations to which I have referred and to reach a conclusion based on these considerations, but this problem which I am called upon to solve must be decided by the objective standard of legal principles as these have been developed and must be confined to the narrow issue of whether this form of insemination constitutes adultery in the eyes of the law. If it is not adultery, although a grave breach of the marriage contract, that is a matter for the Legislature if it be thought that a separate legal remedy should be provided.

[Lord Wheatley concluded that the following propositions emerged from English and Scottish case law:]

> 1. For adultery to be committed there must be two parties physically present and engaging in the sexual act at the same time. 2. To constitute the sexual act there must be an act of union involving some degree of penetration of the female organ by the male organ. 3. It is not a necessary concomitant of adultery that male seed should be deposited in the female's ovum. 4. The placing of the male seed in the female ovum need not necessarily result from the sexual act, and if it does not, but is placed there by some other means, there is no sexual intercourse. ...

If artificial insemination by a donor without the husband's consent is to be deemed adultery, the first question which seems to call for a decision is whether the donor whose seed has been used has himself been guilty of adultery. If the answer is in the affirmative, the further question arises, at what point of time has he done so? If it be at the point when the seed is extracted from his body, certain interesting considerations would arise. I gather that seed so obtained can be retained for a considerable time before being used, and in some cases it may not be used at all. If the donor's seed is taken merely to lie *in retentis* it surely cannot be adultery if that seed is never used. Thus, if his adultery is to be deemed to take place at the time of the parting with the seed, it can only be an adultery subject to defeasance in the event of the seed not being used. Such a statement need only be stated for its absurdity to be manifested. If, on the other hand, his adultery is deemed to take place when the seed is injected into the woman's ovum, this latter act may take place after his death, and in that case the woman's conduct would constitute not only adultery but necrophilism. Such a proposition seems to me to be equally absurd. The third alternative is that the whole process should be regarded as an act of adultery, but as this might in certain cases result in the act covering a period of say two years, and be committed partly during the lifetime and partly after the death of the donor, I cannot distinguish between the absurdity of such a proposition and the absurdity of the other alternatives. Senior counsel for the pursuer appreciated the illogicality and absurdity of these consequences of the proposition that the donor had committed adultery, and accepted that he had not. This then forced him to argue that the wife could commit adultery by herself. One need not consider the interesting point whether the administrator could be said to commit adultery, because the administrator might be a woman or the seed might be self-injected by the wife herself operating the syringe. The idea that a woman is committing adultery when alone in the privacy of her bedroom she injects into her ovum by means of a syringe the seed of a man she does not know and has never seen is one which I am afraid I cannot accept. Unilateral adultery is possible, as in the case of a married man who ravishes a woman not his wife, but self-adultery is a conception as yet unknown to the law. The argument of pursuers' counsel was that adultery meant the introduction of a foreign element into the marital relationship. That, however, seems to me to beg the question, because what has still to be determined is what is the foreign element? For the reasons which I have already explained, that foreign element is the physical contact with an alien and unlawful sexual organ, and without that element there cannot be what the law regards as adultery. The introduction of a spurious element into the family, with all its consequences, may be the result of such conduct, but it not a necessary result, and it is by the means and not by the result that this issue is to be judged. If artificial insemination by a donor were to be regarded as adultery, then I opine the view that it would be adultery whether the seed germinated or not, and yet in the latter case there would be no resultant adulteration of the strain. At the root of the argument for the pursuer was the proposition that impregnation is at the basis of adultery, and it was argued that the view of the English Judges that there must be penetration indicated that there must be the possibility of insemination. Whatever the moral and ethical aspects of that argument may be, the Courts have now accepted that adultery can take place when the possibility of insemination has been excluded either by natural causes or artificial expedients, and so that argument must fail.

It accordingly follows, in my opinion, that artificial insemination by a donor does not constitute adultery according to our law. ...

P. (S.E.) v. P. (D.D.)

(2005), 259 D.L.R. (4th) 358 (B.C. S.C.)

[A wife petitioned for divorce on the basis that her husband had committed adultery. The petition was not defended and the husband provided an affidavit stating that he had had "voluntary sexual intercourse with a man" at a specified location and on a specific date. The court declined to grant the divorce without a hearing and requested the wife to make submissions on the issue of whether some sexual activities between a married man and another man could constitute adultery. The Attorney General of Canada intervened to support the wife's submissions that adultery should not be limited to sexual intercourse between persons of opposite sexes.]

GARSON J.: — 10 The current *Divorce Act* does not define "adultery." Rather, adultery has been defined by the courts on a case-by-case basis. As mentioned above, until the 1985 amendment of the 1968 *Divorce Act*, a homosexual act was expressly stated to be a ground for granting a divorce. Once a homosexual act was removed as an express separate ground for divorce by the enactment of the 1985 *Divorce Act*, the question could arise, as it has in this case, whether a spouse's sexual act outside of the marriage with someone of the same gender is adultery within the meaning of the current *Divorce Act*. ...

Adultery in the Common Law

20 ... The courts held that adultery had to be strictly proven and insisted on a requirement that there be penetrative sexual contact: *Babineau v. Babineau*, [1924] 4 D.L.R. 951 (N.B. C.A.).

21 In *Orford v. Orford* (1921), 58 D.L.R. 251 (Ont. H.C.), the common law meaning of adultery was discussed, as well as the historical rationale for its prohibition. The issue before the court was whether artificial insemination, without consent of the husband, was adultery and the court concluded that it was. ...

22 In 1982, when the issue was what meaning should be given to the words "homosexual act" in the list of grounds for divorce under the *Divorce Act*, the Ontario Supreme Court held in *Guy v. Guy* (1982), 35 O.R. (2d) 584 (H.C.) that "homosexual act" was to be given a very broad meaning. The court held that s. 3(b) of the 1968 *Divorce Act* required only a positive, physical act between at least two persons of the same sex having as its object, whether satisfied or not, the gratification of the sexual drives or propensities or preferences of the parties. There was no need to prove any vaginal contact or sodomy to establish such an act.

...

25 In *B. (Y.) v. B. (J.)* (1989), 66 Alta. L.R. (2d) 193 (Q.B.), the Alberta Court of Queen's Bench found that adultery was the only form of sexual conduct that constituted grounds for divorce, as specified in the *Divorce Act, 1985* and that this excluded homosexual conduct.

26 Although there is some uncertainty in the common law as to the precise definition of adultery, until now the courts in Canada have generally said that the act of adultery is between persons of the opposite sex.

American Approach

27 Some American courts have developed a different approach.

28 In the case of *S.B. v. S.J.B.*, 258 N.J. Super. 151, 609 A.2d 124, 1992 N.J. Super. LEXIS 275 (U.S. N.J. Super. Ch. 1992), from the Superior Court of New Jersey, the court said:

> All laws dealing with the termination of a marriage must first be looked at through the eyes of the injured spouse. Other than eighteen month continuous separation (*N.J.S.A. 2A:34 — 2d*) all grounds for divorce are bottomed in some type of "fault" concept which give the aggrieved spouse the right to seek termination of the marriage. ... An extramarital relationship viewed from this perspective is just as devastating to the spouse irrespective of the specific sexual act performed by the promiscuous spouse or the sex of the new paramour. The homosexual violation of marital vows could be well construed as the ultimate in rejection. ...
>
> What is important is to define, in human terms, those acts which constitute adultery so as to give rise to a termination of the marriage. Accordingly this court finds that adultery exists when one spouse rejects the other by entering into a personal intimate sexual relationship with any other person, irrespective of the specific sexual acts performed, the marital status, or the gender of the third party. It is the rejection of the spouse coupled with out-of-marriage intimacy that constitutes adultery.

29 American cases subsequent to *S.B. v. S.J.B.* addressing the issue of whether adultery may include a homosexual act outside of marriage have generated mixed results. ...

31 The Supreme Court of New Hampshire reached a different conclusion in *In re Branchflower*, 150 N.H. 226 (U.S. N.H. 2003). There, the majority found that to include homosexual acts in the definition of adultery would be contrary to legislative intent given the plain and ordinary meaning of adultery...

32 Several American decisions have classified heterosexual non-coitus events as adultery: *Rosser v. Rosser*, 355 So. 2d 717, 1977 Ala. Civ. App. LEXIS 749 (U.S. Ala. Cir. Ct. App. 1977); *Doe v. Doe*, 286 S.C. 507, 334 S.E.2d 829 (U.S. S.C. Ct. App. 1985); and *Menge v. Menge*, 491 So. 2d 700 (U.S. La. Ct. App. 5th Cir. 1986). ...

Current Common Law Definition of Adultery

43 Returning to the case before me, the historical justification for civil and, in fact, criminal penalties for adultery was the societal interest in ensuring the line of heredity was not adulterated. While it is not for this court to engage in a searching review of evidence of current societal views, it is clear, based on the legislative and common law developments legalizing same-sex marriage, that there has been an evolution of societal values such that the societal interest in marriage is focussed largely on the forming of relationships characterized by emotional and economic interdependence. As was stated by the Law Commission of Canada, marriage is now an institution to provide an orderly framework in which people can express their commitment to each other, receive public recognition and support, and voluntarily assume a range of legal rights and obligations. The evolution of societal values concerning same-sex marriage has not been without controversy or opposition. However, I consider Parliament's enactment of the *Civil Marriage Act* to be a legislative statement of the current values of our society consistent with the *Charter* that I am obliged to use as a guide to my consideration of the current common law definition of adultery. Individuals of the

same sex can now marry and divorce and the common law would be anomalous if those same-sex spouses were not bound by the same legal and social constraints against extra-marital sexual relationships that apply to heterosexual spouses.

44 I conclude that the definition of adultery used in our courts should reflect views that are consistent with the *Civil Marriage Act* and should be harmonized with the values enunciated in the *Charter*. If necessary to achieve this result, an incremental change in the definition of adultery should be made. ...

45 I agree with counsel that in this case it is unnecessary to engage in a specific s. 15 *Charter* analysis, that is whether under the *Charter* the provisions of the *Divorce Act* are discriminatory and therefore unconstitutional.

46 I turn next to the question of the definition of what sexual acts constitute adultery and whether this court should attempt to define adultery.

47 The traditional definition of adultery included the requirement that the sexual activity be intercourse. Because sexual relations might involve no penetration at all, this requirement could serve to deny a divorce to a man or a woman whose partner is having a sexual affair with a person of the same sex. However, the uncertainty about precisely what would constitute adultery in a same-sex relationship is not a reasonable basis for denying spouses the ability to divorce on the basis of same-sex sexual activity.

48 In the modern understanding of marriage, the wrong for which the petitioner seeks redress is something akin to violation of the marital bond. Viewed from this perspective, the heterosexual nature of the sexual acts is not determinative. Intimate sexual activity outside of marriage may represent a violation of the marital bond and be devastating to the spouse and the marital bond regardless of the specific nature of the sexual act performed.

49 In this case, the evidence of an intimate sexual relationship outside of Mr. and Ms. P's marriage is sufficient to grant the divorce on the grounds of adultery, notwithstanding that the act alleged was a same-sex sexual act. Adultery may include same-sex sexual acts where as here the evidence supports a finding that such has occurred.

50 In this case I do not consider it is necessary or desirable for me to define what type of intimate sexual activity constitutes adultery. Questions about the meaning of adultery in same-sex marriages should be clarified over time on a case-by-case basis, just as those questions have been resolved on a case-by-case basis in the context of heterosexual marriages.

Disposition

51 On the basis of the evidence before me, I am satisfied that Mr. P committed adultery and accordingly Ms. P is granted an order for divorce as petitioned for.

NOTES AND QUESTIONS

1. For further discussion of the issue raised in the *Orford* and *Maclennan* cases, see Tallin, "Artificial Insemination" (1956), 34 Can. Bar Rev. 1; Hubbard, "Artificial Insemination: A Reply to Dean Tallin" (1956), 34 Can. Bar Rev. 425; Payne, "Artificial Insemination Heterologous and the Matrimonial Offence of Adultery" (1961), 40 N.C.L.R. 111; Lang, "Does Artificial Insemination Constitute Adultery?" (1966), 2 Man. L.J. 87; and Fullerton, "Artificial Insemination" (1979), 2 Fam. L. Rev. 31.

2. Consent is a necessary ingredient of adultery. When a woman is sexually assaulted she does not commit adultery: *Redpath v. Redpath*, [1950] 1 All E.R. 600 (C.A.) and *Barnett v. Barnett*, [1957] P. 78, [1957] 1 All E.R. 388 at 82 [P.]. See also: *T. v. T.* (1969), 1 R.F.L. 23, [1970] 2 O.R. 139, 10 D.L.R. (3d) 125 (H.C.) at 128 [D.L.R.]. A woman may also be so drunk that she will be held not to have consented to the sexual intercourse: *Cunningham v. Cunningham* (1966), 11 F.L.R. 399 (Qld. S.C.).

3. The *P. v. P.* case was followed in *Thebeau v. Thebeau* (2006), 27 R.F.L. (6th) 430 (N.B. Q.B.), where a husband petitioned for divorce on the basis of his wife's adultery. Justice Wooder reasoned (paras. 8 and 12 to 14):

8 The *Divorce Act* applies to spouses. To confine the statutory right to divorce on the basis of adultery only to spouses whose partners engage in heterosexual extra-marital activity would be discriminatory in more than one respect. Homosexual spouses should be bound by the same legal constraints as heterosexual spouses. Homosexual violation of marriage vows should have the same consequences under the *Divorce Act* as heterosexual violation.

12 The consequence of infidelity, at least in the context of the *Divorce Act*, should not be confined to heterosexual spouses. To do so grants license to homosexual spouses to be sexually unfaithful and to violate vows, untrammeled by the prospect of a fault-based dissolution of their marriage. That is not equal treatment.

13 The definition of adultery must be consistent with the governing legislation and the values enshrined in the Charter. The dynamic nature of the common law and the judicial recognition of the obligation to ensure that it keeps in step with both permit this court to apply a definition of adultery as a ground of divorce regardless of whether the sexual misconduct is homosexual or heterosexual.

14 The evidence in this case satisfies me that the respondent has engaged in intimate sexual acts outside of the marriage. That is sufficient, in my view, to grant the divorce on the ground of marriage breakdown due to adultery and the divorce judgment will issue under section 8(2)(b)(i) of the *Act*.

4. What homosexual acts should qualify as adultery? How much guidance do the *P. v. P.* and *Thebeau v. Thebeau* cases give? Was it wise for the judges in those cases to refuse to articulate a comprehensive definition? Should they at least have given some indication of the nature of the extra-marital sexual conduct that occurred in those cases so that a definition can develop on a case-by-case basis?

5. Does it follow from the *P. v. P.* and *Thebeau v. Thebeau* cases that heterosexual acts short of intercourse can also constitute adultery? If so, what acts qualify? When Monica Lewinsky performed oral sex on President Clinton, did he have "sexual relations with that woman"? Did the President commit adultery?

6. Is sexual intercourse between a married, but separated, person and a third party adultery? See *Horvath v. Fraess* (1997), 36 R.F.L. (4th) 32 (Sask. Q.B.).

7. In *Fleming v. Fleming* (2001), 19 R.F.L. (5th) 274 (Ont. S.C.J.), a husband sought leave to amend his application for divorce on the basis of his wife's adultery to seek damages from his wife for committing the tort of deceit and for "breach of fiduciary relations". He claimed that, unbeknownst to him, his wife had engaged in two lengthy affairs during the marriage. Justice Mckinnon accepted (at para. 13) that "the spousal relationship is such that the law may impose a duty upon a spouse to warn the other of hazardous sexual activity that might expose the other to harm or illness", but concluded (at para. 14) that any principles requiring disclosure "fall far short of imposing an obligation upon a spouse to disclose extra-marital affairs".

(b) Proof of Adultery

(i) Standard and Nature of Proof

SHAW v. SHAW

(1971), 4 R.F.L. 392, 7 N.S.R. (2d) 77, 1971 CarswellNS 26 (T.D.)

DUBINSKY J.: — At the conclusion of the hearing in this case I granted a *decree nisi* in the divorce petition by Mrs. Shaw on the ground of cruelty. I reserved my decision on the counter-petition by Mr. Shaw on the ground of adultery.

Harold Bellefontaine, the co-respondent named in the counter-petition, denied that he had committed adultery with Mrs. Shaw, the respondent by the counter-petition.

I am on safe ground in saying that there is no *direct* evidence of any adulterous relationship between Mrs. Shaw and Mr. Bellefontaine. It follows, therefore, that if adultery is to be found herein on the part of the respondent (the respondent by the counter-petition), it must be inferred from the proven facts.

Power on Divorce, 2nd ed., 1964, p. 425 states as follows:

> Since it is almost never possible to adduce direct evidence of the act of adultery its commission is permitted to be proven by evidence of acts or a course of conduct which convinces the court that it should infer that it did occur.
>
> The inference can be drawn although both parties deny their guilt. The drawing of the inference must always be with caution and evidence that creates only a suspicion of adultery is insufficient.
>
> It is now settled that the standard of proof required in a divorce action wherein no question of legitimacy arises is not that applicable to criminal cases where the prosecution must prove guilt beyond a reasonable doubt, but is the standard required in civil actions where the preponderance of probabilities determines the issues. ... Where, as is usually the case, the evidence is circumstantial, it is not necessary that the facts should be inconsistent with any other rational conclusion than that the defendant is guilty. In such a case, and speaking generally of the standard of proof in an action for divorce, it is sufficient if the circumstances are such as would lead the guarded discretion of a reasonable or just man to that conclusion. ...
>
> It is impossible to lay down any general rule defining the circumstances which are sufficient in an action for divorce to justify a finding of adultery, except that the circumstances must be such as lead by fair and reasonable inference to that conclusion. Each case depends on its own particular facts. Evidence of familiarities between the parties and of facts showing opportunity for the commission of adultery raise a *prima facie* case that adultery has been committed, but the inference should always be drawn with extreme caution and it has been held should not be drawn unless there is proof of an inclination to commit adultery.

It would, in my opinion, be a reasonable and guarded inference from the facts that Mrs. Shaw and Mr. Bellefontaine, a married man with two children, were seeing so much of each other that the *opportunities* for her to commit adultery were present. However, Lord Atkin in *Ross v. Ellison (Ross)*, [1930] A.C. 1 at 23, points out:

> That there were opportunities for committing adultery is nothing; *there must be circumstances amounting to proof that the opportunities would be used.* (The italics are mine.)

... I would regard it as a sorry day if a married person could not have and enjoy the warm friendship of one of the opposite sex, without being stamped with the stigma of impropriety.

In two fairly recent cases, where the same sort of situation existed, I did draw the inference that adultery had been committed. In each of these cases there was something which led me to find as I did. In the first case there was evidence that on one occasion the respondent and co-respondent, who were both present at a party, were found lying fully clothed on the bed of a darkened bedroom. This uncontradicted piece of evidence led me to conclude that they were there for an amorous purpose. This incident, coupled with other evidence, led me to infer that adultery had taken place between the respondent and co-respondent.

In the other case there was introduced a letter which had been written by the respondent to the co-respondent and which referred to the great love that existed between them, as well as to other things. That letter, when added to other evidence which had been given, led me to infer that adultery had been committed.

In each of these two cases I had in mind what Lord Buckmaster said in *Ross v. Ellison (Ross), supra*, at p. 7:

> Adultery is essentially an act which can rarely be proved by direct evidence. It is a matter of inference and circumstance. It is easy to suggest conditions which can leave no doubt that adultery has been committed, but the mere fact that people are thrown together in an environment which lends itself to the commission of the offence is not enough unless it can be shown by *documents, e.g., letters and diaries, or antecedent conduct that the association of the parties was so intimate and their mutual passion so clear that adultery might reasonably be assumed as the result of an opportunity for its occurrence.* (The italics are mine.)

. . . . .

In short, keeping in mind the authorities quoted above and reviewing all the evidence given in the present case touching upon the allegation of adultery, I am not led to the conclusion that adultery was committed by Mrs. Shaw and Mr. Bellefontaine. Accordingly, I dismiss the counter-petition.

NOTES AND QUESTIONS

1. Direct evidence of adultery is obviously rare. In contested cases, the finding that the respondent has committed adultery is usually an inference drawn from circumstantial evidence. In *Burbage v. Burbage* (1985), 46 R.F.L. (2d) 33 (Ont. H.C.), Stortini L.J.S.C. stated (at 37): "In my view, once opportunity and intimacy are established on a balance of probabilities, there is a burden on the alleged adulterers to call evidence in rebuttal sufficient to dislodge the preponderant evidence." In *Burbage* the wife admitted that she spent a lot of time with the co-respondent and that she had spent several nights at his house. However, she and the co-respondent asserted that they had not had sexual intercourse because back surgery had rendered the co-respondent impotent. The judge, finding that the husband had established his wife's adultery, suggested that the co-respondent could have undergone a medical examination and either submitted a medical report or called the doctor to testify.

2. It is not necessary to name the third party in an application based on adultery. See *Family Law Rules*, O. Reg. 114/ 99, r. 36(3). In *d'Entremont v. d'Entremont* (1992), 44 R.F.L. (3d) 224 (N.S.C.A.), the affidavit of the respondent husband acknowledging uncondoned adultery with an unnamed person was sufficient evidence to prove adultery. If the third party is named, that person has to be served with the application and has all the rights of a respondent: *Family Law Rules*, O. Reg. 114/ 99, r. 36(3).

(ii) Section 10 of the Ontario Evidence Act

Section 23(1) of the *Divorce Act* incorporates by reference the provincial laws of evidence. Accordingly, the *Evidence Act*, R.S.O. 1990, c. E.23, applies to divorce proceedings in Ontario. By virtue of s. 8, parties to an action and their spouses are competent and compellable witnesses. However, s. 11 provides that persons cannot be compelled to disclose any communication between themselves and their spouses during the marriage. Moreover, s. 10 stipulates:

> The parties to a proceeding instituted in consequence of adultery and the spouses of such parties are competent to give evidence in such proceedings, but no witness in any such proceeding, whether a party to the suit or not, is liable to be asked or bound to answer any question tending to show that he or she is guilty of adultery, unless such witness has already given evidence in the same proceeding in disproof of his or her alleged adultery.

Section 10 applies wherever a divorce application or counter-claim relies on adultery to establish marriage breakdown. The cases exploring whether the section applied in other circumstances were recently reviewed in *Brazeau v. Brazeau* (2008), 56 R.F.L. (6th) 194 (Ont. S.C.J.) where a wife refused to answer questions on examination with respect to an alleged affair. She had applied for an equalization of the net family properties under Part I of the *Family Law Act* and there was a serious disagreement between the parties as to the date of separation. The husband wanted to show that the wife was involved with another man to buttress his argument that the parties had separated on the date chosen by him. Justice Hennessy concluded that s. 10 of the *Evidence Act* did not apply because this was not a "proceeding instituted in consequence of adultery".

The protection given by s. 10 can obviously be waived by a witness. Where an oral hearing occurs, it is advisable for counsel to inform the witness of the protection granted by s. 10 before the witness is sworn. After the witness is sworn, it is prudent to establish that the witness is aware of the protection and has expressly waived it before asking the relevant questions. See *Elliott v. Elliott*, [1933] O.R. 206, [1933] 2 D.L.R. 40 (H.C.) and *Welstead v. Brown* (1951), [1952] 1 S.C.R. 3, 102 C.C.C. 46 at 23 [S.C.R.]. Where a spouse files no answer to a divorce application, it is also possible to establish adultery by affidavit evidence alone. The rules formerly specified that where the respondent's or a third party's affidavit acknowledged the adultery, it had to stipulate that the deponent was aware that there was no obligation to give evidence of the adultery and that the evidence was willingly provided. The *Family Law Rules*, O. Reg. 114/99 have not retained these requirements, but the old practice of ensuring that the deponent is aware of s. 10 of the *Evidence Act* is still prudent.

NOTES AND QUESTIONS

1. Despite the statutory protection, the court may consider a party's failure to present evidence in disproof of adultery in deciding if the adultery has been established: *Fogel v. Fogel* (1976), 24 R.F.L. 18 (Ont. H.C.); affirmed (1979), 9 R.F.L. (2d) 55 (Ont. C.A.). Does this tend to defeat the legislative policy behind the legislation?

2. The effect of s. 10 is to prevent a party from commencing a proceeding on the ground of adultery unless the adultery can be proved by independent evidence or unless one of the adulterers consents to give evidence. Is s. 10 an outdated anomaly that should be repealed? The rule against self-incrimination in adultery cases has been repealed in England and several provinces. The Ontario Law Reform Commission urged its repeal in Ontario. See *Report on the Law of Evidence* (Ottawa: Ministry of the Attorney General, 1976) at 105–112. See also Rosen, "The Privilege Against Incrimination as to Adultery. Should it be Abolished?" (1960), 23 M.L.R. 275.

(3) Cruelty

KNOLL v. KNOLL

1 R.F.L. 141, [1970] 2 O.R. 169, 1970 CarswellOnt 101 (C.A.)

[The wife appealed a judgment dismissing a petition under the 1968 *Divorce Act* based on the husband's cruelty. Evidence at trial indicated that the husband drank heavily and that the wife left the matrimonial home because of the husband's abusive conduct towards her after he drank. Corroborated evidence indicated that the husband assaulted his wife on a number of occasions and that he was very rude and disrespectful when inebriated. The wife's doctor testified at trial that the marital situation had ruined the wife's nerves. She had high blood pressure, was completely rundown, and had lost 19 lbs. before she left the home. Medication had been prescribed. The wording of s. 3(d) of the 1968 Act was virtually identical to that in s. 8(2)(b)(ii) of the current Act.]

SCHROEDER J.A.: — ... It is evident that the learned Judge held and gave effect to the view that cruelty within the meaning of s. 3(d) of the *Divorce Act* was legal cruelty as defined in *Russell v. Russell*, [1897] A.C. 395 at 467, and in Ontario in *Bagshaw v. Bagshaw* (1920), 48 O.L.R. 52, 52 D.L.R. 634, and in many English and Canadian cases in which the principle there enunciated has been consistently followed and applied, a rule which required proof of conduct of such a character as to cause danger to life, limb or health (bodily or mental), or as to give rise to a reasonable apprehension of such danger. He must have concluded that the concept of cruelty as laid down in those cases was unaffected by the provisions of s. 3 of the *Divorce Act*. ...

In enacting the *Divorce Act* of 1968, Parliament has expressed the public will to soften the rigours of the marriage bonds as recognized in English canon law and founded upon the thesis that the general happiness of married life was secured by the indissolubility of the marriage bond, even though in individual cases its principles operated with great severity. Unhappy spouses were required to sleep in their beds as they had made them except in those extreme cases as outlined in Lord Stowell's judgment in *Evans v. Evans* (1790), 1 Hag. Con. 35, 161 E.R. 466.

Over the years the courts have steadfastly refrained from attempting to formulate a general definition of cruelty. As used in ordinary parlance "cruelty" signifies a disposition to inflict suffering; to delight in or exhibit indifference to the pain or misery of others; mercilessness or hard-heartedness as exhibited in action. If in the marriage relationship one spouse by his conduct causes wanton, malicious or unnecessary infliction of pain or suffering upon the body, the feelings or emotions of the other, his conduct may well constitute cruelty which will entitle a petitioner to dissolution of the marriage if, in the court's opinion, it amounts to physical or mental cruelty "of such a kind as to render intolerable the continued cohabitation of the spouses". That is the standard which the courts are to apply, and in the context of s. 3(d) of the Act that standard is expressed in language which must be taken to exclude the qualifications laid down in *Russell v. Russell, supra,* and in the numerous other cases which have followed and applied the ancient ecclesiastical rule in matrimonial disputes. ...

Care must be exercised in applying the standard set forth in s. 3(d) that conduct relied upon to establish cruelty is not a trivial act, but one of a "grave and weighty" nature, and not merely conduct which can be characterized as little more than a manifestation of incompatibility of temperament between the spouses. The whole matrimonial relations must be considered, especially if the cruelty consists of reproaches, complaints, accusations, or constant carping criticisms. A question most relevant for consideration is the effect of the conduct complained of upon the mind of the affected spouse. The determination of what constitutes cruelty in a given case must, in the final analysis, depend upon the circumstances of the particular case, having due regard to the physical and mental condition of the parties, their character and their attitudes towards the marriage relationship.

In the present case it is the cumulative effect of the acts of the defendant upon the petitioner which must be considered and given proper weight. The wife's return to her home after a day's work only to find her husband in an inebriated state, given to quarrelsomeness and abuse, heaping insult upon insult and indignity upon indignity, was clearly conduct amounting to mental cruelty of such a kind as to render intolerable the continued cohabitation of the spouses. I cannot be convinced that our community standards require a wife to tolerate such an intolerable situation. ...

GILBERT v. GILBERT

(1980), 18 R.F.L. (2d) 240, 39 N.S.R. (2d) 241, 1980 CarswellNS 45 (T.D.)

[In 1978, the combined effect of working, looking after her young daughter and maintaining a home became too much for the wife. She suffered from loss of sleep; she lost weight and was eventually admitted to hospital suffering from heart palpitations. After her discharge, she began to see a psychologist regularly. On 27th October 1979, the wife left the family home with her daughter, stating that life with her husband had become intolerable. The wife petitioned for divorce, alleging mental cruelty. Her principal complaint was that the husband had a domineering personality and often criticized her. The husband opposed the petition.]

HALLETT J.: — ... I formed the impression from the evidence and from my observation of the respondent that the worst that can be said about the respondent is that he is a very smug and self-satisfied person, and I accept the petitioner's evidence that she found it intolerable to continue living with him as far as she was concerned, but I do not think that the acts of which she complains constituted mental cruelty. The acts complained of were not grave and weighty but merely reflected a concern he had for the family's financial affairs and concern he had to see that his wife and child developed their personalities. It has been said many times that in the test as to whether the actions of a spouse constitute cruelty one must look at what effect the spouse's actions have had on the petitioner, not what effect they might have on a person of a different temperament. I accept that as a proper principle, but the conduct must be grave and weighty, and there is nothing in the evidence that measures up to this test of cruelty. I can understand that the petitioner was unhappy and that her husband's personality contributed to her unhappiness, but I do not feel his conduct amounted to mental cruelty of such a kind as to render intolerable the continued cohabitation of the parties. ...

The practice of the court in granting divorces on flimsy evidence in uncontested cases involving mental cruelty has, in my view, led petitioners and their counsel to overlook the fact that a petitioner must prove both that the conduct of the respondent was cruel and that it rendered cohabitation intolerable: *Luther v. Luther* (1978), 26 N.S.R. (2d) 232, 5 R.F.L. (2d) 285, 40 A.P.R. 232 (C.A.).

The acts of cruelty must be grave and weighty. The petitioner has testified that she could not stand living with the respondent and left. However, I am not satisfied that the evidence supports her allegations that he treated her with *mental cruelty* in that there was nothing in the evidence to show acts of a *grave and weighty nature* as necessary to establish this ground for divorce. The evidence shows the parties were of very different personalities, the petitioner somewhat shy and reserved and the respondent self-confident and self-satisfied. Such personality clashes cannot be elevated to form the basis for a decree to be granted on the ground of mental cruelty, notwithstanding the fact that one must look at the acts of the respondent in such a way as to ascertain what effect those acts had on *this* petitioner. I am not satisfied that the difficulties the petitioner had over the last year of their marriage can be attributed to conduct of the respondent that constituted mental cruelty. I am satisfied that pressures were present over which the respondent had little or no control. These pressures had an effect on the petitioner and she found she could not continue living with him and left.

The petition is dismissed. ...

DELANEY v. DELANEY

(1971), 5 R.F.L. 44, [1972] 1 O.R. 34, 1971 CarswellOnt 104 (C.A.)

SCHROEDER J.A. (orally): — ... The parties were married on 10th May 1969 and lived together until 13th July 1970, when the appellant deserted the respondent under the circumstances hereinafter mentioned.

It is alleged by the appellant that she and her husband had intercourse only four or five times within the first eight weeks of the marriage, but that, since that time, no further acts of intercourse took place; that the husband had persistently refused to gratify her wishes, although she requested him to have intercourse with her on numerous occasions during the remainder of the period of their life together. She suggested that he seek medical advice or other professional counselling, but he refused to do so.

In this case the marriage has admittedly been consummated, since there were four or five acts of sexual intercourse between the parties in the first and second month of the marriage. It would appear, and, indeed, there is nothing in the evidence to suggest the contrary, that this young woman had the normal sex drive, and the husband's abnormal reaction to her repeated invitations could have no other effect upon a normal healthy young woman of 21 years of age than to convince her that she was a total failure, wholly inadequate, perhaps a hopeless case. The erosion of her self-esteem, the feelings of despair and frustration, which would be thus engendered in her, could well, and, in this case, did have unwholesome consequences upon the petitioner's mental and physical health. Her father, who gave evidence, stated that she had become in his opinion a "nervous wreck". She lost a great deal of weight and her general physical health was impaired. The wife was brought face to face, therefore, with the alternative of having to live out her years under these intolerable conditions in a marriage state filled with mental anguish and despair, or to seek to put an end to it by divorce proceedings without further delay.

... The conduct on the part of the husband was clearly calculated to render intolerable the continued cohabitation of the spouses within the meaning of s. 3(d) of the *Divorce Act*. ...

NOTES AND QUESTIONS

1. As *Knoll* and *Gilbert* illustrate, the courts held that s. 3(d) of the *Divorce Act* of 1968 incorporated both a subjective and objective test. The objective test was considered necessary to ensure that mere incompatibility did not become a basis for divorce whereby the parties could avoid the three- or five-year waiting period under s. 4(1)(e). Nevertheless, the objective element of the test was downplayed in the years immediately preceding the repeal of the 1968 Act. Divorces were often granted, especially in uncontested cases, on the basis of evidence that revealed little more than incompatibility. See, for example, *Mes v. Mes* (1981), 24 R.F.L. (2d) 257 (Ont. H.C.) and Professor McLeod's annotation to the case in those reports. Should a more rigorous application of the test for cruelty be used under the new Act in light of the fact that a divorce can be obtained after a one-year separation? Conversely, is there any point in refusing to grant a divorce on the basis of cruelty because the divorce can readily be obtained on an alternative basis anyway?

2. In *Wright v. Wright* (2001), [2001] S.J. No. 408, 2001 CarswellSask 453 (Sask. Q.B.), Justice Ryan-Froslie quoted from the *Knoll* case and stated (at para. 46) that the comments relating to cruelty were still applicable. In refusing to grant a divorce on the basis of the husband's cruelty where there was evidence of shouting and mutual name-calling, the Justice concluded (at para. 50):

> Human relationships are prone to ups and downs. D.S.W. and D.M.W. are very different types of individuals. Those differences point more to incompatibility than to cruelty. The matters complained of by D.S.W. have either not been proven looking at the evidence as a whole or I find them to be evidence of incompatibility as opposed to cruelty.

As the husband and wife had separated over a year before the hearing, the court granted the wife's application for a divorce on the alternative basis of living separate and apart. See also *B. (Y.) v. B. (J.)* (1989), 20 R.F.L. (3d) 154 (Alta. Q.B.), where the court refused to find cruelty although the husband had confessed to his wife that he was a "practicing homosexual".

3. The courts have not given great weight to previously decided cases dealing with similar conduct. As a result, similar conduct may satisfy the test in one case and not in another. For example, refusing to have sexual intercourse constituted cruelty in *Delaney* and *Lewis v. Lewis* (1982), 44 N.B.R. (2d) 268 (N.B. Q.B.), but it did not in *Markus v. Markus* (1970), 3 R.F.L. 306, [1971] 2 W.W.R. 35, 16 D.L.R. (3d) 520 (Sask. Q.B.); *Ebenal v. Ebenal* (1970), 2 R.F.L. 180, [1971] 1 W.W.R. 473, 15 D.L.R. (3d) 242 (Sask. Q.B.); affirmed (1971), 3 R.F.L. 303 (Sask. C.A.); and *Boivin v. Massicote* (1977), 4 R.F.L. (2d) 315 (Que. S.C.). What circumstances might convince the court that refusing to have sexual intercourse is not cruelty?

4. Can a divorce be granted on the basis of s. 8(2)(b)(ii) of the *Divorce Act* in the following situation? A husband suffers from premature ejaculation. He refuses to seek or accept medical help despite his wife's requests and despite his awareness of the obvious emotional and mental stress caused to the wife. See *Katopodis v. Katopodis* (1979), 27 O.R. (2d) 711 (C.A.). Compare *Rouleau c. Wells* (1980), 124 D.L.R. (3d) 766 (Que. S.C.).

5. The respondent need not intend to be unkind or cruel for a court to conclude that his or her conduct was cruel. Nor is mental illness a defence to a divorce application on the basis of cruelty: *Castillo v. Castillo* (1986), 3 R.F.L. (3d) 423 (N.B. Q.B.). How is intent to be hurtful, to embarrass, etc., if present, nevertheless relevant? See *Emmerson v. Emmerson* (1970), 2 R.F.L. 147 (B.C. S.C.); *Wittstock v. Wittstock*, 3 R.F.L. 326, [1971] 2 O.R. 472, 18 D.L.R. (3d) 264 (C.A.); and *Thordarson v. Thordarson* (1978), 5 R.F.L. (2d) 92 (Ont. C.A.).

6. In almost every case where a divorce is granted on the basis of cruelty the parties will be living separate and apart. In some circumstances, however, a woman may succeed in establishing cruelty even if she continues to

cohabit with her husband. In *Horne v. Horne*, 5 R.F.L. 394, [1972] 3 W.W.R. 153 (B.C.S.C.), McIntyre J. stated (at 395):

> The presence of small children needing her care might influence a mother to "tolerate the intolerable". A woman without funds and without means of earning a living in a remote area far from help and friends, might also find herself in the same situation.

See also *MacDonald v. MacDonald* (1975), 23 R.F.L. 303 (Man. Q.B.); *Pongor v. Pongor* (1976), 27 R.F.L. 109 (Ont. C.A.); and *Boulos v. Boulos* (1980), 14 R.F.L. (2d) 206, 24 Nfld. & P.E.I.R. 370 (Nfld. T.D.).

7. The courts are usually willing to consider conduct after separation to determine whether cruelty has been established. See, e.g., *Storr v. Storr* (1974), 14 R.F.L. 346 (N.S. C.A.) and *Greggain v. Hunter* (1984), 31 Sask. R. 311 (U.F.C.).

4. Bars to Proceedings

(1) Introduction

Section 11 of the *Divorce Act* resembles s. 9 of the 1968 Act. The wording of s. 11 indicates that it is the duty of the court to ascertain whether or not any of the relevant bars exist, even if neither party raises this issue. See *Money v. Money* (1987), 5 R.F.L. (3d) 375 (Man. C.A.) and *Kaur v. Brar* (2003), 35 R.F.L. (5th) 380 (Ont. S.C.J.). However, this duty may be of more theoretical than practical significance in an undefended divorce, especially one involving only affidavit evidence.

(2) Collusion

Section 11(1)(a) of the 1985 *Divorce Act* retains collusion as an absolute bar to an application for divorce. Section 11(4) defines the term in essentially the same manner as it was defined in the 1968 Act. The following article examined the extent to which the 1968 statutory definition altered the common law concept of collusion.

SOPINKA, "THE DIVORCE ACT, 1968: COLLUSION CONFINED"

(1969), 47 Can. Bar Rev. 31–39 (Footnotes omitted)

In the past, judicial definition of collusion exhibited three levels, ranging from the most restrictive to the more expanded definition:

Level one	The most restrictive "a corrupt agreement or conspiracy to which the petitioner is a party, to obtain a divorce by means of manufactured evidence, or some fraud or deceit practised on the court".
Level two	The restrictive definition was expanded by extending it to apply to any agreement to withhold or abandon a defence otherwise open to one of the respondents or to suppress evidence.
Level three	Levels one and two were further expanded to include an agreement in which, in consideration of a promise to bring and conduct a divorce proceeding, on valid grounds, the plaintiff was provided with substantial benefits in the form of maintenance, costs, division of marital property and the like if the agreement could be characterized as a bribe to bring proceedings.

Courts have had no difficulty in classifying as collusive, agreements under level one because the presentation of a false case clearly perverted or tended to pervert the course of justice. Such agreements are manifestly included in the statutory definition in the *Divorce Act*.

Agreements coming under level two presented more difficulty. Here the grounds for a divorce exist but may be subject to defences open to one of the parties such as condonation, connivance, adultery by the plaintiff or petitioner, lack of domicile and the like. If a party agrees that these defences will be suppressed in whole or in part the court is prevented from getting at the truth and may grant a divorce which, but for the agreement, would not have been granted. The result is a subversion of the course of justice. *Prima facie*, therefore, such agreements were properly characterized as collusive in the past, and, it is submitted are collusive under the *Divorce Act* because they are entered into "for the purpose of subverting the administration of justice" and "to deceive the court". ...

It is only a *prima facie* case, however, which may be rebutted by evidence that satisfies the court that the agreement did not suppress any defence having a reasonable chance of success and was entered into merely to save the parties the time and expense of protracted litigation or otherwise to "smooth the asperities of litigation". If a judge is satisfied that there has been such a full and frank disclosure of the facts that he is able to come to the conclusion that the decree would have been granted if defended, it seems highly unreasonable to refuse a decree simply on the basis of the existence of the agreement.

Agreements of the type classified under the third level referred to above which provide for the institution of divorce proceedings in return for financial benefits presented the greatest difficulty to the courts in the past.

[After discussing some of the cases where agreements of the type classified under the third level were held to be collusive, Sopinka concludes:]

The rationale of these cases is that the court must be satisfied that the plaintiff has received a real injury and genuinely seeks relief. If the plaintiff is only nominally seeking relief which is actually desired by the defendant wrongdoer then the court will refuse to allow the wrongdoer to obtain the divorce.

This reasoning had some justification in administering a divorce law based exclusively on the matrimonial offence concept. A divorce was only to be granted to the innocent against the guilty. If the court found that the situation in substance as opposed to form was reversed then it refused the decree. The *Divorce Act* however has departed from the matrimonial offence concept. It introduces the marriage breakdown concept and enables the so-called guilty spouse to divorce the innocent. ...

A departure from the matrimonial offence concept would therefore suggest the elimination altogether from the definition of collusion the type of agreement outlined under level three. It seems futile to analyze the motives of the petitioner to see whether it is the injured party who seeks relief when the injured party may be divorced against his or her will in certain circumstances and in others a divorce may be granted on grounds which involve no matrimonial offence at all.

While the change in the basic concept of divorce suggests the narrowing of collusion as to exclude agreements under level three it is submitted that an examination of the definition itself clearly leads to that conclusion. An agreement for financial benefits to the petitioner in consideration of the commencement of proceedings for divorce, where valid grounds exist, (especially if disclosed to the court) cannot, it is submitted be characterized as being "for the purpose of subverting the administration of justice." Such an agreement "in no way distorts the grounds upon which relief is sought, nor does it provide for the suppression of material facts". It is submitted that the saving clause of the definition was inserted to make it abundantly clear that such agreements were to be excluded. It cannot be interpreted to refer to the usual separation agreement *simpliciter*, which makes no mention of divorce. A statutory exclusion would hardly be necessary to cover such an agreement. No case has found such an agreement to be collusive. ...

In summary, it appears that in order to eliminate the uncertainty in the law of collusion which kept the parties at arms length, hampered reconciliation and discouraged settlement of support, custody and property issues, Parliament has narrowed the definition of collusion. It is the author's conclusion that Parliament intended to remove the taint of collusion from those troublesome agreements by which divorce proceedings are agreed to be brought in return for financial benefits by way of support or for the division of marital property and costs. Such an agreement could not, of course, provide for the fabrication or manufacturing of evidence, the withholding of a just defence or the suppression of evidence.

NOTES AND QUESTIONS

1. In *Gillett v. Gillett* (1979), 9 R.F.L. (2d) 97, 9 Alta. L.R. (2d) 238 (T.D.), the court expressly adopted the views of Sopinka regarding agreements that he classified under Level Three.

2. For a rare recent example of a case in which the court refused to grant a divorce because of collusion between the parties, see *Wei v. Cao* (2008), 2008 CarswellBC 415 (S.C.) where the husband and wife "backdated" the date of separation in their joint claim for divorce so that it would appear that they had been living separate and apart for over a year.

3. The bar of collusion has caused problems in some "immigration marriages" where a person agrees to marry another solely to allow the latter to obtain favourable immigration status. For example, Justice Dunn refused to grant a divorce in *Kaur v. Brar* (2003), 35 R.F.L. (5th) 380 (Ont. S.C.J.) where the marriage was "a collusive attempt to defraud immigration authorities" (para. 13). See also *Singh v. Singh* (1975), 25 R.F.L. 20 (B.C. S.C.) and *Johnson v. Ahmad* (1981), 22 R.F.L. (2d) 141 (Alta. Q.B.). Compare *Fernandez (Alacrio) v. Fernandez* (1983), 34 R.F.L. (2d) 249 (Man. Q.B.). These cases were recently reviewed in *Merchant v. Dossani* (2007), 2007 Carswell-Alta 988, 39 R.F.L. (6th) 404 (Q.B.).

If there is a "collusive marriage", why is the attempt to end it collusive? What purpose is served by insisting that an "immigration marriage" continue?

(3) Condonation

The purpose of the bar of condonation is to prevent a spouse who agrees to resume or continue cohabitation with a partner who has committed a "matrimonial offence" from holding that offence over the other's head forever afterwards. However, if condonation is an absolute bar it may discourage attempts at reconciliation. The innocent spouse may fear losing the right to an immediate divorce as a result of a failed attempt at reconciliation. This was obviously more significant in the past when the grounds were limited. The current *Divorce Act*, much like the 1968 Act, retains condonation as a bar to a divorce application that relies on adultery or cruelty but reduces it to a discretionary bar and suspends its application for up to 90 days during cohabitation for the purpose of reconciliation. See ss. 11(1)(c) and 11(3).

WATKINS v. WATKINS

(1980), 14 R.F.L. (2d) 97, 1980 CarswellNfld 8 (Nfld. T.D.)

[The husband petitioned on the basis of his wife's adultery. After the petition was issued, the couple had sexual intercourse. Justice Goodridge dealt with the issue of condonation as follows.]

GOODRIDGE J.: — ... It used to be considered that sexual intercourse between spouses taking place after a known act of adultery amounted to condonation of that act. This is no longer necessarily the case.

Under the present law of condonation there are three essential elements. These are: (a) knowledge of the matrimonial offence; (b) an intention to forgive; and (c) the restoration into the marriage of the guilty spouse. ...

As to the questions of fact that arise out of the three points, my finding is as follows:

While there would appear to have been knowledge by the innocent spouse of the adultery of his wife, I am somewhat doubtful that he was aware of the extent of the adultery. Apart from admitted acts of intercourse, I imagine that he entertained suspicions only. This of course is not relevant in this case, as when the sexual intercourse took place between the spouses after the adultery the respondent was either clearly pregnant or had already given birth to a child of whom the petitioner was not the father.

On the evidence, there was clearly no intention on the part of the petitioner to forgive. The sexual intercourse took place evidently solely with a view to personal satisfaction. The respondent testified that while she participated in the intercourse she was not an instigator of the intimacy and it would appear was not an altogether enthusiastic participant.

Quite apart from the first two considerations, however, there was clearly no intention to restore the respondent into the marital relationship. Reconciliation was clearly the farthest thing from the minds of the spouses. She was about to have or had already had a child by an adulterous relationship. The parties were not living nor proposing to live as man and wife and in fact were formulating plans for a separate existence and discussing matters such as custody of the children.

On the facts of the case I find that the subsequent intercourse between the spouses did not amount to condonation of the adultery of the respondent and therefore I award the decree. ...

In addition to that, even if there was condonation, I may still grant the decree if I am of the opinion that the public interest would be better served thereby.

In this case a child has been born of whom the petitioner was not the father. I cannot hold otherwise than that the public interest would not be served by my refusing the decree, for to do so would be to require that there be interjected into the marriage a foreign element, namely, a fourth child conceived in adultery, a situation that should not be imposed upon the petitioner without his consent, and there is no such consent. ...

NOTES AND QUESTIONS

1. Continued or resumed cohabitation may not lead to a finding of condonation. First, s. 11(3) of the *Divorce Act* provides that condonation does not include the continuation or resumption of cohabitation for a period of, or periods totalling, not more than 90 days if such cohabitation is continued or resumed with reconciliation as its primary purpose. Second, continued or resumed cohabitation may not establish that an actual reconciliation has occurred. For example, a wife may return to the matrimonial home simply because she has no other place to go: *Khader v. Khader* (1975), 20 R.F.L. 365 (Ont. C.A.). Third, sometimes the courts appear to require a successful

reconciliation before they are willing to find condonation. In *Einarson v. Einarson*, 4 R.F.L. 355, [1971] 5 W.W.R. 478, 20 D.L.R. (3d) 126 (B.C. S.C.), the wife returned to live with her husband after obtaining a *decree nisi*. Both spouses hoped that they would be able to salvage the marriage. Although they cohabited for over a year, the court found that the attempt had degenerated into a "loveless co-existence" after about two months. The court held that, as there had been no reconciliation, the wife had not condoned the husband's cruelty.

2. Notwithstanding condonation, s. 11(1)(c) of the *Divorce Act* empowers a court to grant the divorce if "the public interest would be better served by granting the divorce". A similar power existed under s. 9(1)(c) of the 1968 *Divorce Act*. Marriage breakdown alone was considered sufficient reason to conclude that the decree would be in the public interest in most cases, including *Saunders v. Saunders* (1975), 22 R.F.L. 210 (Man. Q.B.). This factor was fortified by the need to bring stability to the lives of the children of the marriage in *Getson v. Getson* (1970), 2 R.F.L. 91 (N.S. T.D.). The liberal interpretation of the public interest adopted in the cases means that condonation is rarely a bar to divorce.

3. Under the traditional doctrine of revival, condonation was always conditional upon the other spouse not committing a further matrimonial offence. If a matrimonial offence were committed after condonation, the earlier offence would be revived. The offence that revived the earlier offence did not necessarily have to be of the same nature or degree as the earlier offence, nor did it have to be of itself a ground for the matrimonial relief sought by the innocent spouse: *Beard v. Beard* (1945), [1946] P. 8 (Eng. P.D.A.). Section 9(2) of the 1968 Act abolished the doctrine of revival. See now s. 11(2) of the *Divorce Act*. Can you think of any reasons why the legislature would abolish the doctrine?

4. Notwithstanding the abolition of the doctrine of revival, it appears settled that the court may examine a respondent's condoned conduct to determine if a subsequent act or course of conduct amounts to cruelty. See, e.g., *Raney v. Raney* (1973), 1 O.R. (2d) 491 (S.C.); *Storey v. Storey* (1973), 10 R.F.L. 170, 4 Nfld. & P.E.I.R. 229 (P.E.I. T.D.); and *Ifield v. Ifield* (1975), 24 R.F.L. 237, 66 D.L.R. (3d) 311 (Sask. Q.B.) at 319 [D.L.R.]

(4) Connivance

Like condonation, connivance is only a bar if a divorce is sought in the circumstances described in s. 8(2)(b) of the *Divorce Act*. Connivance is not defined in the Act but it has a relatively well-established meaning at common law.

MADDOCK v. MADDOCK

[1958] O.R. 810, 1958 CarswellOnt 129 (C.A.)

[Two drivers for Canada Bread became friends. They and their wives associated together frequently. After about two years, one of the wives told her husband that his friend had asked her to go away with him and that she intended to agree if the marriage did not improve. Thereafter, the marriage deteriorated and the wife suggested that the couple separate. The husband agreed and they signed a separation agreement. While the agreement was silent as to who should remain in occupation of the matrimonial home, apparently it was agreed that the husband should move out. He remained in the house until the following day, when he moved with the few belongings to which he was entitled under the agreement. As he was moving out, he met his friend going into the house with his clothes. The husband denied any knowledge of the friend's intention to move in or of any arrangement between them. The trial judge on these facts found connivance. In his reasons for judgment he said:

> Now, this would appear to me to be more than a coincidence. It seems to me to lead to the almost inescapable conclusion that there must have been some understanding between the plaintiff and the male defendant.

> It would be hard otherwise to believe that a male defendant, apart from some understanding with the husband, would have the temerity to move in his belongings while the husband was removing his from the matrimonial home.

In the present case — if I understood the evidence correctly, and I believe I did, — the plaintiff and the male defendant were actually brushing past each other as one was taking his things from the house and the other was bringing his things into the house.

The inference, it seems to me, is clear that the understanding between the plaintiff and the male defendant was that the plaintiff would move out of his home and that the male defendant would move in.

Certainly, it appeared to me that the plaintiff recklessly permitted the adultery, which he has alleged, to take place between his wife and the male defendant; and, indeed, that he facilitated the commission of such adultery.]

SCHROEDER J.A.: — ... I think it is clear from the learned trial Judge's reasons that he attached the most vital significance to the fact that the co-respondent was moving his personal belongings into the Gore St. house at the same time as the plaintiff was moving out, and despite the latter's emphatic denial, he refused to believe that this was a purely coincidental occurrence. ...

With the greatest deference to the opinion of the learned trial Judge, I am unable to place a construction upon the evidence which would support his conclusion that the plaintiff was guilty of connivance which precluded his right to a decree dissolving the marriage.

It is of the very essence of connivance that the person complaining of the misconduct should have consented or wilfully contributed to the commission of the adultery or have promoted it in some other way, so that it would appear that he had what has been frequently described in the authorities as "a corrupt intention". ...

It is well recognized, of course, that a petitioner may connive at adultery otherwise than by giving an express consent. If, with a corrupt intention, he stands by and permits the act to take place he may be guilty of connivance by acquiescence.

... It may be that the plaintiff was too easily prevailed upon to yield to his wife's desire for a separation, and perhaps his failure to protest when he saw the defendant moving into the home as he was leaving it, is open to criticism. It must be borne in mind, however, that he had entered into a formal separation agreement with his wife and that he was bound, by the covenant to which he had subscribed, to live separate and apart from her. Even if he had taken steps on that occasion to prevent the co-respondent from moving into his late home, what would have prevented this man from returning to it as soon as the plaintiff's back was turned? The circumstance which gave rise to the suspicion in the learned trial Judge's mind must be weighed against the positive statements of the plaintiff that he did not know that the co-respondent had arranged to move into his house. It is evident, however, that the defendant wife knew and that she acted with complete independence and in arrant and shameless disregard of her husband's wishes or his sensibilities. I should think that if there had been a guilty arrangement entered into between the plaintiff and the co-respondent as the learned Judge suggests, the plaintiff would have taken great pains to avoid even the slightest appearance of evil, and the fact that the co-respondent's act of moving into the premises coincided in the point of time with the plaintiff's moving out is equally, if not more, suggestive of his innocence in the matter. It is also noteworthy that he made no attempt to conceal this fact when testifying, although the action was unopposed. ...

LAIDLAW J.A.: — It will be convenient and helpful to state certain propositions or principles of law respecting connivance. ...

1. Connivance may consist of any act done with corrupt intention of a husband or wife to promote or encourage either the initiation or the continuance of adultery of his or her spouse, or it may consist of passive acquiescence in such adultery.

2. Corrupt intention of the husband or wife seeking a divorce is an essential ingredient of connivance, and the conduct of the husband or wife seeking the divorce must show that he or she, as the case may be, willingly consented to the adultery of the other spouse.

3,   The issue is whether on the facts of the particular case, the husband or wife seeking the divorce was or was not guilty of the corrupt intention of promoting or encouraging either the initiation or the continuance of the adultery of the other spouse.

4.   Acts done by a husband or wife seeking a divorce or by any person employed by him or her, as the case may be, to keep a watch on the other spouse to see whether or not his or her suspicions of adultery are well-founded or unfounded, do not necessarily constitute connivance and, likewise, if one spouse does nothing without lulling into a sense of security, the other spouse about whom he or she, as the case may be, is suspicious, but merely watches her, he is not necessarily guilty of passive acquiescence amounting to connivance.

5.   "The Court should not allow its judgment to be affected by importing, as principles of universal application, pronouncements made with regard to wholly different circumstances and be led to a conclusion contrary to the justice of the case": *Churchman v. Churchman*, [1945] P. 44 at p. 52.

6.   There is a presumption of law against the existence of connivance and the Court should not find a spouse guilty of connivance unless the evidence shows clearly that all the essential ingredients thereof exist in the particular facts under consideration.

      ...

I am satisfied that in the particular circumstances of this case the plaintiff's conduct does not show that he had a "corrupt intention" to encourage or promote the adultery of his wife and therefore he was not guilty of connivance. ...

[Justice Lebel dissented, holding that the inference of passive connivance drawn by the trial judge was correct.]

FLEET v. FLEET

7 R.F.L. 355, [1972] 2 O.R. 530, 1972 CarswellOnt 153 (C.A.)

GALE C.J.O. (orally): — This is an appeal from a judgment dismissing a petition for divorce by reason of the petitioner's connivance.

The trial Judge held that the conduct of the petitioner in not making her presence known immediately upon arrival at the scene where her spouse was committing adultery was connivance. It is our unanimous view that he erred in that conclusion, particularly when regard is had to the evidence of both the petitioner and a corroborating witness. I refer to the petitioner's evidence as follows:

> MR. CLARK: Mrs. Fleet at the time you spotted the car, was this action in progress? [Sexual intercourse between the respondents.] A. Yes Sir.
>
> Q. And is it correct to inform this Court that you just witnessed the completion of it, and as they sat there talking? A. That is correct.

The petitioner's evidence was corroborated by a witness who had accompanied the petitioner to the scene of the misconduct. He stated that the said act had already commenced as he and the petitioner drove into the road overlooking the gravel pit where the car occupied by the respondents was located. On that evidence we are of the view that connivance was not proven and the petitioner ought to have been granted a decree *nisi*. We also point out that it would not be connivance even if the misconduct had not commenced at the time the petitioner and her witness arrived.

The learned trial Judge appeared to be of the opinion that at any time a petitioner becomes aware that the adultery may take place it is incumbent upon the petitioner to stop it or become disentitled to any relief by reason of connivance. In our view, that is not the law and I refer to *Maddock v. Maddock*. ...

NOTES AND QUESTIONS

1. What is the basic difference between connivance and condonation?

2. Section 11(1)(c) of the *Divorce Act* authorizes a court to grant a divorce notwithstanding connivance if this serves the public interest. Should the courts adopt the same approach in determining the public interest in this context as they have in relation to condonation?

(5) Reasonable Arrangements for the Support of Children

ORELLANA v. MERINO

(1998), 40 R.F.L. (4th) 129, 1998 CarswellOnt 2533 (Ont. Gen. Div.)

CAMPBELL J.: — This is an application for divorce *simpliciter*. There are two children of this marriage. The parties separated in July 1990. The girls have lived with their mother since separation and, pursuant to an order of Webster Prov. J. of December 12, 1990, the applicant has custody of the children and the respondent is required to pay $50 per month per child.

The respondent left Canada in 1991 until he returned in August 1995. The respondent has exercised very little access to the girls since then. He has not exercised access at all since the summer of 1996. He is in arrears of child support and the order is filed with the Family Responsibility Office.

When the respondent attended at the applicant's lawyer's office for service of the divorce documentation, he declined to disclose his address. His attendance for service was arranged by the applicant who, although she is unaware of his present address, obviously has a means of communicating with him.

On the 1st of June, 1998, I stayed this divorce on the basis that I was not satisfied that s. 11 of the *Divorce Act* ... had been addressed. I decided that appropriate financial arrangements had not been made for the support of the children. Although the respondent appears to be gainfully employed, there is no current information as to his present ability to pay support.

Counsel for the applicant, by way of a letter directed to me (rather than an affidavit of the applicant) advises *inter alia* that

(a) she does not have sufficient information to bring a support motion before the court in an attempt to obtain child support in accordance with the current Guidelines;

(b) The Respondent has exercised very little access to the children. The Applicant is currently engaged to be married and her partner acts as a father to the children. The Applicant's partner is prepared to support the children. ...

(c) The Applicant has built a life for herself and the children with the help of her current partner. She wishes this divorce so that she and her partner can marry and unite their family.

It would place an undue hardship on the Applicant to require her to determine the Respondent's current financial situation prior to granting her divorce. If she is unable to obtain this information she will remain indefinitely tied to a man who is no longer a part of her life or her children's.

Counsel seeks to have the court exercise its discretion and grant the divorce, despite the principles of the new *Child Support Guidelines*, SOR/ 97-175 and s.11 of the *Divorce Act*. [The *Guidelines* came into effect May 1, 1997. By virtue of s. 15.1(3) of the *Divorce Act*, child support orders must accord with the *Guidelines*. Regarding the *Guidelines* generally, see Chapter 8, *CHILD SUPPORT*. In 1997, s. 11(1)(b) of the *Divorce Act* was amended to stipulate that the courts must have regard to the *Guidelines* in determining whether the parents have made reasonable arrangements for child support.]

In the past, there has been much criticism of the courts with regard to inconsistent child support orders. The *Child Support Guidelines* clearly intend to offer consistency to Canadian children by requiring Canadian parents to meet their financial obligation to their children in a fair, consistent and predictable manner. What the applicant seeks would, in my view, represent a complete abrogation of the court's obligation and a direct contravention of the intent and principles of the *Child Support Guidelines*.

A support order of $100 per month for two children would be required of any non-custodial parent earning only $9,000 per year. There is no evidence whatsoever to indicate that Mr. Merino is only earning an income of that level. Minimum wages for a 40 hour work week offers a yearly income of over $14,000.

It is not for the applicant to choose not to bother to try to obtain reasonable support. The applicant offers no reason whatsoever why she has not sought to inform the Director of the Family Responsibility Office of this man's return and present employment or why she has not attempted to update an order that is seven-and-a-half years old.

Although the applicant's present partner has obviously treated the children as his own, and is apparently willing to "help", the primary financial obligation remains with the natural parents of these children.

Unless the applicant's partner intends to adopt the children (with or without Mr. Merino's consent), the respondent's obligation to his daughters continues.

The court is not persuaded to act on a letter from counsel to exercise its discretion to allow Mr. Merino to avoid his obligation to his daughters due to some reluctance by the applicant (the basis of which is as yet unknown) to ensure that her daughters obtain an appropriate level of support.

The divorce was stayed on the 1st of June, 1998. There is nothing properly before the court upon which the court could or is willing to exercise its "discretion" to change that status.

McLEOD, "ANNOTATION"

(1998), 40 R.F.L. (4th) 129

In *Orellana v. Merino*, Campbell J. refused to grant a wife's application for divorce because he was not satisfied that reasonable financial arrangements had been made for the support of the children. Although his decision not to grant the divorce is correct on the facts of the case, his comments on when a judge may decline to grant a divorce under s. 11(1)(b) of the *Divorce Act* are more problematic.

Pursuant to s. 11(1)(b) of the Act, a judge must stay the granting of a divorce unless he or she is satisfied that reasonable arrangements have been made for the children's support. The purpose behind s. 11(1)(b) of the *Divorce Act* is to force the parents to address the issue of child support before obtaining a divorce.

Granting a divorce does not affect a child's right to support. A parent can obtain child support after divorce under the *Divorce Act* and a child can obtain support under provincial child-support legislation. Although it makes sense to force a payor who seeks a divorce to prove that he or she has discharged his or her child-support obligation, different considerations apply where a custodial parent seeks a divorce.

Practically, a custodial parent has to support a child in his or her care. Although a non-custodial parent may be required to pay child support, a custodial parent must make up any shortfall from personal resources. If a custodial parent does not make adequate arrangements with the other parent for the support of a child, he or she makes sacrifices, the child does without or the State provides welfare assistance. Section 11(1)(b) of the *Divorce Act* is intended to minimize the chance that either of the latter two contingencies will occur.

If a custodial parent is able to support the child and is prepared to do so, a court should grant the custodial parent's application for divorce regardless of whether the non-custodial parent is paying sufficient child support. The child's needs will be met and the State will not be called upon to support the family. No public interest justifies denying the custodial parent's application for a divorce.

A custodial parent may be prepared to maintain a child because it is not worth his or her time and money to seek support from the other parent or because the other parent is content to leave the parent and child alone if he or she is not required to pay child support. Either of these may be a good reason in a particular case not to pursue the issue of child support if a custodial parent has sufficient resources to maintain the child.

In *Orellana v. Merino*, the wife failed to explain her reason for not claiming increased child support from her husband or why the outstanding child-support order remained appropriate. This was an error in judgment. A lawyer drafting an affidavit in support of a divorce must address child support. Campbell J. was correct to stay the wife's application for divorce in the first instance to force her to explain her inaction.

The *Divorce Act* puts an onus on a petitioner to explain why a judge does not have to worry about the children's financial needs. There must be some evidence before a judge that the children's needs will be met. A petitioner's divorce affidavit or testimony must address child support. If the support paid is less than the Guidelines amount, a petitioner must explain why. If the explanation is reasonable, a court should grant the divorce. Judges are not charged with ensuring that every non-custodial parent pays Guidelines support before granting a divorce, just that reasonable arrangements for child support have been made. In deciding what is reasonable a court must consider the Guidelines.

In *Zarebski v. Zarebski* (1997), 29 R.F.L. (4th) 93 (Ont. Gen. Div.), Campbell J. granted a mother's application for a divorce notwithstanding the fact that she had no information about the father's whereabouts or his income. Rather than prolong the divorce proceedings, she was prepared to support the children herself. Campbell J. stated that the mother's solution was not "ideal" but "reasonable arrangements" do not have to be "ideal".

The wife's lawyer [in *Orellana*] responded to the stay by sending the judge a letter outlining her client's position. This is not an acceptable way to provide information to a judge in divorce proceedings. Campbell J. is correct to reject the lawyer's letter explaining why her client did not seek increased spousal support as sufficient evidence to discharge the onus under s. 11(1)(b) of the *Divorce Act*. A lawyer or party cannot send a letter to a judge and expect the judge to treat the letter as evidence. Evidence in divorce proceedings may be by *viva voce* testimony or an affidavit. It is a small matter for the lawyer to take the evidence in the letter and put it into an affidavit for the wife to swear.

Even then, it is questionable whether Campbell J. would have granted the divorce. Campbell J. appears to be of the view that pursuant to s. 11(1)(b), a petitioner must prove that the non-custodial parent pays Guidelines support or explain why not. The wife opted for "why not". She stated that she did not have sufficient information to justify an application to increase child support and that her new partner, whom she planned to marry, could and would support the children. Campbell J. was not convinced. With respect, it is submitted that the wife's explanation, if contained in an affidavit, should be sufficient to satisfy the onus under s. 11(1)(b) of the *Divorce Act*. The children's needs will be met and the State will not be called upon to contribute to child support.

The possibility that the husband is paying insufficient support should not be determinative of whether Campbell J. grants the divorce. If the husband wanted the divorce, Campbell

J. could reasonably stay the divorce until the husband proved that he was honouring his child-support obligations. A person should not be allowed to seek relief if he or she is not honouring related legal obligations.

By denying the wife a divorce, Campbell J. prevents her and her new partner from regularizing their relationship and marrying. The wife does not have sufficient information to bring a support application and should not have to spend money needed to support herself and the child to pursue the husband for child support if she has a reasonable alternative. ...

It is submitted that Campbell J. was correct in rejecting a lawyer's letter as information to satisfy s. 11(1)(b) of the *Divorce Act*. The Act requires a petitioner to adduce evidence that reasonable arrangements for child support have been made. A letter from counsel is not such evidence. However, the suggestion that the information contained in the letter would be insufficient evidence to justify a divorce if properly before the court should be approached with caution.

WILLENBORG v. WILLENBORG

(2001), 23 R.F.L. (5th) 447, 2001 CarswellSask 792 (Sask. Q.B.)

McINYTRE J.: — This is an application for a judgment of divorce brought on motion by the respondent [husband]. A petition was issued in 1994 in which the petitioner [wife] sought *inter alia*, divorce and child support in the amount of $500.00 per month. There are three children of the marriage ...:

There is an order of June 29, 1994 in which the respondent is to pay interim child support to the petitioner for the support of Ashley and Autumn in the amount of $250.00 per month per child. The material on file indicates that at that time Amber was in her father's care. There was a subsequent interspousal contract of October 18, 1994.

The affidavit in support of the present motion for a judgment of divorce indicates that he continues to pay $250.00 per month per child for the two children who remain in the care of their mother. He indicates that he had custody of and solely supported their daughter Amber who recently became self-supporting. ...

When this matter came on I expressed concern as to whether I could be satisfied that reasonable arrangements had been made for the support of the children of the marriage, having regard to the applicable Guidelines. Counsel was requested to make submissions in this regard and attempt to obtain financial information as to the petitioner's circumstances. A letter was filed from the petitioner, together with documentation which indicated that her 2000 earnings consisted of $19,621.81 in gross employment income and $6,000.00 in taxable child support.

With the enactment of the Guidelines effective May 1, 1997, any child support order made thereafter is non-taxable to the recipient and non-deductible to the payor and there is a presumptive rule that the appropriate amount of child support will be determined in accordance with the applicable table and based upon the income of the payor. As noted, the objectives of the Guidelines include establishing a fair standard of support based upon the financial means of the spouses and to ensure consistent treatment of spouses and children who are in similar circumstances.

The respondent's income is $59,000.00. If he were paying child support in accordance with the Guidelines, he would pay, absent s. 7 expenses, $766.00 per month non-deductible/non-taxable. He is paying $500.00 per month to the petitioner which is taxable income in the hands of the petitioner. After paying tax on her child support, the petitioner is actually receiving approximately $350.00 per month. The actual cost to the respondent is approximately $325.00 per month.

In doing a comparison of the two child support regimes using the ChildView, Version 2001.2, software program, by ChildView Inc., it would indicate that the petitioner's present monthly cash flow taking into account the child support, GST credits and child tax benefits received and allowing for CPP, EI and income taxes is $2,146.00 per month. If the respondent were paying child support in a table amount in accordance with the Guidelines, the petitioner's net cash flow would be $2,640.00 per month. This is a difference of $494.00 per month or $5,930.00 per annum. ...

In this instance the parties have a child support arrangement in place which is less than half of what Parliament presumes to be a reasonable child support arrangement. On its own that is not a reasonable arrangement having regard to the Guidelines. There is nothing in the material before me to indicate whether there are other facts and circumstances which the Court ought to take into account which might make the present arrangement reasonable having regard to the Guidelines. There will be an order staying the granting of any judgment of divorce until either reasonable arrangements have been made or the Court can be satisfied that the present arrangement satisfies the criteria of s. 11(1)(b). If the parties should chose to agree upon a new arrangement then the matter of the application for judgment of divorce may be resubmitted to the Court. If either party wishes to have an oral hearing and present evidence to the Court in an effort to persuade the Court that the present arrangement constitutes a reasonable arrangement for the support of the children, having regard to the applicable Guidelines, then such arrangements may be made with me through the office of the local registrar.

NOTES AND QUESTIONS

1. What should be the court's response where the custodial parent receives social assistance and the other spouse can pay more than agreed, either formally or informally? In "Annotation" (1987), 8 R.F.L. (3d) 216 Professor McLeod argues (at 218):

> It is not the concern of the law of support to protect the public purse. ... If welfare is providing for the child as well as the payor could, there is no family law reason for the court to interfere. It should not allow "Treasury"-related considerations to affect divorce proceedings to change marital status.

Do you agree? The "public-purse-protection" history of s. 11(1)(b) is noted and criticized in Thompson, "'Getting Blood From a Stone' Or How to Find Ability to Pay When There Isn't Any" (1995), 12 C.F.L.Q. 117 at 163–175.

2. In *McIllwraith v. McIllwraith* (1999), 210 N.B.R. (2d) 391 (Q.B.), the husband earned only $15,000 per year. Under an informal agreement that had been in operation for four years, he purchased clothes worth $700 a year for his daughter and also spent about $500 per year on trips so that the child could spend almost every long weekend and school holiday at his home. Under the *Guidelines*, the husband would be required to pay $118 per month to his wife as child support. Justice Guerette considered the arrangement reasonable, granted the divorce, and incorporated the agreement into a court order using ss. 15.1(7) and (8) of the *Divorce Act*. He suggested (at para. 20)

> When parties request a court to confirm their private support arrangements because they deem them to be satisfactory for their situation, a court should be loathe to change them. Such arrangements, when freely entered into, are an important manifestation of their wishes to resolve issues between themselves and should accordingly be given appropriate weight by the court.

Professor Thompson notes in "Who Wants to Avoid the Guidelines? Contracting Out and Around" (2001-2002), 19 C.F.L.Q. 1 at 43, that not all courts take this deferential view in applying s. 11(1)(b) of the *Divorce Act*. He adds (*ibid*):

> In my view, the correct approach is that taken by Justice Guerette. If the parties are able to agree upon something "reasonably close" to the table amount, then squeezing out that extra few dollars to achieve "certainty and consistency" sacrifices the objective of encouraging settlement.

For further analysis of s. 11(1)(b), see Maur, "Child Support Below the Guidelines: Why a Bird in the Hand Isn't Always Worth Two in the Bush" (2008), 27 C.F.L.Q. 201.

3. In *Shore-Kalo v. Kalo* (2007), 41 R.F.L. (6th) 115 (Man. Q.B.), the court granted the wife's application for divorce even though the husband, who had no income because he was finishing his education, was not paying any child support for the children in her care.

4. In *Marinovic v. Marinovic* (1989), 20 R.F.L. (3d) 404 (Ont. H.C.), Salhany L.J.S.C. held that s. 11(1)(b) of the *Divorce Act* does not preclude the granting of a motion for a divorce judgment in advance of the disposition of a claim for child support. In effect, he concluded that leaving child support for future judicial determination can constitute making reasonable arrangements for child support. For other cases dealing with the issue of severance of the divorce application from other issues, see *Kramer v. Kramer* (2004), 2004 CarswellOnt 345 (S.C.J.); *K. (D.K.) v. K. (A.J.)* (2006), 2006 CarswellBC 2531 (S.C.); *Yung v. Yung* (2006), 2006 CarswellSask 531 (Q.B.); and *Fowler v. Szabo-Fowler* (2006), 2006 CarswellSask 106 (C.A.).

5. Reconciliation and Conciliation

(1) Duty of Lawyer

Examine s. 9(1) of the *Divorce Act*. The duty imposed upon every legal advisor by this provision does not apply "where the circumstances of the case are of such a nature that it would clearly not be appropriate". What circumstances fall within this exception? Section 9(1)(a) requires a lawyer acting on behalf of a spouse in a divorce proceeding to draw to the attention of the spouse "those provisions of this Act that have as their object the reconciliation of spouses". Which provisions are envisioned? It is also a lawyer's duty, under s. 9(1)(b), to inform the spouse of the marriage counselling or guidance facilities known to the advisor that might be able to assist the spouses to achieve a reconciliation. Finally, each legal advisor is required to discuss with the spouse "the possibility of the reconciliation of the spouses".

Section 9(2) of the *Divorce Act* was introduced in 1985 to encourage the use of mediation to resolve corollary matters. According to the Department of Justice in *Evaluation of the Divorce Act: Phase II: Monitoring and Evaluation* (Ottawa: Department of Justice, Bureau of Review, 1990) at 123, this provision "represents a compromise response to the much stronger request by the divorce mediation community for a mandatory visit to a divorce mediator where custody and access are in dispute". The Department of Justice concluded that most lawyers discussed the possibility of mediation with their clients, but that there was little evidence to suggest that it was encouraged.

Bill C-22, which died on the Order Paper when the 2nd Session of the 37th Parliament ended on November 12, 2003, would have amended s. 9(2) so that it would apply in any application under the Act and not just in divorce proceedings. It would also have required the lawyer to "discuss with the spouse or former spouse the obligation to comply with any order under this Act".

(2) Duty of the Court

Section 10(1) of the *Divorce Act* requires the court "before considering the evidence, to satisfy itself that there is no possibility of the reconciliation of the spouses, unless the circumstances of the case are of such a nature that it would clearly not be appropriate to do so". In cases where the evidence is presented entirely by affidavit, the courts are generally content with a statement in the affidavit or affidavits that there is no possibility of reconciliation. Where oral evidence is presented, the court itself can direct inquiries to the spouses in open court to determine if reconciliation is a possibility.

Where one spouse denies that there is a possibility of reconciliation, the court usually concludes that there is no such possibility even if the other spouse expresses a fervent and sincere hope that there will be a reconciliation: *McDermid v. McDermid* (1989), 21 R.F.L. (3d) 47 (Sask. C.A.); *Pires v. Pires* (2005), CarswellBC 3358 (B.C. S.C.); and *Gerth v. Gerth* (2007), 2007 CarswellBC 694 (B.C. S.C.). See also *Roadburg v. Braut* (1994), 4 R.F.L. (4th) 96 (B.C. C.A.), where the court concluded that the failure to make a formal inquiry about the possibility of reconciliation was not an error. The circumstances of that case indicated that such an inquiry would have been pointless.

If the possibility of reconciliation appears to exist, the court is obliged by s. 10(2) of the *Divorce Act* to adjourn the proceedings and may nominate a marriage counsellor to assist the parties to achieve a reconciliation. Where the proceedings are adjourned, either spouse may apply after 14 days for a resumption of the proceeding: s. 10(3). The Manitoba Court of Queen's Bench held in *Nash v. Nash* (1976), 28 R.F.L. 41 (Man. Q.B.) that (under a similar provision in the 1968 Act) the proceedings must then be resumed even if the other spouse insists this is premature.

By virtue of s. 10(4) of the *Divorce Act*, a counsellor nominated by the court under s. 10 is not compellable or competent to disclose any admissions or communications made to him or her as nominee. Section 10(5) makes it explicit that evidence of anything said or any admission or communication made in the course of assisting spouses to achieve a reconciliation is not admissible in any legal proceedings. The Ontario Court of Appeal held in *R. v. Pabani* (1994), 17 O.R. (3d) 659 (C.A.); leave to appeal refused (1994), 33 C.R. (4th) 405n (S.C.C.), that s. 10(5) only applies to statements made to counsellors appointed under the *Divorce Act*. However, the Alberta Court of Appeal held in *B. (L.M.) v. B. (I.J.)* (2005), 18 R.F.L. (6th) 237, 2005 ABCA 100 (C.A.), that the section precluded the admission into evidence in divorce proceedings of communications of admissions made during marital counselling sessions, even if these sessions occurred before the divorce proceedings. See also *Albertson v. Albertson* (2007), 2007 CarswellOnt 6302 (S.C.J.); additional reasons at (2007), 2007 CarswellOnt 5929 (S.C.J.). Even if s. 10(5) does not apply, a common law privilege may preclude the admission in matrimonial proceedings of statements made during counselling sessions or during reconciliation attempts. See *Robson v. Robson*, [1969] 2 O.R. 857 (Ont. H.C.) and *Pabini*. The Ontario Court of Appeal held in *Pabini* that the common law privilege did not apply in criminal proceedings instituted against the husband for the murder of his wife.

6. Effective Date of Divorce

Under the 1968 *Divorce Act*, the court originally granted a decree *nisi* of divorce. One of the spouses then had to apply, generally after three months, for a decree absolute. The necessity to make application for a decree absolute does not exist under the 1985 *Divorce Act*. Generally, the divorce "takes effect" on the 31st day after the day on which the judgment granting the divorce is rendered: s. 12(1). If an appeal is launched the divorce takes effect when the appeal process is exhausted: s. 12(3)–(6).

In *Canada (Minister of Social Development) v. Riddell* (2006), 2006 CarswellNat 6120 (Can. Pen. Apps. Bd.), a court granted a divorce on November 14, 2001. The Canada Pension Appeals Board held that the divorce became effective "at the stroke of midnight on December 14, 2001" and that the wife became a divorced person before the husband's death at 5:00 A.M. on December 15. This meant that the wife could not qualify as the husband's "survivor" for the purposes of the Canada Pension Plan. See also *H. (A.) v. H. (D.S.)* (2003), 2003 CarswellBC 1474 (C.A. [In Chambers]).

Under s. 12(2) a court may order that the divorce is effective in less than 31 days. This power exists only if, *inter alia*, the court is "of the opinion that by reason of special circumstances the divorce should take effect earlier than the thirty-first day after the day on which the judgment is rendered". In *Mascarenhas v. Mascarenhas* (1999), 44 R.F.L. (4th) 131 (Ont. Gen. Div.); affirmed (2000), 18 R.F.L. (5th) 148 (Ont. Div. Ct.), the husband intended to marry his common law partner, who was pregnant, in Niagara Falls on the way back to their home in North Carolina. Without further explanation, the court noted (at 134): "An immediate divorce was granted by this Court during the proceedings." Indeed, most of the cases under the 1968 Act in which the normal waiting period was abridged involved a cohabitation arrangement where children had been or were about to be born.

Should the desire to remarry as soon as possible be a "special circumstance"? It was held not to be in *Hansford v. Hansford* (1972), 9 R.F.L. 233, [1973] 1 O.R. 116, 30 D.L.R. (3d) 392 (H.C.) and *Hughes v. Hughes* (1975), 24 R.F.L. 265, 10 Nfld. & P.E.I.R. 170 (P.E.I. S.C.). But see *Bowler v. Bowler* (1977), 4 R.F.L. (2d) 27 (Ont. H.C.) and *Lester v. Lester* (1983), 26 Man. R. (2d) 249 (Q.B.). In *Arsenault v. Arsenault* (2001), 15 R.F.L. (5th) 12 (Ont. S.C.J.), both the husband and wife applied for a divorce and the wife asked, with the husband's agreement, that it be effective immediately. The wife, who was pregnant, wished to marry in Cuba about a week later and she and the groom had already purchased non-refundable tickets for themselves and some other members of the wedding party. The court refused to consider these "special circumstances", noting (para. 15) that "s. 12(2)(a) was not enacted as a refuge for the foolhardy". Do you agree with this result?

NOTES AND QUESTIONS

1. The appeal referred to in s. 12(3)–(6) is an appeal from the granting of the divorce itself. Therefore, a divorce can take effect even if an appeal relating to corollary relief is taken. See *Fullarton v. Fullarton*, 5 R.F.L. 356, [1972] 1 O.R. 782 (C.A.) and *Chadderton v. Chadderton* (1972), 8 R.F.L. 374, [1973] 1 O.R. 560 (C.A.).

2. In *Fraser v. Fraser* (1989), 23 R.F.L. (3d) 30 (Ont. H.C.), the court concluded that it had the power under s. 10 of the *Divorce Act* to order a stay of the judgment of divorce where the parties had reconciled after the judgment was granted but before it took effect. The 1968 Act expressly empowered the court to rescind the *decree nisi* in such circumstances, but this provision was dropped from the 1985 Act. See also *Alexa v. Alexa* (1995), 14 R.F.L. (4th) 93 (B.C. S.C.), where a divorce was set aside when the husband died before it took effect.

3. For a review of the jurisprudence on the question of whether there are any circumstances in which a divorce can be set aside after it has become effective, see *Revie v. Canada (Minister of Social Development)* (2006), 2006 CarswellNat 5901 (Can. Pen. Apps. Bd.).

4

FAMILY PROPERTY

1. Introduction

When a spousal relationship ends, a major economic adjustment is almost inevitably necessary. The interrelated issues of support and property rights need to be negotiated or litigated. Statutory entitlement to family property in the common law provinces is a fairly recent development and is still confined to married persons in most provinces. As we will see, the property rights of unmarried cohabitees without a domestic contract are determined in most provinces in accordance with the common law.

In Ontario, the *Family Law Act* (the *FLA*), which came into force on March 1, 1986, fundamentally changed the law governing the property rights of spouses on marriage breakdown and on death. In order to understand the operation of this legislation, one must have a basic grasp of the historical background.

(1) Historical Background

(a) *The Law Prior to the* Family Law Reform Act, 1978

The enactment of Part I of the *Family Law Reform Act, 1978* was the first comprehensive attempt in Ontario to eliminate the inequities produced by the system of separate property. The norm of separate property was itself introduced in the 19th century by a series of *Married Women's Property Acts* as a response to the doctrine of unity of legal personality. According to this doctrine, the husband and wife became one legal personality upon marriage. In effect, the common law treated the husband as that legal personality. A wife did not have an independent right to contract, to sue or be sued, or to make a will. The husband acquired the right to manage and control all the wife's freehold lands and he was entitled to the rents and profits. A wife was unable to dispose of the land without his consent. If the husband predeceased her, all rights in the freeholds were resumed by her. If she predeceased him, the husband acquired rights as life tenant in all her freeholds of inheritance of which she died solely seised provided the husband had issue born alive by the wife capable of inheriting her freeholds. This was called curtesy and was abolished in Ontario by s. 48 of the *Succession Law Reform Act, 1977*. The wife's leaseholds belonged to the husband during coverture and he had absolute power to dispose of them during his lifetime. All other personalty held by the wife, except jewellery and clothing "suitable to her rank", vested absolutely in the husband. He could dispose of it *inter vivos* or by will.

The common law compensated to some extent for the wife's loss of legal personality. A husband was liable for his wife's ante-nuptial debts, her torts, and for debts incurred by her after marriage to procure necessaries of life. On her husband's death, a wife was entitled by virtue of her dower (abolished by s. 70 of the *Family Law Reform Act, 1978*) to an estate for life in a third of all the freehold estates of inheritance of which he had been seised in possession at any time during the marriage.

To some extent, the law of equity made it possible for a wife to acquire and hold property independently through the concepts of a married woman's separate estate and restraint upon anticipation. These developments, which appear to have had little impact in Canada, enabled the propertied classes in England to keep the family property intact by preserving it from falling into a daughter's husband's hands.

The *Married Women's Property Acts* of the 19th century whittled away at the concept of unity of legal personality. In part, they gave wives the right to acquire and hold property. They established a separate property regime under which marriage created no property rights apart from the inchoate rights of dower and curtesy and the contingent rights created by the law of succession. In brief, a husband and wife were to be treated as strangers for the purposes of determining the ownership of property.

The system of separate property often resulted in hardship when the marriage ended. The traditional roles assumed by marriage partners and the social mores meant that property acquired during the marriage was usually paid for by the husband and taken in his name. In such a situation, it belonged to him absolutely. This economic inequality meant that a wife frequently had no property on marriage breakdown.

Prior to the passage of family property law reforms, the courts had various tools available to mitigate the harshness of the separate property regime. One of these was an old rule called the presumption of advancement, whereby the law presumed that a husband who paid for property taken in his wife's name or who transferred property into his wife's name intended to make a gift to her. This presumption could be rebutted: *Bible v. Bible* (1974), 15 R.F.L. 105 (Ont. C.A.). Nevertheless, it was a useful device whereby a wife could claim legal and equitable title to property in her name regardless of the financial contributions to its acquisition. See, for example, *Maysels v. Maysels* (1974), 14 R.F.L. 286, 3 O.R. (2d) 321 (C.A.); affirmed (1975), 19 R.F.L. 256, 17 N.R. 111 (S.C.C.). The presumption of advancement could also be used in situations where property was held jointly by a husband and wife and the husband provided the purchase price. In this situation, it buttressed the presumption that beneficial interests followed the legal estates. See, for example, *Lindenblatt v. Lindenblatt* (1974), 18 R.F.L. 247, 4 O.R. (2d) 534 (H.C.). In any event, Canadian courts generally gave great weight to the paper title where title was held jointly. See, e.g., *Kearney v. Kearney*, [1970] 2 O.R. 152, 10 D.L.R. (3d) 138 (C.A.), where the wife was the sole contributor to the purchase price of a home held jointly by the spouses. The court found that the beneficial ownership was also held jointly, even though the presumption of advancement never applied when a wife made the financial contributions.

Neither the presumption of advancement nor the presumption that the beneficial interest followed the legal interest could be used to assist a wife where the title to the property was taken in the husband's name alone. It was in this situation that the concept of separate property worked the greatest hardship. For a short time, some judges attempted to find in s. 12 of the *Married Women's Property Act* (repealed S.O. 1978, c. 2, s. 82) a broad, discretionary power to adjust existing property rights between spouses. Development of this approach — frequently labelled "palm-tree justice" — was effectively precluded by the Supreme Court of Canada in *Thompson v. Thompson*, [1961] S.C.R. 3, 26 D.L.R. (2d) 1. Thereafter, the judiciary's chosen means of recognizing the contribution of a non-titled spouse to the acquisition of property was through the use of trust concepts — in particular, the resulting and constructive trusts.

The concept of resulting trust was sufficiently malleable to enable the courts to achieve equitable results in some situations. Through a resulting trust analysis, a non-titled spouse could be declared to have an interest in the matrimonial home based on a direct contribution to the purchase price: *Re Whiteley* (1974), 4 O.R. (2d) 393, 48 D.L.R. (3d) 161 (C.A.). In this situation, it was well-established that a presumption of resulting trust arose. This presumption could be rebutted by evidence of a contrary intention on the part of the contributing spouse or displaced by a presumption of advancement (see above). In the decade before the legislative reforms, the courts extended the presumption of resulting trust to situations where the contribution of the non-titled spouse to the acquisition of the property was an indirect one. Most often this involved paying for household expenses, while the title holder acquired the family home. See, for example, *Madisso v. Madisso* (1975), 21 R.F.L. 51, 11 O.R. (2d) 441 (C.A.); leave to appeal refused (1975), 11 O.R. (2d) 441n (S.C.C.). Similarly, a contribution in the form of labour during construction of the home could be recognized through a resulting trust: *Trueman v. Trueman*, 5 R.F.L. 54, [1971] 2 W.W.R. 688 (Alta. C.A.).

However, problems remained. Traditionally, the resulting trust arose where a person without legal title contributed to the purchase price. In this limited situation, equity presumed that the contributor did not intend a gift. The presumed intention of the contributor created a trust under which the beneficial interests were proportionate to the financial contributions of the parties. Once the presumption of resulting trust was extended to situations involving indirect financial or non-financial contributions, this "historical anchorage" was lost: Laskin J., dissenting, in *Murdoch v. Murdoch*, [1975] 1 S.C.R. 423 at 454. The courts became more and more concerned with the actual intentions of the parties in order to determine if the contribution to family life should be considered a contribution to the acquisition of property. Increasingly, judges suggested that the resulting trust depended on a common intention of the spouses to share the beneficial interest. Not only was this a departure from the traditional analysis, but a resulting trust analysis that emphasized the common intention of the spouses seemed very artificial in family situations. While the matrimonial relationship was harmonious, the parties did not usually address themselves to the issue of property ownership. After the relationship faltered, evidence regarding intention was often conflicting and self-serving. Where the contribution was indirect, it also became increasingly difficult to quantify the extent of the beneficial interest held by the non-titled spouse. Finally, it should be emphasized that contributions through household management and child-raising were not treated as relevant contributions giving rise to a presumption of resulting trust. The contribution to family life by a homemaker was left wholly out of account. Professor Cullity, a leading authority on the law of trusts concluded in "The Matrimonial Home — A Return To Palm-Tree Justice: Trust Doctrines Based On (a) Intent And (b) Unjust Enrichment" (1979), 4 E. & T.Q. 277 at 286:

> It seems beyond dispute that the traditional principles of resulting trusts are inadequate to deal with problems concerning the ownership of matrimonial property. If they are applied strictly, the consequences may be quite fortuitous and manifestly unjust. If an attempt is made to extend the principles to indirect contributions, the inquiry quickly ceases to have much contact with reality and the principles themselves become distorted.

For many, the notorious *Murdoch* case illustrated the inability or unwillingness of the courts to use equitable principles to achieve justice between spouses on marriage breakdown. For some four years after their marriage in November 1943, the Murdochs worked on ranches as a hired couple earning $100 per month plus room and board. In 1947, the husband and his father-in-law purchased a guest ranch for $6,000. The husband paid half of the purchase price. Mr. Justice Martland (Judson, Ritchie and Spence JJ. concurring) stated (at 427) that Mr. Murdoch paid his portion out of his own assets. Laskin J. pointed out (at 441) that an indeterminate part of the husband's share of the purchase price of this first property came from savings from the earnings of the couple, which were received by the husband.

The couple operated the guest ranch as a joint venture with the wife's father until 1951. During this time, the husband held an outside job that required him to be away from home during the day for some five months of the year. Therefore, the wife accompanied guests on park hikes and fishing and hunting trips. She also did other necessary chores around the ranch. This ranch was sold in 1951 and Mr. Murdoch received $3,500 from the proceeds of sale.

With this money and a loan from Mrs. Murdoch's mother, the husband, by a series of transactions involving ranches, acquired a valuable ranch registered in his name alone. Until separation in 1968, the wife continued to assist in the operation of the various ranches, partly because the husband maintained his outside employment. At trial, the wife testified (at 443) that she was involved in "haying, raking, swathing, mowing, driving trucks and tractors and teams, quietening horses, taking cattle back and forth to the reserve, dehorning, vaccinating, branding, anything that was to be done".

After separation in 1968, Mrs. Murdoch claimed an interest in the ranch in her husband's name. The majority of the Supreme Court applied a resulting trust analysis. Accepting the trial judge's analysis of the facts, the majority held that Mrs. Murdoch could not establish a financial contribution. Insofar as the claim rested on a contribution through physical labour, the majority accepted the trial judge's finding that Mrs. Murdoch had not made a substantial contribution to the acquisition of the ranch in that "what the appellant had done, while living with the respondent, was the work done by any ranch wife". Because the wife's contribution could be characterized as the performance of the usual duties of matrimony, it could not by itself raise the presumption of resulting trust. In other words, she did what she did simply because she was married to Mr. Murdoch; not because she expected to gain an interest in any property in his name.

Laskin J. dissented. He clearly disagreed with the trial judge's assessment of the facts. He held that the wife had made a modest financial and a substantial physical contribution to the acquisition of the ranch. Although he indicated that the principles of resulting trust could be adapted to cover the situation, he urged the use of the constructive trust as a remedial device in property disputes on marriage breakdown. In particular, he identified the following weaknesses in a resulting trust analysis (at 454):

> What complicates the application of a presumption of a resulting trust, in its ordinary signification arising from the contribution of purchase money to the acquisition of property, is that in the case of husband and wife the contribution may relate only to a deposit on property which has to be carried on mortgage or instalment payments for many years; that where the spouses have lived together for some years after the acquisition, without any thought having been given to formalizing a division of interests claimed upon the breakdown or dissolution of the marriage, the presumption (as a mere inference from the fact of payment of money) is considerably weakened if not entirely dissipated; and that there is no historical anchorage for it where the contribution of money is indirect or the contribution consists of physical labour. Attribution of a common intention to the spouses in such circumstances (where evidence of the existence of such an intention at the material time is lacking) and resort to the resulting trust to give it sanction seem to me to be quite artificial.

The use of the constructive trust as a remedial or restitutionary device in property disputes was approved by three Supreme Court Justices in *Rathwell v. Rathwell*, 1 R.F.L. (2d) 1, [1978] 2 S.C.R. 436; adopted by a majority in *Pettkus v. Becker*, [1980] 2 S.C.R. 834, 8 E.T.R. 143; and finally used in a unanimous judgment in *Sorochan v. Sorochan*, 2 R.F.L. (3d) 225, [1986] 2 S.C.R. 38.

Although the constructive trust analysis might have effectively eliminated the harshness of the separate property regime on marriage breakdown, it developed too late to stem the tide of legislative reform. Eventually, all the legislatures in the common law provinces enacted comprehensive matrimonial property regimes. In Ontario, certain very limited reforms were accomplished by the *Family Law Reform Act*, S.O. 1975, c. 41 (repealed S.O. 1978, c. 2, s. 78). In addition to destroying the vestiges of unity of personality, this Act abolished the presumption of advancement between husband and wife. It also provided that where the husband and wife took property as joint tenants, the presumption was that the beneficial interest was also held jointly. (See now s. 14 of the *FLA*.) A final provision of the Act was inserted to preclude the characterization of a spouse's contribution to the acquisition of property as that of a "reasonable spouse in the circumstances" when applying the concept of resulting trust.

(b) The Family Law Reform Act, 1978

The 1978 Act featured deferred sharing of some assets coupled with considerable judicial discretion. It provided for the general retention of separate property during the marriage coupled with the division of family assets and, in certain circumstances, non-family assets on marriage breakdown. The norm for the division of family assets was that of equal division, although there was authority to divide these assets unequally. Non-family assets were divided only in limited circumstances, particularly where a non-titled spouse made a contribution of "work, money or money's worth in respect of the acquisition, management, maintenance, operation or improvement of property, other than family assets, in which the other has or had an interest." See *Leatherdale v. Leatherdale*, 30 R.F.L. (2d) 225, [1982] 2 S.C.R. 743, where the court held that the wife made an indirect financial contribution to her husband's R.R.S.P. and Bell Canada shares by using her income for family expenses thereby freeing up some of her husband's income.

Family assets were defined to include the matrimonial home and all other assets "ordinarily used or enjoyed by both spouses or one or more of their children while the spouses are residing together for shelter or transportation or for household, educational, recreational, social or aesthetic purposes". The courts held that casual or occasional use for the purposes listed was not sufficient, but that the use had to be "in the course of the customary mode of life of the person concerned": *Taylor v. Taylor* (1978), 6 R.F.L. (2d) 341 at 353 (Ont. U.F.C.). Nor was an intention to use the asset for the purposes listed sufficient to render it a family asset. Thus, a pension or funds in an RRSP were not family assets: *Leatherdale, supra*. This result was viewed as a major flaw in the scheme for property division in the Act (see *A Brief to the Attorney-General of Ontario Respecting the Family Law Reform Act* (Toronto: Ontario Status of Women Council, 1983) at 13).

In addition to the property regime described above, the *Family Law Reform Act* of 1978 introduced substantial changes to the law governing possession of the matrimonial home, support, and domestic contracts. Parts II (Matrimonial Home), III (Support Obligations), and IV (Domestic Contracts) of the *FLA* are modeled on the corresponding provisions of the 1978 *FLRA*.

While the 1978 reforms relating to support, matrimonial homes, and domestic contracts thus proved to be generally acceptable, a number of problems relating to the division of assets under Part I of the *Family Law Reform Act* soon became apparent. First, entitlement varied depending on the nature of the assets accumulated by the spouses. As the concept of marriage as a partnership in which each spouse contributes in various ways to the financial gain of both spouses became increasingly accepted, it seemed odd that only assets used for family purposes were subject to the general rule of equal division. Second, the Act did not distinguish between property acquired before or after marriage. Again, this seemed to conflict with the partnership concept whereby only the property to which the non-owning spouse has contributed in some way should be shared. Third, the Act provided for considerable judicial discretion. In essence, judges were authorized to divide family assets unequally and to divide non-family assets in accordance with their views of equity or fairness. The guidelines for the exercise of this discretion were vague. Fourth, the fact that there was no *prima facie* right to share equally the value of pensions built up during the marriage caused great concern since a pension is often the major asset held by an employed spouse. Finally, Part I did not apply when the marriage ended because of the death of a spouse. This meant that a spouse whose marriage broke down could be in a better position than a widower or widow.

(c) The FLA

By the mid-1980s there was general agreement that the property regime established under the 1978 Act was in need of reform. There was, however, disagreement over the nature of the reform required. Some individuals and groups favoured limited reforms, such as the inclusion of pensions in the pool of family assets and the extension of the regime to marriages ended by the death of a spouse. Others wanted more fundamental change. In the end, the latter view prevailed. On March 1, 1986 the FLA came into force. Part I of the Act introduced a modified version of the regime proposed by the Ontario Law Reform Commission in 1974. Deferred sharing of the economic gain achieved by both spouses during the cohabitation under the marriage became the norm in Ontario. Briefly, a deferred sharing regime involves the retention of separate property while the marriage is an ongoing concern. Once the marriage has broken down, the profits of the marriage are divided equally between the two spouses.

Part I of the FLA is the subject of most of this chapter. However, the next two sections examine the exclusion of unmarried cohabitees from the statutory regime and the continued development of the common law.

FURTHER READING

For summaries of the common law treatment of married women's property, see Hovius and Youdan, *The Law of Family Property* (Toronto: Carswell, 1991) c. 2; Holcombe, *Wives and Property: Reform of the Married Women's Property Law in Nineteenth-Century England* (Toronto: University of Toronto Press, 1983) c. 2; and McCaughan, *The Legal Status of Married Women in Canada* (Toronto: Carswell, 1977) at 5–10. Regarding the 19th century reforms, see also Backhouse, "Married Women's Property Law in Nineteenth-Century Canada" (1988), 6 Law and History Review 211.

(2) Coverage of the Statutory Family Property Regime

Unmarried couples, both opposite-sex and same-sex, are not presently covered by Part I of the FLA. In its *Report on the Rights and Responsibilities of Cohabitants under the Family Law Act* (Toronto: 1993), the Ontario Law Reform Commission recommended that the legislature amend the definition of "spouse" in s. 1(1) of the FLA to include unmarried, opposite-sex cohabitees who cohabit continuously for at least three years or who cohabit in a relationship of some permanence and are the parents of a child. It had serious doubts that the exclusion of unmarried opposite-sex couples could withstand a challenge based on s. 15 of the *Canadian Charter of Rights and Freedoms*. It also stressed four policy reasons for the inclusion of opposite-sex unmarried couples: 1) the functional similarities between married couples and opposite-sex cohabiting couples, 2) the reasonable expectations of persons involved in cohabitation, 3) the desirability of compensating each partner for contributions to the family's economic well-being, and 4) the desirability of alleviating pressure on social assistance. Under its proposal, cohabiting opposite-sex couples would, like their married counterparts, be able to contract out of the statutory regime through an appropriately drafted domestic contact.

Regarding same-sex cohabiting couples, the Commission concluded that it lacked sufficient information to recommend their inclusion in the statutory property regime. In particular, it speculated (at 3) that "the expectations that same-sex partners bring to their relationship may be different from the assumptions made by heterosexual couples and that there may be less likelihood that same-sex couples will encounter the economic inequalities that have been common in traditional heterosexual relationships". It recommended that only those who registered their partnerships as a Registered Domestic Partnership (under a proposed scheme) should be subject to the legislation. The Ontario legislature did not implement the Commission's recommendations.

In the late 1990s, individuals in various provinces began to use the *Charter* to challenge the exclusion of unmarried couples from the family property regimes. These challenges were generally successful in the lower courts. Indeed, the main reason given in the legislative debates in Saskatchewan for the extension of that province's family property regime to unmarried couples was that the courts were dictating this action. See Hovius, "Property Division for Unmarried Cohabitees in the Common Law Provinces" (2003-2004), 21 C.F.L.Q. 175, at 203-204. When the Nova Scotia Court of Appeal held in *Walsh v. Bona* (2000), 5 R.F.L. (5th) 188, that the omission of unmarried opposite-sex couples from the *Matrimonial Property Act*, R.S.N.S. 1989, c. 275, constituted unjustified discrimination on the basis of marital status contrary to s. 15 of the *Charter*, the legislature responded by enacting a registered domestic partnership scheme. Under this scheme, two individuals, whether of the same sex or of opposite sexes, who are cohabiting or intend to do so can formally register a "domestic-partner declaration". Registration accords the domestic partners the same rights and obligations as spouses under various statutes, including the *Matrimonial Property Act*. By allowing cohabitees to opt into the family property regime, the province clearly hoped that the courts would conclude that it had remedied the alleged unjustified discrimination. At the same time, the Attorney General of Nova Scotia appealed the finding of discrimination in *Walsh v. Bona* to the Supreme Court of Canada.

It is fair to say that the Supreme Court of Canada's decision in *Walsh v. Bona* (reproduced below), surprised many observers. The court's holdings in *Miron v. Trudel* (1995), 13 R.F.L. (4th) 1, and *M. v. H.* (1999), 46 R.F.L. (4th) 32, (reproduced in Chapter 6, *SPOUSAL SUPPORT*) appeared to call into question the constitutionality of all legislation that differentiated between married and unmarried couples or between unmarried opposite-sex couples and same-sex couples.

WALSH v. BONA

(2002), 32 R.F.L. (5th) 81, 2002 CarswellNS 511, 2002 CarswellNS 512 (S.C.C.)

BASTARACHE J. (MCLACHLIN C.J.C. and IACOBUCCI, MAJOR, BINNIE, ARBOUR, LEBEL JJ. concurring): —

I. Introduction

1 This case involves a *Charter* challenge to the Nova Scotia *Matrimonial Property Act*, R.S.N.S. 1989, c. 275 (*"MPA"*), and asks whether its failure to include unmarried cohabiting opposite sex couples from its ambit violates s. 15(1). The challenge revolves around the definition of "spouse" in s. 2(g) of the *MPA*, which is limited to a man and a woman who are married to each other.

2 The question before this Court, then, is whether the exclusion from the *MPA* of unmarried cohabiting persons of the opposite sex is discriminatory. In my view, it is not. The distinction chosen by the legislature does not affect the dignity of unmarried persons who have formed relationships of some permanence and does not deny them access to a benefit or advantage available to married persons. It is, therefore, not discriminatory within the meaning of s. 15(1).

II. Factual Background

3 Susan Walsh and Wayne Bona lived together in a cohabiting relationship for a period of 10 years, ending in 1995. Two children were born out of this relationship, in 1988 and 1990 respectively. Walsh and Bona owned a home as joint tenants, in which Bona continued to reside after the separation, assuming the debts and expenses associated with the property. In 1983, Bona received as a gift from his father a cottage property which was sold after separation for $20,000. Approximately $10,000 was used to pay off the respondent's debts. Bona also retained 13 acres of surrounding woodland in his own name, valued at $6,500. The total value of assets retained by Bona at the date of separation including the house, cottage, lot, vehicle, pensions and RRSPs, was $116,000, less "matrimonial" debts of $50,000, for a net value of $66,000.

4 The respondent Walsh claimed support for herself and the two children. She further sought a declaration that the Nova Scotia *MPA* was unconstitutional in failing to furnish her with the presumption, applicable to married spouses, of an equal division of matrimonial property. Her claim for a declaration was rejected by the chambers judge, whose decision was reversed on appeal.

5 My colleague, Justice L'Heureux-Dubé, chooses not to make reference to the *Law Reform (2000) Act*, S.N.S. 2000, c. 29 ("*LRA*"), in the course of her analysis. I mention it as a new contextual consideration but, as will become clear below, my conclusion on the constitutionality of the *MPA* does not depend on the existence of the *LRA*.

6 In response to the Court of Appeal judgment, the Nova Scotia legislature introduced legislation, Bill No. 75, "*An Act to Comply with Certain Court Decisions and to Modernize and Reform Laws in the Province*," on November 6, 2000, that effectively amends the definition of "spouse" to "partner". Heterosexual and same-sex partners are both included in the definition of partner, and these may be either registered under the *Vital Statistics Act*, R.S.N.S. 1989, c. 494, or unregistered. Only registered partnerships are eligible for the benefits of the *MPA* and other legislation: "*LRA*".

7 Walsh's counsel advised the Court that subsequent to leave to appeal having been granted, Walsh and Bona have settled the litigation between them respecting the division of property.
...

VI. Analysis

A. Does the MPA Discriminate?

[Justice Bastarache applied the framework suggested in *Law v. Canada (Minister of Employment & Immigration)*, [1999] 1 S.C.R. 497 (S.C.C.), for assessing claims based on s. 15(1). This involved three inquiries. First, did the impugned law (a) draw a formal distinction between the claimant and others on the basis of one or more personal characteristics, or (b) fail to take into account the claimant's already disadvantaged position within Canadian society resulting in substantially differential treatment on the basis of one or more personal characteristics? Second, if so, was this differential treatment based on one or more of the grounds listed in s. 15(1) or on a ground analogous thereto? Third, if there was such differential treatment, did it amount to substantive discrimination? There was little discussion about the first two inquiries because the Attorney General conceded that 1) the *Matrimonial Property Act* drew a formal distinction between persons on the basis of a personal characteristic; namely, marital status; and 2) marital status was a ground of differentiation analogous to those listed in s. 15(1) of the *Charter*. Regarding the third inquiry, Justice Bastarache reasoned as follows.]

33 It is with respect to the third broad inquiry that the appellant argues the Court of Appeal erred. In *Law, supra*, Iacobucci J. set out four non-exhaustive factors for consideration of whether impugned legislation violates a claimant's human dignity:

    (a) pre-existing disadvantage, stereotyping or vulnerability of the claimant;

    (b) correspondence between the claim and the actual need or circumstances of the claimant;

    (c) the ameliorative purpose or effect of the impugned law on other groups in society; and

    (d) the nature and scope of the interest affected. ...

35 I agree with the appellant that the examination of pre-existing disadvantage and the nature of the interest affected is dependent on the proper characterization of the relationships involved. In my view, the most important aspect of this question is not whether the situation in which Walsh and Bona found themselves at the time of trial was similar to that of married persons, but whether persons entering into a conjugal relationship without marrying are in fact entering into a relationship on the same terms as persons who marry. On the one hand, we have persons who choose to marry and thereby indicate their intention to assume all of the legal rights and responsibilities that the *MPA* attributes to persons who have that status. On the other, we have persons who cannot be presumed to have accepted all of the obligations of marriage. This is a significant aspect of the context in which the respondent's claim of discrimination arises.

36 The respondent Walsh argues and the Court of Appeal held that the *MPA*, by excluding unmarried spouses from its purview, serves to perpetuate the view that unmarried couples are less deserving of recognition and respect in Canadian society. I cannot agree. As this Court reasoned in *Law, supra*, consideration of whether the differential treatment is discriminatory must always be done in a purposive and contextual manner. ...

38 In the present case, then, the inquiry can be stated as whether a reasonable heterosexual unmarried cohabiting person, taking into account all of the relevant contextual factors, would find the *MPA's* failure to include him or her in its ambit has the effect of demeaning his or her dignity.

39 As this Court has stated on numerous occasions, the equality guarantee is a comparative concept. It requires the location of an appropriate comparator group from which to assess the discrimination claim. The two comparator groups in this case are married heterosexual cohabitants, to which the *MPA* applies, and unmarried heterosexual cohabitants, to which the *MPA* does not apply. Although in some cases certain functional similarities between these two groups may be substantial, in this case it would be wrong to ignore the significant heterogeneity that exists within the claimant's comparator group. The contextual analysis of the respondent's claim reveals that reliance solely on certain "functional similarities" between the two groups does not adequately address the full range of traits, history, and circumstances of the comparator group of which the claimant is a member.

40 It is indeed clear from the evidence that some cohabitants have specifically chosen not to marry and not to take on the obligations ascribed to persons who choose that status (see: Z. Wu, *Cohabitation: An Alternative Form of Family Living* (2000), at pp. 105-6, 116, 120-21; and University of Alberta Law Research and Reform Institute, *Survey of Adult Living Arrangements: A Technical Report* (1984), at pp. 64–72). In his study of alternative family forms, Professor Wu makes several conclusions, which include: (1) that common law relationships tend to be of much shorter duration than married relationships; (2) that cohabitation can be a "trial marriage"; (3) that cohabitation can be a deliberate substitute for legal marriage; (4) that persons who do not marry tend to have less conventional attitudes toward marriage and family and reject the institution of marriage on the basis of personal choice. These findings are indicative not only of the differences between married couples and co-

habiting couples, but also of the many differences among unmarried cohabitants with regard to the manner in which people choose to structure their relationships.

41 This Court has recognized both the historical disadvantage suffered by unmarried cohabiting couples as well as the recent social acceptance of this family form. ...

42 Since *Miron, supra*, significant legislative change has taken place at both the federal and provincial levels. Numerous statutes that confer benefits on married persons have been amended so as to include within their ambit unmarried cohabitants. Nevertheless, social prejudices directed at unmarried partners may still linger, despite these significant reforms. In light of those social prejudices, this Court recognized in *Miron, supra*, that one's ability to access insurance benefits was not reducible to simply [a] matter of choice. L'Heureux-Dubé J., in her concurring judgment, reasoned as follows, at para. 102:

> To recapitulate, the decision of whether or not to marry is most definitely capable of being a very fundamental and personal choice. The importance actually ascribed to the decision to marry or, alternatively, *not* to marry, depends entirely on the individuals concerned. For a significant number of persons in so-called "non-traditional" relationships, however, I dare say that notions of "choice" may be illusory. It is inappropriate, in my respectful view, to condense the forces underlying the adoption of one type of family unit over another into a simple dichotomy between "choice" or "no choice". Family means different things to different people, and the failure to adopt the traditional family form of marriage may stem from a multiplicity of reasons — all of them equally valid and all of them equally worthy of concern, respect, consideration, and protection under the law. [Emphasis in original.]

43 Where the legislation has the effect of dramatically altering the legal obligations of partners, as between themselves, choice must be paramount. The decision to marry or not is intensely personal and engages a complex interplay of social, political, religious, and financial considerations by the individual. While it remains true that unmarried spouses have suffered from historical disadvantage and stereotyping, it simultaneously cannot be ignored that many persons in circumstances similar to those of the parties, that is, opposite sex individuals in conjugal relationships of some permanence, have chosen to avoid the institution of marriage and the legal consequences that flow from it. As M. Eichler posited:

> Treating all common-law relationships like legal marriages in terms of support obligations and property division ignores the very different circumstances under which people may enter a common-law union. If they choose to marry, they make a positive choice to live under one type of regime. If they have chosen not to marry, is it the state's task to impose a marriage-like regime on them retroactively? (M. Eichler, *Family Shifts: Families, Policies, and Gender Equality* (1997), at p. 96)

To ignore these differences among cohabiting couples presumes a commonality of intention and understanding that simply does not exist. This effectively nullifies the individual's freedom to choose alternative family forms and to have that choice respected and legitimated by the state.

44 Examination of the context in which the discrimination claim arises also involves a consideration of the relationship between the grounds and the claimant's characteristics or circumstances. ...

45 Consideration of the extent to which the impugned legislation properly accommodates the claimant's circumstances begins with the *MPA* and the changes it brought about. The purpose of the *MPA* is revealed in its preamble and through the debates of the House of Assembly at the time it was introduced. On second reading of the *MPA* Bill on May 8, 1980, the legislative purpose was described as follows:

> The intent and purport of the legislation, Mr. Speaker, is to be found in the preamble ... The intent, by virtue of the introduction and, hopefully, *the ultimate passage of this legislation, is to establish clearly that marriage is a partnership and that that partnership carries with it an understanding of equality*, and equality in all senses and, as it relates to this particular piece of legislation, equality at the time any such marriage should come to an end, by reason either of separation, divorce or upon

death. [Emphasis added.] (Nova Scotia, House of Assembly Debates and Proceedings, 80-44, May 8, 1980, at p. 2011)

46 The *MPA* created a regime of "deferred sharing," replacing the regime of absolute separate property. The new legislative scheme deems married persons to have agreed to an economic partnership wherein both pecuniary and non-pecuniary contributions to the marriage partnership are considered to be of equal worth. The *MPA* provides *inter alia* that property acquired by each spouse before and during the marriage constitutes a pool of assets, which may be divided, regardless of legal title, in equal shares upon marriage breakdown, divorce or death of either spouse. It also provides each spouse with an equal right of possession in the matrimonial home, without regard to title, and provides that no sale or mortgage of the matrimonial home may occur without the consent of both spouses. ... As a whole, then, the *MPA* is designed to ensure the economic partnership between married persons by affording protections to the non-title holding spouse both during the marriage and at its end, whether due to divorce or death.

47 The respondent is correct in noting that the *MPA* was designed to remedy the wrongs of the past and to support the equality of both spouses as a result of their joint commitment to share equally in the matrimonial assets. ...

48 ... Thus the *MPA*, by deeming all marriages to be economic partnerships, imposes a significant alteration to the *status quo* of an individual's proprietary rights and obligations. Moreover, these statutorily created proprietary restrictions and obligations arise at the time of the marriage and continue throughout the duration of the marriage until separation or death. The decision to marry, which necessarily requires the consent of each spouse, encapsulates within it the spouses' consent to be bound by the proprietary regime that the *MPA* creates.

49 Unmarried cohabitants, on the other hand, maintain their respective proprietary rights and interests throughout the duration of their relationship and at its end. These couples are free to marry, enter into domestic contracts, to own property jointly. In short, if they so choose, they are able to access all of the benefits extended to married couples under the *MPA*. Though my conclusion in this case is no way dependent upon the existence of the *LRA*, this new legislation offers another means by which unmarried cohabitants can access these benefits. The *LRA* is tailored to persons who, for myriad reasons, choose not to marry but who nevertheless consent to be bound legally to the same regime of economic partnership with all of the rights and obligations that it entails. The general principle is that, without taking some unequivocal consensual action, these cohabiting persons maintain the right to deal with any and all of their property as they see fit.

50 The *MPA*, then, can be viewed as creating a shared property regime that is tailored to persons who have taken a mutual positive step to invoke it. Conversely, it excludes from its ambit those persons who have not taken such a step. This requirement of consensus, be it through marriage or registration of a domestic partnership, enhances rather than diminishes respect for the autonomy and self-determination of unmarried cohabitants and their ability to live in relationships of their own design. As Iacobucci J. phrased it in *Law*, at para. 102, "[t]he law functions not by the device of stereotype, but by distinctions corresponding to the actual situation of individuals it affects." ...

52 Following the reasoning of McLachlin J. in *Miron*, *supra*, Walsh argues that there may be many factors that preclude certain individuals from marrying and thereby availing themselves of the *MPA*, even though their relationships have all the functional markings of a marriage. By excluding from its ambit unmarried couples, whom the respondent submits are the functional equivalents of married couples, the *MPA* has the effect of perpetuating the view that these alternative family forms are less deserving of recognition and respect.

53 In *Miron, supra*, this Court held the denial of insurance benefits to unmarried spouses to be discriminatory within the meaning of s. 15(1). In that case, the impugned legislation denied automobile insurance benefits to persons in circumstances similar to married persons. Short of agreeing to marry, the cohabitants had no ability to control the availability to each other of the benefits. Moreover, the extension or denial of these benefits had no impact on the rights and obligations of the spouses vis-à-vis each other. The discriminatory distinction at issue in *Miron, supra*, concerned the relationship of the couple as a unit, to third parties. The marital status of the couple should have had no bearing on the availability of the benefit.

54 In the present case, however, the *MPA* is primarily directed at regulating the relationship between the parties to the marriage itself; parties who, by marrying, must be presumed to have a mutual intention to enter into an economic partnership. Unmarried cohabitants, however, have not undertaken a similar unequivocal act. I cannot accept that the decision to live together, without more, is sufficient to indicate a positive intention to contribute to and share in each other's assets and liabilities. It may very well be true that some, if not many, unmarried cohabitants have agreed as between themselves to live as economic partners for the duration of their relationship. Indeed, the factual circumstances of the parties' relationship bear this out. It does not necessarily follow, however, that these same persons would agree to restrict their ability to deal with their own property during the relationship or to share in all of the other's assets and liabilities following the end of the relationship. As Eichler, *supra*, points out, at pp. 95-96:

> There is a distinct difference between a young couple living together, having a child together, and then splitting up, and an older couple living together after they have raised children generated with another partner. If a middle-aged couple decide to move in together at the age of fifty-five and to split at age sixty, and if both of them have children in their thirties, the partners may wish to protect their assets for themselves and for their children — with whom they have had a close relationship for over thirty years — rather than with a partner with whom they were associated for five years.

55 In my view, people who marry can be said to freely accept mutual rights and obligations. A decision not to marry should be respected because it also stems from a conscious choice of the parties. It is true that the benefits that one can be deprived of under a s. 15(1) analysis must not be read restrictively and can encompass the benefit of a process or procedure, as recognized in *M v. H, supra*. It has not been established, however, that there is a discriminatory denial of a benefit in this case because those who do not marry are free to take steps to deal with their personal property in such a way as to create an equal partnership between them. If there is need for a uniform and universal protective regime independent of choice of matrimonial status, this is not a s. 15(1) issue. The *MPA* only protects persons who have demonstrated their intention to be bound by it and have exercised their right to choose.

56 The respondent Walsh argues that the choice to marry, to enter into a domestic contract or to register a partnership under the *LRA* still does not address her situation, nor does it address the circumstances of those individuals whose unmarried partner either refuses to marry or to register their domestic partnership. For these persons, as Walsh argues, the decision is not entirely within their control. Similarly, she argues that maintaining the proprietary *status quo* in unmarried cohabiting relationships unduly disadvantages both the non-title holding partner, who have historically been women, as well as the children of the relationship. The respondent argues that protection of women and children from the potentially dire economic consequences of marriage breakdown is one of the main purposes of the *MPA*. Excluding unmarried cohabitants, then, constitutes a denial of equal protection of women in conjugal relationships and the children of those relationships, the persons whom the legislation was specifically designed to protect.

57 On this basis, the respondent submits that the only constitutionally acceptable formula is to extend the ambit of the *MPA* to all unmarried cohabitants, while providing consenting

couples the opportunity to opt out, as the current *MPA* does with regard to married couples. The problem with that proposition, in my view, is that it eliminates an individual's freedom to decide whether to make such a commitment in the first place. Even if the freedom to marry is sometimes illusory, does it warrant setting aside an individual's freedom of choice and imposing on her a regime that was designed for persons who have made an unequivocal commitment encompassing the equal partnership described in the *MPA*? While there is no denying that inequities may exist in certain unmarried cohabiting relationships and that those inequities may result in unfairness between the parties on relationship breakdown, there is no constitutional requirement that the state extend the protections of the *MPA* to those persons. The issue here is whether making a meaningful choice matters, and whether unmarried persons are prevented from taking advantage of the benefits of the *MPA* in an unconstitutional way.

58 Persons unwilling or unable to marry have alternative choices and remedies available to them. The couple may choose to own property jointly and/or to enter into a domestic contract that may be enforced pursuant to the *Maintenance and Custody Act*, R.S.N.S. 1989, c. 160, s. 52(1) and the *Maintenance Enforcement Act*, S.N.S. 1994-95, c. 6, s. 2(e). These couples are also capable of accessing all of the benefits of the *MPA* through the joint registration of a domestic partnership under the *LRA*.

59 It is true that certain unmarried couples may also choose to organize their relationship as an economic partnership for the period of their cohabitation. Similarly, some couples, without making a public and legally binding commitment, may simply live out their lives together in a manner akin to marriage. In these cases, the law has evolved to protect those persons who may be unfairly disadvantaged as a result of the termination of their relationship.

60 Firstly, provincial legislation provides that an unmarried cohabitant or "common-law partner" may apply to a court for an order of maintenance or support: *Maintenance and Custody Act*, s. 3. The court is empowered to take into consideration a host of factors pertaining to the manner in which the parties organized their relationship as well as the particular needs and circumstances of both of the parties.

61 For those couples who have not made arrangements regarding their property at the outset of their relationship, the law of constructive trust remains available to address inequities that may arise at the time of the dissolution. The law of constructive trust developed as a means of recognizing the contributions, both pecuniary and non-pecuniary, of one spouse to the family assets the title of which was vested wholly in the other spouse. ... After the enactment of the *MPA*, the law of constructive trust remained and remains as a recourse for unmarried partners who find themselves unfairly disadvantaged *vis-à-vis* their former partner. Those situations where the fact of economic interdependence of the couple arises over time are best addressed through the remedies like constructive trust as they are tailored to the parties' specific situation and grievances. In my view, where the multiplicity of benefits and protections are tailored to the particular needs and circumstances of the individuals, the essential human dignity of unmarried persons is not violated.

62 All of these factors support the conclusion that the extension of the *MPA* to married persons only is not discriminatory in this case as the distinction reflects and corresponds to the differences between those relationships and as it respects the fundamental personal autonomy and dignity of the individual. In this context, the dignity of common law spouses cannot be said to be affected adversely. There is no deprivation of a benefit based on stereotype or presumed characteristics perpetuating the idea that unmarried couples are less worthy of respect or valued as members of Canadian society. All cohabitants are deemed to

have the liberty to make fundamental choices in their lives. The object of s. 15(1) is respected.

63 Finally, it is important to note that the discriminatory aspect of the legislative distinction must be determined in light of *Charter* values. One of those essential values is liberty, basically defined as the absence of coercion and the ability to make fundamental choices with regard to one's life: *R. v. Big M Drug Mart Ltd.*, [1985] 1 S.C.R. 295 at p. 336 (S.C.C.); *R. v. Oakes*, [1986] 1 S.C.R. 103 (S.C.C.); *New Brunswick(Minister of Health & Community Services) v. G. (J.)*, [1999] 3 S.C.R. 46, ¶117 (S.C.C.). Limitations imposed by this Court that serve to restrict this freedom of choice among persons in conjugal relationships would be contrary to our notions of liberty.

64 Accordingly, I do not find that s. 2(g) of the *MPA* violates s. 15(1) of the *Charter*. Having found no discrimination in this particular case, it is unnecessary to proceed with a s. 1 analysis.

[Justice Gonthier, in concurring, expressly adopted the reasons given by Justice Bastarache, but stated that additional comments were warranted to emphasize the importance of the choice to marry. Because marriage was founded on the consent of the parties, he considered it fitting that the attributes, rights and obligations that gave marriage its unique character should not be conferred on unmarried couples (para. 201):

> It is by choice that married couples are subject to the obligations of marriage. When couples undertake such a life project, they commit to respect the consequences and obligations flowing from their choice. The choice to be subject to such obligations and to undertake a life-long commitment underlies and legitimates the system of benefits and obligations attached to marriage generally, and in particular, those relating to matrimonial assets. To accept the respondent Walsh's argument — thereby extending the presumption of equal division of matrimonial assets to common law couples — would be to intrude into the most personal and intimate of life choices by imposing a system of obligations on people who never consented to such a system. In effect, to presume that common law couples want to be bound by the same obligations as married couples is contrary to their choice to live in a common law relationship without the obligations of marriage.

Justice Gonthier also stressed that legislatures were entitled to define and promote marriage which "gives structure to the family, providing it with the stability best suited to the education and rearing of children". Although the Justice acknowledged that there had been a growing recognition that cohabiting opposite-sex couples should be subject to the same support regime as married couples, for him it did not follow that the regime of equal sharing of matrimonial assets should also apply to all couples. He stated that entirely different principles underlay the support and matrimonial property regimes. Support was based on need and dependency. A property regime applied regardless of need and spouses chose to be governed by it, either directly through contract or indirectly through marriage. Justice Gonthier concluded (para. 204): "To invoke s. 15 of the *Charter* to obtain spousal assets without regard to need raises the spectre of forcible taking in disguise, even if, in particular circumstances, equitable principles may justify it."

In her dissent, Justice L'Heureux-Dubé stated that the analysis should be confined to the law as it stood at the time that Walsh commenced her legal action. She expressed (para. 77) the fear that pronouncing on the constitutional validity of the legislation in force in Nova Scotia at the time of the appeal, including the system of domestic registered partnerships, might stultify the process underway in the various provinces whereby they were extending the benefits of the statutory family property regime to unmarried couples.

Justice L'Heureux-Dubé stressed that the broad fundamental purpose of the guarantee of equality was the recognition of the innate dignity of each human being. She concluded that the distinction drawn in the *Matrimonial Property Act* constituted discrimination on the basis of marital status because it undermined the dignity of unmarried cohabitees. She articulated several ways in which it did so. First, the omission of unmarried couples from the *Matrimonial Property Act* exacerbated the pre-existing disadvantages faced historically by them. Instead of being able to rely on a statutory presumption of equal contribution and equal sharing of property, unmarried cohabitees without legal title were forced to make their claims in equity with all the attendant expense and problems of proof.

The Justice also believed that marital status was unrelated to the goal underlying the *Matrimonial Property Act*. In her view (para. 104), a basic goal of matrimonial property regimes was a redistribution of economic resources to alleviate economic burdens that arose on the breakdown of a family. These needs were not tied to marriage but existed whenever any long-term relationship of dependency ended. She continued:]

(e) Recognizing Contributions to Non-marital Relationships — The Purpose of the MPA

105 In para. 35 of his reasons, my colleague stresses the importance of distinguishing between the intentions of married persons and heterosexual unmarried cohabitants upon entering into their respective relationships. ... In effect, the appellant's position was that it was constitutionally justified in treating two different relationships differently, most notably by giving effect to the intentions of those entering into the two types of conjugal relationships involved. The Court of Appeal instead chose to focus on whether the complete non-recognition of the contributions made by heterosexual unmarried cohabitants to their relationship constituted discrimination. Given the purpose of the *MPA*, I believe that the Court of Appeal's focus on this crucial point was sound. ...

(i) Purpose of the MPA — Recognizing a Need

117 The goal of matrimonial property regimes, and indeed the goal of family law generally, is a redistribution of economic resources on the breakdown of the family. While the relationship is a going concern, this redistribution is presumed to occur automatically. Family law only steps in on dissolution to distribute resources and alleviate economic burdens: see G. G. Blumberg, "The Regularization of Non-marital Cohabitation: Rights and Responsibilities in the American Welfare State" (2001), 76 *Notre Dame L. Rev.* 1265, at p. 1266. The preamble, this Court's previous statements concerning the goals of matrimonial property and similar legislation, the prevention of poverty, and the use of public funds all point to one purpose for the *MPA*, that of recognizing the problems that erupt at the end of the relationship and redistributing wealth to ensure that these problems are resolved. Infused in this interpretation is the notion that both parties have contributed to the relationship and that, in recognition of this contribution, wealth will be presumed to be distributed to each party equally.

(ii) The Needs of Heterosexual Unmarried Cohabitants

118 This brings me to the central theme of this factor. I hold that heterosexual unmarried cohabitants experience similar needs as their married counterparts when the relationship comes to an end. In this sense, the relationships are functionally equivalent. Since the purpose of the *MPA* is to recognize this need and to alleviate it, limiting the recognition to married cohabitants implies that the needs of heterosexual unmarried cohabitants are not worthy of the same recognition solely because the people in need have not married. Further, the *MPA* equal presumption is based on the recognition of the contribution made by both spouses to the family. Functionally, spouses contribute to various types of families. Failing to recognize the contribution made by heterosexual unmarried cohabitants is a failure to accord them the respect they deserve. This failure diminishes their status in their own eyes and in those of society as a whole by suggesting that they are less worthy of respect and consideration. Their dignity is thereby assaulted: they are the victims of discrimination. ...

126 The increased incidence of heterosexual unmarried cohabitation as a means by which children are raised and socialized and as a form of economic, emotional and social interdependence dictates some form of recognition of the functional equality displayed by both heterosexual married and unmarried cohabitants. The family is no longer an institution reserved for married persons. In essence, the family is a matrix of relationships through which values are transmitted, members are socialized, and children are raised. Disregarding the matrix because two of its members are unmarried fails to take into account the social reality that the same incidents of interdependence are faced by both the married and the unmarried living together in these relationships. ...

132 By denying functionally equal relationships benefits based on a status wholly unrelated to their needs, the *MPA* ends up drawing an inappropriate distinction. ...

133 The equivalency of functions described above gives rise to identical needs upon the breakdown of the family relationship. As both marital and non-marital cohabitation can be characterized by emotional, social, and economic inter-dependence, it follows that the termination of these relationships generates similar problems. ...

137 One complaint that could arise from the extension of the benefits accorded married cohabitants under the *MPA* to heterosexual unmarried ones involves the fact that the latter are, on average, relationships of shorter duration than marriages. It is argued that, as a result, a greater percentage of unmarried cohabitants do not leave their relationship in a similar state of mutual interdependence as does the average married cohabitant on the dissolution of marriage. Assuming this to be true, there are several responses to this objection.

138 First of all, the matter of whether attenuated or no benefits should be offered to certain heterosexual unmarried cohabitants is a matter best left to the legislature. They are the ones best able to decide at what point benefits ought to be extended. In the case of marriage, the legislature has chosen to extend the presumption to all married cohabitants regardless of the duration of their relationship or the lack of mutual interdependence. It is well known that some marriages, like some unmarried cohabitation relationships, are of short duration. Despite this, the legislature nevertheless offered the benefit to all married cohabitants.

139 Further, the *MPA* has built-in devices to allow courts to rebut the presumption of equal sharing where appropriate to do so. Section 13 of the *MPA* lists certain factors the court may consider in delineating a smaller share of the assets including, at para. (d), the "length of time that the spouses have cohabitated." ...

(f) Choosing to Marry and Choosing to Cohabit — Effect on Dignity

141 One of the appellant's main submissions was that the deliberate non-recognition of the contribution made by heterosexual unmarried cohabitants to their relationships is done as a means of giving effect to the intentions of those entering into such relationships. In a different vein, the appellant also argues that marriage involves a considered choice to enter into a relationship that, by its very nature, is infused with certain legal rights. The same cannot be said, it is asserted, for those who enter into unmarried relationships. Based on this belief, legislation that fails to extend its benefits to heterosexual unmarried cohabitants merely gives effect to their intentions. In fact, it serves to enhance their dignity by respecting their choice not to be bound by the rigours associated with marriage.

142 With the greatest respect, such an argument fundamentally misconceives the reasons people enter into relationships in the first place. It is an assumption based on scant evidence at best. I will in fact show that the *MPA* has nothing to do with consensus and everything to do with recognizing the needs of spouses (as discussed earlier).

143 I believe it to be highly problematic to conceive of marriage as a type of arrangement people enter into with the legal consequences of its demise taken into account. In the first place, most people are not lawyers. They are often not aware of the state of the law. Worse, many maintain positive misconceptions as to what obligations and rights exist in association with marriage and other relationships: Canada Law Reform Commission, *Studies on Family Property Law*, *supra*, at p. 267. The Law Reform Commission in Nova Scotia accepted that there is anecdotal evidence that unmarried partners believe that the *MPA* applies to them after one year of cohabitation: Law Reform Commission of Nova Scotia, *Final Report: Reform of the Law Dealing with Matrimonial Property in Nova Scotia*, *supra*, at p. 22.

144 Even assuming that people contemplating marriage are, as a whole, fully aware of their legal rights and obligations as married people, it is a mistake to base the obligations imposed by the *MPA* on the partners' perceived consensus to be bound by these obligations through marriage. Commenting on both the choice of marriage and the choice not to marry, the Law Reform Commission in Tasmania wrote the following:

> Sometimes two people choose to live together in absolute freedom and choose not to marry, just to avoid the responsibilities of marriage. But, although this is becoming more common, it affects a small minority of de facto relationships, and we believe that the vast majority of people who live together without marrying do so without thought of the legal consequences. It is we think, fanciful to think that any more than a handful of people organise their *personal* lives in this way in order to achieve specific legal consequences. [Emphasis in original.] (Law Reform Commission of Tasmania *Report on Obligations Arising From De Facto Relationships*, No. 36 (1977), at p. 5.)

145 Couples do not think of their relationship in contract terms. ...

147 Recognizing the obvious limits to conceptualizing the obligations flowing from marriage as a form of consensus, the legislature in Nova Scotia first enacted its matrimonial property legislation without regard for the wishes of married cohabitants at the outset of their relationship. Section 5(1) of the *MPA* explicitly states that the matrimonial property regime applies to spouses who entered into marriage "before or after the first day of October, 1980". ...

148 If I am incorrect in concluding that the source of the obligations in the *MPA* is not based on the choice of marriage, it does not follow that heterosexual unmarried cohabitants enter into their relationships specifically to avoid those legal obligations. In other words, the choice argument fails from both sides: many unmarried partners do not choose to cohabit or remain unmarried so as to avoid the legal consequences of marriage.

. . . . .

157 Based on the above comments, it is my view that the argument that the claimant's dignity was not violated by legislation enacted to respect her choice (and the choice of all heterosexual unmarried cohabitants) fails. This argument fails to account for the fact that the *MPA* rights are not based on choice or consensus. Moreover, it is incorrect to paint each unmarried cohabitant with the same brush as regards the "choice" to cohabit. For many, choice is not an option. For those where choice is in fact an option, few structure their lives by marrying or not marrying to take advantage or avoid particular legal obligations. The *MPA* does not therefore promote the dignity of the claimant. In fact, its failure to appreciate the absence of choice many cohabitants face with its concomitant exploitative features demeans the dignity of heterosexual unmarried cohabitants.

[Justice L'Heureux-Dubé found that the existing remedies available to unmarried cohabitees were inadequate. She noted (paras. 164–169) that the principles relating to the determination of the appropriate remedy for unjust enrichment and to the quantum of entitlement under a constructive trust were complex and uncertain.

Finally, L'Heureux-Dubé J. concluded (paras. 174–188) that the *Matrimonial Property Act*'s limitation of the equality rights of heterosexual unmarried cohabitees could not be justified under s. 1 of the *Charter*. First, she did not think that there was a sufficiently important objective underlying the Act and its exclusion of heterosexual unmarried couples. In her view, the true objective was the protection of married individuals from the harmful economic effects of family breakdown to the exclusion of all unmarried couples. This was not a constitutionally permissible objective because the state could not promote marriage over other functionally equal forms of intimate relationships. Second, she concluded that the means chosen to achieve any possible, constitutionally permissible objectives were not proportional. In particular, there was no rational connection between these objectives and the exclusion of unmarried heterosexual cohabitees.]

NOTES AND QUESTIONS

1. References to Nova Scotia's domestic partnership registration scheme pop up from time to time in the reasons in *Walsh v. Bona*. Do you think that the scheme's existence had any impact on the decision?

2. In her review of the social science data, Justice L'Heureux-Dubé noted (at para. 156) that the average length of a non-marital cohabitation relationship in Canada is only three years. To what extent, if any, does that statistic affect the argument that such relationships should be covered by a statutory family property regime?

3. Justice L'Heureux-Dubé concluded in *Walsh v. Bona* that a major goal of Nova Scotia's family property regime was to address the needs of the economically weaker spouse at the end of the relationship. Note, however, that the preamble to Nova Scotia's *Matrimonial Property Act* suggests that the family property regime is instituted to recognize the contributions that each spouse makes to the relationship. Also, unlike British Columbia's family property legislation, Nova Scotia's statute does not list the needs of a spouse as a factor to be considered in determining the appropriate division of assets (although it does list a child's needs). This led Justice Gonthier to conclude (para. 203): "While spousal support is based on need and dependency, the division of matrimonial assets distributes assets acquired during marriage without regard to need." Part I of Ontario's *FLA* also indicates that the rationale underlying its deferred equal sharing of net family properties is based on presumed equal, past contributions to the family rather than the future needs of the spouses. See s. 5(7). Does this make any difference to the question of whether the legislation should apply to unmarried couples?

4. Justice Bastarache suggested in *Walsh v. Bona* that the decision to get married is a decision to choose to be covered by a marital property regime and that the decision not to marry is a rejection of the regime. Do you find this convincing? Do couples generally know the legal consequences of marriage?

5. Family property regimes such as Ontario's leave little room for judicial discretion to vary the sharing of the gain that accrued during the marriage. As you examine the cases dealing with Ontario's regime, consider whether it would be desirable to modify it if it were extended to unmarried couples.

6. A family property regime such as Ontario's depends upon a clear identification of the start of a couple's economic partnership. Would this present a difficulty if it were extended to unmarried couples? A related question is whether the regime should apply to all couples as soon as they cohabit. Would it be permissible or appropriate to specify that the regime applies only to couples who have cohabited for at least three years?

7. The Supreme Court of Canada's decision in *Walsh v. Bona* raises the possibility that *Taylor v. Rossu* (1998), 39 R.F.L. (4th) 242 (Alta. C.A.) was wrongly decided. In the latter case, the Alberta Court of Appeal upheld a *Charter* challenge to the *Domestic Relations Act* on the basis that the legislation unjustifiably discriminated on the basis of marital status because it imposed support obligations only on married persons. The court noted that a clear majority of the Canadian jurisdictions had extended support obligations to some common law couples, but it was especially influenced by the Supreme Court of Canada's decision in *Miron v. Trudel* (1995), 13 R.F.L. (4th) 1 (S.C.C.).

8. All the common law provinces now have legislation extending support obligations to unmarried couples, including same-sex couples, if certain prerequisites are met. As we shall see in Chapter 6, *SPOUSAL SUPPORT*,

the support order may be geared to compensation for past contributions as well as need and may provide for a lump sum or a transfer of property.

On the other hand, most provinces, including Ontario, have limited their family property regimes to married couples. In these provinces, an individual involved in a common-law relationship who wishes to assert a claim in relation to property held by a partner has, in the absence of a contract, access only to the common law and equitable remedies analyzed in the next section of this casebook. Some provinces such as Nova Scotia and Manitoba allow common law couples to register their common law relationships with the result that they are covered by the family property regime. Manitoba, Saskatchewan, the Northwest Territories and Nunavut have extended their family property regimes to include some unmarried couples even without registration of their relationships. See generally Hovius, "Property Rights for Common-Law Partners" in Shaffer, ed. *Contemporary Issues in Family Law: Engaging with the Legacy of James G. McLeod* (Carswell, 2007).

9. Prior to the S.C.C. decision in *Walsh v. Bona* the momentum was clearly towards extending statutory property regimes to unmarried couples. This was being done either through ascription of the status of spouse or a system of registered domestic partnerships. Jurisdictions were moving in this direction largely in response to court challenges and in anticipation of a holding by the S.C.C. that such an extension was constitutionally mandated. Now that the S.C.C. has surprised the prognosticators by determining that it is constitutionally permissible to restrict the coverage of a matrimonial property regime to married persons, will the trend towards the extension of statutory property regimes to unmarried couples continue? Note that the majority in the S.C.C. gave positive reasons why such regimes should be confined to married couples. Indeed, it went so far as to write that the state should, in the interest of liberty, respect the individual's freedom to choose alternative family forms by not imposing all of the rights and obligations of married persons on unmarried cohabitees.

(3) Remedies for Common Law Partners

BECKER v. PETTKUS

19 R.F.L. (2d) 165, [1980] 2 S.C.R. 834, 1980 CarswellOnt 299, 1980
CarswellOnt 644

DICKSON J. (LASKIN C.J.C., ESTEY, MCINTYRE, CHOUINARD and LAMER JJ. concurring): — The appellant Lother Pettkus, through toil and thrift, developed over the years a successful bee-keeping business. He now owns two rural Ontario properties, where the business is conducted, and he has the proceeds from the sale, in 1974, of a third property located in the province of Quebec. It is not to his efforts alone, however, that success can be attributed. The respondent Rosa Becker, through her labour and earnings, contributed substantially to the good fortune of the common enterprise. She lived with Mr. Pettkus from 1955 to 1974, save for a separation in 1972. They were never married. When the relationship sundered in late 1974 Miss Becker commenced this action, in which she sought a declaration of entitlement to a one-half interest in the lands and a share in the bee-keeping business.

[While Miss Becker's claim was essentially dismissed at trial, the Ontario Court of Appeal awarded her a one-half interest in the lands owned by Mr. Pettkus and in the bee-keeping business.]

II Resulting trust

This appeal affords the court an opportunity to clarify the equivocal state in which the law of matrimonial property was left, following *Rathwell v. Rathwell*, [1978] 2 S.C.R. 436.

...

Broadly speaking, it may be said that the principles which have guided development of recent Canadian case law are to be found in two decisions of the House of Lords: *Pettitt v.*

Pettitt, [1970] A.C. 777, [1969] 2 W.L.R. 966, [1969] 2 All E.R. 385; and *Gissing v. Gissing*, [1971] A.C. 886, [1970] 3 W.L.R. 255, [1970] 2 All E.R. 780. In neither judgment does a majority opinion emerge. Though it is not necessary to embark upon a detailed analysis of the two cases, the legacy of *Pettitt* and *Gissing* should be noted. First, the decisions upheld the judicial quest for that fugitive common intention which must be proved in order to establish beneficial entitlement to matrimonial property. Second, the Law Lords did not feel free to ascribe or impute an intention to the parties, not supported by evidence, in order to achieve "equity" in the division of assets of partners to a marriage. Third, in *Gissing* four of the Law Lords spoke of "implied, constructive or resulting trust" without distinction.

A majority of the court in *Murdoch v. Murdoch*, [1975] 1 S.C.R. 423, 13 R.F.L. 185, [1974] 1 W.W.R. 361, 41 D.L.R. (3d) 367, adopted the "common intention" concept of Lord Diplock in *Gissing* [at p. 438]:

> Difficult as they are to solve, these problems as to the amount of the share of a spouse in the beneficial interest in a matrimonial home where the legal estate is vested solely in the other spouse, only arise in cases where the court is satisfied by the words or conduct of the parties that it was their common intention that the beneficial interest was not to belong solely to the spouse in whom the legal estate was vested but was to be shared between them in some proportion or other.

In *Murdoch* it was held that there was no evidence of common intention. In *Rathwell*, *supra*, common intention was held to exist. Although the notion of common intention was endorsed in *Murdoch* and in *Rathwell*, many difficulties, chronicled in the cases and in the legal literature on the subject, inhered in the application of the doctrine in matrimonial property disputes. The sought-for "common intention" is rarely, if ever, express; the courts must glean "phantom intent" from the conduct of the parties. The most relevant conduct is that pertaining to the financial arrangements in the acquisition of property. Failing evidence of direct contribution by a spouse, there may be evidence of indirect benefits conferred: where, for example, one partner pays for the necessaries while the other retires the mortgage loan over a period of years, *Fibrance v. Fibrance*, [1957] 1 All E.R. 357.

The artificiality of the common intention approach has been stressed. Professor Donovan Waters in a comment in (1975) 53 Can. Bar Rev. 366 stated [at p. 368]:

> ... In other words, this "discovery" of an implied common intention prior to the acquisition is in many cases a mere vehicle or formula for giving the wife a just and equitable share in the disputed asset. It is in fact a constructive trust approach masquerading as a resulting trust approach. ...

In *Murdoch v. Murdoch* Laskin J. (as he then was) introduced in a matrimonial property dispute the concept of constructive trust to prevent unjust enrichment. It is imposed without reference to intention to create a trust, and its purpose is to remedy a result otherwise unjust. It is a broad and flexible equitable tool which permits courts to gauge all the circumstances of the case, including the respective contributions of the parties, and to determine beneficial entitlement. ...

Although the resulting trust approach will often afford a wife the relief she seeks, the resulting trust is not available, as Professor Waters points out, at p. 374: "where the imputation of intention is impossible or unreasonable". One cannot imply an intention that the wife should have an interest if her conduct before or after the acquisition of the property is "wholly ambiguous", or its association with the alleged agreement "altogether tenuous". Where evidence is inconsistent with resulting trust, the court has the choice of denying a remedy or accepting the constructive trust.

Turning then to the present case and common intention, the evidence is clear that Mr. Pettkus and Miss Becker had no express arrangement for sharing economic gain. She conceded there was no specific arrangement with respect to the use of her money. ...

With respect to the period from 1955 until the spring of 1961, the trial judge found:

> Now the plaintiff claims a share in the said farm on the ground that at the beginning of their relationship they had implicitly agreed to carry on a common enterprise, the plaintiff paying the living ex-

penses and the defendant doing the saving. I am sure that the plaintiff would not have voiced such a proposition explicitly at the time, bent as she was on marriage, for fear of scaring away a prospective husband. *I find that her contribution to the household expenses during the first few years of their relationship was in the nature of risk capital invested in the hope of seducing a younger defendant into marriage.*

Moreover, the evidence does not clearly show that from 1955 to May 1961 the plaintiff contributed more than the defendant to the overall expenses of the household, so that *I find that the $12,000 accumulated by the defendant was due to his superior salary, his frugal living and his off-job gains from repairs.* It is to be noted that the plaintiff made also some savings. (The italics are mine.)

Whatever the passage may lack in point of gallantry, the words italicized represent findings of fact by the trial judge, negating common intention . ...

In the view of the Ontario Court of Appeal, speaking through Wilson J.A., the trial judge vastly underrated the contribution made by Miss Becker over the years. ...

The trial judge held there was no common intention, either express or implied. It is important to note that the Ontario Court of Appeal did not overrule that finding.

I am not prepared to infer, or presume, common intention when the trial judge has made an explicit finding to the contrary and the appellate court has not disturbed the finding. Accordingly, I am of the view that Miss Becker's claim grounded upon resulting trust must fail. If she is to succeed at all, constructive trust emerges as the sole juridical foundation for her claim.

III Constructive trust

The principle of unjust enrichment lies at the heart of the constructive trust. "Unjust enrichment" has played a role in Anglo-American legal writing for centuries. Lord Mansfield, in the case of *Moses v. MacFerlan* (1760), 2 Burr. 1005, 97 E.R. 676, put the matter in these words: "the gist of this kind of action is that the defendant, upon the circumstances of the case, is obliged by the ties of natural justice and equity to refund the money". It would be undesirable, and indeed impossible, to attempt to define all the circumstances in which an unjust enrichment might arise. ... The great advantage of ancient principles of equity is their flexibility: the judiciary is thus able to shape these malleable principles so as to accommodate the changing needs and mores of society, in order to achieve justice. The constructive trust has proven to be a useful tool in the judicial armoury. ...

How then does one approach the question of unjust enrichment in matrimonial causes? In *Rathwell* I ventured to suggest there are three requirements to be satisfied before an unjust enrichment can be said to exist: an enrichment, a corresponding deprivation and absence of any juristic reason for the enrichment. This approach, it seems to me, is supported by general principles of equity that have been fashioned by the courts for centuries, though, admittedly, not in the context of matrimonial property controversies.

The common law has never been willing to compensate a plaintiff on the sole basis that his actions have benefitted another. Lord Halsbury scotched this heresy in the case of *Ruabon SS. Co. Ltd. v. London Assce.*, [1900] A.C. 6 (H.L.) with these words, at p. 10: "I cannot understand how it can be asserted that it is part of the common law that where one person gets some advantage from the act of another a right of contribution towards the expense from that act arises on behalf of the person who has done it." Lord Macnaughten, in the same case, put it this way, at p. 15: "There is no principle of law that a person should contribute to an outlay merely because he has derived a benefit from it". It is not enough for the court simply to determine that one spouse has benefitted at the hands of another and then to require restitution. It must, in addition, be evident that the retention of the benefit would be "unjust" in the circumstances of the case.

Miss Becker supported Mr. Pettkus for five years [while he saved towards the purchase of a farm]. She then worked on the farm for about 14 years. The compelling inference from the facts is that she believed she had some interest in the farm and that that expectation was reasonable in the circumstances. Mr. Pettkus would seem to have recognized in Miss Becker some property interest, through the payment to her of compensation, however modest. [This comment refers to the fact that, when Miss Becker first left in 1972, Mr. Pettkus threw $3,000 on the floor and told her to take the money, a 1966 Volkswagen, 40 beehives containing bees, and "get lost".] There is no evidence to indicate that he ever informed her that all her work performed over the 19 years was being performed on a gratuitous basis. He freely accepted the benefits conferred upon him through her financial support and her labour.

On these facts, the first two requirements laid down in *Rathwell* have clearly been satisfied: Mr. Pettkus has had the benefit of 19 years of unpaid labour, while Miss Becker has received little or nothing in return. As for the third requirement, I hold that where one person in a relationship tantamount to spousal prejudices herself in the reasonable expectation of receiving an interest in property and the other person in the relationship freely accepts benefits conferred by the first person in circumstances where he knows or ought to have known of that reasonable expectation, it would be unjust to allow the recipient of the benefit to retain it.

I conclude, consonant with the judgment of the Court of Appeal, that this is a case for the application of constructive trust. As Wilson J.A. noted [at R.F.L. p. 348]: "The parties lived together as husband and wife although unmarried, for almost 20 years, during which period she not only made possible the acquisition of their first property in Franklin Centre by supporting them both exclusively from her income during 'the lean years', but worked side by side with him for 14 years building up the bee-keeping operation which was their main source of livelihood."

Wilson J.A. had no difficulty in finding that a constructive trust arose in favour of the respondent by virtue of "joint effort" and "team work", as a result of which Mr. Pettkus was able to acquire the Franklin Centre property, and subsequently the East Hawkesbury and West Hawkesbury properties. The Ontario Court of Appeal imposed the constructive trust in the interests of justice and, with respect, I would do the same.

. . . . .

VI Causal connection

The matter of "causal connection" was also raised in defence of Miss Becker's claim, but does not present any great difficulty. There is a clear link between the contribution and the disputed assets. The contribution of Miss Becker was such as enabled, or assisted in enabling, Mr. Pettkus to acquire the assets in contention. For the unjust enrichment principle to apply it is obvious that some connection must be shown between the acquisition of property and corresponding deprivation. On the facts of this case, that test was met. The indirect contribution of money and the direct contribution of labour is clearly linked to the acquisition of property, the beneficial ownership of which is in dispute. Miss Becker indirectly contributed to the acquisition of the Franklin Centre farm by making possible an accelerated rate of saving by Mr. Pettkus. The question is really an issue of fact: Was her contribution sufficiently substantial and direct as to entitle her to a portion of the profits realized upon sale of the Franklin Centre property and to an interest in the Hawkesbury properties and the bee-keeping business? The Ontario Court of Appeal answered this question in the affirmative, and I would agree.

VII Respective proportions

Although equity is said to favour equality, as stated in *Rathwell*, it is not every contribution which will entitle a spouse to a one-half interest in the property. The extent of the interest must be proportionate to the contribution, direct or indirect, of the claimant. Where the contributions are unequal, the shares will be unequal.

It could be argued that Mr. Pettkus contributed somewhat more to the material fortunes of the joint enterprise than Miss Becker but it must be recognized that each started with nothing; each worked continuously, unremittingly and sedulously in the joint effort. Physically, Miss Becker pulled her fair share of the load: weighing only 87 pounds, she assisted in moving hives weighing 80 pounds. Any difference in quality or quantum of contribution was small. The Ontario Court of Appeal in its discretion favoured an even division and I would not alter that disposition, other than to note that in any accounting regard should be had to the $2,600 and the car, which Miss Becker received on separation in 1974. ...

I would dismiss the appeal with costs to the respondent.

[MR. JUSTICE RITCHIE agreed with this conclusion, but preferred a resulting trust analysis. He reasoned, in part:]

I should make it plain at the outset that in my opinion contributions made by one spouse and freely accepted by the other for use in the acquisition and operation of a common household give rise to a rebuttable presumption that, at the time when the contributions were made and accepted, the parties both intended that there would be a resulting trust in favour of the donor to be measured in terms of the value of the contributions so made. ...

[W]hatever her motives may have been, the respondent's intention in making the contributions was to benefit the appellant and it is clear that they were acquiesced in and indeed freely accepted by him to be applied for and toward the maintenance and operation of a joint household.

[MARTLAND J., BEETZ J. concurring, expressed agreement with the reasons of RITCHIE J. However, he explained why he could not accept the application of a constructive trust in this situation. In particular, he noted:]

In my opinion, the adoption of this concept involves an extension of the law as so far determined in this court. Such an extension is, in my view, undesirable. It would clothe judges with a very wide power to apply what has been described as "palm tree justice" without the benefit of any guidelines. By what test is a judge to determine what constitutes unjust enrichment? The only test would be his individual perception of what he considered to be unjust.

As stated in the reasons of my brother Ritchie, the determination of this appeal in the respondent's favour can be made in accordance with existing authority and without recourse to the concepts of unjust enrichment and constructive trust.

SOROCHAN v. SOROCHAN

2 R.F.L. (3d) 225, [1986] 2 S.C.R. 38, 1986 CarswellAlta 714
, 1986 CarswellAlta 143

DICKSON C.J.C. [For the Court]: — In this appeal, the court is called upon to consider whether the appellant, Mary Sorochan, is entitled to an interest in the farmland owned by the respondent. The central issue is whether a court can impose a constructive trust in a situation where a "common law" wife has contributed her labour for a number of years to preserving and maintaining a farm and doing all of the domestic labour, despite the fact that her spouse already owned the property prior to the date cohabitation commenced.

I Facts

Mary and Alex Sorochan lived together for 42 years, between 1940 and 1982, on a farm in the Two Hills district of Alberta. During this time, they jointly worked a mixed farming operation and had six children. They never married. Mary Sorochan did all of the domestic labour associated with running the household and caring for the children. In addition, she worked long hours on the farm. The family lived in modest circumstances.

At the time the parties began living together, Alex Sorochan was the owner, along with his brother, of six one-quarter sections of farmland. In 1951, the land was divided between the two brothers and the respondent became the registered owner of three one-quarter sections. From 1942 to 1945, and from 1968 to 1982, the respondent worked as a travelling salesperson. During these periods, Mary Sorochan often assumed responsibility for doing all of the farm chores on her own. In 1982, due to the failing health of the appellant and the deteriorating relationship between the couple, Mary Sorochan moved to a senior citizen's home. She subsequently commenced this legal action for an interest in the farm upon which she had worked for 42 years.

II Judgments

Alberta Court of Queen's Bench

At trial, Purvis J. of the Alberta Court of Queen's Bench, relying on *Pettkus v. Becker*, [1980] 2 S.C.R. 834, 19 R.F.L. (2d) 165, 8 E.T.R. 143, 117 D.L.R. (3d) 257, 34 N.R. 384 (Ont.), held that "the law of constructive trust can be extended to cover situations such as the one disclosed in the evidence in these proceedings". He found that Alex Sorochan was enriched by his association with Mary Sorochan and that she had suffered a corresponding deprivation. Purvis J. also found that there was no juristic reason justifying the enrichment. Mary Sorochan had prejudiced herself with the reasonable expectation of receiving an interest in the property and Alex Sorochan knew of that expectation. Purvis J. noted, in particular, that in 1971 Mary Sorochan had asked the respondent to transfer land into her name.

Accordingly, Purvis J. ordered the transfer of one of the three quarter sections of land into the name of Mary Sorochan, upon her undertaking to transfer title forthwith to her six children. He also ordered Alex Sorochan to pay $8,000 in cash forthwith to Mary Sorochan and a further $12,000 within one year, the latter sum to be reduced to $7,000 if paid within six months.

Alberta Court of Appeal

The Court of Appeal reversed the trial judge's order and rejected the finding of a constructive trust in favour of Mary Sorochan. Lieberman J.A., for the court, held that the trial judge had erred in his interpretation of *Pettkus v. Becker*, stating [at p. 120]:

> Plaintiff's counsel argues that a constructive trust has been created here by reason of the unjust enrichment of the defendant as a result of the plaintiff's labours, but she has been unable to point out any accumulation of assets by the couple during the relevant period.
>
> In *Pettkus* Dickson J., as he then was, said at p. 183:
>
> > For the unjust enrichment principle to apply it is obvious that some connection must be shown between the acquisition of property and corresponding deprivation. On the facts of this case, that test was met. The indirect contribution of money and the direct contribution of labour is clearly linked to the acquisition of property, the beneficial ownership of which is in dispute.
>
> Unfortunately, the facts in the case at bar do not fall within that principle. There is no link between the acquisition of the property in question and the plaintiff's labour.

III Unjust Enrichment

... Before a constructive trust can be imposed in this case, the court must find that there has been an unjust enrichment. In *Pettkus* and *Rathwell*, the court outlined three requirements that must be satisfied before it can be said that an unjust enrichment exists. These include:

(a) an enrichment;

(b) a corresponding deprivation; and

(c) the absence of any juristic reason for the enrichment.

In the present appeal, the appellant worked on the farm for 42 years, during which time she received no remuneration from the respondent. She did all of the household work, including the raising of their six children. In addition, she looked after the vegetable garden, milked the cows, raised chickens, did farmyard chores, worked in the fields, hayed, hauled bales, harvested grain and helped to clear the land of rocks. She also sold garden produce, milk and eggs to pay for food and clothing for the family and for the schooling of the youngest child. On numerous occasions when Alex Sorochan was engaged in his sales activities, Mary Sorochan was left with sole responsibility for the operation of the farm.

The trial judge held that there was "clear evidence of enrichment" to the respondent. The Court of Appeal found that Mary Sorochan "performed all the work of a diligent farm wife". In my view, it is clear that the respondent derived a benefit from the appellant's many years of labour in the home and on the farm. This benefit included valuable savings from having essential farm services and domestic work performed by the appellant without having to provide remuneration. ...

In addition, through the appellant's years of labour, the farm was maintained and preserved as valuable farm land. It did not deteriorate in value through neglect or disuse, as it no doubt would have in the absence of Mary Sorochan's faithful and long years of labour. The appellant's maintenance and preservation of the land, therefore, conferred a significant benefit on the respondent. ...

On the other side of the coin, the labour done by Mary Sorochan during those 42 years constituted for her a corresponding deprivation. The trial judge concluded that this was the case. Moreover, the case law indicates that the full-time devotion of one's labour and earnings without compensation can readily be viewed as a deprivation. ...

The third condition that must be satisfied before a finding of unjust enrichment can be made is also easily met on the facts of this case. There was no juristic reason for the enrichment. Mary Sorochan was under no obligation, contractual or otherwise, to perform the work and services in the home or on the land. In *Pettkus*, the court held that this third requirement would be met in situations where one party prejudices himself or herself with the reasonable expectation of receiving something in return and the other person freely accepts the benefits conferred by the first person in circumstances where he or she knows or ought to have known of that reasonable expectation.

Mary Sorochan came to live with Alex Sorochan on his farm. Together they worked the land, had six children and held themselves out to the community as married. In my view, Mary Sorochan had a reasonable expectation of receiving some benefit in return for her 42 years of domestic and farm labour. Indeed, it was reasonable for her to believe that this would take the form of an interest in the property. In 1951, when the two brothers split their joint ownership of the land, Mary Sorochan was asked to sign the conveyancing documents to bar any dower entitlement to the lands ceded to Alex Sorochan's brother. At the time of their first child in 1941, Mary Sorochan asked Alex Sorochan to get married. She testified at trial that he responded "later on". In 1971, she asked him to transfer part of the land into her name, which he refused to do. These incidents convince me that Alex Sorochan knew or ought to have known that Mary Sorochan had a reasonable expectation of obtaining some share in the land in return for her long-term commitment to working the farm and raising their six children.

In my view, to deny Mary Sorochan any form of relief would be unjust. I conclude, therefore, that the three preconditions for unjust enrichment have been satisfied in this case.

IV Constructive Trust

The constructive trust constitutes one important judicial means of remedying unjust enrichment. Other remedies, such as monetary damages, may also be available to rectify situations of unjust enrichment. We must, therefore, ask when and under what circumstances it is appropriate for a court to impose a constructive trust. ...

In this regard, the first issue to be considered is the causal connection requirement, upon which the Court of Appeal's decision turned. Relying on the decision in *Pettkus*, the Court of Appeal held, and the respondent now submits, that before a constructive trust can be imposed, some connection must be shown between the deprivation and the actual *acquisition* of the property in question. Alex Sorochan already owned the land at the time Mary Sorochan moved in with him; it is maintained, therefore, that she did not contribute in any way to the acquisition of the farm.

It is understandable that this issue could be a source of confusion. Since the early constructive trust cases involved situations where there was some acquisition of property, there was a tendency to treat a particular manifestation of a general principle as the rule itself. ...

In my view, the constructive trust remedy should not be confined to cases involving property acquisition. While it is important to require that some nexus exist between the claimant's deprivation and the property in question, the link need not always take the form of a contribution to the actual acquisition of the property. A contribution relating to the preservation, maintenance or improvement of property may also suffice. ...

In the present case, Mary Sorochan worked on the farm for 42 years. Her labour directly and substantially contributed to the maintenance and preservation of the farm, preventing asset deterioration or divestment. There is, therefore, a "clear link" between the contribution and the disputed assets. ...

In addition to the causal connection requirement, it is often suggested that the reasonable expectation of the claimant in obtaining an actual interest in the property as opposed to monetary relief constitutes another important consideration in determining if the constructive trust remedy is appropriate. ... A reasonable expectation of benefit is part and parcel of the third precondition of unjust enrichment (the absence of a juristic reason for the enrichment). At this point, however, in assessing whether a constructive trust remedy is appropriate, we must direct our minds to the specific question of whether the claimant reasonably expected to receive an actual interest in property and whether the respondent was or reasonably ought to have been cognizant of that expectation. As concluded above, Mary Sorochan did have a reasonable expectation in obtaining an interest in the land and Alex Sorochan was aware of her expectation in this regard.

In assessing whether or not an *in rem* remedy is appropriate, a final consideration in this case is the longevity of the relationship. The appellant worked the farm for 42 years of her life. In my opinion, this constitutes a further compelling factor in favour of granting proprietary relief.

Under these circumstances, I conclude that it was appropriate for the trial judge to provide relief, at least in part, by way of constructive trust.

V The Appropriate Remedy

There remains the question of the appropriateness of the trial judge's remedial orders. After considering the equities and the circumstances of the parties, he awarded Mary

Sorochan title to one third of the farm property by way of constructive trust, on the condition that she transfer title forthwith to her six children. This portion of the farm had an assessed market value of $40,000 in 1983. The total value of the farm was approximately $138,000. It appears that the trial judge's order for proprietary relief was motivated by Mary Sorochan's desire to devise an interest in the lands she had worked for 42 years to her children. This further explains the condition stipulated by the trial judge that title be transferred forthwith to her children, a matter to which I shall return below. The trial judge allowed Alex Sorochan to retain full title to the other two-thirds of the farm, which included the home quarter. In so doing, Alex Sorochan could continue to live on the farm and derive his income from the land.

In addition to the constructive trust remedy, the trial judge made an order for monetary relief for $20,000 (to be reduced to $15,000 if paid within six months). In my opinion, it was open to the trial judge to make this type of lump sum award. The statement of claim of Mary Sorochan had requested not only proprietary relief, but as well "such further Order that this Honourable Court may deem just".

To remedy the unjust enrichment, therefore, the trial judge relied in part on the constructive trust device and in part on a straightforward monetary award.

The quantum of the trial judge's award has not been challenged by either party, except insofar as the respondent contends that no remedy whatsoever should have been granted. Under these circumstances, and bearing in mind that the trial judge is much better situated to assess what is fair and just in light of the particular facts of each case, I am inclined to defer to the trial judge's ruling in all but one respect.

In my view, the trial judge erred when he made Mary Sorochan's entitlement to the land contingent on her immediate transfer of title to her children. Mary Sorochan is the one who suffered the deprivation and it is she who is entitled to the remedy — not her children. She may well decide to transfer title to the land to her children, but this will be her decision alone to make. ...

PETER v. BEBLOW

(1993), 44 R.F.L. (3d) 329, 1993 CarswellBC 44, 1993 CarswellBC 1258 (S.C.C.)

CORY J. (concurring) (L'HEUREUX-DUBÉ and GONTHIER JJ. concurring): — The issue in this appeal is whether the provision of domestic services during 12 years of cohabitation in a common law relationship is sufficient to establish the proprietary link which is required before the remedy of constructive trust can be applied to redress the unjust enrichment of one of the partners in the relationship. Further, consideration must be given to the extent to which the remedy of constructive trust should be applied in terms of amount or proportion.

Factual Background

In April 1973, the respondent asked the appellant to come and live with him. That same month, the appellant, together with her 4 children, moved into the respondent's home in Sicamous, B.C. At the time, 2 children of the respondent were living in the home. The parties continued to live together in a common law relationship for over 12 years, separating in June 1985. During this entire time the appellant acted as the wife of the respondent. She was a stepmother to his children until 1977 while they remained in the home. As well, she cared for her own children, the last one leaving in 1980.

During the 12 years, the appellant cooked, cleaned, washed clothes, and looked after the garden. As well, she worked on the Sicamous property, undertaking such projects as painting the fence, planting a cedar hedge, buying flowers and shrubs for the property, and building a rock garden. She built a pig pen. She kept chickens for a few years, butchering and cooking them for the family. During the winters, the appellant shovelled snow, chopped wood, and made kindling. The respondent did not pay the appellant for any of her work. Both the appellant and the respondent contributed to the purchase of groceries and household supplies, although the respondent contributed a greater share.

In the first year of the relationship the appellant did not undertake outside work and spent 8 hours a day doing housework and work on the Sicamous property. In subsequent years, she took part-time work as a cook from June to October. During these months she worked some six hours a day at a rate of $4.50 per hour. Except for one winter when she worked at a bakery, the appellant received unemployment insurance benefits in the winter months.

Throughout the relationship, the respondent worked on a more or less full-time basis as a grader operator. His work frequently took him out of town to various locations in British Columbia.

Before he met the appellant, the respondent had lived in a common law relationship with another woman for 5 years. When she left his home he hired housekeepers. The last housekeeper he had before the appellant came to his home was paid at a rate of $350 per month.

The trial judge accepted the appellant's testimony that the respondent had asked her to live with him because he needed someone to care for his 2 children. This need arose when the welfare authorities expressed some concern that the respondent left the children alone when he was working away from home.

When the parties met, the appellant had savings of $100. In 1976, she purchased a property in Saskatchewan for $2,500. She sold this property in 1980 for $8,000 and purchased a property at 100 Mile House for $6,500. She used the remainder of the sale proceeds for a trip to Reno. At the time of trial, the appellant still owned the 100 Mile House property.

The respondent had purchased the Sicamous property in 1971 for $8,500. Some $900 was paid in cash and the balance of $7,600 was secured by a mortgage. The respondent was able to pay off the mortgage in 1975. The estimated market value of the Sicamous property as of 1987 was $17,800. The property's assessed value in that year was $23,200. In that same year, the respondent rented the property. The tenants were given an option to purchase it for $28,000. The option was not exercised.

With the passage of time, the respondent began to drink heavily and became verbally and physically abusive to the appellant. As a result, the appellant moved out of the Sicamous home on June 7, 1985. At the time of the trial, she was on welfare and lived in a trailer court in Sicamous. The respondent, by that time, had retired and was living on a houseboat in Enderby, B.C. The Sicamous house and property were vacant.

The appellant brought an action claiming that the respondent had been unjustly enriched over the years of the relationship as a result of the work which she performed in his home without payment of any kind. She sought to have a constructive trust imposed on her behalf in respect of the Sicamous property or, in the alternative, monetary damages as compensation for the labour and services she provided to the respondent.

Position of the Respondent

The respondent conceded that there was an unjust enrichment but contended that there was no corresponding deprivation suffered by the appellant. It was said that she was adequately compensated for her services by the respondent's provision of free shelter and a large portion of the groceries.

Second, it was argued that the domestic services provided by the appellant did not establish any causal link to or proprietary interest in the Sicamous property.

The Court of Appeal clearly agreed with the respondent on these issues. With respect, I believe they erred in reaching these conclusions.

Should the Remedy of Constructive Trust be Applied to the Case at Bar?

1. Enrichment

It should not be forgotten that the trial judge specifically found that there had been an enrichment to the respondent "since he obtained the services of the Plaintiff as a housekeeper, homemaker and in fact stepmother without compensation." Indeed, it was conceded before us that the respondent was enriched by the work and contributions of the appellant.

2. A Corresponding Deprivation

It is again important to first consider the finding of the trial judge on this issue. He stated:

> The plaintiff was deprived of any compensation for her labour since she devoted the majority of her time and energy and some of the monies she earned towards the benefit of the Respondent, his children and his property.

That finding would seem in itself to warrant the conclusion that the appellant suffered a deprivation which corresponds to the enrichment of the respondent.

Indeed, I would have thought that if there is enrichment, that it would almost invariably follow that there is a corresponding deprivation suffered by the person who provided the enrichment. There is ample support for the proposition that once enrichment has been found, the conclusion that the plaintiff has suffered a corresponding deprivation is virtually automatic . ... In *Everson v. Rich* (1988), 16 R.F.L. (3d) 337, the Saskatchewan Court of Appeal, applying *Sorochan*, stated, at p. 342:

> The spousal services provided by the appellant were valuable services and did constitute a benefit conferred upon the respondent. The provision of those services was a detriment to the claimant by virtue of the use of her time and energy.

I agree with this reasoning. As a general rule, if it is found that the defendant has been enriched by the efforts of the plaintiff, there will, almost as a matter of course, be deprivation suffered by the plaintiff. ... Particularly in a matrimonial or long term common law relationship it should, in the absence of cogent evidence to the contrary, be taken that the enrichment of one party will result in a deprivation of the other.

Business relationships concerned with commercial affairs may, as a result of the conduct of one of the corporations involved, result in a court's granting a constructive trust remedy. The constructive trust has been appropriately used to redress a gain made through a breach of trust in a commercial or business relationship (See, for example, *Canadian Aero Service Ltd. v. O'Malley*, [1974] S.C.R. 592.) Yet how much closer and trusting must be a long term common law relationship. In marriages or marriage-like relationships commercial matters and a great deal more will be involved. Clearly, parties to a family relationship will, in a commercial sense, share funds and financial goals. More importantly, couples, such as the parties to this case, will strive to make a home. By that I mean a place that provides safety, security, and love, and which is as well frequently the place where children may be cared for and nurtured. In a relationship that involves living and sleeping together, couples will share their worst fears and frustrations and their fondest dreams and aspirations. They will plan and work together to achieve their goals. Just as much as parties to a formal marriage, the partners in a long term common law relationship will base their actions on mutual love and trust. They too are entitled, in appropriate circumstances, to the relief provided by the remedy of constructive trust.

This remedy should be granted despite the fact that family will seldom keep the same careful financial records as business associates. Nonetheless, fairness requires that the constructive trust remedy be available to them and applied on an equitable basis without a minute scrutiny of their respective financial contributions. Indeed, in a situation such as the one presented in this case, it may be very difficult to assess the value of making a house a home and of sharing the struggle to raise children to become responsible adults.

In the present case, although there was no formal marriage, the couple lived and worked together in the most intimate of relationships. They shared work and the monies which they earned. The amount of the contributions may have been varied and unequal. Yet the very fact that, in addition to her household work, the appellant contributed something of the income from her outside employment indicates that there was a real sharing of income. As a result of the relationship, the Sicamous property was looked after and maintained. None of this could have been achieved without the efforts of the appellant.

Certainly, it cannot be said that the relationship was so short-lived that it should not give rise to mutual rights and obligations. Twelve years is not an insignificant period of time to live in a relationship based on mutual trust and confidence. In those circumstances, there is a strong presumption that the services provided by one party will not be used solely to enrich the other. Both the reasonable expectations of the parties and equity will require that upon the termination of the relationship, the parties will receive an appropriate compensation based on the contribution each has made to the relationship.

The respondent asserts that because the appellant loved him she could not have expected to receive compensation or an interest in the property in return for the contributions she made to the home and family. However, in today's society it is unreasonable to assume that the presence of love automatically implies a gift of one party's services to another. Nor is it unreasonable for the party providing the domestic labour required to create a home to expect to share in the property of the parties when the relationship is terminated. Women no longer are expected to work exclusively in the home. It must be recognized that when they do so, women forgo outside employment to provide domestic services and child care. The granting of relief in the form of a personal judgment or a property interest to the provider of domestic services should adequately reflect the fact that the income earning capacity and the ability to acquire assets by one party has been enhanced by the unpaid domestic services of the other. Marcia Neave in "Three Approaches to Family Property Disputes — Intention/ Belief, Unjust Enrichment and Unconscionability", in T.G. Youdan, ed., *Equity, Fiduciaries and Trusts* (Scarborough, Ont.: Carswell, 1989), lucidly sets out the position in this way, at p. 254:

> The characterization of domestic services as gifts reflects a view of family relationships which is now out-dated and has a differential impact on women, since they are the main providers of such services. Women no longer work exclusively in the home. Those who do so sacrifice income that could otherwise be earned in paid work. Couples who decide that one partner, usually the woman, will forgo paid employment to provide domestic services and provide child care, presumably believe that this arrangement will maximize their economic resources. Grant of relief, whether personal or proprietary, to the provider of domestic services would recognize that the income-earning capacity of one partner and his ability to acquire assets have been enhanced by the unpaid services of the other and that those services were only provided free because it was believed that the relationship would continue.

This same reasoning has been recently applied in the context of divorce in *Moge v. Moge*, [1992] 3 S.C.R. 813. It is appropriate to recognize that the same principle should be applied to long term common law relationships.

In the present case it cannot be said, as the respondent suggests, that the contributions of the appellant were minor or that they were compensated by the provision of free accommodation. It is true that the appellant did not devote all of her energy to the home or family business as did Mary Sorochan. ... However, the mere fact that the appellant was able to engage in part-time employment does not detract from the fact that she provided extensive and valuable services to the respondent for which she was not compensated.

It cannot be forgotten that the trial judge recognized that the appellant worked to create a "home" for the respondent. The nature and extent of her efforts were clear from the evidence, but one rather touching indication of her dedication is that she helped the children to make Christmas gifts. The value of the commitment of a homemaker, such as the appellant, should not be underestimated. The partner who provides domestic services often works far in excess of 40 hours per week in order to provide a "home". Women who work in the home may have given up a career or a type of work which would enable them to improve their earning capacity. These are matters which should be taken into account when considering both the benefits conferred and the deprivation suffered by a claimant who has been a partner in a long-term common law relationship.

The balancing of benefits conferred and received in a matrimonial or common law relationship cannot be accomplished with precision. Although it may well be essential in a commercial relationship to closely scrutinize the contributions made by each of the business partners to the acquisition of property, such an approach would be unrealistic and unfair in the context of a family relationship. Ordinarily, the trial judge will be in the best position to assess all the evidence presented and to estimate the contribution made by each of the parties. The nature of the relationship, its duration, and the contributions of the parties must be considered. Equity and fairness should form the basis for the assessment. There was ample evidence presented in this case to justify the finding of the trial judge that there had been a deprivation suffered by the appellant.

3. Absence of Juristic Reason for the Enrichment

In *Becker v. Pettkus, supra*, Dickson J. had this to say, at p. 849, with regard to juristic reasons for the enrichment:

> ... I hold that where one person in a relationship tantamount to spousal prejudices herself in the reasonable expectation of receiving an interest in property and the other person in the relationship freely accepts benefits conferred by the first person in circumstances where he knows or ought to have known of that reasonable expectation, it would be unjust to allow the recipient of the benefit to retain it.

The test put forward is an objective one. The parties entering a marriage or a common law relationship will rarely have considered the question of compensation for benefits. If asked, they might say that because they loved their partner, each worked to achieve the common goal of creating a home and establishing a good life for themselves. It is just and reasonable that the situation be viewed objectively and that an inference be made that, in the absence of evidence establishing a contrary intention, the parties expected to share in the assets created in a matrimonial or quasi-matrimonial relationship, should it end. ...

It is not necessary that there be evidence of promises to marry or to compensate the claimant for the services provided. Rather, where a person provides "spousal services" to another, those services should be taken as having been given with the expectation of compensation unless there is evidence to the contrary. ...

In the case at bar, the trial judge appropriately drew the inference that, in light of the duration of the relationship and the appellant's contribution to the home and property, she would reasonably have had an expectation of sharing the wealth she helped to create. He concluded that:

> ... there is no juristic reason for the enrichment. She was under no obligation to perform the work and assist in the home without some reasonable expectation of receiving something in return other than the drunken physical abuse which she received at the hands of the Respondent.

When a claimant is under no obligation, contractual, statutory, or otherwise, to provide the work and services to the recipient, there will be an absence of juristic reasons for the enrichment. ...

In summary, then, there was unjust enrichment of the respondent by the work of the appellant. The appellant suffered a corresponding deprivation. There was no juristic reason for the enrichment, that is to say, there was no obligation of any kind upon the appellant to provide the services to the respondent. It follows that the trial judge was correct in his finding that there had been an unjust enrichment, a corresponding deprivation, and no juristic reason for providing the enriching services. It remains to be considered what remedy should have been provided in the circumstances. Would a monetary judgment have been appropriate or should the remedy of constructive trust have been granted?

The Appropriate Remedy

In *Sorochan v. Sorochan*, it was noted that, although the constructive trust provides an important judicial means of remedying unjust enrichment, there are other remedies available, such as monetary damages. The first question to be resolved is which remedy is appropriate in the circumstances of this case? In *Sorochan* it was said that the court must consider whether there is a causal connection between the deprivation suffered by the plaintiff and the property in question, because in order to justify the imposition of a constructive trust a court must be satisfied that there is a "clear proprietary relationship" between the services rendered and the disputed assets. ...

In addition to the causal connection requirement, Dickson C.J. stated that the claimant must have reasonably expected to receive an interest in the property and that the respondent ought to have been aware of that expectation. He also observed that, in considering whether a constructive trust is the appropriate remedy, the duration of the relationship should be taken into account.

The difficulty of establishing a causal connection between unjust enrichment arising from the provision of domestic services and the property has been the subject of scholarly debate (see, for example: Ralph E. Scane, "Relationships 'Tantamount to Spousal', Unjust Enrichment, and Constructive Trusts" (1991) 70 Can. Bar Rev. 260; Keith B. Farquhar, "Causal Connection in Constructive Trusts" (1986–88) 8 Est. & Tr. Q. 161; Berend Hovius and Timothy G. Youdan, *The Law of Family Property* (Scarborough, Ont.: Carswell, 1991); Ian Narev, "Unjust Enrichment and De Facto Relationships" (1991) 6 Auckland U.L. Rev. 504). As Professor Ralph Scane (*supra*, at p. 289) put it, the difficulty with looking for a causal connection in such cases is "that the unjust enrichment created by receipt of the benefit of [domestic] services ... seeps throughout all of the assets of the defendant". Thus, the contributions which indirectly created accumulated family wealth for the parties cannot be traced to any one property. However, I do not think that the required link between the deprivation suffered and the property in question is as difficult to establish as it may seem . ...

It seems to me that in a family relationship the work, services, and contributions provided by one of the parties need not be clearly and directly linked to a specific property. As long as there was no compensation paid for the work and services provided by one party to the family relationship, then it can be inferred that their provision permitted the other party to acquire lands or to improve them. In this case the work of the appellant permitted the respondent to pay off the mortgage and, as well, to purchase a houseboat and a cabin cruiser. In the circumstances, the trial judge was justified in applying the constructive trust to the property which he felt would best redress the unjust enrichment and would treat both parties in a just and equitable manner. ...

I agree with my colleague that there is a need to limit the use of the constructive trust remedy in a commercial context. Yet I do not think the same proposition should be rigorously applied in a family relationship. In a marital or quasi-marital relationship, the expectations the parties will have regarding their contributions and interest in the assets acquired are, I expect, very different from the expectation of the parties engaged in a commercial transaction. As I have said, it is unlikely that couples will ever turn their minds to the issue of their expectations about their legal entitlements at the outset of their marriage or common law relationship. If they were specifically asked about their expectations, I would think that most couples would probably state that they did not expect to be compensated for their contribution. Rather, they would say, if the relationship were ever to be dissolved, then they would expect that both parties would share in the assets or wealth that they had helped to create. Thus, rather than expecting to receive a fee for their services based on their market value, they would expect to receive, on a dissolution of their relationship, a fair share of the property or wealth which their contributions had helped the parties to acquire, improve, or to maintain. The remedy provided by the constructive trust seems to best accord with the reasonable expectations of the parties in a marriage or quasi-marital relationship. Nevertheless, in situations where the rights of *bona fide* third parties would be affected as a result of granting the constructive trust remedy it may well be inappropriate to do so. (See Berend Hovius and Timothy G. Youdan, *The Law of Family Property*, at p. 146.)

It follows that in a quasi-marital relationship in those situations where the rights of third parties are not involved, the choice between a monetary award and a constructive trust will be discretionary and should be exercised flexibly. Ordinarily both partners will have an interest in the property acquired, improved, or maintained during the course of the relationship. The decision as to which property, if there is more than one, should be made the subject of a constructive trust is also a discretionary one. It too should be based on common sense and a desire to achieve a fair result for both parties.

There will, of course, be situations where an award for a monetary sum may be the most appropriate remedy. For example, where the relationship is of short duration or where there are no assets surviving its dissolution, a monetary award should be made. Professors Berend Hovius and Timothy G. Youdan (*Law of Family Property*, at p. 147) provide the following list of factors which I think are helpful in determining that a monetary distribution may be more appropriate than a constructive trust:

> (a) is the "plaintiff's entitlement ... relatively small compared to the value of the whole property in question";
>
> (b) is the "defendant ... able to satisfy the plaintiff's claim without a sale of the property" in question;
>
> (c) does "the plaintiff [have any] special attachment to the property in question"; and
>
> (d) what "hardship might be caused to the defendant if the plaintiff obtained the rights flowing from [the award] of an interest in the property."

In this case the appellant contributed to the maintenance and the preservation of the home. She painted the fence, planted the cedar hedge, installed the rock garden, and built the chicken coop. Nevertheless, her principal contribution was made through the provision of domestic services. Her work around the house and in caring for the children saved the respondent the expense of hiring a housekeeper and someone to care for the children. As a result, he was able to use the money which he had saved to purchase other property and to pay off the mortgage on the Sicamous property.

The trial judge found that since the respondent was now retired and living on a War Veteran's Allowance, a monetary award would be "impracticable, probably unrealistic and would not be reasonable under the circumstances" and imposed a constructive trust upon the Sicamous property. I think he was correct in doing so. It could reasonably be inferred that, given the work she had done, the appellant would expect to receive a share in the Sicamous property when the relationship ended. Further, although there was no specific evidence that the appellant had formed an emotional attachment to the property, it would not have been unreasonable for the trial judge to have inferred this in light of the work which she had done on the property. In addition, the property was vacant at the time of the trial and the respondent was retired and living on his veteran's pension in another community. Clearly, he has no particular attachment to the property. A monetary award would be meaningless. Therefore, it was both reasonable and appropriate to choose the Sicamous property as the object of the constructive trust. In the circumstances of this case, the application of the constructive trust remedy was eminently suitable.

Was the Amount of the Appellant's Interest Reasonably Determined?

There are, generally speaking, two methods of evaluating the contribution of a party in a matrimonial relationship. The first method is based upon the value received. This can be thought of as *quantum meruit*, that is, the amount the defendant would have had to pay for the services on a purely business basis to any other person doing the work that was provided by the claimant. Alternatively, it can be based upon what is termed "value surviving," which apportions the assets accumulated by the couple on the basis of the contributions made by each. Value surviving is the approach that has been traditionally employed in cases of constructive trust. However, there is no reason why *quantum meruit* or the value received approach could not be utilized to quantify the value of the constructive trust. The remedy should be flexible so that it can be readily adapted to the situation presented in any given case. In many cases the cost of retaining and presenting expert evidence as to the value of the property may be beyond the reach of the parties and at times clearly impractical. This in itself indicates the need for maintaining flexibility in the remedy.

Here, the trial judge undertook the same type of *quantum meruit* analysis employed in *Herman v. Smith* (1984), 42 R.F.L. (2d) 154 (Alta. Q.B.). That is, he calculated the appellant's contributions on the basis of what the respondent would have been required to pay a housekeeper. It has to be noted that his calculations were favourable to the respondent in that he used the amount paid prior to the commencement of the common law relationship as a basis for the calculation and then reduced it by 50 percent to allow for the value of the accommodation that the appellant received from the respondent. This was a fair means of calculating the amount due to the appellant.

Nonetheless, I would observe that the value surviving approach will often be the preferable method of determining the quantum of a claimant's share. This method will usually be more equitable and will more closely accord with the expectation of the parties as to how the assets which they have accumulated should be divided upon termination of the relationship. Further, the utilization of the value surviving method will avoid the difficult task of assigning a precise dollar value to the services provided by someone who has dedicated him- or her-self to raising children and caring for a home. Instead, the contributions of the parties can more accurately be expressed as a percentage of the accumulated wealth existing at the termination of the relationship. Thus, for pragmatic reasons, the value surviving method may be the preferable one in many cases. No matter which method is used, equity and fairness should guide the court in determining the value and contributions made by the parties. In this case awarding the Sicamous property to the appellant reflected a fair assessment of her contribution to the relationship. ...

McLACHLIN J. (LA FOREST, SOPINKA and IACOBUCCI JJ. concurring): — I have had the advantage of reading the reasons of Justice Cory. While I agree with his conclusion and with much of his analysis, my reasons differ in some respects on two matters critical to this appeal: the issues raised by the requirement of the absence of juristic reason for an enrichment and the nature and application of the remedy of constructive trust.

In recent decades, Canadian courts have adopted the equitable concept of unjust enrichment, *inter alia*, as the basis for remedying the injustice that occurs where one person makes a substantial contribution to the property of another person without compensation. The doctrine has been applied to a variety of situations, from claims for payments made under mistake to claims arising from conjugal relationships. While courts have not been adverse to applying the concept of unjust enrichment in new circumstances, they have insisted on adhering to the fundamental principles which have long underlain the equitable doctrine of unjust enrichment. ...

The basic notions are simple enough. An action for unjust enrichment arises when three elements are satisfied: (1) an enrichment, (2) a corresponding deprivation, and (3) the absence of a juristic reason for the enrichment. These proven, the action is established and the right to claim relief made out. At this point, a second doctrinal concern arises: the nature of the remedy. "Unjust enrichment" in equity permitted a number of remedies, depending on the circumstances. One was a payment for services rendered on the basis of *quantum meruit* or *quantum valebat*. Another equitable remedy, available traditionally where one person was possessed of legal title to property in which another had an interest, was the constructive trust. While the first remedy to be considered was a monetary award, the Canadian jurisprudence recognized that in some cases it might be insufficient. This may occur, to quote Justice La Forest in *International Corona Resources Ltd. v. LAC Minerals Ltd.*, [1989] 2 S.C.R. 574, at p. 678, "if there is reason to grant to the plaintiff the additional rights that flow from recognition of a right of property." Or to quote Dickson J., as he then was, in *Becker v. Pettkus*, [1980] 2 S.C.R. 834, at p. 852, where there is a "contribution [to the property] sufficiently substantial and direct as to entitle [the plaintiff] to a portion of the profits realized upon sale of [the property]." In other words, the remedy of constructive trust arises where monetary damages are inadequate and where there is a link between the contribution that founds the action and the property in which the constructive trust is claimed.

Notwithstanding these rather straightforward doctrinal underpinnings, their application has sometimes given rise to difficulty. There is a tendency on the part of some to view the action for unjust enrichment as a device for doing whatever may seem fair between the parties. In the rush to substantive justice, the principles are sometimes forgotten. Policy issues often assume a large role, infusing such straightforward discussions as whether there was a "benefit" to the defendant or a "detriment" to the plaintiff. On the remedies side, the requirements of the special proprietary remedy of constructive trust are sometimes minimized. ...

Such difficulties have to some degree complicated the case at bar. At the doctrinal level, the simple question of "benefit" and "detriment" became infused with moral and policy questions of when the provision of domestic services in a quasi-matrimonial situation can give rise to a legal obligation. At the stage of remedy, the trial judge proceeded as if he were making a monetary award, and then, without fully explaining how, awarded the appellant the entire interest in the matrimonial home on the basis of a constructive trust. It is only by a return to the fundamental principles laid out in cases like *Becker v. Pettkus* and *LAC Minerals* that one can cut through the conflicting findings and submissions on these issues and evaluate whether in fact the appellant has made out a claim for unjust enrichment, and if so what her remedy should be.

1. Is the Appellant's Claim for Unjust Enrichment Made Out?

I share the view of Cory J. that the three elements necessary to establish a claim for unjust enrichment — an enrichment, a corresponding deprivation, and the absence of any juristic reason for the enrichment — are made out in this case. The appellant's housekeeping and child-care services constituted a benefit to the respondent (1st element) in that he received household services without compensation, which, in turn, enhanced his ability to pay off his mortgage and other assets. These services also constituted a corresponding detriment to the appellant (2nd element) in that she provided services without compensation. Finally, since there was no obligation existing between the parties which would justify the unjust enrichment and no other arguments under this broad heading were met, there is no juristic reason for the enrichment (3rd element). Having met the three criteria, the plaintiff has established an unjust enrichment giving rise to restitution.

The main arguments on this appeal centred on whether the law should recognize the services which the appellant provided as being capable of founding an action for unjust enrichment. It was argued, for example, that the services cannot give rise to a remedy based on unjust enrichment because the appellant had voluntarily assumed the role of wife and stepmother. It was also said that the law of unjust enrichment should not recognize such services because they arise from natural love and affection. These arguments raise moral and policy questions and require the court to make value judgments.

The first question is: Where do these arguments belong? Are they part of the benefit-detriment analysis, or should they be considered under the third head — the absence of juristic reason for the unjust enrichment? The Court of Appeal, for example, held that there was no "detriment" on these grounds. I hold the view that these factors may most conveniently be considered under the third head of absence of juristic reason. This court has consistently taken a straightforward economic approach to the first two elements of the test for enrichment: *Becker v. Pettkus, supra; Sorochan v. Sorochan*, [1986] 2 S.C.R. 38; *Peel (Regional Municipality) v. Ontario*, [1992] 3 S.C.R. 762 (hereinafter *"Peel"*). It is in connection with the third element — absence of juristic reason for the enrichment — that such considerations may more properly find their place. It is at this stage that the court must consider whether the enrichment and detriment, morally neutral in themselves, are "unjust".

What matters should be considered in determining whether there is an absence of juristic reason for the enrichment? The test is flexible, and the factors to be considered may vary with the situation before the court. For example, different factors may be more relevant in a case like *Peel, supra*, at p. 803, a claim for unjust enrichment between different levels of government, than in a family case.

In every case, the fundamental concern is the legitimate expectation of the parties: *Becker v. Pettkus, supra*. In family cases, this concern may raise the following subsidiary questions:

> (i) Did the plaintiff confer the benefit as a valid gift or in pursuance of a valid common law, equitable, or statutory obligation which he or she owed to the defendant?
>
> (ii) Did the plaintiff submit to, or compromise, the defendant's honest claim?
>
> (iii) Does public policy support the enrichment?

In the case at bar, the first and third of these factors were argued. It was argued first that the appellant's services were rendered pursuant to a common law or equitable obligation which she had assumed. Her services were part of the bargain she made when she came to live with the respondent, it was said. He would give her and her children a home and other husbandly services, and in turn she would look after the home and family.

This court has held that a common law spouse generally owes no duty at common law, in equity, or by statute to perform work or services for her partner. ...

Nor, in the case at bar, was there any obligation arising from the circumstances of the parties. The trial judge held that the appellant was "under no obligation to perform the work and assist in the home without some reasonable expectation of receiving something in return other than the drunken physical abuse which she received at the hands of the Respondent." This puts an end to the argument that the services in question were performed pursuant to obligation. It also puts an end to the argument that the appellant's services to her partner were a "gift" from her to him. The central element of a gift at law — intentional giving to another without expectation of remuneration — is simply not present.

The third factor mentioned above raises directly the issue of public policy. While it may be stated in different ways, the argument at base is simply that some types of services in some types of relationships should not be recognized as supporting legal claims for policy reasons. More particularly, homemaking and childcare services should not, in a marital or quasi-marital relationship, be viewed as giving rise to equitable claims against the other spouse.

I concede at the outset that there is some judicial precedent for this argument. Professor Marcia Neave has observed generally that "analysis of the principles applied in English, Australian and Canadian courts sometimes fails to confront this question directly. ... Courts which deny or grant remedies usually conceal their value judgments within statements relating to doctrinal requirements." (Marcia Neave, "Three Approaches to Family Property Disputes — Intention/Belief, Unjust Enrichment and Unconscionability," in T.G. Youdan, ed., *Equity, Fiduciaries and Trusts* (Scarborough, Ont.: Carswell, 1989), at p. 251). ... On the judicial side, the view of the respondent is pointedly stated in *Grant v. Edwards*, [1986] 2 All E.R. 426, at p. 439, per Browne-Wilkinson V.-C.:

> Setting up house together, having a baby and making payments to general housekeeping expenses ... may all be referable to the mutual love and affection of the parties and not specifically referable to the claimant's belief that she has an interest in the house.

Proponents of this view, Professor Neave, *supra*, at p. 253, argues, "regard it as distasteful to put a price upon services provided out of a sense of love and commitment to the relationship. They suggest it is unfair for a recipient of indirect or non-financial contributions to be forced to provide recompense for those contributions." To support this position, the respondent cites several cases. ...

It is my view that this argument is no longer tenable in Canada, either from the point of view of logic or authority. From the point of view of logic, I share the view of Professors Hovius and Youdan that "there is no logical reason to distinguish domestic services from other contributions" (*The Law of Family Property* (Scarborough, Ont.: Carswell, 1991), at p. 136). The notion that household and childcare services are not worthy of recognition by the court fails to recognize the fact that these services are of great value, not only to the family, but to the other spouse. As Lord Simon observed nearly thirty years ago: "The cock bird can feather his nest precisely because he is not required to spend most of his time sitting on it" ("With All My Worldly Goods," *Holdsworth Lecture* (University of Birmingham, 20th March 1964), at p. 32). The notion, moreover, is a pernicious one that systematically devalues the contributions which women tend to make to the family economy. It has contributed to the phenomenon of the feminization of poverty which this court identified in *Moge v. Moge*, [1992] 3 S.C.R. 813, per L'Heureux-Dubé J., at pp. 853-54.

Moreover, the argument cannot stand with the jurisprudence which this and other courts have laid down. Today courts regularly recognize the value of domestic services. This became clear with the court's holding in *Sorochan*, leading one author to comment that "[t]he Canadian Supreme court has finally recognized that domestic contribution is of equal value as financial contribution in trusts of property in the familial context" (Mary Welstead, "Domestic Contribution and Constructive Trusts: The Canadian Perspective" [1987] Denning L.J. 151, at p. 161). If there could be any doubt about the need for the law to honestly recognize the value of domestic services, it must be considered to have been banished by *Moge v. Moge, supra*. While that case arose under the *Divorce Act*, R.S.C. 1985, c. 3 (2nd Supp.), the value of the services does not change with the legal remedy invoked.

I cannot give credence to the argument that legal recognition of the value of domestic services will do violence to the law and the social structure of our society. It has been recognized for some time that such services are entitled to recognition and compensation under the *Divorce Act* and the provincial Acts governing the distribution of matrimonial property. Yet society has not been visibly harmed. I do not think that similar recognition in the equitable doctrine of unjust enrichment will have any different effect.

Finally, I come to the argument that, because the legislature has chosen to exclude unmarried couples from the right to claim an interest in the matrimonial assets on the basis of contribution to the relationship, the court should not use the equitable doctrine of unjust enrichment to remedy the situation. Again, the argument seems flawed. It is precisely where an injustice arises without a legal remedy that equity finds a role. This case is much stronger than *Rawluk v. Rawluk*, [1990] 1 S.C.R. 70, where I dissented on the ground that the statute expressly pronounced on the very matter with respect to which equity was invoked.

Accordingly, I would agree with Cory J. that there are no juristic arguments which would justify the unjust enrichment, and the third element is made out. Like him, I conclude that the defendant was enriched, to the detriment of the plaintiff, and that no justification existed to vitiate the unjust enrichment claim. The claim for unjust enrichment is accordingly made out and it remains only to determine the appropriate remedy.

2. Remedy — Monetary Judgment or Constructive Trust?

The other difficult aspect of this case is the question of whether the remedy which the trial judge awarded — title to the matrimonial home — is justified on the principles governing the action for unjust enrichment. Two remedies are possible: an award of money on the basis of the value of the services rendered, i.e., *quantum meruit*; and the one the trial judge awarded, title to the house based on a constructive trust.

In Canada the concept of the constructive trust has been used as a vehicle for compensating for unjust enrichment in appropriate cases. The constructive trust, based on analogy to the formal trust of traditional equity, is a proprietary concept. The plaintiff is found to have an interest in the property. A finding that a plaintiff is entitled to a remedy for unjust enrichment does not imply that there is a constructive trust. As I wrote in *Rawluk, supra,* for a constructive trust to arise, the plaintiff must establish a direct link to the property which is the subject of the trust by reason of the plaintiff's contribution. This is the notion underlying the constructive trust in *Becker v. Pettkus, supra,* and *Sorochan v. Sorochan, supra,* as I understand those cases. It was also affirmed by La Forest J. in *LAC Minerals, supra.*

My colleague Cory J. suggests that, while a link between the contribution and the property is essential in commercial cases for a constructive trust to arise, it may not be required in family cases. ...

I doubt the wisdom of dividing unjust enrichment cases into two categories — commercial and family — for the purpose of determining whether a constructive trust lies. A special rule for family cases finds no support in the jurisprudence. Neither *Pettkus,* nor *Rathwell,* nor *Sorochan* suggests such a departure. Moreover, the notion that one can dispense with a link between the services rendered and the property which is claimed to be subject to the trust is inconsistent with the proprietary nature of the notion of constructive trust. Finally, the creation of special rules for special situations might have an adverse effect on the development of this emerging area of equity. The same general principles should apply for all contexts, subject only the demonstrated need for alteration. ...

Nor does the distinction between commercial cases and family cases on the remedy of constructive trust appear to be necessary. Where a monetary award is sufficient, there is no need for a constructive trust. Where a monetary award is insufficient in a family situation, this is usually related to the fact the claimant's efforts have given her a special link to the property, in which case a constructive trust arises.

For these reasons, I hold the view that in order for a constructive trust to be found, in a family case as in other cases, monetary compensation must be inadequate and there must be a link between the services rendered and the property in which the trust is claimed. Having said this, I echo the comments of Cory J. ... that the courts should exercise flexibility and common sense when applying equitable principles to family law issues with due sensitivity to the special circumstances that can arise in such cases.

The next question is the extent of the contribution required to give rise to a constructive trust. A minor or indirect contribution is insufficient. The question, to quote Dickson J. in *Becker v. Pettkus, supra*, at p. 852, is whether "[the plaintiff's] contribution [was] sufficiently substantial and direct as to entitle her to a portion of the profits realized upon sale of the ... property." Once this threshold is met, the amount of the contribution governs the extent of the constructive trust. ... Cory J. advocates a flexible approach to determining whether a constructive trust is appropriate, an approach "based on common sense and a desire to achieve a fair result for both parties". ... While agreeing that courts should avoid becoming overly technical on matters which may not be susceptible of precise monetary valuation, the principle remains that the extent of the trust must reflect the extent of the contribution.

Before leaving the principles governing the remedy of constructive trust, I turn to the manner in which the extent of the trust is determined. The debate centres on whether it is sufficient to look at the value of the services which the claimant has rendered (the "value received" approach), or whether regard should be had to the amount by which the property has been improved (the "value survived" approach). Cory J. expresses a preference for a "value survived" approach. However, he also suggests ... that "there is no reason why *quantum meruit* or the value received approach could not be utilized to quantify the value of the constructive trust." With respect, I cannot agree. It seems to me that there are very good reasons, both doctrinal and practical, for referring to the "value survived" when assessing the value of a constructive trust.

From the point of view of doctrine, "[t]he extent of the interest must be proportionate to the contribution" to the property: *Becker v. Pettkus, supra*, at p. 852. How is the contribution to the property to be determined? One starts, of necessity, by defining the property. One goes on to determine what portion of that property is attributable to the claimant's efforts. This is the "value survived" approach. For a monetary award, the "value received" approach is appropriate; the value conferred on the property is irrelevant. But where the claim is for an interest in the property one must of necessity, it seems to me, determine what portion of the value of the property claimed is attributable to the claimant's services.

I note, as does my colleague, that there may also be practical reasons for favouring a "value survived" approach. Cory J. alludes to the practical problems with balancing benefits and detriments as required by the "value received" approach, leading some to question whether it is the least attractive approach in most family property cases (see *Davidson v. Worthing* (1986), 6 R.F.L. (3d) 113, McEachern C.J.S.C.; Hovius and Youdan, *supra*, at pp. 136ff). Moreover, a "value survived" approach arguably accords best with the expectations of most parties; it is more likely that a couple expects to share in the wealth generated from their partnership, rather than to receive compensation for the services performed during the relationship.

To summarize, it seems to me that the first step in determining the proper remedy for unjust enrichment is to determine whether a monetary award is insufficient and whether the nexus between the contribution and the property described in *Becker v. Pettkus* has been made out. If these questions are answered in the affirmative, the plaintiff is entitled to the proprietary remedy of constructive trust. In looking at whether a monetary award is insufficient, the court may take into account the probability of the award's being paid, as well as the special interest in the property acquired by the contributions: per La Forest J. in *LAC*

Minerals. The value of that trust is to be determined on the basis of the actual value of the matrimonial property — the "value survived" approach. It reflects the court's best estimate of what is fair, having regard to the contribution which the claimant's services have made to the value surviving, bearing in mind the practical difficulty of calculating with mathematical precision the value of particular contributions to the family property.

I turn now to the application of these principles to the case at bar. The trial judge began by assessing the value received by the respondent (the *quantum meruit*). He went on to conclude that a monetary judgment would be inadequate. The respondent had few assets other than his houseboat and van, and no income save for a War Veteran's Allowance. The judge concluded, as I understand his reasons, that there was a sufficiently direct connection between the services rendered and the property to support a constructive trust, stating that "[the appellant] has shown that there was a positive proprietary benefit conferred by her upon the Sicamous property." Accordingly, he held that the remedy of constructive trust was made out. This approach accords with principles discussed above. In effect, the trial judge found the monetary award to be inadequate on the grounds that it would not be paid and on the ground of a special contribution to the property. These findings support the remedy of constructive trust in the property.

The remaining question is the quantification of the trust. The trial judge calculated the *quantum meruit* for the housekeeping for 12 years at $350 per month and reduced that figure by 50% "for the benefits she received." The final amount was $25,200. He then reasoned that, since the services rendered amounted to $25,200 after appropriate deductions, it follows that the appellant should receive title to the respondent's property, valued at $23,200. The missing step in this analysis is the failure to link the value received with the value surviving. As discussed above, a constructive trust cannot be quantified by simply adding up the services rendered; the court must determine the extent of the contribution which the services have made to the parties' property.

Notwithstanding the trial judge's failure to make this link, his conclusion that the appellant had established a constructive trust entitling her to title to the family home can be maintained if a trust of this magnitude is supported on the evidence. This brings me to a departure from the methods used below. The parties and the Court of Appeal appear to have treated the house as a single asset rather than as part of a family enterprise. This led to the argument that the appellant could not be entitled to full ownership in the house because the respondent had contributed to its value as well. The approach I would take — and the approach I believe the trial judge implicitly to have taken — is to consider the appellant's proper share of all the family assets. This joint family venture, in effect, was no different from the farm which was the subject of the trust in *Becker v. Pettkus*.

With this in mind, I turn to the evidence on the extent of the contribution. The appellant provided extensive household services over a period of 12 years, including care for the children, while they were living at the house and maintenance of the property. ... The trial judge held that while the respondent worked in the construction business:

> ... he would be away from home during the week and would return on the weekend whenever possible. While he was absent, the Plaintiff would care for the property in the home and care for the children while he was away. ...

> In effect, the Plaintiff by moving into the Respondent's home became his housekeeper on a full-time basis without remuneration except for the food and shelter that she and the children received until the children left home.

The respondent also contributed to the value of the family enterprise surviving at the time of breakup; he generated most of the family income and helped with the maintenance of the property.

Clearly, the appellant's contribution — the "value received" by the respondent — was considerable. But what then of the "value surviving"? It seems clear that the maintenance of the family enterprise through work in cooking, cleaning, and landscaping helped preserve the property and saved the respondent large sums of money, which he was able to use to pay off his mortgage and to purchase a houseboat and a van. The appellant, for her part, had purchased a lot with her outside earnings. All these assets may be viewed as assets of the family enterprise to which the appellant contributed substantially.

The question is whether, taking the parties' respective contributions to the family assets and the value of the assets into account, the trial judge erred in awarding the appellant a full interest in the house. In my view, the evidence is capable of supporting the conclusion that the house reflects a fair approximation of the value of the appellant's efforts as reflected in the family assets. Accordingly, I would not disturb the award.

NOTES AND QUESTIONS

1. Would Becker have succeeded if Pettkus had explicitly told her, when the relationship began, that all property acquired as a result of their efforts would belong to him exclusively? See *Spence v. Mitchell* (1993), 1 R.F.L. (4th) 28 (Ont. Gen. Div.); *Harper v. Harper* (1995), 166 A.R. 212 (Q.B.); and *Hughes v. Miller* (2007), 2007 CarswellBC 373 (C.A.). Compare *MacFarlane v. Smith* (2003), 35 R.F.L. (5th) 112 (N.B. C.A.).

2. The *Becker v. Pettkus* case had a sad and tragic postscript. Pettkus did everything he could not to satisfy the judgment. When he was finally ordered to sell his bee farm to pay, he allowed the bees to starve to death to reduce the farm's value. In the end, he paid about $80,000 but much of this went to cover Becker's legal fees. Becker's bitterness and disillusionment led to her suicide in 1986. She left a note explaining that her action was a protest against the slowness and failure of the legal system.

3. The emphasis on "reasonable expectations" in *Pettkus v. Becker* and *Sorochan v. Sorochan* is problematic. Is it consistent with Justice Dickson's castigation of the role of intention in the context of resulting trust? Is it sufficient that the claimant has a reasonable expectation of receiving some benefit or must there be an expectation of payment or of receiving an interest in specific property? See Hovius and Youdan, *The Law of Family Property* (Toronto: Carswell, 1991) where the authors suggest (at 124):

> [A]ll that is necessary is the parties' reasonable expectations of benefiting from the property of each of them. Such an expectation will typically exist in spousal relationships, and in other relationships in which the lives and economic well-being of the parties are integrated; and it should be presumed to exist in such relationships except where the evidence establishes a contrary intention, for example, that a contribution was in fact made as a gift in the sense that it was made for the exclusive benefit of the other party.

How did the S.C.C. deal with the concept of reasonable expectation in *Peter v. Beblow*?

4. Out of a concern to maintain doctrinal integrity, Justice McLachlin proceeded in *Peter v. Beblow* on the basis that unjust enrichment principles ought to be the same in commercial and family cases. In the end, was there much difference between her position and that of Cory J.?

5. In Hovius and Youdan, *The Law of Family Property* (Toronto: Carswell, 1991), the authors state (at 106):

> Now that the general principle of unjust enrichment (along with its range of remedies, including constructive trust) is available to deal flexibly with non-financial and indirect financial contributions, the resulting trust should be restricted to direct financial contributions and voluntary transfers. In particular, contributions by way of labour or services and improvements to property (whether by money spent or by labour) should not be dealt with by resulting trusts. Even direct contributions to the payment of a mortgage and similar indebtedness owed by the other party are, because of the need for flexibility, more suitably dealt with by the general principle of unjust enrichment.

Do you agree?

For examples where resulting trusts were found based on contributions to the purchase price of property acquired within the context of a common law relationship, see *Billinghurst v. Reader* (1997), 151 D.L.R. (4th) 753 (Ont. Gen. Div.); *Fancy v. Quilty* (1998), 37 R.F.L. (4th) 409 (Nfld. T.D.); and *Forbes v. Chen* (2003), 42 R.F.L. (5th) 344 (B.C. C.A.). See also *Huscroft v. Bodor* (2004), 50 R.F.L. (5th) 65, 5 E.T.R. (3d) 170 where the British

Columbia Supreme Court found that a woman held her joint interest in a house under a resulting trust for the man who had paid the purchase price. Compare *Spence v. Michell* (1997), 33 R.F.L. (4th) 147 (Ont. C.A.) where the presumption of resulting trust was rebutted and the court concluded that the man had gifted a home to his common-law partner.

NOWELL v. TOWN ESTATE

(1997), 30 R.F.L. (4th) 107, 1997 CarswellOnt 3460 (Ont. C.A.)

[Nowell, the female plaintiff, and Town, a married man, had an affair for 24 years. Throughout the affair, the man's marriage and family responsibilities continued. Nowell and Town maintained separate residences and never cohabited. Thirteen years after the relationship began, Town, by then a prominent and successful artist, purchased a farm. Town and Nowell spent most weekends at the farm. Nowell contributed to life at the farm, including cooking, cleaning, gardening and organizing social events. She was not paid for those services. Nowell also assisted with Town's art exhibits, but third parties usually paid her for this work.

Town often assured Nowell that he would look after her. During the relationship, he gave her many works of art. She subsequently sold most of them for over $120,000. After the relationship ended, Nowell was left essentially destitute and she demanded a settlement of $100,000. Town, who by then had assets worth at least $20 million, delivered certain works of art to Nowell. She subsequently sold many of them, obtaining over $125,000.

Nowell brought an action after Town died for a declaration that he had been unjustly enriched as a result of the services she performed during their relationship. She sought the imposition of a constructive trust against his estate, or damages. The trial judge dismissed the action. He found that Nowell had contributed much to Town's life, but that Town, in turn, had enriched her life. In addition to receiving gifts of substantial value, Nowell benefitted personally and professionally from the opportunity to participate in Town's social and artistic life. Nowell appealed.]

BY THE COURT: — In our view, the trial judge misapprehended the evidence concerning the nature of the relationship between the appellant and Mr. Town. Theirs was not a "casual" relationship. The nature of that relationship as testified to by the appellant is amply corroborated by the testimony of the other witnesses. The relationship lasted for twenty-four years, and for the last thirteen years resembled a quasi-spousal relationship.

This error was material to the finding by the trial judge that there was no unjust enrichment, and that the appellant had been fully compensated over the years by Mr. Town and others. The appellant clearly made out a claim for unjust enrichment — an enrichment, a corresponding deprivation, and the absence of any juristic reason for the enrichment, see *Peter v. Beblow* (1993), 44 R.F.L. (3d) 329 at 337 (S.C.C.). The appellant made Mr. Town the focal point of her life and there was clear evidence of an enrichment to him and a corresponding financial deprivation to her. The many services performed by the appellant were capable of founding an action for unjust enrichment: *Peter v. Beblow, supra* at pp. 337–41.

The trial judge made no express finding that the transfer of $100,000 worth of paintings to the appellant at her request constituted a final settlement of any claim that the appellant may have had. In our view, this transfer did not constitute a final and binding settlement of her rights. At the time she wrote the letter relied upon by the respondent, the appellant was 52 years of age and had been left essentially destitute after a relationship of over twenty years. On the other hand, Mr. Town had assets of between $20 and $50 million. In this respect, we think that the trial judge also erred in failing to take into account the evidence of the many assurances over the years by Mr. Town that he would look after the appellant. Admittedly, as the trial judge said, these assurances did not "in themselves" create a legal relationship. These assurances were, however, cogent evidence of the nature of the relationship and had to be considered along with the other substantial body of evidence.

We have considered the appropriate order to be made in light of these errors. In our view, it would not be in anyone's interest to order a new trial. We are also not persuaded that the appellant's claim for 20% of the estate on the basis of a constructive trust was made out. The appellant is, however, entitled to a monetary award as compensation for unjust enrichment: see *Peter v. Beblow*, at p. 343. Although it is difficult to quantify what amount is appropriate in these circumstances, giving the matter our best consideration, we think that a proper disposition is to allow the appeal, set aside the order below and award the appellant the amount of $300,000. The appellant is entitled to her costs of the appeal and the trial before Justice Jarvis.

McLEOD, "ANNOTATION"

(1997), 30 R.F.L. (4th) 108

The reasons for judgement of the Ontario Court of Appeal in *Nowell v. Town Estate* are disappointing. The case provided the Ontario Court of Appeal with an opportunity to clarify a number of issues in the law of unjust enrichment, including:

1. whether the law of unjust enrichment applies differently between "spouses" than between strangers;

2. when a person has received fair value for benefits conferred;

3. whether the compensation for benefits conferred must come from the defendant;

4. how a court values personal services in unjust enrichment cases; and

5. the nature of the causal connection between benefits conferred and property necessary to impose a remedial constructive trust to redress unjust enrichment.

Unfortunately, the Court of Appeal did not expressly comment on any of these issues. Instead, the court substituted its opinion of what was reasonable compensation for Nowell's contributions for that of the trial judge. ...

The trial judge and the Court of Appeal agreed that whether Nowell was entitled to relief depended on whether Town had a juristic right to retain the benefit of Nowell's services without further accounting. The trial judge held that there was no unjust enrichment, but the Court of Appeal disagreed.

Is there a rule for "family law" and another rule for everyone else?

The trial judge in *Nowell v. Town Estate* did not view Nowell and Town as "cohabiting" or involved in a "spousal" relationship. The Ontario Court of Appeal took exception with the trial judge's characterization of the parties' relationship. The court stated that the relationship was not "casual" but "quasi" spousal. Courts should not use "pretend legalese". "Quasi" is not a term of art, nor is it a word capable of easy definition. At best, it means "sort of" or "like" or "almost". If the relationship in *Nowell v. Town Estate* was "quasi" spousal, it was non-spousal.

Why then did the Court of Appeal go out of its way to institutionalize the couple's relationship by labeling it "quasi" spousal (whatever this means)? Presumably, the inference is that there are different unjust enrichment rules for "spouses" than for other people. A quasi spouse (like a common law spouse) is under no obligation to render services to a partner and there is a presumption that such services will be compensated. As a result, there is an almost automatic unjust enrichment following the breakdown of an informal family. Nowell's efforts to support Town's career and Town personally are a valuable benefit to Town. The issue is whether Nowell received fair value for the benefits she conferred.

In *Peter v. Beblow* ... the Supreme Court of Canada held that a party to a "spousal" relationship does not receive fair value for benefits conferred if the other partner to the relationship retains most of the family property when the relationship ends. The trial judge held that the case was not like *Peter v. Beblow*. By this he meant that there was no merging of the parties' economic, social and emotional lives.

By labelling the relationship "quasi" spousal, the Court of Appeal is trying to take advantage of the bias in favour of providing relief to family partners when a relationship breaks down. Notwithstanding the Court of Appeal's repeated statements in other cases that it will not review a trial judge's determination of facts or exercise of discretion unless the conclusion reached is perverse, this is what the court did in *Nowell v. Town Estate*. The court relabeled the Town/Nowell relationship with a "non-label" which looked like a label that carried a presumptive right to relief.

The couple formed a symbiotic relationship which met each of their needs and interests. Nowell received an entry to a world and lifestyle that she might not have been able to achieve on her own. She also received valuable gifts throughout the relationship. The legislators created matrimonial property rights for married couples. The Supreme Court of Canada extended similar rights to unmarried couples. The reasons in *Nowell v. Town Estate* come close to asserting an almost automatic right to relief to long-time lovers.

Fair value for benefits conferred

In most cases, a defendant defends an unjust enrichment case by alleging that the plaintiff received fair value for benefits conferred. In *Peter v. Beblow* ... the British Columbia Court of Appeal held that if a person got as much money as he or she gave and received corresponding "personal" services to those rendered, he or she received fair value for benefits rendered. The Supreme Court of Canada rejected this analysis and held that in deciding whether a spouse received fair value for services rendered, a court had to look at the totality of the parties' relationship. By pooling their resources and efforts, the parties contribute equally yet differently to the overall success of the relationship. Accordingly, they should each share in the financial resources of the relationship as well as the non-financial resources. The same policies that promote division of matrimonial property upon marriage breakdown, promote sharing family property upon breakdown of an informal family.

In a "family" or "spousal" context, the determination of whether a person received fair value for benefits conferred involves an analysis of what was acquired by the "family" unit and how it was distributed between the "spouses" when the relationship ended. Town amassed a substantial estate during the course of the parties' relationship and retained almost all of it when the relationship ended. If *Nowell v. Town Estate* is a "family" or "spousal" case, it is arguable that she did not receive a fair share of the family resources.

The trial judge adverted to the nature of Nowell's relationship with Town. There is no indication that he missed any aspect of the relationship. He appreciated that Town had benefitted from Nowell's efforts. He assessed Nowell's recovery under the relationship and held that she had received fair value for benefits conferred. He held that the cash and property Nowell received during the relationship, plus the additional $100,000 she received upon relationship breakdown, was adequate compensation for any benefits conferred. Accordingly, Town was not unjustly enriched by her efforts. The Court of Appeal held that the trial judge was wrong in his conclusion and awarded Nowell $300,000. Why? Why not $200,000, $400,000 or a round million dollars? ...

Conclusion

... When a relationship ends, the spouse with the larger net worth can expect to transfer money or property to the spouse with the lesser net worth, regardless of legal niceties. In *Nowell v. Town Estate*, the Ontario Court of Appeal extends the class of relationships to which this philosophy applies to long-term committed affairs. Why? What is so important about this relationship that society should intervene to impose a bargain on the parties that they did not make for themselves?

WYLIE v. LECLAIR

(2003), 38 R.F.L. (5th) 227, 2003 CarswellOnt 1966 (Ont. C.A.)

[Wylie and Leclair cohabited as a common law couple for about fifteen years and had two children. Justice Lafrance-Cardinal held that a monetary award was appropriate to remedy the unjust enrichment that would otherwise occur and that the quantum of that award should be determined by assessing the value received. She then set out the assets and liabilities of the couple at the commencement of cohabitation and at separation. Ultimately, she awarded Leclair $150,000. Wylie appealed.]

MACPHERSON J.A., for the court: — ...

2) Unjust enrichment

11 The trial judge held that Wylie was unjustly enriched by Leclair's domestic services during their fifteen-year relationship. Although Wylie initially appealed this holding, during oral argument he conceded that some award under this rubric was appropriate.

12 The trial judge awarded Leclair $150,000 under this heading. Wylie contends that this award was far too high and that a proper award would have been something in the $35,000–$70,000 range. I agree.

13 The trial judge correctly held that a monetary award, rather than a constructive trust, was an appropriate remedy: see *Peter v. Beblow*, [1993] 1 S.C.R. 980 (S.C.C.). She also held, again correctly, that the 'value received' approach should be employed to calculate the monetary award: see *Peter v. Beblow* at 999 and *Bell v. Bailey* (2001), 148 O.A.C. 333 at 341 (Ont. C.A.).

14 Unfortunately, there is virtually nothing in the trial judge's reasons to indicate that she applied the 'value received' approach to quantification. On the contrary, both her reasons and her conclusion establish that the trial judge was intent on attempting to provide an equalization of net family property in the context of a relationship — common law — to which it did not apply. ...

17 ... [I]t appears that the trial judge thought that Parliament's failure to provide for equalization of net family property for common law spouses was a "lacuna" in legislation that needed to be addressed. In my view, these comments are significant in the context of this case. The trial judge essentially awarded an equalization of net family property. These *obiter* comments of the trial judge can be seen as informing her approach to the calculation of her unjust enrichment award.

18 In *Walsh v. Bona*, ... the Supreme Court of Canada upheld Nova Scotia's legislation that provides equalization to married spouses but not to common law spouses. ... Accordingly, there is no presumption that the net family property of common law spouses should be equalized upon breakdown of the relationship.

19 ... The value of the benefits that Leclair and Wylie received from each other were not assessed or set-off. A set-off analysis would have been particularly relevant in light of findings of the trial judge that Leclair lived rent-free for the duration of her fifteen-year relationship with Wylie and had made no contribution during the first three years of their relationship.

20 Accordingly, I conclude that the trial judge erred in assessing Leclair's damages based on principles relating to the equalization of net family property rather than on a 'value received' basis. ...

22 ... In my view, the $150,000 awarded by the trial judge is far too high. In argument, Wylie's counsel suggested a range of $35,000 to $70,000. On the basis of my review of the record, I am inclined to think that the higher number in this range reflects a fair assessment of quantum on the unjust enrichment issue. Accordingly, I would award Leclair $70,000.

THOMAS v. FENTON

(2006), 29 R.F.L. (6th) 229 (B.C. C.A.)

[A man and woman began to cohabit in 1975. In 1978, the woman purchased a house for $44,000, with $12,000 down and a $32,000 mortgage. After the couple moved in, the man commenced extensive renovations. The woman purchased most of the materials for the renovation and she gave the man a $4,000 van in recognition of his efforts. Throughout the relationship, the man and woman did not intermingle their finances or property. The woman made the mortgage and property tax payments and paid the telephone bills and most of the hydro bills. She also purchased a substantial portion of the groceries. By 1986, the relationship deteriorated and the couple's interactions gradually decreased. In 1998, the man and woman began to live in separate areas of the house.

The woman executed an agreement to sell the house for $382,000 in 2004. The purchaser intended to knock down the existing house and build a significantly more substantial one. The woman paid off the mortgage of $120,892 and received some funds. The remaining proceeds of sale were placed in trust, pending determination of the man's claim to an interest based on unjust enrichment.

The trial judge found that the man made a substantial contribution to the renovation of the house and modest contributions to the housekeeping and gardening. The judge concluded that the woman would be unjustly enriched if she retained all the proceeds of sale and he awarded the man $57,625, representing a 25% interest in the "value survived" in the house. The woman successfully appealed. Justice Kirkpatrick, for the court, reasoned as follows.]

15 The appellant's most forceful and persuasive submission, with which I agree, is that the trial judge did not give adequate consideration to the benefits conferred on Mr. Thomas by Ms. Fenton in his analysis as to whether she was unjustly enriched by Mr. Thomas' renovations and repairs to the home. ...

17 The relationship in this case extended over approximately 30 years. The marital aspects of the relationship had abated by 1998, 23 years after the relationship began. Even so, by any definition, it was a long relationship.

18 Accepting that there was in this case an enrichment and a corresponding deprivation, it was nevertheless necessary for the trial judge to analyze whether there was an "absence of juristic reason" for the conferred benefits and the corresponding deprivation. ...

19 In *Ford v. Werden* (1996), [1997] 2 W.W.R. 245, 78 B.C.A.C. 126 (B.C. C.A.), this Court remarked on the necessity in each case of determining whether there is no juristic reason for the enrichment. Newbury J.A. held at paras. 16-17:

¶ 16 In any event, the fact that "spousal services" can be and are now regarded by Canadian courts as valuable and compensable does not in my view remove the necessity of determining on the facts of each case whether there is no juristic reason for the enrichment — i.e., whether the enrichment is "unjust" or, in the terms advanced by Cory, J., whether one party's expectation to share in the other's property is a "legitimate" one. In situations involving "traditional" common law marriages, these are not difficult questions — the court is generally confronted with one party (usually a woman) who has subverted her economic independence to the greater good of the family, foregoing opportunities to maximize her own income stream or asset base in the expectation that the relationship will last and she will be in a position to share in the income stream of her husband and in the appreciation of his assets. The courts rightly regard it as unjust to permit the husband thereafter to walk away from the relationship, taking with him all his assets and his entire income stream, enlarged or improved as it is by the common law wife's efforts.

¶ 17 It is a different matter, however, to apply these assumptions to relationships that are not the stereotypical or "traditional" type of common law marriage. ... In these non-traditional relationships, each party confers "benefits" on the other without expecting to be paid — except perhaps in kind by reciprocal services. The very nature of the relationship as a kind of partnership between two independent persons necessarily implies mutual duties and obligations that for legal purposes might be described as "gifts" in the sense that they are rendered outside of the realm of contractual, common law, equitable or statutory obligation and without a known expectation of compensation. A clearer example (in the sense that it is less clouded with moral and policy considerations) of such a relationship occurs where two persons room together and divide the household tasks between them: the law does not, as far as I know, permit one to sue the other for the "benefits" conferred, even though they are not conferred pursuant to a legal obligation. In this context, neither person expects to compensate or to be compensated.

20 In the case at bar, the uncontroverted evidence was that Ms. Fenton purchased the house for herself. She alone paid all of the mortgage payments. She refused any monetary contribution from Mr. Thomas. He paid her no rent. He earned very little income. She paid for substantially all of the groceries, some of his clothing and substantially all of the hydro expenses. She paid the house insurance and property taxes in respect of the property. She purchased a $4,000 van for Mr. Thomas in recognition of his contributions.

21 It is not disputed that Mr. Thomas provided his time and labour in effecting the renovations and repairs to the home (although the amount of time expended by him was very much in issue). However, Ms. Fenton paid for the materials and supplies that were used in the renovation. Given that the renovations were completed in about 1986, Ms. Fenton says that when the parties separated in 2004, any value that Mr. Thomas' improvements had added to the property had been spent.

22 Ms. Fenton concedes that if the parties had separated soon after 1986, Mr. Thomas' claim might have been justified. However, she says that after 1986 she conferred substantially greater benefits on Mr. Thomas than he conferred on her. She provided him with essentially free housing and groceries. He performed some minor repairs on a clothes dryer and a sliding door. He cut down and replaced three cedar trees. He did some washing and housecleaning. They together rebuilt the driveway to the home.

23 From the foregoing discussion in *Ford*, it is clear that a broad view of the relationship must be taken to determine whether or not a juristic reason for the enrichment exists. In this case, the trial judge was confronted with evidence in which both Ms. Fenton and Mr. Thomas bestowed benefits on the other. The trial judge appears to have concluded that the

conferring of the benefits by Mr. Thomas (and the resultant deprivation) related specifically to the renovations was automatically without juristic reason.

24 However, looking at the whole of the relationship, there is nothing unfair or unjust in this arrangement. Ms. Fenton provided Mr. Thomas with essentially free room and board for almost 30 years. For 23 years of the relationship, Mr. Thomas provided some modest services. The renovations completed by him in 1986 were enjoyed by them both. By the time the relationship ended in 2004, the value of Mr. Thomas' renovation work was essentially exhausted. Although Ms. Fenton continues to rent the home pending determination of Mr. Thomas' claim, it will be demolished when the rezoning application is approved.

25 In my opinion, the trial judge erred in failing to give adequate consideration to the benefits conferred on Mr. Thomas by Ms. Fenton. It is manifestly clear that Ms. Fenton bestowed far more on Mr. Thomas than he bestowed on her. Had the trial judge undertaken the requisite global analysis of the circumstances of these parties, I think he would have concluded that there was a juristic reason for Ms. Fenton's enrichment and that the claim for unjust enrichment could not succeed.

26 Given this conclusion, it is unnecessary to address the applicability of the "value survived" approach to the assessment of Mr. Thomas' interest in the subject property.

27 I would allow the appeal and dismiss Mr. Thomas' claim.

PEGLER v. AVIO

(2008), 2008 CarswellBC 169, 49 R.F.L. (6th) 145 (S.C.)

[Pegler was 51 years old at the time of trial and Avio was 65. They met in 1990 when Avio was Pegler's economics professor at the University of Victoria. Avio had been previously married and had two adult children. When Pegler and Avio moved in together in January 1992 their personal financial circumstances were significantly different. Pegler had a modest car and a provincial disability pension, awarded to her because of her multiple sclerosis. Avio earned over $80,000 annually in employment income and owned a mortgaged house, a University of Victoria pension (the "UVIC Pension") then worth approximately $232,000, a car, and a few minor investments. In addition, he was entitled to, and ultimately received, an inheritance of approximately US$250,000 and proceeds from a lawsuit of approximately US$445,000.

Although Pegler and Avio discussed the possibility of marriage before and after they moved in together, Avio was unwilling to marry unless a marriage contract suitable to him was concluded and, between 1992 and 1996, he produced and proposed many forms of possible agreement. These proposals varied in detail, but all contemplated that Pegler would accrue an interest in the family home and the UVIC Pension over time. Avio insisted, however, that the inheritance and lawsuit funds were sequestered assets in which Pegler would never accrue an interest of any kind. Pegler sought legal advice and declined to sign any of the draft marriage contracts. By the time the couple's son was born in 1997 such discussions had come to an end.

Pegler worked outside the home for about a year before her son was born and was also able to contribute financially to the household in a modest way through her provincial pension. Avio paid for the vast majority of family living costs, including property taxes, home renovations and home maintenance, throughout the entire period of cohabitation. By 2005, Pegler's health deteriorated and it became necessary for Avio to undertake more family duties than he had before, including significant family driving. This, in turn, increased his level of irritability and stress. Increasing tension and friction caused Pegler to leave the family home with her son in 2006. She lived with her sister as her health had deteriorated significantly.

At separation, Pegler had few assets. Avio owned a home (the couple had changed houses during their cohabitation) worth about $1.1 million, the UVIC Pension valued at over $1.3 million, and mutual funds and RRSPs with a value of approximately $650,000. The mutual funds and RRSPs were largely acquired using his inheritance and lawsuit funds.

Pegler brought an action based on unjust enrichment, seeking a compensatory monetary award, based on a value survived approach, representing an equal or near equal share in the current value of Avio's assets after deduction of his pre-relationship wealth, inheritance funds, and lawsuit proceeds. Avio conceded that she was entitled to monetary compensation and child and spousal support orders but disputed the extent of her entitlement.]

DICKSON J.: ...

Legal Principles [Governing Unjust Enrichment]

53 When an unjust enrichment is established, the court must go on to consider the nature of the appropriate remedy in the circumstances of the case. In so doing, flexibility and common sense are exercised and the requirements of justice and good conscience are taken into account. ...

54 In some circumstances, a constructive trust will be imposed as a remedy for unjust enrichment if a monetary remedy would be inadequate. The remedy of constructive trust is available to give effect to the reasonable expectations of the parties where there is a link between the contribution at issue and the property in which the constructive trust is claimed. ...

55 Where a constructive trust is imposed, its extent must be proportional to the extent of the claimant's direct or indirect contribution. ... The great value of domestic services must not be distinguished from that of other forms of contribution, however, and proportionality may be estimated when quantification in exact dollar amounts cannot occur.

56 In cases of unjust enrichment in the family law context, the "value survived" approach to valuation of contributions to the net worth of both parties is generally adopted. This approach accounts for the amount by which the property at issue is acquired, improved and maintained by the parties' respective contributions. It may also accord best with their reasonable expectations, as it is common for a couple to expect to share in the wealth generated by their partnership. ...

57 The value survived approach to valuation may be adopted regardless of whether the appropriate remedy in an unjust enrichment claim is one of constructive trust or monetary damages. It is particularly appropriate in cases where there has been a long-term marriage-like relationship in which the property at issue has appreciated in value. In such cases, the value survived approach enables both parties to share in the increased value of the properties brought about by their joint contributions. ...

58 The court can assess a monetary award based on the value survived approach in cases involving direct and indirect contributions in various ways. In some cases, the plaintiff may be awarded a percentage of the net increase in value of property based on a mathematical approach that accounts for factors such as interest rates on financial contributions. In others, a dollar figure reflecting the court's view of the parties' relative contributions to the property's increase in value may appropriately be assessed. ...

Application of the Law to the Facts

Was Dr. Avio unjustly enriched by Ms. Pegler's domestic and childcare contributions over the course of their spousal relationship? If so, what is a fair compensatory monetary award?

81 I conclude that, as he concedes, Dr. Avio was unjustly enriched by Ms. Pegler's domestic and childcare contributions over the course of their spousal relationship. The three necessary elements are established, as is a link between her contributions to the joint family enterprise and the acquisition, improvement or maintenance of the Windsor House and the UVIC Pension. Ms. Pegler is entitled to a compensatory award in the sum of $440,000 in connection with the increased net value in the Windsor House and $400,000 in connection with the increased value in the UVIC Pension. She is, however, not entitled to a share of Dr. Avio's mutual funds or RRSPs.

82 As is apparent from my findings of fact, I am satisfied that Ms. Pegler's domestic and childcare contributions to the joint family enterprise were substantial. Although she did not contribute to the acquisition of the Rockland House she certainly did contribute to its ongoing maintenance and improvement and, latterly, to that of the Windsor House. In so doing, Ms. Pegler worked hard to provide Dr. Avio with a well-run household and thus enabled him to pursue his career comfortably while enjoying the many benefits of an enriched family life. In these circumstances, it was reasonable for all concerned to expect Ms. Pegler to receive a significant proportion of the increased value in the family home.

83 The high value of Ms. Pegler's domestic and childcare contributions is evidenced by, amongst other things, the negative effect on Dr. Avio when, due to her illness, they were somewhat reduced. Although it is impossible to quantify the value of Ms. Pegler's indirect contributions with mathematical precision, in my view they were roughly equivalent to Dr. Avio's direct financial contributions in connection with the family homes.

84 The compensatory award of $440,000 is assessed on the basis of the value survived approach to valuation of the parties' respective contributions to net worth. It incorporates a deduction of $144,000 from the $1,122,000 value of the Windsor House in recognition of Dr. Avio's equity in the Rockland House when the spousal relationship began. This deduction leaves a balance of $978,000 in net increased value, from which I decline to deduct renovations costs and property taxes paid by Dr. Avio because they are part of his roughly equivalent direct financial contribution to the joint family enterprise. While some of the funds expended came from his inheritance account or lawsuit proceeds, he chose to apply them in this manner. ...

86 The $440,000 award of compensation is just over 45 percent of the $978,000 increased net value figure, despite my finding that Ms. Pegler's indirect domestic contributions were roughly equivalent in value to Dr. Avio's direct financial contributions in connection with the family homes. This adjustment reflects the fact that Dr. Avio also made valuable, though relatively modest, indirect domestic contributions which must be taken into account.

87 The $400,000 award of compensation in connection with the UVIC Pension is also assessed on the basis of the value survived approach to valuation. Given her substantial indirect contributions to the joint family enterprise, including consultation with and support of Dr. Avio in professional matters, it was reasonable to expect Ms. Pegler would receive a significant proportion of the increased value of the UVIC Pension, especially following Joe's birth.

88 In addition to providing Dr. Avio with a well-run family home while he pursued his career, Ms. Pegler sacrificed her own career to provide Joe with full-time care. In so doing, amongst other things, she lost the opportunity to contribute to an employee pension plan and

benefit from its appreciation in value over time. In these circumstances, ... the touchstone of justice and good conscience requires that Ms. Pegler be allowed to share in the pension of her mate.

89 Like the Windsor House award, the $400,000 UVIC Pension compensatory award incorporates a deduction for Dr. Avio's pre-relationship equity. In this case, the sum of $232,000 is deducted from the $1,360,000 current value, leaving a balance of $1,128,000 in increased net value. The $400,000 awarded represents approximately 35 percent of that sum, which accounts for the fact that Dr. Avio's proportional contribution to the value of the UVIC Pension was somewhat higher than Ms. Pegler's indirect contribution, especially prior to Joe's birth. It also accounts for the full pre-tax nature of the pension's valuation. ...

91 Ms. Pegler concedes that she is not entitled to share in the value of Dr. Avio's inheritance or lawsuit proceeds based on her claim for unjust enrichment. I agree. She did not contribute toward their acquisition, improvement or maintenance and has no reasonable expectation of entitlement to a share.

92 Dr. Avio's mutual funds and RRSPs have a value roughly equivalent to the amounts he received for his inheritance and lawsuit. I conclude that Ms. Pegler is not entitled to a share of their value. ...

NOTES AND QUESTIONS

1. As the *Pegler v. Avio* case illustrates, courts in British Columbia have sometimes used the "value surviving" or "value survived" approach when quantifying the monetary award. The British Columbia Court of Appeal sanctioned this approach in *Pickelein v. Gillmore* (1997), 27 R.F.L. (4th) 51, 1997 CarswellBC 307 (C.A.); additional reasons at (1997), 27 R.F.L. (4th) 51n (C.A.) and in *Shannon v. Gidden* (1999), 1 R.F.L. (5th) 105 (B.C. C.A.). In *Pickelein*, the court noted that the "value received" approach would have resulted in the dismissal of both parties' claims since their contributions to the respective properties over the years were equal. The "value survived" approach allowed both parties to share in the increased value of the properties brought about by their joint contributions. In *Panara v. Di Ascenzo* (2005), 16 R.F.L. (6th) 177 (Alta. C.A.), the Alberta Court of Appeal endorsed the B.C.C.A.'s approach.

However, relying on the comments in *Peter v. Beblow*, the Ontario Court of Appeal concluded in *Bell v. Bailey* (2001), 20 R.F.L. (5th) 272 that a court should not determine the size of a monetary award using the "value survived" approach. The trial judge had first determined that a woman should be granted a 45% interest in the increase in values of a man's house and RRSP. He then translated this into a monetary award, after deducting certain benefits received by the woman. The appellate court stated (at para. 38) that, once the trial judge found that a monetary award was adequate, "the issue of constructive trust should have left the table" and the monetary award should have reflected the value of the woman's contributions on a "value received" basis. Nonetheless, the court acknowledged (at para. 37) that "the value received calculation of a monetary award may, to some degree, reflect the extent to which the value of the asset was enhanced by the claimant's direct and indirect contributions". Because of this last comment, it may appear that the difference between the results under the two approaches is not great. Note, however, the following statement by Justice Weiler in *Roseneck v. Gowling* (2002), 35 R.F.L. (5th) 177 (Ont. C.A.); additional reasons at (2003), 223 D.L.R. (4th) 229 (Ont. C.A.); additional reasons at (2003), 38 R.F.L. (5th) 180 (Ont. C.A.), at para. 33:

> When monetary compensation is ordered, the claimant is given the "value received" by the other party. The value conferred on the property is irrelevant. When a constructive trust is imposed, the claimant receives an interest in the property and receives the "value survived" of the contribution. In the latter instance regard is had to the extent to which the property has been improved in deciding the property interest.

The Ontario cases were recently discussed in *Taylor v. Guindon* (2005), 2005 CarswellOnt 3183 (S.C.J.); additional reasons at (2005), 2005 CarswellOnt 5311 (S.C.J.).

Why is this issue of practical significance? Which approach is likely to result in a higher award, especially where the claimant's contribution consists of domestic services?

2. Did the court in the *Pegler v. Avio* case consider the benefits that Pegler received during the relationship? Was the fact that Pegler suffered from multiple sclerosis and was unlikely ever to be self-sufficient influential?

3. In *Belvedere v. Brittain Estate* (2009), 2009 CarswellOnt 14, 60 R.F.L. (6th) 249 (C.A.), a woman, who was on leave from her position as a flight attendant, sold her home and car when she went to live with her partner and his young child. The man paid almost all expenses and gave the woman various gifts. The woman used her airline privileges to arrange numerous trips for the couple. The man occasionally suggested that the couple should have a cohabitation agreement under which he would arrange for a transfer of some or all of his RRSPs to the woman in the event of his death. However, when he died in a farm accident after living with the woman for two years, there was no agreement and he had not designated the woman as a beneficiary under the RRSPs which were worth almost $2 million. Nor did the man provide for her in his will. He left the bulk of his $6 million estate to his child.

The woman brought an action based on unjust enrichment against the man's estate. The trial judge awarded her $1.75 million, a sum equal to approximately the after-tax value of his RRSPs. The Ontario Court of Appeal allowed the estate's appeal, concluding that unjust enrichment had not been established:

> 46 ... [I]t is ... clear that the conferring of a benefit does not, by itself, constitute unjust enrichment. ... Rather, what is required, and what the trial judge failed to do in this case, is to balance the benefits conferred and received by the parties to determine whether the claimant's contribution is sufficient to entitle her to compensation.

> 47 As it stands, the trial judge's conclusion that Ms. Belvedere "suffered deprivation exceeding the lifestyle she enjoyed" is not supported by the evidence. While it is clear that Mr. Brittain benefited from Ms. Belvedere's care and companionship in the ways discussed above, it is equally clear that she, too, benefited significantly from the relationship. On Ms. Belvedere's own evidence she was "breaking even" financially during their relationship. She added that in terms of her happiness, "it went up 500 percent".

The appellate court went on to note (paras. 56–60) that, if unjust enrichment existed, the appropriate remedy was a damage award calculated on a "value received" basis. On this basis the amount awarded was patently unreasonable.

4. In *Becker v. Pettkus*, Justice Martland predicted that the acceptance of the remedial constructive trust would result in "palm tree justice". Has he been proved correct?

5. Recall that Justice L'Heureux Dubé in *Walsh v. Bona* described the equitable remedies available to unmarried cohabitees as inadequate and uncertain. In his annotation to the case, Professor Thompson states ((2003) 32 R.F.L. (5th) 87, at 92):

> Thanks in part to *Peter v. Beblow*, the law in this area has become more incoherent, inconsistent and unpredictable. Vague tests of "juristic reason" and "direct link" and "value received/ survived" leave much room for subjective and stereotyped interpretations of roles and contributions. More structure is needed to guide this remedial discretion, perhaps borrowing more liberally from the well-developed procedures and rules of the matrimonial property regimes.

Do you agree?

Sharing the Economic Gain of a Marriage

(1) Overview

The key feature of the property regime established by Part I of the *Family Law Act* is that spouses are entitled to an equal share of the total financial product of the marriage, determined by calculating the net family property (defined in s. 4(1)) of each spouse, when the relationship ends. The basic premise underlying the regime is that both spouses make a vital and essentially equal contribution to the economic viability of the family unit and hence to the acquisition of wealth by the unit. This premise is reflected in the Preamble and is clearly articulated in s. 5(7).

The regime only applies to those who qualify as spouses as that term is defined in s. 1(1). The good faith requirement in paragraph (b) of this definition has been interpreted to mean that the claimant must have intended to be validly married according to the applicable law: *Harris v. Godkewitsch* (1983), 41 O.R. (2d) 779 (U.F.C.); *Reaney v. Reaney* (1990), 28 R.F.L. (3d) 52 (Ont. H.C.); and *Debora v. Debora* (1998), 43 R.F.L. (4th) 179 (Ont. C.A.). In *Reaney*, the man knew that he was already married to another woman at the time he went through the marriage ceremony. He also realized that, according to Ontario law, he lacked the capacity to marry. Accordingly, he did not qualify as a "spouse" under s. 1(1). The Deboras were married in a religious ceremony that did not comply with the *Marriage Act*, R.S.O. 1990, c. M.3. The man advised the woman that he wished to continue receiving a widower's pension and, therefore, their marriage should not be registered with the authorities for some time. Seven years later, the couple married in a civil ceremony. The Ontario Court of Appeal held that the woman only became a "spouse" for the purposes of Part I of the *FLA* after the second ceremony. It stated (at 184) that a person who participated in a marriage ceremony knowing that it did not comply with the provincial law could not claim to be acting "in good faith" even if he or she believed the ceremony created a marriage. For a critical comment, see McLeod, "Annotation" (1998), 43 R.F.L. (4th) 179.

The deferred sharing of financial gain during the relationship is superimposed on the separate property regime. Ownership of property between spouses is determined by the ordinary rules of property law, as modified to a minor extent by s. 14. Section 10 provides a procedure whereby ownership or possessory rights of the spouses may be determined at any time in accordance with these modified rules. The Ontario Court of Appeal confirmed in *Miller v. Miller* (1996), 20 R.F.L. (4th) 191 that s. 10 is procedural only, a vehicle for determining and enforcing substantive rights that have their origins elsewhere.

Until a court orders otherwise, spouses are generally free to deal with their separate property. However, there are some significant and, to some extent, uncertain exceptions to this general rule. First, Part II of the *FLA* places restrictions on dealings with a matrimonial home to protect the possessory rights of the non-owning spouse. These restrictions and the law governing possession of a matrimonial home are examined in Chapter 5, *THE FAMILY HOME*. Second, where a spouse intentionally or recklessly depletes his or her net family property, the court may determine that equalization of the net family properties is unconscionable and may vary the equalization entitlement to favour the other spouse. See s. 5(6) of the *FLA*, analyzed later in this chapter. Finally, there may be circumstances where a court can use the *Fraudulent Conveyances Act*, R.S.O. 1990, c. F.29, to set aside some transfers that reduce a spouse's assets. See *Stone v. Stone* (2001), 18 R.F.L. (5th) 365 (Ont. C.A.), described later in this chapter.

When certain events (often referred to as "triggering events") occur, the spouse whose net family property is less than that of the other spouse is entitled to one-half the difference between them. The triggering events set out in s. 5(1) of the *FLA* occur when a divorce is granted, when a marriage is declared a nullity, or when the spouses are separated and there is no reasonable prospect of resumed cohabitation. Under s. 5(2), a surviving spouse is also entitled to one-half of the difference between his or her net family property and that of the deceased spouse. The estate cannot make an equalization claim even if the surviving spouse's net family property is greater than that of the deceased. Rules are established by s. 6 to govern the relationship among equalization claims, rights under a will, and rights on intestacy under the *Succession Law Reform Act*, R.S.O. 1990, c. S.26. Finally, s. 5(3) permits one spouse to apply to the court under s. 7 to "have the difference between the net family properties divided as if the spouses were separated and there were no reasonable prospect that they would resume cohabitation" if "there is a serious danger that one spouse may improvidently deplete his or her net family property."

Only s. 5(3) permits equalization claims during an ongoing marriage relationship. It provides a remedy where one spouse, by reason of disease, addiction to drugs or senility, is not competent to make sensible day-to-day decisions regarding the management of his or her property. The subsection also applies where one spouse is about to gamble away property on a speculative and unwise venture or if one spouse wants to make inordinate gifts to third parties. This was confirmed in *Stone v. Stone* (2001), 18 R.F.L. (5th) 365 (Ont. C.A.), where Justice Feldman stated (para. 30): "One of the effects of s. 5(3) of the Act is to provide a remedy to a spouse in those circumstances where the other spouse seeks to divest himself or herself of his or her property in anticipation of death and in order to defeat the spouse's claim to equalization."

Where a court makes an order for a sharing of economic gains based on s. 5(3), neither spouse may make a further application under s. 7 in respect of the marriage: s. 5(4). This provision effectively precludes equalization claims, even if one of the other triggering events later occurs, unless a domestic contract provides otherwise.

In many situations, but especially when an application for equalization of net family properties is based on s. 5(3), it may be prudent to apply for a preservation order under s. 12 of the *FLA*. As Granger J. explained in *Lasch v. Lasch* (1988), 13 R.F.L. (3d) 434 at 438 (Ont. H.C.), the purpose of an order under s. 12 is to ensure that there are sufficient assets held at trial by the spouse with the greater of the two net family properties to satisfy the equalization payment due to the other spouse. In the absence of an order under s. 12, the owning spouse generally remains free to deal with his or her property, other than a matrimonial home, after the valuation date. Therefore, a spouse who is owed an equalization sum under s. 5 is in a vulnerable position. By the time a court order for payment is made under s. 9, there may be few assets held by the other spouse and it may be difficult to enforce the judgment. Orders under s. 12 are intended to prevent this situation. Accordingly, a s. 12 order should be made in equalization proceedings wherever there is a real risk that the ability of a spouse to satisfy an equalization payment is likely to be impaired by his or her dealings with property prior to trial. For an analysis of s. 12, see Hovius and Youdan, *The Law of Family Property* (Toronto: Carswell, 1991) at 235–240. See also *Gaudet (Litigation Guardian of) v. Young Estate* (1995), 11 R.F.L. (4th) 284 (Ont. Gen. Div.); *Webster v. Webster* (1997), 37 R.F.L. (4th) 347 (Ont. Gen. Div.); and *Both v. Both* (2008), 53 R.F.L. (6th) 65 (Ont. S.C.J.).

Where a triggering event other than that specified in s. 5(3) occurs, entitlement to an equalization of net family properties arises independent of court action. The wording of s. 5(1) suggests, for example, that as soon as the spouses separate without reasonable prospect of resumed cohabitation, the spouse with the lesser of the two net family properties is entitled to one-half the difference between the two. The occurrence of a triggering event, therefore, creates a statutory entitlement to the sum of money necessary to equalize the net family properties. To enforce this entitlement, a spouse may bring an application under s. 7 and the court is then empowered by s. 9 to make various orders to ensure that this sum is realized in a fair and effective manner.

Statutory entitlement to equalization of net family properties upon a triggering event is not absolute. It is subject to the power of a court to award a greater or lesser amount under s. 5(6). Enforcement of the entitlement may also become statutorily-barred if a s. 7 application is not commenced within the limitation periods set by s. 7(3). Note, however, that a court may extend the period under s. 2(8). For a recent case explaining when such an extension should occur, see *Poirier v. Alie* (2007), 39 R.F.L. (6th) 193 (Ont. S.C.J.).

It is clear from the wording of s. 5 and s. 7(2) that the statutory entitlement under s. 5 does not create any interest by one spouse in the property of the other. In *Canada (Attorney General) v. Ristimaki* (2000), 4 R.F.L. (5th) 167 (Ont. S.C.J.), Justice Low described the entitlement as follows (para. 16): "[W]hile it may be possible to say that as of the date of separation, one spouse is the creditor of the other to the extent of the sum required to equalize their net family properties, there is no transfer of property by operation of the *Family Law Act* even though a court may ultimately order [under s. 9(1)] a transfer either absolutely or as security in order to give effect to the provisions of the *Act*." See also *Nevarc Holdings Ltd. v. Orchid Communications Inc.* (1990), 28 R.F.L. (3d) 330 (Ont. Gen. Div.). For commentary on the question whether the creditors of a spouse or deceased spouse's estate have priority over a spouse who is owed an equalization sum, see Hovius and Youdan, *The Law of Family Property* (Toronto: Carswell, 1991) at 211–214.

Regarding the impact of bankruptcy on claims under Part I of the *FLA*, see Klotz, "Bankruptcy Issues in Family Law" (1992), 14 Adv. Q. 18; Merchant and Vogel, "The Bankruptcy Dodge" (1993), 9 C.F.L.Q. 161; Klotz, "Bankruptcy Problems in Family Law" in L.S.U.C., *Family Law: Rules, Fairness and Equality* (Special Lecture Series, 1993); Ontario Law Reform Commission, *Report on Family Property Law* (Toronto: 1993) at 16–18; Goldwater, "Bankruptcy and Family Law" (1997-98), 15 C.F.L.Q. 139; and Klotz, "Pitfalls and Pointers in High Debt Cases" (1997-1998), 15 C.F.L.Q. 187. See also *Janakowski v. Janakowski* (2000), 7 R.F.L. (5th) 117 (Ont. S.C.J.).

When the parties cannot settle the equalization entitlement, an application under s. 7 is required. Section 7(1) permits the court to "determine any matter respecting the spouse's entitlement under section 5". Where an application is made under s. 7, each party must serve on the other and file with the court a statement of property in accordance with s. 8. The practice relating to the form and delivery of the statement required is governed by Rule 13 of *the Family Law Rules*, O. Reg. 114/ 99. See also *Buttrum v. Buttrum* (2001), 15 R.F.L. (5th) 250 (Ont. S.C.J.); additional reasons at (2002), 31 R.F.L. (5th) 277 (Ont. S.C.J.), where Aitkin J. discusses the lawyer's role in ensuring that such statements are properly filled out. Because accurate determination of the equalization entitlement depends on accurate disclosure of the spouses' assets and liabilities, the courts have frowned on inadequate statements and have sometimes used costs as a penalty. Another possibility is that a court will make certain assumptions about the net family property of a spouse who fails to provide adequate information. In *Burnett v. Burnett* (1999), 50 R.F.L. (4th) 223 (Ont. S.C.J.), the husband, who lived in Switzerland, avoided complete financial disclosure and ultimately did not appear at trial. The court attributed a value of $12 million to the husband's business assets largely on the basis of two letters to his brother regarding his will. The resulting equalization payment was over $6.5 million, with pre-judgment interest of $225,315.63.

The key to determining entitlement under s. 5 is obviously the calculation of each spouse's net family property so that one-half of their difference can be determined. The definition of "net family property" in s. 4(1) suggests the following analysis for calculating a spouse's net family property.

Calculation of A Spouse's Net Family Property

Step 1. Determine the valuation date in accordance with the definition in s. 4(1).

Comment: This date determines what property interests, debts and liabilities are considered in the calculation. It also fixes the time for valuing them.

Step 2. List the property interests owned by the spouse on the valuation date and determine their values at that time. Total the values.

Comment: If only one spouse owns an asset, including the matrimonial home, it is listed only in the calculation of that spouse's net family property. If spouses hold property interests jointly, include the value of the joint interest in each of the spouse's net family properties.

Step 3. Determine if any of the spouse's property interests are excluded by s. 4(2). Deduct the value of any excluded property interests from the total reached in Step 2.

Comment: To ensure that only the gain attributable to the joint efforts of both spouses during the marriage relationship is shared, certain property interests are excluded.

Step 4. Calculate the amount of the spouse's debts and liabilities on the valuation date. Deduct the total of these debts and liabilities from the figure determined under Step 3.

Comment: Since the net family properties of the spouses are intended to represent the net financial product of their marriage relationship, s. 4(1) permits a spouse to deduct debts and other liabilities on the valuation date from the value of included property.

Step 5. Deduct the marital property deduction. Determine the marital property deduction of the spouse by adding up the values of all property interests, other than those in a matrimonial home, that the spouse owned at marriage and then subtracting from that total the value of the debts and other liabilities of the spouse on the date of the marriage other than those directly related to the acquisition of a matrimonial home.

Comment: Since only the gain during the marriage is shared, the Act allows a marital property deduction. The cases indicate that this number can be a negative one, resulting in what is effectively an addition to the spouse's net family property. For policy reasons, there are special rules governing the matrimonial home. The special treatment of debts and liabilities at marriage directly related to the matrimonial home originally developed through case law, but will become part of the statutory definition of net family property if and when the amendments to the *FLA* contained in Bill 133 (not yet proclaimed.)

Step 6. If the result is a negative number, it is deemed to be zero by s. 4(5).

Comment: The mathematical calculation of a spouse's net family property will result in a negative figure if the debts at the valuation date plus the marital property deduction is greater than the value of the spouse's included property at the valuation date. Section 4(5) represents a policy choice by the legislature to the effect that debts on the valuation date and losses since marriage are shared only to the extent that they are offset by the existence of included property.

Once the net family property is determined for both spouses, the entitlement of the spouse with the lesser of the two net family properties is determined by deducting the smaller of the two figures from the larger and dividing this amount by two.

Under s. 5(6) of the *FLA*, a court may award a spouse a greater or lesser amount "if the court is of the opinion that equalizing the net family properties would be unconscionable" having regard to the factors listed. Section 5(7) helps to emphasize that equalization of net family properties is the norm and provides the rationale for this general rule.

As indicated above, the final result of the equalization of the net family properties is that one spouse is entitled to a monetary sum. Section 9 of the *FLA* then empowers the court, in an application under s. 7, to make various orders to ensure that this sum is realized in a fair and effective manner.

It should be noted that spouses can opt out of Part I of the Act or modify the rules applicable to their relationship by entering into a domestic contract. Part IV of the Act provides a framework within which couples are allowed great freedom to determine the property rights arising out of their relationships. See Chapter 9, *DOMESTIC CONTRACTS*.

NOTES AND QUESTIONS

1. In *Weinstein v. Weinstein (Litigation Guardian of)* (1997), 30 R.F.L. (4th) 116 (Ont. Gen. Div.), a wife made a will leaving her estate to her grandchildren. Subsequently, she became mentally incapacitated due to Alzheimer's disease. The husband applied for an equalization of the spouses' net family property under s. 5(3) of the *FLA* and received $2.5 million. When the husband died, his will left the bulk of his estate to The University of Western Ontario. The grandchildren successfully argued that the original order equalizing the net family properties should be set aside because they had not received notice of the proceeding. For a critical comment, see McLeod, "Annotation" (1997), 30 R.F.L. (4th) 117.

2. Courts have awarded interim advances against the expected equalization payments in many cases, even though there is no express authority to do so in the *FLA*. Justice Lane reviewed the cases in *Zagdanski v. Zagdanski* (2001), 19 R.F.L. (5th) 458 (Ont. S.C.J.); appeal quashed (2002), 2002 CarswellOnt 614 (Ont. C.A.).

3. In *Maljkovich v. Maljkovich Estate* (1995), 20 R.F.L. (4th) 222 (Ont. Gen. Div.); affirmed (1997), 33 R.F.L. (4th) 24 (Ont. C.A.); leave to appeal refused (1998), 111 O.A.C. 200 (note) (S.C.C.), the husband murdered his wife following separation and while they were negotiating property matters. He filed an election under s. 6 of the *FLA*, but Jennings J. ruled (at 231) that "based on considerations of public policy, the applicant cannot be permitted to profit from his wrong by making an election under section 6". The judge suggested (*obiter*, at 231) that the husband's application would also have failed even if he had launched it on the basis of s. 5(1) before the murder. Do you agree? See Professor McLeod's annotation to the case on page 222. For a general discussion regarding the effect of a spouse's death after separation, see Atin, "Application for Equalization: Death of Separated Spouses" (2003-2004), 21 C.F.L.Q. 175.

4. As noted above, the rationale for Ontario's family property regime is to recognize past, equal contributions to the accumulation of wealth during the marriage. The regime limits judicial discretion, relying on fairly hard and fast rules to determine the spouses' rights at the end of their marriage. Finally, it is characterized by deferred sharing of the value of the gain during the relationship rather than an actual division of property.

The family property regimes in some of the other provinces do not have these features. The *Family Relations Act*, R.S.B.C. 1996, c. 128, for example, provides that, upon certain triggering events, both spouses are entitled to equal interests as tenants-in-common in each family asset. Some family assets are specifically listed, but the category includes any property owned by one or both spouses and "ordinarily used by a spouse or a minor child of either spouse for a family purpose". For the purposes of characterizing property, it is irrelevant whether it was acquired before or after the marriage. "Business assets" and "ventures" are not family assets and so remain separate property unless the non-owning spouse contributes directly or indirectly to them. While there is a statutory presumption in favour of equal sharing of family assets, a court is empowered to make a reapportionment "on the basis of fairness" in light of a number of factors. The threshold for the exercise of judicial discretion is lower than in Ontario's *FLA*. Also, one factor listed in s. 65(1)(e) of the *Family Relations Act* refers to "the needs of each spouse to become or remain economically independent and self sufficient". Thus, the division of property is meant not only to ensure that past contributions are rewarded, but to provide for future needs. See generally, Farquar, "Matrimonial Property and the British Columbia Court of Appeal" (1988), 23 U.B.C. L. Rev. 30 and Law Reform Commission of British Columbia, *Working Paper on Property Rights on Marriage Breakdown* (1989).

As you examine Ontario's family property regime, consider whether there should be more judicial discretion and whether future financial need should be a factor in deciding whether there should be an unequal division of the wealth generated during the couple's cohabitation.

5. For a critical examination of some of the technical defects in the Ontario family property regime, see Raphael, "The Need to Reform the Division of Property Provisions in the *Family Law Act*" (1999), 21 Adv. Q. 380. Some of these will be remedied if and when the amendments to the *FLA* contained in Bill 133 are adopted.

(2) Calculating the Net Family Property

(a) Determining the Valuation Date

Section 4(1) of the *FLA* defines "valuation date" as the earliest of five dates. In the context of a marriage breakdown, the earliest of these is almost always the date on which the spouses separated and there was no reasonable prospect of resumed cohabitation. Pinpointing that date may be difficult because, as Killeen L.J.S.C. pointed out in *Czepa v. Czepa* (1988), 16 R.F.L. (3d) 191 (Ont. H.C.) at 196, the course of marital discord is rarely simple and each case has its own unique facts. In some circumstances, the date of separation may be an issue. More often, there will be legitimate dispute over when there was no longer a reasonable prospect of resumed cohabitation.

There is extensive case law examining the concept of "living separate and apart" in the context of divorce proceedings. The cases decided under the *FLA* generally apply the concept of separation in the same way in determining the valuation date. See, for example, *Oswell v. Oswell* (1990), 28 R.F.L. (3d) 10 (Ont. H.C.); affirmed (1992), 43 R.F.L. (3d) 180 (Ont. C.A.) and *Torosantucci v. Torosantucci* (1991), 32 R.F.L. (3d) 202 (Ont. U.F.C.). In these cases the judges accepted that spouses can be separated without a reasonable prospect that they will resume cohabitation, notwithstanding that they both live under one roof. See also *Harbour v. Harbour* (2000), 6 R.F.L. (5th) 225 (Ont. S.C.J.), which illustrates that determining whether the spouses are living separate and apart under the same roof may be especially difficult where a marriage gradually deteriorates and *Button v. Button* (2000), 8 R.F.L. (5th) 20 (Ont. S.C.J.); additional reasons at (2000), 2000 CarswellOnt 2070 (Ont. S.C.J.), where Justice Kitely reviewed the case law and stressed (at para. 76) that "caution must be exercised when determining the date of separation absent any physical separation." Is it possible to have one date on which the spouses begin to live separate and apart for the purposes of the *Divorce Act*, but a different valuation date for the *FLA*?

CARATUN v. CARATUN

(1987), 9 R.F.L. (3d) 337, 1987 CarswellOnt 348 (Ont. H.C.); affirmed (1992), 1992 CarswellOnt 287 (Ont. C.A.); leave to appeal refused (1993), 46 R.F.L. (3d) 314 (note) (S.C.C.)

[Mrs. Caratun, the petitioner, moved out of the family home on July 18, 1981, and cohabitation never resumed. She argued, however, that the valuation date should be set at some point in 1984 because there was a reasonable possibility of reconciliation until that time.]

VAN CAMP J.: — ...

VALUATION DATE

... The parties separated on 18th July 1981 and have not reconciled. The problem arises as to whether there was then any reasonable prospect that they would resume cohabitation. The evidence shows that the respondent led the petitioner to believe that there was such a prospect of reconciliation until January 1984. As late as July 1984, the respondent was walking in and out of her home at will to see his child and was portraying himself to an outsider as the man of the house. Following the separation in 1981, in order to obtain an agreement with respect to custody, the respondent saw the petitioner frequently and had sexual relations with her. Persuaded by him, the petitioner withdrew her application for custody on the ground that there was an attempt to reconcile. In March 1982 the petitioner acknowledged that the respondent was a fit father and that there was a possible reconciliation. From the date of separation, however, the respondent had put off the resumption of cohabitation on the ground that he could not cohabit with her as long as she had an order for custody and, subsequently, he postponed it again until she had some weight off and, finally, until she would stop smoking. I find that there was never any intention on the respondent's part to reconcile and that there was no reasonable prospect that they would resume cohabitation after the separation in July 1981.

One reason for the postponement of the valuation date after separation until the date when there was no reasonable prospect of resumption of cohabitation would be that only on

that latter date would each of the spouses make plans for their assets as a separated person. In this case the petitioner was showing the tendency that the psychologist referred to as "her tendency to believe that what she wants will come true and disregards the signs to the contrary". I find that there was no reasonable prospect that they would resume cohabitation after July 1981. The unfairness of his leading her to think to the contrary might be assessed in deciding whether equalization is unconscionable, but she suffered no monetary loss thereby.
...

NOTES AND QUESTIONS

1. Why might Mrs. Caratun have argued in favour of the later valuation date? How does the date affect the equalization claim?

2. In *Torosantucci v. Torosantucci* (1991), 32 R.F.L. (3d) 202 (Ont. U.F.C.), Beckett U.F.C.J. described the question of a reasonable prospect of resumed cohabitation this way (at 206):

> A reasonable prospect of reconciliation must be more than wishful thinking on the part of either party. There must be more than residual affection that may linger by one or both of the parties. ... The question is whether a reasonable person, knowing all the circumstances, would reasonably believe that the parties had a prospect or expectation of resuming cohabitation.

3. The case of *Davis v. Davis* (2002), 35 R.F.L. (5th) 48 (Ont. S.C.J.) involved unusual facts. The wife and children lived in Midland. The husband, an "uncontrolled philanderer", worked in Toronto and spent two or three weekends a month in the Midland home. This pattern continued even after a spousal and child support order was made on consent in 1985. When the wife applied for equalization of net family properties many years later, the husband argued that the claim was foreclosed by the time limit set in s. 7(3)(b) of the *FLA* because the couple had separated without a reasonable prospect of resumed cohabitation in 1985. The Justice concluded, however, that the valuation date was April 16, 2001, the day when the husband refused his wife's request that he end his latest affair.

4. In *Fleming v. Fleming* (2001), 19 R.F.L. (5th) 274 (Ont. S.C.J.), the husband sought to argue that separation would have occurred about 13 years earlier if he had been aware of the wife's affair. Justice Mackinnon held that this argument was irrelevant under the *FLA* where there was no discretion to alter the valuation date. In addition, the Justice refused to allow the husband to bring claims for damages for the torts of deceit and breach of fiduciary duty. Justice Mackinnon concluded that the wife had no legal duty to disclose the affair to her husband.

5. In its *Report on Family Property Law* (Toronto: 1993), the Ontario Law Reform Commission noted (at 52): "A rigidly defined valuation date may have substantial financial consequences if the value of an asset alters significantly between the triggering event and the court order of an equalization payment." After reviewing the situation in other provinces, the Commission stated (at 56-57):

> The different models for determining a valuation date adopted in common law provinces represent varied attempts to resolve the tension between the need to achieve consistency and predictability, and the desire to ensure that individuals receive fair treatment. In British Columbia, the great flexibility adopted by the courts has generated criticism of the inconsistencies that have resulted. In Ontario the rigidity of the valuation date appears to have redirected litigation into the factual question of when separation occurs, or into trust claims. This has the disadvantage of embroiling the courts in complicated factual and legal issues which bear little relation to the real problem faced by the parties — a substantial fluctuation in the value of assets accumulated during the relationship.

In the end, the Commission recommended no change to the definition of "valuation date" in Ontario's family property regime. Instead, it suggested amendments to the *FLA* to make it clear that a court could deviate from an equal sharing of net family properties where some changes in property values after the valuation date made equal sharing unfair.

The extent to which such changes in value can currently be considered under s. 5(6) of the *FLA* will be examined later in this chapter.

(b) The Concepts of Property, Ownership and Value

(i) Property

The calculation of a spouse's net family property under the *FLA* requires a determination of the value of all non-excluded property owned by a spouse on the valuation date. This determination may involve some complex issues. What is "property"? Note the definition in s. 4(1). What is meant by ownership? More particularly, does ownership for the purpose of Part I include beneficial ownership? If so, do the trust concepts continue to be relevant? Finally, what is meant by "value"? These issues are explored in the cases and materials that follow. Because pensions are very important practically and give rise to special difficulties, they will be the subject of a separate section.

HOVIUS AND YOUDAN, *THE LAW OF FAMILY PROPERTY*

(Toronto: Carswell, 1991) 241-242 (Footnotes omitted)

There is no simple answer to the abstract question, what is property? The subject-matter of property is not, of course, restricted to tangible things such as land and chattels but extends to intangibles such as shares, money in a bank and goodwill of a business. There is, moreover, no closed list of the possible subjects of property. In addition, there is no comprehensive definition, in the sense of a set of "necessary and jointly sufficient conditions", that enables one to determine whether something is property. The law operates pragmatically in characterizing things as property so that something may be property in one context but not in another.

Certain characteristics are commonly associated with private property. The right to alienate provides an example. The presence or absence of such a characteristic is indicative whether or not something is property. But such characteristics are not conditions of property. Therefore, the absence of a common characteristic does not mean that something is necessarily not property.

Despite the indeterminacy in the term "property", it may be stated that property is a concept that is concerned with access to wealth and control over it. Moreover, assistance in determining its meaning in a particular context may, indeed must, be derived from that context. The *Family Law Act* gives some explicit direction by providing a definition of "property".

... More generally, the meaning of the term "property" in the context of Part I of the *Family Law Act* must be determined after taking account of the purposes of the *Family Law Act* generally and Part I in particular.

BRINKOS v. BRINKOS

(1989), 20 R.F.L. (3d) 445, 1989 CarswellOnt 252 (Ont. C.A.)

CARTHY J.A.: — In this proceeding for divorce and related relief, the husband appeals from the refusal of the trial judge to include in "net family property" the wife's entitlement to the income from a trust for her lifetime. ... The trial judge held that a future interest in income from property does not fall within the equalization scheme of the *Family Law Act*, S.O. 1986, c. 4.

When the wife was a small child her parents established a bank account for her and made gifts to that account through the years. At the date of marriage, June 1965, the value of that account was $224,475. Following the marriage but prior to 1972, the father made additional contributions of $71,750. On 1st January 1972 the wife settled a trust with her mother and brother as trustees. By the terms of the trust, the wife was granted an inalienable life interest in the net income from the trust property. In addition, a discretionary power was vested in the trustees to encroach upon the capital. At the time of the settlement the gifts from her parents with accumulated interest totalled $305,175 and were transferred into the trust. In January 1980 the father made a further gift, this time to the trust, in the amount of $100,000. On the date of separation, September 1982, the assets of the trust had a market value of $609,933. ...

The parties agreed that the sum of $224,475 was property "owned on the date of marriage", and was thus a deduction from the calculation of net family property of the wife under s. 4(1). The disagreement arises as to the treatment of the interest of the wife in the future income stream as of the date of separation. The trial judge found that this interest is not "property" within the meaning of s. 4(1). He, therefore, did not have to consider the further question of whether those portions of the income stream attributable to the $71,750 contribution and the $100,000 contribution are "excluded property" under s. 4(2) of the Act. ...

The basic position of the wife is that the scheme of the Act is to divide accumulated assets between the spouses but to leave future income as the basis for any support order. Thus, one should be restrictive in applying the definition of "property" to avoid it being divided twice, once for its capitalized value, and what remains for support. ... Alternatively, if it is property, there is no power in the wife to dispose of it, and it, therefore, has no market value to add to "net family property".

The trial judge found the language of s. 4(1) to be reasonably capable of two interpretations and adopted the construction contended for by the wife as more consistent with the intention of the legislature.

I cannot agree that the subsection raises interpretative doubt on its face. The opening language of s. 4(1) is plain, direct and broad, firmly embracing a present interest in future income from the trust corpus. The arguments put against that plain meaning relate to the consequences flowing from such an interpretation, but, on my analysis, the concerns expressed are either unreal or can be resolved within the general intent of the Act.

Taken from the beginning, the $224,475 was "property" as it came into the marriage, as admitted by the parties, and it never changed its character. It grew through gifts, capital gains, and some reinvestment of income by the wife, but it remained "property". When the trust was settled, the "property" was divided into two portions, the corpus and the income entitlement. The present value of the expectancy of the wife's heirs to the corpus is considerably less stripped of the income and that difference in the value did not disappear; it was retained by the wife as a presently vested entitlement in respect to personal property.

... [T]he life interest in this case is property in itself, and under the particular definition must certainly be a vested interest in the settled estate, which is clearly personal property. Thus, the life interest is itself property, as generally understood, and an interest in property under this definition.

In this case, the interest is a vested one. ...

The words "vested" and "contingent" should, in my view, be read in their legal sense as developed in the law of real property and estates. This legal meaning was succinctly put by MacKinnon L.J. in *Re Legh's Resettlement Trusts*, [1938] Ch. 39 at 52, [1937] 3 All E.R. 823 (C.A.):

> As I understand the rules of law upon such a problem, a future estate or interest is vested when there is a person who has an immediate right to that interest upon the cessation of the present or previous interest. But a future interest is contingent if the person to whom it is limited remains uncertain until the cessation of the previous interest.

A related proposition put forward by the wife is that her interest in this trust cannot be property because, by its terms, it is incapable of being transferred. *Jowitt's Dictionary of English Law*, 2nd ed. (1977), contains this definition of "property" at p. 1447:

> In its largest sense property signifies things and rights considered as having a money value, especially with reference to transfer or succession, and to their capacity of being injured. Property includes not only ownership, estates, and interests in corporeal things, but also rights such as trade marks, copyrights, patents, and rights *in personam* capable of transfer or transmission, such as debts.

Jowitt cannot have intended to exclude from property anything rendered inalienable by choice or agreement. The last three lines of this definition must be taken to mean that the item under consideration be intrinsically capable of transfer. This would exclude personal income because it is inseparable from the personal effort required to attract it; it does not exclude a vested entitlement to income even though it is not marketable. This remains property without a market value, but with a very real value to the owner.

In the present case, the fund of money and investments was originally capable of transfer and was transferred into the trust. Before transfer, it had a value within the marriage, and after transfer, despite the provision as to inalienability, the income entitlement had value within the marriage. Its character as property of a spouse did not change and, sensibly, fits as an item to be shared on dissolution under the philosophy of the Act.

. . . . .

The argument was put that the Act contemplates separating assets for immediate division from income for future support. It is said that any interpretation which puts the present value of income into the assets invites confusion and duplication of benefits. This argument again shows the danger of interpreting language which describes entitlement by looking to potential results. If this income is not part of net family property and remains with the wife, it presents a larger pool of assets for justifying future support payments to the husband, but if divided, it diminishes the justification for any such application. Any court analyzing such an application for support would see the whole picture and exercise its discretion in keeping with the philosophy of the Act — to be even-handed and fair in its treatment of the spouses. Double recovery would be obvious and difficult to justify.

[The court permitted the wife to exclude, under s. 4(2) of the *FLA*, the present value of her right to the trust income attributable to the post-marriage gifts of $71,750 and $100,000. Ultimately, she had to include $263,154 as the value of the right to income from that part of the trust not attributable to those gifts. As noted earlier, she also had a deduction of $224,475 for the value of the bank account at marriage.]

DaCOSTA v. DaCOSTA

(1992), 40 R.F.L. (3d) 216, 1992 CarswellOnt 257 (Ont. C.A.)

LABROSSE J.A.: — This is an appeal by the husband from the judgment of Granger J., dated October 18, 1990, awarding an equalization payment to the wife. The wife cross-appeals for prejudgment interest and costs.

The main issue in this appeal is the husband's interest in the capital of the estate of Henry W. Biddle (the "estate"). The trial judge valued the interest at $596,783. This accounted for a substantial part of the equalization payment. ...

The parties were married on October 17, 1980, and they separated on March 27, 1987.

The husband is 64 years of age. He is the adopted great-grandson of the late Henry W. Biddle, who died in Pennsylvania in 1923, leaving a substantial estate. Until 1972 Pennsylvania did not recognize adopted children for the purpose of testamentary dispositions. The law was changed by the decision of the Supreme Court of Pennsylvania, as a result of which natural and adopted children were accorded equal treatment: *In re Tafel's Estate*, 449 Pa. 442, 296 A.2d 797 (Pa. 1972).

Before this decision the husband had been excluded from any payments from the estate. The change in the law led the trustees of the estate to make an application to include the husband as a beneficiary of the estate. This application was opposed by the husband's two brothers (the natural children). It was rejected at trial but was eventually successful on appeal to the Supreme Court of Pennsylvania. ... As a result, the husband has been sharing in distributions of the estate's income since 1976.

On the death of Henry Biddle's sole surviving grandchild, Isabella Sage, now 87 years of age, the capital of the estate will be distributed among the surviving great-grandchildren.

Husband's Interest in the Capital of the Estate

The husband's position is that the Supreme Court of Pennsylvania dealt only with his right to share in the income of the estate and that the issue of whether he has an interest in the capital of the estate has never been adjudicated. If he should survive Isabella Sage, he will be required to litigate his right to share in the capital of the estate. At the present time he has, at best, a possible right to a contingent interest, that is to say, an interest contingent upon surviving Isabella Sage and upon successfully asserting his right in the Pennsylvania courts to a share of the capital of the estate. Whatever interest he may have is so uncertain that it cannot come within the definition of property. ... From the material before us, it is my understanding that on the death of Isabella Sage, the trustees of the estate will be obliged to file an accounting with the Pennsylvania courts setting out the status of the estate and make recommendations as to who should be entitled to share in the capital or remainder of the estate. Under the law in Pennsylvania, the trustees could not recommend persons other than those who have been sharing the income. Anyone objecting to the trustees' recommendation may file an objection, necessitating a court ruling.

However, if there are objections, it seems clear on the basis of the expert evidence that the husband will overcome them. His interest is not subject to the usual contingency of litigation. It has already been decided that he was a child for the purpose of sharing in the distribution of income. To reach a different conclusion for purposes of the distribution of capital, on the basis of *res judicata* or on the basis that the will expressly excluded an adopted child, would be illogical.

Is the Husband's Interest "Property" under s. 4(1) of the Act?

. . . . .

In my view, the trial judge's conclusion was correct. The husband's interest in the estate is a contingent interest and it is "property" within the definition of s. 4(1).

Lastly, on this issue the husband submits that if his interest in the capital of the estate is found to be "property," it should be substantially discounted. Since, it is contended, he will have to assert a claim to a capital interest in the Pennsylvania courts, whether he will be entitled to any interest, and the amount thereof, is unknown. The trial judge failed to allow any discount in this respect or, further, for the possibility that the husband may predecease Isabella Sage.

I have already dealt with the first part of this argument. The contingency that he will have to assert his claim has not been established, nor is it realistic to doubt that he will succeed if it should prove necessary for him to litigate this question. ...

With respect to the last part of the argument, there was evidence as to the proper discount to apply to account for the possibility of the husband predeceasing Isabella Sage. The trial judge did not deal with this contingency in his reasons, or in his calculations, to arrive at the equalization payment. It is not in dispute that an adjustment must be made. The amounts used by the trial judge for the value of the husband's interest in the capital of the estate were $596,783 as of March 27, 1987 (valuation date), and $179,442 as of October 17, 1980 (date of marriage), for the purpose of deduction under s. 4(1)(b). The parties agree that these amounts should be reduced to $530,730 and $165,135 respectively.

No other discount is applicable. ...

LOWE v. LOWE

(2006), 22 R.F.L. (6th) 438 (Ont. C.A.)

[When a husband separated from his wife in 2004, he was receiving two monthly disability benefits under the *Workman's Compensation Act*, R.S.O. 1980, c. 539. The first was payable for life and the amount was based on the extent to which the workplace injury had impaired the husband's earning capacity. The second was intended to supplement his low income and was payable to age 65.

When the husband and wife could not agree on the appropriate treatment of the husband's benefits in calculating his net family property under the *FLA*, the wife applied for a determination of the issue. The applications judge concluded that the husband's entitlement to receive workers' compensation benefits in the future constituted an interest in property. She also found that this interest did not fall within the exclusions listed in s. 4(2). Accordingly, she held that the capitalized value of the husband's future benefits had to be included in his net family property. The husband appealed.]

SHARPE J.A.: [for the court] ...

11 The issue to be decided on this appeal is whether the entitlement to a future income stream derived from WSIB disability benefits must be capitalized and included in family property. There appears to be no decision of this court dealing directly with the appropriate treatment of disability benefits pursuant to s. 4 of the FLA. There are, however, many trial level decisions dealing with the issue. This extensive body of case law does not follow a consistent line of analysis. However, the result in most cases has been to exclude the capitalized value of disability benefits from family property for equalization purposes, in some cases because these benefits are not "property" or, in cases finding that they are property, because they are excluded as damages. ... For the following reasons, I have concluded that the result reached in the majority of the cases is the correct result and accordingly I would allow the appeal.

12 The definition of "property" in the FLA, s. 4 is admittedly broad. It includes, for example, a stream of income derived from a trust: see *Brinkos v. Brinkos* (1989), 69 O.R. (2d) 225 (C.A.). However, the definition of property is not without limits. In *Pallister v. Pallister* (1990), 29 R.F.L. (3d) 395 (Ont. Gen. Div.), at 404-405, Misener J. acknowledged the apparently "all-encompassing nature of the definition of 'property'" but pointed out that as "property in law is simply a right or collection of rights" identified by "no single criterion or even a discrete number of criteria", interpretation is required to contain the category of property within limits appropriate to achieve the purpose and object of the legislation as a whole:

> It seems to me therefore that when the word appears in legislation defined in the broadest possible way, the limits are to be found through a consideration of the scope of that legislation, and the objects it seeks to accomplish. If the definition of the right or rights as property is consistent with the scheme of the legislation and advances its objects, then it should be so defined. If either of those attributes is absent, then, unless the right or rights under consideration fall within a category that has been legally recognized as property heretofore, it should not be so defined.

13 I agree with this approach. It is consistent with the "modern approach" to statutory interpretation, set out in R. Sullivan, *Sullivan and Driedger on the Construction of Statutes*, 4th ed. (Toronto: Butterworths, 2002) at p. 1 and adopted by the Supreme Court of Canada (see *Bell ExpressVu Ltd. Partnership v. Rex*, [2002] 2 S.C.R. 559 (S.C.C.) at para. 26):

> the words of an Act are to be read in their entire context and in their grammatical and ordinary sense harmoniously with the scheme of the Act, the object of the Act, and the intention of Parliament.

14 As Misener J. put it at 406, this purposive and contextual method of statutory interpretation allows "the courts to insure that the broad definition employed is kept within the bounds of the scope of the Act." In keeping with the "modern" approach to statutory interpretation, s. 4 should not be read as including any and every interest, even those bearing no relationship to the marriage partnership, simply because that interest is not specifically excluded. While the scheme of the FLA is to give a broad definition to property and then exclude certain specific types of property, I agree with Misener J. that the definition of property itself must be given meaningful content and that meaningful content imposes limits on the definition of property limits apart from the specific exclusions. Misener J. held, at 405, that the wife's monthly benefits from an Armed Forces Disability Pension, found on the facts to amount to a permanent pension, were not "property" within the meaning of s. 4:

> The *Family Law Act* purposely eschews any attempt to equalize all the assets owned at the date of separation. Rather it seeks only to equalize the assets the accumulation of which occurred during the marriage, and then only those assets that can fairly be said to bear some relationship to the partnership that the marriage is said to create. Accordingly, there is provision in Section 4(1) for the deduction of the value of property owned on the date of the marriage on the ground that that value was acquired prior to the marriage, and in Section 4(2) for the exclusion of property acquired by gift or inheritance after the date of the marriage and for the exclusion of the right to damages for personal injuries suffered after the date of the marriage, on the ground that the acquisition of that property bears no relationship to the marriage partnership.

15 The disability pension bore no relationship to the marriage partnership but rather arose because of a disability that impeded the recipient's capacity to earn a livelihood. It followed, reasoned Misener J., that the stream of benefits to be received post separation should not be capitalized and included as family property for purposes of equalization. The benefits would be taken into consideration with respect to spousal support, but they fell outside the category of "property" and could be distinguished from a pension earned as part of a spouse's remuneration during the marriage.

16 More recently, in *Hamilton v. Hamilton*, [2005] O.J. No. 3050 (Ont. S.C.J.), Aitken J. reached a similar conclusion with respect to Canada Pension Plan ("CPP") and private insurance disability pensions after a detailed and comprehensive review of the authorities. I find Aitken J.s' analysis compelling and agree with her conclusion that disability benefits should not be considered family property for equalization purposes.

17 I agree with Aitken J.'s statement at para. 113 that "the purpose of the disability payments is to replace in whole or in part the income that the person would have earned had he or she been able to work in the normal course." This makes disability benefits "more comparable to a future income stream based on personal service" than to either a retirement pension plan (explicitly included in family property by s. 4(1)), or to a future stream of payments from a trust (held to constitute property in *Brinkos*). A retirement pension is, as Wilson J. put it in *Clarke v. Clarke*, [1990] 2 S.C.R. 795 (S.C.C.), at 814, "analogous" to a savings account and has value even when not in pay, while a disability plan has value only as income protection in the event of accident or illness. It is true that, in some case, disability benefits may be properly categorized as property in that they are "part and parcel of an overall employee pension benefit plan totally funded by the company": see *McTaggart v. McTaggart* (1993), 50 R.F.L. (3d) 110, ¶19 (Ont. Gen. Div.). Ordinarily, however, disability benefits replace income during the working life of the employee and therefore are appropri-

ately treated as income for purposes of equalization and spousal support. As Aitken J. put it at para 115, "a disability pension is simply the flip side of employment or self-employment income." I adopt Aitken J.'s analysis at para 124:

> Future disability benefits to be paid following the valuation date fall outside the concept of net family property for many reasons. They are paid due to an on-going personal characteristic or condition of a spouse, namely that spouse's state of health and impairment. Entitlement must be earned each day after the valuation date through the disability continuing. In that sense the rights are created on a very current basis, they are not created in advance of the period for which they relate. Entitlement has not gelled as of the valuation date; there is no accumulation of benefits as of that date. Disability benefits are not payable to a spouse due to the joint contributions of both spouses in one form or other to the marriage partnership. Disability benefits are intended to replace income on an on-going basis, as and when the need for such an income replacement arises; they are not intended to be a form of savings available regardless of what the future holds. They exist to support the person who cannot work, and that person's dependents. They are of the same nature as the income that the person would earn, if not disabled. Just as we do not consider that a person owns on the valuation date his or her future employment or self-employment income not yet earned or the ability to earn that income, we should not consider that a person owns on the valuation date his or her future disability payments not yet earned or the inability to earn an income with the concomitant entitlement to receive the disability benefits. We should treat those future disability benefits just as we treat future employment insurance benefits, social assistance benefits, student loans, payments from health care insurance plans and the like. These are all potential income sources that are payable if certain conditions exist. All of these potential income sources following the valuation date will be relevant to the issue of support, just as the earned income of the parties will be relevant to the issue of support.

18 I also agree with the point made by Lally J. in *Mead v. Mead* (1990), 2 O.R. (3d) 49 (Ont. Gen. Div.) (adopted in *Hamilton* at para. 111) that disability benefits are distinguishable from other pensions in that they cannot realistically be valued if not in pay as of valuation day. It would be anomalous to include as property a disability benefit in pay the day before separation but to exclude a disability benefit not in pay until the day after separation. It seems to me that this serves to reinforce the point that disability benefits are, for purposes of family property and support, more readily dealt with as income rather than as property. They should be taken into account in relation to spousal support but excluded from consideration in relation to equalization of family property. ...

24 It might be argued that the husband's permanent disability pension, payable for life, should be included as property as it is a fixed entitlement, apparently not contingent on the husband establishing disability on an on-going basis. I would reject this argument. It seems to me preferable from the perspective of clarity and predictability to treat all disability benefits the same whether they are calculated strictly in terms of lost income or as compensation for impairment to earning capacity. However, as I have already indicated, disability payments that form part and parcel of an employee pension benefit plan may be on a different footing. In the end, the central point is that disability benefits represent income replacement and, from the perspective of family property and spousal support, are more appropriately treated on the same basis as income for employment.

NOTES AND QUESTIONS

1. As the *Brinkos* and *DaCosta* cases indicate, beneficial interests in express trusts are clearly property within the definition of s. 4(1). It is also implicit in the reasoning of the Supreme Court in *Rawluk v. Rawluk* (1990), 23 R.F.L. (3d) 337 (reproduced below) that a beneficial interest under a resulting trust is property for the calculation of a spouse's net family property. On the other hand, a spouse who is a trustee does not generally have a property interest that has value even though he or she has the legal interest in the property. For example, in *Skrlj v. Skrlj* (1986), 2 R.F.L. (3d) 305 (Ont. H.C.), the wife held money in two bank accounts for her children. None of it was included in her net family property.

2. Does the decision in *Lowe v. Lowe* cast doubt on the holdings in the *DaCosta* case? After all, it might be argued that the husband's interest in the Biddle estate in *DaCosta v. DaCosta* "bore no relationship to the marriage partnership". Or did the Ontario Court of Appeal in *Lowe v. Lowe* intend to limit this qualification to an assessment of those interests that traditionally have not been labeled "property"?

3. The Ontario Court of Appeal distinguished the *Lowe v. Lowe* case in *Maphangoh v. Maphangoh* (2007), 39 R.F.L. (6th) 46 (Ont. C.A.) where a husband, at the age of 56, became entitled to a disability pension under the federal government's pension plan about six years after he left the civil service. Absent the disability, the husband would have had to wait until he reached 60 before being entitled to an unreduced pension. At trial, the husband was already past that age. Although the benefits were still labeled as payable under a disability plan, the trial judge concluded that the husband's future entitlement had "the attributes of a retirement pension and is not a disability pension or disability income" and was, therefore, "property" within the meaning of the *FLA*. The Ontario Court of Appeal agreed, noting: "The disability pension was, in essence, an entitlement to take early retirement without penalty." It also pointed out that only the value of the pension entitlement at age 60 was included in the husband's net family property.

4. Many interests are considered "property" for the purposes of determining a spouse's net family property under the *FLA*. Pensions, Registered Retirement Savings Plans (RRSPs), retirement allowances, entitlement to compensation for unused sick days, stock options, interests in discretionary trusts, milk quotas, entitlement to a pay equity award covering a period before the valuation date, interests in discretionary trusts, entitlement to severance pay referable to compensation for lost wages during cohabitation, and the right to receive future payments under a non-competition agreement have all been valued and included in the equalization calculation.

5. In *Arvai v. Arvai* (2001), 14 R.F.L. (5th) 223, the Ontario Court of Appeal confirmed that the correct approach under the *FLA* is to include the value of all non-excluded assets owned by a spouse in the determination of his or her NFP. The trial judge had removed a GMC pickup truck from the calculation of the husband's NFP, but had required him to pay one-half of the proceeds that he had received from the sale of the truck after the valuation date to his wife. On appeal, Simmons J.A. stated (at para. 27):

> Given that the GMC pickup was owned on the date of separation, the correct method of accounting for its value would have been to include it in the equalization calculation. Errors in applying the equalization provisions ... can occur when assets are dealt with in isolation. For example, had Mr. Arvai's net family property, excluding the 1989 GMC pickup, been deemed to be zero because it amounted to a negative figure, treating the vehicle separately could have resulted in an error. While it is generally preferable not to depart from the scheme of computation prescribed by the *Family Law Act*, it does not constitute reversible error to deal separately with an asset omitted from the equalization calculation where doing so does not ultimately give rise to an error in that calculation. ... In this case, no such error has been demonstrated. The trial judge did not therefore err in requiring Mr. Arvai to account separately for half of these proceeds.

In practice, a spouse's credits under the Canada Pension Plan are generally ignored in the calculation of the equalization claim even though they are valuable property interests: Justice Aston in *Bennett v. Bennett* (2003), 46 R.F.L. (5th) 256, ¶68 (Ont. S.C.J.). This is because the legislation governing the CPP mandates an equal division of the credits built up by the spouses during their relationship. A proposed amendment to s. 4(2) of the *FLA* contained in Bill 133 (not yet proclaimed) would ensure that this practice is sanctioned by statute.

6. In *Ross v. Ross* (2006), 34 R.F.L. (6th) 229 (Ont. C.A.), the husband, at separation on August 31, 2001, held 175,000 stock options of the corporation that employed him. On December 12, 2001, the Board of Directors granted the husband an additional 245,000 options (the "December 2001 options") in appreciation of his efforts and in light of the corporation's positive performance in the past year. The husband exercised the December 2001 options in January and April 2005, realizing a net after-tax capital gain of $652,313.00. In determining the husband's net family property, the trial judge concluded that the value of 2/3 of the December 2001 options should be included in addition to the value of the 175,000 options that the husband already held at separation. She reasoned that these options were granted to the husband for work done during 2001 and that 2/3 of them had been earned before separation.

The husband's appeal was dismissed, Justice Borins dissenting. Justice Rouleau, O'Connor A.C.J.O. concurring, reasoned that employee stock options were employment related benefits that ought to be included in a spouse's net family property if, on the valuation date, the spouse had earned the right to the options. In each case, it had to be determined whether, as at the date of separation, the spouse was entitled as of right to stock options that were only conferred later or whether the benefit received after the separation was *ex gratia*. The answer to this question would depend on the evidence and, specifically, how the benefit arrangements were structured. In this case, although the granting of stock options was discretionary, Justice Rouleau noted that the employer had fairly regularly issued options to the husband. This suggested that what had started as a discretionary benefit had become an integral part of the husband's employment compensation. There was, therefore, an evidentiary basis for the trial judge's finding that a substantial portion of the December 2001 stock options related to work carried out by the husband prior to the date of separation.

Justice Rouleau added that, although the trial judge did not put it this way, her inclusion of a portion of the December 2001 options in the husband's net family property could be interpreted as meaning that, as of the date of separation, the husband had earned 2/3 of the as yet non-issued stock options and that, on a balance of probabilities, he was entitled as of right to that benefit. In other words he was, within the meaning of s. 4(1) of the *FLA*, the owner of property that consisted of a right to receive those earned stock options. Justice Rouleau stated that this finding was available to the trial judge on the evidence and, in the circumstances, best achieved the *FLA*'s primary goal of ensuring that each spouse received a fair share of the net financial gain during the relationship.

In his dissent, Justice Borins stressed that an asset that did not exist on the valuation date could not form part of a spouse's net family property. This was so even if a subsequently acquired asset was connected in some manner to a spouse's employment during the marriage. Justice Borins noted that the husband did not own the December 2001 options on the valuation date. Indeed, they did not exist on that date. Nor did the husband have a right on the valuation date to receive any additional options from his employer. At most, Justice Borins stated, the husband had an expectation that the Board of Directors would later exercise their discretion to give him an unspecified number of stock options.

See also *Patterson v. Patterson* (2006), 36 R.F.L. (6th) 268 (Ont. S.C.J.); additional reasons at (2007), 38 R.F.L. (6th) 434 (Ont. S.C.J.) where a husband received a bonus from his employer, CIBC, over three months after the valuation date. Nonetheless, Justice McLaren held that 2/3 of the after-tax value of the bonus should be included in the husband's net family property. What property interest, if any, did the husband own on the valuation date in relation to the bonus? For a critical analysis of the case, see Franks, "Case Comment on *Patterson v. Patterson*" (2007), 36 R.F.L. (6th) 326.

CARATUN v. CARATUN

(1992), 42 R.F.L. (3d) 113, 1992 CarswellOnt 287 (Ont. C.A.); leave to appeal refused (1993), 46 R.F.L. (3d) 314 (note) (S.C.C.)

McKINLAY J.A.: — ...

Contribution towards the Obtaining of Appellant's Dental Licence

The reasons of the trial judge make it quite clear that Dr. Caratun's primary objective in marrying Mrs. Caratun and fathering their child was to assist him in immigrating to North America to practise dentistry. Mrs. Caratun worked extremely hard over a number of years in Israel and in Canada to assist Dr. Caratun in attaining his ultimate objective. Two days after [he learned that he had passed his final exam and was qualified to practise dentistry in Ontario], he rejected Mrs. Caratun as his wife, at a time when family assets were next to non-existent but his future income-earning ability was substantial.

Facts such as these raise difficult legal questions, given the purpose of the F.L.A., on the one hand, and its specific provisions, on the other. The combining of spousal efforts over a number of years to provide for the education and professional qualification of one spouse is not unusual in our society. The inevitable result, if there is a separation on attaining the joint objective, is that one family member is left with no assets and often very little in the way of educational or professional qualifications with which to sustain herself or himself in the future. The extreme unfairness of the situation is patent, but the possibility of a legal remedy is far from settled law.

Dental Licence as "Property"

Mrs. Caratun's position at trial, which was accepted by the trial judge, was that Dr. Caratun's dental licence is property within the meaning of that word as defined in s. 4(1) of the F.L.A. ...

That definition is broadly framed, and includes all conceivable types of property in the traditional common law sense. However, it does not, by its terms, extend the meaning of property beyond those limits. The contrary argument is that in construing that definition one must keep in mind the F.L.A. policy of marriage partnership, which requires, on final separation, the equal division of wealth accumulated during the marriage; and that a licence to practise a particular profession constitutes wealth in the matrimonial context.

Two important cases at the trial level have reached opposite conclusions on this issue — the trial decision in this case and the decision of Killeen L.J.S.C. in *Linton v. Linton* (1988), 11 R.F.L. (3d) 444, 29 E.T.R. 14, 64 O.R. (2d) 18, 49 D.L.R. (4th) 278 (H.C.). Both decisions include detailed and thoughtful analyses of this issue, and substantial reference to authorities, both Canadian and American. The American decisions are so varied as to be of little assistance. Although all purport to be based on the wording of the particular statute involved, they reach varying results based on statutes with very similar wording.

In determining the issue of whether a professional licence constitutes "property," the cases and the numerous articles written on the subject concentrate primarily on two aspects of the problem: first, the nature or characterization of a licence, and, second, the difficulty of valuing a licence in the family property context.

(i) Characterization of Licence

The broad definition of property in the F.L.A. clearly encompasses many forms of intangibles — a classification into which a licence must fall if it is to be considered property. The common law has never had any difficulty in dealing with property evidenced by pieces of paper representing bundles of rights — such as a share certificate with its attendant rights to dividends, voting privileges, and distribution of assets on corporate dissolution. If a licence to practise a profession is property, what are its attendant rights? Apart from possible benefits, such as the right to join professional groups and clubs — which are not relevant in this context — the only real right conferred on the holder of the licence is a right to work in a particular profession. That right, assuming it is held at the time of separation, is a present right to work in the future, and it will continue for as long as the holder of the right is professionally and personally able to perform the activity involved. It is the nature of the right given by the licence which, in my view, causes insurmountable difficulties in treating such a licence as property for matrimonial purposes. Those difficulties arise, first, because it is not a right which is transferable; second, because it requires the personal efforts of the holder in order to be of any value in the future; and, third, because the only difference between such a licence and any other right to work is in its exclusivity.

(a) Non-transferability

One of the traditional indicia of property is its inherent transferability. That transferability may, of course, be precluded either by law or by contract. In contrast, the right or licence to practise a particular profession is, by its very nature, a right personal to the holder, incapable of transfer. It is very different in nature from the professional practice which may be built up by the licensee after attaining the licence. The practice itself is clearly capable of transfer for value, although the market is limited to other licensees. Where spouses separate before a practice has been built up, there is nothing available for transfer. ...

It is clear that many rights or things which are restrained from transfer by law are, by agreement or otherwise, inherently transferable and are of value to their owners. Such rights or things fall within the normal legal definition of property, and would clearly fall within the statutory definition of property in the F.L.A. However, rights or things which are inherently non-transferable, such as the right to practise a profession, clearly do not constitute property in any traditional sense.

(b) Requirement of Personal Efforts of the Licensee

Under the F.L.A. the types of property included in the statutory definition are very broad-ranging. The definition is in the F.L.A. for the purpose of determining the value of the property to be included in arriving at "net family property" to be equalized under s. 5. I see no way in which that definition can be interpreted to include work to be performed by either spouse in the future. It goes without saying that without the personal efforts of the licensee, the licence will produce nothing. The only provisions in the F.L.A. that allow one spouse to share in the fruits of the other spouse's future labours are the support provisions, which do not form a part of the equalization payment under s. 5.

The policy of the F.L.A. emphasizes principles of partnership during marriage, and self-sufficiency following its termination. When the marriage ends, the partnership ends. Placing a value on future labours of either spouse for purposes of the equalization payment would frustrate those policy objectives.

(c) Right To Work in General

The only difference between a professional licence and the ability and right of any individual to perform a particular type of work is in the exclusive nature of a professional licence. Only those who have successfully survived the rigors of professional training have the right to practise their profession. Nonetheless, the difference between the right to practise a profession and the right to work at any job which requires special skill or knowledge is a right which differs only in scope, but not in substance. A plumber, carpenter, or an electrician spends a substantial period of time in apprenticeship before becoming proficient at his trade; a salesman spends a substantial period of time developing a clientele in order to enhance his income; a business executive may spend a substantial period of time in university and then working his way up the corporate ladder to attain his level of income. Should the law consider all of these attainments as property for the purposes of determining the equalization payment under the F.L.A.? Clearly not. I see no interpretation of the F.L.A., either specifically under s. 4, or generally, which would allow the court to treat such attainments as property.

(ii) Valuation of Licence

It is clear from the considerations referred to above that there are substantial difficulties, both practical and conceptual, in treating licences as "property." In addition, the valuation of such a right would be unfairly speculative in the matrimonial context. A myriad of contingencies, including inclination, probability of success in practice of the profession, length of physical and mental capability to perform the duties of the profession, competition within the profession, and many others, all render a fair valuation of the licence unusually difficult. But a further potential inequity arises: support orders may be varied if circumstances change, but no amendment of an equalization payment is possible regardless of changed circumstances.

The valuation approach approved by the trial judge in this case was to compare the appellant's actual professional income since attaining his dental licence up to September 1986 with the average earnings of an honours university graduate of the same age during the same period. His future professional income from 1986 until his expected retirement age of 65 was determined, based on his actual income level adjusted by the rate of growth of income for dentists according to the American Dental Association. The difference between his projected future earnings and those of honours graduates was valued at an annual discount rate of 2.5 per cent according to the *Rules of Civil Procedure*. Based on this approach, a valuation of the dental licence as of valuation date, July 18, 1981 was found to be $379,965. This valuation did not take into account any of the contingencies of the type referred to above. Another method of valuation, which resulted in the figure of $219,346, was to compare the expected career earnings of the average dentist obtaining his licence in July 1981 and retiring in November 2013, to the average earnings of honours university graduates for the same period.

Either valuation approach is logical, if the licence is "property." However, it would be equally logical to treat a university degree as property, and then value that degree by comparing incomes of university graduates with those of high school graduates. In the matrimonial context, the fallacy lies in treating a licence as property on valuation date, when most of its value depends on the personal labour of the licensed spouse after the termination of the relationship. That future labour does not constitute anything earned or existing at the valuation date.

For all of the above reasons, it is my view that a professional licence does not constitute property within the meaning of s. 4 of the F.L.A. ...

Unequal Division of Net Family Assets

The trial judge considered a possible method of compensating Mrs. Caratun would be to order an unequal division of net family assets pursuant to s. 5(6), treating the respondent's contribution to her husband's professional training as a "circumstance relating to the acquisition, disposition, preservation, maintenance or improvement of property." Since I am of the view that the licence does not constitute property within the F.L.A., an unequal division of net family property would not solve this dilemma, as the parties had accumulated next to nothing in the way of family assets at the date of separation.

Compensatory Support

The partnership theory of marriage espoused by the F.L.A. and any ordinary sense of fairness require that some form of compensation be afforded the respondent in this case for her substantial contribution towards the career aspirations of her husband. The need for a remedy is made even more pronounced in this case because Dr. Caratun separated from his wife immediately upon obtaining his licence. Nonetheless, any such remedy must be provided in accordance with the provisions of the relevant statutory provisions.

... [I]n this case the applicable legislation is the corollary relief provisions of s. 11(1) of the *Divorce Act*, S.C. 1967-68, c. 24, R.S.C. 1970, c. D-8 (the "old *Divorce Act*") ... [The section gave a broad discretion to the courts to order spousal support if they thought it "fit and just to do so" in light of the "conduct ... condition, means and other circumstances" of the spouses.] The wording in the old *Divorce Act* is somewhat different from the wording of the support provisions of the F.L.A. However, s. 11(1) is expressed in broad terms and encompasses all of the relevant factors outlined under the provisions of the F.L.A.

In this case it is clear from the facts found by the trial judge that the respondent made a significant contribution to the marriage relationship, and more particularly to the ability of the appellant to attain his dental licence. Although the evidence did not disclose the dollar terms of the economic consequences of the relationship to Mrs. Caratun, it is clear that she gave up the practice of her profession in Israel and came to this country, where she worked as a waitress and hairdresser, to assist her husband to attain his professional objective. Mrs. Caratun sacrificed, or at least delayed, her personal career advancement to assist her husband in furthering his. Both of their future lives were affected substantially as a result. His income-earning ability and future prospects have been enhanced significantly. While she is not destitute, her income-earning ability and future prospects have been diminished significantly.

I am of the view that a compensatory support order pursuant to s. 11(1) of the old *Divorce Act* is appropriate in this case. The trial judge took all of the relevant factors into consideration in arriving at the amount of $30,000, which she considered an appropriate amount to reflect the respondent's contribution to the obtaining of the appellant's dental licence, and awarded that amount in a lump sum. I see no reason to disturb that decision.

NOTES AND QUESTIONS

1. Do you find the reasoning in *Caratun v. Caratun* convincing? For a critical comment on the case, see McCallum, "*Caratun v. Caratun*: It Seems That We Are not All Realists Yet" (1994), 1 Can. J. Women & Law 197.

(ii) Ownership

RAWLUK v. RAWLUK

(1990), 23 R.F.L. (3d) 337, 1990 CarswellOnt 217, 1990 CarswellOnt 987 (S.C.C.)

[Jacqueline Rawluk claimed a beneficial one-half interest in a number of assets in her husband's name by way of a remedial constructive trust because she wanted to share in the post-valuation date increase in value of the assets. It was common ground that, but for the equalization of net family properties available under the *FLA*, Mrs. Rawluk's direct and indirect contributions to the acquisition of these properties would have warranted the imposition of a constructive trust. However, the husband argued that this avenue of redress had been foreclosed by the enactment of Part I of the *FLA*. The trial judge awarded Mrs. Rawluk a one-half interest in the contested properties and the Ontario Court of Appeal affirmed that decision. The Supreme Court of Canada dismissed the husband's further appeal in a 4-3 decision.]

CORY J. (DICKSON C.J.C., WILSON and L'HEUREUX-DUBÉ JJ. concurring): — At issue in this appeal is whether the doctrine of constructive trust can be applied to determine the ownership of assets of married spouses under the provisions of the *Family Law Act, 1986*, S.O. 1986, c. 4.

[After a discussion of the history of constructive trust and of the major Canadian cases, Cory J. continued:]

These cases show that in Canada the doctrine of remedial constructive trust has been accepted for almost a decade as an important remedial device whose prime function is to remedy situations of unjust enrichment. It is clear that at the time that the *Family Law Act, 1986*, was enacted, the constructive trust was widely recognized as the pre-eminent common law remedy for ensuring the equitable division of matrimonial property. The validity and importance of the remedy designed, as it is, to achieve a measure of fairness between married persons and those in a marital relationship, must have been well known to the framers of the legislation. It would seem unlikely that they would, without a precise and specific reference, deprive parties of access to such an equitable remedy. ...

In my view, far from abolishing the constructive trust doctrine, the *Family Law Act, 1986*, incorporates the constructive trust remedy as an integral part of the process of ownership determination and equalization established by that Act.

Provisions of the *Family Law Act, 1986*, which Indicate that the Constructive Trust Doctrine should Continue to Play a Role in Determining the Assets of Spouses and their Division

It is trite but true to state that as a general rule a legislature is presumed not to depart from prevailing law "without expressing its intentions to do so with irresistible clearness" (*Goodyear Tire & Rubber Co. v. T. Eaton Co.*, [1956] S.C.R. 610 at 614, 56 D.T.C. 1060, 4 D.L.R. (2d) 1). But even aside from this presumption, when the structure of the *Family Law Act, 1986*, is examined and the ramifications of a number of its provisions are studied, it becomes apparent that the Act recognizes and accommodates the remedial constructive trust.

At the outset, the Act's preamble recognizes not only the need for the "orderly and equitable settlement of the affairs of the spouses", but also "the equal position of spouses as individuals within marriage" and the fact that marriage is a "form of partnership". These fundamental objectives are furthered by the use of the constructive trust remedy in appropriate circumstances. It provides a measure of individualized justice and fairness which is essential for the protection of marriage as a partnership of equals. Thus the preamble itself is sufficient to warrant the retention and application of this remedy.

In addition, various provisions of the Act lead to the same conclusion.

(a) Sections 4 and 5

Sections 4 and 5 of the *Family Law Act, 1986*, create a two-step property division process that emphasizes the distinction between the determination of legal and equitable ownership and the equalization of net family property. These sections require a court first to determine individual "ownership piles" and then to equalize the spouses' assets by ordering the spouse with the larger ownership pile to pay money to the spouse with the smaller pile.

Before property can be equalized under s. 5 of the *Family Law Act, 1986*, a court is required by s. 4 to determine the "net family property" of each spouse. Under s. 4(1) this is defined as "the value of all the property ... that a spouse owns on the valuation date". "Property" is defined in the same subsection as "any interest, present or future, vested or contingent, in real or personal property". This all-encompassing definition is wide enough to include not only legal but beneficial ownership. The appellant has conceded that "property" as defined under s. 4(1) includes a beneficial interest arising from an express or resulting trust. I see no reason why the remedial constructive trust should not be included in the list of equitable principles or remedies that may be used to calculate the beneficial ownership of net family property.

It is important in this respect to keep in mind that a property interest arising under a constructive trust can be recognized as having come into existence not when the trust is judicially declared but from the time when the unjust enrichment first arose. ...

... As a result, even if it is declared by a court after the parties have already separated, a constructive trust can be deemed to have arisen when the duty to make restitution arose. It should therefore be considered as part of the property owned by the beneficiary at valuation date.

(b) Section 5(6)

Section 5(6) of the *Family Law Act, 1986*, allows a court to "award a spouse an amount that is more or less than half the difference between the net family properties if the court is of the opinion that equalizing the net family properties would be unconscionable". The Court of Appeal observed that if a post-valuation date increase or decrease in property values is significant enough to render a simple equalization unconscionable, a court might utilize s. 5(6) to remedy the resultant inequities. I need not and do not express any opinion as to whether s. 5(6) could be used in that way or whether the Court of Appeal's observation is correct. I have assumed solely for the purposes of argument that s. 5(6) might be available in some cases as an alternative remedy for dealing with post-valuation date changes in value. Even so, the section does not have the effect of supplanting the constructive trust remedy. The constructive trust is used in the matrimonial property context to allocate proprietary interests, a function that is totally distinct from the process of determining how the value of matrimonial property should be distributed under the equalization process.

Under the Act a court is, as a first step, required to determine the ownership interests of the spouses. It is at that stage that the court must deal with and determine the constructive trust claims. The second step that must be taken is to perform the equalization calculations. Once this is done, a court must assess whether, given the facts of the particular case, equalization is unconscionable. The s. 5(6) analysis, even if it could be considered, would be a third step — a last avenue of judicial discretion which might be used in order to bring a measure of flexibility to the equalization process. This step in the process, if it could be used, would have to be kept distinct from the preliminary determinations of ownership.

(c) Section 10

Section 10 of the *Family Law Act, 1986*, reinforces the Act's emphasis on the importance of individual ownership, even within a regime of deferred sharing. This section allows a spouse to apply to a court to determine a question of ownership or possession prior to equalization, and thus to assert some degree of control over matrimonial property during cohabitation. ...

The creation under s. 10 of a proprietary remedy that can be commenced during cohabitation provides further evidence that the Ontario legislature could not have intended the provisions of the *Family Law Act, 1986*, to completely supersede the remedial constructive trust. Section 10 enables non-titled spouses to assert control over matrimonial property during cohabitation to the extent that their beneficial interests entitle them to do so. Even if the appellant's argument that the *Family Law Act, 1986*, equalization provisions replace the constructive trust remedy were to be accepted, this would not prevent a deserving spouse from obtaining a declaration of constructive trust in his or her spouse's property during cohabitation pursuant to s. 10. Certainly such an application will not necessarily be followed by separation and equalization of property.

Since a spouse can thus obtain a constructive trust remedy prior to separation, it would be inconsistent to deny a spouse the same remedy when it is sought after a separation. To take such a position would encourage spouses to apply for a constructive trust interest early in a marriage, perhaps thereby creating unnecessary marital stress, fostering costly litigation and penalizing those spouses who waited until separation to enforce their common law rights. It is unlikely that the legislature intended a spouse's rights to depend on whether or not a constructive trust had been declared before or after the separation.

(d) Section 14

... The appellant argues that the provisions of s. 14 expressly preserve the doctrine of resulting trust and by implication abolish all other non-express trusts. I cannot accept that contention. Section 14 is, I believe, intended not to specifically preserve but rather to modify the resulting trust doctrine as it applies in the context of the *Family Law Act, 1986*. If anything, the combination of these modifying provisions and the legislature's silence on the subject of remedial constructive trust supports the view that the constructive trust is maintained in an unmodified form.

Conclusion

The review of the cases decided by this court from *Murdoch v. Murdoch* ... to *Sorochan v. Sorochan* ... demonstrates the importance that has been attached to the use of the remedy of constructive trust to achieve a division of property that is as just and equitable as possible. A marital relationship is founded on love and trust. It brings together two people who strive and sacrifice to attain common goals for the benefit of both partners. When it is terminated and acquired assets are to be divided, then in this of all relationships the concept of fairness should predominate in making decisions as to ownership. This was the fundamental equitable principle underlying the application of the constructive trust remedy to matrimonial cases. Where the application of the principle would achieve the goal of fairness it should not be discarded unless the pertinent legislation makes it clear that the principle is to be disregarded.

The *Family Law Act, 1986*, does not constitute an exclusive code for determining the ownership of matrimonial property. The legislators must have been aware of the existence and effect of the constructive trust remedy in matrimonial cases when the Act was proposed. Yet neither by direct reference nor by necessary implication does the Act prohibit the use of the constructive trust remedy. Indeed, the foregoing review of the provisions of the Act supports the view that the constructive trust remedy is to be maintained. The Act's two-step structure and its individual provisions indicate that the constructive trust remedy still has an important role to play in the determination of matrimonial property disputes in Ontario. The application of the remedy in the context of the *Family Law Act, 1986*, can achieve a fair and just result. It enables the courts to bring that treasured and essential measure of individualized justice and fairness to the more generalized process of equalization provided by the Act. That vital fairness is achieved by means of a constructive trust remedy and recognition of ownership.

In this case fairness requires that the dedication and hard work of Jacqueline Rawluk in acquiring and maintaining the properties in issue be recognized. The equitable remedy of constructive trust was properly applied.

McLACHLIN J. (dissenting) (LA FOREST and SOPINKA JJ. concurring): — ... It is not disputed that apart from the statute, this would be an appropriate case for the court to declare a constructive trust entitling the wife to a half interest in the property. This leaves the question of whether the *Family Law Act, 1986*, changes the situation.

The answer to this question depends on the answer to two sub-issues. The first concerns the nature of the doctrine of constructive trust. Is it a concept of substantive property law, automatically vesting in the wife a half interest in the property at the time of separation? Or is it a remedial device, to be applied only where other remedies for unjust enrichment are unavailable or inadequate?

If the doctrine of constructive trust is a remedial device, the further question arises of whether the doctrine should be applied where a statute already provides a remedy for the alleged unjust enrichment.

As I see the problem, the issue in this case is not whether the *Family Law Act, 1986,* ousts the remedy of constructive trust. I agree with Cory J. that it does not. In my view, the real question which must be answered is whether the doctrine of constructive trust, as it has been developed by this court, finds application where a statute already provides a remedy for the unjust enrichment complained of.

III. Decision on the Issues

I would answer the questions posed above as follows:

1.   The doctrine of constructive trust, as it has developed in Canada, is not a property right but a proprietary remedy for unjust enrichment; as such, the availability of other remedies for the unjust enrichment must be considered before declaring a constructive trust.

2.   The doctrine of constructive trust should not be applied in this case because the *Family Law Act, 1986,* provides a remedy for the unjust enrichment of the husband to the detriment of the wife.

. . . . .

This case poses the question of whether the doctrine of constructive trust should be applied where there exists a comprehensive statutory scheme providing a remedy for the situation where one spouse holds exclusive title to property to which the other spouse has contributed.

The *Family Law Act, 1986,* sets up a comprehensive statutory scheme which recognizes the contributions of both spouses to the acquisition, preservation, maintenance or improvement of property during the marriage. It addresses the question of unjust enrichment between spouses by providing for a monetary equalization payment based on the value of the "net family property" at the valuation date, i.e., the time of separation (s. 5(1)). ...

The question may be put thus: given that there was an unjust enrichment arising from the fact that the property to which the wife contributed was in the husband's name, does the *Family Law Act, 1986,* provide a remedy, which makes it unnecessary to resort to the doctrine of constructive trust? In my opinion, the answer to this question must be affirmative.

Both the statutory remedy and the remedy of constructive trust are, on the facts of this case, directed to the same end. The purpose of a constructive trust, as already discussed, is to permit a party without title to receive compensation for his or her contribution to the acquisition and maintenance of property standing in the other's name. The purpose of the *Family Law Act, 1986,* is the same: it sets up a scheme to equalize the property holdings of each party to a marriage, regardless of who holds legal title. The only difference for the purposes of this case is that the *Family Law Act, 1986,* provides for the equalization to be accomplished by a payment of money based on the value of the property at the time of separation (a remedy *in personam*), while the doctrine of constructive trust would give a beneficial interest in the land which persists to the date of trial (a proprietary remedy).

If the doctrine of unjust enrichment is to be applied in this case, it is not for the purpose of rewarding the wife for her contribution to the property held in the husband's name, but for the purpose of permitting her to share in the increase in value of the property after separation. But this cannot support a claim for a constructive trust for two reasons.

First, the Act contemplates the problem that assets may increase or diminish in value between the date of separation and trial; s. 5(6)(h) permits the trial judge to vary the equal division of property as at separation, on the basis of circumstances relating to the disposition or improvement of the property. I agree with Cory J. that this step of the process is distinct from the preliminary determinations of ownership.

Second, it would appear that the elements necessary to establish a constructive trust are not present where the enrichment occurs as a result of appreciation of the market value of the land after separation. Under the statute, the wife already receives a payment sufficient to give her 50 per cent of the family property, valued at the date of separation. There is no unjust enrichment there. What then of the fact that because of delays in obtaining judgment, the value of the property held in the hands of the husband increases pending trial? True, this is an enrichment of the husband. But there is no corresponding deprivation to the wife giving rise to an injustice. The husband is not being enriched at her expense or because of her efforts. In these circumstances, the first two requirements of a constructive trust posited in *Pettkus v. Becker* — unjust enrichment of one party and corresponding deprivation of the other — are absent.

In the final analysis, the *Family Law Act, 1986*, provides complete compensation for the wife's contribution to the date of separation. Any disproportionate enrichment must occur because of the increase in value due to changing market conditions after that date. But that does not constitute an unjust enrichment under the principles set forth in *Pettkus v. Becker*, given that the wife made no contribution after that date. As a matter of legal principle, the legislature having provided a remedy for the unjust enrichment which would otherwise have occurred in this case, it is not for this court to impose an additional equitable remedy aimed at correcting the same wrong.

I add that application of the remedy of constructive trust to the statutory scheme may pose practical problems. The scheme under the Act is relatively clear and simple; the basic rule is equality between the spouses, an equality effected by an equalization payment from one spouse to the other, based on the value of the property at the valuation date, usually the date of separation. In most cases the parties can ascertain without difficulty what payment must be made, thereby settling their affairs without lengthy litigation. Grafting the remedy of constructive trust on to this scheme would add uncertainty and promote litigation featuring detailed inquiries into how much each party contributed to the acquisition, preservation, maintenance and improvement of the property to the end of having the court declare a constructive trust in one of the parties. Moreover, property rights which third parties have acquired in the interval may be adversely affected. One returns to Professor Water's warning that to employ constructive trust where personal remedies suffice threatens to upset the operation of other doctrines.

One must also consider the converse situation to that of this case — the situation where instead of increasing in value after separation, the property loses value. Is the amount recoverable by the spouse lacking title to be diminished accordingly? One judge has said yes, imposing a beneficial constructive interest in the property on the wife as at separation, against her wishes and at the behest of the husband: *McDonald v. McDonald* (1988), 11 R.F.L. (3d) 321, 28 E.T.R. 81 (Ont. H.C.). So we arrive at the anomaly of the equitable remedy of constructive trust being applied against the wishes of the party found to have been unfairly treated, at the behest of the party who has been unjustly enriched. What does this leave of the maxim that he who seeks the aid of equity must come with clean hands? The fallacy at the root of such an approach is that of treating the *remedy* of constructive trust as though it were a *property interest*, which for the sake of consistency must be imposed regardless of the circumstances or of other remedies. ...

V. Conclusion

I would set aside the judgments of the Court of Appeal and the trial judge, and refer the matter back to the trial judge to determine whether an adjustment should be made under s. 5(6)(h) of the *Family Law Act, 1986*, to reflect the increase in value of the land held in the husband's name since separation, and to adjust the amount of the equalization payment due to the wife, on the basis that she is not entitled to a constructive trust vesting her with a beneficial half interest in the property as at the date of separation.

NOTES AND QUESTIONS

1. Under the *FLA*, aside from extraordinary circumstances that might be brought within s. 5(6) (discussed later in this chapter), the quantity and quality of spousal contributions to the marriage partnership are non-issues. Does *Rawluk v. Rawluk* once again establish the importance of contributions — their quantity, quality, value, connection to property, etc. — even on marriage breakdown?

2. Part I of the *FLA* is designed to operate with limited judicial discretion. The continued relevance of the constructive trust introduces flexibility, but it does so by increasing judicial discretion. Do you agree with Justice Cory's statement in the *Rawluk* case that "a measure of individualized justice and fairness ... is essential for the protection of marriage as a partnership of equals"? Can this flexibility be provided by s. 5(6) of the *FLA*?

3. In cases such as *Sorochan* and *Peter v. Beblow* (reproduced earlier in this chapter), the Supreme Court of Canada stressed that the constructive trust was a remedy and not a substantive property right. Professor Farquhar observes in "Unjust Enrichment — Special Relationship — Domestic Services — Remedial Constructive Trust: *Peter v. Beblow*" (1993), 72 Can. Bar Rev. 538 at 550-551:

> The chief implication of this position is that, because it is remedial, it cannot arise until a court has made the appropriate ruling. Thus, unless the court exercises a discretion to make the order retroactive, third-party dealings with the property in question, prior to the order, may place the plaintiff at risk. If, by contrast, the constructive trust is seen as substantive, it would arise at the moment of the unjust enrichment and the plaintiff would thereafter be protected by its proprietary nature. The truly remedial nature of the constructive trust following unjust enrichment seemed to be cemented by the decision in *LAC Minerals Ltd. v. International Corona Resources Ltd.*, [1989] 2 S.C.R. 574, and as a result the decision in *Rawluk v. Rawluk* came as a surprise.

4. In "*Rawluk v. Rawluk*: What Are the Limits of the Remedial Constructive Trust?" (1990), 9 Can. J. Fam. L. 152, Professor Sheppard suggests that there is a middle ground between the views adopted by Justices Cory and McLachlin in *Rawluk v. Rawluk* (at 161):

> Cory J. took the view that the enactment of the statutory regime for marital property did not affect the availability of the remedial constructive trust. He seemed to say that courts should grant a remedial constructive trust to any spouse who applies and is entitled to it, because it is more just and equitable than the statutory scheme. On the other hand, McLachlin J. went to the opposite extreme; in her view, a court should never grant a remedial constructive trust over a family asset to a spouse who also has a remedy by way of an equalization payment under the Act. The courts should keep the remedial constructive trust only for a party who is not entitled to an equalization payment.
>
> Another approach may be worth considering, because it reconciles the two views, and is consistent with the result in *Rawluk v. Rawluk* and with other authorities. According to this view, the statutory equalization payment is the rule of general application, and a claimant should be entitled to it as of right. The remedial constructive trust is an equitable remedy, which means that before granting it, a court should decide two questions: (1) Is the equalization payment an adequate remedy in the circumstances? and (2) Since equitable remedies are discretionary, should the court exercise its discretion to grant the [remedy] after weighing the equitable considerations? If the answer to either question is negative, the court should refuse the declaration of constructive trust, leaving the claimant to the statutory equalization payment. It is respectfully submitted that this principle will eventually emerge as the ratio of *Rawluk v. Rawluk*. These two principles are fundamental to equity jurisdiction. They also meet the concerns expressed in the majority and dissenting reasons for judgment in the *Rawluk* case.

Many of the cases after *Rawluk* do indeed consider, at least implicitly, what the result would be under the relevant matrimonial property legislation before determining whether a married defendant has been unjustly enriched or which remedy is appropriate. It was done explicitly in *Joshi v. Joshi* (2001), 21 R.F.L. (5th) 60 (Ont. S.C.J.). Cases such as *Docherty v. Docherty* (1992), 42 R.F.L. (3d) 87 (Ont. Gen. Div.); affirmed (1994), 1994 CarswellOnt 457, 8 R.F.L. (4th) 155 (C.A.) illustrate that it is not easy to establish a constructive trust in the context of claims under Part I of the *FLA*.

5. Do you agree with the result in the *McDonald* case discussed by Justice McLachlin (as she then was)? See also *Amsterdam v. Amsterdam* (1991), 31 R.F.L. (3d) 153 (Ont. Gen. Div.); *Arshinoff v. Arshinoff* (1993), 1993 CarswellOnt 1551 (Gen. Div.); and *Socan v. Socan* (2005), 20 R.F.L. (6th) 418 (Ont. S.C.J.). Justice Herman reviewed the cases on the availability of a "reverse constructive trust" in *Serra v. Serra* (2007), 36 R.F.L. (6th) 66 (Ont. S.C.J.); reversed in part (2009), 2009 CarswellOnt 513, 61 R.F.L. (6th) 1 (C.A.) and concluded (para. 74) that the case law was "inconclusive". In its decision, the Ontario Court of Appeal did not address the question of whether a person can ask the court to impose a constructive trust because he or she has been enriched by the efforts of another.

6. One can infer from the Ontario Court of Appeal's comments in *Rawluk v. Rawluk* (1987), 10 R.F.L. (3d) 113 (at 116) that decreases in value can trigger s. 5(6) of the *FLA*. The dissenters in the Supreme Court of Canada stated (at 378 R.F.L.) that both decreases and increases can be considered. The majority (at 366) explicitly left the question open. In *Serra v. Serra* (2009), 2009 CarswellOnt 513, 61 R.F.L. (6th) 1 (C.A.) (reproduced below), the Ontario Court of Appeal recently used s. 5(6) to adjust the equalization sum where the value of a husband's business decreased dramatically after the valuation date.

7. In *Gallant v. Gallant* (1998), 42 R.F.L. (4th) 353, the Manitoba Court of Appeal held that there should be an unequal division of the marital property owned at separation because of a subsequent substantial decrease in the value of the husband's property. As a result there was no need to consider the constructive trust argument. Commenting on the *Rawluk case* and the resultant situation in Ontario, Huband J.A. stated (at 360-361):

> It is not for me to say that the majority decision was wrong and the minority reasons were correct in the *Rawluk* case with respect to the Ontario legislation. I do observe, however, that the existence of parallel remedies, each of a completely different nature, creates uncertainty and promotes litigation. ... Given the broader discretionary power given to the court under ... *The Marital Property Act* in Manitoba, in my opinion we need not consider any alternative remedy, and the legal gymnastics of resort to an inappropriate parallel remedy can be avoided in this jurisdiction.

8. The Law Reform Commission of British Columbia's draft legislation, modeled on the Ontario scheme, explicitly directed the courts to consider "a significant change in the value of assets between the valuation date and the date of trial other than changes caused by either of the spouses": *Working Paper on Property Rights on Marriage Breakdown* (Vancouver: Ministry of the Attorney General, 1989) at 126. Commenting on the developments in Ontario, the Commission observed (at 126, footnote 8): "It is a sign that the legislation is defective, at least in part, when the courts must resort to common law tools that were intended to be replaced by the legislation." In its *Report on Family Property Law* (Toronto: 1993), the Ontario Law Reform Commission recommended the following amendments to the *FLA* to deal with fluctuations of value between the valuation date and the trial:

> 1) the addition of a separate provision empowering a court to vary an equalization payment if an asset has fluctuated in value, if necessary to prevent an inequitable result;
>
> 2) the adoption of a specific prohibition against the application by a spouse for a declaration of resulting trust with respect to property owned by his or her spouse, based on the common or presumed intention of the spouses regarding his or her contribution, either direct or indirect, to the acquisition, preservation, or enhancement of the property; and
>
> 3) the adoption of a specific prohibition against the application by a spouse for a declaration of a remedial constructive trust with respect to property owned by his or her spouse, as restitution for his or her contribution, either direct or indirect, to the acquisition, preservation, or enhancement of that property.

The *Family Law Act*, S.P.E.I. 1995, c. 12, which is very similar to the *FLA*, specifically permits a court to award a spouse an amount that is more or less than half the difference between the net family properties "if the court is of the opinion that equalizing the net family properties would be inequitable because of a substantial change after the valuation date in the value of any property included in either spouse's net family property". The court used this provision in *Ballum v. Ballum* (1999), 49 R.F.L. (4th) 176 (P.E.I. T.D.).

9. Once a court decides to grant a remedy for unjust enrichment in the context of an equalization claim, it must then factor the remedy into the calculation of each party's net family property. This is illustrated in an interesting way in *Rarie v. Rarie* (1997), 32 R.F.L. (5th) 232 (Ont. C.A.). The wife and husband cohabited for about 38 months prior to their marriage in 1989. They separated approximately 28 months later. At separation, the husband apparently had a negative NFP, although lack of disclosure made it difficult to determine if this was accurate. The trial judge concluded that the husband was unjustly enriched by his wife's efforts which included working for the husband's business for about 30 months. He next determined that a monetary award was appropriate and valued the

wife's contributions at $600 per month for a total of $39,600. The Ontario Court of Appeal concluded that the award should stand, but that the trial judge should have gone on to factor the monetary award into the calculation of the equalization sum under the *FLA*. For the purpose of disposing of the matter without a rehearing, the appellate court proceeded on the basis that the net family property of each spouse was zero, prior to factoring in the award for unjust enrichment. It then noted (at para. 10) that the interest in the unjust enrichment award should be recognized as coming into existence when the unjust enrichment first arose. Accordingly, the wife had an asset (her interest in the unjust enrichment award) worth $39,600 at the valuation date. However, since a large portion of this asset was attributable to her efforts during the period of cohabitation before marriage, she could deduct 38 × $600 or $22,800 as the value of property owned by her on marriage. This left her with an NFP of $16,800. Since the husband's NFP was zero, the wife owed him an equalization sum of $8,400 which was deducted from the $39,600 awarded as a remedy for unjust enrichment.

Because the husband's NFP in the *Rarie* case was negative, the monetary award that he was required to pay had no impact on the value of his NFP. Assume, however, that he had had a positive NFP. How would the award have affected it?

10. In the *Rawluk* case, the motive behind the wife's constructive trust claim was to share in the increased value of her husband's property. Another situation in which it may be advantageous for a spouse to seek a declaration of constructive trust is where he or she contributed to property held by the other spouse at the marriage. If the claim succeeds, the spouses, in effect, share the deduction of the value of the property at marriage in calculating their net family properties. Consider the following example. A man and woman cohabit before marriage and the woman contributes to the acquisition of an investment property that is in the man's name. The man and woman then marry while the man still holds the property. The man will get the full benefit of the value of this property at marriage as part of his marital property deduction unless the woman is able to establish that he held a portion of the beneficial interest in trust for her.

In *Fair v. Jones* (1999), 44 R.F.L. (4th) 399 (N.W.T. S.C.); additional reasons at (1999), 48 R.F.L. (4th) 279 (N.W.T. S.C.) an unjust enrichment claim based on pre-marital contributions was successful. The case involved the application of Part III of the *Family Law Act*, S.N.W.T. 1997, c. 18 modeled on Part I of Ontario's *FLA*. Justice Vertes stated (at 417): "There is no juristic reason why the respondent should have the sole benefit of the 'commencement date' value for this property without some recognition of the petitioner's contribution." See also *Caravan v. Caravan* (2004), 2 R.F.L. (6th) 260 (N.L. T.D.) and *Panara v. Di Ascenzo* (2005), 16 R.F.L. (6th) 177 (Alta. C.A.).

In Ontario, the situation is more complicated where the pre-marital contribution by the non-titled spouse is to a matrimonial home because, as will be seen in the next section of the casebook, the value of a matrimonial home at marriage cannot be deducted in calculating a spouse's NFP. This situation arose in *Roseneck v. Gowling* (2002), 35 R.F.L. (5th) 177 (Ont. C.A.), where the husband purchased a home prior to marriage. When the wife moved into the home, she contributed about $89,000 to its renovation. Following marriage, title to the home was transferred into the names of the husband and wife. It was their main asset at the end of their relationship about four years later. The husband purchased the wife's share of the equity in the home for about $53,500. The trial judge found that, at the date of the marriage, the husband was unjustly enriched by the wife's pre-marital contribution in money towards the renovation of the matrimonial home. As a remedy, she ordered that monetary compensation of almost $89,000 be paid to the wife and included in her pre-marital property holdings. This permitted her to deduct this amount from the value of the assets that she held at separation in calculating her NFP. The trial judge declined to grant the remedy of constructive trust because this would have resulted in the wife having an interest in the matrimonial home before the marriage, the value of which could not be deducted as part of her pre-marital property.

The Ontario Court of Appeal allowed the husband's appeal. It concluded that the trial judge erred by focusing first on the situation at marriage (paras. 27–30):

> The calculation [of a spouse's NFP] begins by ascertaining the property that a spouse owns as at the date of separation. Here, title to the matrimonial home was held in joint tenancy as at the date of separation. ...

> In ascertaining whether unjust enrichment exists the court should examine whether a benefit should be *retained*. ...

> It is not until the end of the relationship or an application is made to the court for relief that the court ascertains whether justice does not permit the benefit to be retained.

Having regard to the joint interest of the parties in the property at the time of separation, she [the wife] no longer suffered a corresponding deprivation. She had received an interest in the property that was equal to [the husband's] interest.

The appellate court also found that, even if the date of marriage were chosen as the relevant date, the elements of unjust enrichment would not be made out because there was a juristic reason for the enrichment:

> In relation to ... the absence of any juristic reason for enrichment, it is the legitimate expectation of the parties that is of fundamental concern: *Peter v. Beblow* at paras. 9 and 10 of the reasons of McLachlin J. There is no suggestion in the evidence that [the wife] expected to be reimbursed for the money she put into the home. The legitimate expectation of the parties was, on [the wife's] evidence, that she was contributing to what would become "our home for the future". Thus, at the date of the marriage, [the wife] expected that she was contributing to a joint venture. The fact that her expectation was fulfilled after marriage does not mean that there was an absence of any juristic reason for her deprivation at the date of the marriage. (Para. 31)

Finally, the Ontario Court of Appeal noted (paras. 32–35) that, even if one were to accept that all of the elements of unjust enrichment existed, the appropriate remedy was a constructive trust with respect to one-half of the matrimonial home.

Justice Blishen applied *Roseneck v. Gowling* in *Browstein v. Hanson* (2003), 45 R.F.L. (5th) 67 (Ont. S.C.J.) where the wife also contributed financially before marriage to the renovation of a house in the husband's name. However, in *Browstein v. Hanson*, the husband sold this house after the marriage and used the proceeds to purchase another house, the title to which was placed in joint names. Because the property was no longer the couple's matrimonial home, its value at marriage could be deducted from the husband's net family property. The court's refusal to find unjust enrichment meant that the husband alone had the benefit of the value of the first home at marriage.

11. By virtue of s. 14 of the *FLA*, a presumption of resulting trust arises where one spouse makes a direct contribution to the purchase price of property registered in the name of the other: *Hamilton v. Hamilton* (1996), 92 O.A.C. 103 (C.A.). Similarly, the presumption of resulting trust arises where one person makes a gratuitous transfer of property to his or her spouse. The presumption of resulting trust was influential in *Belisle v. Belisle* (2000), 13 R.F.L. (5th) 262 (Ont. S.C.J.); *Launchbury v. Launchbury* (2001), 15 R.F.L. (5th) 106 (Ont. S.C.J.); affirmed (2005), 2005 CarswellOnt 1335 (Ont. C.A.); *Dubin v. Dubin* (2003), 34 R.F.L. (5th) 227 (Ont. S.C.J.); *Perks v. Perks* (2003), 35 R.F.L. (5th) 435 (Ont. S.C.J.); and *Nussbaum v. Nussbaum* (2004), 9 R.F.L. (6th) 455 (Ont. S.C.J.).

Where property is held by spouses as joint tenants, s. 14 indicates that the presumption is that they also hold the beneficial interest in the property as joint tenants. In that situation, a presumption of resulting trust does not arise even if one of the spouses may have paid for the purchase price or gratuitously conveyed the property into the names of the spouses as joint tenants. In *LeCouteur v. LeCouteur* (2005), 18 R.F.L. (6th) 386 (Ont. S.C.J.), a husband placed some inherited money into a bank account that he held jointly with his wife. The court held that, on the facts, the husband had failed to rebut the presumption of joint ownership created by s. 14. However, the husband in *Witzel v. Witzel* (2004), 2004 CarswellOnt 555 (S.C.J.) was able to convince Justice Aston that he did not intend to gift one-half of an inheritance to his wife when he placed it into a joint bank account.

12. The presumption of advancement still arises when a parent transfers property into his or her child's name or pays the purchase price for property registered in the child's name. In *Pecore v. Pecore* (2007), 37 R.F.L. (6th) 237 (S.C.C.) and *Saylor v. Madsen Estate* (2007), 279 D.L.R. (4th) 547 (S.C.C.), the Supreme Court of Canada confirmed that this presumption only applies while the child is still a minor and that it can be rebutted by establishing, on a balance of probabilities, that the parent did not intend to make a gift.

(iii) Value

HOVIUS AND YOUDAN, *THE LAW OF FAMILY PROPERTY*

(Toronto: Carswell, 1991) 291–299 (Edited footnotes appear at the bottom of the excerpt.)

Valuation of Property

1. Introduction

Despite the importance of the valuation of property for the working of Part I of the [FLA], the Act does not define "value" nor prescribe any particular method of valuation. In fact, the Act gives very little guidance as to how property is to be valued. It simply refers to the "value" of property in the definition of "net family property" in section 4(1) and the "value" of excluded property in section 4(2).

The Act also gives no explicit guidance as to onus of proof with respect to property valuation.[4] ... In *Menage v. Hedges*, Fleury U.F.C.J. dealt with the onus of proof as follows:

> The Act does not state on whose shoulders lies the burden of establishing the value of the net family property. The only reference to onus of proof can be found in s. 4(3) dealing with excluded property. The entire scheme of the Act and the new Rules of Civil Procedure (and by analogy of the amended Unified Family Court Rules) is to ensure full and fair disclosure so as to foster an early settlement of all the issues raised in the proceedings. Section 8 clearly imposes an obligation on each party to serve and file a sworn statement disclosing particulars of a party's property, debts and other liabilities. In many cases, the filing of a statement in compliance with this section may constitute the first notice to the other party of the existence of certain assets or debts. Because the property or debts being described are that of the deponent and presumably may have been or may still be under his control, the primary onus of establishing the values referred to in the statement should reside on the deponent. In the absence of any contest by the opposing party, it may not be necessary for the deponent to call further evidence to justify the valuations arrived at, but where a real issue is raised as to the figures used the onus is on the deponent to establish on a balance of probabilities the accuracy of his sworn statement. Because of the nature of the claims made in proceedings of this type, it is only reasonable to consider each party as having to discharge the civil burden of proof concerning the value of his or her respective assets and debts.[6]

2. Times for Valuation

The Act does deal expressly with the time as of which property is to be valued. The definition of "net family property" requires the valuation of property owned on the "valuation date", subject to the exclusion of the value of excluded property owned "on the valuation date" and the deduction of the value of property "calculated as of the date of the marriage". ...

The inflexible tying of valuation to the dates of valuation prevents the use of hindsight in determining values as at those dates. In *Menage v. Hedges* the valuation of the husband's loan portfolio could only take account of experience of recovery of loans up to the valuation date; evidence of payment performance after the valuation date was irrelevant. In *Harry v.*

---

[4] *Cf.* s. 4(3). ...

[6] (1987), 8 R.F.L. (3d) 225 at 243-244 (Ont. U.F.C.). *Cf. Crutchfield v. Crutchfield* (1987), 10 R.F.L. (3d) 247 at 253 (Ont. H.C.); affirmed (4 April 1990), CA 768/ 87 (Ont. C.A.) where it was held that the husband was not entitled to any discount from the value of his dentist's practice with respect to tax liabilities: "The onus to adduce such evidence was on the husband, and he failed to meet it. Therefore, I make no allowance for any such potential tax."

Harry[15] the appraisal by one valuator of company shares was flawed because it was "based in part on financial statements of the company after valuation date". In *Heon v. Heon*[16] the valuation of a nursing home business at the date of marriage on October 18, 1970 could take account only of the facts known at that date:

> Although the nursing home industry has recently experienced rapid growth, the fair market value on October 18th, 1970 cannot consider growth in subsequent years unless it was predictable at that time.[17]

As Granger J. recognized in *Heon v. Heon*, facts occurring after the valuation date should be taken into account to the extent that they were predictable at that date. Evidence of subsequent events may, therefore, be relevant in "assessing the fundamental assumptions underpinning the opinions"[18] given as to value. ...

3. Methods of Valuation: General Considerations

Apart from the provisions dealing with valuation dates, the Act does not give any directions about the valuation of property for the purpose of the Act. In the absence of statutory prescription of any particular method of valuation, there is no one "right" method of valuing property. In general, choice of appropriate methods of valuation depends on the particular asset under consideration, the particular purpose for which valuation is sought, and the evidence relating to value available in a particular case.[20] Walsh J., in *Rawluk v. Rawluk*, expressed a flexible view of property valuation for the purpose of the *Family Law Act*:

> While the Act speaks of value, it contains no definition of that term nor, indeed, guidelines of any kind to assist in the determination of its meaning other than the provision contained in s. 4(4) that when value is required to be calculated as of a given date, it shall be calculated as of close of business on that date. Absent any statutory direction, "value" must then be determined on the peculiar facts and circumstances as they are found and developed on the evidence in each individual case. While this approach does not lead to uniformity and predictability of result, it does recognize the individuality inherent in each marriage and case and permit the flexibility so often necessary to ensure an equitable result.[21]

Each judge should not, however, feel completely free to determine the method of valuation that appears most suitable in the circumstances of the particular case. The interests of justice demand reasonable predictability and this requires a large measure of uniformity in the methods of valuation adopted. There should not be unalleviated rigidity, nor should there be unpredictable exercise of individual discretion.

Ordinarily, the appropriate measure of value is the fair market value of the asset in question: "the highest price obtainable in an open and unrestricted market between informed and prudent parties, acting at arm's length and under no compulsion."[22] The fair market value measure of value has indeed been used in numerous cases dealing with a variety of types of

---

15 (1987), 9 R.F.L. (3d) 121 (Ont. Dist. Ct.).

16 (1989), 69 O.R. (2d) 758 (H.C.).

17 *Ibid.* at 766. See also *Martin v. Martin* (1988), 17 R.F.L. (3d) 78 (Ont. H.C.). ...

18 *Woeller v. Woeller* (1988), 15 R.F.L. (3d) 120 at 131 (Ont. Dist. Ct.).

20 For example, where evidence of sales of comparable properties is available, fair market value may be proved by such evidence. Where such comparisons are not available, fair market value may need to be proved by other methods, such as by capitalization of earnings produced by the property.

21 (1986), 3 R.F.L. (3d) 113 at 122 (Ont H.C.); affirmed (1987), 10 R.F.L. (3d) 113 (Ont. C.A.); which was affirmed (1990), 23 R.F.L. (3d) 337 (S.C.C.).

22 *Heon v. Heon, supra,* note 16 at 766 per Granger J.

property.[23] Some cases suggest fair market value is the only measure of value for the purpose of Part I of the *Family Law Act*. This view gives rise to difficulty in two distinct situations. The first is where the asset in question does not have a market value. The view that fair market value is the only measure of value has the result in this situation that no value can be attributed to the asset in question. ...

This view is wrong in principle. The fact that a particular item has no exchange value is relevant as a factor in determining whether that item is property but once it is decided that something is property, there is no reason why one particular measure of value should be taken to be the only way of valuing it. The view [that fair market value is the only measure of value] has, moreover, been rejected by the Ontario Court of Appeal in *Brinkos v. Brinkos*[29] and by the myriad of cases in which value has been placed on pension rights, assets which are generally not transferable and for which no market exists. ...

It may be concluded, therefore, that ordinarily fair market value is the appropriate measure of value. Another method of valuation should, however, be used both where the property has no fair market value and where fair market value is an inappropriate measure of value for the property in question. As Fleury U.F.C.J. said, in *Menage v. Hedges* in approving the view of a valuator, S.R. Cole:

> He recommends that fair market value be retained as an initial guide in assessing the value of property but that the court retain its freedom to depart from fair market value concepts where this would result in an inequitable valuation. The court could then use the concept of fair value to correct obvious inequities arising out of a servile application of the fair market value approach.[34]

NOTES AND QUESTIONS

1. A number of cases have confirmed that one should generally determine the property's value on the valuation date without the benefit of hindsight, although subsequent events that could reasonably be contemplated at that time can be factored into the calculation. See, e.g., *Best v. Best* (1999), 49 R.F.L. (4th) 1 (S.C.C.) and *Pacheco v. Pacheco* (2001), 13 R.F.L. (5th) 442 (Ont. S.C.J.) (both dealing with a pension). The case law is reviewed in *Dababneh v. Dababneh* (2003), 48 R.F.L. (5th) 55 (Ont. S.C.J.); additional reasons at (2004), 2004 CarswellOnt 654 (Ont. S.C.J.). In *Ruster v. Ruster* (2003), 44 R.F.L. (5th) 436, the Ontario Court of Appeal applied the same approach to the determination of the value of property at marriage.

In *Ross v. Ross* (2006), 34 R.F.L. (6th) 229 (Ont. C.A.), the Ontario Court of Appeal specifically agreed (para. 39) with the following approach:

> In valuing an asset as of the valuation date, only facts known or reasonably foreseeable on that date should be taken into account. It is inappropriate to look to events that occurred after the valuation date if they were not reasonably foreseeable on the valuation date. Nevertheless, post-valuation events can be looked at to confirm or challenge the reasonableness of inferences drawn based on the information available on the valuation date.

2. Bill 133 (not yet proclaimed) would create a "net family law value" for certain employment pensions and stipulate that that value be determined in accordance with a formula set under the *Pension Benefits Act*.

---

[23] See e.g., *Dibbley v. Dibbley* (1986), 5 R.F.L. (3d) 381 (Ont. H.C.) (accountant's partnership interest); *Crutchfield v. Crutchfield, supra*, note 6 (dentist's practice); *Corless v. Corless* (1987), 5 R.F.L. (3d) 256 (Ont. U.F.C.) (lawyer's partnership interest); *Heon v. Heon, supra*, note 16; *Woeller v. Woeller, supra*, note 18; *Black v. Black* (1988), 18 R.F.L. (3d) 303; *Lessany v. Lessany* (1988), 17 R.F.L. (3d) 433 (Ont. Dist. Ct.) (all concerned with shares in private companies); *Crawford v. Crawford* (1987), 6 R.F.L. (3d) 308 (Ont. H.C.) and *Martin v. Martin, supra*, note 17 (both concerned with land).

[29] (1989), 69 O.R. (2d) 225 (C.A.).

[34] *Supra*, note 6 at 245.

SENGMUELLER v. SENGMUELLER

(1994), 2 R.F.L. (4th) 232, 1994 CarswellOnt 375 (Ont. C.A.)

[In proceedings under the *FLA*, the husband was ordered to make an equalization payment of $368,556.06. The trial judge deducted $137,697.69 in calculating the husband's net family property to account for notional disposition costs. The wife appealed the decision to deduct the notional disposition costs.]

McKINLAY J.A. (for the court): — ... At the time of trial Mr. Sengmueller had approximately $26,000 of non-taxable assets with which to satisfy the equalization payment of $368,556.06. The balance of his assets at that time consisted primarily of an R.R.S.P., two parcels of real estate (one of which included the matrimonial home), and Film Sound Services Ltd., the business from which he earned his livelihood. Their value as at valuation date, April 21, 1988, was found to be $85,272, $250,000, $375,000, and $161,854 respectively, less the trial judge's finding as to the tax cost of realization in amounts of $38,789, $36,911, $35,862, and $26,134 respectively. ...

Notional Costs of Disposition

The trial judge, in valuing net family property, deducted as a debt or other liability under s. 4(1) of the Act amounts estimated as taxes (but not other types of costs of disposition, such as real estate commissions), which would be exigible if the assets involved were realized upon. Counsel for Mrs. Sengmueller argues that he was in error in so doing, relying on the decisions of this court in *McPherson v. McPherson* (1988), 63 O.R. (2d) 641, and in *Starkman v. Starkman* (1990), 75 O.R. (2d) 19. In deducting tax costs, the trial judge relied on *Heon v. Heon* (1989), 69 O.R. (2d) 758 (H.C.).

The *McPherson* case, decided under the *Family Law Reform Act*, R.S.O. 1980, c. 152, involved shares held by the husband in a private company. The husband and wife acted as true partners in the company, although their shareholdings did not reflect that fact. Evidence was adduced before the trial judge to show the tax implications to the husband of satisfying the award out of earnings and/ or assets of the company. The trial judge, in arriving at the amount payable to the wife, ignored the tax consequences. On appeal to this court, a deduction for taxes was allowed.

In my view, it is equally appropriate to take such costs into account in determining net family property under the *Family Law Act* if there is satisfactory evidence of a likely disposition date and if it is clear that such costs will be inevitable when the owner disposes of the assets or is deemed to have disposed of them. In my view, for the purposes of determining net family property, any asset is worth (in money terms) only the amount which can be obtained on its realization, regardless of whether the accounting is done as a reduction in the value of the asset, or as a deduction of a liability: the result is the same. While these costs are not liabilities in the balance-sheet sense of the word, they are amounts which the owner will be obliged to satisfy at the time of disposition, and hence, are ultimate liabilities inextricably attached to the assets themselves. This is consistent with *McPherson* but goes beyond it.

If assets are transferred in specie or are realized upon to satisfy the equalization payment, the amount of tax and other disposition costs is easily proven, assuming the availability of a preliminary calculation of the equalization payment. The real problem arises when the equalization payment is satisfied with liquid assets not subject to disposition costs, and there are other assets to be valued for the purposes of s. 4(1) which will inevitably be subject to disposition costs at some time in the future. Two questions then arise: First, in what circumstances should disposition costs be deducted, and second, how should the amount of the deduction be calculated?

Counsel for Mrs. Sengmueller takes the position that both *McPherson* and *Starkman* stand for the following propositions, to quote from his factum: "In valuing an asset, an allowance for taxes should not be made where it is not clear if the asset will ever be disposed of, or where the payor does not have to dispose of an asset that would attract liability in order to make the equalization payment." I agree with the first proposition but not with the second.

Support for the first proposition is found in *McPherson*. Finlayson J.A. commenced his analysis with the following comment, at p. 645:

> It makes little sense, in my view, to visit the entire costs of the disposition on one spouse when dealing with a division of a non-family asset: they, like the benefits, are to be shared equally.

After discussing some of the cases which have grappled with this issue, he stated further, at p. 647:

> The cases appear to turn on their own facts and if I might hazard a broad distinction, an allowance should be made in the case where there is evidence that the disposition will involve a sale or transfer of property that attracts tax consequences, and it should not be made in the case where it is not clear when, if ever, a sale or transfer of property will be made and thus the tax consequences of such an occurrence are so speculative that they can safely be ignored.

The result in that appeal (decided, as I have said, under the *Family Law Reform Act*) was that income tax liability was deducted in calculating the value of the business involved. The reasons give us the following guidance: first, that as a basic principle the entire costs of disposition of assets should not be visited on one spouse and that those costs, like benefits, should be shared equally; and second, that this principle should be departed from only where the timing of disposition, and thus disposition costs, is "so speculative" that such costs "can safely be ignored." The basic principle is very easy to apply; unfortunately, the exception is not. ...

In *Heon v. Heon*, decided under the *Family Law Act, 1986*, Granger J. distinguished the objectives under the *Family Law Reform Act* from those under the *Family Law Act, 1986*, and concluded that the appropriate procedure was to value all assets as of valuation day as if there were an actual sale on that day with taxes and other disposition costs deducted. However, Catzman J.A., speaking for the court in *Starkman*, considered that a fairer method of arriving at the equalization payment than that applied in *Heon v. Heon* was to require clear evidence of the likely fact of disposition of an asset before allowing deduction of disposition costs.

The reasons in the *Starkman* case indicate that the appeal was argued on the basis that it was necessary to realize on the R.R.S.P. and on the company shares involved in order to meet the equalization payment. It was clear that the evidence adduced did not satisfy that position and there was no evidence of any other likely date of disposition. In my view, the decision went no further than that.

In general terms, this court in *Starkman* approved the application under the *Family Law Act, 1986* of the approach recommended by Finlayson J.A. in *McPherson*. If the evidence satisfies the trial judge, on a balance of probabilities, that the disposition of any item of family property will take place at a particular time in the future, then the tax consequences (and other properly proven costs of disposition) are not speculative, and should be allowed either as a reduction in value or as a deductible liability.

R.R.S.P.s, in particular, are taxable in full, regardless of the time of realization, whether they are cashed in total, or taken by way of annuity.

In dealing with a business, one should fairly consider the nature of the business, the possible requirement that the business could only operate if the owner spouse continued to be involved, any shareholder agreement which required sale of his or her shareholding in specified circumstances, and myriad other possible considerations in the individual case. Different considerations would be relevant in dealing with other types of assets.

By requiring evidence of the expected time of the disposition, and by making a present value calculation, courts could avoid inevitable unfair results flowing from the application of the approach used in *Heon v. Heon*, and from the approach suggested by the appellant.

A short unsophisticated example will point out the possibility for gross unfairness if paying spouses could only deduct disposition costs when disposition of the assets is necessary to satisfy the equalization payment. On separation, a husband's assets consist solely of liquid non-taxable bonds totalling $850,000. He has been paying tax annually on the interest, and accruing the balance. His wife's assets consist of an R.R.S.P. worth $500,000, a parcel of real property worth $500,000, for which she paid $100,000, and liquid non-taxable bonds in the amount of $150,000. The calculation of their assets and liabilities (without taking disposition costs into account) results in the wife being required to pay an equalization amount to the husband of $150,000. From a practical standpoint, she must satisfy the equalization payment to her husband from the bonds, because she cannot meet the test of needing to sell the real property or the R.R.S.P. to satisfy the equalization. A few years later she, being of retirement age and wishing to maintain her standard of living to the extent possible, needs to sell the real property and take the R.R.S.P. in the form of an annuity. In so doing, her ultimate tax liability will be substantially in excess of the amount *she was required to pay to her husband* as an equalization sum.

The decision in *Heon*, in my view, points out a different possibility of unfairness. For example, apply the *Heon* approach of a notional disposition on valuation day, and assume that the parties in the above example were both in their early forties. The wife could deduct the full amount of tax which would have been payable on disposition of her R.R.S.P. and realty *as if* she had disposed of them on valuation day, resulting in a deduction of tax of approximately $350,000, and real estate commission of approximately $25,000. *Her husband would have to pay to her* an equalization payment of approximately $37,500 — a difference of $187,500 from the result applying the approach pressed by counsel for Mrs. Sengmueller. This result would obtain even if she had no intention of disposing of those assets for some substantial period of time.

It would be much fairer to require her to adduce evidence (see s. 4(3) of the Act) from which the trial judge could assess the likely time of disposition, the likely disposition costs at that time, and the present value of those costs as at the valuation date. The deduction allowed would be substantially less than would be the case if assets were valued *as if* disposed of on valuation day. It is true that such calculations are not exact, but courts have never refused to make assessments merely because the evidence available is less than precise.

From the *McPherson* case I glean three rules to apply in all cases:

(1) apply the overriding principle of fairness, i.e., that costs of disposition as well as benefits should be shared equally;

(2) deal with each case on its own facts, considering the nature of the assets involved, evidence as to the probable timing of their disposition, and the probable tax and other costs of disposition at that time, discounted as of valuation day; and

(3) deduct disposition costs before arriving at the equalization payment, except in the situation where 'it is not clear when, if ever,' there will be a realization of the property.

Under the *Family Law Act* it does not matter whether the third rule is applied as part of the valuation of the asset involved or whether the deduction is made as an inevitable liability which exists on valuation day, although it is not payable until some time in the future.

[The court affirmed the trial judge's decision.]

NOTES AND QUESTIONS

1. There is a general consensus that, in the absence of special circumstances, there should be a discount for the spouse's future tax liability in determining the value of a pension. Although some pre-*Sengmueller* decisions had refused to discount the value of an RRSP, it is now generally accepted that RRSPs should be treated in the same way. See, e.g., *Aguanno v. Aguanno* (2002), 30 R.F.L. (5th) 14 (Ont. S.C.J.).

2. In *Brosseau v. Shemilt* (1995), 16 R.F.L. (4th) 129 (Ont. Gen. Div.), a major portion of the equalization payment was to be satisfied by a transfer of the husband's RRSP to the wife. The effect of the rollover provisions in the *Income Tax Act* was that this transfer would have no immediate tax consequences and the wife would eventually have to pay tax on the proceeds of the RRSP. As a result, the husband's RRSP was not discounted as of the date of valuation. Should the possibility that the spouses will have different tax rates when each receives funds from an RRSP be considered in such a case? If so, how?

3. What guidance did the Ontario Court of Appeal give in the *Sengmueller* case regarding the extent to which taxes payable some time in the future should be discounted? For commentary, see *Mannarelli v. Mannarelli* (1998), 41 R.F.L. (4th) 117 at 124 (Ont. Gen. Div.). Should there be any consideration of the costs of disposition including taxes if it is unclear when, if ever, a spouse will dispose of the property?

4. For further reference, see Cole and Freedman, *Property Valuation and Income Tax Implications of Marital Dissolution* (Toronto: Carswell) (looseleaf service).

(c) Deductions and Exclusions

HOVIUS AND YOUDAN, *THE LAW OF FAMILY PROPERTY*

(Toronto: Carswell, 1991) 314-315 (Footnotes omitted)

A property regime such as that established by Part I of the *Family Law Act* is based on the premise that both spouses make an essential and basically equal contribution to the economic viability of the family unit and hence to the acquisition of wealth by the unit. The total financial product of the marriage as an economic partnership is, therefore, generally shared equally when the relationship ends. It follows that the norm of equal sharing should be applied only to the net value of those property rights which constitute the economic product of the constructive collaboration of husband and wife, not to the gross value of all property held by the spouses at the end of the relationship. While this principle may be readily accepted, actual identification of the shareable financial product presents difficulty and may lead to differences of opinion. Least controversial is the treatment that should be accorded to the debts and liabilities of the spouses at the end of their relationship. In order to determine the financial product of their marriage relationship, the debts and liabilities of the spouses should generally be deducted from the value of their property. Similarly, account should be taken of pre-marital property since its existence cannot be attributed to the partnership effort. However, there are a number of issues relating to pre-marital property that have caused considerable debate. Should a spouse be given credit for pre-marital property that has decreased in value or been used to purchase consumables during the marriage? Should the increase in value of any pre-marital property be considered part of the product of the relationship? Finally, property may be acquired during the marriage in such a way, for example, by inheritance, that its value does not originate in the joint efforts of the spouses. Should it, nonetheless form part of the financial product of the marriage? If some credit is to be given for acquisition of property in this way, should it be for the value at the date of acquisition or its value at the end of the relationship?

In Ontario, the legislature's response to these and related issues is revealed in the definition of "net family property". ...

FOLGA v. FOLGA

(1986), 2 R.F.L. (3d) 358, 1986 CarswellOnt 279 (Ont. H.C.)

[At the time of the marriage, the husband owned a house (referred to as "Frederick Street" in the reasons for judgment). The parties lived in this house for three years following the marriage. It was then sold and the husband purchased another house, which became the family home.]

GRAVELY L.J.S.C. (orally): — ... The respondent [the husband] claims a deduction for the equity in Frederick Street pursuant to s. 4(1)(b) of the *Family Law Act*. The petitioner says that there should be no deduction because Frederick Street was the matrimonial home. By the terms of s. 4(1)(b), the value of an interest in a matrimonial home may not be deducted. ...

The term "matrimonial home" also is defined in s. 4(1). ...

Section 18 is in Pt. II of the Act, and that part of the Act deals with issues relating to the matrimonial home. ...

Once spouses occupy a property as a matrimonial home they acquire all the rights set out in Pt. II. For a property to be treated as a matrimonial home as defined in s. 18, the spouses have to be either living in the property or to have been living in it at the time of separation. It appears also that to qualify for a deduction under s. 4(1), the matrimonial home must be as defined by s. 18 at the valuation date.

These definition sections then suggest the status of a matrimonial home is not immutable and a spouse may lose the protection given by the matrimonial home status and that a spousal owner may regain the right to deduct under s. 4(1)(b). Here it appears that although Frederick Street was once the matrimonial home it is no longer so under s. 4(1) or 18 since the parties were not ordinarily resident in it at the date of separation. Not being a matrimonial home, it now qualifies for deduction under s. 4(1)(b).

Counsel for the petitioner argues vigorously against this conclusion. He suggests the whole thrust of law reform in this area has been towards protection of the benefits of the matrimonial home for both spouses and that I should not be restricted to the definition of "matrimonial home" contained in the Act.

I do not think I can go beyond the definition in the statute. The words "matrimonial home" are technical words in the context of the statute and the definitions are very specific. Part II of the Act gives very extensive rights to spouses in relation to a matrimonial home, and I assume the legislature intended to substitute those specific rights for the more general concepts set out in the former legislation.

The respondent then will be able to deduct his former equity in Frederick Street of $12,000 for the purpose of determining his net family property.

NOTES AND QUESTIONS

1. The Ontario Court of Appeal in *Nahatchewitz v. Nahatchewitz* (1999), 1 R.F.L. (5th) 395; additional reasons at (1999), 1999 CarswellOnt 3076, confirmed that only the property occupied as the family residence on the valua-

tion date qualifies as a matrimonial home for the purpose of Part I of the *FLA*. The court specifically disapproved of *Miller v. Miller* (1987), 8 R.F.L. (3d) 113 (Ont. Dist. Ct.), where Misener D.C.J. was faced with a fact situation similar to that in *Folga* and ruled that the husband could not include the value of the home he brought into the marriage in the calculation of his pre-marital property deduction.

The Ontario Court of Appeal also held in *Nahatchewitz v. Nahatchewitz* that the value of the deduction relating to a previous family residence owned at marriage was not discounted to reflect real estate fees paid on its disposition approximately one year after marriage. Justice Heeney reluctantly followed this holding in *Pocs v. Pocs* (2001), 2001 CarswellOnt 2448 (S.C.J.), but such a discount from the marital deduction occurred in *Reinhardt v. Reinhardt* (2004), 8 R.F.L. (6th) 340 (Ont. S.C.J.); additional reasons at (2004), 2004 CarswellOnt 4374 (S.C.J.) and *Yeates v. Yeates* (2007), 2007 CarswellOnt 2107 (S.C.J.); affirmed (2008), 2008 CarswellOnt 3842 (C.A.); leave to appeal refused (2009), 2009 CarswellOnt 340, 2009 CarswellOnt 339 (S.C.C.).

2. In his annotation to the *Folga* case, Professor McLeod supports the conclusion but he acknowledges that it reveals "one of the glaring inconsistencies" in the Act. He concludes (at 360):

> The pre-marital home exclusion from deduction will likely only catch the unwary. If the home is sold and another (or the same) acquired the day after [marriage], the deduction remains for the cash brought in. If the home is kept and not occupied until years later, but is in fact the family residence on the valuation date, the deduction is lost. Perhaps the most startling scenario arises where a pre-marital home is sold and a new home acquired relying almost exclusively on financing without using the proceeds of the earlier sale. The cash is deductible and the net value of the home, after deducting debts (s. 4(1)) is likely to be negligible. If the purpose of the Act was fairness, it falls short. If it was to protect the largest asset for most families or somehow give the home a talismanic effect in law, its operation is erratic.

COLLIER v. TORBAR

(2002), 27 R.F.L. (5th) 304, 2002 CarswellOnt 2443 (Ont. C.A.)

SHARPE J.A. (for the court): —

1 Before the parties were married, the respondent wife purchased land by means of a loan that met the requirements of a housing loan under the *Income Tax Act*, R.S.C. 1985 (5th Supp.), c. 1. She built a house on the land, which later became the parties' matrimonial home. The issue on this appeal is the appropriate treatment of the housing loan in calculating the wife's net family property. ...

Facts

3 In 1991, the respondent wife purchased land on which she later built a house. The purchase of the land was financed by a loan from Triad International Freight Forwarding Ltd., which the wife and her business partner owned and operated. The loan was not secured by a mortgage, but took the form of a housing loan that met the requirements of s. 15(2.4) of the *Income Tax Act*. Under s. 15(2.4), the amount of a loan received from a corporation by a shareholder of the corporation need not be included in the shareholder's income where the shareholder is an employee of the corporation and the loan is made to enable or assist the employee to acquire a dwelling.

4 The wife's housing loan was transferred to Linda Collier Holdings Ltd., which was owned by the wife's mother and was created to buy out the interest of the wife's business partner.

5 In the spring of 1994, the parties began cohabiting. The parties were married on July 15, 1995. The wife's house became the parties' matrimonial home. When the parties married, the wife owed $513,748 to Linda Collier Holdings Ltd. on account of the housing loan. The parties separated on April 30, 1997. ...

6 There is no dispute that in calculating the wife's net family property, the wife must include the valuation date value of the matrimonial home and may not deduct its marriage date value. Section 4(1) of the *Family Law Act* provides that a spouse must include the valuation date value of all property owned on the valuation date. Section 4(1)(b) provides that a spouse must deduct from this value the marriage date value of all property owned on the marriage date, except a matrimonial home.

7 The issue in this case is whether the amount of the housing loan must be deducted from the marriage date value of the property owned by the wife on the marriage date. Section 4(1)(b) provides that a spouse must deduct debts and other liabilities from the marriage date value of property owned on the marriage date. The result of deducting marriage date debts from the marriage date value of property owned on the marriage date is that a spouse's marriage date debts increase the spouse's net family property. Requiring the wife to deduct the amount of the housing loan from the marriage date value of the property she owned on the marriage date would increase her net family property by $513,748, the amount of the housing loan.

8 The wife submits that this result would be harsh and inequitable since she is already required to include the valuation date value of the matrimonial home and is not permitted to deduct the marriage date value of the home. She submits that this result could not have been intended by the *Family Law Act*. The husband concedes that if the loan on the matrimonial home had been secured by a mortgage, the amount of the loan would not be deducted from the marriage date value of the property owned by the wife on the marriage date. However, the husband submits that since the loan was not secured by a mortgage, the loan must be treated the same as any other debt not tied to the matrimonial home.

9 The trial judge accepted the wife's argument and held that the amount of the housing loan should not be deducted from the marriage date value of the property owned by the wife on the marriage date. The trial judge found that housing loans under the *Income Tax Act* "are clearly in the nature of an alternative type of mortgage. Like a mortgage, they must be either paid off on the sale of the home or transferred to another home. I see no reason to treat them any differently than a conventional mortgage."

Issue

10 The issue on this appeal is whether the trial judge erred in holding that the wife was not required to deduct the amount of the housing loan from the marriage date value of the property she owned on the marriage date for the purpose of calculating her net family property.

Analysis

11 One interpretation of s. 4(1)(b) would require a spouse to include a pre-marriage debt in the calculation of his or her net family property even where the debt was incurred to acquire a matrimonial home. In *Menage v. Hedges* (1987), 8 R.F.L. (3d) 225 (Ont. U.F.C), Fleury U.F.C.J. reluctantly held that he was bound to adopt this literal interpretation. The husband had borrowed $35,000 from his father to purchase the matrimonial home. Fleury U.F.C.J. held that he had no option but to include the debt in calculating the husband's net family property. At p. 255, he described this result as one of "the shortcomings" of the *Family Law Act*. ...

12 In subsequent cases, courts have distinguished *Menage v. Hedges* where the loan takes the form of a mortgage secured against the matrimonial home: *DaCosta v. DaCosta* (1990), 29 R.F.L. (3d) 422 (Ont. Gen. Div.); varied on other grounds (1992), 7 O.R. (3d) 321 (C.A.), *Hulme v. Hulme* (1989), 27 R.F.L. (3d) 403 (Ont. H.C.), *Reeson v. Kowalik* (1991), 36

R.F.L. (3d) 396 (Ont. Gen. Div.). ... But see *Leeson v. Leeson* (1990), 26 R.F.L. (3d) 52 (Ont. Dist. Ct.), where the court followed *Menage v. Hedges* even though the loan took the form of a mortgage secured against the matrimonial home.

13 In *DaCosta v. DaCosta*, Granger J. held that where the debt is secured against the land in the form of a mortgage, it should not be deducted from the marriage date value of property owned on the marriage date. At p. 448, Granger J. stated:

> In my opinion, to exempt the value of the matrimonial home from the value of Mr. DaCosta's property as of 6th October 1980 but require him to reduce the value of his other property by the amount of the mortgage would ignore that the mortgage was attached to the land. Such an interpretation would lead to an absurd result and would not be in keeping with the avowed intent of the [*Family Law Act*], which is to equalize the value of wealth accumulated during the period of cohabitation.

. . . . .

16 The decisions in *DaCosta v. DaCosta*, *Hulme v. Hulme*, *Reeson v. Kowalik* and *Menage v. Hedges* all recognize the unfairness of deducting the amount of a debt incurred to purchase a matrimonial home from the marriage date value of property owned on the marriage date. Section 4(1)(b) of the *Family Law Act* imposes a special burden on the spouse who brings a matrimonial home into the marriage by not permitting the spouse to deduct the marriage date value of the home in calculating his or her net family property. The legislature must have determined that the special character of a matrimonial home justified this special burden.

17 However, to require the spouse to deduct a debt incurred to purchase the matrimonial home from the marriage date value of property owned on the marriage date would impose a double burden. The spouse would receive no benefit for the marriage date value of the matrimonial home and would be further burdened by the marriage date amount of any debt attributable to the home. I agree with the reasoning in *DaCosta v. DaCosta*, *Hulme v. Hulme* and *Reeson v. Kowalik* that the *Family Law Act* should be interpreted so as to avoid this obvious unfairness.

18 As noted above, the husband has conceded that if the loan on the matrimonial home had been secured by a mortgage, the amount of the loan would not be deducted from the marriage date value of the property owned by the wife on the marriage date. The wife submits that the trial judge correctly found that a housing loan that meets the requirements of the *Income Tax Act* is sufficiently similar to a mortgage that the amount of the housing loan should not be deducted from the marriage date value of property owned on the marriage date. In the alternative, the wife submits that *Menage v. Hedges* should be overruled and that no debt incurred to acquire a matrimonial home, whether secured by a mortgage or not, should be deducted from the marriage date value of property owned on the marriage date.

19 In my view, the trial judge correctly held that if the amount of a loan secured by a mortgage should not be deducted from the marriage date value of property owned on the marriage date, then the wife's housing loan should also not be deducted from that value. On the one hand, a housing loan under s. 15 of the *Income Tax Act* is not registered against a home and does not diminish the owner's equity in the home, since the owner is free to dispose of the home without the constraints imposed by a mortgage to protect the security of the lender. However, a housing loan must be documented to satisfy the *Income Tax Act* and the borrower is subject to significant income tax consequences when disposing of the home. In my view, these constraints represent a sufficient link between the debt and the matrimonial home to bring the case within the principle from *DaCosta v. DaCosta*, *Hulme v. Hulme* and *Reeson v. Kowalik*.

20 Because of the foregoing conclusion, it is not strictly necessary to address the wife's alternative submission that no debts incurred to acquire a matrimonial home, whether or not

secured by a mortgage, should be deducted from the marriage date value of property owned on the marriage date. However, since the issue was argued before us, I offer the following comments. Although there is much to be said for treating all debts on the same basis regardless of the legal form they take, unsecured and undocumented family loans may require different treatment. In general terms, it seems to me that if the borrower can demonstrate that he or she is subject to some legal or financial constraint linking the debt to the matrimonial home, the debt should not be deducted from the marriage date value of other property owned by the borrower. While I do not wish to rule out the possibility of similar treatment for other debts incurred to purchase a matrimonial home, courts must closely scrutinize unsecured and undocumented family loans to ensure the integrity of the equalization provisions of the *Family Law Act*.

NOTES AND QUESTIONS

1. In his annotation to the *Collier v. Torbar* case, Professor McLeod stated (27 R.F.L. (5th) 304 at 304 and 308):

> The Court of Appeal's decision ... appears to be the first obvious chink in the Court of Appeal's strict constructionist interpretation of Part I of the *Family Law Act*. ...
>
> The Court of Appeal's decision ... is reasonable and intellectually defensible. Unfortunately, it strains the words of the *Family Law Act* to the breaking point in order to avoid an illogical result. The question is how far the court is prepared to go to achieve a "fair" result. So far, the court's refusal to introduce a broad discretion into the equalization accounting under Part I of the Act has limited the amount of matrimonial property litigation. If the court decides to expand the role of discretion in property division, the volume of cases will increase as in British Columbia, where the Court of Appeal actively promotes a broad discretion in property cases.

He also suggested (at 307) that the Ontario Court of Appeal in essence accepted the wife's alternative submission that debts incurred to acquire a matrimonial home before marriage should never be deducted from the marriage-date value of property owned at marriage.

2. Must a spouse deduct the value of a collateral mortgage secured against a matrimonial home from his or her pre-marital property if the loan was arranged before marriage to purchase other assets? In other words, is the purpose or the form of the loan determinative? See *Nagy v. Nagy* (2002), 27 R.F.L. (5th) 383 (Ont. S.C.J.), where Justice Marshman held that the debt had to be deducted.

3. A possible objection to the approach in the *Collier v. Torbar* case is that the spouse who borrows money to purchase the matrimonial home before marriage will be in a more advantageous position than one who pays cash for the home and acquires other pre-marital property through borrowing. This may not seem fair in light of the fact that in both situations the spouse's net worth at marriage may be identical. However, this result merely reflects the fact that a spouse who acquires pre-marital property other than a matrimonial home is in a better position under the *FLA* than one who owns the matrimonial home at marriage. The fundamental issue that must be confronted is whether the special treatment accorded the matrimonial home in the rules governing the pre-marital property deduction and the exclusion of property is justified. Is it fair or logical that a spouse who buys the matrimonial home before marriage should be treated differently from one who brings money into the marriage and then buys the matrimonial home? Is it reasonable that a spouse who inherits $200,000 after marriage and uses it to purchase stocks can exclude the stocks from the calculation of his or her net family property but if the money is used to purchase a matrimonial home then its value must be included?

4. When proclaimed, Bill 133 will confirm the holding in the *Collier v. Torbar* case by repealing clause (b) in the existing definition of "net family property" and substituting the following: "(b) the value of the property, other than a matrimonial home, that the spouse owned on the date of the marriage, after deducting the spouse's debts and other liabilities, other than debts or liabilities related directly to the acquisition or significant improvement of a matrimonial home, calculated as at the date of the marriage".

5. The special rules relating to the matrimonial home appear to be based on the premise that both spouses contribute significantly to this asset's preservation and maintenance. If so, there may have to be adjustments to the equalization payment where this is not the case. For example, one spouse may have inherited the home only months before the valuation date. In this situation, the initial effect of the inheritance has not been significantly eroded by

spousal efforts affecting family and home. Section 5(6), particularly paragraph (h), might be invoked to justify granting the owning spouse a greater share of the net family properties. Similarly, where the matrimonial home is brought into a short marriage it seems unfair to allow the non-owning spouse to have equal benefit of the pre-marital value. Indeed, paragraph (e) of s. 5(6) appears to have been included specifically to deal with this situation. Of course, all the circumstances must be considered in determining if equal sharing of the net family properties would be unconscionable. Regarding the application of s. 5(6) where one spouse owns the matrimonial home before a short marriage, see Hovius, "Unequal Sharing of Net Family Properties under Ontario's *Family Law Act*" (2008), 27 C.F.L.Q. 147 at 177–181. Where the spouses cohabit for more than five years, paragraph 5(6)(e) is not applicable and the court will be more hesitant to adjust the equalization payment on the basis that one spouse brought the matrimonial home into the marriage: *Cassidy v. Cassidy* (1996), 17 R.F.L. (4th) 403 (Ont. Gen. Div.).

6. In its *Report on Family Property Law* (Toronto: 1993), the Ontario Law Reform Commission recommended that the legislature end the special treatment of the matrimonial home for the purposes of Part I of the *FLA*. When the Northwest Territories legislature adopted legislation modeled on Part I of Ontario's *FLA*, it did not provide for the exclusion of the value of the matrimonial home from the pre-marital property deduction. See Part III of the *Family Law Act*, S.N.W.T. 1997, c. 18.

The deduction in respect of pre-marital property can be taken even where the property no longer belongs to the spouse on the valuation date or cannot be traced into other property owned by the spouse. See, e.g., the *Folga* case reproduced above. By way of contrast, an exclusion under s. 4(2) of the *FLA* is permitted only if the property described in paragraphs 1 to 4 still belongs to the spouse on the valuation date or can be traced into property, other than the matrimonial home, that belongs to the spouse on the valuation date. Other important consequences also flow from the distinction between exclusions and deductions. These are explored in the cases, notes and questions that follow.

MITTLER v. MITTLER

(1988), 17 R.F.L. (3d) 113, 1988 CarswellOnt 303 (Ont. H.C.)

McKINLAY J.: — ...

Property and debts of Mr. Mittler on date of marriage

At the date of marriage Mr. Mittler owned property and owed one debt. ...

Counsel for Mr. Mittler argues that, although those properties had a net value of $115,000 at the time of marriage, that amount, reflected in 1985 dollars by using the Consumer Price Index, would be equivalent to $367,270 on valuation date. It is this latter amount which Mr. Mittler claims should be deducted in calculating his net family property. It must be acknowledged that failing to account for inflationary increases in value raises possible inequities, such as inequities between the application of the definition of net family property under s. 4(1) and the application of s. 4(2), which excludes certain properties from the calculation of net family property. The problem can be best illustrated by a simple example. Assume that a painting was obtained by inheritance shortly before marriage in 1964, the value at marriage being $30,000, and the value at valuation date being $150,000. If one deducts the value in 1964 dollars for the purpose of determining net family property, then there is an amount of $120,000 at valuation date which must be shared between the spouses. Now assume that the same painting was obtained by inheritance by one of the spouses shortly after the marriage in 1964, the value at that time being $30,000 and the value at

valuation date being $150,000. In that situation, the full value of the painting —
$150,000 — would be excluded from the calculation of net family property by virtue of s.
4(2)1.

Of course, there are many types of assets which may be owned by a spouse on the date
of marriage which either will have disappeared long before valuation date, or will have
changed so substantially as to be unrecognizable as the original asset; for example, a young
corporation operated at the time of marriage may grow significantly in size and complexity
prior to valuation date. Such is the situation with Mr. Mittler's companies in this case. To
deduct the valuation date value of such assets would be clearly inequitable to the non-owning spouse.

Counsel for Mr. Mittler, however, argues that the effect of inflation alone, and not the
effect of other types of changes in the value of assets, should be taken into consideration,
and there is some logic and fairness in such an approach. The legislature obviously intended
that assets owned by a spouse at the time of marriage should be exempt, at some value, from
the effect of the statutorily imposed "partnership". The question is, what is the "value" to be
exempt? Growth in the value of assets in excess of that attributable to inflation alone must
surely have been intended to form part of net family property. To hold otherwise would lead
to importing impossibly complicated problems into an already complicated procedure, and
would often lead to gross inequities. However, such considerations would not arise if only
the purely inflationary element were considered.

But what does the statute say? Paragraph (b) of the definition of "net family property" in
s. 4(1) of the F.L.A. requires the deduction of:

> "net family property"
>
>> (b) the *value of property*, other than a matrimonial home, that the spouse owned on the date
>> of marriage, after deducting the spouse's debts and other liabilities, *calculated as of the date
>> of the marriage*. [emphasis added]

It is argued that the above definition only requires that the *calculation* (that is, the deducting of debts and other liabilities from property) be done as of the date of marriage, and
that the calculation does not determine the *value* to be deducted. I have difficulty accepting
that argument. On a grammatical reading of the definition, it is clear that what is being
calculated is the "value of property", and that that value is calculated as of the date of marriage. There is no suggestion anywhere in s. 4(1) that the result of that calculation should be
altered to reflect the effect of inflation.

I conclude with some reluctance that the legislature has directed the court, in deducting
the value of property owned at the date of marriage, to deduct only the value based on date
of marriage dollars. Although proceeding thus will often create apparent inequities, I consider that this practice is required by the text of s. 4(1). ...

OLIVA v. OLIVA

(1988), 12 R.F.L. (3d) 334, 1988 CarswellOnt 208 (Ont. C.A.)

[Mr. Oliva's relatives, who were also his business partners, provided the down payment
for several rental properties both before and after the marriage. The remainder of the
purchase price was raised through mortgages on the properties and rental income was then
used to pay off the mortgages. The trial judge held that the husband had an interest in the
properties equal to that of each of his relatives and that he had acquired his initial interest in
the properties by way of gift. Regarding the properties acquired before the marriage, he
permitted the husband to deduct the value of his interest at marriage. Regarding the proper-

ties acquired after the marriage, the husband was allowed to exclude only the value of the original gift at the time it was made. McDermid L.J.S.C. reasoned ((1986), 2 R.F.L. (3d) 188 at 205-206):

> Tony Oliva is not entitled to have excluded his share of the value of the properties in excess of the down payment since that portion of their value was acquired with income from the properties, which income was not expressly excluded by the donors from his net family property.

The husband appealed.]

The decision of the appellate court was as follows: — ... While we might have found that none of the properties was a gift but all were part of the business and partnership activities among the partners, we are not disposed to interfere with any of [the] findings of fact. It follows that the deductions made by the local judge with respect to the properties acquired before marriage based upon s. 4(1) will stand. Under that section, the net family property is determined after deducting the value of the property owned on the date of marriage and that is the procedure the local judge followed. With respect to the two properties found to be gifts after the marriage, the position is different. There, s. 4(2) provides that, with respect to property acquired by gift after marriage, "the value of the ... property that a spouse owns on the valuation date does not form part of the spouse's net family property". It follows that the whole value including any appreciation therein after the date of the gift cannot be included. The local judge excluded only the actual value of the gift at the time it was made.

We believe therefore that the judgment must be amended to determine the net family assets of the husband so as to exclude the value of those two properties as of the valuation date. Section 4(2)2 provides that income from the property, unless expressly otherwise stated in the gift, will be included. It follows that any income from those properties used to pay or reduce the interest or principal of the mortgages or used in any other way to increase the equity or value of those two properties should not be excluded. There is no evidence of income being used for any purpose other than reduction of the mortgage.

We are not aware of the precise figures that will result and if counsel cannot agree we refer the matter back to the local judge of the Supreme Court to make that determination. In all other respects the appeal including the appeal as to costs will be dismissed. ...

HO v. HO

(1993), 1 R.F.L. (4th) 340, 1993 CarswellOnt 287 (Ont. Gen. Div.)

FERRIER J.: — ... (b) *Exclusions*

During the course of the marriage, the husband's father and mother made substantial cash gifts to either the husband or the wife, or both.

The husband's evidence and position is that any funds advanced by his father to the wife were intended for him and that they were advanced to the wife solely for tax purposes — the explanation being that because the husband was employed and the wife was not, she was in a much lower tax bracket, and if the funds were transferred to her, the interest income thereon would attract much less tax than if the funds were transferred to him. Thus, there is no issue that the funds were gifts. The only issue is whether or not they were gifts to the husband or gifts to the wife. ...

The effect of the wife's evidence is that her father-in-law simply gifted the funds to her. I accept the evidence of the husband that the funds were transferred to Mrs. Ho for tax purposes. That does not end the matter, however. Mr. Ho cannot have it both ways. The funds are either his wife's or his. If they are his, then there would be no basis upon which Mrs. Ho would have to pay tax on the interest derived from the funds. Clearly, if Mr. Ho had been asked by the Department of National Revenue, in 1989, whose funds they were, he most certainly would have answered "my wife's." That answer would have been true and he cannot now, in the face of the separation and the *Family Law Act*, reverse the facts.

Accordingly, I find that the gifts referred to ... have been established by the wife.

From the $200,000 received by the wife in November and December 1988, she advanced approximately $146,000 to her husband, in April 1989, to permit the husband to invest in the property on Queen Street. An issue arises as to whether or not the advance to the husband was a loan or a gift. As I have above determined, these funds were the sole property of the wife. She readily advanced the funds to her husband and no loan documentation was undertaken. She was quite willing to assist her husband in his investment endeavours. ...

I note as well that the husband indicated that he had forgotten about the balance of the $200,000 which had been forwarded by his father to his wife. If he were truly the owner of those funds, I find it quite unlikely that he would forget about the approximately $50,000 still in his wife's bank account. His lack of attention to those funds tends to support the wife's contention that the $200,000 gift was a gift without any qualifying understandings or conditions.

I accept the evidence of the wife that she expected to be repaid the $146,000. The husband did not suggest that the $146,000 advanced to him by the wife was a gift. He could not do so because of his position in reference to the $200,000 gift from Mr. Ho, Sr. As well, because of this position, the husband gave no evidence concerning his alleged obligation to repay the money.

The wife's counsel indicated that, in any event, the situation in reference to the $146,000 is "a wash." In other words, the husband's net family property statement would show it as a liability and the wife's would show it as a receivable. To this extent, counsel for the wife is correct. However, because the funds were a gift from Mr. Ho, Sr., and because the wife is able to trace those funds to the receivable due from her husband, the value of the asset (the receivable) may be excluded under the *Family Law Act*. This is the correct treatment of the $146,000.

As to the balance of the exclusions sought by the wife, although to some extent there was a commingling of funds, I am satisfied, on the basis of the evidence of the wife and the copies of her bank account statements, that she has succeeded in tracing the $5,400 amount in reference to the Honda and the $10,000 Canada Savings Bond purchased November 1, 1989. Beyond those items and the $146,000 loan to the husband, the funds received from Mr. Ho, Sr. have been commingled with other funds to such an extent that it is not possible to trace the items claimed by the wife, as set out in Exhibit 20. Accordingly, the wife is entitled to exclusions totalling $161,400.

The husband seeks to exclude the sum of $20,000, which was in his bank account at the date of separation, having been received from his father two weeks previously. In my view, the husband's position in this respect is correct. The husband is unable to establish any other exclusions. ...

CARTIER v. CARTIER

(2007), 47 R.F.L. (6th) 436, Ont. S.C.J. (Footnotes omitted)

[A husband's mother gave him valuable farmland during the marriage. Eventually, the husband sold this land and used the proceeds of almost $1 million to acquire four investments that he held jointly with his wife. After separation, he sought to exclude the value of his interests in these investments from his net family property.]

E. DUCHARME J.:

A. Overview

1 This application raises a question about s. 4(2).1 of the *Family Law Act*: If a spouse who receives a gift from a third party during the marriage transfers the gifted property into joint names with the other spouse, is the spouse who received the gift originally permitted to exclude one half of the value of the joint property, or property into which the gifted property can be traced, from his or her net family property upon separation?

2 In some cases in which the issue has arisen courts have held that property otherwise excluded under s. 4(2).1 or 4(2).5 of the Act may not be deducted in the computation of a spouse's net family property, if the spouse used or intended to use the gift or inheritance for the purposes of the family.

3 The contrary view, and the one I believe to be the correct one, is that when a spouse transfers gifted or inherited property into joint names, thereby conferring an interest in the other spouse, the transferring spouse loses the exclusion *only* to the extent of the gift he or she made to the other spouse, provided that the result intended by the transfer is joint ownership.

4 On the facts of this case, and for the reasons that follow, I have concluded that the respondent husband, Marc Joseph Cartier, is entitled to exclude from his net family property statement his half interest in the value on the valuation date of the four jointly held properties that lie at the heart of this dispute. ...

23 In his Answer to Mrs. Cartier's Application, Mr. Cartier pleaded that he understood "the effect" of his gift of a half interest in the matrimonial home to Mrs. Cartier and of holding jointly with her the properties traceable to the sale of the farmland. Unlike the situation in some of the cases placed before me, Mr. Cartier has not sought to set aside any conveyance to his wife, nor has he tried to prove that his wife held her half interest in the properties in trust for him. He has merely pleaded, and testified, that he intended his wife to have a 50% interest in the properties he and she owned jointly. I accept Mr. Cartier's testimony on the subject without the slightest doubt or hesitation. ...

25 Counsel for Mrs. Cartier argued that in the opening sentence of subsection 4(2) emphasis should fall upon the word "owns": "The value of the following property that a spouse *owns* on the valuation date does not form part of the spouse's net family property. ..." A spouse must first prove that he or she owns the property before seeking to exclude it from net family property. According to this argument, it is impossible to say on these facts what each spouse owned of the impugned properties, because they held them jointly.

26 I do not accept this position. I do not believe Mrs. Cartier's testimony that she and her husband had, in effect, an undefined, indivisible 100% ownership in each of the properties. I believe Mr. Cartier's evidence that he intended his wife to share with him equally the benefits flowing from his mother's gift to him. I accept Mr. Cartier's evidence on this point, because it is the most consistent with the known, uncontradicted facts, including those relating to the transfer of ownership in and the disposition of the matrimonial home. When it came to the matrimonial home, the parties were certainly of like minds. They were to be joint tenants, and they were to share the value of the home equally, 50/50. ...

33 As subsection 4(2) makes clear, a spouse may deduct the value of the gift received during marriage only if he or she still owns the property in question on the valuation date, or if it can be traced into other property owned by the claiming spouse on the valuation date. On Mrs. Cartier's own telling, the properties in question represent proceeds gained directly by her and Mr. Cartier from the sale of the gifted property. I see no reason, therefore, why Mr.

~~Cartier should be prohibited from deducting the value of his joint interest in those properties. To conclude otherwise, to find that Mr. Cartier cannot have his exclusion because he has a joint ownership interest, rather than a sole segregated ownership interest, is illogical. It would also be manifestly unfair.~~

34 I reiterate: that Mrs. Cartier has an equal property interest with her husband in the proceeds of the gifted property has nothing to do with Mr. Cartier's personal right to deduct the value of what he has left of the proceeds of the gifted property. And in my view it makes no difference in law that Mr. Cartier did not segregate and keep entirely to himself in one or more separate accounts the proceeds of the sale of the farmland.

35 On all the evidence, I conclude that Mr. Cartier gave Mrs. Cartier a half interest in the jointly held assets and retained his own half interest. In arriving at this conclusion, I acknowledge that the presumption of the resulting trust in s. 14 of the Act is not a presumption of a gift of one half, but merely a presumption of an intention "to own the property as joint tenants."

36 Still, if spouses own property as joint tenants, or if they have a joint interest in property, then they share and ought to share that asset equally. Accordingly, Mr. Cartier shall lose his exclusion only to the extent of his gift to Mrs. Cartier of one half interest in each of the four properties. ...

NOTES AND QUESTIONS

1. The difference between a pre-marital property deduction and an exclusion is dramatically illustrated by *Black v. Black* (1988), 18 R.F.L. (3d) 303 (Ont. H.C.). Under the terms of the will of the husband's grandparents, one half of the residue of their estates was directed to be held in trust by the husband's father for the husband and his younger brother until the latter reached 25 years of age. At that time each brother would receive an equal share of the *corpus* of the trust. When the husband married in 1964, the value of his share in the *corpus* of the trust was $468,050. The husband received his share of the *corpus* in 1969 and its value on the valuation date was $6.2 million. The husband claimed that these assets were inherited after the marriage and that he was, therefore, entitled to exclude their entire value of $6.2 million in calculating his net family property. But the court concluded that the husband inherited the assets prior to the marriage and that he was only entitled to a pre-marital property deduction of $468,050.

2. Although McKinlay J. did not refer to it in *Mittler v. Mittler*, the legislative history of the *FLA* reinforces her conclusion that the amount of the pre-marital property deduction is fixed at the time of the marriage, with no indexing or credit system for simple inflation. The presentation of the Canadian Bar Association — Ontario Branch to the Standing Committee on the Administration of Justice regarding the draft bill specifically alluded to the fact that inflation might drastically reduce the value of the pre-marital deduction in a long marriage. Although the Association suggested changes, including the possibility of adjusting the value of the deduction in accordance with the Consumer Price Index during the marriage, the Committee did not adopt them. See Ontario, Standing Committee on Administration of Justice, *Transcripts* (1st Session, 33rd Parl., Nov. 25, 1985) J-12, at 5.

For the argument that an increase in the value of pre-marital property solely due to inflationary pressures should not be shared, see McLeod, "Annotation" (1984), 39 R.F.L. (2d) 2 at 2-3 and Law Reform Commission of British Columbia, *Working Paper on Property Rights on Marriage Breakdown* (Vancouver: Ministry of the Attorney General, 1989) at 77–83. For additional comment, see Botsford, "Net Family Property and the Use of Constant Dollar Values" (2000), 17 C.F.L.Q. 327.

3. The courts have generally concluded that the pre-marital property deduction can be a negative figure, thereby becoming, in effect, an addition to the spouse's net family property. The cases are reviewed in *McAndrew v. Rooney-McAndrew* (2003), 47 R.F.L. (5th) 120 (P.E.I. C.A.), where the court also explains how this approach accords with the general policy underlying the legislation.

4. The onus of proving a deduction or exclusion is on the person claiming it: s. 4(3) of the *FLA*. The onus of proof may be significant in many situations because evidence regarding the existence of pre-marital property or the acquisition of property by gift is often stale or uncertain. It has been especially important in cases involving alleged

debts owed to relatives or where one spouse asserts that gifts or inheritances can be traced into property still owned on the valuation date. The concept of tracing will be further examined below.

5. There are many cases dealing with the issue of whether moneys advanced by one spouse's parents during the marriage are a gift or a loan. On first impression, it may be thought that it makes no difference in the calculation of a spouse's NFP whether an advance from a parent is a gift or a loan. If it is a gift, it can give rise to an exclusion. If it is a loan, the amount owing on the valuation date can be deducted. Consider, however, a situation where the money has been used to pay off the mortgage on the matrimonial home or one where the money was used to fund a world cruise for the family.

Generally, the courts are suspicious when it is only after separation that the recipient spouse alleges a loan. Even where they conclude that there is a debt owing on the valuation date, they may discount it for the possibility that it will be years before repayment will occur. The case law on both the characterization of the transaction as a gift or loan and the question of discounting any family debt is reviewed in *Traversy v. Glover* (2006), 30 R.F.L. (6th) 372 (Ont. S.C.J.).

6. The cases appear to accept that property may be partially acquired by gift and partially by purchase and that the portion of the value of the property attributable to the gift after marriage is excluded from net family property. See, e.g., *Leslie v. Leslie* (1987), 9 R.F.L. (3d) 82 (Ont. H.C.); *McDonald v. McDonald* (1988), 11 R.F.L. (3d) 321 (Ont. H.C.); *Cotter v. Cotter* (1988), 12 R.F.L. (3d) 209 (Ont. H.C.); and *Andreoli v. Andreoli* (1990), 27 R.F.L. (3d) 142 (Ont. Dist. Ct.). Explain how the analysis of the Ontario Court of Appeal in the *Brinkos* and *Oliva* cases support the general proposition that property interests may be partially acquired by gift for the purpose of s. 4(2)1. See also the note on tracing, below.

7. The increase in value of excluded property from the date of acquisition to the valuation date may be due to factors other than capital appreciation. Consider the following example. Five years after his marriage a husband inherits a rental property valued at $50,000. He immediately sells GICs, acquired through a payroll deduction plan during the marriage, to finance renovations of the property costing $50,000. At separation, some five years later, the property is worth $150,000. Can the husband exclude the entire value of the property? Should there be some form of apportionment?

8. The special treatment (in s. 4(2)2 of the *FLA*) of income from property received as a gift or inheritance from a third party after the marriage highlights the general rule that income from excluded property is included in net family property.

A Brief Note on Tracing

As indicated in the *Cartier* and *Ho* cases, above, paragraph 5 of s. 4(2) of the *FLA* provides for the exclusion from a spouse's NFP of the value of property, other than a matrimonial home, into which property excluded under paragraphs 1 to 4 can be traced. The word "trace" is not defined in the Act and the question arises whether the term is to be taken as referring to the common law and equitable rules of tracing or whether it is being used in a special sense. The early cases under the *FLA* generally assumed the former. However, these tracing rules were developed to deal with situations such as a trustee's wrongful disposition of trust property. Such situations are hardly analogous to a claim for an exclusion under a matrimonial property regime. At the very least there are difficulties in adapting these rules to fit the general scheme of the *FLA*. Accordingly, some courts have begun to use more liberal tracing rules.

In some situations, tracing may be quite straightforward. Consider the following example. A husband inherits $25,000 under his father's will and places this money into a bank account that never has any other funds in it. Using moneys from this account, he purchases a truck for $22,500. He never makes any other withdrawals. At the valuation date, the husband's truck is worth $15,000 and there is $2,580 in the bank account. The husband has retained all the transaction slips and receipts documenting these events. He can exclude the value of the truck and most of the moneys in the bank account in calculating his NFP. He does have to include $80 as income on the money in the bank account unless his father stipulated that income from the legacy was to be excluded from the husband's NFP. See paragraph 2 of s. 4(2).

However, the situation is almost always more complicated. There are often a series of transactions involving excluded property or it is mixed with non-excluded property. The husband in the earlier example might place the legacy in a joint account that the family uses to make general purchases. Alternatively, he might place it in an account in his name and a number of deposits and withdrawals might then follow. Assume, for example, that he places it in an account in his name that already has $25,000 of his employment income in it. He then uses $22,500 to buy a truck with money from the account. The following month, he withdraws $25,000 to pay for a luxury cruise for the whole family. There are no further transactions involving the account and, on the valuation date, there is $2,580 in the account. Can the husband exclude any or all or none of the value of the truck? Can he trace any of the money left in the account to the legacy? In *Mittler v. Mittler* (1988), 17 R.F.L. (3d) 113 (Ont. H.C.); additional reasons at (1988), 1988 CarswellOnt 2519 (H.C.), the court referred to the "first in, first out" (FIFO) principle from *Clayton's Case* as still relevant to this type of situation. If this principle were applied, the husband would not be able to exclude any of the value of the truck. However, the Ontario Court of Appeal in *Ontario (Securities Commission) v. Greymac Credit Corp.* (1986), 55 O.R. (2d) 673 (C.A.); additional reasons at (October 20, 1986), Doc. CA 306/ 85 (Ont. C.A.); affirmed (1988), 31 E.T.R. 1 (S.C.C.), confined the application of the rule in *Clayton's Case* essentially to its facts. It refused to apply the FIFO rule to a contest between two innocent beneficiaries injured by the unauthorized withdrawals by a trustee from a mixed fund. Instead, it ruled that the beneficiaries shared on a *pro rata* basis. Several courts have relied on the *Greymac* case to justify the application of a *pro rata* approach to the determination of the extent of an exclusion under s. 4(2) of the *FLA*.

In *Goodyer v. Goodyer* (1999), 168 D.L.R. (4th) 453 (Ont. Gen. Div.), the husband received about $140,000 from his father during the marriage. This money was placed into an investment account. From time to time, the account borrowed money to provide additional funds for investment in mutual funds. The units of the mutual funds were frequently bought and sold. Regularly, the husband used some money from the investment account for the family's living expenses. To complicate matters further, he eventually transferred the account into the names of himself and his wife as joint tenants. After that, in June 1996, the husband mortgaged another property and injected an additional $150,000 into the investment account because the family was eating into the capital. At that point, the investment account had a total value of $282,867 (including units purchased with the $150,000 capital injection) and there was $64,427 owing on the husband's loan. On the valuation date, a year later, the value of the account was $248,279 and there was $117,131 owing on the loan.

In analyzing the husband's claim for an exclusion from his net family property, Justice Perkins indicated (para. 70):

> If *Ontario (Securities Commission) v. Greymac Credit Corp.* represents the law of tracing generally in trust cases, on the basis that a pro rata approach is more sensible and just, it must also be the law for family law cases where tracing is to be carried out under subs. 4(2) of the *Family Law Act*. There is no reason to resort to the old legal fiction in these circumstances, even though the *Family Law Act* has a bias against exclusions. Once an exclusion for gift property is established, the amount of the exclusion should be calculated in accordance with the new rule as set out in *Ontario (Securities Commission) v. Greymac Credit Corp. Mittler v. Mittler* must be taken to have been overruled on this point.

The Justice next dealt with the interest and dividends that had been paid into the investment account during the marriage (para. 72):

> The account was credited with interest and dividends over the years, some of which were attributable to the original capital and some of which resulted notionally from the injection of loan funds, but none of the interest and dividends is entitled to be excluded from the equalization calculation under

> subs. 4(2) par. 2, because there was no express statement by Henry Barron [the father] that the income from his gift was to be excluded. In any event, the interest and dividend credits were in fact used up, as shown by the sharply declining net equity position with only a minimal decline in the loan. I realize that this is a last in, first out accounting of the dividends and interest, but this makes sense — the husband, the wife and their broker intended the capital to be maintained as much as possible in order to generate future income. A deliberate choice was made to spend the interest and dividends and not pay the loan off. I think that I should give effect to actual intent to allocate the interest for daily living expenses, rather than rely on a presumption or a legal fiction.

Finally, the Justice turned to the apportionment of the value of the investment account that could be traced to the original gift of $140,000. In fixing the portion of the equity in the investment account that could be traced, the Justice looked at June 1996 "when the net value of the asset had reached its lowest point" because "the husband cannot exclude an amount greater than he actually had at any given point". (para. 73). At that time, following the injection of the $150,000 from the mortgage, the account had assets of $282,427 and owed $64,427 on the loan. The Justice therefore concluded that the funds from the mortgage accounted for 68.66% of the equity while the original gift accounted for 31.34% of the equity in the investment account just after the injection of the $150,000. This was the ratio used by the Justice in determining what portion of the equity in the account on the valuation date was attributable to the original gift. Thus, the original gift could be traced to $41,101.78 (31.34% of the equity in the account at separation). Because the husband had gifted a joint interest in the account to his wife, his exclusion was reduced to $20,550.89.

The *pro rata* approach to the determination of the extent of an exclusion under s. 4(5) of the *FLA* was also applied in *Wolfe v. Wolfe* (2003), 43 R.F.L. (5th) 223 (Ont. S.C.J.), where a husband placed about $50,000 inherited money into a bank account into which his wages were regularly deposited. On the valuation date, the account had $16,552.61 in it. The Justice allowed the husband to exclude $10,345.40 on the basis that the original inheritance of $50,000 represented five-eighths of the moneys deposited.

As indicated above, the judges in the *Goodyer* and *Wolfe* cases struggled with the application of the concept of tracing where excluded funds had been commingled with non-excluded funds. Another, perhaps even more common, hurdle faced by a spouse who seeks to establish that a property interest held on the valuation date can be traced back to an inheritance is the fact that people do not usually keep detailed records of their financial transactions during their married life. As a result, the spouse claiming that a property held on the valuation date can be traced back to an excluded property may be unable to produce the documents demonstrating the chain of transactions. Frequently, this leads to the loss of the exclusion. See, e.g., *Launchbury v. Launchbury* (2001), 15 R.F.L. (5th) 106 (Ont. S.C.J.); affirmed (2005), 2005 CarswellOnt 1335 (Ont. C.A.). However, a possible liberalization of the evidentiary requirements is suggested in *Bennett v. Bennett* (1997), 34 R.F.L. (4th) 290 (Ont. Gen. Div.); affirmed (1999), 1999 CarswellOnt 2139 (Ont. C.A.); leave to appeal refused [1999] 3 S.C.R. v. The husband inherited $40,000 and shortly afterwards purchased some farmland (Parcel "C") for $35,000. There was evidence of the inheritance and the later purchase, but there was no evidence of where the funds were in the interim. The husband admitted that they might have been intermingled with family funds in a joint bank account. Justice Metivier reasoned (at 305):

> With respect to parcel "C" and the tracing of inherited funds which went to purchase it, I find the proximity of the two events (the inheritance and the purchase) to be such that, on a reasonable balance of probabilities, the inherited funds were used for this purchase. Strict tracing rules would not provide for this result but common sense and a reasonable view of how this couple could have found the amount of money required for the purchase of the land leads to a conclusion that the strict tracing rules should be relaxed. Professor McLeod, in an annotation to *Berdette v. Berdette* (1991), 33 R.F.L. (3d) 113 (Ont. C.A.), is of the view that such rules could be relaxed where there is no trustee-beneficiary equity and relationship. Equity and the facts of this case call for it.

The tracing only leads to a particular asset, that being parcel "C". There is available therefore an exclusion for the value of that property as of the date of separation, s. 4(2)2, *Family Law Act*. That exclusion is valued at $27,750.

See also *McIsaac v. McIsaac* (2004), 1 R.F.L. (6th) 293 (Ont. S.C.J.); additional reasons at (2004), 2004 CarswellOnt 270 (Ont. S.C.J.) and various Alberta cases such as *Harrower v. Harrower* (1989), 21 R.F.L. (3d) 369 (Alta. C.A.); *Roenisch v. Roenisch* (1991), 32 R.F.L. (3d) 233 (Alta. C.A.); *Brokopp v. Brokopp* (1996), 19 R.F.L. (4th) 1 (Alta. C.A.); and *Timms v. Timms* (1997), 29 R.F.L. (4th) 392 (Alta. Q.B.); additional reasons at (1997), [1998] 4 W.W.R. 458 (Alta. Q.B.). A strict approach is still evident in *Fotheringham v. Fotheringham* (2004), 2 R.F.L. (6th) 288 (Ont. S.C.J.).

In its *Report on Family Property Law* (Toronto: 1993), the Ontario Law Reform Commission recommended (at 77):

[S]ection 4 of the *Family Law Act* should be amended to provide that all gains or losses in the capital value of an asset listed in section 4(2) and income earned on such an asset must be included in the net family property of its owner. The Commission further recommends that gains or losses in the capital value of an excluded asset should be defined as the change in value occurring between the later of the date of the marriage and the date of the receipt, and the valuation date.

In effect, the above recommendation will end the "exclusion" of assets from net family property. Rather, all assets will be included in the calculation, but a spouse will be able to deduct from her [sic] net family property the value of an asset of the type listed in section 4(2) at the later of the date of marriage or the date of receipt.

Implementation of the Commission's recommendations would, of course, eliminate the tracing requirement.

For further reading, see Zylberman and Burke, "Tracing Exclusions in Family Law" (2006), 25 C.F.L.Q. 67.

(d) Sample Problems

Calculate the net family property for each spouse in the following fact situations.

1. A daughter, on the death of her mother, inherits her parents' home. Shortly thereafter she marries and she and her husband move into the home. They live in the home until separation. At the time of the marriage, this is the wife's only asset and she has no liabilities. The home is valued at $100,000 at the time of the marriage. The husband has assets valued at $150,000 at that time and liabilities of $50,000. Six years later the spouses separate with no reasonable prospect of resumed cohabitation. At that time the home is valued at $125,000. The wife still has no other assets and no liabilities. The husband now has assets valued at $250,000 and liabilities of $150,000. None of his property is excluded under s. 4(2).

2. The facts are identical to #1 above, except that the wife inherits the home valued at $100,000 after the marriage and the spouses begin to live in it after that date.

3. The facts are identical to #2 above, except that the spouses never move into the home. Instead the wife rents it out and uses the income to rent an apartment for herself and her husband.

4. The facts are identical to #1 above, except that the spouses only live in the home for one year and then move into a rented apartment. The home is then rented to a third party.

5. At marriage, Henry has clothes, furniture and a car. The total value of these items (made up almost entirely of the car's value) was $9,000. He also has shares in a gold mine worth $1,000. Wendy, Henry's wife, has property at marriage with an estimated value of $25,000 (mostly because of an employee's pension). She also has a student loan on which she owes $15,000.

    When they separate without reasonable prospect of resumed cohabitation, Henry has mutual funds in an RRSP valued at $50,000 and he owns a BMW worth $25,000 (given to him last year by his father). The shares in the gold mine are now worth $26,000, while Wendy's pension is worth $250,000. Each spouse has a separate bank account with $10,000 in it. In addition, there is a joint bank account with $4,000 in it. During the marriage, each spouse's pay is deposited into this account. Wendy also has a ring (given to her by Henry on the couple's fifth anniversary) worth $10,000 and she is the registered owner of a Honda Civic worth $12,000. Although money for the purchase of the Honda came from the couple's joint bank account, this car is always treated as Wendy's and referred to it as such. Finally, the couple has a home worth $200,000 registered in joint tenancy and furniture worth $10,000. There is a mortgage of $100,000 for which each spouse is responsible. All of the money for the various household purchases such as the furniture came from the couple's joint bank account.

6. Harry, aged 45, and Wanda, aged 40, get married. Each of them already owns a home valued at approximately $250,000. They decide to move into Harry's house because it is better landscaped. Wanda rents out her house. At marriage, Harry has furniture worth $20,000, a Lexus valued at $50,000 and an employment pension worth $300,000. He has no debts. Wanda's pension is worth $320,000 at marriage and she also has a car worth $20,000, a bank account with $20,000 in it, and furniture worth $10,000.

    When they separate four years later with no prospect of resumed cohabitation, they are still living in Harry's house. It is now worth $350,000. His pension is valued at $400,000, his furniture at $30,000 and his Lexus at $35,000. There is $30,000 in a joint bank account. Wanda's house, which is still rented out, is now worth $350,000. She also has furniture worth $10,000, a pension valued at $430,000, and her Honda Civic is worth $5,000.

7. A wife has no assets or liabilities on marriage. However, she inherits her parents' home two years after the marriage. At that time it is valued at $200,000. The home is never used as the family residence. The wife mortgages the home immediately and spends the $100,000 raised by the mortgage renovating the home. It is valued at $360,000 when the wife and husband separate five years later without reasonable prospect of resumed cohabitation. At that time, the balance on the mortgage is $80,000. The wife has other assets valued at $50,000 on separation and no other liabilities. At the time of the marriage, the husband had no assets. He owed $3,000 on a student loan. On separation, the husband had assets valued at $130,000 and liabilities of $33,000. The student loan was paid off by the husband during the first two years of marriage.

8. At the time of the marriage, the husband owns a Ford Mustang valued at $5,000 and the wife has a bank account with $5,000 in it. Two years later, the wife is given a BMW as a graduation gift by her father. She sells it and uses the proceeds to buy a Chevrolet Cavalier and some furniture. The husband inherits a home four years after the marriage. At that time it is valued at $400,000. Shortly after, the husband sells shares for $100,000 and uses the proceeds to renovate the house. The shares were

purchased during the marriage by the husband through an employee-share plan. The house, which is never used as the family residence, is valued at $460,000 when the spouses separate without reasonable prospect of resumed cohabitation.

Other than the house, the husband has the following assets on separation: a Volvo station wagon valued at $21,000, a Canada Savings Bond valued at $11,000, and Bell Canada shares valued at $25,000. The wife's assets on separation are as follows: the Chevrolet valued at $2,000, furniture (purchased with the proceeds from the sale of the BMW) valued at $12,000, and an RRSP with $40,000 standing to her credit. The matrimonial home is jointly owned and is valued at $380,000. It has a mortgage with a balance of $104,000. Finally, the couple's joint bank account to which they both contribute has a balance of $12,500 on separation.

(3) Variation of the Equalization Payment

HOVIUS, "UNEQUAL SHARING OF NET FAMILY PROPERTIES UNDER ONTARIO'S *FAMILY LAW ACT*"

(2008), 27 C.F.L.Q. 147 (Some footnotes have been edited and others omitted)

1. Introduction

... Under s. 5(6) of the FLA, a court may award a spouse "an amount that is more or less than half the difference between the net family properties if the court is of the opinion that equalizing the net family properties would be unconscionable" having regard to the factors listed. ...

2. Threshold of "Unconscionable"

... The appropriate threshold for judicial variation of the equalization payment was the focus of much of the debate surrounding the bill that ultimately became the FLA. Women's rights groups argued strongly against the Canadian Bar Association of Ontario — Family Law Section's recommendation that the word "inequitable" should replace "unconscionable" in s. 5(6), believing that any increase in judicial discretion would be used to reduce the share of the spouse who had not acquired property during the marriage — traditionally, the wife. In the end, the legislature decided to stick with the word "unconscionable" rather than revert to "inequitable", the threshold used in the predecessor legislation [the *Family Law Reform Act*] in connection with a possible unequal division of family assets.

The courts have fairly consistently acknowledged that the standard for an unequal sharing of NFPs is a tough one to meet and the results in the cases, on the whole, prove this. While the Ontario Court of Appeal has not written extensively about the meaning of "unconscionable", it has generally signaled that unequal sharing should be limited to exceptional circumstances. In *MacDonald v. MacDonald*, the Court overturned a lower court's adjustment to the equalization payment because the husband had contributed less to the family's welfare than his wife, stating: "Unconscionable conduct is well established in the law to be conduct which is harsh and shocking to the conscience."[1] More recently, the Court said that "s. 5(6) reapportionment is only available on those rare occasions when a party is able to

---

[1]   *MacDonald v. MacDonald* (1997), 33 R.F.L. (4th) 75 (Ont. C.A.) at para. 17.

meet the high threshold required to establish unconsionability".[2] The Court has also recently accepted that "the 'unconscionable' threshold is higher than 'unfairness', 'harshness' or 'injustice'".[3] This lends support to those lower court decisions where judges expressly concluded that, even though the equal sharing of the NFPs might be unfair, there should be no adjustment because such sharing was not unconscionable.[4] ...

One of the longest judicial discussions of the concept of "unconscionable" can be found in the trial judgment in *Braaksma v. Braaksma* where Justice Beckett examined various dictionary meanings and concluded: "It is clear that by using the word 'unconscionable' in s. 5(6) rather than the word 'inequitable' ..., the legislature intended a much stricter test than mere unfairness, harshness or injustice."[5] Ultimately, Justice Beckett concluded that equal sharing of the NFPs in that case would be "grossly unfair, unreasonable, and repugnant to anyone's sense of justice to the level of unconscionability".[6] Justice Beckett's reasoning was referred to recently in *LeVan v. LeVan*, where Justice Backhouse stated:

> "Unconscionability" is a much more difficult test to meet than "fairness" and, as a result, the courts have only minimal discretion to order anything other than an equal division of family property. Unconscionable conduct has been defined as, among other things, conduct that is harsh and shocking to anyone's sense of justice, or shocking to the conscience of the court.[7]

Similarly, Justice S.M. Rogers suggested in *Weddel v. Weddel* that the threshold is "more than hardship, more than unfair, more than inequitable" and must "reach the extent of outrageous".[8] Justice Webber of the Prince Edward Island Court of Appeal reviewed many of the Ontario cases dealing with the meaning of "unconscionable" in this context in *Murphy v. Murphy* and concluded:

> While these cases show various ways in which the issue of unconscionability may be approached, they also indicate that the onus of proving the need for an unequal division is on the person seeking it and the factual foundation must show significantly more than an inequity if assets are divided equally. The facts must show that an equal division would in the circumstances shock the conscience of the court.
>
> The evolution of the law in this regard is consistent with the social goal of reducing litigation and encouraging settlement. The Legislature appears to have intended that judges be given the power to adjust the division of assets where not to do so would clearly "shock the conscience of the court" but not be given the power to "fine tune" the division of assets between parties. While the decision on

---

2   *von Czielik v. Ayuso* (2007), 36 R.F.L. (6th) 231 (Ont. C.A.) at para. 30. See also *LeVan v. LeVan* (2008), 51 R.F.L. (6th) 237 (Ont. C.A.); additional reasons at (2008), 51 R.F.L. (6th) 261 (Ont. C.A.); leave to appeal refused (2008), 2008 CarswellOnt 6207, 2008 CarswellOnt 6208 (S.C.C.) where Justice Borins stated (at para. 63): "The court's authority to order unequal division is severely restricted to those circumstances that are 'unconscionable' and that fall within the specific circumstances set out in clauses (a) through (h) of s. 5(6)".

3   *Roseneck v. Gowling* (2002), 35 R.F.L. (5th) 177 (Ont. C.A.) at para 39.

4   See, e.g., *Heal v. Heal* (1998), 43 R.F.L. (4th) 88 (Ont. Gen. Div.) at para. 27; *Higgins v. Higgins* (2001), 19 R.F.L. (5th) 300 (Ont. S.C.J.) at para 30; *Conway v. Conway* (2005), 16 R.F.L. (6th) 23 (Ont. S.C.J.); and *Azimi v. Mirzaei* (2007), 2007 CarswellOnt 2999 (S.C.J.); affirmed (2007), 2007 CarswellOnt 8304 (C.A.).

5   (1992), 41 R.F.L. (3d) 304 (Ont. U.F.C.) at para. 15; affirmed (1996), 25 R.F.L. (4th) 307 (Ont. C.A.). The Ontario Court of Appeal upheld the trial judgment awarding the couple's only asset, the matrimonial home, to the wife.

6   *Ibid.* at para. 17.

7   *LeVan v. LeVan* (2006), 32 R.F.L. (6th) 291 (Ont. S.C.J.), at para. 258; additional reasons at (2006), 32 R.F.L. (6th) 359 (Ont. S.C.J.); affirmed (2008), 51 R.F.L. (6th) 237 (Ont. C.A.); additional reasons at (2008), 51 R.F.L. (6th) 261 (Ont. C.A.); leave to appeal refused (2008), 2008 CarswellOnt 6207, 2008 CarswellOnt 6208 (S.C.C.).

8   (2006), 2006 CarswellOnt 3901 (S.C.J.) at para 22.

whether or not to exercise this power is a discretionary one, there is a very high standard that must be met before a judge is empowered to exercise that discretion.[9]

Even if it is accepted that the threshold is a high one, determining whether it is met still involves a value judgment. Justice G.A. Campbell acknowledged this recently:

> Almost all cases which deal with "unconscionability" cite the difficulty in defining that term. "Unconscionable" has generally been strictly interpreted, for example, as meaning "shocking the conscience of the court" ..., "shockingly unfair", and "patently unfair or inordinately inequitable". Despite the strict interpretation of subsection 5(6), it remains difficult to advise a client as to whether a particular result will be unconscionable. This is because what might shock the conscience of one judge, might not shock the conscience of another. Thus, what is indeed "unconscionable" is a somewhat subjective standard and is largely fact driven.[10]

The creation of a high threshold for the variation of an equalization payment accords with the intent of the legislature when it enacted s. 5(6) of the FLA. It also has some practical benefits. It promotes certainty and predictability. As noted by various commentators, the high threshold helps to explain why there is less litigation concerning property rights following separation in Ontario than there is in a province such as British Columbia where courts have greater discretion. However, setting a high threshold means that individualized justice is restricted. General rules that produce a fair result in the vast majority of cases may cause injustice or unfairness in particular circumstances. In its 1993 *Report on Family Law*, the OLRC recognized that maintaining a high threshold carried a price, but recommended against lowering the standard for fear of "increased inconsistency and unpredictability of results".[11]

3. Extent of Court's Power under Section 5(6)

Almost from the time that the FLA came into effect in 1986, there has been debate over the extent of a court's power under s. 5(6) of the FLA. This issue arose mainly in the context of an "intentional or reckless depletion of ... net family property", one of the listed situations in s. 5(6). A classic example of such a situation is provided by *Harry v. Harry*.[12] In that case the husband gifted shares valued at $170,800 to his daughter a few days before separation. District Court Judge Mossop found that the husband wished "to create another impediment to the legitimate claims of the wife".[13] However, the remedial options available were limited by the fact that there was (and still is) no provision within the Act authorizing judges to claw back gifts or transfers. Using s. 5(6), the judge added one-half of $170,800 to the equalization payment owing to the wife so that she was in the same position as she would have been if the husband had not made the gift.

However, in some situations involving intentional depletion of a spouse's NFP, the application of s. 5(6) presents difficulty. Consider the following:

> *Example 1*: When marital problems first arise, a husband gives assets valued at $100,000 to his daughter to prevent his wife from sharing in their value. On separation one year later, his NFP is $25,000. The wife has an NFP of $20,000.

Equalization of the NFPs in this situation would mean that the husband owed the wife $2,500. In light of the husband's intentional depletion of his NFP, a court is likely to conclude that simple equalization would be unconscionable. But, what does s. 5(6) permit the

---

9   (2003), 40 R.F.L. (5th) 234 (P.E.I. C.A.).

10 *Aukstuolyte v. Balchun* (2005), 2005 CarswellOnt 3482 (S.C.J.) at para. 29.

11 OLRC, *Report on Family Property Law* (1993) at 68 [1993 *Family Property Report*].

12 (1987), 9 R.F.L. (3d) 121 (Ont. Dist. Ct.).

13 *Ibid.* at 126.

court to do in response? It has always been accepted that a court can use the provision to allow the wife in this situation to retain her property and award her $5,000; that is, the difference between the spouses' NFPs. However, the wife would then still be $47,500 worse off than if the husband had not made the gift. Some cases decided soon after the enactment of the FLA suggested that a court could use s. 5(6) in this situation to award the wife an equalization sum of $25,000; that is, in effect grant her 100% of the spouses' NFPs. Indeed, there was some speculation that a court might have the authority under s. 5(6) to go further and order the husband to pay the wife $52,500 to place her in the same position as she would have been without the gift.

However, statements in several Ontario Court of Appeal cases cast doubt on a court's authority to use s. 5(6) of the FLA to do anything more than deal with the difference between the spouses' NFPs.[14] As a result, commentators began to adopt this restrictive interpretation although at least one lower court judge refused to accept it.

The Ontario Court of Appeal revisited and settled the extent of a court's authority under s. 5(6) of the FLA in its 2007 decision in *von Czieslik v. Ayuso*.[15] In that case, a husband gifted property to a friend through a series of transactions before the couple's final separation. This reduced his NFP by approximately $190,000. The wife first learned of these transactions after the separation, prompting her to apply for an unequal division of the NFPs. At trial, Justice Stewart calculated that the husband's NFP was $74,385 and that the wife's was $63,919. She found that the husband had intentionally depleted his NFP by $190,000 and that an equal sharing of the remaining NFPs would be unconscionable. However, because Justice Stewart believed that her power under s. 5(6) of the FLA was limited to the reapportionment of the difference between the spouses' NFPs, she awarded the wife only $10,466.

The Ontario Divisional Court upheld the trial judgment, ... [but the] Ontario Court of Appeal allowed the wife's further appeal and awarded her $74,385, a sum equal to the value of the husband's NFP. Justice Lang, for the court, concluded that the grammatical and ordinary meaning of s. 5(6) of the FLA, read in context and in light of the goals underpinning the statutory scheme, indicated that a court could award an amount of money that was greater than the difference between the spouses' NFPs. She stressed that permitting a court to award an amount up to the whole of an offending spouse's NFP provided a "real, substantial, and meaningful remedy for the unconscionable conduct".[16]

After the *von Czieslik v. Ayuso* case, it is clear that a court can award one spouse an amount that is greater than the difference between the NFPs. This is obviously important in situations where a spouse intentionally depletes his or her NFP, but still has a sizeable NFP remaining. However, it is also clear that a court cannot use s. 5(6) to order a payment greater than the total value of the payor's NFP. In her reasons, Justice Lang explicitly identified the latter limitation on the court's power several times and applied it in the case itself. Although the husband's unconscionable behaviour had decreased the equalization payment by $95,000, the wife's award was limited to only $74,385 because this was the value of the husband's NFP. ...

---

14 Particularly influential was the first sentence in para. 42 in *Stone v. Stone* (2001), 18 R.F.L. (5th) 365 (Ont. C.A.) where Justice Feldman, in giving several reasons why the *Fraudulent Conveyances Act*, R.S.O. 1990, c. F.29, applied, stated: "Fourth, section 5(6) of the *Family Law Act* only empowers the court to order an unequal division of the difference in value of net family property."

15 *Supra* note 2. For additional analysis, see Hovius, "Case Comment on *von Czieslik v. Ayuso*" (2007), 38 R.F.L. (6th) 30.

16 *Ibid.* at para. 35.

4. Application of s. 5(6) where NFPs are Equal

After *von Czieslik v. Ayuso*, it is clear that a court can resort to s. 5(6) of the FLA even where the spouses' NFPs are equal. Justice Lang expressly stated that, in this "unusual situation", a court may award an amount "to the wronged spouse that is greater than zero, up to a maximum of the value of the offending party's net family property."[17] In so doing, she effectively overruled a second reason for the Ontario Court of Appeal's rejection of the appeal in the earlier case of *Berdette v. Berdette*.[18] ...

6. Section 5(6) Factors: The Passive Ones

(a) Failure to Disclose Debts or Liabilities at Marriage

The first paragraph listed in s. 5(6) refers to "a spouse's failure to disclose to the other spouse debts or other liabilities existing at the date of marriage". This paragraph is a holdover from the 1974 *Family Property Report* in which the OLRC recommended that a spouse's pre-nuptial deduction could not be negative. As a result, a spouse who entered the marriage with more debts than assets could use income earned during the marriage to pay off the debts without a resulting increase in his or her "residuary estate". [This was the term used by the OLRC to describe the equivalent of NFP.] The OLRC thought that this might be unjust where the other spouse did not know of the existence of the debts at marriage. It, therefore, proposed that this might be a circumstance where the court should adjust the equalization payment.

The force of this rationale for the inclusion of paragraph (a) is considerably weakened now that it is clear that a pre-marital property deduction can be a negative figure.[19] The fact that a spouse pays off a pre-marital debt during the marriage is now always reflected in that spouse's NFP. There is no longer a need to resort to s. 5(6) to do justice, whether or not that spouse disclosed the debt prior to marriage.[20] This probably explains why s. 5(6)(a) of the FLA has been so insignificant in the case law. ...

(b) Gifts Between Spouses

Section of s. 5(6)(c) of the FLA ... has had little impact, in large part because there is no clear rationale for it. Like paragraph (a), paragraph (c) appears to have originated in the 1974 recommendations of the OLRC. Under the proposed scheme, a spouse could deduct, in the computation of the "residuary estate" (NFP), the lesser of the value of a gift received from the other spouse at the time of its receipt or its value at the valuation date. The OLRC then proposed that, where such a deduction produced an unjust result, the court should be able to include all or a portion of the gift's value in the donee's "residual estate". Thus, this factor was proposed to benefit donor spouses where the donee's deduction caused injustice.

Under the FLA, however, the value of a gift from one spouse to another is included in the donee's NFP, provided that it is still held on the valuation date. In most circumstances

---

[17]   *Ibid.* at para. 49.

[18]   (1991), 33 R.F.L. (3d) 113 (Ont. C.A.); leave to appeal refused [1991] 3 S.C.R. v.

[19]   The Ontario cases are reviewed in *McAndrew v. Rooney-McAndrew* (2003), 47 R.F.L. (5th) 120 (P.E.I. C.A.).

[20]   There may, however, be situations where the spouse uses significant amounts of income received during the marriage merely to pay the interest on a pre-marital debt. Such payments will not be reflected in the spouse's NFP. Perhaps resort to s. 5(6)(a) would then be warranted if the spouse did not disclose the debt.

where the gifted property is still held on the valuation date, the spouses will, therefore, share its value equally. This mirrors the situation where no gift is made. Consider the following:

> *Example [2]*: Two years before separation, a wife gives a car to her husband. It is worth $10,000 on the valuation date. The husband has other included assets valued at $50,000 and deductions of $10,000. His NFP is, therefore, $50,000. The wife has included assets worth $60,000 and no deductions. Her NFP is $60,000. She owes her husband an equalization payment of $5,000.

It is difficult to understand how the wife's gift in this example could possibly lead to the conclusion that equalization of the NFPs is an injustice to the wife. She leaves the relationship with exactly the same financial gain she would have had if she had not made the gift. If she had kept the car, her NFP would have increased by $10,000 and the husband's would have decreased by that amount. The wife would have owed an equalization payment of $15,000, but she would have owned a car worth $10,000.

There is, however, one situation where the value of an inter-spousal gift is not shared even if it still exists at the valuation date. Consider the following:

> *Example [3]*: A husband has investments worth $100,000 at marriage and no debts. On the valuation date, these investments are worth only $75,000 but the husband also owns a car worth $25,000 that was a gift from his wife. The husband's NFP = $100,000 (value of assets on the valuation date) - $100,000 (pre-marital property deduction) = $0. Assume that the wife's NFP = $100,000. Unless an adjustment is made under s. 5(6), the wife will owe the husband an equalization payment of $50,000.

In this example, the value of the gift offsets a loss that would otherwise not have been shared because of s. 4(5) of the FLA. Perhaps the wife could argue that this is unconscionable. Whether one is sympathetic to this argument depends, at least in part, on one's view of the fairness of s. 4(5). ...

(c) Disproportionately Larger Amount of Family Debts

Section 5(6)(f) of the FLA requires the court to take into account "the fact that one spouse has incurred a disproportionately larger amount of debts or other liabilities than the other spouse for the support of the family". On first impression, the paragraph seems unnecessary, at least as it relates to debts in existence on the valuation date. After all, a spouse's debts and liabilities on the valuation date, whether or not they relate to financial provision for the family, are deducted in calculating the NFP. Although the responsibility for payment of these debts remains with the debtor spouse, their deduction in this way causes both spouses to share the financial burden equally. ...

There is, however, one situation where a spouse's debt may not be fully deducted from the value of that spouse's assets in the NFP calculation. Consider the following:

> *Example [4]*: On the valuation date, a wife has assets valued at $10,000. She owes her mother $15,000 as repayment of a loan used to pay for children's clothing and furniture. Assuming that the wife has no pre-marital property deduction, her NFP would be -$5,000 but for s. 4(5) of the FLA which deems it to be $0. Her husband has acquired some assets during the marriage and has no debts. His NFP is $20,000. The husband owes the wife an equalization payment of $10,000.

The payment of $10,000 will leave the husband in this example with a gain of $10,000 while the wife's net gain will only be $5,000 once she repays her mother. However, s. 5(6)(f) provides a means by which the family debts in Example [4] can be effectively shared. The wife has incurred a disproportionately larger amount of debt for the support of the family than the husband and it is arguably unconscionable simply to equalize the NFPs. Therefore, a court may order the husband to pay $12,500 so that the husband and wife share the net gain of $15,000 equally. ...

Although the history of the FLA indicates that s. 5(6)(f) was designed to deal with situations where the debtor spouse's NFP is deemed to be $0 by s. 4(5), courts have also used the paragraph where debts or expenditures are incurred to support the family after separation.[21] Obviously, such debts or expenditures have no effect on the size of the NFPs. Section 5(6)(h) is often also called into play to justify the adjustment, particularly where one spouse incurs expenses related to a jointly owned matrimonial home.[22] Despite this trend, one may well question whether the fact that a spouse goes into debt to support the family after separation is relevant to a fair distribution of the financial product of the marriage. In any event, it seems more appropriate to deal directly with the failure to provide support through a retroactive support order rather than an adjustment of the equalization payment. There are also ways, other than an adjustment to the equalization sum, to deal with post-separation expenditures relating to jointly owned property.[23]

(d) Written Agreement That is Not a Domestic Contract

Section 5(6)(g) of the FLA provides that a court should consider "a written agreement between the spouses that is not a domestic contract". The requirement that the agreement must be in writing may cause concern. Consider the following situation:

> *Example [5]*: During cohabitation, a husband and wife agree orally that the husband has no interest in the matrimonial home registered in the wife's name and that he will never share in its value. The wife, relying on the agreement, uses an inheritance to make substantial improvements to the home.

In reliance on the oral agreement, the wife has turned property that would have been excluded from her NFP into included property.[24] Although the agreement may not be considered under paragraph (g), it may be (depending on all the circumstances) unconscionable to allow the husband to share in the increased value of the home attributable to the improvements. As a result, a court may well hold that the wife's detrimental reliance on the oral agreement is a "circumstance relating to the ... improvement of property" that can be taken into account under s. 5(6)(h).[25] ...

One of the few cases where s. 5(6)(g) played a role is *Braaksma v. Braaksma* where the Ontario Court of Appeal upheld an unequal sharing of the NFPs.[26] The trial judge relied partly on s. 5(6)(g), concluding that the husband's transfer of the matrimonial home to the wife by a gift of deed was a "written agreement between the spouses that was not a domestic contract". The most important factor, however, appears to have been the gift itself and the circumstances in which it was made. ...

---

21 See, e.g., *Perrin v. Perrin* (1988), 17 R.F.L. (3d) 87 (Ont. Dist. Ct.); *Hohn v. Hohn* (1995), 1995 CarswellOnt 2044 (Ont. Gen. Div.); *Macedo v. Macedo* (1996), 19 R.F.L. (4th) 65 (Ont. Gen. Div.); and *Ahern v. Ahern* (2007), 2007 CarswellOnt 5733 (S.C.J.). In *LeVan v. LeVan, supra* note 2, the Ontario Court of Appeal cited (at para. 74), with apparent approval, *Perrin v. Perrin* and *Macedo v. Macedo* as examples of cases where post-separation circumstances were considered.

22 See, e.g., *Hohn v. Hohn, ibid.* and *Macedo v. Macedo, ibid.*

23 See, e.g., *Higgins v. Higgins* (2001), 19 R.F.L. (5th) 300 (Ont. S.C.J.); *Gill v. Jhajj* (2003), 37 R.F.L. (5th) 338 (Ont. S.C.J.); *Tessarolo v. Tessarolo* (2005), 2005 CarswellOnt 3085 (S.C.J.); additional reasons at (2005), 2005 CarswellOnt 4013 (S.C.J.); *Patterson v. Patterson* (2006), 36 R.F.L. (6th) 268 (Ont. S.C.J.); additional reasons at (2007), 38 R.F.L. (6th) 434 (Ont. S.C.J.); and *Rezel v. Rezel* (2007), 37 R.F.L. (6th) 445 (Ont. S.C.J.).

24 The exclusion is lost because an inheritance cannot be traced into a matrimonial home: s. 4(2), FLA.

25 See *Belman v. Belman* (1995), 26 O.R. (3d) 56 (Gen. Div.) at para. 38.

26 *Supra* note 5.

7. Section 5(6) Factors: The Active Ones

(a) Debts Incurred Recklessly or in Bad Faith

A spouse's debt on the valuation date is a deduction in the calculation of his or her NFP. As a result, while that spouse continues to be solely responsible for any personal debt, the spouses, in effect, share the debt.[27] However, in determining whether to adjust the equalization sum, s. 5(6)(b) of the FLA directs the court to consider "the fact that debts or other liabilities claimed in reduction of a spouse's net family property were incurred recklessly or in bad faith". Obviously, this paragraph is relevant only where the debts are still in existence on the valuation date. If the debts have already been paid, paragraph (d), dealing with intentional or reckless depletion of NFP, may be invoked. Indeed, s. 5(6)(b) may reasonably be viewed as a specific example of the reckless or intentional depletion of NFP. Accordingly, the case law dealing with paragraph (d) provides additional insight into the appropriate application of paragraph (b). Not surprisingly, the two paragraphs often come into play together because a spouse who recklessly depletes NFP by using income or assets for such things as gambling may well also have some debts relating to this activity on the valuation date.[28]

Running up excessive gambling debts is probably the classic example of incurring debt recklessly. In *Naidoo v. Naidoo*,[29] the husband had a personal debt of about $13,000. Justice Howden found that the husband, who earned a substantial income as a doctor, had been losing about $20,000 annually because he persisted in a gambling habit despite his wife's objections. The Justice explained that a gambling debt did not automatically result in an unequal sharing of NFPs:

> In law, speculative activity including gambling *per se* does not equate to unconscionability and reckless deprivation of N.F.P. ... Gambling must be considered in light of other factors, such as the amounts ... involved, the proportion of family means put at risk, the parties' incomes, the resources that the parties brought into the marriage, and the conduct of the parties including whether the risk or deprivation was condoned.[30]

In the result, the Justice concluded that the equalization sum due to the wife should be increased by $6,500 so that the personal debt was not shared.

Section 5(6)(b) was also used in *Abaza v. Abaza* where some of the husband's debts related to "escort services".[31] The case is most notable because Justice Aitken only disallowed, through an adjustment to the equalization sum, those debts that were incurred before the wife's private investigator confirmed her suspicions regarding the husband's activities. The Justice reasoned: "Once she became aware of what he was doing, she had the choice of triggering the valuation date ... or seeking recourse under s. 5(3)."[32]

---

[27] This is no longer the case when the debt causes a spouse's NFP to drop below $0 because s. 4(5) of the FLA deems a negative NFP to be $0.

[28] Section 5(6)(b) and s. 5(6)(d) are considered together in *Jukosky v. Jukosky* (1990), 31 R.F.L. (3d) 117 (Ont. Gen. Div.); affirmed (1996), 1996 CarswellOnt 1121 (C.A.); *Thompson v. Thompson* (1993), 1993 Carswell-Ont 1750 (Gen. Div.); *Ferguson v. Kalupnieks* (1997), 27 R.F.L. (4th) 437 (Ont. Gen. Div.); *McCoy v. Hucker* (1998), 1998 CarswellOnt 2919 (Gen. Div.); additional reasons at (1999), 1999 CarswellOnt 10 (Gen. Div.); and *Naidoo v. Naidoo* (2004), 2 R.F.L. (6th) 362 (Ont. S.C.J.); additional reasons at (2004), 2004 CarswellOnt 2723 (S.C.J.).

[29] *Ibid.*

[30] *Ibid.* at para 29.

[31] (2001), 16 R.F.L. (5th) 1 (Ont. S.C.J.).

[32] *Ibid.* at para. 75.

The fact that a spouse incurs debt for an unwise investment should not, by itself, generate an unequal sharing of NFPs. In *Dibbley v. Dibbley*,[33] the husband's NFP was substantially reduced by a number of debts relating to an unsuccessful development scheme. Justice Rosenberg concluded: "While Mr. Dibbley may not have been wise in his investment practices, I cannot say even with the benefit of hindsight that he was so reckless as to justify an unequal distribution".[34] However, in *Thompson v. Thompson*,[35] the court adjusted the equalization sum to reflect the debt incurred by the husband to finance a failed driving-range. Describing the husband as "a very poor money manager", Justice Rutherford stressed that the husband dealt with this particular debt and others related to the home in a secretive and misleading manner that deprived his wife of the opportunity to bring the couple's financial situation under control.

Where the debts relate to an unrealistically high family lifestyle, courts will generally not use s. 5(6) to adjust the equalization sum. In *McCoy v. Hucker*,[36] for example, Justice Ferrier concluded that debts relating to unwise and excessive expenditures on the family were not incurred by the husband recklessly or in bad faith. It was specifically noted that the husband did not benefit from the expenditures to any greater degree than the other family members. ...

In applying s. 5(6)(b), courts should remember that Part I of the FLA generally maintains the separate property system until one of the triggering events occurs. In other words, a spouse is generally entitled to deal with his or her property as he or she sees fit. As long as a debt is not incurred so as to reduce NFP intentionally or with reckless disregard for the impact on the family's finances, its existence should not result in an adjustment to the equalization sum. Imposing a requirement that a debt be "reasonable" ... invites bitter *ex post facto* assessments of the conduct of each spouse during the relationship.

(b) Intentional or Reckless Depletion of NFP

(i) **Gifts to Third Parties**: Paragraph (d) of s. 5(6) of the FLA directs the court to consider "a spouse's intentional or reckless depletion of his or her net family property". An illustration of the type of situation that clearly falls within this paragraph is provided by *Harry v. Harry*,[37] discussed earlier. Recall that the husband transferred shares valued at $170,800 to his daughter for no consideration a few days before the separation. The judge found that the husband intended to defeat "the legitimate claims of the wife"[38] and concluded that equalization of the NFPs would be unconscionable. To remedy the situation, $85,400 was added to the equalization sum owed to the wife.

Obviously, not all gifts to relatives or friends constitute intentional or reckless depletion of the donor's NFP so as to render the equalization of the remaining NFPs unconscionable. Key considerations are the motivation of the donor, the timing of the gift, and the quantum of the gift in relation to the value of the property owned by the donor.[39] Gifts to new roman-

---

33 (1986), 5 R.F.L. (3d) 381 (Ont. H.C.).

34 *Ibid.* at para. 40. See also *Cowan v. Cowan* (1987), 9 R.F.L. (3d) 401 (Ont. H.C.); additional reasons at (1987), 9 R.F.L. (3d) 401 at 409 (Ont. H.C.); affirmed (1988), 13 R.F.L. (3d) 381 (Ont. C.A.).

35 *Supra* note 28.

36 *Supra* note 28.

37 *Supra* note 12. See also *von Czieslik v. Ayuso, supra* note 2.

38 *Harry v. Harry, ibid.* at 126.

39 See *Mittler v. Mittler* (1988), 17 R.F.L. (3d) 113 (Ont. H.C.); additional reasons at (1988), 1988 CarswellOnt 2519 (H.C.); *Balogh v. Balogh* (1996), 24 R.F.L. (4th) 181 (Ont. C.A.); leave to appeal refused (1997), 215 N.R. 399 (note) (S.C.C.); and *Helmy v. Helmy* (2000), 12 R.F.L. (5th) 68 (Ont. S.C.J.). See also *Stone v. Stone,*

tic partners before separation have sometimes resulted in requests for an unequal division of NFPs, with mixed results. The claim succeeded in *Hutchings v. Hutchings*,[40] but it failed in *Biant v. Sagoo* where Justice Perkins suggested: "It would be a novel proposition that a philandering spouse is responsible under section 5(6) for paying to the other spouse a sum equal to the cost of an affair, either direct costs (jewellery and such) or indirect costs (diminished profits from business)".[41]

(ii) Unsuccessful Investments or Business Ventures: Unsuccessful investments or business ventures do not usually amount to intentional or reckless depletion of NFP.[42] In particular, it is not enough for the spouse who seeks an unequal sharing of the NFPs to show that poor judgment or poor management resulted in a loss. Rather, the claimant must establish that the other spouse knowingly made bad investments in order to waste assets or was totally indifferent to the consequences of a foolish decision. This approach is in keeping with the wording of the paragraph since it refers to "intentional" or "reckless" depletion. The courts also appear influenced by the fact that the claimant spouse would have been entitled to share in any gain if the speculative investment had worked out. Since gains are shared, losses should be shared in the absence of *male fides*. Finally, the active or passive concurrence of the claimant spouse in the investment decision will militate against a finding that the other spouse intentionally or recklessly wasted assets so as to justify an adjustment to the equalization sum.

(iii) Wasteful or Extravagant Spending: Wasteful or excessive spending is a third way in which a spouse can intentionally or recklessly deplete NFP. A spouse may, for example, react to marital problems by cashing in bonds to pay for a gambling spree in Las Vegas in an attempt to ensure that the other spouse will not share in the value of the bonds in the event of a separation.[43] However, extravagant spending does not necessarily amount to intentional or reckless depletion of NFP so as to render equalization of the NFPs unconscionable.[44] This is particularly so where the goods are purchased for use by the family as a whole. Another key factor is whether the other spouse concurs in the expenditures or the adoption of an extravagant lifestyle. Overall, judges exhibit a natural reluctance to analyse the spending habits of the spouses during cohabitation.

(iv) Limited Effectiveness of S. 5(6) as Remedy: Even as interpreted in *von Czieslik v. Ayuso*, s. 5(6) of the FLA provides only limited protection for a spouse where the other spouse dissipates or depletes his or her NFP. While Part II of the FLA imposes significant restrictions on the powers of an owning spouse to deal with a matrimonial home, the owning spouse can generally deal with other property prior to the valuation date as he or she wishes.

---

supra note 14, where the Ontario Court of Appeal applied the *Fraudulent Conveyances Act* to gifts made by a husband in anticipation of his death.

[40] (2001), 20 R.F.L. (5th) 83 (Ont. S.C.J.).

[41] (2001), 2001 CarswellOnt 1517 (S.C.J.) at para. 126; additional reasons at (2001), 20 R.F.L. (5th) 284 (Ont. S.C.J.). See also *Lackie v. Lackie*, *supra* note 12.

[42] For cases involving unsuccessful claims for unequal sharing of NFPs based on failed investments or business ventures, see *Jahnke v. Jahnke* (1995), 1995 CarswellOnt 2213 (Gen. Div.); additional reasons at (1996), 1996 CarswellOnt 982 (Gen. Div.); *Coscarella v. Coscarella* (1999), 1999 CarswellOnt 4606 (S.C.J.); additional reasons at (2000), 2000 CarswellOnt 146 (S.C.J.); *Fraser v. Fraser* (2004), 8 R.F.L. (6th) 125 (Ont. S.C.J.); and *Boisvert v. Boisvert* (2007), 40 R.F.L. (6th) 158 (Ont. S.C.J.).

[43] The facts in *Weddel v. Weddel* (2006), 2006 CarswellOnt 3901 (S.C.J.) are somewhat similar to this hypothetical.

[44] Such claims failed in *McCoy v. Hucker*, *supra* note 28; *Roseneck v. Gowling*, *supra* note 3; and *McLean v. McLean* (2004), 2004 CarswellOnt 4234 (S.C.J.); additional reasons at (2004), 2004 CarswellOnt 4412 (S.C.J.).

If the owning spouse recklessly or intentionally depletes his or her NFP, an unequal sharing of the remaining NFPs may result. However, this may be an ineffective remedy. Consider the following example:

> *Example [6]*: When marital problems first surface, a wife gives $100,000 to her daughter in an attempt to limit her husband's equalization claim. On separation one year later, her NFP is $20,000. The husband's NFP is $10,000.

In light of the wife's depletion of her NFP, a court might well conclude that equalization of the NFPs would be unconscionable and order the wife to pay $20,000 to the husband.[45] However, this provides only a partial remedy because the husband would have received an equalization payment of $55,000 if the wife had not made the gift.

The husband might turn to the *Fraudulent Conveyances Act*[46] to attack the gift to the daughter. In *Stone v. Stone*, the Ontario Court of Appeal sanctioned the use of this statute to set aside property transfers made with the intent of defeating a spouse's entitlement under Part I of the FLA.[47] However, the court stressed that a spouse must have an existing claim against the other spouse at the time of the impugned conveyance.[48] In the case itself, the Court relied on the fact that the wife, if she had known of the dying husband's intention to transfer substantial assets to his children, could have applied under s. 5(3) of the FLA for equalization of the NFPs. Depending on the contextual facts in Example [6], a court might give s. 5(3) a sufficiently expansive interpretation so as to grant the husband standing under the *Fraudulent Conveyances Act*.[49] The other requirements of this Act would, of course, also have to be met.[50]

The need to rely on the *Fraudulent Conveyances Act* with its 16th century language to deal with 21st century attempts by spouses to avoid a family property regime is unfortunate. It would be preferable, as recommended by the OLRC in 1993, to add specific anti-avoidance provisions to Part I of the FLA that give courts specific authority to reverse gifts or transfers made with the intention of subverting the legislation.[51] Such provisions exist in other provinces such as Manitoba.[52] Until the legislature acts, Ontario lawyers will have to rely upon s. 5(6) of the FLA, the *Fraudulent Conveyances Act*, and the law of trusts.[53]

(c) Short Period of Cohabitation

One of the factors that has fairly often resulted in an unequal sharing of the NFPs is listed in s. 5(6)(e) of the FLA. That paragraph stipulates that the court must consider "the

---

[45] Recall that it was held in *von Czieslik v. Ayuso* that this is the maximum that a court can order.

[46] R.S.O. 1990, c. F.29.

[47] *Supra* note 14.

[48] *Ibid.* at para. 25.

[49] In "Setting Aside Pre-Separation Transfers Designed to Diminish Spousal Claims" (2005), 20 N.C.D. Rev. 20, Klatz suggests, at 24, that the courts are likely to act whenever one spouse intends to defeat the other's claim "in such a manner that the court considers inappropriate, unfair or fraudulent".

[50] See *ibid.*

[51] 1993 *Family Property Report, supra* note 11.

[52] *Family Property Act*, C.C.S.M. c. F25, ss. 6(7)–6(11).

[53] Arguments based on the law of trusts could take two forms. First, the aggrieved spouse might argue that he or she had a beneficial interest in the transferred property. Any equitable remedies for breach of trust should then be available. Second, in some circumstances, it might be possible to argue that the transferee holds the property in a secret trust for the transferor. If this argument succeeds, the value of the transferor's beneficial interest will fall into his or her NFP.

fact that the amount a spouse would otherwise receive ... is disproportionately large in relation to a period of cohabitation that is less than five years". After a series of conflicting lower court cases, the Ontario Court of Appeal held in *MacNeill v. Pope* that pre-marital cohabitation by the spouses is to be considered in computing the period of cohabitation.[54] The courts have also generally held that the reason why the cohabitation ends does not justify disregarding its short length.[55]

Where spouses cohabit for only a short time, the financial gain accruing during the relationship is likely to be relatively small. However, the special treatment of the matrimonial home in the calculation of the owner's NFP may result in a large equalization payment even in a short relationship. This is because the FLA does not allow a spouse to deduct the value of the matrimonial home at marriage in the NFP computation. Where the marriage lasts a long time, the non-owning spouse's contribution to the home's maintenance arguably[56] justifies this exception to the general rule whereby only the financial gain accruing during cohabitation is shared. Where, however, the spouses cohabit for a short period; it may be unconscionable for the non-owning spouse to share equally in the pre-marital value of the home.

The case of *Harris v. Harris* provides an extreme example.[57] The couple cohabited for a total of 13 weeks. Because the husband brought a newly-constructed home into the relationship, the equalization payment due to the wife was over $400,000. Although Justice R.F. Scott accepted that the wife made a contribution to the relationship by, *inter alia*, buying groceries and choosing some of the finishes for the home; the Justice decided that it would be unconscionable for the wife to receive any equalization sum. Instead, the wife was awarded $10,000 on the basis that the husband had been unjustly enriched by her efforts relating to the home's construction.

Where one spouse brings a matrimonial home into a relationship that lasts less than five years, courts often do adjust the equalization sum. The Ontario Court of Appeal has twice affirmed such results, but without analysis.[58] Justice Heeney set out the rationale for an adjustment in *Kucera v. Kucera*:

> It seems to me that s. 5(6) ... is designed to deal with the scenario that presents itself before this court. If the normal principle of sharing equally the wealth accumulated during the marriage were to be applied, it would rarely be seen to be unconscionable whether the marriage lasted 10 months or 10 years. Marriage is a form of partnership, and it is inherently fair that wealth accumulated during the life of the partnership should be shared equally.

> Where the Act potentially becomes unfair is where the special provisions [relating to the matrimonial home] come into play. This is because the equalization process does not only share wealth accumulated during the marriage, but also shares the value of one specific asset, the matrimonial home, that was accumulated prior to the marriage. In very short marriages, this represents an unjustifiable windfall to the non-titled spouse. So long as the marriage is of a duration of less than five years, s. 5(6) is available to redress the unfairness.[59]

---

[54] (1999), 43 R.F.L. (4th) 209 (Ont. C.A.).

[55] See, e.g., *Futia v. Futia* (1990), 27 R.F.L. (3d) 81 (Ont. H.C.); *Clayburn v. Clayburn* (1997), 29 R.F.L. (4th) 12 (Ont. Gen. Div.); and *Harris v. Harris* (2005), 2005 CarswellOnt 3684 (S.C.J.).

[56] The OLRC recommended that the special treatment be ended. See 1993 *Family Property Report, supra* note 11 at 84-85. When the Northwest Territories legislature adopted legislation modeled on Part I of Ontario's FLA, it did not provide for the exclusion of the matrimonial home from the pre-marital property deduction. See Part III of the *Family Law Act*, S.N.W.T. 1997, c. 18.

[57] *Supra* note 55.

[58] *Knapp v. Knapp* (1996), 1996 CarswellOnt 2042 (C.A.) and *Rivers-Eshkibok v. Eshkibok* (2003), 2003 CarswellOnt 2290 (C.A.).

[59] (2005), 16 R.F.L. (6th) 250 (Ont. S.C.J.) at paras. 18 and 19.

However, occasionally courts conclude that equalization of the NFPs is not unconscionable even though a spouse brings a matrimonial home into the marriage and the relationship is shorter than five years.[60] The Ontario Court of Appeal has affirmed one of these cases, again without analysis.[61] Perhaps the case in which the claim for an adjustment was strongest was *Linov v. Williams*,[62] where each of the spouses owned a home before they married. The couple moved into the husband's home and so it became the matrimonial home. When the relationship ended about four years later, the wife was able to deduct the value of her home at marriage in calculating her NFP while the husband received no deduction relating to his home. As a result, the husband owed the wife an equalization sum of $128,000. Justice Backhouse refused to adjust this amount, noting that the period of cohabitation was fairly close to five years and adding:

> One goal of the *Family Law Act* is to promote certainty of result, thereby decreasing the potential for litigation. Some may consider it unfair that the wife's home is a deduction whereas the husband's is not. However, the *Family Law Act* allows deductions for all assets at the date of the marriage, including real estate assets. A matrimonial home is treated differently. There is no unconscionability in this case in applying the statutory scheme.[63]

In rebuttal, it might be pointed out that s. 5(6) is also part of the FLA and that the legislature did intend for courts to adjust the equalization sum in some circumstances. Indeed, the inclusion of paragraph (e) in s. 5(6) appears to have been specifically designed to deal with situations where the special treatment accorded to the matrimonial home in calculating the premarital property deduction may cause inequity.[64]

In determining whether to adjust the equalization sum because one spouse brought a matrimonial home into a short relationship, courts consider such factors as the size of the sum, the proportion that is attributable to the home's value at marriage, the length of the relationship, and the contributions of the spouses to the family relationship. Where judges decide that there should be an adjustment, they often refer to these same factors in deciding its extent. Sometimes, the equalization sum is reduced to zero. More often, the adjustment is less severe and is simply announced after an examination of some or all of the factors listed above. Some judges prefer a more formulaic approach. Sometimes the equalization sum is adjusted so that only the increase in the value of the home during the marriage is shared.[65] In *Sarcino v. Sarcino*, the cohabitation lasted 42 months.[66] Noting that the wife would have received 100% of the equalization sum after 60 months, Justice Taliano decided that the most appropriate award was 42/60ths of the presumptive entitlement. This formula both limits the "cliff effect" of the rather arbitrary five year rule and provides an objective method for determining the extent of the adjustment.

Section 5(6)(e) of the FLA has had little influence in situations other than those where one spouse loses a deduction for the pre-marital value of the matrimonial home. Where

---

60 See *Murphy v. Murphy* (1987), 17 R.F.L. (3d) 422 (Ont. Dist. Ct.); affirmed (1991), 1991 CarswellOnt 2496 (C.A.); *Kozuch v. Kozuch* (1992), 1992 CarswellOnt 3529 (Gen. Div.); and *Linov v. Williams* (2007), 2007 CarswellOnt 1463 (S.C.J.).

61 *Murphy v. Murphy* (1991), 1991 CarswellOnt 2496 (C.A.).

62 *Supra* note 60.

63 *Ibid.* at para. 36.

64 In its *Working Paper on Property Rights on Marriage Breakdown* (1989), the Law Reform Commission of British Columbia speculated (at 101) that the "inclusion of paragraph (e) probably relates to the special treatment accorded to the matrimonial home in Ontario".

65 See, e.g., *Rivers-Eshkibok v. Eshkibok*, *supra* note 58.

66 (1999), 1999 CarswellOnt 819 (Gen. Div.).

spouses cohabit for only a short time, the financial gain accruing during the relationship is likely to be relatively small and equal sharing will be fair. There may, however, be exceptional cases where one spouse wins a lottery, acquires a large return on an investment or earns an exceptionally large income during a short marriage. If, for example, the husband is the heavyweight champion of the world who earns $25 million for the one match that occurs during a marriage that lasts ten months, the equalization payment due to his wife may be "disproportionately large" in relation to the period of cohabitation and it may be unconscionable for the wife to share equally in this enormous financial gain. It is certainly arguable that the wife has not made a sufficiently significant contribution during the short relationship to either the family unit or the heavyweight's earning capacity to justify such a large equalization sum.

There are no Ontario cases dealing with heavyweight champions, but the case of *Reid v. Reid* did involve a major adjustment in favour of a "super spouse".[67] The couple cohabited for 34 months, almost half of which occurred before the marriage. Because of a high tech boom, the wife's exercise of her share options resulted in a significant financial gain during the marriage and her NFP was almost $337,000. The wife was also the primary caregiver for the couple's child and she earned considerably more employment income than the husband. The husband's NFP was about $23,500. Justice Snowie concluded that the presumptive equalization sum was disproportionately large in relation to the short period of cohabitation. The Justice awarded the husband only 15% of the difference between the NFPs.

(d) Other Circumstances

(i) **General**: Section 5(6)(h) of the FLA directs courts to consider "any other circumstance relating to the acquisition, disposition, preservation, maintenance or improvement of property" in determining whether equalization of the NFPs would be unconscionable. Although this "catch-all" provision is the broadest paragraph in s. 5(6), it does not allow a court to consider anything and everything. Only circumstances relating to the acquisition etc. of property fall within the scope of the paragraph. Accordingly, it would not be appropriate to take into account the needs of the spouses.[68]

It would also be improper for a court to deviate from the norm of equal sharing out of sympathy for an innocent party whose spouse engaged in matrimonial misconduct leading to marriage breakdown. This does not mean that courts cannot take into account the conduct of the spouses. Conduct that has an impact on the financial product of the relationship is relevant. A specific example, explicitly covered by s. 5(6)(d), is a spouse's intentional or reckless depletion of his or her NFP. Failure to contribute in any significant way to the familial responsibilities identified by s. 5(7) of the FLA can also arguably be considered under s. 5(6)(h) since this affects the ability of the spouses to acquire or maintain property. [See below.] ...

(ii) **Bringing Matrimonial Home into Relationship**: The fact that the FLA does not allow a spouse to include the value of the matrimonial home in the computation of the premarital property deduction may seem unfair to the owning spouse, but it is unlikely to lead to an adjustment of the equalization sum unless the relationship lasts for less than five years.

---

67 (2003), 50 R.F.L. (5th) 170 (Ont. S.C.J.); additional reasons at (2005), 2005 CarswellOnt 389 (S.C.J.).

68 The legislation in some provinces specifies that a court should consider the needs and means of the spouses in determining whether equal sharing should be varied. None of the paragraphs in s. 5(6) of the FLA encompass this factor. This reinforces the point, also implicit in s. 5(7), that the goal underpinning Part I of the FLA is to recognize the past contributions of the spouses to the financial product of their relationship. A sharing of the NFPs may well provide the financial resources needed for each spouse to begin an independent existence, but this is an indirect effect rather than the goal of such sharing.

There are several cases in which the relationship ended shortly after the five year anniversary and the spouse who brought a matrimonial home into the marriage requested an adjustment. Unless there were other factors leading to a finding that equalization of the NFPs would be unconscionable, this plea failed.[69] This is not surprising because the spouse was essentially arguing that the legislation itself dictated an unconscionable result.

(iii) Using Gift or Inheritance to Acquire or Improve Matrimonial Home: The special treatment of a matrimonial home in the rules relating to exclusions can also result in requests for an adjustment of the equalization sum. ... This special treatment of matrimonial homes appears to be based on the premise that both spouses contribute significantly to their preservation and maintenance. Arguably, therefore, there can be an adjustment to the equalization sum where this premise is not borne out. For example, a spouse may use inherited money to acquire a matrimonial home mere months before the valuation date. In this situation, the initial effect of the inheritance has not been significantly eroded by spousal efforts affecting family and home and paragraph (h) of s. 5(6) may be invoked.

Although there are no cases dealing precisely with the scenario described in the previous paragraph, judges are generally reluctant to use s. 5(6) to adjust the equalization sum where a gift or inheritance finds its way into a matrimonial home. ... The wife in *Clewlow v. Clewlow* inherited the matrimonial home only three years before the separation.[70] Nonetheless, her claim for unequal sharing of the NFPs was rejected by Justice Marshman who stated:

> It can certainly be argued that it is unfair that Mr. Clewlow benefits to such a great degree from Mrs. Clewlow's inheritance but the unfairness arises because s. 4(2) specifically excludes a matrimonial home from inherited property which can otherwise be excluded. It cannot be said that it is unconscionable to equalize the net family properties in accordance with the principles of the Act. In any event, I would not find an equal division to be unconscionable in these circumstances. The parties cohabited for close to 20 years. They had three children. Each contributed to the relationship in accordance with his or her ability. I have no doubt that Mr. Clewlow's difficulty with alcohol contributed to his lack of ability to maintain a job for any great length of time but he did work for a significant time during the marriage. ...[71]

. . . . .

(iv) Disparity in Contributions Before Valuation Date: Section 5(7) of the FLA indicates that NFPs are presumed to result from the joint and equal, albeit different, contributions of the spouses during their relationship. The courts have (fairly) consistently accepted that two consequences follow. First, the fact that one spouse earns most or even all of the money used to acquire property during the marriage does not by itself justify an unequal sharing of the NFPs. This accords with the legislature's statement in s. 5(7) that a non-financial contribution to family life is as significant as financial provision and with the general motive for adopting the legislation. Second, s. 5(6) does not generally require or, indeed, permit a court to assess whether one spouse contributed more than the other or more than the "average spouse" to the responsibilities that are inherent in family life. Justice Osborne confirmed this in the Ontario Court of Appeal decision in *Brett v. Brett*:

> None of the factors set out in s. 5(6)(a) to (h) require the court to examine the spouses' respective contributions to household management, child care, and financial provision. If this was to be an area of specific inquiry to determine if the equalization of net family properties would be unconscionable, the factors listed in s. 5(6) would have been expanded. ... In establishing the equalization of net family properties in the *Family Law Act*, the Legislature did not intend for the courts to undertake a

---

69 See, e.g., *Cassidy v. Cassidy* (1996), 17 R.F.L. (4th) 403 (Ont. Gen. Div.); *MacNeill v. Pope, supra* note 54; and *Williams v. Williams* (2006), 2006 CarswellOnt 7943 (S.C.J.).

70 (2004), 2004 CarswellOnt 3397 (S.C.J.).

71 *Ibid.* at para. 22.

post-mortem examination of the sharing of responsibilities to determine if equalizing the spouse's net family properties would be "unconscionable".[72]

Nevertheless, there are some situations where the contributions of spouses, financial or otherwise, are assessed and compared. This tends to occur where one of the other circumstances listed in s. 5(6) is being considered. For example, if one spouse argues that there should be unequal sharing of the NFPs in light of the short period of cohabitation, a court is likely to assess, openly and directly, the relative contributions of the spouses to determine whether the equalization sum is "disproportionately large" within the meaning of s. 5(6)(e). Also, cases involving claimed intentional or reckless depletion of NFP often concern spouses with gambling, alcohol or drug addictions and the contributions of these spouses to the relationship is, indirectly at least, considered.

Unequal sharing of the NFPs may also be appropriate where there is a gross disparity in contributions during cohabitation or where one spouse has abdicated his or her responsibilities to the family. There was some support in the early cases for the view that s. 5(7) of the FLA deems the spouses' contributions to be equal and so precludes an unequal sharing where one spouse, in fact, contributes little or nothing to family life.[73] However, this approach was dealt a blow by *LeBlanc v. LeBlanc*[74] where the Supreme Court of Canada upheld an unequal division of marital property under New Brunswick's *Marital Property Act*.[75] In that case, the husband was an alcoholic who contributed little to family life over a period of 26 years.

Although the New Brunswick legislation, in contrast to s. 5(7) of the FLA, does not expressly state that equal contribution to familial responsibilities is inherent in the marital relationship and although its threshold for unequal division is "inequitable" rather than "unconscionable"; some Ontario judges concluded that the reasoning in *LeBlanc v. LeBlanc* should still apply. For example, Justice Granger expressly stated in *Berdette v. Berdette* that "gross disparity" in contributions should affect the sharing of NFPs where "the disparity arises from a *mala fides* failure to contribute or an abdication which is not accepted by the other spouse".[76] Although Justice Granger found a gross disparity in contributions that might have justified unequal sharing in favour of the wife, he held that there should be no adjustment because the wife had given the husband a one-half interest in the two main properties owned by the couple. This decision was upheld on that basis on appeal.[77] The question of whether the husband's abdication of responsibilities could be considered was fully argued, but the Ontario Court of Appeal specifically left the issue "open until it is necessary to decide it".[78] That Court has still not definitively determined the issue, although its approval of the consideration under paragraph (h) of the abdication of family responsibilities after separation[79] suggests that such abdication before separation is relevant. Indeed,

---

[72] (1999), 46 R.F.L. (4th) 433 (Ont. C.A.). In *MacDonald v. MacDonald* (1997), 33 R.F.L. (4th) 75 (Ont. C.A.), the Ontario Court of Appeal overturned an unequal sharing of NFPs that the trial judge favoured because the wife contributed more, especially financially, to the relationship.

[73] See, e.g., *Waters v. Waters* (1986), 1986 CarswellOnt 1509 (Ont. Dist. Ct.).

[74] (1988), 12 R.F.L. (3d) 225 (S.C.C.).

[75] S.N.B. 1980, c. M-1.1.

[76] (1988), 14 R.F.L. (3d) 398 at 413 (Ont. H.C.); additional reasons at (1988), 16 R.F.L. (3d) 360 (Ont. H.C.); affirmed (1991), 33 R.F.L. (3d) 113 (Ont. C.A.).

[77] *Berdette v. Berdette, supra* note 18.

[78] *Ibid.* at para. 39.

[79] See *Scherer v. Scherer* (2002), 26 R.F.L. (5th) 183 (Ont. C.A.); additional reasons at (2002), 2002 CarswellOnt 1562 (C.A.).

the latter is arguably more relevant to a fair sharing of the financial gain during the relationship because it will obviously affect the size of that gain.

The Ontario Court of Appeal's conclusion in *MacDonald v. MacDonald* that "the test of unconscionability was far from met on the undisputed facts of this case"[80] can also be interpreted as supporting the view that abdication of responsibilities before separation can lead to unequal sharing. The trial judge in that case awarded a greater share of the NFPs to the wife because she was the main financial provider. The Court of Appeal, in overturning the decision, noted that the husband had looked after the couple's children and had "contributed significantly through his labour to improvements to the matrimonial home".[81] There was no need to note the husband's contributions unless abdication of responsibilities would have justified the result at trial.

Similarly, the Ontario Court of Appeal's dismissal of the husband's appeal in *Jukosky v. Jukosky* also impliedly suggests that grossly disproportionate contributions to family life can lead to an adjustment of the equalization sum.[82] The trial judge relied on a number of factors — including the husband's "total disregard of his obligations as a husband and father"— to find that equal sharing of the NFPs would be unconscionable. He reduced the equalization sum to be paid by the wife by 50%. The Court of Appeal simply noted that there was no reason to interfere with this result and that "the findings of fact to justify unequal division are all founded on the evidence".[83]

There have been a number of lower court decisions in addition to *Jukosky v. Jukosky* where the equalization sum has been adjusted on the basis of gross disparity in spousal contributions. In *Sullivan v. Sullivan*, Goodearle U.F.C.J. found "that the contribution made to the family unit during these several years [while the husband returned to school and later tried to establish a consulting business] was staggeringly uneven in all three major areas of contribution to family".[84] He concluded that the husband should not share equally in the NFPs. Similarly, in *Giba v. Giba*, an alcoholic husband who had rarely worked during the relationship and who had damaged the matrimonial home and assaulted his wife and son, was denied any share of the NFPs.[85] In contrast, Justice Metivier ordered equal sharing in *Valenti v. Valenti* even though the husband in that case also had problems with alcohol and was abusive.[86] The Justice took note of the husband's financial contribution to the family through gifts from his parents and the labour he contributed to significant repair and renovation projects.

If a spouse's failure to contribute to the family unit results from ill-health or a disability, a court is unlikely to adjust the equalization sum. ...

(v) Abdication of Responsibilities & Other Conduct After Valuation Date: Initially, the issue of whether events after the valuation date could be considered in the application of s. 5(6) of the FLA sharply divided the courts. The Ontario Court of Appeal apparently settled the matter in *Merklinger v. Merklinger*, concluding that a court could take into account the economic consequences of a spouse's post-separation conduct.[87] In that case, the husband's conduct caused the wife to lose her cottage after separation and he then purchased it

---

[80] *Supra* note 21 at para 17.

[81] *Ibid.*

[82] *Supra* note 28.

[83] *Ibid.* at para. 2.

[84] (1986), 5 R.F.L. (3d) 28 (Ont. U.F.C.) at para. 36.

[85] (1996), 1996 CarswellOnt 2948 (Ont. Gen. Div.).

[86] (1996), 21 R.F.L. (4th) 246 (Ont. Gen. Div.); affirmed (1998), 41 R.F.L. (4th) 289 (Ont. C.A.).

[87] (1996), 26 R.F.L. (4th) 7 (Ont. C.A.).

at a discount from the bank. In addition, he failed to support his wife and a dependent child after the separation. At trial, Justice Ferrier found that it would be "outrageous" and, therefore, unconscionable if the wife had to pay any equalization sum. The Court of Appeal upheld the decision, simply noting: "In light of the economic effect of the husband's conduct on the wife, particularly in reference to the cottage, we agree with the trial judge's conclusion. ..."[88]

After the *Merklinger* decision, more judges began to hold that abdication of familial responsibilities after separation, particularly failure to provide financial support, can result in an adjustment of the equalization sum. This approach received approval in *Scherer v. Scherer* where the Ontario Court of Appeal upheld a refusal to extend a limitation period so as to allow a husband to apply for equalization of NFPs.[89] ...

Despite this trend in the cases, one may question whether abdication of spousal responsibilities after separation should be considered. Recall that the basic goal underpinning Part I of the FLA is to ensure that the spouses receive a fair return on the contributions made during their partnership, a partnership that ends on the valuation date. The fact that one of them shirks responsibilities after separation has little bearing on the calculation of fair compensation for the execution of familial responsibilities prior to the separation. At the very least, there needs to be some relationship between the shirking of familial responsibilities and "the acquisition, disposition, preservation, maintenance or improvement of property" for the purposes of s. 5(6)(h). Not visiting one's children is unlikely to qualify. Failure to provide support may. For example, lack of financial provision may cause the other spouse to dispose of property. It may also leave the other spouse solely responsible for the maintenance of jointly held property.

In any event, there are alternative and, arguably, more appropriate remedies to redress the injustice caused when one spouse fails to provide support after separation. Retroactive child and spousal support is possible under both the FLA and the *Divorce Act*. An order tailored to accord with the policy and factors designed to deal with support is preferable to an adjustment of the equalization payment that is really a disguised retroactive support order. There are also other ways to deal with post-separation expenditures relating to jointly owned property.[90]

(vi) Market Driven Changes in Property Values after Valuation Date: In 1993, the OLRC recommended that Ontario adopt a provision to deal expressly with post-valuation date increases or decreases in the value of the spouses' property: "Part I of the *Family Law Act* should be amended to grant courts the discretion to vary the equalization payment to recognize a substantial post-valuation date change in value of an asset if necessary to ensure an equitable result, having regard to the cause of the fluctuation".[91] Note the reference to a "substantial" change and the recommendation for a lower threshold ("inequitable") than the one ("unconscionable") set by s. 5(6) of the FLA. The legislature did not act on this recommendation and so the courts are left to determine whether fluctuations in value after the

---

[88] *Ibid.* at para 2.

[89] (2002), 26 R.F.L. (5th) 183 (Ont. C.A.); additional reasons at (2002), 2002 CarswellOnt 1562 (C.A.).

[90] See, e.g., *Higgins v. Higgins, supra,* note 23; *Gill v. Jhaji, supra* note 23; *Tessarolo v. Tessarolo, supra* note 23; *Patterson v. Patterson, supra* note 23; and *Rezel v. Rezel, supra* note 23.

[91] 1993 *Family Property Report, supra* note 11 at 71 and 144. When Prince Edward Island enacted family property legislation generally modeled on Ontario's, it adopted the OLRC's recommendation. See s. 6(6) of the *Family Law Act,* S.P.E.I. 1995, c. 12. For an example of a case where s. 6(6) was used to adjust the equalization of NFPs, see *Ballum v. Ballum* (1999), 49 R.F.L. (4th) 176 (P.E.I. T.D. [In Chambers]) (husband's business suffered setbacks). The provision was also considered in *Creelman v. Creelman* (2000), 2000 CarswellPEI 100 (T.D.), although ultimately the court concluded that an equal sharing should prevail.

valuation date can be considered under s. 5(6)(h) of the FLA. Of course, even if they are relevant, adjustment of the equalization sum will only occur where equal sharing of the NFPs would be unconscionable. ...

Whether post-separation changes in value can be considered under s. 5(6)(h) of the FLA is a question to which the Ontario Court of Appeal was expected to provide a definitive answer in its recent decision in *LeVan v. LeVan*.[92] The main, preliminary issue in the *LeVan* case was the validity of a pre-nuptial agreement. Once Justice Backhouse set aside the contract at trial, she had to determine the wife's equalization sum. Her calculations suggested that it was slightly over $10 million, but the husband argued that this would result in the transfer of most, if not all, of his current net worth because of a dramatic drop in the value of his shares in a family business after the valuation date. He, therefore, asked for an adjustment under s. 5(6). Justice Backhouse concluded that the market driven decease in the value of the husband's business could not provide a basis for an adjustment of the equalization sum because "had the Legislature intended that post-valuation date increases and decreases in value might form the basis of a s. 5(6) application, I think it likely, given the frequency of these events, that it would have included a provision to this effect". Nevertheless, she went on to note that, if she could have considered the decrease in the value of the shares, she would have found an equalization sum of $10 million to be unconscionable. Ultimately, she awarded the wife $5.3 million because this was "all that is requested".

The Ontario Court of Appeal affirmed this result.[93] Writing for the Court, Justice Borins explored the question of whether any post-valuation date events can be considered under s. 5(6) of the FLA and concluded: "[T]here does seem to be room within s. 5(6) to consider post-separation circumstances in limited situations, such as where the conduct of one spouse post-separation has resulted in a significant depletion of assets".[94] Next, he stated: "Nevertheless, the cases that have considered post valuation date fluctuations in a spouse's net family property are uniform that this factor does not come within the stipulated grounds in s. 5(6)".[95] Immediately after this questionable summary of the case law, Justice Borins gave his answer to the question at hand: "However, *in the context of this case*, for the reasons that follow, I am of the view that it is not appropriate *in this case* to consider the decrease in the value of the husband's assets subsequent to the valuation date" (emphasis added).[96] Justice Borins then identified three specific reasons for this answer. First, the husband's conduct in relation to the marriage contract had "put him into the situation of having his property and the value of his shares subject to the equalization provisions of the *FLA*".[97] Second, Justice Borins stated that "the husband could have disposed of his shares to hedge against the setting aside of the contract, but he chose not to do so".[98] Finally, the Justice noted that, under Part I of the FLA, the wife became "an ordinary unsecured creditor" at separation who was owed an equalization sum and that "no one would suggest that any ordinary creditor share the burden of a debtor's reversal of fortune".[99]

The fact that Justice Borins stated that it was not appropriate "in the context of this case" to consider the decrease in the value of the husband's assets subsequent to the valuation date

---

[92] *Supra* note 2.

[93] *LeVan v. LeVan, supra* note 7.

[94] *Ibid.* at para. 75.

[95] *Ibid.*

[96] *Ibid.* at para. 75.

[97] *Ibid.* at para. 76.

[98] *Ibid.* at para. 77.

[99] *Ibid.* at para. 79.

leaves open the possibility that there may be some circumstances in which it would be appropriate to consider such decreases under s. 5(6)(h) of the FLA. Unfortunately for those seeking guidance from the Court, the Justice gave little indication as to when decreases in value may be relevant so as to render equal sharing of the NFPs unconscionable. Nonetheless, the three specific reasons for the conclusion on the facts of the case contain some clues. The first reason only relates to situations where there is a domestic contract and so will often not be a factor. The third reason is arguably present whenever s. 5(6) is invoked. By that time, a triggering event has occurred so that one spouse owes the other an equalization sum. If this were, in and of itself, sufficient to preclude consideration of fluctuations in value after the valuation date; then Justice Borins' reference to "the context of this case" and his consideration of the other two reasons for the conclusion would be unnecessary. This leaves the ability of the owning spouse to divest himself or herself of the property as a possible key determinant in future cases. Often, the owning spouse will be able to divest of the property so as to avoid (additional) losses. However, there may be some situations where the owning spouse is precluded by law from doing so. For example, a matrimonial home is covered by the restrictions contained in Part II of the FLA. If the non-owning spouse refuses to consent, the owning spouse cannot dispose of an interest in it. In addition, a spouse's assets may be subject to a preservation order obtained by the non-owning spouse under s. 12 of the FLA. In both of these situations the non-owning spouse is preventing the owning spouse from disposing of assets and it is questionable whether the non-owning spouse should be described as "an ordinary creditor" in these situations. Thus, the owning spouse's argument that there should be an adjustment to the equalization sum in this situation is strong and there are powerful arguments for distinguishing the *LeVan* case.

In the end, the Court of Appeal's comments in the *LeVan v. LeVan* case on the question of whether market-driven, post-valuation date changes in the value of property can lead to an unequal sharing of NFPs are disappointing. They are focused on the particular facts of that case and provide limited general guidance. They do, nonetheless, suggest that it will continue to be difficult to obtain adjustments to the equalization sum based on post-valuation date fluctuations in property values. Those who believe such fluctuations are relevant to the fair distribution of the NFPs should still push for a legislative amendment. ...

SERRA v. SERRA

(2009), 2009 CarswellOnt 513, 61 R.F.L. (6th) 1 (C.A.)

BLAIR J.A.:

Introduction

1 The important issue raised on this appeal is whether, and if so, in what circumstances, a market-driven post-valuation date change in the value of a spouse's assets may be taken into account in determining whether an equalization of family property is unconscionable under s. 5(6) of the *Family Law Act*. This legal question has not previously been decided by this Court. A second issue is whether — if the decline in value of the appellant's principal asset may be taken into account — the equalization of family property would be unconscionable in the circumstances of this case.

2 Barbara and Harold Serra were married in 1976. They separated 24 years later, in November 2000, and were divorced in 2003.

3 Mr. Serra carried on what had been a very profitable textile business in Ajax, Ontario, known as Ajax Textiles. The success of that business enabled him and his wife to live in

what the trial judge described as a "luxurious lifestyle". At the time of separation Mr. Serra's shareholdings in the business — the principal asset in question — were valued at between $9.5 million and $11.25 million. By the time of trial, however, the value had decreased to somewhere between $1.875 million and $2.6 million — a drop of approximately $8 to $9 million. This dramatic change was not due to any fault on the part of Mr. Serra, who has done everything in his power to keep his failing business afloat. The change is attributed entirely to shifting market forces that have adversely affected the Canadian textile industry generally. It pre-dates the economic downturn that is currently bedevilling the Canadian and world economies and is therefore not the product of a temporary recession inevitably followed by an economic rebound.

4 At trial, Mr. Serra argued that equalizing his and his wife's net family properties on the basis of the separation-date value of his assets would be "unconscionable" as contemplated by s. 5(6) of the FLA. It would require him to make an equalization payment of $4,129,832.50 — an amount that exceeds his total net worth (and on one view of the evidence, could be as much as twice his total net worth). The trial judge ruled, however, that she could not take a market-driven post-separation date decline in the value of a spouse's assets into account under s. 5(6) and ordered the large equalization payment. In my respectful view, she erred in taking this approach, and I would allow the appeal for the reasons that follow.

. . . . .

[The wife commenced her action in December 2002. Among other things, she claimed periodic support, a trust interest in her husband's shares in the business, an interim and permanent restraining order prohibiting him from disposing of or otherwise dealing with any of his property and assets, and a preservation order with respect to all of his property and assets. In late December 2002, the husband was ordered to pay interim spousal support of $12,500 per month, maintain the expenses of the Florida condominium, amounting to $60,000 per year; and pay a further $7,500 per month to be characterized as either support or capital by the judge hearing the motion for interim relief. At the trial, the latter payments were characterized as advances on the equalization sum.]

29 These payments [under the interim order] could only be made if Ajax Textiles remained in business. Mr. Serra made every effort he could to facilitate this. He testified that in order to keep Ajax Textiles running, he depleted his $2 million loan account with Ajax Textiles, borrowed more than $1 million, laid off employees, rolled back salaries, reduced shifts, closed the Marine Division, sold corporate assets, increased corporate debt, obtained alternate financing after the Chartered Banks declined to lend further funds, mortgaged his own home, cashed in his and his new wife's RRSPs and his life insurance polices, and injected all of the proceeds into Ajax to keep it operational. He is financially strapped and left without any further assets to encumber or sell. ...

32 In August and September, 2004, the interim restraining and preservation orders that were originally before Justice Sachs in December, 2002, were dealt with. On August 26, at the instance of the respondent, the court ordered that Mr. Serra take no steps to sell the Florida property. On September 16, again at the request of the respondent, Justice Karakatsanis granted a preservation order, requiring the appellant (a) to preserve all property in which he had an interest, directly or indirectly, and over which he could exercise any control, directly or indirectly, and (b) to provide Ms. Serra with at least 30 days notice of any intended disposition. Needless to say, this order had an impact on Mr. Serra's ability to dispose of, preserve, maintain or improve the textile business and hence on the value of his indirect shareholding position in it.

33 Mr. Serra testified that his shares had no current value at the time of trial on a liquidation basis and that there were no prospective buyers for the textile business. In fact, all but two of the approximately ten dye houses that formerly operated in Ontario have gone out of business. This evidence was undisputed. ...

The Section 5(6) Issue: Recognizing Post-Separation Changes in Value

38 ... The appellant relies in particular upon paragraph 5(6)(h) ... He says that the marked post-separation date decline in value of the textile business and therefore of his common shares in it, in combination with the respondent's trust claims to an interest in those shares, the preservation order she obtained, and the significant interim support and capital payments he was required to make (and which could only be made out of an operating Ajax Textiles), are all circumstances relating to the disposition, preservation and maintenance of Ajax Textiles and, therefore, of his property assets. In these circumstances, it would be "unconscionable" to order an equalization of net family properties based upon a separation-date valuation of his interest in the business; to do so would be to require him to make an equalization payment that exceeds his total net worth, perhaps significantly.

39 The scope of the exception in s. 5(6) — and, in particular, whether its factors encompass post-valuation date fluctuations in the value of family property assets — has been the subject of considerable controversy amongst family law professionals. This is perhaps because the exception appears to fly in the face of what is seen as the essential characteristic of present-day family law legislation in Ontario, namely, the promotion of certainty, predictability and finality in the determination of support obligations and property division and the removal of judicial discretion in those areas to the extent possible. The great concern ... is to dispel any interpretation of the *Family Law Act* that might suggest the courts are empowered to deal with the division of family property on the basis of "discretionary fairness." On this view, expanding the discretion in the hands of the judiciary in family law matters is anathema to Ontario's legislative scheme and the development of any trend in that direction would be worrisome.

40 In my opinion, however, the concern is overblown, especially on the facts of this case, and misses the distinction between factors that may legitimately be considered under s. 5(6) and a finding of unconscionability under that provision.

41 Whereas other provinces have chosen different mechanisms for giving effect to the policy underlying modern family law legislation — that is, the equal division of family property in recognition of equal contributions to marriage — Ontario deliberately chose a fixed valuation date approach. For most practical purposes, that date is the date of separation. There is no discretion in the court to vary the valuation date. Hence the debate about whether courts can vary an equalization payment if the value of the asset has changed significantly after the valuation date.

42 Judges have tended to limit the application of the s. 5(6) factors to circumstances arising from misconduct on the part of the spouse who owns the asset in question or against whose favour the unequal distribution is to be made. Indeed, the general view to this point appears to be that post-valuation date variations in value are not to be taken into account under s. 5(6). One commentator has gone so far as to suggest that equal sharing of net family property is so clearly the norm in Ontario that some practitioners believe it "might as well be written in stone". ...

46 In my opinion, a court may take into account a post-separation date change in the value of a spouse's assets, and the circumstances surrounding such a change, for purposes of determining under s. 5(6) of the *Family Law Act* whether equalizing net family properties would be unconscionable. An order for an unequal division of net family properties is ex-

ceptional, however, and may only be made on such a basis (i) where the circumstances giving rise to the change in value relate (directly or indirectly) to the acquisition, disposition, preservation, maintenance or improvement of property (s. 5(6)(h)), and (ii) where equalizing the net family property would be unconscionable, having regard to those circumstances (taken alone or in conjunction with the other factors mentioned in s. 5(6)).

47 In this regard, the threshold of "unconscionability" under s. 5(6) is exceptionally high. The jurisprudence is clear that circumstances which are "unfair", "harsh" or "unjust" alone do not meet the test. To cross the threshold, an equal division of net family properties in the circumstances must "shock the conscience of the court". ...

49 However, it does not follow that because the threshold is exceptionally high the factors to be taken into account in assessing whether that threshold has been crossed should not include post-separation changes in the value of a spouse's assets and the circumstances surrounding that change. In an article published after the trial decision in LeVan, but before the argument on appeal, Professor Bala stated:

> It is submitted that while the outcome in *LeVan* may well be correct, the courts should interpret the vague, general words of s. 5(6)(h) to include the factor of a post-separation decline in property values that renders an equalizing of net family properties as evaluated on separation date to be unconscionable. It seems inappropriate for there to be judicial recognition only of post separation increases in property values, with post-separation declines ignored, even in situations of "unconscionability." While in some circumstances it is appropriate to expect the titled spouse to dispose of the assets after separation or bear the full risk of not doing so, there are circumstances when such a disposition would be unreasonable.

50 I agree. This is precisely one of those situations. ...

52 The rationale behind the statutory direction in s. 5 of the *Family Law Act* that net family property is to be shared equally — with the rare exception provided in s. 5(6) — is set out in s. 5(7) of the Act.

53 This rationale is affirmed in the preamble of the Act. ...

54 There is a jurisprudential theme running through the cases to the effect that relief may only be granted under s. 5(6) where there has been fault-based conduct on the part of the asset-owning spouse, that is, that the word "unconscionable" embraces factors relating to "unconscionable conduct" only: see, for example, *von Czieslik v. Ayuso* (2007), O.R. (3d) 88 (C.A.). ... In *von Czieslik*, for instance, Lang J.A. noted in *obiter*, "the legislative restriction of s. 5(6)'s application to certain enumerated circumstances, none of which have to do with ownership, but all of which relate to fault-based conduct on the part of the other spouse" (at para. 29).

55 Respectfully, I do not think this proposition is correct. First, it is clear that not all of the enumerated circumstances in s. 5(6) relate to fault-based conduct on the part of a spouse. Three of them — 5(6)(a), (b) and (d) — do. Four of them — 5(6)(c), (e), (f) and (g) — do not. One — 5(6)(h), the general basket clause at issue here — may or may not arise in conduct-related circumstances. Accordingly, there is no basis for concluding that the general basket clause in the list must take its colour and meaning from a previous list of specific conduct-based factors and, therefore, that the "circumstances" referred to must themselves embody fault-based conduct. That is not the case.

56 Secondly, neither the purpose or object of the s. 5 equalization payment scheme, the s. 5(6) exception, nor of the Act itself call for such an interpretation. The design of the legislation is to promote the goals of certainty, predictability and finality in the resolution of property matters following the breakdown of marriage. This, in turn, is founded on the central premise articulated in s. 5(7). ...

57 Thus, to ensure adherence to the policy choices made by the Legislature, and reflected in s. 5(7) and the preamble of the Act, equalization of net family properties is the general rule. As with most rules, however, there are exceptions — in this case, the high-threshold unconscionability provisions of s. 5(6). This exception is expressly contemplated by the caveat "subject only to the equitable considerations set out in subsection (6)" set out in s. 5(7). Judicial discretion with respect to equalization payments is therefore severely restricted, by statutory design, but it is not eliminated altogether since there is discretion to order an unequal payment. ...

58 There is no principled reason that I can see, given the language of the Act and its purpose or objects, to confine the word "unconscionable" in s. 5(6) only to circumstances arising from fault-based conduct on the part of one of the spouses. Although unconscionable conduct is obviously an appropriate consideration in determining whether equalizing the net family properties would be unconscionable, in my opinion the true target of the limited exception to the general rule is a situation that leads to an unconscionable result, whether that result flows from fault-based conduct or not. ...

60 The marked downturn in the textile industry is a "circumstance relating to" (at least) the "disposition, preservation [and] maintenance" of Ajax Textiles — the shares of which are Mr. Serra's major asset — within the meaning of s. 5(6)(h). So, too, are several other factors characterizing this case: the preservation order obtained by Ms. Serra, her ongoing claim for a trust interest in the assets, and the significant interim payments Mr. Serra was ordered to make and which could only be made if he kept Ajax Textiles operating as a viable business. Eight of the existing ten comparable businesses in Ontario had gone out of business. There were no buyers for Ajax Textiles, and Mr. Serra testified that the company's liquidation value was zero by the time of trial. This is not a case, then — like *LeVan*, for instance — where the owner of the diminishing asset could have sold it in a falling market in order to preserve at least some of its value. Nor, I emphasize, is it a case of a temporary decrease in the value of an asset resulting from a temporary economic recession; the difficulties in the domestic textile industry were well embedded before the onset of the current economic downturn.

61 The sale of Ajax Textiles was not a workable solution in the circumstances of this case for other reasons as well. Ms. Serra claimed an interest in the company. She consistently refused to agree to the disposition of the Florida condominium which was costing Mr. Serra $5,000 each month pursuant to the order of Sachs J. In addition he was required to pay Ms. Serra monthly support of $12,500 and an additional $7,500 per month (support or capital — to be determined later) by the same order. His only source of income to comply with those obligations was what he could derive from the continued operation of the business. He therefore engaged in the assiduous attempts outlined above (para. 29) to preserve and maintain the business, depleting whatever other assets he may have had in the process. Even in these efforts he was affected by the preservation order that had been obtained because he required the prior permission of Ms. Serra for any actions he planned to take in relation to those assets.

62 In my respectful view, therefore, the trial judge erred in refusing to take into account the market-driven downward impact on the value of Mr. Serra's interest in Ajax Textile, in combination with the other factors mentioned above, in considering the application of s. 5(6) of the *Family Law Act*. These are all factors to be considered in the s. 5(6) analysis. ...

The Section 5(6) Issue: Unconscionability

64 It is worth emphasizing that the legal issue in question here is whether a market-driven decline in value of a spouse's assets post-separation may be considered as a factor in deter-

mining whether an equalization of net family property is unconscionable under s. 5(6). Concluding that it may be considered as a factor does not lead necessarily to a finding on the facts that an equalization order would be unconscionable. This is an important distinction, in my view, and may sometimes be overlooked in the heat of the debate over finality and certainty versus discretionary fairness.

65 Although a purely market-driven decline in the value of Mr. Serra's principal asset is at the heart of these proceedings, this case is not about whether a significant post-separation drop in the value of an individual's stock portfolio, precipitated by a deep but temporary recession, will amount to unconscionability. Such an occurrence may well be a factor for consideration under s. 5(6)(h), but whether it would be sufficient by itself to constitute "unconscionability" is quite another matter. Each case must be determined on its own facts. In the circumstances here, however, I am satisfied that an equalization of net family property would be unconscionable, given the dramatic downward turn in Mr. Serra's fortunes and the factors giving rise to, and surrounding, it.

66 This is not a situation where any of the other factors listed in clauses (a) through (g) of s. 5(6) come into play to be weighed in the analysis against the market-driven decrease in value. For example, there is no fault-based conduct on the part of Mr. Serra that could — if it existed — be evaluated in the s. 5(6) analysis against the market-driven factors affecting his assets, as there was in such cases as *LeVan, von Czieslik* and others. ... Nor — for reasons mentioned above — is this a situation like *LeVan* where Mr. Serra could have disposed of the business (or of his shares in it) as a hedge against their downward trend in value, another factor that could otherwise be considered in the mix. It was necessary to keep Ajax Textiles afloat to enable him to continue to meet the interim support and capital obligations he had been ordered to pay.

67 In these circumstances, an equalization of net family property that requires Mr. Serra to pay more than his total net worth (and arguably as much as twice his net worth) because of a marked decline in the value of his major asset post-separation — over which he had absolutely no control and in spite of his best efforts to save the business in the face of Ms. Serra's trust claims, the preservation order and the need to comply with his support obligations — is, in my view, unconscionable. In so concluding, I have taken into account that Ms. Serra is not a woman without means. The trial judge found she left the marriage "with assets worth a considerable amount." She has net family property of about $1 million in addition to her interest in the Florida property. She has lived, and continues to live, a life of relative luxury, 6 months in Canada and 6 months in Florida. The trial judge found she had been "very well compensated" for her contributions to the business during the course of the marriage.

What is the Appropriate Way to Craft a Remedy?

69 Since the threshold for an unequal division of net family property is unconscionability, some would argue that the appropriate disposition in such circumstances is simply to roll back the award in favour of the recipient spouse to the point where it is just shy of "unconscionable". Justice Backhouse adopted this position at trial in *LeVan* and Mr. Epstein initially advanced that argument before us. Backhouse J. said (at paras. 272–274): "The virtue of this approach is that the court adheres as closely as possible to the statutory scheme and does not engage in a value driven exercise which the Legislature clearly intended should not apply." ...

70 I concede that this approach ... has a certain attraction. Respectfully, however, I do not agree with it. I say this for two reasons. First, I do not accept that it represents an interpretation of s. 5(6) that is more consistent with the Act. Secondly, an order that is just shy of

unconscionable remains — by jurisprudential definition — an order that is at least unfair, unjust and inequitable, if not worse. Courts do not make orders deliberately, in the exercise of their discretion, that are unfair, unjust and inequitable; that is the antithesis of what courts stand for.

71 Section 5(6) does not call for an award that is just short of unconscionable. It provides that the court may award a spouse "an amount that is more or less than half the difference between the net family properties" if "equalizing the net family properties *would be unconscionable*", (emphasis added) In short, the threshold that an applicant must cross in order to open the door to an unequal division is — as I have said earlier in these reasons — exceptionally high. That is because of the policy underlying the Act encouraging finality, predictability and certainty and minimizing the exercise of judicial discretion to the extent possible, also referred to earlier. Once the threshold has been crossed, however, and the rare resort to judicial discretion under the Act is in play, the court should exercise its discretion as it normally does: by doing what is just, fair and equitable in the circumstances. Such an approach, in my opinion, is (a) true to the language of s. 5(6) itself, (b) reflective of the wording in s. 5(7) establishing that the presumed equal contribution of the spouses leading to the normal equal division of net family property is subject only to the "equitable" considerations set out in s. 5(6); and (c) consistent with the call in the preamble of the Act for "the orderly and equitable settlement of the affairs of the spouses upon the breakdown of the partnership."

What is the Appropriate Award in this Case?

73 On this issue, the appellant submits that the appropriate award in the circumstances of this case would be to require Mr. Serra to make an equalization payment of $1.5 million which, after credit for the capital payments he has already made, nets out to a payment due now of $656,000. This is arrived at by taking Mr. Serra's net family property at the date of trial as $4.5 million (after taking into account the decreased value of the textile business, based on the KPMG valuation as of November, 2004) and valuing Ms. Serra's at $1.5 million. The difference between the two net family properties is $3 million, one-half of which is $1.5 million. From that amount must be deducted credit for capital payments already made by Mr. Serra. The balance is $656,000 — a far cry from the net of almost $3.3 million ordered by the trial judge. ...

75 Having regard to all the circumstances, and bearing in mind that the court is exercising a fairness function in this narrow context, I have concluded that the net outstanding equalization payment should be fixed at $900,000. I say this for a number of reasons.

76 I accept that the amount of Mr. Serra's net equalization payment must be reduced substantially from the amount ordered by the trial judge. However, I would not reduce it mechanically to the suggested $656,000 by simply applying the reduced trial-date valuation of Ajax Textiles. Instead, I would make an upward adjustment of approximately $250,000 in that amount. I do so to give better effect in particular to these considerations: (i) the possibility, however remote, of a modest turn around in the fortunes of the Ajax Textiles business; (ii) the length of the Serra's marriage; (iii) the principle of dividing matrimonial property in a way that recognizes the equal contribution of spouses to the accumulation of wealth during a marriage; and, (iv) a desire not simply to substitute a trial-date valuation for the separation-date valuation in the circumstances of this case.

77 The Legislature chose the date of separation, principally, as the valuation date for purposes of establishing the equalization of net family property in Ontario. In doing so, it gave effect to the "equal contribution to the marriage" tenet by measuring the accumulation of wealth during the marriage as the difference between the value at separation and the value of

property brought into the marriage. The same theory does not apply to post-separation date valuations because what happens to an asset after that point — whether its value goes up or down — is not related to contributions within the marriage context. In addition, a trial-date valuation is somewhat random in that it depends upon the time it takes the parties to get ready for trial and the vagaries of the trial scheduling system. As well, it may be open to manipulation by parties seeking the most advantageous timing. I note that there is no suggestion on the record here that Mr. Serra sought to manipulate the timing of the trial for these purposes. Notwithstanding this, and while there may be cases where it would be appropriate to apply a straight trial-date valuation approach in these kinds of circumstances, I do not think this is one of them.

78 Mr. and Ms. Serra had a long-term marriage of over 24 years. While it seems unlikely that Ajax Textiles will ever return to its highly profitable heydays, Mr. Serra testified that he was optimistic he could make the business profitable once again. It seems unfair — particularly given the length of the marriage, the principles underlying the *Family Law Act*, and Ms. Serra's sometimes role in the business — to saddle her with the entire downside of the business' decline while Mr. Serra retains at least the possibility, however remote, of enjoying some upside in the future. At the time of trial, Mr. Serra's shareholdings in the business were valued at between $1.875 million and $2.6 million. The adjustment I propose represents roughly 10%–15% of that range — depending on where one settles on the spectrum — and is designed to reflect the foregoing factors while still recognizing the dramatic negative impact of the decline in the textile business on Mr. Serra's net worth. ...

NOTES AND QUESTIONS

1. In *Redman v. Korchinski* (2006), 33 R.F.L. (6th) 36 (Man. C.A.), the trial judge concluded that the husband had dissipated assets by gambling away almost $44,000 in the three months after his release from hospital following a third party's criminal assault and by turning a minor problem in the basement of the family home into a major one through a botched repair job. As a result, he ordered the husband to pay $31,945.50 under *The Family Property Act*, C.C.S.M., c. F25. Section 1(1) of that Act defined "dissipation" as "the jeopardizing of the financial security of a household by the gross and irresponsible squandering of an asset". The trial judge specifically stated that the fact that the husband might well have had little control over his actions because the assault had impaired his abstract reasoning, memory and self-control was irrelevant.

The Manitoba Court of Appeal allowed the husband's appeal. It held that there had to be some mental element in dissipation, however slight that requirement might be. Because of the husband's injury, he simply could not comprehend that his actions were irresponsible.

2. Several times in the *Serra* case Justice Blair stressed that each case has to be decided on its facts and that the instant case was not about whether a significant post-separation drop in the value of assets "precipitated by a deep but temporary recession" triggered s. 5(6) of the *Family Law Act*. How much guidance did the court provide for lawyers currently (early 2009) negotiating cases where spouses separated in the summer of 2008 before the major collapse of the world's stock markets and the smaller, but significant, fall in house prices? Why should it matter whether the drop in values is only temporary?

3. The decline in the markets in the fall of 2008 was dramatic and quick. Can one nevertheless argue that the spouse who held stock or owned realty should have cut his or her losses by disposing of assets?

(4) Implementation of the Equalization Entitlement

HOVIUS AND YOUDAN, *THE LAW OF FAMILY PROPERTY*

(Toronto: Carswell, 1991) 449–459 and 463–468

1. Introduction

To determine a spouse's entitlement under section 5, the net family properties of the spouses must be calculated. Once this is done, the spouse with the lesser of the two net family properties is entitled to one-half the difference between them unless the court awards a greater or lesser amount under section 5(6). The end result is that one spouse owes the other a monetary sum (which will be referred to as the equalization sum in this chapter). Section 9 then empowers the court to make various orders to ensure that this sum is realized in a fair and effective manner.

Section 9 is, therefore, an implementation provision that only comes into play after the court has determined the equalization sum under section 5. The section cannot be used to short circuit the process by, for example, removing assets from the net family properties and dividing them equally. Although section 9(1)(d) does empower the court to order the transfer of property from one spouse to the other, this can only be done after the equalization sum has been calculated based on all included property owned by each spouse on the valuation date.[1]

The range of options available under section 9 is extensive:

> ... (1) the whole amount can be ordered paid forthwith; (2) if necessary, to avoid hardship, the whole amount can be paid in instalments not exceeding ten years; (3) security may be imposed for the whole or part of the amount; (4) to satisfy all or part of the amount, property may be transferred to the receiving spouse absolutely, for life, or a term of years; (5) to satisfy all or part of the amount, property can be placed in trust or vested in a spouse absolutely, for life, or a term of years; (6) to satisfy all or part of the amount, any property may be partitioned or sold.[2]

The section, therefore, provides the court with considerable flexibility enabling it to balance the interests of the debtor spouse and creditor spouse while choosing the most appropriate method of satisfying the equalization sum in a particular case. In addition, section 11(2) empowers the court to make special orders regarding operating businesses or farms to avoid their sale or the serious impairment of their operations. ...

2. Payment Forthwith

Section 9(1)(a) establishes the court's power to order that one spouse pay to the other the amount to which the latter is entitled under Part I. Since the entitlement created by section 5 itself is to a sum of money, the inclusion of this power naturally follows. Indeed, it is the legislature's decision not to confine the court's power to orders for immediate payment that requires explanation.

The legislature clearly recognized that an order requiring immediate payment of the equalization sum could cause hardship for the debtor spouse in some circumstances. Hence, it empowered the court, if necessary to avoid hardship, to delay the payment for a period of up to ten years or to order payment by instalments during a period not exceeding ten years. This concern is reinforced by section 11(1) which forbids the court from making an order

---

[1] *Marsham v. Marsham* (1987), 7 R.F.L. (3d) 1 (Ont. H.C.).

[2] *Ibid.* at 20.

that would require or result in the sale of an operating business or farm or that would seriously impair its operation unless there is no reasonable alternative method of satisfying the award. While certain of the additional powers listed in section 9(1) can, therefore, be explained on the basis that the debtor spouse should not suffer undue hardship in the realization of the equalization sum, others are included for the benefit of the creditor spouse. If the court could only render a money judgment, the creditor spouse would in all cases have to rely for enforcement on the general debtor-creditor law. This could lead to future enforcement problems. In an attempt to avoid these potential problems, the legislature empowered the court to order that property be transferred from one spouse to the other or that it be sold to satisfy the order. The power to order that security be given for the performance of an obligation imposed by the implementation order can be explained on the same basis. In summary, the legislature enabled the courts to choose the most appropriate method of satisfying the equalization sum in each individual case in light of the interests of both the debtor spouse and the creditor spouse.

Many reported cases indicate that the judges begin their assessment of the appropriate method of satisfying the equalization sum with a preference for orders for immediate payment of the entire equalization sum. Such a preference seems reasonable since section 5 itself creates an entitlement to a sum of money. Of course, judges should remain open to the possibility that additional or alternative orders may be necessary to ensure that the equalization sum is realized in a fair and effective manner.

3. Security

Under section 9(1)(b) a court may order that security be given for the performance of an obligation imposed by the implementation order. Such security may include a charge on property, which can then be registered to ensure priority over subsequently acquired interests of third parties.[12] The awarding of security pending payment in full is particularly appropriate where a court orders deferred payment or payment by instalments pursuant to section 9(1)(c) and there is some concern whether the money will be paid.

Where an order for security has been made, the court has authority under section 13 to vary or discharge the order on the application of either party. Variation or discharge might be appropriate in a number of circumstances including situations where the obligation has been satisfied or where a valid case is made for the disposition of property involved or the transfer of the charge to another piece of property. ...

Section 13 also empowers a court, on notice to all persons having an interest in the property, to direct the sale of property for the purpose of realizing the security or charge imposed.

4. Deferred Payment or Instalment Payments

(a) When permitted

Section 9(1)(c) permits the court to order that the equalization sum be paid in instalments during a period not exceeding ten years or that payment of all or part of the sum be delayed for a period not exceeding ten years. This power can only be exercised, however, "if necessary to avoid hardship". Thus, the creditor spouse is entitled to immediate satisfaction of the equalization sum unless this would cause hardship to the debtor spouse.

Where the equalization sum is created mainly by the inclusion of the value of a pension in the debtor spouse's net family property, this spouse may not be able to raise the money

---

[12]   See s. 2(11).

necessary to make the payment immediately since the value of the pension will usually not be accessible. ...

Immediate satisfaction of the equalization sum may also cause hardship where the debtor spouse's major assets comprise a business or farm which is the source of this spouse's livelihood. In this context, s. 11(1) must be considered. It prohibits a court from making an order under s. 9 that would require or result in the sale of an operating business or farm or that would seriously impair its operation unless there is no reasonable alternative method of satisfying the equalization sum. Where immediate satisfaction of the equalization sum would have this effect, deferred payment or payment by instalments may represent a reasonable alternative method by which the sum could be realized. In *McDougall v. McDougall*,[16] the wife was entitled to an equalization sum of $63,980.93. Almost all of the husband's assets consisted of shares in a farming operation conducted by himself, his father and his brother. Finding that the immediate payment of the equalization sum would probably necessitate a sale of the husband's interest in the farm business and that the husband had "no employment or other economic prospects outside that business",[17] Killeen D.C.J. concluded that "the fair order is to direct that the defendant pay the equalization sum in five yearly instalments".[18] He also ordered that post-judgment interest be paid on the equalization sum which was to be secured against the husband's shares.

In some situations the solution adopted in *McDougall v. McDougall* will not be economically feasible. This was the conclusion reached by Craig J. in *Leslie v. Leslie*.[19] ...

The situations analyzed above represent perhaps the most obvious examples where immediate satisfaction of the equalization sum could cause hardship. However, such hardship could arise in other circumstances and for other reasons.[23] Deferral for a short period of time has, for example, been ordered in some cases to allow the debtor spouse to liquidate assets in an orderly fashion or otherwise raise the necessary funds.

(b) Corollary orders

If the court orders deferred payment or payment by instalments, it may make certain corollary orders under section 9(2) either at the time the original order is made or, on motion, at a later time. It can order that the debtor spouse furnish the other spouse with specified financial information, which may include periodic financial statements. It can also require the debtor spouse to permit inspections of specified property by or on behalf of the other spouse.

(c) Variation

Section 9(3) permits the court to vary the order for deferred payment or payment by instalments where "there has been a material change in the circumstances of the spouse who has the obligation to make instalment or delayed payments". While it might be anticipated that most applications for variation will be made by the debtor spouse for additional deferment of the payment or a reduction in the instalments because of deteriorating financial

---

[16] (1989), 23 R.F.L. (3d) 320 (Ont. Dist. Ct.).

[17] *Ibid.* at 326.

[18] *Ibid.*

[19] (1987), 9 R.F.L. (3d) 82 (Ont. H.C.).

[23] Where the creditor spouse is granted exclusive possession of the matrimonial home owned exclusively or partly by the debtor spouse, immediate satisfaction of the equalization sum may also cause hardship. See *Ward v. Ward* (1990), 26 R.F.L. (3d) 149 (Ont. C.A.).

circumstances, there might well be situations where a creditor spouse could successfully invoke the court's jurisdiction. For example, accelerated payment might be appropriate if the debtor's circumstances have improved. Also, in cases where deferred payment or payment by instalments was ordered to allow the debtor spouse to continue to operate a business or farm, the financial position of this spouse may be deteriorating to such an extent that there is a legitimate concern whether the order will ever be fulfilled. Section 9(3) appears to be broad enough to allow the court to order sale of the debtor's assets so that the equalization sum can be realized before the value of these assets declines even further. The financial statements and inspections of property contemplated by section 9(2) might serve to alert the creditor spouse to the need for a variation order on this basis.

Even if a material change in circumstances is established, section 9(3) explicitly prohibits the court from varying the amount of the equalization sum. Also, subsection (4) provides that the power to vary the order does not permit the court to postpone payment beyond the original ten year period.

(d) Interest

Section 9 does not specifically empower the court to order the payment of interest on deferred payments or payments by instalments. However, payment of interest has been ordered in several cases, presumably pursuant to sections 139 and 140 of the *Courts of Justice Act, 1984.*[27]

As a general principle, interest should normally be payable from the date of the order providing for deferred payment or payment by instalments. Otherwise, the creditor spouse's payment will be diminished by the effect of inflation and there will be a *de facto* unequal sharing of net family properties. Moreover, delay in the realization of the equalization sum is obviously detrimental to the creditor spouse who is denied the use of the money in the interim. Unless there is good reason why this detriment should be borne solely by the creditor spouse,[31] compensation in the form of interest is appropriate.

5. Property Orders

(a) Introduction

Under section 9(1)(d) the court is empowered to make a number of orders dealing directly with the spouses' property where "appropriate to satisfy an obligation imposed by the order". ...

(b) Transfer of property

Section 9(1)(d)(i) has provided the basis for what has become known as an "if and when" order regarding the portion of the equalization sum attributable to a pension held by the debtor spouse to prevent the hardship that could result if immediate payment of the sum was required. Under such orders, the court directs that the debtor spouse hold a portion of the pension in trust for the other, with payments generally to commence once the pension is received.

---

27 S.O. 1984, c. 11. [See now ss. 129 and 130 of the *Courts of Justice Act*, R.S.O. 1990, c. C.43.]

31 Where, for example, the creditor spouse is granted exclusive possession of a matrimonial home owned partly or wholly by the debtor spouse and the creditor spouse is not required to pay occupation rent, interest on the deferred payment of the equalization sum might not be appropriate. While the creditor spouse is denied the benefit of immediate payment, he or she has the use of an asset owned by the debtor spouse. This should be taken into account in determining whether any interest should be payable and, if so, the rate.

Except for these special orders relating to pensions, orders requiring the transfer of property to satisfy the equalization sum have been infrequent. In several cases, however, the courts have ordered a transfer of the debtor spouse's interest in a jointly owned matrimonial home to the creditor spouse. In *Oliva v. Oliva*[36] the husband owed the wife an equalization sum of $28,729.10. His most substantial asset was a partnership interest in a hairdressing business and McDermid L.J.S.C. found that it was most unlikely that his partners would consent to the sale of any partnership property to pay the equalization sum. Immediate satisfaction of the equalization sum could, therefore, only be achieved by looking to the husband's equity in the jointly owned matrimonial home. Rather than order the sale of that asset and payment out of the husband's share of the proceeds, McDermid L.J.S.C. acceded to the wife's request that the court order the husband to transfer his interest in the matrimonial home and its contents to the wife in satisfaction of $24,750.00 of the total sum owing. The balance was to be paid within one year with interest. In this way the equalization sum could be realized and the wife and children could continue to reside in the matrimonial home. ...

... [The] concern that a transfer of property requires an accurate valuation of the property at the time of trial is a legitimate one. Certainly, the court cannot simply adopt the value that was used in calculating the net family properties because there may well have been a change in the property's value since the valuation date. While the requirement for yet another valuation introduces even more complexity and difficulty into the equalization process, a transfer of property to satisfy the equalization sum should remain an option as long as the court has sufficient evidence to allow it to assess the present value of the property in a realistic fashion.

One further complication that may be introduced by the transfer of property should be noted. A transfer of property may necessitate a reassessment of the treatment of notional sale costs and taxes payable on the disposition of the property in calculating the net family property of the transferor. If property is transferred between the spouses, there will be no immediate sale and the transferor will not have to pay commission to a real estate agent. It would, therefore, be inappropriate to take these notional sales costs into account in the calculation of the transferor's net family property. Moreover, the "rollover" provisions in the *Income Tax Act* may apply so that there are no immediate tax consequences for the transferor. Instead, there may be future tax consequences for the transferee who steps into the transferor's shoes for tax purposes. These consequences should be considered in determining how much of the equalization sum is satisfied by the transfer.

(c) Sale of Property

Subparagraph (ii) of section 9(1)(d) empowers the court to order the partition or sale of any property "if appropriate to satisfy an obligation imposed by the order". The most common order made under this subparagraph requires the sale of property held jointly by the spouses with payment of all or some of the equalization sum to be made out of the debtor spouse's share of the proceeds. Since a sale of jointly held property will frequently be required in any event so that both spouses can realize their ownership interest, ordering the sale under section 9(1)(d) and stipulating that the equalization sum be paid out of the proceeds interferes little with the property rights of the debtor spouse while it ensures payment without future enforcement problems. Orders for the sale of property owned exclusively by the debtor spouse with payment of the equalization sum out of the proceeds interfere more significantly with the proprietary interests of this spouse. However, they too may be appro-

---

[36] *Oliva v. Oliva* (1986), 2 R.F.L. (3d) 188 (Ont. H.C.); varied (1988), 12 R.F.L. (3d) 334 (Ont C.A.).

priate in some cases to avoid future enforcement problems which might be anticipated if the court simply imposed an obligation to pay a sum of money. ...

6. Special Powers Relating to Operating Businesses or Farms

As previously noted, section 11(1) prohibits a court from making an order under section 9 that would require or result in the sale of an operating business or farm or that would seriously impair its operation unless there is no reasonable alternative method of satisfying the equalization sum. In some circumstances, deferred payment or payment by instalments may be a reasonable way in which the debtor spouse can satisfy the equalization sum while continuing to operate a business or farm. In *Leslie v. Leslie*,[70] the Court concluded that any form of deferred payment was not economically feasible and it carefully designed an order requiring the sale of some farm property to permit payment of the equalization sum without undue impairment of the farm operation.

Section 11(2) provides for additional orders whereby the equalization sum may be satisfied without a sale or serious impairment of a business or farm operation. Under paragraph (a), a court may order that the debtor spouse pay the other spouse a share of the profits from the business or farm. If the business or farm is incorporated, paragraph (b) empowers the court to order "that one spouse transfer or have the corporation issue to the other shares in the corporation".[71]

The prohibition created by section 11(1) is obviously not absolute. A court is prohibited from making an order under section 9 that would require or result in the sale of an operating business or farm or that would seriously impair its operation only if there is a reasonable alternative method of satisfying the equalization sum. The effect of section 11(2) is to expand the range of alternatives the court may consider. But if none of these is viewed as a reasonable way of satisfying the award, then the court may make an order for immediate satisfaction of the equalization sum even if this order would bring the business or farm operation to an end.

There are no reported cases in which the special powers granted by section 11(2) have been utilized. This may be explained partly by the fact that the courts have looked first to the various options provided by section 9(1) itself, including deferred payment or payment by instalments. Where one of these represents a reasonable way of satisfying the equalization sum without a forced sale of the farm or business, there is no need to examine the possible use of section 11(2). On the other hand, where none of these other options is economically feasible, it is unlikely that an order for the sharing of profits in some way will be either, particularly if the creditor spouse is to be compensated for the loss of the use of the capital represented by the equalization sum. Moreover, an order under section 11(2) would require the spouses to continue their economic relationship to some extent and thus provide fertile ground for future dispute.[74] This will be enough to make such orders unattractive to both parties in most circumstances. In conclusion, orders under section 11(2) are likely to remain rare.

---

[70] *Supra*, note 19.

[71] Regarding the use of such orders and the impact of a provision in the articles of incorporation providing that no shares may be transferred without the consent of the board of directors, see Mannering and Hainsworth, "Private Corporations — Keeping Control in the Wake of the *Family Law Act, 1986* (Ontario)" (1990), 6 C.F.L.Q. 23.

[74] Such disputes might involve the determination of the business' or farm's profits or allegations that the business or farm is not being operated efficiently. See, generally, McLeod, "Annotation" (1986), 2 R.F.L. (3d) 2 and Law Reform Commission of British Columbia, *Working Paper on Property Rights on Marriage Breakdown* (1989) at 132-133.

7. Prejudgment Interest

There is no provision in the *Family Law Act* regarding prejudgment interest. However, sections 137–140 of the *Courts of Justice Act, 1984*[75] apply. Pursuant to section 138(1), "[a] person who is entitled to an order for the payment of money is entitled to claim and have included in the order an award of interest thereon at the prejudgment interest rate, calculated from the date the cause of action arose to the date of the order". Section 140(1) then empowers the court "where it considers it just to do so" to disallow such interest, allow it at a higher or lower rate, or allow it for a period other than that provided in section 138. Thus, a successful litigant has a *prima facie* right to prejudgment interest and the onus is upon the party to persuade the trial Judge to exercise his or her discretion to the contrary.

NOTES AND QUESTIONS

1. For some additional cases where one spouse was ordered to transfer property to another to satisfy all or part of the equalization payment, see *Burnett v. Burnett* (1997), 33 R.F.L. (4th) 356 (Ont. Gen. Div.); *Best v. Best* (1997), 31 R.F.L. (4th) 1 (Ont. C.A.); reversed on another point (1999), 49 R.F.L. (4th) 1 (S.C.C.); *Harbour v. Harbour* (2000), 6 R.F.L. (5th) 225 (Ont. S.C.J.); *Kennedy v. Sinclair* (2001), 18 R.F.L. (5th) 91 (Ont. S.C.J.); *Aning v. Aning* (2002), 30 R.F.L. (5th) 237 (Ont. S.C.J.); *McIsaac v. McIsaac* (2004), 1 R.F.L. (6th) 293 (Ont. S.C.J.); additional reasons at (2004), 2004 Carswell 270 (S.C.J.); and *Bauer v. Bauer* (2005), 2005 CarswellOnt 2278 (S.C.J.). In *Best*, the S.C.C. commented (paragraph 109) that the choice of the appropriate implementation method was "highly contextual and fact-based".

2. Regarding the tax consequences of property transfers between spouses on marriage breakdown and the way in which such transfers may be used to minimize the tax consequences of the breakdown, see Cole and Freedman, *Property Valuation and Income Tax Implications of Marital Dissolution* (Toronto: Carswell) (looseleaf service). ...

4. The leading case on prejudgment interest is *Burgess v. Burgess* (1995), 24 O.R. (3d) 547 (C.A.). The court reviewed the case law and held that, as a general rule, a payor spouse is required to pay prejudgment interest on an equalization payment owing to a payee spouse in order to encourage timely settlement of equalization claims. The court also confirmed that, as indicated in *McQuay v. McQuay* (1992), 8 O.R. (3d) 111, 39 R.F.L. (3d) 184 (Div. Ct.), the principles for awarding prejudgment interest on equalization payments are not identical to those used in commercial cases. It approved a line of lower court decisions indicating that no prejudgment interest will be awarded "where, for various reasons, the payor spouse cannot realize on the asset giving rise to the equalization payment until after the trial, does not have the use of it prior to trial, the asset generates no income, and the payor spouse has not delayed the case being brought to trial." For some additional cases dealing with the issue of prejudgment interest, see *Nahatchewitz v. Nahatchewitz* (1999), 1 R.F.L. (5th) 395 (Ont. C.A.); additional reasons at (1999), 1999 CarswellOnt 3076 (Ont. C.A.); *Clegg v. Clegg* (2000), 9 R.F.L. (5th) 290 (Ont. S.C.J.); affirmed (2001), 18 R.F.L. (5th) 62 (Ont. C.A.); *Taylor v. Taylor* (2002), 29 R.F.L. (5th) 424 (Ont. C.A.); *Huot v. Kaszap* (2006), 2006 CarswellOnt 8400 (S.C.J.); and *Debora v. Debora* (2007), 33 R.F.L. (6th) 252 (Ont. C.A.).

5. For some additional cases where the equalization payment was deferred or ordered to be paid by installments, see *Best, supra; MacDonald v. MacDonald* (1997), 33 R.F.L. (4th) 75 (Ont. C.A.); and *Balcerzak v. Balcerzak* (1998), 41 R.F.L. (4th) 13 (Ont. Gen. Div.). In each of these cases post-judgment interest was ordered.

6. Reluctance to make one spouse a minority shareholder in a corporation controlled by the other is illustrated in *Faulkner v. Faulkner* (1998), 166 D.L.R. (4th) 378 (Alta. C.A.).

7. A court cannot, under provincial matrimonial property legislation, order transfers of property located on land reserved for Indians under the federal *Indian Act*. However, the value of that property can be included in the net family properties and a court can require a monetary payment to equalize the spouses' net family properties. See *George v. George* (1996), 24 R.F.L. (4th) 155 (B.C. C.A.) where a compensation order adjusted the division of

---

[75] S.O. 1984, c. 11. The Ontario Court of Appeal confirmed the applicability of this statute's provisions regarding prejudgment interest in *Starkman v. Starkman* (1990), 28 R.F.L. (3d) 208 at 216. [See now ss. 127–130 of the *Courts of Justice Act*, R.S.O. 1990, c. C.43.]

family assets located on a reserve. See also *Dunstan v. Dunstan* (2002), 26 R.F.L. (5th) 67 (B.C. S.C. [In Chambers]).

Under the *First Nations Land Management Act*, S.C. 1999, c. 24, First Nations that enter into a Framework Agreement on First Nation Land Management with the federal government are required by s. 17(1) to "establish general rules and procedures, in cases of breakdown of marriage, respecting the use, occupation and possession of first nation land and the division of interests in first nation land".

Recently, the House of Commons gave first reading to a bill that, if enacted, would become the *Family Homes on Reserves and Matrimonial Interests or Rights Act*. This legislation was first introduced in March 2008. It received second reading and was referred to committee in May 2008, but died on the Order Paper before committee study began. The proposed legislation would provide a framework for all First Nations governed by the *Indian Act* to develop and adopt their own matrimonial property rules. The bill also sets forth a detailed regime that would apply in situations where First Nations did not adopt such rules. The rules in the default regime would impose restrictions on what the holder of a right or interest in a family home could do with it during the relationship, permit a court to make exclusive possession orders, and would provide for equal sharing of the value of a right or interest in a family home at the end of the relationship. The default regime would apply to married persons and common law partners. For analysis of and commentary on the proposed legislation, see Ruru, "Finding Solutions for the Legislative Gaps in Determining Rights to the Family Home on Colonially Defined Indigenous Lands" (2008), 41 U.B.C.L. Rev. 315.

(5) Pensions

LAW COMMISSION OF ONTARIO, *DIVISION OF PENSIONS UPON MARRIAGE BREAKDOWN*, FINAL REPORT

(December 2008)

[The full report is available online at the Law Commission of Ontario's web site.]

I. An Overview of Pensions in Ontario

Broadly speaking, the subject of this report is the treatment of a spouse's interest in a pension plan upon marriage breakdown. Our principal concern in that regard is with occupational pension plans that provide lifetime periodic (usually monthly) benefit payments to former employees following their retirement, with a particular focus on defined benefit plans, as it is in relation to interests under those types of plans that the main problems that have been identified arise. Generally, the report will not deal with other kinds of private arrangements aimed at providing an income on retirement, such as personal or group Registered Retirement Savings Plans (RRSPs), or with government-provided social welfare schemes, such as the federal Old Age Security program, although it will deal with certain matters related to the *Canada Pension Plan* (CPP).

Types of Pension Plans and Employee Coverage

Occupational pension plans are most commonly established by an employer, although in some cases, a plan may be established jointly by one or more employers and one or more trade unions. In the construction industry, where employer-employee relationships tend to be transient, the plan might be established solely by a union. Plans covering public sector employees are usually established by legislation.

In terms of the nature of the benefit provided, there are two main types of occupational pension plan, the defined benefit plan and the defined contribution plan. Under both kinds of plan the employer is required to make contributions, but both may also require employees to make contributions (in which case the plan is labelled "contributory").

Under a defined contribution plan, the contributions made by the employer and by the employee, if any, are set at a fixed amount or rate; those contributions are invested and the sum of accumulated contributions and returns on their investment is used to purchase an annuity when the employee retires. (Because of this aspect, such plans are sometimes referred to as "money purchase plans".) In contrast, the amount of the pension benefit under a defined benefit plan has no immediate relation to the contributions and investment yield, but rather is determined according to a set formula. ...

A typical defined benefit formula might provide that the annual pension amount is equal to the product obtained when the employee's number of years of service with the employer is multiplied by a specified percentage and then applied against the average salary earned by the employee during some specified number of years in which his employment income was the greatest or during some specified number of years immediately preceding retirement. For example, a plan might provide that the yearly pension income would be equal to years of service times two per cent times the average salary of the employee during his five highest years of earnings. A member of such a plan who had 25 years of service at retirement and who earned an average of $80,000 during his most remunerative years would have an annual pension income of $40,000.

The type of defined benefit plan described in the preceding paragraph is often referred to as a "best average" or "final average" earnings plan. Other common types include the flat benefit plan and the career earnings plan. In a flat benefit plan, the formula does not refer to earnings or percentages; rather, the multiplier is simply the years of service and the multiplicand is a flat dollar amount. (For example, if the flat dollar amount is $80 a month, an employee who retired after thirty years' service would have a monthly pension of $2,400, or $28,800 annually.) Under a career earnings plan, the multiplier is a bare percentage (that is, it is not a function of years of service) and the multiplicand is the aggregate of the employee's earnings during the entire period of her membership in the pension plan. (For example, if the percentage in the benefit formula is two per cent and the retiring employee had earned $1,250,000 over the course of her career with the employer, her pension income would be $25,000 per year.)

Benefits under defined benefit plans are usually "integrated" with the CPP, meaning that the pension amount that was calculated using the basic defined benefit formula is reduced to reflect the assumed receipt of CPP benefits. Effectively, in such cases, the basic formula indicates what the employee can expect to receive in total from both sources, the occupational pension and the CPP benefit.

There are some plans, called hybrid plans, which combine features of defined benefit and defined contribution plans. This type of plan may provide a retiring employee with a benefit equal to the greater of the amount determined under a defined benefit formula and the amount of contributions and investment yield, or it might provide a benefit equal to the total of the defined benefit amount and what was accumulated under the defined contribution part of the plan. In some cases, an employer might convert a defined benefit plan into a defined contribution plan, with the employee's benefits earned up to the conversion date being determined under the defined benefit formula and benefits thereafter being the amount of subsequent contributions and returns on investment.

A study prepared for the Ontario Expert Committee on Pensions (OECP) cited a report prepared by Statistics Canada indicating that roughly 34% of employees in Ontario jurisdiction were members of an occupational pension plan as of 2005.[14] Noteworthy, however, is the public sector-private sector divide on this score; while 80% of public sector employees were members of an occupational pension plan, only 25% of private sector employees had such coverage. Also interesting is the fact that while the number of defined contribution plans is slightly greater than the number of defined benefit plans, defined benefit plans collectively have far more members, although membership in defined contribution plans has been increasing at a much faster rate than membership in defined benefit plans. ...

With respect to the demographics of pension plan membership, while currently the number of males who are members of a pension plan (928,000) is slightly greater than the number of females (832,000), it appears that over the long term the number of males has not been growing, while the number of females has been increasing fairly dramatically; further, the percentage of pension plan members who are members of a defined benefit plan as opposed to some other type of plan is approximately 80% for both sexes. [The Commission goes on to note, that, for various reasons, average pension income for females is still substantially lower than that for males.] ...

Jurisdictional and Legislative Framework

Under the *Constitution Act, 1867*, occupational pensions, like other aspects of employment and labour law, are a matter of property and civil rights and so generally their regulation would fall under provincial legislative jurisdiction. However, in the case of some industries, including atomic energy, banking, inter- and extra-provincial transportation on land or water, aviation and telecommunications, as well as the federal public service and employment in the three territories, Parliament has jurisdiction. With respect to most employees who are employed in Ontario and who are members of a pension plan within provincial regulatory jurisdiction, the province's *Pension Benefits Act*[28] (PBA) requires the plan to be registered and establishes minimum standards relating to, among other things, entitlements under the plan and plan administration and funding. (Section 6 of the PBA makes it illegal to administer a plan that has not been registered.) The federal counterpart to the PBA is the *Pension Benefits Standards Act, 1985*[29] (PBSA), although it does not apply to employees of the federal government.[30] ...

Putting aside federal jurisdiction plans (where registration, if required, would be under the PBSA) and those multi-jurisdictional plans registered under another jurisdiction, most pension plans covering Ontario employees are required to be registered under the PBA. However, some such plans are not required to be registered at all because they are exempted from the PBA, either directly or through exclusion from the PBA definition of "pension plan". These include group RRSPs and the plans that cover members of the Legislative Assembly and the provincial judiciary, as well as plans that only provide benefits that exceed

---

[14] Richard Shillington, *Occupational Pension Plan Coverage in Ontario*, statistical report prepared for the Ontario Expert Commission on Pensions, Infometrica Limited, 2007, p. 14.

[28] R.S.O. 1990, c. P.8.

[29] R.S.C. 1985, c. 32 (2nd Supp). Section 25 of the PBSA generally makes federally-regulated pensions subject to provincial matrimonial property laws. Despite this, it appears that some administrators of federally-regulated plans refuse to follow provincial law; see Thomas G. Anderson, "Pensions" in *Federation of Law Societies of Canada 2006 National Family Law Program*, p. 5.

[30] See subsections 4(4) to (6) of the PBSA and section 4 of the *Pension Benefits Standards Regulations, 1985* (SOR/87-19) and Schedule I to the regulations. Pensions for federal public servants are provided under the *Public Service Superannuation Act* (R.S.C. 1985, c. P-36). There are several other statutes providing pension plans for persons who might broadly be described as employees of the federal government, such as, for example, the *Royal Canadian Mounted Police Superannuation Act* (R.S.C. 1985, c. R-11).

the maximum benefit limits applicable to plans registered under the federal *Income Tax Act* (ITA) or that only permit contributions in excess of the contribution limits for plans registered under the ITA. The latter type of plan is sometimes referred to as a "supplementary employee retirement plan" (SERP) because it supplements benefits provided for by another plan and membership in it is conditional on being a member of that other plan. Such plans are sometimes established by employers in order to provide relatively high income earners with a pension commensurate with the income they enjoyed before retirement, as the ITA limits mean that the plan to which the SERP is supplemental will pay a pension that is smaller than that which would otherwise result from the application of the basic defined benefit formula.

Registration of a pension plan under the ITA is not compulsory, but it does confer certain advantages. Contributions made by employers and employees are deductible in calculating income subject to taxation; further, plan earnings are exempt from taxation and employees are not taxed on benefits until the pension is in pay. However, as was alluded to in the preceding paragraph, there are limits on the quantum of benefits that can be provided and on the amount of contributions that can be made in the case of plans registered under the ITA.

Timing of Retirement

The PBA generally requires that a pension plan provide for a "normal retirement date" of not later than one year after the employee reaches the age of 65. This does not mean that the employee must retire at that date; it simply means that the employee is entitled to retire and begin receiving a full pension at that date. She could instead decide to continue working, although she could not both be in receipt of a pension and be continuing to accrue service credits under the same plan.

Alternatively, an employee might decide to retire before reaching the normal retirement date. Under the PBA, an employee who is within 10 years of that date may, upon termination of employment, elect to begin receiving an early retirement pension. The PBA implicitly permits the monthly amount payable under an early retirement pension to be reduced from the amount that would have been payable had the employee waited until normal retirement age to begin receiving the pension, reflecting the fact that a pension taken earlier will likely be in pay longer. Some plans, however, offer an unreduced early retirement pension to employees who meet a specified threshold based on age or years of service or some combination of the two. (For example, a plan might offer an unreduced early retirement option to an employee who satisfies a "factor 90" qualification, whereby the sum of his age and years of service equals at least 90.)

Because defined benefit plan pensions are typically integrated with CPP benefits and CPP benefits usually do not commence until age 65, it is not uncommon for defined benefit plans to offer so-called "bridging benefits" to employees who take an early retirement pension. These benefits supplement the pension being paid under the plan for a temporary period that ends when the employee begins to receive CPP benefits, with the effect that the total monthly amounts being received by the employee before age 65 and after remain roughly the same.

Vesting, Locking-in and Portability

A pension benefit is said to be "vested" when the plan member has an enforceable right to receive a pension upon reaching retirement age; at the point at which the benefit is vested, it can no longer be lost, even if the employee's employment is terminated prior to his reaching retirement age (although where the termination is the result of death, the right to a pension is replaced by a death benefit, as to which, see below). The vesting rules under the PBA were changed as of January 1, 1987, but on a prospective basis only. As a result, vesting of benefits accrued prior to 1987 occurred once the individual was at least 45 years of age and had been a member of the pension plan for at least 10 years, while vesting for benefits accrued after 1986 occurs once the individual has been a member of the plan for two years.

At the same point at which a pension benefit becomes vested, the member's benefits are "locked in". The locking-in rules have two aspects. The first is that even if the member resigns from employment or has her employment terminated, she cannot obtain a refund of contributions made to the pension plan in respect of her employment; the contributions must remain in the plan fund, to be used to provide income in retirement. The second aspect is that during the member's lifetime the pension entitlement cannot be commuted or surrendered in return for an immediate lump sum payment; even if her employment ends long before she is ready to retire, she cannot choose to withdraw the value of her accrued entitlement from the plan instead of taking it as a deferred pension payable when she reaches retirement age. There are, however, certain "portability" exceptions to the locking-in rules that provide the former employee who is not entitled to an immediate pension with alternatives to a deferred pension from the plan. These exceptions, like the locking-in requirement itself, reflect the social policy concern that pension funds be used to provide an income for the employee in retirement; they allow an amount equal to the commuted value of the pension benefit to be transferred to another pension plan (if the other plan will accept the transfer) or "a prescribed retirement savings arrangement" (such as a locked-in retirement income fund) or to be applied to the purchase of a deferred life annuity.

The same rationale lies behind the rules that moneys payable under a pension plan cannot be assigned or attached, set out in, respectively, sections 65 and 66 of the PBA. These prohibitions are subject to certain exceptions in the family law context; subsection 66(4) creates an exception to the prohibition on attachment in the case of support orders (to a maximum of 50 per cent of the amount payable under the plan), while subsection 65(3) establishes a broader exception covering any FLA court orders or "domestic contracts" (a term that would include a separation agreement following marriage breakdown). However, while subsection 65(3) contains no limit on the amount of pension moneys that can be assigned, the exception must be read in conjunction with section 51, which limits the reach of orders and contracts made under the family property provisions of Part I of the FLA.

Limits re: FLA Part I Domestic Contracts and Orders

Section 51 of the PBA, which specifically addresses marriage breakdown, imposes both temporal and quantitative restrictions on the effect of domestic contracts and orders made under Part I of the FLA insofar as pensions are concerned.

Subsection 51(1) provides that such a contract or order cannot require payment of a pension benefit before the date that the spouse who was a member of the pension plan in question actually begins to receive the benefit or the date on which she reaches the normal retirement date under the plan, whichever date is earliest. However, where the member's employment is terminated, subsection 51(5) gives the non-member spouse the same options in relation to his interests as established by the contract or order that are available to the member in relation to the member's interests (such as, for example, transfer of his share of the commuted value of her pension to a "prescribed retirement savings arrangement").

Under subsection 51(2), a domestic contract or Part I order cannot give the non-member spouse more than 50 per cent of the benefits accrued during the period when she and the member were spouses. Regulations under the PBA prescribe the manner in which the benefits so accrued are to be calculated.[57] This "50 per cent rule", like the locking-in rules and

---

[57] See section 56 of the *General* regulation under the PBA.

the prohibitions against assignment and attachment, is rooted in the view that a pension exists to provide retirement income for the pension plan member. However, it has been seen as a potential obstacle to the full implementation of certain kinds of family property settlement arrangements involving pensions, a point which is discussed in more detail below.

Death Benefits

Under section 48 of the PBA, pension plans must provide a pre-retirement death benefit where a plan member whose right to a pension has vested dies before reaching retirement. The entitlement, which is payable to the member's spouse provided that the member and the spouse were not living separate and apart at the date of death, is either a lump sum payment equal to the commuted value of the pension or a pension having an equivalent commuted value. A spouse may waive his right to the death benefit. In that case (as well as in the case where the member had no spouse with whom she was living at the date of death), if the member had designated a beneficiary, the beneficiary would be entitled to a lump sum payment; where no beneficiary had been designated, the lump sum would be paid to the member's estate.

It should be noted that under subsection 48(13), the entitlement to a death benefit is subject to the rights of a former spouse established by a domestic contract or order made under Part I of the FLA.

If a former member in receipt of a pension has a spouse with whom he is cohabiting on the day the pension payments are due to commence, the PBA requires that the pension be a "joint and survivor pension". Such a pension is payable during the joint lives of the spouses, as opposed to being payable only during the member's lifetime. The PBA implicitly permits the initial amount payable under a joint and survivor pension to be reduced from the amount that would have been payable had the pension been for the employee's life alone; this is because of the possibility that the pension will be in pay for a longer period. The amount payable to the surviving spouse of the former member must be at least 60 per cent of the amount that was being paid to the former member while both were alive.

Section 46 of the PBA allows the member and the spouse, acting jointly, to waive the right to a joint and survivor pension prior to the commencement of the pension payments. Where such a waiver is given, the pension will be paid as a single life pension (that is, it will continue only for as long as the member lives).

Inflation and Indexing

Even relatively low levels of inflation can have a profound impact on the real value of a given sum of money. An annual inflation rate of a mere two per cent would reduce the purchasing power of a dollar to just 75 cents in 15 years; such a reduction would occur in just 10 years at an inflation rate of three per cent. Obviously this could have a very adverse effect on a pensioner who is afforded no inflation protection; if the pensioner lives for many years after retirement (as she surely hopes to do), her standard of living could be severely eroded in her later years. ...

Fortunately, despite the lack of statutory compulsion many pension plans provide inflation protection in the form of indexing, whereby the monthly pension amount is adjusted annually to compensate, to some extent at least, for the effect of inflation. Such protection may be contractual, in the sense that indexation is a matter of entitlement under the pension plan, as is typically the case in the public sector.

With private sector plans, *ad hoc* indexing is more common; while the employer purportedly does not offer inflation protection as of right, the amounts of pensions in pay are occasionally adjusted upwards to preserve (or more precisely, perhaps, restore) their real value (or at least some of it).

Funding

The PBA provides that a defined benefit pension plan must be funded; in other words, the plan's assets must be sufficient to pay for its liabilities, as determined by a triennial actuarial valuation. The valuation must be done both on a solvency basis, under which assets and liabilities are valued as if the plan is terminated on the date of the valuation, and on a "going-concern" basis, under which valuation proceeds on the assumption that the plan will be continuing. Where liabilities exceed assets under either type of valuation, "special payments" will be required; these are payments, additional to the employer's usual contributions, which are required to be made to the pension plan in order to eliminate the solvency deficiency or going-concern unfunded liability, as the case may be. Under the PBA, a solvency deficiency can be amortized over a five-year period, while a going concern unfunded liability can be amortized over a 15-year period. ...

II. Ontario's Family Property Legislation

[An overview of Part I of the *Family Law Act* (FLA) is omitted.]

Pensions as Family Property

... [P]ension entitlements are treated as family property for equalization purposes. The term "property" is defined in subsection 4(1) of the FLA as including "... in the case of a spouse's rights under a pension plan that have vested, the spouse's interest in the plan including contributions made by other persons." The reference to vesting formed the basis for early decisions holding that rights that had not yet vested at the point of marriage breakdown were not included, but "the weight of authority" now favours the view that unvested rights do constitute property, although this may not have been the Legislature's intention. The reference to contributions made by persons other than the member spouse appears to have been intended to ensure that employer contributions are taken into account in placing a value on the pension rights where the rights have vested; however, while that is certainly appropriate in the case of a defined contribution plan, the amount of contributions, whether made by the employer or the employee, is generally not a relevant consideration in valuing rights under a defined benefit plan, for reasons that are explained below.

The inclusion of the value of pension interests in the member spouse's net family property had the highly laudable goal of achieving greater fairness between the spouses following the collapse of their marriage, but it has also proven highly problematic insofar as rights under defined benefit pension plans are concerned.

III. Valuation of Rights under a Pension Plan

Valuation of rights under a defined contribution plan generally poses few problems; the value for net family property purposes is simply the aggregate of the contributions made during the marriage and the returns on investment of those contributions as of the valuation date. With a defined benefit plan, however, this "contributions approach" plainly does not provide an appropriate value, because what the plan member is entitled to by way of a pension has no immediate relation to the accumulated contributions and investment yield; rather, the pension entitlement is determined according to a set formula, typically based on years of service multiplied by some specified percentage of the average of the member's earnings in his final few years of employment. Equating the value of such an entitlement to the sum of contributions made plus the return on their investment is likely to understate considerably its true worth. A different approach must be used.

Present Value

To produce a figure that can appropriately be attached to a defined benefit pension for equalization purposes requires that its "present value" (sometimes called "present-day capitalized value") be determined. The present value of a stream of payments that are to begin at some point in the future may be thought of as the amount that one would have to invest today so that as of the date the payments begin the original investment plus accumulated earnings would be exactly sufficient to cover all of the payments that are to be made as they come due. In the particular context of marriage breakdown and defined benefit pensions, the present value as of the valuation date is the amount that would have to have been invested on that date in order for the original investment and accumulated earnings to be just adequate to fund the monthly benefits when the pension comes into pay. Of course, this figure is necessarily the product of conjecture. On the valuation date, the person performing the valuation does not know when the pension payments will begin (given that the date of retirement is unknown on that date) or even whether they ever will begin (given the possibility that the employee will die first) or if they do begin how long they will last (given that the date of death is unknown), nor does she know how much any given investment will ultimately earn (given that tomorrow's interest rates and inflation levels are unknown); lacking omniscience concerning the future, the valuator must make speculative assumptions about all of these variables. As the Supreme Court of Canada has noted, ascertaining a present value is "a matter of educated guesswork, undertaken by actuaries".[131]

Methods of Valuation

Although there seems to be little doubt today that the present value approach is to be preferred over the contributions approach in valuing rights under a defined benefit pension plan, at least some uncertainty regarding the methodology used to calculate a present value continues to exist. Neither the FLA nor the PBA provide any guidance as to how pension rights should be valued for purposes of calculating net family property, and so the question of how it should be done has been left to be answered by the parties, their lawyers, actuaries or other pension valuators and, ultimately, the courts. Debate on the issue has typically been framed as a matter of whether to use the "retirement method" or the "termination method". However, there is some ... ambiguity in these terms, and it is not always clear what a court means when it declares that one or the other method is being utilized. Indeed, it has been suggested that in many cases in which the termination method was ostensibly used, the method that was actually being employed was the "real interest method" (also known as the "hybrid termination-retirement method").

Retirement Method v. Termination Method

The retirement method assumes that the employee will continue in her employment with the plan sponsor until reaching some specified retirement age selected by the valuator. Accordingly, the basis on which value is calculated includes projections as to future salary increases, both those that are rooted in inflation and those that are based on promotion or productivity increases, as well as future service credit accruals and possible future enhancements to members' rights under the plan. In contrast, under the termination method, the amount of the future pension entitlement is said to be assessed as if the pension plan member had terminated her employment on the valuation date. This means that only those service credits accrued to the valuation date are taken into account; it would also seem to imply that

---

[131] *Boston v. Boston*, [2001] 2 S.C.R. 413, 17 R.F.L. (5th) 4, at para. 32.

no consideration is given to the possibility of salary increases or plan improvements that may occur after that date.

If one goes strictly by the labels employed by Ontario courts to describe their preferences in valuation methodology, the termination method seems generally to have found much more favour than the retirement method, although the view that it represents the better approach is by no means universal. (Indeed, the Supreme Court of Canada has raised the possibility that the retirement method might provide an appropriate result in at least some circumstances.)[135]

Two main arguments have been advanced in support of the termination method over the retirement method. The first is that by projecting salary levels and service credits that might be earned after the valuation date, the retirement method gives the non-member spouse the "fruits" of the member spouse's post-separation labours and is therefore in conflict with the FLA requirement that value be determined as of the valuation date. How valid an objection this is can be debated. While the retirement method undeniably looks to post-separation events (or rather, assumptions about post-separation events), the "years of service" multiplier used in a defined benefit plan formula does not assign any greater weight to the final years of the member's time with the plan sponsor than to the early years[137] (although the dollar multiplicand employed in the formula obviously would be based on post-separation salary levels).

The second principal objection to the retirement method concerns its highly speculative nature, resulting from the fact that it requires the making of assumptions as to what the member spouse's salary and service credits will be and what plan improvements will have been made by the time he does retire. These assumptions will virtually never have a perfect correspondence with future facts as they unfold and they may not even be close. Still, the termination method also involves the making of many assumptions that may not be borne out by subsequent developments. In order to produce a present value, the termination method, like the retirement method, must employ assumptions about when (and if) the member spouse will retire and about how long he will collect the pension; assumptions are also made about future rates of interest and taxation. Any of these assumptions could turn out to be "incorrect", in the sense that events might unfold differently than was assumed, and in fact they will in that sense almost certainly prove to be incorrect in any individual case, notwithstanding their validity from an actuarial point of view. And, if subsequent events do diverge significantly from what was assumed, the actual value of the pension benefit and the value it had been considered to have had for equalization purposes could deviate quite dramatically, to the great disadvantage of one or the other spouse. For example, if the member spouse collects the pension for a longer period than that on which the valuation was based, the actual value of the pension rights may end up exceeding, perhaps by a quite considerable amount, that which was attributed to them as net family property.

---

135 *Best v. Best*, [1999] 2 S.C.R. 868, 49 R.F.L. (4th) 1, at paras. 88–93. In discussing the possibility that the retirement method might be used in some cases, the Court seemed to suggest that it would be appropriate where the likely retirement date was fairly close at the time of valuation, as there would be a lesser degree of speculation than in the case where retirement would probably only occur at a more remote date.

137 This seems to be the point being made by certain judicial authorities and other sources cited in Berend Hovius and Timothy G. Youdan, *The Law of Family Property*, Carswell, Scarborough, 1991, p. 501.

Do the Courts Really Favour the Termination Method?

In *Bascello v. Bascello*,[140] a number of previous decisions of Ontario courts purporting to apply the "termination method" were reviewed and the conclusion offered that most of those courts were not in fact using a true termination method but the "real interest method". Under this approach, while the valuation is based on the pension entitlement accrued to the valuation date, allowance is made for inflation (at least in the case of fully-indexed plans, as most public sector plans are); it is only non-inflationary increases in salary, such as those stemming from promotions and productivity improvements, that are not taken into account. (The real interest method takes its name from the fact that it allows for inflation by employing a discount based on the difference between inflation rates and nominal interest rates, which over the long term has been relatively constant despite whatever fluctuations were occurring in the nominal rates.)

Another feature of the approach typically employed by Ontario courts that *Bascello* identified as being inconsistent with a pure termination approach lies in the treatment of rights that an employee may have under the pension plan to take early retirement without any reduction in the defined benefit. While courts that purport to apply the termination method do not take into account any actual or assumed post-valuation date employment for purposes of calculating the amount of the pension, in the majority of cases that have dealt with pension plans having an unreduced early retirement option the courts did assume that the employee's employment would continue for the purpose of eligibility to exercise such an option in order to determine the date on which the employee would be most likely to retire.

The impact of this approach can be illustrated with the example of an employee who has twenty-one years of service and who is 45 years old as of the valuation date and whose pension plan establishes a normal retirement date of age 65 but also accords a right to take early retirement without penalty if the employee meets a "factor 90" qualification. A valuation based on a pure termination method would ignore the unreduced early retirement possibility, as the stated premise of the termination method is that the future pension entitlement is assessed as if the pension plan member had terminated her employment on the valuation date, and in that case the employee in our example would reach the normal retirement date before achieving factor 90. Nevertheless, although the amount of her pension entitlement for valuation purposes will be based on her years of service as of the valuation date, most courts will posit continued employment after the valuation date and eventual qualification for an unreduced early retirement pension (in the case of the employee in this example, at age 57) for the purpose of selecting the date on which the employee is most likely to retire. (Objections that the member spouse's employment may terminate prior to retirement because of lay-off or other reasons are typically addressed by using a discount for that possibility.) This can have a very substantial impact on the valuation, because where an employee retires before the normal retirement date, the pension is likely to be in pay for a longer period than it otherwise would, thereby increasing the value.

The approach used in *Bascello* and in the majority of the other cases discussed in that decision appears to have become the dominant approach to pension valuation in Ontario. Although *Bascello* referred to this as the "real interest method", some commentators have labelled it the "hybrid termination-retirement method", as it combines elements of both the termination method (in that termination at the valuation date is assumed in order to determine the amount of the accrued pension benefit) and the retirement method (in that inflation is recognized where the plan is indexed and continued employment is assumed for purposes of eventual eligibility to take early retirement on an unreduced pension). The *Bascello* court

---

[140] (1995), 26 O.R. (3d) 342 (Gen. Div.); additional reasons at (1995), 18 R.F.L. (4th) 362 (Ont. Gen. Div.); further additional reasons at (1996), 1996 CarswellOnt 2898 (Gen. Div.).

was highly critical of this terminology, arguing that the expressions "termination method", "retirement method" and "hybrid termination-retirement method" did not adequately convey the actuarial assumptions being utilized; it recommended instead that the method of valuation be described in terms of whether allowance was being made for full, partial or no indexing prior to retirement. With respect, however, a description of the sort espoused in *Bascello* is also inadequate, in that it fails to give any indication of how unvested unreduced early retirement rights are to be treated. Perhaps it is simply not possible to devise terms that are at once both reasonably concise and comprehensively significative [sic]. In any event, although the labels "termination method", "retirement method" and "hybrid termination-retirement method" may not be entirely satisfactory, they do at least impart some idea of the underlying principles, with "hybrid" suggesting a middle ground between two conflicting and more radical approaches. For that reason, those terms will be used in this report.

In its *1993 Standard of Practice for the Computation of the Capitalized Value of Pension Entitlements on Marriage Breakdown for Purposes of Lump Sum Equalization Payments*, the Canadian Institute of Actuaries referred to both the "termination method" and the "retirement method", indicating that the choice of method would depend on the jurisdiction in which the division or equalization of family property was taking place. That terminology does not appear in section 4300 of the Institute's *Standards of Practice*, which superseded the original marriage breakdown standard, but it would appear that the choice of method continues to be left as a matter for the law of the jurisdiction concerned rather than a subject of professional prescription. The current standard indicates that an actuary might produce more than one figure in valuing a pension because of the treatment of possible future salary increases, both those that are inflation-based and those that are productivity-based; it also states, insofar as the age of retirement is concerned, that an actuary would usually report a number of different values based on a range of retirement ages, including the normal retirement date, the earliest age at which the member could elect an unreduced pension assuming termination of employment at the valuation date and the earliest age at which the member could elect such a pension assuming that employment continues beyond the valuation date. Obviously, the current standard is flexible enough to accommodate use of any of the termination method, the retirement method or the hybrid method.

Despite *Bascello* and a number of other cases that seem to reject, in substance if not in name, the termination method (at least in its pure form), this area of the law cannot be regarded as entirely settled. In *Salib v. Cross*,[153] decided after *Bascello*, the Ontario Court of Appeal approved the trial court's use of a quite stringent termination approach. ... On the other hand, as was noted above, the Supreme Court of Canada in *Best v. Best* indicated that the retirement method might be appropriate in some circumstances. Thus, it appears that while the hybrid termination-retirement method is the most frequently used, a court has discretion to employ the termination method or the retirement method if it thinks that that method produces the fairest result in a particular case. However, this means that some uncertainty about how a defined benefit pension should be valued for family law purposes continues at a fundamental level.

Pre-Marriage Accruals

One valuation issue in respect of which there is certainty concerns the situation in which the member spouse joined the pension plan prior to the marriage. This requires setting a value on the pension rights not only as of the date of separation but also as of the date on

---

[153] (1995), [1995] O.J. No. 4147, 27 O.R. (3d) 255, 18 R.F.L. (4th) 218 (C.A.); affirming (1993), [1993] O.J. No. 2093, 15 O.R. (3d) 521 (Gen. Div.).

which the spouses married, because the FLA requires that the value of property owned on the marriage date be deducted in calculating net family property. Two approaches for addressing this situation have been put forward, the *"pro rata* approach" and the "value added approach". Under the former, the separation date value is multiplied by the quotient obtained when the number of years of pensionable service during the marriage is divided by the total number of years of pensionable service as of separation. In contrast, the value added approach involves separate actuarial valuations for the marriage date and the separation date. (In other words, the marriage date value is not simply a derivative of the separation date value.) The *pro rata* approach tends to produce a higher value as of the marriage date than the value added approach, which necessarily results in a lower value being attributed to the portion of the pension that accrued during the marriage, and some have argued that the failure to provide a separate valuation as of the marriage date is not in accord with what the FLA requires; however, the *pro rata* method was approved by a majority of the Supreme Court of Canada as generally being the fairer approach in *Best v. Best*.[158]

Valuation Assumptions: The Age of Retirement

As has been noted, the assumption that is made concerning the age at which the employee is likely to retire can have a very substantial impact on the valuation of the member spouse's rights under a defined benefit plan; the earlier the retirement date, the longer the pension payments will continue to be made and hence the greater the value attributed to those rights. This leads to the possibility that the member spouse and the non-member spouse will put forward opposing, self-interested positions as to the likely retirement date. The member spouse, desiring a lower value, may assert that he does not plan to retire until the normal retirement date or later, while the non-member spouse, wanting a higher value, may contend that the member always intended to retire at the earliest date on which an unreduced pension could be taken.

In several cases decided soon after the coming-into-force of the FLA, it was held that where there is a conflict in the evidence that is presented in relation to the likely retirement date, it should be presumed that an employee will retire at the earliest date on which she would become eligible to take an unreduced pension. In other early cases, courts ruled that in the event of such conflict valuation should proceed on the basis that the employee would retire at the mid-point between the earliest unreduced pension date and the normal retirement date. However, in two 1996 decisions,[161] the Ontario Court of Appeal rejected these approaches, holding that a trial court must make a finding respecting the likely date of retirement on a balance of probabilities on the basis of the evidence before it. This stance appears to have been given implicit approval by the Supreme Court of Canada in the *Best* case.[162] ...

Such considerations may seem to favour the establishment of a statutory presumption based on the mid-way point between the earliest date on which the member can retire on an unreduced pension and the normal retirement date set out in the plan. However, there are numerous situations in which such a presumption would not be workable or would produce inequitable results. Some plans do not have an unreduced early retirement option. Some plans offer such options, but attach conditions at some ages and not at others. Some plans put a limit on the accrual of service credits, leading to the possibility that the limit would be

---

[158] Note 135, para. 87.

[161] The Court rejected the use of a presumption of the earliest unreduced retirement date in *Kennedy v. Kennedy* (1996), [1996] O.J. No. 764, 19 R.F.L. (4th) 454 (C.A.) and the use of a mid-way point presumption in *Huisman v. Huisman* (1996), [1996] O.J. No. 2128, 21 R.F.L. (4th) 341 (Ont. C.A.).

[162] Note 135, para. 103-104.

reached before the mid-point. Some plans may to some extent subsidize early retirement at ages earlier than the "unreduced" age, imposing a reduction that is less than a full actuarial reduction, such that the value of the reduced pension could actually be greater than the pension that would be available when the member reaches the earliest age at which an unreduced pension can be taken. And in some cases the member may have joined the plan at a very late stage in her working life, making it virtually inconceivable that she would retire at the mid-way point. Given the complexity and diversity of pension plan options and the multitude of different factual circumstances that could arise, the LCO is not convinced of the merits of a presumption regarding retirement age. In our view, any issue as to when a member will retire should continue to be treated as a question of fact, resolved on the basis of the evidence according to the balance of probabilities.

Other Valuation Assumptions

Just as assumptions regarding the date on which the member spouse is likely to retire will affect the value attributed to the member's pension rights (in that the earlier the retirement date, the longer the pension is likely to be in pay and accordingly the higher its value), assumptions regarding the date on which the member spouse will die will also affect the value (in that the earlier the date of death, the shorter the period in which the pension will be in pay and accordingly the lower its value). However, pension valuators generally do not attempt to make individual-specific predictions about death; rather, they rely on mortality tables, which purport to indicate the probability of death within one year at each age in the human life span for a large population (typically, 1,000 persons). Using such a table, the valuator takes into account the probability of the member surviving to any given year.

... Paragraph 4330.02 of the Canadian Institute of Actuaries' *Standards of Practice* states that actuaries should assume death rates in accordance with a mortality table prescribed by the Institute's Practice Standards Council, modified where warranted if the member is in poor health. At the date of writing the prescribed table is a group annuity mortality table; however, the LCO understands that the Institute is reviewing this matter.

Another assumption that a pension valuator might make concerns income tax. The fact that the pension will be subject to taxation when it comes into pay means that its actual worth to the member will be something less than its before-tax value, and the Ontario Court of Appeal has held that valuation of a pension should reflect a deduction for the tax that is likely to be paid. The Canadian Institute of Actuaries' *Standards of Practice* specifies that where tax is to be taken into account, the deduction should be based on the member's average (as opposed to marginal) rate of tax, calculated on the basis of her anticipated income once retired but assuming continuation of the existing taxation rules as to rates, brackets and other matters.

As was noted above, the present value of the member spouse's rights under a defined benefit plan as of the valuation date is the amount that would have to have been invested on that date in order for the original investment and accumulated earnings to be just adequate to fund the monthly benefits when the pension comes into pay. Determining this amount requires the making of assumptions respecting interest rates in order to project a notional investment yield. In that regard, the *Standards of Practice* prescribe different approaches for indexed and non-indexed pensions. ...

Do So Many Assumptions Rob Valuation of Its Legitimacy?

It is quite evident that valuation of a pension involves the making of many assumptions. As was noted above, any of these assumptions could turn out to be "incorrect", in the sense that events might unfold differently than was assumed; in fact they will in that sense almost certainly prove to be incorrect in any individual case, however sound the assumptions may have been from an actuarial standpoint. But does this make valuation illegitimate?

If subsequent events do diverge significantly from what was assumed, the ultimate real value of the pension benefit and the value it had been considered to have had for equalization purposes could deviate quite dramatically; understandably, this can cause resentment on the part of the "loser" spouse. However, if rights under defined benefit pension plans are to be considered property for purposes of the FLA equalization regime, they obviously must be valued, and given that the contributions method is plainly not an appropriate valuation method for such plans, it is difficult to see how these rights could be valued without resort to assumptions. ...

One should also keep in mind that many assets, and not just rights under a pension plan, could ultimately prove to have a greater or lesser value than that which was attributed to them at equalization. ... If pensions are to remain within the equalization regime, they must be valued, and with valuation comes the risk (indeed, virtual inevitability) of post-equalization changes in value, as it does with any property. The real problem with equalization insofar as pensions are concerned lies not in their valuation, but with settlement.

IV. Settlement

If the value of one spouse's net family property exceeds the value of the other spouse's net family property, that other spouse will be entitled to an equalization payment amounting to half the difference. Where the spouse with the higher-valued net family property is in that position because of the value of her rights under a pension plan, there are, under Ontario law as it currently stands, essentially three options insofar as satisfaction of the equalization entitlement is concerned.

Trade of Cash or Other Assets

Under the first option, sometimes labeled as "valuation and accounting", the member spouse retains exclusive rights to the pension and defrays the equalization obligation with cash or other property owned by her. This option, where it can be taken, has some significant advantages over other approaches. Usually it presents little or no risk to either of the spouses, and it provides them with a "clean break", which is generally desirable and particularly so where the marriage breakdown is accompanied by animosity; it also avoids the administrative burdens imposed on pension plan administrators by some of the other options (as to which, see below). However, this will not be a viable solution if the member spouse has insufficient money or other liquid assets to satisfy the equalization debt, which means that it is probably not an option if most of the value of her net family property resides in rights under a pension plan. Someone who is "pension rich but cash poor" will likely not have enough in the way of non-pension assets to make an equalizing swap.

... [T]he FLA does give a court the authority in cases of hardship to order that the equalization entitlement be paid in instalments over a period of not more than ten years or that all or part of the payment be delayed for such a period, but there are problems associated with such a course of action. It will not be viable if the member spouse does not have an adequate income unburdened by other obligations (such as, for example, support), to make the payments, and in any event, the other spouse may have concerns about the security of his entitlement to the instalment payments or deferred payment over such a lengthy period. Further, postponing the achievement of equalization in this way can hardly be said to provide a clean break, thus eliminating one of the primary benefits of the asset trade option.

Another problem with the valuation and accounting approach stems from the possibility of "double dipping". This refers to the situation in which the member spouse was the equalization debtor and traded cash or other assets to satisfy the debt, only to find later that the non-member spouse is looking to the pension in pay for support. (Double dipping could also be said to exist where no such trades occur at equalization because the net value of the member's pension and other family assets does not exceed the value of the non-member spouse's net family property and where the non-member spouse subsequently applies for support on the basis of the pension income.) Understandably, the member may find this unfair, feeling that the pension was already taken into account in the family property settlement and should not later be regarded as income available for support purposes.

A majority of the Supreme Court of Canada in *Boston v. Boston*[182] held that, as a general matter, double dipping was inappropriate and that only that part of the pension earned after separation should be taken into account in determining the member spouse's support obligation; however, it also recognized exceptions to this principle, such as where a support order is rooted in need rather than compensation or where, despite the fact that the order is compensatory, the non-member spouse has made reasonable efforts to use his assets to produce income but still suffers from economic hardship as a result of the marriage breakdown. Of course, following the breakdown of a lengthy marriage, such grounds for spousal support are fairly common, and while the Court may have felt that it was pronouncing a quite limited exception to the general rule that double dipping was inappropriate, one commentator observed that the dispensation was "wide enough to almost eat the rule itself". It may be that the exception is too broad and should be narrowed. But perhaps one should first consider whether double dipping vis-à-vis a pension really is wrong in principle.

The Supreme Court's assertion that double dipping in respect of a pension, as opposed to other income-producing properties, should generally be avoided was based on its view that a pension is different from other assets, such as investments, because a pension, once it is in pay, is being "liquidated", whereas an investment can pay out income without thereby causing depletion of the asset itself. The LCO respectfully suggests that this rationale is flawed.
...

So far as double dipping is concerned, it is the LCO's view that there is no difference in principle between a member spouse giving cash to meet an equalization debt in hopes of keeping her pension income intact and a shareholder spouse giving cash to meet an equalization debt in hopes of keeping his dividend income intact. It follows that the issue of double dipping is not unique to pensions; it is relevant in the case of any income-producing asset that has been taken into account in the equalization process. Accordingly, in this report the LCO will not be making recommendations as to whether double dipping should be prohibited or the exceptions to the "rule" against double dipping narrowed; these are issues for a project looking at generic family property law, and not one whose scope is limited to pensions.

"If and When" Arrangements

In most cases where an asset trade is not a practical solution, the parties will likely have to enter into what is commonly known as an "if and when" arrangement. Such an arrangement defers satisfaction of the equalization requirement until the pension is in pay, utilizing a trust imposed through the vehicle of a domestic contract or court order. The trust may be imposed on the plan member, requiring him to pay part of each pension payment received over to the non-member spouse; alternatively, it may be imposed directly on the plan administrator, who is obligated to divide the pension payments at source. The latter course avoids some of the drawbacks of the former, in that contact between the former spouses is not required and potential enforcement difficulties inherent in a trust that is personal to the

---

[182] Note 131.

member spouse are avoided. Unfortunately, however, there are numerous other problems attendant on both forms of an "if and when" arrangement.

The most obvious drawback to an "if and when" approach is that the non-member spouse loses the benefit of immediate satisfaction of her equalization entitlement. The view that this is necessarily unfair to the non-member spouse is perhaps not compelling, given that the "property" that led to the equalization entitlement is itself not immediately accessible and given as well that the FLA contemplates the possibility that equalization payments could be postponed for or spread out over as many as ten years in any event. Undeniably, however, the non-member spouse is disadvantaged by the fact that control as to when the entitlement finally is satisfied is outside of her control, for the pension will become payable only when the member spouse elects to receive it; the member may decide to retire at the "normal retirement date", but he might also decide to retire at an earlier or a later date. This may have an adverse impact on the income that is eventually received, and in any case it obviously can complicate financial planning for the non-member spouse, as she does not know when the pension income (and thus her sharing of it) will commence.

Another concern is that "if and when" orders in the form in which they are often made do not appear to be entirely in accord with the intention behind the FLA equalization provisions. (The same concern does not arise with respect to domestic contracts requiring an "if and when" division, as parties are generally free to contract out of the FLA.) The requirement to value net family property, including pension rights, implies that where equalization is to be achieved through resort to the member spouse's pension, payments to the non-member spouse should end once the equalization debt has been satisfied. But many "if and when" arrangements do not seem to do this, instead appearing to provide for indefinite sharing, dividing the pension according to the ratio of the present value of the rights at separation to the present value of the rights at retirement or to the ratio of pensionable time while the marriage was ongoing to total pensionable time. One might infer that the latter type of division is often being used to avoid, for both spouses, the risks associated with equalization valuations, which, as previously noted, employ numerous speculative assumptions about the future that virtually ensure that the present value attributed to the pension rights will significantly and perhaps even wildly overstate or understate their ultimate real value. ...

A further difficulty stems from section 51 of the PBA, which provides that no more than 50 per cent of pension benefits that accrued during marriage can be assigned under a domestic contract or court order. For purposes of this limitation, the *General* regulation under the PBA essentially prescribes a strict termination method of valuation;[195] this raises the possibility that a non-member spouse's entitlement under an "if and when" agreement or order, at least where based on a time ratio, will exceed what can be paid out to her under the PBA. As a consequence, pension plan administrators upon whom a trust is imposed by such an agreement or order may find themselves unable fully to carry out the trust obligation, leaving the parties to determine how to satisfy the portion of the non-member spouse's entitlement that exceeds the 50 per cent limit.

This points to another problem with "if and when" arrangements; they not only have drawbacks for the parties, but they also impose burdens on those responsible for administering pension plans that are subject to such arrangements. Administrators are effectively required to calculate the value of the non-member spouse's share in accordance with the PBA regulation to determine whether the agreement or order creates a conflict with the PBA and, if it does, to advise the parties that they are bound to refuse to divide the pension payment in full conformity with what was agreed to or ordered. Other problems faced by administrators include orders and agreements that are unclear or that fail to deal comprehensively with

---

[195] R.R.O. 1990, Reg. 909, s. 56.

potential issues or that purport to divide benefits in a way that is not consistent with the provisions of the pension plan. ...

There are several other potential difficulties that have been identified with respect to "if and when" agreements and orders. The non-member spouse's entitlement to share in the pension payments will, of course, end when the member spouse dies; some suggest that if that occurs prior to retirement, the non-member spouse could end up having received nothing. There is also the risk that other possible future occurrences, such as the winding up of the plan due to failure on the part of the plan sponsor to meet funding requirements, could significantly reduce the amount of pension benefits that both parties had assumed would be available (though payments from the Pension Benefits Guarantee Fund could mitigate the loss to some extent). Finally, there could be taxation issues; if the payments made to the non-member spouse come directly from the member spouse, they will be made from after-tax dollars; while adjustments could be made to reflect this, if the member spouse's marginal tax rate is higher than that of the non-member, the tax that is paid will be greater than if the payments made to the non-member came directly from the pension plan.

Lump Sum Transfer on Termination

Generally speaking, there is under Ontario law at present no ability to effect an immediate transfer of a share of the member's interest under a pension plan to her spouse in order to achieve a family property settlement following marriage breakdown; currently, where an asset trade is not an option, the parties will usually have to resort to an "if and when" arrangement, with all its drawbacks. However, there is one situation in which such a transfer of a share of the member's interest to the non-member spouse can be effected — that being where the member's employment is terminated — because in that situation subsection 51(5) of the PBA gives the non-member spouse rights that parallel those of a member entitled to a deferred pension. ...

Settlement: Proposals for Reform

Obviously, the current situation is unsatisfactory; no one would disagree that it demands reform. But what form should reform take? Ideally, a pension division regime should treat parties to a broken marriage fairly, enable them to make a "clean break", recognize that pensions are family property, recognize as well that they are a very atypical form of property, meet the social objective of ensuring that individuals have a reasonable income if and when they retire, take account of the view that pensions represent deferred compensation for wage-earners, offer flexibility according to differing needs and circumstances, provide certainty to the parties and contain costs, obviate to the extent possible the need for litigation and minimize financial and other burdens that may be placed on pension plan administrators. These are a diverse set of objectives, raising the possibility that a reform proposal that meets some of them may not meet others.

Among the Canadian jurisdictions that have enacted legislation to divide pensions upon marriage breakdown, a majority have favoured an approach that is usually called the "Immediate Settlement Method" (ISM),[205] whereby there is an immediate (loosely speaking) deter-

---

[205] Alberta, Saskatchewan, Manitoba, Quebec, New Brunswick and the territories all use a version of the ISM; it is also the method used under the federal *Pension Benefits Division Act* (S.C. 1992, c. 46, Sch. II), which applies to federal government employees. Under the federal PBSA, which applies in respect of federal jurisdiction private sector employees, pension division is generally governed by the relevant provincial family property law; however, the PBSA does allow a member to make an assignment to a former spouse or common law partner that has the effect of making both ISM and DSM solutions accessible.

mination of the non-member spouse's share of the value of the member's pension and an immediate transfer of an amount out of the fund of the member's pension to a locked-in RRSP or other vehicle that will eventually provide a retirement income (in other words, the sort of settlement that is currently possible in Ontario only where the member's employment is terminated).

Three provinces[206] have adopted an alternative approach, the Deferred Settlement Method (DSM). Under this approach, the non-member spouse becomes a "kind of member" of the member's pension plan, but actual division of the pension is postponed until some future point (generally, when the pension comes into pay), at which time the non-member spouse receives his share in the form of a separate pension from the plan. ...

The Arguments: ISM v. DSM

Among the reasons offered in support of adopting the ISM approach are the following:

- the ISM provides a "clean break" between the parties, quickly and completely severing their affairs, whereas the DSM will require that the parties continue to have dealings with one another;

- the ISM represents a simple and easy-to-apply approach in comparison to the DSM;

- the ISM is much less burdensome and costly for pension plans than the DSM;

- as the majority of Canadian jurisdictions have adopted the ISM approach, its adoption by Ontario would promote uniformity in the law; and

- the DSM allows the non-member spouse to share in post-separation increases in the value of the member's pension.

On the other hand, those who favour the DSM argue that

- it is appropriate that the non-member spouse share in post-separation increases in the value of the member's pension because the ultimate value of a pension is largely paid for by contributions made in the earlier part of the member's career;

- with the DSM, it is not necessary to calculate the present value of the member's pension; thus, the "guesswork" inherent in determining present value — and thus the risk of significantly overvaluing or undervaluing the pension as a result of assumptions that have to be made in order to arrive at a present value — is avoided;

- the ISM, as it exists in almost all other Canadian jurisdictions, uses a commuted value approach in valuing the member's pension entitlements, and hence produces a relatively low value for the transfer out of the fund for the non-member spouse;

- related to the preceding point, adoption of the ISM would exacerbate economic inequality as between the sexes; and

- the ISM typically results in the non-member spouse being given a lump sum to invest in a locked-in retirement vehicle, but very often the non-member spouse is unsophisticated and inexperienced in investment matters; this can cause stress and lead to the making of improvident decisions that may not produce enough income for support in old age.

---

[206] British Columbia, Nova Scotia and Newfoundland and Labrador use a DSM approach.

V. Other Issues

Canada Pension Plan *Credits*

Credits under the CPP fall within the FLA definition of "family property, making them subject to the equalization regime, although it appears that the point is largely ignored in practice, with CPP credits simply being omitted from the calculation of net family property.[212] Therein, however, lies a trap for the unwary and the overtrusting.

The CPP provides for a division of credits upon marriage breakdown, with credits earned during the marriage by a spouse being divided equally between him and the other spouse; where an application for division is made, the federal authorities are required to divide the credits unless the two spouses have agreed that there should be no division and the family legislation of the province in question permits such agreements. While some other provinces have enacted permissive legislation of this nature,[213] Ontario has not done so. This has sometimes led to instances where a party agreed under an equalization settlement not to apply for a credit split, only to make such an application at a later date. ...

Common Law Spouses

... Part I of the FLA does not apply to couples who are in a common law relationship. The LCO does not intend in this report to address the issue of whether they should be covered by Part I, as that is an issue that goes beyond pensions. ...

VI. The LCO'S Assessment of the Issues

A. Pensions and the FLA Equalization Regime

1. Should Pensions Be Taken Out of the Equalization Regime?

For purposes of this report, the LCO has assumed continuation of the main features of the family property provisions of the FLA. ... Thus, we have looked into the question of whether pensions should continue to be subject to the FLA equalization regime based on the current generic features of that regime.

Removing pensions from the equalization regime could lead to unfairness between spouses who are in the same net asset position. Consider a pension plan member who has debts of $200,000, a pension valued at $150,000 and other assets valued at $50,000 and whose spouse has assets of $10,000 and debts totaling $10,000. If the pension is divided outside the equalization regime, the member would lose half the value of his pension to the non-member spouse, even though both parties are in the same position so far as net family property is concerned, whereas if the pension rights are included in the equalization process, he would retain the entire pension because his net family property would be zero. (This is not to suggest that the non-member spouse, depending on the circumstances, may not have a valid claim for support. However, the purpose of Part I of the FLA is to put the spouses in an equal position with respect to family property, not to address support needs. Support is dealt with in Part III of the FLA.)

The LCO also notes that dividing a pension outside the equalization regime may result in the parties having less flexibility in relation to other family property. For example, it is not

---

[212] See Hovius and Youdan, note 137, p. 488.

[213] The legislation of Alberta, British Columbia, and Saskatchewan expressly provides that parties may contract out of the CPP division of credits provisions. Article 422 of the *Civil Code of Québec* allows a court to order that there not be a partition of earnings registered under the Québec Pension Plan.

unusual for a couple to have only two substantial assets, an interest under a pension plan on the part of one spouse and a matrimonial home owned jointly. In such a situation, dividing the pension outside the equalization regime would likely necessitate sale of the matrimonial home, whereas dealing with all family property under the equalization regime may make it more likely that the non-member spouse can keep the matrimonial home if he feels that that is preferable to selling it and dividing the proceeds.

Finally, the LCO observes that it is difficult to see a policy justification for excluding pensions from the equalization regime when other retirement vehicle assets, such as RRSPs, are not excluded. Accordingly, the LCO recommends as follows:

1. The interest of a pension plan member whose rights have vested continue to be considered "family property" for purposes of the Family Law Act (FLA) and therefore subject to the FLA equalization regime.

2. Should Rights that Have Not Vested Be Treated as Property?

... [T]he LCO sees no reason not to include unvested rights under a pension plan as "property" for purposes of the equalization regime — while such rights may be contingent, that does not mean that they do not have value. An amendment to the FLA definition to eliminate any implication that rights that have not vested are not included (which could be achieved simply by deleting the words "that have vested") would be desirable, as it would make the text of the Act consonant with the actual state of the law. Accordingly, the LCO recommends as follows:

2. The FLA be amended to indicate that rights under a pension plan that have not vested are also "family property".

B. Valuation of Rights Under a Defined Benefit Pension Plan

As was discussed above, there are three main methods of pension valuation for family law purposes: the termination method, the retirement method and the hybrid termination-retirement method (hereinafter referred to as the "hybrid method"). The termination method and the hybrid method both take *as a starting point* the dollar amount of the pension accrued to the valuation date (generally, the date of separation), that is, without assuming further service and without projection for future salary increases or plan improvements. However, the hybrid method, unlike the termination method, does provide for inflation (where benefits are indexed) and it assumes future service for purposes for rights to ancillary benefits that have not vested at the time of separation because the member has not accrued sufficient service but that will vest eventually if the member continues in employment. (An example would be a right to take early retirement on an unreduced pension if the member meets a "factor 90" qualification where, at the time of separation, the member's age and service credits do not yet add up to 90.) The retirement approach assumes future service for purposes of these rights, but also projects future salary increases, including those not related to inflation, such as those stemming from promotion, as well as enhancements to plan members' rights that might be made in the future. As was noted above, Ontario courts generally seem to favour the hybrid method (notwithstanding some inconsistency in the terminology used in many of the decisions), but as a matter of law the question cannot be regarded as entirely settled.

In its 1995 *Report*, the OLRC argued that the retirement method should be prescribed as the only approach to valuation of rights under a defined benefit pension plan for family law purposes.[221] However, the LCO observes that in doing so, the OLRC seems to have seen the choice as one solely between the termination method and the retirement method; the issuance of the *Report* appears to have preceded any general recognition of a third way ... In any case, the LCO is of the view that the hybrid method is the most appropriate; moreover it recommends that the FLA be amended to provide that it be used in valuing rights under a pension plan for family law purposes, thereby eliminating any lingering uncertainty in this area.

Although some might object that in considering future service for purposes of rights to ancillary benefits such as an unreduced early retirement pension, the hybrid method effectively gives the non-member spouse a share in post-separation increases in the value of the member's pension, the LCO notes that the accumulation of sufficient service credits to result in the vesting of such rights is in part the result of service credits that were earned during the period of marriage. On the other hand, the retirement method plainly could result in the non-member spouse inappropriately sharing in post-separation increases in value, as is most obvious where it is assumed that there will be improvements to the pension plan or that the member will experience significant promotions subsequent to the marriage breakdown. With respect to the latter, while the LCO acknowledges the argument that post-separation career successes may, to some extent at least, have their genesis in decisions taken and roles assumed during the marriage, the retirement method makes no distinctions in that regard. Further, it is far more speculative than either of the other two methods; indeed, in projecting plan improvements and future promotions, the retirement method employs conjecture at a profound level. On balance, the LCO believes that the hybrid approach strikes the fairest balance as between the parties. Accordingly, the LCO recommends as follows:

3. The FLA be amended to provide that for purposes of valuation, rights under a defined benefit pension plan should be assessed using the hybrid termination-retirement method.

C. Settlement: Defined Benefit Pension Not Yet in Pay

1. Assessing the Arguments

In the LCO's view, many of the arguments made in support of or against the ISM or DSM overstate the case. While there is no doubt that the ISM provides a "clean break", it is simply incorrect to suggest that the DSM would force the former spouses to continue to have dealings with each other. The DSM model presumes that the non-member spouse becomes a quasi-member of the member's pension plan; any communication regarding the plan in relation to this would be with the plan administrator — there would be absolutely no need for the former spouses to have contact with each other. Still, it must be acknowledged that with the DSM, the break is not complete. Obviously there would continue to be a financial link between parties, in that the amount of the pension received by the non-member or quasi-member spouse would be a function of the amount of the member's pension when it came into pay. The link may be a silent one, but it is still a link.

The arguments about post-separation increases in pension value are also overstated, on both sides. Proponents of the DSM who argue that the value of a pension is paid for disproportionately through contributions made in the early part of the member's career may be correct in that assertion, but this ignores the point that for family law purposes the value of a defined benefit plan pension (unlike that of a defined contribution plan pension) is not a matter of the amount of contributions and the yield on their investment. (That is why it is the present value method, rather than the contributions method, that is used to assess the worth

---

[221] Ontario Law Reform Commission (OLRC), *Report on Pensions as Family Property: Valuation and Division* (Ministry of the Attorney General, Toronto, 1995), pp. 104–106.

of the member's rights.) On the other hand, it is surely incorrect to assert that no part of the post-separation increase in the value of the member's pension can ever be attributed to the married years. Simply looking at the matter from a mechanical perspective, eligibility to take an unreduced pension would in many cases never have been attained (and certainly not attained as early as it was) had the pensionable service earned during marriage not been counted. And the economic and other contributions made by the non-member spouse to the marital partnership may well have been the foundation on which the member's post-separation success was built. ...

With respect to the argument that adoption of a DSM approach means that determination of the pension's present value is rendered unnecessary, the LCO acknowledges that the assumptions used in determining present value will usually mean that the pension will turn out to have been undervalued or overvalued in comparison with what is ultimately paid out. However, we are also of the view that this ignores the fact that the value of virtually any property, as determined at the separation date, might turn out to be considerably more or less than its value at some subsequent point. While this may cause resentment on the part of one or the other spouse, the risk of its happening is inherent in a regime that requires family property to be valued for equalization purposes. ...

The LCO acknowledges the validity of the concern that providing a lump sum to a non-member spouse for placement in an RRSP could be very daunting for someone untutored in investment matters (or perhaps, in light of recent events, even for individuals who consider themselves quite sophisticated when it comes to stocks and financial instruments). However, this same concern can arise in cases where resort to pension division is unnecessary because the member spouse is able to pay off his equalization debt by trading other assets — indeed, the concern may be all the greater, since in that scenario there is nothing that would require the non-member spouse to convert the asset that was traded into a vehicle that will provide income in later years. In our view, given that in most cases equalization is achieved through an asset swap rather than pension division, the inexperienced investor concern, while not without validity, does not provide a compelling reason to reject the ISM. We note as well that the concern could in any event be addressed through the establishment of a new provincial retirement fund, as discussed in section E, below.

We are not persuaded that adoption of the ISM would exacerbate economic inequality as between the sexes. As was noted above ..., the number of males who are members of Ontario jurisdiction pension plans is only slightly greater than the number of female members, and male membership has not been growing while female membership has been increasing substantially; further, the percentage of pension plan members who are in a defined benefit plan is virtually the same for men and women. Choosing between the competing proposals for reform of the law relating to pension division upon marriage breakdown is thus unlikely to have a negative (or positive) effect on women particularly. ... In the LCO's view, the choice between the ISM and the DSM is not one between a change in the law that is likely to promote economic equality between the sexes and a change that is likely to perpetuate or worsen existing inequalities.

The LCO does agree with critics of the ISM that, as implemented in other Canadian jurisdictions, it tends to produce an artificially low value for the pension and is thus unfair to the non-member spouse (whether that person be male or female). However, we also agree with critics of the DSM that the DSM is much more complicated by comparison with the ISM and that it imposes burdens on pension plans and plan administrators that the ISM does not. (While arguably the weight of those burdens has been somewhat exaggerated, the problems posed for defined benefit plans by the current economic situation suggests a need to be very cautious about adding to the difficulties they face.) This has led us to make a twofold recommendation:

- The ISM should be the main pension division settlement mechanism, available in all cases of marriage breakdown, but with a proviso that the member's equalization debt is satisfied only to the extent of the value transferred out of the plan to the benefit of the non-member spouse;

- A DSM option should be available on a limited basis, namely,

  a) where the member is within ten years of the normal retirement date in the plan and both the member and the non-member spouse agree; and

  b) where, despite the fact that the member is not within ten years of the normal retirement date, the member, the non-member spouse and the pension plan administrator agree that the pension be divided using the DSM.

2. Some Alternative ISM Approaches

The reason that critics of the ISM argue that it is unfair to the non-member spouse is because it generally uses the commuted value approach to value the member's pension, and thus the transfer-out for the benefit of the non-member spouse. The commuted value approach, in assuming immediate termination of plan membership, ascribes no value to unvested ancillary benefits, such as a right to take an unreduced early retirement pension where the eligibility requirements have not yet been met; this may produce a lower value — and thus a lower transfer amount for the benefit of the non-member spouse — than a valuation utilizing some other method, such as the hybrid method discussed above. ... In that regard, the LCO did consider whether an ISM using the hybrid method of valuation rather than the commuted value method would be feasible. However, such an approach could result in plans paying out more by way of transfer for the benefit of the non-member spouse than would be justified by the value that the member's pension ultimately achieves (as where the member terminates employment shortly after separation without ever having qualified for an unreduced early retirement pension); the shortfall would either have to be absorbed by the plan or recovered from the member's already diminished future pension.

The LCO also considered whether it would be practical to require that a second commuted value calculation and transfer-out be undertaken at the time that the member reaches a "trigger date" (retirement or pre-retirement death or termination of employment), with the aim of supplementing the amount originally transferred to the benefit of the non-member spouse based on any subsequent increase in the value of the member's pension. However, we concluded that this approach would be overly complex and produce burdens for plan administrators, particularly in the case of members who ended up having more than one former spouse.

On balance, the LCO believes that the ISM with a transfer based on commuted value is the most appropriate solution. We also note that the commuted value does not always produce a lower value than the hybrid method, and we would point out that in any case under the LCO's proposal the member would remain liable for any difference between the amount transferred from the fund of the plan for the benefit of the non-member spouse and her equalization debt. Finally, we believe that our proposal that a DSM option be available on a limited basis will provide an appropriate settlement for parties who do not experience marriage breakdown until fairly late in the member's career. The DSM, which produces a financial result that is likely to be more in keeping with the expectations of both parties had they not separated, may be a particularly fitting solution (despite the burdens imposed on the plan administrator) when retirement is relatively close at hand, as that is when those expectations would be at their most definite and pronounced. (And the LCO sees no reason why the DSM should not be an option in other cases if the plan administrator is willing to shoulder the burdens that that approach involves.)

3. Transfer Destinations

The PBA gives a plan member who terminates employment and who is entitled to a deferred pension but who wishes to transfer his rights out of the plan three options: transfer to another pension plan (if the other plan is willing to accept the transfer), transfer to "a prescribed retirement savings arrangement" (essentially, a "locked-in" retirement vehicle) or purchase of a deferred annuity. The LCO believes that options corresponding to the first two of these should be available to the non-member spouse in the case of an ISM resolution. ... (The third option, purchase of a deferred annuity for someone who is not a pension plan member, may raise problems under section 147.4 of the ITA.)

Transfer to a locked-in retirement vehicle may make sense for some non-member spouses who feel they have the expertise to manage their own investments or who feel that they can readily access such expertise from other sources. However, many non-member spouses who do not have their own pension plans may be lacking in the investment knowledge and experience that is required to self-administer an RRSP or even to choose someone else who is suitably skilled to administer it for them. Creation of a new public fund into which transfer moneys could be paid might provide a good alternative for non-member spouses in that position, in that it would give them some advantages comparable to those enjoyed through membership in a large pension plan, namely, the pooling of resources and risk, the power of substantial investment capital and professional, expert fund management and administration. ...

Generally speaking, it seems unlikely that pension plan administrators would favour establishing a credit in the member's pension plan for the non-member spouse, essentially making him or her a member. However, there may be cases where the plan administrator is willing to do this, and there is no reason not to allow it where that is the case. Accordingly, the LCO recommends as follows:

4. Subject to the other recommendations in this section, where a member of a defined benefit pension plan is an equalization debtor to his or her spouse and wishes to satisfy the equalization debt through resort to his or her interest in the pension plan, legislation provide that the immediate settlement method of division applies, under which the member could require the plan administrator to transfer a pro rata share of the commuted value of the member's pension as of the separation date from the fund of the member's plan to

> (a) the fund of a plan of which the non-member spouse is a member, if the administrator of that plan agrees;
>
> (b) a retirement savings arrangement of the type prescribed for purposes of clause 42(1)(b) of the Pension Benefits Act;
>
> (c) the fund of the member's plan (that is, for credit to the non-member spouse's account), if the administrator of the member's plan agrees; or
>
> (d) if the government considers it appropriate to establish a provincial retirement fund, that fund. ...

Where the amount that would otherwise be transferred exceeds the member's equalization debt, the amount to be transferred shall be reduced to the amount of the equalization debt. If the amount that is transferred is less than the member's equalization debt, the member remains liable for the difference.

Under specified circumstances, the DSM would be available, as set out in Recommendations 6 and 7.

5. Where the immediate settlement method applies, the non-member spouse's pro rata share shall be based on the formula

$$1/2 \times A/B \times CV$$

where A is the pensionable service accrued while the parties were married, B is the member's pensionable service and CV is the commuted value as of the separation date.

4. Limited Availability DSM Option

Because it poses greater burdens on pension plan administrators than the ISM by effectively creating two pensions to be administered, the LCO does not believe that a DSM solution should generally be available to the parties as of right. However, where the marriage breakdown occurs at a point when the member's retirement is likely to be fairly imminent, the LCO believes that the parties should have the option of sharing the pension when it comes into pay, as it is much more likely in that case that both parties had formed assumptions about their financial future that were predicated very firmly and specifically on receipt of income from the member's pension. (The DSM would also be available in other cases if the pension administrator agrees, since in that case the administrator is obviously willing to take on the burdens.) ...

Where the DSM option is elected, the sharing between the former spouses of the member's pension should be seen as having taken the place of the equalization debt. There is an inherent risk in this form of division that the total amount paid to the non-member spouse will prove either to be less than or in excess of what is owed to her as a result of the equalization obligation, and both parties should bear that risk equally. Accordingly, the LCO recommends as follows:

6. If on the date of separation the member spouse is within ten years of the normal retirement date established under the plan, the parties may agree, as an alternative to settlement using the ISM, to have the member's pension entitlements divided between the member and the non-member spouse so that each is entitled to receive a separate pension. The non-member spouse would become a quasi-member of the plan, with an ability to enforce his or her entitlements under the plan and a right to receive from the plan administrator information concerning the member's pension and his or her share.

Generally, the non-member spouse would begin receiving a pension when the member retired and began receiving his or her pension, but where the member did not retire by the normal retirement date established under the plan, the non-member spouse would have the option of having his or her pension commence on the member's normal retirement date.

Where the non-member spouse will be commencing his or her pension at the same time as the member, the member's service credits shall be divided according to the formula

$$1/2 \times A/B$$

where A is the pensionable service accrued while the parties were married and B is the member's total pensionable service at retirement. The member's pension would be calculated using the benefit formula provided by the plan and his or her service credits as reduced. To determine the amount of the non-member spouse's pension, there would be an initial calculation using the benefit formula provided by the plan and the service credits transferred to him or her; that amount would then be adjusted to ensure that the actuarial present value of his or her pension, when added to the actuarial present value of the member's pension, equals the actuarial present value of the member's total pension before adjustment.

Where the member does not retire or otherwise begin receiving his or her pension by the normal retirement date established under the plan and the non-member spouse elects to have his or her pension commence without further delay, the non-member spouse's pension shall be based on the accrued amount of pension computed as at the normal retirement date, using the formula

$$1/2 \times A/C$$

where A is the pensionable service accrued while the parties were married and C is the member's pensionable service as of the normal retirement date. There could be an actuarial adjustment for the non-member's age.

When the member retires, he or she will receive a pension based on the plan's benefit formula calculated at the actual retirement date less the dollar amount of the pension payable to the non-member spouse.

Where the DSM option is selected, no survivor pension shall attach to the non-member spouse's pension.

The election of the DSM option (and any election by the non-member spouse to commence his or her pension before the member retires) shall be accomplished using forms prescribed in regulation or otherwise authorized by government. Plan administrators could not be held liable for any loss resulting from an action taken by them in good faith in reliance on a form submitted to them. They would also be allowed to charge a fee to offset the initial and ongoing costs incurred by them as a result of the election of these options.

Legislation would provide that where this option is selected, the member's equalization obligation, to the extent that it was based on the value of the pension, is deemed to have been satisfied (that is, even if the total amount that is ultimately paid out to the non-member spouse is less than the member's equalization debt). It should also provide that the non-member spouse's estate will owe nothing to the member or his or her estate if the total amount ultimately paid out to the non-member spouse exceeds the member's equalization debt.

. . . . .

7. Where the member is not yet within ten years of the normal retirement date, the parties may elect the DSM option if the plan administrator agrees.

6. Defined Benefit Plan Coverage

... Subject to some exceptions, the LCO recommends that the settlement options apply only in respect of plans that are registered under the PBA. However, they should be available as well in the case of private sector plans in the federal employment law jurisdiction, as the federal PBSA, which applies to such plans, makes provincial family property law apply in respect of the division of pensions on marriage breakdown. (The federal *Pension Benefits Division Act*, which has its own pension division scheme, applies to federal public sector plans.) ...

Accordingly, the LCO recommends as follows:

8. Recommendations 4 to 7 apply to

(a) a defined benefit pension plan, other than any class of defined benefit plan that is prescribed by regulation;

(b) subject to the regulations, a hybrid plan, insofar as it provides a defined benefit;

if the pension is not in pay and

(c) the plan is registered under the Pension Benefits Act or the substantive provisions of that Act apply to it;

(d) the plan is registered under the federal Pension Benefits Standards Act;

(e) the plan is not registered under the Pension Benefits Act but it is supplemental to a plan that is so registered and

(i) it provides for the accrual of pension benefits in a gradual and uniform manner, and

(ii) neither the formula for the employer's contributions to the plan fund nor the pension benefit provided is at the discretion of the employer; or

(f) the plan is a member of such other class of defined benefit plan as is prescribed.

D. Settlement Options and Defined Contribution Plans

While valuation of a member's interest in a defined contribution plan generally does not raise problems, some stakeholders suggested that Ontario law should provide for immediate division as a settlement option regardless of whether the pension plan is a defined benefit plan or a defined contribution plan, and the LCO sees no reason why the ISM option it is recommending should not be available in the case of both types of plans. However, there would seem to be no advantages for either party in the non-member spouse becoming a quasi-member of his spouse's defined contribution plan; given this, and the fact that a DSM approach does inevitably impose some burdens on plan administrators, the LCO is not recommending that the DSM option described in Recommendation C.3 be available in the case of defined contribution plans. Accordingly, the LCO recommends as follows:

9. The ISM option discussed in Recommendations 4 and 5 also be available where a spouse is a member of a defined contribution plan, but the DSM option should not be available.

E. A New Provincial Retirement Fund?

As discussed in section C, the LCO is recommending in the case of ISM settlements three transfer options for non-member spouses who become entitled to a transfer following pension division, with a possible fourth option: transfer to a provincial retirement fund, if the government decides to establish such a fund. Where the non-member spouse has her own plan, or where the administrator of the member's plan is willing to establish a pension account in that plan for the non-member spouse, a transfer to (or within) the plan will likely be the preferred option. However, for many of those who do not have their own plan (or who will not be offered an account in the member's plan) transfer into an RRSP may not be [an] attractive course, particularly for those who are unsophisticated or inexperienced in investment matters. For these persons, transfer to a large fund offering the pooling of resources and risk, the investment power of large amounts of capital and expert management may be preferable. ...

10. Ontario may wish to consider establishing a retirement fund into which non-member spouses who are entitled to a transfer pursuant to a pension division (see Recommendation 4, above) may place the transferred amount. The plan could also receive transfers from pension plans that wish to divest themselves of their "lost members". The plan would be a capital accumulation fund, that is, the benefit ultimately paid out to the individual would be based on the amount originally paid into the fund plus the yield on the fund's investment of that amount.

F. The 50 Per Cent Rule

The LCO acknowledges that the rule that a court order or domestic contract dealing with family property cannot entitle the non-member spouse to more than 50 per cent of the member's pension benefits reflects a legitimate pension plan (and indeed, societal) objective, namely, to enhance the likelihood that plan members will have a reasonable income for retirement. (We would note, however, that this objective is rather undermined by the fact that support orders can attach up to 50 per cent of the member's pension income; this could result in the member losing 100 per cent of his pension, half to equalization and half to support, as occurred in *Gauthier v. Gauthier.*)[236] While we are not recommending abolition of the rule, we are concerned about the possibility that its unqualified application could in some cases prevent implementation of one or the other of the settlement options being recommended in Section C, even though (if the recommendations are adopted) the approach taken was in accordance with settlement mechanisms specifically made available to the parties by legislation. As the LCO believes that its recommendations concerning settlement will provide a fair method of dividing the pension asset where equalization cannot be achieved without resort to the pension, we believe that a settlement that is in accord with the legislated ISM or DSM approach should be deemed to be in compliance with the 50 per cent rule. Accordingly, the LCO recommends as follows:

11. A settlement that is in accord with the ISM or DSM settlement regime be deemed to comply with the 50 per cent rule.

G. Canada Pension Plan *Credits*

There is little doubt that, as a matter of law, CPP credits constitute "family property" under the FLA, although it seems, as was indicated above, that the point is often ignored in practice. While some stakeholders suggested that the definition of "family property" should accordingly be amended so as to exclude CPP credits, the LCO can see no justification in principle for holding that rights under an occupational pension plan are "family property" while CPP credits are not. However, the LCO is of the view that parties should be able to waive the right to a split of such credits.

The CPP, which is federal legislation, permits the provinces to enact legislation allowing such a waiver, but Ontario has not thus far seen fit to do so. The LCO has noted that there have been instances in which a party to an equalization settlement agreed, in return for other consideration, not to apply for a credit split, only to make such an application at a later date; in the absence of Ontario legislation permitting a waiver, the federal authorities have no choice but to carry out the split where such an application is made. The LCO sees no reason why Ontario should not eliminate this avenue for double dealing. Accordingly, the LCO recommends as follows:

12. Ontario enact legislation permitting parties to waive the right to a split of CPP credits.

H. Common Law Relationships

The LCO has assumed, for purposes of this report, that the family property provisions of the FLA will generally continue not to apply common law relationships. In doing so, we offer no opinion as to whether the exclusion of such relationships from coverage under Part I of that Act should continue. The question of whether the family property provisions should apply to common law relationships is one that extends well beyond pension interests, and generally speaking the LCO believes that it would be inappropriate to address it in the context of a project that is limited to pensions.

Having said that, however, we see no reason why common law partners who separate should not be able to access the settlement mechanisms that we are recommending be made

---

[236] (2003), 23 R.F.L. (6th) 94 (Ont. S.C.J.).

available to married couples should they wish to do so. ... Accordingly, the LCO recommends as follows:

13. Where a common law relationship ends and one or both spouses is a member of a defined benefit pension plan, they may agree to have one or both pensions divided in accordance with the regime described in section C.

A Note On Bill 133

The *Family Statute Law Amendment Act, 2008* (Bill 133) has been passed but is not yet proclaimed in force. It will make significant changes to the way in which an interest in a pension is valued under Part I of the FLA and to the options available for satisfying the portion of an equalization payment attributable to that interest.

Bill 133 will amend the definition of "property" in s. 4(1) of the FLA by repealing the current clause (c) and replacing it with the following: "(c) in the case of a spouse's rights under a pension plan, imputed value, for family law purposes, of the spouse's interest in the plan, as determined in accordance with section 10.1, for the period beginning with the date of the marriage and ending on the valuation date". Under a new s. 10.1 of the FLA, the "imputed value" of a spouse's interest in a pension plan to which the *Pension Benefits Act* applies would be determined in accordance with a new s. 67.2 of the latter Act. In turn, s. 67.2(4) would define the "imputed value" of an interest in a pension as "that portion of the preliminary value that is attributed, in accordance with the regulations" to the marriage. Section 67.2(1) would specify that the "preliminary value" is to be determined in accordance with the regulations and s. 67.2(2) would add that, for defined benefit plans, the "preliminary value" includes "such adjustments as may be prescribed for ancillary benefits and other entitlements". The member of the plan or his or her spouse would be able to apply to the plan administrator for a statement of the "imputed value" of the member's interest in the plan and the administrator would be obligated to provide it. As of the time of writing, none of the all important regulations have been made public and they are likely yet to be drafted.

Bill 133 will also make an immediate settlement method available for pensions covered by the *Pension Benefits Act*. Where the pension is not yet being paid out on the valuation date, an order under s. 10 of the FLA, a domestic contract or a family arbitration award could provide for a transfer of a lump sum from the pension plan to another pension plan (if the administrator of the other plan agrees to accept it) or to a "prescribed retirement savings arrangement". See proposed s. 67.3 of the *Pension Benefits Act*. The transfer of the lump sum could also be implemented by "leaving it in the plan to the credit of the eligible spouse". However, this latter option would only be available "in such circumstances as may be prescribed and only if the administrator agrees to it". The maximum amount that could be transferred would be "50 per cent of the applicable net family value of the pension".

Where, and only where, a member spouse is already receiving the pension benefits on the valuation date; Bill 133 will provide for a division of the pension benefits by the plan administrator where a court order, domestic contract or a family arbitration award so specified. The plan would then pay benefits directly to each spouse. Again, the formula for division could not provide that the non-member spouse receive more than 50 per cent of the net family law value of the pension. See proposed s. 67.4 of the *Pension Benefits Act*.

The provisions in Bill 133 dealing with pensions have been welcomed because they would simplify and clarify the law relating to the division of pensions on marriage breakdown and allow an immediate settlement of the pension. However, there are some concerns. First, the legislature is being asked to approve a skeletal framework in advance of knowing the content of the all-important regulations. Second, unlike the Ontario Law Commission's proposal, Bill 133 will provide a single value — the net family law value — for both the calculation of net family property under Part I of the FLA and for determining the amount that could be transferred out of the pension plan. In a comment in *The Lawyers Weekly* of February 20, 2008, actuaries Jay Jeffrey and Kelley McKeating argue:

> Plan sponsors are comfortable with a requirement to transfer out half of the termination commuted value to a spouse because this is half of what they'd have to transfer out anyway if the member left the plan. But, requiring the plan to transfer out half the hybrid-termination value would cause unacceptable and unaffordable financial damage to the plan.
>
> There are really two pension values — one to be used to determine the value of a pension for family property purposes, the other to be used to determine the maximum lump sum available to assist in settling the equalization obligation.
>
> So the problem with Bill 133 is this. It requires the same value to be used for both purposes. Inevitably, this will result either in a significant financial penalty to the non-member spouse or in unacceptable financial damage to the pension plan.
>
> Surprisingly, given the complexity of the issue, there's a simple solution. Delink the two values. Use the termination commuted value to determine the lump sum available from the plan to assist in settling the equalization obligation. Use the hybrid-termination method to determine the pension component of net family property.

Jeffrey and McKeating fear that, unless this delinking occurs, the prescribed net family law value will be the termination commuted value to ensure that the pension plans can realistically afford to make the transfers after marriage breakdown. To drive home their point that this will shortchange spouses of plan members, Jeffrey and McKeating provide the following example:

> Let's look at a typical 45-year-old teacher with 20 years of teaching experience going through a separation. According to the Ontario Teachers' Pension Plan, the average retirement age for a teacher in 2005 was 57. The actual gross value of this individual's pension, taking into account the pension earned to separation at age 45 and assuming retirement at age 57, is $405,000. [This would be the value using the "retirement method".] The termination commuted value is $255,000. A typical "intermediate" value under the hybrid-termination method [most often used currently in calculating net family property under Part I of the FLA] is $340,000.

Other concerns with the pension provisions in Bill 133 include the elimination of flexibility in valuation of pensions. Currently, lawyers and judges can consider special circumstances such as a plan member's shortened life expectancy and the fact that a plan may become insolvent.

For further reading, see Anderson, "Pension Basics for Family Lawyers, Part I: Overview of Pensions in Canada" (2007), 26 C.F.L.Q. 43 and Anderson, "Pension Basics for Family Lawyers, Part II: Canadian Models for Dividing Pensions When a Relationship Ends" (2007), 26 C.F.L.Q. 91.

5

THE FAMILY HOME

1. Introduction

(1) Significance of the Family Home

HOVIUS, "THE MATRIMONIAL HOME: AN ANALYSIS OF PART II OF THE *FAMILY LAW ACT, 1986*"

(1988), 16 R.F.L. (3d) 31 (Footnotes omitted)

The matrimonial home occupies a special position in family property. It is usually the single item of property of greatest value owned by either or both spouses during their relationship. Moreover, it is the focal point of family life and so couples tend to view it as an asset belonging to both spouses, at least while the relationship is an ongoing one. In order to reflect this perception, the Ontario Law Reform Commission recommended the adoption of the basic principle of co-ownership in the matrimonial home, a principle that would entitle the husband and wife to equal shares secured by their joint control of the asset. While the Ontario legislature did not follow this recommendation, the *Family Law Act, 1986* does contain special provisions regarding the matrimonial home in determining the net family property of each spouse and alters the traditional property law governing ownership where one spouse dies owning an interest in the home as a joint tenant with a third person (s. 26(1)).

But the matrimonial home is more than a valuable asset. It is the shelter and focal point of the family. As a result, the spouses often develop deep emotional attachment to it. This may be especially true for a spouse who has functioned as a full-time homemaker during the relationship. Moreover, the right to occupy the matrimonial home satisfies one of the basic needs of individuals in our society, namely, the need for accommodation. It is, therefore, not enough to ensure that the spouses share the value of the matrimonial home when the relationship ends. In her critical analysis of American law dealing with the economic consequences of divorce, Lenore Weitzman notes that an equal division of marital property, however defined, frequently results in the forced sale of the couple's family residence. This compounds the financial dislocation and impoverishment of women and children generated by divorce. Where the spouses' only significant tangible asset is the matrimonial home and it is sold on the breakdown of the relationship so that the proceeds can be shared equally, often the custodial parent's share will be insufficient to acquire suitable accommodation. While this problem might be remedied by more generous support payments, the loss of the matrimonial home will invariably necessitate a move to a new accommodation. This may well disrupt a child's schooling or neighborhood and friendship ties, thereby creating additional stress and dislocation at the very time when the child most needs continuity and stability. For these reasons, Pt. II of the *Family Law Act, 1986* recognizes that the right to occupy the matrimonial home is important and that it cannot be governed by reference to ownership alone.

(2) Historical Background

Even before the legislative reforms in the 1970s, the courts developed special rules governing the occupational rights in the family residence. Certain rights of occupation were vested by law in both spouses as a result of the rights and duties that flowed from the marital relationship itself.

While the law recognized that a spouse had occupational rights in the matrimonial home, these rights were so limited, so uncertain, and so inadequately protected that legislative reform proved necessary. The main problems regarding occupation rights in the matrimonial home prior to the legislative reforms can be summarized as follows. First, a non-owning spouse's right to occupy was dependent on good behaviour as a spouse. Second, even where the right clearly existed, it could be extinguished by unilateral dealings with the matrimonial home by the owning spouse. Third, the courts had developed few guidelines to determine when a non-owning spouse should be given exclusive possession and they were slow to exclude the owning spouse even where the latter had committed a matrimonial offence. Finally, the relationship between a co-owner's *prima facie* right to partition or sale and the spousal right to occupation presented difficulties.

Further Reading

For further reading regarding the law prior to the legislative reforms, see Cullity, "Property Rights During the Subsistence of Marriage" in Mendes da Costa, ed., *Studies in Canadian Family Law* (Toronto: Butterworths, 1972) and Ontario Law Reform Commission, *Report on Family Law: Part IV: Family Property Law* (Ottawa: Ministry of the Attorney General, 1974) at 35–38.

(3) Overview of Part II of the *Family Law Act*

Part II of the *Family Law Act* (*FLA*) is modeled on Part III of the *Family Law Reform Act, 1978*, which was enacted in 1978 to replace the limited rights briefly described above. Both spouses are given an equal right to possession of a matrimonial home, regardless of its ownership: s. 19(1). When only one of the spouses has an interest in the home, the other spouse's right of possession is a personal right that can only be asserted against the owning spouse: s. 19(2)(a). Adultery or the commission of another matrimonial offence by the non-owning spouse no longer ends that spouse's right to occupy the matrimonial home. However, this right terminates when the marriage ends unless a separation agreement or court order provides otherwise: s. 19(2)(b). Despite this general rule, a spouse who has no interest in a matrimonial home but is occupying it at the time of the other spouse's death, whether under a court order or otherwise, is entitled to retain possession against the spouse's estate, rent free, for 60 days after the spouse's death: s. 26(2).

Notwithstanding each spouse's equal right to possession, a court is authorized by s. 24 to grant exclusive possession to one spouse. Such an order can be made in favour of either spouse regardless of which spouse owns the matrimonial home. A court order for exclusive possession can provide that the non-owning spouse's possession will continue following the dissolution of the marriage. Orders made under Part II can be registered against land under the *Registry Act* and the *Land Titles Act*: s. 27.

Registration gives notice to third parties that they are dealing with a matrimonial home. The significance of this fact will become apparent when the restrictions on the titled spouse's power to dispose of or encumber an interest in the matrimonial home are analyzed. These restrictions, which are important not only to the spouses themselves but to all third parties who acquire interests in property that could be a family residence, are imposed to protect a non-titled spouse's right to possession. As well, any spouse with a right to possession in a matrimonial home is granted a right of redemption and relief against forfeiture in certain proceedings by third parties: s. 22.

Section 26(1) provides that if a spouse dies owning an interest in a matrimonial home as a joint tenant and not with the other spouse, the joint tenancy is deemed to have been severed immediately before the time of death. As a result, the joint tenancy becomes a tenancy in common and the surviving joint tenant loses the benefit of the right of survivorship. The deceased's interest falls into his or her estate, rather than passing to the surviving tenant. The expropriatory nature of this provision was noted and confirmed in *Fulton v. Fulton* (1994), 17 O.R. (3d) 641 (C.A.). The Ontario Law Reform Commission recommended its repeal in its *Report on Family Property Law* (Toronto: 1993) (at 132).

Part II of the *FLA* only applies to matrimonial homes that are situated in Ontario: s. 28(1). This is in keeping with the territorial limitation on provincial legislative power over property and civil rights imposed by the words "in the Province" contained in s. 92(13) of the *Constitution Act, 1867*. As well, it is a general principle of private international law that only the jurisdiction where an immovable is situated has the power to determine the rights and interests in that property. Although Part II does not apply to a family residence situated outside the province, such a residence may still qualify as a matrimonial home for the purpose of calculating a spouse's net family property under Part I. That Part simply incorporates by reference the definition of matrimonial home contained in Part II. The definition does not itself exclude property situated outside of Ontario. Nor does s. 28(1) specify that property situated outside of Ontario is not a matrimonial home. As a result, a cottage in Quebec was characterized as a matrimonial home in determining the spouses' net family properties under Part I in *Perrier v. Perrier* (1987), 12 R.F.L. (3d) 266 (Ont. H.C.).

(4) Occupation Rights of Common Law Partners

HOVIUS AND YOUDAN, *THE LAW OF FAMILY PROPERTY*

(Toronto: Carswell, 1991) 580–585

Part II of the *Family Law Act* awards possessory rights to spouses and provides certain protection for those rights. The general definition of "spouse" in section 1(1) applies to determine who is covered by Part II. It stipulates that a spouse is "either of a man or woman who (a) are married to each other, or (b) have together entered into a marriage that is voidable or void, in good faith on the part of the person asserting a right under this Act". [This definition was amended in 2005 to refer to "two persons".] Therefore, persons who cohabit without going through any marriage ceremony are not covered by Part II.

The support obligations established by Part III of the *Family Law Act* do apply to certain cohabitees. Section 30 stipulates that every spouse has a duty to support the other spouse "in accordance with need, to the extent that he or she is capable of doing so". In Part III, a spouse includes "either of a man and woman who are not married to each other and have cohabited (a) continuously for a period of not less than three years, or (b) in a relationship of some permanence, if they are the natural or adoptive parents of a child".[36] [This definition was amended in 2005 to refer to "two persons".] Section 34(1) lists the types of orders that a court may make in an application for support. One of these is an order for exclusive posses-

---

[36] Section 29.

sion of the matrimonial home.[37] In *Young-Foong v. Leong-Foong*[38] it was accepted that a cohabitee who fell within the extended definition of spouse could be granted an order for exclusive possession of the matrimonial home under this provision. However, a more recent Ontario District Court decision[39] held that, by definition, unmarried cohabitees cannot have a matrimonial home. Accordingly, the Court concluded that orders for exclusive possession of a matrimonial home could only be made if the dependant seeking exclusive possession as part of a support order was a spouse within the more restricted and traditional meaning of that term set out in section 1(1). This conclusion, based as it is on the definition of matrimonial home, appears to be the correct one.[40] In any event, the issue is of limited practical significance since a court can secure exclusive possession of the family residence for a cohabitee in a support application through the power granted by section 34(1)(c). It authorizes the court to require the respondent to transfer any property to the dependant absolutely, for life or for a term of years. A similar power is granted to a court under the *Succession Law Reform Act*[41] where a deceased, whether testate or intestate, has not made adequate provision for the proper support of a dependant who may, in some circumstances, be an unmarried cohabitee.[42] In addition, the court under that Act can order that a dependant be granted the possession or use of any specified property for life or a more limited period.[43]

In summary, the legislation in Ontario does not provide unmarried cohabitees with rights of occupation in the family residence corresponding to those of a spouse. Although the courts are authorized to make the exceptional orders referred to in the [previous] paragraph on an application for support by an unmarried cohabitee under the *Family Law Act* and the *Succession Law Reform Act*, the occupation rights of such cohabitees are generally determined by reference to the common law.

At common law, possessory rights of unmarried persons flow generally from proprietary rights. Where, for example, the legal ownership is in both parties, they both have an equal right to live in the home. Absent agreement, neither co-owner can exclude the other. Where domestic violence has occurred, however, it may be possible for the victim indirectly to obtain exclusive possession at least until an application for partition or sale is heard. Although there is no express authority in the *Criminal Code* for imposing exclusive possession as a condition on a peace bond, some judges have done so.[44] Also, an order restraining one

---

37 Section 34(1)(d).

38 (1980), 1 F.L.R.A.C. 718 (Ont. Master); appeal dismissed (1980), 1 F.L.R.A.C. 721 (Ont. H.C.). In his short reasons, O'Leary J. stated, *obiter dictum*: "I am of the view that someone not a spouse for purposes outside Pt II [of the *Family Law Reform Act*, dealing with support], could be given exclusive possession of property owned by the one responsible for support if in the circumstances she could not reasonably be otherwise supported." Justice O'Leary did not specifically address the problem created by the definition of "matrimonial home".

39 *Czora v. Lonergan* (1987), 7 R.F.L. (3d) 458 (Ont. Dist. Ct.).

40 See, however, Bala and Cano, "Unmarried Cohabitation in Canada: Common Law and Civilian Approaches to Living Together" (1989), 4 C.F.L.Q. 147 where the authors express agreement (at 184-185) with the *obiter dicta* in *Young-Foong v. Leong-Foong*.

41 R.S.O. 1990, c. S.26, s. 63(2)(c).

42 See s. 57.

43 Section 63(2)(d). See, e.g., *Re Nalywayko* (1984), 17 E.T.R. 151 (Ont. Surr. Ct.) where an unmarried cohabitee was granted a one-half interest in a bungalow owned by the deceased cohabitee and the right to live in it for three years.

44 See Orlando, "Exclusive Possession of the Family Home: The Plight of Battered Cohabitees" (1987), 6 R.F.L. (3d) 83, fn. 47. [In *Fayant v. Yaroski* (2001), 20 R.F.L. (5th) 34 (Sask. Q.B.); additional reasons at (2001), 2001 CarswellSask 669 (Q.B.) Justice Hunter noted (para. 59) that a common law partner, Joan, was able to

spouse from molesting, annoying or harassing the other is available to unmarried cohabitees under section 46 of the *Family Law Act* if they satisfy the requirements of the extended definition of spouse contained in Part III of the Act. Such orders may have the effect of preventing a co-owner from exercising possessory rights.[45] Finally, it may be possible for one co-owner to be granted an interim injunction excluding the other pending partition or sale proceedings.[46]

In the absence of a legal or equitable interest in the property, the cohabitee's status will often be that of a bare licensee who must leave within a reasonable time once notice to quit is given.[47] In England, however, the courts have been developing the contractual licence as a method of conferring greater occupational rights on the non-owning cohabitee.[48] ...

There is a certain unreality and artificiality about the use of the contractual licence to secure occupation rights for unmarried cohabitees in some of the English cases. Often, one is forced to conclude that there was never any real agreement between the parties and that the courts are, in fact, imposing one in order to do justice. Rather than wait for the courts in Ontario to manipulate traditional legal concepts in a similarly creative fashion, the provincial legislature should enact laws to deal with the occupational rights of cohabitees, particularly where there are children of the relationship. Perhaps the time has come for the Ontario legislature to extend the occupational rights accorded to spouses and the protection of those rights established by Part II of the *Family Law Act* to, at least, unmarried cohabitees who satisfy the extended definition of spouse found in Part III of the Act.

NOTES AND QUESTIONS

1. In *Williams v. Hudson* (1997), 33 R.F.L. (4th) 111 (Ont. Gen. Div.), Justice de P. Wright reviewed the conflicting case law regarding whether s. 34(1)(d) of the *FLA* permits a court to grant an exclusive possession order to an unmarried cohabitee as part of a support order. The court granted leave to appeal to the Divisional Court on the basis of the uncertainty, but it appears that the appeal was not pursued. See also *Bathie v. Munro* (2002), 2002 CarswellOnt 3621 (S.C.J.), where Justice Kiteley decided that there was no need to determine the issue because no exclusive possession order was warranted in any event.

2. In *Guénette v. Brisebois* (2004), 2004 CarswellOnt 4132 (S.C.J.), the court held that the common law partner had no right to occupy her partner's house after their relationship ended. See also *Fayant v. Yaroski* (2001), 20 R.F.L. (5th) 34 (Sask. Q.B.); additional reasons at (2001), 2001 CarswellSask 669 (Q.B.) where the court ordered a woman to leave her partner's home after it rejected her argument that she was a spouse for the purposes of *The Family Property Act*, S.S. 1997, c. F-6.3.

---

continue to occupy the home owned by her partner only because he was charged with assaulting her and "prohibited from attending at or near where Joan resided".]

45 Such an order could, for example, specify that one of the cohabitees is not to have any contact with the other who brought the application. Even though both parties would continue to have equal right of possession, the one subject to the order would be unable to exercise the right without violating the order.

46 See, for example, *Hersog v. Hersog* (1975), 22 R.F.L. 380 (B.C. S.C.). Although the case involved married co-owners, there is no reason why an interim injunction pending partition or sale proceedings could not be granted in similar circumstances where the parties are not married to each other.

47 On licences generally, see Megarry and Wade, *The Law of Real Property*, 5th ed. (1984) ch. 14 and Cheshire and Burn, *Modern Law of Real Property*, 14th ed. (1988) ch. 18. See also Moriarty, "Licences and Land Law: Legal Principles and Public Policies" (1984), 100 L.Q.R. 376 and Dewar, "Licences and Land Law: An Alternative View" (1986), 49 M.L.R. 741.

48 For further analysis of the use of the contractual licence and the related doctrines of constructive trust and proprietary estoppel in recent English cases, see Chapter 8, "Developments in England and Australia" of Hovius and Youdan, *The Law of Family Property* (Toronto: Carswell, 1991). See also Holland, *Unmarried Couples: Legal Aspects of Cohabitation* (1982) at 75–82, and Bala and Cano, *supra*, note 40 at 181–183.

3. In *Joyce v. O'Neill* (2008), 2008 CarswellOnt 7965 (Ont. S.C.J.), the judge granted a common law partner temporary exclusive possession of the family home through an injunction that would last until her claim to an interest in the home by way of constructive trust was decided.

4. An unmarried partner, including a same-sex partner, can apply for exclusive possession of the family residence in some provinces that do not extend the statutory rules for the sharing family property to common law partners. See, e.g., *Family Law Act*, R.S.N.L. 1990. In those Canadian jurisdictions that have extended their family property regimes to include unmarried couples, the special rules governing possession of the family residence also apply to such couples. See, e.g., Part III of *The Family Property Act*, S.S. 1997, c. F-6.3.

The recent legislation enacted in various provinces to provide emergency relief where there is domestic violence empowers the courts to grant temporary exclusive possession orders even if the parties are not married. See *Protection Against Family Violence Act*, S.A. 2000, c. P-27; *The Domestic Violence and Stalking Prevention, Protection and Compensation Act*, S.M. 1998, c. 41; *Domestic Violence Intervention Act*, S.N.S. 2001, c. 29; *Victims of Family Violence Act*, R.S.P.E.I. 1988, c. V-3.2; and *The Victims of Domestic Violence Act*, S.S. 1994, c. V-6.02. Similar legislation was enacted in Ontario as the *Domestic Violence Protection Act, 2000*, S.O. 2000, c. 33, but it was never proclaimed into force and would be repealed by *An Act to amend various Acts in relation to certain family law matters and to repeal the Domestic Violence Protection Act, 2000* (Bill 133) (not yet proclaimed in force, May 2009).

5. Bill 133 would re-enact s. 46 of the *Family Law Act* so that a restraining order could be made against a person cohabiting with the applicant or who has cohabited with the applicant. In other words, the section's application would not be limited to spouses or former spouses as defined in s. 29 of the Act.

6. The *Residential Tenancies Act, 2006* and its regulations define "spouse" to include some common law partners. They provide specific rights to a spouse where the other spouse is the sole tenant and dies or vacates the rental unit without notice to the landlord. However, the non-tenant partner is not granted any rights vis-à-vis a partner who is the sole tenant.

7. In *Report on the Rights and Responsibilities of Cohabitants under the Family Law Act* (Toronto: 1993), the O.L.R.C. recommended that the definition of "spouse" in s. 1(1) of the *FLA* be amended to include unmarried persons of the opposite sex who have cohabited continuously for a period not less than three years or in a relationship of some permanence if they are the parents of a child. Part II of the Act would then be applicable to these couples. It also recommended the extension of the rights and obligations under the *FLA*, including Part II, to Registered Domestic Partnerships. Such partnerships could involve persons of the same sex. One of the consequential amendments suggested by the Commission was the replacement of the term "matrimonial home" with the term "family home".

8. Recall the Supreme Court of Canada's decision in *Walsh v. Bona* (2002), 32 R.F.L. (5th) 81 (reproduced in the previous chapter). Although the court did not expressly consider the rights of possession in a family residence, can one infer from the reasons that there is no constitutional obligation to extend Part II of the *FLA* to unmarried cohabitees, whether of the same or opposite sex?

2. Identification of a Matrimonial Home

It is important to be able to identify a matrimonial home because this asset is accorded special treatment in the calculation of net family properties under Part I of the *FLA* and the rights granted in Part II apply only to matrimonial homes. The definition of matrimonial home is contained in s. 18. Note also the definition of "property" in s. 17.

Under s. 39(1) of the *Family Law Reform Act, 1978* any property occupied by the spouses as a family residence at any time during their marriage qualified as a matrimonial home. The Act also expressly provided in s. 39(2) that the definition of matrimonial home could be applied, notwithstanding that its application resulted in there being more than one matrimonial home. Where the couple occupied one property as a family residence and then moved to another, both properties were matrimonial homes so long as they were still owned by one or both spouses. The definition in s. 18(1) of the *FLA* makes it clear that this is no longer the situation.

Section 18(2) and (3) of the *FLA* are virtually identical to s. 39(3) and (4) of the 1978 Act. These latter two subsections were considered in the first case that follows.

HARTLING v. HARTLING

(1979) (Ont. H.C.)(unreported)

[Under the *Family Law Reform Act, 1978*, a matrimonial home was a family asset unless a domestic contract provided otherwise. In this case, the wife applied for an equal division of family assets and claimed that certain properties were matrimonial homes. Only the portion of the reasons dealing with the identification of the couple's matrimonial homes is reproduced here.]

McDERMID L.J.S.C.: — ... In this case, a separate appraisal was submitted for the value of the farmhouse and one acre of land. I have no hesitation in finding, in this case, that the farmhouse and one acre of land constituted the matrimonial home of Mr. and Mrs. Hartling since it was property in which Mr. Hartling had an interest and it was occupied by Mr. Hartling and Mrs. Hartling as their family residence from July 1974 until at least sometime in November 1974. Section 39(4) was designed specifically to deal with the situation present in this case, namely that where the residence is situate on a farm, in this case comprising approximately 200 acres, where only a small portion, in this case 1 acre, was "necessary to the use and enjoyment of the residence". I therefore find that the farm house and one acre constitute a family asset and that the remaining portion of the farm property is a non-family asset.

On the evidence, Mr. and Mrs. Hartling also occupied a two bedroom apartment in a building of 108 apartment units at 112 Baseline Road, London, Ontario, known, I believe, as the Valhalla Apartments. At the time Mr. and Mrs. Hartling lived in this building, it was owned by Comgord Limited, a corporation in which Mr. Hartling owned 50% of the common shares. From Mr. Hartling's evidence I would conclude that the fair market value of the two bedroom unit in which they resided was $16,000.00.

Mr. Ledroit, on behalf of Mrs. Hartling, urges that by virtue of ss. 39(3) and 3(b)(ii) the apartment unit is also a "family asset" and that she is entitled to one-half its fair market value, or $8,000.00.

There is no evidence in this case that the mere ownership of shares in Comgord Limited entitled Mr. Hartling, or any other shareholder, to occupy an apartment unit in the building in question. I infer from the evidence that he occupied it pursuant to a lease, in the normal way, there being no evidence to the contrary. Although s. 39(3) is not specifically so worded, it would appear to me to be more applicable to a condominium corporation.

There is no doubt then that within the provisions of s. 39(1), Mr. Hartling had a leasehold "interest" in the property, i.e., the apartment unit, and that it was occupied by him and Mrs. Hartling as their family residence. It therefore constitutes a matrimonial home. However, I emphasize that Mr. Hartling's interest in the unit arises not from his ownership of shares in the corporation but from his status as a lessee.

Although there was evidence adduced to establish the fair market value of the apartment unit as part of the apartment building, there was no evidence adduced to establish the value of the leasehold interest, if any. In my opinion, it would be that value, if any, in which the spouses are entitled to share and not the fair market value of the rental unit since, as I have indicated, Mr. Hartling was not entitled to occupy the apartment unit merely as a result of owning shares of the corporation which owned that unit ....

DEBORA v. DEBORA

(2006), 33 R.F.L. (6th) 252 (Ont. C.A.)

[A man and woman met in 1985 and began to live together in 1986. A company in which the man was the sole shareholder purchased a cottage as an investment in 1993. The man and woman became husband and wife in 1994 and separated in 1995. During the marriage, the husband and wife used the cottage as a recreational residence and entertained family and friends there. On the wife's application for an equalization of the net family properties under the *Family Law Act*, the trial judge, relying on ss. 18(1) and 18(2), concluded that the cottage was a matrimonial home. Once the cottage was characterized as a matrimonial home, the husband received no deduction from his net family property for its value at marriage. The appellate court upheld this result. Justice Weiler, for the court, reasoned as follows.]

1 There is no issue on this appeal that the cottage property owned by the appellant's numbered company was ordinarily occupied as a residence by him and his spouse. The issue is whether the trial judge erred in holding that the appellant had an interest in the cottage property sufficient to render it a matrimonial home pursuant to the *FLA*. ...

14 The appellant submits that as a shareholder has no interest in the assets of a corporation, he had no interest in the cottage. Rather, it is his ownership of the shares in the company that are subject to equalization. Using this approach, the value of the shares of the company as at the date of marriage would be deducted from his net family property. Only the increase in value of the shares of the corporation from the date of the marriage to the date of separation would be used to calculate net family property. Assuming that as of the date of marriage the value of the shares was equal to its sole asset, the cottage, the value of the shares at the date of marriage would be $840,000. At the date of separation the cottage had a value of $1-million. Thus, the difference of $160,000 would be subject to equalization. As a result the appellant submits that the trial judge erred in piercing the corporate veil and in valuing the cottage as a matrimonial home whose entire value of $1 million dollars at the date of separation was subject to equalization and part of the appellant's net family property.

15 The question of whether the appellant has an interest in the cottage property requires me to consider how s. 18(2) of the *Family Law Act* and its statutory predecessor, s. 39(3) of the *Family Law Reform Act* (R.S.O. 1980, c. 152) (the *FLRA*), should be interpreted. As well, the evolving jurisprudence at common law as to when a court is entitled to pierce the corporate veil must be considered. ...

17 The appellant contends that s. 18(2) primarily applies to a situation where a matrimonial home is a co-operative apartment or where the purpose of putting the home in the name of the corporation is to defeat the *FLA*. In this regard, the appellant's submission echoes the obiter comments of the motion judge in *CMLQ Investors Co. v. 530995 Ontario Ltd.* (1995), 17 R.F.L. (4th) 31 (Ont. Gen. Div.).

18 I disagree with this interpretation. The plain wording of the subsection does not limit a spouse's interest to a condominium or co-operative apartment and I can think of no reason to so limit it in this manner. The simple device of holding a house in the name of a personally owned corporation prior to the date of marriage would deprive the other spouse of the rights associated with the matrimonial home: an equal right to possession; the requirement that the consent of the other spouse to alienate or encumber the home be obtained; and the full value

of the home being included in the calculation of a spouse's net family property on separation. Such an interpretation would defeat the desired effect of the *FLA*, which regards the matrimonial home as a unique asset and gives it a special treatment.

19 In *Mancini v. Mancini* (1982), 31 R.F.L. (2d) 418 (Ont. U.F.C.), Steinberg U.F.C.J. interpreted s. 39(2) of the *FLRA*, a provision nearly identical to the present s. 18(2) of the *FLA*. He focused on the phrase "entitling the owner to occupy a housing unit," and held that if the owner of a share or shares in the corporation has a controlling interest so as to enable him to vote his shares so as to give him a right of residence, then the owner has an "interest" in the property for the purposes of the statute. In other words, legal control over the corporation amounts to legal control over the residence for the purposes of the matrimonial home provisions. Alternatively, he held that if a company has passed a resolution entitling its owner to reside in the home, it would be a matrimonial home. ...

23 The reasoning in *Mancini, supra*, accords with the purposes of the *FLA* respecting the treatment to be afforded to a matrimonial home and I would adopt it. If the owner of shares in a corporation has a controlling interest that would enable him to vote his shares so as to give him a right of residence, then the owner has an "interest" in the property for the purposes of the statute.

24 The interpretation of s. 18(2) I propose also accords with the evolving common law jurisprudence as to when the corporate veil should be pierced. Simply put, there is no one all-encompassing rule as to when a court will pierce the corporate veil. A contextual approach is required. A court will not enforce the "separate entities" principle when it would yield a result too flagrantly opposed to justice, convenience or would defeat the desired effect of legislation ... Here the interpretation proposed by the appellant would defeat the desired effect of the legislation. ...

25 An important consideration that affects whether the corporate veil will be pierced is whether the interests of third parties would be affected. ...

26 Here, ... the husband is the sole shareholder and director of the corporation and there is no concern that piercing the corporate veil may adversely affect the interests of innocent third parties.

29 In the appeal before us, the appellant is the sole shareholder and controls the numbered company. This company did not pay for the renovations and did not pay the ongoing expenses for the cottage property. Money from the couple's joint bank account was used to pay ongoing expenses. The appellant's attempt to deduct expenses related to the cottage as a business expense was rejected. The corporation is the *alter ego* of the husband and is being used by him to try to defeat the legitimate claim of his wife. ...

DaCOSTA v. DaCOSTA

(1990), 29 R.F.L. (3d) 422, 1990 CarswellOnt 314 (Ont. Gen. Div.); affirmed
(1992), 1992 CarswellOnt 257 (Ont. C.A.)

[In August 1986 Mr. DaCosta used $149,613, which he had inherited after the marriage, together with other investments to purchase a hobby farm, the Cedar Dee Farm, for $380,000. Although the marriage was in difficulty by October 1986, Granger J. concluded that the valuation date was March 27, 1987. When the Cedar Dee Farm was purchased, the spouses expected that Mr. DaCosta would operate the farm and that the family would use it as a weekend retreat.]

GRANGER J.: — ... There can be no doubt that at any given time spouses may have more than one matrimonial home, i.e., cottage, hobby farm or condominium. In this case it was the intention of the spouses to use Cedar Dee Farm as a weekend retreat. It had a beautiful house, swimming pool and stables for riding horses. The issue is whether it was ever "ordinarily occupied" by Mr. and Mrs. DaCosta as a matrimonial home. Again the evidence of Mrs. DaCosta is less than satisfactory. She claims to have cooked meals and moved furniture at Cedar Dee. I do not believe her on this aspect of the case. Prior to the closing of the purchase of Cedar Dee, Mrs. DaCosta attended at the farm on two occasions. After the closing she attended at the farm on no more than three occasions. They did not stay overnight at the farm nor did they do any cooking at the farm. Mrs. DaCosta did not attend at the farm after the end of October 1986. It was after this date that the furniture which would allow the farm to be used as a matrimonial home was delivered from the garage at 291 Oriole Parkway. After the furniture was delivered to the farm, Mr. DaCosta spent considerable time at the farm. I find it impossible to reconcile Mrs. DaCosta's position that Cedar Dee Farm was ordinarily used as a matrimonial home and her failure to attend at the farm between 1st November 1986 and 27th March 1987. Surely, if it was being used as a matrimonial home, she would have attended at the farm. In my view, because of the stress in the marriage, Mrs. DaCosta by her own choice never used Cedar Dee Farm as a matrimonial home. In order to be a matrimonial home, it must be ordinarily occupied by the spouses at the time of separation. In this case it was never occupied as a matrimonial home. They may have intended to occupy it as a matrimonial home but they never carried out their intention, notwithstanding that they had an opportunity to carry out such an intention. Accordingly, Mr. DaCosta is entitled to exclude from the value of Cedar Dee Farm as of valuation day the sum of $149,613 which he inherited from his mother, grandmother and great aunt after his marriage to Mrs. DaCosta: s. 4(2)1 and 5 of the F.L.A.

GOODYER v. GOODYER

(1999), 168 D.L.R. (4th) 453, 1999 CarswellOnt 37 (Ont. Gen. Div.)

PERKINS J.: — This case raises some interesting and difficult issues:

1. Is a housing unit occupied by the wife's mother within the spouses' matrimonial home a part of their matrimonial home as defined in subs. 18(1) of the Family Law Act? This has important implications in this case because the home was (or may have been) a gift or inheritance, and if this part of the home is not within the matrimonial home as intended by the Act, the husband will be able to claim an exclusion from his net family property. [The other issues are omitted.]

Extent of the matrimonial home: is the "granny flat" included?

Facts

I have used a popular term to describe the wife's mother's accommodations within the house occupied by the spouses as their matrimonial home. In fact the unit was not sealed off from the rest of the house, although it did have an entrance at the rear of the house, which Mrs. Johnston used for her comings and goings. The area she occupied was on the ground floor of the house and included a bedroom, living room, bathroom and kitchen. It was an area of about 500 sq. ft. in a house of slightly less than 3000 sq. ft. (not including basement), or roughly 1/6 of the living area. (Numbers up to 800 sq. ft. were given for Mrs. Johnston's living area, but the diagram that was accepted as accurate by the parties shows an area of 500 sq. ft. at the very most.) The connection to the other rooms on the ground floor was through two doorways that had doors on them, but the doors could not be locked. The husband and wife (and Ashley [the husband's minor son from a previous marriage]) had their living room and kitchen on the ground floor as well and their bedrooms and bathroom upstairs. No renovations were done to accommodate Mrs. Johnston's needs. There was no rent charged for use of the area, though Mrs. Johnston did contribute to some household charges such as cable TV.

Mrs. Johnston's kitchen was actually the laundry room of the house and it was used by the wife (and I suppose other members of the family) when laundry had to be done. Mrs. Johnston's toaster oven sat on top of the dryer. This room also contained a freezer that was used for the whole family. The wife's evidence was that she often entered her mother's area to spend time with her in her living room and that the wife and family visitors also sometimes used the main floor bathroom for convenience rather than running upstairs. The husband corroborated this as he said that the wife's use of the main floor bathroom was a point of irritation — he didn't think it was right to impinge on Mrs. Johnston's space in this way. There was also evidence that the mother came occasionally into the main floor kitchen and dining room used by the spouses to eat and for socializing, though the wife admitted that there was not a lot of interaction between the husband and Mrs. Johnston. Nevertheless the husband acknowledged that they all gathered for cards on the main floor once or twice a week. Ashley sometimes went into Mrs. Johnston's area to use her VCR.

Law

The husband's first argument focuses on the words "ordinarily occupied by the person and his or her spouse as their family residence" in subs. 18(1). The husband says that the "granny flat", as I have called it, was not ordinarily occupied by the spouses and was not part of *their* family residence. Further, the argument goes that the granny flat was "normally used for a purpose other than residential", "residential" meaning residential for the spouses. In other words, quarters that were rented out to a tenant would not qualify as part of the spouses' matrimonial home and neither does this living area, submits the husband.

I have not been given any comparable cases and have not found any. My decision must be based entirely on an analysis of the statutory language.

Dealing first with subs. 18(1), I think the evidence shows here that the spouses did occupy the area in question as part of their ordinary mode of life. To occupy something ordinarily does not require constant or continual occupancy, nor does it require occupancy of every square metre. In this case, the evidence shows that Mrs. Johnston's bathroom, "kitchen" (really the family laundry room) and living room were all occupied from time to time on a free and easy basis by various members of the family, including the spouses and Ashley. Ashley's use of the area, while a dependent minor living with his father, is attributable to his father, in my view.

That leaves only the bedroom, about which there was no evidence of direct use by the wife, the husband or Ashley. However, I do not think that anything turns on that. The great majority of the area was used by various family members. The entire area was used by Mrs. Johnston as a resident of the family home and I do not see that subs. 18(1) was intended to exclude from the spouses' matrimonial home parts of the home used for residential purposes primarily or even exclusively by an extended family member who was not even paying rent. I think the word "family" in the phrase "ordinarily occupied by the person and his or her spouse as their family residence" is not meant as an exclusive word, leaving out parents, children or other close relations of either of the spouses. If Ashley were no longer a dependent minor, or if a niece or cousin were living in the home, should the provision be interpreted to subtract their exclusive use areas from the spouses' matrimonial home? "Family" is not defined in the *Family Law Act* for the purpose of s. 18 and nothing in the context of s. 18 requires that it be given a restrictive meaning as sought by the husband.

Nor does subs. 18(3) assist the husband, in my view. It talks about uses "other than residential", but does not qualify the word "residential" with a phrase such as "by the spouses". This area was used only for residential purposes, albeit primarily by Mrs. Johnston. Subs. 18(3) comes into play only if the area is "normally used for a purpose other than residential". There is no such use here.

I note that the only cases found by counsel that even come close to this one involve portions of the matrimonial home that were rented out to parties at arms' length from the spouses, and even they are in the majority against the husband: *Solonynko v. Solonynko* (1978), 1 F.L.R.A.C. 211 (Ont. H.C.); *C. v. C. (No. 1)* (1979), 11 R.F.L. (2d) 356 (Ont. Co. Ct.); *C. v. C. (No. 2)* (1979), 11 R.F.L. (2d) 364 (Ont. Co. Ct.). But see *Kozlowski v. Kozlowski* (1984), 39 R.F.L. (2d) 34 (Ont. H.C.) — house used 75% for commercial boarding house operation is a matrimonial home only to the extent of 25%; and see the commentary in Mamo, Alfred P., *Matrimonial Property Law in Canada*, O-148–O-150.

The husband's argument to exclude the "granny flat" from the spouses' matrimonial home must fail. He is not entitled to exclude any portion of the home from his net family property. ...

NOTES AND QUESTIONS

1. A leasehold interest is a species of personal property, not realty. Why can a leasehold interest nevertheless qualify as a matrimonial home? Can a mobile home be a matrimonial home? See *Caldwell v. Caldwell* (1978), 1 F.L.R.A.C. 143 (Ont. Dist. Ct.). Can a sailboat be a matrimonial home? See *Clark v. Clark* (1984), 40 R.F.L. (2d) 92 (Ont. H.C.).

2. The term "family residence" connotes something more than simple occupation of a dwelling. It must be the residence around which the couple's normal family life revolves: *Taylor v. Taylor* (1978), 6 R.F.L. (2d) 341 at 350 (Ont. U.F.C.). A Florida condominium was held not to be a matrimonial home as it had only recently been purchased, and the family occupied it only to ready it for future use. Compare the Taylor case with *LeCouteur v. LeCouteur* (2005), 18 R.F.L. (6th) 386 (Ont. S.C.J.), where the court held that a condo was a matrimonial home even though the couple continued to own another home in which they had lived for many years and even though they separated five days after moving into the condo.

3. In *Clarke v. Read Estate* (2000), 12 R.F.L. (5th) 305 (Ont. S.C.J.); additional reasons at (2001), 2001 CarswellOnt 597 (Ont. S.C.J.), the wife, shortly before the marriage, transferred ownership of her house to a trust of which her daughter was the beneficiary. The husband and wife then lived in the house for ten years until the wife died. Justice Planet found (at para. 37) that "the Property does not come within the definition of a matrimonial home under the F.L.A. and further that [the wife] did not have an interest in the Property". Was this case rightly decided in light of *Debora v. Debora*?

4. Other cases where the courts concluded that only the farm house and a small parcel of contiguous land constituted the matrimonial home include *Youngblut v. Youngblut* (1979), 11 R.F.L. (2d) 249 (Ont. H.C.) and *Dudley v. Dudley* (1981), 22 R.F.L. (2d) 337 (Ont. H.C.). Compare *Perks v. Perks* (2003), 35 R.F.L. (5th) 435 (Ont. S.C.J.), where the family residence was located on approximately 23 acres. The surrounding land was largely unused, but the family did occasionally use parts for activities such as baseball games and hikes. The husband allowed a local farmer to use four acres to grow a hay crop "to enable the parties to gain a farm tax credit". Justice Ingram stated (at para. 21): "While Mr. and Mrs. Perks did not frequently make a physical presence throughout the property, it would be wrong to suggest that it was 'normally used for a purpose other than recreational'." The Justice concluded (at para. 21) that the use of some of the property by the neighbouring farmer "could not be characterized as a commercial enterprise but rather a simple method of getting a tax advantage". The entire 23 acres were characterized as part of the matrimonial home.

5. A husband and wife live in an apartment unit in a five-unit building owned by the husband. The other four units are rented out to third parties. Identify the couple's matrimonial home. See *Young v. Young* (1981), 21 R.F.L.

(2d) 388 (Ont. C.A.); *Kozlowski v. Kozlowski* (1984), 39 R.F.L. (2d) 34 (Ont. H.C.); and *Fekete v. Begovic* (2008), 2008 CarswellOnt 709, 51 R.F.L. (6th) 424 (S.C.J.).

6. Cases in which a couple had more than one matrimonial home include *Battye v. Battye* (1989), 22 R.F.L. (3d) 427 (Ont. H.C.); affirmed (1993), 48 R.F.L. (3d) 130 (Ont. C.A.). This case suggests that judges readily conclude that cottages are matrimonial homes. Justice McKeown simply stated (at 431):

> The evidence was that Mr. and Mrs. Battye and their two sons attended regularly at the cottage in the early years of the marriage and, to a much lesser extent, in the last couple years of the marriage. It is clearly a matrimonial home.

7. In *Ledrew v. Ledrew* (1993), 46 R.F.L. (3d) 11 (Ont. Gen. Div.), the wife owned a cottage which was used by the family on weekends and in the summers during the early 1980s. By 1985, some four years before separation, the husband and wife no longer spent any time together at the cottage. Justice Smith concluded (at 17):

> ... [T]here is no evidence forthcoming that the parties occupied the premises as a family residence after 1985. Even if, in the early 1980s, the White Cottage could have been categorized as the family's vacation residence, it had ceased to have that use or character for a number of years prior to separation. I find the White Cottage not to be a matrimonial home under s. 18(1) of the *Family Law Act*.

8. Where the spouses have more than one matrimonial home, they may designate one to be a matrimonial home in accordance with s. 20 of the *FLA*. If they register the designation of one home, is the other one still a matrimonial home?

9. Can a couple effectively opt out of Part II of the *FLA* by jointly designating their only residence as a matrimonial home under s. 20 and then cancelling the designation? Can one spouse unilaterally defeat the other spouse's rights under Part II by designation and cancellation?

3. Orders for Exclusive Possession

Section 24 of the *FLA* allows the court to make exclusive possession orders regarding the matrimonial home and its contents. Such orders may be made on a temporary or interim basis (s. 24(2)). Final orders for exclusive possession for any period that the court directs are also possible. Such orders may continue even after the marriage relationship ends (s. 19(2)(b)). Section 24(1) confers upon the court ancillary powers respecting the following: contents of the home; release of other property that is also a matrimonial home from the application of Part II; payments in the nature of occupation rent; fixing the obligation to repair and maintain the home and to pay liabilities arising in respect of the property; and the authorization of dispositions or encumbrances of the home, subject to the right of the spouse who is granted exclusive possession. Any of the orders set out in s. 24(1) can be made regardless of the ownership of the matrimonial home and its contents and despite the provision in s. 19(1) that both spouses have an equal right to possession.

Section 24(3) sets out the factors that the court should consider in deciding whether to make an order for exclusive possession. Section 24(4) provides further guidance to the court by specifying criteria for the determination of the best interests of a child. The factors listed in s. 24(3) and (4) indicate that the court has considerable discretion in determining applications for exclusive possession.

Orders for exclusive possession can be registered against land under the *Registry Act* and the *Land Titles Act*. See s. 27 of the *FLA*. Section 24(5) creates the offence of contravening an order for exclusive possession. Section 24(6) grants arrest powers in relation to this offence to the police.

The first six cases that follow involve applications for exclusive possession on an interim or temporary basis. The last two deal with applications for such orders on a long-term basis. Is there a difference in approach?

PIFER v. PIFER

(1986), 3 R.F.L. (3d) 167, 1986 CarswellOnt 289 (Ont. Dist. Ct.)

SALHANY D.C.J.: — On 15th May 1986 the plaintiff obtained an order from the Honourable Judge E.G. McNeely granting her interim interim custody of the infant children and interim interim exclusive possession of the matrimonial home and contents. The defendant appeared on that application but was unrepresented by counsel and did not file any affidavit material. Because of the allegations contained in the affidavit of the plaintiff, the order was granted.

The matter was adjourned until 29th May 1986 when it was heard by the Honourable J.V. Scott. Counsel retained by the defendant appeared on his behalf but had not had the opportunity to file material. On consent, the order of Judge McNeeley was extended to 12th June 1986 in order to enable the defendant to file his material.

In the meantime, the defendant has launched his own application for interim interim custody and exclusive possession of the matrimonial home and contents. In his affidavit, he refutes most of the allegations made by the plaintiff against him. He says that he is better suited to look after the children, that the plaintiff should be required to leave the matrimonial home and that he should be entitled to return to the home and look after the children. Alternatively, he says that the material filed by both him and the plaintiff is so conflicting that it is impossible for this court to come down on the side of one or the other so as to determine whether an order of exclusive possession should be made under s. 24 of the *Family Law Act, 1986*, until, at least, cross-examinations have been conducted of the parties.

Counsel for the plaintiff argued that pending cross-examinations, the status quo should be maintained and that the plaintiff and children should be allowed to remain until the return of the motion. I have difficulty with that submission. The order made by Judge McNeeley granting the plaintiff exclusive possession has to be characterized essentially as an *ex parte* order because there was only the affidavit material of the plaintiff and the babysitter, Linda Gregoire, before him for consideration. In my view, it would be unfortunate if one spouse could create a status quo by deciding to jump the gun and obtain an order *ex parte* on material that the other spouse does not have an opportunity to refute. What I must do at this stage is to assess all of the affidavit material before me and determine whether it supports a case for exclusive possession by either party or none at all. If it does not, then the existing order for exclusive possession should be dissolved and the defendant allowed to return to reside in the matrimonial home. ...

Turning now to the material before me, the parties were married on 11th December 1976 in Milwaukee, Wisconsin. They have two young daughters, Laura, aged 6, and Jennifer, aged 4. The plaintiff is a nurse and the defendant an accountant. Apparently, they enjoyed a relatively comfortable life-style until the defendant decided to go into business for himself and purchased a Go-Camping franchise which involved rental and sales of motor homes and travel trailers. Unfortunately, the business lasted only a few months and the defendant found himself unemployed. To assist in the family finances, the plaintiff decided to seek employment first in February 1984 in a doughnut shop and later in May 1984 as a nurse at the K-W Hospital where she remains today. The defendant sought and obtained work in the accounting department of a law office and later with a chartered accountant. Since February 1986 he has attempted to establish his own accounting business.

The material indicates that until the plaintiff began to work, she assumed most of the responsibility for looking after the children. After she began work, the parties shared that responsibility with the defendant taking an active role particularly when the plaintiff was working shift work at the hospital. In April it was decided to hire a babysitter, Linda Gregoire, so that the defendant could devote more time to his new business.

The main allegation of the plaintiff is that the defendant has, over the last four months, started to drink heavily at home starting in the afternoon around 4:00 p.m. until he passes out around 10:00 p.m. There is also an allegation that he smokes heavily, leaving live cigarettes in the ashtrays, and leaves on a propane heater after he has gone to bed. She also says that the arguments between them have increased in frequency since he began to drink heavily and this affects the children and frightens the babysitter. The allegations of excessive drinking are supported by the babysitter in her affidavit. Although the defendant concedes drinking alcohol, he denies that it is to excess and also denies that he is endangering his family by the use of cigarettes or the propane heater.

The balance of all of the material indicates to me that there is a great deal of stress and strain in this household which is obviously affecting the children. There is no doubt in my mind that it would be in the best interests of the children if they were relieved of that stress by the separation of their parents. If it were not for the serious allegations of drinking and bizarre conduct by the defendant, as supported by the affidavit of Linda Gregoire, I might have considered granting him interim interim exclusive possession and custody because of the fact that he has more time to devote to looking after the children. However, because of those allegations, I am of the view that it would be in the best interests of the children that the plaintiff have custody of them and exclusive possession of the matrimonial home.

[The court awarded interim custody and exclusive possession to the wife.]

PERRIER v. PERRIER

(1989), 20 R.F.L. (3d) 388, 1989 CarswellOnt 248 (Ont. H.C.)

KOZAK L.J.S.C.: — On 18th May 1989 this court heard competing motions wherein both parents claimed interim custody of the children and interim exclusive possession of the matrimonial home.

The parties are husband and wife who reside at 421 Westbury Crescent in the city of Thunder Bay with their two children, a daughter, Aaren Nicolle, born 18th February 1978, and a son, Patrick Byron, born 1st March 1982. They have been married some 16 years. The husband is employed at the Thunder Bay Terminals, whereas the wife is enrolled at university as a full-time nursing student and in addition is employed on a part-time basis at the McKellar Hospital. Both parents, because of their careers, have shared in the raising of the children.

It is admitted that the marriage has deteriorated as a result of constant arguments, and that such arguments are having a detrimental effect upon the children because they have reached the stage of becoming volatile if allowed to go unchecked. Both feel that the other is to blame.

Matters came to a head as a result of an incident which occurred on 30th April 1989 and 1st May 1989 concerning the manner in which the mother disciplined the daughter for missing dancing classes. The husband responded by commencing a petition for divorce which was issued on 12th May 1989 and this was accompanied by a motion for an *ex parte* order for interim custody and exclusive possession of the matrimonial home on 15th May 1989, which was granted until the return date of these motions.

In seeking interim custody of the children and interim exclusive possession of the matrimonial home, the husband alleges that the wife has been extremely abusive towards the daughter and that she has exhibited some violence towards the daughter and himself. Counsel for the husband indicated that the party that was granted interim exclusive possession of the matrimonial home should also have interim custody of the children in that it is in the best interests of the children to remain in the matrimonial home. The wife states that the husband has grossly exaggerated the argument with the daughter and says that her disciplinary measures on that occasion were no more grievous than disciplinary measures imposed by the husband on previous occasions, none of which the wife classifies as child abuse.

The materials disclose that on 30th April 1989 the mother, feeling that Aaren had lied to her about attending dancing classes and feeling that the daughter was being insolent, attempted to hit her across the buttocks with a wooden dancing stick. Inadvertently the daughter was hit across the hand. The mother then held the daughter by the neck, but without pressure, so that she could speak to her. There is nothing to substantiate the husband's claim that the child's head was hit against the wall, causing a lump. The next afternoon the school called to say that Aaren was sick to her stomach and should be picked up.

The next day the daughter was again sick to her stomach, with the father stating the cause to be that the mother expressed a hatred for the child, whereas the mother states that the illness was caused because the husband countermanded her order and permitted the daughter to go to a soccer practice.

The material discloses certain other incidents between mother and daughter concerning the doing of homework, going skiing, and the use of strong language which I considered to be anything but supportive of extreme child abuse.

The parties' descriptions of the pushing and shoving as described in their supplementary affidavits do not contain that element of violence or volatility that would prompt a court to exclude either one from the matrimonial home. ...

Section 19(1) of the *Family Law Act* provides that both spouses have an equal right to possession of a matrimonial home. In seeking interim exclusive possession of the home, there is an onus on the party claiming exclusive possession to satisfy the court that the criteria as set out in s. 24(3) of the *Family Law Act* exist so as to warrant the making of such an order. The husband relies upon his allegations of violence committed by the wife against himself and the daughter. I do not categorize the disciplinary measures which the wife employed against the daughter as being acts of violence of a type that should exclude a mother from a matrimonial home. Similarly, the confrontations between husband and wife which involved some pushing and shoving by both parties can hardly be classified as acts of violence. The husband also relies upon the best interests of the children. It may very well be in the best interests of the children to continue to reside in the matrimonial home but this factor only applies to exclusive possession of the home where the person claiming it has interim custody of the children.

With respect to the issue of interim custody, I find that both motions have some merit; however, it would not be in the best interests of the children to be under the custody, care and control of any one parent under the present circumstances at this stage of the proceedings. I do not consider the wife's disciplinary actions against the daughter to be abusive so as to deprive her of her right to custody of the children, by finding that the best interests of the children lie with the father. The parties have done a good job of sharing the task of raising the children and, in the absence of an interim custody order by this court, the parties will continue to have joint custody, care and control of the children pending the trial of this matter.

An interim custody order, along with interim exclusive possession of the matrimonial home, based on the materials filed, appears to be more calculated towards the gaining of a tactical legal advantage as opposed to determining what is in the best interests of the children. The court should not allow this to take place. Neither party should have to consider himself a failure at this point, nor should there be a winner-loser mentality at this early stage. In this case, neither party has persuaded the court as to the relative merits of their claims for interim custody and interim possession.

The mother should not be excluded from the matrimonial home or deprived of custody based on the materials filed by the husband.

Accordingly, there will be no order as to custody and both motions with respect to interim possession of the matrimonial home are hereby dismissed. The status quo which prevailed prior to the *ex parte* order of 15th May 1989 is therefore restored. Hopefully the parties, in sharing the matrimonial home and the custody of the children, will see fit to live in tranquility pending trial. In this regard there will be an order that the parties:

(1) not dissipate any assets;

(2) not molest, harass or annoy each other or the children; [and]

(3) subject themselves to a psychological assessment.

There is no reason why the parties cannot get this matter ready for trial in short order. ...

DYCK v. DYCK

(2005), 2005 CarswellSask 379 (Q.B. [In Chambers])

BAYNTON J.:

1 The parties were married on May 29, 1999 in Melfort, Saskatchewan. They have resided at 717 Murray Crescent in Warman, Saskatchewan since May 2000 where they now live with their three children, Kadin Gerald James Dyck, born September 8, 2001 and Daylin Nelson Dyck and Rylan Neil Dyck, both born September 2, 2003. In November 2000, the father was seriously injured in an automobile accident and continues to suffer from the injuries he received in it and a subsequent accident in December 2004. Early in 2004, the mother established a spa and tanning business in Melfort. In January of 2005, with the assistance of the father, she opened a spa in Warman.

2 Although there is considerable dispute in the evidence over the issue of how much time the mother spends in Melfort each week, it appears that she has been spending at least two or more days plus every other weekend in Melfort attending to her business there. The father spends a couple of days a week attending to the Warman business. Because of his injuries, he has not otherwise been employed and has been more available to attend to the children in the home than has been the mother. In November of 2004, the parents hired a nanny to assist with the care of the children. The father says this was done to enable him to spend some time at the Warman business. The mother says that it was done because the father could not look after the children without assistance.

3 The parents have not been getting along. On May 9, 2005, the dispute escalated into an incident which resulted in the mother obtaining an emergency intervention order under *The Victims of Domestic Violence Act*, S.S. 1994, c. V-6.02. The father was evicted from the home and was prohibited from communicating with the mother or the three children for a period of 30 days. A rehearing respecting that order was directed and in a lengthy fiat dated May 26, 2005, Madam Justice M.-E. Wright confirmed the order but varied it so that it did not pertain to the three children. I consider that her findings of fact constitute issue estoppel and in any event are adopted by me in accordance with the principle of comity. She continued the order primarily on the ground that the complainant subjectively perceived that she would be physically harmed, not on the nature of the conduct of the respondent. The order

expires today. The three children have not seen their father since May 9, 2005 except for two brief periods.

4 Each of the parties have applied for various forms of relief. The father applies for an order for the exclusive possession of the matrimonial residence and for an order that the three children continue to reside in it with him. He does so on the ground that he has been the children's primary caregiver as a stay at home dad. ... The mother applies for interim custody of the three children, for exclusive possession of the matrimonial residence and household goods and for an interim restraining order against the father respecting herself, the residence and the two businesses. ...

7 There is no further basis for the restraining order that is sought by the mother. Her application respecting it is dismissed. It is imperative that the parents co-operate and communicate with one another, either directly or through their respective counsel, to ensure that the value of the two ongoing businesses are not put in jeopardy by their ongoing matrimonial dispute.

8 The primary issue I must determine is which parent shall have exclusive possession of the matrimonial residence in Warman. ... In the case before me, the resolution of this matter will have a significant impact on which parent will be the one who provides the children with their primary residence. The mother wants the father out of the residence and given the status of an access parent. The father proposes an interim "nesting" arrangement under which both parents would have exclusive but separate access to the residence. He offers to vacate the residence for a couple of days a week and on alternate weekends to permit the mother to be with the children in the home on the days she is not in Melfort where she is required to stay overnight. He submits that this arrangement would disrupt the children as little as possible in the interim until a more permanent solution can be worked out.

9 Both parents claim to be the primary parent of the three children and that this "status quo" should be maintained. In the rather unique circumstances of this case where the mother has more work related responsibilities outside the home than does the father, each claim is credible. The substantial body of affidavit evidence adduced by and on behalf of each of them is conflicting to say the least. It is impossible to determine this issue without the benefit of a trial. To the credit of the parties, their counsel have agreed to co-operate to obtain an expedited home study at the expense of the parents. Conceivably, the recommendations of such a study could be available to the parties and to the court within the next month or two if a privately funded assessor is utilized.

10 Although I doubt that a "nesting" arrangement is seldom a feasible solution, it has been ordered in other cases in several instances. It is an extension of the concept of shared parenting. ...

11 The "nesting" aspect of shared parenting appears to be predicated on the theory that it is better to inconvenience the parents than the children by requiring the parents to come and go to the children rather than requiring the children to come and go to the respective parents. ...

12 One of the primary objectives of a chambers judge facing a host of interim applications on the heels of a separation, is to redirect the focus of the litigants. The desire to punish one another and the fear of the unknown in the future, drive such litigants to seek control of their lives by getting an interim court ruling in their favour. This interim ruling is often used by the "winning" parent to restrict the access of the other parent to the children or to take positions that are contrary to the best interests of the children. It often "sets the stage" for what will follow even though the ruling may be based on unreliable and conflicting evidence that has not been tested and verified by means of a trial. Instead of focussing their efforts and resources on winning an interim application, litigants are better advised to focus on arriving at a more permanent and rational resolution that maximizes the best interests of all those involved.

13 This approach is certainly in the best interests of the children, the ones who are most affected by the litigation yet have no say in it. It is for this reason in this particular case, that I decline to make an order that will escalate the conflict rather than dampen it. The order I intend to make will put each of the parents "on trial". Their conduct toward one another and toward their children will be open to scrutiny by the assessor and by the court if the matter is not resolved short of a trial or a pre-trial conference. Another compelling reason in this case to attempt to dampen the conflict is to preserve the two ongoing businesses so that their value will remain available to the parents and indirectly to the children. If the parents engage in a prolonged and high level conflict that precludes co-operation with one another respecting the operation of the businesses, those businesses are almost certain to fail.

14 I am satisfied that this is one of those cases where, until a home study can be completed, a "nesting" arrangement of shared parenting will work and will be in the best interests of the children. Although what I will order is not what either parent seeks, it will provide the least disruption to the children until cooler heads can prevail. It is also better for each parent than an order that the other parent have the exclusive possession of the residence and the primary residence of the children. If either of the parents fail to make the "nesting" arrangement work, particulars of that failure will be available to the home study assessor and to the court.

15 If the parents through their counsel are able to work out the particulars of the "nesting" arrangement and reduce it to writing, that arrangement shall prevail. Failing such an agreement, and until further order, the three children shall continue to reside in the matrimonial residence and the parents will split the exclusive possession of the residence on a one and three period schedule. It attempts to suit the Melfort work schedule of the mother yet provide the children with the benefit of each parent being in the home no less than 13 days of each four week period. It will also provide the father with one full weekend in the residence with the children.

16 On the first period following this fiat commencing on June 15, the father shall have exclusive possession of the residence for five days and nights from Wednesday at 9:00 a.m. until Monday at 8:00 a.m. and the mother shall have exclusive possession for the following day and night from Monday at 9:00 a.m. to Tuesday at 8:00 a.m. On the second, third and fourth periods following this fiat, the father shall have exclusive possession for three days and nights from Tuesday at 9:00 a.m. to Friday at 8:00 a.m. and the mother shall have exclusive possession for four days and nights from Friday at 9:00 a.m. to Tuesday at 8:00 a.m. The one and three periods will continue to repeat until the "nesting" arrangement is terminated.

17 The one-hour intervals between the exclusive possession periods will provide the parents with a sufficient degree of separation to enable them to leave and enter the residence without meeting one another and risking a confrontation. They will have to make arrangements with the nanny or family members to ensure that the children are supervised during these one-hour intervals. The father has gratuitously agreed to sleep elsewhere in the house and not to enter the master bedroom at any time so that it will be exclusively available to the mother. She is granted leave to change the locks or to otherwise secure it as she deems advisable.

18 Unless otherwise agreed in writing between the parents and until further order, their access to the children with one exception shall be restricted to those times that coincide with their respective periods of exclusive possession of the residence. Each parent shall have telephone access to the children for a period not exceeding 15 minutes between the hours of 7:00 and 8:00 p.m. on any evening. This shall not preclude a parent from taking the children

out of the residence on an outing during this time provided it is not done so regularly as to preclude reasonable telephone access.

VOLLMER v. VOLLMER

(1998), 1998 CarswellOnt 1819 (Ont. Gen. Div.)

[The husband and wife had been living in separate households within the matrimonial home for at least two years. In affidavits that had not yet been tested by cross-examination, each accused the other of being verbally abusive and threatening. Each had called the police on one occasion. The wife's two children, a girl aged 17 from a previous relationship and a boy aged 7, lived in the home also.]

AITKEN J.: — ... The parties are in agreement that Ms. Vollmer will have custody of both children and will provide their primary residence. They also agree that the matrimonial home should be listed for sale and sold as quickly as possible. These are very important factors which affect my determination of whether Ms. Vollmer should be given interim exclusive possession of the matrimonial home. ...

Although the evidence regarding the parties' conduct is contradictory in terms of whose behaviour is more aggressive or abusive, both are alleging behaviour which if witnessed by the children would be harmful to their well-being. Children are entitled to live in an environment where they are not being constantly exposed to anger, hostility, lack of respect, stress and fear. There are enough allegations in the affidavits of both parties to suggest that this is the environment in which Matthew and Agata are now residing. Being exposed to such an environment is not in their best interests.

There is no suggestion that either Agata or Matthew want to reside with Mr. Vollmer. Both are in the middle of their school year and it would be disruptive for the children to move until the end of their school year.

Ms. Vollmer does not have any family in the Ottawa area with whom she can stay. Mr. Vollmer has his parents and two brothers in the area. Although he states he could not stay with either his parents or his brothers, I assume that they could offer some assistance on a very short-term basis. ...

An order for interim exclusive possession of a matrimonial home should not be given lightly when it will have the effect of forcing one party out of the matrimonial home. The court must be concerned with giving one party an inappropriate advantage over the other party in terms of a claim for custody or access or in terms of a claim for exclusive possession or eventual ownership of a matrimonial home. The court must also be concerned with putting too great a financial burden on a family.

In this case, the parties agree that Ms. Vollmer will have custody of the two children. Mr. Vollmer is not seeking equal time sharing for either of the children. All he wants is reasonable, unsupervised access to Matthew and the right to be consulted on major decisions affecting Matthew. He acknowledges that Agata will have whatever contact with himself that she wishes. An order granting Ms. Vollmer interim exclusive possession of the matrimonial home would not prejudice the access rights he is seeking.

The parties agree that the matrimonial home is to be listed for sale and sold as quickly as possible. Therefore an interim order for exclusive possession of the matrimonial home would be a temporary measure in effect only until the home can be sold and would not give either party any advantage in terms of any claim for long-term exclusive possession of the matrimonial home or eventual ownership of the home.

In all of these circumstances, and for the primary purpose of protecting the children from living on a daily basis in an environment of anger, stress and possible violence, I order Mr.

Vollmer to move out of the matrimonial home by May 1st, 1998. Thereafter, Ms. Vollmer will have interim exclusive possession of the matrimonial home until its sale. ...

KOONING v. KOONING

(2005), 2005 CarswellOnt 3539 (Ont. S.C.J.)

TULLOCH J.:

1 Based on the materials filed and submissions of counsel, I am satisfied that this mater proceed by way of a motion prior to a case conference being held due to the urgency of the current situation.

Overview

2 The parties were married for a ten-year period and have been separated since either January 2005, according to the applicant [wife], or June 20, 2005, according to the respondent. In any event, on June 20, 2005, the applicant moved out of the matrimonial home and the respondent was charged with criminal harassment as against her.

3 The parties are the parents of three children, all of whom are currently residing with the applicant at her mother's residence. The respondent continues to reside in the matrimonial home. ...

6 The applicant submits that during the marriage she has been subjected to psychological, emotional and verbal abuse which eventually culminated in frightening and irrational behaviour on the part of the respondent. This resulted in criminal harassment charges being laid against him. She submits that as a parent, the respondent was uninvolved in the raring [sic] of his children. ...

7 She submits that she should be given sole custody of the children with reasonable access to the respondent; as well, that she and the children should be allowed to return to the matrimonial home and have exclusive possession of the matrimonial home.

8 The respondent, on the other hand, contests the position taken by the applicant and submits that the applicant moved out of the matrimonial home on June 20, 2005 and is currently living in a home that she co-owns with her mother. He submits that he has no alternative accommodations available to him if he is ordered out of the matrimonial home.

9 He further submits that he has been a fully involved co-parent to the children and so he should be given joint custody of the children. In the interim he wants an order for the appointment of Janice King Watson to conduct an investigation and report to the Court. ...

Analysis

10 The first issue that I will deal with is that of the exclusive possession of the matrimonial home. Section 24(3) of the *Family Law Act* outlines the criteria which must be considered. ...

11 In the case at hand, I find that it would be in the best interest of the children affected for them to be back in the matrimonial home. The ages of the children are 14 years for the oldest, William Jeffery, and 11 years for the twins, John Patrick and Andrew Michael. The children should remain in the matrimonial home until the home can be sold as this will enable them to remain in a familiar environment, maintain their established friendships and resume attending the same school. This, I feel, would cause minimal disruptive effects to them. I also accept as a fact that the applicant mother has been the primary caregiver of the

children throughout the marriage. As such the primary residence of the children should be with her. In light of the acrimony between the parties and the resultant criminal charges, I feel that it is necessary for the parties to remain separate and apart. The applicant and the children will therefore be allowed to move back into the matrimonial home and the respondent will have to find alternate accommodations. ...

12 Accordingly, I will make the following interim, interim order: ...

> 2. The primary residence of the children of the marriage shall be with their mother, the applicant.

> 3. The applicant shall have exclusive possession of the matrimonial home until the home is sold. The respondent shall vacate the matrimonial home within seven days of this order.

> 4. The respondent father shall have reasonable access of the children of the marriage on reasonable notice. The matter of access may be revisited by either party upon confirmation of the father's new residence. Either party may bring the matter back into Court on four days notice to address the issue of access. ...

HILL v. HILL

(1987), 10 R.F.L. (3d) 225, 1987 CarswellOnt 238 (Ont. Dist. Ct.)

FITZGERALD D.C.J.: — The parties to this proceeding are the applicant wife and the respondent husband. Under the *Family Law Act* the wife, aged 69, seeks interim relief from her husband of the same age by way of exclusive possession of the matrimonial house, support and costs. There is no lack of money available in the short term to either party but it is apparent that the husband's business is the major asset and income producer in a marriage which lasted some 40 years. Within two years of marriage in August 1947, the wife gave up her employment as a clerk and has since devoted herself to running the matrimonial house and raising two sons born in 1951 and 1954.

The husband formed his own business firm in 1950. At first the wife assisted in that business but after the birth of the second child ceased to be active in the firm. The business has prospered. The parties enjoyed a generous lifestyle but their interests diverged. Mrs. Hill devoted her energies to the house while Mr. Hill devoted his to the business. Eventually Mrs. Hill indicated that she would seek a separation.

The response to this was delivery to Mrs. Hill by one of her sons of a handwritten statement of what would happen if she proceeded with her intention. These included:

> We will evict you from house and cottage

> You will have no money for 2 or 3 years until support awarded

> You will die penniless and be buried in an indigent grave ...

> You will be up against ... best lawyers — money no object — we are going to drag this out

> No more medical payments by G.O. Hill

> We will take the car away

> How are you going to pay litigation costs?

It is apparent that "we" refers to Mr. Hill and at least one of his sons. The effect of this document was intimidating in the extreme and constitutes harassment of a particularly invidious character.

In addition on this application two affidavits were sworn by friends of Mrs. Hill who, since the separation was contemplated, received anonymous notes identified by a handwriting expert as being written by Mr. Hill. These vindictive missives are of some relevance in support of Mrs. Hill's contention that her husband has undertaken a deliberate campaign of what I regard as psychological warfare against her and her friends in the hope of undermining her resolve to obtain a fair settlement on separation. ...

Meanwhile the wife alleges that she continues to be harassed by the husband and that his conduct and attitude have driven her to seek psychiatric help. This harassment has been subtle. It consisted of changing the pattern of delivery of money for household and personal expenses as well as the delay in coming to grips with the legal proceedings.

On the other hand Mr. Hill did pay all the usual household expenses and did continue to supply Mrs. Hill with money. He spent only part of his time in the matrimonial home preferring to spend his time at the family cottage. He did use the home for his noon hour siesta and slept there some week nights. She reports that he frequently tells her such things as "the judge and the lawyers say you are crazy to leave me" and "The judge is going to send you to an asyilum [*sic*] where you will be locked up for several months and observed through a one-way mirror". As a result of such actions and his underhand communications with her friends, the wife has begun to fear what her husband may do next and has begun absenting herself from home when he is there. Now that winter is approaching he will probably spend more time at home.

The report of Dr. Sheppard indicates that anxiety over the domestic situation, while not a cause of her neck pain, is a contributing factor. He says: "I believe that the continued cohabitation of Mrs. Hill and her husband is having a detrimental effect on her psychological state" and "since her decision to separate ... the symptoms have been worse". ...

In the short term both parties have the financial resources to find alternate accommodation. I find it is *not* feasible for the two of them to occupy the same dwelling having regard to the psychological warfare being waged by the husband against the wife and its effect upon her. Which of them should give up the house? ...

As to para. (c) [of s. 24(3) of the *Family Law Act*], the husband is worth at least $2 3/4 million and has available cash exceeding $150,000. The wife is worth $275,000 including cash of $39,000. If she is to maintain her lifestyle and finance an action involving the valuations necessary to a successful prosecution of her claim she can least afford to move.

As to para. (e) there is no evidence whatever from either party except that the respondent husband's two sons have physical room for his accommodation.

Paragraph (f) refers to "violence". In my view the violence in this context must be such that it makes continuation of joint cohabitation in the matrimonial dwelling impractical. Violence in my view includes psychological assault upon the sensibilities of the other spouse to a degree which renders continued sharing of the matrimonial dwelling impractical. Where, as here, the conduct of the husband in written and spoken communication to the wife is calculated to produce and does in fact produce an anxiety state which puts the wife in fear of her husband's behaviour and impinges on her mental and physical health, violence has been done to her emotional equilibrium as surely as if she had been struck by a physical blow. ...

In my view the sense and purpose of the *Family Law Act*, which is a remedial statute and hence to be liberally construed, must surely include in the meaning of violence that violence causing injury to a spouse which can be achieved by words and deeds and is not restricted to the violence which can be achieved solely by physical abuse. ...

In my view it is the conduct of Mr. Hill which has rendered the matrimonial home incapable of being shared. His is the lesser emotional attachment to the home. His is the lesser continuous use of the home. He will be the least inconvenienced by finding alternate accommodation. His are the greater resources to do so. ...

For all the foregoing reasons it is "an equitable settlement of the affairs of the spouses" (preamble to the Act) that Mrs. Hill have interim exclusive possession of the matrimonial home and contents and I so order. ...

McLEOD, "ANNOTATION"

(1987), 10 R.F.L. (3d) 225

In *Hill v. Hill* FitzGerald D.C.J. takes the unusual course of making an order for interim exclusive possession which has the effect of ordering the husband out of the home. Although there is no question that the court has power to make such orders, the power appears to be rarely exercised. In fact, the analysis adopted and conclusion reached probably accord with the expectations of most people.

In effect, FitzGerald D.C.J. held that it is appropriate to make an order for interim exclusive possession where, on the facts, continued cohabitation is intolerable. In such circumstances if no order is made the weaker party will be forced to leave. In deciding whether continued cohabitation is intolerable the cruelty jurisprudence under the *Divorce Act* ... would seem to be relevant.

In deciding whether the requirements of s. 24 of the *Family Law Act* ... have been met, FitzGerald D.C.J. held that "violence" is not restricted to physical violence but includes emotional and psychological harm. It would seem that any deliberate conduct that makes home life impossible or threatens the security of the other spouse falls within the concept of "violence" and justifies an order for exclusive possession.

Having decided that continued cohabitation is physically impossible and that one of the parties is in an unequal position, the court must decide who should receive possession. The easy answer would be that the "innocent" party should remain and the guilty party should leave. Such a simple causal link may not, however, reflect the reality of the entire marriage. FitzGerald D.C.J. has adopted a more neutral analysis focusing on which of the parties has the greater need for the home and which party is better able to function without the home. To decide these questions the court must take into account the emotional and physical state of the parties, the financial situation of the parties and the roles adopted in marriage. ...

CICERO v. CICERO

(1978), 1 F.L.R.A.C. 49, 1978 CarswellOnt 76 (Ont. U.F.C.)

GRAVELY U.F.C.J.: — ... There is a very serious dispute about what is to happen to the matrimonial home. Mrs. Cicero wants to live there with the children without her husband being present and Mr. Cicero wants the place sold and the proceeds divided equally.

It seems clear on the evidence that the parties are unable to live together in the same place, at least at the present time. It is clear also that the property is a jointly owned home and is a family asset within the meaning of that term in the *Family Law Reform Act. Prima facie,* then the husband is entitled to realize on his interest in the home and have it sold unless an order is made under s. 45 of the Act [the predecessor section of s. 24 of the *Family Law Act*].

I have carefully considered all of the evidence that was presented and I am satisfied that in this case the only reasonable disposition is an order for exclusive possession under s. 45 of the Act. ...

This house is a modest house, probably the most modest, I would think, that could accommodate this family. The three bedrooms are occupied, one of them by an older child who is unable to remove himself from the care of his mother because of his medical condition.

The family has its roots in this area of the city. This is an Italian community and the children have known no other area. The children are near the school and they come home for lunch. The wife's relatives are nearby and can provide assistance to the wife as she may need it and it may be that that assistance might eventually extend to babysitting if the wife is able to find employment in the future.

There is no suggestion that there is any suitable alternative accommodation.

I am satisfied that it would not be in the interests of the children for the present situation to be changed in the reasonably foreseeable future and that it would be to their benefit to remain in the matrimonial home.

In regard to the economics of the situation, this property has been paid for. The maintenance is low. Even insofar as Mr. Cicero is concerned, I am not satisfied that his interests would be helped substantially by any sale of the premises.

He should understand that the order I am going to make does not provide for any change of the title. His interest in the property is still there and at some future time he can realize on that interest, perhaps at a profit.

There will be an order under s. 45 for exclusive possession of the matrimonial home in Mrs. Cicero. I do not propose at this time to attach a time limit to the possession order. The section provides for such an order to extend for life, but circumstances could change at any time, and, if so, a variation or a discharge order may be made under s. 46 of the Act. ...

ROSENTHAL v. ROSENTHAL

(1986), 3 R.F.L. (3d) 126, 1986 CarswellOnt 288 (Ont. H.C.)

McMAHON L.J.S.C.: — ... The matrimonial home is located as I have indicated at 1905 Labelle Street, in the city of Windsor. By agreement of counsel, its estimated value is $130,000 with a present mortgage of $85,000 to $86,000.

The three sons are residing with the petitioner [the wife] in this home. Michael is in attendance at St. Clair College, and pursuant to the minutes of settlement that were formulated into the decree nisi, the respondent is paying $300 a month toward the support and maintenance of Michael [aged 21]. Jeffrey and Mark [aged 21 and 23 respectively], although not working, are in receipt of income, one through Unemployment Insurance, and the other as a result of a work related injury. Both of these young men are paying to their mother the sum of $30 per week; however, in her financial statement, the petitioner has indicated that the cost of groceries is $175 per week. It is quite clear that the amount being paid for room and board does not even cover the individual cost of groceries to each of these young people.

They are accordingly being subsidized by their parents. The shelter costs, as indicated by the material filed, would include the monthly mortgage payment, the taxes, the utilities, the insurance, and annual repairs. On a monthly basis, this results in a cost of some $1,541.50. ...

Certainly, Mark and Jeffrey cannot be considered to be children affected by this application. As I have indicated by agreement, the respondent is already paying the sum of $300 for the support of Michael so that he might continue his education.

Paragraphs (b), (d), (e) and (f) [of s. 24(3) of the *Family Law Act*] in my view have no application to support the claim for exclusive possession by the wife.

The respondent is presently residing in a one-bedroom apartment, paying rent in the amount of $600 per month.

There is no question that Mrs. Rosenthal finds herself to be the aggrieved party in this unfortunate situation. The evidence of her doctor, heard by the court as a result of an application for an adjournment, clearly identifies the emotional stress that the petitioner is suffering as a result of the marital breakdown. However, the court must be bound by the provisions of the statute.

Mrs. Rosenthal in her evidence stated quite clearly that in her view, her choice of living standards should not in any way be affected by her husband's situation. This, of course, is an entirely unrealistic view of the result of a marital breakdown.

It is axiomatic that two people can live cheaper together than they can apart and this is something that Mrs. Rosenthal unfortunately must face. Her attempts to maintain the standard at which she was living prior to the marital breakdown must be viewed in the light of the moneys that are available to maintain that standard. Even during cohabitation, it is apparent that these two parties were living beyond their means, despite the relatively large joint income enjoyed by them. When one considers the financial statements filed by both parties, it becomes readily apparent that there are not sufficient funds to continue the occupation of the marital home.

Pursuant to the provisions of the statute, each party is entitled to a one-half interest in the matrimonial home. In order to have the court set aside that statutory right of the respondent, Mrs. Rosenthal must establish on the balance of probabilities that she falls within the provisions of s. 24(3). On the totality of the evidence, she has failed to satisfy the court that she has met this requirement. Unfortunate as it may be, it is the view of the court that the present situation cannot continue and it is in the best interest of both parties that the matrimonial home be sold for the best available price and that the excess moneys would, in accordance with the statute, be divided between them and form a portion of each net family property.

This will, of course, require Mrs. Rosenthal to acquire other accommodations, be it an apartment or a less expensive dwelling, either by rental or ownership. It is, of course, laudable that Mrs. Rosenthal might wish to have the three sons continue to reside with her. If that is their choice, then of course the sons, who are in receipt of income, would be required to pay their fair share of maintaining such accommodation.

The court is cognizant of the adverse effect that this determination will have upon Mrs. Rosenthal; however, as I have indicated, the court is bound by the provisions of the statute. There is no legal obligation upon this respondent to maintain Mark and Jeffrey in a style to which they have been accustomed. It is, for example, noted that each of the three boys owns and operates their own motor vehicle, as does Mrs. Rosenthal. To require Mr. Rosenthal to pay for the continuing occupation of the family unit in the matrimonial home would in effect be requiring him to support and maintain both Mark and Jeffrey under the present circumstances. Even apart from that, I am satisfied after review of the financial statements filed by both parties, that Mr. Rosenthal is entirely incapable of paying the amount that would be required to continue their occupancy of the matrimonial home at the price that I have indicated.

NOTES AND QUESTIONS

1. How are the issues of custody and exclusive possession inter-related? Why might a court be reluctant to determine these issues on an interim basis, especially when the couple is still living under the same roof?

2. For other examples of court-ordered "nesting" arrangements, see *Squitti v. Squitti* (March 6, 1995), Doc. # Thunder Bay 84-95 (Ont. Gen. Div.) digested at [1995] W.D.F.L. 869 (Ont. Gen. Div.) and *Blumer v. Blumer* (2004), 1 R.F.L. (6th) 16 (B.C. S.C.).

3. In *Kutlesa v. Kutlesa* (2008), 2008 CarswellOnt 1657, 52 R.F.L. (6th) 164 (S.C.J.), Justice Pazaratz relied on *Hill v. Hill* to hold that "violence" can include "psychological warfare" and "intimidation and emotional abuse".

The court issued a temporary exclusive possession order where a husband wished to return to a "nanny suite" in the matrimonial home some 15 months after separation. He had left threatening text messages for his wife, who had mental issues that were aggravated by his aggressiveness, in an apparent attempt to intimidate her into a settlement.

4. As noted earlier in considering the position of unmarried cohabitees, several provinces have enacted legislation to provide emergency relief for married and unmarried persons where there is domestic violence. Typically, the remedies include an order requiring a respondent to vacate a residence or an order granting an applicant temporary exclusive possession of a residence. Such legislation usually permits short-term orders without notice to the other party (*ex parte* orders) where family violence has occurred and the circumstances are serious or urgent. Police officers may be specifically directed to remove the other party from the residence. See *Protection Against Family Violence Act*, R.S.A. 2000, c. P-27; *The Domestic Violence and Stalking Act*, C.C.S.M., c. D93; *Domestic Violence Intervention Act*, S.N.S. 2001, c. 29; *Victims of Family Violence Act*, R.S.P.E.I. 1988, c. V-3.2; and *The Victims of Domestic Violence Act*. S.S. 1994, c. V-6.02. Similar legislation was enacted in Ontario as the *Domestic Violence Protection Act, 2000*, S.O. 2000, c. 33, but it was never proclaimed into force and would be repealed by Bill 133.

Court-ordered eviction from one's home without an opportunity to present evidence or argument obviously raises concerns regarding procedural fairness. See *C.(A.L.G.) v. Prince Edward Island* (1998), 157 D.L.R. (4th) 523 (P.E.I.T.D.), where certain aspects of Prince Edward Island's legislation were found to infringe s. 7 of the *Charter*. See also *Dolgopol v. Dolgopol* (1995), 127 Sask. R. 237 (Q.B.) and *Bella v. Bella* (1995), 132 Sask. R. 17 (Q.B.) where the reviewing judges concluded that the justices of the peace had acted in the absence of the urgency needed for *ex parte* orders.

5. Where one spouse finds it necessary to seek an interim exclusive possession order, it may be prudent in some circumstances to also obtain an order under s. 46 of the *Family Law Act* restraining the other spouse from molesting, annoying or harassing the applicant. Regarding restraining orders and their enforcement, see *Scono v. Scono* (1984), 41 R.F.L. (2d) 57 (Ont. H.C.); *Colley v. Colley* (1991), 31 R.F.L. (3d) 281 (Ont. U.F.C.); *Hamilton v. Hamilton* (1996), 92 O.A.C. 103 (C.A.); *Chau v. Jiang (Guardian of)* (1997), 34 R.F.L. (4th) 249 (Alta. Q.B.); *Cole v. Cole* (1998), 40 R.F.L. (4th) 54 (Ont. Gen. Div.); and *Ciffolillo v. Nieweglowski* (2007), 2007 CarswellOnt 6695 (S.C.J.).

Bill 133 would repeal the existing s. 46 and replace it with a new provision that would, *inter alia*, clarify the criteria required for a restraining order, make breach of an order a criminal offence, and ensure that orders are in a standard form that would make them easier to understand and enforce.

6. Financial circumstances are likely to militate against long-term orders for exclusive possession in many situations. In addition to *Rosenthal*, see *Norlander v. Norlander* (1989), 21 R.F.L. (3d) 317 (Sask. Q.B.); *Venslovaitis v. Venslovaitis* (1989), 1989 CarswellOnt 1347 (Ont. H.C.); *Balogh v. Balogh* (1996), 24 R.F.L. (4th) 181 (Ont. C.A.); *Dolman v. Dolman* (1998), 38 R.F.L. (4th) 362 (Ont. Gen. Div.); and *Harbour v. Harbour* (2000), 6 R.F.L. (5th) 225 (Ont. S.C.J.). In *Venslovaitis*, Morrissey J. stated (at para. 40):

> It has not been established that a move from the matrimonial home would have disruptive effects. The evidence satisfies me that the two younger children are good students and suffer from no physical, emotional or learning disability. They will, in my opinion, be able to adapt to new surroundings. The respondent failed to prove that there was no other suitable and affordable accommodation available for the respondent and the two children in her care. The matrimonial home's equity represents a substantial asset in which both parties have an interest. It would be unfair to the petitioner to withhold from him his interest in this major asset since the capital is required by him to set up another residence. The proceeds of the sale will likewise assist the respondent in setting up another residence.

Where there is no need to sell the home to realize its capital value and the parties can afford the carrying charges, a court will more readily delay sale and make an exclusive possession order. See, e.g., *Elliot v. Elliot* (1995), 10 R.F.L. (4th) 424 (Ont. Gen. Div.).

7. The cases generally suggest that, before a court will order exclusive possession overriding ownership rights for any significant period based on the best interests of a child, there must be some evidence to indicate that a move will significantly disrupt the life of the particular child or children involved. An example is *Crane v. Crane* (1986), 3 R.F.L. (3d) 428 (Ont. H.C.). The husband had custody of two children. He sought an order for exclusive possession of the jointly owned matrimonial home for two years so that the youngest child could continue attending the local elementary school. Mossop L.J.S.C. ordered the home sold and the proceeds divided. He stated (at 433-434): "The evidence relating to the criteria to be considered by the court in the legislation is either non-existent or very sparse in the case at bar so I must assume that there will be no great negative effects to the parties or the children in

refusing to grant exclusive possession to the husband as he requests." See also *Silver v. Silver* (1984), 41 R.F.L. (2d) 344 (Ont. H.C.); affirmed (1985), 49 R.F.L. (2d) 148 (Ont. C.A.); *Hart v. Hart* (1985), 46 R.F.L. (2d) 274 (Nfld. U.F.C.); *Nicol v. Nicol* (1989), 21 R.F.L. (3d) 236 (Ont. H.C.); and *Scanlan v. Scanlan* (1990), 25 R.F.L. (3d) 241 (Ont. H.C.).

In *James v. James* (1994), 3 R.F.L. (4th) 226 (Ont. Gen. Div.), Walsh J. granted indefinite exclusive possession of the matrimonial home to the wife who had custody of three children. He reasoned (at 230):

> As the children have all continuously resided in the home since 1987 and are now well settled into the neighbourhood with friends and schools close by, and given the difficulties disclosed in the official Guardian's report [the children were angry and needed counselling to help them re-establish a relationship with their father], the best interests of the children clearly require that they remain in the matrimonial home and be sheltered from the disruptive effects of a forced move to new surroundings, new schools, and new friends for as long a period as possible.

See also *Elliot v. Elliot* (1995), 10 R.F.L. (4th) 424 (Ont. Gen. Div.) (exclusive possession to mother and two children until oldest child graduated from elementary school mainly because child had problems and would not adjust well to moving) and *Yeates v. Yeates* (2007), 2007 CarswellOnt 2107 (S.C.J.); affirmed (2008), 2008 CarswellOnt 3842 (C.A.); leave to appeal refused (2009), 2009 CarswellOnt 340, 2009 CarswellOnt 339 (S.C.C.) (exclusive possession to mother and three children for three years where oldest two children had special needs).

8. The courts are generally reluctant to grant long-term exclusive possession orders where an emotional attachment to the home appears to be the only factor favouring such an order. In *D. v. D.* (1979), 13 R.F.L. (2d) 279 (Man. C.A.), the husband sought partition and sale of a jointly-held matrimonial home that had been occupied by the wife since separation. The couple's children were now adults who lived on their own. The wife sought to retain possession on the basis that the home was a "symbol, a centre, a concourse for family gatherings" (at 281). The Manitoba Court of Appeal held that the trial judge had correctly ordered partition and sale. It stated (at 281):

> We have no doubt that this sentimental attachment is sincere and deeply felt. But ought it to prevail over the right of a joint tenant to obtain the benefit of an asset he owns, particularly when he has no other significant assets? To give effect to the wife's contention for keeping the home unsold could deny to the husband the fruits of this asset for years ahead, perhaps even for the span of the wife's lifetime.

Similarly, Justice H.M Pierce, citing *Balogh v. Balogh* (1996), 24 R.F.L. (4th) 181 (Ont. C.A.), emphasized in *Stemberger v. Stemberger* (2007), 42 R.F.L. (6th) 353 (Ont. S.C.J.), that there must be a compelling reason for granting a long-term exclusive possession order and that "the mere preference by the spouse to remain in the matrimonial home" does not suffice.

9. As noted by the Supreme Court of Canada in *Lamb v. Lamb* (1985), 46 R.F.L. (2d) 1, an exclusive possession order may affect the quantum of spousal support. If the dependent spouse is granted possession of a home, his or her financial needs may be significantly reduced as may be the means of the other spouse.

The relationship between the equalization claim under Part I of the *FLA* and an order for exclusive possession of a matrimonial home is perhaps less obvious, but often no less important. In particular, orders for possession in favour of a spouse who does not have an ownership interest in the home may affect the other spouse's ability to satisfy an equalization claim through the payment of a monetary sum. As a result, a court may use its power to delay payment of all or part of the equalization sum for a period up to ten years: *Porter v. Porter* (1986), 1 R.F.L. (3d) 12 (Ont. Dist. Ct.); *Nicol v. Nicol* (1989), 21 R.F.L. (3d) 236 (Ont. H.C.); and *Ward v. Ward* (1990), 26 R.F.L. (3d) 149 (Ont. C.A.). Some courts have used s. 9 to transfer the entire interest in the matrimonial home to one spouse as a means of satisfying part or all of the equalization sum. See, e.g., *Oliva v. Oliva* (1986), 2 R.F.L. (3d) 188 (Ont. H.C.); varied (1988), 12 R.F.L. (3d) 334 (Ont. C.A.); *McCutcheon v. McCutcheon* (1986), 2 R.F.L. (3d) 327 (Ont. Dist. Ct.); *Bell v. Bell* (2000), 6 R.F.L. (5th) 52 (Ont. S.C.J.); and *Harbour v. Harbour* (2000), 6 R.F.L. (5th) 225 (Ont. S.C.J.). However, such orders can only be made where the transfer of property is an appropriate means for satisfying the equalization payment. See *Hoar v. Hoar* (1993), 45 R.F.L. (3d) 105 (Ont. C.A.).

10. In *Derrickson v. Derrickson* (1986), 26 D.L.R. (4th) 175, the Supreme Court of Canada held that the provisions of the *Family Relations Act*, R.S.B.C. 1979, c. 121, relating to the ownership and possession of immovable property could not apply to lands on an Indian reserve. In the companion case of *Paul v. Paul* (1986), 26 D.L.R. (4th) 196 (S.C.C.), the court also concluded that exclusive possession orders relating to family residences on such lands could not be made under the provincial legislation. For analysis of these decisions, see Bartlett, "Indian Self-Government, Equality of the Sexes, and the Application of Provincial Matrimonial Property Laws" (1986), 5

Can. J. Fam. L. 188; Mossman, "Developments in Property Law: The 1985-86 Term" (1987), 9 Supreme Court L.R. 419 at 430 ff.; and Turpel, "Home/Land" (1991), 10 Can. J. Fam. L. 17.

Under the *First Nations Land Management Act*, S.C. 1999, c. 24, a First Nation that enters into a Framework Agreement on First Nation Land Management with the Government of Canada is required by s. 17(1) to "establish general rules and procedures, in cases of breakdown of marriage, respecting the use, occupation and possession of first nation land and the division of interests in first nation land". These rules are likely to deal with possession of a family residence and so fill the vacuum created by cases such as *Derrickson*.

Recently, the House of Commons gave first reading to a bill that, if enacted, would become the *Family Homes on Reserves and Matrimonial Interests or Rights Act*. This legislation was first introduced in March 2008. It received second reading and was referred to committee in May 2008, but died on the Order Paper before committee study began. The proposed legislation would provide a framework for all First Nations governed by the *Indian Act* to develop and adopt their own matrimonial property rules. The bill also sets forth a detailed regime that would apply in situations where First Nations did not adopt such rules. The rules in the default regime would impose restrictions on what the holder of a right or interest in a family home could do with it during the relationship, permit a court to make exclusive possession orders, and would provide for equal sharing of the value of a right or interest in a family home at the end of the relationship. The default regime would apply to married persons and common law partners. For analysis of and commentary on the proposed legislation, see Ruru, "Finding Solutions for the Legislative Gaps in Determining Rights to the Family Home on Colonially Defined Indigenous Lands" (2008), 41 U.B.C.L. Rev. 315.

11. A spouse's right to claim an exclusive possession order under the *FLA* is lost upon divorce. See *Miller v. Miller* (1996), 20 R.F.L. (4th) 191 (Ont. C.A.) and *Finnie v. Finnie* (December 21, 1998), Doc. Goderich 408/ 97 (Ont. Gen. Div.). These cases cast serious doubt on the suggestion in *Luyks v. Luyks* (1998), 38 R.F.L. (4th) 464 at 466 (Ont. Gen. Div.) that a court has the authority under s. 24 to grant possession to a non-owning widow beyond the period set in s. 26(2) of the FLA.

12. Where one spouse remains in the matrimonial home on separation without a court order and the other has an ownership interest in the property, the latter may later seek occupation rent. The spouse who stayed in the home may respond with a claim for reimbursement of expenses. The cases dealing with occupation rent are reviewed in *Higgins v. Higgins* (2001), 19 R.F.L. (5th) 300 (Ont. S.C.J.) and *Cripps v. Cripps* (2007), 2007 CarswellNB 10 (Q.B.). For a case involving a claim for occupation rent by an unmarried cohabitee, see *Howarth v. Doucette Estate* (2001), 2001 CarswellBC 1918 (B.C. S.C. [In Chambers]).

In *Szuflita v. Szuflita Estate* (2000), 4 R.F.L. (5th) 313 (Ont. S.C.J.); additional reasons at (2000), 2000 CarswellOnt 1792 (Ont. S.C.J.), an estate unsuccessfully claimed occupation rent when a widow stayed in the matrimonial home following the death of the owning husband.

4. Partition and Sale of a Family Home

Many married couples own the matrimonial home as joint tenants. As a result, the *Partition Act* may be relevant when the relationship breaks down. Section 2 of that Act provides that "all joint tenants" may apply for a division of the property they co-own. The *Partition Act* in Ontario can be traced back to 1868, to the British *Partition Act*. It, therefore, significantly pre-dates the *FLA* and was not designed specifically to address issues between spouses. Rather, it was, and is, a general statute that deals with the rights of all persons who own, or have an interest in, property together.

Section 10 of the *FLA* also authorizes orders for the partition of property owned jointly by married partners. Ontario courts have puzzled over which statute should be used in specific situations, and at what point in the family litigation. Can a spouse who is a joint owner invoke the *Partition Act* and ask the court to make an order for partition and sale of the matrimonial home before *FLA* proceedings have been completed? Or, does the *FLA* govern the division of property owned jointly by spouses? When, specifically, should s. 10 of the *FLA* be used?

The Ontario Court of Appeal discussed these issues in *Martin v. Martin* (1992), 39 R.F.L. (3d) 360. It held that s. 10 of the *FLA* is restricted to cases in which there is a real dispute about the ownership of the property. The kinds of disputes that arise between spouses are often trust claims (where one spouse is the titled owner, but the other claims a beneficial interest on the basis of a constructive or resulting trust). If there is such a dispute, s. 10 allows the court to determine title and then, if appropriate, resolve the dispute by ordering partition and sale of the property. As Professor McLeod pointed out in his annotation to *Martin*, it is difficult to see how a court could make an order for sale of jointly owned property before trial pursuant to s. 10. If there is a genuine dispute about ownership, the matter must be tried before any decision can be made about selling the property. And, if there is no genuine dispute about ownership of the property, s. 10 does not apply in the first place.

Having held that the *Partition Act* and not s. 10 of the *FLA* applies where there is no dispute between the spouses about the ownership of the jointly held property, the court in *Martin* also commented on whether the *Partition Act* can be invoked prior to a trial of other *FLA* issues. One spouse may, for example, wish to use the *Partition Act* to force an early sale of the jointly held matrimonial home. The court in *Martin* made it clear that courts should be cautious about ordering the partition and sale of the home before the determination of any applications under the *FLA* for equalization of net family properties or exclusive possession of the matrimonial home:

> Although there is clear jurisdiction under the *Partition Act* to order the sale of the parties' matrimonial home, I do not wish to be taken to have endorsed the wholesale issuance of these orders. In my view, an order directing the sale of a matrimonial home before trial should only be made in cases where, in all of the circumstances, such an order is appropriate. Orders for the sale of a matrimonial home made before the resolution of *Family Law Act, 1986* issues (particularly the determination of the equalization payment) should not be made as a matter of course. See *Binkley v. Binkley* (1988), 14 R.F.L. (3d) 336 (Ont. C.A.). In addition, spousal rights of possession (s. 19) and any order for interim exclusive possession should be taken in account.

Orders for partition and sale prior to the trial of the issues under the *FLA* should, therefore, only occur where there is no prejudice to either spouse and where a sale is the likely result at trial. Pre-trial orders for partition and sale of a jointly owned matrimonial home are, therefore, unlikely where one spouse has applied for exclusive possession. If an order for exclusive possession in favour of one joint tenant is granted, it effectively defers partition and sale until the order expires or is discharged under s. 25 of the *FLA*. See *Nicol v. Nicol* (1989), 21 R.F.L. (3d) 236 (Ont. H.C.). For a review of the cases dealing with the partition and sale of a jointly held matrimonial home prior to trial, see *Young v. Hansen* (2003), 1 R.F.L. (6th) 445 (Ont. S.C.J.); *Kereluk v. Kereluk* (2004), 9 R.F.L. (6th) 385 (Ont. S.C.J.); additional reasons at (2004), 2004 CarswellOnt 5037 (S.C.J.); *Salomon v. Salomon* (2007), 2007 CarswellOnt 1909 (S.C.J.); and *Trush v. Trush* (2007), 44 R.F.L. (6th) 69 (Ont. S.C.J.).

The *FLA* also grants the court the power to order the sale of the jointly owned property pursuant to s. 9 of the Act to implement an equalization sum. This jurisdiction exists only where an equalization of net family properties is claimed.

In summary, a court has no power under the *FLA* to order a partition and sale of a jointly owned matrimonial home unless there is an application for either equalization of net family properties or for the determination of ownership. Where a spouse only wants a jointly owned matrimonial home sold, the *Partition Act* is the applicable legislation. This rarely occurs because there is usually also a claim for equalization of the spouses' net family properties.

Where the joint owners of property are common law partners, Parts I and II of the *FLA* do not apply and so the only recourse is to the *Partition Act*. That Act provides for the orderly division of the value of property and is not concerned with other important considerations that arguably should be addressed when an unmarried couple separates. For example, a court cannot consider whether it would be best for the couple's children to delay the sale so that they can continue to reside in it. The Ontario Court of Appeal confirmed in *Latcham v. Latcham* (2002), 27 R.F.L. (5th) 358 (Ont. C.A.) that the courts have very limited discretion to refuse an application for partition and sale under the *Partition Act*. The party opposing the application must show that the applicant is guilty of malicious, vexatious or oppressive conduct. This is a high hurdle. In conclusion, unmarried partners must resort to the *Partition Act* if they want to realize the equity in their jointly owned property. Where one of them applies for partition and sale under that Act, the court can only refuse to grant the application on very narrow grounds.

It is not uncommon for one joint tenant, whether the couple is married or not, to want to purchase the other's interest and keep the home. It is clear, however, that the court does not have jurisdiction under the *Partition Act* to force one joint tenant to sell to the other: *Osborne v. Myette* (2004), 2004 CarswellOnt 3331 (S.C.J.). Nor does the *FLA* allow a court to do so. While s. 9 of that Act does allow a court to transfer a property interest from one spouse to another as partial or full satisfaction of an equalization entitlement, a court cannot use that section to transfer property from one spouse to the other if the effect is to create a new debt.

It is also questionable whether a court can grant one joint tenant a right of first refusal where it orders the sale of a jointly held matrimonial home. The Ontario Court of Appeal held in *Martin v. Martin, supra*, that neither spouse should be given such a right. See also *Amaral v. Amaral* (1993), 50 R.F.L. (3d) 364 (Ont. Gen. Div.); additional reasons at (1993), 50 R.F.L. (3d) 384 (Ont. Gen. Div.). However, see *Willemze-Davidson v. Davidson* (1997), 98 O.A.C. 335 (Ont. C.A.) and *Pastway v. Pastway* (1999), 49 R.F.L. (4th) 375 (Ont. Gen. Div.) where a spouse was granted an opportunity to purchase the matrimonial home.

5. Dealings with a Matrimonial Home

As indicated in the last chapter, Part I of the *FLA* continues the separate property regime between spouses, subject to a system of deferred sharing of gains. Until a court orders otherwise (for example, by transferring the property under s. 9(1) or by making a preservation order under s. 12), the owning spouse is able to dispose of his or her assets subject only to the possibility that the transaction will be set aside under the *Fraudulent Conveyances Act*, R.S.O. 1990, c. F-29. The position with regard to the matrimonial home is different. While ownership between the spouses is unaltered, a spouse who disposes of or encumbers an interest in a matrimonial home must ensure that the transaction complies with s. 21.

The primary purpose of s. 21 is to provide some protection for the possessory rights of the non-owning spouse established by Part II of the Act. However, because the section also applies where the spouses are co-owners of the matrimonial home, it sometimes serves to protect the proprietary interest of one spouse against the other. In *Kozub v. Timko* (1984), 45 O.R. (2d) 558, 39 R.F.L. (2d) 146, the Ontario Court of Appeal held that a similar provision in the *Family Law Reform Act, 1978* applied where the wife, who owned the matrimonial home in joint tenancy with her husband, conveyed her interest in the home to her son. The husband did not learn of this conveyance until after the death of the wife. The court set aside the conveyance and held that it did not sever the joint tenancy between the husband and wife. The court left for future determination the question of whether a conveyance by one joint tenant of the interest in a matrimonial home to himself or herself had to comply with s. 42(1) of the *Family Law Reform Act, 1978* (now s. 21(1) of the *FLA*). The sole purpose and effect of such a conveyance is to sever the joint tenancy. It does not have any impact on the possessory rights established by Part II of the *FLA*, but causes the other spouse to lose the right of survivorship in the home. After a series of conflicting lower court decisions, the Ontario Court of Appeal held in *Horne v. Evans* (1987), 8 R.F.L. (3d) 195, that s. 42(1) of the *Family Law Reform Act, 1978* (now s. 21 of the *FLA*) did not apply to a conveyance by one joint tenant of the matrimonial home to himself or herself.

Section 21(1) of the *FLA* prohibits a spouse from disposing of or encumbering an interest in the matrimonial home unless at least one of four statutory conditions is met. Does s. 21(1) apply where the owning spouse merely rents out a room in the matrimonial home for a two-month period? Does it apply where the owning spouse mortgages the matrimonial home?

Any attempt by a spouse to dispose of, or place a direct encumbrance on, his or her interest in the matrimonial home without the consent of the other spouse violates s. 21. However, transactions which might indirectly lead to an execution directed against a spouse's interest in a matrimonial home are not caught. In *Bank of Montreal v. Bray* (1997), 33 R.F.L. (4th) 335, the Ontario Court of Appeal held that the renewal of an unsecured guarantee, given by the husband without the wife's consent, did not amount to an encumbrance of an interest in the matrimonial home. The Bank of Montreal could, therefore, enforce the guarantee against the husband's interest in the jointly owned matrimonial home. See also *First City Trust Co. v. McDonough* (1993), 50 R.F.L. (3d) 197, 15 O.R. (3d) 586 (Gen. Div.) and *Enterprise Newfoundland & Labrador Corp. v. Kawaja* (1997), 29 R.F.L. (4th) 116 (Nfld. T.D.). These cases were distinguished in *Walduda v. Bell* (2004), 7 R.F.L. (6th) 205 (Ont. S.C.J.), where the wife's sister funded her family litigation through loans, then obtained consent judgments against the wife, and finally registered both judgments against the jointly owned matrimonial home. Justice Crane accepted (at para. 27) that the two sisters were "two bodies, one head" who intended to thwart the husband's occupation of the home with the couple's three children. The Justice set aside the writs of execution.

Because s. 21 only applies to spouses, a party who agrees to sever the divorce from the corollary relief claims may be vulnerable to dealings with the matrimonial home before these claims are dealt with. See *Love v. Baker* (1997), 30 R.F.L. (4th) 370 (Ont. Gen. Div.).

Examine the statutory conditions set out in s. 21(1). Notice that s. 21(1)(b) only refers to a separation agreement. This is because a purported release of possessory rights in a matrimonial home in a marriage contract is unenforceable (s. 52(2)) and does not affect the restrictions on alienation contained in s. 21. By virtue of s. 21(1)(c), a spouse can dispose of or encumber an interest in a matrimonial home if a court order has authorized the transaction or has released the property from the application of Part II. Section 23(b) empowers a court, upon application by a spouse or person having an interest in the property, to "authorize the disposition or encumbrance of the matrimonial home if the court finds that the spouse whose consent is required, (i) cannot be found or is not available, (ii) is not capable of giving or withholding consent, or (iii) is unreasonably withholding consent". For some cases examining when a court will find that a spouse is unreasonably withholding consent, see *Mills v. Andrewes* (1982), 31 R.F.L. (2d) 47 (N.S. T.D.); *Robbins v. Robbins* (1983), 35 R.F.L. (2d) 108 (Ont. Master); *Clarkson v. Lukovich* (1986), 2 R.F.L. (3d) 392 (Ont. H.C.); varied (1988), 14 R.F.L. (3d) 436 (Ont. C.A.); *Allesandro Building Corp. v. Rocca (No. 2)* (1987), 9 R.F.L. (3d) 422 (Ont. H.C.); *Borsch v. Borsch* (1987), 9 R.F.L. (3d) 444 (Ont. H.C.); *Royal Bank v. King* (1991), 35 R.F.L. (3d) 325 (Ont. Gen. Div.); and *Proc v. Proc* (1992), 42 R.F.L. (3d) 418 (Ont. Gen. Div.). An order releasing property from the application of Part II of the *FLA* may be made under s. 24(1)(b). Where the court grants exclusive possession of a matrimonial home to one spouse, it may release another property that is a matrimonial home from the application of Part II. In this situation s. 21(1)(c) would allow the owning spouse to deal with the other property without the other's consent. Why is s. 21(1)(d) superfluous? Examine s. 20(4).

To identify the potential remedies available when s. 21(1) of the *FLA* is violated, see ss. 21(2), 23(d) and 24(1)(g). In light of the wording of s. 21(2), it would appear that a transaction that does not comply with s. 21(1) is valid unless set aside by a court. Justice Taliano confirmed (at para. 19) this point in *Chornley v. Chornley* (2003), 48 R.F.L. (5th) 49 (Ont. S.C.J.). On the effect of such a transaction and the circumstances in which a court should set it aside, see *Van Dorp v. Van Dorp* (1980), 30 O.R. (2d) 623 (Co. Ct.); *Mills v. Andrewes, supra*; *Robbins v. Robbins, supra*; *Bank of Montreal v. Norton* (1983), 36 R.F.L. (2d) 268 (Ont. H.C.); *Kozub v. Timko, supra*; *Robinson v. Royal Bank* (1995), 26 O.R. (3d) 627 (Gen. Div.); *Maimets v. Williams* (1997), 29 R.F.L. (4th) 207 (Ont. C.A.); *Parker v. Parker* (1997), 32 R.F.L. (4th) 289 (Ont. Gen. Div.)); *Banton v. Banton* (1998), 164 D.L.R. (4th) 176 (Ont. Gen. Div.); additional reasons at (1998), 164 D.L.R. (4th) 176 at 244 (Ont. Gen. Div.); *McCaskie v. McCaskie* (2002), 26 R.F.L. (5th) 401 (Ont. S.C.J.); and *Roby v. Roby (Trustee of)* (2003), 43 R.F.L. (5th) 193 (Ont. S.C.J.).

Section 21(2) provides protection for the person who acquires an interest in a matrimonial home for value, in good faith and without notice that the property was a matrimonial home. "Notice" for the purpose of this subsection includes both actual and constructive notice that the property is a matrimonial home: *Stoimenov v. Stoimenov* (1985), 44 R.F.L. (2d) 14 (Ont. C.A.). See also *767648 Ontario Ltd. v. Engel* (1993), 46 R.F.L. (3d) 382 (Ont. Gen. Div.); affirmed (1994), 1 R.F.L. (4th) 144 (Ont. C.A.). In *Stoimenov*, the court distinguished between the two types of notice as follows (at 21): "Actual notice means knowledge of the very fact required to be established, whereas constructive notice means knowledge of other facts which put a person on inquiry to discover the fact required to be established."

To facilitate conveyancing, s. 21(3) of the *FLA* specifies that a statement by the person making the disposition or encumbrance verifying certain facts is deemed to be sufficient proof that the property is not a matrimonial home in the absence of notice to the contrary. For a case requiring that such a statement strictly comply with the wording of the statute, see *Bank of Nova Scotia v. Halef* (2003), 42 R.F.L. (5th) 251 (N.S. C.A.). In *Stoimenov*, the Ontario Court of Appeal held that the notice referred to is notice of the falsehood of the facts set out in the statement rather than notice that the property is a matrimonial home. The analysis in *Stoimenov* suggests the following relationship between subsections (2) and (3). Where an affidavit is given, the onus is on the spouse seeking to set aside the transaction to establish that the third party had notice of the falsehood. Once this is done, the transaction can be set aside unless the third party proves that despite notice of the falsehood he or she was without notice of the fact that the property was a matrimonial home. As *Stoimenov* demonstrates, notice of the falsehood may in some circumstances amount to notice that the property is a matrimonial home. For recent cases applying the two step analysis from *Stoimenov*, see *McCaskie v. McCaskie, supra* and *Roby v. Roby (Trustee of), supra*.

Section 21(3) of the *FLA* differs from its predecessor in the *Family Law Reform Act, 1978*. In that statute the person to whom the disposition or encumbrance was made could rely on the affidavit unless he or she had "*actual* notice" (emphasis added) to the contrary. By deletion of the word "actual" in the new provision, either actual or constructive notice of the inaccuracy of the facts contained in the affidavit will now negate the effect of the affidavit. This was confirmed in *McCaskie v. McCaskie, supra*, at para. 35. As a result of this changed wording, persons dealing with property that might be a matrimonial home must approach the affidavit with more caution. Under the *Family Law Reform Act, 1978* a person who suspected that the property was a matrimonial home could still rely on an affidavit even if it contained false statements, provided the person did not have actual knowledge of the falsehood. Now, however, the facts that lead the person to suspect that the property is a matrimonial home could very well also amount to constructive notice of the falsehood of the statement. As a result, a solicitor acting for a party who is acquiring an interest in or receiving the benefit of an encumbrance of property that could be a matrimonial home should investigate what that party knows regarding the use of the property and the marital status of the other party in order to assess whether the affidavit can be safely relied upon.

Where the court is precluded by s. 21(2) from setting aside the transaction, the wronged spouse may be able to obtain another remedy under s. 24(1)(g). That paragraph empowers the court to direct the person who made a false statement under s. 21(3) (or a "person who knew at the time he or she acquired an interest in the property that the statement was false and afterwards conveyed the interest") to substitute other real property for the matrimonial home. Alternatively, the court can direct such persons to set aside money or security to stand in the place of the matrimonial home. Why are these remedies unlikely to be effective?

6. Right to Redemption and Relief Against Forfeiture

Section 22 of the *FLA* is intended to give a spouse who has a right to possession by virtue of s. 19 the same right of redemption or relief against forfeiture as the other spouse. In an action by a mortgagee for foreclosure, possession, and payment on the convenant, s. 22(1) gives a spouse, who has a right to possession by virtue of s. 19, a statutory right of redemption and a statutory right to seek relief against the acceleration clause equal to that of the spouse who is directly liable to the mortgagee. See *Maritime Life Assurance Co. v. Karapatakis* (1979), 9 R.F.L. (2d) 265, 7 R.P.R. 229 (Ont. H.C.), which dealt with the equivalent provision in the *Family Law Reform Act, 1978*. To exercise the rights given by s. 22 effectively, the spouse must comply with the statutory and regulatory provisions governing the exercise of similar rights by the owning spouse.

To ensure that the non-owning spouse is in a position to exercise the substantive rights given by s. 22, s. 22(1) provides that any person proceeding to realize upon a lien, encumbrance or execution, or attempting to exercise a forfeiture against the matrimonial home, must give notice to both spouses. The proper procedure for giving such notice in an action for foreclosure, possession and payment on the covenant by a mortgagee is detailed in *Maritime Life Assurance Co. v. Karapatakis*, above.

6

SPOUSAL SUPPORT

1. Introduction

Spousal support was historically gendered and fault-based: "innocent wives" obtained orders for maintenance or alimony from "guilty husbands". Even if entitlement were found, there were few guidelines for the exercise of discretion about the amount and the duration of the payment, resulting in inconsistent outcomes.

Provincial law offered various avenues of support for wives in Ontario prior to 1978. The most common way in which a wife obtained support after the marriage was through summary proceedings in Provincial Court (Family Division) under the *Deserted Wives' and Children's Maintenance Act*, R.S.O. 1970, c. 128. Desertion coupled with a failure to maintain was the sole basis for an order under this Act, but a dependent wife was deemed deserted where she was living separate and apart by reason of the husband's cruelty or uncondoned adultery. Adultery by the wife, if not condoned, was an absolute defence. Any acts that made her a deserter would also preclude relief.

Wives of more wealthy husbands obtained support through the common law action for alimony in the High Court. A husband's liability was conditional upon his misconduct in the form of adultery, cruelty, or desertion. Matrimonial misconduct on the part of the wife was a defence.

Provincial law, contained in the *Matrimonial Causes Act*, R.S.O. 1970, c. 265, also governed support in nullity actions. This legislation exhibited the same basic features as alimony and deserted wives' maintenance: only the woman could obtain support, there was no expectation that women would maintain themselves, and misconduct in the form of adultery by the woman provided a complete defence.

The passage of the federal 1968 *Divorce Act* created a new, gender-neutral, remedy of spousal support, available to spouses of either sex, based on the needs and means of the parties. The Act, however, gave limited guidance to the courts in dealing with support. It simply directed the court to make an order "if it thinks it fit and just to do so having regard to the conduct of the parties and the condition, means and other circumstances of each of them." Nevertheless, the Act introduced significant reforms. It permitted husbands to obtain maintenance in appropriate cases, although this rarely occurred; and it no longer barred maintenance for a spouse who had been guilty of marital misconduct. Spousal support was no longer fault-based.

By the mid- to late-1970's most of the provinces had followed suit, and had passed legislation that eliminated misconduct as a basis for spousal support, and that allowed either spouse to apply for, and receive, support. As discussed in Chapter 1, the concurrent jurisdiction of the federal and provincial governments regarding spousal support needs to be kept in mind. Federal legislation dealing with the establishment of grounds and procedures for obtaining a divorce clearly falls within s. 91(26) of the *Constitution Act, 1867*. The authority of the Parliament of Canada to enact legislation dealing with support and custody on divorce rests on the "rational, functional connection" between such "corollary relief" and the establishment of grounds and procedures for obtaining a divorce. On the other hand, the provinces have authority under s. 92(13) of the *Constitution Act, 1867* to deal generally with the rights and obligations of private individuals towards one another. Therefore, provincial legislation can deal with the support obligations of married persons during their marriage, upon separation, and even on divorce. To the extent that provincial legislation deals with the latter topic, the potential for conflict between provincial and federal legislation arises. Often, the provincial legislation will indicate that its support provisions do not apply in divorce proceedings. See, e.g., s. 36(1) of Ontario's *Family Law Act* (the *FLA*). Note also s. 36(3). Provincial legislation, and only provincial legislation, can deal with the support obligations of persons who cohabit but do not get married.

Part II of the *Family Law Reform Act, 1978* was the Ontario legislature's initial response to the need for reform of the law of spousal support. The Act abolished the action for alimony, and repealed the *Deserted Wives' and Children's Maintenance Act* and those parts of the *Matrimonial Causes Act* dealing with support. It created equal, mutual support obligations. The duty of a spouse to support himself or herself was also statutorily recognized. The concept of fault as the basis for spousal support was abolished, although in extreme circumstances fault could still be considered in determining quantum. In place of fault, the legislation substituted need as the basic determinant of entitlement and provided the courts with factors to consider in determining the amount. For the first time, unmarried, opposite-sex cohabitees could claim support if their relationship met certain statutory criteria. In addition to altering the substantive law of support, Part II of the *Family Law Reform Act, 1978* contained provisions to facilitate the enforcement of support orders.

In 1986, Part III of the *FLA* replaced Part II of the 1978 *Family Law Reform Act*. Although there were some significant changes, the basic features of the support law introduced by the *Family Law Reform Act, 1978* were retained. Part III of the *FLA* is now the sole basis for spousal support under provincial law in Ontario.

There were significant amendments to the *Divorce Act* in 1985. Section 15.2(6) (s. 15(7) until the numbers were altered by S.C. 1997, c. 1) of the current *Divorce Act* sets out the objectives that the court is to keep in mind in determining spousal support. Section 15.2(4) (previously s. 15(5)) identifies the factors that the court is to consider. The objectives and factors are arguably difficult to reconcile, and are not easily applied. The legislation does not, on its face, make it clear whether the objectives and factors can be applied on an individual basis, or whether they were meant to be applied all at once in each case. As we will see in this Chapter, the broad nature of the objectives and factors led to Supreme Court of Canada decisions clarifying their proper application to the issue of entitlement to spousal support.

Between 1980 and 2000, the theoretical basis for spousal support entitlement in Canada underwent major shifts. The Supreme Court of Canada released three decisions (*Pelech v. Pelech* (1987), 7 R.F.L. (3d) 225 (S.C.C.); *Richardson v. Richardson* (1987), 7 R.F.L. (3d) 304 (S.C.C.); and *Caron v. Caron* (1987), 7 R.F.L. (3d) 274 (S.C.C.)) in the late 1980's, which became known as "the Pelech trilogy". Some read the trilogy to say that spousal support entitlement had to be grounded in the marriage itself ("causal connection"), and that need unrelated to the marriage did not result in entitlement. As we will see in this Chapter, the trilogy was actually about variation of existing spousal support orders in which there was a termination date. It was never a statement about the initial entitlement of a spouse to support. Nonetheless, the trilogy had a huge impact on spousal support entitlement *ab initio* until the Supreme Court of Canada decision in *Moge v. Moge* (1992), 43 R.F.L. (3d) 345 (S.C.C.). *Moge* became the leading case on the issue of spousal support entitlement in longer term marriages and Justice L'Heureux-Dubé's reasoning established the concept of spousal support as compensation for roles taken on during the marriage. It did not address the issue of entitlement in shorter marriages, or in marriages in which a spouse was not necessarily entitled to compensation, but had need of support anyway. In 1999, the Supreme Court addressed this aspect of entitlement in *Bracklow v. Bracklow* (1999), 44 R.F.L. (4th) 1

(S.C.C.). *Bracklow* was a broad statement about the possible bases for spousal support, and created a framework for theories of spousal support that is now well-established in Canadian law.

As a result of these two milestone cases, the Canadian discussion about the basis for entitlement was well underway by 2000. The unanswered questions that remained were "how much support should be paid?" and "for how long"? Decisions continued to vary widely in both quantum and duration. The resulting unpredictability in spousal support awards was unsatisfactory for lawyers and clients alike. There was a real need for more certainty in spousal support outcomes.

With the publication of the draft federal *Spousal Support Advisory Guidelines* in March, 2006 and the final version, in July, 2008, spouses, judges and lawyers across the country can now discuss quantum and duration on a more consistent, principled basis. The SSAG have been controversial in some quarters (most notably Quebec), but most Canadian jurisdictions have welcomed the formulas for spousal support quantum and duration contained in the SSAG. The SSAG provide a range of amounts, and a durational range, in individual cases, based largely on the length of cohabitation, and the incomes of the parties, as well as on the number and ages of the children of the marriage. They link the amount of support and the length of time support is to be paid. This allows spouses to agree to arrangements that restructure the support. For example, the parties can agree to pay a smaller amount for a longer time or a larger amount for a shorter time, depending on what suits the circumstances of the parties. The SSAG do not, as discussed in detail in this Chapter, determine entitlement. They do offer, however, an extremely useful starting point for most discussions about spousal support, once entitlement has been established. The SSAG have therefore ushered in a new era of comparative certainty regarding quantum and duration of spousal support awards.

2. Who Can Apply Under the *Family Law Act?*

The *FLA* contains two different definitions of "spouse". Section 1 of the Act defines "spouse" as "either of two persons who, (a) are married to each other, or (b) have together entered into a marriage that is voidable or void, in good faith on the part of a person relying on this clause to assert any right." This definition applies to all sections of the Act. For the purposes of support only, s. 29 expands this definition to include unmarried cohabitees who have cohabited continuously for three years or more, or who are the natural or adoptive parents of a child together and cohabited "in a relationship of some permanence". Determining who is a spouse for the purposes of this section has not always been straightforward. Defining the commencement and end of cohabitation; determining the continuity of cohabitation; and determining the permanence of a relationship have all engendered litigation.

STOIKIEWICZ v. FILAS

(1978), 7 R.F.L. (2d) 366, 21 O.R. (2d) 717, 1978 CarswellOnt 327 (U.F.C.)

STEINBERG U.F.C.J.: — This is an application brought by Krystina Stoikiewicz against Stanley Filas, pursuant to which she has claimed: (1) maintenance for herself; (2) maintenance for her child Gerry Filas, born 4th July 1972; and (3) custody of the said child.

Mr. Filas did not attend at the hearing, and there seems to be no issue in respect of the custody and maintenance of the child. However, Krystina Stoikiewicz and Stanley Filas were never married. Therefore, to qualify for maintenance as a dependant under the *Family Law Reform Act*, 178 (Ont.), c. 2, the applicant must fall within the definition of "spouse" contained in s. 14(b)(i) of the Act. ... [Section 14(b)(i) specified that "spouse", for the purpose of support, included "either of a man and woman not being married to each other who have cohabited 1. continuously for a period of not less than five years, or 2. in a relationship of some permanence where there is a child born of whom they are the natural parents, and have so cohabited within the preceding year".]

The relevant facts of the case are as follows:

(1)   On 2nd September 1972 the parties began to reside in the same apartment. The respondent owned the building in question and had been living in a separate apartment therein. Prior to the respondent moving in with the applicant, they had been engaging in sexual relations, and she became pregnant. According to the applicant, "when I was pregnant, we fix the room up in the back and share the apartment".

(2)   The respondent never shared a bedroom with the applicant, but slept separately from her in a room in the same apartment.

(3)   The respondent never paid the applicant any support or maintenance for herself or the child. His contribution to the household, according to the applicant, was that he bought all of the furniture.

(4)   When the respondent found out that the applicant was pregnant, he gave her an engagement ring, which she still wears.

(5)   While the parties shared the apartment, the applicant received Mother's Allowance, which is a provincial welfare benefit.

(6)   The nature of their personal relationship was described by the applicant as follows:

> Q. Mrs. Stoikiewicz, did you live with Mr. Filas as husband and wife? A. That's the way it was.
>
> Q. Did you share the same bedroom? A. No.
>
> Q. I see. Did you have sexual relations with each other? A. Yes.
>
> Q. Was it frequent or just occasional? A. Occasional. From time to time.
>
> Q. Did you cook his meals? A. I cooked for him.
>
> Q. And did he treat your child Gerry as his son? A. Yes.
>
> Q. And who bought the groceries? A. I did.
>
> Q. Did he give you money to buy groceries? A. No.
>
> Q. You used your own money, did you? A. Yes.
>
> Q. Where did you get that money from? A. I took it from Mother's Allowance.
>
> Q. Now, did you live with him for about five or six years, on Mother's Allowance? A. I paid him $100 a month rent, for which I have receipts; but because he really wanted $200 a month rent, for that reason I was also doing washing and ironing and other things.

The issue, therefore, is whether the relationship between the spouses was such so as to amount to a cohabitation within the meaning of s. 14(b)(i). There is much to support a positive finding in that regard. For example: (1) the respondent gave the applicant an engagement ring; (2) they lived in the same apartment and engaged in occasional sexual relations; and (3) the applicant cooked and washed for the respondent.

Indeed, if the parties had been married they would not have been considered to be living "separate and apart" within the meaning of s. 4(1)(e) of the *Divorce Act*, R.S.C. 1970, c. D-8.

There are, however, other aspects of their relationship which could support a negative finding, i.e., that the parties were not cohabiting with each other within the meaning of the *Family Law Reform Act*. These are that: (1) the applicant paid the respondent rent each month; and (2) the applicant did not look to the respondent for her support, but rather to the provincial government.

There are today many men and women living together without (for the lack of a better phrase) the benefit of clergy. There are many reasons for this — but it is safe to say that many couples who do so, do so in order that they can retain their personal freedoms unencumbered by the obligations which both the law and traditional morality impose on married spouses. Section 14(b)(i) is an intrusion upon that liberty, and thus, in my view, it ought to be strictly construed.

The intent of the *Family Law Reform Act* is to view the marriage relationship, for its purposes, primarily in the nature of an economic partnership. ...

Maintenance benefits under the Act flow from the intermeshing of the relative productivities of each of the spouses, together with their economic needs, resulting from the way they have divided up their respective duties and obligations in the marriage, as defined in s. 4(5) of the Act. [See now s. 5(7) of the *FLA*.] All this is premised upon the fact that each spouse has a duty to support and provide for the other. ...

It is my view that unmarried persons cannot be found to be cohabiting within the meaning of s. 14(b)(i) unless it can be determined that their relationship is such that they have each assumed an obligation to support and provide for the other in the same manner that married spouses are obliged to do. ...

In my view, the applicant has never cohabited with the respondent within the meaning of s. 14(b)(i) of the *Family Law Reform Act*. The evidence is clear that, although from time to time the parties were intimate, their economic life was on an arms-length basis. Any household services that the applicant provided to the respondent were in satisfaction of a portion of the rent. Neither of the parties looked to the other for support or assistance outside of their unusual rental agreement.

Accordingly, the applicant's claim for spousal maintenance is dismissed. ... [Custody was awarded to the mother and child support of $75 per week was ordered.]

HAZLEWOOD v. KENT

(June 20, 2000), Doc. 7621/99, [2000] O.J. No. 5263 (Ont. S.C.J.)

WILDMAN J. — This is a motion for temporary spousal support by the applicant. The sole issue which I have been asked to determine on this motion is whether or not the applicant is entitled to support as a spouse under the provisions of the *Family Law Act*. Specifically, the parties require a ruling as to whether their living arrangements can be considered "cohabitation" within the meaning of that Act as they only lived together on weekends.

The Facts

2 The applicant and respondent were never married. They had a relationship from approximately March of 1991 to July of 1998 of which two children were born. Throughout this time, the applicant lived in her own home and the respondent lived in his own home. The applicant's material indicates that they did not "live together". I assume by this she means that they did not live together exclusively as the issue of whether or not they "live together"

or "cohabited" is the issue that she has put forward for determination by this Court. On weekends, the respondent would come to stay with the applicant in her home where she was residing with the children. It is common ground that these weekend "visits" were more or less continuous throughout their relationship.

3 The parties agree that their relationship was exclusive. Neither had any other spouse or intimate partner throughout the time that they were together.

4 After the birth of their first child in 1993, the applicant gave up her full-time job to remain at home to raise their son. Since March of 1994, the respondent has provided her with $1500.00 per month to assist with her expenses.

5 Following separation, the respondent started paying child support in accordance with the Child Support Guidelines. Interestingly, the guideline amount is also approximately $1500 per month. ...

Discussion

7 Counsel for the respondent has conceded that these parties had a relationship of some permanence and that they are the natural parents of the two children, Michael (born April 22, 1993) and Jordan (born March 19, 1995).

8 The entire argument in this case revolves around the meaning of the word "cohabit" and whether or not the weekend relationship qualifies as "cohabitation" within the meaning of the Act.

9 Counsel have conducted a very thorough review of the case law in Ontario. I have been referred to at least 24 relevant cases.

10 It is clear that a finding of cohabitation does not turn exclusively on the amount of time that the parties spent living under the same roof. There are cases where parties live under one roof but are not found to be cohabiting. There are also cases where parties maintain separate residences but are found to be cohabiting. Where there is any suggestion of a common residence at some point in the relationship, it is necessary to look at the particular circumstances of each case to determine whether or not the time spent sharing living quarters is sufficient to constitute "cohabitation" in the legal sense.

11 Almost all the cases start with a reference to *Molodowich v. Penttinen* (1980), 17 R.F.L. (2d) 376 (DCO). In that case, the applicant moved to Thunder Bay to stay with the respondent in his apartment in 1973. The applicant subsequently obtained her own apartment and the respondent gave up his apartment in 1974 to move in with her. Later the same year, the applicant and respondent moved into a new home that he had been building. In finding that the parties were spouses under the extended definition of the Family Law Reform Act, Judge Kurisko found that cohabitation had begun even before January 1974 when the respondent physically moved into the applicant's apartment.

12 At p. 381 of the decision, Judge Kurisko sets out a very useful seven-part test to apply to analyze whether "cohabitation" or "consortium" exists.

> 1. *Shelter*:
> a) Did the parties live under the same roof?
> b) What were the sleeping arrangements?
> c) Did anyone else occupy or share the available accommodation?
>
> 2. *Sexual and Personal Behaviour*:
> a) Did the parties have sexual relations? If not, why not?
> b) Did they maintain an attitude of fidelity to each other?
> c) What were their feelings toward each other?
> d) Did they communicate on a personal level?

e) Did they eat their meals together?

f) What, if anything, did they do to assist each other with problems or during illness?

g) Did they buy gifts for each other on special occasions?

3. Services:

What was the conduct and habit of the parties in relation to:

a) preparation of meals;

b) washing and mending clothes;

c) shopping;

d) household maintenance; and

e) any other domestic services;

4. Social:

a) Did they participate together or separately in neighbourhood and community activities?

b) What was the relationship and conduct of each of them toward members of their respective families and how did such families behave towards the parties?

5. Societal:

What was the attitude and conduct of the community toward each of them and as a couple?

6. Support (economic):

a) What were the financial arrangements between the parties regarding the provision of or contribution toward the necessaries of life (food, clothing, shelter, recreation, etc.)?

b) What were the arrangements concerning the acquisition and ownership of property?

c) Was there any special financial arrangement between them which both agreed would be determinant of their overall relationship?

7. Children:

What was the attitude and conduct of the parties concerning children?

14 What is clear is that the applicant and respondent had an exclusive personal relationship of which there were two children born. Although they continued to enjoy a sexual relationship together after the birth of the children, the respondent had his own room at the applicant's residence. I can only assume that, if he had "his own room", he also kept personal items in this room. It is acknowledged, for example, that the respondent had a computer at the applicant's home to use on the weekends when he was there. There is a reference to him leaving personal reading material in his bedroom which suggests a certain comfort level beyond that of a "visitor". There is a reference to the applicant making the respondent's bed after he had left which implies that she was responsible for the household chores including cleaning his room.

15 The respondent indicates in his material that when he did spend the weekends, he would care for the children as a father. The "family" spent the weekend sharing common activities such as eating, going to parks, movies, or shopping. The respondent indicates that he and the applicant did attend social and business functions as a couple but details are not provided. He acknowledges that he left the applicant's telephone number with coworkers and others so that he could be reached on weekends. He completed an application naming the applicant as

his spouse to maintain her and the children on his health benefits from approximately November 19, 1993 forward.

16 The couple approached a financial planner in 1993 who prepared a 20 page report for them. Although the report is not before me as proof of the contents, it does provide some useful narrative to corroborate the state of mind of the couple. The report contains comments such as:

- You have two homes and, indeed, two separate lifestyles, and the process of merging them will, by choice, be gradual.

- You are retaining both houses for now, in the hopes that you can obtain a better price when the real estate market improves, and you have not decided which of the two will be sold.

- As you plan to marry, it would be a good idea to ensure that your wills are worded accordingly. ...

38 One of the strongest indicia of an intention to be treated as a family is the existence of children born to the couple. When this is combined with an element of financial support by one party to the other, an altering of the roles in the relationship as a result of the birth of the children and some time spent together on a regular basis, this relationship should be considered to be "cohabitation in a relationship of some permanence" within the meaning of the *Family Law Act*. The amount of residence sharing which is necessary to support a spousal finding where there are children and ongoing financial support is probably less than would be required if either of these important factors were absent. Although these two criteria are not determinative of the question for all cases, their existence is very persuasive to the Court in assessing whether or not a family unit has been established. ...

[The court found that the couple had cohabited and ordered the man to pay $400 monthly as interim spousal support.]

McEACHERN v. FRY ESTATE

(1993), 1993 CarswellOnt 3632, [1993] O.J. No. 1731 (Gen. Div.)

SHEPPARD, J. — In this application, the applicant seeks an award under S. 58 of the *Succession Law Reform Act* for support from the Estate of the respondent on the basis that she had cohabited with the deceased continuously for a period of not less than three years.

2 Jean McEachern and Harry Fry knew each other before their respective spouses died in 1975. In April 1976 Harry telephoned Jean and asked her out. Jean was 48 years old at the time. Harry was 62. They were constant companions and lovers for over 15 years until Harry's death in 1991.

3 When they first met, Harry owned a farm in Aurora where he raised horses and cattle. Jean owned a house in Barrie where she has been and presently is employed by Barrie Raceway. Jean is presently the Race Secretary earning $30,000 annually. Jean owned her own home throughout her years with Harry and continues to own her own home today. Early in their relationship the two would spend weekends together and occasionally time during the week. Generally, they did not spend more than two consecutive nights together. As time went on they spent pretty well all their free time together. Jean would often have to work on Saturday at the raceway. After work she would go to Harry's farm for the remainder of the weekend and occasionally stay through to Monday or Tuesday.

4 In 1988, Harry disposed of his horses and cattle and thereafter Harry spent more time at Jean's house. Each kept his or her clothes and personal items at each other's residence. In

February 1989, Harry sold his farm and bought a house in Aurora. Jean helped Harry select the house and furniture and the two discussed Jean moving to the house when she retired. While Harry was alive, Harry and Jean conducted their lives in much the same fashion as any couple would where each person has his or her own career. Each pursued his or her personal interests and career, retiring together to his place or her place to spend their free time together. Jean estimated that after Harry sold the farm he spent approximately sixty percent (60%) of his time living at her house in Barrie.

5 Throughout Harry's marriage to his first wife and while he was living on his farm and later his house in Aurora, Harry had the services of a cleaning lady. However, when his cleaning lady was not available, Jean would do Harry's laundry, clean his house and prepare meals for him. Indeed she prepared meals for his farm hands when that was required as well. Harry looked after Jean. She estimated that Harry spent between $2500.00 to $3000.00 annually on clothes for her. He bought her a fur coat. He contributed to the upkeep of the Barrie house. He paid for gardening expenses and snow removal. He purchased groceries for them; he gave Jean $50.00 per week for miscellaneous household expenses; and he paid for repairs to her car.

6 Counsel for the respondent pointed out that each maintained separate residences, that there were no joint bank accounts, that each owned his or her own car, that they never bought a house together, that they never married, that they never lived together all the time and Harry did not introduce Jean to others as Mrs. Fry. As to how Jean was known to others, some referred to Jean as Mrs. Fry and Harry did not object. The affidavit of Anthony Arkell filed in support of the application stated that he was a neighbour of Harry Fry for 30 years. He and his wife became very good friends with Harry and later with Jean. Mr. Arkell and his wife moved from the farm beside Harry's farm but they still would see Harry and Jean about twice a month. They would go out together for an evening and were often guests of Jean and Harry both in Barrie at Jean's house and in Aurora at Harry's farm and later at his house. It was obvious to Mr. and Mrs. Arkell that Harry and Jean were living together. Once the Arkells, Harry and Jean and others vacationed together in Ireland for two weeks and Harry and Jean stayed together in the same room. In Mr. Arkell's view, Harry and Jean seemed very close and fond of one another. Harry and Jean regularly vacationed together:

9 Harry and Jean would celebrate their "anniversary" near Easter of each year.

10 Mutual friends considered Harry and Jean a couple. After Harry's death, their friends who were originally just Harry's friends continued to include Jean in their activities. ...

15 The question is: can it be said that Harry and Jean did not cohabit because each maintained his and her separate residences while they "co-existed" for the 15 year term of their relationship? In my view and on the basis of the authorities, this fact, although of itself significant, loses its significance when a broader view is taken of their relationship. Harry and Jean lived together as husband and wife in every sense of the word. They were as committed to each other as any married couple. Each depended on the other. Their respective lives, although at times separate, revolved around and included the other.

16 I do not see that the fact that each maintained a separate residence throughout their relationship as terribly significant when one looks at the fact that when Harry and Jean established a relationship, she was 48 and he was 62 and each had been married and had children. Obviously, they found love and companionship in each other. Had they not, then I should think they would not have spent all their free time together at either Jean's place or Harry's place. And it has to be remembered that Jean maintained a job in Barrie which is far enough from Aurora as to make the prospect of travelling back and forth daily unattractive. ...

21 Whether or not a couple have cohabited continuously is both a subjective and an objective test. What was the intention of the parties as gleaned from the facts and how were they

regarded by others? Intention of the parties is important. In today's world where often both spouses work sometimes in different cities and where work can keep them apart for often long periods of time, one must look at the relationship generally and not specifically item by item to see if the parties were in fact cohabiting in the legal sense or merely living together for the time being for whatever purpose. When you find as here a fifteen year period of companionship and commitment and an acceptance by all who knew them as a couple, surely you must have continuous cohabitation. It has been said that cohabitation is a state of mind. In my view Harry recognized this and when he prepared his Will in 1990 when interest rates were as high as they were, he probably felt that he had provided for Jean as he said he would. [The latter comment referred to the fact that Harry's will directed his executors and trustees to set aside and invest the sum of $75,000, known as "Jean's Trust", and to pay to Jean until her death or remarriage the net income earned on the capital or $5,500.00 per year, whichever was greater. Where the income earned on the capital in any year was less than $5,500.00, the deficiency was to be made up out of the capital. The court ultimately ordered spousal support of $1,900 per month from Harry's estate to be paid to Jean, such amount to include the payment provided for in the will.]

SANDERSON v. RUSSELL

(1979), 9 R.F.L. (2d) 81, 24 O.R. (2d) 429, 1979 CarswellOnt 381 (C.A.)

MORDEN J.A.: — ... It is submitted by Bessie Sanderson, the respondent in this appeal, that she and Milton Russell, the appellant, not being married to each other, lived together as husband and wife from July 1971 to May 1977, and that, therefore, they cohabited "continuously for a period of not less than five years" as required by s. 14(b)(i)1 [of the *Family Law Reform Act*. Note that under the *FLA* the required period of continuous cohabitation is now three years as opposed to five.] It is Mr. Russell's position that, apart from a four or five-day separation in February 1976, there was such cohabitation, but because of this period of separation there was not the requisite period of continuous cohabitation required by the Act. This defines the first issue to be resolved. ...

Was there continuous cohabitation for not less than five years?

The appellant submits that, because he had moved out of the home he was sharing with the respondent from a Friday to the following Tuesday in February 1976, he did not cohabit continuously with the respondent for a period of not less than five years. As indicated, there is no issue that, apart from this long weekend, the parties did not cohabit for the whole of the period from July 1971 to May 1977.

The evidence concerning the February 1976 interlude is sparse. The respondent said that they had had a fight because the appellant went to a dance at a singles club and stayed to the end of it. The appellant said that he moved out because they could not agree on anything. He moved out of the house they were living in, taking his clothes and a small bed. He made a deposit of $100 on an apartment. At the urging of her parents, the appellant said that he went back to speak to the respondent and they were reconciled.

Morton Prov. J. described this episode as "nothing more than a temporary lovers' quarrel" which did not constitute a break in the cohabitation. Couture Co. Ct. J. agreed with this conclusion.

Undoubtedly the meaning of "cohabited continuously" will be tested from different vantage points in a great variety of situations. "Cohabit" is defined in s. 1(b) of the Act as meaning "to live together in a conjugal relationship, whether within or outside marriage". Put into more everyday language this means to live together as husband and wife, or, as His

Honour Judge Honey put it in *Feehan v. Attwells*, Ont., 19th February 1979 (not yet reported), to live together "in a 'marriage-like' relationship outside marriage". Without in any way attempting to be detailed or comprehensive, it could be said that such a relationship has come to an end when either party regards it as being at an end and, by his or her conduct, has demonstrated in a convincing manner that this particular state of mind is a settled one. While the physical separation of parties following "a fight" might, in some cases, appear to amount to an ending of cohabitation, the test should be realistic and flexible enough to recognize that a brief cooling-off period does not bring the relationship to an end. Such conduct does not convincingly demonstrate a settled state of mind that the relationship is at an end.

The question will often be largely one of fact. In this case I think the conclusion that there was no break in the cohabitation is the correct one. ...

LABBE v. McCULLOUGH

(1979), 23 O.R. (2d) 536, 1979 CarswellOnt 1439 (Prov. Ct.)

WEISMAN PROV. CT. J.: — The applicant, Darlene Labbe, seeks support from the respondent, Steve McCullough, pursuant to the *Family Law Reform Act*, 1978 (Ont.), c. 2 (The Act).

The respondent is a musician who tours the country with a musical group. He met the applicant in January of 1976, while performing in Kirkland Lake, Ontario. In March of 1977, the applicant moved to Toronto, where the respondent resides with his parents, in order to be near him and to further her career as a model. She rented an apartment in her own name and resided there until May of that year. The respondent was performing in other parts of the country during this entire three-month period except for a four-week span which he spent with Miss Labbe in her apartment. He continued to leave all his worldly possessions at his parents' except for those personal effects that were needed for his daily use.

In May of 1977, Miss Labbe moved to North Bay. Mr. McCullough resided with her for two weeks in July of that year while he was recuperating from a broken hand. A child, Katrina, was conceived during that two-week period. When the applicant informed the respondent that she was pregnant in August, he terminated the relationship.

While there was no formal engagement, there was some talk of marriage some day.

[Judge Weisman set out the facts and reasoning of *Stoikiewicz v. Filas* and distinguished the case in one line: "There are no such peculiar economic arrangements in the matter before me." He continued:]

I find on the evidence that the parties, while not married to each other, cohabited for a four-week period between March and May of 1977, and again for a two-week period in July of 1977. In making this finding I adopt the common definition of "cohabit" found in the fifth edition of the Concise Oxford Dictionary, i.e., "live together". I further find that Katrina was conceived in July of 1977, and that the applicant and respondent are the child's natural parents. Darlene Labbe filed her application on June 13, 1978, which is within one year of the date on which the parties last cohabited.

These findings satisfy four of the five conditions set out in s. 14(b)(i), para. 2. It now becomes important to decide whether the parties cohabited "in a relationship of some permanence".

The following evidence would lead to a conclusion that theirs was not a relationship of some permanence:

1. They cohabited for only six weeks out of a total period of 19 months;

2. The apartment in Toronto and all its contents belonged exclusively to Darlene Labbe;

3.   The respondent at all times left all his possessions in his parents' home.

The following evidence would lead to a conclusion that theirs was a relationship of some permanence:

1.   The parties knew each other's whereabouts at all times between January, 1976 and August of 1977

2.   The applicant moved to Toronto in part to be with the respondent;

3.   The respondent went to North Bay to be with the applicant while he recovered from his broken hand; [and]

4.   There was some talk of marriage some day.

In deciding this matter, I place great weight on the fact that the parties discussed the possibility of marriage some day. In my view, this gives the relationship a touch of permanence. The Legislature has used the words "some permanence" and I cannot find that there was no permanence to the relationship between Miss Labbe and Mr. McCullough.

The length of time the applicant and respondent cohabited was very brief. This, however, goes to the quantum of support that the respondent must provide, and not to his liability to do so. ...

In my opinion, notwithstanding the tender age of the child, Katrina, in view of the brief and sporadic nature of the parties' cohabitation, the respondent should not be required to support the applicant for a lengthy period.

Accordingly, after assessing the needs of the applicant, and the respondent's ability to meet those needs, I have decided to order the respondent to provide support for the dependant spouse in the amount of $150 per month in advance for a period of 12 months commencing on April 1, 1979.

NOTES AND QUESTIONS

1. The current *Family Law Act* defines spouses so that the support provisions apply to same-sex couples in exactly the same manner as opposite-sex couples. The legislative amendments to this section were prompted by the Supreme Court of Canada decision in *M v. H* (1999), 46 R.F.L. (4th) 32, 1999 CarswellOnt 1348, 1999 CarswellOnt 1349 (S.C.C.); reconsideration refused (2000), 2000 CarswellOnt 1914, 2000 CarswellOnt 1913 (S.C.C.). The majority decision in M v. H. remains an important and thoughtful application of s. 15 of the *Charter*. Substantively, however, the case has been eclipsed by the general acceptance of same-sex couples in Canada over the decade since its release, and by the now clearly worded s. 29. Justice Gonthier's dissenting judgment remains worthwhile reading, however, for an appreciation of how legal and social attitudes have shifted in Ontario in the past 10 years or so. There were, at the time, concerns expressed that the gay and lesbian community may have different views regarding support obligations than have been traditionally accepted in the heterosexual community. See, for example, the Ontario Law Reform Commission *Report on the Rights and Responsibilities of Cohabitants under the Family Law Act* (Toronto: 1993) which recommended against ascribing spousal status under the *FLA* to all same-sex couples who cohabited for at least three consecutive years. The Commission urged the government to acquire more information concerning same-sex relationships, including information about the attitudes and expectations within the gay and lesbian community.

2. Do you agree with the conclusions in *Hazlewood v. Kent* and *McEachern v. Fry Estate*? How does one distinguish between an affair and cohabitation?

3. *Sanderson v. Russell* was applied in *Dicks v. Zavitz* (1979), 13 R.F.L. (2d) 179 (Ont. Prov. Ct.) where a woman and man were found to have cohabited continuously despite numerous separations lasting from three days to six weeks. The court held that the woman had never initiated the separations with the intent of ending the relationship but was merely demonstrating that she would not comply with the man's sadistic demands.

In *Harris v. Godkewitsch* (1983), 41 O.R. (2d) 779 (Prov. Ct.) the applicant was denied support. The applicant had entered the relationship with the respondent on the basis that she could come and go as she pleased. The applicant would occasionally absent herself without notice or the respondent's blessing. On one occasion, she went to Paris, France, for four months. Prior to her departure, she indicated to friends that she would be there at least a year and might never return. It was held that the applicant failed to prove that she did not intend to end the continuous relationship with the respondent when she left for Paris. As a result, the period of continuous cohabitation was interrupted by her action.

4. In Alberta, the *Adult Interdependent Relationships Act*, S.A. 2002, c. A-4.5, indicates that persons are "adult interdependent partners" if (a) they have lived in a relationship of interdependence (i) for a continuous period of at least three years or (ii) of some permanence if there is a child of the relationship; or (b) they have entered into an adult interdependent partner agreement in accordance with the *Adult Interdependent Partner Agreement Regulation*, Alta. Reg. 141/2003. Two persons, whether of the same sex or of opposite sexes, who live together in a non-conjugal relationship as well as those who live together in a conjugal relationship can therefore qualify as "adult interdependent partners". The Alberta *Family Law Act*, S.A. 2003, c. F-4.5 allows the court to make an order for support if adult interdependent partners have separated, or if one partner is refusing unreasonably to support the other. Do you think the Ontario law should be expanded to impose support obligations on people who are living in relationships of interdependence, regardless of whether the relationship is conjugal? See *Beyond Conjugality: Recognizing and Supporting Close Personal Adult Relationships* (Ottawa: 2001), in which the Law Reform Commission of Canada proposed (at ix) a new approach to the "legal recognition and support of the full range of close personal relationships among adults".

5. Pursuant to the *Civil Code* in Quebec, only married partners are "spouses", entitled to spousal support upon breakdown of the relationship. At the time of writing (2008), there is a constitutional challenge in the Quebec Superior Court asserting that the *Civil Code* unfairly discriminates against unmarried cohabitees. In *Walsh v. Bona* (2002), 32 R.F.L. (5th) 81 (S.C.C.) reproduced in Chapter 4, the Supreme Court of Canada determined that provincial legislation that does not grant unmarried couples the same property rights as married couples is constitutional. The court's reasoning was that the decision to marry, or not to marry, should be respected, and that the court should not impose the property rules that apply to married couples on those who have chosen not to marry. Do you think this reasoning will prevail regarding spousal support in Quebec?

Recall that Quebec is the jurisdiction with the highest proportion of unmarried cohabitees of all of the provinces (see Chapter 1).

6. In *Brebric v. Niksic* (2002), 215 D.L.R. (4th) 643, 27 R.F.L. (5th) 279 (Ont. C.A.); leave to appeal refused (2003), 181 O.A.C. 200 (note) (S.C.C.), a man and a woman cohabited outside marriage for about 18 months before the man died in a motor vehicle accident. The woman commenced an action against the driver of the van in which the man had been a passenger, claiming damages pursuant to s. 61 of the *FLA*. That section provided a right of action to, *inter alia*, the spouse of a person who was killed by the fault or neglect of another in circumstances where the deceased would have been entitled to recover damages. The section adopted the extended definition of "spouse" contained in s. 29. The woman also brought a motion for a declaration that s. 61 was unconstitutional because the adopted definition of spouse unfairly discriminated against her contrary to s. 15 of the *Canadian Charter of Rights and Freedoms* and a further declaration that she was entitled to make a claim under s. 61. The motions judge granted the van's driver's motion for summary judgment dismissing the action for damages.

The Ontario Court of Appeal dismissed the woman's appeal. It reasoned that, because the woman's attack on the definition was based on the fact that it drew a distinction on the basis of the duration of common law relationships, the appropriate comparison was between unmarried persons cohabiting for three years or more and those cohabiting for less than three years. It held that the definition did subject these two groups to differential treatment on the basis of a personal characteristic. However, the court reasoned that the woman's claim faltered since the differential treatment was not based on a ground listed in s. 15(1) or a ground analogous to those listed. In particular, it held that a person's status as one who cohabited with another for less than three years was not an analogous ground. That status, it noted, was not immutable. Rather, it was inherently fluid and transitory since it changed with the passage of time and lasted a maximum of three years. Furthermore, the court stated that this variable status had not historically been a basis for stereotyping or a demeaning proxy for merit-based decision-making.

The court also found that the woman's claim failed the final step in the s. 15 analysis because the differential treatment did not constitute discrimination. It stated that the impugned definition gave equal recognition to married and common law spousal relationships and was not based on any moral disapproval of unmarried persons who cohabited for fewer than three years. It concluded that the three-year period was a reasonable attempt to target only those relationships of sufficient duration and demonstrated stability so as to justify the imposition of ongoing private support obligations.

In light of the fact that the appellate court concluded that there was no infringement of s. 15, it was not strictly necessary to determine whether the definition could be saved under s. 1 of the *Charter* as a reasonable limit on equality rights. However, the court noted that the legislature chose the three-year period of cohabitation as a reasonable indicator of the kind of common law relationship that ought to attract ongoing private obligations. It stated (at para. 31):

> Although the three-year minimum period of cohabitation may not correspond precisely with the characteristics of all common law relationships, any deleterious effects of the definition of "spouse" are outweighed by the advantages of having an objective standard by which individuals and the courts can determine when state-imposed support obligations and rights of action arise.

3. When and Where are Applications brought under the *Family Law Act*?

A support application under Part III of the *FLA* must be brought in the Family Court of the Superior Court of Justice in those parts of Ontario serviced by a specialized court that handles only family law cases. In the other areas, they may be brought in the Ontario Court of Justice or the Superior Court of Justice. It should be noted that the Ontario Court of Justice does not have the same powers in making support orders as the other courts mentioned (see s. 34(2)). These limitations on the court's power should be considered in determining where the application is brought. It should also be recalled that the Ontario Court of Justice has no jurisdiction to hear applications under Parts I or II of the Act (Property and the Matrimonial Home).

Section 33 does not specify that the spouses must be separated before a support application is made. In *Galea v. Galea* (1980), 15 R.F.L. (2d) 191 (Ont. Prov. Ct.), the wife applied for support under the *Family Law Reform Act*, 1978 even though the parties were still cohabiting. The parties agreed on the quantum of support and that there should be an attachment of the husband's wages in order to ensure that it was paid. The court made the order as requested even though it observed (at 192): "... this order is not due to a separation of the parties and to make sure that some of the income of the respondent goes into the hands of the wife and children rather than the hands of the race track ...". It might also be possible to bring a support application on the eve of separation to provide funds so that the applicant can move out and relocate. Do you think the courts would entertain support applications where the spouses are still cohabiting but one of them believes that the other is not providing sufficient funds for the needs of the household?

An application for support under the *FLA* must be brought while the parties are still spouses. Therefore, an application cannot be made for support pursuant to the *FLA* after divorce. Until fairly recently, the Act contained a limitation period, but this has been abolished. Also, the general limitation period set in the *Limitations Act, 2002*, S.O. 2002, c. 24, Sch. B does not apply: s. 16(1)(c).

Section 36(1) provides that, where a divorce proceeding has been commenced, an application for support under the Act that has not been adjudicated is stayed unless the court orders otherwise. If a marriage is terminated by divorce and the question of support is not adjudicated in the divorce proceeding, an order for support made under the *FLA* "continues in force according to its terms": s. 36(3). It should also be noted that it is possible to claim support as alternative relief under the *FLA* in a divorce proceeding. In this way, if the divorce is not granted, the court can still deal with the alternative claim for relief.

4. Applications for Spousal Support under the *Divorce Act*

Section 15.2(1) of the *Divorce Act* specifies that either or both spouses may apply for a spousal support order. Applications may be made in the divorce proceeding itself to the court that has jurisdiction to grant the divorce. Once such an application is made, the court has authority to grant interim support: s. 15.2(2). Final orders may be made at the trial of the divorce proceeding. See ss. 2 ("divorce proceeding") and 15.2(1). As the Parliament of Canada's jurisdiction over support is ancillary to its legislative jurisdiction over divorce, the power to order support under the *Divorce Act* ceases if the court refuses to grant the divorce: *Lietz v. Lietz* (1990), 30 R.F.L. (3d) 293 (N.B. Q.B.). See also *Ninham v. Ninham* (1997), 29 R.F.L. (4th) 41 (Ont. Gen. Div.), where the court stayed the divorce under s. 11(1)(b) of the *Divorce Act*. The wife advanced a spousal support claim under that Act or, alternatively, under the *FLA*. Justice Aston concluded (at 53): "Regardless of which legislation is applicable, the considerations and the result are the same in this particular case."

Applications for support can also be made in a separate corollary relief proceeding following the divorce. See ss. 2 ("corollary relief proceeding") and 15.2(1). For this purpose, s. 15 stipulates that "spouse" includes a former spouse. Section 4 specifies when a court has jurisdiction to hear and determine a corollary relief proceeding. It should be noted that the courts had held under the *Divorce Act* of 1968 that they had jurisdiction to make a maintenance order after the granting of the divorce as well as at the time the decree was granted: *Zacks v. Zacks*, 10 R.F.L. 53, [1973] S.C.R. 891; *Ouellet v. Ouimet* (1975), 7 N.R. 1 (S.C.C.); and *Lapointe v. Klint* (1974), [1975] 2 S.C.R. 539, 20 R.F.L. 307. However, they were quite reluctant to exercise this jurisdiction (see Steel, "The Award of Maintenance Subsequent to Decree Nisi: A Question of Jurisdiction or Discretion?" (1981), 19 R.F.L. (2d) 33). To some extent, this reluctance reflected a recognition of the limited nature of Parliament's constitutional authority over support. Since Parliament's jurisdiction is ancillary to its power over divorce, there should arguably be a connection between the divorce and the need for support: *Wark v. Wark* (1986), 2 R.F.L. (3d) 337 (Man. C.A.). See also *Murphy v. Murphy* (1994), 10 R.F.L. (4th) 102 (Man. C.A.) at 105. Such a connection may become tenuous if the application for support is not made until some time after the divorce.

In *Delaney v. Delaney* (1995), 11 R.F.L. (4th) 155 (B.C.C.A.), the parties separated in 1982 and a court awarded the wife periodic support under the British Columbia *Family Relations Act*. The divorce judgment of 1988 was silent regarding support. In 1991, the husband obtained a "Final Order" under the *Family Relations Act* specifying that all support would terminate later that year. In 1993, a court granted the wife periodic support under the *Divorce Act* in a corollary relief proceeding. This order was upheld on appeal. The British Columbia Court of Appeal confirmed that (i) a support order can be made under the *Divorce Act* after the divorce is granted even if no such support was awarded at the time of the divorce, and (ii) any order made under the *Family Relations Act* does not preclude a support order under the *Divorce Act*.

The Ontario Court of Appeal held in *Rothgiesser v. Rothgiesser* (2000), 2 R.F.L. (5th) 266 (Ont. C.A.) and *Okmyansky v. Okmyansky* (2007), 38 R.F.L. (6th) 291 (Ont. C.A.) that an Ontario court only has jurisdiction to deal with a corollary relief proceeding if there has been a Canadian divorce. See also *Leonard v. Booker* (2007), 286 D.L.R. (4th) 451, 44 R.F.L. (6th) 237 (N.B. C.A.). The Quebec Superior Court disagreed in *M. (O.) v. K. (A.)* (2000), 9 R.F.L. (5th) 111 (Que. S.C.).

Under the 1968 *Divorce Act*, it was unclear whether either party could ask for a determination of support or whether only the spouse seeking support could apply. The wording of s. 15.2(1) of the current Act suggests that either spouse can apply. See *Strong v. Strong* (1987), 5 R.F.L. (3d) 209 (Ont. H.C.); *Clayton v. Clayton* (1989), 19 R.F.L. (3d) 430 (Ont. Div. Ct.);

and *Callison v. Callison* (1989), 22 R.F.L. (3d) 123 (B.C. C.A.). Compare *Rehn v. Rehn* (1988), 13 R.F.L. (3d) 440 (Ont. U.F.C.). There are several reasons why one spouse might apply for a support order in favour of the other spouse. There may be an existing order under provincial legislation that the payor spouse thinks is too high. If a new order is made under the *Divorce Act*, the previous order will cease to be operative. An order under the *Divorce Act* may also be sought to effectively override the support provisions of a domestic contract that the payor spouse considers too onerous (see Chapter 9, *DOMESTIC CONTRACTS*).

5. Determining Spousal Support Entitlement

(1) Introduction

Under both the *FLA* and the *Divorce Act*, the court must determine whether a spouse is entitled to support. This is a two-step process. Once the initial hurdle of technical entitlement has been passed (either establishing a valid marriage, or a form of marriage in good faith, or establishing the requirements of s. 29 of the *FLA*), the second, and more substantive entitlement issue has to be resolved: on the facts of an individual case, is the spouse entitled to support? Although the two pieces of legislation contain different language, Ontario courts have applied the same theories of entitlement regardless of which legislation is being considered. The language of both pieces of legislation supports this approach. Case law regarding entitlement under the *Divorce Act* is therefore often used to support discussions of entitlement under the *FLA*, and *vice versa*.

Spousal support entitlement theory has been the subject of intense academic and judicial commentary over the past 20 years or more. Understanding modern thinking about spousal support entitlement requires some knowledge of the jurisprudence which emerged from the Supreme Court of Canada in the 1980s and 1990s.

During the 1980s and early 1990s, many wives settled for spousal support for only very short periods (four to five years in many cases), even if the marriage had lasted a long time. The primary reasons for this were that litigation is expensive; and at that time, the outcomes on spousal support were difficult to predict. A woman could spend considerable time and money on an application for spousal support, without much certainty of a result that justified her investment. There were sometimes secondary reasons, too, such as a trade-off regarding the children (custody of the children might be exchanged for a promise to limit spousal support). Often, the consent court order or agreement containing a termination date of some four or five years would prove to be inadequate and the support recipient would come back to court, looking for an extension on the spousal support arrangement. It was this situation that the Supreme Court was attempting to address in the cases that follow (*Messier v. Delage*; *Pelech v. Pelech*; *Richardson v. Richardon*; *Caron v. Caron*).

Justice Lamer's dissent in *Messier v. Delage* (1983), 35 R.F.L. (2d) 337 (S.C.C.) can now be seen as the initial source of the court's thinking about variation of spousal support agreements between 1983 and 1992. It was followed by *Pelech*, *Richardson* and *Caron* (known together as "the *Pelech* trilogy"). In the *Pelech* trilogy, the court held that in cases in which the recipient was returning to court and asking to extend the spousal support beyond the term she had originally agreed to, she must demonstrate a material change in circumstance and, further, establish that the change in her circumstances was somehow "causally connected" to the marriage.

Despite the context in which the Supreme Court of Canada articulated the requirement of a causal connection, the idea that need had to be related to the marriage relationship was attractive, most likely for its seeming simplicity. Some writers and trial court judges soon adopted the concept as a way to determine entitlement on initial applications for spousal support. An important aspect of the history of spousal support law in Canada is the influence of Professor James McLeod. After *Pelech* was released, Professor McLeod, who at that time was the editor of the *Reports of Family Law*, published an annotation that affected the thinking of many practitioners and trial judges. Professor McLeod in 7 R.F.L. (3d) 226, at 232:

> The reasons of Wilson J. in *Pelech, Richardson and Caron* confirm a basic support model. In order to obtain support, a claimant must prove:
>
> (1) need;
>
> (2) that the need arises for a legally acceptable reason; and
>
> (3) that the need/ inability is causally connected to the marriage. ...
>
> The reasons purport to spell out a support model which emphasizes the individualistic nature of the support obligation. People enter marriage as individuals and leave it as such. Following marriage breakdown, the parties should be free to make new lives for themselves without an ongoing contingent liability. Where a spouse is unable to relate his/ her inability to achieve self-sufficiency to the marital relationship, there is no reason to burden the other spouse with the support obligation. Based on the support model postulated in *Pelech, Richardson and Caron*, support is not to be awarded to compensate for systemic gender-based inequality in the workplace or society. Rather, it is to be awarded to minimize the economic loss incurred by a spouse from the roles adopted in marriage. If a spouse cannot prove his/ her income or job position has suffered as a result of the marital relationship, no support should be awarded.

This interpretation of the reasons in *Pelech* suggested that trial judges should be looking at the causal connection as a determining factor in initial applications for support. The idea was new, but it dovetailed with emerging, and perhaps optimistic, social notions of women's ability to become full, independent participants in working life outside the home after having children. It seemed like a natural progression to many at the time, flowing out of social change and the Supreme Court's decisions in the trilogy. It took the Supreme Court of Canada decision in *Moge v. Moge* to restrict the trilogy to its facts, and to create a theory of spousal support that made more sense in the actual circumstances many women found themselves in following longer marriages.

(2) "Causal Connection"

BALA, *ENTITLEMENT TO SPOUSAL SUPPORT: ASKING THE TOUGH QUESTIONS*

Schaffer, M. ed., *Contemporary Issues in Family Law: Engaging with the Legacy of James G. McLeod*, Toronto, Carswell, 2007 (Footnotes omitted)

The first significant occasion for the Supreme Court of Canada to address the issue of entitlement to support after the adoption of major family law reforms of the latter part of the twentieth century was in its 1983 decision in *Messier v Delage*. The Court was clearly divided over the issue of entitlement. During the twelve years of living together the woman had assumed primary responsibility for the care of the two children of the marriage and had dropped out of the labour force. Following separation the woman received child and spousal support, and furthered her education, but was still unable to find significant employment. After five years of paying spousal support, the man claimed that his former wife was no longer entitled to spousal support as she should have been self-supporting. The four member majority held that the former wife was still entitled to continued spousal support. In the majority judgment, Chouinard J. highlighted the discretionary nature of spousal support decisions, but also emphasized that at some point (undefined by the Court), the woman would no longer be entitled to look to her former husband for support. ...

In 1987 the Supreme Court decided the spousal support "Trilogy", *Pelch, Richardson and Caron*. These cases all dealt with the power of a court under the 1968 *Divorce Act* to override spousal support provisions of a separation agreement that was entered into with independent legal advice and was not unconscionable. Justice Wilson wrote the majority judgments, articulating a test that allowed a court to exercise its "relieving power" only if after the agreement was made there had been a "radical change in circumstances flowing from an economic pattern of dependency engendered by the marriage." She referred to the need to establish a "causal connection between the changed circumstances and the marriage." While it is clear that the decisions dealt with the issue of the effect of a separation agreement on a later spousal support claim, Wilson J. had concurred in the dissent in *Messier v. Delage*, and some of her statements in the Trilogy could have been interpreted as being premised on a view that entitlement to support should be based on establishing a relationship between need and roles assumed in the marriage.

. . . . .

After *Pelech* was decided, many and probably most, spousal support decisions adopted some form of the "causal connection" test, with at least 15 reported decisions in the RFL's making explicit reference to [Professor James] McLeod's *Annotation to Pelech*, and many others clearly relying on it as establishing the law. It is apparent that after *Pelech*, or more accurately after McLeod's Annotation, it was more difficult for women to get spousal support, and limited term orders were more common.

In terms of policy analysis, the "causal connection" test can in some ways be viewed as an appropriate response to a "partnership of equals model" of marriage, but in articulating this general theory of spousal support, Prof. McLeod had a narrower and more focused vision of spousal support than what was recognized by the relevant provisions of either the 1968 or 1986 *Divorce Acts*. Further, the test that he was promoting was itself one of the narrower versions of the concept of "causal connection." Prof. McLeod placed great emphasis on self-sufficiency and gave lesser weight to the long-term consequences of women assuming primary domestic roles than other commentators who were writing at that time about differing formulations of a "causal connection" approach to spousal support.

An example of the influence of the causal connection test and the attitude of Prof. McLeod towards it is provided by a case decided about a year after the Trilogy, the Ontario case of *Bast v. Bast* [(1988), 13 R.F.L. (3d) 98 (Ont. H.C.)]. In his brief written decision, which Prof. McLeod thought merited reporting and annotation in the RFL's, Salhany L.J.S.C. simply accepted (without explicit reference to either *Pelech* or Prof. McLeod) that a former spouse was only entitled to support for as long as she could establish that she had a need "causally connected" to the marriage. The judge concluded that spousal support should terminate for a 45 year old woman three and a half years after her divorce, even though the woman had stayed at home during a 21 year marriage and had been the primary caregiver of the couple's two children. At the time of the application she was earning $14,000 and her former husband was making $40,000. The judge accepted that her period out of the work force "created a causal connection between the marriage and her dependency," but held that her lower standard of living was no longer the "fault" of her former husband and hence she should no longer be liable for her support. Prof. McLeod wrote approvingly in his Annotation that the "decision should put to rest the fears that the notion of causal connection [will] deny relief to 'traditional' spouses." Many would argue that a woman in her mid-forties who has been out of the labour force for 21 years will have suffered a loss of experience, seniority and job skills that will significantly affect her income, and will presumptively entitle her to spousal support for the rest of her working life.

In the years following the Trilogy, there was great controversy in the legal profession and academic community about the "causal connection" test and Prof. McLeod's views about the law of spousal support. McLeod was criticized as articulating an approach that was insensitive to the needs of women, and that was not consistent with the terms of the *Divorce Act*. While Prof. McLeod was out-spoken in his opinions, he was always prepared to give others a platform to air their disagreements with him, and all of the 1989 volume of the *Canadian Family Law Quarterly*, which he edited, was devoted to articles on the law of spousal support, many sharply critical of his approach. In the late 1980s and early 1990s articles were written by many other family law scholars in various journals, and while the majority clearly disagreed with the narrow interpretation of entitlement to spousal support that Prof. McLeod had propounded, his views were invariably a reference point that needed to be addressed.

MESSIER v. DELAGE

(1983), 35 R.F.L. (2d) 337, 1983 CarswellQue 60, 1983 CarswellQue 99 (S.C.C.)

[Michel Messier, the appellant in the Supreme Court, and Jocelyn Delage, the respondent, were married in 1962 and separated in February 1974. In 1975 Delage petitioned for divorce. A decree nisi was granted on 10th September 1975. It awarded custody of the two children of the marriage to the petitioner who was granted maintenance of $1,600 per month for herself and the children. The decree was made absolute on 30th December 1975. At the time of the divorce Delage, who had not worked outside the home during the marriage, was enrolled in a program of studies leading to a Master's degree in translation. In 1979 Messier applied for a variation of the spousal support order on the basis that Delage was no longer entitled to look to him for financial provision even though she had been unable to find full-time employment. He stressed that Delage had five years following separation in which to reorganize her life; that she now had a Master's degree in translation, and at the age of 38 and in good health was fully able to support herself; and that she was no longer required to stay home to look after the children since the only child in her custody was 15 years old. Finally, he pointed out that Delage had earned $5,000 in 1978 as a freelance translator.

The trial judge reduced the amount of spousal support and stipulated that the husband's obligation to pay such support should end in about six months. The Court of Appeal reversed the judgment of the Superior Court in part by striking that portion of the trial court's order setting a time limit on the spousal support. Messier appealed to the Supreme Court of Canada. He argued that the decision of the Court of Appeal effectively meant that the support obligation between former spouses survived the divorce indefinitely, thereby ignoring "the evolution in the status of married women", "the equality of treatment between the sexes established by the *Divorce Act*", and the trend to emphasize the duty to support oneself after marriage breakdown apparent in recent judicial decisions as well as in reformed provincial support legislation. Justice Chouinard, for a bare majority, held that the trial judge had disregarded the actual circumstances of the parties and that the Court of Appeal had acted properly.

JUSTICE LAMER, dissenting with JUSTICES MCINTYRE and WILSON, reasoned in part:]... This appeal raises a question of importance at the present time in view of the current economic situation, the difficulty in finding work and the resulting high rate of unemployment. Should a divorced spouse who is working always bear the consequences of all this and provide for the needs of his unemployed former spouse, or is it for the government, if it cannot remedy, at least to alleviate the effects, and to what extent? ...

Purpose of maintenance awarded to one of the spouses following a divorce

In my opinion, the purpose of maintenance is to reduce in material terms the consequences resulting from breaking the marriage bond. Maintenance will be awarded to a spouse who cannot provide for her own needs. The division of functions in traditional society has meant that it is nearly always the wife who is in this position. It was almost impossible for her, without proper training after several years of not earning her living, to find employment and so be able to provide for her own needs.

The evolution of society and of the status of women both require us to re-examine what the nature of maintenance should be. Formerly the ex-wife would, more often than not, remain a burden to her former husband indefinitely. ...

Women cannot on the one hand claim equal status without at the same time accepting responsibility for their own upkeep.

Furthermore, quite apart from the fact that the woman rather than the man is the recipient of maintenance, the divorce itself is intended to dissolve the marriage bond, whereas separation only changes the living arrangements. If the divorce terminates the marriage, it is desirable that the *Divorce Act* should apply to ensure the termination of all relations, even those that are financial, provided this must be borne in mind — that such a thing is possible.

In a working paper ((No. 12), *Maintenance on Divorce* (1975)) the Canada Law Reform Commission suggested the following at p. 30:

> We suggest that the period following divorce should be characterized in law as a time of economic transition for both spouses from the arrangements that were suitable to the marriage when one spouse may have made financial provision for both, to the single state when each should be, as before marriage, financially self-reliant. The law should require the former spouse who does not have an economic need created by the marriage to assist the one who has such a need to become financially rehabilitated. ...

Although the principles endorsed by the commission are not law, I agree with them. ...

[After reviewing the post-divorce events, Lamer J. continued.] Are these changes sufficient for a petition to cancel the maintenance?

The respondent contended that the fact she had obtained a university degree is not in itself a guarantee of employment. She has made a definite effort to become self-supporting. This is in no way a case of a lazy person who refuses to work. However, the circumstances are such that, as she has no employment, she is still entitled to receive a pension from her former husband.

The question in the case at bar is whether the ability to work is in itself a determining factor which justifies canceling the maintenance or whether, in addition, the respondent must actually be working.

The courts have hitherto held that the ability to work is a significant factor in determining the quantum of maintenance. ...

However, I would go further.

In my view the evolution of society requires that one more step be taken in favour of the final emancipation of former spouses. To me, aside from rare exceptions, the ability to work leads to "the end of the divorce" and the beginning of truly single status for each of the former spouses. I also consider that the "ability" to work should be determined intrinsically and should not in any way be determined in light of factors extrinsic to the individual, such as the labour market and the economic situation.

As maintenance is only granted for as long as it takes to acquire sufficient independence, once that independence has been acquired it follows that maintenance ceases to be necessary. A divorced spouse who is "employable" but unemployed is in the same position as other citizens, men or women, who are unemployed. The problem is a social one and it is therefore the responsibility of the government rather than the former husband. Once the spouse has been retrained, I do not see why the fact of having been married should give the now single individual any special status by comparison with any other unemployed single person. In my view, the duty of a former spouse is limited in the case of retrainable persons to the retraining period and the discretion conferred on the judge in s. 11(2) to determine what is fit and just is not a bar to this conclusion, which the evolution of society has now made necessary. The rule is not absolute and remedy under s. 11(2) is never completely excluded to compensate for the financial negative effects of the marriage, but I would only make an exception to it in, to use the words of Bergeron J., "very special circumstances". That is not the case here.

PELECH v. PELECH

(1987), 7 R.F.L. (3d) 225, 1987 CarswellBC 147, 1987 CarswellBC 703 (S.C.C.)

[In *Pelech v. Pelech*, the parties married in 1954 and had two children. The wife did not enter the labour force, but did assist her husband in his business by acting as receptionist and bookkeeper. When they divorced in 1969 they entered into a settlement agreement, having each received independent legal advice. The agreement was incorporated into the divorce decree and the husband paid the amount specified, a total of $28,760 over a period of thirteen months. Over the following years, the wife's physical and psychological problems increased to the extent that she was unable to work. By 1982, her settlement sum was gone and she was on welfare. The husband prospered and his net worth increased from about $128,000 in 1969 to $1,800,000 in 1984. The wife applied to vary the original support order. The trial judge allowed the application because there had been a gross change in circumstances and ordered support of $2,000 per month. The British Columbia Court of Appeal overturned this decision and the wife appealed further.

The Supreme Court of Canada denied the appeal, emphasizing the policy of promoting individual autonomy in setting the contractual terms for all issues arising out of a marriage breakdown. Justice Wilson, Dickson C.J.C. and Justices McIntyre, Lamer and LeDain concurring, reasoned in part:]

... [A]s I stated at the outset, the *Hyman* principle that parties cannot by contract oust the jurisdiction of the court in matters of spousal maintenance is an established tenet of Canadian law. The question thus becomes the nature and extent of the constraint imposed on the courts by the presence of an agreement which was intended by the parties to settle their affairs in a final and conclusive manner. ...

It seems to me that where the parties have negotiated their own agreement, freely and on the advice of independent legal counsel, as to how their financial affairs should be settled on the breakdown of their marriage, and the agreement is not unconscionable in the substantive law sense, it should be respected. People should be encouraged to take responsibility for their own lives and their own decisions. This should be the overriding policy consideration.

The test of radical change [as a basis for overriding a contractual support waiver] is an attempt to carve a fairly narrow exception to the general policy of restraint. It fails, however, in my opinion in one important particular. It makes the mere magnitude of the change the justification for the Court's intervention and takes no account of whether or not the change is in any way related to the fact of the marriage. In order to impose responsibility for changed circumstances on a former spouse it seems to me essential that there be some relationship between the change and the marriage... . In the case of a wife who has devoted herself exclusively to home and children and has acquired no working skills outside the home, this relationship is readily established. The former spouse in these circumstances should have a responsibility for a radical change in his ex-wife's circumstances generated as a consequence of her total dependency during the period of the marriage. By way of contrast, a former spouse who simply falls upon hard times through unwise investment, business adversity, or a life style beyond his or her means should not be able to fall back on the former spouse, no matter how radical the change may be, simply because they once were husband and wife.

Absent some causal connection between the changed circumstances and the marriage, it seems to me that parties who have declared their relationship at an end should be taken at their word. They made the decision to marry and they made the decision to terminate their marriage. Their decisions should be respected. They should thereafter be free to make new lives for themselves without an ongoing contingent liability for future misfortunes which may befall the other. It is only, in my view, where the future misfortune has its genesis in the fact of the marriage that the court should be able to override the settlement of their affairs made by the parties themselves. Each marriage relationship creates its own economic pattern from which the self-sufficiency or dependency of the partners flows. The assessment of the extent of that pattern's post-marital impact is essentially a matter for the judge of first instance. The causal connection between the severe hardship being experienced by the former spouse and the marriage provides, in my view, the necessary legal criterion for determining when a case falls within the "narrow range of cases" [where a court should override a final agreement relating to spousal support.]. ... Accordingly, where an applicant seeking maintenance or an increase in the existing level of maintenance establishes that he or she has suffered a radical change in circumstances flowing from an economic pattern of dependency engendered by the marriage, the court may exercise its relieving power. Otherwise, the obligation to support the former spouse should be, as in the case of any other citizen, the communal responsibility of the state.

VIII. Disposition Of The Appeal

The dependency of the appellant Mrs. Pelech on social assistance is evidence of the extremity of her need. In addition, there are the observations of Wong L.J.S.C. at trial that her impoverishment is dire and her future prospects limited if not non-existent. However, although I agree with him that her present state evidences "a gross change in circumstances" since the time of the original order incorporating the minutes of settlement in 1969, no link is found by the trial judge between the change of circumstances and her former marriage to Mr. Pelech. Indeed, quite the contrary. Wong L.J.S.C. found that the psychological problems which have resulted in her inability to care for herself pre-dated the marriage and contributed to its failure. He specifically rejected the submission that they stemmed from the marriage or from the behaviour of the respondent during it. Wong L.J.S.C. also rejected the submission that the agreement was improvident and unconscionable. He found that it was entered into freely by Mrs. Pelech on the advice of counsel and was perfectly fair at the time it was made. He found, however, that the basic premise on which it was entered into, namely that Mrs. Pelech would be able to work and support herself, had not materialized.

While I realize that Mrs. Pelech's present hardship is great, to burden the respondent with her care fifteen years after their marriage has ended for no other reason than that they were once husband and wife seems to me to create a fiction of marital responsibility at the expense of individual responsibility. I believe that the courts must recognize the right of the individual to end a relationship as well as to begin one and should not, when all other aspects of the relationship have long since ceased, treat the financial responsibility as continuing indefinitely into the future. Where parties, instead of resorting to litigation, have acted in a mature and responsible fashion to settle their financial affairs in a final way and their settlement is not vulnerable to attack on any other basis, it should not, in my view, be undermined by courts concluding with the benefit of hindsight that they should have done it differently.

For these reasons I would dismiss the appeal. I would make no award as to costs.

[Justice La Forest gave separate, concurring reasons. He stressed that all aspects of the marital relationship should, as much as possible, come to an end on divorce and that financial ties should continue only if necessary to provide for a former spouse whose needs were related to the marriage relationship. Thus the trial judge had erred in taking into account changes that were not attributable to the marriage or the settlement. He concluded: "This is not a case, as in my view *Richardson* [reproduced below] is, where the poverty of the spouse results from the marriage."]

RICHARDSON v. RICHARDSON

(1987), 7 R.F.L. (3d) 304, 1987 CarswellOnt 315, 1987 CarswellOnt 963 (S.C.C.)

[The parties married in 1967 and separated in 1979. They had two children. The wife worked full-time until the birth of the second child in 1974. Apart from two jobs of very short duration in 1974 and 1976, the wife did not thereafter work outside the home. The husband was a sergeant in the police force. *Family Law Reform Act* proceedings were settled in 1981 with the assistance of legal advice by minutes of settlement. They provided that the spouses would share equally the repayment of a $20,000 debt to the wife's mother, that the husband would assume additional debts of about $10,000 accumulated during the marriage, and that the wife would release her interest, worth about $11,000, in the matrimonial home to the husband. The settlement also specified that the wife would have custody of one child and the husband the other and that the husband would pay spousal support of $175 per month for one year and child support of $300 per month. The written settlement stipulated that it was a final and conclusive settlement of all claims between the parties. Two years later, the wife commenced divorce proceedings. Now on welfare, she sought spousal support and increased child support. The trial judge did not increase the child support, but awarded spousal support of $500 per month and indexed the support to keep up with inflation. The Ontario Court of Appeal struck the spousal support award and the indexing clause, but increased child support to $500 per month. Justice Grange, speaking for a unanimous court, stated:

> The trial judge granted maintenance to the wife notwithstanding the minutes of settlement upon the grounds that there had been a change of circumstance entitling the wife to that allowance. We can see no change of circumstance in either the wife or the husband that would justify that allowance. It is possible that the parties contemplated when limiting the support for the wife to the one-year period that the wife would, during that period, not only seek, but obtain employment. Indeed there is some suggestion in the evidence of the husband that that was so. The difficulty with that assumption, however, is that when the solicitor for the wife was examined in the previous proceedings, he was not permitted to give the substance of his advice to the wife and consequently, we do not know whether or not that was her contemplation at the time.

The wife appealed further.]

WILSON J. (DICKSON C.J.C., McINTYRE, LAMER and LE DAIN JJ. concurring): — The issue in this case is when is it "fit and just" for a judge to make an order for spousal maintenance under s. 11(1) of the *Divorce Act*, R.S.C. 1970, c. D-8 in an amount different from that agreed upon by the parties in an antecedent settlement agreement. ...

In approaching this case the court should have regard to the principles enunciated in *Pelech v. Pelech* ... that a court should vary a settlement agreement only where there has been a radical change in the circumstances of a former spouse and that change is the result of a pattern of economic dependency generated by the marriage relationship. I appreciate that that principle was stated in the context of a s. 11(2) application and that this case involves s. 11(1). I appreciate also that the wording of the two subsections is different. Section 11(1) provides that the court may make the order it thinks fit and just having regard to the condition, means and other circumstances of the parties. Section 11(2) states that an order made under s. 11(1) may be varied if the court thinks it fit and just to do so having regard to any change in the conditions, means or other circumstances of the spouses. Nevertheless, in my view, despite the difference in the statutory language, when a court is confronted with a settlement agreement reached by the parties the same criteria should be applied under both sections. The underlying rationale is the same under both, namely 1) the importance of finality in the financial affairs of former spouses and 2) the principle of deference to the right and responsibility of individuals to make their own decisions. ...

In my view, the only difference under the two subsections is that in a s. 11(1) application the change being considered will have occurred between the signing of the agreement and the application for the decree nisi whereas in the s. 11(2) application the change will have occurred between the granting of the decree nisi and the application for variation.

Given that the *Pelech* test is applicable in a s. 11(1) as well as a s. 11(2) application, the test is not met on the facts of this case. No event has occurred which the appellant is peculiarly unable to deal with because of a pattern of economic dependency generated by the marriage. At the time the separation agreement was concluded Mrs. Richardson was unemployed and Mr. Richardson was a sergeant in the Ottawa police force earning approximately $40,000 per annum. The same conditions existed when the divorce proceeding was heard. Not only had there been no change of circumstances, as the Ontario Court of Appeal found, but it was also questionable whether Mrs. Richardson's position at the time could be attributed to a pattern of economic dependency developed during the marriage. As has already been mentioned, Mrs. Richardson was married in 1967 and worked continuously as a clerk-typist until the birth of her second child in 1974. She worked for one month in 1974 and for three months in 1976. The couple separated in November 1979. In sum, she was employed more often than not during the marriage. Moreover, the period of time from her last employment until the date of separation was not that great. In this sense it cannot be said that the marriage atrophied her skills or impaired their marketability. ...

... As discussed in *Pelech*, the courts in making an award of spousal maintenance are required to analyze the pattern of financial interdependence generated by each marriage relationship and devise a support order that minimizes as far as possible the economic consequences of the relationship's dissolution. Financial provision may be temporary or permanent. Spousal maintenance is the right of the spouse and a spouse can therefore contract as to the amount of maintenance he or she is to receive. Where this happens the court will be strongly inclined to enforce that contract: see *Pelech v. Pelech*.

... [I]f the court's concern is that the child is being inadequately provided for, then that concern should be addressed by varying the amount of child support. ... Accordingly, in the circumstances of this case Mrs. Richardson's support payments should not be increased simply because she has custody of a child. The Court of Appeal adopted the proper route and increased the child support payments. This part of the order is not being contested.

Counsel for the appellant also relies on another ground of appeal. He argues that the parties in this case limited the period of spousal maintenance because it was their common expectation that Mrs. Richardson would be employed within that period of time. This expectation did not materialize and therefore the judge hearing the petition for divorce was free to make the order he considered "fit and just" without regard to the minutes of settlement entered into by the parties. Counsel argues, in effect, that the lost or failed expectation represents a change of circumstances from those anticipated by the parties justifying a departure from the settlement agreement under s. 11(1) of the *Divorce Act*. ...

However, the evidence of the parties' expectation in this case is unclear. ...

In the absence of evidence of a common expectation of the parties it seems to me that the minutes of settlement entered into by the parties freely and on the advice of independent legal counsel (which are not unconscionable in the substantive law sense) should be respected subject to the principle enunciated in *Pelech*. The possibility that Mrs. Richardson would not be employed at the end of the one-year period was not unforeseeable. Although she had clerk-typist skills she had not been recently employed. It is not as though Mrs. Richardson had been guaranteed a specific job and through a series of unexpected events that job fell through. ...

Having regard to Mrs. Richardson's circumstances at the time of the agreement including her skills, her previous record of employment and the fact that no employment position had been guaranteed to her, it cannot be said that the possibility of her being unemployed was completely outside the reasonable contemplation of the parties. I do not believe therefore that Mrs. Richardson is entitled on that ground to be relieved from the clause in the minutes of settlement which provides for the cessation of her maintenance at the expiry of the one-year period.

[The appeal was dismissed, La Forest J. dissenting. In his dissent, La Forest J. held that the test enunciated in *Pelech* to deal with variation applications under s. 11(2) of the *Divorce Act* should not apply to s. 11(1). In variation applications, a judge was being asked to vary an order which had accepted that the agreement was fit and just. Therefore, the judge's authority was confined to considering circumstances that had since intervened. Under s. 11(1), the judge had to determine whether the support provision in the agreement was "fit and just". Although the existence of the agreement was an important fact to consider, the judge was not bound by it. La Forest J. stated (at 319): "To allow separation agreements the kind of compelling weight argued for in this case is effectively to rewrite the Act so as to provide that where such an agreement exists, the trial judge's discretion is solely to vary the agreement in those cases only where radical or ... catastrophic changes have occurred since it was made." He pointed out that neither the *Divorce Act* nor the various provincial statutes adopted the proposition that separation agreements were to have binding force unless radical changes occurred.

Turning to the facts of the case, La Forest J. concluded (at 325) that Mrs. Richardson's present situation flowed directly from the division of functions during the marriage:

> During the years she stayed home with the children, her skills would ... not only have atrophied; she would not have been able to gain the new skills that are so necessary today in her field as well as in others. ... Mrs. Richardson is now in her mid-forties and must find time and energy to care for a child, factors that are by no means negligible in assessing her competitive position as against younger people with recent training.

Justice La Forest considered these factors sufficient to justify the trial judge's decision.]

NOTES AND QUESTIONS

1. The third case in the trilogy handed down on June 4, 1987, was *Caron v. Caron* (1987), 7 R.F.L. (3d) 274 (S.C.C.). In that case, the parties were married in 1964 and separated in 1978. Two years later, with the advice of independent legal counsel, they concluded a separation agreement that settled property matters and provided for the payment of support to the wife until such time as she "shall remarry or cohabit as man and wife with any person for a continuous period of time in excess of ninety (90) days". The agreement provided also that the quantum of support could be varied "by a court if circumstances changed." The essential parts of the agreement were incorporated into the decree nisi of divorce. After the divorce, the former wife cohabited with a man for more than three months and the former husband ceased the support payments. The former wife, who went onto social assistance, applied for renewed support. Her variation application was denied at trial and the appellate court affirmed this judgment. The Supreme Court of Canada unanimously dismissed the former wife's appeal. It concluded that the paragraph providing for termination of support was valid and enforceable and had been properly invoked by the respondent. It also held that the paragraph allowing for variation was limited to quantum and did not authorize reinstatement of support where the right to such support had been forfeited.

The Supreme Court of Canada also held that the power to vary maintenance under s. 11(2) of the 1968 *Divorce Act* should not be exercised in this situation. Wilson J. (Dickson C.J.C., McIntyre, Lamer, and Le Dain JJ. concurring) stated (at 282):

> [T]he court's power to vary maintenance in a divorce decree is very limited where the provisions in the decree are the result of a negotiated settlement freely entered into by the parties on the advice of independent legal counsel. The approach of the courts is to respect such settlements wherever possible and to exercise their power of intervention under the *Divorce Act* only in the case of a radical

change in circumstances related to a pattern of economic dependency of one party on the other generated by the marriage relationship: see *Pelech*. We have no evidence in this case of such a change in
circumstances.

2. In *Richardson*, Wilson J. felt that it was questionable whether Mrs. Richardson's situation could be attributed to a pattern of economic dependency developed during the marriage. Justice La Forest specifically disagreed.
Which view is more convincing?

3. The Supreme Court of Canada in *Miglin v. Miglin*, [2003] 1 S.C.R. 303, 34 R.F.L. (5th) 255, eventually
adopted a new approach to final agreements dealing with spousal support. See Chapter 9, *DOMESTIC
CONTRACTS*.

(3) More Modern Bases For Spousal Support

MAUR AND BALA, "SPOUSAL SUPPORT LAW IN CANADA: THE CONTINUING IMPORTANCE OF THE BASIS FOR ENTITLEMENT"

Paper presented at the National Family Law Institute, July, 2008 (Footnotes omitted)

The 1992 Supreme Court of Canada decision in *Moge* [(1992), 43 R.F.L. (3d) 345
(S.C.C.), excerpts reproduced below] dealt with entitlement to compensatory support in the
case of longer term marriages with children, while the 1999 decision in *Bracklow* [(1999),
44 R.F.L. (4th) 1 (S.C.C.), excerpts reproduced below] considered needs-based entitlement
for ill spouses at the end of a shorter marriage. Both cases extended the boundaries of entitlement, and discussed the social implications of spousal support in sometimes vague but
expansive terms. In *Moge* the Court clearly rejected a narrow view of causal connection and
accepted that a spouse who stayed out of the labour force for significant periods to look after
children was entitled to support to compensate for the long term effects on her earning potential of the role she assumed in marriage, this support might well be indefinite. Justice
L'Heureux-Dubé recognized that entitlement to support is to reflect the roles adopted during
marriage rather than arising out of the status of spouse:

> The equitable sharing of the economic consequences of marriage or marriage breakdown, however, is
> not a general tool of redistribution which is activated by the mere fact of marriage. ... Presumably,
> there will be the occasional marriage where both spouses maximize their earning potential by work-
> ing outside the home, pursuing economic and educational opportunities in a similar manner, dividing
> up the domestic labour identically, and either making no economic sacrifices for the other or, more
> likely, making them equally. In such a utopian scenario there might be no apparent call for compensa-
> tion. The spouses are able to make a clean break and continue on with their respective lives. ... In
> most marriages in which both partners make economic sacrifices and share domestic responsibilities,
> or where one spouse has suffered economic losses in order to enable the other spouse to further a
> career, their roles should be considered in the spousal support order.

Justice L'Heureux-Dubé argued that the inadequacy in spousal support awards had
played a significant role in the post-separation impoverishment of women, and recognized
that in long term marriages the disadvantages that a woman suffered as a result of the role
which she assumed in marriage could well result in the right to compensatory support for
life; in *Moge* the marriage was 17 years and the support was continued for longer than that
by the Court.

In *Bracklow*, the Court discussed three different conceptual bases that may be used to
establish a post-separation entitlement to spousal support: a contractual approach, which is
rarely relevant and received little attention in *Bracklow*; a compensatory approach, which
was developed in *Moge*, but was not relevant on the facts of *Bracklow*; and needs-based
approach. The non-compensatory needs-based approach is based on various provisions of

the *Divorce Act*, most notably s. 15.2(6)(c) which provides that spousal support may be ordered to relieve "hardship" that might arise from the "breakdown of the marriage". Justice McLachlin wrote:

> ... [S]pouses may have an obligation to meet or contribute to the needs of their former partners where they have the capacity to pay, even in the absence of a contractual or compensatory foundation for the obligation. Need alone may be enough...

> ... Mr. Bracklow cites L'Heureux-Dubé J.'s statement in *Moge*, that "marriage *per se* does not automatically entitle a spouse to support"... That is true. To hold otherwise would swing the pendulum too far back and completely ignore the independent, clean-break model of marriage. But, in certain circumstances, marriage *may* give rise to an obligation. It is not the bare fact of marriage, so much as the *relationship* that is established and the expectations that may reasonably flow from it that give rise to the obligation of support under the statutes.

Justice McLachlin went on to observe that the roles and relative independence of the parties during marriage and the length of the marriage were factors to be taken into account in assessing the quantum and duration of any non-compensatory spousal support obligation.

In June 2006, the Supreme Court revisited the issue of entitlement to support in *Leskun v. Leskun* [(2006), 34 R.F.L. (6th) 1 (S.C.C.), excerpts reproduced below]. The parties had a 20 year marriage, with one child. During the marriage the wife had provided support to the husband while he gained further educational qualifications, which eventually contributed to him pursuing a lucrative career in business. The wife worked throughout much of the marriage, but shortly before separation, she was informed by her employer that her position was to be terminated due to corporate restructuring. A year before separation the husband had been transferred by his employer to the United States, and it was expected that the wife would join him. The husband, after learning that his wife would be terminated from her employment, returned home, ostensibly to help his wife negotiate with her employer a better severance package or alternate employment, but he arrived to tell her that he had been having an affair and the marriage was over. At the time of the trial, she was in her mid 50's; she was awarded spousal support, subject to "review" by the former husband "both as to entitlement and quantum", as there was uncertainty about whether her former employer would offer her another job and there was an expectation that she would regain employment.

Four years after the separation, the former husband brought a review application, seeking to terminate support, arguing in part that the woman had not taken sufficient steps to become self-sufficient, as she could have at least part-time employment. The judge rejected his application, recognizing that the separation, and the deaths and illness of a number of her close relatives had resulted in the "emotional devastation" of the woman, which, combined with her age (late 50's by that point), the narrowness of her previous employment experience and a pre-existing back injury, rendered her unable to become self-sufficient. That decision was upheld by the British Columbia Court of Appeal, though Southin J.A. observed that the woman was "bitter to the point of obsession with his misconduct and in consequence has been unable to make a new life. Her life is this litigation." Justice Southin nevertheless held that support was appropriate because the woman's inability to support herself was "a failure resulting at least in part from the emotional devastation of misconduct by the other spouse". This comment suggested that his fault in ending the marriage might be a factor in determining spousal support issues.

The Supreme Court of Canada in *Leskun* clearly rejected the idea that marital misconduct or fault itself should be a factor in awarding support, but accepted that in all of the circumstances of the case, including the woman's emotional devastation at the end of the marriage, support should be continued. Justice Binnie observed that marital misconduct is not itself a basis for spousal support, as compensation for harm is not a factor under Canada's divorce law. However, the Court accepted that emotional suffering arising from one spouse's wrongdoing — or any other type of emotional trauma — can be a factor when judges determine how much support will be paid.

> Misconduct, as such, is off the table as a relevant consideration. ... Consequences [however] are not rendered irrelevant because of their genesis in the other spouse's misconduct.

The Supreme Court emphasized that the woman had made significant economic contributions to the marriage and to her husband's career, and due to the "unfortunate" combination of circumstances was unable to become self-sufficient. There was a concern that the woman was simply being manipulative and refusing to seek employment, and Binnie J observed: "Clearly, where incapacity is alleged some independent evidence, including medical evidence would be highly desirable." However, the Supreme Court accepted the findings of the trial judge that this was not a case of refusal to become self-sufficient, but rather a situation of incapacity.

While *Moge*, *Bracklow* and *Leskun* have laid the foundation for the current law of entitlement to spousal support, as a result of the vagueness of the doctrines articulated, there has continued to be controversy in the case law and commentary about issues of spousal support. Although the SSAG has clearly helped to reduce the range of uncertainty in regard to issues of quantum and duration of spousal support, the issue of entitlement remains contentious, and can be difficult to resolve in some cases.

The Importance of the Basis for Entitlement

Cases in which spousal support entitlement is an issue can be hard to resolve. There may be big differences of opinion about entitlement issues. Unless there is a significant award at stake, the financial and emotional costs of litigation about entitlement-related issues may outweigh the potential benefit of a relatively small award. As a consequence, most of the cases on entitlement to spousal support are ones in which the payor's income is relatively high, and the difference in spousal incomes is quite substantial. In cases where the means of the recipient are limited, $100 or $200 per month in spousal support might make a significant difference to how the recipient is able to manage, yet may be too small to litigate over if the legal issue of entitlement itself remains less than clear. Clarification of the entitlement issues could therefore potentially benefit recipients in lower income situations.

Overall, spousal support entitlement is one of the core issues in family law, one that arises frequently. It attracts an emotional response from clients, and challenging commentary in the media. It is clearly an issue of financial, social and emotional importance to the public in general, and to separating spouses in particular. It deserves the clearest boundaries we can come up with as a profession.

In cases at either end of the spectrum, answers to the question of entitlement may be relatively easy to answer. Marriages longer than 20 years in which the applicant was not employed at the time of separation but had the primary domestic or child care responsibilities, will almost certainly result in compensatory support if there is any ability to pay, and the award will likely be indefinite. Marriages of short duration, less than five years, where there are no children will almost certainly result in at most short-term awards to bridge the transition back to single life, even if one spouse was not employed for much of the marriage. But most divorce cases involve marriages that fall in the middle of the spectrum. They may be "medium-term" in length, or may have appear to be partly "traditional" and partly "modern." The support may be analyzed as either (or both) compensatory or needs-based.

MOGE v. MOGE

(1992), 43 R.F.L. (3d) 345, 1992 CarswellMan 143, 1992 CarswellMan 222 (S.C.C.)

[The parties were married in Poland in the mid-1950s and moved to Canada in 1960. They had three children. The wife had limited education and no special skills or training. She generally worked evenings, cleaning offices, to supplement her husband's income as a welder. On separation in 1973, the court awarded the wife custody and spousal and child support. In 1980, a court ordered the husband to continue paying $150 per month to support his wife and remaining dependent child. The wife was laid off from her job cleaning a hotel in 1987 and she failed to find new employment. On the wife's application, the court increased spousal support to $200 per month and child support to $200 per month. By then, the husband had remarried and was earning approximately $2,000 per month. The wife later resumed part-time work and in 1989 the husband, who was now earning about $2,200 per month, obtained an order terminating the support. On appeal, the Manitoba Court of Appeal reinstated the spousal support at $150 per month. The husband appealed that decision. The wife did not appeal the quantum.]

L'HEUREUX-DUBÉ J. (LA FOREST, GONTHIER, CORY and IACOBUCCI JJ. concurring): — At the heart of this appeal lies the question of spousal support. Specifically, the court is asked to determine the circumstances under which spousal support ought to be varied or terminated pursuant to s. 17 of the *Divorce Act*. ... In a broader sense, however, this case turns upon the basic philosophy of support within the Act as a whole. ...

V. The Trilogy And Its Jurisprudence

The position of Mr. Moge before this court is that his support obligation to his ex-wife should be terminated on the basis of the reasoning in the so-called "trilogy." He submits that though those cases specifically concerned situations in which the parties had set out their respective rights and obligations following the dissolution of the marriage by agreement, the court was advocating a model of support to be relied upon even in the absence of a final settlement.

That model, he says, is characterized by such notions as self-sufficiency and causal connection. Effectively, his position is that his ex-wife should have been self-sufficient by now and, if she is not, no link may be drawn between that lack of self-sufficiency and the marriage. In other words, her current financial position is no concern of his. ...

Early on, Professor J.G. McLeod expressed the view that the trilogy cases apply beyond their facts and espoused the model Mr. Moge asks this court to apply. ...

With respect, I cannot agree. A careful reading of the trilogy in general, and *Pelech* in particular, indicates that the court has not espoused a new model of support under the Act. Rather, the court has shown respect for the wishes of persons who, in the presence of the statutory safeguards, decided to forgo litigation and settled their affairs by agreement under the 1970 *Divorce Act*. In other words, the court is paying deference to the freedom of individuals to contract. ...

Professor Julien D. Payne ... best identifies the flaws of the early interpretation of the trilogy in "Further Reflections on Spousal and Child Support After *Pelech, Caron* and *Richardson*" (1989) 20 R.G.D. 477, when he states, at p. 487:

> Professor McLeod's proposed extension of *Pelech, Caron* and *Richardson* to non-consensual situations and to provincial statutes as well as the new *Divorce Act, 1985*, virtually eliminates the significance of statutory criteria, whatever their form and substance, and at the same time closes the door to

the wise exercise of judicial discretion that can accommodate a diverse range of economic variables on marriage breakdown or divorce.

> Notwithstanding the common law's recognition of a spousal agency of necessity, it must not be forgotten that current spousal support laws are of statutory origin. Furthermore, subject to over riding constitutional doctrines, the sovereignty of Parliament . . . remains paramount. Judge-made law may explain, but cannot override, statute law.

In addition, there are diverse appellate rulings in Canada that endorse the view that the principles articulated in the trilogy should not be applied to non-consensual situations. ...

In light of my reading of *Pelech*, I decline to accede to Mr. Moge's argument that this court has already determined the basis on which entitlement, or continuing entitlement, to spousal support rests in the absence of a settlement agreement intended by the parties to be final under the Act.

Since this case is not one which involves a final agreement entered into between the parties in order to settle the economic consequences of their divorce, I leave for another day the question of causal connection under the Act, which was discussed in the trilogy in the particular context of a final settlement under the 1970 *Divorce Act*.

The present appeal not only does not involve a final settlement agreement but deals specifically with a variation application following a support order at the time of divorce, a question to which I will now turn.

VI. Spousal Support

(1) The Act

Although subss. (4) and (7) of s. 17 [now s. 17(4.1) and (7)] of the Act are the two subsections directly applicable to this appeal, s. 15(2), (4), (5), (6), and (7) [now s. 15.2(1), (3), (4), (5), and (6)], and s. 17(1), (3), (6), (8), and (10) [now s. 17(1), (3), (4.1), (6), and (10)] of the Act are also relevant to the analysis. ...

(2) Introduction

Before dealing squarely with the main issue raised by this appeal, there are a number of preliminary observations that I wish to make.

The first has to do with the argument raised by Mr. Moge that, quite apart from the trilogy, the Act espouses a self-sufficiency model as the only basis of spousal support. ... Mrs. Moge disagrees. She points out that self-sufficiency is only one of many objectives which the Act directs a court of competent jurisdiction to consider in exercising its discretion under ss. 17(4) and 17(7), and that even then, the objective of self-sufficiency in s. 17(7) is modified by such terminology as "in so far as practicable." She further submits that there is now appellate court jurisprudence which recognizes that in cases such as her own, self-sufficiency will not be practicable, largely due to the residual effects of being outside the labour market for a protracted period of time.

The self-sufficiency model advanced by Mr. Moge has generally been predicated on the dichotomy between "traditional" and "modern" marriages. Often, in order to draw the line after which no more support will be ordered, courts have distinguished between "traditional" marriages in which the wife remains at home and takes responsibility for the domestic aspects of marital life, and "modern" ones where employment outside the home is pursued. ... [C]ourts have frequently been more amenable to finding that "traditional" marriages survive the so-called "causal connection" test than "modern" ones. ...

There are, however, many cases which do not fall easily into either category. These cases pose difficulties for courts which attempt to make assessments based on two clear stereotypes, especially when determining the question of self-sufficiency. ...

Given the concerns I harbour about making a spouse's entitlement to support contingent upon the degree to which he or she is able to fit within a mythological stereotype ..., the distinction between "traditional" and "modern" marriages does not seem to me to be as useful as perhaps courts have indicated so far. While it may reflect flexibility on the part of courts and constitute an attempt to achieve fairness, I am of the view that there are much more sophisticated means which may be resorted to in order to achieve the objectives set out in the Act. ...

The second observation I wish to make is that, in determining spousal support, it is important not to lose sight of the fact that the support provisions of the Act are intended to deal with the *economic* consequences, for both parties, of the marriage or its breakdown. Marriage may unquestionably be a source of benefit to both parties that is not easily quantified in economic terms. Many believe that marriage and the family provide for the emotional, economic, and social well-being of its members. It may be the location of safety and comfort, and may be the place where its members have their most intimate human contact. Marriage and the family act as an emotional and economic support system as well as a forum of intimacy. In this regard, it serves vital personal interests, and may be linked to building a "comprehensive sense of personhood." Marriage and the family are a superb environment for raising and nurturing the young of our society by providing the initial environment for the development of social skills. These institutions also provide a means to pass on the values that we deem to be central to our sense of community.

Conversely, marriage and the family often require the sacrifice of personal priorities by both parties in the interests of shared goals. All of these elements are of undeniable importance in shaping the overall character of a marriage. Spousal support in the context of divorce, however, is not about the emotional and social benefits of marriage. Rather, the purpose of spousal support is to relieve economic hardship that results from "marriage or its breakdown." Whatever the respective advantages to the parties of a marriage in other areas, the focus of the enquiry when assessing spousal support after the marriage has ended must be the effect of the marriage in either impairing or improving each party's economic prospects.

This approach is consistent with both modern and traditional conceptions of marriage in as much as marriage is, among other things, an economic unit which generates financial benefits. ... The Act reflects the fact that in today's marital relationships, partners should expect and are entitled to share those financial benefits.

Equitable distribution can be achieved in many ways: by spousal and child support, by the division of property and assets, or by a combination of property and support entitlements. But in many, if not most, cases the absence of accumulated assets may require that one spouse pay support to the other in order to effect an equitable distribution of resources. This is precisely the case here, as the parties are not wealthy; for the most part, all they appear to possess are their respective incomes.

Fair distribution does not, however, mandate a minute, detailed accounting of time, energy, and dollars spent in the day-to-day life of the spouses, nor may it effect full compensation for the economic losses in every case. Rather, it involves the development of parameters with which to assess the respective advantages and disadvantages of the spouses as a result of their roles in the marriage, as the starting point in determining the degree of support to be awarded. This, in my view, is what the Act requires.

A third point worthy of emphasis is that this analysis applies equally to both spouses, depending on how the division of labour is exercised in a particular marriage. What the Act requires is a fair and equitable distribution of resources to alleviate the economic consequences of marriage or marriage breakdown for both spouses, regardless of gender. The reality, however, is that in many, if not most, marriages, the wife still remains the economically disadvantaged partner. There may be times where the reverse is true and the Act is equally able to accommodate this eventuality.

These caveats having been made, the question of spousal support which lies at the heart of this appeal must be dealt with first by examining the objectives of the Act.

(3) The Objectives of the Act

Parliament, subject always to overarching constitutional norms, may set down any principles it wishes to govern spousal support. The task, then, is to determine the principles embodied in ss. 15 and 17 of the Act. ...

I fully agree with Professor Payne, who has commented on these objectives in *Payne on Divorce*, 2d ed. (Toronto: Butterworths, 1988), at p. 101, that:

> Judicial implementation of the newly defined policy objectives should, to some degree, result in a shift from the narrow perspective of a 'needs' and 'capacity to pay' approach, particularly in cases where one of the spouses has substantial means: see *Linton v. Linton* (1988), 11 R.F.L. (3d) 444, Killeen L.J.S.C. (Ont. S.C.) [now affirmed (1990), 1 O.R. (3d) 1 (C.A.)]. It may also have an impact on the types of orders that will be used to effectuate one or more of the applicable policy objectives. In this context, it should be observed that the four policy objectives defined in the *Divorce Act*, 1985 are not necessarily independent of each other. They may overlap or they may operate independently, depending upon the circumstances of the particular case. *Legislative endorsement of four policy objectives manifests the realization that the economic variables of marriage breakdown and divorce do not lend themselves to the application of any single objective.* Long-term marriages that ultimately break down often leave in their wake a condition of financial dependence, because the wives have assumed the role of full-time homemakers. The legitimate objective(s) of spousal support in such a case will rarely coincide with the objective(s) that should be pursued with respect to short-term marriages. Childless marriages cannot be treated in the same way as marriages with dependent children. The two-income family cannot be equated with the one-income family. A 'clean break' accommodated by an order for a lump sum in lieu of periodic spousal support can often provide a workable and desirable solution for the wealthy, for the two-income family and for childless marriages of short duration. Rehabilitative support orders by way of periodic spousal support for a fixed term may be appropriate where there is a present incapacity to pay a lump sum and the dependent spouse can reasonably be expected to enter or re-enter the labour force within the foreseeable future. *Continuing periodic spousal support orders may provide the only practical solution for dependent spouses who cannot be reasonably expected to achieve economic self-sufficiency.* There can be no fixed rules, however, whereby particular types of orders are tied to the specific objective(s) sought to be achieved. In the final analysis, the court must determine the most appropriate kind(s) of order, having regard to the attendant circumstances of the case, including the present and prospective financial well-being of both the spouses and their dependent children. ... [Emphasis added.]

All four of the objectives defined in the Act must be taken into account when spousal support is claimed or an order for spousal support is sought to be varied. No single objective is paramount. The fact that one of the objectives, such as economic self-sufficiency, has been attained does not necessarily dispose of the matter. ...

Many proponents of the deemed self-sufficiency model effectively elevate it to the preeminent objective in determining the right to, quantum, and duration of spousal support. In my opinion, this approach is not consonant with proper principles of statutory interpretation. The objective of self-sufficiency is only one of several objectives enumerated in the section and, given the manner in which Parliament has set out those objectives, I see no indication that any one is to be given priority. Parliament, in my opinion, intended that support reflect the diverse dynamics of many unique marital relationships. ...

It is also imperative to realize that the objective of self-sufficiency is tempered by the caveat that it is to be made a goal only "in so far as is practicable." This qualification militates against the kind of "sink or swim" stance upon which the deemed self-sufficiency model is premised. ...

That Parliament could not have meant to institutionalize the ethos of deemed self-sufficiency is also apparent from an examination of the social context in which support orders are made. In Canada the feminization of poverty is an entrenched social phenomenon, ...

It would be perverse in the extreme to assume that Parliament's intention in enacting the Act was to financially penalize women in this country. And, while it would undeniably be simplistic to identify the deemed self-sufficiency model of spousal support as the sole cause of the female decline into poverty, based on the review of the jurisprudence and statistical data set out in these reasons, it is clear that the model has disenfranchised many women in the courtroom and countless others who may simply have decided not to request support in anticipation of their remote chances of success. The theory, therefore, at a minimum, is contributing to the problem. I am in agreement with Professor Bailey, ["*Pelech, Caron*, and *Richardson*" (1989-90), 3 C.J.W.L. 615, at 633], that:

> The test is being applied to create a clean break between the spouses before the conditions of self-sufficiency for the dependent partner have been met, *and will undoubtedly cause an increase in the widespread poverty (at least relative poverty) of women and children of failed unions.* [Emphasis added.]

In the result, I am respectfully of the view that the support model of self-sufficiency which Mr. Moge urges the court to apply, cannot be supported as a matter of statutory interpretation, considering, in particular, the diversity of objectives set out in the Act.

(4) Doctrine and Jurisprudence

A burgeoning body of doctrine and, to some extent, jurisprudence is developing both abroad as well as in Canada which expresses dissatisfaction with the current norms along which entitlement to spousal support is assessed. This body of doctrine, in particular, proposes, instead, a scheme based on principles of compensation. ...

The theory, however, is not new, as is evident from the Law Reform Commission Working Papers and Report, 1972-1976. Antecedents of the compensatory spousal support model may be found in portions of the Law Reform Commission of Canada's Working Paper 12, *Maintenance on Divorce* (Ottawa: Information Canada, 1975). The commission recommended, *inter alia*, that the mere fact of marriage not create a right of maintenance and that the economic disabilities incurred due to marriage and the eventuality of children be compensated. ...

Legislative support for the principles of compensation may be found in ss. 15(7)(a)–(c) and 17(7)(a)–(c), which are extremely broad in scope and which direct the court, in making or varying a support order, to recognize any economic advantages or disadvantages arising from the marriage or its breakdown, to apportion between the spouses any financial consequences arising from the care of children over and above those consequences which have already been made the subject of child support, and to relieve economic hardships arising from the marriage. As a matter of statutory interpretation, it is precisely the manner in which compensatory spousal support is able to respond to the diversity of objectives the Act contains that makes it superior to the strict self-sufficiency model.

Although the promotion of self-sufficiency remains relevant under this view of spousal support, it does not deserve unwarranted pre-eminence. After divorce, spouses would still have an obligation to contribute to their own support in a manner commensurate with their abilities. ... In cases where relatively few advantages have been conferred or disadvantages incurred, transitional support allowing for full and unimpaired reintegration back into the labour force might be all that is required to afford sufficient compensation. However, in many cases a former spouse will continue to suffer the economic disadvantages of the marriage and its dissolution while the other spouse reaps its economic advantages. In such cases, compensatory spousal support would require long-term support or an alternative settlement which provides an equivalent degree of assistance in light of all of the objectives of the Act. ...

Women have tended to suffer economic disadvantages and hardships from marriage or its breakdown because of the traditional division of labour within that institution. Historically, or at least in recent history, the contributions made by women to the marital partnership were non-monetary and came in the form of work at home, such as taking care of the household, raising children, and so on. Today, though more and more women are working outside the home, such employment continues to play a secondary role and sacrifices continue to be made for the sake of domestic considerations. These sacrifices often impair the ability of the partner who makes them (usually the wife) to maximize her earning potential because she may tend to forgo educational and career advancement opportunities. These same sacrifices may also enhance the earning potential of the other spouse (usually the husband), who, because his wife is tending to such matters, is free to pursue economic goals. This eventually may result in inequities. ... Hence, while the union survives, such division of labour, at least from an economic perspective, may be unobjectionable if such an arrangement reflects the wishes of the parties. However, once the marriage dissolves, the kinds of non-monetary contributions made by the wife may result in significant market disabilities. The sacrifices she has made at home catch up with her and the balance shifts in favour of the husband who has remained in the workforce and focused his attention outside the home. In effect, she is left with a diminished earning capacity and may have conferred upon her husband an embellished one.

The curtailment of outside employment obviously has a significant impact on future earning capacity. According to some studies, the earning capacity of a woman who stays at home atrophies by 1.5 per cent for each year she is out of the labour force. ... Richard Kerr's *An Economic Model to Assist in the Determination of Spousal Support* (Ottawa: Paper prepared for the Department of Justice and Status of Women Canada, 1992), came to a similar conclusion. He posits that "[f]or women whose labour force interruptions have lasted for 10 years or longer, the cumulative present value of post re-entry earning losses will typically exceed $80,000," over and above any loss incurred during the interruption itself. The figure is relative to women who have not interrupted their careers in such a fashion. He adds that "[e]ven labour force interruptions lasting as little as two years can have significant long-term costs in terms of lost earnings ($30,000 or more)" (p. 1). Labour force interruptions are common and this accentuates the need for compensation. ...

Often difficulties are exacerbated by the enduring responsibility for children of the marriage. The spouse who has made economic sacrifices in the marriage also generally becomes the custodial parent, as custody is awarded to the wife 75 per cent of the time, to both parents jointly in 13 per cent of cases, and to the husband alone in less than 8 per cent of divorces. ... The diminished earning capacity with which an ex-wife enters the labour force after years of reduced or non-participation will be even more difficult to overcome when economic choice is reduced, unlike that of her ex-husband, due to the necessity of remaining within proximity of schools, not working late, remaining at home when the child is ill, etc. The other spouse encounters none of these impediments and is generally free to live virtually wherever he wants and work whenever he wants.

The doctrine of equitable sharing of the economic consequences of marriage or marriage breakdown upon its dissolution, which, in my view, the Act promotes, seeks to recognize and account for both the economic disadvantages incurred by the spouse who makes such sacrifices and the economic advantages conferred upon the other spouse. Significantly, it recognizes that work within the home has undeniable value and transforms the notion of equality from the rhetorical status to which it was relegated under a deemed self-sufficiency model, to a substantive imperative. Insofar as economic circumstances permit, the Act seeks to put the remainder of the family in as close a position as possible to the household before the marriage breakdown. ...

The equitable sharing of the economic consequences of marriage or marriage breakdown, however, is not a general tool of redistribution which is activated by the mere fact of marriage. Nor ought it to be. It is now uncontentious in our law and accepted by both the majority and the minority in *Messier v. Delage* ... that marriage *per se* does not automatically entitle a spouse to support. Presumably, there will be the occasional marriage where both spouses maximize their earning potential by working outside the home, pursuing economic and educational opportunities in a similar manner, dividing up the domestic labour identically, and either making no economic sacrifices for the other or, more likely, making them equally. In such a utopian scenario there might be no apparent call for compensation. The spouses are able to make a clean break and continue on with their respective lives. Such cases would appear to be rare. In most marriages in which both partners make economic sacrifices and share domestic responsibilities, or where one spouse has suffered economic losses in order to enable the other spouse to further a career, their roles should be considered in the spousal support order.

The Act refers to economic advantages and disadvantages flowing from marriage or *its breakdown*. ... Sections 15(7)(a) and 17(7)(a) of the Act are expressly compensatory in character while ss. 15(7)(c) and 17(7)(c) may not be characterized as exclusively compensatory. These latter paragraphs may embrace the notion that the primary burden of spousal support should fall on family members, not the state. In my view, an equitable sharing of the economic consequences of divorce does not exclude other considerations, particularly when dealing with sick or disabled spouses. While the losses or disadvantages flowing from the marriage in such cases may seem minimal in the view of some, the effect of its breakdown will not, and support will still be in order in most cases. We must recognize, however, ... that family law can play only a limited role in alleviating the economic consequences of marriage breakdown. ...

As economic consequences have to be shared in an equitable manner by both partners, it is my view that the Act, while envisaging compensation for the economic advantages and disadvantages of marriage or marriage breakdown, does not necessarily put the entire burden of such compensation on the shoulders of only one party. I stress here that in the discussion of spousal support one must not lose sight of the fact that the real dilemma in most cases relates to the ability to pay of the debtor spouse and the limits of support orders in achieving fair compensation and alleviating the economic burdens of the disadvantaged spouse. While the disadvantages of the kind I mention hereunder are compensable, though not necessarily automatically or fully compensated in every case, the ultimate goal is to alleviate the disadvantaged spouse's economic losses as completely as possible, taking into account all the circumstances of the parties, including the advantages conferred on the other spouse during the marriage.

The four objectives set out in the Act can be viewed as an attempt to achieve an equitable sharing of the economic consequences of marriage or marriage breakdown. At the end of the day, however, courts have an overriding discretion and the exercise of such discretion will depend on the particular facts of each case, having regard to the factors and objectives designated in the Act.

(5) The Exercise of Judicial Discretion

The exercise of judicial discretion in ordering support requires an examination of all four objectives set out in the Act in order to achieve equitable sharing of the economic consequences of marriage or marriage breakdown. This implies a broad approach with a view to recognizing and incorporating any significant features of the marriage or its termination which adversely affect the economic prospects of the disadvantaged spouse. Not all such elements will be equally important, even if present, to the awarding of support in each case. However, it may be useful to canvass some of the most common compensable advantages and recognized disadvantages which the Act envisages. They are not to be taken as exhaustive but only as examples of some of the losses and gains one spouse, usually the wife, incurs and confers which may be useful for the courts to consider in the exercise of their discretion.

The financial consequences of the end of a marriage extend beyond the simple loss of future earning power or losses directly related to the care of children. They will often encompass loss of seniority, missed promotions, and lack of access to fringe benefits, such as pension plans, life, disability, dental, and health insurance. ... As persons outside of the workforce cannot take advantage of job retraining and the upgrading of skills provided by employers, one serious economic consequence of remaining out of the workforce is that the value of education and job training often decreases with each year in comparison to those who remain active in the workforce and may even become redundant after several years of non-use. All of these factors contribute to the inability of a person not in the labour force to develop economic security for retirement in his or her later years.

The most significant economic consequence of marriage or marriage breakdown, however, usually arises from the birth of children. This generally requires that the wife cut back on her paid labour force participation in order to care for the children, an arrangement which jeopardizes her ability to ensure her own income security and independent economic well-being. In such situations, spousal support may be a way to compensate such economic disadvantage.

If child-care responsibilities continue past the dissolution of the marriage, the existing disadvantages continue, only to be exacerbated by the need to accommodate and integrate those demands with the requirements of paid employment. In that regard, I adopt without reservation the words of Bowman J. in *Brockie v. Brockie* (1987), 5 R.F.L. (3d) 440 (Man. Q.B.); affirmed (1987), 8 R.F.L. (3d) 302 (Man. C.A.):

> To be a custodial parent involves adoption of a lifestyle which, in ensuring the welfare and development of the child, places many limitations and burdens upon that parent. A single person can live in any part of the city, can frequently share accommodation with relatives or friends, can live in a high-rise downtown or a house in the suburbs, can do shift work, can devote spare time as well as normal work days to the development of a career, can attend night school, and in general can live as and where he or she finds convenient. A custodial parent, on the other hand, seldom finds friends or relatives who are anxious to share accommodation, must search long and carefully for accommodation suited to the needs of the young child, including play space, closeness to daycare, schools and recreational facilities, if finances do not permit ownership of a motor vehicle, then closeness to public transportation and shopping facilities is important. A custodial parent is seldom free to accept shift work, is restricted in any overtime work by the daycare arrangements available, and must be prepared to give priority to the needs of a sick child over the demands of an employer. After a full day's work, the custodial parent faces a full range of home making responsibilities including cooking, cleaning and laundry, as well as the demands of the child himself for the parent's attention. Few indeed are the custodial parents with strength and endurance to meet all of these demands and still find time for night courses, career improvement or even a modest social life. The financial consequences of all of these limitations and demands arising from the custody of the child are in addition to the direct costs of raising the child, and are, I believe, the factors to which the court is to give consideration. ...

It is important to note that families need not fall strictly within a particular marriage model in order for one spouse to suffer disadvantages. For example, even in childless marriages, couples may also decide that one spouse will remain at home. Any economic disadvantage to that spouse flowing from that shared decision in the interest of the family should be regarded as compensable. Conversely, the parties may decide or circumstances may require that both spouses work full time. This in and of itself may not necessarily preclude compensation if, in the interest of the family or due to child-care responsibilities, one spouse declines a promotion, refuses a transfer, leaves a position to allow the other spouse to take advantage of an opportunity for advancement, or otherwise curtails employment opportunities and thereby incurs economic loss. ...

A spouse may contribute to the operation of a business, typically through the provision of secretarial, entertainment, or book-keeping services, or may take on increased domestic and financial responsibilities that enable the other to pursue licences, degrees, or other training and education. ... To the extent that these activities have not already been compensated for pursuant to the division of assets, they are factors that should be considered in granting spousal support.

Although the doctrine of spousal support which focuses on equitable sharing does not guarantee to either party the standard of living enjoyed during the marriage, this standard is far from irrelevant to support entitlement. ... Furthermore, great disparities in the standard of living that would be experienced by spouses in the absence of support are often a revealing indication of the economic disadvantages inherent in the role assumed by one party. As marriage should be regarded as a joint endeavour, the longer the relationship endures, the closer the economic union, the greater will be the presumptive claim to equal standards of living upon its dissolution. ...

In short, in the proper exercise of their discretion, courts must be alert to a wide variety of factors and decisions made in the family interest during the marriage which have the effect of disadvantaging one spouse or benefiting the other upon its dissolution. In my view, this is what the Act mandates, no more, no less.

Such determination demands a complex and, in many cases, a difficult analysis. The same, of course, might be said of the evaluation of damages in contract or in tort. However, this complexity does not excuse judges from hearing relevant evidence or from fully applying the law. There are no easy recipes, nor are there neat compartments on which to rely, as families and family relationships are not simple. But there are few matters more important before the courts, given the repercussions on the future of the parties themselves and, in particular, their children. ...

Given the principles outlined above, spousal support orders remain essentially a function of the evidence led in each particular case. In some cases such evidence might come in the form of highly specific expert evidence which enables parties to present an accurate picture of the economic consequences of marriage breakdown in their particular circumstances. (See *Ormerod v. Ormerod* (1990), 27 R.F.L. (3d) 225 (Ont. U.F.C.), and *Elliot v. Elliot* (August 4, 1992), Doc. Hamilton-Wentworth V-178/ 91, [1992] O.J. No. 1665 [Ont. U.F.C.]; [reported at (1992), 42 R.F.L. (3d) 7, 95 D.L.R. (4th) 614 (Ont. U.F.C.); reversed (1993), 48 R.F.L. (3d) 237 (Ont. C.A.); leave to appeal refused (1994), 3 R.F.L. (4th) 290 (note) (S.C.C.)].) Although of great assistance in assessing the economic consequences of marriage breakdown in a particular marriage, such evidence will not be required, nor will it be possible, in most cases. For most divorcing couples, both the cost of obtaining such evidence and the amount of assets involved are practical considerations which would prohibit or at least discourage its use. Therefore, to require expert evidence as a sine qua non to the recovery of compensation would not be practical for many parties, not to mention the use of court time which might be involved. It would be my hope, therefore, that different alternatives be examined.

One proposal put forth by Professor Rogerson would be for Parliament to consider enacting a set of legislative guidelines. ...

One possible disadvantage of such a solution lies in the risk that it may impose a straitjacket which precludes the accommodation of the many economic variables susceptible to be encountered in spousal support litigation.

Another alternative might lie in the doctrine of judicial notice. The doctrine itself grew from a need to promote efficiency in the litigation process and may very well be applicable to spousal support. ...

Based upon the studies which I have cited earlier in these reasons, the general economic impact of divorce on women is a phenomenon, the existence of which cannot reasonably be questioned and should be amenable to judicial notice. More extensive social science data are also appearing. Such studies are beginning to provide reasonable assessments of some of the disadvantages incurred and advantages conferred post-divorce. ... While qualification will remain difficult and fact-related in each particular case, judicial notice should be taken of such studies, subject to other expert evidence which may bear on them, as background information at the very least. ...

In all events, whether judicial notice of the circumstances generally encountered by spouses at the dissolution of a marriage is to be a formal part of the trial process or whether such circumstances merely provide the necessary background information, it is important that judges be aware of the social reality in which support decisions are experienced when engaging in the examination of the objectives of the Act. ...

VII. Application To The Case At Bar

Since this appeal involves an application for a variation order, here an order for the termination of support by Mr. Moge to Mrs. Moge, s. 17(4) of the Act applies.

As a necessary preliminary condition to making such an order, s. 17(4) of the Act requires that the court be satisfied that "there has been a change in the condition, means, needs or other circumstances of either former spouse ... for whom support is or was sought occurring since the making of the support order or the last variation order made in respect of that order."

That there has been a change in the circumstances of the parties since the last support order was not seriously contested and I agree with both the trial judge and the Court of Appeal that the threshold requirements of s. 17(4) of the Act are satisfied.

The sole remaining consideration is whether the application of Mr. Moge to terminate support ought to have been granted in this case. In my view, it should not have, and the majority of the Court of Appeal was right in finding an error of principle on the part of the trial judge. ...

The four objectives of spousal support orders under s. 17(7) of the Act, as explicated above and applied by the Court of Appeal, are met in this case. For this reason, the following specific findings are in order based on the evidence in the record:

1. Mrs. Moge has sustained a substantial economic disadvantage "from the marriage or its breakdown" within the meaning of s. 17(7)(a) of the Act.

2. Mrs. Moge's long-term responsibility for the upbringing of the children of the marriage after the spousal separation in 1973 had had an impact on her ability to earn an income so as to trigger the application of s. 17(7)(b) of the Act.

3. Mrs. Moge continues to suffer economic hardship as a result of the "break down of the marriage" within the meaning of s. 17(7)(c) of the Act.

4. Mrs. Moge has failed to become economically self-sufficient notwithstanding her conscientious efforts.

These findings are irrefutable even in the absence of expert evidence relating to the appropriate quantification of spousal support. It follows that in view of all of the objectives of spousal support orders set out in s. 17(7) of the Act, continuing support is in order in this case. Accordingly, there was no error in the Court of Appeal. ...

McLACHLIN J. (concurring) (GONTHIER J. concurring): — I have read the reasons of L'Heureux-Dubé J. and would dispose of the appeal as she proposes. I wish to add, however, the following comments.

It seems to me important to emphasize that this is, first and last, a case of statutory interpretation. It is interesting and useful to consider how different theories of support yield different answers to the question of how support should be determined. However, in the end the judge must return to what Parliament has said on the subject. Parliament has enacted that judges considering applications for variation of support consider four different factors [set out in s. 17(7)]. ...

The first thing the judge must consider are "economic advantages or disadvantages ... arising from the marriage or its breakdown." This heading brings in many of the considerations which my colleague discusses. It clearly permits the judge to compensate one spouse for sacrifices and contributions made during the marriage and benefits which the other spouse has received.

The second factor which the judge must consider is the "apportionment" of the "financial consequences" of the care of children. This heading also raises compensatory considerations. If a spouse, either before or after separation, has or continues to incur financial disadvantage as a result of caring for a child of the marriage, he or she should be compensated.

The third thing which the judge's order should do is grant relief from any economic hardship arising from the breakdown of the marriage. The focus here, it seems to me, is not on compensation for what the spouses have contributed to or gained from the marriage. The focus is rather post-marital need; if the breakdown of the marriage has created economic hardship for one or the other, the judge must attempt to grant relief from that hardship.

Finally, the judge's order must "in so far as practicable" promote the economic self-sufficiency of each former spouse within a reasonable period of time. This subhead raises the question of the degree to which ex-spouses should be expected to become self-sufficient, a contested point on this appeal. Several things about this subhead should be noted. First, unlike the first three factors, this one is stated in qualified language, beginning with the conditional phrase "in so far as practicable." Second, economic self-sufficiency is not to be required or assumed; the verb used is "promote." By this language Parliament recognizes that actual self-sufficiency, while desirable, may not be possible or "practicable."

Considering the factors together, the judge's task under s. 17(7) of the statute is to make an order which provides compensation for marital contributions and sacrifices, which takes into account financial consequences of looking after children of the marriage, which relieves against need induced by the separation, and, to the extent it may be "practicable," promotes the economic self-sufficiency of each spouse. Neither a "compensation model" nor a "self-sufficiency model" captures the full content of the section, though both may be relevant to the judge's decision. The judge must base her decision on a number of factors: compensation, child care, post-separation need, and the goal, insofar as practicable, of promoting self-sufficiency.

The need to consider all four factors set out in s. 17(7) rules out the strict self-sufficiency model which Mr. Moge urged upon this court. The trial judge erred, in my respectful opinion, in giving no weight to the first three factors of s. 17(7) and in imposing a categorical requirement of self-sufficiency.

The majority of the Court of Appeal correctly rejected the view that there is an absolute obligation for a spouse to become self-sufficient and that there is a time after which one spouse should no longer have to support another. They placed considerable emphasis on the need to compensate Mrs. Moge for her contributions as homemaker and mother during the course of the marriage, and the permanent economic disadvantage she suffered as a consequence. ... Having concluded that Mrs. Moge's earning potential had been diminished in this way by her contribution to the marriage, the Court of Appeal found she was entitled to an order of maintenance to supplement her own income. This conclusion represented a proper application of s. 17(7) of the *Divorce Act*, and I would dismiss the appeal from its decision. ...

BRACKLOW v. BRACKLOW

(1999), 44 R.F.L. (4th) 1, 1999 CarswellBC 532, 1999 CarswellBC 533 (S.C.C.)

[The parties married in 1989 after living together for four years. It was a second marriage for both and the wife brought two children into the relationship. The husband knew that the wife had health problems when the relationship started. At the start of the relationship the wife left a job with full health and disability benefits because she wanted to get a management position. The husband supported this decision. A year later the wife found new employment, but her health deteriorated and she found the overtime stressful. The husband told her to leave this job and she did so after about a year. She worked at temporary jobs until she secured a full-time position in late 1990. In October 1991, she had to give up that job because of psychiatric problems that led to her hospitalization. She was repeatedly readmitted to hospital after that time and never worked again. The wife suffered from bipolar mood disorder, obsessive compulsive disorder and fibromyalgia, which was aggravated by the stress of the marriage breakup.

The wife provided two-thirds of the household expenses for the first two years of the relationship as she earned more money and her two children were living with them. The couple later split the expenses evenly. After the wife became unemployed, the husband provided for the family. The couple separated in 1992 and divorced in 1995.

The husband's income at the time of trial was $3,764 per month and his portion of his new household expenses was $2,284 per month. The wife lived in subsidized housing and received $787 monthly in disability benefits. It was unlikely that she would ever work again. The wife obtained an interim order for spousal support of $275 per month, which was increased to $400 per month. The wife's application for permanent support was dismissed and the interim support order was terminated. The trial judge reasoned that no economic hardship befell the wife as a result of the marriage or its breakdown since she was in no different circumstances than if she had never married. The British Columbia Court of Appeal, characterizing the relationship as a non-traditional marriage in which each spouse paid his or her own way, upheld the decision. The wife appealed.]

McLACHLIN J. (for the court): —

I. Introduction

What duty does a healthy spouse owe a sick one when the marriage collapses? It is now well-settled law that spouses must compensate each other for foregone careers and missed opportunities during the marriage upon the breakdown of their union. But what happens when a divorce — through no consequence of sacrifices, but simply through economic hardship — leaves one former spouse self-sufficient and the other, perhaps due to the onset of a debilitating illness, incapable of self-support? Must the healthy spouse continue to support the sick spouse? Or can he or she move on, free of obligation? That is the question posed by this appeal. It is a difficult issue. It is also an important issue, given the trend in our society toward shorter marriages and successive relationships. ...

V. Issue

Is a sick or disabled spouse entitled to spousal support when a marriage ends, and if so, when and how much? More precisely, may a spouse have an obligation to support a former spouse over and above what is required to compensate the spouse for loss incurred as a result of the marriage and its breakdown (or to fulfill contractual support agreements)? I would answer this question in the affirmative. ...

VI. Analysis

A. *Entitlement to Support*

The lower courts implicitly assumed that, absent a contractual agreement for post-marital assistance, entitlement to support could only be founded on compensatory principles, i.e., reimbursement of the spouse for opportunities foregone or hardships accrued as a result of the marriage. I conclude, however, that the law recognizes *three* conceptual grounds for entitlement to spousal support: (1) compensatory; (2) contractual; and (3) non-compensatory. These three bases of support flow from the controlling statutory provisions and the relevant case law, and are more broadly animated by differing philosophies and theories of marriage and marital breakdown.

(1) The Historical Perspective: ... The new legislation, while changing much, did not entirely supplant the traditional obligations to support. Legal equality did not translate into actual or substantive equality, and in its absence, one spouse might still be obliged to support the other. Accordingly, the *Divorce Acts* of 1968 and 1986 and provincial family support and property legislation recognized that in many circumstances one spouse might still be required to provide support for the other upon marriage breakup. The new philosophy of spousal equality brought to the fore the idea that parties' agreements on support should influence their rights and obligations during the marriage and upon its breakup, as well as the idea that compensatory support should be awarded where it would be just to compensate a spouse for his or her contributions to the marriage or for sacrifices made or hardships suffered as a result of the marriage. Contractual support obligations, while not new, were given new emphasis by statutory stipulations that the courts take into account support agreements, express or implied, between the parties. The propriety of compensatory support was recognized by this Court in *Moge* [[1992] 3 S.C.R. 813] as flowing from the 1986 *Divorce Act*. While a few cases prior to *Moge* had acknowledged that support criteria extended beyond needs and capacity to pay, the reasons of L'Heureux-Dubé J. in *Moge* offered the first comprehensive articulation of the view that when a marriage ends, spouses are entitled to be compensated for contributions to the marriage and for losses sustained as a consequence of the marriage. The same reasons, however, made it clear that compensatory considerations were not the only basis for support. Judges must exercise their discretion in light of the objectives of spousal orders as set out in s. 15.2(6), and after having considered all the factors set out in s. 15.2(4) of the *Divorce Act*. By directing that the judge consider factors like need and ability to pay (as explored below), the new *Divorce Act* left in place the possibility of non-compensatory, non-contractual support.

(2) Modern Marriages: Marriage and Marriage Breakdown: In analysing the respective obligations of husbands and wives, it is critical to distinguish between the roles of the spouses during marriage and the different roles that are assumed upon marriage breakdown.

To begin, when two spouses are married, they owe each other a mutual duty of support: 1986 *Divorce Act*. Marriage, as this Court has said, is a joint endeavour: *Moge, supra*, at p. 870. The default presumption of this socio-economic partnership is mutuality and interdependence. This comports with the statutes and with the reasonable expectations of Canadian society. Thus the *Family Relations Act* [of British Columbia] states: "A spouse is responsible and liable for the support and maintenance of the other spouse..." (s. 89(1)). Parties, of course (subject to the Act), may alter this expectation, either through explicit contracting (usually before the union is made with a prenuptial agreement), or through the unequivocal structuring of their daily affairs, to show disavowal of financial interweaving. The starting presumption, however, is of mutual support. We need not elevate to contractual status the marital vows of support "in sickness and health, till death do us part" to conclude that, absent indications to the contrary, marriages are generally premised on obligations and expectations of mutual and co-equal support.

When a marriage breaks down, however, the situation changes. The presumption of mutual support that existed during the marriage no longer applies. Such a presumption would be incompatible with the diverse post-marital scenarios that may arise in modern society and the liberty many claim to start their lives anew after marriage breakdown. This is reflected in the *Divorce Act* and the provincial support statutes, which require the court to determine issues of support by reference to a variety of objectives and factors.

The reason that a general presumption of post-marital support would be inappropriate is the presence in the latter half of our century of two "competing" theories of marriage and post-marital obligation: Carol J. Rogerson, "Spousal Support After *Moge*" (1996-97), 14 C.F.L.Q. 289; Carol J. Rogerson, "Judicial Interpretation of the Spousal and Child Support Provisions of the *Divorce Act, 1985* (Part I)" (1991), 7 C.F.L.Q. 155.

The first theory of marriage and post-marital obligation is the "basic social obligation" model, in which primary responsibility falls on the former spouse to provide for his or her ex-partner, rather than on the government. This model is founded on the historical notion that marriage is a potentially permanent obligation (although it revises the archaic concept of the wife's loss of identity with the voluntary secession of autonomy of two, co-equal actors as the basis for the ongoing duty). The payment corollary of this theory has been referred to as the "income replacement model", because the primary purpose of alimony payments, under the basic social obligation model, is to replace lost income that the spouse used to enjoy as a partner to the marriage union. The advocates of this theory vary in degree of fidelity. For example, some espouse permanent and indefinite support under this model. Others argue that the goal should be not just to meet the dependent spouse's post-marital needs, but to elevate him or her as closely as possible to the standard of living enjoyed during the marriage. Yet others, like Rogerson, contend that the social obligation entitlement to spousal support need not translate into a permanent obligation.

At the other end of the spectrum lies what may be termed the "independent" model of marriage. This model sees each party to a marriage as an autonomous actor who retains his or her economic independence throughout marriage. The parties, while they "formally" commit to each other for life at the time of their vows, regard themselves as free agents in an enterprise that can terminate on the unilateral action of either party. The theory of spousal support that complements this model is the "clean-break" theory, in which a former spouse, having compensated in a restitutionary sense any economic costs of the marriage on the other spouse, moves on with his or her life, possibly to enter into more such relationships. Again, the proponents vary in their degree of allegiance. Some prefer to characterize the clean-break model as encompassing "transitional support", in addition to straight restitution, due to the general dislocation costs of unwinding the partnership.

The independent, clean-break model of marriage provides the theoretical basis for compensatory spousal support. The basic social obligation model equally undergirds what may be called "non-compensatory" support. Both models of marriage and their corresponding theories of spousal support permit individual variation by contract, and hence provide a third basis for a legal entitlement to support.

These two theories (and I recognize that I paint with broad strokes, creating these two anchors for sake of simplicity) represent markedly divergent philosophies, values, and legal principles.

The mutual obligation model of marriage stresses the interdependence that marriage creates. The clean-break model stresses the independence of each party to the union. The problem with applying either model exclusively and stringently is that marriages may fit neither model (or both models). Many modern marriages are a complex mix of interdependence and independence, and the myriad of legislative provisions and objectives discussed below speak varyingly to both models. As *Payne on Divorce* (4th ed. 1996), at pp. 269-70, puts it, "The economic variables of marriage breakdown and divorce do not lend themselves to the application of any single objective".

The independent, clean-break model of marriage and marriage breakdown reflects a number of important policies. First, it is based on the widely accepted modern value of the equality and independence of both spouses. Second, it encourages rehabilitation and self-maximization of dependent spouses. Third, through its acceptance of a clean break terminating support obligations, it recognizes the social reality of shorter marriages and successive relationships.

These values and policies support the compensatory theory of support (and, to some extent, the contractual theory as well). The basic premise of contractual and compensatory support is that the parties are equal. As such, when the relationship ends, the parties are entitled to what they would receive in the commercial world-what the individuals contracted for and what they have lost due to the marriage, and its breakdown. Insofar as marriage may have created dependencies, it is the duty of dependent spouses to strive to free themselves from their dependencies and to assume full self-sufficiency, thereby mitigating the need for continued compensation.

The mutual obligation theory of marriage and divorce, by contrast, posits marriage as a union that creates interdependencies that cannot be easily unraveled. These interdependencies in turn create expectations and obligations that the law recognizes and enforces. While historically rooted in a concept of marriage that saw one spouse as powerful and the other as dependent, in its modern version the mutual obligation theory of marriage acknowledges the theoretical and legal independence of each spouse, but equally the interdependence of two co-equals. It postulates each of the parties to the marriage agreeing, as independent individuals, to marriage and all that it entails — including the potential obligation of mutual support. The resultant loss of individual autonomy does not violate the premise of equality, because the autonomy is voluntarily ceded. At the same time, the mutual obligation model recognizes that actual independence may be a different thing from theoretical independence, and that a mutual obligation of support may arise and continue absent contractual or compensatory indicators.

The mutual obligation view of marriage also serves certain policy ends and social values. First, it recognizes the reality that when people cohabit over a period of time in a family relationship, their affairs may become intermingled and impossible to disentangle neatly. When this happens, it is not unfair to ask the partners to continue to support each other (although perhaps not indefinitely). Second, it recognizes the artificiality of assuming that all separating couples can move cleanly from the mutual support status of marriage to the absolute independence status of single life, indicating the potential necessity to continue support, even after the marital "break". Finally, it places the primary burden of support for a needy partner who cannot attain post-marital self-sufficiency on the partners to the relationship, rather than on the state, recognizing the potential injustice of foisting a helpless former partner onto the public assistance rolls.

Both the mutual obligation model and the independent, clean-break model represent important realities and address significant policy concerns and social values. The federal and provincial legislatures, through their respective statutes, have acknowledged both models. Neither theory alone is capable of achieving a just law of spousal support. The importance of the policy objectives served by both models is beyond dispute. It is critical to recognize and encourage the self-sufficiency and independence of each spouse. It is equally vital to recognize that divorced people may move on to other relationships and acquire new obligations which they may not be able to meet if they are obliged to maintain full financial burdens from previous relationships. On the other hand, it is also important to recognize that sometimes the goals of actual independence are impeded by patterns of marital dependence, that too often self-sufficiency at the time of marriage termination is an impossible aspiration, and that marriage is an economic partnership that is built upon a premise (albeit rebuttable) of mutual support. The real question in such cases is whether the state should automatically bear the costs of these realities, or whether the family, including former spouses, should be asked to contribute to the need, means permitting. Some suggest it would be better if the state automatically picked up the costs of such cases: Rogerson, "Judicial Interpretation of the Spousal and Child Support Provisions of the *Divorce Act*, 1985 (Part I)", *supra*, at p. 234, n. 172. However, as will be seen, Parliament and the legislatures have decreed otherwise by requiring courts to consider not only compensatory factors, but the "needs" and "means" of the parties. It is not a question of either one model or the other. It is rather a matter of applying the relevant factors and striking the balance that best achieves justice in the particular case before the court.

With these theories and policy concerns of marriage and marriage breakdown in mind, I turn to the pertinent statutes. They reveal the joint operation, in different provisions, of both legal paradigms, and hence the compensatory, non-compensatory, and contractual foundations for an entitlement to post-marital spousal support.

(3) The Statutes: The *Divorce Act* and the provincial support statutes are intended to deal with the economic consequences of the marriage breakdown for both parties. See, e.g., *Family Law Act*, R.S.O. 1990, c. F.3, preamble, which characterizes its purpose as "to provide in law for the orderly and equitable settlement of the affairs of the spouses upon the breakdown of the partnership". The statutes require a fair and equitable distribution of resources to alleviate these consequences, regardless of gender. ... As this Court pointed out in *Moge, per* L'Heureux-Dubé J., the *Divorce Act* is premised on the doctrine of the equitable sharing of the economic consequences of the marriage and its breakdown. It is not confined to one type of marriage or one type of support.

Moge, supra, sets out the method to be followed in determining a support dispute. The starting point is the objectives which the *Divorce Act* stipulates the support order should serve: (1) recognition of economic advantage or disadvantage arising from the marriage or its breakdown; (2) apportionment of the financial burden of child care; (3) relief of economic hardship arising from the breakdown of the marriage, and (4) promotion of the economic self-sufficiency of the spouses; s. 15.2(6). No single objective is paramount; all must be borne in mind. The objectives reflect the diverse dynamics of the many unique marital relationships.

Against the background of these objectives the court must consider the factors set out in s. 15.2(4) of the *Divorce Act*. Generally, the court must look at the "condition, means, needs and other circumstances of each spouse". This balancing includes, but is not limited to, the length of cohabitation, the functions each spouse performed, and any order, agreement or arrangement relating to support. Depending on the circumstances, some factors may loom larger than others. In cases where the extent of the economic loss can be determined, compensatory factors may be paramount. On the other hand, "in cases where it is not possible to determine the extent of the economic loss of a disadvantaged spouse ... the court will consider need and standard of living as the primary criteria together with the ability to pay of the other party": *Ross v. Ross* (1995), 168 N.B.R. (2d) 147, N.B. C.A. at p. 156, *per* Bastarache J.A. , (as he then was). There is no hard and fast rule. The judge must look at all the factors in the light of the stipulated objectives of support, and exercise his or her discretion in a manner that equitably alleviates the adverse consequences of the marriage breakdown.

The *Divorce Act* and *Family Relations Act*, through their various provisions, accommodate both models of marriage and marriage breakdown outlined above. While the law has evolved to accept compensation as an important basis of support and to encourage the self-sufficiency of each spouse when the marriage ends, where compensation is not indicated and self-sufficiency is not possible, a support obligation may nonetheless arise from the marriage relationship itself. Turning to the specific provisions, the factors judges must consider in resolving support issues reveal the three different conceptual bases for spousal support obligations — contractual, compensatory, and non-compensatory. The judge must consider them all, and any or all of them may figure in the ultimate order, as may be appropriate in the circumstances of the case. ...

While the statutes contemplate an obligation of support based on the grounds of contract and compensation, they do not confine the obligation to these grounds. The "ability and capacity of, and the reasonable efforts made by, either or both spouses to support themselves" (*Family Relations Act*, s. 89(1)(d)), suggests a concern with need that transcends compensation or contract. Even if a spouse has foregone no career opportunities or has not otherwise been handicapped by the marriage, the court is required to consider that spouse's actual ability to fend for himself or herself and the effort that has been made to do so, including efforts after the marriage breakdown. Similarly, "economic circumstances" (s. 89(1)(e)) invites broad consideration of *all* factors relating to the parties' financial positions, not just those related to compensation. The same may be said for the broad injunction of the *Divorce Act* that the court consider the "condition, means, needs and other circumstances of each spouse". To be sure, these factors may support arguments based on compensation for what happened during the marriage and its breakdown. But they invite an inquiry that goes beyond compensation to the actual situation of the parties at the time of the application. Thus, the basic social obligation model may equally be seen to occupy the statutory provisions.

Section 15.2(6) of the *Divorce Act*, which sets out the objectives of support orders, also speaks to these non-compensatory factors. The first two objectives — to recognize the economic consequences of the marriage or its breakdown and to apportion between the spouses financial consequences of child care over and above child support payments — are primarily related to compensation. But the third and fourth objectives are difficult to confine to that goal. "[E]conomic hardship ... arising from the breakdown of the marriage" is capable of encompassing not only health or career disadvantages arising from the marriage breakdown properly the subject of compensation ..., but the mere fact that a person who formerly enjoyed intra-spousal entitlement to support now finds herself or himself without it. Looking only at compensation, one merely asks what loss the marriage or marriage breakup caused that would not have been suffered but for the marriage. But even where loss in this sense cannot be established, the breakup may cause economic hardship in a larger, non-compensatory sense. Such an interpretation supports the independent inclusion of s. 15.2(6)(c) as a separate consideration from s. 15.2(6)(a). Thus, Rogerson sees s. 15.2(6)(c), "the principle of compensation for the economic disadvantages of the *marriage breakdown* as distinct from the disadvantages of the marriage" as an explicit recognition of "non-compensatory" support ("Spousal Support After *Moge*", *supra*, at pp. 371-72 (emphasis in original)).

Similarly, the fourth objective of s. 15.2(6) of the *Divorce Act* — to promote economic self-sufficiency — may or may not be tied to compensation for disadvantages caused by the marriage or its breakup. A spouse's lack of self-sufficiency may be related to foregoing career and educational opportunities because of the marriage. But it may also arise from completely different sources, like the disappearance of the kind of work the spouse was trained to do (a career shift having nothing to do with the marriage or its breakdown) or, as in this case, ill-health.

In summary, nothing in the *Family Relations Act* or the *Divorce Act* suggests that the only foundations for spousal support are compensatory. Indeed, I find it difficult to confine the words of the statutes to this model. It is true that in 1986 the *Divorce Act* was amended to place greater emphasis on compensation. This represented a shift away "to some degree" from the "means and needs" approach of the 1968 Act: *Payne on Divorce, supra*, at p. 267. But while the focus of the Act may have shifted or broadened, it retains the older idea that spouses may have an obligation to meet or contribute to the needs of their former partners where they have the capacity to pay, even in the absence of a contractual or compensatory foundation for the obligation. Need alone may be enough. More broadly, the legislation can be seen as a sensitive compromise of the two competing philosophies of marriage, marriage breakdown, and spousal support.

(4) The Case Law: Turning to the jurisprudence, Mr. Bracklow cites L'Heureux-Dubé J.'s statement in *Moge, supra*, that "marriage *per se* does not automatically entitle a spouse to support" (p. 864). That is true. To hold otherwise would swing the pendulum too far back and completely ignore the independent, clean-break model of marriage. But, in certain circumstances, marriage *may* give rise to an obligation. It is not the bare fact of marriage, so much as the *relationship* that is established and the expectations that may reasonably flow from it that give rise to the obligation of support under the statutes. This Court in *Moge, per* L'Heureux-Dubé J., emphasized that the court must consider all the objectives of support and all the factors relating to its award. These include non-compensatory factors, like need and means. Indeed, L'Heureux-Dubé J. expressly alluded to the propriety of non-compensatory support in *Moge*. She held that although the 1986 *Divorce Act* shifted the focus of support toward self-sufficiency and compensation, it did not eliminate the traditional consideration of "means and needs". Although *Moge* was primarily concerned with a claim for compensatory support, L'Heureux-Dubé J. noted that in other cases, like those of sick or disabled spouses, a support obligation might well lie even in the absence of a compensatory underpinning. She pointed out that while some of the provisions of the *Divorce Act* are compensatory in character, "[they] may not be characterized as exclusively compensatory" (p. 865). ...

Following *Moge's* broad view of causation in compensatory support and the concomitant acceptance of the availability of non-compensatory support, courts have shown increasing willingness to order support for ill and disabled spouses. Sometimes they have done this as a "transition" to self-sufficiency: *Parish v. Parish* (1993), 46 R.F.L. (3d) 117 (Ont. Gen. Div.). But more often, they have frankly stated that the obligation flows from the marriage relationship itself. Collecting cases, Rogerson explains in "Spousal Support After *Moge*", *supra*, at p. 378 (footnotes omitted):

> The [more dominant] approach, ... particularly in cases of earning capacity permanently limited by age, illness or disability, and the one generally supported by the developing Court of Appeal jurisprudence, has been to award continuing support without regard to the source of the post-divorce need. On this approach, which I earlier referred to as the "basic social obligation" approach, causal connection arguments have been rejected not only in determining entitlement to support, but also in assessing the extent of the obligation. The message coming from the cases adopting this approach appears to be that one takes one's spouse as one finds him or her, subject to all his or her weaknesses and limitations with respect to income-earning capacity; and a spouse with higher earning capacity has a basic obligation to make continuing provision for a spouse who is unable to become self-sufficient at the end of the marriage. One is simply not allowed to abandon a spouse to destitution at the end of a marriage if one has financial resources which might assist in relieving the other spouse's financial circumstances. [Emphasis added.]

Rogerson concludes that "the non-compensatory principle ... has come to play ... a large role in the subsequent case law, providing in many cases a very generous basis for support" (p. 384): see, e.g., *Ashworth v. Ashworth* (1995), 15 R.F.L. (4th) 379 (Ont. Gen. Div.) (non-compensatory permanent support ordered for disabled spouse who, on the judge's findings of fact, *benefitted* from the marriage, as opposed to needing any compensation). "The current approach is typically justified by reference, first, to *Moge's* rejection of the applicability of the causal connection test, and second, to the fact that the spouse who is ill suffers disadvantage from the *breakdown* of the marriage and the loss of financial support from the other spouse" (Rogerson, "Spousal Support After *Moge*", *supra*, at pp. 378-79 (emphasis in original)).

To permit the award of support to a spouse disabled by illness is but to acknowledge the goal of equitably dealing with the economic consequences of marital breakdown that this Court in *Moge*, *supra*, recognized as lying at the heart of the *Divorce Act*. It also may well accord, in my belief, with society's sense of what is just. ... Divorce ends the marriage. Yet in some circumstances the law may require that a healthy party continue to support a disabled party, absent contractual or compensatory entitlement. Justice and considerations of fairness may demand no less.

In summary, the statutes and the case law suggest three conceptual bases for entitlement to spousal support: (1) compensatory, (2) contractual, and (3) non-compensatory. Marriage, as this Court held in *Moge* (at p. 870), is a "joint endeavour", a socio-economic partnership. That is the starting position. Support agreements are important (although not necessarily decisive), and so is the idea that spouses should be compensated on marriage breakdown for losses and hardships caused by the marriage. Indeed, a review of cases suggests that in most circumstances compensation now serves as the main reason for support. However, contract and compensation are not the only sources of a support obligation. The obligation may alternatively arise out of the marriage relationship itself. Where a spouse achieves economic self-sufficiency on the basis of his or her own efforts, or on an award of compensatory support, the obligation founded on the marriage relationship itself lies dormant. But where need is established that is not met on a compensatory or contractual basis, the fundamental marital obligation *may* play a vital role. Absent negating factors, it is available, in appropriate circumstances, to provide just support.

B. Quantum of the Award

The parties segregate entitlement and quantum for purposes of analysis in their submissions on how the Court should exercise its discretion. While I am content to deal with the case in this manner, it must be emphasized that the same factors that go to entitlement have an impact on quantum. In terms of the underlying theories, there is no strong distinction. The real issue is what support, if any, should be awarded in the situation before the judge on the factors set out in the statutes. For practical purposes, however, it may be useful to proceed by establishing entitlement first and then effecting necessary adjustments through quantum. As Rogerson notes, "What is emerging as the dominant approach offers a very broad basis of entitlement, with quantum operating as the only obvious limitation" ("Spousal Support After *Moge*", *supra*, at p. 383 (footnotes omitted)), going on to note that "[i]n most of the cases, the amounts awarded to ill or disabled spouses provide only a very modest or basic standard of living, and do not result in anything approaching equalization of income or even the marital standard of living".

On quantum (which refers both to the amount of support payments and their duration), both parties advance different "rules" for calculation. Mrs. Bracklow segregates the amount of the monthly payments and their duration. She argues that since the basis of support is her "need", that "need" determines the (minimum) amount of the monthly support payment to which she is entitled. The only issue, in her submission, is of duration — how long should Mr. Bracklow continue to meet that need? Her answer is that he must continue as long as her need persists, on the ground there is no principled reason to terminate non-compensatory support while need persists.

Mr. Bracklow, for his part, identifies length of the marital relationship as the critical factor in determining the amount of support. He sees the length of the marital relationship as a proxy for interdependency (and hence the moral obligation of non-compensatory support), relying on the comment in *Moge* that "[a]s marriage should be regarded as a joint endeavour, the longer the relationship endures, the closer the economic union, the greater will be the presumptive claim to equal standards of living upon its dissolution" (p. 870).

Both these arguments miss the mark in that they fix on one factor to the exclusion of others. The short answer to Mrs. Bracklow's argument is that need is but one of a number of factors that the judge must consider. Similarly, the short answer to Mr. Bracklow's contention is that the length of the marital relationship is only one of a number of factors that may be relevant. While some factors may be more important than others in particular cases, the judge cannot proceed at the outset by fixing on only one variable. The quantum awarded, in the sense of both amount and duration, will vary with the circumstances and the practical and policy considerations affecting particular cases. Limited means of the supporting spouse may dictate a reduction. So may obligations arising from new relationships in so far as they have an impact on means. Factors within the marriage itself may affect the quantum of a non-compensatory support obligation. For example, it may be difficult to make a case for a full obligation and expectation of mutual support in a very short marriage. (Section 15.2(4)(a) of the *Divorce Act* requires the court to consider the length of time the parties cohabited.) Finally, subject to judicial discretion, the parties by contract or conduct may enhance, diminish or negate the obligation of mutual support. To repeat, it is not the act of saying "I do", but the marital relationship between the parties that may generate the obligation of non-compensatory support pursuant to the Act. It follows that diverse aspects of that marital relationship may be relevant to the quantum of such support. As stated in *Moge*, "At the end of the day ..., courts have an overriding discretion and the exercise of such discretion will depend on the particular facts of each case, having regard to the factors and objectives designated in the Act" (p. 866).

Fixing on one factor to the exclusion of others leads Mrs. Bracklow to an artificial distinction between amount and duration. The two interrelate: a modest support order of indefinite duration could be collapsed into a more substantial lump-sum payment. It also leads her to the false premise that if need is the basis of the *entitlement* to the support award, then the quantum of the award must meet the total amount of the need. It does not follow from the fact that need serves as the predicate for support that the quantum of the support must always equal the amount of the need. Nothing in either the *Family Relations Act* or the *Divorce Act* forecloses an order for support of a portion of the claimant's need, whether viewed in terms of periodic amount or duration. Need is but one factor to be considered. This is consistent with the modern recognition, captured by the statutes, of the variety of marital relationships in modern society. A spouse who becomes disabled toward the end of a very short marriage may well be entitled to support by virtue of her need, but it may be unfair, under the circumstances, to order the full payment of that need by the supporting spouse for the indefinite future.

Mr. Bracklow's fixation on the length of the marital relationship leads to other difficulties. He elevates this Court's observation in *Moge* about general expectations in long-term marriages to an immutable rule constraining the factors applicable to determining quantum of support. And he introduces "morality" into the calculation of quantum. This is unnecessary, because the statutes already state what the judge should consider. It is also unhelpful, because it does not in the end explain why the length of the marital relationship should serve as the sole "moral" determinant of support, to the exclusion of need and other factors. The flexible mandate of the statutes belies such rigidity.

Mr. Bracklow makes a final policy argument. In an age of multiple marriages, he asserts, the law should permit closure on relationships so parties can move on. Why, he asks, should a young person whose marriage lasts less than a year be fixed with a lifelong obligation of support? When can a former spouse finally move on, knowing that he or she cannot be drawn back into the past by an unexpected application for support?

Again the answer is that under the statutes, the desirability of freedom to move on to new relationships is merely one of several objectives that might guide the judge. Since all the objectives must be balanced, it often will not be possible to satisfy one absolutely. The respondent in effect seeks a judicially created "statute of limitations" on marriage. The Court has no power to impose such a limitation, nor should it. It would inject a rigidity into the system that Parliament and the legislatures have rejected. Marriage, while it may not prove to be "till death do us part", is a serious commitment not to be undertaken lightly. It involves the potential for lifelong obligation. There are no magical cut-off dates.

VII. Application

... Refocusing the facts of this case through the correct juridical lens suggests that while the early years of the Bracklows' union might indicate the atypical partnership of strict independence (rebutting the presumption of intra-marital mutual interdependency), by the end the Bracklows had established a more interdependent relationship. In addition to adjusting their expenses to a more even ratio, it is evident that Mr. Bracklow covered Mrs. Bracklow's needs in the early stages of her illness. Accordingly, it follows that divorce *did* in fact render Mrs. Bracklow in a state of economic hardship, as contemplated by s. 15.2(6)(c) of the *Divorce Act.*

Bearing in mind the statutory objectives of support and balancing the relevant factors, I conclude that Mrs. Bracklow is eligible for support based on the length of cohabitation, the hardship marriage breakdown imposed on her, her palpable need, and Mr. Bracklow's financial ability to pay. While the combined cohabitation and marriage of seven years were not long, neither were they (by today's standards) very short. Mrs. Bracklow contributed, when possible, as a self-sufficient member of the family, at times shouldering the brunt of the financial obligations. These factors establish that it would be unjust and contrary to the objectives of the statutes for Mrs. Bracklow to be cast aside as ineligible for support, and for Mr. Bracklow to assume none of the state's burden to care for his ex-wife.

I leave the determination of the quantum of support to the trial judge, who is in a better position to address the facts of this case than our appellate tribunal. My only comment on the issue is to reiterate that all the relevant statutory factors, including the length of the marital relationship and the relative independence of the parties throughout that marital relationship, must be considered, together with the amount of support Mr. Bracklow has already paid to Mrs. Bracklow. I therefore do not exclude the possibility that no further support will be required, i.e., that Mr. Bracklow's contributions to date have discharged the just and appropriate quantum. Absent settlement between the parties, these issues are for the trial judge to resolve.

VIII. Disposition

I would allow the appeal, set aside the judgment of the Court of Appeal, and remit the matter to the trial judge for assessment in conformity with these reasons of the quantum of the award on the basis that Mrs. Bracklow is legally eligible for post-marital support.

[When the matter returned to the trial judge, the wife's disability payments had increased to $846.44 per month. Her rental housing was subsidized and she lived very modestly. However, she had debts totalling over $8,000. The husband's income had risen to about $71,000 per annum and he was prospering. However, he was now supporting his unemployed new wife. The ex-wife sought an award of $400 per month indefinitely, while the husband argued that he had already satisfied any support obligation he might have had. The judge, reasoning that a time limit was appropriate because the wife's support entitlement was based on non-compensatory grounds arising out of a relatively short marriage awarded $400 per month for five years, with the time beginning to run on March 15, 1995. The arrears under this order stood at $16,000 at the date of the judgment in *Bracklow v. Bracklow* (1999), 181 D.L.R. (4th) 522, 3 R.F.L. (5th) 179 (B.C. S.C.) and the court ordered them to be paid at the rate of $400 per month after March 15, 2000.]

LESKUN v. LESKUN

(2006), 34 R.F.L. (6th) 1, 2006 CarswellBC 1492, 2006 CarswellBC 1493 (S.C.C.)

[Madam Justice McLachlin's statement in *Bracklow* that "[t]here are no magical cut-off dates", was an invitation to further litigation on the issue of when support should end in cases where entitlement is based on need. The question is a reasonable one: how long is an ill spouse entitled to support? In *Leskun v. Leskun*, the applicant wife suffered from physical and emotional illnesses that disabled her from working. Her emotional illness had been exacerbated by the fact that the marriage ended when the husband had an affair.

Four years after the separation, the former husband brought a review application, seeking to terminate support, arguing in part that his former wife had not taken sufficient steps to become self-sufficient. In particular, he asserted that she could have at least obtained part-time employment. The judge rejected the application, recognizing that the separation and the deaths and illnesses of a number of the former wife's close relatives had resulted in "emotional devastation", which, combined with her age (late 50's by that point), the narrowness of her previous employment experience and a pre-existing back injury, rendered her unable to become self-sufficient. That decision was upheld by the British Columbia Court of Appeal, though Southin J.A. observed that the woman was "bitter to the point of obsession with his misconduct and in consequence has been unable to make a new life. Her life is this litigation." Justice Southin nevertheless held that support was appropriate because the woman's inability to support herself was "a failure resulting at least in part from the emotional devastation of misconduct by the other spouse". This comment suggested that fault might be a factor in determining spousal support. There was much media speculation that the decision signaled a return to fault-based spousal support. The husband appealed to the Supreme Court of Canada.]

The judgment of the Court was delivered by

1 BINNIE J.: — This appeal comes to us largely on the strength of a statement in the majority judgment of the Court of Appeal for British Columbia that while a court dealing with spousal support under the *Divorce Act*, R.S.C. 1985, c. 3 (2nd Supp.), is directed not to take into account "any misconduct of a spouse in relation to the marriage" (s. 15.2(5)), it is nevertheless appropriate to take into account the fact the failure to achieve self-sufficiency resulted "at least in part from the emotional devastation of misconduct by the other spouse": (2004), 31 B.C.L.R. (4th) 50, 2004 BCCA 422, at para. 56. Southin J.A. described the respondent wife (who is self-represented) as "bitter to the point of obsession with his misconduct and in consequence [she] has been unable to make a new life. Her life is this litigation." [para. 54] The misconduct consists essentially in the facts that after 20 years of marriage, during which the wife worked, and financially contributed to her husband's continuing education, and bore his child, she was in short order afflicted with a significant back injury and the elimination of her job, and was soon after abandoned by the appellant husband, who announced that he wanted a divorce to marry someone else and live in Chicago. He had, his counsel acknowledged, been "carrying on behind his wife's back", for some time.

2 I agree with the appellant and with the concurring opinion of Newbury J.A. in the B.C. Court of Appeal that the majority judgment wrongly suggests that a court can achieve indirectly what Parliament has said the court is not to do directly. The needs and circumstances of the claimant spouse will of course be relevant to a failure to achieve the objective of self-

sufficiency. It is the attribution of fault to the other spouse that is deemed by Parliament to be irrelevant to the issue of spousal support in a regime designed to deal with the consequences of marital breakdowns on a no-fault basis.

3 However, there were a number of other factors, unrelated to the observations about misconduct, that led the B.C. Court of Appeal unanimously to dismiss the appellant husband's claim for a reduction in support payments. The judgment under appeal can and should be sustained on that basis. I would therefore dismiss the appeal.

Facts

4 The parties were married in 1978. They had one daughter who has a child. Both the daughter and the grandchild reside with the respondent wife, who is currently 59 years old. She and the appellant husband, who is about ten years younger, met while both were working at the Toronto-Dominion Bank. The respondent had two children from her first marriage. The appellant helped to raise them. The respondent continued to work at the bank for most of the marriage except for interruptions from time to time to help the appellant advance his education. He obtained an MBA from the University of Western Ontario and worked towards qualification as a Certified General Accountant. These educational qualifications substantially boosted his income earning capacity. To meet the family's needs while the appellant was studying, the respondent cashed in her RRSPs and obtained the return of her pension contributions, both of which in the long run contributed to her present financial problems.

5 In 1993, the appellant left the bank and joined Motorola, which in April 1998 moved him to Chicago as its local Director of Program Management. It was expected that the respondent would move to Chicago to join him. In September of that year, however, the appellant returned to Vancouver to inform her that he wanted a divorce, which was obtained in 1999. Pending resolution of a number of issues, the appellant agreed to pay the respondent $2,250 per month as interim support.

6 When the issue of permanent spousal support eventually went to trial, Collver J. was confronted with serious uncertainty about the wife's financial prospects: [2000] B.C.J. No. 1085 (Q.L.), 2000 BCSC 1912. Firstly, as mentioned, the respondent had injured her back in 1995 (when she and the appellant were lifting a generator at their home). This required surgery. Her recovery was incomplete. Secondly, the month prior to the marital break-up, the respondent learned that her position at the TD Bank was about to be eliminated. Shortly thereafter she applied for long-term disability benefits arising out of her back injury. The benefits were granted but then discontinued in the fall of 1999. (Subsequent to the trial, the respondent received a severance award from the TD Bank of $83,000.)

7 In his decision, the trial judge held that the respondent had been disadvantaged by the marriage. The interruption in her career did not enhance her position at the bank and, as stated, she had cashed in her RRSPs and pension contributions to meet the family needs. Further, following the marital breakdown, the combined incomes of the appellant and his new wife enabled them to enjoy a standard of living that the respondent could not possibly maintain on her own. The respondent's ability to attain economic self-sufficiency was in some doubt. Collver J. held that she needed, and was entitled to, support until she had resolved outstanding issues with the TD Bank. He therefore ruled that: "Spousal support of $2,250 per month will continue until Sherry Leskun returns to full employment, when both entitlement and quantum will be reviewed" (para. 25b). However, the formal order issued over a year later did not put the condition so specifically and simply provided as follows: "The Plaintiff shall pay spousal support to the Defendant in the sum of $2,250.00 per month ... until further Order of this Honourable Court, *and the Plaintiff shall be at liberty to apply*

for an Order reviewing both entitlement to and quantum of spousal support". [Emphasis added; para. 2.]

Analysis

15 The appellant says the Court of Appeal erred (i) in taking into account spousal misconduct in determining whether the respondent is entitled to spousal support; (ii) in failing to give meaningful effect to the respondent's "duty or obligation to pursue the goal of self-sufficiency"; (iii) in taking into account the appellant's capital in determining his ability to pay spousal support; and (iv) in apparently treating his application as a s. 17(1) *variation* of the original order, thus imposing on him a requirement to demonstrate changed circumstances, instead of a *review* pursuant to a condition set out in the s. 15.2 order, which imposes no such onus. The respondent, who as stated is self-represented, provided a scalding reply on each point. In this Court, we were greatly assisted by the *amicus curiae*. I propose to address the appellant's objections in order.

A. Relevance of Spousal Misconduct

16 The appellant objects that the majority decision of the B.C. Court of Appeal wrongly relied on his alleged misconduct to exonerate his former wife from the consequences of her failure to achieve economic self-sufficiency. The appellant did not challenge the finding that the respondent was not self-sufficient. His point is that in the five years that elapsed between the marital break-up and the hearing before Morrison J. she *ought* to have moved on emotionally and become self-sufficient financially.

17 There is some merit in his complaint that his self-represented wife failed to put on the record documentary support corroborating her alleged job hunting efforts or to file medical evidence to support a finding of continued inability to achieve self-sufficiency. She filed considerable documentary evidence on lesser matters. Nevertheless the Chambers judge heard the respondent and after reading the record was satisfied on that point. The finding of fact was upheld on appeal.

18 Self-sufficiency is one of the goals set out in s. 15.2(6) of the *Divorce Act*. ...

19 In forceful submissions, counsel for the appellant says that the court should not encourage unemployment self-induced by a spouse's "scorched earth" policy and warns that if the court is to permit "a claim that a spous[e]'s adulterous conduct has left the non-offending spouse so bitter and emotionally traumatized as to be unable to return to work", the court will not only be "opening the floodgates" but create a "legal tsunami" of review or variation applications which would not only "be the return to fault in the *Divorce Act*" but lead to a "weakening, I guess, of the Canadian economy".

20 I believe that stripped of the rhetoric, the appellant has a valid point of statutory interpretation. Prior to the 1985 Act, s. 11 of the *Divorce Act*, S.C. 1967-68, c. 24, directed the court to have "regard to the *conduct of the parties* and the condition, means and other circumstances of each of them" in exercising its discretion in making an award of spousal support. The 1985 Act sought to eliminate misconduct, as such, as a relevant consideration. Section 15.2(5) of the *Divorce Act* now provides that in making an interim or final order for spousal support, "the court shall not take into consideration any misconduct of a spouse in relation to the marriage". In addition, s. 17(6) of the *Divorce Act* instructs the court not to consider any conduct in a variation application that could not be considered in the making of the initial order. These provisions make it clear that misconduct should not creep back into the court's deliberation as a relevant "condition" or "other circumstance" which the court is to consider

in making or varying a spousal support order (s. 15.2(4)). Misconduct, as such, is off the table as a relevant consideration.

21 There is, of course, a distinction between the emotional consequences of misconduct and the misconduct itself. The consequences are not rendered irrelevant because of their genesis in the other spouse's misconduct. If, for example, spousal abuse triggered a depression so serious as to make a claimant spouse unemployable, the consequences of the misconduct would be highly relevant (as here) to the factors which must be considered in determining the right to support, its duration and its amount. The policy of the 1985 Act however, is to focus on the consequences of the spousal misconduct not the attribution of fault.

22 Section 15.2(4) states that in making a spousal support order "the court shall take into consideration the *condition, means, needs and other circumstances of each spouse*". ... Certainly the "condition ... needs and other circumstances" includes the capacity of the respondent to be self-sufficient for whatever reason. Whether or not the claimed inability or incapacity of the claimant spouse is credible is for the trial judge to determine. It is not helpful to cast about to assign blame.

23 A break-up in the circumstances found here will perhaps inevitably precipitate a period of shock and emotional trauma for the jilted spouse, but Parliament has concluded that the attempt to get to the bottom of all the rights and wrongs that contributed to the break-up is likely impossible and in any event irrelevant to the task of sorting out the financial consequences. As to the "legal tsunami", I agree with the *amicus curiae* that for the most part parties will realize "that the only way out [of the financial difficulties consequent on the break-up] is if they pull themselves up by their own bootstraps".

24 If the misconduct point were to be viewed in isolation, the appellant is correct, but the point cannot be viewed in isolation. The fact is that both the Chambers judge and Newbury J.A., who differed from her colleagues on the relevance of the misconduct, cited numerous other factors (also referenced by the majority judgment) to reject the appellant's attempt to extricate himself from any further financial responsibility for his former wife. Newbury J.A. observed that

> Mrs. Leskun is now 57 years of age and her affidavit evidence points to various family difficulties and to her medical problems and those of her family. A court cannot ignore these difficulties, which have been exacerbated by the breakdown of the Leskuns' marriage. For this reason, and not because of any self-imposed disability, I would reluctantly uphold the order of the Court below and dismiss the appeal. [para. 63]

I agree. I would add the point made by the Chambers judge about the narrowness of the respondent's work experience, and underline the difficulty of someone now approaching 60 years of age to re-enter the labour force after a lengthy absence and with few marketable skills outside the limits of her former job at the bank, now eliminated.

B. The Respondent's Alleged "Duty" to Become Self-Sufficient

25 Counsel for the appellant framed his point in this way:

> The emotional states of the payor or recipient and their idiosyncrasies should be irrelevant to the duty to pursue self-sufficiency, in the absence of some objective clinical, medical or psychiatric evidence, obviously.

> The duty to be self-sufficient is inversely proportionate to the means of the payor. Persistence in unremunerative employment or unrealistic or unprotective career aspirations should not be countenanced.

> Self-induced reduction in income should not be encouraged or rewarded. And income levels prior to this self-induced reduction should be attributed.

26 Subsection 15.2(6)(d) of the *Divorce Act* provides that one of the objectives of the spousal support order is to, *"in so far as practicable*, promote the economic self-sufficiency of each spouse within a reasonable period of time". This Court has rejected characterizing this objective as a duty, see *Moge v. Moge*, [1992] 3 S.C.R. 813 at p. 853, and *Bracklow v. Bracklow*, [1999] 1 S.C.R. 420, at paras. 31-32, 35-36 and 43. The respondent advanced a number of reasons why, despite alleged efforts, she had been unable to return to the workforce. She was believed.

27 Failure to achieve self-sufficiency is not breach of "a duty" and is simply one factor amongst others to be taken into account. As stated in *Moge* and repeated in *Bracklow*: "[A]t the end of the day ..., courts have an overriding discretion and the exercise of such discretion will depend on the particular facts of each case, having regard to the factors and objectives designated in the Act." (*Moge*, at p. 866, *Bracklow*, at para. 53.)

28 Clearly where incapacity is alleged some independent evidence, including medical evidence would be highly desirable. But it is not essential. Newbury J.A. commented that "[h]aving seen Mrs. Leskun, who appeared on her own behalf, I would have thought she was employable at least on a part-time basis in the banking industry." [para. 62] The Chambers judge approached the respondent's evidence with a measure of scepticism but at the end of the day she had to reach a conclusion on the evidence before her. She said the respondent's inability to move on was "unfortunate". It was not a breach of some alleged duty. It was a regrettable fact of life which could not be ignored in a contextual analysis of the position of these parties. I see no error in the treatment of this issue by the Chambers judge.

Conclusion

43 For the foregoing reasons, I would dismiss the appeal without costs, save and except that the respondent is entitled to be reimbursed for her actual out-of-pocket expenses incurred to respond to the appeal in this Court.

NOTES AND QUESTIONS

1. The Supreme Court confirmed in *Leskun* that, while one of the objectives of the *Divorce Act* is to promote self-sufficiency, there is no duty on spouses to become self-sufficient. Contrast this with *Walsh v. Walsh* (2007), 36 R.F.L. (6th) 262 (Ont. C.A.); leave to appeal refused (2007), 2007 CarswellOnt 5948, 2007 CarswellOnt 5949 (S.C.C.). Ms. Walsh, like Ms. Leskun, represented herself. Ms. Walsh also exhibited symptoms of emotional illness, and like Ms. Leskun, had no medical diagnosis of her condition. Ms. Walsh was similarly obsessed with her husband's infidelity and had made the litigation her main occupation. In *Walsh*, however, the Ontario Court of Appeal had no difficulty with the emphasis placed by the trial judge on the objective of self-sufficiency:

> The application judge terminated spousal support primarily because of what he characterized as the "flagrant circumstances" where the mother has had ample time to obtain employment outside the home but has chosen not to do so. Section 17(7) of the *Divorce Act* provides that an order varying a spousal support order, should consider among other factors "(d) in so far as practical, promote the economic self-sufficiency of each former spouse within a reasonable period of time". The authorities are clear that the judge is to take into account all of the relevant factors set out in s. 17(7).

> There was a basis in the record for the application judge's conclusion both that there had been a material change in circumstances and that a time-limited spousal support order was appropriate. Unless, it can be said that the judge gave unreasonable emphasis to the self-sufficiency factor, this court has no basis for interfering. The application judge set out at length the history of the proceedings and the conduct of the mother that led him to find that the self-sufficiency factor was of particular importance in this case. However, he also considered all the circumstances including the availability of child support; the mother's allegation that her medical condition prevented her from obtaining employment (he drew an adverse inference against the mother because of the lack of medical evidence); that she had obtained employment in the recent past; and that the intention of the parties during the marriage was that the mother would stay at home until the children were in school.

We are satisfied that the application judge did not make an unreasonable finding and did not place unreasonable emphasis on the self-sufficiency factor. We would therefore not give effect to this ground of appeal.

Given their factual similarities, can the outcomes in these two cases be reconciled?

2. *Walsh* and *Leskun* are cases in which the basis for entitlement to support was largely need based (and not compensatory). In compensatory cases, the amount of support tends to be higher, and the duration longer. The basis for the support order is therefore critical to the practical outcome. If the court characterizes the case as a needs-based one, the result may be very different than it would be if the support is compensatory.

In *Shields v. Shields* (2008), 53 R.F.L. (6th) 9 (Alta. C.A.), the Alberta Court of Appeal overturned a trial decision that had ordered indefinite spousal support after a relatively long marriage in which there were three children. The wife entered the marriage with few job skills, and was leaving it in the same condition, after having devoted her time to raising the children. The husband, meanwhile, had prospered and had a large income. In a decision which appears to echo the old causal connection theory of support entitlement, the appellate court decided that spousal support should end after eight years. It noted:

> 27 The chambers judge found that the respondent did not sacrifice employment opportunities as her employment prospects as an unskilled person were always minimal. Consequently, the spousal support order appears to be based on a needs model designed to increase the respondent's standard of living above what she would have with just her employment income. ...

> 29 The chambers judge erred when he did not sufficiently consider the fact that the mother was only 34 years old at the time of separation, that the matrimonial property had been divided equitably, that the couple had a modest standard of living while together, that there was no longer a need for child care and that the mother had achieved a degree of self sufficiency with full time employment at a level consistent with her work skills. ...

> 32 After a fifteen year marriage followed by an eight year separation, and taking into account the appropriate factors, a spousal support order ought to provide the mother with a realistic time frame to return to the workforce and acquire adequate income to achieve self sufficiency. At $1000.00 per month, the eight years from the date of separation to the date when the chambers judge heard this matter, in our view, was a realistic time frame for the mother to be compensated for the economic disadvantage she sustained and to allow her to re-enter the job market in order to earn income leading toward financial self sufficiency. Put another way, given the factors in this case, a spousal support order of $1000.00 per month for an eight year duration complies with the spousal support objective of recognizing the respondent's economic disadvantage arising from the marriage and its breakdown, while also encouraging the respondent to complete her transition to self sufficiency by positioning her to earn an adequate income and adapt her lifestyle accordingly.

In *Fisher v. Fisher* (2008), 47 R.F.L. (6th) 235 (Ont. C.A.) (reproduced below), the Ontario Court of Appeal limited support to a period of seven years following a 19-year marriage. There were no children, which may explain the court's finding that the basis for the award was primarily need, and not compensation. However, there were compensatory elements to the support claim. The case received sharp commentary from prominent Toronto practitioner Philip Epstein at the Law Society of Upper Canada's Family Law Summit, June, 2008 (*Spousal Support — Fisher v. Fisher*):

> The parties were married in 1985, when the wife was 22 and the husband 23 years of age. They separated in 2004, when they were 41 and 42 years of age respectfully [sic]. It is of fundamental importance in analyzing this decision to understand there were no children of the relationship. There were, however, other potentially compensatory elements. ...

> The trial judge made clear findings of fact that would entitle Mrs. Fisher to compensatory support. While it is a very significant and virtually overwhelming fact in this case that the parties did not have children, the wife did help put the husband through school, obviously pooled her income with his and the parties did live a comfortable lifestyle on a combined income of at least $120,000 per year. There would hardly be any question that the end of this marriage created a significant economic disadvantage to Mrs. Fisher and an economic hardship. ...

3. Another important issue in spousal support cases is whether the recipient's need should be assessed subjectively or objectively. If it is assessed on the basis of the standard of living enjoyed during the marriage, the recipient can expect a higher award. If it is assessed objectively, the court will be looking at whether the recipient has enough

money to keep him or her out of poverty, thereby often resulting in a lower award. The basis of entitlement may influence this choice. In need-based cases, courts tend to assess need more objectively. In compensatory cases, courts tend to assess need on the basis of the marital standard of living. See, for example, *Allaire v. Allaire* (2003), 35 R.F.L. (5th) 256 (Ont. C.A.) where the appellate court, in upholding a "compensatory spousal support in the amount of $2,500 monthly" for an indefinite period, stated (paras. 20 & 21):

> It is clear from the trial judge's reasons that the award is designed not only to redress the economic consequences of the breakdown of the marriage, but also to compensate Ms. Allaire for the likely permanent economic results of having to postpone her post-secondary education. It is an amount that properly seeks to adjust the economic disparity between the two households based on the former joint standard of living.
>
> Mr. Allaire's submits that any disadvantages flowing from the marriage must defer to the fact that Ms. Allaire now earns a reasonable income that makes her "self-sufficient". This ignores the reality that self-sufficiency is not a free-standing concept. It must be seen in the context of the standard of living previously enjoyed by the parties. Where, as here, the economic consequences of the marital relationship were to permanently reduce Ms. Allaire's income, it is inappropriate to consider Ms. Allaire's annual income of $68,000 as "sufficient" without considering whether Mr. Allaire can financially assist her to live a lifestyle closer to what they shared as a couple.

4. A compensatory award is meant to compensate the recipient for career opportunities lost during the marriage as a result of the roles taken on during the marriage (most often child-rearing, but also supporting the payor in furthering his or her education). While need remains an important determinant of the amount of support in compensatory cases, compensatory support will often continue when need has become less of an issue. For example, compensatory support may still be appropriate even when the recipient has a new partner, although the amount may be reduced. See *Levandusky v. Levandusky* (2003), [2003] O.J. No. 2783, 39 R.F.L. (5th) 134 (Ont. S.C.J.); additional reasons at (2003), 2003 CarswellOnt 2613 (S.C.J.). See also *M. (K.A.) v. M. (P.K.)* (2008), 50 R.F.L. (6th) 165 (B.C. S.C.) where Justice Barrow stated (para. 72):

> What then of the effect of re-partnering? Although not free of doubt, I consider that the fact of re-partnering has no effect on entitlement and should have little effect on quantum at least initially, given the compensatory nature of the entitlement. As the recipient spouse's new relationship matures, however, the concept of "merger over time", which partially animates the determination of quantum and duration of support, would, if applied to the second union, suggest a growing obligation on the new spouse to support the former spouse of the first union. To the extent that is so, it would be reasonable to reduce the obligation of the first paying spouse over time.

5. Section 15.2(5) of the *Divorce Act* specifies that the court "shall not take into consideration any misconduct of a spouse in relation to the marriage" in making a spousal support order. See also s. 17(6). Thus, marital misconduct is no longer a factor to be considered. Do you agree with the Supreme Court of Canada's conclusion in *Leskun v. Leskun* that these provisions do not preclude the indirect consideration of a spouse's conduct that may have had an impact on the spouse's present ability to support himself or herself?

Section 33(10) of the *Family Law Act* stipulates that the obligation to provide support exists without regard to "the conduct of either spouse, but the court may, in determining the amount of support, have regard to a course of conduct that is so unconscionable as to constitute an obvious and gross repudiation of the relationship". This subsection has been narrowly interpreted and so conduct is very rarely considered. See *Morey v. Morey* (1978), 8 R.F.L. (2d) 31 (Ont. Prov. Ct.) for a general discussion of the predecessor subsection in the *Family Law Reform Act* and *Freid v. Freid* (1982), 30 R.F.L. (2d) 342 (Ont. Co. Ct.); *MacDonald v. MacDonald* (May, 1991), unreported [Ont. Gen. Div.]; *Krigstin v. Krigstin* (1992), 43 R.F.L. (3d) 334 (Ont. Gen. Div.); and *Belleville v. White* (2002), 35 R.F.L. (5th) 1 (Ont. S.C.J.) for a few cases where a recipient spouse's conduct affected the award.

6. Determining the Support Application — How Much and For How Long?

(1) Introduction

Once entitlement and the basis for it has been determined, a court must consider how much support to order and, if periodic, for how long. Until the publication of the *Spousal Support Advisory Guidelines*, it was hard to find consistent principles driving these important determinations. The writers of the SSAG considered many factors in arriving at the formulas contained in the SSAG for determining how much should be paid, and for how long.

ROGERSON AND THOMPSON, *SPOUSAL SUPPORT ADVISORY GUIDELINES*

(Department of Justice Canada, Ottawa: July, 2008) (Full version is on Departmental web site)

Executive Summary

The *Spousal Support Advisory Guidelines* were developed to bring more certainty and predictability to the determination of spousal support under the federal *Divorce Act*. The Advisory Guidelines project has been supported by the federal Department of Justice. The Advisory Guidelines were released three years ago, in January 2005, in the form of a Draft Proposal and have been used across Canada since then. Comments and feedback were provided and some revisions made. This document is the final version.

The *Spousal Support Advisory Guidelines* are very different from the *Federal Child Support Guidelines*. They **have not been legislated** by the federal government. They are informal guidelines that will operate on **an advisory basis only**. The Advisory Guidelines will be used to determine the amount and duration of spousal support within the existing legal framework of the Divorce Act and the judicial decisions interpreting its provisions. The Guidelines are not legally binding and their adoption and use will be voluntary. They are intended as a practical tool to assist spouses, lawyers, mediators and judges in determining the amount and duration of spousal support in typical cases. The various components of the Guidelines — the basic formulas, restructuring, and exceptions — are intended to build upon current practice, reflecting best practices and emerging trends across the country. The process of developing the Advisory Guidelines is described in Chapter 2.

An overview of the structure of the Guidelines is found in Chapter 3.

The Advisory Guidelines **do not deal with entitlement**, just amount and duration once entitlement has been found. A mere disparity of income that would generate an amount under the Guidelines does not automatically lead to entitlement. As is set out in Chapter 4, there must be a finding (or an agreement) on entitlement, on a compensatory or non-compensatory or contractual basis, before the formulas and the rest of the Guidelines are applied. The basis of entitlement is important, not only as a threshold issue, but also to determine location within the formula ranges or to justify departure from the ranges as an exception. Entitlement issues also arise frequently on review and variation, especially applications to terminate support.

Some limitations on the application of the Guidelines are dealt with in Chapter 5. The Advisory Guidelines have been developed specifically for use under the federal *Divorce Act*. **Provincial/territorial laws** differ in some respects and any use of these Guidelines in the provincial/territorial context must take account of these distinctive statutes, especially on matters of entitlement for unmarried couples and agreements. A **prior agreement** may limit the application of the Guidelines, as the Advisory Guidelines cannot be used to override existing agreements, especially agreements that time limit or waive spousal support.

There are two basic formulas in the proposal: the *without child support* **formula** and the *with child support* **formula**. The dividing line between the two is the absence or presence of a dependent child or children of the marriage, and a concurrent child support obligation, at the time spousal support is determined. Both formulas use **income sharing** as the method for determining the amount of spousal support, not budgets. The formulas produce **ranges** for the amount and duration of support, not just a single number. The precise number chosen within that range is a matter for negotiation or adjudication, depending upon the facts of a particular case.

The starting point under both formulas is the definition of **income** used in the *Federal Child Support Guidelines*, subject to some minor adjustments for spousal support purposes, explained in Chapter 6.

The *without child support* **formula**, set out below, is built around two crucial factors: the gross **income difference** between the spouses and the **length of the marriage**. Both the amount and the duration of support increase incrementally with the length of the marriage, as can be seen in the summary box below. The idea that explains this formula is **merger over time**: as a marriage lengthens, spouses more deeply merge their economic and non-economic lives, with each spouse making countless decisions to mould his or her skills, behaviours and finances around those of the other spouse. The gross income difference measures their differential loss of the marital standard of living at the end of the marriage. The formulas for both amount and duration reflect the idea that the longer the marriage, the more the lower income spouse should be protected against such a differential loss. Merger over time captures both the compensatory and non-compensatory spousal support objectives that have been recognized by our law since *Moge* and *Bracklow*.

The *Without Child Support* Formula

Amount ranges from 1.5 to 2 percent of the difference between the spouses' gross incomes (the **gross income difference**) for each year of marriage (or, more precisely, years of cohabitation), up to a maximum of 50 percent. The maximum range remains fixed for marriages 25 years or longer at 37.5 to 50 percent of income difference. (The upper end of this maximum range is capped at the amount that would result in equalization of the spouses' net incomes-the **net income cap**.)

Duration ranges from .5 to 1 year for each year of marriage. However, support will be **indefinite (duration not specified)** if the marriage is **20 years or longer** in duration or, if the marriage has lasted 5 years or longer, when the years of marriage and age of the support recipient (at separation) added together total 65 or more (the **rule of 65**).

Chapter 7 contains examples of the application of the *without child support* formula and the ranges it produces for marriages of different lengths and incomes.

Cases with dependent children and concurrent child support obligations require a different formula, the *with child support* **formula**, set out in Chapter 8. These cases raise different considerations: priority must be given to child support; there is usually reduced ability to pay; and particular tax and benefit issues arise. The rationale for spousal support is also different. Where there are dependent children, the primary rationale is compensatory, as both *Moge* and *Bracklow* made clear. What drives support is not the length of the marriage, or marital interdependency, or merger over time, but the presence of dependent children and the need to provide care and support for those children. This parental partnership rationale looks at not just past loss, but also at the continuing economic disadvantage that flows from present and future child care responsibilities, anchored in s. 15.2(6)(b) of the *Divorce Act*.

There are three important differences between the *without child support* formula and the *with child support* formula. First, the with child support formula uses the **net incomes** of the spouses, not their gross incomes. Second, this formula divides the **pool** of combined net incomes between the two spouses, not the gross income difference. Third, the upper and lower percentage limits of net income division in the with child support formula **do not change with the length of the marriage**.

Set out below is a summary version of the **basic *with child support* formula**, used to determine the amount of spousal support to be paid where the payor spouse pays both child and spousal support to the lower income recipient spouse who is also the parent with custody or primary care of the children.

The Basic *With Child Support* Formula for Amount

1.   Determine the individual net disposable income (INDI) of each spouse:

  • Guidelines Income minus Child Support minus Taxes and Deductions = Payor's INDI

  • Guidelines Income minus Notional Child Support minus Taxes and Deductions Plus Government Benefits and Credits = Recipient's INDI

2.   Add together the individual net disposable incomes. By iteration, determine the range of spousal support amounts that would be required to leave the lower income recipient spouse with between 40 and 46 percent of the combined INDI.

Net income computations like these require computer software. Basic to this formula is the concept of **individual net disposable income**, an attempt to isolate a **pool** of net disposable income available after adjustment for each spouse's child support obligations. This is done by deducting or backing out their respective **contributions to child support**. The details of these calculations are set out in Chapter 8, along with several examples.

Duration under this basic *with child support* formula also reflects the underlying parental partnership rationale. Initial orders are **indefinite (duration not specified)**, subject to the usual process of review or variation. The formula does, however, provide a **durational range** which is intended to structure the process of review and variation and to limit the cumulative duration of spousal support. The durational limits under this formula can be thought of as "soft" time limits. There are two tests for duration and whichever produces the longer duration at each end of the range is to be employed:

  • First is the **length-of-marriage** test, which is modelled on the duration under the *without child support* formula, i.e. one-half to one year of support for every year of marriage, and which will likely govern for most marriages of ten years or more.

  • Second is the **age-of-children** test. The lower end of the durational range is until the youngest child starts full-time school. The upper end of the durational range is until the last or youngest child finishes high school. This test will typically apply to marriages of less than ten years.

Shared and split custody situations require slight variations in the computation of individual net disposable income, as the backing out of child support obligations is a bit more complicated. There is also a different, hybrid formula for cases where **spousal support is paid by the custodial parent**. Under this formula, the spouses' Guidelines incomes are reduced by the grossed-up amount of child support (actual or notional) and then the *without child support* formula is applied to determine amount and duration. Finally, there is one more hybrid formula for those spousal support cases where the child support for **adult children** is determined under section 3(2)(b) of the *Child Support Guidelines*.

The formulas provide ranges for the amount and duration of spousal support. The location of a precise amount or duration within those ranges — what we refer to as **using the ranges** — will be driven by the **factors** detailed in Chapter 9: the strength of any compensatory claim; the recipient's needs; the age, number, need and standard of living of any children; the needs and ability to pay of the payor; [the need to preserve] work incentives for the payor; property division and debts; and self-sufficiency incentives.

Restructuring allows the amount and duration under the formulas to be traded off against each other, so long as the overall value of the restructured award remains within the total or global amounts generated by the formula when amount and duration are combined. Chapter 10 shows how restructuring can be used in three different ways:

- to **front-end load** awards by increasing the amount beyond the formula's range and shortening duration;
- to **extend duration** beyond the formula's range by lowering the monthly amount; or
- to formulate a **lump sum** by combining amount and duration.

"**Ceilings**" and "**floors**" in Chapter 11 define the boundaries of the typical incomes to which the formulas can be applied. The **ceiling** is the income level for the payor spouse above which any formula gives way to discretion, set here at a **gross annual income for the payor of $350,000**. The **floor** is the income level for the payor below which no support is usually paid, here set at **$20,000**. To avoid a cliff effect, there is an **exception** for cases where the payor spouse's gross income is **more than $20,000 but less than $30,000**, where spousal support may not be awarded or may be reduced below the low end of the range. An additional exception is also necessary, to allow an award of spousal support **below the income floor** in particular cases. Any formula, even with restructuring, will have its limits and there will always be exceptional cases. Because the Guidelines are only advisory, departures are always possible on a case-by-case basis where the formula outcomes are inappropriate. The Guidelines do contain a short list of **exceptions** in Chapter 12, intended to identify common categories of departures:

- compelling financial circumstances in the interim period;
- debt payment;
- prior support obligations;
- illness and disability [of the recipient spouse];
- the compensatory exception in short marriages without children;
- reapportionment of property (British Columbia);
- basic needs/hardship under the without child support and custodial payor formulas;
- non-taxable payor income;
- non-primary parent to fulfil parenting role under the custodial payor formula;
- special needs of a child; and
- section 15.3 for small amounts and inadequate compensation under the with child support formula.

(2) Working With the Formulas Under The SSAG

ROGERSON AND THOMPSON, *Spousal Support Advisory Guidelines*

(Department of Justice Canada, Ottawa: July, 2008) (Full version is on
Departmental web site)

Content of the Advisory Guidelines

The Advisory Guidelines are based on what is called "income sharing". Contrary to popular conception, income sharing does not necessarily mean equal sharing. It simply means that spousal support is determined as a percentage of spousal incomes. The percentages can vary according to a number of factors. The Advisory Guidelines offer two basic formulas that base spousal support on spousal incomes and other relevant factors such as the presence or absence of dependent children, and the length of the marriage. The formulas deal with the amount (sometimes referred to as quantum) and duration of spousal support once entitlement to support has been established. The formulas generate ranges of outcomes, rather than precise figures for amount and duration, which may be restructured by trading off amount against duration.

The Guidelines are advisory only and thus always allow for departures from the outcomes generated by the formulas on a case-by-case basis where they are not appropriate. While we have tried to specify exceptions to assist the parties and the courts in framing and assessing any departures from the formulas' ranges, they are not exhaustive of the grounds for departure. There is still considerable room for the exercise of discretion under the Advisory Guidelines but it will be exercised within a much more defined structure than existed before - one with clearer starting points. Budgets, which are currently the primary tool in spousal support determinations, increasingly play a reduced and less central role. ...

1 Background — The Current Law Of Spousal Support

1.3 The Problem of Spousal Support and the Need for Guidelines

The culture of spousal support after Bracklow was one that emphasized individualized decision making and an absence of rules. Multiple theories of spousal support competed with each other while, on the ground, spousal support cases were negotiated and argued under an amorphous needs-and-means framework dominated by budgets. "Need" means many different things to different people and many different theories of spousal support can be couched in the language of need. The guidelines project sprang from the growing concern expressed by lawyers and judges that the highly discretionary nature of the current law of spousal support had created an unacceptable degree of uncertainty and unpredictability.

Similar fact situations could generate a wide variation in results. Individual judges were provided with little concrete guidance in determining spousal support outcomes and their subjective perceptions of fair outcomes played a large role in determining the spousal support ultimately ordered. Appeals were often be of little help because appeal courts frequently dispose of appeals with little explanation, deferring to trial judges on issues of quantum and duration. Lawyers in turn had difficulty predicting outcomes, thus impeding their ability to advise clients and to engage in cost-effective settlement negotiations.

And for those without legal representation or in weak bargaining positions, support claims were simply not pursued. Despite a very broad basis for entitlement under the existing law, many spouses did not claim spousal support, being unwilling to engage in the difficult and costly process required.

More generally, the uncertainty and unpredictability that pervaded the law of spousal support was undermining the legitimacy of the spousal support obligation. The widely differing understandings of the nature of the spousal support obligation generated concerns about unfair outcomes at both ends of the spectrum. In some cases awards were perceived as too low, in others as unjustifiably high.

The Advisory Guidelines were a response to these concerns. They were developed for the purpose of bringing more certainty and predictability to spousal support determinations. They incorporate the basic principles of compensation and need that the Supreme Court of Canada has identified as the bases for spousal support under the *Divorce Act* but provide a more structured way of implementing those principles through formulas based on income sharing, i.e. formulas based on sharing specified percentages of spousal incomes. ...

2 The Guideline Project

2.1 The Nature of the Guidelines: Informal and Advisory

There are many preconceptions about what spousal support guidelines are and how they work. Any talk of spousal support guidelines immediately brings to mind the *Federal Child Support Guidelines*. As we emphasized in the introduction, this comparison should be resisted. These Advisory Guidelines are very different.

Unlike the *Federal Child Support Guidelines*, the Spousal Support **Advisory Guidelines** do not involve formal legislative reform. They have not been legislated by the federal government. They are intended to be **informal** guidelines that operate on an advisory basis only, within the existing legislative framework. ...

3 An Overview Of The Advisory Guidelines

3.2 Preliminary Issues — The Applicability of the Advisory Guidelines

. . . . .

3.2.3 Application to provincial/territorial law

The Advisory Guidelines were specifically developed under the federal *Divorce Act* and intended for use under that legislation. Provincial/territorial support law is governed by specific statutory regimes. However, in practice there is much overlap between federal and provincial/territorial support laws.

The broad conceptual framework for spousal support articulated by the Supreme Court of Canada in *Moge* and *Bracklow* has been applied under both provincial and federal legislation. Indeed *Bracklow*, which combined claims under the *Divorce Act* and provincial legislation, made no real distinction between the two. Given this overlap, the Advisory Guidelines have been used under provincial/territorial support legislation.

There are some distinctive features of provincial/territorial spousal support laws that need to be taken into account when using the Advisory Guidelines. Many provincial/territorial laws have specific provisions governing entitlement, for example provisions determining which non-marital relationships give rise to a spousal support obligation. Like other issues of entitlement discussed above, this must be a threshold determination before the Advisory Guidelines are applied to determine amount and duration of support. We also note that the list of specific factors to be considered in determining spousal support does vary from statute to statute, with some provincial/territorial legislation making explicit reference, for example, to factors such as property and conduct, although the impact of these differences in wording on spousal support outcomes is unclear.

Provincial laws differ from the *Divorce Act* in their application to unmarried couples but this should not cause any difficulties with respect to the operation of the Advisory Guidelines. Although we conveniently refer to "length of marriage" as a relevant factor in the operation of the formulas, the formulas actually rely upon the period of spousal cohabitation (including any periods of pre-marital cohabitation), thus easily meshing with provincial/territorial legislation. ...

3.3 The Formulas

3.3.5 Length of marriage

Under the Advisory Guidelines length of marriage is a primary determinant of support outcomes in cases *without* dependent children. Under the *without child support* formula the percentage of income sharing increases with length of the marriage; the same is true for duration of support.

Length of marriage is much less relevant under the *with child support formula*, although it still plays a significant role in determining duration under that formula.

Given the relevance of length of marriage under the Advisory Guidelines, it is important to clarify its meaning. **While we use the convenient term length of marriage, the more accurate description is the length of the cohabitation, which includes periods of pre-marital cohabitation, and ends with separation.**

3.3.6 Ranges

The Advisory Guidelines do not generate a fixed figure for either amount or duration, but instead produce a **range of outcomes** that provide a starting point for negotiation or adjudication. Ranges create scope for more individualized decision-making, allowing for argument about where a particular case should fall within the range in light of the *Divorce Act's* multiple support objectives and factors. Ranges can also accommodate some of the variations in current practice, including local variations in spousal support cultures. ...

3.3.7 Ceilings and floors

As with the *Federal Child Support Guidelines*, the *Spousal Support Advisory Guidelines* establish ceilings and floors in terms of the income levels to which they are applicable. Both the ceiling and the floor have been set by reference to the annual gross income of the payor. The ceiling has been set at a gross annual income for the payor of $350,000 and the floor at a gross annual income of $20,000. ...

3.4 After the Formulas Have Been Applied

Under the Advisory Guidelines there is still much room for flexibility to respond to the facts of particular cases. First, there is considerable room for discretion in the fixing of precise amounts and durations within the ranges generated by the formulas. Second, there is the ability to restructure the formula outcomes by trading off amount against duration. Third, the other is the possibility of departing from the formula outcomes by relying upon exceptions.

3.4.1 Using the ranges

The location of a precise amount or duration within those ranges will be driven by the factors detailed in Chapter 9: the strength of any compensatory claim, the recipient's needs, the age, number, needs and standard of living of any children, the needs and ability to pay of the payor, work incentives for the payor, property division and debts, and self-sufficiency incentives.

3.4.2 Restructuring

Although the formulas generate separate figures for amount and duration, the Advisory Guidelines explicitly recognize that these awards can be restructured by trading off amount against duration.

In *Bracklow* the Supreme Court of Canada explicitly recognized that the amount and duration of awards can be configured in different ways to yield awards of similar value (what the Court called quantum). Thus the Court noted that an order for a smaller amount paid out over a long period of time can be equivalent to an order for a higher amount paid out over a shorter period of time.

Restructuring can be used in three ways:

- to **front-end load** awards by increasing the amount beyond the formulas' ranges and shortening duration;

- to **extend duration** beyond the formulas' ranges by lowering the monthly amount; and

- to formulate a **lump sum** payment by combining amount and duration.

When restructuring is relied upon to resolve issues of inappropriate formula outcomes, awards remain consistent with the overall or global amounts generated by the Advisory Guidelines. **Restructuring thus does not involve an exception or departure from the formulas.** Restructuring works best when duration is clearly defined, and will thus have its primary application under the *without child support* formula. ...

3.4.3 Exceptions

The formulas are intended to generate appropriate outcomes in the majority of cases. We recognize, however, that there will be cases where the formula outcomes, even after consideration of restructuring, will not generate results consistent with the support objectives and factors under the *Divorce Act*. The informal, advisory nature of the Guidelines means that the formula outcomes are never binding and departures are always possible on a case-by-case basis where the formula outcomes are found to be inappropriate. The Advisory Guidelines do, however, itemize a series of exceptions which, although clearly not exhaustive, are intended to assist lawyers and judges in framing and assessing departures from the formulas. The exceptions create room both for the operation of competing theories of spousal support and for consideration of the particular factual circumstances in individual cases where these may not be sufficiently accommodated by restructuring. [Recall that the exceptions were listed in the Executive Summary, above.] ...

7 The Without Child Support Formula

7.1 The Basic Structure of the Without Child Support Formula

The *without child support* formula is set out in the box below in its most basic form. The formula is in fact two formulas — one for amount and one for duration. The formula generates **ranges** for amount and duration, rather than fixed numbers. There are two crucial factors under the formula:

- the gross income difference between the spouses, and

- the length of the marriage, or more precisely, as will be explained below, the length of the period of cohabitation.

Both amount and duration increase incrementally with the length of marriage.

The *Without Child Support* Formula

Amount ranges from 1.5 to 2 percent of the difference between the spouses' gross incomes (the **gross income difference**) for each year of marriage (or more precisely, year of cohabitation), up to a maximum of 50 percent. The range remains fixed for marriages 25 years or longer, at 37.5 to 50 percent of income difference. (The upper end of this maximum range is capped at the amount that would result in equalization of the spouses' net incomes — the **net income cap**).

Duration ranges from .5 to 1 year for each year of marriage. However support will be **indefinite (duration not specified)** if the marriage is **20 years or longer** in duration or, if the marriage has lasted five years or longer, when years of marriage and age of the support recipient (at separation) added together total 65 or more (the **rule of 65**).

A simple example illustrating the basic operation of the without child support formula will be helpful at this point before we venture further into its more complex details. The primary purpose of this example is to show the basic calculations required under the formula and to give a sense of the outcomes the formula generates.

Example 7.1

Arthur and Ellen have separated after a 20-year marriage and one child. During the marriage Arthur, who had just finished his commerce degree when the two met, worked for a bank, rising through the ranks and eventually becoming a branch manager. He was transferred several times during the course of the marriage. His gross annual income is now $90,000. Ellen worked for a few years early in the marriage as a bank teller, then stayed home until their son was in school full time. She worked part time as a store clerk until he finished high school. Their son is now independent. Ellen now works full time as a receptionist earning $30,000 gross per year. Both Arthur and Ellen are in their mid forties.

Assuming entitlement has been established in this case, here is how support would be determined under the *without child support* formula.

To determine the **amount** of support:

- Determine the gross income difference between the parties: $90,000 - $30,000 = $60,000
- Determine the applicable percentage by multiplying the length of the marriage by 1.5-2 percent per year: 1.5 × 20 years = 30 percent to 2 × 20 years = 40 percent
- Apply the applicable percentage to the income difference: 30 percent × $60,000 = $18,000/year ($1,500/month) to 40 percent × $60,000 = $24,000/year ($2,000/month)

Duration would be indefinite (duration not specified) in this case because the length of the marriage was 20 years.

Thus, assuming entitlement, spousal support under the formula would be in the range of $1,500 to $2,000 per month for an indefinite (not specified) duration. This formula amount assumes the usual tax consequences, i.e. deductible to the payor and taxable to the recipient. It would also be open to the normal process of variation and review.

An award of $1,500 per month, at the low end of the range, would leave Ellen with a gross annual income of $48,000 and Arthur with one of $72,000. An award of $2,000 per month, at the high end of the range, would leave Ellen with a gross annual income of $54,000 and Arthur with one of $66,000. In Chapter 9 we deal with the factors that determine the setting of a precise amount within that range.

On first glance, this formula no doubt looks like an entirely new approach to spousal support, far removed both from the *Divorce Act* and its spousal support objectives and factors and from the principles of compensatory and non-compensatory support that the Supreme Court of Canada articulated in *Moge* and *Bracklow*. ...[However,] the formula is a "proxy measure" for factors such as economic disadvantage, need, and standard of living that are currently used to determine spousal support outcomes. ...

7.5 *The Formula for Duration*

As with amount, duration under the *without child support* formula increases with the length of marriage. [Recall that the term "length of marriage" actually means the period of cohabitation in the application of the formulas.] Subject to the provisions for indefinite support (duration not specified), the formula generates ranges for duration with the ends of the ranges determined as follows:

- **a minimum duration of half the length of the marriage and**
- **a maximum duration of the length of the marriage.**

It is important to remember ... that any periods of interim support are to be included in the durational ranges.

The ranges for duration under the *without child support* formula are admittedly very broad, allowing for an award at the top end of the range that is effectively double in value that at the bottom end. This will be particularly significant in medium-length marriages. Given the uncertainties in the current law on duration, it was not possible to come up with tighter ranges.

The formula also provides for indefinite support (duration not specified) in two circumstances:

- when the marriage has been 20 years or longer in length; or
- when the marriage has lasted five years or longer, **if the years of marriage plus the age of the support recipient at the time of separation equals or exceeds 65 and (the rule of 65).**

The "rule of 65" recognizes that length of marriage cannot be the only factor in determining the duration of spousal support in marriages without dependent children. **Age** is also a significant factor as it affects the ability to become self-supporting. ...

7.5.3 The "rule of 65": the age factor and indefinite support

The *without child support* formula provides that indefinite (duration not specified) support will be available even in cases where the marriage is shorter than 20 years **if the years of marriage plus the age of the support recipient at the time of separation equals or exceeds 65**. In a shorthand expression, we described this as the"rule of 65".

Thus, if a 10-year marriage ends when the recipient is 55, indefinite (duration not specified) support will be available because years of marriage (10) plus age (55) equals 65. Note that this is only a "rule" about duration, as the amount of support would be limited by the length of the marriage, i.e. 1.5 to 2 per cent per year or 15 to 20 per cent of the gross income difference in a 10-year marriage.

In reality, given the ages of the parties in the cases covered by the rule of 65, there will likely be significant changes in the amount of support ordered upon the retirement of one or both of the spouses. This refinement to the formula for duration is intended to respond to the situation of older spouses who were economically dependent during a medium length marriage and who may have difficulty becoming self-sufficient given their age.

The "rule of 65" for indefinite (duration not specified) support is not available in short marriages (under 5 years in length). The assumption in the current law is that short marriages generate only limited support obligations.

In the Draft Proposal, we struggled with the issue of whether an age component should always be required for indefinite (duration not specified) support — i.e. whether the "rule of 65" should apply even in long marriages. Under a 20 year rule with no age requirement, for example, a 38 year-old spouse leaving a 20 year marriage would be entitled to indefinite (duration not specified) support. Some would argue that indefinite (duration not specified) support is not appropriate for a spouse who is still relatively young and capable of becoming self-sufficient. If the "rule of 65" were generally applicable, support would not become indefinite (duration not specified) even after a 20 year marriage unless the recipient were 45 years of age or older.

Several considerations led us to the conclusion that a 20-year rule without any age requirement was the more appropriate choice. First, a spouse who married young and spent the next 20 years caring for children could be more disadvantaged than someone who married when they were older and had been able to acquire some job skills before withdrawing from the labour force. As well, under the current law it would be very difficult to impose a time-limit on support after a 20 year marriage, even if self-sufficiency and an eventual termination of support were contemplated at some point in the future. The typical order would be an indefinite order subject to review and/or variation. An order for indefinite support (duration not specified) under the Advisory Guidelines is no different. ...

7.6 Making the Formula Concrete — Some Examples

7.6.1 A short-marriage example

In cases of short marriages, marriages of less than 5 years, the *without child support* formula generates very small amounts for a very short duration. The formula will always generate time-limits in these cases.

Example 7.2

Karl and Beth were married for only four years. They had no children. Beth was 25 when they met and Karl was 30. When they married, Beth was a struggling artist. Karl is a music teacher with a gross annual income of $60,000. Beth now earns $20,000 per year, selling her work and giving art lessons to children. Entitlement is a threshold issue before the Advisory Guidelines apply. On these facts, given the disparity in income and Beth's limited income at the point of marriage breakdown, entitlement is likely to be found.

The conditions for indefinite (duration not specified) support do not apply and duration would be calculated on the basis of .5 to 1 year of support for each year of marriage.

To determine the amount of support under the formula:

- Determine the gross income difference between the parties: $60,000 - $20,000 = $40,000
- Determine the applicable percentage by multiplying the length of the marriage by 1.5-2 percent per year: 1.5 × 4 years = 6 percent to 2 × 4 years = 8 percent
- Apply the applicable percentage to the income difference: 6 percent × $40,000 = $2,400/year ($200/month) to 8 percent × $40,000 = $3,200/year ($267/month)
- **Duration** of spousal support = (.5-1) × 4 years of marriage = 2 to 4 years

The result under the formula is support in the range of $200 to $267 per month for a duration of 2 to 4 years.

In practice, this modest award would likely be converted into a lump sum using **restructuring**, discussed in Chapter 10.

7.6.2 Some medium-length marriage examples

In medium-length marriages (5 to 19 years), the formula generates increasing amounts of support as the marriage increases in length, moving from relatively small percentages at the shorter end of the spectrum to relatively generous amounts after 15 years, when awards of 30 percent of the gross income difference become possible. Except where the rule of 65 is applicable, the formula generates time limits of varying lengths depending on the length of the marriage. The ranges for duration are, however, very wide, leaving much opportunity to respond to the facts of particular cases.

This category covers a diverse array of cases raising a variety of support objectives. Current law is at its most inconsistent in its handling of these cases. This area posed the greatest challenges to developing a single formula that would yield appropriate results. We concluded that our formula based on merger over time provided the best starting point. But not surprisingly, it is in these cases that there will be the most frequent need to rely upon restructuring to massage the formula outcomes and where there will likely be the greatest resort to exceptions.

Example 7.3

Bob and Susan have been married 10 years. They married in their late twenties and Sue is now 38. Bob is employed as a computer salesman and Sue is a hairdresser. Both worked throughout the marriage. There were no children. Bob's gross annual income is $65,000; Sue's is $25,000.

Entitlement is a threshold issue before the Advisory Guidelines are applicable. An argument might be made that there is no entitlement to support: Sue is employed full time and could support herself, and there is no compensatory basis for support. However, Sue will suffer a significant drop in standard of living as result of the marriage breakdown and, at an income of $25,000, will likely experience some economic hardship. Current law would suggest an entitlement to at least transitional support on a non-compensatory basis to allow Sue to adjust to a lower standard of living.

The case does not satisfy the conditions for indefinite (duration not specified) support. The marriage is under 20 years and the case does not fall within the "rule of 65" for indefinite support because Sue's age at separation plus years of marriage is below 65 (38+10=48).

To determine the **amount** of support under the formula:

- Determine the **gross income difference** between the parties: $65,000 - $25,000 = $40,000
- Determine the **applicable percentage** by multiplying the length of the marriage by 1.5-2 percent per year: 1.5 × 10 years = **15 percent** to 2 × 10 years = **20 percent**
- Apply the applicable percentage to the income difference: 15 percent × $40,000 = $6,000/year (**$500/month**) to 20 percent × $40,000 = $8,000/year (**$667/month**)

Duration of spousal support = (.5-1) × 10 years of marriage = 5 to 10 years

The result under the formula is support in the range of $500 to $667 per month for a duration of 5 to 10 years.

Consistent with current law, the formula essentially generates modest top-up support for a transitional period to assist Sue in adjusting from the marital standard of living.

An award of $500 per month, at the low end of the range, would leave Sue with a gross annual income of $31,000 and Bob with one of $59,000. An award of $667 per month, at the high end of the range, would leave Sue with a gross annual income of $33,000 and Bob with one of $57,000. In a marriage of this length the formula does not equalize incomes.

Some might find the amounts generated by the formula too low, even at the high end of the range. An argument could be made that, consistent with current law, any transitional order should put Sue somewhat closer to the marital standard of living for the period of gearing down. As will be discussed in Chapter 10, a **restructuring** of the formula outcome is possible to produce larger amounts for a shorter duration. ...

7.6.3 Some long-marriage examples

In cases of long marriages (20 years or longer) the formula generates generous levels of spousal support for indefinite periods, reflecting the fairly full merger of the spouses' lives. The long marriages covered by the *without child support* formula fall into two categories: those where there have been children who are no longer dependent and those where the couple did not have children.

Example 7.1 provides an example of the formula's application to a long marriage with children where the wife was a secondary earner. *Example 7.5*, presented below, involves the familiar scenario of a very long traditional marriage.

Example 7.5

John and Mary were married for 28 years. Theirs was a traditional marriage in which John worked his way up the career ladder and now earns $100,000 gross per year, while Mary stayed home and raised their two children, both of whom are now grown up and on their own. Mary is 50 years of age and has no income. John is 55.

Entitlement to spousal support is clear on these facts and thus the Advisory Guidelines are applicable. Because the length of the marriage is over 25 years, the maximum range for amount applies — 37.5 to 50 percent of the gross income difference (capped at equalization of net incomes).

The range for amount on an income difference of $100,000 after a 28 year marriage would be:

37.5 percent × $100,000 = $37,500/year (**$3,125/month**) to 50 percent × $100,000 = $50,000/year (**$4,167/month, capped at $4048**)

Duration is indefinite (duration not specified) because the marriage is 20 years or over in length.

The formula results in a range for support of $3,125 to $4,048 per month for an indefinite (unspecified) duration, subject to variation and possibly review.

An award of $3,125 per month, at the low end of the range, would leave Mary with a gross income of $37,500 per year and John with one of $62,500. An award of $4,048 per month, at the high end of the range, would equalize the net incomes of the parties.

... [T]he order is open to variation over time in response to changes in the parties' circumstances, including increases in Mary's income or the imputation of income to her if she fails to make reasonable efforts to contribute to her own support. John's retirement would also likely be grounds for variation. ...

8.0 The *With Child Support* Formula

The dividing line between the two proposed formulas under the Advisory Guidelines is the presence of a child support obligation [to a child of the relationship]. Where the spouses have not had children or the children have grown up and are on their own, the *without child support* formula will apply. Where a spouse is paying child support, the *with child support* formula will apply.

From a technical perspective, there must be a different formula for spousal support in these cases, a formula that takes into account the payment of child support and its priority over spousal support as set out in s. 15.3 of the *Divorce Act*. Further, because of tax and benefit issues, we have to use net rather than gross incomes. Practically, the payment of child support usually means reduced ability to pay spousal support. And, theoretically, there are different rationales for the amount and duration of spousal support where there are still dependent children to be cared for and supported.

This category of cases dominates in practice, in support statistics and in jurisprudence. Any guidelines must generate a workable formula for amount and duration for this category, a formula that can adjust across a wide range of incomes and family circumstances. For the most part, marriages with dependent children will involve spousal support paid by a parent who is also paying child support to the recipient spouse. The basic formula in this chapter is constructed around this typical situation. Variations on the basic formula are required to accommodate cases of shared and split custody. There are also a sizeable number of cases where the spouse paying spousal support has primary parental responsibility for the children. In these custodial payor situations, an alternative formula must be constructed. Finally, we have added one more hybrid formula, applicable in cases where the only remaining children are away at university or otherwise have their child support determined under section 3(2)(b) of the Child Support Guidelines.

The *with child support* formula is thus really a family of formulas, adjusted for different parenting arrangements.

8.1 The Compensatory Rationale for Spousal Support

Where there are dependent children, the primary rationale for spousal support is compensatory. After *Moge*, spouses must, as Chief Justice McLachlin put it in *Bracklow*, "compensate each other for foregone careers and missed opportunities during the marriage upon the breakdown of their union." The main reason for those foregone careers and missed opportunities is the assumption of primary responsibility by one spouse for the care of children during the marriage. Where one spouse, in a marriage with children, has become a full-time homemaker or has worked outside the home part time or has worked as a secondary earner, there will be disadvantage and loss at the end of the marriage, usually warranting compensatory support. This compensatory rationale is encompassed by the first of the four objectives of spousal support, in s. 15.2(6)(a) of the *Divorce Act*.

Under compensatory theory, it is usually necessary to estimate the spouse's disadvantage or loss by determining what the recipient's career or employment path might have been, had the recipient not adopted his or her role during the marriage — not an easy task. The ideal evidence would be individualized economic evidence of earning capacity loss, but few litigants can afford such evidence and often it would be highly speculative. Some spouses never establish a career or employment history. For others, their pre-marital and marital choices were shaped by their future expected role during marriage. And there are short marriages, where past losses are relatively small and most of the spouse's child-rearing and any associated losses are still to come in the future.

... [A]fter *Moge*, courts had to develop proxies to measure that loss where there was no clear and specific career or employment path. Need became the most common proxy, calculated through the conventional budget analysis. Sometimes standard of living was used, with the post-separation position of the recipient spouse measured against the marital standard or some reasonable standard of living. In practice, crude compromises were made in applying the compensatory approach.

More recently, what we have called the **parental partnership** rationale has emerged in the literature and in the case law. On this approach, the obligation for spousal support flows from parenthood rather than the marital relationship itself. It is not the length of the marriage, or marital interdependency, or merger over time, that drives this theory of spousal support, but the presence of dependent children and the need to provide care and support for those children. Unlike the conventional compensatory approach, parental partnership looks at not just past loss, but also the continuing economic disadvantage that flows from present and future child-care responsibilities. For shorter marriages with younger children, these present and future responsibilities are more telling. Further, the parental partnership rationale better reflects the reality that many women never acquire a career before marriage, or mould their pre-marital employment in expectation of their primary parental role after marriage.

The parental partnership rationale is firmly anchored in one of the four statutory objectives in s. 15.2(6) of the *Divorce Act*, where clause (b) states a spousal support order should:

"apportion between the spouses any financial consequences arising from the care of any child of the marriage over and above any obligation for the support of any child of the marriage." The 1997 implementation of the *Federal Child Support Guidelines* has reinforced this rationale. Under the Guidelines, only the direct costs of child-rearing — and not even all of them — are included in child support. The indirect costs of child-rearing were left to be compensated through spousal support, as was recognized by the 1995 Family Law Committee's *Report and Recommendations on Child Support*. Principal amongst these indirect costs is the custodial parent's reduced ability to maximize his or her income because of child-care responsibilities. Now that child support is fixed under the *Child Support Guidelines* and determined by a different method than before 1997, spousal support has to be adjusted to reflect the concerns identified by the parental partnership model.

With the implementation of the *Federal Child Support Guidelines* came the increased use of computer software. The software regularly and graphically displays information like net disposable income, monthly cash flow and household standards of living. This information has made spouses, lawyers, mediators and courts more conscious of the financial implications of child and spousal support, in turn reflected in the use of these concepts in determining the amount of spousal support. Before the *Federal Child Support Guidelines*, and even afterwards for a while, most courts were not prepared to award more than 50 percent of the family's net disposable income to the recipient spouse and children, leaving the single payor spouse with the other 50 percent. With the new software, many courts began consciously to allocate more than 50 percent of a family's net disposable income to the recipient spouse and children, and even as much as 60 percent, as in the Ontario Court of Appeal decision in *Andrews v. Andrews* [(1999), 50 R.F.L. (4th) 1 (Ont. C.A.)] and in numerous trial decisions across the country.

These cases also reveal a non-compensatory element found in some decisions where both child and spousal support are paid to the same parent. There is a household standard of living element within the parental partnership rationale that should be openly acknowledged. Both child and spousal support go into the same household, to support the standard of living of both parent and child. In some cases, spousal support is used as a residual financial remedy to shore up the standard of living that the children experience in the recipient's household.

8.2 Background to the Basic Formula

There is no simple way to construct a formula for spousal support where the support payor is also paying child support. First, child support must be determined, as it takes priority over spousal support in assessing the payor's ability to pay. Second, child support is not taxable or deductible, but spousal support is taxable to the recipient and deductible for the payor. Third, child and spousal support must be determined separately, but it is very difficult in any formula to isolate spousal finances cleanly from support of children.

This formula for cases with child support — the *with child support* formula — differs from the *without child support* formula set out in Chapter 7. First, the *with child support* formula uses **the net incomes** of the spouses, not their gross incomes. Second, the *with child support* formula divides the **pool** of combined net incomes between the two spouses, not just the difference between the spouses' gross incomes. Third, in the *with child support* formula, the upper and lower percentage limits for net income division **do not change with the length of the marriage**.

Unlike the *without child support* formula, this formula must use **net income**. While gross income would be simpler to understand, calculate and implement, nothing remains simple once child support has to be considered. Different tax treatment demands more detailed after-tax calculations, and ability to pay must be more accurately assessed. Net income computations will usually require computer software, another unavoidable complication.

Thanks to that same computer software, many lawyers had become familiar with net disposable income or monthly cash flow calculations before the release of the Draft Proposal. Judges were using such calculations to underpin their spousal support decisions. In the software programs, these numbers included child and spousal support to produce what can be called **family net disposable income** or monthly cash flow. This larger pool of net income is then divided between the spouses. Often, more than 50 percent of this family net disposable income is allocated to the recipient spouse and children by way of combined child and spousal support, or sometimes as much as 60 percent and occasionally even more. Under the formula proposed here for spousal support, we divide a different and smaller pool of net income, after removing the spouses' respective child support obligations — what we call **individual net disposable income** or **INDI**.

We considered using the more familiar family net disposable income as the basis for the *with child support* formula, rather than this newer variation of individual net disposable income. In the end we opted for individual net disposable income. First, the family net disposable income of the recipient spouse includes both child and spousal support, bulking up the recipient's income in a somewhat misleading fashion and masking the impact of spousal support upon the recipient parent's individual income. Second, allocating family NDI between spouses blurs the distinction between child and spousal support, between child and adult claims upon income. Individual NDI attempts to back out the child support contributions of each spouse, to obtain a better estimate of the income pool that remains to be divided between the adults. Third, after separation, the spouses see themselves, not as one family, but more as individuals with distinct relationships with their children and their former spouses. Fourth, separating out each spouse's individual net disposable income, after removal of child support obligations, produced a more robust and sophisticated formula, one that adjusted better across income levels and numbers of children.

8.3 The Basic Formula

Set out ... below is a summary of how this basic *with child support* formula works. Remember that this formula applies where the higher income spouse is paying both child and spousal support to the lower income spouse who is also the primary parent. By primary parent, we mean the spouse with sole custody or the spouse with primary care of the children in a joint custody arrangement.

The Basic With Child Support Formula for Amount

1. Determine the **individual net disposable income (INDI)** of each spouse:

  - Guidelines Income *minus* Child Support *minus* Taxes and Deductions = Payor's INDI
  - Guidelines Income *minus* Notional Child Support *minus* Taxes and Deductions *plus* Government Benefits and Credits = Recipient's INDI

2. Add together the individual net disposable incomes. By iteration, determine the range of spousal support amounts that would be required to leave the lower income recipient spouse with between 40 and 46 per cent of the combined INDI.

8.3.1 Calculating individual net disposable income

Basic to this formula is the concept of **individual net disposable income**, an attempt to isolate a **pool** of net disposable income available after adjustment for child support obligations.

The starting point is the Guidelines income of each spouse. ... In the interests of uniformity and efficiency, we basically use the same definition of income as that found in the *Federal Child Support Guidelines*. Next, we deduct or back out from each spouse's income their respective **contributions to child support**.

For the child support **payor**, that is usually the table amount, plus any contributions to special or extraordinary expenses, or any other amount fixed under any other provisions of the *Federal Child Support Guidelines*. For the child support **recipient**, a **notional table amount** is deducted, plus any contributions by the recipient spouse to s. 7 expenses. In reality, the recipient will likely spend more than these amounts through direct spending for the children in her or his care. But by this means we make an adjustment, however imperfect, for the recipient's child support obligation. A formula could be constructed without this notional child support number, but such a formula would have adjusted to the number of children and income levels with less precision and with less transparency about the role of the recipient parent.

Second, **income taxes and other deductions** must be subtracted from the incomes of both the payor and the recipient to obtain net incomes. As spousal support is transferred from one spouse to another, because of tax effects, the size of the total pool of individual net disposable income actually changes slightly, which complicates these calculations. The current software does these calculations automatically, as differing hypothetical amounts of spousal support are transferred, a process called "iteration".

Clearly permissible **deductions** are federal and provincial income taxes, as well as employment insurance premiums and Canada Pension Plan contributions. Union dues and professional fees are already deducted from Guidelines income under the adjustments of Schedule III to the *Federal Child Support Guidelines*. Deductions should be recognized for certain benefits, e.g. medical or dental insurance, group life insurance, and other benefit plans, especially those that provide immediate or contingent benefits to the former spouse or the children of the marriage.

More contentious are **deductions for mandatory pension contributions**. We concluded that there should not be an automatic deduction for such pension contributions, but the size of these mandatory deductions may sometimes be used as a factor to justify fixing an amount towards the lower end of the spousal support range.

We reached this conclusion after considerable discussion. Like EI, CPP and other deductions, pension contributions are mandatory deductions, in that the employee has no control over, and no access to, that money. But, unlike other deductions, pension contributions are a form of forced saving that permit the pension member to accumulate an asset. Further, after separation, the spouse receiving support does not usually share in the further pension value being accumulated by post-separation contributions. Finally, there are serious problems of horizontal equity in allowing a deduction for mandatory pension contributions by employees. What about payors with non-contributory pension plans or RRSPs or those without any pension scheme at all? And what about the recipient spouse — would we have to allow a notional or actual deduction for the recipient too, to reflect her or his saving for retirement? In the end, we decided it was fairer and simpler not to allow an automatic deduction for pension contributions.

Third, we **do include** in each spouse's income the amounts identified for **government benefits and refundable credits**. Included are the Child Tax Benefit, the National Child Benefit Supplement, the GST credit, the refundable medical credit, the Child Disability Benefit, the various provincial benefit and credit schemes, and the new Universal Child Care Benefit. Under the *Federal Child Support Guidelines* these benefits and credits are generally not treated as income. For the reasons set out in Chapter 6 on Income above, a different approach is warranted for spousal support purposes. [Chapter 6 is omitted from this text.]

8.3.2 The Basic Formula: Dividing Individual Net Disposable Income

Once the individual net disposable income (INDI) of each spouse has been determined, the next step is to add together these individual net disposable incomes. Then we have to iterate, i.e. to estimate hypothetical spousal support repeatedly, in order to determine the amount of spousal support that will leave the lower income recipient spouse with between 40 and 46 percent of the combined pool of individual net disposable income. ...

We found that a range of 40 to 46 percent of individual net disposable income typically covered spousal support outcomes in the middle of the very wide range of outcomes now observed in most Canadian provinces. To capture the **middle** of the range on a national basis means that some areas will find the upper bound (46 percent) a bit low and other areas will consider even the lower bound (40 percent) at the higher end of their local range. ...

8.4 Amounts of Spousal Support: Examples of the Basic Formula

At this point it helps to give a few examples of the ranges of monthly spousal support generated by this basic formula. Then we will move to the issue of duration. For illustration purposes, we assume that these parents and children all live in Ontario, as the use of one jurisdiction simplifies the exposition of the formula's operation.

In the earlier Draft Proposal, the formula calculations were done partially with software and partially by hand. With the release of the Draft Proposal, Canada's three major family law software suppliers incorporated the Spousal Support Advisory Guidelines into their programs, so that the calculations can be done easily and with greater precision. In addition, the ranges for amount have changed since the January 2005 release of the Draft Proposal, due to changes in child support table amounts in May 2006, various changes to federal and provincial taxes and changes in child benefits. The result is that the numbers in these examples are different from those set out in the Draft Proposal.

Example 8.1

Ted and Alice have separated after 11 years together. Ted works at a local manufacturing plant, earning $80,000 gross per year. Alice has been home with the two children, now aged 8 and 10, who continue to reside with her after separation. After the separation, Alice found work, less than full time, earning $20,000 gross per year. Alice's mother provides lunch and after-school care for the children, for nothing, when Alice has to work. Ted will pay the table amount for child support, $1,159 per month. Alice's notional table amount would be $308. There are no s. 7 expenses (if there were, the spousal amounts would be lower).

Under the formula, Ted would pay spousal support in the range of $474 to $1,025 per month.

Using the *family* net disposable income figures (or the similar monthly cash flow figures) more familiar to current software users, spousal support of $1,025 monthly along with the child support would leave Alice and the children with $4,003 per month and Ted with $2,976 per month, or 57.4 per cent of the family's net disposable income in favour of Alice and the children. At the lower end of the range, with spousal support of $474 per month, the net disposable income of the family would be split 52.6/47.4 in favour of Alice and the children, leaving Ted with $3,326 monthly and Alice and the children with $3,684. The amount of spousal support is obviously affected by the **number of children**. If Ted and Alice had only one child, the spousal support range would be higher, from $888 to $1,463 per month. If the couple had three children, Ted's ability to pay would be reduced, bringing the range down to $79 to $626 monthly. Four children would lower that range even further, down to a range from zero to $222 per month.

The spousal support range will also be lowered by any payment of section 7 expenses. In our *Example 8.1*, if Alice were paying child care expenses of $8,000 per year for the two children and Ted paid his proportionate share of the net cost, the formula range would reduce to $319 to $925 per month for spousal support.

Example 8.2

Bob and Carol have separated after eight years of marriage and two children, now aged 4 and 6, who are both living with Carol. Bob earns $40,000 gross annually at a local building supply company, while Carol has found part-time work, earning $10,000 per year. Carol's mother lives with Carol and provides care for the children when needed. Bob pays the table amount of $601 per month for the children. Carol's notional table amount of child support would be $61 per month. There are no s. 7 expenses.

Under the formula, Bob would pay spousal support in the range of zero to $34 per month.

Again, by way of comparison to the more familiar numbers, if Bob were to pay child support of $601 and spousal support of $34 monthly, at the upper end of the range, he would be left with $1,951 per month, while Carol and the two children would have family net disposable income of $2,325 monthly, or 54.4 percent of the family's net disposable income.

Example 8.3

Drew and Kate have been married for four years. Drew earns $70,000 gross per year working for a department store. Kate used to work as a clerk in the same store, but she has been home since their first child was born. The children are now 1 and 3, living with Kate. Kate has no Guidelines income (and hence there is no notional table amount for her). Drew will pay the table amount of $1,043 per month for the two children.

Under the formula, Drew would pay spousal support to Kate in the range of $908 to $1,213 per month.

If Drew were to pay spousal support of $1,213 monthly, he would have $2,394 per month, while Kate and the children would have family net disposable income of $3,084 monthly, or 56.3 percent of the total family NDI. At the lower end of the range, spousal support of $908 per month would leave Drew with $2,604 in family NDI, while Kate and the children would have $2,780 monthly, or 51.6 percent of the family's NDI.

The formula generates ranges for the amount of spousal support. ...

8.5 Duration under the Basic Formula

8.5.2 The length-of-marriage test for duration

The first test for duration is the same as the test for duration under the *without child support* formula. It will typically be the applicable test for longer marriages, marriage of ten years or more. The **upper end** is one year of support for each year of marriage, subject to the provisions under the *without child support* formula for indefinite (duration not specified) support after 20 years of marriage. The **lower end** is one-half year of support for each year of marriage. If the children are already in school at the time of separation, then the lower end of the range will always be determined by this *length-of-marriage* test.

Once again, we emphasize that these "softer" time limits are intended to structure the process of review and variation of initial orders that are indefinite in form; they are not intended to give rise to time-limited orders, at least not initially. ...

We can use *Example 8.1* above to explain this test. Ted and Alice cohabited for 11 years during their marriage and are now in their late thirties or early forties, with two children, aged 8 and 10 at separation. The initial support order would be indefinite (duration not specified), but it would be expected that the ultimate, cumulative duration of the award would fall somewhere within the range of 5.5 years (lower end) to 11 years (upper end). The maximum outside time limit would be 11 years. Reviews and variations in the meantime may bring support to an end before 11 years, and certainly the amount may have been reduced significantly during this period. But if support is still in pay after 11 years, there would be an expectation, barring exceptional circumstances, that support would be terminated at that point on an application for review or variation. ...

8.5.3 The age-of-children test for duration

The second test for duration under the basic *with child support* formula is driven by the age of the children of the marriage. It usually operates where the period of time until the last or youngest child finishes high school is greater than the length of the marriage. These are mostly short or short-to-medium marriages, typically (but not always) under 10 years in length. The current case law is inconsistent and erratic on duration for these marriages, ranging from indefinite orders without conditions, to indefinite orders with short review periods and sometimes stringent review conditions, and even occasionally to time limits. Despite the language of indefinite support, the reality in most cases is that support does not continue for long, as re-employment, retraining, remarriage and other changes often intervene to bring spousal support to an end.

We too have struggled with duration for this category of cases. On the one hand, many of these custodial parents face some of the most serious disadvantages of all spouses, especially mothers with little employment history who have very young children in their care, all of which militates in favour of no time limits or very long time limits. On the other hand, many recipient spouses do have good education and employment backgrounds, are younger, and are emerging from shorter marriages and briefer periods out of the paid labour market, all indicators of quicker recovery of earning capacity. Inevitably, as under the current law, this means that reviews are a critical means of sorting out the individual circumstances of the recipient spouses.

The **upper end of the range** for spousal support under this test is the **date when the last or youngest child finishes high school**. Relatively few cases will reach this outside time limit and those that do will likely involve reduced amounts of top-up support by that date. Hence, extensions beyond that date would involve cases that fall within any of the exceptions described in Chapter 12, like the exception for the special needs of a child or the exception under s. 15.3 of the *Divorce Act*.

The **lower end of the range** under this test is also tied to the age of the youngest child and schooling, once again reflecting the parental partnership model. In shorter marriages, spousal support should continue at least until the **date the youngest child starts attending school full-time**. The school date will vary from province to province and from school district to school district, based upon the availability of junior kindergarten, the age rules governing school registration and the program the child takes. ...

8.5.4 The use of the two tests for duration: whichever is longer

In most cases, only one of the two tests, either the *length-of-marriage* test or the *age-of-children* test, will apply to determine both the upper and lower ends of the range. In general, the *length-of-marriage* test applies for longer marriages, marriages of ten years or more, while the *age-of-children* test applies for shorter marriages, those under ten years. But the two tests must be used together, **as it is the longer of the two tests that applies for each end of the range**. Remember that this is a range for duration, and that the actual outcome in any particular case will be worked out within that range over a series of orders or agreements, by way or review or variation of an initial order or agreement. ...

8.6 Shared Custody

The basic formula is constructed around the typical fact situation, where the higher income spouse pays child and spousal support to the lower income spouse who has the primary care of the children. Here we address custodial variations, the first being shared custody.

Where the spouses have **shared custody**, the starting point for the calculation of child support under s. 9(a) of the *Federal Child Support Guidelines* is the straight set-off of table amounts for the number of children subject to shared custody, as set out in the Supreme Court decision in *Contino v. Leonelli-Contino* [(2005), 19 R.F.L. (6th) 272 (S.C.C.)]. That amount is then adjusted, usually upwards, but occasionally downwards, based upon s. 9(b) (increased costs of shared custody and actual spending on children by the spouses) and s. 9(c) (other circumstances, including relative incomes, income levels, assets and debts, household standards of living, any reliance upon previous levels of child support paid). The *Contino* decision was handed down after the release of the Draft Proposal, but the shared custody formula anticipated that outcome. The majority in *Contino* emphasised that there is no presumption in favour of the full table amount for the payor, nor is there any presumption in favour of the straight set-off, under section 9.

Under the basic *with child support* formula, child support is deducted from the payor's income and then that child support amount plus a notional amount for child support is deducted from the recipient's income, to obtain individual net disposable income. Shared custody requires some changes to this basic formula.

Assume for the moment that the payor is paying only the straight set-off amount of child support in a shared custody case. If we were only to deduct the smaller set-off amount of child support for the payor spouse in a shared custody situation, that would misrepresent and understate the payor parent's contribution to child support. Shared custody assumes that both parents spend directly upon the child in their shared care. The full table amount (plus any s. 7 contributions) is thus deducted from the payor spouse's net disposable income. For the recipient, the notional table amount (plus any contribution to s. 7 expenses) is deducted from his or her income. This would be done in the calculation of INDI, even though the child support paid by the payor and received by the recipient would be the straight set-off amount.

If the straight set-off of child support is calculated as above, it turns out that the spousal support ranges are basically the same in these shared custody situations as in sole custody situations. Shared custody arrangements do not result in any automatic lowering of spousal support. It was important that the shared custody formula not provide any false financial incentives to encourage shared custody litigation, while at the same time providing ample room within the range to adjust for the realities of shared parenting.

Example 8.4

Peter and Cynthia have separated after nine years together. Peter works as a reporter at the local television station, earning $65,000 gross per year, while his wife Cynthia works for a local arts organization, earning $39,000 gross per year.

Peter and Cynthia share custody of their two children, aged 8 and 7 on a week about, 50/50 basis. In these circumstances, there could be entitlement issues, but we will assume entitlement here for exposition purposes.

First, assume Peter only pays the straight set-off amount of child support, i.e. $972 - $584 = $388. We would deduct from Peter's income the full table amount of $972, of which $584 is spent by him directly for the children in his care and $388 is paid as child support to Cynthia. Cynthia's income would still be reduced by her notional table amount of $584. If Cynthia receives the full amount of the child benefits, and assuming entitlement, then the range for spousal support would be **zero to $142 per month**.

. . . . .

8.7 *Split custody*

In a **split custody** situation, more significant changes to the basic formula are required. If each parent has one or more children in their primary care or custody, then s. 8 of the *Federal Child Support Guidelines* requires a set-off of table amounts, with each spouse paying the table amount for the number of children in the other spouse's custody. But this means that each parent will also be considered to support the child or children in their care directly, out of their remaining income. Thus, in the split custody situation, a notional table amount must be deducted from each parent, not just the recipient but the payor as well.

Since there is one child in each household, there are no economies of scale and accordingly larger proportions of their incomes are devoted to child support, leaving a smaller pool of INDI to be divided by way of spousal support. Again, as with shared custody, this would be done in the calculation of INDI, even though the child support paid by the payor and received by the recipient would be the set-off amount directed by the s. 8 formula.

Example 8.5

Take the case of Peter and Cynthia again, and assume that each parent has custody of one child, same incomes, same facts. Peter's one child table amount would be $601 per month, Cynthia's $358 per month. Under s. 8 of the *Federal Child Support Guidelines*, these table amounts would be offset, with Peter paying Cynthia $243 per month. In calculating Peter's individual net disposable income, for spousal support purposes, the full one child amount is deducted, twice, once for the table amount effectively paid to Cynthia and once for the notional amount spent directly on the child in his care. Similarly, in calculating Cynthia's INDI, a double deduction of her one-child table amount is made, once for the amount effectively paid to Peter for the child in his care, plus a notional table amount for the child in Cynthia's own care.

The actual child support paid by Peter to Cynthia would be $243, the one-child set-off amount under s. 8. Using the split custody formula for spousal support, Peter would pay spousal support to Cynthia in the range of **zero to $445 per month**.

. . . . .

8.9 *A Hybrid Formula for Spousal Support Paid by the Custodial Parent (The Custodial Payor Formula)*

The basic formula for marriages with dependent children assumes that the higher income spouse pays both child and spousal support to the recipient parent, who also has sole custody or primary care of the children. The spousal support to be paid must then adjust for the payor's child support payments. The shared and split custody situations may change the math, but both still involve the higher income spouse paying both child and spousal support to the recipient. A different formula is required where the higher income spouse paying spousal support is also the parent with sole custody or primary care of the children. Now spousal support and child support flow in opposite directions. The *without child support* formula does not apply, however, as it assumes no dependent children. While we could have left this situation as an exception, with no formulaic solution, it is common enough that we constructed a formula to guide outcomes in this situation.

Either of the two formulas could be used as a starting point and then modified to accommodate custodial payors. We chose to start from the *without child support* formula for custodial payors. In this situation the recipient parent does not have the primary care of children and thus more closely resembles the single recipient in the *without child support* formula. The primary rationale for the payment of spousal support in these cases will be merger over time, rather than parental partnership. That said, a number of lower income recipient spouses in this situation will continue to play an important role in their children's lives and any formula must be able to adjust in such cases. The other advantage of the *without child sup-*

port formula is ease of calculation, but the formula will have to be modified to back out child support and to take into account tax implications.

Most of these cases will involve older children and longer marriages, where the husband is the higher-income payor and the parent with primary care. In many of these cases, the non-custodial wife may have a sizeable compensatory claim from her past role in child-rearing, which will be reflected in the range for spousal support, and the location of any amount within that range. In these cases involving older children and longer marriages, the children will cease to be children of the marriage within a few years and the wife will cross-over into the *without child support* formula, as is explained below in Chapter 14 on variation and review. In a subset of custodial payor cases, there will be illness or disability issues for the non-custodial spouses, many of which can be accommodated within the ranges or re-structuring, but exceptions will be made in some cases. ... There is a small minority of custodial payor cases that involve young children, shorter marriages and husbands claiming spousal support from their wives.

Formula for Spousal Support Paid by Custodial Parent
(The *Custodial Payor* Formula)

1. Reduce the payor spouse's Guidelines income by the **grossed-up notional table amount** for child support (plus a gross-up of any contributions to s. 7 expenses).

2. If the recipient spouse is paying child support, reduce the recipient's Guidelines income by the **grossed-up amount of child support paid** (table amount plus any s. 7 contributions).

3. Determine the **adjusted gross income difference** between the spouses and then quantum ranges from 1.5 percent to 2 percent for each year of marriage, up to a maximum of 50.

4. **Duration** ranges from .5 to 1 year of support for each year of marriage, with the same rules for indefinite (duration not specified) support as under the without child support formula.

In reducing gross incomes by grossed-up amounts for child support, this formula does the same thing conceptually as the basic *with child support* formula — it establishes the spouses' available incomes after their child support obligations are fulfilled. To gross up the child support will require a calculation of the gross value of the non-taxable child support, using the appropriate marginal tax rate for the payor or recipient spouse.

Example 8.6

Matt earns $100,000 gross per year and has custody of two teenage children. Anna earns $30,000 gross per year. The spouses separated after 16 years together. There are no s. 7 expenses.

Assume entitlement to spousal support has been established.

First, Matt's income is reduced by the table amount for two children, $1,404, grossed-up to $2,525 per month or $30,300 annually. Matt's reduced income would thus be $69,700. Anna is required to pay child support at the table amount of $444 per month, grossed-up to $625 monthly or $7,500 annually. Anna's reduced income would be $22,500. After a 16-year marriage, Anna would receive a range of 24 to 32 percent of the adjusted gross income difference of $47,200.

Under the custodial payor formula, Matt would pay spousal support in a range from $944 to $1,259 per month, for a duration of 8 to 16 years.

. . . . .

[Chapter 9, which deals with the determination of the precise amounts and time periods within the ranges created by the formulas, is omitted. Recall from the Executive Summary, above, that the suggested factors are: the strength of any compensatory claim; the recipient's needs; the age, number, need and standard of living of any children; the needs and ability to pay of the payor; the need to preserve work incentives for the payor; property division and debts; and self-sufficiency incentives.]

10 Restructuring

10.1 The General Concept: Trading Off Amount Against Duration

Under the Advisory Guidelines there are several mechanisms that allow outcomes to be adjusted in response to the facts of particular cases. ... [T]here is considerable flexibility in the fixing of precise amounts and durations within the ranges generated by the formulas. Here we discuss a second mechanism for flexibility — the ability to "restructure" the formula outcomes by trading off amount against duration. In Chapter 12, ... we discuss the third method — that of departing from the formula outcomes by relying upon exceptions.

Although the formulas generate separate figures for amount and duration, the Advisory Guidelines explicitly recognize that these awards can be "restructured" by trading off amount against duration. The only limit is that the overall value of the restructured award should remain within the global — or total — amounts generated by the formula when amount is multiplied by duration.

While the terminology of restructuring is new, the concept of trading off amount against duration is an established feature of current spousal support practice. Such tradeoffs are commonly made in separation agreements and consent orders. In *Bracklow* the Supreme Court of Canada acknowledged that such an adjustment can also be made by judges, explicitly recognizing that the amount and duration of awards can be configured in different ways to yield awards of similar value (or quantum). Thus the Court noted that an order for a smaller amount paid out over a long period of time can be equivalent to an order for a higher amount paid out over a shorter period of time.

Under the Advisory Guidelines a certain degree of adjustment of amount against duration will occur when precise amounts and duration are being fixed within the ranges. .... However, in particular cases an appropriate award will require an adjustment beyond the limits of the formula's ranges. Restructuring allows the formula to continue to act as a tool to guide such deviations from the ranges because the overall value of the award remains within the global amounts set by the formula. In this way restructuring differs from exceptions, ... which involve an actual departure from the global range of outcomes suggested by the formula.

When restructuring is relied upon to resolve issues of inappropriate formula outcomes for amount or duration, awards remain consistent with the overall or global amounts generated by the Advisory Guidelines.

Restructuring can be used in three ways:

- first, to **front-end load** awards by increasing the amount beyond the formulas' ranges and shortening duration

- second, to **extend duration** beyond the formulas' ranges by lowering the monthly amount; and

- third, to formulate a **lump sum** payment by combining amount and duration.

Restructuring was a crucial component in the development of the Advisory Guidelines, particularly the development of the *without child support* formula. It was the only way in which some of the results generated by the formula could be rendered consistent with current practice. **Restructuring is thus an important aspect of a SSAG analysis after the formulas have been applied to generate ranges for amount and duration.**

In practice, restructuring has often been ignored. In many cases, particularly short marriages under the *without child support* formula, courts have found the amounts generated by the formula too low and have then simply concluded that the Advisory Guidelines do not yield an appropriate outcome and are of no further use. The failure to consider restructuring is unfortunate because it means that an important element of flexibility is not being utilized.

The structure and guidance provided by the Guidelines are thus being lost in a number of cases where these benefits would otherwise be available.

10.2 How Does Restructuring Work? Some Examples

We now provide some examples of the different ways restructuring might be used and set out the basic calculation of the "global ranges" generated by the formulas. **Note that the calculations provided in these examples are very simplified** and do *not* take into account the time-value of money or the various future contingencies that could affect the value of awards over time. In practice, more sophisticated calculations may take such factors into account. Computer software programs may assist in some of the calculations required by restructuring. If periodic payments are converted into a lump sum, the different tax consequences must be taken into account in arriving at a comparable lump sum.

Despite such software programs, however, there will also be a certain amount of guesswork involved in restructuring. But this is already familiar to family law lawyers who frequently make trade-offs between amount and duration in settlement negotiations and spousal support agreements. Restructuring by means of a lump sum payment or an increase in amount above the formula amounts will also require a finding of ability to pay on the payor's part.

Our examples focus on the first and second uses of restructuring. We have assumed that the third use of restructuring — converting a periodic order to a lump sum in a short marriage — is familiar and straightforward, and so we have not provided a specific example.

... [T]he primary use of restructuring will be under the *without child support* formula which generates fixed time limits. Our examples reflect this. ...

10.2.1 Example 1: restructuring by front-end loading

Our first example involves front-end loading to increase the amount outside the formula's range by reducing duration. This involves choosing a durational limit at the low end of the formula's range or below it. Front-end loading may be appropriate in shorter marriages under the *without child support* formula where the monthly formula amounts are relatively modest. Restructuring will provide a generous but relatively short transitional award. Under current practice, spousal support awards in such cases will be shaped by the goal of cutting the ties between the parties fairly quickly and allowing them to go their separate ways. Front-end loading may also be desirable in cases where the recipient spouse needs significant support for a short period to undertake a program of retraining or education, or where the recipient spouse has a low base income.

Example 10.1

Here we return to the case of Bob and Susan in *Example 7.3*, who were married 10 years and had no children. They are both in their late thirties and employed full time. Bob's gross annual income as a computer salesman is $65,000; Sue's as a hairdresser is $25,000.

Under the *without child support* formula a 10 year marriage such as this gives rise to a range for amount of 15 to 20 percent of the gross income difference. Under the formula, spousal support would be in the range of $500 to $667 per month (or $6,000 to $8,000 per year) for a period of 5 to 10 years.

Given the parties' ages and employment situations and the length of the marriage, the appropriate award in this case would likely be one that cut the ties between the parties fairly quickly. The monthly amounts generated by the formula might also appear low when assessed against current practice. Both of these concerns could be met by providing transitional support at a higher level than the formula allows, for example $1,300 per month (which represents roughly 39 percent of the income difference) for only 3 years, rather than the 5 year minimum duration under the formula.

Restructuring requires the calculation of the global or total amounts generated by the formula when amount is multiplied by duration. On the facts of this example, the simplified calculation of the minimum and maximum global awards under the *without child support* formula would be as follows:

- low end of global range (low end of range for monthly amount × low end of range for duration in months)

  $500 per month for 5 years ($500 × 60 months) = $30,000

- high end of global range (high end of range for monthly amount × high end of range for duration in months)

  $667 per month for 10 years ($667 × 120 months) = $80,040

  The global range in this example would therefore be between $30,000 and $80,040.

  The proposed award of $1,300 per month for three years, which has a total value of $46,800 ($1,300 × 36 months), would be permissible under restructuring as it falls within the global ranges generated by the formula, even though it falls outside the formula's specific ranges for amount and duration.

Although this example uses a fixed monthly amount for the duration of the restructured award, it would also be possible to restructure using step-down awards, as long as the total amount of the award falls within the range set by the formula. In the example above, restructuring would allow an award of $1,500 per month for the first year, 1,000 per month for the second year, and $750 per month for the third year. The total value of the award — $39,000 — falls within the global amounts generated by the formula.

10.2.2 *Example 2: restructuring by extending duration and reducing amount*

Our second example shows the use of restructuring to extend duration by cutting back on amount. Depending on how much of an extension of duration is required, this can be accomplished either by choosing an amount at the lower end of the formula's range for amount or by setting an amount below the formula's range. This use of restructuring might be desirable in medium-length marriages where the recipient spouse will have long-term need and would be better off with modest supplements to income over a longer period of time than with more generous payments over the time period suggested by the formula.

Example 10.2

Brian and Gail were married for 15 years and had no children. Both are 45. Gail is a phys ed teacher earning $70,000 gross per year. Brian worked as a trainer in the early years of the marriage but was forced to stop working because of a debilitating illness. He now receives CPP disability of $10,000 per year.

For a 15-year marriage, the *without child support* formula generates an amount ranging from 22.5 to 30 percent of the gross income difference. Here the formula results in a range for spousal support of $1,125 to $1,500 per month (or $13,500 to $18,000 per year), for a duration of from 7.5 to 15 years.

An award of 15 years' duration would take Brian to the age of 60. The desirable result in this case might be to provide support until Brian reaches age 65 when he will start to receive pension benefits. Restructuring would permit this.

On the facts of this example, the simplified calculation of the minimum and maximum global awards under the without child support formula would be as follows:

- low end of global range (low end of range for monthly amount × low end of range for duration in months)

  $1,125 per month for 7.5 years ($1,125 × 90 months) = $101,250

- high end of global range (high end of range for monthly amount × high end of range for duration in months)

$1,500 per month for 15 years ($1,500 × 180 months) = $270,000

The global range in this example would therefore be between $101,250 and $270,000.
Because of Brian's need and the length of the marriage, absent restructuring, this would likely be a case where the award would tend towards the upper end of the ranges for both amount and duration. Using restructuring, the award could be extended to 20 years to take Brian to age 65 if the amount were set at the lowest end of the formula's range: $1,125 per month. In this case, the total amount of the award ($1,125 × 240 months) would equal the maximum global amount set by the formula, $270,000.

Although this example extends duration for a defined period, it might also be possible to use restructuring to extend duration indefinitely, recognizing, however, that the total value of an indefinite (duration not specified) award cannot be calculated with precision. A certain amount of guesswork would inevitably be involved in determining how low the amount of the indefinite award should be set to achieve some rough equivalence with the formula amounts.

. . . . .

[Chapters 11, 12, and 13 are omitted. Chapter 11 deals with ceilings and floors. Recall from the Executive Summary that the ceiling is set at $350,000 of gross payor income and the floor is set at $20,000 of gross payor income. Above the ceiling and below the floor, the formulas do not operate.

Exceptions are covered in Chapter 12. Recall that the exceptional situations include: compelling financial circumstances in an interim period, a couple's debts exceed assets and a paying spouse must pay off a disportionate share of the debts, a payor has prior support obligations, the recipient spouse suffers an illness or disability, the recipient spouse has a strong compensatory claim in a short marriage without children, the formula range will not provide sufficient funds for the recipient to meet basic needs and the payor has the ability to pay, the payor receives income on a non-taxable basis, a recipient is not the primary parent but must play an important parenting role under the custodial payor formula, a child has special needs, and the couple has three or more children or there are large child expenses under s. 7 of the *Child Support Guidelines*.

Chapter 13 deals with the issue of self-sufficiency. It explains how the objective to promote the economic self-sufficiency of each spouse "in so far as is practicable" under s. 15.2(6)(d) of the *Divorce Act* can be considered under the SSAG.]

14 Variation, Review, Remarriage, Second Families

14.2 Applications to Reduce Spousal Support Because of Changes in Income

The largest category of variations and reviews consists of applications seeking a reduction in spousal support based upon a change in the income of one party or the other. One of three reasons provides the foundation for the application:

I. the payor spouse's income goes down;

II. the recipient spouse's income goes up; or

III. the payor spouse applies to reduce or terminate support on the grounds that the recipient spouse ought to have a higher income.

In each of these three situations the Advisory Guidelines can be used to determine the amount of support. In some situations, the Advisory Guidelines can even result in the termination of spousal support, if the amount of support falls to zero with little or no prospect of future change.

In situations (i) and (iii), difficult questions of imputing income can arise. In situation (i), there can be questions about the good faith and reasonableness of the payor spouse who alleges an income reduction, which in turn may call for imputing income to the payor. In situation (iii), income may have to be imputed to a recipient spouse who has failed to maximize earning capacity, as has been discussed above in Chapter 13 on self-sufficiency.

Under the *without child support* formula, as the gross income difference between the spouses narrows, spousal support will be reduced. Similarly, under the *with child support* formula, as the disparity between the spouses' net incomes is reduced, so too is the amount of spousal support required to bring the income of the lower income recipient spouse up to the desired percentage. In some cases with children, this may mean the end of entitlement, but in others it may just reflect a current inability to pay and the postponement of payment of spousal support, consistent with section 15.3 of the *Divorce Act*. At some point, as the disparity in spousal incomes narrows under either formula, entitlement may disappear.

We provide below some examples of how the Advisory Guidelines would apply to variation or review applications in this category.

Example 14.1

In *Example 7.2* John and Mary had been married for 25 years in a traditional marriage, with two grown-up children. Mary had no income, but John was earning $100,000 gross per year. Now assume that John has lost his previous job and changed employers, with a reduction in his annual gross income down to $80,000, while Mary still has no income.

On a variation application by John, the range for spousal support would be reduced, under the *without child support* formula, from the initial $3,125 to $4,167 (capped at $4,046) per month, down to $2,500 to $3,333 (capped at $3,216) per month.

Example 14.2

In *Example 8.1* Ted was earning $80,000 gross per year at the end of an 11-year marriage, with two children aged 8 and 10, while Alice was working part time, earning $20,000 gross per year. Now assume that Alice has found a full-time job, increasing her gross annual income to $35,000, while Ted still earns $80,000.

On a variation or review under the *with child support* formula, Alice's increase in income would reduce the range for spousal support, from the original $474 to $1,025, down to $52 to $741 per month.

Example 14.3

Again using *Example 6.1* above, now assume that the children are 13 and 14 and Alice is still working part-time, but Ted alleges that Alice was offered a full-time job by her employer and she turned it down.

Upon review or variation, a court might decide to impute the full-time income of $35,000 per year to Alice and to reduce support to the same range as above, of $52 to $741 per month. Or a court might not be prepared to go to that full amount, instead imputing a slightly lower income, such as $30,000, which would produce a range of $163 to $846 per month.

14.3 The Payor's Post-Separation Income Increase

There are two possible formulaic extremes here. At one extreme, one could decide that any post-separation income increase of the payor spouse should not affect the amount of spousal support. After all, some would suggest, the recipient is entitled to a sharing of the marital standard of living, but no more. Certainly, this bright-line method would be predictable and administratively simple. At the other extreme, one could argue that the formulas should just continue to be applied to any income increase for the payor. This again would offer a predictable result, but one which the basic principles of spousal support would not justify in all cases. This approach is most compelling after a long traditional marriage.

Under the current law, it is impossible to maintain either of these approaches to the exclusion of the other. Some rough notion of causation is applied to post-separation income increases for the payor, in determining both whether the income increase should be reflected in increased spousal support and, if it should, by how much. It all depends on the length of the marriage, the roles adopted during the marriage, the time elapsed between the date of separation and the subsequent income increase, and the reason for the income increase (e.g. new job vs. promotion within same employer, or career continuation vs. new venture). The extent of sharing of these post-separation increases involves a complex, fact-based decision.

We can propose one formulaic limit in these cases: the upper limit upon any increased spousal support ought to be the numbers generated by the formulas. As the following examples show, that upper limit offers some help in defining a range of possible results after a post-separation income increase.

Example 14.4

In *Example 7.1*, Arthur and Ellen were married for 20 years and had one grown-up child. At the time of the initial order, Arthur earned $90,000 gross per year and Ellen earned $30,000, both working full time. Under the without child support formula, spousal support was indefinite (duration not specified), in the range of $1,500 to $2,000 per month. Arthur's income increases to $110,000 gross per year, while Ellen's remains unchanged.

A court, on an application for variation, might order that none, some or all of Arthur's post-separation income increase be taken into account. If all the increase were taken into account, the formula would define the upper limits of any varied spousal support within a range of $2,000 to $2,666 per month.

Example 14.5

The arithmetic becomes more complicated under the *with child support* formula. When the payor spouse's income increases, then child support will usually increase too, if requested. Let's go back once again to Ted and Alice in Example 6.1. At the time of the initial order, Ted earned $80,000 gross per year and Alice earned $20,000, after 11 years together. Their two children were aged 8 and 10 at that time. Spousal support under the formula was in a range from $474 to $1,025 monthly. Assume Ted's income subsequently increases, to $100,000 gross per year. His child support for two children will rise from $1,159 to $1,404 per month.

If none of Ted's increase were taken into account for spousal support purposes, then Ted would pay child support of $1,404 and the range for spousal support would remain unchanged at $474 to $1,025 per month. The result would be that Alice's percentage of family net disposable income would drop, as would her percentage of INDI, calculated using Ted's new income. At the other extreme, the full amount of the increase might be taken into account under the spousal support formula, generating a new and higher range of $961 to $1,715 per month.

14.4 The Recipient's Reduced Income After Separation

Suppose the recipient loses employment after the initial order, or suffers an illness or disability, or otherwise suffers a reduction in income. If either of the income-sharing formulas were applied, any reduction in the recipient's income after separation would lead to an increase in the spousal support payable. Once again, as with the payor's post-separation increase, some notion of causation seems to operate under the current law, requiring another complex, fact-based decision. While a formulaic solution is thus not possible, the same upper limit can be applied, i.e. the upper limit upon any increased spousal support ought to be the numbers generated by the formulas.

Example 14.6

In *Example 7.1*, Ellen was working full time and earning $30,000 gross per year at the time of the initial determination. Assume Ellen has been reduced to part-time hours and now earns $20,000 gross per year, while Arthur's income is unchanged at $90,000.

The initial range of spousal support was $1,500 to $2,000 monthly, where it would remain if none of Ellen's income reduction were taken into account. The range could rise as high as $1,750 to $2,333 monthly if the full amount of Ellen's reduction were considered.

. . . . .

14.6 The Payor's Remarriage or Re-partnering

The payor's remarriage or re-partnering usually is **not** grounds for a reduction in spousal support under the current law, apart from some exceptional cases. Where there were ability to pay limitations upon the support previously ordered, the payor's remarriage or re-partnering may even improve the payor's ability to pay, as a result of the sharing of expenses with the new spouse or partner. There is no need for any formulaic adjustment here.

14.7 The Recipient's Remarriage or Re-partnering

The remarriage or re-partnering of the support recipient does have an effect on spousal support under the current law, but how much and when and why are less certain. There is little consensus in the decided cases. Remarriage does not mean automatic termination of spousal support, but support is often reduced or suspended or sometimes even terminated. Compensatory support is often treated differently from non-compensatory support. Much depends upon the standard of living in the recipient's new household. The length of the first marriage seems to make a difference, consistent with concepts of merger over time. The age of the recipient spouse also influences outcomes.

In particular fact situations, usually at the extremes of these sorts of factors, we can predict outcomes. For example, after a short-to-medium first marriage, where the recipient spouse is younger and the support is non-compensatory and for transitional purposes, remarriage by the recipient is likely to result in termination of support. At the other extreme, where spousal support is being paid to an older spouse after a long traditional marriage, remarriage is unlikely to terminate spousal support, although the amount may be reduced.

An ability to predict in some cases, however, is not sufficient to underpin a formula for adjustment to the new spouse's or partner's income. Ideally, a formula would provide a means of incorporating some amount of gross income from the new spouse or partner, to reduce the income disparity under either formula. Any such incorporation could increase with each year of the new marriage or relationship. Where the recipient remarries or re-partners with someone who has a similar or higher income than the previous spouse, eventually — faster or slower, depending upon the formula adopted — spousal support would be extinguished. Where the recipient remarries or re-partners with a lower income spouse, support might continue under such a formula until the maximum durational limit, unless terminated earlier.

We have been unable to construct a formula with sufficient consensus or flexibility to adjust to these situations, despite considerable feedback that a formula would be desirable. In this final version, we still have to leave the issues surrounding the recipient's remarriage or re-partnering to individual case-by-case negotiation and decision making.

14.8 Second Families

Second families — or, more accurately, subsequent children — raise some of the most difficult issues in support law. We have already addressed prior support obligations for prior spouses and prior children as an exception under both formulas in Chapter 12. We have also addressed remarriage and re-partnering in this Chapter. Under this heading, we consider a different issue, that of support for subsequent children.

By "subsequent children", we mean children who are born or adopted after the separation of the spouses. For the most part, subsequent children will be an issue upon variation or review, but it is possible that these issues can arise at the point of the initial determination of spousal support.

Since the coming into force of the *Federal Child Support Guidelines*, courts have struggled with these issues in the child support setting, left largely to discretionary decision making, mostly under the undue hardship provisions in the *Child Support Guidelines*. The issues do not get any easier when the potential conflict between child support and spousal support is added to the mix.

The first-family-first philosophy is the most common approach. On this view, the payor's obligations to the children and spouse of the first marriage take priority over any subsequent obligations. Most who adopt the first-family-first principle will acknowledge a narrow exception: where payment of first-family support would drive the second family onto social assistance or otherwise into poverty, relief may be granted, but only in extreme cases. Other than this narrow exception, first-family-first provides a simple rule for child and spousal support: no change for subsequent children.

If child support is the only issue, there is a strong second philosophy that runs through the cases: to determine child support in a way that treats all the payor's children equally. This is usually done through the use of household standard of living calculations. This equal-treatment-of-children approach gives greater weight to the interests of subsequent children, but gives no guidance to balancing the demands of spousal support to a first spouse vs. support for subsequent children. There is a tendency on this approach to give reduced weight to spousal support, given the concern for equal treatment of the payor's *children*. Reduced spousal support is often used as a means of adjustment between the households.

In the absence of any clear policy in the *Federal Child Support Guidelines* on this issue, it is difficult, if not impossible to articulate any related policy on spousal support vs. subsequent children. For now, again with some regret, we must leave the issues of quantum and duration to discretion or case-by-case decision making. Any changes in child support policy on second families would have important implications for spousal support issues.

(3) The Courts And The SSAG

YEMCHUK v. YEMCHUK

(2005), 16 R.F.L. (6th) 430, 2005 CarswellBC 1881 (B.C. C.A.)

PROWSE J.A.: —

Nature Of Appeal

1 Mr. Yemchuk is appealing from the decision of a trial judge, made October 29, 2004, ... dismissing his claim for spousal support on the basis that he had not established any need for such support. Mr. Yemchuk is seeking spousal support, including retroactive support, until Ms. Yemchuk's anticipated retirement date in November 2007. ...

Issues On Appeal

3 Suffice it to say that the principal issue on appeal is whether the trial judge erred in finding that Mr. Yemchuk was not entitled to spousal support. The determination of that issue requires this Court to consider whether the trial judge erred in:

a) failing to properly consider and apply the provisions of the *Divorce Act*, R.S.C. 1985, c. 3 (2nd Supp.), as amended, (the "Act") and the relevant authorities relating to spousal support;

b) failing to properly take into account the significant disparity in respective standards of living of the parties following the breakdown of the marriage;

c) finding that Mr. Yemchuk's retirement was an irrelevant consideration in determining entitlement to spousal support;

d) finding that Mr. Yemchuk had not established any need for support by adopting an unduly restrictive interpretation of the concept of "need" and by imputing income to Mr. Yemchuk with respect to the lump sum payment Mr. Yemchuk received as his share of Ms. Yemchuk's employment pension.

4 In the event this Court concludes that Mr. Yemchuk is entitled to spousal support, there is an issue as to the quantum of that support. With respect to that issue, counsel provided submissions regarding the use, if any, this Court should make of the proposed Spousal Support Advisory Guidelines: A Draft Proposal, (Ottawa, Dept. of Justice: 2005) (the "Advisory Guidelines") in determining the issue of quantum.

5 If spousal support is awarded, there is also an issue as to the date on which payments should commence. ...

Background

7 The parties were married in July 1966 and separated in May 2001 after 35 years of marriage. ...

8 At the time of the order under appeal, Mr. Yemchuk was 63 years of age and Ms. Yemchuk was 61. (They are now 65 and 63.) Their only child is in his 30's and is self-supporting.

9 Mr. Yemchuk retired in 1997 after having been employed for 32 years as a chemical engineer. Ms. Yemchuk, who is a registered nurse, works full-time for the federal government as a Labour Affairs Officer. She faces mandatory retirement in November 2007 when she turns 65. Both parties worked throughout the marriage.

Decision Of The Trial Judge

14 The trial judge ... noted that Mr. Yemchuk was seeking support in an amount approaching equalization in the incomes of the parties based primarily on the length of the marriage and the disparity of standards of living experienced by the parties on marriage breakdown. Ms. Yemchuk took the position that income should be attributed to Mr. Yemchuk as if he had invested the $132,000 pension payout in an annuity, rather than in the short-term investments recommended by his investment counsellors. In her submission, if income was attributed to Mr. Yemchuk on that basis, he was able to meet his expenses with the income available to him. It followed, in Ms. Yemchuk's view, that Mr. Yemchuk had no need for support, and, therefore, no entitlement to support.

15 The trial judge accepted Ms. Yemchuk's position that Mr. Yemchuk's entitlement to support could only be justified on the basis of need. He went on to attribute income of between $800 and $1,000 to Mr. Yemchuk on the basis that this is the amount Mr. Yemchuk would have received if he had invested the $132,000 in an annuity. The trial judge did not accept that Mr. Yemchuk was entitled to account only for the interest he actually received on his investment of that fund. ...

16 The trial judge also found that the fact that Mr. Yemchuk had retired early from employment, and the reasons for his retirement were irrelevant to the issue of spousal support.

Discussion

Standard of Review

17 The standard of review applicable to orders of spousal support is set forth in *Hickey v. Hickey*, [1999] 2 S.C.R. 518, at paras. 11 and 12). In summary, an appellate court should not interfere with a support order (or an order refusing support) unless the reasons for judgment disclose an error in law or in principle, a serious misapprehension of the evidence, or unless the judgment is clearly wrong.

a) The Act, Moge and Bracklow

18 An original application for spousal support is dealt with in s. 15.2 of the Act. ...

19 The two leading authorities which are almost invariably referred to in cases dealing with spousal support are *Moge v. Moge*, [1992] 3 S.C.R. 813, and *Bracklow v. Bracklow*, [1999] 1 S.C.R. 420, both of which were referred to in the reasons of the trial judge. In brief, the *Moge* decision focuses primarily on the compensatory aspects of spousal support, but makes it clear that need continues to be a basis for an order of spousal support in appropriate cases. The *Bracklow* decision expands upon the discussion of spousal support in *Moge* and identifies three fundamental bases for an award of spousal support: compensatory, contractual and non-compensatory (needs-based). There are many authorities and learned articles which discuss these decisions at length. I will refer to them only to the extent necessary to dispose of this appeal. Suffice it to say at this point that the trial judge found that the compensatory and contractual bases for spousal support did not apply in this case, and that the only basis upon which an award of support could be founded was need. Having determined that income in the range of $800-$1,000 per month should be attributed to Mr. Yemchuk, the trial judge found that Mr. Yemchuk was not in need of spousal support.

b) Application of the Act and the Authorities

20 In *Bracklow*, Madam Justice McLachlin (as she then was), speaking for the court, noted (at para. 18) that trial judges "must exercise their discretion in light of the objectives of spousal orders as set out in s. 15.2(6), and after having considered all the factors set out in s. 15.2(4) of the *Divorce Act*." As a matter of convenience and clarity in this case, I will discuss the factors in s. 15.2(4) first, since the evidence in relation to those factors lays a foundation for determining whether the objectives set out in s. 15.2(6) mandate an order of support in this case. Clearly both s. 15.2(4) and (6) have to be considered in determining whether an order of support should be made, and if so, the quantum and duration of that support.

21 Under s. 15.2(4) of the Act, in making an order for spousal support, the court is directed to take into account the means, needs and other circumstances of each spouse including the length of the time the spouses cohabited (15.2(4)(a)) and the functions performed by each

spouse during cohabitation (15.2(4)(b)). (There is no agreement relating to support in this case, so ss. 15.2(4)(c) is not relevant.)

22 Here, the relatively modest assets of the parties were divided equally between the parties as of the date of the triggering event as set forth in the order of Madam Justice Satanove. The results of that division are described in paras. 10 and 11, *supra*. I note that those amounts had diminished by the date of the spousal support application for reasons which are not entirely clear (particularly in the case of Ms. Yemchuk), but which are probably referable, in part, to the fact that both parties were living beyond their income.

23 Mr. Yemchuk also received a lump sum payment of $132,000 for his one half share of Ms. Yemchuk's pension, which must be regarded as offset by an equal value of the pension to her as of the date of the triggering event. Ms. Yemchuk and Mr. Yemchuk also shared the income stream from Mr. Yemchuk's pension from which they each received approximately $22,000 (gross) per year ($1,833 per month).

24 In terms of income, the trial judge found that Ms. Yemchuk's income for spousal support purposes was $75,000, of which $55,500 was income from employment. Because of the uncertain state of some of the financial evidence, including some confusion between the use of net and gross income, I am not prepared to find that the trial judge erred in finding that Ms. Yemchuk's income was $75,000 for the purpose of determining spousal support.

25 The trial judge found that Mr. Yemchuk's total income for spousal support purposes, apart from attributed income, was $37,632, including payments of $300 per month from his elderly mother for rent on the two bedroom apartment they share and $300 per month investment income relating to his share of Ms. Yemchuk's pension.

26 The trial judge noted that Mr. Yemchuk claimed expenses of $46,000 per year and that Ms. Yemchuk claimed expenses of $69,000 per year. Counsel for Mr. Yemchuk invited the trial judge not to embark on a detailed analysis of the parties' expenses and he accepted that invitation. I, too, am satisfied that no benefit will be derived from a detailed analysis of those expenses and I do not propose to conduct one. I note, however, that Mr. Yemchuk's listed expenses are very modest. At the level of expenses claimed by both parties, each of them is encroaching on capital. It is clear, however, that Ms. Yemchuk has had considerably more income at her disposal than has Mr. Yemchuk, attributable mainly to the fact that she is employed and he is not. It is also apparent that Ms. Yemchuk has been disposing of her capital at a greater rate than Mr. Yemchuk for reasons which are not disclosed in the evidence.

27 I turn now to the length of the parties' cohabitation and the functions played by both spouses during cohabitation. As earlier noted, the parties cohabited as a married couple for 35 years prior to their separation. This is a long marriage by any measure. They both worked throughout the marriage and progressed in their careers. Ms. Yemchuk deposed that she worked part-time for three years early in the marriage after the birth of their son, but, apart from that, there is no evidence that the child-rearing or household responsibilities fell more on one party than the other. The exception is the period following Mr. Yemchuk's retirement when he deposes he took over primary responsibility for selling their homes and running the household for the four years they lived together thereafter prior to the separation. Mr. Yemchuk contributed his income to a joint account from which most household expenses were paid and Ms. Yemchuk also maintained a separate account from which she paid personal expenses and made contributions to their adult son. In general terms, it appears that both parties contributed their time, efforts and income to their mutual benefit and that they were able to maintain a comfortable, but not extravagant, standard of living.

28 With these considerations in mind, I turn to the objectives of a spousal support order set out in s. 15.2(6) of the Act. While the authorities are clear that all objectives must be consid-

ered in determining whether an order of support is warranted, the most relevant factors in this case are: (a) the economic advantages or disadvantages to the spouses arising from the marriage or its breakdown (a provision described in *Moge* as "expressly compensatory in character"); and (c) relieving any hardship of the spouses arising from the breakdown of the marriage (described in Moge as not being exclusively compensatory).

29 Here there is a significant disparity in the economic circumstances and standard of living of the spouses which I am satisfied arises directly from the marriage breakdown and resulted in hardship to Mr. Yemchuk disproportionate to that experienced by Ms. Yemchuk. Mr. Yemchuk is living in a rented two-bedroom apartment with his elderly mother who contributes to her room and board. His listed monthly expenses are modest. Ms. Yemchuk is living on her own in a rented apartment. Her listed monthly expenses are not extravagant, but are considerably higher than those of Mr. Yemchuk ($5,800 as compared with $3,800). ...

30 When Ms. Yemchuk retires, it appears that the disparity between the parties' means and needs and their respective standards of living will narrow, and it is for that reason Mr. Yemchuk is not seeking support once Ms. Yemchuk has retired.

31 It is apparent that the principal reason for the disparity in the means and circumstances of the parties upon marriage breakdown was Mr. Yemchuk's retirement in 1997. While the trial judge considered the reason for Mr. Yemchuk's retirement to be irrelevant, I do not agree. In my view, it is apparent that Mr. Yemchuk retired in large part because his wife had to relocate in order to maintain her employment with the Federal Government and had been offered employment in Manitoba. Subsequently, she was offered similar employment in British Columbia. The parties sold their homes and moved to accommodate the wife's employment situation on both occasions. The second move also enabled them to be closer to their son. There is no suggestion that Ms. Yemchuk objected to Mr. Yemchuk's retirement, or that he had the opportunity which she enjoyed of readily finding employment in a new jurisdiction, particularly given the fact that he was 57 years of age at the time of their first move.

32 At the time of his retirement, Mr. Yemchuk received a pay-out of $60,000 and a generous pension reflecting his 32 years of service. Ms. Yemchuk received the benefits from his retirement during the time they continued to live together, and from the division of assets upon their marriage breakdown.

33 As a result of the marriage breakdown, there is no question that Mr. Yemchuk was significantly disadvantaged in relation to Ms. Yemchuk. She continued to enjoy the benefit of a full salary, the ability to continue to contribute to her pension and other benefits, and, in addition, the benefit of sharing in Mr. Yemchuk's pension upon the division of assets. Her income of $75,000 was more than twice that of Mr. Yemchuk at $37,000. (I have already referred to her disproportionately higher level of monthly expenses.) She was also enjoying a higher standard of living than was Mr. Yemchuk. To reiterate, the breakdown of the marriage had a disproportionately negative effect on Mr. Yemchuk than it did on Ms. Yemchuk.

34 Thus, after considering the objectives and factors mandated by the Act, and having particular regard to the length of the marriage, and the working partnership the parties enjoyed during the marriage (as best that can be determined from the evidence), it is difficult to rationalize the trial judge's conclusion that Mr. Yemchuk was not entitled to spousal support.

35 In that regard, I adopt, as apposite, the following extract from the judgment of Madam Justice L'Heureux-Dubé, speaking for the majority, at p. 870 of the *Moge* decision:

> Although the doctrine of spousal support which focuses on equitable sharing does not guarantee to either party the standard of living enjoyed during the marriage, this standard is far from irrelevant to support entitlement (see *Mullin v. Mullin*, [1991] P.E.I.J. No. 128, and *Linton v. Linton*, [1990] O.J.

No. 2267). Furthermore, great disparities in the standard of living that would be experienced by spouses in the absence of support are often a revealing indication of the economic disadvantages inherent in the role assumed by one party. *As marriage should be regarded as a joint endeavour, the longer the relationship endures, the closer the economic union, the greater will be the presumptive claim to equal standards of living upon its dissolution.* ...

In short, in the proper exercise of their discretion, courts must be alert to a wide variety of factors and decisions made in the family interest during the marriage which have the effect of disadvantaging one spouse or benefiting the other upon its dissolution. In my view, this is what the Act mandates, no more, no less. (Emphasis added.)

36 This statement from *Moge* was made in the context of a judgment which was primarily focused on compensatory support. In *Bracklow*, however, where the issue before the court was one of entitlement, Madam Justice McLachlin makes it clear that an application for spousal support should not be analyzed on the basis that there is only one model of support that applies. In other words, the courts should not seek to pigeon-hole the application before them into one of the three predominant models of support identified in *Bracklow*, but should bear in mind all of the factors and objectives listed in the Act in determining whether there is an entitlement to support. The Bracklow decision also points out that there is a close relationship between entitlement to support and quantum of support. ...

37 In this case, the trial judge accepted the submission of counsel for Ms. Yemchuk that "need" was the sole basis upon which a spousal support order could be based. In my view, he erred in so doing. By finding that the reason for Mr. Yemchuk's retirement was irrelevant, he ignored Mr. Yemchuk's retirement as a compensatory factor in determining entitlement to support.

38 In my view, Mr. Yemchuk's retirement is highly relevant as it is the single most important factor which resulted in the disproportionate effect of the marriage breakdown on the parties. Had Mr. Yemchuk foreseen that marriage breakdown was on the not-so-distant horizon at the time he retired, he may well have reconsidered his decision to forego his full salary and benefits and follow Ms. Yemchuk to Manitoba and British Columbia so that she could further her career. While this event happened in the late stages of the marriage, it is no less relevant to the fact that upon the termination of the marriage, Ms. Yemchuk retained her employment and ongoing earning power, while Mr. Yemchuk did not. The subsequent equal division of assets did not make up for that loss, as is evident from the parties' respective financial circumstances following their separation. In my view, the cause and effect between Mr. Yemchuk's retirement and the subsequent disparity in economic circumstances of the parties is obvious and should have been taken into consideration by the trial judge.

39 This is so whether or not Ms. Yemchuk actively encouraged Mr. Yemchuk to retire. She took the benefits of his retirement and, in my view, she must also share in the drawbacks.

40 The circumstances and effect of Mr. Yemchuk's retirement raised a compensatory aspect to his claim for spousal support which was overlooked by the trial judge, perhaps because it was not the focus of the submissions before him.

41 I am also satisfied that the trial judge erred in viewing Mr. Yemchuk's "need" for support from too narrow a perspective. He treated "need" as solely a question of whether Mr. Yemchuk could meet his stated expenses with the income available to him. After attributing $800–$1,000 per month to Mr. Yemchuk, the trial judge found that Mr. Yemchuk could meet his expenses and, therefore, was not entitled to support.

42 Before elaborating on the concept of "need", I will discuss the question of whether the trial judge erred in the manner in which he attributed income to Mr. Yemchuk.

43 As earlier noted, Mr. Yemchuk invested the $132,000 lump sum payment he received for his share of Ms. Yemchuk's pension in short term investments yielding approximately

$3,600 over the first year (June 2003-June 2004). He did so, on the advice of investment counsellors, on the basis that it would not make economic sense to invest it in an annuity at that time given the low interest rates. The trial judge, however, imputed income to Mr. Yemchuk based on the rate of return which he would have received had he invested the lump sum in an annuity. In that regard, I am satisfied that there is evidence to support the trial judge's finding that the rate of return on an annuity would have been in the range of $800–$1,000 per month.

44 The question is whether the trial judge erred in the circumstances of this case in imputing income to Mr. Yemchuk on the basis of the rate of return he could have received if he had purchased an annuity, rather than on the actual rate of return he achieved based on investment advice. Mr. Yemchuk's argument is that if he had purchased an annuity, not only would he have jeopardized his future security in relation to that of Ms. Yemchuk by locking in this investment at a low rate of return (contrary to the advice he has received from experts), but he would also have been forced to encroach on the capital of that sum. Given the length of the marriage, the fact that he is no longer employed and able to contribute to a pension, and the fact that Ms. Yemchuk's interest in her own pension is growing by virtue of her continued contributions and increases in her earnings (her pension is based on her best five consecutive years of earnings), Mr. Yemchuk submits that the trial judge's decision in this regard has placed him in a disadvantaged position in terms of his future security in relation to Ms. Yemchuk. In other words, while Ms. Yemchuk is accumulating capital in relation to her pension, his capital is being depleted. He is seeking an order to enable him to maintain his capital in this asset for the relatively short period until Ms. Yemchuk retires.

45 It is not uncommon for a court to impute income to a spouse who has received a lump sum as part of the division of family assets between the parties and who is seeking spousal support. There are circumstances, however, in which the court will decline to do so. One example is where a party (usually the wife) wishes to use the proceeds, or a portion thereof, to purchase a home for herself and a child or children of the marriage, does not have other funds available to do so, and the court is satisfied that it is reasonable to permit her to use her capital for that purpose rather than to produce income.

46 In my view, this case presents another example of a situation in which the imputation of income is not justified. Here, the length of the marriage, the age of the parties, and their overall financial circumstances, support the proposition that both of them should be permitted to preserve the capital in Ms. Yemchuk's pension, to the extent possible, until Ms. Yemchuk retires. Mr. Yemchuk is seeking to do so by investing in short term investments until interest rates rise or until Ms. Yemchuk retires so that he will not be forced to encroach on capital. Ms. Yemchuk is doing so by her continued contributions to her pension and her ongoing years of service which will accrue to her benefit alone. Mr. Yemchuk finds himself in a disadvantaged position in relation to Ms. Yemchuk only because he retired early. Ms. Yemchuk shared in the benefit of the $60,000 lump sum payment he obtained at that time, and she now shares in his pension income. In my view, the decision of the trial judge to impute income to Mr. Yemchuk in these circumstances resulted in Mr. Yemchuk bearing the full burden of a decision made by the parties which, at the time it was made, was intended to be for their mutual benefit.

47 I also note that, in imputing income to Mr. Yemchuk of between $800–$1,000 per month, the trial judge appears to have overlooked the fact that Mr. Yemchuk's statement of gross income took into account the $300 on investments that he had actually earned on the lump sum (which he did not object to being included in his income). In other words, if any amount was to be imputed to Mr. Yemchuk, it should only have been $500–$700 per month. On the trial judge's analysis of need, increasing Mr. Yemchuk's income (before tax) by that amount

would not have enabled him to meet his modest expenses without a further incursion into capital.

48 Further, even if attribution of income were justified in these circumstances, the trial judge's treatment of Mr. Yemchuk's need for support was unduly restrictive. In *Myers v. Myers* (1995), 17 R.F.L. (4th) 298 (B.C.C.A.), for example, Mr. Justice Finch (as he then was), speaking for the Court, stated at para. 10:

> ... "Need" or "needs" are not absolute quantities. They may vary according to the circumstances of the parties and the family unit as a whole. "Need" does not end when the spouse seeking support achieves a subsistence level of income or any level of income above subsistence. "Needs" is a flexible concept and is one of several considerations which a trial judge must take into account in deciding whether any order for spousal support is warranted.

49 In considering the concept of "need" in the context of a long-term marriage involving a sharing of resources, I am satisfied that it should take into account the relative standards of living of the spouses following the marriage breakdown. In many cases, like this one, where the parties have relatively modest assets at their disposal and no realistic prospect of increasing those assets given their retirement (and pending retirement), it is often not possible to replicate the standard of living enjoyed by the parties when they were living together. The most a support order can do is to attempt to alleviate a significant disparity in their relative standards of living following marriage breakdown.

50 While equalization of the standards of living of the parties is not a stated objective of spousal support, in long-term marriages in which the parties have approached their roles as a partnership where each contributed their various resources, both economic and non-economic, to the relationship, equality of standard of living (which is not the same as equality of income) may well be the just result. (I leave aside those cases in which the parties, or one of them, are wealthy, since other considerations may apply.)

51 In the result, I am satisfied that, not only was there a compensatory aspect to Mr. Yemchuk's claim for support which was overlooked by the trial judge, but that Mr. Yemchuk also demonstrated a need for support, taking into account the economic consequences of the marriage breakdown, and the significant disparity in the relative standards of living of the parties following the breakdown.

52 In summary, I conclude that Mr. Yemchuk has established entitlement to spousal support.

53 The next issue, therefore, is the quantum of support. (Duration is not in issue since Mr. Yemchuk is seeking support only until Ms. Yemchuk retires, which, as earlier noted, is anticipated to be in November 2007.)

c) Quantum of Support

. . . . .

56 In approaching the issue of quantum, one of the questions I considered was whether Ms. Yemchuk's income from Mr. Yemchuk's pension should be taken into account. The concern I had was whether including that income in Ms. Yemchuk's overall income gave rise to the possibility that Mr. Yemchuk was seeking to "double dip". In other words, having "lost" 50% of his pension income to Ms. Yemchuk through the division of assets, was he seeking to regain it though an order of spousal support?

57 After considering this issue, I conclude that Mr. Yemchuk's pension income should be treated in the same manner in the hands of both parties. Either it should be included in income, because it is in fact an income stream in the parties' hands, or it should be excluded from both parties' income on the basis that it had already been divided between them as property. In these circumstances, I am satisfied that it should be included as income to both

parties since that accords with practical realities. I do not consider that this results in "double dipping" as that concept is discussed in the leading case of *Boston v. Boston*, [2001] 2 S.C.R. 413.

58 For the purposes of determining the quantum of spousal support, therefore, I accept the trial judge's finding that Ms. Yemchuk's income is $75,000 and Mr. Yemchuk's income is $37,000.

59 Based on my earlier analysis, I conclude that an award of spousal support in this case should attempt to alleviate the disproportionate economic hardship Mr. Yemchuk suffered as a result of the marriage breakdown reflected in the disparity between the relative standards of living of these spouses. I must also have regard, however, to the fact that Ms. Yemchuk is still employed and has expenses related to employment which Mr. Yemchuk does not. Any award I make must be in keeping with this fact.

60 This brings me to the question of whether, and to what extent, I should rely on the Guidelines in determining the quantum of support. In answering that question, I will briefly describe the Guidelines, as I understand them.

(e) The Spousal Support Guidelines

61 In my view, the best source of the history and nature of the Advisory Guidelines is the report prepared by Professors Carol Rogerson and Rollie Thompson dated June 2005 entitled Spousal Support Advisory Guidelines: A Draft Proposal (which I commend for its clarity to any writer embarking on this subject).

62 An important point to make at the outset of this discussion is that the proposed Advisory Guidelines are just that — proposed advisory guidelines. They are in a draft form and are subject to ongoing consultation with various interest groups. Further, unlike the Federal and Provincial Child Support Guidelines (which, in fact, are not guidelines at all, but form part of the substantive law), there is no plan to draft legislation to implement these Advisory Guidelines as law. Rather, their purpose is to be advisory only, with a view to bringing more certainty and predictability to the determination of spousal support under the Act. They are a response to what has been perceived as a significant lack of predictability in spousal support awards, which commentators suggest are even less predictable following the *Bracklow* decision.

63 It is also important to note that the Advisory Guidelines do not deal with entitlement to support, but are only relevant to issues of quantum and duration of support once entitlement has been resolved. Nor do they address situations in which there are prior agreements between the parties dealing with spousal support.

64 It should also be stressed that the Advisory Guidelines are intended to reflect the current law, rather than to change it. They were drafted by the authors after extensive analyses of the authorities regarding spousal support across the country, particularly the *Moge* and *Bracklow* decisions and those following thereafter. ... While decisions can undoubtedly be found in which the result would not accord with the Advisory Guidelines, I am satisfied that their intention and general effect is to build upon the law as it exists, rather than to present an entirely new approach to the issue of spousal support. For that reason, ... I have no hesitation in viewing the Advisory Guidelines as a useful tool to assist judges in assessing the quantum and duration of spousal support. They do not operate to displace the courts' reliance on decided authorities (to the extent that relevant authorities are forthcoming) but to supplement them. In that regard, they do not constitute evidence, but are properly considered as part of counsels' submissions.

65 The Advisory Guidelines set out two basic formulas for the determination of spousal support: the "without child support formula" and the "with child support formula". Since Mr. and Ms. Yemchuk have no dependent children, the "without child support formula" is the relevant formula in this case. Both formulas use income sharing as the method for determining spousal support, rather than budgets. Given the dubious and unhelpful nature of the budgets which are presented in many cases (a fact commented upon in the authorities from time to time), the move away from a budget-laden analysis is appealing. This is particularly so in cases, such as this one, in which compensatory and non-compensatory factors come into play.

66 The formulas set out in the Advisory Guidelines are also useful in that they provide ranges for the quantum and duration of support, rather than precise numbers. This is designed to provide flexibility by permitting individual factors relevant to spousal support to be taken into account. ...

68 The without child support formula is set forth as follows (at vi):

The *Without Child Support* Formula

Amount ranges from 1.5 to 2 percent of the difference between the spouses' gross incomes (the **gross income difference**) for each year of marriage (or, more precisely, years of cohabitation), up to a maximum of 50 percent. The range remains fixed for marriages 25 years or longer at 37.5 to 50 percent of income difference.

Duration ranges from .5 to 1 year for each year of marriage. However, support will be **indefinite** if the marriage is **20 years or longer** in duration or, if the marriage has lasted 5 years or longer, when the years of marriage and age of the support recipient (at separation) added together total 65 or more (the **rule of of 65**).

69 In using this formula, a spouse's income is determined in the same manner as in the Federal Child Support Guidelines.

70 Under these proposed Advisory Guidelines, the amount of support which would be payable by Ms. Yemchuk to Mr. Yemchuk ranges from $1,190 per month to $1,580 per month (in rounded figures). At the low end of the range, Mr. Yemchuk's annual gross income would be $51,250 and Ms. Yemchuk's income would be $60,750. At the high end of the range, Mr. and Ms. Yemchuk would each have income of approximately $56,000.

71 The only authorities to which the Court was referred with respect to the quantum of support relate to the basic principles of support which I have referred to earlier in these reasons. As Madam Justice McLachlin indicated in *Bracklow*, the considerations in determining quantum of support are interrelated to those applied in determining entitlement. In that regard, I have found that Mr. Yemchuk's claim for support rests on both compensatory principles (relating to the circumstances and consequences of his early retirement) and need. I have also found that equitable sharing of the economic hardship arising from the breakdown of the marriage, including a reduction of the disparity in relative standards of living of the parties is the most important principle applicable to spousal support in this case. The ranges of support set out in the Advisory Guidelines are a factor which I have considered in attempting to give effect to these principles, after taking into account the overall financial circumstances of the parties. In that regard, the expense lists of the parties are of limited assistance, particularly since Mr. Yemchuk has clearly restricted his expenses to a very basic level reflecting the significantly reduced standard of living he is experiencing as a result of the breakdown of the marriage. Ms. Yemchuk's list may more closely reflect the standard of living during the marriage, but it involves a running and increasing deficit which reflects her attempt to maintain a standard of living which is not sustainable now that the parties are living separate lives. Unfortunately, both parties have reason to be concerned about their future security.

72 Taking into account the fact that Ms. Yemchuk has increased needs for additional income to support her expenses relating to employment (including clothing, transportation expenses and significant compulsory employee deductions, not including pension and income tax), I conclude that the appropriate quantum of support in this case is $1,100 per month, reduced to $800 per month as of June 1, 2005 when Mr. Yemchuk became entitled to his Old Age Security Pension. These payments shall be made on the first day of each and every month (or in equal instalments on the first and fifteenth day of every month if Ms. Yemchuk is paid bi-monthly) up to and including the last day of the month preceding Ms. Yemchuk's retirement.

Conclusion

78 I would allow the appeal and set aside the order of the trial judge. I would make an order that Ms. Yemchuk pay spousal support to Mr. Yemchuk in the amount of $1,100 per month commencing February 1, 2004 and continuing on the first day of each and every month thereafter (or in equal instalments on the first and fifteenth day of each month if Ms. Yemchuk is paid bi-monthly) up to and including the first day of June, 2005, at which time the payments shall decrease to $800 per month, to be paid up to and including the last day of the month preceding Mr. Yemchuk's retirement. I would order that the arrears of spousal support arising under this order in the amount of $20,000 be paid by Ms. Yemchuk to Mr. Yemchuk on or before November 1, 2005.

FISHER v. FISHER

(2008), 47 R.F.L. (6th) 235, 2008 CarswellOnt 43 (C.A.)

The judgment of the Court was delivered by

1 S.E. LANG J.A.: — This appeal challenges both the amount and duration of spousal support awarded following an almost nineteen-year marriage.

2 The trial judge ordered the respondent, Robert Fisher, to pay the appellant, Anita Fisher, $2,600 spousal support from March 1 to December 1, 2006; $1,800 for the calendar year 2007; and $1,050 for the calendar year 2008. The order makes no award of support for 2009; however, it provides that, after January 1, 2009, either party may "seek a review of both entitlement and/or quantum ... without the need to establish a material change in circumstances." The trial judge declined to make support retroactive, leaving the appellant with the $2,000 monthly interim support she was awarded for the period from October 1, 2004, until the end of trial. The order also requires the respondent to disclose his income to the appellant on an annual basis. It does not contain a reciprocal provision for the appellant to disclose her income to the respondent.

3 The appellant challenges the trial judge's factual findings. She also argues that the trial judge erred in his application of the law by time-limiting/reviewing support, by failing to order support payable from the date of the interim order, by failing to apply the *Spousal Support Advisory Guidelines: A Draft Proposal* (Ottawa: Department of Justice, 2005) (the Guidelines), and by reducing the amount of support based on the respondent's obligations to his second family.

4 For the reasons that follow, I would allow the appeal and set aside those parts of the divorce order dealing with the quantum of spousal support and the review order. In their place, I would order spousal support in the amount of $3,000 monthly beginning October 1, 2004. I would step down spousal support on April 1, 2008, to $1,500 and terminate it on September 1, 2011. This would provide the appellant with seven years of spousal support,

subject of course to any variation order made in accordance with s. 17 of the *Divorce Act*, R.S.C. 1985, c. 3 (2nd Supp.).

Background

5 The parties married in August 1985, when the appellant was 22 and the respondent 23 years of age, and separated in April 2004, when they were 41 and 42 years of age respectively. There were no children of the marriage.

6 Initially, the appellant contributed her earnings from clerical entry-level employment to assist with the parties' expenses during the two years necessary for the respondent to complete his Honours Bachelor of Arts. The parties then moved from Waterloo to London so that the respondent could obtain his Bachelor of Education. The appellant sought new employment and continued to contribute to the parties' expenses.

7 Following graduation, the respondent taught high school for eleven years, earning $65,000 in his final year. In 1999, the respondent accepted employment in London with the Ontario Secondary School Teachers' Federation (O.S.S.T.F.) at an increased salary. Over the three years prior to separation, the respondent earned increasing amounts of income. By 2003, he was earning $81,800. In February 2004, the respondent accepted a position with the O.S.S.T.F. in Toronto at an annual salary of $120,000, plus car allowance and benefits. The parties separated two months later. The respondent earned approximately $132,000 in 2005 and $140,000 in 2006, both amounts including car allowance and benefits.

8 The respondent began a relationship with his current partner, who then lived in the United States. Although the new partner was a physiotherapist, she left her profession to stay at home with her two pre-school-age children. During this time, she worked part time as a day care aide.

9 In 2005, the new partner and her children moved to Canada to join the respondent. Until she married the respondent and obtained the necessary immigration status, the new partner was prohibited from employment in Canada. As well, she needed to retrain to meet Ontario physiotherapist qualifications. However, even though both children attended school full time, the new partner elected not to retrain, but instead to stay at home. Her only apparent contribution to the family income is the U.S. $700 monthly child support she receives from the children's biological father, who earns U.S. $70,000 annually. The trial judge also imputed $10,000 of notional annual income to her based on her prior U.S. day care employment.

10 The respondent's support of his partner's decision to stay at home means that he voluntarily assumes most of the financial responsibility for his new family, which he argues adversely affects his ability to support the appellant.

11 The appellant had a high school education when the parties married. During the marriage she took university courses, mostly through distance education. After separation, she returned to university and was one and a half credits short of completing her Bachelor of Fine Arts degree at the time of trial.

12 Although the trial judge found that the appellant worked full time throughout the marriage, the parties agree that her work, until 1999, was often part time, or seasonal, with periods of absence from the work force. It is conceded that, from 1984 to 1999, the appellant was only employed full time approximately half the time. However, she did work full time in the area of advertising sales during the last years of the marriage.

13 For the most part, the appellant earned an average annual income of $30,000. For about two years before separation, she had a commission job that provided a base salary of

$35,000 with a total income of $41,000, including commissions. This was the highest income she ever earned.

14 The separation came as a shock to the appellant, who had planned to leave her employment to join the respondent in a new home they had purchased to accommodate his Toronto employment. Several months after separation, the appellant became clinically depressed. She took disability leave from October 2004 to September 2005, for which she received $19,500 of gross disability benefits from her insurer. The appellant has since returned to full-time employment. At the time of trial, she earned $30,000 annually.

15 The parties equalized their assets, including the proceeds of sale of the matrimonial home and the respondent's pension, with the respondent paying the appellant an equalization payment of approximately $102,000. From this, the appellant bought a $191,000 home, which the trial judge found was a "huge 'step down'" in lifestyle that resulted from the respondent's "decision to terminate their marriage." In contrast, the respondent bought a $328,000 home in Ajax for himself and his new family, as a result of which he has significant expenses.

Trial judgment

16 Both at trial and on appeal, the respondent argued that spousal support should be terminated and the appellant considered self-sufficient at her current $30,000 income. The appellant argued for support at $3,000 monthly, retroactive to October 2004, and ongoing indefinite support of $3,500, reviewable on or after September 1, 2012. While entitlement to support was agreed upon both at trial and on appeal, the trial judge discussed, and counsel argued, the principles regarding entitlement that are also relevant to the issue of quantum.

17 The parties agree that the experienced trial judge correctly canvassed the legal principles. He recognized the factors and objectives set out in s. 15.2 of the *Divorce Act*. He reviewed the seminal authorities, including *Moge v. Moge*, [1992] 3 S.C.R 813, regarding compensatory support, and *Bracklow v. Bracklow*, [1999] 1 S.C.R. 420, regarding needs-based support. He considered questions of economic disadvantage, economic hardship, self-sufficiency and the reduction in the appellant's standard of living. He concluded that the appellant "fits entirely within the jurisprudential criteria of having suffered an 'economic disadvantage' by Mr. Fisher's decision to [end] the marriage."

18 While the trial judge did not come to an explicit conclusion regarding the issue of self-sufficiency, he cited a series of cases providing transitional support following mid-range marriages where the recipient spouse would be able to achieve self-sufficiency. From this and his later analysis, it is apparent that he determined that it was practicable for the appellant to become self-sufficient from her earnings, or to adjust her standard of living, by December 2008 — subject to the 2009 review also provided by his order.

19 In the trial judge's view, the respondent's obligations to his second family were a significant issue. In his thorough analysis, the trial judge recognized the need to balance obligations to two families. ...

20 The trial judge concluded that the respondent's decision to support his second family "is a reality that must be taken into account" when assessing the quantum of support payable to the appellant.

21 The trial judge also considered cases dealing with time-limited support and implicitly concluded that any economic disadvantage suffered by the appellant as a result of the marriage was not sufficient to warrant indefinite support. The trial judge's analysis again referred to *Moge*, as well as the decisions of this court in *Kent v. Frolick* (1996), 23 R.F.L. (4th) 1 (Ont. C.A.) and *Krauss v. Krauss* (1991), 33 R.F.L. (3d) 233 (Ont. C.A.), for the

principle that time-limited support should only be ordered in "unusual" or "unique circumstances" or in the particular circumstances of the parties. On this issue, the trial judge summarized the principle: "[C]ourts appear to continue to make time-limited orders only where, because of a young age, short marriage or other factors, a dependent spouse is capable of achieving self-sufficiency, or where a spouse has sustained very little, if any, economic disadvantage as a result of the breakdown of the marriage. (para. 33)"

22 In the result, he concluded:

> I am persuaded that based upon the case law — *Moge*, the *Krause* factors, *Bracklow* and *Huisman* — Ms. Fisher's relative youth, her good health, the fact that she has no dependents and has no (significant) debt, and her past and present work record/ethics/opportunities, this case is indeed one that is "unusual." *I speculate that over the next few years Ms. Fisher will become entirely self-sufficient and, like Mr. Fisher, perhaps enter into a new relationship* (or partnership) whereby her day-to-day expenses can at least be shared. (para. 69) (Emphasis added)

Issues

23 The appellant argues that the trial judge erred in making factual findings that materially affected his decision, including that:

a) the appellant was employed full time throughout the marriage;

b) the appellant would earn enough income to be self-sufficient in the next few years; and

c) the appellant would find a new partner to share her expenses.

24 The appellant also argues that the trial judge's award fails to apply properly the objectives of s. 15.2(6) of the *Divorce Act* to recognize the appellant's economic disadvantages arising from the marriage or its breakdown, to relieve against the hardship she suffered as a result of the breakdown and to recognize the appellant's limited ability to achieve economic self-sufficiency. In particular, the appellant argues that the trial judge erred by:

a) reducing the respondent's obligation to pay support by reason of his obligations to his second family;

b) refusing to order that increased support begin effective October 1, 2004, the date of the interim support order;

c) time-limiting the appellant's support, subject to a review order; and

d) failing to award support based on the Guidelines.

Analysis

Standard of Review

25 Based on the standard of review of a support order set out by L'Heureux-Dubé J. in *Hickey v. Hickey*, [1999] 2 S.C.R. 518, at paras. 10-11, I am mindful that the discretionary decision of the trial judge, who in any event is very experienced, is entitled to considerable deference and should not be interfered with absent an error in principle, a significant misapprehension of the evidence, or unless the award is clearly wrong.

Findings of fact

a) Full-time employment

26 As I have indicated, it was common ground that the appellant did not work full time throughout the marriage. Accordingly, the trial judge erred in finding that she worked full time. Such a finding likely affected his determination of the quantum of the appellant's support.

b) Sufficient employment income

27 The appellant testified about her employment income. At its highest, the appellant's testimony included an expression of her "hope" that her income would increase to $35,000 in a couple of years. On this evidence, the trial judge concluded that the appellant "predicts that after about three years her [$30,000] income will increase and her employment position will solidify." (para. 67) The appellant argues that this finding is not supported by the evidence because a "prediction" invokes more certainty than does a "hope".

28 The trial judge's uncertainty about the appellant's prospects is reflected in another part of his reasons, also challenged by the appellant, when he said: "I speculate that over the next few years Ms. Fisher will become entirely self-sufficient". The appellant argues that the trial judge was not entitled to base his decision on speculation.

29 In my view, while the choice of the word "speculate" was unfortunate, when considered in the context of the trial judge's reasons as a whole, the trial judge meant no more than that he anticipated the appellant's income might return to the $40,000 level once she was able to build a commission base in her new employment. It was likely precisely because the trial judge recognized this uncertainty that he provided for a subsequent review of the support order. Accordingly, while different terminology would have been preferable, I am not persuaded that any misstatement by the trial judge on this point materially affected his decision.

30 However, the uncertainty regarding the appellant's employment income is relevant to both the review order and the trial judge's analysis of the appellant's self-sufficiency, which I will discuss in detail later.

c) A new partner

31 In his reasons, the trial judge also "speculate[s]" that the appellant would "perhaps enter into a new relationship (or partnership) whereby her day-to-day expenses can at least be shared." (para. 69) It is conceded that this comment was not supported by the evidence. Indeed, there was no evidence that the appellant even had a relationship with any potential partner. In my opinion, the trial judge's unwarranted comment was an error that contributed to his decision to provide what he described as a "type of time-limited review spousal support order."

Conclusion on findings of fact

32 The errors regarding the appellant's employment and potential new relationship, particularly when considered in combination with the discussion that follows about the impact of the respondent's second family on his support obligation, and the circumstances in which "termination/review" orders are appropriate, lead to the conclusion that the trial award must be set aside. It is not necessary that the matter be returned for a new trial because there are no factual disputes that would justify the delay and expense that would necessarily be incurred. Accordingly, it falls to this court to assess the appropriate quantum of spousal support.

Application of the law

Factors and objectives

33 It is helpful to begin by setting out the factors and objectives of ss. 15.2(4) and (6) of the *Divorce Act* regarding an order of spousal support. ...

34 I will deal with each of the relevant factors and objectives in turn, mindful, as was the trial judge, of the admonition that no one objective predominates; rather, it is important to balance all four objectives in the context of the circumstances of the particular case: ... After this, I will balance the considerations that emerge to determine an appropriate quantum of support.

Factors

15.2 (4)(a) Length of the cohabitation

35 A determination of the "condition, means, needs and other circumstances of each spouse" includes consideration of the length of the parties' cohabitation. The Guidelines, which I will discuss later, observe that "in parts of the country it is difficult to time-limit support after 15 years of marriage." Indeed, in other cases involving lengthy marriages, many courts have imposed indefinite orders for support. See *Andrews v. Andrews* (1999), 50 R.F.L. (4th) 1 (Ont. C.A.); *Adams v. Adams* (2001), 15 R.F.L. (5th) 1 (Ont. C.A.); *Desramaux v. Desramaux* (2002), 28 R.F.L. (5th) 25 (Ont. C.A.). Indefinite support is appropriate after a long-term marriage because the dependent spouse is often of an age that makes it difficult to achieve economic self-sufficiency.

36 Even though this marriage was lengthy, the trial judge decided that an indefinite order was not appropriate. In making this determination, the trial judge considered the appellant's employment position and relative youth. For reasons that I will expand on later, I see no reason to interfere with the trial judge's determination on this point.

15.2(4)(b) Functions performed during cohabitation

37 The appellant and the respondent remember their functions during the marriage somewhat differently, and the trial judge does not appear to have made a factual finding on this issue. However, even accepting the appellant's testimony that she assumed a somewhat greater proportion of non-economic responsibilities during the marriage, the evidence also indicated that the respondent fully participated in household chores. In any event, the appellant does not argue that any assumption of household responsibilities negatively affected her career goals or advanced those of the respondent.

15.2(4) Other circumstances

38 The court is required, as it did in this case, to consider other factors, including the means and needs of the parties. One important factor in this case is the respondent's responsibility, if any, for his "new" or second family. The appellant does not take issue with the trial judge's review of the law on this point; rather, her concern lies with the application of the law to the facts of this case.

39 While courts generally recognize a "first-family-first" principle (which provides that a payor's obligations to the first family take priority over any subsequent obligations), inevitably new obligations to a second family may decrease a payor's ability to pay support for a first family.

40 In each case, obligations toward second families must be considered in context. For example, where spouses with a child separate, and one remarries and produces another child, the obligations to the second child will affect support for the first family because the payor has an equal obligation to both children. However, that is not this case.

41 In this case, the respondent voluntarily assumed significant responsibility for his second family when he knew, or should have known, of his pre-existing obligation to his first family. He assumed this obligation even though the second family is capable of contributing to its own support provided the respondent's new partner completed her qualifications to practise as a physiotherapist in Ontario. In addition, the second family receives child support from the children's biological father. This is not a case where the respondent was obliged to support his new family, at least beyond the temporary legal obligation based on their initial immigration status. In any event, there was no evidence that the respondent's obligations to his first family would impoverish his second family. In these circumstances, the respondent's endorsement of his second wife's preference to remain at home cannot be relied upon to reduce his support obligation to his first family.

42 I now turn to consider the objectives set out in s. 15.2(6).

Objectives: Section 15.2(6)

15.2(6)(a) Economic advantages or disadvantages from the marriage or its breakdown

43 The concept of economic advantage or disadvantage arising from the marriage is the foundation for the principles of compensatory support familiar from their detailed discussion in *Moge*.

44 In this case, the parties formed a relationship of financial interdependence, which began when the respondent partly depended on the appellant's assistance to complete his education. This permitted the respondent to begin his career at a young age, and to advance that career during the marriage and after its breakdown. This was no doubt an economic advantage to the respondent.

45 With the respondent's support and encouragement, the appellant chose an educational program in fine arts, which accorded with her personal interests. There was no evidence that this choice, or any other choice made during the marriage, deprived the appellant of any other education or retraining that she otherwise would have pursued to improve her income-earning potential. Indeed, the appellant is content with her current career, which is a continuation of the career she followed during the marriage. In those circumstances, the marriage did not put her at a disadvantage regarding her career.

46 This brings me to the appellant's primary contention on this appeal, namely, that she was economically disadvantaged not by the marriage, but by its breakdown, and in particular by her loss of the parties' standard of living, past and future.

47 As the trial judge noted, the appellant's standard of living was significantly reduced when she moved to a small townhouse (a disadvantage also suffered by the respondent in view of his similar loss of the matrimonial home and the diminution in capital). Specifically, the trial judge found that the appellant "lost not only her future dream and the large financial salary increase in which she was led to believe she would share, but she also lost the comfortable middle-class lifestyle to which they both had been accustomed." (para. 60) In addition, the appellant was economically disadvantaged by the reactive depression she suffered after the separation. The resulting interruption to her employment reduced her income, at least in the short term.

48 It follows that the economic disadvantages from the marriage breakdown were more pronounced for the appellant, particularly regarding the reduction in her standard of living.

15.2(6)(c) Economic hardship

49 It is also necessary to consider whether the appellant suffered economic hardship from the marriage breakdown. The trial judge thoroughly canvassed the case law that discusses the distinction between economic hardship and economic disadvantage. There appears to be ongoing uncertainty about whether 'hardship' refers to an inability to meet basic needs or whether it should be more liberally interpreted to refer to an inability to meet the recipient's needs considered in their context.

50 In this case, if defined literally, as did the trial judge, the appellant did not suffer "hardship" because, even on her $30,000 income, the appellant could provide for her basic needs. However, if defined liberally, she did suffer the economic hardship of a reduction in her standard of living.

51 While it may be preferable to consider hardship in the relative context of the particular parties, I need not determine that issue on this record. Instead, I will discuss any economic hardship arising from the appellant's reduced standard of living under the objective of self-sufficiency because it is under that rubric that the issue is raised in the appellant's argument.

15.2(6)(d) Self-sufficiency

52 Section 15.2(6)(d) of the *Divorce Act* promotes the objective of economic self-sufficiency only if it is "practicable" to do so and where the objective can be realized "within a reasonable period of time".

53 Self-sufficiency, with its connotation of economic independence, is a relative concept. It is not achieved simply because a former spouse can meet basic expenses on a particular amount of income; rather, self-sufficiency relates to the ability to support a reasonable standard of living. It is to be assessed in relation to the economic partnership the parties enjoyed and could sustain during cohabitation, and that they can reasonably anticipate after separation. See *Linton v. Linton* (1990), 1 O.R. (3d) 1 (C.A.) at 27-28. Thus, a determination of self-sufficiency requires consideration of the parties' present and potential incomes, their standard of living during marriage, the efficacy of any suggested steps to increase a party's means, the parties' likely post-separation circumstances (including the impact of equalization of their property), the duration of their cohabitation and any other relevant factors.

54 Self-sufficiency is often more attainable in short-term marriages, particularly ones without children, where the lower-income spouse has not become entrenched in a particular lifestyle, or compromised career aspirations. In such circumstances, the lower-income spouse is expected either to have the tools to become financially independent or to adjust his or her standard of living.

55 In contrast, in most long-term marriages, particularly in traditional long-term ones, the parties' merger of economic lifestyles creates a joint standard of living that the lower-income spouse cannot hope to replicate, but upon which he or she has become dependent. In such circumstances, the spousal support analysis typically will not give priority to self-sufficiency because it is an objective that simply cannot be attained. See *Linton* at 27.

56 The relevance of standard of living as a measure of dependency in long-term marriages is best encapsulated by L'Heureux-Dubé J. in the following passage from *Moge*:

> Although the doctrine of spousal support which focuses on equitable sharing does not guarantee to either party the standard of living enjoyed during the marriage, this standard is far from irrelevant to support entitlement. ... Furthermore, great disparities in the standard of living that would be exper-

ienced by spouses in the absence of support are often a revealing indication of the economic disadvantages inherent in the role assumed by one party. As marriage should be regarded as a joint endeavour, the longer the relationship endures, the closer the economic union, the greater will be the presumptive claim to equal standards of living upon its dissolution. ...

57 In this case, I have already noted that the appellant's claim is largely a needs-based one arising from the financial dependence that developed mainly in the latter years of the marriage when the respondent's income began to increase significantly. By the time of separation, the parties' anticipated sharing an average *joint* income of about $125,325.

58 Yet the respondent submits that the appellant should be considered self-sufficient on the basis of her current $30,000 income. I reject this submission. It is not only obvious that the appellant would need more than her $30,000 income to maintain her pre-separation standard of living, she would still require support even if that income increased to $41,000. Accordingly, the goal of self-sufficiency based on her income-earning capacity is not practicable in a reasonable time. However, that does not end the matter.

59 The question remains whether it is reasonable to expect the appellant to gradually adjust her standard of living to one commensurate with her own income. The answer depends on a balancing of all the objectives and factors, which I will address under quantum of support.

Summary of objectives

60 In summary, the appellant suffered no established economic disadvantage arising from the marriage either by the assumption of child-care responsibilities or in any other way that compromised her career or educational aspirations. Any minimal disadvantage cannot be compared to that of a long-term traditional spouse who made career sacrifices to the significant advantage of the other spouse. While the appellant's economic assistance at the beginning of the parties' marriage provided an advantage to the respondent, the primary basis for the appellant's support claim is framed as an inability to attain self-sufficiency in light of the marital standard of living.

61 Before turning to quantum of support, it is necessary to first address whether a review order was appropriate in this case and whether the support order should have applied from the date of the interim order.

Review order   CLASS (Necessary)

62 On the language of the order in this case, the appellant would receive her last support payment on December 1, 2008. After January 1, 2009, she would be permitted to apply for a review.

63 A review allows an application for support without the need to prove the material change in circumstances required in a section 17 variation application. Unless the review is restricted to a specific issue, it is generally equivalent to an initial application for support and necessitates a complete rehearing of every issue from entitlement to quantum. Thus, a review, particularly one relatively proximate to the time of the originating order, causes unnecessary and significant expense for the parties, not only emotionally, but also financially. ...

70 Review orders in effect turn an initial order into a long-term interim order made after trial. Accordingly, they should be the exception, not the norm. They are appropriate when a specified uncertainty about a party's circumstances at the time of trial will become certain within an identifiable timeframe. When one is granted, it should include specifics regarding the issue about which there is uncertainty and when and how the trial judge anticipates that

uncertainty will be resolved. [The court cited *Leskun v. Leskun* (2006), 34 R.F.L. (6th) 1 (S.C.C.) on this point].

71 In any other case, a trial judge should issue a final order based on a preponderance of the evidence called by the parties. In the family law context, a final order will always be subject to variation, which will suffice to protect against future events. A variation is available not only when there is an unexpected change in circumstances, but also when an anticipated set of specified circumstances fails to materialize. This is particularly the case where an initial order specifies a trial judge's anticipation that the recipient spouse will or should be able to earn a given income within a particular timeframe. This flexibility is to be contrasted with a review order, which invariably places the burden on the applicant, albeit in the context of an initial application.

74 Accordingly, I conclude that the imposition of the review order constituted an error in principle on the facts of this case.

Commencement date for support

75 The appellant obtained an interim support order of $2,000 monthly commencing in October 2004, which is when she began her disability leave. The award continued through the January 2006 trial. At trial, the appellant requested that the final support order be retroactive to October 2004.

76 In my view, the trial judge erred in refusing that relief. I say this for three reasons. First, as was established at trial, the appellant was in need of support and the respondent had the ability to pay. While the trial judge referred to the $12,000 debt the appellant incurred in this period, he saw this as offset by the $19,500 of disability insurance. However, in my view, retroactive support to replace an interim support order should not be restricted to situations where the recipient spouse has incurred a crippling amount of debt. Rather, retroactive support should be available when the recipient establishes at trial that he or she was entitled to a greater amount of interim support, the respondent had the ability to pay, and the imposition of retroactive support would not create undue hardship for the payor.

77 Second, the interim motion judge limited the amount of interim support partly because she was sceptical about the appellant's reasons for leaving her employment. However, the trial evidence established that the appellant did not wilfully leave her employment, but rather, that she was disabled by depression. Even if the appellant could have resumed her employment earlier with the help of the medication that she refused at the time, she still would have needed support to offset the diminution in her lifestyle resulting from the loss of the parties' combined incomes.

78 Finally, the interim support award was based on the premise that the appellant earned $48,000, or would have earned that amount had she not taken disability leave from her employment. However, the trial judge ultimately determined that the appellant never earned, or had the ability to earn, $48,000 at that time.

79 In these circumstances, the appellant was entitled to an appropriate level of spousal support from the October 2004 date of commencement of interim support.

80 This decision to award a final order of support commencing from the date of the interim award also accords with the structure of the Guidelines, which explicitly apply to interim orders. This is important because, as I will discuss, if the Guidelines are applied to final orders, but not retroactively to interim orders, or the period between separation and the commencement of support is otherwise not accounted for, the Guidelines' recommendations for duration of support will be distorted.

81 In addition, a refusal to order support payable from the date of interim support will provide one party with an incentive to delay a final hearing and the other party with an incentive to insist on its expedition. Either incentive may result in increased procedural costs. Thus, achievement of the Guidelines' objectives of discouraging litigation manoeuvring between the parties, while promoting an equitable result for the parties, mandates an earlier commencement date for final support where feasible.

82 Accordingly, I would allow the appeal on this issue and order increased support commencing October 1, 2004. I turn now to the questions of amount and duration of support.

Quantum — Amount and Duration

83 This assessment must be completed in the context of the legal principles carefully reviewed by the trial judge, including the factors relevant to whether support should be indefinite or limited-term.

84 The factors and objectives require a balancing of the parties' circumstances, including the duration of the parties' cohabitation, their ages, their incomes and prospective incomes, the effects of equalization, the stages of their careers, contributions to the marital standard of living, participation in household responsibilities, the absence of child-care obligations, the respondent's increased cost of living arising from his new employment, the parties' reasonable expectations, the respondent's rapid pre- and post-separation increases in income, the appellant's limited claim for compensatory support and her greater need for transitional support.

85 In reaching his decision to limit the duration of support, the trial judge referred to several authorities and specifically referenced the appellant's "relative youth, her good health, the fact that she has no dependents and has no (significant) debt, and her past and present work record/ethics/opportunities". As I have said, I agree with the trial judge that indefinite support was not indicated on the facts of this case.

86 In this case, the appellant's dependency on the marital standard of living was not entrenched in the manner it would have been in a traditional marriage where the parties enjoyed a gradually increasing standard of living. The respondent's substantial income increases started in approximately 2002. This provided the parties with a better standard of living during the last years of their marriage than they enjoyed in the many preceding years, a standard of living that would have increased further commensurate with the respondent's 2004 income.

87 In this circumstance, Professor Rogerson's observation in "Spousal Support Post-*Bracklow*: The Pendulum Swings Again?" is apt: "Such discrete [limited-term] obligations may also arise in longer relationships where both parties have worked throughout the relationship and the lower-income spouse is understood to have only a limited claim to non-compensatory, transitional support to cushion the drop in standard of living occasioned by the marriage breakdown." (p. 259)

88 To provide the appellant with a reasonable transition following her nineteen-year marriage, it is my view that the appellant will need support for seven years, beginning with the year of separation. In my view, a seven-year order complies with the spousal support objective of recognizing the appellant's economic disadvantage arising from the marriage and its breakdown, while also encouraging the appellant to complete her transition to self-sufficiency, whether by reason of earning a higher income or, more likely, by adapting her lifestyle to her then income.

89 To achieve an equitable result regarding the amount of support, I have averaged the parties' incomes for the last years. In the respondent's case, I use his increasing income in

the three years prior to separation, as well as his substantially increased income in the year of separation, even though it was largely received post-separation. This results in an average salary for the respondent of $89,825, which allows for the parties' expectation that they would have shared those increases but for the separation.

90 For the appellant, as with the respondent, I use her income earned in the three years prior to separation and in the year of separation which produces an average income of $35,500.

91 On the basis of these averages, in my view, the appropriate amount of transitional and compensatory support for the appellant is reflected by an award of $3,000 monthly for a three and a half year period from October 1, 2004, to March 1, 2008, followed by a further three and a half years at $1,500 monthly from April 1, 2008 until September 1, 2011. I would then terminate support. Such an award cushions the appellant's drop in standard of living caused by the marriage breakdown.

92 While I have assessed the amount and duration of spousal support based on the circumstances involved, it is helpful to consider the reasonableness of this award by reference to the Guidelines. As noted, the trial judge's omission of any reference to the Guidelines in the trial reasons is the final issue raised in this appeal.

Spousal Support Advisory Guidelines

93 Since it is clear that the Guidelines were put to the trial court, the appellant argues that the trial judge erred in failing to take them into account in determining the quantum of support. In fairness to the trial judge, at the time of trial, the Guidelines were released only one year earlier and were not yet the subject of widespread commentary.

94 The Guidelines were drafted under the aegis of the federal Department of Justice by the highly-regarded family law professors, Carol Rogerson and Rollie Thompson. The objective of the Guidelines is to bring certainty and predictability to spousal support awards under the *Divorce Act*. For this purpose, they employ an income-sharing model of support, that if proven viable, will reduce the need to rely on the labour-intensive, and thus expensive, budget-based evidence employed in a typical case. In this way, in a manner quite different from the Child Support Guidelines (CSGs), the Guidelines aspire to reduce the expense of litigation of spousal support by promoting resolution for the average case.

95 In the seminal case of *Yemchuk v. Yemchuk* (2005), 16 R.F.L. (6th) 430 (B.C.C.A.), at para. 64, Prowse J.A. aptly characterized the Guidelines as a "useful tool." She recognized that, unlike the CSGs, the Guidelines are neither legislated nor binding; they are only advisory. The parties, their lawyers, and the courts are not required to employ them. As well, the Guidelines continue to evolve; they are a "work in progress" subject to revision. Those revisions, as with the Guidelines themselves, will follow after broad consultation by the authors with a wide range of interested constituents.

96 Importantly, the Guidelines do not apply in many cases. They specifically do not apply at all in certain enumerated circumstances, including where spouses earn above $350,000 or below $20,000. Furthermore, they only apply to initial orders for support and not to variation orders. They are thus prospective in application. They do not apply in cases where a prior agreement provides for support and, obviously, in cases where the requisite entitlement has not been established. They will not help in atypical cases. As well, there will be regional variations, as well as rural and urban variations, that may be seen to merit divergent results based on variations in cost of living or otherwise. Importantly, in all cases, the reasonableness of an award produced by the Guidelines must be balanced in light of the circumstances of the individual case, including the particular financial history of the parties during the marriage and their likely future circumstances.

97 Accordingly, the Guidelines cannot be used as a software tool or a formula that calculates a specific amount of support for a set period of time. They must be considered in context and applied in their entirety, including the specific consideration of any applicable variables and, where necessary, restructuring.

98 Importantly, the Guidelines do not impose a radically new approach. Instead, they suggest a range of both amount and duration of support that reflects the current law. Because they purport to represent a distillation of current case law, they are comparable to counsel's submissions about an appropriate range of support based on applicable jurisprudence. However, if the Guidelines suggest a range that conflicts with applicable authorities, the authorities will prevail.

99 Counsel on this appeal advise that in London, where this support order was made, the Guidelines are widely used by the bar as a starting point for the purpose of assessing an appropriate level of spousal support, or for checking the validity of a proposed settlement. This is consistent with the finding of Professors Rogerson and Thompson set out in "The Advisory Guidelines 31 Months Later", which provides an extensive review of how the Guidelines have been applied in courts across Canada.

100 Other appellate courts have accepted the Guidelines as a "cross-check" or "starting point" for spousal support that "will help in the long run to bring consistency and predictability to spousal support awards", encourage settlement and allow parties to "anticipate their support responsibilities at the time of separation." [The Justice here cited *C. (J.D.E.) v. C. (S.M.)* (2006), 27 R.F.L. (6th) 19 (N.B.C.A.).]

101 However, Quebec courts have not been as accepting of the application of the Guidelines, mainly on the basis that an "individual analysis" is required in assessing spousal support, as opposed to the adoption of a "mathematical formula". [Here, the Justice footnoted *G. (C.) c. V. (G.)*, [2006] J. Q. No. 5231 (Que. C.A.) and several trial decisions.] This concern is satisfied by the structure of these reasons, which first address the quantum of support in the traditional manner, and then assess the reasonableness of that support against the range drawn from the Guidelines. Nonetheless, I am optimistic that, with experience, the Guidelines will become accepted as a reliable tool for resolution of many cases, subject always to the important caveat that due consideration be given to the parties' individual circumstances.

102 In addition, when considered in their entirety and subject to their limitations, the Guidelines also assist in informing an appellate standard of review. In *Redpath v. Redpath* (2006), 33 R.F.L. (6th) 91 (B.C.C.A.), at para. 42, Newbury J.A. commented: "Now that [the Guidelines] are available to provide what is effectively a "range" within which the awards in most cases of this kind should fall, it may be that if a particular award is substantially lower or higher than the range and there are no exceptional circumstances to explain the anomaly, the standard of review should be reformulated to permit appellate intervention."

103 In my view, when counsel fully address the Guidelines in argument, and a trial judge decides to award a quantum of support outside the suggested range, appellate review will be assisted by the inclusion of reasons explaining why the Guidelines do not provide an appropriate result. This is no different than a trial court distinguishing a significant authority relied upon by a party.

104 I turn to the application of the Guidelines. The "Without Child Support Formula" purports to incorporate both compensatory and non-compensatory support objectives by focusing on a combination of the difference in the parties' gross incomes and the length of their

cohabitation. This approach is consistent with a party's needs serving as a proxy for dependency. The formula is set out in section 5.1 of the Guidelines:

> **Amount** ranges from 1.5 to 2 percent of the difference between the spouses' gross incomes (the **gross income difference**) for each year of marriage, (or, more precisely, years of cohabitation), up to a maximum of 50 percent. The range remains fixed for marriages 25 years or longer at 37.5 to 50 percent of income difference.
>
> **Duration** ranges from .5 to 1 year for each year of marriage. However support will be **indefinite** if the marriage is **20 years or longer** in duration or, if the marriage has lasted five years or longer, when years of marriage and age of the support recipient (at separation) added together total 65 or more (the **rule of 65**).

105 According to Professors Rogerson and Thompson, trial judges and lawyers often overlook or ignore the integral component of duration of marriage. The Guidelines use duration to categorize cohabitation: a short-term cohabitation is one of less than five years; a medium-term cohabitation is from five to nineteen years and a long-term cohabitation is twenty years or longer.

106 However, under the Guidelines, a medium-term marriage becomes a long-term one (giving rise to indefinite support) if the parties' years of marriage, plus the age of the support recipient at the date of separation, equals or exceeds sixty-five. This refinement recognizes that an economically-dependent older spouse may have trouble thereafter attaining self-sufficiency.

107 While the "rule of 65" does not apply in this case, the general principle that it adopts in classifying marriage based on a spouse's age at separation is still relevant. This is because age is a strong indicator of an individual's ability to become self-sufficient.

108 In circumstances such as these, where the marriage falls just outside of the Guidelines' classification of a "long-term" marriage, a court may still decide that an indefinite support order is appropriate. Similarly, a court may decide that limited-term support is appropriate even though the period of cohabitation is twenty years or more. This is because, as the Guidelines note, while courts should consider the age of the parties and the duration of the marriage, they must also consider all other relevant circumstances.

109 In recognition of the symbiotic relationship between amount and duration, the Guidelines emphasize:

> Amount and duration are interrelated parts of the formula-they are a package deal. Using one part of the formula without the other would undermine its integrity and coherence. As discussed below, *the advisory guidelines provide for restructuring, which allows duration to be extended by lowering the monthly amount of support.* (p. 39) [Emphasis added]

110 In this case of a medium-term nineteen-year marriage, the Guidelines provide a range of support. At the low end of the range, the appellant would receive 28.5% of the parties' income differential of $54,325, or $1,290 monthly ($15,483 annually). At the high end of the Guidelines' range, the appellant would receive 38% of the differential, or $1,720 monthly ($20,644 annually). In accordance with the formula for duration, support would be payable for a period ranging from 9.5 to nineteen years.

111 The award I consider appropriate in this case, at least initially, both exceeds this range for amount and falls below the range for duration. Thus, I turn to the provisions for restructuring, which essentially involve converting the specific ranges of support to a lump sum amount (without consideration for present values). In this case, this conversion results in a broad support range from a low of $147,088, to a high of $392,236.

112 This global range can be compared to the trial award as a "litmus test of reasonableness". The trial award, including interim support, but assuming termination in December 2008, totals a lump sum of $94,200, an amount that falls far below the Guidelines, although

I recognize that this does not account for what may have been the final result after a review hearing.

113 In comparison, the support award that I propose in these reasons would total $189,000. This figure falls within the Guidelines global range, albeit toward the low end of that range.

Result

114 In the result, I would allow the appeal, set aside paragraphs 2 and 3 of the divorce order and substitute an order for spousal support of $3,000 monthly commencing October 1, 2004, and continuing to March 1, 2008. Thereafter I would award support of $1,500 monthly from April 1, 2008, terminating after a final payment on September 1, 2011. I would also vary paragraph 5 of the order to make reciprocal the obligation to disclose annual incomes to the other spouse as long as support is payable.

115 This termination order is designed to provide the appellant with support to enable her to become financially independent, or adjust to a lower standard of living within seven years. It also assumes that the respondent will maintain his income in a manner consistent with his current employment. The order is, of course, subject to variation by reason of a material change in circumstances. ...

NOTES AND QUESTIONS

1. In determining a spouse's income for the purposes of assessing his or her capacity to pay spousal support, a court may be asked to consider income from a pension that has already been shared in whole or in part as property. This issue of "double dipping" is especially significant in provinces such as Ontario where *"in specie"* pension division is less common than in other provinces. The Supreme Court of Canada dealt with this issue in *Boston v. Boston* (2001), 17 R.F.L. (5th) 4 (S.C.C.). The case involved a husband and wife who separated in 1991 after a 36-year marriage during which the wife was a homemaker and the primary caregiver for the couple's seven children. In 1994, the husband and wife agreed to a judgment determining the property and support issues arising out of their relationship. The husband retained his employment pension worth $333,329 after tax on separation. He kept some other assets and assumed certain debts so that his assets, including the pension, had a net value of approximately $385,000. The wife received assets worth about $370,000. At the time, the husband's employment income was about $115,476 and he agreed to pay the wife $3,200 per month in spousal support, indexed to the cost of living. The parties divorced in 1995 and the husband remarried in 1996.

In 1997, the husband retired and began to receive an indexed employment pension of almost $7,600 per month and Canada Pension Plan benefits of about $431 per month. In early 1998, the husband applied to reduce the amount of spousal support. He claimed that his retirement, his reduced income and the systematic depletion of his pension as capital amounted to a material change in circumstances. By this time, the wife's assets were worth about $493,000. The wife's stated needs were $3,400 per month and she had little income aside from the spousal support. An expert calculated that if the wife purchased a $250,000 life annuity, it would produce $18,025 per year for life. The husband's assets, other than his pension, exceeded his debts by only $7,000. The husband's submission was that, considering the earlier division of assets, the wife had an obligation to contribute to her own support and only the unshared portion of his pension should be considered when determining support in light of the changed circumstances. This portion, earned after the separation, was about $2,300 per month.

The motions judge found that she had jurisdiction to vary the support order as there had been a material change in circumstances due to the husband's retirement and resultant drop in income. She next concluded that the wife had an obligation to use her assets in an income-producing way. Otherwise, the wife would augment her estate while the husband's only substantial asset from the marriage was being liquidated. The motions judge reduced the support to $950 per month, not indexed, and also rescinded any arrears.

In the wife's appeal to the Ontario Court of Appeal, the parties accepted that there had been a material change in circumstances. The appellate court found that the wife needed support and that the husband had the ability to pay. It examined the total assets of the wife that could be liquidated and estimated that she could earn a yearly investment of about $15,000 plus Canada Pension Plan benefits. It concluded that the amount of variation made by the motions judge was unreasonable and substituted an order of support for $2,000 per month, indexed. It also ordered payment of arrears, if any. The husband's appeal to the Supreme Court was allowed, L'Heureux-Dubé and LeBel JJ. dissenting. The court restored the order of the motions judge, but ordered that the amount payable be indexed.

Significantly, Justice Major, for the majority, concluded that support should be reduced because a significant portion of the pension which now provided the husband's income had already been shared in the equalization of the net family properties. He stated that it would be inequitable to allow the wife to reap the benefit of the pension first on the determination of her property entitlement and again as a source of income:

> 34 The term "double recovery" is used to describe the situation where a pension, once equalized as property, is also treated as income from which the pension-holding spouse (here the husband) must make spousal support payments. Expressed another way, upon marriage dissolution the payee spouse (here the wife) receives assets and an equalization payment that take into account the capital value of the husband's future pension income. If she later shares in the pension income as spousal support when the pension is in pay after the husband has retired, the wife can be said to be recovering twice from the pension: first at the time of the equalization of assets and again as support from the pension income.

> 35 Double recovery appears inherently unfair in cases where, to a large extent, the division or equalization of assets has addressed the compensation required. In equalizing the spouses' net family properties, the husband or wife as the case may be must include the future right to the pension income as "property" on his or her side of the ledger. This means that the pension-holder must, on separation or divorce, transfer real assets of equal value to the pension to the other spouse in order to retain the pension under the property accounting. ...

> 54 When a pension is dealt with by the lump-sum method, the pension-holding spouse (here the husband) must transfer real assets to the payee spouse (here the wife) in order to equalize matrimonial property. The wife can use these real assets immediately. Under a compensatory spousal support order or agreement, the wife has an obligation to use these assets in an income-producing way. She need not dedicate the equalization assets to investment immediately on receiving them; however, she must use them to generate income when the pension-holding spouse retires. The ideal would be if the payee spouse generated sufficient income or savings from her capital assets to equal the payor spouse's pension income. In any event, the payee spouse must use the assets received on equalization to create a "pension" to provide for her future support.

> 55 This requirement is based on the principle that, as far as it is reasonable, the payee spouse should attempt to generate economic self-sufficiency. Self-sufficiency is only one factor of many that is weighed. It is obvious that in most cases of long-term marriage, the goal of self-sufficiency is decidedly difficult to attain, particularly for spouses who remained at home during the marriage. Self-sufficiency will often not be practicable largely due to the residual effects of being outside the labour market for a protracted period of time. In addition, there are factors to consider such as age, education and parenting responsibilities. Consequently, it is often unreasonable to expect the payee spouse to earn an income from employment after separation or divorce.

> 56 However, where the payee spouse receives assets on equalization in exchange for a part of her former spouse's pension entitlement, she must use those assets in a reasonable attempt to generate income at least by the time the pension starts to pay out. The reason for this requirement is clear. The payee spouse cannot save the assets that she receives upon equalization and choose instead to live on the liquidation of the payor spouse's pension when he retires. If she were permitted to do so, the payee spouse would accumulate an estate while the payor spouse's estate is liquidating.

In par. 65, Justice Major added:

> 65 Despite these general rules, double recovery cannot always be avoided. In certain circumstances, a pension which has previously been equalized can also be viewed as a maintenance asset. Double recovery may be permitted where the payor spouse has the ability to pay, where the payee spouse has made a reasonable effort to use the equalized assets in an income-producing way and, despite this, an economic hardship from the marriage or its breakdown persists. Double recovery may also be permitted in spousal support orders/agreements based mainly on need as opposed to compensation, which is not the case in this appeal.

In his dissent, Justice LeBel suggested that, in the end, the case remained a very straightforward matter of the assessment of the needs and means of the former spouses in the context of the dynamic relationship that arose from the marriage and its breakdown. He concluded that the wife was entitled to a reasonable standard of living without having to "engage in a massive programme of liquidation of assets".

The reported cases subsequent to the Supreme Court of Canada's decision in *Boston v. Boston* frequently make use of the exceptions to the general rule against "double dipping". Double recovery from a pension is often justified on the basis of support principles such as need and compensation. See, e.g., *Cymbalisty v. Cymbalisty* (2003), 44 R.F.L. (5th) 27 (Man. C.A.), where the court stated:

> 26 The motions judge's rejection of the double recovery argument is consistent with the manner in which the *Boston* principles have been interpreted and applied in subsequent decisions of the courts. Professor Carol J. Rogerson, in "Developments in Family Law: The 2000-2001 Term" [(2001), 15 S.C.L.R. (2d) 307] commented (at p. 350):

> Over the long run, it is possible that the exception might replace the rule, in which case the response to "double dipping" generated by the majority ruling will be little different in practice from that favoured by the dissent — a flexible, case-by-case approach in which the entire pension may be considered for support purposes if, after reasonable use of equalized assets, a trial judge in his or her discretion decides that there is remaining need or disadvantage. *Boston* is unlikely to bring the desired degree of certainty to this area of law, and legislative reform remains a priority.

> 27 That viewpoint was a prophetic one. In cases where the payor spouse has retired on pension and sought a reduction of the spousal support obligation, courts across the country have found circumstances and factors that support continuing need or disadvantage and permit double recovery.

The issue of "double dipping" will arise less often if proposed changes to the Ontario *Family Law Act* are passed into law. As noted in Chapter 4: *FAMILY PROPERTY*, one of the major reforms proposed in Bill 133 is a mechanism for an immediate division of pensions directly at source upon marriage breakdown. The Bill received First Reading in the Ontario Legislature in November, 2008.

2. Prior to the decision in *Leskun v. Leskun* (2006), 34 R.F.L. (6th) 1 (S.C.C.), many family law practitioners resolved spousal support duration by agreeing to a "review" which could be triggered after the passage of a specified time or upon the happening of a particular event (such as the recipient earning a higher income). Judges, too, often used review orders as a way to provide for immediate support without ruling that support would go on indefinitely.

Review orders are attractive because they side-step a difficult legal issue. An indefinite order cannot be changed except through a variation proceeding where the applicant must establish a "material change in circumstance" (see s. 17 of the *Divorce Act*, and s. 35 of the *Family Law Act*). Proving that there has been a "material change" is not easy. The change has to be one that was not foreseen at the time the original order was made: *Willick v. Willick* (1994), 6 R.F.L. (4th) 161 (S.C.C.) and *B. (G.) c. G. (L.)* (1995), 15 R.F.L. (4th) 201 (S.C.C.). Many changes are arguably foreseeable as of the date the original order is made. An example is provided in *L.G. v. G.B.*. The wife was "seeing" a new partner at the time the original order was made. She eventually cohabited with him and the husband applied to end spousal support. The Supreme Court of Canada held that the wife's new relationship did not constitute a material change because it was within contemplation at the time the order was made that the wife might enter into a long-term relationship with this partner. Review orders, properly used, provide for specific triggers that allow either or both parties to return to court to have support examined afresh without having to establish a "material change".

However, the problem is that review orders, in effect, create long-term "interim" orders. This is objectionable to some because it allows the issue of support to be readily revisited and there is little guidance for the "reviewing" court as to how the support issue should be revisited and what evidence is relevant. On a variation application, only evidence regarding events occurring after the original order is generally relevant. Unlike some reviews, a variation proceeding does not allow the parties to re-litigate the entire case. Because of these concerns, the Supreme Court of Canada in *Leskun* said that review orders were to be the exception rather than the rule. They were only to be used when important facts are truly uncertain:

> 36 Review orders under s. 15.2 have a useful but very limited role. As the amicus pointed out, one or both parties at the time of trial may not, as yet, have the economic wherewithal even to commence recovering from the disadvantages arising from the marriage and its breakdown. Common examples are the need to establish a new residence, start a program of education, train or upgrade skills, or obtain employment. In such circumstances, judges may be tempted to attach to s. 15.2 orders a condition pursuant to s. 15.2(3) of the *Divorce Act*, that entitles one or other or both of the parties to return to court for a reconsideration of a specified aspect of the original order. This will properly occur

when the judge does not think it appropriate that at the subsequent hearing one or other of the parties need show that a change in the condition, means, needs or other circumstances of either former spouse has occurred, as required by s. 17(4.1) of the *Divorce Act*.

39 ... [However] a trial court should resist making temporary orders (or orders subject to "review") under s. 15.2. ... Insofar as possible, courts should resolve the controversies before them and make an order which is permanent subject only to change under s. 17 on proof of a change of circumstances. If the s. 15.2 court considers it essential (as here) to identify an issue for future review, the issue should be tightly delimited in the s. 15.2 order. This is because on a "review" nobody bears an onus to show changed circumstances. Failure to tightly circumscribe the issue will inevitably be seen by one or other of the parties as an invitation simply to reargue their case. That is what happened here. The more precise condition stated in the reasons of the trial judge was excessively broadened in the formal order. This resulted in a measure of avoidable confusion in the subsequent proceedings.

After the *Leskun* case, some trial and appellate courts have been reluctant to use review orders. Recall the comments of the Ontario Court of Appeal in *Fisher v. Fisher* (2008), 47 R.F.L. (6th) 235 (Ont. C.A.), excerpts reproduced above. For a critical comment on this aspect of the case, see Philip Epstein's annotation preceding it in the *Reports of Family Law*. Review orders or agreements, however, remain an important tool where there is uncertainty about how a specific event will unfold or specific fact will develop. For some post-*Leskun* cases using review orders, see *Wetmore v. Wetmore*, 2007 BCSC 1177 (S.C.) and *Lucik v. Lucik*, 2008 BCSC 531 (S.C.).

7

CUSTODY AND ACCESS

1. Introduction

Legislative Authority: Custody of and access to the children of separated parents is governed by both the *Divorce Act* (*DA*) and, in Ontario, the *Children's Law Reform Act* (*CLRA*). Married couples who separate will use the *CLRA* if no divorce is claimed and the *DA* if a divorce is claimed along with the custody or access claim. Only the *CLRA* governs parents who are not married, whether they are living common law or not.

The *DA* provides less legislative guidance to the court than the *CLRA* as to the basis for orders for custody of or access to children. Section 16 of the *DA* requires a court to take into account "only" the best interests of the child in any application for custody of or access to a child. It goes on to deal with past conduct (s. 16(9)) and maximum contact (s. 16(10). The *CLRA*, by contrast, sets out a long list of factors in s. 24 that the court is required to take into account in determining the best interests of a child. The governing principle under both pieces of legislation is the same, however: the court must resolve the issues in the best interests of the children. The substantive outcome is therefore affected very little by the particular legislation governing a case.

Who Can Apply: Under the CLRA, anyone, including a person who is not a spouse or a parent, can make an application for custody of, or access to, a child and may commence an application independent of any application commenced by the parents of a child (s. 21). Under the *DA*, a person other than the spouses may make an application, but only with leave of the court (s. 16(3)). In practice, it is most common for parents to apply for custody or access, but occasionally relatives and family friends apply for custody of or access to children pursuant to either piece of legislation. Generally, courts have held that third parties applying for access must demonstrate that they already have a close relationship with the child. Further, Ontario courts frequently defer to the parents' wishes in cases of third party applications for access, but will grant access to third parties if severing the relationship will adversely affect the child (see *Bowles v. Coggins* (2008), 52 R.F.L. (6th) 224 (Ont. C.J.).

What is Custody? What is Access? Used in its broadest sense, custody of a child denotes the totality of rights and duties in relation to children. Section 20(2) of the *CLRA* specifies: "A person entitled to custody of a child has the rights and responsibilities of a parent in respect of the person of the child and must exercise those rights and responsibilities in the best interests of the child." Section 20(2) refers to "rights and responsibilities ... in respect of the person of the child". The Act contains special rules relating to the property of the child and distinguishes between custody of the child and guardianship of the property of the child (see ss. 47–60).

While the parents of the child are cohabiting, both are entitled to custody (s. 20(1) of *CLRA*). Either of them, with or without the consent of the other, "may exercise the rights and accept the responsibilities of a parent on behalf of them in respect of the child" (s. 20(3)). The law assumes, therefore, that a mother and father will act with the necessary co-operation and trust. If a dispute does arise between cohabiting parents regarding the upbringing of the child, s. 21 of the *CLRA* appears broad enough to permit either of them to apply to a court for a resolution of the specific issue. See the comments of Justice Belch in *Lyon v. Lyon* (2004), 49 R.F.L. (5th) 122 (Ont. S.C.J.), at para. 48.

Access to a child is the right of a person to visit with a child, but also includes the important right to information about a child. Adults who want to be part of a child's life often want information about the child that is normally only available to parents. The *CLRA* provides that persons with access have "the same right as a parent" to information regarding the health, education and welfare of a child (s. 20(5)). This means that an access parent or a non-parent who is granted access to a child is entitled to make inquiries of the child's doctor, dentist, teacher, therapist, and the like. The *DA* contains a more restrictive provision regarding information. Pursuant to s. 16(5), only a spouse who is granted access has the right to "make inquiries" and "be given information" as to the child's health, education and welfare, but the section does not state that this right is the same as a parent's. It is often more beneficial for non-spouses who want access to a child to make the application pursuant to the *CLRA*, to take advantage of the expanded right of information about a child.

Of course, the terms "custody" and "access", and their generally assigned meanings, often do not adequately cover the many issues that can arise in a child's life when parents separate. Does an access parent have the right to take a child to certain religious events without the permission of the custodial parent? If the parents share joint custody, how are they to resolve issues such as which school the children will attend? Can one parent restrict the contact the other allows the children to have with extended family? Issues of this type, which are not central to the resolution of the larger issues of custody and access, are often referred to as "incidents of custody". There are certainly numerous cases where a court has determined an incident of custody after parents separate. In one of the earliest reported cases under the *CLRA*, *Chauvin v. Chauvin* (1987), 6 R.F.L. (3d) 403 (Ont. Dist. Ct.), Judge Killeen relied on s. 21 of the *CLRA* to order that two boys, who were in their mother's sole custody, should attend a French language school. In that case, the mother had transferred the children to an English language school and the father objected. For some more recent cases, see *Bachor v. Lehmann-Bachor* (2001), 14 R.F.L. (5th) 238 (Alta. C.A.) (access father not allowed to take child to "Dedication Ceremony" in his church); *P. (N.S.) v. P. (M.A.)* (2003), 42 R.F.L. (5th) 106 (Alta. Q.B.) (deciding that five-year-old, whose parents had joint custody, could accompany mother and grandmother to Disneyland and could also attend French immersion school); *Lyon v. Lyon*, above (deciding child, subject to joint custody order, should attend a private school and keep the surname of "Lyon"); *Prest v. Cole* (2003), 49 R.F.L. (5th) 168 (N.S. S.C.) (mother with sole custody of child not allowed to relocate with child to British Columbia); and *Miyasaki v. Rustia* (2004), 4 R.F.L. (6th) 92 (Ont. S.C.J.) (father and grandmother could use photo and name of child with special needs to promote Foundation seeking research funds).

When parents separate, they may come to an understanding or agreement regarding custody of the children. Section 20(4) of the *CLRA* stipulates that "where the parents of a child live separate and apart and the child lives with one of them with the consent, implied consent or acquiescence of the other of them, the right of the other to exercise the entitlement to custody and the incidents of custody, but not the entitlement to access, is suspended until a separation agreement or order otherwise provides". Where the parents cannot agree on custody or access, either can apply for a court order under s. 21 of the *CLRA*. Such an application may be made even if there is initially an agreement between the parents. The court has authority to disregard the terms of the agreement if it is in the best interests of the child to do so (see s. 56(1) of the *Family Law Act*).

The Best Interests Test: Professor Mnookin argues in "Child Custody Adjudication: Judicial Functions in the Face of Indeterminacy" (1975), 39 Law and Contemporary Problems 226, that the best interests test in custody cases does little more than give broad discretion to the courts. What is best for a child is indeterminate, in his view, for two reasons. First, it is difficult and sometimes impossible to predict the effects of a particular alternative for the child with any certainty. Current psychological theories are generally incapable of yielding such predictions, primarily because this requires the anticipation of the future behaviour of the persons involved and the effect of such behaviour. Second, even if reliable predictions could be made, the decision-maker must assign some measure of utility to each possible outcome:

> Deciding what is best for a child poses a question no less ultimate than the purposes and values of life itself. Should the judge be concerned with the economic "productivity" of the child when he grows up? Are the primary values of life in warm, interpersonal relationships, or in discipline and self-sacrifice? Is stability and security for a child more desirable than intellectual stimulation? These questions could be elaborated endlessly. And yet, where is a judge to look for a set of values that should inform the choice of what is best for the child? Normally, the custody statutes do not themselves give content or relative weights to the pertinent values. And if the judge looks to society at large, he finds neither a clear consensus as to the best child rearing strategies nor an appropriate hierarchy of ultimate values.

Other commentators have also argued that the best interests of the child test is inherently vague, and inevitably permits or even requires judges to decide cases based on their personal values, beliefs or ideology. For a brief account of the origins of the principle and a review of the critical commentary, see Bala, "The Best Interests of the Child in the Post-Modern Era: A Central But Paradoxical Concept" in Harold Niman and Gerald P. Sadvari, ed., *Family Law: "Best Interests of the Child"* (Toronto: Law Society of Upper Canada, 2000) 1. On the limitations of social science research in this area, see Shaffer, "Joint Custody, Parental Conflict and Children's Adjustments to Divorce: What the Social Science Literature Does and Does Not Tell Us" (2007), 26 C.F.L.Q. 285 and Kushner, "Judges and Child Custody Evaluators Beware: Methodological Limitations Inherent in the Research About Children and Divorce" (2009), 28 C.F.L.Q. 33.

In *Young v. Young* (1993), 49 R.F.L. (3d) 117 (S.C.C.), Justice L'Heureux-Dubé (dissenting) noted the concerns regarding the "best interests" concept and responded (at 199 and 206):

> Custody and access decisions are pre-eminently exercises in discretion. Case-by-case consideration of the unique circumstances of each child is the hallmark of the process. ... The wide latitude under the best interests test permits courts to respond to the spectrum of factors which can positively and negatively affect a child. Such discretion also permits the judge to focus on the needs of the particular child before him or her, recognizing that what may constitute stressful or damaging circumstances for one child may not necessarily have the same effect on another. ...

> It should not be assumed that a grant of discretion is an invitation to exercise personal prejudice, as it is well established in the jurisprudence that discretion in every instance must be exercised judicially and in conformity with the objectives and standards of the legislation. The application of the best interests test, if done in an individual case according to irrelevant or improper criteria, remains subject to the normal process of review on appeal.

In the same case, Justice McLachlin commented on the best interests of the child test as follows (at 149-150):

> ... The express wording of s. 16(8) of the *Divorce Act* requires the court to look *only* at the best interests of the child in making orders of custody and access. This means that parental preferences and "rights" play no role.

> ... Parliament has recognized that the variety of circumstances which may arise in disputes over custody and access is so diverse that predetermined rules, designed to resolve certain types of disputes in advance, may not be useful. Rather, it has been left to the judge to decide what is in the "best interests of the child", by reference to the "condition, means, needs and other circumstances" of the child. Nevertheless, the judicial task is not one of pure discretion. By embodying the "best interests" test in legislation and by setting out general factors to be considered, Parliament has established a legal test, albeit a flexible one. Like all legal tests, it is to be applied according to the evidence in the case, viewed objectively. There is no room for the judge's personal predilections and prejudices.

There are various ways in which judicial discretion in custody cases can be limited. The first is to direct judges to consider a non-exhaustive list of factors deemed relevant to a child's best interests. The second is to create prescriptive rules or legal presumptions in favour of or against defined classes of claimants, such as primary caregivers. A third method is to apply legal presumptions favouring specific custody arrangements, such as joint custody. Finally, the legislation can proscribe the consideration of a specific factor such as marital misconduct. See generally, Ehrcke, "Limiting Judicial Discretion in Custody Proceedings on Divorce" (1987), 6 Can. J. Fam. L. 211. As you study the statutory provisions and the case law, consider the extent to which any of these methods have been utilized in Canada.

Nature of Custody and Access: The traditional custody order entrusts sole custody to one parent after separation and allows access by the other. In *Kruger v. Kruger* (1979), 11 R.F.L. (2d) 52 (Ont. C.A.), Thorson J.A. indicated (at 78) that the effect of such an order "is to clothe that parent, for whatever period he or she is awarded custody, with full parental control over, and ultimate parental responsibility for, the care, upbringing and education of the child, generally to the exclusion of the right of the other parent to interfere in the decisions that are made in exercising that control or carrying out that responsibility". Thus, the non-custodial parent who has a right to access has been traditionally considered to have no voice in the upbringing of the child. In accordance with this view the non-custodial parent with access has the right only to visit the child or be visited by the child in accordance with the order. While the right to access includes the right to manage the child during a visit and to consent to emergency medical treatment, it does not allow the parent to influence the child's life style, education or religion. See *McCutcheon v. McCutcheon* (1982), 29 R.F.L. (2d) 11, 41 N.B.R. (2d) 263 (Q.B.); *Glasgow v. Glasgow (No. 2)* (1992), 51 N.S.R. (2d) 13 (Fam. Ct.); and *McLean v. Goddard* (1994), 3 R.F.L. (4th) 117 (N.S. Fam. Ct.).

This description of the traditional custody and access order has never been universally accepted and must be reassessed in light of recent developments. First, the cases noted above such as *Chauvin v. Chauvin* indicate that a non-custodial parent can obtain judicial scrutiny of a decision made by the custodial parent. Second, both the *CLRA* and the *DA* provide that in the absence of a contrary court order the parent with access has the right to make inquiries and to be given information regarding the health, education and welfare of the child (see s. 20(5) of the *CLRA* and s. 16(5) of the *DA*). While these statutory provisions only expressly provide for a right to be given information, the Manitoba Court of Appeal stated in *Abbott v. Taylor*, 2 R.F.L. (3d) 163, [1986] 4 W.W.R. 751, that similarly worded Manitoba legislation impliedly gave the non-custodial parent with access a right to participate in the process of making important decisions regarding the child. While the custodial parent continued to have ultimate authority to make such decisions, the court suggested that the parent with access had a right to be consulted. Finally, a majority of the British Columbia Court of Appeal held in *Young v. Young* (1990), 29 R.F.L. (3d) 113 at 209; varied (1993), 49 R.F.L. (3d) 117 (S.C.C.), that the custodial parent cannot unilaterally prevent the access parent "from sharing his or her religious views with the child, whether that sharing takes the form of discussions, observance or other activities related in some way to those views". See also *Hockey v. Hockey* (1989), 21 R.F.L. (3d) 105 (Ont. Div. Ct.).

In *Young v. Young* (1993), 49 R.F.L. (3d) 117 (reproduced below), the Supreme Court of Canada was divided sharply regarding the appropriate role of the access parent. The case involved a custodial mother who wanted to limit the access rights of a father who was a Jehovah's Witness and, in particular, to restrict the extent to which he could share his religious views and observances with his children. Justices McLachlin and Sopinka emphasized the importance of the continued involvement of non-custodial parents in the lives of their children, reflected in s. 16(10) of the *DA* which provides for a presumption of maximum contact. Justice McLachlin wrote (at 151):

> The custodial parent's wishes are not the ultimate criterion for limitations on access. ... The only circumstance in which contact with either parent can be limited is where the contact is shown to conflict with the best interests of the child.

> ... Given the interest of the child in coming to know his or her access parent as fully as possible, judges may well be reluctant to impose limits on what the access parent may say or do with the child in the absence of some evidence suggesting that the activity may harm the child.

In her view, although a custodial parent seeking to restrict access does not have to prove harm, it is an important factor. Moreover, she indicated (at 157) that generally expert evidence should be adduced in an application to restrict access.

Because he concluded that the restrictions affected the father's freedom of religion, Justice Sopinka went further (at 166–169):

> The policy favouring activities that promote a meaningful relationship is not displaced unless there is a substantial risk of harm to the child. ... Harm ... in this context, connotes ... a substantial risk that the child's physical, psychological or moral well-being will be adversely affected.

The position of Justices McLachlin and Sopinka, emphasizing the importance of a meaningful relationship between the child and the access parent, contrasts with the views of Justice L'Heureux-Dubé (La Forest J. and Gonthier J. concurring). In lengthy reasons reviewing various aspects of custody and access, she favoured an analysis that characterized the access parent (at 184) as "a passive bystander who is excluded from the decision-making process in matters relating to the child's welfare, growth and development". She specifically stated (at 184) that neither s. 16(5) nor any of the other provisions of the *DA* conferred any authority on the non-custodial parent to participate, even through consultation, in the major decisions of a child's life. While acknowledging (at 183) that an access parent could ask a court to review a custodial parent's decision on the basis that it was not in the best interests of the child, she stressed (at 187) that the courts should generally support those decisions since custodial parents were "uniquely situated to assess, understand, ensure, and promote the needs of the child".

Her willingness to respect the views of the custodial parent extended to requests for restrictions on the activities of the access parent. She began (at 184) by rejecting the proposition that the custodial parent could never forbid certain types of contact between the access parent and the child. "For example, a custodial parent, aware of sexual or other abuse by the non-custodial parent, would be remiss in his or her duty to the child not to cut off access by the abuser immediately, with or without a court order." She also indicated (at 212) that judges who are asked by a custodial parent to place restrictions on the access parent should recognize that the "custodial parent normally has the best vantage point from which to assess the interests of the child, and thus will often provide the most reliable and complete source of information to the judge on the needs and interests of that child". She questioned (at 213) the role of mental health experts in determining the child's best interests and concluded that the evidence of experts was generally unnecessary. Thus, Justice L'Heureux-Dubé would have judges determine whether any restrictions on access are appropriate by applying a best interests test, placing considerable reliance on the evidence of the custodial parent.

The two justices whose views were decisive to the outcome in *Young v. Young* and the companion case of *Droit de la famille — 1150* (1993), 49 R.F.L. (3d) 317 (S.C.C.) were Justices Cory and Iacobucci. They wrote very brief judgments indicating that in *Young* the proper application of the best interests of the child test did not support forbidding Mr. Young from discussing his religion with the children, while it did support restrictions on the father's religious activities in *Droit de la famille*.

The split in the Supreme Court was again evident in *Gordon v. Goertz* (1996), 19 R.F.L. (4th) 177, where a majority rejected Justice L'Heureux-Dubé's view that the courts should presume that a custodial parent's decision to move with a child is in the child's best interests.

Joint Custody: While orders for sole custody to one parent and access to the other continue to be used in most cases, the court has authority under both the *CLRA* and the *DA* to deviate from this model. Parents, obviously, can also agree on other forms of custody arrangements. There are several variants under which both parents continue to be actively and meaningfully involved in the upbringing of the child. Often the term "joint custody" is used to describe all of these arrangements although the term is most appropriate to describe a situation where both parents continue to have, at all times, joint legal responsibility for the child's upbringing. Courts in the 1990s also began to develop orders involving "parallel parenting", whereby each parent has final decision-making authority in some areas of a child's life. See "Joint Custody and Other Options", below.

The trend in custody cases has been away from sole custody for one parent with access for the other. In 2002, for the first time, orders granting mothers sole custody did not represent the majority of all custody awards in divorce cases. Still, they occurred in 49.7% of the cases, while fathers received sole custody in 8.5% of the awards and almost 42% of the awards contained some form of joint custody. There was considerable regional variation, with joint custody awards representing over 68% of all awards in divorce cases in Alberta and only 32% and 25% in Ontario and Quebec divorce cases respectively. See Statistics Canada, *Divorces, 2001 and 2002* (Ottawa: 2003) and The Vanier Institute of the Family, *Profiling Canada's Families III* (Ottawa: 2004).

In most forms of joint custody, the child still resides primarily with the mother. In *Phase 2 of the Survey of Child Support Awards: Final Report* (Department of Justice Canada, 2005), Dr. Bertrand, Dr. Hornick, Ms. Paetsch, and Professor Bala report that parents had shared custody in accordance with the definition in the *Child Support Guidelines* (the child spends at least 40% of the time with each parent) in only 6.2% of the divorce cases involving child support orders. The child resided primarily with the mother in almost 80% of the cases, although the authors note a trend toward more children sharing time more or less equally with both parents.

Use of New Terminology: Some cases suggest that the courts should refrain from using the traditional terms to describe living and decision-making arrangements after separation. In *Abbott v. Taylor*, above, the trial judge avoided the use of the terms "custody" and "access", choosing instead to order that the child live with the mother at certain times and with the father at other times. Additionally, he conferred on the mother "the prime responsibility for making any major decisions as to the education or medical matters or religious matters". The Manitoba Court of Appeal concluded (at 172) that it was acceptable to use "ordinary language in expressing the responsibilities which each parent should exercise with respect to the child". Twaddle J.A. explained, for the court (at 171-172):

> The language of custody orders has ordinarily followed the language of the statute. Custody has, however, several aspects. If effect can be given to the statutory intention by the use of language more easily understood by the parties to the proceedings and the child whose custody is in issue, there can be no objection to it provided all the responsibilities of custody are conferred on the parents between them. I do not prescribe this choice of language, but approve of it when required in the best interests of the child.

The mother's appeal was allowed only to the extent that the court substituted "ultimate responsibility" for "prime responsibility" in the order.

In *M. (T.J.) v. M. (P.G.)* (2002), 25 R.F.L. (5th) 78 (Ont. S.C.J.), Justice Aston stated (para. 21):

> The words "custody" and "joint custody" are often used as shorthand descriptors. However, I am convinced that many custody and access trials could be avoided if parents had to first describe, without using the words "custody" or "joint custody", what specific rights and responsibilities they wish to have, or are willing to share with the other parent. The phrase "joint custody" is emotionally charged. The parent who does not have the child on a day-to-day basis, still typically the father, pursues the Holy Grail of joint custody to avoid being reduced to the status of a mere visitor to the child. This case is typical. Inevitably, the issue is framed as a question of parental rights rather than an allocation of parental responsibilities.

A move away from the traditional terminology may be beneficial in several respects. Use of the term "custody" suggests that one parent has possession, almost akin to ownership. It also implies that there is a "winner" and a "loser". Finally, the development of new language to describe the residential and decision-making arrangements after breakdown may encourage the parents and the courts to focus on the wide range of possible options that could ensure continued involvement by both parents. See, generally, Payne, "The Dichotomy Between Family Law and Family Crises on Marriage Breakdown" (1989), 20 R.G.D. 109 at 118–126. The current uncertainty and debate over the legal effect of a traditional custody and access order provides another reason to abandon the old labels and focus directly on what role each parent should play in the child's life. At the very least, judges should spell out the intended effect of any order, even if the traditional labels are used. This will ensure that an order is given its intended effect and perhaps minimize further litigation.

Abduction of Children — The Hague Convention: Abduction of children by their parents, enforcement of custody and access orders, and wrongful removal of children from one jurisdiction to another are important topics which are only dealt with in an interstitial way in this chapter. However, a brief description of the *Convention on the Civil Aspects of International Child Abduction* (the Hague Convention) is warranted. This convention was adopted in 1980 and came into effect in 1983 to deal with the increasing problem of international child abduction by a parent. A parent who lost a custody battle, or who was afraid of doing so, could fairly easily take the child and seek out a friendly forum in which to apply for custody. Foreign custody orders were not enforceable at common law, and a court would assert jurisdiction to determine custody on the basis of the abducted child's presence in the forum. Thus, a forum-shopping abductor could obtain legal custody in the new jurisdiction and the left-behind parent's only remedy was self-help in the form of re-kidnapping.

The Hague Convention deals exclusively with civil and not criminal aspects of international child abductions. It does not address the merits of custody disputes; rather, it provides a mechanism for ensuring that custody decisions take place in the State of the child's habitual residence. The objectives of the Hague Convention, set out in Article 1, are "to secure the prompt return of children who have been wrongfully removed to or retained in any Contracting State," and "to ensure that rights of custody and of access under the law of one Contracting State are effectively respected in the other Contracting States". Article 12 provides that where a child has been "wrongfully" removed to or retained in Canada, an order will be made for return of the child to the country of his or her habitual residence, unless the application for return has been brought more than a year after the wrongful removal or retention and the child is now settled in his or her new environment. Further, limited exceptions to the rule of automatic return are set out in Articles 13 and 20.

The Hague Convention deters the wrongful removal and retention of children by depriving the abductor of any practical or juridical consequences of the removal. In focussing on prompt return as a primary objective, the Hague Convention makes it clear to potential abductors that the removal of a child to another Contracting State will likely have little value. In the event of removal or retention, the Convention seeks to secure the immediate return of the child into his or her habitual residence.

It is not necessary that the left-behind parent have a custody order; it is sufficient that under the laws of the child's habitual residence that parent had "rights of custody" within the meaning of the Hague Convention at the time of the wrongful removal or retention. The Hague Convention does not attempt to harmonize the rules regarding recognition and enforcement of foreign custody orders but to restore the *status quo* by providing for immediate return of the child.

The Hague Convention is based on the interests of children collectively rather than focussing on the best interests of a particular child. It assumes that the abduction of a child will generally be against his or her best interests and proceeds to recognize the need for international mechanisms to secure a child's return following an abduction.

Because most decisions relating to custody and access are based on the best interests of the child principle, it can be difficult for courts to apply the Hague Convention. In effect, the courts must exercise a degree of self-denial.

Canada was one of the first countries to sign and ratify the Hague Convention. All ten provinces and three territories have enacted implementing legislation, mainly incorporating the text of the Hague Convention into their law. Quebec's implementing legislation is distinctive in that it does not incorporate the text of the Convention but instead adopts the principles of the Convention using somewhat different language.

For further reading on the Hague Convention, see McLeod, "Hague Convention on the Civil Aspects of International Child Abduction" and McLeod, "Enforcement of Custody and Access Orders" in McLeod, ed., *Child Custody Law and Practice* (Toronto: Carswell, looseleaf service); MacPhail, "Responses to Inter-Jurisdictional Custody and Access Breaches" (2004), 23 C.F.L.Q. 123; and Brodkin, "The Application of the Convention — From the Practitioner's Perspective" (2004), 23 C.F.L.Q. 219.

The Hague Convention does not directly apply to custody and access disputes containing an inter-provincial rather than an international dimension. Legislative reforms in most provinces have addressed the intertwined issues of territorial jurisdiction and enforcement of custody and access orders where a child has moved across a provincial border. For an examination of the rules and principles that apply to determine 1) territorial jurisdiction to deal with the merits of a dispute with inter-provincial aspects and 2) whether custody and access orders made in one province should be recognized and enforced in another, see Hovius, "Territorial Jurisdiction and Civil Enforcement Issues in Interprovincial Custody and Access Disputes in Canadian Common Law Provinces" (2002-2003), 20 C.F.L.Q. 155. For an examination of the criminal and civil remedies available where one parent abducts a child and crosses a provincial or international border, see MacPhail, "Responses to Inter-Jurisdictional Custody and Access Breaches" (2004), 23 C.F.L.Q. 123.

Parental Alienation: When parents separate, it is not uncommon for either or both parties to make threats to steal the children's affections. Often these threats are not carried out, but reflect the hurt and anger felt around the time of separation. In a significant number of cases, however, a parent may carry out the threat to alienate the children from the other parent. Such cases often feature dramatic evidence of allegations of abuse of the children made by the alienating parent against the other parent. Because of the seriousness of the allegations, investigations are required. Investigations take time, and in that time, the alienating parent may continue to convince the children not to see the other parent. Because children who are denied contact with a parent may suffer emotional illness as adults, Family Court judges generally listen carefully to any evidence that one parent is attempting to influence the children not to have contact with the other parent.

These cases are always serious, and always a challenge for counsel. This chapter includes some commentary and case law discussing how Ontario judges deal with parental alienation.

The timely and appropriate resolution of custody of, and access to, children is critically important for individual families, but on a broader scale, has large societal effects. Children who have an interruption in their contact with one or both parents report having significantly less happy childhoods and find it harder to form stable relationships as adults (C. Williams, "Family Disruptions and Childhood Happiness" (2001), *Canadian Social Trends*, Statistics Canada Catalogue 11-008). Judges, lawyers, mental health professionals and others involved in the resolution of custody cases continue to search for ways to minimize the impact on children of the separation of their parents. The sum of the social science research is that children should have as much contact with both parents as is consistent with their best interests — however "best interests" may be defined. The work of the legal system in this aspect of family law is to try to define "best interests", both in a broad sense, and in individual cases.

2. Institutional Framework

Avoiding Litigation: Considerable effort is being placed on avoidance of litigation in custody and access disputes. A number of Canadian jurisdictions have instituted education courses to facilitate more effective resolution of parenting disputes. For example, voluntary courses have been available in Alberta since 1993. In 1996, a pilot project was introduced in Edmonton whereby any parent who wished to litigate a custody or access dispute had to attend an educational seminar. It was conducted two nights per week and covered six hours. Course evaluations were sufficiently positive that the program has been extended across the province and all Albertans in urban areas must now attend a "Parenting after Separation" course before bringing an application relating to child support, custody or access. For discussion of such programs, see Arbuthnot *et al.*, "Does Mandatory Divorce Education for Parents Work?" (1996), 34 Fam. and Conciliation Courts Rev. 60; Cossman and Mykitiuk, "Reforming Child Custody and Access Law in Canada: A Discussion Paper" (1998), 15 Can. J. Fam. L. 13 at 63–66; and Special Joint Committee on Child Custody and Access, *For the Sake of the Children* (Ottawa: Government of Canada, 1999) at 28–30. The Special Joint Committee recommended that

> [A]ll parents seeking parenting orders, unless there is agreement between them on the terms of such an order, be required to participate in an education program to help them become aware of the post-separation reaction of parents and children, children's developmental needs at different ages, the benefits of co-operative parenting after divorce, parental rights and responsibilities, and the availability and benefits of mediation and other forms of dispute resolution, provided such programs are available.

The vast majority of custody and access disputes are in fact resolved through negotiation, settlement conferences, and mediation. Only a small portion of parents, perhaps as low as three per cent, rely on judges to resolve their disputes. See Bureau of Review, *Evaluation of the Divorce Act* (Ottawa: Department of Justice, 1990).

Section 9(2) of the *DA* requires that the lawyer acting in the divorce proceeding discuss "the advisability of negotiating the matters that may be the subject of ... a custody order" and inform the client "of the mediation facilities ... that might be able to assist the spouses in negotiating those matters". See also s. 9(3).

Section 31(1) of the *CLRA* authorizes the court, at the request of the parties, to appoint a person selected by the parties to mediate any aspect of a custody dispute. Mediation conducted pursuant to this section can be either "open" or "closed", at the option of the parties.

See s. 31(4) and (7). In "open" mediation, what goes on and is said during mediation can be revealed if a settlement is not reached. In "closed" mediation, the opposite occurs and everything is confidential. The latter type is prevalent.

The Special Joint Committee reported in *For the Sake of the Children*, at 32, that Quebec legislation requires divorcing parents to attend at least one information session about the benefits of mediation. If the parents then decide to use mediation, they are entitled to up to six sessions at public expense. The legislation permits opting out of the process, including the information session, in cases of domestic violence. The committee recommended (at 33) that "divorcing parents be encouraged to attend at least one mediation session to help them develop a parenting plan for their children". It added:

> Where there is a proven history of violence by one parent toward the other or toward the children, alternative forms of dispute resolution should be used only when the safety of the person who has been the victim of the violence is assured and where the risk of violence has passed. The resulting parental plan must focus on parental responsibilities for the children and contain measures to ensure safety and security for parents and children.

For further reading regarding mediation of custody and access disputes, see Bailey, "Unpacking the 'Rational Alternative': A Critical Review of Family Mediation Claims" (1988), 8 Can. J. Fam. L. 61; Austin, Jaffe, and Hurley, "Incorporating Children's Needs and Views in Alternative Dispute Resolution Approaches" (1992), 8 C.F.L.Q. 69; Irving and Benjamin, *Family Mediation* (Toronto: Sage Pub., 1995); Phegan, "The Family Mediation System: An Art of Distributions" (1995), 40 McGill L.J. 365; Landau *et al.*, *Family Mediation Handbook*, 2nd ed. (Toronto: Butterworths, 1997); Goundry *et al.*, *Family Mediation in Canada: Implications for Women's Equality* (Ottawa: Status of Women Canada, 1998); Irving and Benjamin, "Child Custody Disputes, Family Mediation and Proposed Reform of the *Divorce Act*" (1999), 16 C.F.L.Q. 413; Noble, *Family Mediation: A Guide for Lawyers* (Toronto: Canada Law Book, 1999); Baris, M.A. *et al.*, *Working with High-Conflict Families of Divorce: A Guide for Professionals* (Northvale, New Jersey: Jason Aronson Inc., 2001); and Taylor, A., *Family Dispute Resolution: Mediation Theory and Practice* (San Francisco: 2002, Jossey-Bass).

Arbitration of custody and access disputes is a more recent and less used innovation than mediation. In "Incorporating Children's Needs and Views in Alternative Dispute Resolution Approaches" (1992), 8 C.F.L.Q. 69, the authors suggest arbitration is particularly suitable to deal with specific issues relating to post-separation childcare arrangements. As examples, they mention (at 77-78) "access disputes that centre on whether or not to include mid-week overnight visits or what time the weekend begins". They list (at 78) the following advantages of arbitration:

1.   a time-limited and cost-effective procedure that promises clients some movement towards a decision;

2.   protecting parents from using an assessment or mediation to stall for time and maintain the status quo;

3.   focusing on parents' strengths and specific plans rather than on wide-ranging allegations;

4.   avoiding raising negative topics about early history of parents and marital conflict that are usually outlined in an assessment;

5.   clients feel that they have been heard in an informal setting (relative to court) and by a mental health professional with experience in children's and parents' adjustment to separation and divorce; and

6.   arbitration can take careful consideration of children's wishes without disclosing the exact nature of their wishes to their parents.

In *Hodge v. Legault* (1998), 36 R.F.L. (4th) 211 (Ont. Gen. Div.), the court held that, where the parents agree to arbitration and choose the arbitrator, an arbitration award should be enforced unless the parent contesting its validity clearly shows that the award is not in the child's best interest. See also *Lenney v. Lenney* (1996), 24 R.F.L. (4th) 381 (Alta. Q.B.) where the parents had agreed to joint custody and the mediation of any disputes. The court refused to deal with a mother's application for sole custody until mediation had been tried.

A more recent innovation that incorporates aspects of arbitration is the use of Parenting Coordinators. Parenting Coordinators are commonly used in large centres in the United States and are becoming more common in Ontario. A Parenting Coordinator is often a mental health professional, but can be a lawyer. All Parenting Coordinators must take training, and must, pursuant to the Ontario *Arbitration Act*, have 14 hours of domestic violence screening training. A Parenting Coordinator is used to resolve minor disputes, such as small one-time variations to the residency schedule to accommodate vacations or other special occasions; incidents of custody, such as haircuts, ear piercing, participation in activities; and discipline issues, involving things like bedtimes and homework completion. Parenting Coordinators begin by trying to mediate such disputes between the parents. If the parents cannot agree after a reasonable time of discussion, the retainer contract that they sign empowers the Parenting Coordinator to arbitrate and make a written, final decision. The use of Parenting Coordinators is intended to avoid a return to court for relatively minor adjustments to the parenting regime. The advantages are that these issues can be resolved expeditiously and without the use of lawyers. Also, Parenting Coordinators often help parents learn strategies to communicate without conflict. However, the use of a Parenting Coordinator can be expensive. Parenting Coordinators in the Toronto area charge as much as $300 per hour. If, however, the cost of litigating an issue is taken into account, even this seemingly high rate is a bargain. At the time of writing of this edition, Toronto family law lawyers routinely charge $450 per hour and up. For an excellent discussion of the role and training of Parenting Coordinators, see Baris, J.A. *et al. Working with High-Conflict Families of Divorce: A Guide for Professionals* (Northvale, New Jersey: Jason Aronson Inc., 2001).

The Office of the Children's Lawyer: Given the difficulty of determining a child's best interests, it is not surprising that many parents, lawyers, and judges turn to professionals with expertise in child development. In Ontario, s. 112 of the *Courts of Justice Act*, R.S.O. 1990, c. C.43, authorizes the Office of the Children's Lawyer (OCL), at the court's request, or at the request of any person, to investigate and make a report concerning custody and access. Alternatively, after a request is made for the involvement of the Children's Lawyer, the OCL can decide to appoint a lawyer to represent the interests of the child, without a formal written report being made. Lawyers are appointed to the OCL panel from time to time in all of the various Ontario counties. As cases arise, local members of the bar who have been appointed to the panel will be asked by the OCL to represent the children involved. The Toronto office also employs a staff of full-time lawyers.

Ontario has devoted significant resources to the development of the OCL, and the representation of children in difficult custody and access cases is widespread in Ontario. Representing children raises unusual issues for lawyers. Can the lawyer for a child tell the court what a child has said? If so, how should that evidence be presented? Is child's counsel bound by the same rules of solicitor/client confidentiality? The Ontario Court of Appeal resolved most of these issues in *Strobridge v. Strobridge* (1994), 4 R.F.L. (4th) 169 (Ont. C.A.). It was held that, unless the parties agree otherwise, a lawyer for the OCL cannot both advocate and give evidence about a child's wishes and preferences. Since *Strobridge*, an OCL social worker often assists the OCL lawyer by interviewing the children about their wishes. The social worker then gives evidence and is available for cross-examination by counsel for the parents.

Another OCL response to the *Strobridge* case was to make its participation in a case conditional upon the parents' agreeing that the lawyer would present the child's views to the court. A standard form order, that the parties had to accept if they wanted the OCL to become involved, allowed the OCL's "submissions to include the views and preferences of the child where they can be reasonably ascertained and/or a position based on the interests of the child". Justice Granger strongly disapproved of this practice in *Zelinka v. Zelinka* (October 24, 1995), Doc. 318/95, [1995] O.J. No. 3275 (Gen. Div.). The OCL today still requires a standard form consent order, but the current wording says only that the OCL may make submissions including "the position(s) advanced on behalf of the child(ren)". See *Peltier v. Manderson* (2004), 47 R.F.L. (5th) 359 (Ont. C.J.). Currently, if the position that it wants to put forward requires facts to be adduced that are not going to be put into evidence by one of the parties, the OCL will usually arrange for a social worker to testify rather than having the OCL panel lawyer make submissions that amount to giving hearsay evidence about what the children's preferences.

The OCL continues to be an extremely helpful resource to parents who are litigating the issues of custody and access. Often the involvement of the OCL will resolve the case. Because judges tend to take the recommendations of the OCL lawyer or social worker seriously, many parents will settle the case upon finding out what the recommendations are.

Assessments — Section 30 of the CLRA: Section 30 of the *CLRA* permits the court to appoint "a person who has technical or professional skill to assess and report to the court on the needs of the child and the ability and willingness of the parties ... to satisfy the needs of the child". The differences between an OCL's report and a *CLRA* assessment were explored briefly in *Parniak v. Carter* (2002), 30 R.F.L. (5th) 381 (Ont. C.J.); *Leonardo v. Leonardo* (2002), 35 R.F.L. (5th) 100 (Ont. S.C.J.); and *Van Bilsen v. Van Bilsen* (2003), 48 R.F.L. (5th) 448 (Ont. S.C.J.). In essence, the OCL's report is a social worker's investigation of the facts, often accompanied by a recommendation. A *CLRA* assessment is a mental health professional's clinical assessment of the child and the parents that usually also contains a recommendation. A *CLRA* assessment is more intrusive and time-consuming, but it is also a fuller examination of the situation of the parents and the child. In the following excerpt, Professor Bala explores the role of experts in determining the best interests of a child.

BALA, "THE BEST INTERESTS OF THE CHILD IN THE POST-MODERN ERA: A CENTRAL BUT PARADOXICAL CONCEPT"

Harold Niman and Gerald P. Sadvari, ed., *Family Law: "Best Interests of the Child"* (Toronto: Law Society of Upper Canada, 2000) 1 at 33–42 (Footnotes omitted)

Best interests decisions are intended to formulate a plan that will be "best" for a child's physical, emotional, intellectual and spiritual development. Given the difficulty of making this type of inherently predictive decision, it is understandable that decision-makers often turn for assistance to professionals with expertise in child development and human relations, who may appear to offer the promise of a "scientific basis" for making the decision. Social workers, psychologists and psychiatrists provide a range of different types of assessments to the judges, lawyers and parents who are making best interests decisions. These assessors can provide valuable information and insights about children and parents, and these mental health professionals often play a very significant role in the decision-making process. Their role is not, however, uncontroversial. Like the other professionals involved in these cases, the values, biases and competencies of assessors affect their judgments about the best interests of children. ...

A parent may retain his or her own expert to conduct an assessment, and have that person prepare a report or testify in court. Such an expert is likely to have access to only one parent, and may be tainted with the suspicion that the expert was selected because of known predispositions about child related disputes. While the opinion of an expert retained by one party is admissible, and will sometimes have a decisive effect on a case, typically the opinion of an assessor appointed by the court or with the consent of both parties is likely to be more influential. If the report contains a recommendation, and most of them do, it effectively places a tactical onus on the party seeking to challenge its conclusion. Frequently, this means that a case will be settled on the basis of the court appointed assessor's recommendation and not even proceed to trial, as the party not favoured by the report recognizes that there is little to be gained by taking the case to trial. Judges, however, repeatedly emphasize that it is they, and not assessors, who bear the ultimate responsibility for making a best interests determination in court.

Lawyers may employ a variety of techniques to challenge the recommendation of an assessor. It may be argued that the assessor was unaware of certain facts, or misunderstood their significance. Sometimes the mental health professional will be more directly challenged, either in terms of methodology, judgment or values.

An assessment by a social worker, psychologist or psychiatrist is not needed in every case where child related issues are raised in pleadings. The process of assessment is expensive, and can be intrusive for the child and parents. As observed by the Alberta Court of Appeal in [*Tucker v. Tucker* (1998), 41 R.F.L. (4th) 404 at 413] ...: "an assessment should not be ordered routinely or without good reason. Nor should a child be subjected ... to needless assessments at the whim of the non-custodial parent in the hopes of obtaining a favourable opinion." As recognized by this decision, judges should only order an assessment when there appears to be a genuine contest over a significant child related issue.

Most judges welcome the involvement of mental professionals in seriously contested best interests cases. Some judges, however, are less receptive to involving assessors. In *Mantesso v. Mantesso*, [1991] O.J. No. 643 (Ont. Gen. Div.), Justice Fleury ... observed that the assessment process is time consuming and intrusive, as well as expensive, either for the parties or the government. He went on to comment [at para. 3]:

> I have no doubt that many assessments are conducted without much justification. They are resorted to as a means of defusing a potential conflict over issue of custody and access. They may, in some instances, represent the easy way out for gun-shy lawyers who would rather settle than vigorously defend their client's interests.

Justice Fleury recognized that assessments could facilitate settlements, but ruled that this was not in itself a reason to order them [at paras. 7 and 8]:

> It is true that an assessment may accelerate the settlement of the dispute without resort to the very disruptive and emotionally charged atmosphere of a full trial. Assessors normally manage to elicit information without having to resort to adversarial techniques and this may be conducive to an amicable settlement of the dispute. However they may also be influenced by a variety of undisclosed factors which might have a significant impact on their conclusions. Assessments of this kind are hardly the result of a very scientific analysis. They fall within the realm of behavioral science and are subject to the vagaries of these most imprecise sciences. Assessments are powerful tools which should not be used without good reasons.

The judge suggested that a justification for ordering an assessment would be that the dispute seems so intense that all the relevant evidence might not come out, or if there appears to be a parent-child problem that requires expert analysis.

The approach of Fleury J. in *Mantesso* was further developed by Granger J. in his 1994 Ontario Divisional Court ruling in *Linton v. Clark* (1994), 10 R.F.L. (4th) 92. The mother had custody pursuant to a separation agreement since the parties' separation five years earlier. In response to the mother's request for increased child support and to define access rights, the father applied for custody. In preparing for trial, the mother brought a motion for an assessment, alleging that the children were suffering from emotional problems caused by their visits with the father. The children were already undergoing psychological counselling for behavioural and emotional adjustment problems, including nightmares and sleep terrors. The request for an assessment was dismissed, a decision affirmed by Granger J. [at 101]:

> Assessments should not be ordered in all cases as a vehicle to promote settlement of custody disputes. If the legislature had intended that assessments were to be a vehicle to settle custody disputes the legislation would have mandated assessments in all cases.
>
> In my view, assessments *should be limited* to cases in which there are *clinical* issues to be determined, in order that such assessments can provide expert evidence on the appropriate manner to address the emotional and psychological stresses within the family unit in the final determination of custody.

These judicial comments about "gun-shy" lawyers and about the expense and delay involved in the assessment process are problematic. As Austin and Jaffe, two mental health professionals, note in a critical commentary on *Linton* ["Clinical Comments on *Linton v. Clarke*" (1995), 10 R.F.L. (4th) 92 at 94]: "The court system is not in a good position to criticize custody assessments as being too expensive and slow."

While lawyers and judges have legitimate concerns about the cost and delay of the assessment process, the expense and time for an assessment is relatively minor compared to the costs and delay involved in litigation process as a whole. Although some assessments are of poor quality or biased, this does not justify questioning the value of *most* assessments, including the value of *possibly* promoting settlement. Like judicially supervised pretrial conferences, assessments can serve *either* to facilitate a settlement *or* to ensure a "better trial." Although an assessment often results in a settlement, it is important for assessors to recognize that their role is to provide information and opinions to those who will actually make best interests decisions (whether judges, lawyers or parents), and not to try to coerce the parties into accepting their recommendation as the basis for a settlement.

One can ask also how a judge might apply the "test" of *Linton v. Clark*, namely that there must be a "clinical issue" before an assessment is ordered. The key concept of "clinical issue" is left undefined by Granger J., and indeed arguably was satisfied in that case since the children were already suffering from emotional problems for which they were receiving psychiatric treatment. As Austin and Jaffe note:

> For some judges a clinical reason may imply serious mental health problems for one of the parties or well-defined allegations of child abuse. In reality, any two parents who are prepared to put themselves and their children through the financial and *emotional* cost of a custody trial have a clinical problem.

Although the decisions in *Mantesso* and *Linton v. Clark* represent views that are not uncommon among judges and lawyers, it is submitted that they are in some critical respects inconsistent with Ontario Court of Appeal judgments that continue to place reliance on the recommendations of assessors to decide cases and to emphasize the value of tools like assessments to bring forward evidence of a child's wishes.

In ... *Weaver v. Tate* (1990), 28 R.F.L. (3d) 188, the Ontario Court of Appeal specifically rejected the suggestion of Granger J., in his trial decision in that case, that it was inappropriate for an assessor to make a recommendation about custody:

> Although s. 30 [of the *CLRA*] does not direct that such a recommendation be made, we are of the view that it should be open to an assessor to do so in cases where he or she considers it appropriate and where the court does not direct ... to the contrary.

This ruling suggests that the relatively narrow approach of Granger J. in *Linton v. Clark* does not represent the only judicial view in Ontario, with other judges taking a more receptive approach to the role of assessors in best interests decisions.

Judicial controversy about the role of assessments is not limited to the Ontario courts. Some Supreme Court of Canada best interests decisions also reveal continuing judicial ambivalence about the role of mental health professionals and the knowledge they can bring to the court process. A pair of Supreme Court decisions rendered in 1993 dealt with the circumstances in which a judge should restrict the right of a non-custodial father during access visits to take his child to religious services — in these cases of the Jehovah's Witness faith. In her decision in *Young* (1993), 49 R.F.L. (4th) 117, Madame Justice L'Heureux-Dubé suggested that experts should be used sparingly in cases where the best interests of a child are in dispute:

> ... [E]xpert evidence should *not* be routinely required to establish the best interests of the child. In my view, it is a modern-day myth that experts are always better placed than parents to assess the needs of the child. Common sense requires us to acknowledge that the person involved in day-to-day care may observe changes in the behaviour, mood, attitude, and development of a child that could go unnoticed by anyone else. The custodial parent normally has the best vantage point from which to assess the interests of the child, and thus will often provide the most reliable and complete source of information to the judge on the needs and interests of that child. ...

> In the absence of clear legal presumptions about the best interests of children, judges have increasingly come to rely on the recommendations of experts. ... believing that such experts possess objective, scientific knowledge and can in fact "know" what is in the best interests of the child. However, expert testimony, while helpful in some and perhaps many circumstances, is often inconclusive and contradictory. ... That this should be so is not surprising, since such assessments are both speculative and may be affected by the professional values and biases of the assessors themselves.

The other judges were less sceptical about the role of experts, but also appeared cautious about their role, with Cory and Iacobucci JJ. commenting: "... [W]e also agree with both our colleagues that expert evidence is, while admittedly helpful in some cases, *not always necessary to establish the best interests of the child*; that question can be determined *normally* from the evidence of parties themselves and the testimony, where appropriate, of the children concerned." [Emphasis added.]

While the Supreme Court expressed some doubt about the value of the opinions of mental health professionals in determining the best interests of the child in these 1993 judgments, the 1994 decision of the Supreme Court in *Catholic C.A.S. of Metro Toronto v. C.M.* (1994), 113 D.L.R. (4th) 321 appeared to place great reliance on their opinions. In this child protection case the Supreme Court of Canada held that a child who had been in the care of foster parents for over four years should be made a permanent ward without parental access, with the aim of having the children adopted. Madam Justice L'Heureux-Dubé wrote a unanimous decision for the Court, stating [at 347]: "Within the realm of best interests perhaps the most important factor in the present case, as probably in many others, is regard to the psychological bonding of a child to her or his foster family."

In *C.M.*, the trial judge had actually ordered that the initial temporary wardship order should be terminated and the child returned to her biological mother who had overcome various problems and was able to care adequately for the child. The Supreme Court, however, overruled this trial decision, relying heavily on the evidence of mental health experts, in particular that of a child psychiatrist retained by the child's lawyer. Justice L'Heureux-Dubé referred to this "strong evidence" as establishing the child's wishes and her view of the foster family as her "real family". The psychiatrist also reported on the severe "negative impact" of access visits with the natural mother on the child.

What is noteworthy about *C.M.* for our purposes is the very different attitude towards mental health professionals in comparison to the two earlier decisions. In *C.M.*, the Supreme

Court regarded the experts' assessment of the facts of the case as critically important evidence. Further, Justice L'Heureux-Dubé placed enormous, and quite uncritical weight on "psychological bonding," a concept developed by the very behavioural scientists whose "values and biases" she had challenged in her 1993 decision in *Young*. Nowhere in her judgment in *C.M.* does she even acknowledge the controversial aspects of concepts like "psychological parents" and "bonding." Indeed, American courts dealing with situations like those in *C.M.* have returned children to their biological parents, albeit with much fuller discussions of the competing psychological theories.

While individual judges are giving mixed signals about the value of evidence from mental health professionals in determining the "best interests" of the child, it seems inevitable that both the work of individual assessors and the work of mental health researchers will continue to be very influential for resolving these cases. At the very least, in most contested cases the best way to bring forward the child's views and perspectives will be through the assessment process or by a report from a social worker. Assessments are also a valuable source of information about the parents, and can often have a desirable role in helping parents to make their own best interests decisions rather than leaving judges to make these decisions. Mental health professionals have an important role to play in court proceedings involving children and adolescents, but given the inherently speculative and value-based nature of many of the assessments they are asked to make, it is understandable that their views provoke controversy in the legal profession and among the judiciary. There may also be substantial overlap between what mental health professionals are doing and what is expected of a judge, so a degree of tension between the professions is scarcely surprising, but ultimately their roles are distinct. To be a good professional in one of these disciplines requires an appreciation of the role, competencies, limitations and ambivalences of the other.

Although a child is not a party to a custody and access proceeding, there are various mechanisms that permit a court to ensure that the child's views are taken into account. One of these is through legal representation for the child, a topic explored by Professor Bala in the following excerpt. Some of the others are explored later in this chapter.

BALA, "THE BEST INTERESTS OF THE CHILD IN THE POST-MODERN ERA: A CENTRAL BUT PARADOXICAL CONCEPT"

Harold Niman and Gerald P. Sadvari, ed., *Family Law: "Best Interests of the Child"* (Toronto: Law Society of Upper Canada, 2000) 1 at 26–31 (Footnotes omitted)

It is reflective of the nature of childhood that the child is the one with the greatest stake in best interests litigation, yet the child is not a party to the court process. A range of different strategies are used to try to ensure that judges are presented with information about a child's circumstances, interests and views. In Ontario the government funds the Office of the Children's Lawyer to act on behalf of the child in contested best interests cases. The Office of the Children's Lawyer has social workers and lawyers on staff, as well as a panel of specially trained professionals in private practice who are appointed to act in individual cases.

... In cases where parents have separated and are litigating, pursuant to s. 112 of the *Courts of Justice Act* the court may *request* an investigation to be carried out by a social worker from the Office, and a report made to the court. Under s. 89(3) of the *Courts of Justice Act* the court may *request* that legal representation be provided by the Office for a child. In any case where one or both of the parents requests the involvement of the Children's Lawyer, the judge decides whether to make an order to contact the Office of the Children's Lawyer, and the Office determines whether to provide legal or social work services or both (or not to become involved at all). The Office has to ration access to its "free" services and is most likely to become involved if there is a seriously contested issue related to custody or access, or the case raises safety concerns.

Perhaps understandably there is some controversy over the role of the Office of the Children's Lawyer. Some judges may resist the involvement of an agency that might appear to be encroaching on the judicial role of deciding the child's best interests, while some parents (or their lawyers) will be concerned that the position of the Children's Lawyer may be given too much weight by the court to their prejudice as litigants.

In a decision [*Reynolds v. Reynolds*, [1996] O.J. No. 2230 (Ont. Gen. Div.)] declining the request of a mother to involve the Children's Lawyer, Fleury J. expressed [at para. 2] a concern that doing so may "implicate the children very directly in the litigation ... [and] can cause untold harm to impressionable children who may suddenly feel inappropriately empowered against their parents." In a later decision [*Bazinet v. Bazinet* (1998), 42 R.F.L. (4th) 140 at 141 (Ont. Gen. Div.)], Justice McCartney quoted this passage, and also declined a father's request for involvement of the Children's Lawyer, commenting that if the children's "input ... is required the Court is always at liberty to deal directly with the children if it is deemed necessary."

In times of fiscal restraint, there is undoubtedly a need to limit access to the services of the Office of the Children's Lawyer, and it is for this reason that the Office has the right to determine whether and how to respond to a request for services. There are cases in which it is apparent from the court documents that the issues are relatively straightforward and the outcome quite predictable; these cases may not justify the extra time, expense and intrusiveness that results from involving the Office of the Children's Lawyer. However, in practice in cases that raise serious issues related to custody or access, most judges are receptive to involving the Children's Lawyer.

As suggested by McCartney J. some judges are prepared to meet the child personally and may interview children as an alternative to involving the Office of the Children's Lawyer. In my view, having a trained lawyer or social worker interview a child to ascertain his or her views about a case will generally be less intrusive and traumatic for a child than having a judge conduct an interview with the child. While judicial interviews with a child are authorized by statute, most judges are understandably reluctant to interview a child or have the child testify in a best interests proceeding, recognizing their lack of training with the delicate art of interviewing children. The court or judge's chambers may be an intimidating setting for a child to communicate effectively with a stranger, like the judge. In any event, children caught in a dispute may be reluctant to express their views to a judge, or may suffer later trauma from having been forced by a judge to publicly "take sides." There may also be real procedural concerns about how a judge will make use of the results of any interview that is not conducted in the presence of the parents and counsel. The involvement of the Office of the Children's Lawyer can provide an independent source of information and advocacy about a child's needs and circumstances. Often this voice will push the parents in the direction of settlement, or if a judge is forced to decide a case the social worker or lawyer from the Office of the Children's Lawyer will ensure that all appropriate evidence about the child is before the court.

There were a number of conflicting judicial pronouncements on whether the child's counsel should be representing the child's "best interests" or advocating based upon the wishes of the child (in those cases where children have capacity and are clearly expressing wishes.) The Office of the Children's Lawyer has clarified the position of child's counsel as acting as the "child's legal representative" and "advocate for a child client so that the child's interests are understood and communicated to the parties and to the court." Child's counsel "does not represent the 'best interests' of the child [as that is] the issue to be decided by the courts." [See Wilson McTavish, *Office of the Children's Lawyer — Policy Statement — Role of Children's Counsel* (Toronto: April 3, 1995.]

A major focus of child's counsel is to gather information about a child, including interviewing a child who is old enough to express views. The Policy Statement of the Office directs that where "the information about the child's interests differs from the child's independent and consistent views and preferences, counsel should advance a position on behalf of the child consistent with child's views and preferences." However, if the child's counsel believes that the child is being influenced by one parent, that counsel may decline to advocate for the outcome sought by the child, though counsel should ensure that the wishes of the child are before the court as well as information about how the child may have been influenced by one parent. As recognized by E.M. MacDonald J. [in *Boukema v. Boukema* (1997), 31 R.F.L. (4th) 329 at 348 (Ont. Div. Ct.)]: "it is not the function of the Office of the Children's Lawyer merely to 'parrot' the child's stated wishes ... particularly so when it is apparent that the child's stated wishes have been influenced by one ... parent."

The Official Policy of the Children's Lawyer also provides that in cases in which parents have come to a settlement, child's counsel should not interfere, recognizing that parents who can make their own arrangements are entitled to autonomy. In intact families, children do not have a veto over parental plans, nor should they be permitted to block arrangements just because parents have separated.

In *Strobridge v. Strobridge* (1994), 4 R.F.L. (4th) 169, Justice Osborne of the Ontario Court of Appeal explained how counsel for the child (at that time called the Official Guardian) should bring evidence before the court in a contested case:

> Counsel retained by the Official Guardian is entitled to file or call evidence and make submissions on all of the evidence. In my view, counsel is not entitled to express his or her personal opinion on any issue, including the children's best interests. Nor is counsel entitled to become a witness and advise the court what the children's access-related preferences are. If those preferences should be before the court, resort must be had to the appropriate evidentiary means. ... The Official Guardian, through counsel, will see that evidence going to the issue of the children's best interests is before the courts.

In theory the effect of *Strobridge* is that in contested cases, counsel for a child must be prepared to lead evidence through a social worker from the Office of the Children's Lawyer or other sources about a child's preferences. However, as Osborne J.A. noted: "in many, if not most, cases the parties will agree that counsel representing the children may advise the court of the children's preferences."

NOTES AND QUESTIONS

1. The reported cases continue to indicate that some judges are more likely to order assessments than others. See *Parniak v. Carter* (2002), 30 R.F.L. (5th) 381 (Ont. C.J.); *Leonardo v. Leonardo* (2002), 35 R.F.L. (5th) 100 (Ont. S.C.J.); *Kramer v. Kramer* (2003), 37 R.F.L. (5th) 381 (Ont. S.C.J.); *Brisson v. Brisson* (2003), 45 R.F.L. (5th) 253 (Ont. S.C.J.); and *Sheikh v. Sheikh* (2004), 5 R.F.L. (6th) 456 (Ont. S.C.J.). The biggest area of dispute is whether a judge must first find that there are "clinical issues" before ordering an assessment, or whether the presence of "clinical issues" is only one factor of several that can justify ordering an assessment. "Clinical issues" tend to include things such as obvious mental health issues for either or both parties, or for the children; unusually high conflict between the parents; the special needs of a child; or a parent or child's drug dependancy. If a court must first be satisfied that there are clinical issues, the question whether this threshold is crossed may itself become part of the litigation process. More importantly, an assessment may not be ordered where it would have been helpful. In *Parniak*, Justice Kurkurin concluded: "Although a clinical issue may be an excellent reason for a court to obtain the assistance of a professionally prepared assessment, it is not the only reason that an assessment might be ordered".

2. While the evidence and opinion of experts is accorded great weight in most cases, the ultimate decision must be made by the court. It is an error of law to effectively delegate the decision-making authority to a psychiatrist,

psychologist or social worker: *McClean v. McClean* (1985), 49 R.F.L. (2d) 235, 66 N.B.R. (2d) 65 (C.A.) and *Strobridge v. Strobridge* (1994), 4 R.F.L. (4th) 169 (Ont. C.A.). If the judge is convinced that the best interests of a child require a disposition other than that favoured by the expert, he or she must make an order effectively overruling the expert. The weight given to the expert's testimony or report will be affected by a number of factors such as the following: What are the expert's qualifications? How thorough was the assessment of the parties and child? Did the expert have an opportunity to assess all parties? Did he or she understand the nature of the proceedings? Did any of the parties lie to the expert? How recent was the assessment? Was the expert aware of all relevant facts?

3. For further reading on assessments, see Chisholm, "Preparing Your Client for Assessment or Mediation" (1987), 1 C.F.L.Q. 385; Bala, "Assessing the Assessor: Legal Issues" (1990), 6 C.F.L.Q. 179; Barbara A. Chisholm and H. Christina MacNaughton, *Custody/Access Assessments: A Practical Guide for Lawyers and Assessors* (Toronto: Carswell, 1990); Austin, Jaffe, and Hurley, "Incorporating Children's Needs and Views in Alternative Dispute Resolution Approaches" (1992), 8 C.F.L.Q. 69; Mayers, "Effective Processes in Custody/Access Assessments" (1994), 11 C.F.L.Q. 147; and Bala, "Children, Psychiatrists and the Courts: Understanding the Ambivalence of the Legal Profession" (1995-6), 13 C.F.L.Q. 261.

4. In *New Brunswick v. W. (R.)* (2004), 3 R.F.L. (6th) 444 (N.B. C.A.), the New Brunswick Court of Appeal held that a mother did not have a constitutional right to state-funded legal counsel in a custody dispute. The court held that the *Canadian Charter of Rights and Freedoms* did not apply because there was no state action.

5. In *S. (P.T.), Re* (2004), 8 R.F.L. (6th) 194 (B.C. Prov. Ct.), a court indicated that the boys involved in a custody dispute between their father and a woman appointed as guardian under their deceased mother's will needed a lawyer. However, the province had ceased funding the Family Advocate Program and so the Attorney General refused to appoint a lawyer for the boys. In a further application for an order requiring the appointment of a state-funded lawyer, the court held that it had no jurisdiction to make such an order. In particular, Provincial Judge Brecknell held that s. 7 of the *Charter* did not apply because there was no state action in a private custody dispute. The judge commented (para. 112):

> Unfortunately, as has often been the case in recent years the abdication by the Crown of its moral and ethical responsibility to children by providing assistance to the Court in a family matter where the Court has concluded that a family advocate would be beneficial leaves the Court in the difficult position of trying to ensure the protection of the rights of the Boys while at the same time ensuring that the hearing is conducted fairly and impartially for all the parties.

6. In *F. (M.) c. L. (J.)* (2002), 211 D.L.R. (4th) 350 (Que. C.A.); leave to appeal refused (2002), 317 N.R. 394 (note) (S.C.C.), a court-appointed lawyer represented a boy, aged ten. The mother subsequently brought a motion requesting that this lawyer be removed because she intended to argue for the renewal of visits between the boy and his father rather than urging respect for the boy's wish not to visit his father. The lawyer accepted a psychologist's recommendation that it was in the boy's best interests to renew his relationship with the father. A Superior Court Justice dismissed the motion on the basis that the lawyer's role was to present both the views of the boy and any evidence relating to his best interests so that the court could reach a proper determination. At the hearing of the mother's appeal, the boy's lawyer stated that she would not be able to continue to represent him if she were not entitled to make recommendations or submissions that did not accord with the boy's wishes.

The Quebec Court of Appeal allowed the appeal and directed that the boy's lawyer be replaced. It held that, since the boy was capable of expressing his wishes and of instructing counsel, the lawyer should act as his advocate and urge the court to respect his wishes. It noted that the lawyer had the professional right and duty to advise the boy as to the possible consequences of his wishes and to counsel him as to what she believed to be in his best interests. However, in the court's view, the boy's lawyer had to act as his advocate and simply put forward evidence and make submissions to support his wishes.

7. Regarding the different ways in which children can participate in family law proceedings generally, see Bala, Talwar and Harris, "The Voice of Children in Canadian Family Law Cases" (2005), 24 C.F.L.Q. 221.

3. Factors Relevant to the Custody Decision

(1) Introduction

This section of the casebook focuses on some of the factors used to determine a child's best interests. The following extract stresses that the focus should be on the particular circumstances of each child.

WAKALUK v. WAKALUK

(1976), 25 R.F.L. 292, 1976 CarswellSask 4 (Sask. C.A.)

BAYDA J.A. (dissenting): — ... The issue of custody is without doubt the most important one — and was so treated by counsel at the hearing of this appeal — and the most troublesome. While at the hearing of the appeal the parties concentrated their attention on this issue they were not so minded at the hearing of the petition, even though the issue was far from settled. From the standpoint of custody the hearing of the petition was, in my respectful view, quite unsatisfactory. Virtually no evidence was directed to this issue. The parties primarily concerned themselves with adducing evidence to show whether, on the basis of the many marital battles engaged in by them, one or the other of them should be favoured by the trial judge in his determination of the issue of cruelty.

No one bothered to bring forward much information in respect of the two individuals who of all the persons likely to be affected by these proceedings least deserve to be ignored — the children. We know their names, sex and ages, but little else. Of what intelligence are they? What are their likes? Dislikes? Do they have any special inclinations (for the arts, sports or the like) that should be nurtured? Any handicaps? Do they show signs of anxiety? What are their personalities? Characters? What is the health of each? (This list of questions is not intended as exhaustive or as one that is applicable to all contested cases but only as illustrative of those questions which may be relevant.) In short, no evidence was led to establish the intellectual, moral, emotional and physical needs of each child. Apart from the speculation that these children are "ordinary" (whatever that means) there is nothing on which to base a reasoned objective conclusion as to what must be done for *this* child and *that* child, as individuals and not as mere members of a general class, in order that the welfare and happiness of each may be assured and enhanced.

Nor was any direct evidence led to show which of the parents, by reason of training, disposition, character, personality, experience, identification with a child's pursuits, ability to cope with any special requirements of a child's health, religious observance and such other pertinent factors (again the list is intended as only illustrative of matters which may be relevant), is best equipped to meet the needs of each individual child. The evidence presented on behalf of each side was principally, if not exclusively, geared to do one thing: show how badly one spouse treated the other. Such evidence is hardly a proper basis upon which to make a determination — a crucial one indeed from the standpoint of the children — as to which parent is best suited to meet the needs of the children and upon which to found an order for custody. How inconsiderate one spouse is of the other, or how one spouse reacts towards the other in a marital battle and the ability of a spouse to come out of a marital battle a winner, either actual or moral, are not high-ranking factors, if factors they be at all, in determining where a child's happiness and welfare lie, particularly whether such happiness and welfare are better assured by placement with one parent or the other. ...

NOTES AND QUESTIONS

1. Do s. 24 of the *CLRA* and s. 16 of the *DA* dictate the "child oriented approach" urged by Bayda J.A. in *Wakaluk*? Note that the provincial legislation has a longer list of factors to consider in determining a child's best interest than its federal counterpart.

Bill C-22, which contained amendments to the custody and access provisions of the *DA*, contained the following:

In determining what is in the best interests of the child, the court shall consider all the needs and circumstances of the child, including:

(a) the child's physical, emotional and psychological needs, including the child's need for stability, taking into account the child's age and stage of development;

(b) the benefit to the child of developing and maintaining meaningful relationships with both spouses, and each spouse's willingness to support the development and maintenance of the child's relationship with the other spouse;

(c) the history of care for the child;

(d) any family violence, including its impact on (i) the safety of the child and other family members, (ii) the child's general well-being, (iii) the ability of the person who engaged in the family violence to care for and meet the needs of the child, and (iv) the appropriateness of making an order that would require the spouses to cooperate on issues affecting the child;

(e) the child's cultural, linguistic, religious and spiritual upbringing and heritage, including aboriginal upbringing or heritage;

(f) the child's views and preferences, to the extent that those can be reasonably ascertained;

(g) any plans proposed for the child's care and upbringing;

(h) the nature, strength and stability of the relationship between the child and each spouse;

(i) the nature, strength and stability of the relationship between the child and each sibling, grandparent and any other significant person in the child's life;

(j) the ability of each person in respect of whom the order would apply to care for and meet the needs of the child;

(k) the ability of each person in respect of whom the order would apply to communicate and cooperate on issues affecting the child; and

(l) any court order or criminal conviction that is relevant to the safety or well-being of the child.

The Bill, which died when Parliament was prorogued in late 2002, defined "family violence" to include "behaviour by a family member causing or attempting to cause physical harm to the child or another family member, or causing the child or another family member to reasonably fear for his or her safety or that of another person, but does not include acts of self-protection or protection of another person."

2. What should be the response of the trial judge if he or she does not believe that the parties are presenting the most helpful and relevant information? Is this a situation in which a court-ordered assessment of the child and the parties is especially useful? Would independent representation of the child solve the problem? Should the judge actively seek information from the parties?

In *Gordon v. Gordon* (1980), 23 R.F.L. (2d) 266 (Ont. C.A.), the court stated (at 271):

A custody case, where the best interest of the child is the only issue, is not the same as ordinary litigation and requires, in our view, that the person conducting the hearing take a more active role than he ordinarily would take in the conduct of a trial. Generally, he should do what he reasonably can to see to it that his decision will be based on the most relevant and helpful information available. It is not necessary for us to go into details. In some instances it may well be sufficient for him to put the suggestion to counsel that a particular witness be called or information produced and, if the response is a negative one, to draw the appropriate inference from the absence of the evidence, depending on his assessment of the explanation given for such absence in all the circumstances.

In *Cooney v. Cooney* (1982), 27 R.F.L. (2d) 136, 36 O.R. (2d) 137, the Ontario Court of Appeal considered an appeal of a custody order on the grounds that there was insufficient information before the trial judge upon which he could properly determine the issue of custody and that the trial judge unduly emphasized the wife's adulterous conduct. Justice Cory, for the majority, noted that an appellate court should not lightly disturb the result reached at trial. He continued (at 142):

> It is true that the trial judge indicated that the majority of the evidence was concerned with which party was at fault for the failure of the marriage. On the other hand, he obviously considered that he had heard sufficient evidence and seen enough of the parties to enable him to render his decision. No doubt, from time to time there will be cases which will require the trial judge to seek additional evidence to assist him. This may be a particularly important step if, for example, the child has special gifts or handicaps, unique needs or attachments to one parent. However, there is no indication here that Andrew suffered from an emotional or physical handicap. Rather, he appears to be a bright youngster doing well at school who pursues with relish all the physical activities that one might expect a healthy nine-year-old to enjoy. Clearly, he gets along well with his father and can enjoy skating, skiing and boating with him. Obviously, the trial judge did not consider that additional evidence was required to reach a decision in this case.

In dissent, Justice Wilson quoted at length from Bayda J.A.'s reasons in *Wakaluk*. She stated (at 146): "To make a determination of the custody issue in the absence of an adequate evidentiary foundation on which to apply the 'best interests' test must surely constitute palpable error."

The British Columbia Court of Appeal held in *Cundy v. Irving* (1998), 37 R.F.L. (4th) 401 that the trial judge's extensive questioning of witnesses in a custody and access dispute was appropriate (at 402):

> The judge was ... properly carrying out the kind of inquiry one is often driven to in custody cases, where the court is not concerned with which of two adversaries has the better case, but with the best interests of the child. In that context, a judge will be justified more than he or she otherwise would, in asking questions he or she feels are necessary to make the critical decision concerning which of two parents the child should be placed with.

3. In "Hearing the Voice of Children" (1992), 8 C.F.L.Q. 95, Madam Justice Huddart and Ms. Ensminger stress (at 96) the need for a "child centred approach":

> It is obvious that the best chance of predicting what regime will be in a child's best interests will come if the entire decision-making process is centred on the child. If we learn as much as we can about the children of a relationship, their needs, their affective ties, their capacities, their interests, and as much as we can about the abilities of those adults willing to care for them, we will be able to make orders that will take best advantage of the adult abilities available to fulfill the children's needs.

In turn, this leads them to stress that the views of the child must be heard and considered. They suggest (at 99-100) that this may cause a significant shift in focus:

> ... [W]hat are the questions about which the child's views are needed? In some cases the child herself may identify the important questions. The question of choice of custodial parent may not be the important question or even one that should be posed.

> This approach requires an analysis of the issues. Usually the fundamental issue between the parents in a contested case is one of control. Who is to have the final say when there is disagreement? Who is to control the life of the child? These disputes over control seem to result most frequently from a parent wanting to exclude the other parent from the children's lives in the interest of a second family, or from deep differences in cultural values between the parents, or both.

> A child may have a view on who should have that power, but in many cases the child is more concerned with more ordinary issues — where will he sleep and be fed regularly; where and when can he take his friends to visit; who will help him fix his bike; who will take her to Tuesday soccer practice and Saturday game; can he call his mom if he's with his dad; can she sleep over with her friend when she's spending the weekend with mom; can she still spend Thanksgiving at her grandparents; camp with her cousins — and the myriad of other everyday important things like that.

> No one, least of all the child, expects a judge to order the child's life on a daily basis. But the child does want the judge to understand that her physical, emotional, and social needs are as important as her parents' wishes. Listening to a child talk about her life and her parents' role in it should assist the judge in assessing the parents or other willing adults and their plans. Knowing that the child is going to talk about her needs to the judge might also help the parents make those plans, taking into account

the child's views as to her own needs. A child's talking about her needs will certainly ensure that the decision-making process centres on her.

4. In "The Rap on the Supreme Court, or, What About the Interests of All Children?" in Harold Niman and Gerald P. Sadvari, ed., *Family Law: "Best Interests of the Child"* (Toronto: Law Society of Upper Canada, 2000), Professor Thompson states that the focus on determining the best interests of a particular child leads to case-by-case decision-making without the benefit of "any narrowing presumptions, any procedural burdens, [and] any adversarial formalities". He suggests that this undervalues the interests of all children because it discourages settlement, encourages litigation with an ever-expanding scope, and hides and permits discrimination. He argues (at 213) that the courts should recognize these effects and then "build back into the 'best interests' test some intermediate premises that give some substantive content to that test, in the interests of all children".

5. Partly because custody and access determinations are so fact specific, appellate courts tend to defer to the findings and results at trial. The Supreme Court of Canada addressed the appropriate standard of review in detail in *Van de Perre v. Edwards* (2001), 19 R.F.L. (5th) 396. It stressed that custody and access decisions were inherently exercises in discretion involving a case-by-case consideration of the unique circumstances of each child. It concluded that it was the role of the trial judge to exercise this discretion and that appellate courts could only intervene where the judge erred in law or seriously misapprehended the evidence.

(2) Interim Custody and the Continuity Principle — The *Status Quo*

MARSHALL v. MARSHALL

(1998), 42 R.F.L. (4th) 180, 1998 CarswellNS 183 (N.S. C.A.)

[In an application to vary an interim order, the father, who was unrepresented, agreed that the court should make a final order of custody. The appellate court found that the father's consent was misinformed because the chambers judge suggested that there was little, if any, difference between an interim and final custody order. In its reasons, the court set out the appropriate approach to interim orders.]

ROSCOE J.A. (for the court): — ... The issues before the court at the commencement of the application and those for which the parties prepared were *interim* custody and *interim* child support. The test to apply on an interim custody application is as set out by Justice Kelly in the following passage from *Pye v. Pye* (1992), 112 N.S.R. (2d) 109 (N.S. T.D.) at paragraph 5:

> ... [T]he test in such an application was properly set out in *Webber v. Webber* (1989), 90 N.S.R. (2d) 55, 230 A.P.R. 55 (F.C.), by Daley, J.F.C. at p. 57:
>
>> Given the focus on the welfare of the child at this point, the test to be applied on an application for an interim custody order is: *what temporary living arrangements* are the least disruptive, most supportive and most protective for the child. In short, the *status quo* of the child, the living arrangements with which the child is most familiar, should be maintained as closely as possible. With this in mind, the following questions require consideration.
>>
>> 1. Where and with whom is the child residing at this time?
>>
>> 2. Where and with whom has the child been residing in the immediate past? If the residence of the child is different than in #1, why and what were the considerations for the change in residence.
>>
>> 3. The *short-term needs* of the child including:
>>
>>> (a) age, educational and/ or preschool needs;
>>>
>>> (b) basic needs and any special needs;
>>>
>>> (c) the relationship of the child with the competing parties;

(d) the daily routine of the child.

4. Is the current residence of the child a suitable temporary residence for the child taking into consideration the short-term needs of the child and:

(a) the person(s) with whom the child would be residing;

(b) the physical surrounding including the type of living and sleeping arrangements, closeness to the immediate community and health;

(c) proximity to the preschool or school facility at which the child usually attends;

(d) availability of access to the child by the non-custodial parent and/ or family members.

5. Is the child in danger of physical, emotional or psychological harm if the child were left temporarily in the care of the present custodian and in the present home? (emphasis added)

The focus is on the status quo and the short-term living arrangements for the child. Although in this case the parties had been separated for a few years, and had consented to the first order, the test that should have been applied was the same: if there is no reason to change the existing situation, that situation should continue until the trial. There is authority for variation of interim orders: see *Foley v. Foley* (1993), 124 N.S.R. (2d) 198 (S.C.).

LiSANTI v. LiSANTI

(1990), 24 R.F.L. (3d) 174, 1990 CarswellOnt 219 (Ont. Fam. Ct.)

VOGELSANG PROV. J.: — Because of the unusual history of this proceeding, I thought it best to give some brief written reasons. An *ex parte* motion came before me on 11th January 1990. Being satisfied that the requirements of R. 17 had been met, I granted an interim order that the father, the moving party, would have custody of the two children of the marriage, Andrew and Antonette, who are 4 years old and 9 months old, respectively. The order directed the London Police, among other peace officers, to locate the children and deliver them up to the father. Later that day, a motion to set aside my order was brought before Genest Prov. J. by the wife. Genest Prov. J. purported to "suspend" my order and direct that the issue of interim custody be heard before me at a later date. Thus, this is the third appearance required to resolve the issue.

The husband and wife have been married for about four years and maintained, almost throughout their cohabitation, a matrimonial home in London. The husband, a draughtsman employed by the Ontario government, arrived home from work on 2nd January 1990 to find that his wife and children had gone. Only a few articles of clothing had been taken with them. It appears that the husband called around to find his family's whereabouts. The best he could accomplish was that they might be at the Women's Community House, a "transition" residence for the protection of battered women. In fact, that was their location.

In the affidavit evidence before me there were many substantial disagreements between the parties as to events in the past. Without passing yet on the relevance of those events, it struck me that they could be characterized, in the main, as individually trivial. That was the assessment of the wife's attending physician in his report of 22nd January 1990 but I am not as confident as the physician that the wife's rather precipitous flight to the shelter was "appropriate" in all of the circumstances. ...

As to the merits of the motion as it was argued before me, it is enough to say that the matter was hotly contested. Mr. Winninger pressed his position that the fact that the mother was the primary caretaker of the children in the past should determine the issue. He says that

I should make an inference, from that fact, that there exists a closer emotional bond between her and the children. With great respect to Mr. Winninger, I am unable to do so. There is nothing in the affidavit material which would satisfy me that either the mother or the father is unable to look after these two children in a perfectly acceptable, loving and caring manner in the short time between now and trial; nor is there any undisputed and cogent evidence of a more substantial bond with either parent.

The family lived together in the former matrimonial home until the sudden departure of the mother with the children. She now lives in a transition state and her future accommodation is not assured. However one may characterize the vicious squabbles between the husband and the wife, there is no doubt that their substance is absolutely disputed by the parties. The wife alleges that she was "abused" and Mr. Winninger asserts that she must not be "forced back" to the matrimonial home. It follows, in his argument, that the children must therefore remain in the shelter to avoid a separation from their mother. He says that her position as their mother has created a status quo which should not now be upset.

This is a question of interim custody. There is no reason why, even with extensive discovery, the trial of this action cannot be heard within 12 or 14 weeks. It is not my place to decide the ultimate issue. That is for the trial judge. The only question before me is where the best interests of these children will be assured between now and the trial.

Mr. Mamo argues that the existing status quo for the children is their residence with the father in their accustomed home. The father says in his affidavit that his religious associates of the Jehovah's Witness faith have arranged to assist him with child care while he is at work. Although Mr. Winninger thought that arrangement less than desirable, there is not a tittle of evidence that the father, with this available assistance, could not look after the children completely adequately in their usual surroundings. I agree that the mother unilaterally deprived the children of their accustomed home and the life that they had by removing them when she took her dispute with their father into her own hands. There was no evidence before me of any attempt by the mother to reach an agreement about custody with the father, or to bring an application either for exclusive possession of the matrimonial home or for interim custody of the children prior to her abrupt departure.

Mr. Mamo stresses that the actions of the wife were in contravention of the legislated equal custodial rights of a mother and father set out in s. 20(1) of the *Children's Law Reform Act*. I agree that the departure of the wife and the taking of the children, on substantially disputed grounds, was a complete denial of the husband's custodial rights which cannot stand to her credit on this motion. The best interests of the children, were they ever first considered by her, would have militated against such a result. ...

In the result, there is no clear and cogent evidence which would justify the mother's removal of the children from their accustomed environment. Their best interests, it seems clear to me, can be safeguarded by their father in the former matrimonial home and an interim order will go granting him their custody. The mother should have generous access to the children.

RENAUD v. RENAUD

(1989), 22 R.F.L. (3d) 366, 1989 CarswellOnt 292 (Ont. Dist. Ct.)

BOLAN D.C.J.: — The plaintiff's claim is for custody of the children of the marriage, namely, Melissa Anne Renaud, born 29th July 1985, and Nicole Lea Renaud, born 28th October 1987. The defendant counterclaims for the same relief.

The status of the parties immediately before the separation was that the plaintiff (hereinafter called the wife) had assumed the traditional role in the family of being the primary caregiver for the children and looking after the home. The defendant (hereinafter called the husband) was steadily employed and devoted much of his spare time to raising the children.

Since the separation, the husband has had de facto custody of the children and the wife has had regular access pursuant to the order of the Honourable Judge Perras dated 23rd November 1988. It is important to examine how it came about that the husband obtained de facto custody of the children. ...

I find as a matter of fact that the wife was locked out of the matrimonial home on 14th September 1988 and had no alternative but to leave without the children. The only alternative would have been for her to accede to his consistent demands that she return to live with him in the matrimonial home and that they would "work things out". I accept her evidence that he had slapped her before on two separate occasions and abused her verbally by hurling vile names at her. She was afraid to return to live with him. ...

Both parties are warm and loving parents and both are capable of giving fit and proper care to the children. I cannot say that one home is better for the children than the other or that the plan of one parent for the children is any better than that of the other parent. The issue boils down to which parent should be the primary caregiver.

I am satisfied that the wife has rehabilitated herself from the marriage and is now on firm footing. She sought out and obtained full-time employment. Her plan to raise the children is simplistic but not uncommon with that of many other single mothers who parent their children. She impresses me as an unsophisticated person who is deeply attached to her children and has their best interests at heart.

The husband impresses me as a devoted father who is quite capable of managing the best interests of his daughters. Since the separation, his mother, Solange Renaud, has looked after the children while he is at work. I was impressed with Solange Renaud. She is a 48-year-old widow and has a deep attachment to the children. However, my main concern is the character of the husband. Following the separation, he acted in a mean-spirited manner in not allowing the wife access to the children. The only access she had to the children up to 23rd November was on one occasion when the husband attended with the children at the residence of the wife's brother where she was living. The wife had tried on many occasions to contact the children by telephone but she was repeatedly denied this meagre access. His refusal to deliver to the wife her bicycle is an example of his vindictiveness.

I am also concerned about the husband's fits of anger. During the marriage he was abrasive towards the wife and has continued to be so since the separation. I accept the wife's evidence that he physically assaulted her on two previous occasions during the marriage. I also accept her evidence that he verbally abused her during the marriage and also since the separation. Although the husband during the past year has parented the children in a fit and proper manner, I am not satisfied that it is in their best interests that he continue as the custodial parent.

In my view what is in the "best interests" for these two girls of tender years is that they reside with their mother. She was their primary caregiver from birth up until her banishment from the home by the husband. The husband has proven himself as a good parent; however, in the final analysis the girls are better off with their mother. ...

SPENCER v. SPENCER

(1980), 20 R.F.L. (2d) 91, 1980 CarswellBC 505 (B.C. C.A.)

[The parties separated in December 1979 when the respondent mother left the matrimonial home. Two children, aged approximately six and eight, remained with the father. In April 1980 the trial judge awarded custody to the mother although the father had done an "admirable job" in looking after the children following separation. He concluded that both parties were partly responsible for the separation and that each could provide a suitable home. He decided that the children should reside with the mother because she had been the primary caregiver before separation and could provide "that 'something' that only mothers seem to be able to provide". The Court of Appeal held that the trial judge had erred in stating that "mothers have an edge over fathers" because they are able to spend more time with their children. The court noted (at 97) that the father's employment as a teacher allowed him "to spend a good deal more time with the children than the respondent". The court next addressed the effect of the fact that the children had been with the father since separation.]

TAGGART J.A.: — ... The learned trial judge did not deal with what, in my opinion, is the most important issue in the whole case, namely, whether the lives of the children should be disrupted by taking them from a stable and secure environment to a new environment where they must, so to speak, begin life afresh. He appears to have wholly disregarded the evidence on this issue.

Without placing blame on anyone for the breakup of the marriage, it seems obvious to me and is borne out by the evidence that the departure of the respondent had a staggering effect on the children.

The children have just recovered from the trauma. They have strong roots in the rural community where they live. For years they have lived in the same house. All their friends are there. They are happy and contented.

In the absence of the appellant they are in the constant care of a Mrs. Lambert who lives only a short distance from their home. This is an important relationship and should not be lightly disturbed.

The respondent admits that the children are happy and does not dispute the fact that they live in a stable and secure setting.

In the light of this evidence is it safe to take these children out of this environment? While I have no doubt that the respondent is a good mother and loves her children deeply, I do not think that it is possible to say on the evidence before us that there is not a grave risk in causing the children to be moved out of the Salmon Arm area at this time.

I do not think that it is possible to over-emphasize the need of young children to feel secure in every way. This feeling of security, which they now enjoy, may well be impaired if they are taken away from all their friends and the physical setting with which they are familiar.

I have not overlooked the fact that the learned trial judge, who saw the parties and heard the witnesses, placed stress on the fact that the respondent has a "zest for life" and that the children will not have the advantage of receiving the love and affection that only a mother can give. These are important matters but, in the circumstances of the case at bar, it seems to me that on balance the need of the children not to be uprooted from their stable and secure environment where they are living happily outweighs the need to live with their mother.

To leave the children where they are is not a gamble. To change the status quo is a gamble which I am not prepared to take.

I would allow the appeal and give custody of the children to the appellant, with reasonable and generous access to the respondent. In this respect it is of extreme importance that the children have a strong and continuing relationship with the respondent. I assume that both parties will do everything within their power to achieve this result. This will require great sacrifices on the part of both parents, financially and otherwise, but I am certain that both parties will be willing to bear these burdens.

MOORES v. FELDSTEIN

(1973), 12 R.F.L. 273, [1973] 3 O.R. 921, 1973 CarswellOnt 156 (C.A.); leave to appeal refused [1973] S.C.R. xii (note) (S.C.C.)

[The plaintiff, respondent, sought custody of her daughter. The daughter, within days of her birth, had been delivered by the mother into the care of the appellants, the Feldsteins. The mother hoped that this would lead to reconciliation with her husband, who was not the father of the child. Within months, the mother requested the return of the child but proceedings were not begun until almost two years after the birth of the child and the child was almost four years old when the matter came to trial. The trial judge, finding that the child had not been abandoned and that the mother was not unfit, awarded custody to the mother. The Feldsteins appealed. The Ontario Court of Appeal decision is most important for its application of the "best interests of the child" test in a custody dispute between a parent and non-parents. See generally, Blood Ties, below. The excerpt that follows focuses on the effect of the child's established, stable position with the Feldsteins.]

DUBIN J.A.: — ... After the most anxious deliberation at my command I conclude that the learned trial Judge did fall into error in both such respects, and I would allow the appeal and hold that the child should be left with the Feldsteins. ...

It must be observed that in this case the mother, who has given up a child to the care and custody of others, seeks its return. Under such circumstances it is important in my opinion that the Court consider and give adequate weight to the present position of the child. As Laidlaw J.A. put it in *Re Duffell*, [1950] O.R. 35 at 39 (C.A.); affirmed [1950] S.C.R. 737:

> While the child will obtain great benefits I have mentioned if the plan of the appellant be carried out, I am deeply conscious of the fact that the child cannot be removed from the custody of the respondents, after the great care and devotion given to it for more than twenty months, without much hardship to the child by reason of the change and perhaps much disturbance to its affections. Such a change of custody should not be made lightly. I think that before it is made by order of the Court, the person who asks for the order should show to the satisfaction of the Court that the proposed removal will enure to the welfare of the child. ...

In my opinion, this is an important consideration in this case which, along with others, was overlooked by the learned trial Judge. I cannot help but feel in the circumstances of this case that serious harm may be occasioned by removing this bright, alert little girl from her present surroundings and placing her in the custody and care of someone who would now likely be quite a stranger to her. Unless the result of such a change is shown to be in the interests of the child, I would hesitate to risk the effect of such a disturbance.

This little girl has been with the Feldsteins, as I have already mentioned, for almost four years. In the report of the Official Guardian the little girl is described as follows: this child "is a fair, blue-eyed healthy little girl, appears lively and curious. She is bright and alert and enjoys watching television and reflecting on what she sees ... The child is very fond of singing, loves clothes, and has a strong independent streak ... She has three pet cats and a live rabbit." She is taken to the nearby Church of England on Sundays.

Mrs. Feldstein is described also in the Official Guardian's report "as a very warm-hearted person with a strong motherly instinct". Mr. Feldstein is described to be "a rather aesthetic young man with a sensitive personality who enjoys his home".

The Official Guardian's report went on to say that there was a strong atmosphere of warmth and care in this home, and there could be little doubt that the child receives excellent physical and emotional care. There is a possibility that she might be strongly over-indulged, but the care that she receives would appear to be beyond reproach. ...

I do not feel that I am bound by precedent to return the child to its mother when I have grave concern about its future if I were to do so, merely because the mother now desires her return. In my opinion it would be unfair to the child and not in her interests to expose her to such a risk.

In my view, since the evidence does not show that the child will benefit by the mere fact of its blood relationship with its mother, it cannot be said that the welfare of the child in its broadest sense will best be served by its being returned to her. In its present surroundings it will have the loving care of a father and a mother who will be able to devote their full time to her in her formative years. There will be no risk of the uprooting of the child from its present happy surroundings having a serious effect on her. Without the benefit of omniscience the safest course, in my opinion, is to leave the little girl where she is and where, I have every reason to believe, she will be loved and well cared for.

NOTES AND QUESTIONS

1. On an interim application, courts tend to be reluctant to change an established childcare regime if it is working reasonably well. This was explicitly noted in *James v. Ross* (2003), 49 R.F.L. (5th) 76 (Sask. Q.B.); *Kimpton v. Kimpton* (2002), [2002] O.J. No. 5367, 2002 CarswellOnt 5030 (S.C.J.); and *Winton v. Lofranco* (2004), 7 R.F.L. (6th) 444 (Ont. S.C.J.). The impact of the status quo argument may be undercut if the parent with whom a child does not reside after separation acts quickly. The court may then look upon the situation before separation as the status quo and may well favour the parent who was the primary caregiver before separation. Acting quickly is the key. The longer the interim arrangement lasts, the harder it will be to convince a court that a different residential arrangement is in a child's best interests.

2. As *LiSanti* indicates, the courts sometimes frown on attempts at self-help. See also *Moldowan v. Moldowan* (1979), 13 R.F.L. (2d) 1 (Sask. C.A.); *Miller v. Miller* (1999), 1 R.F.L. (5th) 391 (Ont. C.A.); leave to appeal refused (1999), (sub nom. *W.M. v. D.M.*) 250 N.R. 198 (note) (S.C.C.); and *Donley v. Donley* (2008), 51 R.F.L. (6th) 164 (Ont. S.C.J.). What should Ms. LiSanti have done, in Judge Vogelsang's view? Do you agree with the result in *LiSanti*?

In the recent case of *Donley v. Donley*, the mother secretly left the family home with the couple's two children, took them to her mother's house in a nearby city, and enrolled them in a new school. The husband acted quickly and brought a motion within days. The mother alleged that the father had serious anger management problems and an addiction to pornography. Such allegations usually cause judges to exercise caution until an investigation has occurred. However, Justice Harper, after receiving affidavits and hearing argument, concluded that the mother had failed to prove her allegations and had not established the need to act unilaterally. He stated (paras. 98 & 99):

> There is no reason that Mrs. Donley could not have contacted her lawyer and attempted to negotiate on notice a proper resolve to the custody issue. I also find that Mrs. Donley could have, and should have, come to court first on proper notice to Mr. Donley in order to get a court order prior to up-rooting the children in the dramatic way that she did.

> I find that Mrs. Donley's plan is ill-conceived and self-serving, without regard to the best interests of the children. ...

Declaring that the real *status quo* was for the children to live in the family home in their rural community, he awarded interim custody and interim exclusive possession of the home to the father. See the positive comments on this case in Epstein and Madsen's *This Week in Family Law*, FAMLNWS 2008-13.

The *LiSanti* case should be contrasted with *Sovereign v. Sovereign* (2004), 3 R.F.L. (6th) 190 (Ont. S.C.J.), where Justice O'Neill stated (para. 16): "In my view, a court should be careful not to measure, with too much nicety, the actions taken by a spouse under a situation of alleged domestic violence." The mother and father were divorced and the couple's children lived with the mother. When the father applied for an order allowing the children to live with him, the court made an interim order requiring the mother not to change the children's residence. Shortly thereafter, the mother moved with the children into a shelter some considerable distance away. She alleged that she was being harassed by the father and his family and that a Crown Attorney and victim consultant/advocate had advised her to move into the shelter. The court decided that the children's best interests required them to stay with the mother at her new location, at least on an interim basis.

3. Maintaining the least disruptive environment pending trial may be complicated if one parent moves. In *Howard v. Howard* (1999), 1 R.F.L. (5th) 375 (Ont. S.C.J.), the mother surreptitiously moved to London with three children. Her leaving was not in response to an emergency or for reasons of immediate safety. The father continued to live in the matrimonial home in the village of Nairn some twenty kilometres from London. The children's school was located three doors down from the home. Both parents sought interim custody. The father was a long-distance truck driver who had to be away from home frequently. However, he proposed that his mother, who had looked after the children previously while both parents worked, could assist him. Justice Aston referred to *LiSanti* and stated (at 376):

> I agree wholeheartedly that one of the principles that the court must sustain in these matters is to discourage self-help and, rather, encourage the parties to put the matter before a judge if they cannot resolve custody and access issues between themselves. The fact that the children have been in London with their mother for a little over a month is not to be considered a factor in her favour in the decision now to be made. The only *"status quo"* that counts for anything is the *"status quo"* that existed up to 7 July [the date of the move].

Later, he added (at 378):

> The circumstances under which Ms. Howard established a new residence for the children should not give her an advantage in the decision to be made, but neither should she be punished for leaving as she did. The only consideration is the best interests of the children.

> It is in the best interests of the children to remain in the day-to-day care of their mother but also in their best interests, for now, to return to the matrimonial home in Nairn. That is not Ms. Howard's first choice, but she does claim temporary exclusive possession of the matrimonial home as an alternative and expresses her willingness to return to Nairn if the court determines that to be in the children's best interests. The adjustment of the children to the parental separation may be facilitated if other changes in their lives are deferred and minimized. Mr. Howard is apparently able to live in the rental property he owns in Nairn where his mother now resides.

In the result, the court awarded interim exclusive possession of the matrimonial home and interim custody to the mother on condition that she return to Nairn. See also *Harari v. Harari* (2001), 20 R.F.L. (5th) 59 (B.C. S.C. [In Chambers]), where a mother was granted interim custody, but was required to return her child from Ontario to British Columbia in order to preserve the status quo as much as possible until the trial of the custody dispute. The father faced a criminal charge arising from threats directed at the mother.

In *Leung v. Leung* (1998), 44 R.F.L (4th) 121 (B.C.C.A.), the mother left the matrimonial home and moved from Richmond to a nearby community. The Master granted joint interim custody of two young children to both parents, but ordered that they reside primarily with the mother. The father appealed, arguing that the status quo involved residence in the matrimonial home in Richmond where the children attended school and where their friends and relatives lived. The British Columbia Court of Appeal upheld the decision, partly on the basis that, prior to separation, "the status quo involved the mother having day-to-day care of the children, and access to the father when he was not working" (at 123). Is this a redefinition of "status quo"? Can this case be best understood as illustrating a tendency to favour the primary caregiver?

4. Examine s. 20(4) of the *CLRA*. Where s. 20(4) applies, the parent with whom the child resides has legal custody until a separation agreement or order provides otherwise. In interim proceedings the court is likely to preserve that situation unless it poses some risk for the child.

In *Richer v. Thompson* (1985), 46 R.F.L. (2d) 240 (Ont. Dist. Ct.) the court held that s. 20(4) only applies if there is clear evidence that the parent with whom the child does not reside after separation consents or acquiesces in the arrangement. In that case, the mother took the child without the father's consent on separation. The father took no action for a month because he hoped that a reconciliation could occur. When it became apparent that this would not happen, he seized the child. The mother sought an interim custody order and argued that s. 20(4) applied to give her legal custody that should be maintained until trial. The court held that s. 20(4) was not triggered in these circumstances. Nevertheless, the mother was granted interim custody on the basis that this was in the best interests of the child.

Where s. 20(4) does apply the parent whose custody rights are suspended can only regain custody through a separation agreement or court order. "Self-help" in the form of a seizure of the child or a refusal to return him or her after a visit could be a criminal offence. Section 283(1) of the *Criminal Code* specifies: "Everyone who, being a parent ... of a person under the age of fourteen years, takes, entices away, conceals, detains, receives or harbours that person, whether or not there is a custody order in relation to that person made by a court anywhere in Canada, with intent to deprive a parent ... who has the lawful care or charge of that person, of the possession of that person, is guilty of (a) an indictable offence and is liable to imprisonment for a term not exceeding ten years, or (b) an offence punishable on summary conviction." Consent of the other parent is a defence (s. 284), but consent of the child is not (s. 286). If the action "was necessary to protect the young person from danger of imminent harm or if the person charged with the offence was escaping from danger of imminent harm", then no offence is committed (s. 285). It should also be noted that no proceedings may be commenced under s. 283(1) "without the consent of the Attorney General or counsel instructed by him for that purpose": s. 283(2). Regarding the interpretation and application of these provisions, see *Cook v. R.* (1984), 40 C.R. (3d) 270 (N.S. C.A.); leave to appeal refused (1984), 65 N.S.R. (2d) 90 (S.C.C.); *R. v. Adams* (1993), 19 C.R. (4th) 277 (Ont. C.A.); *R. v. Mendez* (1997), 32 O.R. (3d) 67 (C.A.); and *R. v. Dawson* (1996), 25 R.F.L. (4th) 181 (S.C.C.). See generally, Johnstone, "Parental Child Abduction Under the *Criminal Code*" (1987), 6 Can. J. Fam. L. 271 and Diamond, "Enforcement of Custody and Access Orders" (1989), 4 C.F.L.Q. 303. See also s. 36(2) of the *CLRA*.

5. Consider the following situation: A mother and father have two children, aged four and six. Their relationship is deteriorating and the mother concludes that it is at an end. Without the father's knowledge or consent she takes the children with her and moves into a friend's house. When the father discovers these facts he demands that the mother and children return to the matrimonial home. The mother refuses to comply and will not allow the father to take the children with him.

    (a) Has the mother committed a criminal offence?

    (b) Who has lawful custody of the children?

    (c) Could the father obtain a court order under s. 36(2) of the *CLRA*?

    (d) What alternative courses of action were available to the mother?

6. Where there are concerns about a child's care, a court may be convinced on an interim application that the *status quo* that has existed since separation should not continue until trial. See, e.g., *G. (D.) v. Z. (G.D.)* (1997), 30 R.F.L. (4th) 458 (B.C. Master). In *Sider v. Sider* (2004), 10 R.F.L. (6th) 171 (Ont. S.C.J.), a 12-year-old girl lived with her mother in Markham during the week and with her father in Wellandport on weekends. The custody trial was scheduled to take place in October, but the girl wished to start the new school year in Wellandport. Justice Wildman noted (para. 5) that the safe and usual approach would be to maintain the status quo, but nonetheless the Justice was persuaded to change the arrangement.

7. Professor Bala writes in "The Best Interests of the Child in the Post-Modern Era: A Central But Paradoxical Concept", Harold Niman and Gerald P. Sadvari, ed., *Family Law: "The Best Interests of the Child"* (Toronto: Law Society of Upper Canada, 2000) at 49-50:

> While the courts emphasize that each best interests decision has to be made taking account of all of the circumstances of the parent[s] and children, there are three related factors that are highly predictive of how judges *and* parents decide which parent should have primary responsibility for the care of the children after separation: gender, primary caregiver role and continuity of care.

In most Canadian families that are intact, the mother is the primary caregiver for the children. ... While fathers are more involved with childcare than they were a generation ago, it is still most common for the mother to have primary responsibility for childcare in a family where parents reside together, especially if children are of pre-school age. ... It is not surprising that when parents are in the process of separating, a judge will most frequently decide that the child should live, at least on an interim basis, with the parent who was the primary caregiver when the parents lived together. The primary caregiver, who is usually the mother, provided most of the care when the parents lived together and has the most experience meeting the child's needs. If a case goes to trial, a judge making a best interests decision is also likely to be influenced by a consideration of which parent had primary caregiving responsibilities while the parents and children lived together, and will be reluctant to upset a status quo which may have developed since separation. Further, especially when children are going through the traumatic process of parental separation, most children benefit from stability and continuity of care.

8. Judges deciding interim applications are aware that their decisions often have long-term consequences. Recall that the judge in *Perrier v. Perrier* (reproduced in Chapter 5) declined to make interim custody and interim possession orders partly to avoid making decisions that could determine the final custody arrangements. See also *Bailey v. Bailey* (1987), 5 R.F.L. (3d) 354 (Ont. Dist. Ct.).

In *Stefanyk v. Stefanyk* (1994), 1 R.F.L. (4th) 432 (N.S. S.C.), both parents were still living in the home when the father petitioned for divorce and filed a motion for interim custody of the couple's two children. Justice Saunders concluded that the parents could no longer live together in the home. Acknowledging that there was limited and conflicting evidence, the judge stressed (at 439) that interim orders "are intended to provide a reasonably acceptable solution to difficult problems which the parties are unable, by themselves, to resolve" and that "the trial judge may well come to conclusions substantially different than mine". In the circumstances, the impact of the interim order granting sole custody to the mother was considerably lessened by providing that the unemployed father would return to the home each day to care for the children while the mother went to work.

In several other cases dealing with interim arrangements, the courts have attempted to ensure continued, meaningful involvement by both parents in the child's upbringing. In *Rix v. Rix* (1993), 50 R.F.L. (3d) 22 (P.E.I. S.C.), the judge explicitly declined (at 25) to make an interim custody order, but indicated that the children should remain in the day-to-day care and control of their father with very liberal access by the mother. Presumably such a "non-order" preserved joint custody until trial. There appear to be an increasing number of cases in which some form of joint custody or shared custody is explicitly ordered on an interim basis, See, e.g., *McDonald v. McDonald* (2000), 13 R.F.L. (5th) 143 (Ont. S.C.J.); *Robblee v. Reid* (2003), 34 R.F.L. (5th) 142 (Ont. S.C.J.); and *Collins v. Petric* (2003), 41 R.F.L. (5th) 250 (Ont. S.C.J.).

9. The longer the trial of a custody dispute is delayed, the greater will be the impact of the interim arrangement. Section 26 of the *CLRA* implicitly recognizes this fact by attempting to ensure prompt judicial determination of custody applications under that Act.

10. There are cases in which judges have cautioned that interim custody arrangements, whether by court order or agreement, should not be given undue weight. In *R. v. R.* (1983), 34 R.F.L. (2d) 277 (Alta. C.A.), Kerans J.A. stated (at 284):

> We should remind ourselves that interim custody is just that: a makeshift solution until the correct answer can be discovered. If a judge could tell what is best at the outset, there is no need for an interim order. Interim orders are designed to minimize conflict between parents and cause the least harm to the child pending determination of the cause.

> The interim dispute here was resolved by agreement. The parties sensibly made a working arrangement until trial. It does not follow that, because it worked, that arrangement is the best for the child. And the parties cannot, at trial, be treated as having somehow waived the right to put a different proposal. Indeed, such a view would discourage future litigants from agreeing to workable interim arrangements. I would not encourage turmoil in this way. Also, courts should take care not to permit a new status quo (created by delay) to decide what was not decided by the interim disposition.

Nevertheless, even in *R. v. R.*, Kerans J.A. hastened to add (at 284): "[A]ll other things being equal, it is not in the best interest of a child to substitute an uncertain situation for a certain one." Of course, this is exactly what the parent who has not had interim custody asks the court to do. Other cases in which the courts expressly downplay the significance of the interim order for the final custody decision include *Harden v. Harden* (1987), 6 R.F.L. (3d) 147 (Sask. C.A.); *Stefanyk v. Clancy* (1996), 156 N.S.R. (2d) 161 (S.C.); *Marshall v. Marshall* (1998), 42 R.F.L. (4th) 180 (N.S. C.A.); and *Hamlyn v. Hamlyn* (1999), 50 R.F.L. (4th) 398 (Nfld. U.F.C.).

Clearly, the parent who does not have *de facto* or interim custody should be prepared to present the court with practical, concrete plans for the care of the child if there is to be a realistic possibility of convincing the court that the situation should be altered. That parent should also maintain close contact with the child before trial and the trial should occur as soon as possible.

11. In *Poole v. Poole* (1999), 45 R.F.L. (4th) 56, the British Columbia Court of Appeal emphasized stability and the status quo in overturning a trial judge's decision to grant custody of a seven-year-old girl to her father so that she could rejoin her teenage brothers who lived with the father on the family farm. The court reasoned (at 61-62):

> Directly related to the health and emotional well-being of the child and almost always a consideration when looking at best interests, is an examination of those circumstances which will create the most stable, least disruptive environment for the child. In assessing stability, one must decide what the "status quo" is for a given child. ...

> What is Samantha's status quo in this case? It is significant to note that the mother has been her primary caregiver since birth, and for the last, almost four years (since March 1995), Samantha has been in the sole care and custody of her mother. During those four years, Samantha has established

herself in a home, neighbourhood and school. Samantha participates in recreational pursuits such as swimming and skating and she has established friendships. In reading the transcripts, there is no evidence to indicate that Samantha has not been well looked after by the mother. She is happy, healthy and doing well in various activities.

Madam Justice Stromberg-Stein correctly suggests that the parties seeking to alter a child's status quo must present evidence to show that the status quo is unsatisfactory and not in the best interests of the child and should therefore be changed. Again, after a thorough reading of the transcripts, I was unable to find such evidence.

12. In *Sherrett v. Sherrett* (1987), 6 R.F.L. (3d) 172, the Ontario Court of Appeal concluded that the trial judge had erred in awarding custody of two children to their father while allowing two older children to remain with the mother. However, seventeen months had passed since the trial decision and no motion was made to stay the judgment pending appeal. In the end the court dismissed the appeal because "we are hesitant now to disturb an arrangement which on the surface appears to be working tolerably well without having evidence of what problems would be caused by a further uprooting of the two youngest children".

13. The principle of ensuring stability in children's lives also governs the judicial response to applications for variation of custody orders. The existing order will not be disturbed unless it is demonstrated that there has been a material change in circumstances and that the child's best interests require a change in the order (s. 17(5) *DA* and s. 29 *CLRA*). See *Bubis v. Jones* (2000), 6 R.F.L. (5th) 83 (Ont. S.C.J.).

(3) Conduct

FISHBACK v. FISHBACK

(1985), 46 R.F.L. (2d) 44, 1985 CarswellOnt 270 (Ont. Dist. Ct.)

[The mother had *de facto* custody of two girls aged approximately eight and four since the parties' separation. Misener D.C.J. indicated that he reached his decision to grant custody to the father "with some hesitation, and without the degree of certainty as to its rightness that I would have liked" because Mrs. Fishback was a fit parent and "a mother is more in tune with a child of tender years — especially a girl".]

MISENER D.C.J.: — ... I am certainly satisfied that, from the date of the marriage until the date of the separation, Mr. Fishback did at least as much as Mrs. Fishback in the care of the matrimonial home and in the care of the children. He kept a horse for the children on a farm about one mile away and frequently took the children with him to do the chores and for buggy rides. He looked after the yard, very often with the children as his "helpers". He did a share of the housework and his full share of attending to the children, including the changing of diapers. He has been described by at least one witness as an exceptional father. I accept the validity of that description without any reservation.

According to Mrs. Fishback, matrimonial discord became significant following Heidi's birth for entirely new reasons. She said that Mr. Fishback did not help her enough about the house. Needless to say, I do not believe Mrs. Fishback's testimony as to that. She said that Mr. Fishback was not sympathetic to her migraine headaches. Mrs. Fishback may have suffered some migraine headaches, but I am not satisfied either that it was significant or that Mr. Fishback was not sufficiently sympathetic. She said that Mr. Fishback tried too hard to induce her to go to the Baptist Church. She did not wish to go there. So far as I can determine, she did not wish to go to any church. And finally she said that she found sexual relations with Mr. Fishback insufficiently exciting.

The truth of the matter is that Mrs. Fishback found Mr. Fishback insufficiently exciting. He certainly appeared to me to be a very serious man. He does not consume alcohol. He is totally dedicated to old-fashioned family values. I am sure that he has little interest in going out to the picture shows or to dances or to very much in the way of what is usually called entertainment. He believes he should go to church and that his children should go to Sunday School. He is obviously a religious man, although I am sure not one disposed to publicly proclaim his religious conviction. Having watched him in the courtroom for two days, I am sure that Mr. Fishback never has acquired a reputation for being the life of the party, assuming he has ever been disposed to attend a party. Whether I be right or wrong in that assessment, however, I am sure that the only thing that bothered Mrs. Fishback about her married life was that, in her view, it was just too dull.

She soon found a way to make it more lively. In 1982 Mrs. Fishback renewed acquaintanceship with Mr. Brian Yeoman, a former schoolmate. He was at that time married, separated, and living with one Kim Billson, a young lady who testified before me. He soon separated from Miss Billson and in the spring of 1983 purchased or rented the mobile home directly across the street from the Fishback residence. Mrs. Fishback developed the habit of spending a few hours now and then with Mr. Yeoman in his home alone. Needless to say, her visits soon became a matter of public knowledge. Mr. Fishback questioned their propriety. He was assured that the visits were completely innocent and accused of being mistrustful.

On 4th May 1984 it became clear that Mr. Fishback had been wrongly accused. He came home from his work at about 5:00 a.m. The children were asleep and alone in their home. His wife was not at home. He finally broke into the Yeoman residence and found Mr. Yeoman and his wife in bed together. He woke them up. There was considerable upset. Mrs. Fishback denied that she had had sexual relations with Mr. Yeoman even though they were found in a state of nakedness together in the same bed. Mr. Fishback appears to have been at least half persuaded that he was being told the truth. The marriage continued until the date of the separation on 3rd August. On that date, the confession of adultery was made. Even then Mr. Fishback did not wish his wife to leave. He wanted to have counselling in the hope that they could solve their problems. Mrs. Fishback by this time wanted to end the marriage. And so the separation became final. Mrs. Fishback took the children and on 1st September 1984 set up a household in Woodstock with Mr. Yeoman and the children. Mr. Fishback remained in the matrimonial home.

My concern in deciding who should have custody is confined entirely to the best interests of the children. One conclusion I draw from the facts that I have so far related is simply that Mrs. Fishback was quite prepared — and I think that she consciously thought about it — to deprive the children of the benefit of the constant presence of a good father, of at least a good husband, if not a totally satisfactory one, and of a reasonably harmonious family relationship for no other reason than to find more excitement in life. I am not suggesting that she does not now genuinely love Mr. Yeoman; perhaps she does. Perhaps she is totally dedicated to him. The fact remains that she deliberately sought that state of affairs, knowing full well that the children could never derive a benefit anything close to the loss that they would suffer from it. This factor is not of great significance in determining what is in the present and future best interests of the children, but it certainly is a factor that is entitled to some weight in determining custody because it indicates, at least to some degree, the importance that each parent attaches to the best interests of the children in determining their own future conduct.

The first conclusion at which I have arrived, then, is that Mr. Fishback had shown by his past conduct a total dedication, even to the point of apparently closing his eyes to the obvious, to keeping the family together and to providing a happy marriage for his children. Mrs. Fishback on the other hand has shown that her own desires really have priority to her children. That is of course her privilege, but it inevitably represents an impediment, however slight, to her claim that she is better able to provide for the children now.

I proceed next to the factors that I think are more important but which can be more briefly justified. Except for the last nine months or so, the children have throughout lived at the matrimonial home. Krista spent her first year of school at Tillsonburg. Both children enjoyed a very nice life in a very nice home and acquired good friendships. I am satisfied, in the description given of their reluctance to return to their home in Woodstock at the end of the periods of access, that they have missed that home. Doubtless, Mrs. Fishback is right in saying that they have become more settled in the routine as time goes by. Nevertheless, they obviously had, for a significant period of that nine months, a preference to be with their father. Their preference in itself is of little importance. What is important, however, is that Mr. Fishback clearly commands their affection and respect as much, if not more, than does Mrs. Fishback.

Mr. Fishback is obviously greatly interested in their moral, intellectual and emotional development. He has always shown a greater interest in their education than has Mrs. Fishback. He regularly read to Krista. I accept his testimony that Mrs. Fishback was not much interest[ed] in helping Krista with her learning. He alone sees to their attendance at Sunday School — something they actually enjoy. I was greatly impressed with Mrs. Ella Smith. She is 75 years of age. She is a retired school teacher. She teaches the children Sunday School at the Baptist Church. She in fact owns the farm where Mr. Fishback "boards" his horse. She lives just a mile from the matrimonial home. She has had a lot to do with the children and she dearly loves them. She regularly took Krista to the library when Mr. and Mrs. Fishback were living together. One day she made the mistake of telling Mr. Fishback that Mrs. Fishback was out too much. When Mrs. Fishback heard about that she forbade Mrs. Smith the right to take Krista to the library. To say the least, the punishment inflicted upon Mrs. Smith was at the expense of Krista's welfare, and neither appropriate nor indicative of much concern for Krista. Mrs. Smith bears no malice towards Mrs. Fishback for that. Indeed, she was obviously uncomfortable in the partisan position that she was placed in in testifying — so much so that she apologized to Mrs. Fishback as she left the courtroom for having to choose sides. She testified that, in her view and for the precise reasons she gave, Mr. Fishback was clearly better able to give the children the spiritual, cultural and intellectual assistance and guidance that every child needs. I place considerable weight on Mrs. Smith's assessment because I am satisfied of her dedication to the best interests of the children, of her sense of fairness towards both parties and of her judgment.

I think that Mr. Fishback's proposal for the care of the children, should he receive custody, is somewhat better than the present arrangements that Mrs. Fishback supplies. Mr. Fishback has become acquainted with Lucinda Tye. She is a married woman, without children, and separated from her husband. Mrs. Tye and Mr. Fishback have been keeping company. There is at least the probability that in due course they will marry, and I hope they do. Mrs. Tye testified. I was most impressed with her. She has become well acquainted with the children. She has for some time helped Mr. Fishback almost continuously in their weekend care. The children like her. Mrs. Tye does not stay overnight. Doubtless, Mr. Fishback would consider that immoral and wrong in the absence of marriage, and I am not able to say that he is wrong in that judgment, or, for that matter, that he is right in that judgment. Regardless, he proposes to have Mrs. Tye look after the children in their home at all times when he is unable to be there because of his employment. Mrs. Tye has undertaken in her testimony to do so, even at the expense of foregoing other employment opportunities. I am satisfied that that arrangement will be put in place immediately.

That is not to say that Mrs. Fishback has not so far fully and properly cared for the children in the last nine months. She has, and I am sure that she has cared for them well. But that care has been built around her relationship with Mr. Yeoman. Mr. Yeoman testified. While I do not wish to be at all unfair, I am obliged to say that neither his past performance nor his demeanour as a witness left me fully confident that his present relationship with Mrs.

Fishback will last. They both say that they intend to marry. Needless to say, I hope they do and that it remains a happy one throughout. But I am not confident of the stability of Mrs. Fishback's life from here on in as I am of the stability of Mr. Fishback's. And I think that Mrs. Tye has more to contribute to the total upbringing of the children in non-economic terms than does Mr. Yeoman.

Those are my conclusions that in my view compel me to award the custody of the children to Mr. Fishback.

YOUNG v. YOUNG

(1989), 19 R.F.L. (3d) 227, 1989 CarswellOnt 225 (Ont. H.C.)

[A husband and wife separated in 1985 after about 15 years of marriage. Both worked outside the home during the marriage, but the wife assumed primary responsibility for child care. The children remained with the wife after separation. The son, aged 11, and daughter, aged 13, wished to live with their father. Bolan L.J.S.C. explained why the children should remain in their mother's custody.]

BOLAN L.J.S.C.: — ... Mrs. Young alleges that she was emotionally, physically, verbally and sexually abused by Mr. Young. The emotional and verbal abuse started with small — and at the time — insignificant incidents shortly after marriage. She never knew when Mr. Young was coming home from work. At times, he became sullen and would not talk to her for long periods of time. He never discussed his work with her because he thought she was stupid and would not understand his work. He would make derogatory remarks about school teaching in general; she considered this as a threat to her self-esteem. He told her no one else could or would ever love her. He made derogatory remarks to her in the presence of her friends. There were times when he would not speak to her for days.

Mrs. Young alleges that she was physically abused by Mr. Young on two occasions after separation. She also says she was sexually abused on several occasions starting in 1983. ...

Linda Butler is a doctor of psychology and an expert in the field of clinical psychology. She first saw Mrs. Young on 27th November 1985 and described her as being depressed, anxious and suffering from long-standing emotional and verbal abuse. She had decided to leave the marriage to save herself from the destructive path she was on. She had low self-esteem and she was confused in her thinking.

It was Dr. Butler's impression that Mrs. Young was socially isolated and that she was having difficulty asserting herself. She presented the characteristic symptoms of emotional abuse. She saw her on a weekly basis and made progress reports every two-three months. Over the course of the next year, Mrs. Young's functioning improved particularly at work and with the family. Dr. Butler feels she has made good use of the therapy and that she could continue to resolve whatever issues remain unresolved.

It is Dr. Butler's opinion — based on clinical literature — that if a person is an abuser and does not take therapy that person is likely to be an abuser in another relationship. This becomes relevant if the children should witness an abusive relationship. If children live under conditions where there is an abusive relationship, the children themselves could become abused victims.

Barbara Pressman is an accredited marital and family therapist and an expert on wife abuse and family violence. She saw Mrs. Young for assessment on three different occasions. It was quite clear to her that Mrs. Young had experienced abuse.

Ms. Pressman gave evidence of a "cyclical pattern (behaviour) of abuse." It was her opinion that a male person (a boy) who is abused or who observes abuse can become an abuser — that, in 80 per cent of the time, he will become an abuser. In the case of a girl who observes abuse, she has the potential to become compliant to an abuser.

Ms. Pressman is presently doing rehabilitative work with abusive men. She says there is potential for an abuser to reform provided the person acknowledges that he is an abuser.

Claire Lowry is a doctor of psychology and is an expert in the field of clinical child psychology. Heather and John were referred to her by Dr. Butler. She first saw Heather on 21st May 1987. She expressed the view that Heather had some problems in dealing with her mother (Mrs. Young). She devalued her because she was an abused person (wife) and because she was responsible for the family breaking up. She also looked upon Mrs. Young and cast her as the "bad guy" or the "heavy" — the parent who said "No" to whatever Heather wanted.

Dr. Lowry says the chances of a "rapproachment" between Heather and Mrs. Young are very good. Heather has a real connection with her mother and they can talk to each other.

Dr. Lowry also saw John. He is less sophisticated and has found ways to articulate his problems. He has many strengths and the prognosis is that he can resolve the issues.

Dr. Lowry expressed her concern about the ability of an abuser to parent children. In this particular case she is concerned about Mr. Young's capacity for attachment, his ability to assess the needs of the children and his capacity to "socialize" the children, i.e., social values. On the other hand, Dr. Lowry says that Mrs. Young has a good feel for the children and she has no concerns about her ability to "parent" the children.

This is a summary of the various factors which I must consider in arriving at a proper determination as to which parent is best able to look after the interests of the children.

I am of the view that it is in the best interests of the children that the status quo should prevail and that they remain in the custody of Mrs. Young. There is no compelling evidence to suggest otherwise. I am mindful of the fact that the stated preference of the children should be considered — and I have considered it — however, there are other factors I should look at, notably, the abuse. I accept the evidence of Mrs. Young that she was abused by Mr. Young and I find the abuse to be emotional, verbal, physical and sexual. I find that this emotional and verbal abuse took place during cohabitation and after the separation. Where her evidence of abuse differs with that of Mr. Young, I prefer and accept her evidence. I was impressed with her truthfulness and sincerity as a witness. I cannot say the same for Mr. Young. I found him to be glib and evasive. The relevancy of this finding of abuse is that it goes to Mr. Young's ability to parent the children on a full-time basis. I accept the expert evidence of Dr. Butler and Barbara Pressman that:

1. An abuser who goes without therapy will continue to abuse in another relationship;

2. Children who witness abuse can become abused even though the abuse is not intentionally directed at them;

3. Abused male children often become abusers and abused female children may become compliant to abusers.

I also find that since the separation, Mr. Young did not at times have the children's best interests at heart. Throughout the period of access he manipulated them into obtaining more access for himself by showering them with lavishness, i.e., an unreasonable and incessant bombardment of baseball outings and weekends of fun and games. Furthermore, an incident occurred during the trial which reflects Mr. Young's manipulation of the children. On the weekend following the first week of trial Mr. Young obtained from Mrs. Young's residence (without her knowledge and consent) personal papers with respect to the cottage. Mr. Young had access to John that weekend starting on Friday. Heather was not with Mr. Young that

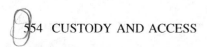

weekend. The only reasonable inference I can draw is that John took the cottage documents and gave them to his father.

I accept Mrs. Young's opinions that the children are too young at this point to give paramountcy to their stated desire — which is to live with Mr. Young. She says perhaps they would be more mature to make this decision when they reach 16.

Heather and John require stability and consistency in their lives. This can best be achieved under the guidance and custody of Mrs. Young. She is best able to provide for the children the nourishment required for their social and moral development.

NOTES AND QUESTIONS

1. Examine s. 24(3) of the *CLRA* and s. 16(9) of the *DA*. Obviously, the conduct of a parent in dealings with the child is relevant. Preventing meaningful contact between the child and the other parent can also be considered. Recall *Renaud v. Renaud*, reproduced in the previous section. See also s. 16(10) of the *DA* which is analyzed later in this chapter. More controversial is the possible consideration of "marital misconduct" and a parent's lifestyle after separation. In *Fishback*, it was asserted that marital misconduct is relevant to a parent's ability to raise the child if it reveals a willingness to place selfish interests ahead of those of the child. See also *Bosch v. Bosch* (1985), 49 R.F.L. (2d) 157 (Sask. Q.B.); *Stephens v. Stephens* (1986), 4 R.F.L. (3d) 200 (B.C. S.C.); and *Dawe v. Dawe* (1987), 11 R.F.L. (3d) 265 (Nfld. T.D.). In *Tyabji v. Sandana* (1994), 2 R.F.L. (4th) 265 (B.C. S.C.), Spencer J. stated (at 269):

> Custody is not awarded in any sense to punish the parent who is deprived of it. There is no contest between parents to see who most deserves the children or who is most responsible for the breakup of the family unit. ... Responsibility for breaking up the marriage, where it lies clearly on one side more than the other, is not necessarily a test for awarding custody. It is relevant only if it shows that one parent or the other pursued, and will probably continue to pursue, his or her self-interest to the detriment of the children, or if it shows that one or the other is less believable on oath, it may result in that parent's evidence bearing upon custody receiving less weight.

Do you agree that marital misconduct should still be considered in this indirect way?

In *Johnstone v. Brighton* (2004), 6 R.F.L. (6th) 294 (Ont. S.C.J.), the mother of a one-year-old began an affair with an American. She used deception to keep it a secret from her husband, the father of the child. Even after she became engaged to the man, she denied under oath for discovery that he was the person with whom she had the affair. In deciding that the child should continue to reside primarily with the mother after her move to Pennsylvania, Justice G.A. Campbell stated (paras. 42 and 43):

> As I commented during submissions, when Mr. Mamo [the father's lawyer] made much of Ann [the mother] and Richard's [the fiancé's] immorality and their lack of "family values", this is a court of law, not a court of morality. ...

> Section 16(9) of the *Divorce Act* enjoins me from "considering" whether Ann's "past conduct" is any worse or different than John's [the father's] admittedly falsifying his income tax returns, his verbally abusing Ann, or his ignoring his wedding vows by walking away from his marriage to Kim [the father's first wife] because he "never really loved her".

In *Somerville v. Somerville* (2007), 36 R.F.L. (6th) 7 (Ont. C.A.), a trial judge found that a father was "arrogant" and "controlling". He also noted that the father had been deceitful regarding his reasons for leaving the marriage and his relationship with another woman. By contrast, the trial judge described the mother, who was awarded sole custody, as "blameless" with respect to the break-up of the marriage. The Ontario Court of Appeal ordered a new trial, noting (para. 13): "It is an error in principle to place undue emphasis on the conduct of a parent and insufficient emphasis on the children's best interests when determining child custody issues."

Conduct after separation is relevant only if it affects a person's ability to parent or to provide a stable, suitable environment for a child. Here again, the determination of what conduct is relevant reflects social and moral values. Attitudes have changed considerably and so older cases must be approached with considerable caution. Today, adultery, homosexual conduct or cohabitation outside marriage have little effect on a custody or access determination.

In *Taylor v. Taylor* (1994), 6 R.F.L. (4th) 423 (B.C. S.C.), it was alleged that the mother had had sexual intercourse with a 15-year-old boy whom she had briefly taken into her home after the separation. Justice A.G. MacKinnon stated (at 426-427):

> I do not find it necessary to make a finding as to whether or not after separation from the respondent, the petitioner had sexual relations with her 15-year-old friend Joshua or with another person. There is no evidence to suggest that such conduct, if it did occur, had, or is likely to have, any adverse effect on the children.

In *F. (T.M.) v. H. (M.)* (2002), 26 R.F.L. (5th) 75, the British Columbia Court of Appeal upheld the award of sole custody of a six-year-old boy to a mother who owned and operated a massage parlour and a pornographic Web site. It should be noted that the father had twice been convicted of assaulting the mother.

The British Columbia Court of Appeal also upheld a trial judge's decision in *Struck v. Struck* (2003), 47 R.F.L. (5th) 405. The trial judge had awarded custody of an infant to a father mostly because of the mother's behaviour. Justice Rowles stated (paras. 50 and 51) that it was open to the trial judge to consider the mother's inability to control her temper, the "succession of cohabiting arrangements" that she had entered since separation, and her financial irresponsibility and dishonesty.

For additional comments on the relevance of conduct, see *Van de Perre v. Edwards* (2001), 19 R.F.L. (5th) 396 (S.C.C.), analysed later in this chapter.

2. Is the fact that one parent smokes (tobacco or marijuana) relevant? In *Bourdon v. Casselman* (1988), 12 R.F.L. (3d) 395 (Ont. Prov. Ct.), a father's access was terminated where he continued to smoke in the presence of his severely asthmatic son. See also *Riss v. Greenough* (2002), 2002 CarswellOnt 3615 (Ont. S.C.J.), where Quinn J. restrained both parents from smoking around the child. In that case, the justice awarded interim custody to the father mainly because the mother drank excessively and smoked marijuana regularly while her new partner used cocaine. Generally, see Wendling, "Smoking and Parenting: Can They Be Adjudged Mutually Exclusive Activities?" (1992), 42 Case Western Reserve Law Review 1025.

3. In "Wife Battery and Determinations of Custody and Access: A Comparison of United States and Canadian Findings" (1990), 22 Ottawa L. Rev. 691, Lorenne Clark concludes (at 708-709):

> ... [A]n analysis of recent Canadian case law involving these issues does not demonstrate that the Canadian judiciary is interpreting the "friendly parent" and "conduct" provisions [s. 16(9) and s. 16(10)] of the *Divorce Act, 1985* or the provisions regulating custody and access determinations in any of the provincial and territorial custody regimes, in a way which appears prejudicial to the protection of the interests of the battered wife. They routinely allow evidence of wife abuse to be admitted ..., solicit expert opinion ..., appear to have no difficulty seeing wife battery as an issue relevant to the considerations of the welfare and best interests of children ..., and give it the weight that it deserves in the sense that they most often award sole custody to the wife in such situations, with access structured to protect the safety of the wife and/ or children.

In "Legal and Clinical Issues in Child Custody Disputes Involving Domestic Violence" (1999), 17 C.F.L.Q. 1, Ms. Kerr and Dr. Jaffe conclude (at 10): "Canadian case law shows that judges are willing to hold ... that domestic violence *is* relevant to custody and access determinations and to accord the existence of spousal abuse significant and appropriate weight in deciding these issues." The relevant legislation and case law is also reviewed in Schnall, "Custody and Access and the Impact of Domestic Violence" (2000-2001), 18 C.F.L.Q. 99 and Shaffer, "The Impact of Wife Abuse on Child Custody and Access Decisions" (2004), 22 C.F.L.Q. 85. In the latter article, the author states (at 87):

> The cases suggested that many judges are becoming increasingly sensitive to issues of wife abuse. This is most apparent in decisions on custody, as abusive men seldom receive custody of their children at the trial stage. However, the case law also provides cause for concern about whether wife abuse is being properly assessed in custody and access determinations. In particular, the case law raises questions about whether courts are properly identifying abuse. It also revealed the need for better training of assessors, as some assessors discounted the impact of violence on children. Finally, the cases revealed access awards to be a source of serious concern. Courts frequently awarded abusive men access on an unsupervised basis, even in cases in which supervision or some restriction on access would appear to have been warranted. This finding is consistent with studies conducted in other jurisdictions which suggest that courts routinely award access to abusive men on the same general terms as men who have not used violence against their spouses.

For several reported cases where pre-separation spousal abuse played an important role in determining custody, see *G. (D.E.) v. G. (D.T.)* (1997), 30 R.F.L. (4th) 320 (Ont. Gen. Div.); *Carton v. Watts* (1998), 42 R.F.L. (4th) 149 (Alta. Prov. Ct.); *Kennedy v. Sinclair* (2001), 18 R.F.L. (5th) 91 (Ont. S.C.J.); affirmed (2003), 42 R.F.L. (5th) 46 (Ont. C.A.); and *Cameron v. Cameron* (2003), 41 R.F.L. (5th) 30 (Man. Q.B.). In *Abdo v. Abdo* (1993), 50 R.F.L. (3d) 171 (N.S. C.A.); *Costa v. Costa* (1994), 4 R.F.L. (4th) 209 (Man. Q.B.); *Alexander v. Creary* (1995), 14 R.F.L. (4th) 311 (Ont. Prov. Div.); *Dixon v. Hinsley* (2001), 22 R.F.L. (5th) 55 (Ont. C.J.); and *D. (R.) v. D. (U.S.)* (2001), 22 R.F.L. (5th) 269 (Y.T. S.C.), the fathers were denied any access because of their abusive treatment of the mothers. Orders for supervised access were made in *Savidant v. MacLeod* (1992), 40 R.F.L. (3d) 443 (P.E.I. C.A.); *Kennedy v. Sinclair* (2001), 18 R.F.L. (5th) 91 (Ont. S.C.J.); affirmed (2003), 42 R.F.L. (5th) 46 (Ont. C.A.) and *H. (H.) v. C. (H.)* (2002), 27 R.F.L. (5th) 63 (Alta. Q.B.). In *Weiten v. Adair* (2001), 21 R.F.L. (5th) 239, the Manitoba Court of Appeal suspended all access until the father completed an anger management course.

Since 2006, the *CLRA* has specifically required a court, in assessing a person's ability to parent, to consider whether the person has ever committed violence or abuse against his or her spouse, a parent of the child, a member of the person's household, or any child. See ss. 24(4) and (5). Recall that Bill C-22 would have amended the *DA* to include specific reference to "family violence" as one of the factors to be considered in determining the best interests of a child.

For additional readings on how allegations of domestic violence should be dealt with in custody and access disputes, see Jaffe, Crooks and Possin, "Common Misconceptions in Addressing Domestic Violence in Child Custody Disputes" (2003), 54 Juvenile & Family Court Journal 57; Shaffer, "The Impact of Wife Abuse on Child Custody and Access Decisions" (2004), 22 C.F.L.Q. 85; Jaffe, Crooks, and Bala, *Making Appropriate Parenting Arrangements in Family Violence Cases: Applying the Literature to Identify Promising Practices* (Ottawa: Department of Justice Canada, Family, Children and Youth Section Research Report No. 2005-FCY-3E, 2005) (available online at the Department's website); Johnston, "A Child-centered Approach to High-Conflict and Domestic-Violence Families: Differential Assessment and Interventions" (2006), 12 J. Fam. Studies 15; Bala, Jaffe and Crooks, "Spousal Violence and Child-Related Cases: Challenging Cases Requiring Differentiated Responses" (2008), 27 C.F.L.Q. 1; and Jaffe, Johnston, Crooks, and Bala, "Custody Disputes Involving Allegations of Domestic Violence: Towards a Differentiated Approach to Parenting Plans" (2008), 46 Family Court Review 500.

4. Allegations of child sexual abuse by a parent occur in a small but significant number of custody and access cases. In "Allegations of Sexual Abuse When Parents Have Separated" (1999), 17 C.F.L.Q. 191, Professor Bala and John Schuman estimate (at 199) that allegations of physical and sexual abuse occur in less than 10% of litigated cases. Where such an allegation is made, the focus of inquiry shifts away from a general analysis of the best interests of the child towards an investigation of whether the abuse actually occurred. For an analysis of the difficult evidentiary and procedural issues that arise in these cases, see Bala and Anweiler, "Allegations of Sexual Abuse in a Parental Custody Dispute: Smokescreen or Fire?" (1987), 2 C.F.L.Q. 343. See also Wilson, "The Ripple Effect of Sexual Abuse Allegation and Representation of the Protecting Parent" (1986-1987), 1 C.F.L.Q. 159.

In general there are few false allegations of child sexual abuse; much more common are false denials by adults. However, experts in the field are coming to recognize that there is a much greater likelihood of falsehood if an allegation of sexual abuse is made in the context of parental separation. Bala and Schuman state (at 199): "Within the group of litigated family law cases that involve abuse allegations, the rate of unproven and unfounded allegations is quite high, probably in the range of 25 to 75 per cent. However, even where the allegation is considered unfounded, the incidence of deliberate fabrication or lying is low." They go on to suggest that most unfounded allegations are the product of miscommunication or misunderstanding. See also Zarb, "Allegations of Childhood Sexual Abuse in Custody and Access Disputes: What Care is in the Best Interests of the Child?" (1994), 12 Can. J. Fam. L. 91.

An unsubstantiated allegation of sexual abuse may still cause a judge to err on the side of caution and limit contact between child and parent, especially where the child disclosed the alleged abuse. See, e.g., *C. (R.M.) v. C. (J.R.)* (1995), 12 R.F.L. (4th) 440 (B.C. S.C.) and *T. (M.) v. T. (J.)* (1997), 33 R.F.L. (4th) 430 (Ont. Gen. Div.). Sometimes, however, judges conclude that the false allegations reflect badly on the accusing parent's ability to parent and reduce that parent's role. See, e.g., *M. (H.B.) v. B. (J.E.)* (1991), 33 R.F.L. (3d) 310 (B.C. S.C.); *Lin v. Lin* (1992), 38 R.F.L. (3d) 246 (B.C. C.A.); *M. (C.A.) v. M. (D.)* (2003), 43 R.F.L. (5th) 149 (Ont. C.A.); *C. (B.A.) v. C. (D.L.)* (2003), 48 R.F.L. (5th) 15 (B.C. C.A.); *Savidis v. Savidis* (2003), 49 R.F.L. (5th) 219 (Ont. S.C.J.); and *B. (S.L.) v. A. (G.)* (2004), 9 R.F.L. (6th) 35 (Alta. C.A.). For their 1999 article, Bala and Schuman reviewed reported Canadian cases between 1990 and 1998 dealing with sexual and physical abuse allegations in the context of parental separation. In 89 of the 196 identified cases, the court concluded that the allegation was clearly unfounded. The accusing party lost custody in 18 cases, although this was sometimes for reasons not directly related to the unfounded allegation. In only one case was the accuser charged (and convicted) for false reporting (mischief) in connection with the false allegation, though in three cases the accuser was cited for contempt of court in connection with denial of access. In a majority of reported cases where the judge found the abuse allegation unfounded, the accusing parent continued to have custody. Of the 51 cases where abuse was proved on the civil standard, access was denied in 21 cases and supervised in 16. The abuser was criminally charged in only three cases.

Lise Helene Zarb points out in "Allegations of Childhood Sexual Abuse in Custody and Access Disputes: What Care is in the Best Interests of the Child?" (1994), 12 Can. J. Fam. L. 91 at 106, that there are several explanations other than malice for unsubstantiated allegations of sexual abuse. She argues that judges should consider these alternative explanations before denying the accusing parent custody. She fears that, if parents face dire consequences for mistakenly alleging abuse, they will be silent and children who have been sexually abused will suffer.

In its *For the Sake of the Children*, the Special Joint Committee recommended (at 90) that "to deal with intentional false accusations of abuse or neglect, the federal government assess the adequacy of the *Criminal Code* in dealing with false statements in family law matters and develop policies to promote action on clear cases of mischief, obstruction of justice or perjury".

5. Bill 133 (not yet proclaimed) contains proposed amendments to s. 21 of the *CLRA*. A new s. 21(2) would require each application for custody or access to be accompanied by an affidavit containing a) the person's proposed plan for the child's care and upbringing; b) information regarding the person's current or previous involvement in criminal proceedings and in family proceedings, including child protection proceedings; and c) any other relevant information. It would also add new ss. 21.1, 22.2, and 22.3 that would apply where an applicant is a non-parent. Among other things, these would require non-parent applicants to file the results of a recent police records check and a form from a Children's Aid Society revealing whether the society has any records relating to the person.

These proposed amendments are a response to the death of Katelynn Sampson. A court granted custody of the seven-year-old to Donna Irving and Warren Johnson, not realizing that Irving had a significant criminal history. She and Johnson now face first-degree murder charges relating to the girls' death.

Twelve family court judges of the Ontario Court of Justice have taken the unusual step of writing to the standing committee studying Bill 133 to warn that these provisions would be "difficult, expensive and burdensome to implement, if they can be implemented at all". Their main concern is that many applications, especially those where the applicants have no legal representation, will be "delayed, deferred, or withdrawn". They suggest that the Office of the Children's Lawyer should conduct an investigation where the parties are unrepresented or when the application is unopposed and the judge fears that key information is missing. See "Family court judges warn bill would have 'unintended consequences'", *Law Times*, April 9, 2009.

(4) Parent's Relationship With a Third Party

RE REID

(1975), 25 R.F.L. 209, 11 O.R. (2d) 622, 1975 CarswellOnt 262 (Div. Ct.)

[Catherine Reid took her three young children from the family home and began to live with Donald Reid (no relation to herself or her husband, Keith Reid). The trial judge awarded custody to the mother and the father appealed.]

GALLIGAN J. (orally): — What has given all members of this court cause for concern is the question of whether it is in the best interests of the children that Donald Reid become their surrogate father. ...

In the opinion of us all, the trial judge is under a very high duty to weigh carefully the suitability of the person who, in a practical sense, will stand in the position of a parent to the children as a result of the custody order that he makes. It is a particularly important duty, in a case such as this, where he has found that the surrogate parent proposed by one parent is fit and suitable to determine that the surrogate parent proposed by the other is also fit and suitable. This duty is one that can be discharged only by the trial judge, because he is the person who must objectively determine the welfare of the children. This duty cannot be delegated to another. In many cases the determination of this issue might well be decisive of the case.

In this case, there was evidence that Donald Reid was harsh with his own children and that basically he did not like children. His wife, Constance Reid, testified for the appellant, as did his son James, and a friend of James, one David Dzwolak. I do not think it appropriate to go into the evidence in any detail, except to say that it has given each member of this court cause to wonder whether it is in the best interests of these children to be in the charge of Donald Reid. ...

For some strange reason known only to the respondent and Donald Reid, Donald Reid did not testify at the trial. No explanation was given as to why he did not testify. In a situation like this, it was open to the trial judge to infer that the reason he did not testify was that if he did testify his evidence would not be helpful to the respondent. It is difficult to understand why the trial judge did not draw that inference, particularly in the light of the uncontradicted evidence of Donald Reid's wife and son.

After giving his reasons for not accepting the evidence of Donald Reid's wife, which reasons on their face are erroneous, the learned trial judge resolved the problem of the suitability of Donald Reid as a person to be a surrogate father to these three children in the following words:

> I am left in the situation that I would have preferred to have seen him [Donald Reid] but my concern on that point is overcome by my respect for the mother and the way she gave evidence, insofar as her concern for her children, and she said unequivocally that she would not permit or tolerate anyone, including Don Reid, to abuse her children and I think that she is that kind of a mother. I think she is an affectionate, warm person. She will be combative if there is any attempt to abuse her children, and I think on that point, I can be assured that she will protect them, and I don't say that with any inference that Don Reid would not conduct himself other than properly with the children, but if there is any suggestion of that, I think it is closed by the mother's protective attitude that I find she would have with respect to her children.

Notwithstanding the great respect that we all have for the trial judge and the appreciation we have for the humane and sympathetic way in which he dealt with this most difficult of problems, we are all of the opinion that he was in serious error in his disposition of this aspect of the case.

He had the duty to determine whether it was in the best interests of these children to live in a home situation in which, for all practical purposes, Donald Reid was their father.

It was his duty to determine whether Donald Reid was a fit and proper person to be their father. However, he did not see or hear Donald Reid testify and he therefore did not have the opportunity to assess for himself Donald Reid's suitability as a surrogate father to these children. In effect, he delegated his responsibility to make that determination to the respondent, who of course cannot be called a disinterested person.

In this case where the scales are so evenly balanced as between the parents, I think the vital inquiry was as to the relative fitness of the surrogate mother and the surrogate father proposed by each parent. That inquiry was not properly made and in my opinion the issue was not properly determined. Accordingly, the order appealed from cannot stand and must be set aside. ... [A new trial was ordered.]

NOTES AND QUESTIONS

1. As the *Reid* case indicates, the character and parenting skills of the person with whom a parent resides or intends to reside are relevant. See also *Doucet v. MacDougall* (2000), 7 R.F.L. (5th) 29 (N.B. C.A.), where the courts were concerned about the mother's new partner's "difficulty with anger management". Most judges, in fact,

will express a desire to hear from the step-parents in any custody trial. Under s. 30(5) of the *CLRA* the court can require a parent's new partner or spouse to attend for assessment by a court-appointed professional.

The stability of the relationship between the parent and the third party can also be considered. See s. 24(2)(f) of the *CLRA*. See also *Bell v. Kirk* (1986), 3 R.F.L. (3d) 377 (B.C. C.A.). In *Van de Perre v. Edwards* (2001), 19 R.F.L. (5th) 396 (S.C.C.), a married member of the Vancouver Grizzlies fathered a child with an unmarried woman who frequented "groupies" bars. The father's wife impressed the psychologist who prepared an assessment as a devoted mother with excellent parenting skills. The psychologist concluded that the father's family unit swung the balance in his favour. Nonetheless, the trial judge awarded custody to the mother. Although he acknowledged the father's wife's positive attributes, he reasoned that the father's affairs posed a serious threat to the stability of his marriage. The Supreme Court of Canada concluded that the trial judge rightly took into account the possibility that the father's marriage might fail.

2. Where the new partner also has children, Holmes J. suggested in *Barnes-Everatt v. Everatt*, [1994] 1994 CarswellBC 1481 (B.C. S.C.) that the court can consider the problems inherent in "blended families".

3. Where one of the parents has entered into a stable relationship with a third party who has good parenting skills, this may be a factor indicating that it is in the best interests of the child to be placed in the custody of that parent.

(5) Tender Years Doctrine, Primary Care-Giving, and Working Mothers

R. v. R.

(1983), 34 R.F.L. (2d) 277, [1983] 5 W.W.R. 385, 1983 CarswellAlta 104 (Alta. C.A.)

[The parents were married in 1974. In 1978 they adopted a baby girl. The mother ceased work to look after the child. In 1981 the mother left the matrimonial home with the child. An interim custody agreement gave custody to the mother. The mother lived and worked in a city 80 kilometers from the family farm where the father continued to live. The child, who was four and a half at the time of trial, was placed in a government approved daycare centre at 8:30 each weekday morning and picked up at the end of the work day. Every second Friday the father picked up the child and took her to the farm until the following Tuesday.

The trial judge in divorce proceedings awarded custody to the father. He concluded that both parents were "more than capable of providing for the material, emotional and spiritual upbringing of the child", but that life with the father on the family farm offered the better choice for the child as long as the mother had "very liberal access". He stressed that the father had much more time to devote to the care of the child during the day. Also, the paternal grandparents lived on the farm and could look after the child during "peak farm work periods".

The mother appealed. One of the grounds put forward was that the trial judge had failed to give any weight to the "tender years doctrine". The essence of this doctrine is captured in the mother's statement at trial: "[F]athers don't make good mothers, there are certain things that a little girl, in fact any little child, I think needs from a mother." The Alberta Court of Appeal, McGillivray C.J.A. dissenting, upheld the trial judge's decision.]

KERANS J.A. (LAYCRAFT J.A. concurring): — ... The next ground offered is that the learned trial judge refused to consider what the mother calls the "tender years principle". He said:

There is no longer, in my view, any historic or traditional right that favours either mother or father. This issue must be decided on the merits of this case.

It is acknowledged for the mother that the learned trial judge was not bound to give the mother custody of a child of tender years just because the child was of tender years; it is argued, however, that he was bound to consider such a disposition for that reason and he refused to do so. In my view, his reasons are misperceived. I understand him simply to reject the "rights" approach to the determination of a custody case in lieu of the "best interests" approach. The classic statement of the "rights" approach was that of Mulock C.J.O. in *Re Orr*, [1933] O.R. 212, [1933] 2 D.L.R. 77 at 80-81 (C.A.):

> ... the general rule is that the mother ... is *entitled* to the custody and care of a child during what is called the period of nurture, namely, until it attains about 7 years of age, the time during which it needs the care of the mother more than that of the father, and then the father as against the mother becomes *entitled* to the custody and care of his child. ... (The italics are mine.)

In my view, the learned trial judge was bound to reject this approach: see *Talsky v. Talsky*, [1976] 2 S.C.R. 292, 21 R.F.L. 27, 62 D.L.R. (3d) 267, 7 N.R. 246.

In an allied argument, the mother suggests that the learned trial judge erred in not giving decisive weight to the tender years "principle" as a "factor". This argument is powerfully close to repeating the error of Mulock C.J.O. If the extreme youth of the child *must be* the deciding factor, then that factor gives the mother an undeniable right.

Should a pre-school child be with the mother? Spence J. (dissenting) in *Talsky* describes the answer "yes" as "common sense". Often, when we invoke common sense, we intend to invoke unstated conventional assumptions. As Einstein rather provocatively said, "common sense is the collection of prejudices acquired by age 18". I suppose that there is no harm in this unless the unstated conventions come to be doubted. That the female human has some intrinsic capacity, not shared by the male, to deal effectively with infant children is an assumption that was once conventionally accepted but is now not only doubted but widely rejected.

As recently as 1955, this rhapsodic commentary by Roach J.A. in *Bell v. Bell*, [1955] O.W.N. 341 at 344 (C.A.), attracted no adverse comment:

> No father, no matter how well-intentioned or how solicitous for the welfare of such a child, can take the full place of the mother. Instinctively, a little child, particularly a little girl, turns to her mother in her troubles, her doubts, and her fears. In that respect, nature seems to assert itself. The feminine touch means so much to a little girl; the frills and flounces and the ribbons in the matter of dress; the whispered consultations and confidences on matters which to the child's mind should only be discussed with Mother; the tender care, the soothing voice; all these things have a tremendous effect on the emotions of the child. This is nothing new; it is as old as human nature. ...

This view confuses cultural traditions with human nature; it also traps women in a social role not necessarily of their choosing, while at the same time freeing men: if only a mother can nurture a child of tender years, then it is the clear duty of the mother to do so; because the father *cannot* do it, he is neither obliged nor entitled even to try. Also, it is seen by some as self-perpetuating; by putting the female child in the custody of somebody who accepts the maternal role model so described, the rule ordains that she will have just such a role model at close hand during her most impressionable years. Thus, the "tender years principle", which at first glance seems only innocently sentimental, is seen by many as part of a subtle, systemic sexual subordination.

In my view, it is no part of the law of Canada that a judge is bound to say that human nature dictates that only females can perform that parental role labelled as "maternal". I do not agree with Roach J.A.; I do not agree with the appellant mother.

Judicial comments about the "tender years" issue must be considered in an historical context. The fact is that there have been substantial changes over the past century in the attitude in our society about the ideal family situation. Once, it was accepted that the husband and father was the decision-maker for the family, even about child-rearing questions and even after a marriage breakdown. The statement by Mulock C.J.O. in 1933, quoted above, was a sign of the emergence of a new attitude. Note, however, that he conceded the right of the father to custody after age seven. In its origins, the "tender years" concept was a way to undermine the traditional model and recognize a new model. The new, "modern" marriage model involved not only the idea of the nuclear family, but also of the marital partnership, where all major decision-making is shared. ... The modern marriage model does not concede any special status to the father and therefore requires a new standard to decide custody cases. The courts adopted the "best interests" approach.

Some divergence in the roles of male and female was accepted in this newer model however. The husband could continue to be the bread-winner and the wife could have a special responsibility as a professional homemaker. This was not to say that she alone was to carry the burden of child-rearing. But there were and are, in this model, a measure of acceptably different parental roles based upon gender. To those who prefer this model, the views of Roach J.A. are simply inadequate.

To others, however, his views are anathema. In what might be called the supra-modern marriage, strenuous efforts are made to avoid *any* role distinction based upon sex. The many tasks of homemaking and child-rearing — indeed, child-bearing — are shared as completely as possible, and not on any gender basis. It follows, of course, that both fathers and mothers must, if this model is to work, acquire the skills and make the commitment which is required for effective parenting.

Taken in this context, the remarks made by judges in the past about "tender years principle" do not come to much. All that can be said in this age of changing attitudes is that judges must decide each case on its own merits, with due regard to the capacities *and* attitudes of each parent. We should take care not to assign to this idea or that (all actually of recent origin and unique to our society) the august status of being the only one consistent with human nature or common sense. And we must continue to recognize that the attitude toward child-rearing of the parties to the marriage which the judge is being asked to dissolve could reflect traditional, modern or supra-modern ideals or, more likely, some confused and contradictory spot on the spectrum between these extremes. For example, there is no point giving a father the custody of a child of tender years if that father believes child-rearing to be "women's work". That would not be in the best interests of the child. And we must remember that our role is not to reform society; our role is to make the best of a bad deal for the child who comes before us for help. ...

On my reading of his judgment, the learned trial judge did not find the father here to be any sort of a radical; he did, however, find him to be, perhaps uniquely, willing to spend a great deal of time with his little daughter. I can see no error in that. ...

The last ground offered by the appellant is that the learned trial judge erred in putting decisive emphasis on the fact that the father had more weekday time available to share with his little daughter than did the mother. There is an irony in this; usually such a complaint is made by the father! Three points are made for the mother:

> (1) It is argued in the factum that the mother is being punished for having to work. This is not fair, as Mr. Babki conceded during argument. Both parents here agreed that both had to work. Maintenance was not an issue. It is mere happenstance that the father has more free weekday time than does the mother. To decide the case on that circumstance is, I concede, collaterally to make the mother a victim of that circumstance. But we must, as I have already said, do what is right for the child, not what is fair to the parents. The mother has no right to demand sympathetic consideration for her circumstances if to do so is not in the best interests of the child. There is no merit to this point.

> (2) It is said that the learned trial judge failed to appreciate that the advantages offered by the father are short-lived: by September next the child will, in any event, be

in kindergarten and thereafter in school during most daylight hours. The learned trial judge was, however, well aware of this point. ...

But, in a case where all else is equal, there is no error in deciding on the basis of the best interest of the child in the short term. This argument has no merit. Further, I detect a certain contradiction in the position of the mother. She says that the judge was wrong to decide the case on the basis of what the situation will be during the brief period before the child goes to school; yet, in invoking the tender years factor, she relies on just that.

(3) It is said that the learned trial judge unfairly deprecates professional child care. To do so would be error. In the absence of cogent evidence on the point, it is surely not fair to criticize those who select a style of child-rearing which is widely accepted now in our society. What the learned trial judge does, however, is something entirely within his province to do: he weighs the quality and quantity of the mother's proposal against that of the father. In this, there is no error.

It is said that the key is not quantity but quality. The quality of time spent with children is obviously more important than quantity (recognizing that in the early bonding period simple quantity is also vitally important). But I understand the learned trial judge here to say that each of the two parents offers time of equal value and the father offers more. I can see no reversible error in relying upon this as a deciding factor.

[In dissent, MCGILLIVRAY C.J.A. stated:] From his reasons it appears to me that the one consideration that weighed with the judge was that the husband, as a farmer, would be able to spend more time with the youngster on a daily basis than the wife would because the wife is working and has the child in a daycare centre during the daytime.

But, in basing his judgment on time available, he has, in my opinion, given no consideration to the proposition that a girl of tender years is best with her mother, when this should be regarded as "... one of the more important factors which must be considered in the granting of custody" (Spence J. in *Talsky* at p. 40). ...

In my opinion the difference in amount of time that one parent can at any given period spend with the child is not of itself a sound criterion on which to base a custody order, particularly when the effect is to overturn the arrangement that the parties themselves had made. Quality not quantity of parental care should be weighed. The judge has held as between the husband and wife that one is not to be preferred to the other. He should have recognized the wife's advantage as a mother in relation to a child of tender years.

I am further of the opinion that the amount of time that can be spent with the youngster by the farmer husband is not a satisfactory basis for overturning the working arrangements that the parties had had, which would be given effect to by giving the wife custody, with the husband to have access for four days in every two weeks. First of all, there must be tens of thousands of children doing very well in daycare centres across the country. Moreover, the child will soon be going to school. The advantage of time available every day to be with the youngster is short lived. Had the mother chosen to go on welfare rather than to work, so as to be able to devote her entire working day to the child, it would appear that the advantage that the husband was found to have possessed by the trial judge would have been more than balanced by the attention the mother could give the child. I cannot bring myself to conclude in this day that custody should be determined by whether the mother has to work or not.

In my respectful view, the learned trial judge has erred in two respects: he is changing what was a workable arrangement, whereby the mother had de facto custody, with the husband having the child for four days every two weeks, and he has overlooked that special bond between a daughter of four and a half and her mother, or has at least not given any or sufficient weight to that factor. ...

HARDEN V. HARDEN

(1987), 6 R.F.L. (3d) 147, 1987 CarswellSask 78 (Sask. C.A.)

[The parties were married in 1978 and separated in 1985 when the father forced the mother to leave. Two children, aged six and three, remained with the father in the home. Before the separation, the father farmed and the mother remained in the home, caring for the children. Following separation, the father and children lived with his parents and the children spent a substantial amount of time with the grandmother while the father worked.

The trial judge awarded custody to the mother, in part because of his view that the custody of young children should be awarded to a mother "unless there is some compelling reason to the contrary". The father appealed, alleging that the trial judge had improperly relied on the tender years doctrine.]

SHERSTOBITOFF J.A. (for the court): — ... The appellant, in advancing his argument against the validity of the tender years doctrine relied on the judgment of Kerans J.A. of the Alberta Court of Appeal in *R. v. R.* ... I agree in large part with what is there said. It is not a part of our law that a court must find that a female, by virtue of her sex alone, is inherently superior as a parent, in the case of a child of tender years, to her husband, and if that is what the trial judge found in this case, he erred. However, an analysis of the judgment and evidence indicates that that was not the governing factor in the case. The parties, after the marriage, presumably by the assent of each of them chose the following roles: the husband as the breadwinner, and the wife as a mother. She did not work during the marriage and one of her primary functions was to care for, raise and nurture the children. The trial judge recognized that this decision and course of action on the part of the parties put the mother into a closer relationship with the children than the father, and all other factors being equal, he properly decided that the mother should have custody of the children. Accordingly, in my view, he reached the right result on the evidence. In a case where the parental roles were reversed, the decision might well be the opposite. Each case must be decided on its own facts. ...

McLEOD, "ANNOTATION"

(1987), 6 R.F.L. (3d) 147 at 148

In *Harden* Sherstobitoff J.A. expressly agrees with the Alberta Court of Appeal and holds that a parent's gender does not, in itself, create a presumption in custody matters. Rather, in all situations, the court is to look to the reality of the particular case in order to determine who has been caring for the child and who is best equipped to meet the child's needs in the future. In many cases, as in *Harden*, custody of young children will be awarded to the mother. However, this will be because on the facts the mother is best equipped to deal with the child's needs.

Although Sherstobitoff J.A. denied the existence of a tender years doctrine, it may also be correct to say that the doctrine has been reformulated. That is, the parent who has had the major input to a young child's development will likely receive custody so long as the task has been reasonably carried out. Whereas in the past this person was regularly the mother because of the nature of the family unit, the change in women's roles in society has created a situation where both parents may share child-rearing responsibilities relatively equally. As well, in some situations, the husband has remained in the home to care for the children. The thrust of the decisions in *R. v. R.* and *Harden* seems to be that, where a parent has had primary childcare responsibilities and has carried them out properly, it will rarely be in the child's best interests for the child to be uprooted and separated from that parent. ...

JANE DOE v. JOHN DOE

(1990), 28 R.F.L. (3d) 356, 1990 CarswellOnt 292 (Ont. Dist. Ct.); affirmed (1990), 1990 CarswellOnt 315, *(sub nom. Doe v. Doe)* 29 R.F.L. (3d) 450 (Ont. C.A.)

[The parties began cohabiting in 1979 and separated in 1987. The child was born in 1985. After the separation the mother and child moved in with the maternal grandmother. From January 1988 to October 1988 the child was in the primary care of the mother. The parties then entered into a joint custody arrangement which provided that the child would spend two weeks with each parent. An assessor's report indicated that the father was far more willing and likely to promote access and that the child should be placed with the father. A second report reached the same conclusion. The father worked full-time and would require full-time child care assistance. The mother was available as a full-time parent and she lived with her family who would help out.

In 1989 the father was awarded sole custody under the *CLRA* largely because of his willingness to promote access. (This aspect of the case will be explored later in this chapter.) Regarding the tender years doctrine, the trial judge concluded that it was at most a common sense rule and could be displaced by the facts of any given case. The mother appealed and obtained a stay pending appeal. Corbett D.C.J. allowed the appeal.]

CORBETT D.C.J.: — ... The appellant submits that the learned trial judge erred in failing to give proper weight to the principle of common sense that children of tender years should be given to the custody of their mother. ...Whether the tender years doctrine is styled a rule of common sense or not, the factual reality is that the bulk of child care, particularly of pre-school age children, is performed by mothers. The reality has not changed with the statutory recognition in s. 20(1) of the *Children's Law Reform Act* that the father and mother of a child are equally entitled to custody of the child. The tender years doctrine reflects that a young child is more likely to be cared for by the child's mother and, if that is the case, it is in the best interests of the child to remain with the mother unless there are other compelling reasons to uproot the child in the child's best interests. I do not find that the learned trial judge erred in his consideration of the tender years doctrine. ...

Counsel for the appellant submits the learned trial judge erred in failing to consider the instability which would result from the custody plan put forward by the respondent. It is submitted that the sum and substance of the respondent's evidence with respect to his custody plan for the child was that she would be cared for by a continuous flow of different nannies or babysitters, a fact which the learned judge failed to fully consider. ... He also submitted the learned trial judge failed to give sufficient weight to the fact that Cathy could be cared for most of the time by her mother.

Counsel for the respondent submitted that the fact that a parent works and requires daycare or babysitting services is a common experience and is not significant. She referred to the learned judge's finding on the evidence given at trial that other caregivers do not detract from the main parent-child attachment, provided the parents are routinely a close part of the child's environment.

In my opinion, the learned trial judge erred in placing custody of a pre-school age child with a working parent requiring nannies, as opposed to that of a parent who works part time on an irregular basis and who lives in a household with other family members.

I agree with the submission of counsel for the appellant that the learned trial judge did not give sufficient weight to the fact that Jane lives on a farm with her mother and her sister. While the learned trial judge noted the child had normal loving relationships with her grandmother and aunt, he failed to refer to the fact that Cathy lived with them and that her grandmother was always available in the home. ...

Without in any way concluding that a working parent cannot be a good parent with the assistance of other caregivers, in my opinion, that is not the issue. In this case, when faced with a choice for a pre-school child between a fit, loving mother who is virtually a full-time parent, and a busy, full-time, fit, loving father who requires full-time child care assistance, it is an error in principle not to award custody to the parent who can devote substantial time to the child, particularly when the mother lives in a household with accessible relatives.

WARCOP v. WARCOP

(2009), 2009 CarswellOnt 782 (S.C.J.)

[The parties were married for a little over four years and had a son who was a year old when they separated. The mother, Gabrielle, resisted allowing overnight access following separation. The father applied for joint custody, while the mother applied for sole custody with generous visitation for the father. One of the mother's main arguments was that the child was young and needed her to nurture him. In the course of awarding joint custody of the now three-year-old boy to the parents with alternating periods of care and control, Justice Gray discussed the tender years doctrine and a possible primary caregiver presumption.]

2 The "tender years" doctrine is apparently dead. However, some of the issues arising in this case suggest that it is not entirely buried.

. . . . .

(b) The Tender Years Doctrine

77 A rule that was rigorously applied for many years came to be known as the "tender years" doctrine. Under that doctrine, a mother was presumptively entitled to custody of a child of tender years, unless exceptional circumstances could be shown. Tender years were generally considered to be seven years of age or less. ...

78 This principle was applied by the Court of Appeal for decades: see *Baker v. Baker*, [1943] O.R. 151 (C.A.), and *Bell v. Bell*, [1955] O.W.N. 341 (C.A.). As recently as 1976, the Supreme Court of Canada regarded the view that children of tender years should be given to the custody of their mother as "a principle of common sense": see *Talsky v. Talsky*, [1976] 2 S.C.R. 292. Even more recently, in 1991, the Court of Appeal unanimously held that "Under the 'tender years doctrine', in order for a court to deprive the mother of a young child of custody, where the child has been in the mother's care and custody, there must be very compelling reasons": see *S.(B.A.) v. S.(M.S.)* (1991), 35 R.F.L. (3d) 400 (Ont. C.A.).

79 Notwithstanding the Supreme Court of Canada's apparent approval of the tender years doctrine in *Talsky, supra*, as a principle of common sense, the Court subsequently re-examined the issue in *Young v. Young*, [1993] 4 S.C.R. 3, where it effectively disapproved of the doctrine.

80 L'Heureux-Dubé J. delivered lengthy reasons, dissenting in the result, in which she extensively canvassed the history of a number of principles of family law. While, as noted, she dissented in the result, none of the other judges took issue with her review of the relevant principles. At para. 36, she stated that "decisions are made according to the best interests of the child without the benefit of a presumption in favour of the mother, or, for that matter, the father." At para. 198, McLachlin J. (as she then was), for the majority, noted that the tender years doctrine had, in the past, been justified on pragmatic grounds, namely, the welfare of the child, and then stated that "so justified, the presumption carried the seeds of its own demise". In the same paragraph, she stated that "courts increasingly looked behind the preference to focus directly upon what was in the child's interest, which was sometimes found to conflict with a maternal preference."

81 Finally, in *Van de Perre v. Edwards*, [2001] 2 S.C.R. 1014, Bastarache J., for a unanimous Court, at para. 34, referred to the doctrine, with obvious disapproval, as "stereotypical".

82 The [Ontario] Court of Appeal has never expressly disavowed the doctrine, and [I have noted] the Court's apparent approval of it in 1991. However, it seems clear that after the decisions of the Supreme Court of Canada in *Young*, in 1993, and *Van de Perre*, in 2001, the doctrine has little, if any, life left.

83 It is likely that the development of the tender years doctrine was influenced by the cultural upbringings of individual judges. Having been raised in family units, they were obviously influenced by the manner in which their own families were raised. However, any predisposition of that sort is now irrelevant. As McLachlin J. stated in *Young*, *supra*, at para. 203:

> There is no room for the judge's personal predilections and prejudices. The judge's duty is to apply the law. He or she must not do what he or she wants to do but what he or she ought to do.

In the same paragraph, she also noted that Parliament, by embodying the "best interests" test, has mandated that it be applied according to the evidence in the case, viewed objectively.

84 Ms. Oliver, for Gabrielle, did not directly place any reliance on the tender years doctrine. However, she urged that I consider that it is in Luke's best interests that he be in the custody of his "primary caregiver" who, she submitted, is her client.

85 There is some authority at the Superior Court level for the proposition that the primary caregiver should be given preference: see *Brotherton v. Brotherton*, [2006] O.J. No. 2844 (S.C.J.); and *Spencer v. Spencer*, [2006] O.J. No. 4144 (S.C.J.). There is some danger, in my view, that any such principle could become a proxy for the now-discredited tender years doctrine. At the time of separation, it is quite likely that very young children have been cared for, primarily, by their mothers. However, empirical evidence suggests that infants form attachments to both parents at approximately the same age, between six and seven months, even though fathers typically spend less time with their infants than do mothers: see *Kelly* (2005), *supra*. Thus, in my view, as mandated by McLachlin J. in *Young*, *supra*, a consideration of giving preference to the primary caregiver must be considered objectively, based on the evidence, and not from the perspective of any predisposition.

In several of the cases reproduced above, one parent appears to have been favoured because he or she would not require paid assistance to care for the children. The following case addressed this point directly. At trial, the judge found that the parents had established an arrangement in which the children, aged five and eight, would spend one day in the father's house and the next in their mother's. The father had remarried and the children were very comfortable with their step-mother. Unfortunately, the mother was forced to move from Winnipeg to Vancouver because of her work. The trial judge found that the children were well-adjusted and that either parent would adequately look after them. He indicated that, if forced to choose, he would choose the mother as the better parent. However, he decided that it would be best for the children to remain in Winnipeg during the school year with generous access to the mother during holidays. He stressed that this would represent continuity and that the step-mother would be available to look after them at all times. The mother's appeal was allowed.

KLACHEFSKY v. BROWN

(1988), 12 R.F.L. (3d) 280, 1988 CarswellMan 40 (Man. C.A.); leave to appeal refused (1988), 54 Man. R. (2d) 160n (S.C.C.)

O'SULLIVAN J.A. (HUBAND J.A. concurring): — ... In my opinion, there is ample material on the record to support the judge's conclusion that on balance Ms. Brown would be the better parent. My perusal of the record satisfies me that he was correct in that assessment. The judge justified departing from his assessment of the two parents by saying [p. 432]:

> With some reluctance, I have determined that it is in the best interests of the children to remain in Winnipeg. In particular, in Winnipeg, there is no need for the reliance on daycare or other hired child caretakers.

In my opinion, the trial judge committed a palpable error in placing undue emphasis on the fact that the mother in Vancouver will require paid assistance to provide care for her children. The younger child is now enrolled in kindergarten where he spends part of the day. Another portion of the day will be spent in a daycare facility, until he graduates to Grade I in six months' time. Both children will be returning home from school around 3:30 p.m. but the mother does not arrive home from work until around 5:30 p.m. She has made arrangements for a competent person to be at the home from 3:00 o'clock on until the mother's arrival. Daycare and home care arrangements of this kind are a fact of life which many parents and children face, and there was no evidence before the judge that the children would suffer the least harm from being exposed to a few hours when they are neither at school nor with their mother. Whether an alternate caregiver is paid or unpaid cannot be decisive of what is in the best interests of the children.

Further, the judge appears to have overlooked the testimony that, in the future, the mother's parents will probably spend their winter holiday time in Vancouver rather than Florida, and the evidence that there is available to the mother extended family in Vancouver.

The learned judge also, in my opinion, committed error in this case by failing to take into account the relative stability of the parents' way of life. Since the separation, the mother has maintained a stable family unit consisting of herself and her two children, with help from her mother and other people with whom she has had good rapport. There is every indication that she could maintain that stable home in Vancouver.

On the other hand, the evidence shows that the home provided by the father, however excellent it has been as found by the learned trial judge, has not been a stable one. [This was a reference to the fact that the father had had brief relationships with two other women prior to meeting the stepmother.] ...

In my opinion, given the judge's conclusions that as between the parents he would prefer Ms. Brown, a preference with which I agree, the judge fell into error in failing to take account the father's record of instability in his home life compared with her stability, and in giving far too much weight to the fact that the mother might have to rely on paid daycare for two hours a day while she looks after the children in Vancouver. ...

PHILP J.A. (dissenting): — ... [T]he trial judge said that his determination must be made "on the basis of what is in the best interests of the children". That is the proper test, and I cannot say that in applying that test he committed palpable error.

My colleagues have come to the opposite conclusion. They are of the view that the appeal should be allowed; that custody of the children should be given to the mother; that the children should be uprooted from their environment since birth in which they have flourished, their neighbourhood, their friends, their extended family, their special "Alternative Program" schooling, and their established sports and cultural activities; and that the children should be bundled off on a voyage in uncharted waters.

The trial judge found that the children are "fond" of the father's new wife. There is evidence to support a stronger finding — that a loving relationship has developed between them. My colleagues would destroy that bond, and, as well, significantly alter the special relationship that exists between the children and their father (and that is surely the practical effect of changing the order as to custody) in order to accommodate the mother who has chosen to put her career interests above all else.

My colleagues have concluded that appellate interference is justified because the trial judge has committed palpable error and has misapprehended the evidence. Three instances are singled out from the evidence of the six-day trial.

Firstly, they say that the trial judge placed undue emphasis on the fact that the mother will require paid assistance to provide care for the children. Her circumstances in Vancouver will require daycare services for the younger child each afternoon, and babysitting arrangements for both children each day after daycare and school closing until the mother returns to work. Those arrangements are not required in Winnipeg. It was the intention of the new wife, after the birth of her child expected a few months after the trial, to remain at home to care for her baby and the children. In determining the best interests of the children, the trial judge was entitled to prefer the care that the new wife was prepared and anxious to provide, and the loving relationship that had developed between the new wife and the children over a period in excess of two years, to that of paid "caregivers". I do not read from the reasons of the trial judge that the decisive factor was whether an alternate caregiver is paid or unpaid. It is a reasonable inference to be drawn that the trial judge looked to the quality and reliability of the care available from the new wife who testified at the trial, and from a daycare facility and a babysitter then available in Vancouver according to the evidence of the mother.

My colleagues have concluded, as well, that the trial judge failed to take into account the relative stability of the parents' way of life. This is the second instance in which they say the trial judge erred, and it is related to the third instance, their conclusion that the trial judge misapprehended the evidence when he said that the new wife "has been for the past two years and will continue to be a good caretaker for the children". ...

There is ample evidence to support the finding that the home provided by the husband and the new wife is a stable one. I do not think the trial judge committed error in failing to arrive at the opposite conclusion on the basis of snippets from the evidence on the father's relationship with two other women, some years ago and prior to this relationship with his new wife.

Nor can I conclude that the trial judge misapprehended the evidence on how long the new wife had filled the role of a "caretaker" for the children. In my view, on any reasonable interpretation of that word, the new wife had performed that role at the time of the trial for at least two years. ...

In this case our duty is clear. The trial judge is an experienced and respected Family Division judge. The evidence was there to support his findings. Those findings, however inelegantly expressed in his oral reasons, are to be respected. ...

NOTES AND QUESTIONS

1. There are now very few cases that explicitly give some weight to the tender years doctrine, even as a "useful rule of common sense". For examples from over a decade ago, see *S. (B.A.) v. S. (M.S.)* (1991), 35 R.F.L. (3d) 400 (Ont. C.A.) and *Lancaster v. Lancaster* (1992), 38 R.F.L. (3d) 373 (N.S. C.A.).

In *Gallagher v. Gallagher* (2000), 9 R.F.L. (5th) 331 (N.B. C.A.), a five-year-old boy lived primarily with his father after the parents separated and a psychologist's report indicated that this should continue. Nonetheless, the trial judge, in making a joint custody order, stipulated that the child would live primarily with his mother. He stated:

> The nurturing requirements for a child of that age are very important and that nurturing comprises a lot more factors than continuity and stability. It involves the love, affection and the general commitment to attend to the child's every need, something *normally done by a mother* for her infant. [Emphasis added by the appellate court.]

The New Brunswick Court of Appeal said (para. 8):

> We have found no authority to support this latter comment in the context in which it was rendered. It relates to the tender years' doctrine, which is no longer applicable to custody decisions. The Supreme Court of Canada has for some time insisted that the best interests of a child is the paramount consideration. Legislation has also dictated that the best interests of the child is the sole consideration in a custody determination.

Nevertheless, the father's appeal was dismissed because this comment "was not the basis of [the] decision".

2. In *Garska v. McCoy*, 278 S.E. 2d 357 (W. Va. S. Ct., 1981) the court stated that there was a presumption that the parent who had been the primary caregiver in the past should obtain custody of children of tender years, unless proven unfit. The court presented a partial list of the caring and nurturing activities that should be explored to identify the primary caregiver:

> ... [T]he preparing and planning of meals; bathing, grooming and dressing; purchasing, cleaning and care of clothes; medical care, including nursing and trips to physicians; arranging for social interaction among peers after school; arranging alternative care; putting the child to bed at night, attending to the child in the middle of the night, waking the child in the morning; disciplining, teaching general manners and toilet training; educating; and teaching elementary reading, writing and arithmetic skills.

The court gave three reasons for creating the primary caregiver preference. First, the court wanted to prevent custody from being used as a bargaining chip or weapon in the non-custody issues underlying the divorce proceedings, such as the level of support payments; second, choosing between parents based solely on their relative degrees of fitness required a precision of measurement that was not possible given the tools available to judges; and third, divorcing couples could rely on the presumption to reach out of court settlements.

To what extent do the cases reproduced above recognize that primary care before separation is a factor in making the custodial decision?

For discussion of the primary caregiver presumption, see Ziff, "The Primary Caretaker Presumption: Canadian Perspectives on an American Development" (1990), 4 International J. L. & Fam. 186; Boyd, "Potentialities and Perils of the Primary Caregiver Presumption" (1990-1991), 7 C.F.L.Q. 1; Pask and McCall, "*K. (M.M.) v. K. (U.)* and the Primary Care-Giver" (1991), 33 R.F.L. (3d) 418; and Hughes, "Mother's Vicarious Hand: Primary Caregiving Reconceived as Relationship and Responsibility" (2002-2003), 20 C.F.L.Q. 467.

3. For commentary on *Klachefsky v. Brown*, see Pask and McCall, "*Klachefsky v. Brown*: A Case of Competing Values" (1989), 4 C.F.L.Q. 73.

(6) Separation of Siblings

The courts accept that it is generally undesirable to separate children of the same family. See also 24(2)(a)(ii) of the *CLRA*. For a case in which the "non-separation of siblings" principle was particularly influential, see *Wereley v. Wereley* (1979), 14 R.F.L. (2d) 193 (Ont. H.C.). More recent cases where the principle played a role include *Lynch v. Lynch* (1995), 12 R.F.L. (4th) 367 (Ont. Gen. Div.); *Clark v. Clark* (1995), 18 R.F.L. (4th) 234 (Sask. Q.B.); and *Sloss v. Forget* (2004), 8 R.F.L. (6th) 380 (Ont. S.C.J.).

The importance of this factor in any given case will depend, of course, on the closeness of the bond between the particular children involved as well as any other relevant circumstances, such as the length of time they have lived apart and become accustomed to other surroundings. For some cases in which it was held that the best interests of the children required separation of siblings, see *Jones v. Jones* (1994), 4 R.F.L. (4th) 293 (Sask. Q.B.); *Poole v. Poole* (1999), 45 R.F.L. (4th) 56 (B.C. C.A.); *Doucet v. MacDougall* (2000), 7 R.F.L. (5th) 29 (N.B. C.A.); and *Levine v. McGrath* (2000), 11 R.F.L. (5th) 337 (Ont. S.C.J.).

(7) Blood Ties

At one time, courts emphasized the blood tie between a biological parent and his or her child in any custody contest involving a non-biological parent. See, e.g, the trilogy of Supreme Court of Canada cases in the 1950s where biological parents recovered custody of their children given up to "strangers" for adoption: *Martin v. Duffell*, [1950] S.C.R. 737, [1950] 4 D.L.R. 1; *Hepton v. Maat*, [1957] S.C.R. 606, 10 D.L.R. (2d) 1; and *McNeilly v. Agar* (1957), [1958] S.C.R. 52, 11 D.L.R. (2d) 721. The trilogy emphasized the right of natural parents to retain or regain custody unless they were shown to be unfit or to have abandoned the child. That approach was significantly altered in the 1980s in *Beson v. Newfoundland (Director of Child Welfare)* (1982), 30 R.F.L. (2d) 438 (S.C.C.); *R. (A.N.) v. W. (L.J.)* (1983), 36 R.F.L. (2d) 1 (S.C.C.); and *K. (K.) v. L. (G.)* (1985), 44 R.F.L. (2d) 113 (S.C.C.). In the last two cases, adoptive parents kept their children in the face of custody applications by biological parents. These cases signified the triumph of a highly individualized "best interests" test even in disputes between biological parents and third parties.

In *K. (K.) v. L. (G.)*, the Supreme Court emphasized the importance of stability and continuity in a child's life. An unwed mother gave up her son for adoption a few days after his birth to a couple carefully chosen by her. Less than three months later the mother requested the child's return. When the couple refused to comply, the mother revoked her consent to the proposed adoption and sought custody. The trial judge awarded custody to the prospective adoptive parents on the basis that the benefits to the child of maintaining his relationship with the biological mother were outweighed by those resulting from maintenance of his present home stability and the existing bond with the couple. This decision was upheld by the Supreme Court of Canada. In delivering the judgment of the court, McIntyre J. stated (at 126):

> I would therefore hold that in the case at bar the dominant consideration to which all other considerations must remain subordinate must be the welfare of the child. This is not to say that the question of custody will be determined by weighing the economic circumstances of the contending parties. The matter will not be determined solely on the basis of the physical comfort and material advantages that may be available in the home of one contender or the other. The welfare of the child must be decided on a consideration of these and all other relevant factors, including the general psychological, spiritual and emotional welfare of the child. It must be the aim of the court, when resolving disputes between rival claimants for the custody of a child, to choose the course which will best provide for the healthy growth, development and education of the child so that he will be equipped to face the problems of life as a mature adult. Parental claims must not be lightly set aside, and they are entitled to serious consideration in reaching any conclusion. Where it is clear that the welfare of the child requires it, however, they must be set aside.

In considering the facts of this case, it should be observed at once that the trial judge found that the adoptive parents, on the one hand, and the mother, on the other, were both capable of providing a satisfactory home for the child. This clearly is not a case where the choice is made easy by clear failure, on one side or the other, to measure up to the required standard. I have read the entire record and it is notable in this case that there is a total absence of the mutual recrimination usually found in such cases. Each party has accepted the proposition that the other can perform the parental duties well, but each seeks custody: the mother because of her love for the child she bore and from whom she has been separated, and the adoptive parents because they have come to look on the child as their own, as a member of their family to whom they have become attached as to their own children.

Stressing the significance of the bond between the child and the prospective adoptive parents, McIntyre J. concluded (at 129) that "there was evidence upon which a finding in favour of the adoptive parents could properly be made".

In a case comment ((1985), 4 Can. J. Fam. L. 514) W.J. Wardell stated (at 516-517):

Rutter's work in the area of maternal deprivation and infant bonding points to the probability that as long as the child's capability to form bonds has been established early in life, then multiple bonding can, and does, take place. The "chief bond" developed with the mother-figure is the strongest bond but basically similar in nature to other bonds the infant forms. It would appear that the critical issue in terms of the young infant's adjustment in later life is whether the infant has formed *any* bonds, not merely whether those bonds have been disrupted. The negative effects of disruption of bonds will depend on such variable factors as the infant's age and gender, the manner of the disruption, the number of times bonding has taken place and been disrupted, and so on. While this thesis lacks full empirical proof, the theory of psychological parenting which is premised on extremely limited bond-forming capability and emphasizes one-caretaker continuity has come under increasing criticism as being overly rigid, restrictive and unrealistic in terms of actual family and kin-group structures.

It is the psychological parenting theory, however, which underlies the *King v. Low* judgments at all three court levels. The "existing parental bonds" which go beyond the mere day-to-day care of the baby are emphasized in the trial judgment. To sever these bonds "would impair its prospects of functioning as a healthy human being as it grows older". This is a reference to Bowlby's maternal deprivation theory and, as noted above, not any longer the last word in child development theory. Had the trial judge taken into account the infant's bonding with its birth mother in hospital, and the benefit to a child of not only knowing but also of actual continued contact with its genetic parentage, and considered these factors in light of the revised bonding theory, he might have come to a different conclusion and awarded the baby to the birth mother. By the time the case reached the Court of Appeal, and certainly by the Supreme Court hearing when the child was three years old, return to the birth mother would be untenable by any theory unless contact had been maintained between families and the transfer effected with the greatest care. Even so, few would argue that after such a passage of time with a child so young, any interests of the child would be served thereby. The best hope for return of the child in the fact situation presented by *King v. Low* is a speedy resolution in a trial court unhampered by overly rigid and possibly outdated child welfare theory. A decision dealing with placement where the child is very young at the onset of the dispute will inevitably result in the award of the child to the caretaker parents by a higher court due to the mere passage of time.

For other cases involving attempts by biological parents to regain custody of children placed for adoption, see Chapter 11, *THE LEGAL CONCEPT OF PARENT: GENETIC PARENTAGE, SOCIAL PARENTAGE, AND ADOPTION.*

The Supreme Court of Canada's 1980s trilogy does not mean that the blood tie is totally irrelevant in a custody dispute. Rather, it becomes one factor in determining the best interests of the child. Some provincial statutes specifically list it as such. See, e.g., s. 24(2)(h) of the *CLRA*. In *Hardcastle v. Huculak* (1987), 11 R.F.L. (3d) 363 (Sask. C.A.), Wakeling J.A. stated (at 366):

Now all things being comparatively equal the welfare of a child is best served in the custody of one or both of his natural parents; there is the advantage of natural parental and filial love, of extended natural family relationships, and of the sense of security which comes from knowing, and knowing of, one's family and one's roots.

Justice Beetz said in *Droit de la famille — 320 (1987)*, (sub nom. *C. (G.) v. V.-F.(T.))* 9 R.F.L. (3d) 263 (S.C.C.) at 291:

> A third person who wished to obtain custody of a child must rebut the presumption to the effect that the parent is in a better position to ensure [the] child's wellbeing. He [or she] must establish on a balance of probabilities that the development of the child is likely to be compromised if he or she remains with the father or mother or returns to live with them. The third person must also show that, unlike the person having parental authority, he or she is able to provide the care and affection needed by the child.

Some more recent decisions have also emphasized the "rights" of biological parents in custody disputes. In *O'Brien v. Thomson* (2004), 1 R.F.L. (6th) 318 (N.S. C.A.), the appellate court upheld a trial judge's award of custody to the father of a four-year-old child who was living with his maternal grandmother. Depicting the case as a contest between "the status quo versus the role and rights of a natural parent in the raising of this child", the trial judge did note that "the paramount consideration ... is the best interests of the child". The Nova Scotia Court of Appeal stated (at para. 26) that the trial judge did not err in "taking Kristopher's father's parental rights into account as he did". The Alberta Court of Appeal stated categorically in *Bowes v. Gauvin* (2001), 20 R.F.L. (5th) 301, that it was an error to apply the best interests of the child test to a custody contest between a father and the child's maternal grandparents. It stated (para. 9) that the fitness test should apply instead and that, quoting from *D. (W.) v. P. (G.)* (1984), 54 A.R. 161 (C.A.); leave to appeal refused (1984), 41 R.F.L. (2d) xxx (S.C.C.), the appropriate principle was that "a stranger to a child ... cannot wrest custody from the lawful guardian of the child without demonstrating that the lawful guardian has either abandoned or neglected the child, or without offering other commanding reasons". The appellate court distinguished (par. 12) the *King* decision on the basis that that case did not deal directly with a contest between a parent and a "legal stranger" to the child. See also *W. (J.) v. C. (J.)* (2003), 49 R.F.L. (5th) 442 (Alta. Q.B.); affirmed (2003), 49 R.F.L. (5th) 450 (Alta. C.A.), where Justice Johnstone stated (para. 23): "The presumption is that the child should be in the custody of the natural parent unless the legal stranger can show that the natural parent is unfit".

For a recent case where grandparents obtained custody in a contest with a parent, see *Rochon v. Jacco* (2003), 42 R.F.L. (5th) 143 (Ont. S.C.J.). The grandparents had looked after the four-year-old child for almost all of her life and she was bonded to them. See also *Crocker v. Sipus* (1992), 41 R.F.L. (3d) 19 (Ont. C.A.), where an aunt and uncle obtained custody in a contest with the father after the mother's death.

NOTES AND QUESTIONS

1. In *Floyd v. Bertrand* (1984), 41 R.F.L. (2d) 458 (Ont. S.C.), the child was living with its mother and the step-father until the mother's death. Master Cork granted interim custody to the biological father on the basis that he would be able to obtain custody at trial and that it was best to move the child sooner rather than later. He added (at 463): "... it is better for the child to be brought up by the biological father, even though it means being separated from the child's half-sisters at an early age." For a reported case in which a step-parent was awarded custody in circumstances similar to Floyd v. Bertrand, see *Fullerton v. Richman* (1983), 40 O.R. (2d) 395 (Fam. Ct.).

Section 61(1) of the *CLRA* allows a "person entitled to custody of a child" to "appoint by will one or more persons to have custody of the child after the death of the appointer". What is the effect of such an appointment? See s. 61(7). If a parent with sole custody of a child specifies in the will that the step-parent is to have custody, does this preclude the other biological parent from applying for custody? If not, how much weight should the court give to the appointment?

2. Section 21 of the *CLRA* permits any person to apply for custody or access. See *Smith v. Hunter* (1979), 15 R.F.L. (2d) 203, 27 O.R. (2d) 683 (H.C.), and *Smith v. Children's Aid Society for Kent (County)* (1980), 29 O.R. (2d) 502 (Co. Ct.). For cases dealing with similar legislation in other provinces, see *Newfoundland (Director of*

Child Welfare) v. T. (B.) (1993), 110 D.L.R. (4th) 160 (Nfld. C.A.); *H. (M.E.) v. F. (R.M.)* (1994), 10 R.F.L. (4th) 77 (Sask. C.A.); *Ochapowace First Nation v. A. (V.)* (1994), 10 R.F.L. (4th) 152 (Sask. C.A.); leave to appeal refused (1995), 12 R.F.L. (4th) 169 (S.C.C.); and *Williams v. Williams* (1995), 13 R.F.L. (4th) 152 (Alta. Q.B.). Section 16(1) of the *Divorce Act* allows a person other than a parent to apply for custody or access in divorce proceedings. However, where the person is not a spouse directly involved in the proceedings, the court must grant leave to apply: s. 16(3). In *M. (R.) v. B. (G.)* (1987), 6 R.F.L. (3d) 441 (Nfld. T.D.); additional reasons at (1987), 64 Nfld. & P.E.I.R. 70 at 74 (Nfld. T.D.) and *Arnink v. Arnink* (1999), 2 R.F.L. (5th) 24 (B.C. S.C. [In Chambers]) it was held that leave should be granted unless the application is clearly frivolous or vexatious.

(8) Race and Culture

VAN DE PERRE v. EDWARDS

(2001), 19 R.F.L. (5th) 396, 2001 CarswellBC 1999, 2001 CarswellBC 2000 (S.C.C.)

[A woman conceived a child during an affair with a married, professional basketball player who had numerous other extra-marital affairs. The mother, who was a Caucasian Canadian, had sexual relations with other professional basketball players. The father and his wife were African-Americans who intended to return to the United States after the father retired. The father's wife was determined to hold their marriage together, partly for the sake of their twin daughters. Prior to the trial of the custody proceedings, the child lived with his mother who depended heavily on her mother and friends for help in caring for him.

The clinical psychologist who prepared a report for the court had some concerns about the mother's personality, but acknowledged that she had acquired appropriate parenting skills and that the child was primarily attached to her. The psychologist described the father as fairly healthy in his psychological functioning and noted that his daughters had a strong, positive attachment to him. The father's wife impressed the psychologist as a devoted mother with excellent parenting skills. The psychologist noted that the child had developed an attachment to the father, the father's wife, and their daughters. She concluded that the father's family unit swung the balance in his favour. The mother's family doctor testified favourably about the mother's parenting skills and the bond between mother and child.

The trial judge awarded custody to the mother and granted the father access for four one-week periods quarterly. He emphasized the mother's parenting skills and the bond between mother and child. Although the trial judge acknowledged the father's wife's positive attributes, he reasoned that he had to determine whether the father alone would be better able to raise the child than the mother. This approach reflected the trial judge's conclusion that the father's affairs posed a serious threat to the stability of his marriage.

On the father's appeal, the British Columbia Court of Appeal invited the father's wife to apply for joint custody with her husband and then granted such a joint custody order. The court stated that the trial judge had failed to engage in the detailed analysis that was required in respect of the backgrounds, personalities, family environments and parenting abilities of each of the parents. It found that the trial judge had essentially ignored concerns about the mother's suitability to raise a child and had become diverted from the central question of the best interests of the child by the father's extra-marital affairs and the parties' attitudes to each other. The appellate court also held that the trial judge erred in concluding that the father's marriage would not last and then assessing the father's ability to parent in isolation from the rest of his family. Finally, and most importantly, it was critical of the trial judge's failure to give weight to the fact that it would be in the child's interest to live with a parent and family who would nurture his identity as a person of colour and would appreciate the day-to-day realities of racism and discrimination that African-Americans faced in North America.

The Supreme Court of Canada stayed the British Columbia Court of Appeal's decision until the disposition of the mother's appeal. In the meantime, the child was spending approximately equal time with his mother in Vancouver and his father and stepmother in North Carolina. Eventually, the Supreme Court unanimously restored the trial decision. In part, the court was concerned about the British Columbia Court of Appeal's failure to apply the proper principles of appellate review. Justice Bastarache, for the court, stated that an examination of the key difficulties in the trial judge's decision identified by the Court of Appeal revealed that there was no scope for appellate intervention. He found that the trial judge had analysed the parenting abilities of the parents and that his reasons explicitly referred to the bonds between the child and the father's wife and between the child and the twins. In addition, he stated that the Court of Appeal had erroneously found that the trial judge focussed on the father's extra-marital affairs and the parties' attitudes to each other. While Justice Bastarache considered responsibility for the affair irrelevant, he stated that the parties' attitudes towards each other were important because these might affect the emotional well-being of the child and because a child should be with someone who wished to foster the relationship between the child and the other parent. Accordingly, he concluded that the trial judge could take into account the fact that the father and his wife both blamed the mother for the relationship and believed that she was a "gold-digger". He also found that the trial judge's assessment of the strength of the father's marriage was warranted because it might affect the parenting help available to him. Turning to the Court of Appeal's criticism of the trial judge for not discussing the mother's conduct even though it was similar to the father's, Justice Bastarache noted that a parent's conduct did not require comment unless it substantially affected the best interests of the child. Finally, Justice Bastarache turned to the Court of Appeal's finding that the trial judge gave no weight to the fact that it would be in the child's interest to live with a parent and family who would nurture his identity as a person of colour.]

36 The Court of Appeal found that the trial judge gave "no consideration" to issues of race and interracial problems that Elijah might face. In fact, the trial judge noted that there had been some testimony at trial related to the race of Elijah and the importance of being exposed to his heritage and culture as the son of an African-American father. Rather than discussing the child's race in detail, however, the trial judge noted that this child is of mixed race and, as such, his Caucasian Canadian heritage must also be considered.

37 The interveners, the African Canadian Legal Clinic, the Association of Black Social Workers and the Jamaican Canadian Association, submit that race is a critical factor in custody and access cases. In my view, the importance of this factor will depend greatly on many factual considerations. The interveners state that there are key tools a Canadian biracial child will need in order to foster racial identity and pride: the need to develop a means to deal with racism and the need to develop a positive racial identity. The corollary to these needs is the parental ability to meet them. The interveners do not state that the minority parent should necessarily be granted custody; rather, the question is which parent will best be able to contribute to a healthy racial socialization and overall healthy development of the child. This question is one of fact to be determined by the courts on a case-by-case basis and weighed by the trial judge with other relevant factors.

38 The interveners submit that, although some studies show that Black parents are more likely to be aware of the need to prepare their children to cope with racism, the main issue is which parent will facilitate contact and the development of racial identity in a manner that avoids conflict, discord and disharmony. But again, this is only one factor to be considered by the trial judge. I would also add that evidence of race relations in the relevant communities may be important to define the context in which the child and his parents will function. It is not always possible to address these sensitive issues by judicial notice, even though

some notice of racial facts can be taken; see *R. v. Williams*, [1998] 1 S.C.R. 1128 (S.C.C.). The weight to be given to all relevant factors is a matter of discretion, but discretion must be exercised with regard to the evidence. In essence, the interveners argue that race is always a crucial factor and that it should never be ignored, even if not addressed by the parties. They favour forced judicial consideration of race because it is essential in deciding which parent is best able to cope with difficulties biracial children may face. This approach is based on the conclusions reached concerning the present state of race relations in Canada. As I have said, racial identity is but one factor that may be considered in determining personal identity; the relevancy of this factor depends on the context. Other factors are more directly related to primary needs and must be considered in priority. ... All factors must be considered pragmatically. Different situations and different philosophies require an individual analysis on the basis of reliable evidence.

39 There is also a distinction between the role of race in adoption cases and those cases involving two biological parents desiring custody; see G. Pollack, "The Role of Race in Child Custody Decisions Between Natural Parents over Biracial Children" (1997), 23 *N.Y.U. Rev. L. & Soc. Change* 603, at p. 617. In adoption cases, the situation might arise whereby the court must make an either/ or decision; in other words, the child is either granted or denied exposure to his or her own heritage. Here, however, we have two biological parents, each of whom shares a part of the race and culture of the child. Of these two biological parents, one will be granted custody and one will be granted access. The result here is that Elijah will have exposure to both sides of his racial and cultural heritage. There was no evidence introduced to suggest that greater exposure to one's racial background through custody as opposed to access is in the better interests of the child in every case. Consequently, cultural concerns are not the same as those involving prospective adoptive parents who do not share the same race and culture as the child. This said, I wish to note that the approach taken in this case is not new. In *H. (D.) v. M. (H.)*, [1997] B.C.J. No. 2144 (B.C. S.C.), (subsequently conf'd by [1999] 1 S.C.R. 328 (S.C.C.)), Bauman J. considered a case involving an adoption dispute between two sets of grandparents: the mother's biological father and her adoptive parents. The mother of the child was aboriginal and the father was African American. The mother's adoptive parents were Caucasian and her biological father was aboriginal. In that case, counsel for the child's biological grandfather argued that the child's aboriginal heritage should be given great weight especially in light of the *Child, Family and Community Service Act*, R.S.B.C. 1996, c. 46, which notes the importance of cultural identity of aboriginal children in consideration of their well-being. Bauman J. stated, at paras. 46 and 47, that the child's

> ... aboriginal heritage and the ability of his biological grandfather to preserve and enhance it are important considerations, but we must not overlook the obvious fact that Ishmael has an African-American background and American citizenship. That heritage is also of importance and it is equally deserving of preservation and nurturing. *This is not a case of taking an aboriginal child and placing him with a non-aboriginal family in complete disregard for his culture and heritage.* ...
>
> ... The submission that Ishmael's aboriginal heritage is virtually a determining factor here, oversimplifies a very complex case. [Emphasis added.]

He next proceeded to consider all factors which impact the best interests of the child, including his aboriginal heritage and, having weighed all these factors, decided that the parenting and family environment of the mother's adoptive parents was superior and better served the child's best interests. This Court upheld this decision. It is therefore clear that, even in adoption cases where it might play a more important role, race is not a determinative factor and its importance will depend greatly on the facts.

40 Race can be a factor in determining the best interests of the child because it is connected to the culture, identity and emotional well-being of the child. New Brunswick, for example,

has adopted legislation prescribing mandatory consideration of "cultural and religious heritage" for all custody determinations (*Family Services Act*, S.N.B. 1980, c. F-2.2, ss. 1 and 129(2)). British Columbia has included similar language in its provisions regarding adoption, but not in those found in the *Family Relations Act* applicable in this case (*Adoption Act*, R.S.B.C. 1996, c. 5, s. 3). The adoption and custody contexts may differ because the adopted child will generally cease to have contact with the biological parent while custody will generally favour contact with both parents. Nevertheless, it is generally understood that biracial children should be encouraged to positively identify with both racial heritages. This suggests the possibility of a biracial identity (i.e. "forming an identity that incorporates multiple racial heritages", see Pollack, *supra*, at p. 619). It is important that the custodial parent recognize the child's need of cultural identity and foster its development accordingly. I would therefore agree that evidence regarding the so-called "cultural dilemma" of biracial children (i.e. the conflict that arises from belonging to two races where one may be dominant for one reason or another) is relevant and should always be accepted. But the significance of evidence relating to race in any given custody case must be carefully considered by the trial judge. Although general public information is useful, it appears to be often contradictory ... and may not be sufficient to inform the judge about the current status of race relations in a particular community or the ability of either applicant to deal with these issues.

41 For the Court of Appeal to intervene, it would have to find a material error. Although Warren J. did not discuss in detail the role that race plays in determining the best interests of the child, he did state that there is an overarching need for the child to be in a stable and loving environment. The limited findings of the trial judge on this issue reflected the minimal weight that the parties themselves placed on the issue at trial. Therefore, notwithstanding the role that race may play in custody determinations, it appears that the trial judge noted that this issue was not determinative and that, in this case, Elijah would be in a more stable and loving environment if custody was granted to the appellant. He clearly considered the mixed race of Elijah and implied that race may impact [the custody decision] in some cases; however, the trial judge obviously was of the view that, even if the biological father provided some benefits as regards fostering a positive racial identity, these benefits did not outweigh the negative findings related to him. By intervening in the consideration of race by the trial judge, the Court of Appeal failed to apply the correct standard of review. It should not have intervened; this issue was given disproportionate emphasis at the initiative of the Court of Appeal.

42 In this case, there was absolutely no evidence adduced which indicates that race was an important consideration. As noted by the appellant in her factum, there was essentially no evidence of racial identity by reason of skin colour or of race relations in Vancouver or North Carolina; there was no evidence of the racial awareness of the applicants or of their attitudes concerning the needs of the child with regard to racial and cultural identity. The issues of race and ethnicity were not argued at trial, nor were written submissions provided in the appeal. The sole evidence relied upon by the respondents in this Court was a blanket statement by Mrs. Edwards that the appellant could not teach Elijah what it was to be Black and the testimony of Dr. Korpach that Elijah would likely be considered to be of Black colour. ...

43 In fact, in this Court, counsel for the respondents stated that "neither of the parties wanted to touch it, because it's so *politically incorrect* to say that race has any bearing" (emphasis added). This is an unacceptable reason for counsel to fail to raise evidence on a factor that he or she believes may impact the best interests of the child. Without evidence, it is not possible for any court, and certainly not the Court of Appeal, to make a decision based on the importance of race. Unfortunately, this is what the Court of Appeal did when Newbury J.A. stated, at para. 50: "If it is correct that Elijah will be seen by the world at large as

'being black', it would obviously be in his interests to live with a parent or family who can nurture his identity. ..." She further stated, at para. 51:

> ... it seems to me likely that being raised in an Afro-American family in a part of the world where the black population is proportionately greater than it is here, would to some extent be less difficult than it would be in Canada. Elijah would in this event have a greater chance of achieving a sense of cultural belonging and identity and would in his father have a strong role model who has succeeded in the world of professional sports.

NOTES AND QUESTIONS

1. For a comment on *Van de Perre v. Edwards*, see Wing-Yun Law, "The Race Issue in Custody Law: Is *Van de Perre* Right?" (2003-2004), 21 C.F.L.Q. 153. The author states that the court's distinction between adoption and custody disputes naively assumes that access parents have enough time and control to make a substantial impression on a child. The author notes (at 170) that access parents often drop out of a child's life. In fact, Edwards stopped seeing his son following the Supreme Court of Canada decision and soon fell behind in his support payments. See *Van De Perre v. Edwards* (2004), 2004 CarswellBC 867, 19 R.F.L. (6th) 442 (B.C. S.C.).

2. Some cases involving children of mixed-race employ a rather simplistic analysis. For example, in *Kassel v. Louie* (2000), 11 R.F.L. (5th) 144 (B.C. S.C.), custody was awarded to a Chinese-Canadian father largely because the child looked Chinese. Others use a more sophisticated analysis, but still emphasize race as a crucial factor. See, e.g., *Camba v. Sparks* (1993), 124 N.S.R. (2d) 321 (N.S. Fam. Ct.); additional reasons at (1994), 1994 CarswellNS 656 (N.S. Fam. Ct.), where the court awarded custody to a black mother largely because she was better able to provide for the racial needs of her bi-racial child.

3. In *Van de Perre*, the Supreme Court of Canada clearly rejected the interveners' arguments that race should be a crucial factor in custody determinations involving bi-racial children and, instead, placed it among a long list of factors to be considered in determining a particular child's best interests. How much guidance does this give to lower courts? Is race ever likely to be determinative under this approach?

4. In *M. (D.) v. L. (A.G.)* (2004), 3 R.F.L. (6th) 79 (Alta. Q.B.), the court awarded an aboriginal father and a non-native mother joint custody of a three-year-old daughter who was to reside primarily with her mother. The court favoured joint custody partly to encourage a strong relationship between father and daughter so that she "could be given the opportunity to understand and develop her First Nations' cultural identity" (para. 18). See also *Brooke v. Grandin* (2003), 37 R.F.L. (5th) 23 (B.C. S.C.), where the court suggested that generous access for the mother could provide the bi-racial child a chance to learn about her Caribbean heritage.

(9) Wishes of the Child

Two basic issues must be considered. What significance should be attached to the wishes of the child? How are the child's wishes to be ascertained?

STEFUREAK v. CHAMBERS

(2004), 6 R.F.L. (6th) 212, 2004 CarswellOnt 4244 (Ont. S.C.J.)

[In his "Annotation" to the case, Professor McLeod states:

> The facts in the case do little more than provide a backdrop for Quinn J.'s discussion of how to inform a presiding judge about a child's views and preferences. The parents were married in 1998, separated in 2000, and divorced in 2002. The divorce judgment established a shared-parenting regime in respect of the parties' seven-year-old son whereby the child would reside with the father three out of four weekends from Friday after school until Monday morning and during the month of July. In spite of this, the parties' practice was that the father exercised access only on alternate weekends from Friday after school until Sunday evening. The mother also pointed out that instead of having the child the month of July, the child was with him for only one week in August. The mother applied to vary the prior order to grant her sole custody and define the father's access to reflect the reality of the

ongoing arrangements, at which point the father insisted on reverting to the judgment regime. The mother alleged that the child preferred to return Sunday evenings. An issue arose during the trial about how to ascertain the child's views and preferences.

In the excerpts from Justice Quinn's reasons that follow, the footnotes have been omitted.]

3.1 Ascertaining the Views and Preferences of Young Children

14 When considering the merits of an application for custody or access and the best interests of a child, the court is required to consider, among other matters, "the views and preferences of the child, where such views and preferences can reasonably be ascertained": see *clause 24(2)(b)* of the *Children's Law Reform Act*. ...

15 There are four primary ways by which the court is able to ascertain the views and preferences of a child caught in the middle of a custody and access war:

(1) through the evidence of trained professionals, such as child psychologists and social workers, who have had contact with the child;

(2) through the evidence of the parties and their lay witnesses who testify about out-of-court statements of the child;

(3) by means of the judge's interviewing the child in chambers;

(4) by permitting the child to testify.

16 Of course, when it comes to very young children, their views and preferences can be difficult to ascertain and are only two factors to consider. After all, the court is not permitted to delegate to very young children the disposition of their fate.

17 And not all custody and access issues require, for their disposition, knowledge of the views and preferences of the child. For example, sometimes common sense or simple notions of fairness will suffice.

3.2 Hearsay Evidence

19 The historical basis for the exclusion of hearsay evidence is that the admission of such evidence does not permit cross-examination; and cross-examination is thought to be the great revealer. ...

23 Out-of-court statements, therefore, must be screened for necessity and reliability before they are admitted for their truth. ...

39 In a custody case, hearsay, in the form of the out-of-court statements of a child, should not be admitted into evidence for the truth of what was said unless the requirements of necessity and reliability have been met. In other words, the *Khan-Smith* tests must be followed. Mr. Dedinsky [the mother's lawyer] submits, however, that the requirements of necessity and threshold reliability should be relaxed in custody cases, as compared to child protection and criminal proceedings. Where the custody case does not involve allegations of abuse, there is some merit to this submission, although I would not lay it down as a rigid rule. The degree of relaxation will depend on all of the circumstances.

40 "Necessity" can be satisfied where it would not be appropriate to call the child as a witness. "Reliability" can be established if the statement under consideration (or a similar utterance) was made to more than one person and those persons will testify. ...

42 In so far as future out-of-court statements of the child are concerned, I think that the best approach is to conduct a *voir dire* for each statement. In the event we encounter a number of statements that, through content or other circumstances, come within the same category, it

might be possible to make one ruling for all. But the best course would seem to be to rule on each statement separately. Nevertheless, in my view, it would be appropriate if I were to make a blanket ruling in respect of "necessity," as it will be seen later that I do not consider it appropriate for the child to be called as a witness. ...

44 Of course, on the *voir dire*, it is for the proponent of the hearsay evidence to establish threshold liability.

3.3 In-Court Testimony of Young Children

45 Mr. Daboll [the father's lawyer] intimated that he might be put in the position of having to instruct his client to authorize the child being called as a witness as part of the father's case. This caused raised eyebrows in every corner of the courtroom. ...

55 Another interesting article to which the court was referred by Mr. Daboll comes from an Australian barrister and solicitor: William J. Keough, "The Separate Representation of Children in Australian Family Law — Effective Practice or Mere Rhetoric?" (2002), 19 Can. J. Fam. L. 371. The author stated, "[c]hildren that are excluded from custody/ access decision making generally feel alienated, angry and fearful." If this statement includes in-court testimony as part of the "decision making," then it seems to run contrary to what I have understood to be a prevailing judicial reluctance to involve young children in custody and access cases as witnesses.

56 Absent some reasonably perceived psychological trauma to the child, the major obstacles to allowing a young child to testify in custody and access cases are twofold:

- first, the typical absence of a developmentally appropriate explanation to the child regarding the need for his or her testimony;
- second, the lack of training of the bench and bar in asking developmentally appropriate questions.

57 Here, although perhaps it is not too late to remove the first obstacle, it is for the second.

3.4 Trial Judge Interviewing Child

58 The prospect of a chambers interview of the child was floated by Mr. Daboll during the argument of these mid-trial issues.

59 *Section 24* of the *Children's Law Reform Act* provides that, in custody and access disputes, two of the criteria to consider are the "views and preferences" of the child. ...

60 *Section 64* of the *Children's Law Reform Act* states that, "where possible," the child is entitled to have his or her views and preferences heard on the issues of custody and access. That section gives to the presiding judge the discretion to interview a child in chambers, with the interview to be recorded. ...

61 *Section 64*, therefore, permits the child to play a direct role in the decision of the court. However, *section 64* neither places a duty on the judge to interview the child, nor identifies specific criteria that must be met before such an interview can take place. Rather, this is a matter for the discretion of the judge. The only requirement is that the interview be recorded, and this would entail the presence of a court reporter. The parents must not be present; however, their counsel may be present at the discretion of the judge.

62 The discretion to conduct a chambers interview is broad. Case law and academics suggest that a judge should only interview a child in chambers where other methods of determining the child's preferences (such as assessments) are unavailable. This suggestion rests on the

assumption that judges are not trained to interview children and that the formality of meeting a judge in chambers creates an intimidating environment in which it will be difficult for the child to speak freely. Ultimately, however, the discretion of whether to interview rests with the judge.

63 The discretion also covers a situation in which parents object to the interview. In *Jandrisch v. Jandrisch*, 3 Man. R. (2d) 135, 16 R.F.L. (2d) 239, [1980] M.J. No. 6 (Man. C.A.), at paragraph 38, the Manitoba Court of Appeal stated that, where the purpose of a chambers interview is to ascertain the wishes of a child, the judge may interview the child "with or without the consent of one or both counsel." In *Hamilton v. Hamilton*, 20 R.F.L. (3d) 152, [1989] S.J. No. 687 (Sask. C.A.), the Saskatchewan Court of Appeal upheld the decision of a trial judge to interview a child despite the objections of his father. And, in *Mannila v. Mannila* (1992), 1992 CarswellOnt 1587 (Ont. Gen. Div.) Justice Erwin W. Stach would have interviewed a child despite objection from the parents but for other considerations that turned him against such a meeting.

64 If a judge does decide to interview the child privately in chambers, the case law provides some clarification of what use may be made of that interview. The primary concern is ensuring that the judge does not allow the comments of the child to be the sole basis of the judgment while disregarding other evidence of what may actually be in the child's best interests. The views or preferences of a child are not to be confused with the child's best interests. However, the judge must make an order that is practical. For example, when dealing specifically with teenagers, an order should reasonably conform with the wishes of the child. Although the preference of a teenager may not be in absolute accord with his or her best interests, a court may defer to the wishes of the child, as it would be undesirable to force a teenager against his or her wishes to live with a parent. Attempting to force a teenager may even be futile. Ultimately, the weight to be attached to any expression of preference depends on the facts and is a function of age, intelligence, apparent maturity, and the ability of a child to articulate a view.

65 In addition, the interview should not be seen as an opportunity to obtain vital information of which the other parties are unaware or cannot challenge.

66 When asked to hold an interview in *Demeter v. Demeter*, 133 D.L.R. (4th) 746, 21 R.F.L. (4th) 54, [1996] O.J. No. 1470, 1996 CarswellOnt 1301 (Ont. Gen. Div.), Justice Christopher M. Speyer listened to all the evidence presented at trial to see whether a current and accurate account of the views and preferences of the children emerged, before deciding whether to meet with the children in private.

67 As another alternative, some judges have held that meeting with the child is not necessarily a matter of attempting to determine the wishes of the child, but may better serve simply to come to a fuller understanding of who the child is for the purposes of determining best interests.

68 Finally, except in the most exceptional circumstances, it is wrong to obtain the confidence of a child by promising that the judge will not disclose the information received. The judge has the discretion to decide whether anything should be disclosed about the results of his or her interview, and to decide what should be said. When making this determination, the court must consider the ability of counsel to make argument at trial or on appeal, fairness to the parties, and potential embarrassment to the children.

69 It is doubtful that very many judges, because of a lack of training in interviewing children, would agree to do so. Although, arguably, a properly conducted interview by the trial judge could be the quickest way to learn of the views and preferences of a child, it might not be the most efficient approach, as it would be desirable for the parties to have this information before embarking on an expensive trial. However, once the trial has commenced, an

interview by the judge would avoid a lengthy adjournment for an assessment under *section 30* of the *Children's Law Reform Act* or an investigation pursuant to *section 112* of the *Courts of Justice Act*, R.S.O. 1990, c. C-43 (as amended).

70 A chambers interview is not feasible at bar, as I have no training or known skill in interviewing children.

3.5 Investigation by Children's Lawyer

72 Section 112 of the *Courts of Justice Act* is authority for the Children's Lawyer to become involved in a case, investigate and make recommendations regarding issues of custody and access. ...

75 May *section 112* be invoked mid-trial? *Section 112* does not say when, in the proceeding, the investigation by the Children's Lawyer is to be conducted. Consequently, the investigation may occur at any stage of the proceeding, including mid-trial (and even mid-appeal).

76 However, before resorting to *section 112*, there should be a clearly identified need that is to be met by the investigation. It would be an abuse of the rule, for example, to order an investigation by the Children's Lawyer with nothing more specific in mind than the hope that it will resolve or narrow the dispute between the parties. Here, I am not convinced that the views and preferences of the child will play much of a role in the decision of the court. For example, on the issue of weekend access, the father currently returns the child on Monday morning directly to the child's school. This may sound benign until one realizes that the father resides in Oakville and the mother in St. Catherines, necessitating a lengthy early-Monday-morning motor vehicle trip. In the end, this particular issue may not require evidence as to the views and preferences of the child. Nonetheless, if I am confronted with an issue for which common sense is insufficient and the wishes of the child, if relevant, cannot be deduced from other evidence, it is still open for me to order an investigation under *section 112*.

77 I am also alive to the prospect that the request by the father for an investigation under *section 112* is merely a "Hail Mary" move by a litigant who may perceive that things are going badly for him in the trial. A request for an investigation made mid-trial requires an explanation why the request was not made earlier and, if that explanation is not forthcoming (as here), the court should harbour a robust suspicion. (In fairness to Mr. Daboll, I point out that he was retained relatively recently, having been preceded by two different solicitors of record and, as a result, was handicapped in offering an explanation.)

3.6 An Assessment

78 Another way of determining the best interests, and even the views and preferences, of the child is by means of an assessment. ...

79 This subsection is permissive in nature. Courts have held that an assessment should only be ordered in cases where there are clinical issues to be determined, either requiring expert analysis or to allow parties to understand the needs of the child.

80 Subsection 30(2) provides:

> (2) When order may be made — An order may be made under subsection (1) on or before the hearing of the application in respect of custody of or access to the child with or without a request by a party to the application.

The words "on or before the hearing" allow the ordering of an assessment mid-trial.

81 Mr. Daboll indicated that his client did not desire an assessment, largely because of the cost involved. (There is some irony in that submission, for I expect the cost of this litigation will prove to be in the tens of thousands of dollars.)

82 In any event, I do not consider an assessment under section 30 to be needed for the same reason that I have eschewed an investigation under *section 112*.

4 Summary of Mid-Trial Rulings

83 The mid-trial rulings are as follows:

> (1) In respect of the hearsay evidence already given by the mother, in the form of out-of-court statements of the child, as no objection was raised at the time, necessity and threshold reliability are deemed to have been admitted by the father.

> (2) Regarding future out-of-court statements, I make a blanket ruling that "necessity" has been established, for I do not consider it appropriate that the child be called as a witness.

> (3) A *voir dire* will be conducted for each such statement to determine threshold liability.

> (4) I will not allow the child to be called as a witness; counsel are not trained to ask developmentally appropriate questions.

> (5) I do not wish to interview the child in chambers because I lack that same training.

> (6) An investigation under section 112 by the Children's Lawyer is unnecessary. I am not convinced that, in the light of the issues presented by this case, the views and preferences of the child will play much of a role in the decision of the court.

> (7) For the same reason, an assessment under section 30 is not needed.

NOTES AND QUESTIONS

1. Section 24(2)(b) of the *CLRA* affirms that the "views and preferences of the child" are relevant. A child's expressed wishes are not, however, binding on the court. What factors determine how much weight is to be given to the child's wishes?

In *Kemp v. Kemp* (2007), 2007 CarswellOnt 1774 (S.C.J.), Justice Blishen stated:

> 36 Although a child's wishes and preferences are just one consideration in determining "best inter-ests", the older the child, the more a custody order requires the co-operation of the child and consider-ation of the child's wishes. ... The weight to be given to the child's stated preference depends on the facts of the case, and is a function of age, intelligence, apparent maturity and the ability of the child to articulate a view.

In *O'Connell v. McIndoe* (1998), 42 R.F.L. (4th) 77 (B.C. C.A.), the trial judge had granted custody of a 13-year-old boy to his mother over the boy's objection. By the time the case reached the appellate court, the boy had run away from his mother's home five times. The appellate court reversed the trial judge, stating (at 81): "In order for custody orders relating to children in their teens to be practical, they must reasonably conform with the wishes of the children." See also *Borgstrom v. Borgstrom* (2004), 2 R.F.L. (6th) 1 (B.C. S.C.), where Justice Mackenzie stated (para. 77): "I am not prepared to make an order against the firm wishes of a 15-year-old." In *Sider v. Sider* (2004), 10 R.F.L. (6th) 171 (Ont. S.C.J.), a 12-year-old girl's wishes to live with her father were influential in determining an interim order. Recall that the wishes of an 11-year-old boy and 13-year-old girl were discounted in *Young v. Young* (1989), 19 R.F.L. (3d) 227 (Ont. H.C.); additional reasons at (1989), 19 R.F.L. (3d) 227 at 238 (Ont. H.C.), reproduced above. In *Boukema v. Boukema* (1997), 31 R.F.L. (4th) 329 (Ont. Gen. Div.); additional reasons at (1997), 1997 CarswellOnt 5151 (Ont. Gen. Div.), Justice E. Macdonald granted sole custody of an 11-year-old child to her father in Toronto rather than her mother in New Jersey even though the child vehemently insisted that she wished to live with her mother. The Justice concluded that the mother had manipulated the daughter and feared that the child's relationship with her father would be threatened if she lived with her mother.

In *Gaulton v. Hynes* (2003), 36 R.F.L. (5th) 114 (N.L. U.F.C.), the court permitted a 16-year-old girl to determine if and when she would see her father. However, in *Chubay v. Chubay* (2001), 20 R.F.L. (5th) 29 (Alta. Q.B.), Justice Veit refused to allow 12- and 13-year-olds to decide whether they would see their father because this would place too heavy a burden on them and the mother might influence their actions.

2. In "Of Better Myths Than the Best Interests of the Child", Harold Niman and Gerald P. Sadvari, ed., *Family Law: "Best Interests of the Child"* (Toronto: Law Society of Upper Canada, 2000), Jeffery H. Wilson states (at 405):

> Children as young as 12 years of age will meet with a judge in chambers and determine their wellbeing. Too many judges avoid telling a 12-year-old what to do.

> That's *incredible* ... We don't let children go prospecting until the age of 18 years under the *Mining Act*, or work in a riding stable until, I believe, the age of 15 under the *Riding Horse Establishment Act*, but the same child will effectively determine where she will live at the age of 12.

3. In "Incorporating Children's Needs and Views in Alternative Dispute Resolution Approaches" (1992), 8 C.F.L.Q. 69, Gary Austin, Peter Jaffe and Pamela Hurley state (at 71-72):

> ... Legal, and thus also clinical criteria for determining the children's best interests include such areas as attachment, parenting ability, length of time in a stable home, plans for care, permanence and stability of the family unit, relationship by blood, and the children's view and preferences if they can be reasonably ascertained. The child's wishes must therefore be weighed in the context of his needs as indicated by the other criteria. A request for a clinician to interview a child alone to determine the child's wishes for the court would today be considered inappropriate. The child's wishes alone may be misleading without a full appreciation of the other factors in the family system that either influence the child or bear directly on his needs.

> A child who expresses a wish with respect to the parent she wants to live with or the amount of time to be spent with the other parent may be identifying a set of arrangements that could indeed be in her best interests. The wish may reflect the actual conditions (e.g., good parenting, strong attachment, etc.) in the family system that influenced the child to make the wish. Examples would include: a child who wants to live with a particular parent because that parent shows more interest and love, has resided consistently in one location, and is more available; or, a child who, several years after the separation, wants to have more access to a parent because that parent can provide activities which interest the child who is now older, the parent is more available now than before the separation, and the child feels a need for more of a connection with that parent. The more congruency between the wish and the evaluation of the child's needs, the more weight the wish would carry in the assessment recommendations.

> The weighing of the child's wishes should be moderated by the chronological and emotional age of the child. The older and more mature the child, the more weight accorded the wishes. Adolescents 16 and over in Ontario are able to act on their wishes as long as the parent in question agrees to the conditions (e.g., is willing to have the child live in his home). Recommending arrangements contrary to the wishes of a 12- to 15-year-old would require considerable justification on the other best interests criteria, such as risk of family violence or parental incompetence, since such adolescents can exert considerable pressure on the family system that may already be vulnerable and strained. Younger children are especially susceptible to other influences, as outlined below, and their wishes need to be carefully viewed in the context of an adult evaluation of the circumstances. More mature children, even some below 12, are able to describe the basis of their wish, weigh the various options, appreciate the effects of enacting their wish on themselves, their parents, other members of their families, and their friendships and can accept some responsibility for those effects. In the final analysis, there is no easy formula to combine age and maturity in weighing wishes but the broader context of needs must always be considered.

4. In *Uldrian v. Uldrian* (1988), 14 R.F.L. (3d) 26 (Ont. C.A.), the court confirmed that, while the *CLRA* requires the judge to consider the views and preferences of a child, the judge has no duty to interview the child. Judge Nasmith in "The Inchoate Voice" (1991-1992), 8 C.F.L.Q. 43 reports (at 64):

> The once prevalent practice of judges conducting private interviews with a child in chambers has pretty much vanished. ... Recently, at a conference of Ontario judges from the Family Division, of the

40 judges in attendance, only two admitted to any recent use of this practice and, in each case, it was not just with the consent of all parties but upon the urging of all parties.

However, in *Gaulton v. Hynes* (2003), 36 R.F.L. (5th) 114 (N.L. U.F.C.), Justice Cook stated (para. 14): "Because Kirsten is 16 as well as being mature and stable, I did not follow *my usual pattern of interviewing a teenager* in Chambers and I did not discourage having her called as a witness" (emphasis added). Interviews in the judge's chambers occurred in *Lindsay v. Lindsay* (1995), 19 R.F.L. (4th) 103 (Ont. Gen. Div.) and *Demeter v. Demeter* (1996), 21 R.F.L. (4th) 54 (Ont. Gen. Div.).

In *Andrusiek v. Andrusiek* (2002), 25 R.F.L. (5th) 8 (B.C. C.A.), the trial judge interviewed a child in Chambers and promised him that he would not reveal his preference. The appellate court stated (para. 24) that this procedure could result in an unfair hearing because the case could be decided on evidence that was unknown to the parties and upon which they did not have an opportunity to cross-examine. Note the stipulations in s. 64 of the *CLRA* regarding these interviews. What problems does s. 64 address? What problems remain?

Justice Harper interviewed a 13-year-old girl in *McAlister v. Jenkins* (2008), 54 R.F.L. (6th) 126 (Ont. S.C.J.). He explained the circumstances and the procedure used:

> 133 At a case conference heard prior to the trial, the children's therapists recommended that I interview the child Stephanie and this was consented to by all parties. Ms. O'Donovan [Stephanie's therapist] stated that it was her opinion that Stephanie needed to talk to the judge as it was very important to her that the judge heard "from her" the problems she was going through, her version of events and her wishes with respect to the custody issues. She further indicated that Stephanie was feeling that no one was listening to her.

> 134 After the submissions of Stephanie's therapist, I agreed to set up an interview with the following structure: the interview was to be held in my chambers; it would be recorded; and the only persons present would be the court reporter, the child's therapist, Sheila O'Donovan, my court services officer, Stephanie and myself.

> 135 I was gowned for the interview. I told Stephanie that I wanted to hear from her about the problems that she was having. At first, Stephanie stated that she was a bit nervous and told me that Sheila O'Donovan had told her to write things down in order that she not forget anything she felt was important. After a few minutes, Stephanie appeared to be comfortable. I told her that everything that was said in this interview would be taken down by the court reporter and a transcript of what was said would be given to her mother, father and Bernadette Davies [the stepmother]. Stephanie appeared to have no difficulty with everyone knowing what took place in the interview.

> 136 I find that Stephanie is an intelligent child, who was 12 years old at the time of the interview. She turned 13 on May 5, 2008.

> 137 Stephanie wanted to make sure that I knew that her mother would not be the same person in front of me that she was with her and her sister. She told me that she would be very nice and that she would deny everything that Stephanie told me. Stephanie insisted that what she was telling me was true and that everything that her mother has done, especially since her parents separated, has made her very angry at her mother. Stephanie's anger at the mother is significantly higher because her mother is lying about what she does to her and her sister.

The interview was a significant, but clearly not the only factor in Justice Harper's decision to end a shared parenting arrangement and to award custody to the father with no access to the mother. The mother and many of her witnesses had strenuously argued that the children had been alienated from her and therefore ought to be removed from the father. The judge ordered a review of the situation in about six months and listed as one of his "expectations" that the mother and step-mother would seek counseling. For a comment on the case, see Epstein, "Case Comment: *L. (J.K.) v. S. (N.C.)* and *McAlister v. Jenkins* (2008), 54 R.F.L. (6th) 163.

5. Courts generally discourage parties from calling children as witnesses. The cases are reviewed in *Collins v. Petric* (2003), 41 R.F.L. (5th) 250 (Ont. S.C.J.) where Justice Perkins refused to allow a father to call his 13-year-old daughter to testify in hopes that she would indicate that she wished to see him. See also *Stefureak v. Chambers*, *supra*.

However, there are some custody and access cases in which children have testified. In *Beck v. Beck* (1993), 48 R.F.L. (3d) 303 (P.E.I. C.A.), the three children testified at trial while the parents were outside the courtroom. Bean Prov. J. stated in *Levine v. Levine* (1993), 50 R.F.L. (3d) 414 (Ont. Prov. Div.) at 420 that there was no need for an independent assessment to reveal the views and preferences of an 11-year-old boy since "he can do that himself by giving evidence at the trial." Children testified in *Gaulton v. Hynes* (2003), 36 R.F.L. (5th) 114 (N.L. U.F.C.);

Hillier v. Hillier (2003), 40 R.F.L. (5th) 112 (B.C. S.C.); additional reasons at (2003), 37 C.P.C. (5th) 122 (B.C. S.C.); and *Neys v. Soden* (2003), 40 R.F.L. (5th) 292 (B.C. S.C.). In the latter case, Justice Craig stated (para. 99):

> I told counsel and the parties during the trial that I would prefer not to hear Brooke [aged 15] testify, and that I questioned whether there was anything her testimony could add to the evidence available through other sources. Brooke testified at the trial, despite these comments.

In *Young v. Young* (1993), 49 R.F.L. (3d) 117 at 213 (S.C.C.), Justice L'Heureux-Dubé (dissenting) suggested: "... [I]t is important to emphasize the importance of the evidence of children ... and ... their testimony alone might ... be a sufficient evidentiary basis upon which to restrict access."

For arguments in favour of hearing the direct testimony of children in custody and access disputes, see Nasmith, "The Inchoate Voice" (1992), 8 C.F.L.Q. 43 at 63–65, and Huddart and Ensminger, "Hearing the Voice of Children" (1992), 8 C.F.L.Q. 95 at 100-101. The latter authors write:

> The child's statement of her views to the judge directly will probably be the most reliable evidence for a court. The judge can observe the child and assess her competency, understanding of the situation, and possible influence, without the screen of a third person. If those views are expressed in the courtroom, the procedural rights of the parents can be respected. As a secondary benefit, the parents will be forced to listen to, if not hear, their child. The child will know that her views are being stated as clearly as she can formulate them, in language she chooses as appropriate to be heard by her parents, without any danger of their being misstated by a well-meaning adult.

> Many participants in the adversary process are loathe to permit children to testify in court. Others seem to assume such testimony is inappropriate and to be discouraged. It is said that such an experience is harmful to the child, particularly if she is required to state a preference between parents. Pressure from parents, the need to choose between parents, fear of hurting an adult one loves and on whom one is dependent and the potential for vengeful retribution from a parent are among the perils cited. As in so much that is written in this area, there are no systematic studies underpinning these conclusions. It may be that the fears are exaggerated. Children whose divorcing parents cannot communicate rationally will usually have seen much more damaging fights than those in a courtroom. But most judges prefer to protect the child from the presumed harm.

> It seems that judges' protective attitudes toward the innocent child involved in a dispute between adults is based on their personal views as to the efficacy and fairness of calling the child as a witness to communicate her needs and wishes. The fear of psychological harm to a child, when measured against the value of a child's evidence, causes a judge to exclude an otherwise competent witness. It may be that the availability of the judicial interview has encouraged this judicial policy.

> We suggest that a child who agrees to give evidence should be restrained from testifying only where it is established on a preliminary motion or voir dire that the potential for psychological harm to the child is such that another method of eliciting the child's views must be found. If the child's views are not relevant, or the child is not competent to give evidence, the question of exclusion on policy grounds will not arise.

6. Recall that the Ontario Court of Appeal held in *Strobridge v. Strobridge* (1994), 4 R.F.L. (4th) 169 that a lawyer acting on behalf of a child in custody and access disputes cannot simply advise the court of the child's views and preferences unless the parties consent. However, as Osborne J.A. noted: "In many, if not most cases, the parties will agree that counsel representing the children may advise the court of the children's preferences."

7. As *Strobridge* indicates, the child's wishes constitute evidence which must be proved in the normal way. The method preferred by most commentators continues to be through an assessment by an independent expert. See, e.g., Huddart and Ensminger, "Hearing the Voice of Children" (1992), 8 C.F.L.Q. 95 at 110–113.

(10) The "Friendly Parent" Principle

JANE DOE v. JOHN DOE

(1990), 28 R.F.L. (3d) 356, 1990 CarswellOnt 292 (Ont. Dist. Ct.); affirmed (1990), 1990 CarswellOnt 315, (sub nom. *Doe v. Doe*) 29 R.F.L. (3d) 450 (Ont. C.A.)

[The facts of this case are set out earlier in this chapter.]

CORBETT D.C.J.: — ... *Risk of harm to child's relation with access parent*
I will next deal with the ground which formed the basis of the learned trial judge's decision, namely, where two parents seeking custody compare closely, having regard to the statutory "best interests" criteria, custody should be given to the parent more likely to support and promote the relationship with the other parent. The appellant submits the learned trial judge erred in awarding custody to the respondent solely on the basis of the expert testimony that the respondent would be better able to promote the appellant's relationship with the child than the reverse. The respondent submits it is in the child's best interest to live with the parent who is prepared to co-operate with respect to access where both parents can equally care for the child.

In considering this matter, the learned trial judge had regard to flexibility respecting access. Although the question of supporting the other parental relation may be considered separately from the question of access, how access has been provided is one area to consider in determining whether the other parental relation is being undermined or is in danger of being undermined. The issue has devastating consequences in that a capable, loving mother has been deprived of custody and a capable, loving father has sought custody solely as a result of conclusions respecting the ability of the mother to support the child's relation with her father. In what circumstances is custody in peril through failure to provide or unwillingness to provide access?

Since lack of co-operation respecting access tends to indicate lack of support of the other parental relation, I will review some of the evidence respecting access. Significantly, the learned trial judge does not discuss access in detail, merely making the general finding that Jane felt unable to be flexible and accommodating to changes requested by John. [Corbett D.C.J. concluded that Jane had been willing to comply with existing court orders but no more.]

In my opinion, provision of reasonable access and compliance with all court orders and relevant agreements is a sufficient standard which should not put custody in peril in the absence of evidence of a detrimental effect on the child or the child's relation with the access parent. The evidence and the findings respecting access fall short of any conduct or standard necessary to deprive a custodial parent of custody as a result of the problems respecting access. ...

There being no findings respecting access, save respecting flexibility, I now turn to the evidence on the positive side, that is, that John is more likely to foster a relationship with the other parent.

I agree with counsel for the appellant, who submits that, on the whole of the evidence at trial, there was insufficient evidence to substantiate the testimony of Drs. Cooper and Sutherland that the appellant would fail to promote a healthy relationship between the respondent and the child. First and foremost, there is no evidence that Jane's attitude or feelings have in fact resulted in any impairment whatsoever of the successful relation between Cathy and her father. There is no evidence of any deleterious effects on Cathy and the evidence is overwhelming that the child was healthy both physically and emotionally and had attained excellent bonds with both her parents.

Second, there is no evidence or finding that the respondent was denigrated by the appellant or her family in the presence of the child. The evidence substantiated hostility by Jane against John, but there is no evidence substantiating any harmful effect on the child. Further, the evidence, if any, respecting the likelihood of its potential effect on the child is too speculative to deprive a parent of custody.

Third, the evidence shows Jane is capable of controlling and does control her feelings against John in relation to Cathy. Evidence of this control is seen in the careful preparation of Cathy to foster pleasant visits with John. An indication of the degree to which Jane is willing and able to control her resentment is evidenced by her dealing with the daily phone calls by John to his daughter from the age of three years. ...

Dr. Cooper's opinion at trial was that Jane still maintained a strongly negative and suspicious opinion of John.

Neither this opinion nor Jane's negative feelings is sufficient to deny custody. Jane's feelings toward John must be related to the actual or likely impact on the child's relationship and on the child herself. No doubt many parents who separate have similar feelings and these may be maintained thereafter. The significant aspect is not the existence of hatred or hostile feelings, but the effects of these feelings in relation to the child.

In my opinion, the learned trial judge erred in law and acted on a wrong principle in depriving a fitting custodial parent of custody on the grounds that the other parent (at this time also custodial) is more likely to support the child's relation with both parents when no findings are made and no evidence is adduced that such failure exists and has resulted or is likely to result in undesirable effects on the child or on the child's relationship with either parent. The existence of antipathy and speculation as to its potential negative effects is not sufficient of itself to deprive a parent of custody. For this reason the appeal should be allowed and custody awarded to the mother. ...

NOTES AND QUESTIONS

1. For cases in which the "friendly parent" principle played a role, see *Renaud v. Renaud* (reproduced earlier in this chapter); *Cormier v. Bell* (2003), 43 R.F.L. (5th) 307 (Ont. C.A.); additional reasons at (2003), 2003 Carswell-Ont 4593 (Ont. C.A.); *C. (B.A.) v. C. (D.L.)* (2003), 48 R.F.L. (5th) 15 (B.C. C.A.); *Savidis v. Savidis* (2003), 49 R.F.L. (5th) 219 (Ont. S.C.J.); *Rutherford v. Rutherford* (2004), 7 R.F.L. (6th) 344 (N.S. S.C.); and *Jamieson v. Jamieson* (2008), 56 R.F.L. (6th) 237 (Ont. C.A.).

2. In *Jarrett v. Jarrett* (1994), 10 R.F.L. (4th) 24 (Ont. Gen. Div.), Eberhard J. wrote (at 29):

I have considered, as a serious blemish in Ms Jarret's parenting record, her inability to cheerfully support access. It is both the law as set out in s. 16(10) of the *Divorce Act* and my considered and passionate belief that, except in the rarest and most extreme circumstances, the one thing that children of separating parents need more than any other single factor in order to emerge healthy and undamaged by the disintegration of their family is the opportunity to know that they are still loved by both parents. ...

[Ms. Jarrett] acts as though access is a favour that she may dole out depending on her plans and convenience and on her judgments as to [the father's] worthiness.

Notwithstanding "this very serious flaw" in the mother's ability to parent, the judge granted custody to the mother and permitted her to move the two boys to British Columbia.

3. In *Dupont v. Dupont* (1993), 47 R.F.L. (3d) 273 (B.C. S.C.) the court considered that the exaggerated criticism of the father's parenting while he had interim custody reflected poorly on the mother's character and the court in *Stefanyk v. Stefanyk* (1994), 1 R.F.L. (4th) 432 (N.S. S.C.) concluded that the mother's more positive description of the father's parenting ability indicated that she was more likely to foster contact between the father and the children.

4. Judges confronted with custodial parents who refuse to comply with access orders often indicate that if interference with access continues, they may reverse custody on the basis that it is in the best interests of the child to know and have contact with both parents. Generally, such threats ring hollow where a child has lived with the custodial parent for an extended period of time. See, e.g., *Cox v. Stephen* (2003), 47 R.F.L. (5th) 1 (Ont. C.A.) (reversing decision to change custody where judge gave insufficient weight to child's attachment to mother). Indeed, the interference with the child's relationship with the access parent may cause the child to refuse to visit that parent and ultimately lead to a termination of access. See *Strobridge v. Strobridge* (1994), 4 R.F.L. (4th) 169 (Ont. C.A.).

However, in *Tremblay v. Tremblay* (1987), 10 R.F.L. (3d) 166 (Alta. Q.B.), a custody order granting custody of two children to the mother was varied a year later because the mother adamantly refused to let the father see the children. See also *Muir v. Sabean* (2003), 47 R.F.L. (5th) 135 (N.S. C.A.); *Struck v. Struck* (2003), 47 R.F.L. (5th) 405 (B.C. C.A.); and *C. (B.A.) v. C. (D.L.)* (2003), 48 R.F.L. (5th) 15 (B.C. C.A.). Recently, courts have become increasingly aware of and concerned about the possibility of parental alienation of a child. Where such alienation occurs after an order or agreement governing custody and access is already in place, the courts will now give very serious consideration to a change in custody. See 7. Parental Alienation, below.

5. At the National Symposium on Women, Law and the Administration of Justice, June 10–12, 1991 in Vancouver, the Workshop on Family Law recommended repeal of s. 16(10) of the *Divorce Act*. Why would it make such a recommendation?

For criticism of the provision, see Boyd, "W(h)ither Feminism? The Department of Justice Public Discussion Paper on Custody and Access" (1995), 12 Can. J. Fam. L. 331 and Cossman and Mytiuk, "Reforming Child Custody and Access Law in Canada: A Discussion Paper" (1998), 15 Can. J. Fam. L. 13, at 49–53.

4. Access

(1) General

BALA, "THE BEST INTERESTS OF THE CHILD IN THE POST-MODERN ERA: A CENTRAL BUT PARADOXICAL CONCEPT"

Harold Niman and Gerald P. Sadvari, ed., *Family Law: "Best Interests of the Child"* (Toronto: Law Society of Upper Canada, 2000) 52–63 (Footnotes omitted)

Access Problems: Another Best Interests Paradox

While the reported case law and literature tend to focus on best interests decisions about custody, problems with access are more frequently a cause of concern for parents and lawyers. In many respects access problems are more intractable for the legal system than custody cases. Custody disputes can be resolved with some degree of finality (subject to variation applications), but access difficulties can involve the constant supervision of often strained human relationships and may last until the children reach an age at which they will make their own decisions. The law is a blunt tool for supervising human relationships and the legal system has great difficulty in dealing effectively with access problems.

Canadian legislation, like s. 16(8) of the *Divorce Act*, establishes the best interests test not only for custody but for access decisions as well. There is, however, a presumption that regular access by the non-custodial parent is in the best interests of children. Most judicial pronouncements base the presumption of access on an assumption that regular contact with the non-custodial parent is best for children, but some decisions characterize access as a "parental right" only to be forfeited in unusual circumstances. Other recent decisions suggest that access is the "right of the child." Somewhat paradoxically, judicial decisions about access that may be intended to promote the best interests of children in general may actually cause the child involved in an access dispute significant emotional distress, in particular if the court must somehow try to enforce its decision.

Although there is surprisingly little good research available on the effects of different patterns of access on children, the available research suggests that *in general* children who have regular contact with the non-custodial parent (usually the father) have better psychological adjustments than children who see the non-custodial parent infrequently or not at all. Most children express a preference for having contact with both parents, and theories of child development would suggest that children will usually benefit from continuing to have contact with both parents after going through the tumult of parental separation.

For a large group of children with separated parents, the access "problem" in their lives is that non-custodial parents (usually the fathers) visit rarely or not at all. In some cases, the father has little contact as soon as separation occurs, while in other cases contact decreases over time, especially when the father forms a new relationship or if contact is disrupted by a parental move. In most cases where the father is an infrequent presence in the child's life, the custodial mother and children want him more involved. There is, however, nothing that the courts can or should do to try to *force* unwilling or reluctant non-custodial parents to visit with their children. Symbolic statements in legislation about the importance of both parents to a child might conceivably encourage some non-custodial parents to be more involved with their children. Education programs for separated parents could have a more significant impact than any legal change on the problem of the "disappearing father."

The legal system focuses on problems that arise in cases where there is difficulty in defining or enforcing access rights of non-custodial parents. The view that access should only rarely be denied was clearly articulated in the 1964 Ontario decision in *Ader v. McLaughlin* (1964), 46 D.L.R. (2d) 12 at 23-24 (H.C.):

> ... access is never refused except in cases where danger to the children is apprehended. The desirability of children knowing both their parents and being able to give a normal account of them has been set out in our courts. ...

The federal Parliament also offered a somewhat circular endorsement of the importance of access in the *Divorce Act* with the inclusion of a "friendly parent" provision [in s. 16(10)]. ...

Subsection 16(10) preserves the discretion of a judge to make the type of access order considered in the best interests of the child before the court, including the complete denial of access in appropriate circumstances. Though not clearly worded, s. 16(10) appears to create a presumption that a significant amount of regular contact with the non-custodial parent is in the best interests of children. The provision clearly focuses on the interests of the child in regard to access rather than parental rights.

... Canadian studies indicate that judges deny access in a relatively small percentage of cases, almost invariably ones where it is demonstrated by the custodial parent that there is a real risk of physical or emotional harm to the child as a result of access, or where the non-custodial parent has not had contact with the child for several years and has no psychological link to the child. In some more recent cases involving serious continuing post-separation spousal abuse, judges considered issues of domestic violence and the risk to the custodial parent that may occur when care of the child is being transferred. There is a growing recognition that psychological or physical injury to the custodial parent, the person with primary responsibility for the child, endangers the child. In some cases the court may order supervised access or supervision of the exchange to minimize risk to the child and custodial parent but maintain the child's relationship with the non-custodial parent.

While access has traditionally been defined as a best interests decision or even the right of a parent, some judges and commentators have started to characterize access as the right of a child. Associate Chief Judge White of the Alberta Family Court wrote [*Knudslien v. Rivard* (1978), 5 R.F.L. (2d) 264 at 269]:

> it is the child who has the *right* to see each parent. It is not necessarily the parent who has a right to see the child. This *right* in the child is one to be protected by the court.

... Despite this rhetorical support for the notion that access is the child's *right*, it may not be practically significant to discuss a child's "right" without thinking about legal remedies. How will children's "right" to access be protected? There may be situations in which it will be possible for a child in a divorce to have independent legal representation to advocate for these rights in negotiations or litigation. However, in most cases, especially in high conflict divorce cases, it is unrealistic to expect a child in the custody of one parent to express independent views about access with the other parent. In high conflict divorce cases it is common for one parent (or both) to pressure the child, subtly or otherwise, into expressing negative attitudes towards the other parent. Although in some cases children will develop their own fear or hatred of one parent, and these feelings need to be recognized and respected, a child's negative attitudes to one parent can also be the reflection of the conscious or unconscious actions of the other parent. There are cases in which "parental alienation" will be present, with one parent (or both parents) causing the children to feel guilty or angry towards the other parent, resulting in the child having negative feelings and expressing an aversion to seeing the other parent.

Perhaps the greatest value of conceptualizing access as a right of the child is symbolic and educational. Professionals and decision-makers can focus on the interests of the children in a dispute, and communicate to parents the desirability of their promoting a harmonious access arrangement to meet their children's needs. ...

The limitations of the legal system are most apparent when a custodial parent is consciously or unconsciously thwarting the visitation rights of the non-custodial parent. This is usually a symptom of a high conflict divorce. Children in these cases are often subjected to loyalty conflicts and may have behavioural or emotional problems associated with the parental conflict. While research suggests that, in general, regular contact with the non-custodial parent has a positive effect on children, in high conflict cases regular access may be very stressful to the children.

This has led some commentators to argue that it would be in the best interests of children for non-custodial parents to have no legally enforceable access rights, with the custodial parent having the right to decide whether access would occur. Although for some children in intractable high conflict cases it might be preferable for their emotional well being not to visit with the non-custodial parent, this type of a legal rule would make it much more difficult to resolve the majority of child related disputes, with custody becoming a "winner-take-all" contest. Further, such a rule would send the wrong message to parents, suggesting that there is no need to try to resolve differences with the other parent. Such a rule would also be contrary to fundamental values about the role of parents in Canadian society.

The paradoxical and problematic nature of court enforced access is illustrated in *McMillan v McMillan* (1999), 44 O.R. (3d) 139 (Gen. Div.), a recent Ontario case in which the custodial mother repeatedly denied the father access to their children. The father had a court order which directed the police to assist the father in exercising his rights of visitation. The police were understandably reluctant to do so, and the father recognized that it would likely be very upsetting to the children for the police to arrive at their home and take them to visit their father. The father finally brought a series of court applications to have the mother found in contempt of court. As is usual in these cases, there were a number of incidents and court appearances, with judges threatening that the mother would be imprisoned if she did not co-operate with the father's access visits. After each court appearance the mother would co-operate for a brief period of time, and then she would again violate the access order.

Finally Justice Quinn found the mother in contempt and sentenced her to five days in jail, commenting [at 145–147]:

> Access is the source of endless conflict in many matrimonial cases. This is not surprising since no matter how detailed and structured the access schedule may be there is still the need for the estranged spouses to achieve some degree of co-operation, consensus and compromise for the schedule to run smoothly. However, the fact that access orders produce so much conflict is a good reason for courts not to treat their breach lightly. ...

> Mr. Crowe, on behalf of Ms. McMillan [the custodial mother], strenuously argued that incarceration would not be in the best interests of the children. I agree. But when would it ever be in the best interests of children to send the custodial parent to jail? To create, repair or enhance the relationship between the access parent and the children? I should think that imprisoning the custodial parent is a very high price to pay if this is the only result sought to be achieved. Of all of the sentencing factors applicable in this case, I think the most important one is the need to preserve the integrity of the administration of justice; and that, as I see it, can only be achieved through a sentence of incarceration. It was also argued on behalf of Ms. McMillan that a jail sentence would deleteriously affect the relationship of the children with their father. This is troubling, but, again, could the same thing not be said in most cases of this nature? In my opinion, a court should be careful not to allow such arguments to declaw the court when it comes to sentencing for contempt in respect of access.

The judge (and father) can only hope that this period in jail will make the mother more co-operative in the future, and that it will not unduly traumatize the children or damage their relationship with their father. This case illustrates that the law is a very blunt instrument for the supervision of delicate human relationships. It is a paradoxical decision that may promote the interests of children in general, by encouraging access, but may be detrimental to the children who were involved in the specific case.

There is significant evidence that mediation and parental education can be helpful to many parents in working out satisfactory access arrangements over time. ...

Issues related to access are particularly likely to be amenable to mediation. The parents have a continuing relationship which may benefit from the negotiation and dispute resolution skills typically developed in mediation. Access issues will not be amenable to solution by the application of a legal standard in court, but rather will be continuously evolving as the child changes. Further, in contrast to economic issues, where one party's gain usually comes directly at the expense of the other, access is not a "zero sum" game. Custodial parents may, through mediation, come to realize that they may actually be better off "giving up" some time with their children, both because they will have more time to pursue their own needs and interests, and because their children will benefit from contact with the other parent.

Access inevitably requires interaction and an on-going relationship between two individuals who may have very negative feelings towards one another. For some parents in high conflict divorces, the struggles over access may reflect deep seated unresolved feelings about the spousal relationship, and individual or couple-based counselling may be needed to resolve emotional issues before mediation can be effective.

Increased use of mediation, counselling and parenting education can help resolve most access disputes, and increased availability of supervision for access or the exchange of care of the children may help deal with some cases where there may be threats to physical or emotional safety. These approaches can help many estranged parents cooperate to promote the welfare of their children by developing appropriate access arrangements. The courts can have a role in urging or even directing parents to take advantage of these resources, if they are available. There will, however, remain a need for recourse to the courts to deal with cases where access should be restricted or denied due to threats to physical or emotional security, and to deal with parents who are too emotionally disturbed or intransigent to resolve access disputes without legal involvement.

NOTES AND QUESTIONS

1. As noted by Professor Bala, research suggests generally that children who have regular contact with both parents do better than children who see the non-custodial parent infrequently or not at all. See Wallerstein and Blakeslee, *Second Chances: Men, Women and Children a Decade after Divorce* (New York: Tichnor and Fields, 1989) and Levanthal, "Divorce, Custody and Visitation in Mid-Childhood" in Galatzer and Kraus, eds., *The Scientific Basis of Child Custody Decisions* (New York: John Wiley, 1999).

2. A parent is almost always granted access. In *Evaluation of the Divorce Act; Phase II: Monitoring and Evaluation* (Ottawa: Ministry of Supply and Services, 1990), the Department of Justice found that the files of divorce cases in four Canadian cities revealed that access was denied in less than three per cent of the cases.

Reported cases where access is denied or ended mostly involve situations where there is a real risk of physical or emotional harm to the child as a result of access or where a parent has lost contact for a number of years. Serious and persistent attempts to undermine the custodial parent may also result in a loss of access: *VandenElsen v. Merkley* (2003), 49 R.F.L. (5th) 416 (Ont. S.C.J.); additional reasons at (2003), 49 R.F.L. (5th) 439 (Ont. S.C.J.).

The cases also indicate that a parent who abuses or harasses the custodial parent risks losing access: *Abdo v. Abdo* (1993), 109 D.L.R. (4th) 78 (N.S. C.A.) (access terminated in part because it affected the abused mother negatively); *Cairns v. Cairns* (1994), 3 R.F.L. (4th) 397 (N.B. Q.B.); affirmed (1995), 10 R.F.L. (4th) 234 (N.B. C.A.) (supervised access only where the father had been abusive before and after separation and used extremely profane and degrading language in his dealings with the mother in front of the child); *Costa v. Costa* (1994), 4 R.F.L. (4th) 209 (Man. Q.B.) (no access until the abused mother was emotionally strong enough to handle the idea that the father would have a continuing role and the father received help to control his anger); *M. (B.P.) v. M. (B.L.D.E.)* (1992), 42 R.F.L. (3d) 349 (Ont. C.A.); leave to appeal refused (1993), 48 R.F.L. (3d) 232 (note) (S.C.C.) (no access for father); and *Roach v. Kelly* (2003), 49 R.F.L. (5th) 177 (Ont. S.C.J.) (father's access terminated where he severely beat the mother's new partner and harassed the family). However, decisions to grant access to fathers who had been convicted of assault were upheld in *Savidant v. MacLeod* (1992), 40 R.F.L. (3d) 443 (P.E.I. C.A.) and *Koning v. Montgomery* (2004), 9 R.F.L. (6th) 154 (Ont. C.A.). In "The Impact of Wife Abuse on Child Custody and Access Decisions" (2004), 22 C.F.L.Q. 85, Professor Shaffer reports on her study of reported cases as follows (at 133):

> The emphasis courts place on contact was evident from the outcome of access claims brought by abusive men. While few abusive men are getting custody of their children, almost all are being granted access. There were only a few notable exceptions to this trend, and these typically involved cases in which the father had been extremely violent towards the mother, had exposed the children to the risk of serious harm, or in which the children were clearly terrorized by the violence.

She also indicates (at 138-139) that most often access was unsupervised, although conditions were frequently imposed in an attempt to limit opportunities for violence or harassment.

There are also cases where the relationship between a child and the non-custodial parent has become so negative that access has become very stressful and the child resists visits. The child's negative attitudes may be due to the attitudes and actions of the custodial parent. In *Katz v. Katz* (1989), 21 R.F.L. (3d) 167 (Ont. U.F.C.), three teenaged children had become alienated from their father and did not wish to see him. Wallace U.F.C.J. concluded that, given the ages of the children, a forced access regime was not in their best interests and she ordered that the father be allowed reasonable access if the children wished to see him. See also *Strobridge v. Strobridge* (1994), 4 R.F.L. (4th) 169 (Ont. C.A.); *Rosenke v. Rosenke* (1998), 36 R.F.L. (4th) 288 (Alta. C.A.); *Lidkea v. Jarrell* (1999), 49 R.F.L. (4th) 324 (Ont. C.A.); *Broz v. Broz* (2001), 18 R.F.L. (5th) 3 (Ont. S.C.J.); *Re E. (B.M.A.)* (2001), 24 R.F.L. (5th) 345 (Alta. Q.B.); and *Warner v. Warner* (2002), 27 R.F.L. (5th) 202 (B.C. S.C.).

3. In *Jennings v. Garrett* (2004), 5 R.F.L. (6th) 319 (Ont. S.C.J.), a mother sought to terminate a father's access to their six-year-old daughter while he obtained long-term psychiatric treatment. Justice Blishen, while continuing supervised access, stated (para. 1):

> Termination of Vanessa's [the child's] right to visit with and know her father is an extreme remedy which should only be ordered in the most exceptional of circumstances. An order for supervised access also requires evidence of exceptional circumstances as it is just a small step away from complete termination of the parent-child relationship.

4. In *McGrath v. Thomsen* (2000), 11 R.F.L. (5th) 174 (B.C. C.A.), the mother of a 10-year-old boy had serious drug addictions. The appellate court upheld an order stipulating that the mother's access was to be at the father's discretion, although it noted that such an order was exceptional.

5. In some cases the courts have concluded that renewed contact between the child and the non-custodial parent is in the child's best interest even if that parent has not seen the child for years. See *Bedard v. Bedard* (1984), 43 R.F.L. (2d) 331 (Man. C.A.); *S. (E.A.) v. B. (K.M.)* (1989), 24 R.F.L. (3d) 220 (Ont. Dist. Ct.); and *Savidant v. MacLeod* (1991), 32 R.F.L. (3d) 266 (P.E.I. T.D.); affirmed (1992), 40 R.F.L. (3d) 443 (P.E.I. C.A.). Contrast these cases with *DeSilva v. Giggey* (1996), 21 R.F.L. (4th) 116 (N.B. Q.B.) and *F. (W.) v. R. (G.)* (1997), 32 R.F.L. (4th) 420 (N.B. Q.B.).

6. What should a custodial parent do if he or she suspects that the access parent has abused the child during a visit? In *Young v. Young* (1993), 49 R.F.L. (3d) 117 (S.C.C.), L'Heureux-Dubé J. (dissenting) suggested (at 184) that "a custodial parent, aware of sexual or other abuse by the non-custodial parent, would be remiss in his or her duty to the child not to cut off access by the abuser immediately, with or without a court order." The majority did not directly address this point, although L'Heureux-Dubé J. mentioned it to illustrate her disagreement with McLachlin J.'s statement (at 150-151) that the custodial parent did not have the right to forbid certain types of contact between the access parent and the child.

In "Canada: Struggling to Find a Balance on Gender Issues" (1994-1995), 33 University of Louisville Journal of Family Law 301, Professor Bala describes (at 305-306) the debate over the proper response of a family lawyer whose client claims that the other parent will abuse the child if a court order is followed:

> It was not only judges who were divided about how to resolve disputes about children, but also lawyers who were ... debating their role in these cases, as was revealed in an important professional discipline decision. A prominent feminist lawyer was charged with professional misconduct as a result of her involvement in a case in which the mother of a three-year-old girl alleged sexual abuse. The trial judge rejected these allegations and ordered the child transferred to her father's custody within ten weeks. Following the order, but before the mother gave over custody, the mother reported further allegations of abuse, which were supported by a social worker. The lawyer in question was retained by the mother to attempt to have the order varied or appealed. The lawyer wrote in a letter that, pending an appeal hearing, the mother "should seriously consider" not allowing the child to be transferred as required by the original court order. The mother then "went underground" with the child, but ultimately contacted the father and eventually voluntarily gave him custody.

> In the meantime, the lawyer was charged with breach of her professional obligations, in particular for "subverting the law by counseling or assisting in activities which are in defiance of it." The Discipline Committee of Ontario's Law Society accepted the principle that a lawyer counseling disobedience of a court order ordinarily is in breach of professional obligations, but this conduct is acceptable if the lawyer:

> > [has a] reasonable and honest belief of ... imminent risk or danger to a child, and that there [is] an immediate application to a court to have the issues determined forthwith. Once that application is made and the facts have been presented before a court of competent jurisdiction however briefly, if that court refuses to act to change an outstanding order, then the obligation of the client is to "trust in the efficacy of the legal system" and adhere to the court order, and then if so advised, to seek a full hearing for a permanent change. (*Law Society of Upper Canada v. Curtis*, LAWYERS WKLY. Sept. 29, 1993, at 1323-018 (full-text).)

This decision did not escape criticism. See, e.g. "Lawyers Can Counsel Clients to Disobey Court Orders", *Lawyers Weekly*, October 15, 1993 at 1 & 10 where Alfred Mamo commented:

> Saying you have to have a reasonable and honest belief ... means nothing. In matrimonial law, people have what they consider to be reasonable and honestly held beliefs about a lot of things.

> Many times clients are looking for a way out of an order that they don't like. Custody and access cases are very emotionally saturated — and I think that as a result counsel is always being asked to try and interpret this sort of thing so as to allow someone to avoid compliance with the order.

An interesting postlude in this story is that Carole Curtis, the lawyer who was the subject of the Law Society proceedings, was appointed a justice of the Ontario Court of Justice in 2008.

In "Enforcement of Access and Alienation of Children: Conflict Reduction Strategies and Legal Responses" (2004), 23 C.F.L.Q. 1, Professor Bala and Nicole Bailey conclude that the cases indicate that a custodial parent may be justified in not permitting a child to go on a visit where there is a risk of harm, but that the parent would be well advised to seek a variation if there are repeated occasions where access is denied. Only in Newfoundland and Labrador is there legislation detailing when denial of access is not wrongful: *Children's Law Act*, R.S.N. 1990, c. C-13, s. 41(4).

7. In *Johnson-Steeves v. Lee* (1997), 33 R.F.L. (4th) 278 (Alta. C.A.), the mother asked a man to father a child on the basis that he would provide support but otherwise she hoped to raise the child on her own. The father paid child support and visited the child for three one-week periods in the first year after the birth. The mother then asked the father to bow out of their lives. The appellate court upheld the granting of an access order.

8. The Nova Scotia Court of Appeal in *Elliott v. Mumford* (2004), 1 R.F.L. (6th) 193 (N.S. C.A.), upheld a lower court's refusal to grant access to a man who lived with the mother and infant child for about six months and maintained contact for the next two years. The woman had just become engaged to another man and the lower court suggested that access for the applicant might cause "confusion" or "turmoil".

9. If it appears likely that the parents can work out the details of the access for the non-custodial parent, the court order may simply grant "reasonable access". Often, however, the order for access will spell out the details regarding the visitation rights of the non-custodial parent. The possible variations in the structure of access orders are limited only by the bounds of the judge's and counsels' creativity. For examples of access orders carefully tailored to meet the particular circumstances of the parties, see *Elbaz v. Elbaz* (1980), 16 R.F.L. (2d) 336, 29 O.R. (2d) 207 (H.C.); *Weiss v. Kopel* (1980), 18 R.F.L. (2d) 289 (Ont. Prov. Ct.); and *Ryan v. Ryan* (1986), 3 R.F.L. (3d) 141, 60 Nfld. & P.E.I.R. 162 (Nfld. T.D.). Regarding the court's authority to stipulate the terms and conditions of access, see ss. 28 and 34 of the *CLRA* and s. 16(6) of the *DA*.

10. Access orders are notoriously difficult to enforce effectively. In an annotation to *Rutherford v. Rutherford* (1986), 4 R.F.L. (3d) 457 (B.C. S.C.), Professor McLeod writes (at 458-459):

> The reasons for judgment in *Rutherford v. Rutherford* highlight the frustration of an access parent who finds his or her access rights interfered with. Ultimately, there is very little one can do to force the custodial parent to provide meaningful access. In many cases, access is an immediate thing for the purposes of a vacation or a special family gathering. Once the custodial parent denies access at that time, the opportunity may not be available at a later date. A custodial spouse's willingness to cooperate in furthering the child's relationship with the access spouse may be affected by many factors including continuing animosity with the other parent or improper linkage of access and support.

> In reality, there is little the court can do to assist the access parent in the face of interference with access by the custodial parent. The judicial process, overall, is too slow and its tools too blunt.

> The denial of access is treated as contempt of court. The normal means of punishment are censure, fine or imprisonment. None of these directly provides access. Fines simply reduce the family income of the lower income family or become a licence to break the law for those that can afford it. Courts are extremely wary of putting a custodial parent in jail, having regard to the best interest of the child. In any event, jailing will only increase the animosity between the spouses and is likely to further erode the access parent's relationship with the child when the child finds out, which is likely to happen.

> In many cases, like *Rutherford*, the courts have indicated that if interference with access continues, they may reverse custody on the basis it is in the best interest of the child to know and have contact with both parents. If one parent will not provide such contact, the other should be given the opportunity. As well, to continue the parental conflict shows an inability to submerge personal desires to benefit the child. In fact, such threats by the courts ring hollow. The more likely scenario is that access will be terminated if it proves sufficiently unsettling to the child, even where the problem may be laid squarely at the feet of the custodial parent.

> Even more insidious to the position of the access parent is the subtle "poisoning" of the child's mind by the custodial parent. If the child receives enough negative information about the access parent, it is likely to affect him. The process may be so subtle and slow that it escapes notice until too late. ...

> As appears clear, the courts are not equipped to respond to the problems involved. Ultimately, it must be questioned whether the problem is properly a legal and justiciable one or whether it should, in part, be turned over to the mental health profession. Where access problems are rooted in parental animosity and are not a response to evidence of abuse or real concern for the child's welfare, which concerns

can be objectively dealt with and responded to, it may well be that thought should be given by judges and legislators to a form of compulsory conciliation to see if the problem can be addressed at its real level: between the parents.

In *Yunyk v. Judd* (1986), 5 R.F.L. (3d) 206, the Manitoba Court of Queen's Bench suggested that there was a third option for dealing with repeated denials of access: to order additional access for the non-custodial parent.

See generally, Bala and Bailey "Enforcement of Access and Alienation of Children: Conflict Reduction Strategies and Legal Responses" (2004), 23 C.F.L.Q. 1. The authors explore both judicial and extra-judicial responses to access problems.

11. In *Frame v. Smith* (1987), 9 R.F.L. (3d) 225 (S.C.C.), a majority of the court concluded that a father did not have a right of action either in tort or for breach of fiduciary duty against the mother and her husband for interfering with his access rights under a court order. The plaintiff claimed both out-of-pocket expenses estimated at $25,000 and damages for severe emotional and psychic distress. For commentary that generally supports Justice Wilson's dissent, see Leon, "The Wisdom of Solomon: A Comment on *Frame v. Smith*" (1988), 3 C.F.L.Q. 397 and Diamond, "Enforcement of Custody and Access Orders" (1989), 4 C.F.L.Q. 303.

12. It is fairly common for judges dealing with access problems to warn a custodial parent that custody may be varied if the situation does not improve. However, in most cases these warnings ring hollow because the application of the best interests test will favour the *status quo*. Indeed, these cases often involve alienated children who do not wish to visit, let alone live with, the access parent.

In *Cox v. Stephen* (2003), 47 R.F.L. (5th) 1 (Ont. C.A.), the trial judge responded to the access problems and the mother's alienating conduct by granting sole custody to the father. Justice Templeton, on appeal, kept the child's primary residence with the mother, but ordered joint custody. The Ontario Court of Appeal upheld this decision, noting that, although the mother's behaviour was inappropriate, the trial judge's decision would have removed the child "from the only home he had ever known".

However, as noted earlier, courts have recently become increasingly aware of and concerned about the possibility of parental alienation of a child. Where such alienation occurs after an order or agreement governing custody and access is already in place, the courts will now give very serious consideration to a change in custody. See 7. Alienation, below.

13. As discussed later in this chapter, some judges have imposed "joint custody" or "parallel parenting" in cases where there have been significant problems with access. Although controversial, these orders do send the implicit message that the parent with whom the child primarily resides must not interfere with the other parent's access or a change in custody may be forthcoming.

14. Separated parents (and the public) frequently view child support and access as two parts of a bargain. The law does not. Generally, denial of access by the custodial parent does not affect the obligation of the other parent to provide child support and that failure to pay support does not affect the right to access.

The adoption of *Child Support Guidelines* affects this issue. The courts have little or no discretion regarding the child support award in the vast majority of cases. It is doubtful that a court can link access and child support under the *Guidelines*, except perhaps when deciding support for adult children or non-biological children under ss. 3(2) and 5. In *A. (J.A.) v. A. (S.R.)* (1999), 45 R.F.L. (4th) 165 (B.C. C.A.), Madam Justice Southin stated (at 171):

> ... [T]he law is believed to be that, even if one parent deliberately and maliciously destroys the relationship between the other parent and the children of their marriage, which is what the respondent has done if the allegations [of child abuse] are false, that other parent must still pay the Guidelines amounts. If that is the law, then the law, on this point, lacks a moral basis.

Do you agree? Generally, see Chapter 8, *CHILD SUPPORT.*

15. In *Ungerer v. Ungerer* (1998), 37 R.F.L. (4th) 41 (B.C. C.A.), there were numerous access problems and the mother served a jail term for contempt. Problems continued and eventually the daughter refused to see her father. The court ended the husband's obligation to pay spousal support in part because of the wife's intransigent refusal to facilitate access, reasoning (at 50) that s. 17(6) of the *DA* was no bar to the consideration of this conduct because it was not "conduct in relation to the marriage".

16. In 1989 the Ontario legislature passed legislation intended to allow more effective enforcement of access orders. See *Children's Law Reform Amendment Act, 1988*, Bill 124. This legislation would, *inter alia*, allow for speedy access to the courts, empower the courts to order compensatory access when access is wrongfully withheld and permit court orders requiring the custodial parent to provide security that would be forfeited if access were wrongfully withheld. The Bill received Royal Assent on June 20, 1989, but has never been proclaimed into force. The main opposition to the Bill came from women's groups claiming that it would simply provide fathers with an institutional means of harassing mothers through motions over minor or imagined interference with access rights. See also *Alberta's Domestic Relations Act*, R.S.A. 2000, c. D-14. Part 8, ss. 65–76.

17. For further reading, see Weisman, "On Access After Parental Separation" (1992), 36 R.F.L. (3d) 35; Kraft, "Rethinking Access for Children Under Age 3" (2004), 22 C.F.L.Q. 37; and Gordon, "Supervised Access: Why, When, How Long?" (2004), 22 C.F.L.Q. 185.

(2) Access for Grandparents

There have been an increasing number of reported cases in which grandparents seek access to their grandchildren. Most of these occur where a grandparent's child is the non-custodial parent and the conflict surrounding the parents' separation has poisoned the relationship. See, e.g., *Parsons v. Parsons* (2002), 29 R.F.L. (5th) 137 (Ont. S.C.J.); additional reasons at (2002), 31 R.F.L. (5th) 373 (Ont. S.C.J.) and *Bowles v. Coggins* (2008), 52 R.F.L. (6th) 224 (Ont. C.J.). However, some cases, such as *Bellamy v. Wendzina* (2004), 49 R.F.L. (5th) 239 (Sask. Q.B.), involve a dispute between grandparents and their own children. In that case, the mother was raising three children as a single mother and already had to deal with access orders in favour of three different fathers. The case of *Chapman v. Chapman* (2001), 15 R.F.L. (5th) 46 (Ont. C.A.), involved an intact two-parent family and the father's mother. See also *Tucker v. Lester* (2002), 29 R.F.L. (5th) 238 (Sask. Q.B.) and *W. (C.) v. T. (D.)* (2004), 4 R.F.L. (6th) 239 (Alta. Prov. Ct.). In *Moreau v. Cody* (1995), 15 R.F.L. (4th) 174 (Ont. Prov. Div.) and *McLellan v. Glidden* (1996), 23 R.F.L. (4th) 106 (N.B. Q.B.), grandparents sought access following the death of a parent.

The leading case in Ontario is *Chapman, supra*, where Justice Abella said:

> A relationship with a grandparent can — and ideally should — enhance the emotional well-being of a child. Loving and nurturing relationships with members of the extended family can be important for children. When the positive relationships are imperiled arbitrarily, as can happen, for example, in the reorganization of a family following the separation of the parents, the court may intervene to protect the continuation of the benefit of the relationship ...

> Larry and Monica Chapman, not Esther Chapman, are responsible for the welfare of the children. They alone have this legal duty. Esther Chapman, as a grandparent, loves her grandchildren and, understandably, wants to maintain contact with them. Nonetheless, the right to decide the extent and nature of the contact is not hers, and neither she nor a court should be permitted to impose their perception of the children's best interests in circumstances such as these where the parents are so demonstrably attentive to the needs of their children. The parents have, for the moment, decided that those needs do not include lengthy, frequent visits with their grandmother. Although the parents' conflict with Esther Chapman is unfortunate, there is no evidence that this parental decision is currently detrimental to the children. It should therefore be respected by the court and the children's best interests left in the exclusive care of their parents.

Unless legislation provides otherwise, grandparents have no special status to claim access and are legal strangers to the child. Most provincial statutes simply permit third parties such as grandparents to apply for access and then indicate that the best interests of the child test applies. See, e.g., s. 21 of the *CLRA*. Under s. 16(3) of the *DA*, grandparents need leave from a court to apply. In "To Grandmother's House We Go? An Examination of Grandparent Access" (2003-2004), C.F.L.Q. 437, Professor Shaffer indicates (at 447-448) that there are two main approaches discernable in the Canadian cases. The dominant approach starts with the assumption that contact with the grandparents is generally in the child's best interests. In effect, the parent or parents must establish a valid objection in light of the child's best interests. In a minority of cases, the courts instead adopt a "parental autonomy" approach that assumes that it is generally in the best interests of a child to respect parental decision making. The parental autonomy approach was evident in *Chapman*, above, where Justice Abela stated (para. 21): "In the absence of any evidence that the parents are behaving in a way which demonstrates an inability to act in accordance with the best interests of their children, their right to make decisions and judgments on their children's behalf should be respected, including decisions about whom they see, how often, and under what circumstances." Under either approach, as Professor Shaffer acknowledges (at 448), a key factor in predicting the outcome in a particular case is whether the grandparents have an existing, healthy relationship with the children. In *Chapman*, for example, Justice Abella emphasized that the children did not have a positive relationship with their grandmother and that visits caused stress.

Where the courts do order access for grandparents, it is usually quite limited and detailed. For example, one weekend day every four or six weeks is fairly typical. However, the ordered access in *Bellamy v. Wendzina*, above, was much more extensive. This might be explained by the fairly close relationship that existed in the past between the grandparents and the children. The children and the mother had lived with the grandparents for several years. Even after the mother and children moved out, the grandparents remained in constant contact with the children and participated in raising them.

The Special Joint Committee "found the testimony of grandparents and their representatives extremely compelling" (*For the Sake of the Children*, at 56) and it recommended (at 57) that the provinces enact a law "to provide that maintaining and fostering relationships with grandparents and other extended family members is in the best interests of children and that such relationships should not be disrupted without a significant reason related to the well-being of the child".

(3) Role of the Access Parent

YOUNG v. YOUNG

(1993), 49 R.F.L. (3d) 117, 1993 CarswellBC 264, 1993 CarswellBC 1269 (S.C.C.)

McLACHLIN J.: — This case raises the question whether a divorced parent, who does not have custody, should be able to offer his children his religious views over the objection of the custodial parent. This issue raises, in turn, the question of the place of the "best interests of the child" standard in the Canadian constitutional system.

The Background

Mr. and Mrs. Young were married in 1974. They had three daughters. In 1987 the Youngs separated. Mrs. Young took custody of the children; Mr. Young had access, subject to court imposed restrictions following from Mrs. Young's objection to his religious activity with the children.

The separation was marked by a protracted series of court battles. It is unnecessary to detail the many disputes over which the parties joined issue before the case finally came on for trial. Suffice it to say that one of those issues was the disagreement between the parents over which religious activities Mr. Young might appropriately undertake with his daughters. Mrs. Young was brought up in the Anglican church. She expressed a wish that her children be brought up in the United Church, although the evidence suggests that religion, particularly organized religion, does not play an important role in the life of Mrs. Young. Mr. Young converted to the Jehovah's Witness faith two years prior to separation from his spouse. He wished, at the very least, to communicate his faith to his children. To this end, he read Bible stories and discussed his beliefs with his children during his periods of access. He also questioned them about religious matters during these periods.

The evidence shows that the older two daughters like their father but, as time went on, came to dislike his religious instruction. There was evidence that by exposing his older children to his religious beliefs, Mr. Young was damaging his relationship with his children and contributing to the stress the children were experiencing in adjusting to their parents' separation. On the other hand, the evidence also established that the children were functioning in an entirely normal fashion, suggesting that neither their mental nor physical health had been adversely affected by the dispute between their parents over Mr. Young's religious instruction, or by that instruction itself.

The trial judge granted custody of the children to Mrs. Young and access to Mr. Young. But Mr. Young's access was again restricted by court order. The order provided that Mr. Young not discuss the Jehovah's Witness religion with the children, not take them to any religious services, canvassing, or meetings, and not expose the children to religious discussions with third parties without the prior consent of Mrs. Young. Both parties were ordered not to make adverse remarks about the other's beliefs. Mr. Young was also enjoined from preventing blood transfusions for the children, should the need arise. The basis of the order was the trial judge's finding (1989), 24 R.F.L. (3d) 193 at p. 211, that "the religious conflict [between the parents] was causing a problem for the children." She wrote, at p. 215:

> There will be certain restrictions because that is necessary to protect the best interests of these children. That can only be done by putting an end to this religious conflict. The respondent has become so involved in enforcing his rights he has completely overlooked the welfare of the children. The respondent can have a meaningful relationship with his children without promoting his religious beliefs. ... If the respondent is seriously interested in retaining a relationship with his children, he will have no difficulty abiding by the restrictions I propose to place on him when he has access.

... Mr. Young appealed. The Court of Appeal (1990), 50 B.C.L.R. (2d) 1, Southin J.A. dissenting in part, set aside the limitations on religious discussion and attendance, on the ground that it is in the best interests of children that they come to know their non-custodial parent fully, including his or her religious beliefs. The majority concluded, at p. 108, that restrictions should not be placed on the freedom of an access parent to discuss religion with his or her child, or to involve the child in religious activities, unless either "the existence of, or the potential for, real harm" to the child was established on the evidence, or the evidence established that the child did not consent to being subject to the access parent's views or practices. ...

A. The Limitations on Mr. Young's Access

1. The Constitutional Validity of the Best Interests of the Child Standard

... Two questions arise. First, what does the "best interests of the child" test require? Second, does this test, properly understood, infringe upon the guarantees of freedom of religion, expression, association, and equality under the *Canadian Charter of Rights and Freedoms*? ...

A. The wording of the Act

Parliament has adopted the "best interests of the child" test as the basis upon which custody and access disputes are to be resolved. Three aspects of the way Parliament has done this merit comment.

First, the "best interests of the child" test is the *only* test. The express wording of s. 16(8) of the *Divorce Act* requires the court to look *only* at the best interests of the child in making orders of custody and access. This means that parental preferences and "rights" play no role.

Second, the test is broad. Parliament has recognized that the variety of circumstances which may arise in disputes over custody and access is so diverse that predetermined rules, designed to resolve certain types of disputes in advance, may not be useful. Rather, it has been left to the judge to decide what is in the "best interests of the child," by reference to the "condition, means, needs and other circumstances" of the child. Nevertheless, the judicial task is not one of pure discretion. By embodying the "best interests" test in legislation and by setting out general factors to be considered, Parliament has established a legal test, albeit a flexible one. Like all legal tests, it is to be applied according to the evidence in the case, viewed objectively. There is no room for the judge's personal predilections and prejudices. The judge's duty is to apply the law. He or she must not do what he or she wants to do but what he or she ought to do.

Third, s. 16(10) provides that in making an order, the court shall give effect "to the principle that a child of the marriage should have as much contact with each spouse as is consistent with the best interests of the child." This is significant. It stands as the only specific factor which Parliament has seen fit to single out as being something which the judge must consider. By mentioning this factor, Parliament has expressed its opinion that contact with each parent is valuable, and that the judge should ensure that this contact is maximized. The modifying phrase "as is consistent with the best interests of the child" means that the goal of maximum contact of each parent with the child is not absolute. To the extent that contact conflicts with the best interests of the child, it may be restricted. But *only* to that extent. Parliament's decision to maintain maximum contact between the child and both parents is amply supported by the literature, which suggests that children benefit from continued access. ...

I would summarize the effect of the provisions of the *Divorce Act* on matters of access as follows. The ultimate test in all cases is the best interest of the child. This is a positive test, encompassing a wide variety of factors. One of the factors which the judge seeking to determine what is in the best interests of the child must have regard to is the desirability of maximizing contact between the child and each parent. But in the final analysis, decisions on access must reflect what is in the best interests of the child. ...

It follows from this that the proposition, put to us in argument, that the custodial parent should have the right to forbid certain types of contact between the access parent and the child, must fail. ...

I conclude that the ultimate criterion for determining limits on access to a child is the best interests of the child. The custodial parent has no "right" to limit access. The judge must consider all factors relevant to determining what is in the child's best interests; a factor which must be considered in all cases is Parliament's view that contact with each parent is to be maximized to the extent that this is compatible with the best interests of the child. The risk of harm to the child, while not the ultimate legal test, may also be a factor to be considered. This is particularly so where the issue is the quality of access — what the access parent may say or do with the child. In such cases, it will generally be relevant to consider whether the conduct in question poses a risk of harm to the child which outweighs the benefits of a free and open relationship, which permits the child to know the access parent as he or she is. It goes without saying that, as for any other legal test, the judge, in determining what is in the best interests of the child, must act not on his or her personal views, but on the evidence.

B. The Constitutionality of the Test

The first question is whether the *Charter* applies. Because of my conclusion later in these reasons that valid orders under the "best interests of the child" standard cannot violate the *Charter*, I find it unnecessary to decide whether the *Charter* applies to an action for access under the *Divorce Act* between two parents. For the purposes of this section, I assume that it does.

The constitutional focus in this case centres on the guarantee of freedom of religion in s. 2(a) of the *Charter* and the guarantee of freedom of expression in s. 2(b) of the *Charter*. The guarantees of freedom of association and equality apply only tangentially, if at all, and were not emphasized in argument.

The respondent says that the legislative provision for the "best interests of the child" violates his religious and expressive freedom. The argument is that in some cases the "best interests of the child" will require a judge to make an order limiting expressive or religious freedom. Therefore, it is submitted, the test is unconstitutional, unless it can be saved under s. 1.

In my view, this argument cannot stand. The reason is that the guarantees of religious freedom and expressive freedom in the *Charter* do not protect conduct which violates the best interests of the child test. ...

2. Whether the Order of the Trial Judge is Valid under the Divorce Act

The question is whether the trial judge correctly applied the "best interests of the child" test set out in s. 16(8) and (10) of the *Divorce Act*.

The trial judge took a custody-oriented approach to the question of whether the father should be allowed to discuss and practice his religion with the children. For her the first question (at p. 205) was "who gets custody and guardianship of the children and what flows from that." She concluded that custody confers on the custodial parent the exclusive "right" to make all decisions with respect to the child's education, health care, and religion. It followed inevitably, at p. 205, from this that she saw the custodial parent as possessing the "sole responsibility for ... the religious instruction of the child." This exclusive right in Mrs. Young to determine the child's religious instruction led directly to her conclusion that Mr. Young should be prevented from discussing his religious ideas with the children. Having concluded that the religious conflict "must stop," she ordered it stopped in the manner which the custodial parent desired, without further discussion of whether another alternative might better serve the interests of the children.

This reasoning departs from the best interest of the child test as outlined earlier in these reasons in three respects. First, it places undue emphasis on the wishes of the custodial parent. The custodial parent is viewed as having the "right" to determine limits on access. In my respectful opinion, this rights-based approach is erroneous. The only question to be considered where limitation of access is in issue is what is in the best interests of the child. While the custodial parent has the obligation to make certain basic decisions as to how the child is educated, which may extend to religious matters, this does not automatically mean that religious contacts with the access parent of a different faith are to be excluded. It is not the wishes of the custodial parent that govern terms of access, but the best interests of the child.

Second, the trial judge failed to consider the benefits which might enure to the children from coming to know their father as he was — that is, as a devoutly religious man devoted to the Jehovah's Witness faith. She made no reference to Parliament's instruction in s. 16(10) that the child shall have as much contact with both parents as is compatible with her best interests.

Thirdly, the trial judge failed to consider adequately whether there was any evidence of a risk of harm to the children which might offset the benefit of full access to their father's values, including those related to religion. While in some circumstances access may be limited on grounds unrelated to harm, in cases such as this, where the issue is whether entirely lawful discussions and activities between the access parent and the child should be curtailed, it behooves the judge to enquire whether the conduct poses a risk of harming the child. While the trial judge alluded to the possibility that if Mr. Young continued to share his religion with the children, he would damage his relationship with the older two, she failed to allude to any other suggestion of harm and failed to consider whether such harm might outweigh the benefit to be gained from a freer, fuller relationship with their father.

The trial judge's undue emphasis on the "rights" of the custodial parent, coupled with her failure to consider the benefits to be gained from unrestricted contact with the access parent or whether those benefits were offset by a greater risk of harm to the children, may have clouded her appreciation of what was in their best interests. It was therefore open to the Court of Appeal to reconsider the matter and seek to give further guidance as to the factors to be considered in determining what is in the child's best interest in cases such as these.

Southin J.A. in the Court of Appeal took a similar but less absolute view of the rights conferred by custody. The custodial parent, according to her, has the "final say" on all matters of religion, although the "right to know" the access parent and the problems with the enforceability of any order restricting the conversation of the access parent led her to conclude that the trial judge's restriction in respect of religious conversations could not stand.

The majority of the Court of Appeal, by contrast, saw the matter less in terms of the custodial parent's "right" to decide all religious matters affecting the children, and more in terms of the best interests of the children. Unfettered by notions of the custodial parent's rights, the majority of the Court of Appeal asked simply what was in the best interests of the child. ...

Thus, for the majority in the Court of Appeal, the prime concern was the best interests of the child. An order for custody vests the custodial parent with the power to determine the child's religious upbringing, to the extent that this parent can require the child to observe a faith until the age of discretion; this is in the child's best interests where the parents cannot agree. A custody order does not, however, give the custodial parent the "right" to limit the access parent's ability to share his or her religious views with the child, unless that is shown on the evidence not to be in the child's best interests. Viewed thus, the notions of custody and access unite in a common purpose of promoting the child's best interests.

The majority held that an access parent's conduct with his child may be limited where the evidence shows the existence of, or potential for, real harm to the child, or where the child does not consent to the instruction. On the latter point, Wood J.A. noted that while it may be in the best interests of the child that the custodial parent be allowed to enforce religious practices against the child's wishes, that rationale did not extend to the access parent. Both limitations on the right to access found by the Court of Appeal are grounded in the best interests of the child. The majority also held that expert evidence, based on scientific criteria, is required to show harm. While, for the reasons discussed earlier, I would not agree as a general proposition that in every case the risk of harm to the child must be established to justify limitations on access, in the context of the dispute in this case, I do not think that the majority of the Court of Appeal erred in placing considerable emphasis on the absence on the evidence of a risk of harm to the child.

I do not share the view of the majority of the Court of Appeal that expert evidence is required in all cases. Nor am I convinced that the failure of the child to consent to instruction necessarily precludes the conclusion that such instruction by the access parent is in the best interests of the child. Apart from these caveats, I substantially subscribe to the views expressed by Wood J.A.

The majority of the Court of Appeal held that the evidence did not establish that harm was being caused to the children. On the issue of the children's consent, Wood J.A. concluded that no order was necessary because Mr. Young had confirmed under oath that he would respect his children's wishes with respect to the activities they objected to — attending services with him and accompanying him on his proselytizing missions. In the end, the majority did not find that it was in the best interests of the children, all factors considered, that even this limited form of religious activity by the access parent be restricted.

If one accepts, as did the majority of the Court of Appeal, that the issue of the children's accompanying Mr. Young to services and in his evangelical efforts is resolved by Mr. Young's undertakings — and I see no reason not to do so given his record of compliance to date — the only issue is whether the order forbidding Mr. Young to discuss religion with his children is valid. Apart from the value of getting to know their father and the difficulty of enforcement which led Southin J.A. to reject this restriction, it is questionable that a proper application of the "best interests of the child" test supports it. Conflict between the parents is, in and of itself, not a sufficient basis for assuming that the child's interests will not be served. There was, in this case, evidence that the children were functioning in an entirely normal fashion, and had not been adversely affected by the dispute between their parents or by their father's religious instruction. We are left, then, with the trial judge's concern that Mr. Young's relationship with his children would deteriorate if he persisted in his religious instruction during his periods of access.

With the greatest respect to the trial judge, this was not, on the record in this case, a sufficient reason for restricting access. Insofar as the possible deterioration of Mr. Young's relationship with his daughters can be considered unfortunate, the alternative — a relationship which prevents them from knowing him as he is — is also undesirable. In these circumstances, any perceived harm to the children cannot be said to outweigh the benefits of unrestricted access. In short, this is not a case where the evidence supports the view that the best interests of the children require further curtailment of the father's communication of religious views and practices than already had been agreed to.

I conclude that the trial judge's orders preventing Mr. Young from discussing religion with his children were not supportable on the evidence. In view of Mr. Young's undertakings, the orders relating to church attendance and proselytizing were unnecessary. The order enjoining the respondent from preventing blood transfusions was unnecessary from a practical point of view. Parents should, of course, not make disparaging comments about the other parent's religion, but the matter might, on the record here, best have been left to the parents' good sense.

L'HEUREUX-DUBÉ J. (dissenting): — I have had the advantage of reading the opinion of my colleague Justice McLachlin. With great deference, I disagree both with her reasons and the result she has reached. Since I do not characterize the issue quite as my colleague does, I will pursue my own analysis.

The main issue in this case, in my view, concerns access by a non-custodial parent to his children whose custody was granted to the other parent. More precisely, this court must determine whether curtailment of access is warranted in the circumstances of this case. The focus of the inquiry is the standard applicable to such a determination. According to the Court of Appeal, the test is one of harm to the children. I disagree. In my view, the only applicable test is the best interests of the children, assessed from a child-centred perspective, a test which is mandated by the *Divorce Act.* ... as well as provincial legislation, and which is universally applied and constitutionally sound. While the respondent, the father in this case, raises the issues of freedom of religion and expression and the infringement of his guarantees under s. 2(a) and (b) of the *Canadian Charter of Rights and Freedoms* (the "*Charter*") due to the trial judge's order restricting access to his children, these questions simply do not arise in the circumstances of this case. If they do, I agree with my colleague that there is no infringement of the *Charter*. ...

Custody

... Despite these changes over time with respect to who is regarded as the appropriate custodial parent, the nature and scope of custody itself have remained relatively constant. The chief feature of such orders was, and still is, the implied, if not explicit, conferral of parental authority on the person granted custody. The long-standing rule at common law is that an order of custody entails the right to exercise full parental authority. In the case of a sole custody order, that authority is vested in one parent to the exclusion of the other.

The power of the custodial parent is not a "right" with independent value which is granted by courts for the benefit of the parent, but is designed to enable that parent to discharge his or her responsibilities and obligations to the child. It is, in fact, the child's right to a parent who will look after its best interests. ...

It has long been recognized that the custodial parent has a duty to ensure, protect, and promote the best interests of the child. That duty includes the sole and primary responsibility to oversee all aspects of day-to-day life and long-term well-being, as well as major decisions with respect to education, religion, health, and well-being. This is reflected in the decision of the Ontario Court of Appeal in *Kruger v. Kruger* (1979), 25 O.R. (2d) 673 at p. 677, in which Thorson J.A. stated:

> In my view, to award one parent the exclusive custody of a child is to clothe that parent, for whatever period he or she is awarded the custody, with full parental control over, and ultimate parental responsibility for, the care, upbringing and education of the child, generally to the exclusion of the right of the other parent to interfere in the decisions that are made in exercising that control or in carrying out that responsibility.

.....

The non-custodial parent retains certain residual rights over the child as one of its two natural guardians, among which is the right to apply to the court for variation of custody and access terms. Various other entitlements have been recognized at common law, including, subject to the best interests of the child, the right to access, the right to contest the child's adoption, the right to claim guardianship of the person of the child upon the death of the custodial parent, and the right to succeed to the child's property, among others. ...

The traditional decision making power of the custodial parent recognized by law is intimately connected to the welfare of the child, as the need for a secure and constant source of parental responsibility in the life of the child is well understood among those who are knowledgeable in the psychology of children. ...

... [A]n important function of the law on divorce or separation is to reinforce the remainder of the family unit so that children may get on with their lives with as little disruption as possible. Courts are not in a position, nor do they presume to be able, to make the necessary day-to-day decisions which affect the best interests of the child. That task must rest with the custodial parent, as he or she is the person best placed to assess the needs of the child in all its dimensions. ... Once a court has determined who is the appropriate custodial parent, it must, indeed it can do no more than, presume that that parent will act in the best interests of the child. As the New Brunswick Court of Appeal stated in *Fougère v. Fougère* (1987), 6 R.F.L. (3d) 314 at p. 316:

> Once courts award custody they must, in our view, support the custodial parent in that parent's reasonable efforts to bring up the children, including the right of the custodial parent to decide questions relating to the religious upbringing of the children.

As has been widely observed by those studying the nature and sources of changes in family institutions, popular notions of parenthood and parenting roles have undergone a profound evolution both in Canada and elsewhere in the world in recent years. ... One of the central tenets of this new vision is that child care both is no longer and should no longer be exclusively or primarily the preserve of women. Society has largely moved away from the assumptions embodied in the tender years doctrine that women are inherently imbued with characteristics which render them better custodial parents. ... Moreover, both economic necessity and the movement toward social and economic equality for women have resulted in an increase in the number of women in the paid workforce. Many people have tended to assume that a natural result of this change would be the concurrent sharing of household and child-care responsibilities with spouses, companions, and, of course, fathers. In addition, the increased emphasis on the participation of fathers in the raising of children and financial support after divorce gave rise to claims by fathers and fathers' rights groups for legislative changes that would entitle them to the benefit of neutral presumptions in custody decisions.

A corollary of the acceptance of neutral parenting roles is the notion that children, after divorce, need to maintain contact with both parents. It is now widely assumed to be self-evident in the child's best interests to ensure the non-custodial parent's involvement in the life of the child. One result of these changes has been the emergence of joint custody awards, which are predicated explicitly on equality of parental responsibilities and the belief that children's interests are served by maximizing the involvement of both parents in decisions concerning the child.

The custody provisions of the Act reflect, to some degree, this evolving view of parental roles. Under the best interests test, courts no longer automatically grant custody according to the tender years doctrine. Instead, decisions are made according to the best interests of the child without the benefit of a presumption in favour of the mother, or, for that matter, the father. Section 16(4) of the Act, for the first time, specifies that a court may make joint custody orders. Section 16(10) of the Act contains the "friendly parent" rule, which directs courts, when granting custody, to take into account the willingness of the parent seeking custody to maximize the contact of the other parent with the child of the marriage. It is clear, then, that the Act envisages contact between the child and each of its parents as a worthy goal which should be, all other things being equal, in the best interests of the child. This is a value which courts have always recognized in generally granting generous access to the non-custodial parent.

Wood J.A., however, has interpreted the Act as reflecting significant changes to the traditional law of custody and access. More specifically, he expressed the view that s. 16(10) of the Act indicates a desire on the part of Parliament to enlarge the concept of access beyond its traditional scope. Therefore, according to him, the traditional decision making power of custodial parents has been curtailed by s. 16, which, taken as a whole, requires a distribution of rights between the parents. ...

Professor Payne, in *Payne on Divorce*, at p. 144, shares the view that the access provisions in the Act do not confer any authority on the non-custodial parent to participate in the major decisions of a child's life. Rather, s. 16(5) of the Act provides that "[u]nless the court orders otherwise, a spouse who is granted access to a child of the marriage has the right to make inquiries, and to be given information, as to the health, education and welfare of the child." It does not mandate that the custodial parent consult with the access spouse when making such decisions with respect to the child. ... Custody, as defined in s. 2(1) of the Act, "includes care, upbringing and any other incident of custody." Payne states, at pp. 145-146:

> The provisions of the *Divorce Act, 1985*, and particularly the definitions of "custody" and "access" in subsection 2(1) of the Act, apparently preclude Canadian courts from reverting to a narrow definition of custody. The word "includes" in the definition of custody necessarily implies that the term embraces a wider range of powers tha[n] those specifically designated in subsection 2(1). ... The opinions expressed in *Kruger v. Kruger, supra*, have thus been statutorily endorsed by the *Divorce Act, 1985*. Consequently, in the absence of a successful application to vary an unqualified sole custody disposition with respect to all or any of the incidents of custody, *the non-custodial spouse with access*

> *privileges is a passive bystander who is excluded from the decision-making process in matters relating to the child's welfare, growth and development. This remains true notwithstanding that subsection 16(10) of the Divorce Act, 1985 provides that the court shall promote "maximum contact" between the child and the non-custodial parent to the extent that this is consistent with the best interests of the child.* [Emphasis added.]

I could not agree more, given the wording of the Act itself and the generally accepted view of custody both before and since its enactment. The Act neither suggests nor requires the division of parental responsibilities between the custodial and access parent. If Parliament had intended such a result, it would have used much clearer and less ambiguous language.

It goes without saying that I do not share the assertion of my colleague that "the proposition, put to us in argument, that the custodial parent should have the right to forbid certain types of contact between the access parent and the child, must fail" [at pp. 150-151]. The proposition is not one of "rights"; it is one of duty and obligation to the child's best interests. For example, a custodial parent, aware of sexual or other abuse by the non-custodial parent, would be remiss in his or her duty to the child not to cut off access by the abuser immediately, with or without a court order. One cannot stress enough that it is from the perspective of the child's interest that these powers and responsibilities must be assessed, as the "rights" of the parent are not a criterion.

The arguments in favour of increased authority over the child by the access parent are closely related to those which support a presumption in favour of joint custody. ... They rest on the premise that the relationship of authority and obligation that existed between each of the parents and the child during the marriage should and can continue, despite the fact that the parents may no longer be willing or able to co-operate on its exercise. While joint custody may remain an ideal solution in proper cases, particularly when parents are willing and able to co-operate, such premises are often based on illusion rather than reality, and may, in the words of Thorston J.A., amount to "a triumph of optimism over prudence" (*Kruger v. Kruger, supra,* at p. 681).

Unlike in other jurisdictions, the Act contains no presumption in favour of joint custody. Nor have Canadian courts generally accepted the view that joint custody is to be preferred in judicial orders as to custody and access. ...

When parents are willing and able to share parenting responsibilities, they usually do so by agreement, which courts generally uphold. ... Courts are also reluctant to interfere with shared parenting arrangements that have survived for a period of time after parental separation or divorce. ...

But the reality of divorce and the circumstances of the parties cannot easily be dismissed. When implementing the objectives of the Act, whether considering joint custody or fashioning access orders, courts, in my view, must be conscious of the gap between the ideals of shared parenting and the social reality of custody and child-care decisions. Despite the neutrality of the Act, forces such as wage rates, job ghettos, and socialization about caregiving still operate in a manner that cause many women to "chose" to take on the caregiving role both during marriage and after divorce. ... Moreover, research uniformly shows that men as a group have not yet embraced responsibility for child care. The vast majority of such labour, both before and after divorce, is still performed by women, whether those women work outside the home or not, and women remain the sole custodial parent in the majority of cases by mutual consent of the parties. ... Nor does a joint custody order in most cases result in truly shared custody. Rather, in day-to-day practice, joint custody tends to resemble remarkably sole custody, as in many such orders care and control remain with one person, ... The person who has performed the primary care-giving role within the marriage, as a rule, retains that obligation upon separation and divorce. Thus, the lived experience of child care for both women and children after divorce has changed much less than we might support or wish. ...

Support for the decisions of the custodial parent in the discharge of his or her responsibilities remains crucial if the child is to flourish. The conferral of decision making authority on the custodial parent acknowledges and reflects the actual day-to-day reality of this task ... In the face of the enduring tasks and obligations of the custodial parent, courts must be wary of any expansion of the traditional rights of the non-custodial parent. The clear risk is that such changes will simply reduce the decision making power of the custodial parent, without any parallel reduction in the responsibilities. This creates no benefit, and may amount to pure disturbance, both to the women who, as a rule, provide the primary care and to the children who must function within such a regime.

The perception that upholding the authority of the custodial parent emphasizes the rights of the parent at the expense of the interests of the child misconceives the problem. It is precisely to ensure the best interests of the child that the decision making power is granted to the custodial parent, as that person is uniquely situated to assess, understand, ensure, and promote the needs of the child. ...

As I stated at the outset, the custodial parent remains the decision-maker in all aspects of the child's life. It is to avoid the spectre of the child as the field upon which the battle of competing parental rights is played out that the law confirms the authority of the custodial parent. This policy serves two functions: it precludes such contests entirely and it provides the necessary support to the parent who bears the responsibility for the child. The wisdom of this approach lies in recognizing the ease with which the interests of the child could be obscured or forgotten were courts to get into the business of parceling out jurisdiction over the emotional, spiritual, and physical welfare of the child between parents who no longer agree. This brings us to the heart of this case, a consideration of the nature of access.

Access

Access rights exist in recognition of the fact that it is normally in the interests of the child to continue and foster the relationship developed with both parents prior to the divorce or separation. This being said, the right to access and the circumstances in which it takes place must be perceived from the vantage point of the child. Wherever the relationship to the non-custodial parent conflicts with the best interests of the child, the furtherance and protection of the child's best interests must take priority over the desires and interests of the parent. ...

I am in agreement with my colleague that s. 16(10) indicates that Parliament has expressed its opinion that contact with each parent is valuable. On the other hand, it must also be recognized that the goal of maximum contact is not absolute and that access may be restricted where there is evidence that such contact would otherwise conflict with the best interests of the child. This limitation on maximum contact is both abundantly clear on a straightforward reading of the section and consistent with the spirit of the Act and its focus on the best interests of the child. In my view, the analysis may and should stop at this point.

As the ultimate goal of access is the continuation of a relationship which is of significance and support to the child, access must be crafted to preserve and promote that which is healthy and helpful in that relationship so that it may survive to achieve its purpose. Accordingly, it is in the interests of the child, and arguably also in the interests of the access parent, to remove or mitigate the sources of ongoing conflict which threaten to damage or prevent the continuation of a meaningful relationship.

Wood J.A. expressed the general concern that access rights remain vulnerable to the caprices of a vengeful custodial parent. In my view, courts should not be too quick to presume that the access concerns of the custodial parent are unrelated to the best interests of the child. Although the myth is that the custodial parent typically attempts to obstruct access of the other parent, studies in Canada, England, and the United States indicate that the problem tends to be quite the reverse. ...

Where there is a genuine problem with access, the non-custodial parent is not without recourse in any case. This stems from the statutory directive to facilitate access where it is in the child's best interests and the role of the judge as the arbiter of those interests in the case of a dispute between the parents. ...

Best Interests of the Child

1. Content of the Rule

... Custody and access decisions are pre-eminently exercises in discretion. Case-by-case consideration of the unique circumstances of each child is the hallmark of this process ... The wide latitude under the best interests test permits courts to respond to the spectrum of factors which can both positively and negatively affect a child. Such discretion also permits the judge to focus on the needs of the particular child before him or her, recognizing that what may constitute stressful or damaging circumstances for one child may not necessarily have the same effect on another.

While the best interests test provides the focus and perspective from which to assess custody and access decisions, the test has nonetheless been subject to evaluation and criticism from various sources. The most common concern is that it is essentially indeterminate and fails to provide the necessary direction and criteria with which to make custody and access decisions. ...

... In the result, a number of presumptions have been suggested to govern the best interests test in custody decisions, the most common of which is the primary care-giver presumption. (See S. Boyd, "Potentialities and Perils of the Primary Caregiver Presumption" [(1991), 7 C.F.L.Q. 1].) This presumption has developed in response to the trend toward joint custody, and the resultant erosion in both the financial resources and the authority of the parent with day-to-day obligations for child rearing. Boyd expresses the concerns underlying this presumption as follows, at p. 6:

> ... a misplaced application of "equality" is evident in legislative and judicial trends toward entrenching fathers' rights in child custody law, such as joint custody and access enforcement. The importance of ensuring "equal" fatherly input into children's lives after family breakdown even if they were not "equally" involved before, has been elevated to arguably too high a level in recent years. The form which this trend often takes — retaining an active and full role for both father and mother in making decisions concerning the child (joint legal custody) — potentially inhibits the autonomy and exercise of discretion by the parent with physical care of the child.

However, as she points out, one of the principal rationales for endorsing this presumption is not to supplant the best interests of the child as the ultimate objective but to ensure that those interests are protected. The presumption explicitly restores the values of commitment and demonstrated ability to nurture as well as continued psychological parenting to the child, factors which may be overshadowed by other considerations in custody disputes. The primary care-giver presumption thus recognizes the obligations and supports the authority of the parent engaged in day-to-day tasks of child rearing.

In assessing all the relevant considerations, courts must be careful that the ideals of parental sharing and equality do not overcome the lived reality of custody and access arrangements, and that the child's needs and concerns are accommodated and not obscured by abstract claims of parental rights. This is not to say that the parent's interests may not coincide with the child's interests or that a court may never validly take a parent's interests into consideration. However, to further the best interests of the child, a recognition of the close relationship between the needs of the child and the needs of the remaining family unit of which he or she is a part is essential. ...

2. Constitutionality of the Best Interests Test

[In this section of her reasons, Justice L'Heureux-Dubé concluded that the best interests test was not unconstitutionally vague because it was not "so uncertain as to be incapable of guiding a consideration of the factors relevant to custody and access determinations". Later she held that the *Charter* could not be used to challenge the trial judge's order on the basis that it infringed the father's freedom of religion. In her view, judicial orders in custody and access disputes do not involve state action and the *Charter* has no application to them. She added that, even if the *Charter* did apply, there would be no infringement of either freedom of expression or freedom of religion where an order restricted parental religious instruction or observance on the basis of the best interests test. That is, she concluded that these freedoms never encompass activities which are not in the child's best interests.]

3. Evidence

One might have thought that the clear and unequivocal language of the Act makes the best interests of the child the only consideration in matters of custody and access, and that the only evidence required for an order limiting access would be evidence indicating that the exercise of access in a particular manner is in the best interests of the child. ... The Court of Appeal, however, ... would elevate the test to one of harm, which the custodial parent must show in order to restrict access to the children by the non-custodial parent. I say at the outset that, even under such a severe test, the appellant has established that restrictions are required. However, the question is whether harm is the test. My answer is a clear no, for the reasons that follow.

As I noted above, the Court of Appeal has equated the alleged absence of harm in this case with the best interests of the child. However, no rationale is proposed for so defining the best interests of the child. Moreover, nothing in the Act mandates or even suggests that "real danger of significant harm to the child" be the sole consideration in matters of custody and access. ...

The harm test by which the Court of Appeal proposes to qualify the best interests test inverts the basic focus of the inquiry into custody and access. Under the best interests test, courts must consider how to best foster the child's overall development and protect the child from conflict and the disruptive effects of divorce at a vulnerable point in his or her life. In contrast, the harm test essentially requires a court to determine how much conflict and stress a child should be required to endure in order that the parent's wishes may prevail. Once the pendulum swings in that direction, it is difficult to control. ... However, the most serious deficiency of the harm test is the following. While the effects of custody and access decisions always remain uncertain to some degree, the harm test places any risk of miscalculation in the degree of stress or conflict occasioned by such decisions squarely on the back of the child, depriving the child of any presumption in his or her favour. Obviously this cannot be correct from the perspective of the interests of the child. To wait until harm has occurred to correct the situation is not only to waive the benefit of prevention, but also to increase the possibility of error. Instead of minimizing the risks, the harm test would maximize them. ...

... [A] number of conclusions about the effects of divorce on children emerge with remarkable consistency in all of the major studies and psychological literature on children after divorce. One of the most important of these is the role of conflict in the welfare of the child. Along with the quality of the relationship with the custodial parent and the ability to maintain contact with the non-custodial parent, there is substantial evidence that continuing conflict is the most important factor affecting the ability of children to readjust to the new family situation after divorce. It appears that, above and beyond the disruption caused by divorce or separation itself, it is the discord and disharmony within the family which are most damaging to children in the aftermath of divorce. ...

I agree with my colleague that expert evidence should not be routinely required to establish the best interests of the child. In my view, it is a modern-day myth that experts are always better placed than parents to assess the needs of the child. Common sense requires us to acknowledge that the person involved in day-to-day care may observe changes in the behaviour, mood, attitude, and development of a child that could go unnoticed by anyone else. The custodial parent normally has the best vantage point from which to assess the interests of the child, and thus will often provide the most reliable and complete source of information to the judge on the needs and interests of that child.

Furthermore, it is important to emphasize the importance of the evidence of children in custody and access disputes, and I would not wish to suggest that their testimony alone might not be a sufficient evidentiary basis upon which to restrict access. Courts have increasingly come to accept and understand in the criminal context that children themselves can be a reliable source of evidence to the judge (*R. v. Khan*, [1990] 2 S.C.R. 531). To disregard their evidence when their own interests are directly at issue would, in my opinion, be at odds with this clear evolutionary trend in the law.

Many legal commentators have noted the degree to which custody and access disputes have become a contest between experts, involving increasing amounts of time and money. ... In the absence of clear legal presumptions about the best interests of children, judges have increasingly come to rely on the recommendations of experts to determine custody and access issues, believing that such experts possess objective, scientific knowledge and can in fact "know" what is in the best interests of the child. However, expert testimony, while helpful in some and perhaps many circumstances, is often inconclusive and contradictory. ... That this should be so is not surprising, since such assessments are both speculative and may be affected by the professional values and biases of the assessors themselves.

Even where such expertise is valuable, there are impediments in such reliance. Assessments may occasion delays in resolving proceedings and may at times constitute a significant disruption in the lives of both parents and children. The cost involved in routinely hiring experts to establish the best interests of the child only increases the expense of custody litigation and is far beyond the resources of most divorcing couples. ...

Given these concerns, while the evidence of experts may form a valuable and necessary part of some custody and access decisions, most of the time they are unnecessary to an ordinary determination of the best interests of the child. Nor does the prospect of access restrictions inevitably require resort to expert opinion, as it may be apparent to the judge from the evidence of the parties and often the children themselves that access should only be granted subject to certain conditions. ...

In summary, as a matter of statutory interpretation, the *Divorce Act* mandates that, in decisions of custody and access, the sole consideration be the best interests of the child. The focus must remain at all times on the child, not the needs or interests of the parents, and parental rights play no role in such decisions except insofar as they are necessary to ensure the best interests of the child.

The custodial parent is responsible for the care and upbringing of the child, including decisions concerning the education, religion, health, and well-being of the child. Parental authority rests with the custodial parent, not for his or her own benefit, but in order to enable that parent to discharge effectively the obligations and responsibilities owed to the child.

As set out in the Act, maximum contact between the child and the non-custodial parent is a worthwhile goal which should be pursued to the extent that it is in the best interests of the child. Generous and unrestricted access, which is the norm, should be favoured except when such access would not be in the best interests of the child. However, ongoing conflict between parents which adversely affects the child must be minimized or avoided, as it is the single factor which has consistently proven to be severely detrimental to children upon separation or divorce.

The best interests of the child must be approached from a child-centred perspective. It is not simply the right to be free of significant harm. It is the right of the particular child in question to the best possible arrangements in the circumstances of the parties, taking into consideration the wide spectrum of factors which may affect the child's physical, spiritual, moral, and emotional well-being, and the milieu in which the child lives.

Where the question of restrictions on access arises, the best interests of the child must be determined by considering the "condition, means, needs and other circumstances of the child" as required by the Act. The totality of these circumstances must be considered. Nothing in the Act suggests that harm should be the controlling factor. To adopt the harm standard would be to invert the focus of the best interests test and place the risk of error on the child, contrary to the objectives of the Act.

Expert evidence, while helpful in some cases, is not routinely required to establish the best interests of the child. That determination is normally possible from the evidence of the parties themselves and, in some cases, the testimony of the children involved.

Freedom of religion and expression are fundamental values protected by the *Charter*. However, the best interests of the child standard in the *Divorce Act* does not offend *Charter* values, but is completely consonant with the underlying objectives of the *Charter*. The *Charter* has no application to private disputes between parents in the family context, nor does it apply to court orders in the area of custody and access. While a child's exposure to different parental faiths or beliefs may be of value, when such exposure is a source of conflict and is not in the best interests of the child, such exposure may be curtailed.

This brings us to the evidence in this case which led to the trial judge's order restricting the respondent's access.

Application to the Case

The majority of the Court of Appeal found no evidence of harm which would support the order made at trial. Even if I were to agree that some measure of harm must be demonstrated before the trial judge is entitled to restrict the respondent's religious activities with the children, a view I do not share, the evidence amply demonstrates the harm such religious activity has brought about. While the rationale underlying the right of access and the objective of maximum contact is to permit the relationship to flourish, in this case the contrary result has occurred, as it has antagonized the children. ...

Although the respondent characterizes this litigation as an attack on his religious freedom, those beliefs are not at risk, as the restrictions place no limits on the respondent's ability to engage in religious practices himself. It is the effect of his practices on the best interests of his three daughters that is in question here.

[The Justice noted that a family court counsellor and a psychologist had reported that the children were under stress because of the religious issues and the litigation that it spawned and unhappy with their access visits because their father made them feel guilty. She also reviewed the letters that the two oldest children had written to the judge.]

In my opinion, this evidence amply demonstrates the stress the children were under; much of it related to the children's resistance to becoming involved in their father's religious practices. The trial judge can in no way be said to have erred in finding that the best interests of these children were served by removing the source of conflict, particularly as the ultimate purpose of the restrictions was to preserve the relationship between the respondent and his children.

Moreover, there was evidence leading the trial judge to conclude that the respondent would not respect the wishes of the children without an order to do so. ...

As the trial judge observed, the respondent was quite unconcerned with the conflict and stress on the children caused by the pursuit of his own religious interests. At the same time as he found the resources to press his claims to religious rights, he apparently did not find the payment of maintenance a top priority. Upon reading the evidence, I cannot disagree with the trial judge that the respondent's concern with religious rights had clearly overtaken the practical realities of parenthood and overshadowed his larger responsibilities to his children in this case.

Since writing these reasons, I have had the opportunity to read the joint reasons of my colleagues Cory and Iacobucci JJ. They invite the following comments.

First, as to the first part of the trial judge's order, contrary to their affirmation, the issue is not moot. It is precisely because the trial judge found as a fact that the respondent could not be trusted for the reasons she outlined, that she issued that order. ...

As to the second part of the order, my colleagues assert that the best interests test does not support an order preventing the respondent from discussing religion with his children, on the ground that it is "difficult to accept that any genuine and otherwise proper discussion between a parent and his or her child should be curtailed by court orders". Otherwise, they suggest, a non-custodial parent who espouses a theory of evolution would be ordered, under the best interests test, not to discuss or explain his or her views to a child in the custody of a parent who is a member of a fundamentalist religion.

However, this scenario has nothing to do with the facts of this case. With respect, to equate the two scenarios is to misapprehend fundamentally the focus of the best interests test. It is not the fact that the parents differ in their fundamental beliefs that warrants the restrictions in this case. It is the finding of fact made by the trial judge, on the basis of evidence she found credible, that continuing conflict over religion, including the respondent's repeated attempts to discuss religious matters with the children against their clearly expressed desires, profoundly disturbed the children and was contrary to their best interests. At the time of trial, the respondent was not engaging in other religious activities with the children, as they had already been curtailed by the interim order almost a year and a half earlier. Therefore, it is *precisely* these continuing "discussions" that were disturbing the children, causing the deterioration of their relationship with their father and which, therefore, had to be curtailed.

I wish to emphasize two points. As I thought I made clear earlier in my reasons, a child's exposure to different parental faiths or beliefs may generally be of value and even of great value; there is no presumption that such exposure is not in the best interests of the child. Rather, the contrary is true. Second, as I also emphasized earlier, generous and unrestricted access should be favoured except where it is not in the best interests of the child. Hence, restrictions such as the trial judge found to be required in the second part of her order will be rare indeed and there is no reason to suppose that, absent a threat to the best interests of the child, any question of such restrictions will arise. However, it is important to acknowledge that in those rare cases where parents cross the line and engage in conduct which constitutes, in the words of my colleagues, "indoctrination, enlistment, or harassment" courts have a duty to intervene in the best interests of children. The evidence strongly suggests that this is just such a case and that is the finding of the trial judge.

LA FOREST J. (GONTHIER J. concurring): (dissenting) — ... I am in agreement with the reasons of Justice L'Heureux-Dubé that the issue of access should be determined on the basis of what is in the best interest of the child. I also agree with her on the constitutional issue. ...

Accordingly, I would allow the appeal and restore the order of the trial judge on all matters except the monetary issues. ...

SOPINKA J.: — I have read the reasons of my colleagues Justice L'Heureux-Dubé and Justice McLachlin and I find myself in agreement with McLachlin J. as to the disposition of the appeal and with most of her reasons. While I agree with McLachlin J. that the ultimate determination in deciding issues of custody and access is the "best interests of the child test," it must be reconciled with the *Canadian Charter of Rights and Freedoms*. General language in a statute which, in its breadth, potentially confers the power to override *Charter* values must be interpreted to respect those values. ... It cannot be done the other way around and allow the best interests test in its broadest interpretation to read down *Charter* rights so as to accommodate this interpretation.

In my view, the test in s. 16(10) of the *Divorce Act* ... and the *Charter* right involved in this case, namely, freedom of religious expression, can best be reconciled by interpreting the best interests test to allow the right to be overridden only if its exercise would occasion consequences that involve more than inconvenience, upset, or disruption to the child and, incidentally, to the custodial parent. The long-term value to a child of a meaningful relationship with both parents is a policy that is affirmed in the *Divorce Act*. This means allowing each to engage in those activities which contribute to identify the parent for what he or she really is. The access parent is not expected to act out a part or assume a phony lifestyle during access periods. The policy favouring activities that promote a meaningful relationship is not displaced unless there is a substantial risk of harm to the child. ...

"Harm" is a term which, in this context, connotes an adverse effect on the child's upbringing that is more than transitory. The impugned exercise by the access parent must be shown to create a substantial risk that the child's physical, psychological, or moral well-being will be adversely affected. Exposure to new experiences and ideas may upset children and cause them considerable discomfort. Anything from starting school to having to go to bed may evoke a strong emotional response. This does not mean that these experiences are not in the long-term best interests of the child. Similarly, conflict between parents on many matters, including religion, is not uncommon, but in itself cannot be assumed to be harmful unless it produces a prolonged acrimonious atmosphere.

I would, therefore, go a step further than my colleague McLachlin J. and conclude that what is in the best interests of the child is the generally applicable test, but in its application to restrict religious expression, risk of substantial harm is not only an important factor but also must be shown.

Interpreted in this way, the statutory test in s. 16(10) of the *Divorce Act* does not constitute a limitation on freedom of religious expression. As my colleague points out, this freedom does not extend to protect conduct which is harmful to others. ...

CORY and IACOBUCCI JJ.: — We have read with great interest the excellent reasons of Justice L'Heureux-Dubé and Justice McLachlin. We are in agreement with their conclusions that the best interests of the child standard provided in ss. 16(8) and 17(5) of the *Divorce Act*, R.S.C. 1985, c. 3 (2nd Supp.), does not violate s. 2(a), (b), and (d), and s. 15 of the *Canadian Charter of Rights and Freedoms* substantially for the reasons given by our colleagues. In this respect, however, we wish to refrain from expressing any opinion on McLachlin J.'s discussion of whether, if an infringement of the *Charter* were found, such an infringement would be so trivial as not to warrant *Charter* protection. We similarly wish to reserve our views on the question discussed by L'Heureux-Dubé J. of whether or not the *Charter* applies to judicial orders made in custody or access proceedings.

We agree, again for many of the reasons she advances, with L'Heureux-Dubé J. that the issue of access to children should be determined on the basis of what is in the best interests of the child. In that respect, we also agree with both our colleagues that expert evidence is, while admittedly helpful in some cases, not always necessary to establish the best interests of the child; that question can be determined normally from the evidence of parties themselves and the testimony, where appropriate, of the children concerned.

We note that the majority of the British Columbia Court of Appeal ... held that the matters of the children attending religious services with the respondent and accompanying him on his proselytizing activities were resolved by the respondent's undertaking to respect his children's wishes in this regard. This leaves as the only remaining issue, whether the order forbidding the respondent from discussing his religion is valid. On this point, we agree with McLachlin J. that a proper application of the best interests of the child test does not support such an order. We find it difficult to accept that any genuine and otherwise proper discussion between a parent and his or her child should be curtailed by court orders. Indeed, curtailment of explanatory or discursive conversations or exchanges between a parent and child should be rarely ordered, in our view. To take an example, suppose custodial parent A is a member of a fundamentalist religion and access parent B is a scientist who espouses the pure Darwinian theory of evolution. We find it unacceptable that parent B should be ordered, under the rubric of the best interests of the child test, not to discuss or explain his views to his child as opposed to being forbidden from indoctrinating or otherwise undermining the religious choice made by the custodial parent for the child or children involved. Surely the best interests of the child test embraces genuine discussion of religious belief, as opposed to indoctrination, enlistment, or harassment, having the aim or effect of undermining the religious decision made by the custodial parent. ...

DROIT DE LA FAMILLE — 1150
[Headnote only]

(1993), 49 R.F.L. (3d) 317, 1993 CarswellQue 64, 1993 CarswellQue 2048 (S.C.C.)

The parents separated in 1984, after cohabiting for three years, and agreed in writing that the mother would have custody of their daughter and that the father would have access. The agreement was incorporated into a court order. The relations between the parents deteriorated following the father's conversion to the Jehovah's Witness religion. The mother, a Roman Catholic, objected to the father indoctrinating their child during his access visits. In 1987 the father brought a motion to have the agreement set aside, and sought custody or increased access. The trial judge stated that the court may intervene when a parent's religious practices harm the child's best interests. He then found that the father's religious fanaticism distressed the child. Although the trial judge held that the father could give the child religious instruction, he concluded that the father could not indoctrinate or involve her in Jehovah's Witness services, conferences, or door-to-door preaching until she was able to decide which religion she preferred. The father appealed, arguing that the child had to suffer real harm for his access rights to be restricted. A majority of the Court of Appeal upheld the trial judgment.

The father appealed.

Held — The appeal was dismissed.

Per L'HEUREUX-DUBÉ J. (LA FOREST and GONTHIER JJ. concurring): — The *Civil Code of Lower Canada* ("CCLC") governs disputes between unmarried parents. According to art. 30, the sole consideration in custody and access cases is the best interests of the child. The child, not the parents, is the focus of the determination. The best interests of the child criterion does not mean simply that the child should not suffer harm; the standard comprises many factors that a court must take into account in determining rights of access, and harm to the child is only one. The child is entitled to an order that will provide the best conditions within which he or she can develop, in accordance with the circumstances of the particular case. Subject to the child's best interests, the right of custody includes the right to make decisions about the child's religious education, until he or she is able to do so. The access parent is not, however, thereby deprived of his or her parental authority: he or she may exercise those parental rights that do not oppose the exercise of custody by the custodial parent. Therefore, the access parent may provide his or her child with a religious education within these limits.

The criterion of the child's best interests set out in art. 30 CCLC and the broad judicial discretion that it entails are not contrary to the Constitution. The court's ability to exercise a broad judicial discretion is closely linked to the promotion of the child's best interests. That criterion refers to all the considerations relating to a child and can be applied to the circumstances of any case. Consequently, it is not vague within the meaning of s. 1 or s. 7 of the *Canadian Charter of Rights and Freedoms.*

The *Charter* does not apply to private conflicts between parents within the context of a family. Nor does it pertain to court orders made to resolve such disputes. Even if the *Charter* were to apply, the access parent's rights to freedom of religion, expression, and association are not absolute, and a court may limit them if they interfere with what is in the best interests of the child. Therefore, the restrictions placed on the access order did not infringe the father's *Charter* rights. Because the trial judge did not err in principle or in his assessment of the evidence, the appeal should be dismissed.

Per CORY and IACOBUCCI JJ. (concurring): — The fundamental issue in custody and access cases is what is in the best interests of the child. Parental differences of opinion about religion and the discussion of these differences with the child will not necessarily harm him or her. These conversations may, in fact, be beneficial. In the case at bar, the trial judge found that the father's religious practices distressed the child and, as a result, he restricted the father's access. The trial judge was in the best position to make findings about the credibility of the witnesses, and to assess the evidence of what was in the best interests of the child. He applied the correct test and the conditions imposed were not so unreasonable as to require intervention.

Per McLACHLIN J. (dissenting) (SOPINKA J. concurring): — Articles 653 and 654 of the *Civil Code of Quebec* ("CCQ") and art. 30 of the CCLC affirm the best interests of the child test in custody and access cases. The analysis in *Young v. Young* of the constitutionality of the best interests criterion set out in ss. 16(8), 16(10), and 17(5) of the *Divorce Act* also applies to the aforementioned articles of the CCQ and the CCLC. Accordingly, the standard and articles are constitutional and do not violate any *Charter* rights.

When a court is deciding whether an access parent should be allowed to share his or her religious beliefs with his or her child, the risk of harm to the child is significant to the determination of what is in the best interests of the child. The trial and appellate court judges erred when they concluded that the child was being harmed by the religious dispute between the parents and that restrictions would be necessary in the best interests of the child. Nothing in the evidence suggested that the parents' religious conflict was creating problems for the child or that the father's teachings were having a detrimental effect on her. In the absence of evidence that suggested that the child was not benefitting from full and free access, the trial judge should not have prohibited the father from sharing his religious values with his daughter.

NOTES AND QUESTIONS

1. Commentators have pointed out that these two decisions provide little guidance, not only because the court was badly split, but also because there was no real effort to reconcile the different results in the two cases. See McLeod, "Annotation" (1994), 49 R.F.L. (3d) 129; Bailey, "Custody, Access, and Religion: A Comment on *Young v. Young* and *D.P. v. C.S.*" (1994), 11 C.F.L.Q. 317; How, "*Young v. Young* and *D.P. v. C.S.*: Custody and Ac-

cess — The Supreme Court Compounds Confusion" (1994), 11 C.F.L.Q. 109; and Bala, "Developments in Family Law: The 1993-94 Term" (1995), 6 The Supreme Court Review (2d) 453.

In their *Annual Review of Family Law, 1995* (Toronto: Carswell, 1995) Professor McLeod and Alf Mamo conclude (at 18) "that most [lower court] judges seem to have formed the view that the cases really have little effect on the prior law. There is authority for almost any position in the two cases and most judges seem to have carried on as before relying on different paragraphs from the cases if they feel the need to reconcile their decision with the cases."

Professor McLeod and Alf Mamo cite the two cases for the following proposition of law in their *Annual Review of Family Law, 2004* (Toronto: Carswell, 2004) (at 64): "Although a custodial parent has the right to determine a child's religion and lifestyle, an access parent has the right to share his or her religion, lifestyle and culture with a child so long as the religious practices or the conflict between parental religions does not pose a risk to the child." Do you agree with this statement?

2. The reasons in the cases do confirm that all custody and access disputes are governed by the best interests of the child test. Can the apparently divergent outcomes in the two cases be explained using this test? Alternatively, was the different wording of the two orders made at trial important?

3. Do you agree with L'Heureux-Dubé J.'s argument against expanding the role of the access parent?

4. Justice Sopinka's opinion is closest to the position described in *Hanson v. Hanson* (1987), 404 N.W. 2d 460 at 463 (N.D.): "[M]ost courts that have considered the question have refused to restrain a noncustodial parent during visitation periods from exposing the minor child to his or her religious beliefs and practices, absent a clear, affirmative showing that these religious activities will be harmful to the child."

5. One of the concerns of the courts is to avoid evaluating the religious beliefs or practices. Is such an evaluation avoidable if a court is asked by the custodial parent to impose restrictions on the basis that exposure to certain beliefs (e.g., that the husband is head of the house) is not in a child's best interests? See *Borris v. Borris* (1991), 37 R.F.L. (3d) 339 (Alta. Q.B.).

6. Both Justice McLachlin and Justice L'Heureux-Dubé indicated in *Young* that the freedom of religion of parents is inherently limited by the best interests of their child. In *B. (R.) v. C.A.S. of Metropolitan Toronto* (1995), 9 R.F.L. (4th) 157 (reproduced in Chapter 10), a majority adopted a broader definition of the freedom. Justice La Forest stated (at 215): "[T]he right of parents to rear their children according to their religious beliefs, including that of choosing medical and other treatments, is [a] ... fundamental aspect of freedom of religion." He went on to conclude (at 216) that any state restrictions on this right had to be justified under s. 1 of the *Charter* even if the state sought to impose them in the interests of the child. Justices Gonthier, McLachlin, Sopinka, and L'Heureux-Dubé concurred with this analysis in the *B. (R.)* case.

7. In *S. (L.L.) v. G. (E.)* (2002), 34 R.F.L. (5th) 442 (Alta. Prov. Ct.), the parents did not have a formal order governing custody or access. However, their son had lived with the father for some time and was being raised in the father's religion. The father did not want the child to visit the mother over Christmas because he had joined a new religious group that considered Christmas a "pagan holiday". The court granted the mother access over Christmas, noting that the mother was not attempting to indoctrinate the child in religious matters and that there was no evidence that participating in the mother's family's Christmas festivities was contrary to the child's best interests.

The custodial mother in *Stubbert v. Ferrare* (2002), 25 R.F.L. (5th) 428 (Ont. S.C.J.); additional reasons at (2002), 2002 CarswellOnt 625 (Ont. S.C.J.), believed that her daughter's exposure to the teachings and observances of her father's religion was interfering with the child's relationship with her mother, her step-father and her half-sister. The girl had suggested that her mother was in danger of going to hell and that her half-sister was a "bastard" because the mother and step-father were not married. The judge, with the father's consent, ordered: "[The father] shall not discuss religious education or religious issues with [his daughter] and he shall ensure that she not attend services or other organized activities at or under the auspices of Frontline Worship Centre".

In *Ackie v. Ackie* (2004), 5 R.F.L. (6th) 1 (Ont. S.C.J.), the mother had joined a cult known as the House of Yahweh, headed by "the greatest teacher in the entire world" who lived in Texas. The father continued to be an adherent of the Seventh Day Adventist faith in which the children were originally raised. When they visited their father, the children sang hymns and attended church. In their mother's home, they were not even allowed to say the words "God" or "Jesus". Justice Marshman granted custody to the father, largely because the mother indicated that she would not allow the children to see their father if they lived with her. The Justice then indicated (para. 22) that the "dogmatic nature of [the mother's] religion causes me grave concerns" and continued (para. 24):

> Although I am tempted to make an order preventing Mrs. Ackie from imposing her religious views on the children, I am not satisfied that there is sufficient evidence that the best interests of the children dictate such a requirement. Mrs. Ackie has indicated that she wants no access to the children if Mr. Ackie is granted custody, but, nonetheless, I am satisfied that it is in their best interests to visit their mother one weekend per month. I am equally satisfied that Mrs. Ackie could not and would not refrain from expressing her religious beliefs to the children and I see no real harm to the children in her doing so.

The mother in *Taman v. Taman* (2004), 5 R.F.L. (6th) 200 (Sask. Q.B.), began to raise her children in accordance with the tenets of the Living Church of God. The conventional Christian holidays such as Christmas and Easter were not recognized and presents on birthdays were forbidden. As a result, access became an issue. The court granted sole custody to the mother. In dealing with access, it stated (paras. 44 and 45):

> Arguably, in Canada, in 2004, Christmas and Easter are treated by the larger society as celebrations which are equal part secular and sacred. It is unreasonable and not in the best interests of the children that [their mother] preclude [their father] having access to the children during Christmas and Easter. It will not harm the children to be exposed to Christmas and Easter celebrations that are common in the larger community. The [father] is specifically restrained from attempting to dissuade the children from the dogma of the Church. However, he is permitted to expose them, but not force them to take part in, mainstream Christian celebrations.
>
> ... [N]on-religious based events such as Halloween and the exchange of gifts on birthdays are anathema to the Church. I conclude it is unreasonable and not in the best interests of the boys that the [mother] forbid the [father], or his extended family, from providing the boys with presents on their birthdays. Halloween, however, presents a different consideration. I accept ... that Halloween has a pre-Christian pagan genesis. Given the boys' ages [approximately 10 and 12], and the [mother's] strong feelings, I conclude it is not an undue hardship nor totally unreasonable to comply with the [mother's] wish that they not take part in this secular festival. Accordingly, I order that the [father] shall not directly or indirectly abet the boys in taking part in Halloween activities.

8. The Alberta Court of Appeal stated in *Bachor v. Lehmann-Bachor* (2001), 14 R.F.L. (5th) 238 (para. 34):

> It has long been recognized that the custodial parent has the sole and primary responsibility to oversee all aspects of the child's day-to-day life and long-term well-being. ... Section 16(5) of the *Divorce Act* gives the access parent a right to be informed of these decisions, but "courts in Canada have never adopted the view that the custodial parent's decisions are subject to the approval of the non-custodial parent". As Ms. Lehmann-Bachor is Cassandra's custodial parent, it is clear that she is responsible for pivotal decisions respecting Cassandra's religion. [The passage quoted is from the dissenting opinion of Justice L'Heureux-Dubé in *Young v. Young*.]

The court concluded that the father, as access parent, could share his beliefs with Cassandra and could take her to religious ceremonies. However, he could not take her to a Dedication Ceremony at his church because this ceremony signified a public commitment by parents to raise the child being dedicated in "God's word and way". This would trench on the mother's right to decide Cassandra's religion.

9. As the *Ackie v. Ackie* case, above, indicates, the religious beliefs of a parent may be a factor in the custody decision itself if they bear on the well-being of the child. See also *Moseley v. Moseley* (1989), 20 R.F.L. (3d) 301 (Alta. Prov. Ct.).

10. Section 20(5) of the *CLRA* and s. 16(5) of the *DA* expressly provide that, in the absence of a contrary court order, the access parent has the right to make inquiries and be given information regarding the health, education and welfare of the child. Are these statutory provisions directed at the custodial parent or do they encompass also individuals such as the child's doctor and school principal?

In *Perrault v. Eady* (2004), 10 R.F.L. (6th) 118 (Ont. C.J.), Justice Duchesneau-McLachlan stated (paras. 17 and 18):

> Under [the *CLRA*], an access parent has as much right to information as the custodial parent from any professional who has dealings with the child, whether it be pertaining to health, education or social behaviour. The father therefore has the right to contact the school, the doctor, the dentist and any

other professional with whom the child is associated including the leader of any extracurricular activity and to obtain any information regarding the child. This includes the right to attend parent-and-teacher interviews and any medical appointment.

In order to avail himself of that right, the father must be advised by the mother of the name, address and telephone number of any such professional.

There are other cases indicating that access parents often have difficulty getting this information. In *Sleiman v. Ontario (Human Rights Commission)* (2003), 34 R.F.L. (5th) 156 (Ont. Div. Ct.), a frustrated access father brought an unsuccessful human rights complaint when the health authorities refused to allow him to see his son's medical records. On an application for judicial review, the court stated (para. 1):

[The father] has a court access order which is silent as to medical records. Without a court order or the consent of the custodial parent he cannot access his son's medical records. His remedy if any is in court, whatever his legal entitlement may or may not be under s. 16(5) of the *Divorce Act* or otherwise.

11. While a custody order may give one parent the authority to decide such matters as the child's religion, medical care, and education, an aggrieved access parent may be able to request a court to overrule a decision dealing with such matters on the basis that it is not in the best interests of the child. In *Chauvin v. Chauvin* (1987), 6 R.F.L. (3d) 403 (Ont. Dist. Ct.), the mother, who had custody of two boys, transferred them from a French school to an English one. The father objected and obtained an order under s. 21 of the *CLRA* requiring the mother to enroll them in a specified French school. Killeen D.C.J. stated (at 411) that "there has to be a strong evidential showing to support a displacement of an educational decision made by a custodial parent, otherwise custody orders and their consequences will be bereft of meaning and effect".

The Supreme Court of Canada allowed an appeal in *S. (L.) c. S. (C.)* (1997), 37 R.F.L. (4th) 344 (S.C.C.), and removed restrictions on the custodial mother's religious activities involving her child. The lower courts had granted custody to the mother who was a Witness of Jehovah, but ordered her not to bring the child to religious ceremonies or on door-to-door proselytizing. The mother was also prohibited from indoctrinating the child. The Supreme Court simply stated: "In the circumstances of this case, given the evidence before us, we are not satisfied that the best interests of the child has been compromised by the practices of the custodial parent." In *Mummery v. Campbell* (1998), 38 R.F.L. (4th) 301 (B.C. S.C.), the court concluded, over the objections of the non-custodial father, that it was in the best interests of an eight-year-old girl to be baptized as she and her mother wished. In light of these cases, could an access parent challenge the custodial parent's decision to require the child to attend a particular church? If so, how would the court make the decision? Would it evaluate the religious belief in question?

12. Sometimes a custodial parent wishes to change a child's surname without the consent of the other parent. Under the *Change of Name Act*, R.S.O. 1990, c. C. 7, a person with lawful custody of a child can apply to the Registrar General of Vital Statistics to change the child's surname. Although a parent with access must be notified of the application (s. 5(6)), his or her consent is not required unless a separation agreement or court order so specifies. In *Silverberg v. Silverberg* (1990), 25 R.F.L. (3d) 141 (Ont. H.C.) (order precluding change as part of original custody order) and *Herniman v. Woltz* (1996), 22 R.F.L. (4th) 232 (Ont. Gen. Div.) (order prohibiting change), Justice Granger held that a court could restrain a parent from changing a child's surname as an incident of custody, either at the time of the original court order or later. See also *Belisle v. Poole* (1994), 2 R.F.L. (4th) 165 (Ont. Gen. Div.) (order prohibiting change); *Hill v. Shimla* (1995), 17 R.F.L. (4th) 316 (Ont. Gen. Div.) (order prohibiting name change without further court order made as part of custody order); *Zho v. Chen* (2000), 11 R.F.L. (5th) 231 (Ont. S.C.J.) (no name change allowed); and *Lyon v. Lyon* (2004), 49 R.F.L. (5th) 122 (Ont. S.C.J.) (order precluding name change).

The *Change of Name Act* does not preclude a custodial parent from informally changing a child's surname without applying for a legal name change: *Longlade v. Moxam* (1989), 20 R.F.L. (3d) 32 (Ont. Fam. Ct.). However, the court suggested that it had the authority to prohibit even an informal change if necessary to protect the child's best interests. In the circumstances of the case, the court dismissed the father's application to vary a custody order to restrain the mother and step-father from informally altering the child's surname for purposes such as registration at school. In *Belisle v. Poole*, *supra*, Zelinski J., although granting an order precluding a formal name change, stated (at 177) that "there does not appear to be any reason why [the child] cannot continue to be enrolled in school by his 'informal' name of Poole, thereby preserving a name at school which is consistent with that of his mother and siblings".

5. Relocation Issues

HOVIUS, "MOBILITY ISSUES IN CUSTODY AND ACCESS CASES"

McLeod, ed., *Child Custody Law and Practice* (Toronto: Carswell, looseleaf) c. 7
(Written in 2004; Footnotes omitted)

(1) Introduction

Canadian courts have increasingly confronted situations where one parent proposes to move with the child and the other parent objects. Various motives may underlie the proposed move. A custodial parent may have become romantically involved with a person who lives in another area and she wishes to join him. A parent who has shared custody may wish to live near his extended family or he may have an opportunity to enhance his career. A parent may have established a second family and her new spouse's employer may seek to transfer him. There may also be situations where the move is desired, in part at least, to preclude the other parent from having frequent contact with the child, perhaps because of continuing conflict between the parents.

Whatever the motive, a proposed move involving any significant distance will likely have considerable impact on the child. A move may entail the loss of familiar surroundings and friends and may require the child to adjust to a new neighbourhood, a different school, and a new social environment. The child's relationship with the parent who remains behind will also be affected, unless there has been no significant relationship between the two. From this parent's point of view, day-to-day involvement in the child's life will be lost and it may appear inevitable that the relationship with the child will erode or even end. This evokes an emotional response and provides considerable motivation for litigation if there is any hope of precluding the move. On the other hand, any order that, in effect, requires a parent to forego the planned move may also have profound economic, social and psychological impact. Mobility cases, therefore, often involve parents who are motivated to litigate because they have much to lose.

The state of the law in Canada also helps to explain why relocation issues continue to be litigated so frequently. In one sense, the law in this area is relatively straightforward and easy to summarize. There is one leading Supreme Court of Canada decision, *Gordon v. Goertz* (1996), 19 R.F.L. (4th) 177. It holds that mobility issues are to be determined in accordance with the best interests of the child and identifies the factors to consider in applying this standard. However, it leaves each case to be determined in accordance with its facts, without the use of presumptions and unhindered by onuses or burdens of proof. This individualized approach makes it difficult to advise parents what the result will be if the matter is litigated. Parents seem willing to take their chances; there have been well over 300 relocation cases [by 2004] in Canada since the *Gordon v. Goertz* decision.

In addition, this appears to be an area of law in which there are an inordinate number of appeals. Despite frequent statements indicating that the scope for appellate review in custody cases is narrow, the success rate in mobility appeals is high. Mobility cases often present the courts with a dilemma in which one of the parents is likely to be profoundly and negatively affected by the decision and in which there is no "correct" answer. Perhaps not surprisingly, appellate courts are fairly easily convinced that the lower courts have failed to give sufficient weight to a factor listed in *Gordon v. Goertz* or have given too much weight to another.

In light of the emphasis in *Gordon v. Goertz* on the desirability of individualized justice in this area, it is perhaps understandable that the appellate courts have made few attempts to create rules or subsidiary guidelines. It is left for lawyers and commentators to mine the voluminous case law for indicators, trends or guides that help predict results. It is certainly possible to identify factors that make it more likely that a court will approve a move and others that make this less likely. However, attempts to identify clear trends in the cases that can be summarized in relatively straightforward propositions seem doomed to fail. In June 2003, Professor Thompson indicated: "[O]ver time, the case law has become less predictable, not more so." Even though this may strike many as an unsatisfactory situation, it is unlikely that the law in this area will change soon. Legislative change is unlikely and the Supreme Court of Canada has shown no inclination to revisit the issues raised in relocation cases. In April 2003, the Supreme Court refused leave to appeal in the controversial and well-publicized case of *Bjornson v. Creighton*, 2003 CarswellOnt 1387 (S.C.C.); 2003 CarswellOnt 1388 (S.C.C.); refusing leave from (2002), 31 R.F.L. (5th) 240 (Ont. C.A.). The Court had earlier refused leave in the *Chilton* and *Woodhouse* cases [*Chilton v. Chilton* (1997), [1996] S.C.C.A. No. 574; refusing leave from (1996), 26 R.F.L. (4th) 124 (B.C.C.A.) and *Woodhouse v. Woodhouse* (1997), [1996] S.C.C.A. No. 402 (S.C.C.)].

(2) The Case Law Prior to *Gordon v. Goertz*

To place *Gordon v. Goertz* in perspective, it is helpful to outline briefly some trends in the prior case law. Although the many reported cases exhibited a variety of approaches, for analytical purposes they may be grouped as follows: (a) cases prior to the Ontario Court of Appeal decision in *Carter v. Brooks* (1990), 30 R.F.L. (3d) 53; (b) *Carter v. Brooks* and cases between 1990 and 1995; and (c) *MacGyver v. Richards* (1995), 11 R.F.L. (4th) 432 (Ont. C.A.) and subsequent cases.

(a) Cases Prior to *Carter v. Brooks*

Well into the 1980s there was considerable support for the proposition that the custodial parent should be permitted to move with a child, provided the custodial parent's plans were reasonable, unless the parent seeking to preclude the move could demonstrate that in the circumstances the move would be harmful to the child. ...

(b) *Carter v. Brooks* and Cases between 1990 and 1995

In *Carter v. Brooks*, the Ontario Court of Appeal in effect ruled that the approach [outlined above] was no longer to be used. The parties in *Carter v. Brooks* had one son, born in 1984. They separated later that same year and the son remained in the care of the mother with the father's tacit approval. A divorce judgment in 1987 contained no provision for corollary relief. The mother remarried in 1988. In 1990 she wished to move from Brantford to British Columbia so that her husband, who had secure employment in Brantford, could pursue an advantageous business opportunity.

The father, who also lived in Brantford, exercised access regularly and frequently. He had a close relationship with his son. When the father learned of the proposed move, he applied for joint custody and an order restraining the mother from removing the child from the County of Brant. The mother brought a cross-application for custody.

At trial, the judge concluded that there was "no serious issue" as to custody and awarded custody to the mother. The only two options under serious consideration were: (1) the child living in British Columbia with the mother; and (2) the child living in Brantford with the mother. Since the judge considered it best that the child live in close proximity with the father, the mother was restrained from removing the child from the jurisdiction.

This result was upheld on appeal. Speaking for the court, Morden A.C.J.O. indicated that the sole matter for consideration was whether the proposed move was in the best interests of the child. The interests of the mother and the new family unit were relevant only in so far as the well being of the mother and the new family had an impact on the boy's best interests. Similarly, the father's interests could only be considered if relevant to the child's best interests. ...

... In its review of the evidence, the appellate court stressed the profound impact of the proposed move on the relationship between the father and his son, the views of the child, the limited financial resources of the father that would not allow him to travel to British Columbia often, and the fact that "there was no real need for the appellant's husband to move." The detailed analysis of the reason for the move and the impact of the move on the relationship between father and son suggested that the key issue was whether the benefit of the move outweighed the detrimental impact on the access relationship.

The decision in *Carter v. Brooks* had an immediate impact on mobility cases, especially in Ontario. Moves were now denied in a significant number of reported cases, although they remained a minority. Professor Thompson in his study of mobility cases between 1985 and 1995 indicated that moves were denied in 40 per cent of reported Canadian cases between 1990 and 1995. [See Thompson, "'Beam Us Up Scotty': Parents and Children on the Trek" (1996), 13 C.F.L.Q. 219.] It was often difficult to predict what the result would be in any particular case. The most important single factor seemed to be the reason for the move. If there was a valid reason and the custodial parent was willing to accommodate the other parent's access, the custodial parent was usually allowed to move with the child. Almost always the two options being considered were to permit the custodial parent to move with the child or to impose a condition on that parent's custody. Rarely was a change in custody even contemplated, let alone ordered.

(c) MacGyver v. Richards and Subsequent Cases

In ... *MacGyver v. Richards*, another three-judge panel of the Ontario Court of Appeal suggested a significantly different approach to mobility cases. As Labrosse J.A. indicated in his concurring reasons, it would have been relatively easy to dismiss the appeal and allow the mother to move with her daughter using the analysis from *Carter v. Brooks*. Instead, Justice Abella, with Grange J.A. concurring, took the opportunity to stress the degree of deference that the courts should accord the custodial parent's decision to move. ...

Although she stated that the ultimate test remained the best interests of the child and adverted to *Carter v. Brooks*, Abella J.A. departed from the analysis in the previous case in several significant ways. First, she sounded a note of caution regarding a court's ability to determine the best interests of any child at any particular time. The speculative nature of the exercise "should give pause to the extent to which judges interpose themselves between the child and the [custodial] parent." Second, she stressed that the child's relationship with the custodial parent was generally far more important to a child than the relationship with the access parent. In her view, the courts should "forcefully acknowledge" that the child's best interests and the interests of the custodial parent are "inextricably tied" together. Third, Justice Abella stated that judges had wrongly been passing judgment on the "necessity" of any move. Her analysis indicated that, as long as the custodial parent was acting "responsibly," there was no further need to explore the reason for the move. Fourth, she suggested that, in effect, the onus was on the access parent to convince the court that there was "substantial evidence" that the move would impair "the child's, not the access parent's, long-term well being". Finally, Abella J.A. reached "the admittedly difficult conclusion that a parent, acting responsibly, should not be prevented from leaving a jurisdiction because the move would interfere with access by the other parent with the child, even if the relationship between the child and the access parent is a good one." Later, she indicated: "There was no evidence [before the trial judge] that a move would impair the child's best interests, only that it would impair access." Thus, impairment of access by itself did not weigh heavily against the move. Of course, other than the effect of the move on the relationship between the child and the access parent, there is usually little to suggest that a move will not be in the child's best interests.

While Justice Abella did not explicitly disagree with either the result or approach in *Carter v. Brooks*, one must conclude that she would have decided the earlier case differently. She would have begun her analysis with "an overwhelming respect" for and "presumptive deference" to Mrs. Brooks' decision to move. She would not have commented on the "necessity" of the move. Impairment of the relationship between the boy and his father would not have been sufficient reason to prevent the move since the mother was acting responsibly.

Professor Thompson's review of the case law [*supra*] subsequent to *MacGyver v. Richards* revealed that the case had considerable impact in Ontario. In eleven mobility cases decided in the first nine months after the 1995 Ontario Court of Appeal decision, ten allowed the custodial parent to move with the child. ...

Three appellate decisions in late 1995 illustrated the uncertain state of the law. The Manitoba Court of Appeal reviewed the mobility cases in *Lapointe v. Lapointe* (1995), 17 R.F.L. (4th) 1. Justice Twaddle, speaking for the Court, described the *Carter* and *MacGyver* decisions as being as different from one another as "oil from water." He generally endorsed the approach adopted in *MacGyver v. Richards*:

> ... In all but unusual cases, the custodial parent is in a better position than a judge to decide what is in the child's best interests. ...

> The alternative approach of *Carter v. Brooks* would lead to uncertainty and inconsistent decisions and tend to immobilize custodial parents in an age when mobility is often necessary for psychological if not economic survival. On the other hand the law as I understand it allows a custodial parent a measure of choice subject to sufficient safeguards to ensure that the custodial parent does not act maliciously, unreasonably or contrary to what is adjudged the best interests of the child in any special circumstances which may be applicable.

In the result, the Manitoba Court of Appeal overturned the trial judge's decision forbidding the mother from removing her two children from Winnipeg. The mother was permitted to move them to Edmonton so that she would be close to her family.

By contrast, the British Columbia Court of Appeal in *Manore v. Manore* (1995), 20 R.F.L. (4th) 68 implicitly disagreed with the approach in *MacGyver*. ... The somewhat confusing reasoning of the New Brunswick Court of Appeal in *Benoît v. Reid* (1995), 171 N.B.R. (2d) 161 appeared also to endorse the *Carter v. Brooks* approach.

The Supreme Court of Canada's Decision in *Gordon v. Goertz*

(a) The Judgment

In *Gordon v. Goertz*, the parents separated in 1990 and their approximately 1-year-old daughter lived with the mother who had been the primary caregiver. The father saw the child frequently. Indeed, an assessment prepared for the custody determination in the divorce proceedings in 1993 indicated that the father had "consistently spent more time with the child" than the mother in the post-separation period. Nevertheless, Carter J. adopted the assessor's recommendation that the mother receive sole custody. She ruled out joint custody because of the continuing hostility between the parents. The father was given generous access, including alternate weekends and mid-week overnight access every other week. The father spent more time with his daughter than allowed under the order, permitting the mother to maintain her busy schedule as a dentist.

In the fall of 1994, the father learned that the mother intended to move in January 1995 from Saskatoon where the parties had been residing to Adelaide, Australia to study orthodontics. He applied for custody or, alternatively, for an order restraining the mother from moving the child from Saskatoon. The mother cross-applied to vary the access provisions of the custody order to permit her to move the child's residence to Australia. Justice Gagne, relying heavily on the judgment of Judge Carter, concluded that the mother was the proper person to have custody and issued an order "that the petitioner [mother] be allowed to move to Australia to study orthodontics and to take the child Samantha with her." The father was granted "liberal and generous access to Samantha in Australia on one month's notice."

The Saskatchewan Court of Appeal upheld the order without hearing the mother's counsel. ...

The father then appealed to the Supreme Court of Canada, seeking a change of custody or, alternatively, an order permitting access on terms that would allow the child to leave Australia. By the time the appeal was heard by the Court, the mother and child had moved to Australia. The Supreme Court of Canada unanimously held that the trial judge correctly continued the mother's custody despite her intended move, but concluded that the order should be varied to provide for access to be exercised in Canada on terms to be negotiated.

Justice McLachlin, with whom five other members of the Court agreed, adopted a two-stage inquiry to determine an application for variation of a custody and access order under the *Divorce Act*. First, the parent seeking the variation must demonstrate a material change in the circumstances of the child since the order. This threshold is met if there has been "(1) a change in the condition, means, needs or circumstances of the child; (2) which materially affects the child; and (3) which was either not foreseen or could not have been reasonably contemplated by the judge who made the initial order." In the case at hand, all three conditions were satisfied since the move would seriously curtail frequent and meaningful contact between father and daughter and the trial judge had clearly assumed that they would live in close proximity.

Turning to the second stage of the inquiry, McLachlin J. stated that the judge must then consider custody and access afresh in light of all the circumstances that presently exist and make an order that reflects the child's best interests. Although the findings of fact made by the judge who made the original order should be considered, it is an error to simply defer to the views of the judge who made the original order or to focus only on the change "isolated from the other factors bearing on the child's best interests."

Justice McLachlin rejected the mother's argument that the inquiry into the best interests of the child should begin with a presumption in favour of the custodial parent. Instead, the Justice specifically endorsed the view of Morden A.C.J.O. in *Carter v. Brooks* that both parents bear an evidentiary burden of showing where the best interests of the child lie and that the judge must "weigh and balance the factors which are relevant in the particular circumstances of the case at hand, without any rigid preconceived notion as to what weight each factor should have." She also approvingly quoted Morden A.C.J.O.'s observation that adopting a general rule that one of the parties would lose unless he or she satisfied a particular burden of proof would undermine the court's role of determining the best interests of the child in the particular circumstances.

She downplayed any differences between *Carter v. Brooks* and *MacGyver v. Richards* regarding the deference to be paid to the custodial parent's plans [para. 32]:

> ... Both cases urge careful consideration of the views of the custodial parent: the court is directed to accord them "a reasonable measure of respect" in *Carter*, and an "overwhelming respect" or "presumptive deference" in *MacGyver*. Despite the stronger language of the majority in *MacGyver*, neither decision proposes a legal presumption in favour of the custodial parent. Most importantly, both cases emphasize that the only and ultimate standard against which to evaluate the evidence is the best interests of the child.

Her own opinion was that the custodial parent's views are "entitled to great respect and the most serious consideration," partly because this parent "may be expected to have the most intimate and perceptive knowledge of what is in the child's interest." "The decision of the custodial parent to live and work where he or she chooses is likewise entitled to respect, barring an improper motive reflecting adversely on the custodial parent's parenting ability."

Ultimately, in McLachlin J.'s view, the only issue is what is in the best interests of the particular child in the circumstances. "Each case turns on its own unique circumstances." Although she acknowledged that this would inevitably produce a "measure of indeterminacy," McLachlin J. believed any "more precise test would risk sacrificing the child's best interests to expediency and certainty."

Justice McLachlin went on to provide [para. 49] a summary of "the law" (in a passage that has predictably been quoted in virtually all subsequent relocation cases):

1.　The parent applying for a change in the custody or access order must meet the threshold requirement of demonstrating a material change in the circumstances affecting the child.

2.　If the threshold is met, the judge on the application must embark on a fresh inquiry into what is in the best interests of the child, having regard to all the relevant circumstances relating to the child's needs and the ability of the respective parents to satisfy them.

3.　This inquiry is based on the findings of the judge who made the previous order and evidence of the new circumstances.

4.　The inquiry does not begin with a legal presumption in favour of the custodial parent, although the custodial parent's views are entitled to great respect.

5.　Each case turns on its own unique circumstances. The only issue is the best interest of the child in the particular circumstances of the case.

6.　The focus is on the best interests of the child, not the interests and rights of the parents.

7.　More particularly the judge should consider, *inter alia*:

(a) the existing custody arrangement and relationship between the child and the custodial parent;

(b) the existing access arrangement and the relationship between the child and the access parent;

(c) the desirability of maximizing contact between the child and both parents;
(d) the views of the child;

(e) the custodial parent's reason for moving, *only* in the exceptional case where it is relevant to that parent's ability to meet the needs of the child;

(f) disruption to the child of a change in custody;

(g) disruption to the child consequent on removal from family, schools, and the community he or she has come to know.

Applying this analysis to the case at hand, Justice McLachlin concluded that the trial judge failed to engage "in the full and sensitive inquiry into the best interests of the child required by s. 17 of the *Divorce Act.*" Nevertheless, such an inquiry indicated that the judge's decision to continue the mother's custody despite her intended move to Australia was correct. "The fact[s] that the child has been in the custody of the mother for some years, that the reasons for initially granting the mother custody have not been shown to have substantially changed, and that a change in custody at this time would be highly disruptive to her, argue in favour of the mother retaining custody." These considerations outweighed the impact of the move on the child's relationship with her father and the disruption caused by removing her from her extended family and community, especially since the father had the means to travel to Australia and the child could return for periodic visits to Saskatchewan once the terms of access were varied.

Justice L'Heureux-Dubé (La Forest J. concurring) agreed with the majority's disposition of the appeal, but not the reasons. Essentially, she believed that a choice had to be made between the approach in *Carter v. Brooks* and the one in *MacGyver v. Richards* and *Lapointe v. Lapointe*. The former left the determination of the best interests of the child in mobility cases "to the discretionary realm of questions of fact where each relevant factor is to be equally considered and where no party bears any specified burden of proof." The latter recognized the "right of the custodial parent to determine the place of residence of the child by placing the burden of proving that the move is not in the child's best interests on the party challenging the legal status quo." She clearly preferred the latter approach, in part because it would provide "much needed clarity and certainty in this difficult area of law and [minimize] the need to resort to protracted negotiations or, even worse, traumatic and costly litigation which, ultimately, cannot but injuriously affect the children."

Justice L'Heureux-Dubé stated that restrictions on the custodial parent's "right to determine where the child should live, should not be inferred from generous or specified access provisions without more." Rather, the burden of proof should shift to the custodial parent only where there is an agreement or court order explicitly precluding a change in the child's residence. In light of her earlier conclusion that "[a]ll decisions as to custody and access must be made in the best interests of children, assessed from a child-centred perspective," one would expect her to go on to conclude that, in this situation, the custodial parent would have to prove that the move was in the child's best interest. Instead, Justice L'Heureux-Dubé stated that "the onus should shift to the custodial parent to establish that the decision to relocate is not made in order to undermine the access rights of the non-custodial parent and that he or she is willing to make arrangements with the non-custodial parent to restructure access, when appropriate, in light of the change of residence of the child." ...

(b) Implications

(ii) Two Options or Three or More?

It should be noted that neither the *Divorce Act* nor any provincial legislation dealing with custody or access gives a court jurisdiction to stipulate where a parent may live. Rather, the courts have authority only to specify that an award of custody is conditional upon the parent living in a certain location or to provide that the custodial parent is prohibited from removing the child from a particular jurisdiction. In other words, a court cannot directly restrict a parent's mobility but can do so only indirectly.

Initially, this distinction may appear to be one of semantics only. An order prohibiting the custodial parent from removing the child from a particular location will effectively limit the parent's mobility as he or she is generally unlikely to move without the child. However, the fact that a court can only indirectly restrict a parent's mobility is significant in at least one respect. It means that a parent can insist that he or she is definitely moving and force the court to choose between two options, allowing the child to move also or providing that the child will reside primarily with the parent who remains behind.

Where the child has been residing primarily with a custodial parent for some time, a court may very well be reluctant to grant custody to the access parent. Often the child will be more detrimentally affected by the loss of frequent, meaningful contact with the custodial parent than the loss of such contact with the access parent. ...

Granting custody to the access parent is likely to occur only in exceptional circumstances such as where there has been shared parenting or the child is an adolescent who prefers to remain in a familiar school and community.

In the vast majority of Canadian mobility cases decided prior to *Gordon v. Goertz* the custodial parent acknowledged that the move was conditional on being able to take the child along. This permitted a court to choose between three possible outcomes: (1) change custody; (2) continue the status quo; and (3) allow the custodial parent to move with the child. Often, the courts simply focused on the last two options only. In contrast, the Supreme Court of Canada in *Gordon v. Goertz* approached the case as requiring simply a choice between the first and the third options. There are two possible explanations. The first entails a rather dramatic departure from the approach in previous mobility cases. The Supreme Court may have been indicating that a mobility case always requires a full-blown custody determination in which the court must choose between allowing the custodial parent to move with the child and awarding custody to the parent who is left behind. In other words, the court may have indicated that conditions regarding a child's residence should only be imposed where a court is prepared to alter custody if the custodial parent in fact moves. ...

The second, and more likely, explanation for the Supreme Court's failure to discuss the possibility of preserving the status quo in *Gordon v. Goertz* is because of the particular facts. Perhaps (although this was not explored in the reasons of either the Saskatchewan Court of Appeal or the Supreme Court) the mother indicated all along that she intended to move with or without the child. Certainly, the possibility of the mother returning immediately to Saskatchewan was fairly remote by the time the case reached the Supreme Court since the mother was already settled in Australia. Indeed, the father's requested remedy no longer referred to this possibility.

In her reasons Justice McLachlin did allude to the possibility of imposing or maintaining a restriction on the child's residence in some circumstances. At one point she indicated that this had been done in cases where the move was "contingent on the retention of custody." Unfortunately, she did not go on to indicate whether another precondition was that the court would transfer custody if the custodial parent in fact moved. Justice L'Heureux-Dubé also did not provide much guidance regarding this issue. She stated that such orders should be made "exceptionally, where there is cogent evidence that the child's best interests could not otherwise be accommodated in any reasonable way".

As explained below, the cases subsequent to *Gordon v. Goertz* have generally continued to explore the possibility of preserving the status quo whenever the parent seeking to move with the child indicates that the move is contingent on being able to take the child. Often, the courts will simply balance the benefits and detriments to the child of the proposed move to decide whether the parent should be permitted to move.

Some cases subsequent to *Gordon v. Goertz* suggest that consideration should perhaps be given to what might be called a fourth option. This involves exploring whether the non-custodial parent might be able to move to the same location as the custodial parent. Other cases indicate that, where the reason for the move is to join a new partner or spouse, there should be some exploration of the possibility of that person moving instead. Although a court cannot order this third party to move, it may decide against the children's move where the new partner can move.

(iii) Carter v. Brooks *Modified? Are Reasons for the Move Relevant?*

The cases of *Carter v. Brooks* and *MacGyver v. Richards* involved situations where trial judges had not changed custody, but had imposed restrictions on the choice of residence. Therefore, the focus in both cases was on the choice between allowing the move and keeping the status quo. In *Gordon v. Goertz*, the Supreme Court of Canada analyzed a different issue: In what circumstances should a custodial parent's relocation result in a transfer of custody to the access parent? However, the Court purported to provide general principles applicable to all mobility cases and the majority's analysis has been adopted in those cases where the real choice is whether to allow the move or maintain the status quo.

As L'Heureux-Dubé J. indicated, the majority's approach in *Gordon v. Goertz* is closer to that of Morden A.C.J.O. in *Carter v. Brooks* than that of Abella J.A. in *MacGyver v. Richards*. Justice McLachlin, in the course of rejecting a presumption in favour of the custodial parent, specifically endorsed the view of Morden A.C.J.O. that both parents bear an evidentiary burden of showing where the child's best interests lie and that the judge must "weigh and balance the factors which are relevant in the particular circumstances of the case at hand, without any preconceived notion as to what weight each factor should have."

However, McLachlin J. did not simply adopt the reasoning from *Carter v. Brooks*. While Morden A.C.J.O. urged judges to accord the views of the custodial parent "a reasonable measure of respect," McLachlin J. suggested that these views were "entitled to great respect and the most serious consideration." This slightly stronger language suggests greater deference to the custodial parent's views.

There are also differences between Morden A.C.J.O.'s list of factors and Justice McLachlin's list. However, it would be a mistake to overemphasize these differences. First, neither list was intended to be exhaustive. Second, some of the differences may be explained by the different options being considered in the two cases. ...

It is tempting to explain the different treatment by Morden A.C.J.O. and Justice McLachlin of the reasons for any move on a similar basis. As noted earlier, *Carter v. Brooks* and the cases applying it emphasized the reason for the proposed move. Where the motive was simply to frustrate access, a move was not permitted. On the other hand, where the move was necessary, for example, to retain employment, this would count heavily in favour of the move. This approach seems to accord with common sense in those situations where the options are continuation of the status quo or allowing the child to move with the custodial parent. Whether the benefits of the move to the child outweigh the detriments will essentially depend on the reasons for the move.

However, where the options are limited to allowing the child to accompany the custodial parent to a new location or transferring custody to the other parent, the reasons for the move are relevant only to the extent that they may reveal something about the custodial parent's capacity to parent. The court must then determine whether the child is better off in the new location with the custodial parent or in familiar surroundings with the access parent. It matters little why the custodial parent is moving, unless the custodial parent is acting irresponsibly by attempting to frustrate access or, perhaps, acting selfishly by putting self-interest ahead of the child's interests. Therefore, on the facts in *Gordon v. Goertz*, it is not surprising that McLachlin J. stated that the custodial parent's reason for moving was relevant "only in the exceptional case where it is relevant to that parent's ability to meet the needs of the child."

It has to be acknowledged, however, that Justice McLachlin indicated at various points that she intended her comments about the reasons for the move to apply in all mobility cases. First, she stated that "applications for ... variation of custody based on relocation of the custodial parent" have "[a]ll too often descended into inquiries into the custodial parent's reason or motive for moving." She specifically cited *Carter v. Brooks* as illustrative. Second, she referred to section 16(9) of the *Divorce Act* to buttress her point. It stipulates that the court "shall not take into consideration the past conduct of any person unless the conduct is relevant to the ability of that person to act as a parent of a child." She inferred that a similar principle applied to present and future parental conduct. Then, significantly and implausibly, she assumed that an examination of the reasons for the proposed move constituted an inquiry into the custodial parent's conduct. Whatever the merits of this assumption (and I suggest that there are none), the comments generally support Justice Abella's view in *MacGyver v. Richards* that, as long as the custodial parent is acting responsibly, there is no further need to explore the reasons for the move.

As explained earlier, lower courts determining whether they should say "yes" or "no" to a proposed move will naturally be tempted to consider and evaluate the reasons for the move. There are several ways in which they may be able to do so without appearing to defy the Supreme Court of Canada. First, an examination of the reasons may be subsumed under an evaluation of the benefits to the child of a move, a clearly relevant issue. Indeed, failing to assess these benefits will almost always result in the conclusion that the status quo should be preserved since the move will be disruptive and will detrimentally affect the relationship between the child and the access parent. Yet, an evaluation of the benefits will inevitably entail exploration of the reasons for the move. If, for example, the trial court in *Gordon v. Goertz* had had to choose between permitting the mother to take the child to Australia and having the mother stay with the child in Saskatchewan, it would have had to assess the benefits of the move to the child. Any benefits to the child would have been derivative of the benefits to the mother. The benefits of the move for the mother could only be discerned by assessing why the mother wanted to go to Australia. Second, Justice McLachlin expressly stated that the reasons for the move should be considered if they are relevant to the custodial parent's ability to parent. This is a fairly flexible test that can be interpreted liberally in individual cases. Certainly, most cases decided after *Gordon v. Goertz* continue to assess the reasons for the move, although the judges are often careful to state that they are not doing so!

In summary, the majority's analysis in *Gordon v. Goertz* is generally similar to that of the Ontario Court of Appeal in *Carter v. Brooks*. Custody and access decisions are to be determined on a case-by-case basis in accordance with the best interests of the individual child in the particular circumstances. There is no legal presumption favouring either parent. However, in assessing the child's best interests the court should accord "great respect" to the views of the custodial parent. The differences in the lists of non-exhaustive factors in the two cases are largely the result of the different options being considered. There is, however, slightly stronger language in *Gordon v. Goertz* regarding the views of the custodial parent. Finally, the comments in *Gordon v. Goertz* about the reasons for the move should cause judges to refrain from expressing an opinion about the "necessity" of a proposed move, but they are unlikely to eliminate the exploration of the reasons where the courts are choosing between maintaining the status quo and permitting a custodial parent to move with the child.

(4) Case Law Subsequent to *Gordon v. Goertz*

... The Ontario Court of Appeal reserved two appeals until the release of the reasons in *Gordon v. Goertz* and heard further submissions from counsel. The extensive reasons in *Woodhouse v. Woodhouse* (1996), 20 R.F.L. (4th) 337 and the two-page endorsement in *Luckhurst v. Luckhurst* (1996), 20 R.F.L. (4th) 373 provide considerable guidance for the interpretation of *Gordon v. Goertz*.

In *Woodhouse*, the mother wished to move from Hamilton, Ontario to Scotland. Under the terms of a separation agreement, the mother had custody of the parties' two sons, aged 4 and 6 at the time of the 1994 trial decision. The father paid child support regularly and exercised access consistently. In 1993, Mrs. Woodhouse gave the father notice, as required by their separation agreement, that she intended to move to Scotland with the children so that they could live there with John Murray, whom she wished to marry. The father responded by applying for custody and, in the alternative, asked the Court to make the mother's custody conditional on residing in the area. While waiting for the application to be heard, the parties entered into an agreement that resulted in a consent order allowing the mother to vacation in Scotland with the children from March 16 to April 11, 1993. Notwithstanding this agreement, the mother did not return to Ontario with the children on April 11. On April 16, the father obtained a court order requiring the mother to return with the children. When this did not occur, he was granted interim interim custody. In the meantime, the mother obtained an order of the Scottish courts granting her interim custody. In those proceedings the mother did not disclose the Ontario proceedings and represented that the children were resident in Scotland. When the mother learned of the order granting the father interim interim custody, she returned with the children to Ontario on the father's undertaking that he would not enforce the order pending the outcome of the original proceedings.

The mother married John Murray upon her return to Ontario. The new husband was a carpenter whose employment prospects in Canada were "very grim," but he had secure employment in Scotland. The mother, who had worked as a dance instructor, sold her dance studio in preparation for the move and she intended to be a full-time homemaker in Scotland.

The parties consented to an assessment. ... The assessor found that the boys had a loving relationship with both parents and that they had a good relationship with Mr. Murray. The assessor, while acknowledging that it was in the best interests of the mother and her new husband to live in Scotland, recommended that the children be in the mother's custody on condition that they stay in the area. He stressed that the emigration of the children would preclude a meaningful relationship with their father.

The trial judge ordered that the children remain in the custody of their mother but restricted their residence to certain municipalities in Southern Ontario. The mother appealed that part of the trial order restricting the children's residence. She argued that the trial judge erred in his application of the best interests test by not giving sufficient weight to her views as the custodial parent and in overemphasizing an assessment that was tainted by a preconceived notion that regular and frequent access was very important.

The Ontario Court of Appeal, Osborne J.A. dissenting, dismissed the appeal with respect to the mobility issue. Significantly, the justices unanimously concluded that McLachlin J.'s reasons in *Gordon v. Goertz* did not limit a court to a choice between only two options in mobility cases; that is, allowing the child to move with the custodial parent or transferring custody to the access parent. Justice Weiler, Houlden and McKinlay JJ.A. concurring, stated: "I interpret McLachlin J.'s words as a recognition that in some cases, including the one she was dealing with, the alternative of maintaining the status quo, as it was at the time of trial, is no longer practicable." Osborne J.A., in dissent, agreed that "McLachlin J. did not intend to rule out consideration of what counsel in their submissions following the release of *Gordon v. Goertz* referred to as the 'third option' — the option of the custodial parent keeping custody but not being allowed to move with the children."

Indeed, all the justices in *Woodhouse* accepted that, where a custodial parent's move is conditional upon being able to retain custody, the court can simply determine whether it is in the child's best interests to preserve the status quo or to allow the custodial parent to move with the child. Justice Osborne specifically indicated that trial judges should determine the true position of the parents at an early stage of the proceedings. "If, as is frequently the case, the custodial parent's position is that she will not move unless the children go with her, and the non-custodial parent claims custody only because of the move, it would not make much sense in these circumstances to embark on a full-blown custody hearing." In other words, the Ontario Court of Appeal confirmed in *Woodhouse v. Woodhouse* that *Gordon v. Goertz* did not alter the practice that prevailed in previous mobility cases.

Interestingly, Osborne J.A., in his dissent, suggested that the Court should explore a fourth option in some cases. Without further analysis, he stated that sometimes "asking the non-custodial parent to move may be more in the child's best interests than requiring the custodial parent to stay." Presumably, this possibility would only be explored where the non-custodial parent indicates a willingness to move if the child does. After all, neither the *Divorce Act* nor any provincial legislation dealing with custody or access gives a court jurisdiction to stipulate where a parent may live. Making access conditional on a move by the access parent will only benefit the child if one can be fairly certain that the access parent will in fact move and continue to exercise access. Otherwise, the child will end up suffering not only the disruption of the move but also the loss of all contact with the access parent. This will rarely be in the child's best interests.

The Ontario Court of Appeal in *Woodhouse v. Woodhouse* accepted that the general principles discernable in the majority's reasons in *Gordon v. Goertz* should also apply where the real choice is between allowing the child to move and maintaining the status quo. Moreover, the Court confirmed that these principles generally support the approach taken by Morden A.C.J.O. in *Carter v. Brooks* rather than that of Abella J.A. in *MacGyver v. Richards*. Justice Weiler quoted extensively from Justice Morden's reasons to explain McLachlin J.'s rejection of any presumption in favour of the custodial parent. ...

Justice Osborne was even more specific, concluding that the majority in *Gordon v. Goertz* "rejected the approach by this court in *MacGyver v. Richards*". ...

Therefore, the *Woodhouse* case confirms that all mobility cases, indeed all custody and access decisions, are to be determined on a case-by-case basis in accordance with the best interests of the particular child in the particular circumstances. While a custodial parent's views normally should be accorded "great respect," there is no procedural or substantive presumption favouring this parent's position. Where the real choice is between allowing the child to move with the custodial parent or maintaining the status quo, the court must weigh "the benefits to the child of the new location" against "the continuance of full contact with the child's access parent, its extended family, and its community." While each case turns on its unique facts, the majority's reasons in *Woodhouse v. Woodhouse* suggest that two key factors will be the economic benefits of the move and the extent to which the child's relationship with the access parent will be detrimentally affected. Regarding the views and wishes of the custodial parent, Justice Weiler concluded that both Morden A.C.J.O. in *Carter v. Brooks* and McLachlin J. in *Gordon v. Goertz* believed these to be "an important factor." She went on to indicate that the weight to be applied to this factor depended on the facts of the particular case. Moreover, her later comments reveal that the custodial parent's assessment of the child's best interests may be discounted if it is flawed in some way. In particular, the mother's conduct in this case raised a suspicion that she did not fully grasp and act upon the best interests of her children.

... [T]he Ontario Court of Appeal indirectly considered and evaluated the reasons for the proposed move in *Woodhouse* under the guise of assessing the economic impact of the options. In the end, the many factors boiled down to a comparison between the benefits of the proposed move to the children and the detrimental effects. Of course, as soon as one begins to identify the possible benefits of a move, one is bound to explore the reasons for the proposed move. In his dissent, Osborne J.A. acknowledged [para. 65] this more forthrightly than did the majority:

> [I]n most cases the reasons for the proposed move will surface because there is a manifest connection between the expected effects of the move and the custodial parent's reasons for proposing the move in the first place. The effect of the proposed move (in this case greater economic security, among other things) will be admissible and will generally be before the court. Nonetheless, *Gordon* makes it clear that there is no burden, or onus, on a custodial parent who is proposing to move to justify the move against a standard of necessity, or any other less onerous standard.

In *Luckhurst v. Luckhurst*, the Ontario Court of Appeal unanimously upheld the decision of Hockin J. permitting the mother to move with her twin sons, her partner and their child from London, Ontario to Cobourg, Ontario. The children's primary residence was with their mother pursuant to a separation agreement that provided for joint custody. The mother applied for an order permitting her to move with the children and the father cross-applied for sole custody. The trial judge granted the mother's application and the father appealed, arguing that the trial judge erred in not directing a trial of the issues and in permitting the children to move ... In upholding the decision on the merits, the [Ontario Court of Appeal] mentioned that the mother's new partner was concerned about the security of his employment in the London area and had obtained a secure position near Cobourg only after making extensive, unsuccessful efforts to find a similar job in the London area. It also noted that the cities were sufficiently close to permit the children to see their father regularly and that the mother had promised to "make reasonable arrangements to assist in the preservation of the quality of the relationship that the children had with their father by driving them to meet him at a halfway point between the two centres." The Court did not change the joint custody regime.

The indeterminacy of the case-by-case approach is illustrated in *Ligate v. Richardson* (1997), 34 O.R. (3d) 423 (C.A.), where various judges disagreed about which outcome was in the child's best interests. The father's expert witness, the trial judge, and a dissenting justice in the Ontario Court of Appeal thought that it was in the child's best interest not to allow her mother to change the child's residence from Toronto to Cambridge, Ontario, a city approximately 100 kilometres away. On the other hand, two members of the appellate court concluded that the trial judge erred by giving little, if any, weight to the views of the custodial parent. This entitled them to take a "fresh look" at the best interests of the child and they found that the move would have limited impact on the relationship between the child and her father. They concluded, therefore, that were "no reasons, compelling or otherwise, why the proposed move to Cambridge should not be allowed." This analysis suggests that a court should not interfere with a custodial parent's decision to move unless, at a minimum, the move will have a significant impact on the child's situation, particularly the relationship between the child and the access parent. Where the move involves a considerable distance, such impact is almost self-evident and the court must assess whether the benefits of the proposed move outweigh the detriments. ...

In *Bjornson v. Creighton* (2002), 31 R.F.L. (5th) 242 (Ont. C.A.), a mother left the family home with her son and immediately sought a custody order. She indicated that she wished to return to her home province of Alberta, where a full-time nursing position was available to her and where she had strong family support. The father asked for a joint custody order and an order prohibiting any change in the ordinary residence of the child. Interim orders were made on consent declaring the father and mother equally entitled to custody, providing that the child reside with the mother for four days and with the father for three days each week, and prohibiting any change in the child's residence. Eventually, the trial judge granted sole custody to the mother but refused to allow her to take the child from Ontario to Alberta on the basis that the child's need to have ready access to the father was not overcome by the advantages of the move.

The father's appeal from the decision awarding sole custody to the mother was dismissed. Justice Austin, for the Court, noted that the father had not originally asked for sole custody and that the trial judge was correct in deciding that joint custody was not appropriate. He noted that the trial judge, on this issue, referred to the father's aggressive style of parenting and his tendency to control and distrust the mother.

However, the Ontario Court of Appeal allowed the mother's appeal on the mobility issue. Justice Austin began his analysis of this issue by noting that two preliminary points arose in applying the guidelines from the Supreme Court of Canada decision in *Gordon v. Goertz* to a case where the issue of custody had not yet been determined. First, the parents could not be classified as "custodial parent" and "access parent" since they were both equally entitled to custody at the outset of the trial. Second, he suggested that the question of custody had to be determined before the question of mobility. "The trial judge appears to have decided the question of mobility first and the question of custody second. With respect, that strikes me as putting the cart before the horse." The order of analysis suggested by Justice Austin was possible in *Bjornson v. Creighton* because the mother had indicated that she was willing to stay in Ontario if this were the only way that she could obtain custody. Thus, the determination of custody did not also determine the mobility issue. If the mother had insisted that she was moving to Alberta, then the only issue to decide would have been whether the child should reside with her in Alberta or with the father in Ontario. The move would simply have been one factor in determining custody and the child's primary residence. Since the father had not applied for sole custody, this might have placed him at a definite disadvantage.

Once the Ontario Court of Appeal determined that the mother should have sole custody, it immediately accorded her the status of custodial parent for the purposes of applying the guidelines from *Gordon v. Goertz* and her views were entitled to "significant weight". ...

Under the telling heading "Best Interests of the Child Include Being With a Well-functioning Parent," Justice Austin also stated that the trial judge erred in focusing only on the mother's employment prospects in Alberta compared with Ontario. The mother wished to move not only to improve her career opportunities, but "to regain the general stability, control and independence that she enjoyed there in her emotional, professional, psychological and social life there." ... Although the "only issue" was what was in the best interests of the child, careful attention had to be paid to the potential negative effects on the child should the custodial parent be restricted from moving and to the potential positive effects on the child should that parent be permitted to relocate. ...

Rather than send the matter back for a new hearing, the Ontario Court of Appeal examined the fresh evidence filed on appeal and determined that the mother should be permitted to take the child to Alberta. The father was awarded access for one month in the summer, one week at Christmas and again at spring break, all such access to take place in Ontario. The father was also awarded two weeks access in Alberta provided that it did not interfere with the child's schooling. The expense of all access was to be borne by the father. The father was only ordered to pay $1 yearly in child support to maintain a minimum support link, on the basis that the mother would be able to support herself and the child once she became established in Alberta. ...

The string of Ontario Court of Appeal decisions in favour of a move was broken in *Young v. Young* (2003), 34 R.F.L. (5th) 214. When the mother and father separated, they were living in Kingston, although they had been planning to move to Ottawa to facilitate the father's consulting business. Shortly after separation, the mother brought an application for custody of the couple's three boys and also sought permission to move to Cornwall. The interim order specified that the children live in Ottawa, with the mother if she moved there and otherwise with the father. The mother moved to Ottawa and the parents agreed to joint custody in partial minutes of settlement. In Ottawa, the boys resided primarily with their francophone mother, although they spent almost equal time with their Anglophone father. The mother obtained a Bachelor of Education degree, but failed to secure a full-time teaching position in a French school in Ottawa. She obtained such a job in Cornwall, a city approximately 100 kilometres away. The mother moved there, commuting to Ottawa on weekends. She brought an application to permit her to move the children, asserting that she would otherwise give up her job and move back to Ottawa.

While the application was pending, a motions judge made an order confirming a new parenting schedule whereby the children lived with their father in Ottawa during the week and with their mother in Cornwall on the weekends. In October 2002, Justice Smith granted the mother's application and ordered that the children's primary residence would be with the mother in Cornwall. Because of the relatively short distance involved, the judge concluded that the move would not unduly disrupt the father's ability to spend time with the children.

He also held that "the financial needs of the children and the family unit will benefit from the applicant being employed as a teacher".

The father appealed. Justice Laskin of the Ontario Court of Appeal stayed the order of Smith J. pending the hearing of the appeal. In allowing the appeal, Justice Laskin ... described the application judge's decision as a "discretionary order" that was, accordingly, entitled to "significant deference." Nevertheless, the reviewing court was justified in interfering with the order because the judge made four interrelated errors. First, he focused almost exclusively on the mother's job opportunity in Cornwall and so failed to engage in the "full and sensitive inquiry" required. Second, he especially failed to take into account the disruption to the children that would be caused by removing them from the family, schools and community they had come to know. Third, by treating the mother as the *de facto* custodial parent and the father as the access parent instead of as joint custodial parents, the judge misapprehended the parenting arrangement that existed before the mother's application. Finally, Justice Smith failed to consider the independent assessment done about a year before the mother's application.

Having concluded that the application judge failed to take into account "many of the important considerations bearing on the ultimate question whether it was in the children's best interests to permit Ms. Young to move to Cornwall with them", the appellate Court was left with two choices. On the one hand, it could assess the evidence and the relevant considerations itself and either affirm, vary, or set aside the order. On the other hand, it could set aside the order and require a new hearing. In contrast to the dispositions in cases such as *Biornson v. Creighton*, the Ontario Court of Appeal preferred the latter approach in *Young v. Young*. Justice Laskin explained: "I would order a new hearing, should Ms. Young desire one. Despite the parties' modest means, that is the sensible solution in this case because many of the findings needed to assess whether the move is in the boys' best interests have not been made."

Professor Thompson began his annotation to the case tentatively: "I will suggest that *Young*, and the other Ontario Court of Appeal decisions make some sense, in light of trial court patterns, real-life custodial arrangements, and the corrosive effects upon the law of *Gordon v. Goertz*." He then made the following preliminary comments about the perceived trend in the Ontario cases. First, he noted that reported Ontario trial decisions between 2000 and 2003 refused to permit requested moves about 50 per cent of the time. Second, he suggested that the "trend" in the Ontario Court of Appeal cases was actually unclear, noting a 2001 Ontario Court of Appeal decision upholding a lower court's refusal to allow a move. Third, he stated: "Trial judges can easily underweigh or overweigh the *Gordon v. Goertz* factors, thereby committing reversible error."

In Professor Thompson's view, the legal form of a custody order does not affect whether the courts will permit a move, but "the real-life, on-the-ground [arrangement] for the child's care" does. He stated ["Annotation" (2003), 34 R.F.L. (5th) 215 at 216]:

> The decided cases have consistently demonstrated that "shared custody" of this kind [the type in place in *Young v. Young*] dramatically changes the results in mobility cases. Although trial judges over the years have said "yes" to moves in 60–70 per cent of mother-custody cases, those proportions are reversed dramatically where custody is truly shared, to only 30–40 per cent in the past few years. Even more interesting, within these shared custody cases, the "no" cases are "ordinary" cases, while the "yes" cases involve unusual facts.

Further, he noted that where a mother is labeled 'the primary caregiver', she will almost always be allowed to move. Therefore, the court's characterization of the actual care arrangements is a key factor in determining the outcome of mobility cases. In *Young v. Young*, the Ontario Court of Appeal insisted that the trial judge had incorrectly characterized the custody arrangements and so had undertaken a faulty analysis.

As the previous paragraph indicates, Professor Thompson believes that there are certain unspoken presumptions at work in the mobility cases. In particular, a mother who is accorded the status of 'primary caregiver' will usually be allowed to move with her child so long as the move is reasonable and she is willing to ensure that the child's relationship with the father continues. ...

In *Burns v. Burns* (2000), 3 R.F.L. (5th) 189 (N.S. C.A.), the parents had joint custody of two children. The children resided primarily with the mother and visited their father every weekend and one weekday per week. The mother wished to obtain a Masters in Social Work and could do so in two years in Ottawa, while it would take much longer if she stayed in Nova Scotia. The mother applied for sole custody of the children and for permission to remove them to Ottawa. She indicated that she would not go without the children. The application was dismissed and the mother appealed. The appeal was allowed. A key preliminary point in the Nova Scotia Court of Appeal's analysis was whether the mother correctly referred to herself as the "primary caregiver." Justice Roscoe, for the Court, noted that the parents had legal joint custody and that the children slept at their father's house three nights a week, but then added [paras. 29, 30, and 33]:

> However, the actual period of time spent with the children is not the only determinant. More importantly, in my opinion, is which parent has taken primary responsibility for all the important decisions concerning the health, safety, education, and overall welfare of the children, since the parties separated four years ago. ...
>
> In addition to the major matters, the primary caregiver is the parent who deals with the countless less significant, but nonetheless obligatory, daily arrangements for the children's clothing, haircuts, hygiene, extracurricular activities and everyday mundane affairs. ...
>
> My assessment of the evidence is that Mrs. Burns has been the primary caregiver and she is therefore the custodial parent whose views are entitled to great respect. She has been an exemplary parent and has assumed substantial responsibility for the care and general welfare of the children, and I believe has significant insight into their emotional, physical and psychological needs.

In the end, the appellate Court concluded that the disruptive effects of the move and the reduction in frequency of the father's access would be more than offset by the long-term economic benefits and increased stability that would flow from the enhancement of the mother's career opportunities. In this regard, Justice Roscoe, for the Court, cited the Ontario Court of Appeal decision in *Woodhouse v. Woodhouse* for the proposition that economic factors were "certainly relevant in this type of case."

In contrast to its decision in *Burns*, the Nova Scotia Court of Appeal in *Doiron v. Mahoney* (2000), 3 R.F.L. (5th) 206 refused to overturn a trial judge's decision granting day-to-day care to a child's father where the mother wished to move. After his birth, the boy lived primarily with his mother in Pomquet. When he was 6, his parents agreed to a consent order whereby they had joint custody, "with *de facto* custody" to the mother. The mother then enrolled in an educational program in Halifax, approximately 200 kilometres away. She made arrangements for her parents to look after her son during the week. She returned to her parents' home every other weekend. On alternate weekends and on Wednesdays, the son stayed with his father who operated a successful business in nearby Antigonish. Later, the mother began a romantic relationship with a man who lived in Halifax and she decided to look for employment there. At the end of June 1999, the son came to live in Halifax with the mother and her new partner. In August, the mother secured a full-time position in Halifax.

The father applied to vary the consent order and the trial judge determined that the parents should remain joint custodians, but that day-to-day care should vest with the father. Justice Wilson clearly compared only two situations: the child living with his mother in Halifax and the child living with his father in the Antigonish area. He concluded that the father's plan served the child's best interests because it would allow the child to stay at his school, continue his extra-curricular activities, and maintain close contact with his extended family. In comparison, the move to Halifax would involve major change and disruption.

Justice Pugsley, for the Nova Scotia Court of Appeal, found that the trial judge made no error that would justify appellate intervention. In his view, the trial judge applied the best interests test and examined all the factors suggested by the Supreme Court of Canada in *Gordon v. Goertz*. In particular, he weighed the views of the mother, knowing that they were entitled to great weight. In the end, he concluded that the mother's plan, involving "a new job, a new home in a new city, with a new partner, and for Jeremy, a major change and disruption from the day-to-day life he had known" compared unfavourably with the father's plan.

In his annotation to the case of *Doiron v. Mahoney* in the *Reports of Family Law*, Professor McLeod suggested that the "trend in mobility cases is that a primary caregiver who has an honest reason for wanting to move and is prepared to recognize the impact the proposed move will have on the child's relationship with the access parent by making access and/ or child-support accommodation will generally be allowed to move with the child over the other parent's objections." He acknowledged that the *Doiron* decision did not fit within this trend and concluded: "It is difficult to believe that the panel of the Court of Appeal that granted the appeal in *Burns* would have dismissed the appeal in *Doiron v. Mahoney*." Thus, the two cases together illustrate the lack of rules in this area and the decision in *Doiron v. Mahoney* shows that sometimes a parent with a good reason to move will not be allowed to relocate with a child even if she is willing to be accommodating. ...

NOTES AND QUESTIONS

1. There is some confusion in the cases as to whether the access parent or the custodial parent must commence proceedings for a variation of an existing custody/ access order where there is a planned relocation. Who has to apply in the following situations? Who has to prove what?

1) A custody/ access order specifies that the mother has custody and that the father has access on Wednesday evenings and every other weekend. There is no non-removal clause in the order and the mother wishes to move with the child to Australia.

2) The parents have joint custody and the order stipulates that the child will live with the father. The mother has generous access. The father wishes to move with the child to a city 200 kilometres away and the mother objects.

3) A custody/access order stipulates that the mother has custody of the child on condition that the child live in the Metro-Toronto area. The mother wishes to move to Windsor with the child.

4) There is no custody/access order, but the child resides with the mother with the approval of the father who sees the child frequently. The mother wishes to move to Sweden with the child.

5) The situation is the same as in #3, but the terms of custody and access are set in a separation agreement.

Another way of looking at these issues is to ask whether the mothers in situations #1, 3, 4, and 5 and the father in situation #2 are legally entitled to move with the child without either the consent of the other parent or the court. If they are, do they nonetheless have a legal obligation to inform the other parent of the move? If so, must there be advance notice?

In *Relocation of Custodial Parents: Final Report* (Ottawa: Status of Women Canada, 1998), Professors Bailey and Giroux recommend (at 8) that the rules governing which parent must commence proceedings should be clarified, especially where there is no non-removal clause in the existing order but the move would interfere with the terms of the access order. They also suggest (at 8-9):

If there is no general requirement that the custodial parent obtain a variation of the terms of the access prior to moving, Canada's law should be amended to require custodial parents to give notice of a proposed move to the other parent or the court. As well, the custodial parent should be required to propose new arrangements for access. The notice requirement should provide for exceptions in cases where notice would create a risk of domestic violence.

See also *For the Sake of the Children* (Ottawa, 1998), where the Special Joint Committee recommended (at 70) an amendment to the *Divorce Act* to require (a) that a parent wishing to relocate with a child, where the distance would necessitate the modification of agreed or court-ordered parenting arrangements, seek judicial permission at least 90 days before the proposed move and (b) that the other parent be given notice at the same time.

2. Courts generally frown on attempts to move first and worry about the consequences later. Where a parent moves a child without consent or court approval, a court will often order a return of the child until the matter can be dealt with in court. At the same time, there is a tendency on interim applications to deny permission to relocate children unless there is an urgent need to move immediately or permission to move will be the inevitable result at trial. See, e.g., *Lehner v. Klanyi* (2001), 21 R.F.L. (5th) 327 (Ont. S.C.J.) and *Hunt v. Hunt* (2001), 21 R.F.L. (5th) 309 (Ont. S.C.J.); additional reasons at (2001), 2001 CarswellOnt 4548 (Ont. S.C.J.). A move prior to trial was allowed in *Roberts v. Young* (2004), 3 R.F.L. (6th) 457 (Ont. S.C.J.).

In *Sodhi v. Sodhi* (2002), 25 R.F.L. (5th) 420 (Ont. C.A.); additional reasons at (2002), 2002 CarswellOnt 1943 (Ont. C.A.), the mother, after being awarded interim custody, unilaterally moved with the children from Ottawa to a city that was a six-hour drive away. The father's motion for an order requiring her to return the children was dismissed on the basis that there was too much "bad blood" between the parents. After lengthy, acrimonious litigation, custody was eventually awarded to the mother on condition that she return to Ottawa with the children. If she failed to move back, the father was to have custody. The Ontario Court of Appeal dismissed the father's appeal, but allowed the mother's cross-appeal from the part of the judgment requiring her to move back. The appellate court ruled that the trial judge's finding that the best interests of the children could best be met by awarding custody to the mother was well supported by the evidence and should not be disturbed. However, it concluded that the trial judge's further order that the mother's custody be conditional upon her return to Ottawa was "difficult to support on the evidence". It found that the conclusion that the mother's employer could easily transfer her to Ottawa was not supported by any convincing evidence and was proved incorrect by fresh evidence filed on appeal. Secondly, and "most importantly," the appellate Court concluded that the trial judge failed to consider the impact of uprooting the children after they had been settled in the new city for a year. Moreover, the passage of another two years since the trial confirmed that the children were doing well in their new community.

In his annotation to the case, Professor McLeod suggested that the result in *Sodhi v. Sodhi* confirms that custody cases are won and lost at the interim stage. "A parent who is not ordered to return a child immediately can rely on the status quo he or she has created after an unauthorized and illegal removal to gain approval for a move that he or she might not have obtained." Indeed, the mother's resort to self-help in the *Sodhi* case ultimately provided the best reason for not returning the children to Ottawa as it led to a three-year period during which they established firm roots in a new community. In the end, the father's problem stemmed from the Court's refusal to order the children's return on the initial interim motion and then the length of time until the trial and the appeal. Given the amount of time that had elapsed, it is not surprising that the Ontario Court of Appeal allowed the mother's cross-appeal. However, the Court missed an opportunity to at least state that it strongly disapproved of unilateral moves and that motions judges should generally order the return of children who are wrongfully removed.

3. Psychologists and psychiatrists who work as assessors appear to generally stress the child's need for meaningful, ongoing regular contact with both parents. As a result, few assessors consider a long-distance move by either parent to be in a child's best interests. Indeed, Professor McLeod suggests in "Annotation to *F. (D.A.) v. O. (S.M.)*" (2004), 4 R.F.L. (6th) 300 at 302 (Alta. C.A.): "Counsel representing a parent who wants to move is generally wise to avoid an assessment if at all possible."

In *Johnstone v. Brighton* (2004), 6 R.F.L. (6th) 294 (Ont. S.C.J.), a father opposed a mother's proposed relocation to Pennsylvania with a five-year-old child to join her fiancé. He retained a clinical psychologist to review recent studies of the effects of relocation on young children. Justice G.A. Campbell refused to allow the father to call the psychologist as an expert witness on the basis that his opinions on "hypothetical" situations was not necessary to decide what was in the best interests of the child. The Justice approached the case as requiring a choice between having the child live with the mother in Pennsylvania or the father in London, Ontario, and chose to allow the relocation of the child's primary residence.

In *Cade v. Rotstein* (2004), 50 R.F.L. (5th) 280 (Ont. C.A.); additional reasons at (2004), 2004 CarswellOnt 829 (Ont. C.A.), the appellate court upheld a trial judge's decision allowing a mother to move to New York with three children despite an expert's report recommending no relocation.

4. What is the effect if a custodial parent announces that he or she is moving, with or without the child? See *Cameron v. Cameron* (2003), 41 R.F.L. (5th) 30 (Man. Q.B.) (relocation allowed despite mother's "intransigence") and *Sloss v. Forget* (2004), 8 R.F.L. (6th) 380 (Ont. S.C.J.); additional reasons at (2005), 2005 CarswellOnt 732 (Ont. S.C.J.) (custody to be altered if mother does move).

5. The case of *Spencer v. Spencer* (2005), 15 R.F.L. (6th) 237 (Alta. C.A.) is significant because the court suggested that it was unfair and inappropriate to ask custodial parents whether they would forego relocation if this were a condition of retaining custody. The Spencers had two children, aged three years and six weeks, when they separated in 2000. The mother became the sole custodial parent and the father exercised access sporadically. In 2005, the father learned that the mother intended to move with her fiancé and the children from Calgary to Victoria where the fiancé's family resided and where he had an attractive job offer. The father then began to see the children every second weekend and applied under s. 17(5) of the *DA* for an order prohibiting the mother from moving the children and for joint custody. The mother brought a cross-application seeking permission to move the children. During the hearing, the mother acknowledged that she would not leave unless she could take the children with her.

The chambers judge determined that it was in the children's best interest to stay in Calgary and ordered that they remain in the mother's sole custody in that city. The mother's appeal was allowed. The court held that the chambers judge erred in assessing the children's best interests by overemphasizing the desirability of maximizing contact with the father and failing to give sufficient respect to the mother's wishes. Moreover, added Paperny J.A.:

> 18 ... it is problematic to rely on representations by the custodial parent that he or she will not move without the children should the application to relocate be denied. The effect of such an inquiry places the parent seeking to relocate in a classic double bind. If the answer is that the parent is not willing to remain behind with the children, he or she raises the prospect of being regarded as self interested and discounting the children's best interests in favour of his or her own. On the other hand, advising the court that the parent is prepared to forgo the requested move if unsuccessful, undermines the submissions in favour of relocation by suggesting that such a move is not critical to the parent's well-being or to that of the children. If a judge mistakenly relies on a parent's willingness to stay behind "for the sake of the children," the status quo becomes an attractive option for a judge to favour because it avoids the difficult decision the application presents.

> 19 Once a material change has been found, *Gordon* directs the judge to be mindful of the status quo prior to the move, but the inquiry cannot stop there. The relevant inquiry is to the children's best interests, evaluated in the new circumstances as found (here, the effect on the children of the mother's relocation with her new husband and child to Victoria if they are allowed to move) compared to its effect on them if they are not allowed to move. The children's best interests must be assessed in the new circumstances, its impact on them if they stay or if they go ...

The appropriate question for the chambers judge, in the Alberta Court of Appeal's view, was whether it was in the best interests of the children to move with their mother to Victoria or to remain in Calgary with their father. If he had asked himself this question, he would have favoured the move. See also *MacPhail v. Karasek* (2006), 30 R.F.L. (6th) 324 (Alta. C.A.); additional reasons at (2006), 33 R.F.L. (6th) 311 (Alta. C.A.); additional reasons at (2008), 50 R.F.L. (6th) 15 (Alta. C.A.); leave to appeal refused (2007), 2007 CarswellAlta 140, 2007 CarswellAlta 141 (S.C.C.).

These two Alberta cases should be contrasted with *Karpodinis v. Kantas* (2006), 27 R.F.L. (6th) 254 (B.C. C.A.); additional reasons at (2006), 2006 CarswellBC 2259 (C.A.); leave to appeal refused (2006), 2006 CarswellBC 2797, 2006 CarswellBC 2798 (S.C.C.). In this case, the parents separated while the mother was pregnant. By consent, the mother had custody and the father's access was scheduled to coincide with his days off from his work as a grocery store shelf stocker. Both parents had family in Vancouver and the child had a close relationship with the father and the paternal grandparents. The mother worked as a shipping manager for a company that was ceasing its Vancouver operations. The company offered the mother a comparable position in Houston, Texas, and the mother sought an order that would allow her to move her three-year-old son. The chambers judge dismissed the application and the mother's appeal was denied. Significantly, Justice Hall, speaking for the B.C.C.A., commented on the principles from *Gordon v. Goertz* as follows (para. 20):

> These principles were enunciated with a view to resolve conflicts between parents where there are only two options: vary the custody order to allow the mother to leave the jurisdiction with the child, or grant custody to the access parent. In other cases, such as the case at bar, the custodial parent states that he or she will not move if the child is not permitted to move to the proposed new location. This

presents another option to a judge hearing such an application, namely maintaining the *status quo* extant before the application.

In the end, Justice Hall concluded (para. 27) that the chambers judge "considered all relevant factors and reached a supportable decision in an admittedly difficult case."

6. The Supreme Court of Canada continues to exhibit no interest in revisiting the issue of relocation. Since June 2004, it has refused six applications for leave to appeal in mobility cases. See Jollimore and Sladic, "Mobility — Are We There Yet?" (2008), 27 C.F.L.Q. 341, for an analysis of these cases.

7. Would you favour the creation of a presumption or a set of presumptions to guide the determination of relocation cases? If so, what presumption would you favour?

8. Regarding the possibility that the relocating parent may be required to pay some or all of the other parent's cost of access, see Chapter 8, *CHILD SUPPORT*.

9. For further reading on relocation, see Bala and Harris, "Parental Relocation: Applying the Best Interests of the Child Test in Ontario" (2006), 22 Can. J. Fam. L. 127; Thompson, "Ten Years after *Gordon*: No Law, Nowhere" (2007), 35 R.F.L. (6th) 307 and Mamo, "A Practitioner's Guide to Mobility Cases" in Shaffer, ed. *Contemporary Issues in Family Law: Engaging with the Legacy of James G. McLeod* (Toronto: Carswell, 2007).

6. Joint Custody and Other Options

MUDIE v. POST

(1998), 40 R.F.L. (4th) 151, 1998 CarswellOnt 3128 (Ont. Gen. Div.)

21 A number of witnesses were called by both sides to attest to the fact that both the applicant [the father] and the respondent [the mother] are loving and caring parents. I am satisfied that they are. Although each has a different view as to how a child should be raised, it is clear on the evidence that the respondent is less tolerant of the applicant's views regarding child rearing than he is of hers.

22 The applicant's background in the military has led him to believe that children should be subject to strict rules and regulations. He believes that children should be punished generally by light physical punishment or by being sent to their room so that they learn not to be a discipline problem. On the other hand, the respondent believes that discussion and reasoning with a child will solve a discipline problem. Over the period of their relationship, the applicant has become more and more receptive to the respondent's approach, taking parenting courses. On the other hand, the respondent has totally rejected any form of physical discipline or social deprivation such as sending a child to his room to discipline him. ...

28 The conduct of both during these custody proceedings has shown a deep lack of maturity and understanding of the effect that it has had on Garrit [the oldest boy]. Although each sought to blame the other for what has gone on, I am satisfied that each must share the blame equally. I also agree with Ms. Stirling's [the assessor's] view that the applicant "must come to terms with the likelihood that his own behaviour has alienated Garrit." ...

31 Historically, custody battles have been an all or nothing proposition. Sole custody orders have been the norm with access to the non-custodial parent through visitation rights. Such orders have granted legal responsibility and physical control to a single custodial parent to the exclusion of the other. A sole custodial order has given the custodial parent the right to decide where the child will live, how the child will be educated, what religion, if any, the child will adopt and what medical and dental care will be provided. The result has been that

the voice of the non-custodial parent in the upbringing of his or her child has been essentially unheard. Any voice of the non-custodial parent in such important decisions affecting the life of "their" child has only been heard where the custodial parent has cared to listen.

32 I pause to stress the word "their" in reference to the child. It is often forgotten that the child, whatever result the court reaches, is the product of both parents. No decision of the court, no matter how limiting in the access granted to the non-custodial parent, can ever take away the fact that the non-custodial parent is still the parent of that child. It is for that reason that where a sole custody order has been made, the losing parent leaves the courtroom, feeling not only alienated from "their" child, but also alienated from the justice system which has adopted the winner-take-all approach to a custody dispute. ...

42 One of the main arguments advanced by those who believe that legal custody should not be separated from physical custody is that it does not work. My experience, after trying custody cases for almost 20 years, is that it does work and works far better to reduce post-trial applications than a sole custody order. Indeed, the frequent applications that are brought in this Court in this jurisdiction after a sole custody order has been made to enforce an access order has led me to the conclusion that joint custody orders are less subject to ongoing litigation than sole custody orders.

43 I have found that the most insidious impediment to the cooperation of equally competent parents is the question of "who should be in control". Far too often parents are prepared to "battle to the end" and to endure the strain and expense of a custody battle, without recognizing the harmful effects on the child, so that they can have the "last word". This attitude has prevailed even where one parent has recognized that the other parent has a valuable contribution to make to the life of the child. It has been my experience that an order for joint legal custody, with clearly defined times for physical custody, has proved to be more effective in settling the dust of battle. Clearly defined periods of legal and physical custody declare the limits of control which each parent will have over the child. More importantly, they ensure that the child will have unimpeded access to the parent who has legal custody during that defined period. ...

46 In this case, Ms. Stirling recommended that sole custody be granted to the respondent although she accepted and recognized that it was in the best interests of Garrit and Parker that the applicant play an important role in their lives. She acknowledged that he has made a genuine effort to improve his parenting skills by taking recommended parenting courses. When asked why she recommended sole custody to the respondent instead of joint custody, she said that it was because she understood the law to be that joint custody could only be awarded where the parties are able to cooperate with one another.

47 I have come to the conclusion that it is in the best interests of the children in this case that there be a joint custody order. I say that because I am convinced that if sole custody were granted to the respondent, she would continue to obstruct the applicant's attempts to develop a relationship with the children. As I said earlier, it was my distinct impression from her evidence that she would prefer that the applicant be entirely out of her life and the life of the children. I am satisfied that if I were to grant her sole custody, she would make every effort to limit the applicant's contact with the children. In my view, the only practical solution to prevent this is to ensure that she is not given absolute control of the children. Indeed, this is a case where neither should be in absolute control.

48 Moreover, I am convinced that once absolute control is removed from the hands of the respondent, the constant bickering between over the parties over "who is telling the truth", "who is telling lies" and "who will the judge believe", will dissipate, if not entirely cease. In short, once the element of absolute control by one or the other is removed and physical custody divided, some peace may come to the lives of these children. I am convinced that

the other alternative will only result in repeated applications to the court by the respondent seeking to restrict the applicant's access to the children and repeated applications by the applicant complaining that that the respondent is trying to frustrate his contact with his children.

[The order stipulated that the boys would reside with their mother and identified specific times when the father would have "physical custody".]

KAPLANIS v. KAPLANIS

(2005), 10 R.F.L. (6th) 373, 2005 CarswellOnt 266 (Ont. C.A.)

1 K.M. WEILER J.A. (for the Court): — On July 8, 2003 Justice E. MacDonald awarded joint custody of the child of the parties' marriage to the appellant mother and respondent father. She further ordered the parties to attend counselling to improve their parenting skills and ordered that decisions with respect to choice of schools, activities and hobbies for the child were to be made by an unnamed counsellor if the parties were unable to agree. ... The mother appeals the order of joint custody and seeks sole custody. ...

2 For the reasons that follow, I would agree with the mother that the order of joint custody should be set aside on the grounds that the trial judge erred in principle in awarding joint custody (a) where there was no evidence of historical co-operation and appropriate communication between the parents, and (b) in the hope that it would improve the parenting skills of the parties. I would also agree that the trial judge exceeded her jurisdiction by making an order that the parties attend counselling and by imposing on them a requirement that, in the event they could not agree, the unnamed counsellor was to decide the matter for them. Inasmuch as an order for joint custody is not appropriate, and the father did not seek sole custody of the child, I would order that the mother be awarded sole custody of the child. I would further order the trial of an issue with respect to the terms of the father's access. Pursuant to s. 112 of the *Courts of Justice Act*, I would request the Children's Lawyer to cause an investigation to be made and to report and make recommendations to the court on all matters concerning access to the child and the father's involvement with the child.

The Custody Appeal

4 The background facts as found by the trial judge and her holding in relation to the issue of custody are as follows. The appellant and the respondent were married on June 6, 1998. The only child of the marriage, a daughter named Victoria, was born on October 11, 2001. The marriage was a tumultuous one. The parties separated two and a half years later on January 12, 2002 when the father left the matrimonial home after he was charged with uttering a death threat to the mother. The charge was subsequently withdrawn largely as a result of an affidavit sworn by the mother. In her affidavit she stated that she was not a victim of violence, that it would be in the best interests of Victoria if her husband were allowed to return to the matrimonial home, and that her husband was "... a good man and no doubt a good father." The father never returned to the matrimonial home and attempts at counselling were unsuccessful. Indeed the counsellor had them leave his office because of the "uncontrollable invective being exchanged by them."

5 The father, who was self-represented at trial, sought a form of joint custody, known as parallel parenting. Parallel parenting envisages that the parents have equal status and exercise the rights and responsibilities associated with custody independently of the other.

6 The mother resisted the father's application on the basis that the parties could not communicate without screaming at each other. In addition to the evidence of the screaming incident in the marriage counsellor's office she led evidence about a screaming incident that was witnessed by a neighbour when the father came to pick up the child at his in-laws' home in which the mother had returned to live.

7 The trial judge held:

> ... My hope is that the parents will put closure on the disappointment and resentments that flow from their failed marriage. They have the support of extended families on both sides including aunts, uncles, grandparents, nieces and nephews. They aspire to raise Victoria in the Greek Orthodox faith into which she was baptized, not after some controversy, in mid 2002. I inferred from the evidence that the parents plan to have Victoria attend both public and Greek school. ...

> It struck me that it is not in the wife's interests to try to communicate and cooperate with the facilitation of access. She would see this as weakening her claim for sole custody, because of the emphasis she puts on their inability to communicate as a justification for a sole custody order. In my view, considerations of the best interests of Victoria in the context of her extended familial relationships, must not preclude joint custody, merely because the parties, fresh from the wounds of their failed marriage, find it difficult to be civil to each other. ...

> [T]heir marriage was short, but as responsible parents to Victoria, they have a long standing obligation, and responsibility to enhance her relationship with both parents. A disposition of sole custody, in favour of the mother, will be used by her to minimize the father's influence and contact. The mother has acknowledged that the father is a good father. For these reasons, Victoria [should] be in the joint custody of her parents.

8 After acknowledging that because Victoria was so young she had not yet been overnight at her father's home, the trial judge ordered a gradual expansion of access to take place over a two-month period and made a detailed order to that effect. In addition the trial judge ordered:

> The parents shall attend counselling on how to improve their communication skills, respecting all matters pertaining to Victoria, including adjustments to scheduled access to accommodate special family events. Decisions about choice of schools, activities and hobbies as Victoria grows older will be made jointly. In the event that they cannot agree, their counsellor who [sic] will decide the matter for them. The costs of such counselling will be split equally between the mother and the father.

Analysis

9 Family law cases are, by their nature, fact-based and discretionary. It is unnecessary to address this court's prior jurisprudence regarding the issue of joint custody to resolve the issue of custody in this appeal.

10 As in any custody case, the sole issue before the trial judge was the best interests of the child. The fact that both parents acknowledged the other to be "fit" did not mean that it was in the best interests of the child for a joint custody order to be made. The evidence before the trial judge should have revealed what bonds the child had with each of her parents and their ability to parent the child. In addition to detailing the mother's current arrangements respecting the care of the child, the evidence should also have indicated what practical plan to care for the child the father proposed to make when he had the child with him and the benefits to the child of such an arrangement. The trial judge had no evidence to this effect. Indeed, as the trial judge acknowledged at the time she made her order, the child had never spent an overnight with the father alone.

11 The fact that one parent professes an inability to communicate with the other parent does not, in and of itself, mean that a joint custody order cannot be considered. On the other hand, hoping that communication between the parties will improve once the litigation is over does not provide a sufficient basis for the making of an order of joint custody. There must be some evidence before the court that, despite their differences, the parents are able to com-

municate effectively with one another. No matter how detailed the custody order that is made, gaps will inevitably occur, unexpected situations arise, and the changing developmental needs of a child must be addressed on an ongoing basis. When, as here, the child is so young that she can hardly communicate her developmental needs, communication is even more important. In this case there was no evidence of effective communication. The evidence was to the contrary.

12 Insofar as the ability of the parties to set aside their personal differences and to work together in the best interests of the child is concerned, any interim custody order and how that order has worked is a relevant consideration for the trial judge and any reviewing court. At trial the father testified that an interim custody order made prior to trial on August 1, provided that the mother have custody and that the father have access on Mondays and Thursdays from 11 to 4 p.m. The father testified that during the time he was with his child, they visited his parents, his niece, Woodbine Centre, McDonald's and Burger King. He also testified that he had sought increased access and had not received it.

13 While the child's best interests are not necessarily synonymous with the child's wishes, the older the child, the more an order as to custody requires the co-operation of the child and consideration of the child's wishes. Here, we are dealing with a very young child, incapable of communicating her wishes. When the child is too young to communicate her wishes, expert evidence may be necessary to enable a judge to determine how the child's psychological and emotional needs would be advanced by the proposed custody order or parenting plan. Ideally, judges conducting a pre-trial would canvass the issue with the parties to alert them to the need to bring forward evidence of how the child's needs will be met by the proposed parenting plan. The assistance of the Children's Lawyer pursuant to s. 112 of the *Courts of Justice Act* ... could also be requested. In this case the trial judge did not have the benefit of expert evidence or input from the Children's Lawyer respecting the child.

14 It may certainly be desirable for parents to take counselling on how to better parent their child and to hire a counsellor or parenting coach to resolve disputes. The order provided by the trial judge was, however, problematic. The legislation does not specifically authorize the making of an order for parental counselling and, while some trial judges have held the court has inherent jurisdiction to make a counselling order, carrying out the order requires the co-operation of the parents. There was no evidence that the parties would be able to agree on whom to appoint. There was no agreed process for the appointment of a counsellor in the event that they could not agree who should be their counsellor. Nor was there any evidence that they were willing to submit their disputes to be decided by a counsellor outside the court process envisaged under the *Divorce Act* and without recourse to it.

15 Having regard to the above factors, the trial judge erred in making an order for joint custody of the child. She further erred in making the orders she did that the parties attend counselling and appoint a counsellor to resolve their disputes. In the absence of any request for sole custody by the father and detailed parenting plan put forward by him, the court's only other choice was to make an order for sole custody of the child to the mother. Accordingly, I would, as indicated, allow the appeal and order that the mother have sole custody of the child. The extent of the father's involvement in the life of the child is a matter that remains to be addressed by way of a new trial on the issue of access, hopefully with the

assistance of the Children's Lawyer. I would therefore order a new trial on the issue of the parties' access.

LADISA v. LADISA

(2005), 11 R.F.L. (6th) 50, 2005 CarswellOnt 268 (Ont. C.A.)

1 K.M. WEILER J.A.: — On January 30, 2004 Justice Linhares de Sousa ordered that the parties have joint custody of their three children, with the eldest child, then about fifteen years and nine months old, residing primarily with the father and the two younger children residing with both parents on an alternating weekly basis. The appellant mother appeals and seeks sole custody of the children. The trial judge also made orders of spousal and child support in favour of the respondent father and the mother appeals these as well.

2 This appeal was heard immediately following the appeal in *Kaplanis v. Kaplanis* ... in which an appeal from an order of joint custody was also taken, and regard should be had to those reasons respecting the issue of joint custody raised here.

3 For the reasons that follow, I would dismiss the appeal with respect to the issue of joint custody. I would allow the appeal in part respecting the orders of spousal and child support. [The reasons with respect to the latter two issues are omitted.]

The Appeal Respecting Custody

4 The parties were married on August 30, 1986 and lived together for approximately sixteen years until they separated in July 2002. They had three children. Alana is now 16 years old, having been born May 6, 1988. Jordan, now 13, was born on April 19, 1991; Jessica, now 9 years old, was born in November 1995.

5 When the parties separated, all three children remained living with their mother in the matrimonial home. Initially, the father resided with his parents and then acquired his own residence in November 2002 when he began exercising overnight weekend access.

6 The parties could not agree on the custody arrangements respecting their children and, after court proceedings began, attempts at mediation failed. At this time Mackinnon J. requested the Children's Lawyer to provide a social work assessment and to make recommendations on the parenting arrangement that would be in the best interests of the three children. The two youngest children remained in the care of their mother while the eldest, Alana, was permitted to move between the care of their mother and father in accordance with her wishes until the trial in December 2003 and January 2004.

7 The trial judge found that the "love, affection and emotional ties between all three children and both their parents were very and equally strong." Throughout most of the marriage, the mother worked outside the home. The father had worked mostly in construction as a labourer as well as a grouter until 1982 when he was diagnosed with Crohn's disease. He underwent surgery for his illness in 1991. He began receiving CPP disability insurance and that has been his consistent source of income since that time. Under this plan, he is able to work up to 90 days without losing his eligibility for disability insurance. ... He dedicated his free time to care for the children and the home. He was home for the children after school, to take them to doctor and dentist appointments and was very actively involved in their sports and school activities. The mother also participated in the children's sporting events and parent teacher meetings to the extent that she was able. The children's maternal grandmother assisted both parents in caring for their children throughout, but as she had to care for an increasingly ill spouse, she was less able to offer assistance. The youngest child, Jessica, had

gone to the same babysitter, Ms. Ryall, since she was an infant and had gone to her home before and after school. In June 2003, when the mother had to go on sick leave from her employment, Ms. Ryall's employment was terminated but it was her intention to re-employ her when she returned to work. The trial judge noted that if the father had the care of the children on alternating weeks there would be no need to have her services during that time because the father would care for Jessica himself.

8 Ms. Savoia, the social worker appointed by the Children's Lawyer, recommended that the children be in the joint custody of their parents.

9 The trial judge also had the benefit of the expressed wishes of the children. Alana did not express a preference to live with one parent or the other but stated she would continue to live with the parent who best met her needs as she saw them at the time. At the time of trial, she was living with her father. Following her parents' separation, she had moved back and forth between her parents as she wished. For example, after moving from her mother's home to her father's home, she moved back in May 2003 for a time because of conflicts with her father over spending time with her boyfriend. She was described as headstrong and defiant and seriously truant from school. In the opinion of Ms. Savoia, who had been appointed by the Children's Lawyer to conduct an assessment, she was a child out of control.

10 Jordan expressed the desire to spend equal time with each parent. He had, on a previous occasion, refused to return to his mother's care against the instructions of both his parents. On another occasion he had defied the wishes of his parents and gone to see his father to get assistance in building a go-cart, a project on which he was working. Jessica was ambivalent. She expressed a desire to spend more time with her father in the first two interviews and then said she was content with the arrangement in existence at trial, residing with her mother and weekend access with her father, in the last interview.

11 At the time of trial, the mother had arranged for counselling for the children and the father had agreed to cooperate with her efforts.

12 The trial judge found:

> Despite the intense conflict between these parents, in emergencies and when the parents have had an opportunity to consider the real interests of their children, they have behaved appropriately, even in each other's presence. Some examples of this are the following. When Alana had her emergency treatment for her fall, the parents were able to work out their differences, although with some sadness on the part of Mr. Ladisa, as to who would stay with Alana and who would care for the other children. When Jordan was adamant that he needed the assistance of his father with his go-cart project, the parents were able to agree on a resolution in the interests of their son. When the parents have been forced together because of their children, such as at parent-teacher meetings, school functions and sports activities, they seem, with perhaps one or two exceptions, to have been able to behave appropriately. According to the testimony of third parties, including teachers, a former hockey coach, other hockey parents and neighbours, the parents have always acted appropriately when together towards each other and towards their children. Their conflict has not been obvious to the observation of these third parties. When the children have forgotten some item at the house of the other parent, arrangements to fetch the item or sports equipment have been worked out. This accommodation even includes the question of the children's confirmation last year. The disagreement was not whether the children should be confirmed but when they should be confirmed that seemed to have some financial consequences.

13 The trial judge also found that both parents had made efforts to meet the financial needs of the children when these needs presented themselves, without consideration of whether the other parent should be paying or without anticipation that one parent would reimburse the other for that expense, and that they had done this at great personal sacrifice to themselves.

14 In the result, the trial judge found that the children needed the parenting that both parents could give them. She therefore ordered that Jordan and Jessica reside with both parents on an alternating weekly basis with the transfer time to be Friday evening at 7 p.m. Each child

was to be free to telephone the other parent while they were in the care of one parent but that, short of an emergency, the parents were to have no direct contact by telephone. Instead, communication between the parents was to be by means of a communication book or by email. School and statutory holidays were to be shared equally and a detailed order was made in this regard. Both parents were permitted to attend school functions and extracurricular activities for the children and both were entitled to receive all medical and school information concerning the children. Both were permitted to travel with the children outside of the Ottawa jurisdiction for vacation purposes upon reasonable notice to the other parent of at least 30 days and the provision of an itinerary.

15 The mother submits that the trial judge erred in her assessment of the evidence respecting the ability of the parties to co-operate with one another in the interests of their children and that the few examples the trial judge cited were flawed and contrary to the weight of the evidence. The mother's position is that a joint custody order is not appropriate as the parties have repeatedly been in conflict. She submits that the trial judge erred in imposing joint custody in these circumstances.

16 In my opinion, it was within the trial judge's discretion to make the order she did respecting Jordan and Jessica. The trial judge's conclusion took into consideration the history of co-parenting by the parties while they were married and the ties that the children had to both their parents. With respect to communication and cooperation, the trial judge considered the evidence of third parties respecting the parents' interaction with their children. She was satisfied that, despite their strife, when necessary, the parents could and had communicated effectively and put the interests of the children ahead of their own. The appellant has not persuaded me that she made a palpable and overriding error in making this finding. The trial judge also had the benefit of the expert evidence of the Children's Lawyer who recommended joint custody. The trial judge's decision also took into consideration the wishes of Jordan, and, although she did not expressly advert to it, the lack of any compelling reason to separate custody of Jordan from that of his sister, Jessica, as well as the mother's evidence that Jessica should not be separated from her for more than a week at a time. In these circumstances, the trial judge did not err in principle in making an order of joint custody regarding Jordan and Jessica.

17 As indicated, Alana was almost sixteen at the time of trial and, in the opinion of Ms. Savoia, she was a child out of control. She indicated she was going to live with whichever parent she pleased and that was precisely what she had done. She attended school sporadically until at least October 2003. It appears from Mr. Ladisa's evidence that she left school altogether two months before trial. I am not prepared to say that the order that the parties have joint custody of Alana was inappropriate at the time it was made. Now that Alana is almost 17, any custody order in respect of her, or requirement that she have her principal residence with one parent, in this case the father, would be moot.

18 Accordingly, for the reasons I have given I would vary paragraph 5 of the trial judge's order to provide that the parties share joint custody of Jordan and Jessica and that no order for custody of Alana be made. ...

SHAFFER, "JOINT CUSTODY SINCE *KAPLANIS* AND *LADISA*: A REVIEW OF RECENT ONTARIO CASE LAW"

(2007), 26 C.F.L.Q. 315 (Footnotes omitted)

1. Introduction

Ever since the courts accepted it as an option, joint custody has been something of a legal lightning rod. Most people agree that joint custody is a perfectly acceptable arrangement where both parents consent to it. But when it comes to the question of whether courts should impose joint custody over the objection of one of the parties, serious conflict erupts. Views range from those who believe joint custody should be the default rule in custody disputes to those who believe it should never be ordered in contested cases. Judges also disagree on when imposed joint custody is appropriate, with some adopting a more permissive view than others.

In *Kaplanis v. Kaplanis*, the Ontario Court of Appeal's most recent foray into the joint custody arena, the court reiterated its cautious approach to joint custody in contested cases. The court held that joint custody should not be ordered in contested cases unless there is evidence that the parents are able to communicate effectively with one another, despite their animosity and personal differences.

In this article, I examine the fate of contested joint custody in the aftermath of *Kaplanis*. In contrast to some early pronouncements that joint custody was "alive and well" and being ordered in 50% of contested cases I found that joint custody was only being ordered in about *one-third* of contested cases.

However, not all of these joint custody orders were consistent with *Kaplanis*. Some courts will order joint custody in cases where the parents are unable to co-operate or communicate if there is a danger that the parent who would otherwise receive sole custody will attempt to exclude the other parent from the children's lives. In these cases, joint custody is ordered as a way of protecting the parent/child relationship.

There are also what I term "outlier cases", in which courts order joint custody where parents are incapable of communication and cooperation and where there is no need to make a joint custody order to protect one parent's relationship with the child. Many of these cases can be explained as reflecting an ideological belief on the part of the trial judge that joint custody arrangements are superior to sole custody, because they are best for children and/or fairest for the parents.

The case law also revealed two intriguing and unexpected trends. First, the *Kaplanis* inquiry into parental communication and co-operation has become the focal point of the courts' analysis of joint custody, sometimes to the exclusion of other salient factors. In many of the cases, the parent seeking joint custody had engaged in conduct that was sufficient in itself to dismiss the joint custody claim. Yet courts seldom dismiss claims on this basis. Instead, courts dismiss these claims on the grounds that the parents lack the ability to communicate and co-operate, as these cases invariably raise communication concerns.

Second, some courts — including the Ontario Court of Appeal — are denying claims for joint custody on the grounds that the parents are unable to communicate or co-operate, yet at the same time are ordering that the child spend equal time, or nearly equal time, with both parents. These orders raise questions that go to the heart of the reasoning in *Kaplanis*. If joint custody requires a certain degree of communication or co-operation, why is it that equal time parenting does not? Is it possible to parent children effectively on an equal time sharing model without having the minimum level of communication required of joint custody?

I examine each of these aspects of the post-*Kaplanis* case law in the pages that follow. I also examine how, under *Kaplanis*, the courts assess whether the parties have the ability to engage in effective communication. I begin, however, with a brief overview of the *Kaplanis* decision and the principles that emerge from it as a way of situating the subsequent discussion.

2. Joint Custody and Kaplanis

In *Kaplanis*, the Court of Appeal reiterated its longstanding disapproval of joint custody orders in contested cases and overturned an order for joint custody of the parties' pre-school aged daughter that had been made at trial. The evidence established that the parties' relationship had been a tumultuous one, both during the marriage and following separation. The child was only three months old at the time the parents separated and she had been in the care of her mother ever since. She was 20 months old at the time of trial. The father, who was self-represented both at the trial and on the appeal, sought an order for "parallel parenting" with the child spending alternate weeks with each parent. The mother sought sole custody. She argued that joint custody would be unworkable as she and the father were unable to communicate with each other without screaming. ...

Despite the mother's concerns about communication, Macdonald J. awarded joint custody, with the father receiving gradually increasing parenting time with the child. In very brief reasons, Macdonald J. held that there had been "no serious evidence of an inability of the father to respond to Victoria's needs when she was in his care" and noted that the mother herself had acknowledged the father to be a good parent. More importantly, Macdonald J. suggested that the mother's concerns about the couple's inability to communicate were more strategic than real. ... Finally, Macdonald J. also expressed the "hope" that "the parents will put closure on the disappointment and resentments that flow from the failed marriage."

Weiler J.A., speaking for the Court of Appeal, held that Macdonald J. had erred in two ways: by awarding joint custody when "there was no evidence of historical co-operation and appropriate communication between the parents" and by ordering joint custody "in the hope that it would improve the parenting skills of the parties." In the most important — and most frequently quoted — passage in the judgment, Weiler J.A. held that before an order for joint custody can be made in contested cases, there must be some evidence that the parents have the ability to communicate effectively with one another with respect to their children. ...

In determining whether parents have demonstrated the "ability to set aside their personal differences and to work together in the best interests of the children", Weiler J.A. held that the existence of an interim custody order and evidence of the parties' communication pursuant to that order would be relevant considerations. On the facts Justice Weiler held that joint custody should not have been ordered in the case, as there was no evidence of effective communication between the parties.

Although Weiler J.A. held that joint custody was not appropriate on the facts of *Kaplanis*, it is clear that the Court of Appeal was not intending to shut the door on joint custody in contested cases altogether. This is clear from Weiler J.A.'s statement that the mere fact that one parent professes an inability to communicate with the other will not preclude an order for joint custody. It is also clear from the Court of Appeal's decision in *Ladisa v. Ladisa* released the same day as *Kaplanis*. In *Ladisa*, the Court upheld a joint custody order made at trial, despite the mother's opposition to joint custody and the existence of a high level of conflict between the parents. The court held that the trial judge had not erred in ordering joint custody because the evidence established that "despite their strife ... the parents could and had communicated effectively and put the interests of the children ahead of their own."

The central message to take away from the *Kaplanis* and *Ladisa* decisions read together is that joint custody can be ordered over the objection of one parent, but only where the court is convinced that the parents have the ability to communicate effectively with one another. Several principles emerge from this holding. First, one parent's opposition to joint custody does not bar a joint custody order. Second, joint custody will seldom (if ever) be in a child's best interests if the parents are not capable of effective communication, as without the ability to communicate they will not be capable of jointly acting in their children's best interests. Third, there must be some evidence before the court that the parents are capable of this type of communication. It is an error to order joint custody in a contested case in the absence of evidence of effective communication, just as it is an error to order joint custody based on an aspiration that the parties will be able to set aside their conflict or as a way of encouraging them to do so.

Finally, as a preliminary matter, joint custody should only be considered where both parents have a strong claim to custody based on the factors courts consider under both the *Divorce Act* and the *Children's Law Reform Act* in custody disputes. If one parent's custody claim is far stronger than the others it will generally be in the children's best interest to be in the custody of that parent regardless of whether the parents are capable of effective communication. Although this is a basic point, in many cases it appears to have been lost in the post-*Kaplanis* world as a result of the emphasis on communication and co-operation in that decision. In both *Kaplanis* and *Ladisa*, the trial judges viewed both parents as having custody claims that were relatively equal. The Court of Appeal's focus on communication and co-operation needs to be situated against that backdrop.

But, *Kaplanis* also leaves important questions unanswered. Although communication and co-operation are the lynchpins of the *Kaplanis* analysis, *Kaplanis* does not tell us what the concepts of "effective communication and co-operation" mean in the custody setting. To put this point another way, how much communication and co-operation do you need in order to make joint custody work? Do you simply need to communicate the barest details of the child's time with you, or can you be even more minimalist and communicate only when something out of the ordinary arises? Does effective communication require any kind of regularity? Does it require parents to communicate about the day-to-day details of their children's lives at all so long as parents are able to discuss major decisions? Does effective communication require parents to adopt a positive — or at least a neutral — tone or can one parent insult or denigrate the other so long as that parent also conveys information about the child? In terms of co-operation, does effective co-operation mean that parents must be able to agree on most issues without recourse to outside decision makers? Does the use of a parenting coordinator, who makes decisions and breaks deadlocks for the parents, count as effective co-operation? Finally, are there situations where, because a child has special needs or because of other similar factors, a higher level of co-ordination and communication is needed in order for joint custody to work?

These questions underscore the point that, although *Kaplanis* tells us there must be evidence of effective communication before ordering joint custody in contested cases, it is not obvious what effective communication and co-operation mean in the joint custody context. In fact, different people will have different views as to the level of communication required to make joint custody work and as to whether the parties in a given case are capable of engaging in effective communication. As I explore in more detail below, to some extent these different views are reflected in the post-*Kaplanis* case law.

(a) Terminology

Before turning to examine the caselaw post-*Kaplanis*, it is important to say a few words about terminology. Terminology in the custody area is a source of extraordinary confusion because the terms used to denote post-divorce parenting arrangements are used inconsistently across cases and because there is some confusion among courts — including the Ontario Court of Appeal — as to what the various terms mean. Some courts, for example, use "joint custody" to refer to arrangements that give both parents shared decision making authority over significant child-rearing issues, what is often called joint "legal" custody in the academic literature. Other courts use joint custody to refer to arrangements in which the parents share the physical care of the child, what the academic literature refers to as joint "physical" custody. Some courts use the terms "joint custody", "shared custody" and "shared parenting" interchangeably, all to refer to arrangements in which both parents spend extensive — if not equal — time with the child. ...

In this article, I will use the terms in the following way. "Shared parenting" will refer to arrangements in which each parent spends extensive amounts of time with the children. ... I use "joint custody" to refer to arrangements in which parents share the authority to make significant decisions over their children's lives — that is, on matters relating to their children's education, health care and religious upbringing. Joint custody has traditionally been understood to mean that the parents must make decisions in each of these areas *jointly*, with the result that parents must resort to the court or another third party decision-maker when they are deadlocked. More recently some courts have made "joint custody" orders in which they have allocated different spheres of decision making to each parent. Under these orders, the parents "share" decision-making in the sense that they each have authority over some aspect of their children's lives but make decisions independently of each other. I include this type of order within my definition of joint custody, but I will specify when decision making authority is split in this way.

The last concept requiring definition is "parallel parenting." Parallel parenting emerged from the mental health professions as a way of permitting both parents to remain involved in their children's lives after separation while minimizing the need for interaction between them. The idea behind parallel parenting is that each parent cares for the child as he or she sees fit during the time the parent has with the child. There is no expectation of consultation between the parents, as each parent is entitled to establish his or her own routines and rules. In terms of decision making authority, each parent is entitled to make day to day decisions when the child is in his or her care. Authority over more significant decisions is typically split between the parties to avoid the need for consultation between them. Although parallel parenting is usually conceptualized as a form of joint custody or shared parenting by the courts, it is important to recognize that parallel parenting refers to a post-divorce parenting *model*, and not to the amount of time the child spends with each parent or to *joint* decision making. Parallel parenting can be used to structure parents' post-divorce interactions regardless of the amount of time the child spends with each parent as a way of defusing parental conflict and keeping parents disengaged.

3. Contested Joint Custody in the Post-*Kaplanis* World: An Overview of the Case Law

... There was an obvious gender dimension to the [67 Ontario] cases [between January 2005 and mid-May 2007 in which one parent sought joint custody and the other opposed it]. With only a very few exceptions, the party making the claim for joint custody was the father and the party opposing joint custody was the mother. In many of these cases, fathers also made claims for sole custody with joint custody being their fall back position.

Joint custody was ordered in only 23 cases, 34% per cent of the total. In almost all of the cases in [which] joint custody orders were made, the courts found the parties to be capable of effective communication and co-operation. But, not all of the cases in which joint custody was ordered were consistent with *Kaplanis*. While the court's conclusion that the parties were capable of effective communication appeared to rest on solid evidence in most of the cases, in at least 10 cases courts were willing to find sufficient communication and co-operation where evidence of communication was meager at best. Sometimes the evidence was so scant, and the interpretation of effective communication so strained, that the case is best viewed as an "outlier" decision, in which the court pays lip service to the *Kaplanis* analysis but the joint custody order appears to be driven by other factors.

On my read of the case law, the 23 cases in which courts ordered joint custody fell into three distinct categories. The first category involved cases that were consistent with *Kaplanis*, as there was evidence that the parties were capable of the kind of communication and cooperation *Kaplanis* demands. The second category involved cases in which the joint custody orders were difficult to reconcile with *Kaplanis* because there was a high level of conflict between the parents on child-related issues. In these cases, the joint custody orders appeared to derive from a concern that the parent who would otherwise receive custody would attempt to exclude the other parent from the child's life. Joint custody in these cases appeared to be about ensuring that both parents' relationships with the child were preserved and protected, not about the ability of the parents to engage in effective communication.

The third category also consisted of cases that were difficult to reconcile with *Kaplanis*. In these cases, courts awarded joint custody even though there was considerable evidence that the parents could not communicate and even though there was no concern that joint custody was needed to preserve one parent's relationship with the child. These cases were more difficult to explain. Some of the cases appear to have arisen from misapplications of *Kaplanis* or from strong ideological convictions that joint custody is a better post-divorce arrangement than sole custody because it is fair to parents and better for children.

Since there were at least 10 joint custody cases that fell in either the second or the third category, the number of contested cases in which the parents are capable of co-operation and communication is smaller than first appears. Removing these cases from the tally, joint custody orders consistent with *Kaplanis* were made in 13 of 67 cases, or in just under 20% of the total. This suggests that if *Kaplanis* is strictly applied, only about *one-fifth* of contested joint custody cases will result in joint custody orders.

By far the largest group in the sample consisted of cases in which the courts refused to order joint custody. In most of these cases, joint custody was refused because the court found that the parties did not have the capacity to co-operate or communicate, or — more accurately — the party seeking joint custody had demonstrated an unwillingness to cooperate with the other parent. There was also another dimension to these cases — in many of them the party seeking joint custody had engaged in conduct that was not in the children's best interests. These cases serve as an important contrast to the cases in which joint custody orders were made because they provide insight into the kind of conduct that courts view as demonstrating an inability — or unwillingness — to engage in effective communication.

To illustrate the impact of *Kaplanis* on Ontario case law, I begin by looking at how courts analyze whether the parties are capable of effective communication and co-operation. Whether they end up ordering joint custody or not, post-*Kaplanis* courts invariably engage in this analysis. ...

(a) Applying Kaplanis: Assessing the Parties' Ability to Communicate

The *Kaplanis* analysis requires courts to assess whether the parties are *capable* of effective communication. In assessing whether parents have this ability, most courts focus on the post-separation conduct of the parents, and specifically on conduct relating to their children. For example, courts will look to see if parents have been able to agree about their children's living arrangements, about schooling, how their children will spend the summer holidays and about extracurricular activities.

Sometimes courts will also examine whether the parties have been able to agree about other areas of dispute, including about financial matters. Courts that do this presumably interpret the parties' ability to agree on any significant issue as some evidence that they are capable of communicating and co-operating when it comes to their children, an assumption that may not always be borne out. Courts will also look at whether the parties have been able to communicate with one another post-separation, whether in person, by phone, by email or through a communication book. Where communication takes place in writing, courts will often scrutinize both the content and the tone of the dialogue to see if it conveys appropriate and adequate information about the child and to see if the communication is being used to denigrate or berate the other parent. Finally, courts will sometimes look to pre-separation conduct, particularly where the post-separation behaviour of the parents is simply a continuation of a pattern of poor communication and co-operation that existed during the marriage.

Although *Kaplanis* suggests that courts should examine whether the parties are *capable* of communication and co-operation, most courts focus on whether or not the parties have *actually* communicated or cooperated since they separated, rather than on whether they are capable of doing so. The assumption courts seem to be making in adopting this approach is that evidence that the parties have been able to agree and to make decisions affecting their children is a good indication — if not the best indication — that they are capable of communicating and co-operating. The emphasis on evidence of actual communication makes good sense. There is a very fine line between courts deciding that parents have the ability to communicate in the absence of any evidence that they have done so post-separation, and ordering joint custody in the "mere hope" that communication between the parties will improve, which *Kaplanis* tells us courts ought not to do.

In a small number of cases, however, courts have considered whether the parties are *capable* of communication and where they have done so they tend to be guided by the degree to which the parents have similar beliefs and value systems. For example, in *Bolduc v. Bolduc* (2006), 2006 CarswellOnt 5004, 31 R.F.L. (6th) 436 (S.C.J.); additional reasons at (2006), 2006 CarswellOnt 6559 (S.C.J.), the court denied a mother's claim for joint custody and awarded the father sole custody of a 3-1/2 year old girl in part because there were "significant differences between the parents on the issues of religion, schooling, nutrition and medical care." The court reasoned that a regime of joint custody would not work because there was "insufficient co-operation and agreement on a number of issues", suggesting that the number and magnitude of the differences between the parents made it unlikely that they would be capable of agreement. Conversely in *Benak v. Benak* (2005), 2005 CarswellOnt 9036 (S.C.J.); additional reasons at (2006), 2006 CarswellOnt 1360 (S.C.J.), the court ordered joint custody in part because there were no significant differences between the parents regarding "religion, schooling, medical care, the geographic area where the children should live, [and the parents'] moral values". In fact, because of the similarity of the parents' views, the court adopted the assessor's opinion that joint custody would work even if there was very little co-operation between the parties. ...

(c) Cases Where the Parties are Not Capable of Communication and Co-operation

Cases in which the parents are not capable of communication or cooperation span a range of situations. In a few of the cases, courts have found parents to be incapable of communicating simply because they have not done so since separation. In most of the cases, however, there is clear evidence of communication problems and lack of co-operation on the part of at least one of the parents, usually the parent seeking joint custody. Obvious examples of problematic communication include refusals by one parent to communicate with the other by not taking phone calls, failing to respond to email or to write in a communication book, or by using the communication book to write derogatory comments about the other parent. Some parents go to greater lengths to thwart communication, making themselves inaccessible by repeatedly changing their cell phone number or by refusing to open an email account. Conduct such as this is obviously incompatible with effective communication.

But many courts have gone beyond the obvious and have interpreted other actions as evidence of faulty communication or co-operation. For example, courts will view a pattern of conduct in which one parent is rude, insulting, argumentative, uncompromising, belligerent or threatening towards the other parent or in which one parent demeans, belittles or harasses the other parent as showing an inability to engage in effective communication. ... At the most extreme end, courts will find communication problems where there is a history of wife abuse or problems of anger management.

Similarly, expressions of contempt or derision for the other parent — particularly when these occur in the courtroom — or conduct which demonstrates a profound lack of respect and trust (such as taping phone conversations) will for many courts signal an inability to co-operate. Courts find it difficult to accept that a parent who has nothing good to say about the other, who shows no respect for the other's parenting abilities, or who is unable to control his or her anger in the courtroom will consult and co-operate. Conduct that undermines the other parent — such as drawing the children into the dispute, encouraging the children to act out or to denigrate the other parent, deliberately making life difficult for the other parent, or making false allegations of child abuse or of other criminal behaviour against the other parent — are also viewed by courts as non-cooperation. So too are refusals to accommodate the reasonable child-related requests of the other parent, such as ensuring that an allergic child's clothing be washed in special detergent to prevent skin reactions or consenting to counseling for the child. Finally, courts will view certain types of unilateral action — such as imposing an access regime on the other parent, refusing to support the children financially or unilaterally deciding to stop paying child support, or engaging in unilateral decision making when a joint custody order is in place — as evidence of an inability to co-operate.

Sadly, cases in which the conduct of the parent seeking joint custody demonstrates an inability to communicate or co-operate with the other parent abound in the post-*Kaplanis* case law. In fact, cases of this sort constitute the *majority* of contested joint custody cases. In many of the cases, the parent's conduct is so extreme that it goes beyond an unwillingness to co-operate with the other parent, or even a desire to act out against that parent, and becomes conduct that demonstrates an inability to act in the child's best interests. ... [I]n many of the cases, the conduct of the parent is so clearly contrary to the child's best interests that the conduct alone should have disentitled the parent from claiming joint custody. Since *Kaplanis*, however, conduct is often discussed as showing problems of parental communication or co-operation, rather than as conduct that itself undermines a custody claim.

There is also a gender dimension to these cases. Overwhelmingly, cases in which courts refuse to grant joint custody because of communication and co-operation problems involve problematic conduct on the part of men. ...

(d) Joint Custody to Protect a Parental Relationship

In a small number of the post-*Kaplanis* cases, joint custody is ordered in the face of high conflict and little communication or co-operation because the parent who would otherwise be awarded sole custody has attempted to exclude the other parent from the children's lives. Although courts often try to justify joint custody orders in these cases in *Kaplanis* terms, the orders are being made on a very different basis — to preserve and protect both parents' relationships with the children. These cases are less about communication and co-operation than they are about ensuring that parent/child relationships are protected.

There may be a slight gender dimension to these cases, although the number of cases was so small that it is not possible to assert this conclusively. In three of the five cases in this category it was mothers who had tried to marginalize the fathers' role in the children's lives. Joint custody was ordered in these cases because granting sole custody to the father would not be in the children's best interests (most often because the mother has been the children's primary caregiver), but there was a need to strengthen the father's role in the children's lives.

Mancini v. Mancini (2006), 2006 CarswellOnt 1080, 25 R.F.L. (6th) 137 (S.C.J.) is a good example of these cases. The parties in *Mancini* had a highly conflicted marriage and separated when their child was two. The high level of acrimony continued after separation and resulted in frequent and protracted litigation, particularly over the father's access to the child. The mother's persistent refusals to allow the father access led to her being found in contempt and in an interim order for joint custody with the child — then 4-1/2 years old — spending alternate weeks with each parent. The mother made a number of complaints to the children's aid society, alleging that the father was physically abusing the child. All of these complaints were investigated and dismissed as unfounded. The mother also sought to have the father charged with various offences in what the court termed an attempt to "use the police ... inappropriately to try to terminate or limit the [father's] access."

The custody trial, held 3 years after separation, lasted 19 days, with both parents testifying that the interim joint custody arrangement was not working. The court, however, found that the joint custody arrangement had been "more successful than the sole custody arrangement which preceded it" because it allowed the father to spend more time with the child. The court made an order for joint custody, noting that if the mother were to have sole custody, "she would try to thwart the [father's] relationship with [the child] and alienate [the father] as much as possible." Although the court suggested that the parties were "able to communicate and co-operate on some level in the best interests of the child" this conclusion is unconvincing in light of the high degree of animosity between the parents.

(e) Joint Custody "Outliers"

In several cases courts have made joint custody orders that are difficult — if not impossible — to reconcile with *Kaplanis* and that cannot be explained as a method of protecting one parent's relationship with the children. In some of these cases, the courts simply get the holding in *Kaplanis* wrong. The joint custody orders in these cases are not consistent with *Kaplanis* because the court has applied the wrong law.

In other cases, the courts find the parties capable of communication and co-operation when the evidence unequivocally points in the opposite direction. In these cases courts fail to identify conduct that is clearly controlling, manipulative or deceitful as evidence of an inability to cooperate or they misread acquiescence or submission by one party as evidence of co-operation. In most of these cases, the court's misreading of the evidence is so glaring that the decisions can only be understood as having being driven by an ideological bias in favour of joint custody. ...

Moyer v. Douglas (2006), 2006 CarswellOnt 8268 (S.C.J.) and *Levesque v. Little* (2006), 2006 CarswellOnt 7404 (S.C.J.); additional reasons at (2007), 2007 CarswellOnt 451 (S.C.J.) are examples of cases that misconstrue the *Kaplanis* holding. In *Moyer*, the court made an order for "parallel parenting" despite explicitly holding that joint custody was not an option in the case because the parents were unable to work co-operatively. *Kaplanis* does not, however, suggest that parallel parenting is appropriate where a couple is too conflicted for joint custody. Instead, the reasoning in *Kaplanis* suggests that neither joint custody (entailing joint decision making) nor parallel parenting (where decision making is allocated between the parties) should be ordered where the parents are incapable of communication or co-operation.

In *Levesque v. Little*, the court ordered joint custody in an extremely high conflict case where there was no possibility that the parties were capable of communication or co-operation. Communication between the parties was so bad that both were subject to peace bonds and restraining orders. The parties had been unable to agree on anything relating to their separation and during the year preceding trial all decisions regarding the children had to be made by court order. Despite finding that there was little possibility that the parties would "begin to communicate in the foreseeable future", the court ordered joint custody, reasoning that "[g]ranting sole custody to one party will likely escalate the tension between them." The court held that although *Kaplanis* discouraged joint custody where the parents could not communicate, it did not preclude courts from making joint custody orders if they were in the children's best interests. ...

Finally, the ideological basis of the court's decision to order joint custody was readily apparent in *Brook v. Brook* (2006), 2006 CarswellOnt 2514 (S.C.J.). ... [T]he father's conduct revealed longstanding problems that were relevant not only to his ability to co-operate and to communicate with the mother, but also to his ability to act as a parent. In *Brook*, the father verbally abused the mother throughout the marriage, and, on one occasion when he believed the mother had been unfaithful, the father chased her around the house with a knife and punched holes in the wall. After separation, the father was charged with threatening the mother with death and entered into a peace bond. The death threat came a year after the father had completed a 25 week course on violence against women. ...

The father's abusive behaviour should have made joint custody a non-starter as conduct undercutting the father's ability to act as parent and as conduct demonstrating an inability to engage in effective communication. As I discussed earlier, most courts view bullying and abusive behaviour as an example of poor communication. However, the court ordered joint custody, finding not only that the parties were capable of sufficient communication but, rather shockingly, that there was no evidence of problematic communication in the case.

There can be no doubt that the court's view of the evidence was coloured by an ideological affinity for joint custody, because the court said as much in explicit terms:

> A non-custodial is frequently perceived in the community as undeserving or unqualified to have custody of his or her child; and this perception is not always accurate. The result is that, sadly, a great many non-custodial parents are unfairly seen as second-class parents. It is not in the best interests of a child to have one of his or her parents viewed in this fashion. The interests of a child are better served by having two parents participate in making the important decisions in his or her life. Therefore, I begin with the rebuttable presumption that an order for joint custody is best for a child and then I look for evidence to the contrary. This means that the initial burden of proof falls on the party opposing a joint custody order to rebut the presumption.

The court's ideological convictions were so strong that the father's conduct in the case was not sufficient to rebut the joint custody presumption.

(f) Two Unexpected Trends

The post-*Kaplanis* case law revealed two interesting and unanticipated trends. The first of these is the over-use of the *Kaplanis* analysis. *Kaplanis* is used in cases where it is clear that joint custody is not in the children's best interests because of problematic conduct of one of the parents. The *Kaplanis* analysis presumes two fit parents who have credible custody claims. Where one parent does not have a strong custody claim, there should be no need to ask about the prospect for parental cooperation. Whether the parents are capable of communicating or not, a parent who behaves in ways that are contrary to the child's best interests should not be granted joint custody. Post-*Kaplanis*, however, many courts ask about "communication" even though joint custody is clearly not in the children's best interests because of one parent's problematic behaviour. In effect, the *Kaplanis* focus on "communication and cooperation" seems to have taken over the analysis of joint custody claims, with the result that courts will deny joint custody on the basis that the parties are incapable of effective communication and co-operation when joint custody should have been denied because of problematic parental conduct.

The second trend concerns the relationship between legal custody — the right to make significant decisions regarding the child — and physical custody — the amount of time each parent spends with the child. Some courts are denying claims for joint custody on the ground that the parents are unable to communicate or co-operate, yet at the same time are ordering that the parents have equal time, or nearly equal time, with the children. Orders such as these raise an obvious question — if joint custody is not in the children's best interests because the parents are incapable of civil communication and co-operation, how is it in the children's best interests to spend equal time in households which do not share information, or worse, which are mired in open conflict? ...

One of the most puzzling examples of this [second] trend is the decision of the Ontario Court of Appeal in *Roy v. Roy* (2006), 2006 CarswellOnt 2898, 27 R.F.L. (6th) 44 (C.A.). In a very short judgment, the Court of Appeal overturned the trial judge's decision to order joint custody but kept the equal time provision of the order intact. The court held that "virtually the entire record" established that the foundation for joint custody was absent due to the "horrendous mistrust" and "enormous antipathy" between the parties. However, the court then held — without elaboration — that "the record amply supports the trial judge's conclusion that '[i]t is in the children's best interests that they spend more or less equal time with each parent.'" ...

Decisions such as these raise fundamental questions about parenting and about the kinds of arrangements that are likely to promote children's well-being following divorce. Equal time parenting arrangements are frequently based on the assumption that it is in the children's best interests to spend as much time as possible with each parent. For some children, this will undoubtedly be true. But the question that arises here is whether this assumption is likely to be true in situations where parents are in such high conflict that there is no prospect of communication or co-operation between them. Will equal time arrangements work well for children if there is no communication and co-ordination between their two households?

At present, the answer to this question remains a matter of speculation. High conflict parents who engage in equal time parenting have not been the subject of empirical study. In fact social scientists have only recently begun to examine families who engage in equal time parenting arrangements. The results of these studies, while preliminary, indicate that equal time parenting is practised by a very small subset of the divorcing population (less than 10%) and that this subset looks very different from the divorcing population as a whole. One distinctive feature of this group is that the parents generally work well with each other and are able to agree on their parenting arrangement without any legal intervention. These studies also suggest that equal time parenting arrangements require a significant degree of co-ordination between households because of the logistical complexities of residing in two places.

The research on the effects of conflict on children's adjustment to divorce is also relevant here. Studies have consistently shown that exposure to parental conflict is harmful to children and a major source of reduced well-being. To the extent that equal time parenting arrangements expose children to conflict they will have a negative impact on children's well-being.

Even if parents are able to contain their conflict the question remains — is it possible to raise children on an equal time model without the minimum level of communication joint custody requires? If parents are unable to co-operate and communicate, how will they handle situations where the child has forgotten possessions at one parent's house? How will the parents ensure that information about the children's school, extracurricular activities, birthday parties and other special events is communicated to each household? Equal time parenting presents high conflict couples a myriad of opportunities to battle one another. It is hard to see how these arrangements can be in the child's best interests where the parents are too conflicted to exercise joint custody.

4. Conclusion

The post-*Kaplanis* case law indicates that Ontario courts take a cautious approach to joint custody in contested cases and tend to make joint custody orders sparingly. For the most part, courts are not making joint custody orders where it is clear that the parties are incapable of cooperation and communication. Some joint custody decisions are ideologically driven but these are very few in number.

The case law does, however, reveal some areas of concern. For one, the case law is full of assessments recommending joint custody in the face of high levels of discord and problematic parental conduct. This is a troubling pattern and one that raises questions about the assumptions assessors bring to their task.

For another, the preponderance of cases involving destructive conduct by parents raises questions about custody presumptions when — or if — custody law reform returns to the political agenda. These cases suggest that a presumption of joint custody — even a rebuttable one — will be contrary to children's best interests in many cases.

Finally, courts should be wary of making orders for equal time parenting where the parents are too highly conflicted to exercise joint custody. It is hard to imagine that children can thrive in an equal time arrangement if even the most basic level of communication is beyond their parents' abilities.

NOTES AND QUESTIONS

1. Should there be an express statutory presumption in favour of joint custody? Although many witnesses before the Special Joint Committee proposed a presumption in favour of joint custody, the committee ultimately decided in *For the Sake of the Children* (at 42) that presumptions favouring any particular form of parenting arrangement could obscure the differences between families. It feared that such a presumption might result in the imposition of joint custody where it was clearly inappropriate such as in families with a history of domestic violence. In "The Language and Ideology of Shared Parenting in Family Law Reform: A Critical Analysis" (2003-2004), 21 C.F.L.Q. 1, Elizabeth Hughes argues, however, (at 15) that the central assumption of equal parental authority is "buried in the text of the *Report*".

2. The terminology in this area of law has not been consistent. Terms such as "joint custody", "shared parenting", and "parallel parenting" are used to describe a variety of arrangements and are sometimes used interchangeably.

In its classic usage, the term "joint custody" "describes an arrangement where both parents have joint legal responsibility for making major decisions concerning their child's welfare involving such matters as the child's education, religious upbringing, and health. The child may reside primarily with one parent or spend an equal amount of time with each parent. The order may stipulate how decisions are to be made when there is no agreement between the parents. In *Johnston v. Johnston* (2004), 49 R.F.L. (5th) 82 (Alta. Q.B.), Justice Mahoney stipulated (para. 27) that, where the parents could not agree on a major decision, they were to refer the matter to "the Family Mediation Services program of the Government of Alberta or other mediation agency to resolve the dispute before making a court application". Justice Aston stated in *M. (T.J.) v. M. (P.G.)* (2002), 25 R.F.L. (5th) 78 (Ont. S.C.J.) at para. 36, that the parents were to make decisions regarding education and religious instruction jointly and that either could apply to the court "by Notice of Application for a summary disposition of any matter upon which they disagree".

The term "shared parenting", although not always used consistently by all judges or commentators, most commonly refers to a situation where the parents jointly exercise parenting authority as set out above and the child resides in each parent's home for approximately equal periods of time, usually on a rotating basis.

In recent years, some judges have imposed "parallel parenting" as a form of legal custody in high-conflict cases. The term has again been used to describe a variety of arrangements, but most frequently "parallel parenting" entails very detailed rules that in effect divide various incidents of custody. Each parent has the equal right to make day-to-day decisions when the child is with him or her, but decision-making with respect to major issues is commonly divided. Thus, one parent may have authority to decide a child's religious instruction while the other determines the child's education. Usually there is no expectation of collaboration and mutual decision making, although the hope is that co-operation between the parents may develop later. Often, parents are directed to communicate through a "communications book" or by e-mail only. As Justice Aston explained in *M. (T.J.) v. M. (P.G.)* (2002), 25 R.F.L. (5th) 78 (Ont. S.C.J.) at para. 20:

> The evolution of the case-law on joint custody orders in Ontario is nicely summarized by Bellamy J. in *Dagg v. Pereira* (2000), 12 R.F.L. (5th) 325 (Ont. S.C.J.), at paras. 39–45. She identifies *Mol v. Mol*, [1997] O.J. No. 4060 (Ont. Gen. Div.) as a significant turning point. In that case, Kruzick J. reviewed a substantial number of cases from across Canada to conclude that "joint custody" can be an appropriate disposition even in cases where parents are openly hostile and unco-operative if crafted as "parallel parenting" instead of "co-operative parenting". Consequently, "parallel parenting" orders have become a form of joint custody, a sub-category if you will, which does not depend upon co-operative working relationships or even good communication between the parents. The concept (consistent with subsection 20(1) of the *Children's Law Reform Act*) is that the parents have equal status but exercise the rights and responsibilities associated with "custody" independently of one another. Section 20(7) ... provides clear authority for the court to deal separately and specifically with "incidents of custody". The form of a "parallel parenting" order addresses specific incidents of custody beyond a mere residential schedule for where children will reside on a day-to-day basis. For example, in *South v. Tichelaar*, [2001] O.J. No. 2823 (Ont. S.C.J.), the court granted "joint custody" but then went on to give the father sole decision-making authority over the children's sporting activities and the mother sole decision-making authority over the dental health of the children.

Justice Aston also suggested (para. 21):

> The words "custody" and "joint custody" are often used as shorthand descriptors. However, I am convinced that many custody and access trials could be avoided if parents had to first describe, without using the words "custody" or "joint custody", what specific rights and responsibilities they wish to have, or are willing to share with the other parent. The phrase "joint custody" is emotionally charged. The parent who does not have the child on a day-to-day basis, still typically the father, pursues the Holy Grail of joint custody to avoid being reduced to the status of a mere visitor to the child. This case is typical. Inevitably, the issue is framed as a question of parental rights rather than an allocation of parental responsibilities.

Often "parallel parenting" orders are used in situations where one parent is being frozen out of a child's life and the courts seek to ensure that the child will have meaningful contact with both parents. For critical commentary, see Epstein and Madsen, "Joint Custody with a Vengeance: The Emergence of Parallel Parenting Orders" (2004), 22 C. F. L.Q. 1. See also the response by Barbara Fidler and Rachel Birnbaum, "Commentary on Epstein and Madsen's Joint Custody with a Vengeance: The Emergence of Parallel Parenting Orders" (2005), 24 C.F.L.Q. 337.

The Ontario Court of Appeal referred to *M. (T.J.) v. M. (P.G.)* with apparent approval in *Ursic v. Ursic* (2006), 32 R.F.L. (6th) 23 (Ont. C.A.); additional reasons at (2007), 2007 CarswellOnt 694 (C.A.) noting (at para. 26): "Many trial courts have recognized that joint custody under a parallel parenting regime may be suitable where both parents love the child and should play an active role in the child's life, yet have difficulty communicating or reaching a consensus on the child's upbringing."

The inconsistency in labelling various custody arrangements does not necessarily create problems as long as the actual order (or agreement) clearly indicates the rights and responsibilities of the parents. However, as noted by the Ontario Court of Appeal in *Segal v. Segal* (2002), 26 R.F.L. (5th) 433 (Ont. C.A.), it may be confusing to order that parents have joint custody and also specify that one of them has final decision-making authority. Such an order is more appropriately described as granting sole custody to one parent but imposing an obligation on that parent to consult the other before making major decisions regarding the child. See also *Tauber v. Tauber* (1999), 43 O.R. (3d) 42 (Gen. Div.); affirmed as to custody (2000), 6 R.F.L. (5th) 442 (Ont. C.A.); additional reasons at (2000), 8 R.F.L. (5th) 441 (Ont. C.A.), where the judge concluded that joint custody was inappropriate because the parents of an 18-month-old child lacked the necessary trust and mutual commitment to co-operate. Justice Jennings awarded custody to the mother but required her to "consult" the father "in a timely manner" prior to making major decisions about the child's health, education, religion or general welfare. The stated intention (at 45) was that "so far as it is possible to do so, all major decisions be consensual and be taken by the wife after consultation with the husband".

3. Recently, in *Warcop v. Warcop* (2009), 2009 CarswellOnt 782 (S.C.J.), Justice Gray made a joint custody order under which a boy of 2 was to spend equal time with his father and mother. The mother strenuously opposed joint custody and there was evidence that the parties had difficulty co-operating shortly after their separation. Justice Gray found that things had improved. The parents were now communicating fairly effectively through e-mails and a log book and co-operating reasonably well. While noting that the Ontario Court of Appeal decisions in *Baker v. Baker* (1979), 8 R.F.L. (2d) 236 (Ont. C.A.) and *Kruger v. Kruger* (1979), 11 R.F.L. (2d) 52 (Ont. C.A.) suggested that joint custody should rarely be imposed on parents, Justice Gray stated (paras. 1 and 94):

> The courts have moved a long way since then. ...

> In the final analysis, in my view, an order for joint custody is not to be rejected based on any rigid standard as formerly reflected in *Baker, supra*. The focus is simply on the best interests of the child. The best interests of the child will obviously not be fostered if the parents are unable to communicate and cooperate in making decisions that affect the child. However, a standard of perfection is not required, and is obviously not achievable. The issue is whether a reasonable measure of communication and cooperation is in place, and is achievable in the future, so that the best interests of the child can be ensured on an ongoing basis. In making this assessment, the Court must be governed by the evidence that has been presented as to the communication and cooperation between the parties to date; the mechanisms that are in place to ensure that it will continue; and the assessment of the judge as to the capabilities of the parties to do so in the future.

In their commentary on the case in 2009-13 TWIFL, Fam. L. Nws. 2009-13 (2009), Philip Epstein and Lene Madsen were particularly troubled that the young boy was expected to adjust to a move roughly every two days. They wrote:

> This case highlights the difficulties that courts are having in determining whether to make a sole custody versus joint custody order particularly when young children are involved. We are uncomfortable with this decision because of the very young age of the child and the schedule that was imposed upon him. ...

> Justice Gray essentially found that *Baker v. Baker* ... and *Kruger v. Kruger* have been overruled by the passage of time. This is a somewhat novel theory of *stare decisis*, but in fairness to Justice Gray, there have been a host of cases since *Baker* and *Kruger* in which the Court of Appeal of Ontario has awarded joint custody when the circumstances were far from exceptional. Justice Gray recognized that the more traditional order in these circumstances would have been a custody order to one parent with generous access to the other. ...

> This decision will significantly encourage those that propose a joint custody presumption and bring joy to fathers' rights groups. It will alarm many on the other side. ...

> Justice Gray has struggled with the concepts of joint custody versus sole custody and tried to make sense of many conflicting decisions. We have the uncomfortable feeling, however, that this case became more of a philosophical discussion about the merits of sole custody versus joint custody and, somehow, the needs of a very young child might not have been as fully considered as they might have been.

4. For futher reading, see Shaffer, "Joint Custody, Parental Conflict and Children's Adjustment to Divorce: What the Social Science Literature Does and Does Not Tell Us" (2007), 26 C.F.L.Q. 221.

7. Parental Alienation

As mentioned in the introduction to this chapter, there are extreme cases in which one parent completely, and insidiously, alienates the affections of the children from the other parent. These cases often include allegations against the estranged parent that are difficult to believe; but, if true, amount to child abuse. The case below is a recent and striking example of the difficulties faced by courts in resolving alienation cases.

The parents were both medical professionals. Their relationship began in 1993; they married in 1996; and they separated in 1998. The three children resided with the mother after the separation. The maternal grandmother was overbearing and clearly influenced the mother's conduct. The mother slowly, and persistently, began to exclude the father from the children's lives. There were several interim court orders granting the father access. For the most part, the mother disobeyed them. An assessment was ordered. The assessor made the difficult recommendation that the children be in the custody of the father because the mother was very unlikely to allow any contact with the father and because the children needed to be "de-programmed" in their attitude towards him.

L. (A.G.) v. D. (K.B.)

(2009), 93 O.R. (3d) 409, 2009 CarswellOnt 188 (S.C.J.)

1 McWATT J: There are two issues to be decided in this trial. First, is who shall have custody of the three female children of the marriage, aged 14, 11 and 9. There has never been any order for the children's custody since the parents separated. They reside with their mother, K.D. The Applicant, A.L. seeks sole custody with no access rights to their mother except for the purposes of counseling. The Applicant alleges that K.D. has and continues to alienate the children from him. He offers this court two choices as a solution. They are:

> 1. Leave the children with the Respondent and ensure that the children will have no relationship with him; or

> 2. Give the Applicant sole custody of the three children and, with counseling and time, the children may have a relationship with both parents.

2 The second issue I must decide is whether K.D. is in contempt of the ... orders made in relation to the children. ... [The reasons relating to that issue are omitted.]

21 Before the couple married, during the marriage and after their separation, there are a number of incidences of note which set the tone of this couple's relationship up to the present time. First, prior to the marriage, A. L. and K. D. would go out together for dinner. K., D's mother, would take care of D [the oldest daughter who was born two years before the parents married]. K. D. would leave the table several times to talk to her mother by phone. A. L. felt that the Respondent's mother controlled the Respondent and used the frequent contacts with her daughter to prevent the couple from having a good time together. The Applicant also noted that the Respondent's mother would complain of chest pains in order to keep her daughter's attention focused on herself rather than on A. L.

22 On one occasion, at the front of K. D's mother's home, the mother quickly exited the home and confronted A. L. insisting "Christine is mine! Christine is mine to help me with her father." While yelling this to A. L., the Respondent's mother was punching the Respondent at the same time. The Respondent's father was very ill at the time and died not long afterwards. A. L. took the Respondent and left the mother's home, but K. D. had the Applicant stop the vehicle at a pay phone where she spoke to her mother for an hour. The couple then went home.

23 K. D's mother accused A. L. of raping the Respondent and impregnating her. K. D. was too afraid to contradict her mother at the time, but eventually told her that she was not raped.

24 A. L. came to learn that K. D's mother seriously and consistently beat the Respondent as she grew up. A. L. saw the mother regularly wear a strap around her neck in her home before they were married. A. L. witnessed the mother drag one of her young grandchildren (K. D's sister's child) from one part of her basement to another part of it. The Applicant was reassured by the Respondent, however, that the mother would never do anything like that to their children.

25 K. D's evidence in a May 9, 2008 affidavit filed in this court starkly describes the kind of upbringing she had and the effect it had on her. She swore the following:

> I have used physical force to discipline my children. I grew up in an immigrant strict Catholic home. I know what it is like to be slapped severely for not obeying your parents. I had bruises for weeks after my beatings. The more severe the beatings became the angrier I became, and the more determined I became to stand my ground. Needless to say, the beatings continued and continued. No one talked to me about the issues ... no one tried to reason with me because my views were not their views. They beat me until I became submissive, but my anger grew inside. That is why we have so many angry children.

26 During their marriage, the police were called to intervene in different situations on three occasions. On the first occasion, in 1998, A. L. was holding J. in his arms. K. D. demanded that he give her the child, grabbed the baby from his arms, put the child on the floor and began to push the Applicant which ended in his falling on the kitchen table and onto the floor. Although no evidence of the parties' weights and heights was led in the trial, my observation of them was that, at least in 2008, A. L. is much larger in height and weight than the Respondent. During the incident, D. was screaming and appeared to be horrified. K. D. disappeared from the kitchen where the incident had taken place only to appear again with abrasions on her knuckles and the police in the house. The police spoke to the couple, A. L. left the house and stayed away for a while. No charges were laid against either party.

27 In the second incident where police were called, the parties were in the bedroom of the Binsgarth home. K. D. pushed the Applicant into the closet doors and called the police. J. was in her crib in the room at the time. The police attended, spoke to the couple and left. No one was charged.

28 On a third occasion, after A. L. had spoken to his lawyer about how the Respondent spoke to him in front of the children, he was advised by counsel, to try and tape the Respondent during such a conversation. While A. L. and his family were in their vehicle going grocery shopping during the incident, he recalled that somewhere near Bloor St. and Castlefrank Rd., he tried to turn on the tape recorder in his pocket. K. D. saw the tape recorder, began to berate the Applicant in front of the children and tried to grab the recorder but could not. A. L. exited the vehicle and K. D. locked all of the doors with herself and the two children inside. A. L. called the police to get the Respondent to open the doors. The police attended and told the couple to cool off. A. L. testified that he did not need to cool off after the incident, but only felt relief that he was separating from the Respondent.

1998–2000

29 The couple separated in late 1998. While A. L. lived on the third floor of his home, he had virtually no contact with his two daughters. He had no time alone with them at all.

30 The Applicant enlisted the assistance of the Catholic priest who had married him and K. D. A. L. converted to Catholicism once the couple had decided to marry. K. D. made no attempts to attend for the arranged counseling.

31 During this period, A. L. made arrangements for counseling with another professional in family matters. On the third meeting, K. D. did not attend. The doctor terminated the counseling.

32 On February 9, 1999, in the Petition for Divorce, the Applicant swore the following:

> (a) The Husband believes that the Wife, without good reason, has deliberately attempted to limit any meaningful involvement he can have with his children. He is concerned that the Wife's overprotective parenting will have negative effects on the children's development. Despite his clear opposition since D. was born, the Wife has continued to choose her mother, who is not in good health, as the caregiver for the children. The Wife's mother openly dislikes the children's father, insists on speak-

ing Polish to her daughter in his presence and will not take any direction from him or even allow him to pick up the children while in her care.

The Petitioner has consistently advised the Respondent that he wishes to have an active role in the raising of the children, including sharing supervision of them at mealtimes, settling them in bed at night, helping decide who their caregivers should be and deciding on their schooling. The Respondent does not accept the Petitioner's parenting input nor agree with his views on encouraging more age-appropriate independent behaviour in the children. As a result, the Petitioner's responsibilities as a father in the ongoing marriage have continued to be eroded. The Petitioner fears if he were to lose custody on separation, that he will have little, if any, meaningful input into the raising of the children, and the children will not develop to their full potential.

Prior to the date of separation, the Wife often demeaned the Husband in front of the children and, since they have been living separate and apart under the same roof, her comments have become increasingly derogatory and inappropriate. When the Husband recently returned from a conference, the Wife told the children in front of him that he had "abandoned" them. The Wife is now attempting to punish the Husband by alienating the children from their father, without any apparent concern for the impact of her conduct on the children.

33 The effects of K. D's behaviour before and after the separation are evidenced most clearly in the words of D. to her father. D., who was five or six years old at the time, told her father, "You're not going to be my daddy anymore. Uncle G. (The Respondent's brother) is going to be my daddy." She also told her father "I'm going to make your life difficult" and "Dad, just do what Mummy says. It's much easier."

34 Whenever A. L. traveled on business during these times, he would call home, but no one would answer his calls.

35 Although separating in November, in December, 1998, the parties resumed their relationship for one night. Their third child, K., was conceived. She was born on September 16, 1999. A. L. had no involvement in K. D's third pregnancy as he was given little information about it. In fact, he found out about the child's birth from D's teacher. He visited the Respondent and the child in the hospital.

36 The Respondent slept with all three children in the master bedroom of the couple's home on Binsgarth.

Court Orders

37 Various orders were made while the couple was separated, but living under the same roof. On March 8, 1999, an order for custody and access set out a schedule for the Applicant to have time with his children. He did not get that access as a result of the Respondent's control over the children.

38 On June 3, 1999, the court ordered an assessment of the family by Dr. Barbara Fidler with a Parent Questionnaire to be filled out by both parties and delivered to Dr. Fidler by June 11, 1999. During the assessment phase of Dr. Fidler's report, the Applicant had access to his children most of the times ordered by this court. Dr. Fidler's Parenting Plan Assessment Report was delivered February 1, 2000.

Dr. Fidler's Report and Evidence at the Trial

39 Dr. Fidler noted K. D's inability to support the children's relationship with their father in 1999 and 2000. Her evidence about this conclusion came from the following observations of and experiences with the Respondent, the Applicant and the children:

(i) K. D. was astonished when Dr. Fidler wanted to see the children with their father;

(ii) K. D. advised that A. L. was not permitted to pick up or drop off the children at her mother's home where they were staying at the time;

(iii) the children did not have any opportunity to spend time alone with their father as K. D. was always present during court ordered access;

(iv) K. D. had a very strong belief that the children could be harmed by A. L.;

(v) K. D's level of vigilance and monitoring was unusual:

(vi) Dr. Fidler noticed a change in D's behaviour when her mother was around, which Dr. Fidler noted as significant behaviour for a 5 year old child;

(vii) Dr. Fidler agreed that D's view of her father was based more on her mother's actions than her father's actions;

(viii) Dr. Fidler had scheduled a visit with K. D. and A. L. during a period of time when the children were supposed to be napping or in school. K. D. changed the children's schedules that day and the children were present. Dr. Fidler explained that they could not have the discussion with the children present;

(ix) K. D. was unable to trust anyone other than her own mother to take care of the children;

(x) K. D. had noteworthy anxiety about the children being apart from her and about her being apart from the children;

(xi) K. D. overprotected the three children to the point of infantilizing all of them. D., at 5 years old was not yet toilet trained. J., at 3 years old, still used a bottle to feed at night; and

(xii) K. D's concerns about A. L's parenting ability were not validated during the assessment.

40 Dr. Fidler concluded, in February of 2000, that

The children are at significant risk for becoming aligned with their mother and in turn alienated from their father. Presently, and given her age, D. is the child most at risk. She is likely to set the stage for her younger siblings, who may follow suit at a younger age than is typical. Clinical intervention is necessary to assist K. D. to understand the complexity of D's feelings and reactions, which are not independent of Mother's, and to assist her to cope with these in a manner minimizing D's loyalty bind and confusion, while at the same time fostering her relationship with her father. Ultimately, D. cannot possibly feel comfortable relating to her father freely and positively given her mother's negative and angry feelings towards him.

K. D. has had significant difficulty complying with Court orders. K. D. has exhibited a notable disregard for authority and remained closed to reason and to opinions that differ from hers. Her concerns, including her perceptions of and her feelings for A. L., his ability to parent, and the children's needs and best interests, provide a rationalization for her noncompliance. Determining consequences for noncompliance consistent with these children's best interests presents a significant challenge.

For one, "make up time" becomes cumbersome to agree upon and implement especially given the parents' animosity and ineffective communication. In addition the three children, each at different developmental stages have very different needs and interests. The parenting plan even if ultimately agreed to, needs to be put into a Court Order. *It is recognized though that a Court Order is likely to be insufficient to ensure implementation and Mother's compliance.* Effective implementation will remain even more difficult if not impossible while the parents remain in the same home. Hopefully, the situation will improve after the physical separation, however, difficulties are likely to continue. A parenting coordinator may assist the family to implement their Court Ordered parenting arrangements.

A recommendation for sole custody to one parent, or for joint custody is contraindicated at this time. The parents remain unable to communicate effectively and thus joint custody is unrealistic. *While the recommended usual schedule has the children living primarily with their Mother, a recommendation for sole custody to her is contraindicated due the significant concerns related to her parenting and her willingness and ability to involve A. L. in the children's lives and decision-making. Further, the results indicate that K. D. may misuse the authority that accompanies sole custody. A. L's input into medical and educational decisions is imperative given not only his knowledge-base, but also given his receptivity to advice and guidance. K. D.'s overprotective parenting and her anxiety and fears are likely to colour her judgment and decision making at times. Also, A. L. is more likely to involve K. D. in major decisions than she is to involve him. Furthermore, he is more likely to foster the children's relationship with her than she is with him.*

41 She dismissed any concerns that A. L. was unable to properly care for the children or that the Applicant had ever sexually abused the children.

2000 to 2006

42 By March 13, 2000, Justice Benotto recommended that Dr. Fidler's Parenting Plan be implemented. She also recommended counseling for D. and the Respondent, noting that the children were at "substantial risk" as a result of their mother's conduct. There is no evidence that K. D. went to any counseling ordered by the court. A. L. arranged for counseling for D. The child went for a time and then the counseling was stopped by the Respondent. D. refused to speak to her father at this time. She was 6 years old.

43 Again, on May 4, 2000, Justice Benotto made an order in this matter appointing a parenting coordinator. The schedule of overnight visits set out by Dr. Fidler and ordered by Justice Benotto on March 13, 2000 was never adhered to by the Respondent. Instead, A. L. had two weekends with his children after March 13, 2000. During the second weekend, the Respondent called constantly to see how the children were doing. D. constantly asked who was calling. After that visit, the children were never brought back to the Applicant's house again.

44 Pursuant to the March 13, 2000 order, A. L. was to have two evenings per week with the children. In the summer, he was to have time with the children. Some of this access took place. By September 2000, however, the Respondent did not give A. L. any time alone with the children.

45 Between 2000 and 2006, the Applicant drove the children to school and back on Tuesdays and Thursdays. He arranged his schedule, as he had done throughout the children's lives, to accommodate this access to them. In fact, the Applicant rarely took his children to school without the Respondent being there for the rides.

46 K. D. also moved away from the Applicant's home after he had chosen to move close to her and the children after the separation. Only after the Respondent's move was A. L. able to take D. to and from school alone. That stopped shortly after it began, however, at the Respondent's whim.

47 Any attempts that A. L. made through professionals to talk to K. D. about parenting the children failed during this period. He finally resolved not to go to court because the court orders made no difference to the Respondent's behaviour. He concluded that it would be better to try and bargain for the children with the Respondent directly. She had warned him, during this period that "If you keep putting pressure on me about the children, you'll get nothing!" He did not go to court between 2000 and 2006.

48 The Applicant was also supposed to have his daughters overnight on Fridays and overnight on alternate Saturdays. On the first day of this court ordered schedule, one of the children was allegedly sick and had to be taken to the hospital. He did not see any of the children. The Applicant never failed to attend for any access dates except when he had to perform surgeries, but did not get his children for overnight Friday and Saturday during the years 2000 to 2006 except the two weekends set out above. The Respondent never gave A. L. a reason for denying this access except at the beginning where the children's illnesses were blamed and the children were also said not to want to go with him. These girls ranged in age from 6 years old to 1 year old at the time. If the Applicant was allowed to see the children, it was at the whim of the Respondent and only when they were all together. On odd

occasions, to shop or help one of the girls with math, K. D. allowed A. L. to be alone with his daughters.

49 A. L. began to accept K. D's rule over the children. Eventually, he was not allowed to see or speak to the children — but was left shouting good night to them through a door of K. D's home. Most times, he was not aware whether they were in the house. He did this for up to two years during this period.

50 During this period, A. L. joined the girls' school bodies in order to find out what his children were doing as the Respondent told him nothing about them. He went to all of their parent/teacher meetings and kept regular contact with their teachers and the principal of their school.

51 While having contact with his children during 2000 to 2006, A. L. noticed the following behaviours and heard the following remarks from his children:

> 1. D's behaviour toward him changed if her mother was not around. She told jokes and seemed more relaxed. When her mother came back into their presence, D. would stop joking and communicating with her father;
>
> 2. J. told her father that K. D. had told her to pack her bags and not to come home if she went to her father's house. (J. was between 6 to 12 years old during this period);
>
> 3. J. told the youngest child, K. that she could "never, never, never go to dad's house";
>
> 4. The girls talked to their father about wearing their "anti-dad coat";
>
> 5. D. once asked her father about doing something with him, "Are we doing that because a judge said that?";
>
> 6. J. and K. would give the Applicant hugs. K. once told her father "Don't tell mummy I did this", referring to a hug and kiss she gave him;
>
> 7. D. was aware that her mother was trying to keep her away from her father. She would whisper things quickly to her father so that her mother could not catch her speaking to him;
>
> 8. By 2006, the kids would neither hug nor kiss their father;
>
> 9. D. showed no affection towards the Applicant. K. eventually stopped looking at her father. J. would not talk to her father except in a monotone;
>
> 10. By 2006, D. had stopped talking to her father completely. By that point, all of the children simply ignored him.

52 Up to 2006, (and in fact to the present), there appears to be no justifiable reason why the Applicant's children have been kept from him or alienated from him to the point where they no longer spoke to him.

2006 to the Trial

59 On July 21, 2006, the Office of the Children's Lawyer (OCL) was appointed to represent the children at the request of the Applicant. A. L. was also given access to the children each Tuesday, Thursday and Saturday. He was never allowed, by the Respondent, to see his children pursuant to this order. There is no evidence in the trial as to why. On one access occasion, A. L. knocked on K. D's door, the Respondent opened the door, said "no" and closed the door.

60 On July 21, 2006, the Applicant was granted telephone access to the children to say goodnight each Monday, Wednesday and Friday. When he called, there was no answer except once during the period covered by this order. On that one occasion, K. D. answered the phone and said she would pass on a message to the children. Initially, when he began calling, there was a message machine at the Respondent's home on which A. L. could leave a message. After a while, the machine was disconnected.

61 By October, 2006, A. L. discovered that the Respondent was moving once again and had not advised him of this pursuant to the order of July 21, 2006.

62 A. L. had no contact with the children from October 2006 to May 2007 except by going to their school on Tuesdays and Thursdays as they were being picked up there by the Respondent. None of the children acknowledged him except the youngest, who smiled. The Respondent would divert the girls' attention away from A. L. by standing in front of him. During this time, A. L. went to the extent of leaving notes for his children on the garage door of their home in order to have some contact.

63 On May 3, 2007, a meeting with the parties and the OCL was cancelled because K. D. took the children. On May 11, 2007, the OCL recommended that D. get counseling and that J. and K. begin seeing their father immediately. A. L. said K. D. refused to respond to anything said at the meeting.

64 On July 17, 2007, the Respondent brought the children to court. Her reason behind this and taking the children to the OCL meeting in May was to have the children tell all involved that it was they who did not want to see their father. As well, however, K. D. herself believed that it would be harmful to the children to have a relationship with their father and to have D. in counseling in order to re-establish a relationship with her father. Yet, she also attested in court to the fact that the Applicant was a good father. She offered no reasons ever validated by any of the professionals involved in this case why A. L. should not be allowed to see his children.

65 On July 17, 2007, two hour supervised visits were ordered every Saturday between A. L. and J. and K. The access was gradually expanded to four hours. The two girls agreed to the expansion of time through the OCL.

66 D. was treated by Ms. Susan Chamberlain between October 2007 and March 2008, but had no access visit with her father. By March, 2008, D. ended counseling sessions with Ms. Chamberlain expressing the opinion that the therapist was "on her father's side".

67 On February 29, 2008, J. and K. agreed to expand their visits with their father to overnights. Both girls attended the first overnight visit. During the second overnight visit on March 7, 2008, J. contacted her mother and asked to go home. The Respondent contacted the police who arrived at A. L's home late that night. Both children returned to their mother's home.

68 After this point, the police were involved on a regular basis. K. D. called them to be present for many of the exchanges saying that she needed witnesses in order to defend herself in court against the allegations of contempt which are part of this trial.

69 The access supervisors and the police were hearing various messages from the two children during access exchanges. At times they said they did not want to see their father. On other occasions they indicated they wanted to see him. On all the evidence, however, I accept that the two younger children were not only warming to their father, contrary to the position of their mother who maintained that they wanted no contact with him, but were showing affection and love toward A. L. and re-establishing a relationship with him. D. never indicated that she would see her father until her mother asked her to attend access visits to supervise the two younger children. In exchange, D. received an Ipod electronic

device. She attended the visits with her father between March, 2008 and May, 2008 and then refused to have further contact with A. L. ...

71 In May, 2008, the OCL met with the parties and suggested access be expanded to alternate weekends and during the week. The Respondent did not agree to the mid-week access proposal. [Problems relating to access continued during June to September of 2008, although the two youngest daughters spent two good weeks with their father at a cottage in August. On September 26, the mother took the three girls to see their father, but they all refused to get out of the car.]

72 Court ordered access has not taken place between A. L. and the 3 children since this time except for one visit between K. and her father in October 2008.

73 Telephone contact with his children, ordered August 21, 2007 did not take place on numerous dates from the date of the order to the trial date. On most occasions, there was no answer when the Applicant called. On other occasions, he spoke with one or two of the children. Other times, the Respondent answered and advised the Applicant that the children did not want to speak to him.

74 Throughout this trial, the Applicant has not had the access to his children ordered by this court. He has complied with directions from the OCL, York Children's Aid Society and his lawyers in participating in counseling and parenting programs to create an atmosphere to assist in the children's development and in order to re-establish a relationship with them. ...

78 It is the position of the Office of the Children's Lawyer that the current situation cannot continue for the children. The children are taken to A. L's home on alternate weekends and sit in their mother's vehicle while their father tries to convince them to come into his home for an access visit. They refuse. The OCL submits that the anxiety and stress created by this arrangement is not in the best interests of the children.

79 The Children's Lawyer's interviews with the children reveal that both J. and K. want a relationship with their father, but have not visited him regularly since September 2008. The Children's Lawyer does not feel that K. D. can change her long-standing inability to support a relationship between the children and A. L. and, if left in her care, the children will have no relationship at all with him. ...

80 The OCL believes that D. will likely be traumatized given her long-standing views of her father and that the only way that a change of custody can be implemented is with the assistance of a specialized program that deals with children who have been alienated from their parents and with intensive therapeutic assistance. The Children's Lawyer supports a plan to address and minimize the damage that has been done to the children to this point in time by placing the children in the care of the parent who can best accomplish it. ...

Analysis

Child Alienation

85 The Applicant alleges that his children have been and are being alienated from him. Dr. Barbara Fidler was qualified as an expert in areas of clinical psychology, custody and access assessments and high conflict custody disputes, including parental alienation cases. She testified about the signs of alienation of children from a parent. Filed as exhibit 8A is Chapter 6 of a book she is publishing on the topic entitled "Understanding Child Alienation and Its Impact on Families". Her research, in part, is derived from the clinical research of others. For example, she refers, in the book, to the work of Richard Gardner and his term "parental alienation syndrome (PAS)". This term is defined as "a form of emotional child abuse almost exclusively seen in separated and divorced families in custody disputes".

86 I note that A. L. is alleging the alienation in this case began from the time each of his three children were born and has continued to the present day.

87 The Respondent did not significantly challenge Dr. Fidler's evidence about the concept and parameters of child alienation nor did she offer any evidence that contradicted the doctor. Although she did not accept Dr. Fidler's assessment dated February, 2000, again, she did not shake Dr. Fidler's evidence in the trial as it related to the doctor's conclusions eight years ago that the children faced a serious risk of aligning with K. D. and being alienated from A. L. She noted as far back as when D. was about 5 years old that she was already aligned with her mother against the Applicant. Dr. Fidler predicted that unless something changed in the family dynamic that the other children would do the same.

88 Dr. Fidler's evidence was that K. D. questioned A. L's ability to care for the children. She expressed a belief that A. L. might do something sexually inappropriate with the children and, as a result, had a high level of vigilance and monitoring when it came to access between the Applicant and the children. This raised a red flag for her 8 years ago regarding alienation of the children. So much so, that she made no recommendation that K. D. have sole custody of the children, which the doctor commented would have been the usual thing to recommend since the children had been with K. D. all of their lives.

89 What gives this eight year old report such weight in this trial is the fact that, on the evidence before me, not much has changed in K. D's behaviour since she was observed by Dr. Fidler. The children have aged and Dr. Fidler's predictions and fears have, in fact been realized. I would go so far as to say that, but for Dr. Fidler's refusal to recommend any form of sole custody of the children to the Respondent, the situation now before me might have been much worse. K. D. would, no doubt, have used the "authority that accompanies sole custody" to shut the Applicant out of his children's lives with greater dispatch. ...

91 As a result, I accept the evidence of Dr. Fidler in relation to conclusions about the parties' family by 2000. And, I accept her evidence about the concept and qualities of child alienation and its effect on families.

92 Pathological child alienation, then, can be summarized from the evidence as follows and as contained in Ex. 8B, p. 20 in the trial:

Table 15 Pathological Alienation: Warning Signs of Behaviours Exhibited by Child, Alienating Parent & Rejected Parent

Child behaviours

- View of parents one-sided, all good or all bad; idealizes one parent and devalues the other
- Vicious vilification of target parent; campaign of hatred
- Trivial, false and irrational reasons to justify hatred
- Reactions and perceptions unjustified or disproportionate to parent's behaviours
- Talks openly to anyone about rejected parent's perceived shortcomings
- Extends hatred to extended family and pets (hatred by association)
- No guilt or ambivalence regarding malicious treatment, hatred, etc.
- A stronger, but not necessarily healthy, psychological bond with alienating parent than with rejected parent
- Anger at rejected parent for abandonment; blames him/her for divorce
- Speech is brittle, a litany; obsessed; has an artificial quality; affect does not match words; no conviction; unchildlike, uses adult language; has a rehearsed quality
- Stories are repetitive and lacking in detail and depth
- Mimics what siblings report rather than own experience
- Denial of hope for reconciliation; no acknowledgement of desire for reconciliation

- Expresses worry for preferred parent, desire to care for that parent; or, defensive denial that child is indeed worried about parent

Alienating Parent Behaviours

- Allows and insists that child makes decisions about contact
- Rarely talks about the other parent; uninterested in child's time with other parent after contact; gives a cold shoulder, silent treatment, or is moody after child's return from visit
- No photos of target parent; removes reminders of the other parent
- Refusal to hear positive comments about rejected parent; quick to discount good times as trivial and unimportant
- No encouragement of calls to other parent between visits; rationalizes that child does not ask
- Tells child fun things that were missed during visit with other parent
- Indulges child with material possessions and privileges
- Sets few limits or is rigid about routines, rules and expectations
- Refuses to speak directly to parent; refuses to be in same room or close proximity
- Does not let target parent come to door to pick up child
- No concern for missed visits with other parent
- Makes statements and then denies what was said
- Body language and nonverbal communication reveals lack of interest, disdain and disapproval
- Engages in inquisition of child after visits
- Rejected parent is discouraged or refused permission to attend school events and activities
- Telephone messages, gifts and mail from other parent to child are destroyed, ignored or passed on to the child with disdain
- Distorts any comments of child that might justify accusations
- Doesn't believe that child has any need for relationship with other parent
- When child calls and is quiet or non-communicative, parent wrongly assumes pressure from target parent, or that child is not comfortable with target parent; evidence of bad parenting; does not appreciate that child is uncomfortable talking to alienating parent about target parent
- Portrays other parent as dangerous, may inconsistently act fearful of other parent in front of child
- Exaggerates negative attributes of other parent, and omits anything positive
- Delusional false statements repeated to child; distorts history and other parent's participation in the child's life; claims other parent has totally changed since separation
- Projection of own thoughts, feelings and behaviours onto the other parent
- Does not correct child's rude, defiant and/or omnipotent behaviour directed towards the other parent, but would never permit child to do this with others
- Convinced of harm, when there is no evidence
- False or fabricated allegations of sexual, physical and/or emotional abuse
- Denigrates and exaggerates flaws of rejected parent to child says other parent left "us," divorced "us" and doesn't love "us"
- Over-involves child in adult matters and litigation
- Child required to keep secrets and spy or report back on other parent
- Child required to be messenger
- Overt and covert threats to withdraw love and affection from child unless other parent is rejected
- Extreme lack of courtesy to rejected parent
- Relocation for minor reasons and with little concern for effects on child

Parental Behaviours that Make Rejection or Alienation More Likely

- Harsh, rigid and punitive parenting style
- Outrage at child's challenge to his/her authority
- Passivity or withdrawal in face of conflict
- Immature, self-centred in relation to child
- Loses temper, angry, demanding, intimidating character traits, but not to level of abuse
- Counter-rejecting behaviour
- Lacks empathic connection to child
- Inept and unempathic pursuit of child, pushes calls and letters, unannounced or embarrassing visits
- Challenges child's beliefs and/or attitudes and tries to convince them otherwise
- Dismissive of child's feelings and negative attitudes
- Induces guilt
- May use force to reassert parental position
- Vents rage, blames alienating parent for brainwashing child and takes no responsibility

93 In the three categories contained in this list, there are stark similarities with the facts of this case. Those similarities have led me to the conclusion that K. D. has conducted a consistent and overwhelming campaign, for more than a decade, to alienate A. L.'s three children from him. ...

The Law

137 The ... test for determining custody of children is the best interests of the child. This court is required to take into consideration the willingness of the person seeking custody to facilitate as much contact between the child and the other parent as is consistent with the best interest of the child.

138 K. D., on all the evidence before me, is incapable and unwilling to support the three children in a relationship with their father. She has demonstrated for the past fourteen years that she will not act in the best interests of her children in this regard. She has assaulted two of the three children and she has further abused all three children by keeping them from their father physically and alienating them emotionally from him.

139 The Applicant, on the other hand, has good parenting skills. Dr. Fidler's 2000 assessment noted that A. L. was "patient, responsive and effective" with the children who were then quite young. Dr. Fidler found no support for allegations by the Respondent that A. L. was an unfit or inept parent. Later, ... the Office of the Children's Lawyer found A. L. to be well prepared for access visits and "excellent" at interacting and engaging the children. ...

143 While the case law generally supports placing a great deal of weight on the views and preferences of children over 12, there are clear exceptions. One is in a case such as this where one parent has undermined the child's relationship with the other parent (*Pettenuzzo-Pettenuzzo-Deschene v. Deschene*, [2007] O.J. No. 3062 (Ont. S.C.J.); *Tock v. Tock*, [2006] O.J. No. 5324 (Ont. S.C.J.). In *Pettenuzzo-Deschene*, Justice Whalen determined that if the court finds that there has been parental alienation, then the child's views cannot be seen as their own. ...

150 The Office of the Children's Lawyer has taken a position different from that expressed by the children. This has been sanctioned where there is evidence that the child's views and preferences were not independent (*Boukema v. Boukema*, [1997] O.J. No. 2903 (Ont. Gen. Div.); *Reeves v. Reeves*, [2001] O.J. No. 308 (Ont. S.C.J.); *Children's Aid Society of the Regional Children's Aid Society of Waterloo (Regional Municipality) v. A. (B.)*, [2005] O.J.

No. 2844 (Ont. C.J.); *Filaber v. Filaber*, [2008] O.J. No. 4449 (Ont. S.C.J.). I am also in agreement with the OCL position that the status quo in this matter cannot be sustained.

Conclusion

151 The three children of the marriage have been alienated from the Applicant over a long period because K. D. is unable to accept that it is in the best interests of the children to have a relationship with their father. She has been given several opportunities to change her behaviour over many years, and refuses to do so. I find that her unrelenting behaviour toward the children is tantamount to emotional abuse as described by Dr. Fidler. The views and preferences of the two older children are not their own. And for the children to have any further contact with the Respondent, significant therapeutic intervention is necessary.

152 It is remarkable that A. L. has not given-in to the Respondent's persistence in keeping his children from him over the last fourteen years and simply gone on with his life without the children as, no doubt, many other parents in the same situation would have and, indeed, have done. It is now time for his and the children's fates to be free from K. D.'s control. She has shown that she cannot be entrusted with it.

153 The best interests of these children require an order for A. L. to have sole custody of them. This court orders the following:

1. The Applicant, A.L., shall have sole custody of the children, D. K. V. D., born November 11, 1994, J. M. A. L., born August 19, 1997, and K. D. M. D. L. born September 16, 1999 ("the children"), and is further granted the authority to make all decisions regarding the children's welfare without consultation.

2. The Respondent shall have no access to the children pending a review of this matter, save and except for the purpose of counseling as also referred to below at paragraph 6.

3. Pursuant to section 17(3) of the *Divorce Act* and section 141 of the *Courts of Justice Act*, the children shall be brought to this courthouse in Toronto on Friday, January 16, 2009 at 10:00 a.m. in courtroom 902 by the Respondent where the transfer of custody shall occur with the assistance, if need be, of the Sheriff and court officers. The Respondent shall not be present or within the premises or vicinity of the premises during the transfer to the Applicant.

4. The Applicant shall have the sole authority to pursue whatever remedy he believes is necessary to enable for the children a transition of least conflict in the actual transfer of physical custody from the Respondent to the Applicant.

5. The Applicant may, in his discretion, utilize the services of Dr. Randy Rand including participation in the Family Workshop for Alienated Children program created by Dr. Randy Rand ("Family Workshop"). For these purposes, the Applicant may transfer the children outside of Canada for treatment and may retain the services of Bill Lane, or any other transport agents, to assist in the transport of the children to the location at which the Family Workshop will be conducted. He is to advise the Respondent of the dates the children will be attending the Family Workshop, but does not have to advise her of the location.

6. The Applicant, the children and the Respondent shall participate in follow-up counseling, commencing no sooner than three months from the date of this order (i.e. to occur after the Family Workshop component including participation by the Respondent in the Family Workshop program for "favoured" parents) with Dr. Yvonne Parnell or, if Dr. Parnell is unable or unwilling to provide counseling for any or all of the Applicant, the Respondent or the children, the parties shall agree on such other

person(s) to provide counseling for each of them, and failing agreement, this court may appoint the person(s) upon special appointment.

7. The Applicant and the Respondent shall ask Dr. Randy Rand and Dr. Yvonne Parnell, or such other person(s) as is engaged or appointed to conduct follow-up counseling, to provide this court with a written report concerning their intervention as described above with the costs of their intervention, and the reports shall be delivered to the parties, through their counsel, and this court on a date to be fixed by April 1, 2009.

8. The Respondent shall be responsible for the costs of all the aforesaid services.

9. The Respondent is to arrange delivery to the Applicant's residence the children's clothing and all their personal belongings, within ten days of this order. She is not to attend at his residence personally. She can make arrangements for delivery through counsel for the Applicant.

10. The Respondent shall send all of the children's clothing and personal belongings to them at the Applicant's address within ten days of the Order, at her expense.

11. Pursuant to section 17(3) of the *Divorce Act* and section 35 of the *Children's Law Reform Act*, and subject to paragraph 2 herein, the Respondent is not to harass, annoy or molest, or attend within 300 meters of, or have any contact with the Applicant or the children. She is not to have any contact, direct or indirect, or cause any contact, direct or indirect, with the children or with the Applicant pending review of this matter, as set out below, and this Order of restraint of contact by the Respondent with the children applies to all places where the children attend, including, without limiting the generality of same, the Applicant's home, the children's schools, the children's church or place of extracurricular activities.

12. The Applicant shall have possession and sole control of the children's passports and birth certificates.

13. The Applicant's passport, previously deposited with the Court, shall be released to the Applicant forthwith.

14. There shall be no restrictions in travel for the Applicant and the children to participate in the Family Workshop. The Respondent's consent to the children's travel out of the country is hereby dispensed with.

15. The Respondent shall co-operate with all aspects of the Family Workshop and sign releases and contractual agreements necessary to fully implement this undertaking.

16. The Applicant shall be entitled to confiscate and prevent the children's use of cell phones, pagers, blackberries, and computers even if such equipment is provided by the Respondent.

17. Pursuant to sections 141 of the *Courts of Justice Act*, R.S.O. 1990, Chap.C.43, and section 36(2) of the *Children's Law Reform Act*, the Sheriff of this court's jurisdiction, York Regional Police, the Ontario Provincial Police, the Royal Canadian Mounted Police, and all enforcement officials to whose attention this order is brought shall assist, as required, for enforcing the provisions of this Order, and shall specifically take all such action as is required to locate, apprehend and deliver the children to the Applicant, including the power of search and entry at any time.

NOTES AND QUESTIONS

1. The Family Workshop for Alienated Children first came to public attention in Ontario as a result of the decision in *L. (J.K.) v. S. (N.C.)* (2008), 54 R.F.L. (6th) 74 (Ont. S.C.J.). A member of the workshop, Dr. Richard Warshak, testified in that case and Justice Turnbull described it in considerable detail. Portions of that description follow:

> 78 Dr. Warshak ... a licenced psychologist qualified to practice psychology in the state of Texas in the United States. He obtained his Ph.D. in clinical psychology in 1978. He is currently a clinical professor in the Department of Psychiatry, Division of Psychology at the University of Texas Southwestern Medical Center. In his private practice as a clinical psychologist, he has undertaken psychological evaluations of children, adults and families, conducted individual psychotherapy with children and adults, led group therapy with children and adolescents, participated in family therapy and undertaken in custody and forensic consultations with mental health professionals, attorneys, courts and parents throughout the world. He has been actively involved in child custody evaluations. ...

> 80 He notes that he works with a team in remedying situations where a child is in conflict with a parent. The associates with whom he works are Dr. Randy Rand, Ed.D., and Dr. Deirdre Rand, Ph.D., who are both qualified psychologists.

> 81 The Family Workshop for Alienated Children is described by Dr. Warshak as a structured, standardized, and highly specialized program developed by Dr. Randy Rand to assist families in which children have become so alienated from one parent and other relatives that they either refuse contact with the alienated parent or show extreme reluctance to spend time with that parent. Dr. Warshak advised that the workshop is an appropriate option to consider when the court has decided that a child needs to be placed with the alienated parent and have restricted contact with the other parent. In such a situation, this program is an option to assist the family in adjusting to the court's orders. In addition, the program offers an avenue by which a parent who is ordered to have limited or no contact with the child can remedy liabilities identified by the court with the goal of gaining additional time with the child. The program, with suitable modifications, may also be appropriate to consider in situations where a child's relationship with a parent is damaged to a less severe degree, but the child's negative attitudes and behavior toward the parent is not a reasonable and proportionate response to that parent's behavior towards the child. Dr. Warshak agreed that the program is not recommended for families wherein the child's alienation is reasonable and warranted by the history of the child's relationship with the rejected parent; this is referred to as "realistic estrangement".

> 85 At the present time the program has the following seven phases:

> > (a) Gaining physical possession of the child;

> > (b) Safely transporting the child to the location of the intervention. In this case, Dr. Warshak has advised the court that in his view the best location for the intervention will be in California where Dr. Rand and his wife have their offices;

> > (c) Orienting the child to the program, which includes assessing any risks that may require immediate attention;

> > (d) Facilitating contact between the child and the rejected parent;

> > (e) Repairing the parent-child relationship;

> > (f) Providing aftercare; and

> > (g) Working with the favoured parent to reestablish contact with the child and support the child's healthy adjustment.

> 86 In the program overview, Dr. Warshak notes that when it is clear to the child and the parents that the court *expects* the child, with the program's help, to repair the relationship with the alienated parent, and that the child's resistance or refusal to spend time with the alienated parent does not determine the outcome, the child will be motivated to participate meaningfully in the intervention. He noted that most children ultimately find the court's order a relief. It relieves them from feeling that they are responsible to support one parent against the other.

> 87 The overview further notes that experience with this program has underscored the importance of the court enforcing its order of no contact between the child and anyone whose influence supports the child's rejection of the alienated parent. It notes that the few cases in which the intervention was undermined or sabotaged all involved situations in which the court's no contact order was violated or

the order allowed contact between the child and people whose influence reinforced the alienation. In this particular case, Dr. Warshak recommended that sole custody be given to the applicant [the mother] with no access to the respondent [father] for at least a period of six months, during which time he will hopefully have undertaken counseling as part of the reintegration of meaningful contact with both parents.

88 Dr. Warshak also noted that transporting the child is an important phase of the program. In most cases of severe alienation, a child will not willingly accompany the unfavoured parent to the work-shop unless there is a familiar adult whose authority the child respects and who does not support the alienation, therefore it is necessary to use law enforcement agents or professional transport agents to safely escort the child to the program site. The transport agents ensure the child's immediate compli-ance with the court's orders. Early compliance is also beneficial because it signals a change from the past wherein the child felt that he or she had the power to dictate to the rejected parent the terms of the relationship. Dr. Warshak has assured the court that the transport agents used in the program are highly skilled professionals, such as juvenile probation officers, social workers or people who have had previous law enforcement experience, and that they operate under a strict program protocol. Dr. Warshak testified that by the time the child and the transport officers reach the program destination, most children have a comfortable and pleasant relationship with the transport officers. All transport agents are bonded and insured and provide a safe, secure and protected pickup and delivery of the child to the program location. He noted that when dealing with reluctant children the transport agents spend approximately one hour with the child to explain their role, the plan and how they will imple-ment it. They clarify to the child that they are legally responsible for enforcing the court's orders or the instructions of the parents. Each child is treated with respect. Using a firm demeanor, delivered in a compassionate and empathetic tone, the transport agents clearly state to the child that he or she needs to cooperate and accompany them. In most cases this is sufficient to enlist children's coopera-tion. He noted that in rare cases, an adolescent chooses not to cooperate and in such cases the trans-port agents use physical restraints to ensure the child's safety. The agents are trained in standard non-violent restraint methods. The children are not treated roughly or with disrespect. Protocols exist for all modes of transportation.

89 Once the child reaches the program destination, specialists meet with the child to explain the role and purpose of the program, the ground rules, and attempt to answer any questions the child may have. At this time, a specialist also evaluates whether or not the child poses a risk of danger, and assess any destructive behaviour that may require immediate attention.

90 It is at this point the contact must be established between the child and the rejected parent. In the case at bar, Dr. Warshak has suggested that LS [the 13 year old boy who had been alienated from his mother] would travel to the United States with the transport agents on one flight and his mother, the applicant, would follow closely after on another flight. In some cases such as the one before this Court, the rejected parent and the child have been out of contact for a long time. Their initial contact during the intervention should occur in a structured and protected manner. In this particular case the program would be conducted in a hotel suite, in a family oriented hotel, which offers opportunities for fun and relaxation. According to Dr. Warshak, the reunion between a severely alienated child and the rejected parent is generally less problematic than most people expect. The court's order, the trans-portation of the child, and the orientation all serve to reinforce the child's cooperation.

91 After the initial contact between the alienated parent and the child, the psychologists begin repair-ing the parent-child relationship. This phase of the workshop helps the parent and child fuel their relationship, and promotes positive feelings and behavior towards the parent. Through the use of audiovisual materials, such as DVDs and slideshows, tailored to the child's developmental level, the child begins to understand how it is possible that he or she has developed an unrealistic and negative view of his or her parent. These materials lay a foundation for the child to recapture a realistic view of the rejected parent and develop the tools necessary to maintain this view. During this "repairing" phase, references to the alienating parent's behavior are usually unnecessary. If the alienating parent's behavior is raised, every attempt is made to cast his or her behavior in the most favourable light so that the child can avoid feeling caught in the middle. ...

In 2009-09 *This Week in Family Law*, Fam. L. Nws., Philip Epstein and Lene Madsen reported that the treat-ment in the *L. (A.G.) v. D. (K.B.)* case was "going well and that the children were opening up to the father". They added: "On the other hand, we understand the child in *L. (J.K.) v. S. (N.C.)* is not doing well at all". They commented on the *L. (A.G.) v. D. (K.B.)* case as follows:

> We remind our readers that this was an extreme case of alienation. It will be hard to imagine a greater degree, and the Court really had only two choices. Leave the children with the mother and thus the father would never have any contact with his children, or intervene in a legal and therapeutic fashion at the same time. Justice McWatt chose the latter and in the particular circumstances of this case we fully support that decision.
>
> What we do deplore is that it took almost 14 years for the issue to be resolved in this case. We have the feeling that if the family justice system had taken hold of this case 10 years ago, the damage caused by the mother would have dramatically lessened, as would the trauma of moving the children from one parent to the other. This case is yet another showing that what we really need is a way of streaming out high-conflict cases and dealing with them on an expedited basis. Alienation cases should be at the top of that streaming list.

2. In *A. (A.) v. A. (S.N.)* (2007), 40 R.F.L. (6th) 248 (B.C. C.A.), the court overturned a trial judgment that left a 10-year-old girl in her mother's custody even though the trial judge stated that the mother and maternal grandmother's emotionally abusive and manipulative behaviour would be detrimental in the long run. The mother was clearly trying to exclude the father from the girl's life and the girl now rejected him. The trial judge feared that a change in custody would be too dramatic for the girl. The British Columbia Court of Appeal stated that the trial judge erred by focusing on the short term in assessing the girl's best interests and in discounting the negative impact of parental alienation.

When the same court later refused the mother's application for a stay while she attempted to appeal to the Supreme Court of Canada, it indicated that the girl had been with the father since the day of the earlier decision and that she was adjusting well. See *A. (A.) v. A. (S.N.)* (2007), 40 R.F.L. (6th) 267 (B.C. C.A. [In Chambers]).

3. Changing custody after many years is obviously a dramatic intervention that will have significant impact on a child's life. It is generally agreed that it is preferable to address the situation as soon as possible. Education of parents shortly after they separate may play a preventative role, as may counselling. Early judicial intervention through careful case management and detailed orders relating to access may serve to disengage the parents and reduce their conflict. Where one parent is clearly responsible for problems relating to access, orders for costs, warnings, and findings of contempt can serve as deterrents. The use of parenting co-ordinators may also help to prevent a high conflict situation. See Bala, Fidler, Goldberg and Houston, "Alienated Children and Parental Separation: Legal Responses in Canada's Family Courts" (2007), 33 Queen's L.J. 79.

4. It is necessary to distinguish between pathological alienation such as occurred in *L. (A.G.) v. D. (K.B.)*, above, and realistic estrangement. In both, the child is resisting or refusing contact with a parent. However, realistic estrangement is an understandable rejection of a parent as a result of the child's experience. The rejected parent may be abusive or have severe parenting deficiencies. Evidence from a mental health professional, preferably appointed by the court, may be needed to provide insights into the reasons for a child's rejection of a parent. See *Stewart v. Stewart* (2006), [2006] O.J. No. 5135, 2006 CarswellOnt 8273 (S.C.J.), where the court ordered an assessment by a psychologist over the mother's objection.

In *McAlister v. Jenkins* (2008), 54 R.F.L. (6th) 126 (Ont. S.C.J.), a mother of two girls asserted that their father was trying to "cut her out" of their lives. Justice Harper ordered an assessment by a psychologist who concluded that the girls were "afflicted with Parental Alienation Syndrome." In the end, the Justice gave no weight to the assessment and concluded that the mother's behaviour was the principal source of the problems in her relationship with the girls. He also noted (paras. 99 and 100):

> I find that the concept of Parental Alienation Syndrome was advanced by Ms. Jenkins almost immediately after she perceived that her role as a mother was being limited with the introduction of Ms. Davies [the stepmother] into the lives of Mr. McAlister and her children. I also find that the advancement of this concept of Parental Alienation Syndrome became a major distraction that prevented many persons and professionals who testified from analysing the issues that were presented, from time-to-time, in the rational, thorough and dispassionate manner that was needed.
>
> Polarization between the mother's camp and the father's camp became the norm rather than the exception for family, friends and professionals. People saw things from the perspective of the camp with which they were aligned.

8

CHILD SUPPORT

1. Introduction

The obligation to pay child support is statute-based. Both the *Divorce Act* and the Ontario *Family Law Act* establish that natural parents and those who stand in place of parents (in the case of the *Divorce Act)* or who have demonstrated a "settled intention" to treat a child as his or her own (in the case of the *Family Law Act*), are liable to pay. The *Child Support Guidelines* (the "CSG"), enacted as a regulation to both the federal *Divorce Act* and the *Family Law Act*, create a comprehensive code that determines the amount to be paid if liability to pay is determined under the legislation. The CSG also contain rules governing the determination of income of the payor.

The *Divorce Act* and the *Family Law Act* differ subtly, but crucially, on the issue of who has an obligation to pay child support. The federal legislation creates an obligation if a party "stands in place of parent" (s. 1). The *Family Law Act* creates an obligation if a party has demonstrated a "settled intention" to treat the child as his or her own (s. 1). The language of the *Family Law Act* thus suggests that a step-parent must have an intention to take on a parental obligation to a child before child support will be ordered. The *Divorce Act*, by contrast, suggests that the court should take a more objective look at the facts, in an effort to determine whether a step-parent stands in place of parent, regardless of intention. The two legislative provisions have not been reconciled and, as will be explored in this chapter, there are two separate legal tracks on the issue of the obligation of non-biological parents to pay child support.

The federal and provincial Acts also say different things about when the obligation to support a child ends. The *Divorce Act* says that the obligation continues as long as a child is a "child of the marriage". "Child of the marriage" is defined as a child under the age of majority or over the age of majority but unable to withdraw from parental charge as a result of illness, disability or "other cause" (s. 1). Courts have interpreted "other cause" to include pursuing education. By contrast, the *Family Law Act* says that the obligation ends when a child is over the age of majority and is not enrolled in a full-time program of education (s. 31). This chapter examines how the courts have dealt with applications to terminate child support under both pieces of legislation.

The CSG contain Tables that set out the basic amount of child support that a payor parent should pay. The number of children involved dictates which Table is applicable and the payor's income then determines the appropriate amount in accordance with the Table. However, the CSG and both the *Divorce Act* and the *Family Law Act* allow adjustments to and deviations from the Table amount in certain circumstances. We discuss these adjustments and exceptions in this chapter.

Finally, this chapter deals with requests for retroactive payments of child support. This issue has become important in recent years and the Supreme Court of Canada and trial and appellate courts across the country have developed principles for dealing with it.

2. Establishing a Support Obligation

(1) Proving Paternity

Section 10 of the *Children's Law Reform Act* provides that the court may make an order for blood or DNA testing. The section is carefully worded. It does not mandate that a party attend for the testing, but rather says that an order permits a party to introduce test results as evidence and that the court is free to draw an adverse inference about paternity if a party fails to participate in the testing.

WILLIAMS v. CRUICKSHANK

(2000), [2000] O.J. No. 5646, 2000 CarswellOnt 5458 (C.J.)

KURKURIN, J.: This case is brought under the *Children's Law Reform Act*, R.S.O. 1990, c. C-12. The applicant is the mother of a child born on 14 February 1995, who is now age five years. The application, which was filed on 29 October 1999 has two claims. The first [is] for child support in accordance with the *Child Support Guidelines*, O. Reg. 391/97, and the second for costs of the application.

2 The respondent is alleged by the applicant mother to be the biological father of the child. He has filed an answer in which he denies that he is a biological parent of the child. The mother brought a motion ... under section 10 ... seeking an order for leave to obtain blood tests and for leave to introduce the results of such tests into evidence in this proceeding.

3 The respondent countered with a motion accompanied by a notice of constitutional question, in which he seeks a declaration that section 10 is of no force or effect for the reason that it is contrary to the Canadian Charter of Rights and Freedoms, being Part I of Schedule B to the *Canada Act 1982*, c. 11 (U.K.) (hereafter "the Charter"). He seeks this declaration under subsection 52(1) of the *Constitution Act, 1982*, being Schedule B to the *Canada Act 1982*, c. 11 (U.K.), which declares its provisions to be the supreme law of Canada and that any law that is inconsistent with its provisions is, to the extent of that inconsistency, of no force or effect.

4 The applicant mother has responded to the motion and the notice of constitutional issue. There is also a response to the notice by the Attorney General for Ontario as intervenor.

5 The respondent's arguments are twofold.

> First:
>
> 1 The possible finding of parentage in these proceedings, being a pronouncement by the state as to his parental status, engages his security interest as well as his liberty interest under section 7 of the Charter.
>
> 2 A finding of parentage by the court would be based on evidence in the form of the blood test results, or based on an inference from the fact of his refusal to participate in the testing.
>
> 3 A finding of parentage would affect the integrity of his family unit, its financial security and the security interest of his child born in wedlock to his present wife.
>
> Second:
>
> 1 A person may be deprived of rights to security and liberty given by section 7 of the Charter so long as such deprivation is in accordance with the principles of fundamental justice.
>
> 2 Here the deprivation is not in accordance with such principles because [the] legislation ... is too vague or ... too overbroad.

6 There is a two-part test here that the respondent must meet on the balance of probabilities. The onus is on the respondent to meet both parts of the test in order to qualify for the remedies sought. ...

8 I am not entirely sure what right to liberty the respondent claims is infringed or denied by section 10. ... He does not specifically refer in his factum, his evidence or his argument to any interference with his right to liberty by operation of section 10. ... Liberty, in terms of section 7 of the Charter does not mean merely freedom from physical restraint. It also encompasses the right to have room for personal autonomy to live one's life and to make decisions that are of fundamental personal importance. Even within this wider concept of freedom, the respondent does not elaborate on how his right to freedom may be affected. I assume his greater interest and arguments, in this case, are directed towards his right to security of his own person, a right guaranteed by section 7 of the Charter.

9 The facts of this case are not unusual or extraordinary, having regard to the issue of paternity. In fact, the respondent admits to one act of sexual intercourse, although before what would be the normal gestation period for the child in question. The applicant claims in her evidence that there were several acts of intercourse with the respondent both prior to and extending into the gestation period. She also claims that, during the time of conception, she was sexually intimate with only one man, namely, the respondent.

10 With this not unusual background and in the context of a claim for child support in which paternity has been put into issue, this court has to consider, among other things, whether it can depart from authorities cited by the parties and, if so, why it should do so.

11 The question of whether ... section 10 ... denies or infringes a person's right of life, liberty and security of the person contained in section 7 of the Charter has been dealt with previously. Most important, from the point of view of this proceeding, is a decision of Justice Robert C. Rutherford in the Ontario High Court of Justice, in the case *Pakka v. Nygard* (1988), 37 C.R.R. 189, 15 R.F.L. (3d) 110, [1988] O.J. No. 1049, the headnote [R.F.L.] of which highlights the decision: "Section 10 of the *Children's Law Reform Act*, which permits a court to grant leave to obtain blood tests, and to admit the results in evidence, does not violate s. 7 of the Canadian Charter of Rights and Freedoms." ...

13 The respondent here has failed in his first of two steps. He has not shown any deprivation, denial or infringement of any of his rights under section 7 of the Charter by virtue of the operation of section 10 of the *Children's Law Reform Act*. Accordingly, there is no need to proceed to a consideration of the second test, nor is there any need to address the claim under subsection 52(1) of the *Constitution Act*.

14 I note that the case of *Pakka v. Nygard* was referred to with approval in the New Brunswick Court of Queen's Bench in *Higgins v. Reid* (1990), 104 N.B.R. (2d) 173, 261 A.P.R. 173, [1990] N.B.J. No. 149, as well as in the later Ontario case of *Silber v. Fenske* (1995), 11 R.F.L. (4th) 145, [1995] O.J. No. 418 (Ont. Gen. Div.). I have not been referred by counsel to any judicial authority that distinguishes this line of cases or overrules them.

15 I am also persuaded by argument of counsel for the intervenor Attorney General for Ontario who develops a theme mentioned in these older authorities. He points out, quite rightly, that the respondent has challenged section 10 ... in his belief that it calls for a pronouncement as to the parental status of the respondent. In fact, section 10 ... does no such thing. It merely provides for a procedure by which evidence — and by today's standards, possibly very high quality evidence — can be brought before the court. It also permits the court to draw such inferences as the court thinks appropriate from a person's refusal to submit to the blood test.

16 The respondent attacks section 10 ..., when one examines his argument, it is the proceeding itself that he claims may be violating his section 7 rights. If a pronouncement is made as to paternity of the child, it will be as a result of the proceeding itself, not because of section 10 of the *Children's Law Reform Act*. It is the nature of the proceeding itself where there is a

claim for child support based on biological parentage and a denial of paternity that evokes the need for a finding of paternity ancillary to the issue of child support.

17 It is unnecessary to deal with the matter of vagueness or the over-broadness. ...

18 The motion of the respondent is, therefore, dismissed on the grounds argued.

NOTES AND QUESTIONS

1. What is the distinction between a finding of paternity in a support application and a declaration of paternity? Does a finding of paternity have any effect outside of the support proceedings? See s. 8(1) 6 of the *CLRA*.

2. Several Canadian cases have indicated that delay in alleging paternity and in claiming child support will not preclude court orders for blood testing and child support. See *H. (S.) v. A. (L.)* (1992), 92 D.L.R. (4th) 310 (Ont. U.F.C.) (blood tests, a finding of paternity and a support order involving a 21-year-old); *D. (J.S.) v. V. (W.L.)* (1995), 11 R.F.L. (4th) 409 (B.C. C.A.) (blood tests ordered where the mother was married to a third party at the time of the birth some 16 years earlier); and *Phiroz v. Mottiar* (1995), 16 R.F.L. (4th) 353 (Ont. Prov. Div.) (the court awarded child support about 15 years after the birth of a child out of wedlock, ruling that there was no limitation period and that the doctrine of *laches* did not apply to a support claim). See also Tweney, "Analyzing Section 10 of the *Children's Law Reform Act*" (1996-97), 14 C.F.L.Q. 49.

3. Where a husband denies that he is the father of a child born to his wife during their marriage and asks for blood tests, some courts are reluctant to grant leave for blood testing unless there are clear grounds for his denial. See *C. (M.) v. C. (L.A.)* (1990), 24 R.F.L. (3d) 322 (B.C. C.A.); *J. (R.) v. M. (S.)* (1990), 25 R.F.L. (3d) 105 (B.C. S.C.); and *G. (F.) v. G. (F.)* (1991), 32 R.F.L. (3d) 252 (Ont. Div. Ct.) In the latter case, Conant J. held that the husband had to rebut the presumption of paternity created by s. 8 of the *CLRA* before leave could be granted. However, in *B. (F.) v. B. (L.)* (2000), [2000] O.J. No. 3833, 2000 CarswellOnt 3689 (S.C.J.), Rogin J. disagreed with this approach, holding that it was too strict. Which view do you think should prevail?

4. In *Silber v. Fenske* (1995), 11 R.F.L. (4th) 145, 1995 CarswellOnt 81 (Gen. Div.), the putative father claimed that the mother lied about using contraception. Courts have generally held that a mother's alleged deception regarding contraceptive measures has no bearing on the father's support obligation. See, e.g., *Boca v. Mendel* (1989), 20 R.F.L. (3d) 421 (Ont. Prov. Ct.); additional reasons at (1989), 1989 CarswellOnt 3600 (Prov. Ct.); *Buschow v. Jors* (1994), 3 R.F.L. (4th) 39 (Sask. Q.B.); and *New Brunswick (Minister of Income Assistance) v. H. (S.)* (1996), 20 R.F.L. (4th) 312 (N.B. C.A.). The judge put it this way in *Boca* (at 425):

> I know of no operative legal principle that would suggest that where a mother decides to have a child and this runs contrary to the wishes of the biological father, it can or should affect the child's right to support from the father or the mother's right to claim child support. There are reasons of public policy to avoid extending the considerations for determining child support into the realm of opinions about abortion or into the realm of singling out responsibility for birth control in each situation or into the realm of measuring the father's enthusiasm about being a father. Very simply, conception is a joint responsibility.

5. This chapter focuses on the factual elements that must be established before an obligation to support a particular child exists and examines the determination of support. It should be noted, however, that children sometimes have a legal duty to support their parents. Section 32 of the *Family Law Act*, as well as legislation in the other provinces, says that adult children have an obligation to support their parents who have "cared for or provided support for" them. Although still quite rare, claims by adults for support from their children succeeded in *Godwin v. Bolcso* (1996), 20 R.F.L. (4th) 66 (Ont. C.A.) and *Dragulin v. Dragulin* (1998), 43 R.F.L. (4th) 55 (Ont. Gen. Div.). See also *Newson v. Newson* (1998), 43 R.F.L. (4th) 221 (B.C. C.A.) where interim support was ordered. The court denied the claim in *Leung v. Leung* (1996), 20 R.F.L. (4th) 48 (Alta. Q.B.) and *Skrzypacz v. Skrzypacz* (1996), 22 R.F.L. (4th) 450 (Ont. Prov. Div.). Christa Bracci examines the legislation and the case law in "Ties That Bind: Ontario's Filial Responsibility Law" (2000), 17 Can. J. Fam. L. 455.

(2) Extended Definition of the Parent-Child Relationship

(a) The Obligation of Step-Parents to Pay Child Support

The jurisdiction of the court to make an order regarding child support under the *Divorce Act* is limited to "child[ren] of the marriage" as defined in s. 2(1) and s. 2(2). To be a "child of the marriage" an individual must be "a child of two spouses or former spouses". Section 2(2) specifies that a "child of two spouses or former spouses" includes "any child for whom they both stand in the place of parents" and "any child of whom one is the parent and for whom the other stands in the place of a parent". The definition of "child of the marriage" in the *Divorce Act* is essentially the same as that which was provided in the 1968 *Divorce Act*, although the latter used the Latin expression "*in loco parentis*" rather than "in the place of a parent".

Provincial legislation also extends the support obligation to some adults who are not biological parents of the child. See, e.g., s. 1(1) of the *FLA*.

CHARTIER v. CHARTIER

(1999), 43 R.F.L. (4th) 1, 1999 CarswellMan 25, 1999 CarswellMan 26 (S.C.C.)

BASTARACHE J. (for the court): — In this appeal, the Court is asked to determine whether a person who stands in the place of a parent to a child within the meaning of the *Divorce Act* ... can unilaterally give up that status and escape the obligation to provide support for that child after the breakdown of the marriage. The Court unanimously decided that a person cannot do so and allowed the appeal at the hearing held on November 12, 1998. The following are the reasons for allowing the appeal.

[The parties began a common law relationship in 1989 and married in June 1991. Their child, Jeena, was born on August 29, 1990. The parties separated in May 1992, later reconciled for a month or two, then permanently separated in September 1992. The wife had a child, Jessica, from a previous relationship. While the parties lived together, the husband played an active role in caring for both children and was a father-figure for Jessica. The parties discussed, but did not proceed with, the husband's adoption of Jessica. The parties amended Jessica's birth registration to indicate, falsely, that the husband was Jessica's natural father and to change her name to his. Following separation, the husband terminated his relationship with Jessica. The trial judge, relying on *Carignan v. Carignan* (1989), 29 R.F.L. (4th) 96, 61 Man. R. (2d) 66 (Man. C.A.), held that a spouse standing in the place of a parent had the right to withdraw unilaterally from that role and so ordered no further support for Jessica. The Manitoba Court of Appeal upheld this portion of the trial decision, but, as indicated at the outset of Justice Bastarache's reasons above, the Supreme Court of Canada allowed the wife's appeal.]

There is one body of case law, exemplified by *Carignan*, supra, that states that a person standing in the place of a parent is entitled to make a unilateral withdrawal from the parental relationship. The other body of case law is typified by *Theriault v. Theriault* (1994), 149 A.R. 210 (Alta. C.A.); it states that a person cannot unilaterally withdraw from a relationship in which he or she stands in the place of a parent and that the court must look to the nature of the relationship to determine if a person in fact does stand in the place of a parent to a child.

Before considering these two lines of authority, I would note that in both cases the courts have engaged upon a historical review of the doctrine of *loco parentis* and taken the view that the words "in the place of a parent" used in the *Divorce Act* were intended to have the same meaning. The doctrine of *loco parentis* was developed in diverse contexts, trust law, tort law, master-apprentice relationships, schoolmaster-pupil relationships, wills and gifts ..., at another time. Alison Diduck, in "*Carignan v. Carignan*: When is a Father not a Father? Another Historical Perspective" (1990), 19 *Man. L.J.* 580, explains how this common law doctrine was applied in family matters, over the years, in various jurisdictions. She concludes, at pp. 601-602, by saying:

> The *in loco parentis* doctrine is a creature of 19th century patriarchy. It evolved during a time when it was a morally offensive notion for a man to be held responsible for another man's child. As Mendes de Costa U.F.J. stated in a 1987 decision, it has "its roots deep in history" and "carries with it connotations of times past" (*Re Spring and Spring* (1987), 61 O.R. (2d) 743 at 748). Notwithstanding Parliament's choice of similar wording in the *Divorce Act, 1985*, it is arguably open to counsel (or to courts) to suggest that Parliament deliberately chose to reject the common law notion of *in loco parentis*, and that the current statute should be interpreted "free from the shadow of earlier authorities". (*Ibid.*, at 749.)

I agree that the policies and values reflected in the *Divorce Act* must relate to contemporary Canadian society and that the general principles of statutory interpretation support a modern understanding of the words "stands in the place of a parent". ...

In my view, the common law meaning of *in loco parentis* is not helpful in determining the scope of the words "in the place of a parent" in the *Divorce Act*.

This being said, it is my opinion that the decision in *Theriault, supra*, provides the proper approach to this issue as it recognizes that the provisions of the *Divorce Act* dealing with children focus on what is in the best interests of the children of the marriage, not on biological parenthood or legal status of children.

In the present appeal, the Court of Appeal, although noting that the decision has not been universally followed, confirmed the judgment in *Carignan* for essentially two reasons. The first reason is that the decision displays a "certain logic and reasonableness" because the modern institution of marriage has substantially departed from its traditional roots. Philp J.A. noted ... that modern marriages are "often fragile and time-limited relationships" and therefore, this raises the question of how many obligations persons must carry with them as they move from relationship to relationship. It would not be logical, in his view, for a step-parent who takes on obligations with respect to a spouse's children to be saddled with this obligation indefinitely while a step-parent who takes on no such obligation is entitled to walk away from the relationship scot-free. The finding in *Carignan* avoids this inconsistency. The second reason ... relates to the fact that the decision in *Carignan* establishes "an understandable and easily determined basis for imposing or excusing responsibility".

The decision in *Carignan, supra*, has been highly criticized ... The most obvious criticism is that it nullifies the effect of the relevant provisions of the *Divorce Act*. If one can unilaterally terminate a relationship where a person stands in the place of a parent to a child, why define such a relationship as giving rise to obligations under the *Divorce Act*? ...

I do not agree with the reasoning in *Carignan, supra*. As noted above, the words "in the place of a parent" must be given a meaning that is independent of the common law concept and reflective of the purposive and contextual approach to statutory interpretation advocated by this Court. Once a person is found to stand in the place of a parent, that relationship cannot be unilaterally withdrawn by the adult. The interpretation of the provisions of the *Divorce Act* relating to "child[ren] of the marriage" should be "given such fair, large and liberal construction and interpretation as best ensures the attainment of its objects": see *Interpretation Act*, R.S.C. 1985, c. I-21, s. 12. The reasoning in *Carignan, supra*, ignores one of the fundamental objectives of the *Divorce Act* as it relates to children. The provisions of the *Divorce Act* that deal with children aim to ensure that a divorce will affect the children as little as possible. Spouses are entitled to divorce each other, but not the children who were part of the marriage. The interpretation that will best serve children is one that recognizes that when people act as parents toward them, the children can count on that relationship continuing and that these persons will continue to act as parents toward them.

What, therefore, is the proper time period for determining whether a person stands in the place of a parent? The term "at the material time" has been interpreted with reference to the parental status to mean "the time of the commencement of the proceedings" (see *H. (L.) v. H. (L.H.)*, [1971] 4 W.W.R. 262 (B.C. C.A.)); "the time of the hearing" (see *Harrington v. Harrington* (1981), 33 O.R. (2d) 150 at p. 159 (Ont. C.A.)); and has also been held to mean "whatever date is appropriate". ...

It is clear that the Court must address the needs of the child as of the date of the hearing or order. The existence of the parental relationship under s. 2(2)(b) of the *Divorce Act* must however be determined as of the time the family functioned as a unit. See Julien D. Payne, *Payne on Divorce* (4th ed. 1996), at p. 148. If the "material time" was to be interpreted as in *H. (L.)*, *supra*, it would be difficult to find a parental relationship in situations where the step-parent has little contact with the child between the separation and the divorce proceedings. This is inconsistent with the purpose of the *Divorce Act*.

The facts of the present case demonstrate why this interpretation is appropriate. Until Mr. Chartier's unilateral withdrawal from the relationship, Jessica saw the respondent as her father in every way. He was the only father she knew. To allow him to withdraw from that relationship, as long as he does it before the petition for divorce, is unacceptable. The breakdown of the parent/child relationship after separation is not a relevant factor in determining whether or not a person stands in the place of a parent for the purposes of the *Divorce Act*. Jessica was as much a part of the family unit as Jeena and should not be treated differently from her because the spouses separated. The "material time" factor does not affect the determination of the parental relationship. It simply applies to the age considerations that are a precondition to the determination of need.

What then is the proper test for determining whether a person stands in the place of a parent within the meaning of the *Divorce Act*? The appellant argued that the test for whether or not a person stands in the place of a parent should be determined exclusively from the perspective of the child. I cannot accept this test. In many cases, a child will be very young and it will be difficult to determine whether that child considers the person as a parental figure. Further, an older child may resent his or her step-parent and reject the authority of that person as a parent, even though, objectively, that person effectively provides for the child and stands in the place of a parent. The opinion of the child regarding the relationship with the step-parent is important, but it constitutes only one of many factors to be considered. In particular, attention must be given to the representations of the step-parent, independently of the child's response.

Whether a person stands in the place of a parent must take into account all factors relevant to that determination, viewed objectively. What must be determined is the nature of the relationship. The *Divorce Act* makes no mention of formal expressions of intent. The focus on voluntariness and intention in *Carignan*, *supra*, was dependent on the common law approach discussed earlier. It was wrong. The Court must determine the nature of the relationship by looking at a number of factors, among which is intention. Intention will not only be expressed formally. The court must also infer intention from actions, and take into consideration that even expressed intentions may sometimes change. The actual fact of forming a new family is a key factor in drawing an inference that the step-parent treats the child as a member of his or her family, i.e., a child of the marriage. The relevant factors in defining the parental relationship include, but are not limited to, whether the child participates in the extended family in the same way as would a biological child; whether the person provides financially for the child (depending on ability to pay); whether the person disciplines the child as a parent; whether the person represents to the child, the family, the world, either explicitly or implicitly, that he or she is responsible as a parent to the child; the nature or existence of the child's relationship with the absent biological parent. The manifestation of the intention of the step-parent cannot be qualified as to duration, or be otherwise made conditional or qualified, even if this intention is manifested expressly. Once it is shown that the child is to be considered, in fact, a "child of the marriage", the obligations of the step-parent towards him or her are the same as those relative to a child born of the marriage with regard to the application of the *Divorce Act*. The step-parent, at this point, does not only incur obligations. He or she also acquires certain rights, such as the right to apply eventually for custody or access under s. 16(1) of the *Divorce Act*.

Nevertheless, not every adult-child relationship will be determined to be one where the adult stands in the place of a parent. Every case must be determined on its own facts and it must be established from the evidence that the adult acted so as to stand in the place of a parent to the child.

Huband J.A., in *Carignan, supra*, expressed the concern that individuals may be reluctant to be generous toward children for fear that their generosity will give rise to parental obligations. I do not share those concerns. The nature of a parental relationship is complex and includes more than financial support. People do not enter into parental relationships with the view that they will be terminated. I share the view expressed by Beaulieu J. in *Siddall* (1994), 11 R.F.L. (4th) 325 (Ont. Gen. Div.) at p. 337:

> It is important to examine the motive behind a person's generosity towards the children of the person they wish to be involved with or are involved with in a relationship. In many cases children are used as pawns by men and, on occasion, women who desire the attention of the children's parent and once the relationship between the adults fail, the children are abandoned. This is not to be encouraged. If requiring men to continue their relationship, financially and emotionally with the children is a discouragement of generosity then, perhaps such generosity should be discouraged. This type of generosity which leaves children feeling rejected and shattered once a relationship between the adults sours is not beneficial to society in general and the children, in particular. After all, it is the court's obligation to look out for the best interests of the children. In too many of these situations the ultimate result is that the child is a mere object used to accommodate a person's selfish and personal interests as long as the relationship is satisfying and gratifying. As soon as things sour and become less comfortable, the person can leave, abandoning both the parent and child, without any legal repercussions. ... It is important to encourage the type of relationship that includes commitment, not superficial generosity. If relationships are more difficult for a person to extricate him- or herself from then, perhaps, more children will be spared the trauma of rejection, bruised self image and loss of financial support to which they have become accustomed.

Huband J.A., in *Carignan, supra*, also expressed the concern that a child might collect support from both the biological parent and the step-parent. I do not accept that this is a valid concern. The contribution to be paid by the biological parent should be assessed independently of the obligations of the step-parent. The obligation to support a child arises as soon as that child is determined to be "a child of the marriage". The obligations of parents for a child are all joint and several. The issue of contribution is one between all of the parents who have obligations towards the child, whether they are biological parents or step-parents; it should not affect the child. If a parent seeks contribution from another parent, he or she must, in the meantime, pay support for the child regardless of the obligations of the other parent. (See *Theriault, supra*, at p. 214; James G. McLeod, Annotation on *Primeau v. Primeau* (1986), 2 R.F.L. (3d) 113 (Ont. H.C.).) ...

Conclusion

The Court of Appeal, by relying on *Carignan, supra*, made a distinction between children born of both parents and stepchildren. As mentioned earlier, the Act does not make such a distinction. Once it is determined that a child is a "child of the marriage" within the meaning of the *Divorce Act*, he or she must be treated as if born of the marriage. ...

Even if a relationship has broken down after a separation or divorce, the obligation of a person who stands in the place of a parent to support a child remains the same. Natural parents, even if they lose contact with their children, must continue to pay child support.

On the facts of this case, the respondent stood in the place of a parent toward Jessica. The respondent represented to Jessica and to the world that he assumed full parental responsibility for her. Mr. Chartier is the only father that Jessica has known owing to the fact that the parties led her to believe that the respondent was in fact Jessica's biological father. The respondent even considered adopting Jessica and the parties had Jessica's birth registration amended to change Jessica's name to correspond to the respondent's. This was done by falsely submitting an application stating that the respondent was Jessica's natural father. After the separation, the respondent continued to have visits with Jessica. Eventually access was terminated with regard to both Jessica and his biological child, Jeena.

The respondent's unilateral withdrawal from the relationship with Jessica does not change the fact that he acted, in all ways, as a father during the time the family lived together. Therefore, Jessica was a "child of the marriage" when the parties separated and later divorced, with all of the rights and responsibilities which that status entails under the *Divorce Act*. With respect to support from the respondent, Jessica is to be treated in the same way as Jeena. ...

P. (G.N.) v. G. (L.A.)

(2001), 198 N.S.R. (2d) 175, 2001 CarswellNS 393 (S.C.)

[A man, P., and woman, G., became engaged in August 1989, intending to marry in the fall of 1990. P. worked for the Department of Fisheries and Oceans and was often away at sea. When G. learned in March 1990 that she was pregnant, the wedding was moved up to August 1990. Twin boys were born in late October of that year, six weeks premature. The couple separated in 1997. Just before the separation, G. told P. for the first time that he was not the boys' father. A DNA analysis performed in 2000 confirmed that P. was not the biological father. Although he was devastated, P. continued to see the boys. He wished to continue his relationship with them, but only as a "friend".

By the time the issue of child support reached the court in a divorce proceeding, the mother was living with C.T. He was the brother of S.T., whom the mother identified as the biological father. She testified that C.T. was acting as the boys' father and that the boys called him "Dad". She stated that she had no intention of seeking support from S.T. and that the twins were unaware of S.T.'s existence.]

BOUDREAU J.: —

10 In the final analysis, I find that Ms. G. did deceive Mr. P. about the paternity of the children in that she kept from him the real possibility, and most likely the probability, that he was not the father of the expected twins. The more difficult question is what to do about it now.

11 Issues

> 1. Did Mr. P. stand in the place of a parent of these children?
>
> 2. Can one stand in the 'place of a parent' without knowing they are doing so; i.e., not making an intentional decision to do so?
>
> 3. How do the *Federal Child Support Guidelines* and the apparent concurrent obligation of others to support these children affect Mr. P.'s obligations of child support?
>
> 4. Do principles of fairness and honesty have any bearing on this case?

The Law

12 The *Divorce Act* does not define who is a "parent" for purposes of the *Act*. It does how-ever define "child of the marriage" to include a child of two spouses or former spouses as follows: "... any child of whom one is the parent and whom the other stands in the place of a parent". This definition incorporates or includes what has been long referred to in the law as the *"in loco parentis"* doctrine, but it is broader than the former common law doctrine.

13 It is the application of that doctrine and the interpretation of the above quoted phrase which is central to the case at bar. ...

14 *Chartier* deals with a step-parent situation, unlike the present case where Mr. P. did not know he was not the biological father of the children. In *Chartier*, the husband knew full well he was not the father of the child in question. I therefore recognize that the fact situa-tions in *Chartier* and the present case are very different; however, in *Chartier*, Bastarache, J., explores contextual and societal policy considerations appropriate or applicable to an analysis of the meaning of 'standing in the place of a parent'. He states at paragraph 21:

> I agree that the policies and values reflected in the *Divorce Act* must relate to contemporary Canadian society and that the general principles of statutory interpretation support a modern understanding of the words "stands in the place of a parent".

... He states the approach to be taken as follows:

> ... it is my opinion that the decision in *Theriault, supra*, provides the proper approach to this issue as it recognizes that the provisions of the *Divorce Act* dealing with children focus on what is in the best interests of the children of the marriage, not on biological parenthood or legal status of children.

15 At paragraph 22, Bastarache, J., then quotes with apparent approval from Kerans, J.A. in the *Theriault v. Theriault* case as follows:

> Our society values parenthood as a vital adjunct to the upbringing of children. Adequate performance of that office is a duty imposed by law whenever our society judges that it is fair to impose it. In the case of the natural parent, the biological contribution towards the new life warrants the imposition of the duty. *In the case of a step-parent, it is the voluntary assumption of that role. It is not in the best interests of children that step-parents or natural parents be permitted to abandon their children, and it is their best interests that should govern.* Financial responsibility is simply one of the many aspects of the office of parent. A parent, or step-parent, who refuses or avoids this obligation neglects or abandons the child. The abandonment or neglect is as real as would be a refusal of medical care, or affection, or comfort, or any other need of a child. [Emphasis added]

17 The question is do those broad principles and obligations apply equally to a situation where a person, in this case a husband, unknowingly stands in the place of a parent because he erroneously believes he is the biological father, having been deceived or misled or is otherwise mistaken.

18 Counsel for Mr. P. points to several cases which allude to the requirement of knowledge and intention in order for an *in loco parentis* relationship to be found to exist between adult and child. In fact Bastarache, J., at paragraph 23 of *Chartier* quotes the following from deWeerdt J., in *Laraque v. Allooloo* (1992), 44 R.F.L. (3d) 10 (N.W.T. S.C.) with apparent approval:

> ... At the risk of being repetitious, *it is well-settled law that it takes a properly informed and deliber-ate intention to assume parental obligations for support of a child, on an ongoing basis, to bring the in loco parentis status in law into being.* Given that premise, it is difficult to conclude that this status is meaningless or can be negated at whim whenever the person *in loco parentis* is visited by second thoughts on the matter or decides to abandon the project altogether. [Emphasis added]

21 In my opinion, the above authorities cited by Mr. P. do not give sufficient consideration to the approach and principles mandated by Bastarache, J., in *Chartier*. ...

22 This approach was followed in the Saskatchewan case of *M. (K.F.) v. M. (M.J.)* (1999), 2 R.F.L. (5th) 113 (Sask. Q.B.) by Kraus, J. He stated at paragraph 7:

> The court in *Chartier* held that the common law definition of *in loco parentis* is no longer the proper definition under the *Divorce Act. The common law emphasis on intention and voluntariness is no longer the proper approach to determining the existence of the relationship. The focus of the inquiry must be on the best interests of the child and not on the biology of parenthood or the legal status of the child. The test to find a relationship where a person stands in the position of a parent is objective review of all relevant factors.* The person may not limit the duration or make the relationship conditional even by express words. *The intention of the person is only one factor to be taken* into account and express intention may be changed by the intention that can be inferred from the person's actions. [Emphasis added]

Analysis

23 There can be no conclusion but that Mr. P. was *de facto* the parent of these twin boys during the entire marriage and for some considerable time after the separation. Some ten years. He fulfilled that role completely because he thought he was the boys biological father. There could be no more complete father and son relationship. I find that, according to *Chartier*, that alone would necessitate a finding that Mr. P. stood in the place of a parent to these children. But even if I were in error in coming to that conclusion, I would find that Mr. P. continued to fulfill the role of father even after he had some doubts about his paternity, and even after a D.N.A. test confirmed he was not the biological father. Mr. P. has testified he wants to continue a close relationship with the boys, but he says he cannot continue as a father, rather as a friend. He therefore wants and requires access rights to the boys. All of these circumstances lead me to find that Mr. P. stands in the place of a parent as intended by the *Divorce Act*. To rule otherwise in these circumstances could set a dangerous precedent for significant upheaval in well and long established family support situations.

24 The question that remains to be decided is what should Mr. P.'s obligation to pay child support be, considering the various provisions of the *Child Support Guidelines* and the factors which would and should apply to the particular circumstances of this case.

25 Section 5 of the *Federal Child Support Guidelines* provides as follows:

> 5. Where the spouse against whom a child support order is sought stands in the place of a parent for a child, the amount of a child support order is, in respect of that spouse, *such amount as the court considers appropriate*, having regard to these Guidelines and any other parent's legal duty to support the child. [Emphasis added]

27 Therefore, the court is mandated in Section 5 to make a discretionary judgement in determining the amount of support it considers appropriate in a case of standing in the place of a parent; however, that discretion is limited to two areas of consideration. The first one is the *Guidelines* themselves; and presumably the reference to *Guidelines* here means primarily the table amount unless there are other issues such as Section 7 expenses or undue hardship claims, etc. The second area of consideration is "any other parent's legal duty to support the child".

28 ... As Professor Julien Payne has stated in a recent article entitled "Child Support Obligations of Multiple Parents" (at page 6):

> A court has discretionary jurisdiction under section 5 of the *Federal Child Support Guidelines* to determine the proper apportionment, if any, of child support between the parent of the child and spouse who stands in the place of the parent. Diverse factors may be considered by the court *but sorting out the extent of the obligation ought not to operate to the detriment of children.* [Emphasis added]

And in referring to the *Chartier* case directly (at page 7):

> ... it is noteworthy that the judgment of the Supreme Court of Canada does not purport to address the implications of section 5 of the *Federal Child Support Guidelines*, which expressly confers a broad

discretion on the court to order child support against a spouse or former spouse who stands in the place of a parent in such amount as the court considers appropriate, having regard to the *Guidelines* and any other parent's legal duty to support the child. In so far as there is no comparable provision whereby a court can take account of "any other parent's legal duty to support the child" when determining the amount of child support to be paid by a biological or adoptive parent, it is arguable that section 5 of the *Federal Child Support Guidelines* impliedly endorses the principle of primary and secondary obligations of child support as between biological or adoptive parents and stepparents or persons who stand in the place of parents to other people's children. Given that *Chartier v. Chartier* does not address the implications of section 5 of the guidelines, there is nothing in the judgment of the Supreme Court of Canada that precludes a court from reducing the amount of support payable by a stepparent to zero, if that is found to be appropriate.

30 Apportionment between various parents with a legal duty to support children must, of necessity, involve the exercise of discretionary jurisdiction and judicial reasoning and judgment. Professor Payne in the above noted article suggests a method of proceeding (at page 10):

> Consequently, when seeking to determine the fair contribution to child support of a stepparent, the court must first determine the appropriate amount specified by the provincial guidelines for that stepparent's liability. The next step would be to determine the legal duty of "any other parent", including that of the non-custodial and custodial parent. If the total amount of "any other parent's" basic financial contribution would be sufficient to provide "a fair standard of support" for the child, the determination of the extent of the stepparent's legal duty could end there and his or her required contribution could be nominal. If the sum of the other parent's basic financial contribution were insufficient to provide a fair standard of support for the child, the stepparent could be called on to top up the available funds to a point where they are sufficient for that purpose.

31 Professor Payne goes on to quote the following from *MacArthur v. Demers*, [1998] O.J. No. 5868 (Ont. Gen. Div.), a decision of Aston, J., of the Ontario Court of Justice (General Division) Family Court which followed a similar approach:

> [para 28] Section 5 of the *Guidelines* only applies if the respondent is not the child's biological parent. The following step-by-step approach offers one way of structuring the exercise of judicial discretion under section 5:
>
> > 1. Determine the guideline amount payable by the respondent. This will involve consideration of the table amount, any section 7 add-ons and any undue hardship adjustment.
> >
> > 2. Determine the "legal duty" of any other non-custodial parent to contribute to the support of the child. As noted above, this will be established by a pre-existing order or agreement or by a guideline calculation. The words in section 5 "any other parent's legal duty to support the child" would include the custodial parent, but the guideline scheme assumes the custodial parent meets this duty by sharing his or her household standard of living with the child.
> >
> > 3. In considering whether it is "appropriate" to reduce the respondent's obligation under the *Guidelines*, once the non-custodial parent establishes that another non-custodial parent (or parents) has (have) a legal duty to support the child, the onus ought to shift to the custodial parent to demonstrate why the respondent's obligation should not be reduced by that of other non-custodial parent(s).
>
> [para 29] The custodial parent might satisfy that onus, in whole or in part, by demonstrating that
>
> > (a) the "legal duty" of the non-custodial parent(s) is (are) unenforceable, or
> >
> > (b) such a reduction is inconsistent with the stated objectives in section 1 of the *Guidelines*.

32 The phrase, "any other parent's legal duty to support the child" has been given liberal or large and purposive interpretation to appropriately reflect the general intent of the *Guidelines* as to what other parent may mean. This is reflected in a recent judgment of P.L.J.

Smith, J., of the Court of Queen's Bench of Alberta in the case of *Nelson v. Nelson*, [1999] A.J. No. 242 (Alta. Q.B.) and summarized by Professor Payne at page 12 of his article:

> She ... concluded that the phrase "any other parent's legal duty to support the child" in section 5 of the Federal Child Support Guidelines "is sufficiently broad to include the legal support obligation of the biological parent of a child, of a former spouse who stood in the place of a parent to the child, *and of a current spouse who stands in the place of a parent to the child*." [Emphasis Added]

33 Mr. P.'s Guideline income has been established at $51,052.00 (Exhibit 4) plus overtime which is estimated to be $5,000.00 for the year 2001. I therefore find his annual income to be $56,000.00 for the purposes of the *Guidelines*. This would ordinarily require basic child support of $754.00 [monthly].

34 I also find there are two other persons, besides Ms. G. and Mr. P., who have a legal duty to support these children. First, and some would say foremost, is the obligation of the biological father, S. T.. Secondly, there is C. T., the person who is now standing in the place of a father to the children. Ms. G. has testified as to Mr. T.'s role with the children and it is definitely as a father and provider. This relationship has existed since the separation in 1997 and continues to the present.

35 Ms. G. has testified that the biological father, S. T., lives in Alberta and is a successful businessman operating a number of Tim Horton franchises in that province. She has stated she has no intention of requesting child support from S. T. or even bringing up the subject with him. It is not clear whether S. T. is aware he is the biological father of these children. Ms. G. is obviously motivated not to make a claim against S. T. because she is presently in a common law relationship with his brother, C. T., and has been since 1997. She would rather place the entire burden of child support on Mr. P., and possibly continue the deception, most probably because of her relationship with C. T.. Ms. G. testified that C. T. earned a net income of $68,000.00 in the year 2000 and is apparently a successful fisherman.

36 On the facts of this case it would be most inappropriate, unjust and unfair to place the entire burden of child support upon Mr. P. In the circumstances, I find that an appropriate amount of child support for Mr. P. is approximately one third of the table amount he would be otherwise required to pay. The basic amount on an annual income of $56,000.00 would be $754.00 and I order Mr. P. to pay the sum of $275.00 per month for the support of these children, effective December 1, 2001. While Mr. P. has paid considerably more child support since 1997, $725.00 per month, this was agreed to prior to the *Guidelines* and is tax deductible for Mr. P.. For that reason I decline to make the present order retroactive.

COLLIS v. WILSON

(2003), 49 R.F.L. (5th) 11, 2003 CarswellOnt 3613 (Ont. S.C.J.)

1 TUCKER J.: — R.C., R.A.C. and L.R.C. appealed the decision of Justice W. Brian Stead, dated 21 August 2001. There were seven grounds of appeal as set out herein.

2 The background is as follows. R.C. resided with C.W. from approximately 1988 until 1991. During their relationship two children were born — R.R.C., born on 29 June 1988, and K.B.C., born on 18 May 1990. Suspicious of K.B.C.'s parentage from about 1996, DNA testing was requested by R.C., which excluded him as the father of the child. C.W. married a Mr. W. after separating from Mr. R.C. and a third son E. was born of that relationship. She and her three sons now reside with a Mr. F. and two of his children. Mr. W. pays $125 for each of the three boys, R.R.C., K.B.C. and E. as child support. ...

7 The [key ground] for appeal [is] as follows: ...

> It is respectfully submitted that the trial judge, The Honourable Mr. Justice W.B. Stead, erred in law and fact in finding that the appellant R.C. should be *in loco parentis* in respect of K.B.C., born May 18, 1990. The appellant states that the respondent wrongly advised the appellant R.C. that he was the father of K.B.C., which misrepresentation he relied on until such time as he initiated paternity testing at his cost. ...

14 ... The ground of appeal centres in the use by Justice Stead of a divorce case — *Chartier v. Chartier*, [1999] 1 S.C.R. 242, 235 N.R. 1, 134 Man. R. (2d) 19, [1999] 4 W.W.R. 633, 193 W.A.C. 19, 168 D.L.R. (4th) 540, 43 R.F.L. (4th) 1, [1998] S.C.J. No. 79 — when trying to ascertain the relationship between Mr. R.C. and K.B.C. The *Divorce Act*, R.S.C. 1985 (2nd Supp.), c. 3, uses words "in place of the parent", while the *Family Law Act*, R.S.O. 1990, c. F-3, speaks to a "settled intention to treat the child as a child of the family". ... In essence the entire picture of the relationship, not just financial or other isolated aspects, must be analyzed in order to determine whether or not a settled intention or *in loco parentis* situation exists and creates a liability for support at law.

15 The appellant argues that it is the repudiation that is relevant in the case of *Chartier v. Chartier*, which is not the situation here. He argues that no settled intention can be formed if the true situation is unknown to the parent in question. I agree that knowledge is an important factor to make such a choice. It is also important to determine the relevant time period of the relationship. Mr. R.C. and his parents both stated that they treated K.B.C. just like R.R.C. Of course, they had no information about K.B.C.'s parentage at the time and presumed that he was their biological child and grandchild respectively. This presumption together with the known and assumed obligation imposed by law on a "parent" to support his child cannot itself give rise to the finding of a settled intention. Unlike cases where there is strong suspicion as to parentage, although the evidence indicated some concern, real doubt did not arise until 1996 when Mr. R.C. was apparently told by Mr. M. that he and not Mr. R.C. was the father of K.B.C. The doubt was only confirmed in 1999.

16 According to Mr. R.C., he confronted Ms. C.W. with that information and it was approximately at that point that access ended for both R.R.C. and K.B.C. Since that time in approximately 1996, other than the birthday party, there has been no contact with K.B.C. or R.R.C. by Mr. R.C., nor any application for access. I do recognize the evidence that support was being paid at some point for K.B.C. I also note that, although there was testimony that he "treated [him] as a son", that in itself is not in law a settled intention to treat a child as a child of the family. It is simply a statement of his belief and understanding of what he believed the situation to be, that K.B.C. was his son. We need to review the entire relationship and find a conscious intention based on knowledge.

17 Accordingly on a review of the law and the evidence and the decision of Justice Stead, I disagree with his finding that Mr. R.C. had a settled intention to treat K.B.C. as a child of the family at any point while he had knowledge of the actual situation. His sporadic access and limited financial support and his total failure to try to have contact with the child since shortly after separation underline this lack of settled intention in our view. We would note a similar situation with Mr. R.C. for R.R.C. except for the present application for access, many years after separation. The mere fact that he pressed the biological factor has given rise to his obligation for support, not his pattern of behaviour or relationship with his son R.R.C. Accordingly, on that ground, I would grant the appeal and amend the support obligation accordingly. In other words, support based on Mr. R.C.'s income will be payable for R.R.C. only in the amount of $308 per month, based upon his income of $35,360, commencing on 1 September 2001.

NOTES AND QUESTIONS

1. As acknowledged in *P. (G.N.) v. G. (L.A.)* and in *R.C. v. C.W.*, above, the case law is divided on whether a man who treats a child as a child of the family because he mistakenly believes that he is the biological father can "stand in the place of a parent" or show "a settled intention to treat a child as a child of his ... family". One can find cases going either way under the *Divorce Act* and the *Family Law Act*, although there appears to be a tendency to hold, as in *R.C. v. C.W.*, that the reference to "settled intention" in the *Family Law Act* dictates that the man must at least have suspicions about a child's parentage. Should the different wording in the two Acts make any difference? Should a common law step-father be able to argue that he did not have a settled intention to treat a child as his own because he mistakenly thought the child was his, while a step-father married to a child's mother cannot do so under the *Divorce Act*?

2. The recent case of *Cornelio v. Cornelio* (2008), 2008 CarswellOnt 8005 (S.C.J.), decided under the *Divorce Act*, attracted a great deal of media attention and commentary. DNA testing had revealed that the ex-husband was not the biological father of 16-year-old twins. He sought to have his support obligation terminated and asked for repayment of the support that he had paid since the separation some ten years earlier. Justice van Rensburg relied heavily on *Chartier v. Chartier* and *Ballmick v. Ballmick* (2005), 18 R.F.L. (6th) 10 (Ont. C.J.) to hold against the ex-husband. The *Ballmick* case, decided under the *Family Law Act*, again involved a man who learned after separation that he had mistakenly assumed that two children were his biological offspring. Justice Maresca there stressed that "family" was not defined by biology but by relationship (para. 21):

> It is the sense of family and bonding between parent and child that is important, not whose DNA is lodged in the child's cells. To permit [the respondent] to repudiate his relationship with these children, built and demonstrated over the entire course of their lives, would be grossly unfair to them. If we are to be sensitive to the realities of these [children's] experience and to act in their best interests, the court must acknowledge the fact that [the respondent] has demonstrated a settled intention to treat them as his own children.

In commenting on the *Cornelio* case in *This Week in Family Law*, Fam. L. Nws. 2009-05 (ECarswell), Philip Epstein and Lene Madsen suggest that the result was "eminently predictable" and state:

> However unpalatable the result for the payor, the right to support is the right of the child, full stop. From a child-focused perspective, there cannot be any other result.

Do you agree that fairness to the payor should not be a factor?

3. Can the parties to a cohabitation agreement or marriage contract stipulate in advance that the step-parent will not be obligated to support a child of a previous relationship? A somewhat similar issue arose in *Jane Doe v. Alberta* (2007), 35 R.F.L. (6th) 265 (Alta. C.A.); leave to appeal refused (2007), 2007 CarswellAlta 941, 2007 CarswellAlta 942 (S.C.C.). The mother became pregnant by artificial insemination against the wishes of her male common law partner. She was willing to take on the sole financial and emotional obligation of raising the child, yet the parties wanted to remain together as partners. They brought an application asking for a declaration that, in accordance with an agreement entered into by the partners, the male partner would not have any obligation to support the child. The chambers judge denied the application, and the male partner appealed. The Court of Appeal found the prospect of the male partner ignoring the child during the term of the relationship to be unrealistic:

> [T]he answer is to be found in the context of the relationship between Jane and John Doe. The "settled intention" to remain in a close, albeit unmarried, relationship thrust John Doe, from a practical and realistic point of view, into the role of parent to this child. Can it seriously be contended that he will ignore the child when it cries? When it needs to be fed? When it stumbles? When the soother needs to be replaced? When the diaper needs to be changed?

4. Is it possible for a man to have a settled intention to treat a child as part of his family without ever cohabiting with the mother? See *Do Carmo v. Etzhorn* (1995), 16 R.F.L. (4th) 341 (Ont. Gen. Div.). In *Cheng v. Cheng* (1996), 21 R.F.L. (4th) 58, the Ontario Court of Appeal allowed a mother to add the father's parents to a claim for child support on the basis that the *FLA* "does not exclude grandparents as persons who may be responsible for support of children". See also *Mitchell v. Mitchell* (1998), 41 R.F.L. (4th) 181 (Sask. Q.B.) and the annotation to the case by Professor McLeod in the R.F.L.'s. In *Monkman v. Beaulieu* (2003), 33 R.F.L. (5th) 169 (Man. C.A.), Justice Steel stated (para. 69), in *obiter dicta*:

> ... [T]he [support] obligation ... *might* fall on a broader category of persons than former stepparents. ...
> The situations where this will occur are likely to be few and far between given that before the obligation can be imposed, a court would have to decide that the adult had, in fact, taken on the role of

parent. In making that decision, a court would examine a number of factors, including intention, on an objective and functional basis. Acts of generosity will not, in and of themselves, result in a legal determination that an the adult has taken on the role of a parent. ...

5. Section 1(1) of the *Family Relations Act*, R.S.B.C. 1996, c. 128 stipulates:

"parent" includes (b) a stepparent of a child if (i) the stepparent contributed to the support and maintenance of the child for at least one year, and (ii) the proceeding under this Act by or against the stepparent is commenced within one year after the date the stepparent last contributed to the support and maintenance of the child.

Section 1(2) then indicates:

For the purpose of paragraph (b) of the definition of "parent" in subsection (1), a person is the stepparent of a child if the person and the parent of the child (a) are or were married, or (b) lived together in a marriage-like relationship for a period of at least 2 years and, for the purposes of this Act, the marriage-like relationship may be between persons of the same gender.

Do you prefer this approach to that of the *Divorce Act* or Ontario's *FLA*?

6. In *Chartier*, the Supreme Court of Canada put an end to the debate over whether a person who assumes a parental role to a partner's child can abandon that role later. In his Annotation to the case, Professor McLeod comments (at 6 in the RFL's):

In *Chartier*, the parties cohabited, married, separated, reconciled and separated again, all within three years. As a result, Mr. Chartier acquires a long-term child-support obligation. Whether that is reasonable is not the question. The Supreme Court of Canada has decided that it is the law. The task facing many lawyers will be to advise their clients on how to prevent that from happening to them. It appears that the only way to prevent a long-term child-support commitment is never to establish a parent-child relationship with a partner's child. Social scientists will have to decide whether that is a good way to force people to interact. ...

Bastarache J.'s reasons are clear on the central issue. A person who assumes the role of a parent to a child cannot abandon that role. The only way out of the parent-child relationship is not to form the relationship in the first place. A person seeking to avoid a parental relationship to a partner's child should minimize the money he or she spends on the child, try not to treat the child in the same way as his or her own child and discourage any attempt by the child to refer to him or her other than by first name. Somehow, that behaviour does not seem to promote the child's best interests.

How did Justice Bastarache respond to this point in *Chartier*? In *Monkman v. Beaulieu* (2003), 33 R.F.L. (5th) 169 (Man. C.A.), Justice Steel discounted this argument. She quoted (at para. 35) the following passages from Alison Harvison Young's "This Child Does Have 2 (Or More) Fathers: Step-parents and Support Obligations" (2000), 45 McGill L.J. 107:

There seems to be very little in the way of empirical evidence, in either the Canadian or the U.S. context, to support such assertions. Will a concern about possible financial liability for support in fact affect conduct during a happy phase of a relationship when a family unit is being formed? Will this really, for example, deter a stepfather from taking a child to soccer practice? If so, it may well be better, as some have suggested, to have this reticence flushed out early in the relationship, thereby preventing the creation of a doomed family unit. Bastarache J. himself expresses this view in *Chartier*. ...

While the question of whether imposing support obligations on step-parents will discourage them from establishing strong relationships with their stepchildren during the marriage remains an open one, *Chartier* will eliminate a related problem created by the pre-*Chartier* line of cases led by *Carignan*: the incentive for step-parents to discontinue contact *after* divorce or separation in order to avoid support obligations.

7. Generally, a court cannot link access and child support under the CSG. In *A. (J.A.) v. A. (S.R.)* (1999), 45 R.F.L. (4th) 165 (B.C. C.A.), Madam Justice Southin stated (at 171):

... [T]he law is believed to be that, even if one parent deliberately and maliciously destroys the relationship between the other parent and the children of their marriage, which is what the respondent has done if the allegations [of child abuse] are false, that other parent must still pay the Guidelines amounts. If that is the law, then the law, on this point, lacks a moral basis.

8. In *Chartier*, the Supreme Court of Canada held that a step-parent cannot unilaterally terminate the relationship with a child, and then use the termination of the relationship as a defence against a child support claim. But what happens if the child, or the custodial parent, unilaterally terminates the relationship? Before the Supreme Court of Canada's reasons in *Chartier* were released, the Saskatchewan Court of Appeal held in *Johb v. Johb* (1998), 40 R.F.L. (4th) 379 that a step-parent's obligation to provide child support was terminated where the custodial parent cut off any relationship between the children and the step-parent. Is this result still possible in light of *Chartier*? Should it make any difference if the child, perhaps a teenager, refuses to have any relationship with the step-parent? Should this be a factor in determining the amount of support? See *H. (K.A.) v. H. (R.S.)* (2001), 23 R.F.L. (5th) 171 (Alta. Prov. Ct.), where Jordan Prov. J. held that the reasoning in *Chartier* was not applicable where a teenager cut off relations between herself and her previous stepfather. The judge stated (at para. 8): "Surely it cannot be the case that when a child herself changes the relationship with the 'payor' that he must continue to be financially responsible for her — especially when the child has relationships with other individuals who have an obligation and a capacity to support her including her mother, her father and her [new] step-father." Up to the time of writing of this edition, *H. (K.A.) v. H. (R.S.)* had not been judicially considered in any reported case.

9. In *Swindler v. Belanger* (2005), 22 R.F.L. (6th) 1 (Sask. C.A.), the step-father admitted that he stood in place of parent during his marriage to the mother. After the mother and step-father separated, the mother reconciled with the child's biological father and married him. Nonetheless, the mother applied for child support against the step-father. The trial judge dismissed the claim. The Court of Appeal allowed the mother's appeal on the basis of the reasoning in *Chartier* and held that the payor's obligation to the child survived separation and the mother's remarriage to the child's biological father.

10. After the Supreme Court of Canada decision in *Chartier*, some cases appear to set a fairly high threshold for the finding that a step-parent has a support obligation. In part, this reflects the fact that such a finding carries with it a substantial support obligation that cannot be unilaterally avoided. See, e.g., *Cook v. Cook* (2000), 3 R.F.L. (5th) 373 (N.S. S.C.); *A. (V.) c. F. (S.)* (2000), 197 D.L.R. (4th) 500 (Que. C.A.); *Neil v. Neil* (2002), 2002 CarswellOnt 2513 (Ont. S.C.J.); and *Morton v. May* (2004), 3 R.F.L. (6th) 95 (N.B. Q.B.). However, other cases, while they may examine similar factors, suggest that a person who interacts with a partner's or spouse's child on a regular and normal basis for any significant period of time is likely to be considered a parent for support purposes. See, e.g., *M. (S.T.) v. F. (M.D.)* (2002), 31 R.F.L. (5th) 82 (Alta. Q.B.). In his critical annotation to this case, Professor McLeod suggests (at 82) that it confirms "the trend that a person who interacts with a spouse's child on a regular basis is likely to be held to be a parent to the child for support purposes and *prima facie* will be ordered to pay the table amount of support for that child". In "The Child Support Obligation of Step-parents" (2001), 18 Can. J. Fam. L. 9, Professor Rogerson reports (at 100) that the threshold "is a moderately easy one to satisfy, particularly where the [non-custodial] biological parent is uninvolved and the children are relatively young at the time the relationship begins".

(b) Extent of the Step-Parent's Obligation

As we have seen, there may be a number of persons legally obligated to support the same child. At one time s. 33(7)(b) of the *FLA* expressly placed primary responsibility for support on the biological parents. There was considerable divergence in the case law regarding how courts were to recognize this primary responsibility. The Ontario Court of Appeal held in *M. (C.) v. P. (R.)* (1997), 26 R.F.L. (4th) 1 that this did not necessarily mean that the biological parents had to pay for more than one-half of the cost of child-rearing. Instead, the court concluded that the courts retained an overriding discretion to determine the appropriate apportionment and suggested that the apportionment should reflect the extent and nature of each parent's involvement with the child. Some cases held that the secondary nature of a step-parent's support obligation should be recognized by imposing a time limit on the obligation: *Spring v. Spring* (1987), 61 O.R. (2d) 743 (U.F.C.) and *A. (D.R.) v. M. (R.M.)* (1997), 30 R.F.L. (4th) 269 (Ont. Gen. Div.). In the last case, Ferrier J. stated (at 274):

> Courts in other provinces have gone further in giving the biological father primary responsibility. Courts in British Columbia, Saskatchewan and New Brunswick have held that where a child's natural father has been providing ongoing support for the child since the disposition of the wife's first marriage and continues to do so ..., the applicant must prove (a) that the support is inadequate and (b) that nothing further can be expected from the natural parent before the court will order support against the

non-biological parent. Further, in these provinces, the courts made these decisions even in the absence of legislative provisions similar to s. 33(7)(b).

The statutory recognition of the primary responsibility of biological or adoptive parents no longer appears in the *FLA*. It was repealed by the *Uniform Federal and Provincial Child Support Guidelines Act, 1997*, S.O. 1997, c. 20. The CSG generally create a standardized formula for determining child support based solely on the payor's income and the number of children. However, in some situations, such as that of step-parents, the courts have a discretion to deviate from the basic calculation. Section 5 of the CSG specifies that, where the party against whom the support order is sought stands in the place of a parent, the court is to order payment of the amount that it considers appropriate "having regard to these guidelines and any other parent's legal duty to support the child". The section lists two specific factors and one of the issues that has arisen is whether the court can consider any others.

Cases applying s. 5 reveal many divergent approaches. Some courts, e.g., the Nova Scotia Supreme Court in *P. (G.N.) v. G. (L.A.)*, above, interpret this section as granting a discretionary power to order the amount that is just and appropriate in all the circumstances. The British Columbia Court of Appeal appeared to endorse this approach in *Dutrisac v. Ulm* (2000), 6 R.F.L. (5th) 132 (B.C.C.A.). See also *Guillemette v. Guillemette* (2008), [2008] O.J. No. 334, 2008 CarswellOnt 434 (S.C.J.), in which Justice Arrell fixed a reduced amount of child support for the step-father without articulating a principle underlying the amount.

Other cases indicate that once step-parents have crossed the threshold of parental status, they are full parents and are considered presumptively liable for child support on the same terms as biological parents. The only issue under this approach is whether the step-parent's obligations should be reduced because of the actual payment of support by a biological parent. "Justice" and "fairness" are not considered. Frequently, there is no reduction where the biological parent is not paying any support. See, e.g., *Kolada v. Kolada* (1999), 48 R.F.L. (4th) 370 (Alta. Q.B.); *Stanton v. Solby* (1999), 49 R.F.L. (4th) 422 (B.C. Master); *B. (S.) v. B. (L.)* (1999), 2 R.F.L. (5th) 32 (Ont. S.C.J.); *O. (T.D.) v. O. (R.G.)* (2000), 6 R.F.L. (5th) 389 (B.C. S.C.); *Bell v. Michie* (1998), 38 R.F.L. (4th) 199 (Ont. Gen. Div.); and *Monkman v. Beaulieu* (2003), 33 R.F.L. (5th) 169 (Man. C.A.). Indeed, Justice Cusinato stated (para. 27) in *obiter dicta* in *Dovicin v. Dovicin* (2002), 29 R.F.L. (5th) 281 (Ont. S.C.J.) that a court has no jurisdiction to reduce a step-parent's obligation unless a biological parent is required to pay child support. Compare these cases to *Oxley v. Oxley* (2003), 1 R.F.L. (6th) 354 (Ont. S.C.J.), where the step-father received a 50% reduction on the basis that the mother of the child, who was heading off to college, should seek support from the biological father. The child had very little contact with her biological father and the failure to pursue him for support during the second marriage had the step-father's tacit approval. In *Millward v. Millward* (2003), 48 R.F.L. (5th) 294 (Ont. S.C.J.), a man in Ontario and a woman in Texas met over the internet and got married. To obtain the consent of her son's father to the move to Canada, the mother agreed not to seek child support from him. The Canadian marriage lasted less than two years and the mother and son planned to return to Texas. The court required the husband to pay the Table amount for one year on the assumption that the mother would be able to obtain support thereafter from the biological father.

Where a biological parent is already providing child support should the step-parent still be ordered to pay the full Table amount? One could argue, as did Master Nitikman in *Gordon v. Paquette* (1998), 36 R.F.L. (4th) 382 (B.C. Master); varied (1998), 1998 CarswellBC 645 (B.C. S.C.); additional reasons at (1998), 1998 CarswellBC 763 (B.C. S.C.), that an affirmative answer is consistent with the policy behind the CSG; namely, that a child should benefit from the income of all of his parents. See also *MacArthur v. Demers* (1998), 166 D.L.R. (4th) 172 (Ont. Gen. Div.) (biological father obligated to pay $150 per month under a separation agreement; court ordered stepfather to pay full Table amount of $545 per month). More often, some adjustment, even if only modest, is made to the step-parent's obligation where the biological parent is paying support. Some cases deduct the full amount being paid from the amount that the step-parent would otherwise have to pay. See, e.g., *Akert v. Akert* (2000), 2000 CarswellSask 334 (Sask. Q.B.) and *Symons v. Taylor* (2000), 10 R.F.L. (5th) 443 (Ont. S.C.J.). Others see this as too much of a reduction and grant a more modest one. See, e.g., *Singh v. Singh* (1997), 1997 CarswellBC 2162 (B.C. Master) and *Squires v. Severs* (2000), 2000 CarswellBC 1150 (B.C. S.C.). In *Cowie v. Makin* (2004), 8 R.F.L. (6th) 1 (Ont. S.C.J.), Justice Langdon limited the step-father's obligation to pay child support to five years in accordance with a separation agreement.

In *Adler v. Jonas* (1999), 48 R.F.L. (4th) 228 (B.C. S.C.), Hardinge J. noted (at 238) that there was a considerable divergence of opinion in the cases regarding the application of s. 5 of the CSG. The Justice set the non-custodial biological parent's support at the Table amount of $141 per month and calculated her share of the extraordinary expenses in accordance with s. 7. Justice Hardinge then suggested the following approach to determining the amount of the step-parent's obligation under s. 5:

> 1) determine the *Guidelines* Table amount, which represents the upper limit of the amount that can be ordered;
>
> 2) determine the legal duty of any other parent, generally the *Guidelines* Table amount; and
>
> 3) decide whether the total contribution of both biological parents will achieve a fair standard of support for the child. If it will, then the court may not require the stepparent to pay any support. If it will not, the stepparent will be required to top up available funds until a fair standard is reached.

In the end, the court ordered the step-father to pay $125 per month on the basis that this amount plus the mother's payment of $141 and the custodial father's notional contribution of $466 per month would provide "a sum equal to that which would have been available to [the child] had her natural parents' marriage not broken down".

The Department of Justice noted in *Children Come First: A Report to Parliament Reviewing the Provisions and Operations of the Federal Child Support Guidelines* (Ottawa, 2002) (Vol. 2 at 49–51) the variety of approaches taken under s. 5 of the CSG. The Department concluded (at 51):

> Courts have adopted a variety of approaches to this issue [determining the quantum of support to be paid by a step-parent]. In light of the resulting inconsistencies some people have argued that the regulations should give judges explicit direction about determining the amount of support for step-children. However, allocating child support among natural parents and step-parents is quite a complex task, which is largely driven by the facts of each case. During consultations, most respondents were concerned that a rigid formula could create unfair results. For these reasons, this section should not be amended.

The CSG and the Tables were amended effective May 1, 2006. Section 5 was left untouched.

Recently, the British Columbia Court of Appeal revisited the application of s. 5 of the CSG in *H. (U.V.) v. H. (M.W.)* (2008), 59 R.F.L. (6th) 25 (B.C. C.A.), a case that is likely to become the leading case on this section even though there were several unusual facts. The mother and father of two children separated in 1992. They shared custody and neither sought a support order. The mother then began a common law relationship with another man (the step-father). The step-father was anxious to assume full responsibility for the children and insisted that the father pay no support. When she learned that the step-father had sexually assaulted one of her children, the mother ended the relationship and sought child support. In 2002, the step-father was ordered to pay the Table amount of $297 per month. The step-father's annual income increased significantly thereafter to about $90,000 and the mother sought to have the support increased to the Table amount of $1,007. She did not seek additional child support from the father who earned about $100,000 annually and was paying about $376 monthly plus some additional expenses. However, the father became involved in the case, presumably because the step-father added him as a party.

The trial judge ordered the father to pay $430 monthly and the step-father to pay the Table amount. The appellate court allowed the step-father's appeal. Justice Newbury, for the Court, stated (paras. 38–43):

> 38 ... although the broad principles of law relating to the existence of child support obligations on the part of stepparents are clear, Canadian courts have differed as to how those obligations, as stated in the Guidelines, are to be determined in practice. I read s. 5 as requiring that the legal duties of support of the "other parent(s)" — in this case, the natural parents — be considered when support is sought from a stepparent. If such duties are to be considered, it seems obvious that they must be quantified if possible. For this purpose, the "other parent(s)" should be before the court, or other evidence satisfactory to the court relating to that parent's status should be adduced. ... Unless that other parent is a stepparent, s. 3 requires that his or her support be the applicable table amount unless custody is being shared, the child is over age 19, or one of the other "discretionary" provisions applies. ... At this stage, the process is not one of "balancing" or even "apportionment": it appears that the natural parent's obligation can be determined only in accordance with the non-discretionary "presumptive rule" of s. 3.
>
> 39 Thus the chambers judge below did err, in my respectful view, in failing to determine whether the father was in fact contributing an amount at least equal to what he would have been required to pay under s. 3 had he been making regular monthly payments in accordance with the Guidelines. Whether or not the father was doing so, the chambers judge should then have ordered him to pay his table amount — although if the mother was content to accept support in the form of the payment of tuition fees or other expenses, she could enter an agreement with him to that effect. She could not, however, choose to give the father a "pass" in favour of pursuing the stepfather for all the support the children required.
>
> 40 Once the duty of the "other parent" had been determined, the chambers judge could proceed to determine the stepfather's obligation, "having regard to" that duty and "these Guidelines". ... [T]he chambers judge's discretion under s. 5 was not "unfettered", but certainly the phrase "these Guidelines" would include the objectives stated in s. 1, which I repeat here for convenience:
>
>> (a) to establish a fair standard of support for children that ensures that they continue to benefit from the financial means of both parents after separation;
>>
>> (b) to reduce conflict and tension between parents by making the calculation of maintenance orders more objective;
>>
>> (c) to improve the efficiency of the legal process by giving courts and parents guidance in setting the levels of maintenance orders and encouraging settlement; and
>>
>> (d) to ensure consistent treatment of parents and children who are in similar circumstances.
>
> Thus a "fair standard of support", objectivity of calculation, and reduction of conflict between parents are relevant to the determination of "appropriate" support by the stepparent. On the other hand, s. 5 does not, in my view, confer a discretion that is so broad as to encompass "all" the circumstances of a case ... or "fairness" to the father arising from a kind of promissory estoppel against the stepparent (as was suggested by the chambers judge in this case).
>
> 41 Given the "children-first" perspective of the Guidelines ..., primacy should be given to the children's standard of living. Where for example the stepparent provided a standard to the children during the period of cohabitation that was materially higher than that which the natural parents can provide by means of their Guidelines amounts, a court might find it appropriate to make an order against the stepparent that is designed to provide the higher standard, or something approximating it, "on top of" the other parents' support. However, where the "piling" of Guidelines amounts would result in a standard beyond one that is reasonable in the context of the standard the children have previously enjoyed, such a "windfall" or "wealth transfer" ... is unlikely to be "appropriate". At the other end of the spectrum, where the three (or more) parents' Guidelines "contributions" together are needed to provide the children with a reasonable standard of living, then both the stepparent and the

non-custodial parent(s) may well be required to pay full Guidelines amounts. Or, where one of the natural or adoptive parents is not present or is unable to pay any support, the stepparent may well have to pay his or her full table amount. The Legislature has left it to the judgment of trial and chambers judges in the first instance to fashion orders that are "appropriate" under s. 5. At the same time, the Guidelines system is not thereby jettisoned in favour of a "wide open" discretion. The inquiry must, like the Guidelines themselves, focus on the children and their needs.

42 In this case, the income levels of the father and stepfather were not very different. When the stepfather was supporting the children, the father was sharing custody and was therefore not expected to contribute funds to the mother for the children's care. Now, the natural parents are able to provide a quite comfortable standard of support — the father by paying his Guidelines amount and the mother by providing her presumed contribution as custodial parent. The chambers judge reasoned that the mother's expenses were slightly more than her Form 89 had indicated — about $2,570 per month from May 1, 2006. In this, he has not been shown to be wrong. Where he erred was in approaching the natural father's obligation as a secondary one, losing sight of the non-discretionary obligation created by s. 3. If the chambers judge had factored in the Guidelines obligations of the natural parents, which come to a total of $2,210 per month, he would have been left with a shortfall of $360 per month. If the stepfather had been ordered to "top up" this amount, the children would have a more than a "fair standard of support" and the other requirements and objectives of the Guidelines would have been met.

43 I would allow the appeal on the basis that the chambers judge erred in his approach to the determination of the stepfather's obligation under s. 5 of the Regulation and the father's obligation under s. 3, and in considering factors that do not come within the wording of s. 5.

In the result, the father was ordered to pay the Table amount of $1,581 per month and the step-father was required to pay $360 monthly.

Sections 33(5) and (6) of the *FLA* permit third parties to be added in support applications. For an example of a case where a step-father added the children's biological father to a mother's application for child support, see *Kaszas v. Guinta* (2001), 20 R.F.L. (5th) 88 (Ont. S.C.J.). The *Divorce Act* does not contain a comparable provision, but some courts have permitted a step-father, against whom a child support order is sought, to add the biological father as a party defendant in divorce proceedings: *Pye v. Pye* (1995), 15 R.F.L. (4th) 76 at 81 (B.C. S.C.); *French v. Stevenson* (1996), 23 R.F.L. (4th) 155 (B.C. Master); and *Cowie v. Makin, supra.* In *Kolada v. Kolada* (1999), 48 R.F.L. (4th) 370 (Alta. Q.B.), Veit J. concluded (at 375) that the Supreme Court of Canada in *Chartier*, "when referring with approval to actions by one custodial parent against another non-custodial parent in a three or more parent situation", indicated that courts might allow the addition of third parties in child support proceedings even if there is no explicit legislative directive. More recently, the cases were reviewed in *Ross v. Ross* (2001), 22 R.F.L. (5th) 426 (Man. Master).

For most situations involving biological or adoptive parents, the *Child Support Guidelines* (analyzed later in this chapter) set a child support figure in accordance with the payor's income. Courts have, for example, no discretion to deviate from the Table amount on the basis that the biological father has no social relationship with the child or may never have had such a relationship. A biological or adoptive parent must pay at least the Table amount, unless a court has discretion to reduce it on the basis of one of the limited areas of discretion under the CSG. While step-parents may, therefore, be able to join biological parents in any application for child support, it appears that biological parents cannot easily add step-parents. In *Pevach v. Spalding* (2001), 19 R.F.L. (5th) 368 (Sask. Q.B.), Justice Wright refused to allow the biological father to add the step-father to a support proceeding under provincial legislation commenced against him by the child's mother. See also *Robinson v. Domin* (1998), 39 R.F.L. (4th) 92 (B.C. S.C.) and Professor McLeod's annotation. This approach was supported in *Wright v. Zaver* (2002), 59 O.R. (3d) 26, 24 R.F.L. (5th) 207 (C.A.).

(3) Age Limits

BALA, "CHILD SUPPORT FOR ADULT CHILDREN: WHEN DOES ECONOMIC CHILDHOOD END?"

1000 Islands Legal Conference, October, 2008 (Footnotes omitted)

Unlike most areas of child support law where the introduction of the *Child Support Guidelines* in 1997 brought a significant degree of predictability and reduced the need to consider the circumstances of individual children and parents, support for adult children remains an area where there is significant judicial discretion and only limited predictability. The facts of individual cases may be significant, as may be the opinions the particular judge about the socially contentious issue of when economic childhood ends, and when and how the adult obligation of self-support begins.

While this remains a contentious and discretionary area, there are some clear trends in the case law. Reflecting the changes in intact families where young adults are living with their parents longer as well as looking to parents for more financial support, compared to a couple of decades ago, the courts in Ontario and other Canadian provinces are now more likely to recognize the obligation to provide support for adult children. Further, the duration of support is now likely to be a somewhat longer, though most support orders terminate when children are in their early twenties, and the obligation to provide support very rarely extends past the mid-twenties of the adult child.

The Social Context: "Delayed Adulthood"

There have been two different social trends related to "coming of age" in Canada that are in some respects in tension with one another, while in other respects reinforcing: the "adultification of youth" and "delayed adulthood." In some ways adolescents in Canada are having "adult" experiences earlier in life than was the cases a few decades ago: the age at which youth have their first experiences with dating, sex, drugs and alcohol has fallen, youth are spending less time with their parents and more with peers, and high schools are placing greater emphasis on "career planning" than in the past. On the other hand, and of particular relevance for the issue of child support for adult children, "delayed adulthood" is reflected in a longer period of post-secondary education and later age of marriage (especially for middle and upper income young adults). Securing good employment requires more education and training, causing increasing numbers of young adults to spend more time in post-secondary institutions. Further, the tuition for many programs has dramatically increased. More time in school and higher tuition costs means higher debt loads. Higher debt loads have caused more young adults to live with their parents while paying off debts rather than living on their own. For a number of economic, social and cultural reasons, increasing numbers of young adults in Canada are delaying "independent living" and continuing to live with their parents, or at least look to them for economic and social support.

The Relevant Statutory Provisions

The authority for a court to order child support for children over the age of majority is found in the *Divorce Act*, and, in Ontario, the *Ontario Family Law Act*, while the *Child Support Guidelines* are to be used to determine the quantum that should be ordered. The *Divorce Act* and the *Family Law Act* determine who is eligible for support; while there is significant overlap in the relevant definitions, there are some significant differences. First, they differ on who can make an application for child support for an adult child. Second, they differ on the circumstances in which child support can be ordered for an adult child. [See s. 2(1) of the *Divorce Act* for its definition of "child of the marriage" and s. 31 of the *Family Law Act*.] The provisions of the *Family Law Act* govern cases where the parties are not obtaining a divorce, most often because the parents were not married to each other.

Determining the amount of support that the child will be entitled to under either legislative scheme is done under the *Child Support Guidelines*, which provide:

> 3. (2) Child the age of majority or over — Unless other[wise] provided under these Guidelines, where a child to whom an order for the support of child relates is the of majority or over, the amount of an order for the support of a child is
>
>> (a) the amount determined by applying these Guidelines as if the child were under the age of majority; or
>>
>> (b) if the court considers that amount to be inappropriate, the amount that the court considers appropriate, having regard to the condition, means, needs, and other circumstances of the child and the financial ability of each spouse to contribute to the support of the child.
>
> 7. (1) Special or Extraordinary Expenses — In a child support order, the court may, on either spouse's request, provide for an amount to cover all or any portion of the following expenses, which expense may be estimated, taking into account the necessity of the expense in relation to the child's best interests and the reasonableness of the expense in relation to the means of the spouses and those of the child and to the family's spending pattern prior to the separation ...
>
>> (e) expenses for post-secondary education.

Eligibility Under the Two Statutes

The *Divorce Act* and the *Family Law Act* differ in some of the criteria for eligibility for support for an adult child. The *Family Law Act* has a narrower and somewhat clearer test, with eligibility only if a young adult child is "enrolled in a full time program of education" and has not voluntarily withdrawn from parental control. The *Divorce Act* has a broader and more discretionary test, allowing for support for young adults "but unable, by reason of illness, disability or other cause, to withdraw from [parental] charge." In practice, there is significant discretion under both pieces of legislation in determining both whether to order support (or cease to require it) and how much support to order.

[Almost] all of the reported case law for support of adult children under the *Divorce Act* deals with cases where the child is pursuing post-secondary studies, and there is only limited practical difference between the two legislative regimes. However, the *Divorce Act* is clearly broader, allowing for support for children who are disabled, pursuing competitive athletic careers or simply unemployed.

Who Can Apply?

The *Divorce Act* allows only spouses and former spouses to apply for support on a child's behalf, as recognized by Johnstone J. in *Wahl v. Wahl* (2000), 2 R.F.L. (5th) 307 (Alta. Q.B.):

> Support is a creation of statute. This means that standing to apply for support, entitlement to support, and form, duration and amount of support are all governed by the enabling support legislation. A child is not a party to divorce proceedings and there is no provision in the *Divorce Act* to allow a child to claim support or apply to vary an outstanding support order.

By way of contrast, the *Family Law Act* states that a "dependant" may apply for the support, which allows a child to make his or her own application. Even under the *F.L.A.*, child support for adult children is normally obtained by the custodial parent, but children can themselves apply. In *Haskell v. Letourneau* (1979), 25 O.R. (2d) 139 (Co. Ct.), Clements Co. Ct.

J. allowed the application of a sixteen year old boy for support from his mother under what is now the *Family Law Act*, and commented:

> ... the concept of the "withdrawal from parental control" at age 16 means a "voluntary" withdrawal; the free choice, indeed, of the child to cut the family bonds and strike out on a life of his own ... It is his choice, freely made, to cut himself away from the family unit. Once this choice is freely made and the responsibility accepted by the child, the family unit has, in effect, been severed and the responsibility of the parents to support the child thus ceases.
>
> If the child is driven from parental control by the emotional or physical abuse in the home brought on due to the circumstances in the home, then surely he cannot be compelled to remain there ... The choice of leaving was not voluntary but of necessity to ensure the physical and mental well-being of the child.

There is not much reported case law on adult children bringing their own support applications under the *F.L.A.*, and while in theory such an application could be brought even if parents continue to reside together, all of the reported cases actually involve situations where the parents are no longer living together. The courts have generally accepted that where a child is 18 or 19 years and still attending high school, there is an onus on the parents to establish that the child has voluntarily withdrawn from "parental control." The courts are generally sympathetic to those young adults who are still in high school and having difficulty in living with either parent if there has been emotional turmoil as a result of parental separation. In *Judd v. Judd* (1995), 16 R.F.L. (4th) 430 (Ont. Prov. Div.), the court held that an 18 year old girl whose parents had separated could bring her own child support application under the *F.L.A.* against her father, despite the fact that she was living with the family of a friend. The court concluded that she could not reasonably be expected to live with either parent, taking into account the negative attitude of her step-mother towards the girl. Guay Prov. Ct. J. observed:

> [I]t is clear that the respondent [daughter] ... did not remove herself from the home of either of her parents simply because she was a rebellious teenager seeking a life of untrammelled freedom. Her departure from each of these homes, I find, was ultimately caused by the break-up of her parents' home and her consequent inability to function in either of the reconstituted units. As such, it cannot be argued that she voluntarily withdrew from parental control. As an eighteen-year-old who is still pursuing her education, she should not be left to her own wits to fund her uncompleted education.

On the other hand, in cases where young adults choose to establish independence, they cannot look to their parents for support; the lack of judicial sympathy is most apparent in cases where the child leaves to live with a boy friend (or girl friend.)

In cases where an order for the support of an adult child has already been ordered under the *Divorce Act*, the child may not bring an additional application against the payor on his or her own behalf under the *Family Law Act* as this could effectively charge the payor parent with two simultaneous orders for support. In the 2008 Saskatchewan case of *Skolney v. Herman* (2008), 2008 CarswellSask 68 (Q.B.), a nineteen year old had moved out of the homes of both of her parents while attending a post secondary college program. She filed an application for support from both of the parents. Previously, a divorce order had ordered that her father pay child support to her mother, with whom the girl had lived after separation. The court held that the girl could not bring her own application under the *Divorce Act*, as only a spouse or former spouse could do so. Further, because there was a child support order in effect under the federal *Divorce Act*, an application for child support could not be brought under the provincial *Family Law Act* due to the constitutional doctrine of paramountcy. McIntyre J. explained:

> [There is] a clear and obvious conflict in operation if the father were the subject of two requirements to pay support, once to his former wife for the maintenance of the "child of the marriage" and again to the child himself as a dependent who has achieved relief under the provincial statute and had the quantum of that support assessed according to the criteria set out in the *Family Law Act* ... Until the provisions in the divorce decree were extinguished, there would continue to be an apparent and actual

conflict if the applicant were allowed to maintain his case and to get an order under provisional law. By virtue of the doctrine of federal paramountcy, only the provision in the divorce decree granted under federal law could prevail.

In summary, [in] order for an application to be made under either Act, the child must display a level of dependence, and as a result, applications are most likely to be made and enforced by the "custodial" (or perhaps better the "residential") parent. In practical terms, that parent is most likely to have the resources and understanding to deal with the court process. However, if there is no child support order under the *Divorce Act*, it is possible for a child to bring his or her own support application under the *Family Law Act*, provided that the child is in attendance at school and can show that there has not be a "voluntary withdrawal from parental control."

Who Can be Paid?

Unlike with the application, which cannot be brought by a child under the *Divorce Act*, both the *Divorce Act* and the *Family Law Act* permit support payments to be made either to the other parent or the child directly. Although payments are usually made to the applicant parent, direct payment to the child may be ordered or arranged by agreement in cases where the child is living away at school or there is a high level animosity between the two parents.

In some cases where the relationship between an adult child and the payor parent is strained, the court may order that payment is to be made to the child or even directly to a post-secondary institution on the child's behalf, in order to emphasize to the child "where the money comes from," and hopefully instil an appropriately appreciative attitude in the child. This will also ensure that there is no benefit to a hostile applicant parent from the support.

In *Colford v. Colford* (2005), 2005 CarswellOnt 1527 (S.C.J.), the court found that the child's mother had negatively influenced her son after the separation, and effectively alienated him from the payor father. By the time that the child was an adult and residing at university, the father brought an application to terminate support. Goodman J continued support, but ordered that support was to be made directly to the child's post-secondary institution. Similarly, in *Rosenberg v. Rosenberg* (2003), 42 R.F.L. (5th) 440 (Ont. S.C.J.); additional reasons at (2003), 2003 CarswellOnt 3250 (S.C.J.), Chapnik J. found that the mother bore much of the responsibility for the breakdown in the relationship between the daughter and her father. The child in this case also lived away at school for most of the year. Accordingly, Chapnik J. ordered that support payments be made directly to the child and to her educational institution.

Adult Child Support: The Four-Step Approach of Wesemann

In the British Columbia case of *Wesemann v. Wesemann* (1999), 49 R.F.L. (4th) 435 (B.C. S.C.), Martinson J. articulated a frequently cited "four-step approach" for determining support for an adult child under the *Divorce Act*, an approach that can also apply with minor adjustments to cases under the Ontario *Family Law Act*.

Step One: Decide whether the child is a "child of the marriage" as defined in the *Divorce Act*? If s/he is not, that ends the matter.

Step Two: Determine whether the approach of applying the *Guidelines* as if the child were under the age of majority ("the usual *Guidelines* approach") is challenged. If that approach is not challenged, determine the amount payable based on the usual *Guidelines* approach.

Step Three: If the usual *Guidelines* approach is challenged, decide whether the challenger has proven that the usual *Guidelines* approach is inappropriate. If not, the usual *Guidelines* amount applies.

Step Four: If the usual *Guidelines* approach is inappropriate, decide what amount is appropriate, having regard to the condition, means, needs and other circumstances of the child and the financial.

Step One involves determining whether or not the child is eligible for support and for how long that support will last. Steps two, three and four are followed to determine the quantum of support that should be ordered. This paper will now address these two issues in order, though the discussion will demonstrate that there is often some overlap between the different steps and issues. ...

The Child's Actual Enrolment in a Full or Part-Time Course of Studies

The significance of whether a student is in full or part-time is in part dependent on whether the proceedings are under the *Divorce Act* or the *Family Law Act*. The Ontario *Family Law Act* requires that the child be "enrolled in a *full time* program of education" and therefore, in proceedings under this Act, child support cannot be ordered for a young adult who is only attending part-time. The issue of part-time studies is more complex in proceedings under the *Divorce Act*. In cases under the *Divorce Act* where a child is only enrolled part-time or is waiting for a suitable program to begin, support may still be ordered. As stated in *Gamache v. Gamache* (1999), 49 R.F.L. (4th) 258 (Alta. Q.B.), "a parent has an obligation to assist the parent on whom the child is dependent through a reasonable transition period." This includes a waiting period before a child is about to begin a post-secondary program. While the courts seem willing to order support during a transition period, this period is not without limit. In *Harder v. Harder* (2003), 41 R.F.L. (5th) 69 (Sask. Q.B.), an eighteen year old young woman who was employed full time but living at home in order to accumulate savings for future education was denied support. Ryan-Froslie J. concluded that:

> Saving money for school and paying off debts does not constitute an "other cause" as contemplated in the *Divorce Act* definition of "child of the marriage". Choosing not to withdraw from her mother's care is not the same as being unable to withdraw from that care.

However, if the child is waiting for school to begin in the near future, then it is likely that support will be ordered.

If the child is only attending school part-time, the judge will likely consider the amount of time spent on the program, and the extent to which it is appropriate for the student to work part-time and provide some, or all, of their own support. In cases where the child could assume a heavier course load, has significant employment while additional attending school part-time, or lives on their own, the court is less likely to grant support. ...

2. Student Loans or Other Financial Assistance

In most cases not involving wealthy parents, the court will also require the child to accrue some level of student debt. However, the courts have been sensitive to the fact that student debt is not the same as support and they are unlikely to require that a child rely primarily on debt if a payor parent was able to pay any support while the child was a minor. The courts are balancing the parent's obligations towards an adult child with an expectation that adult students make a real contribution to their own education.

As recognized by the late Professor McLeod, "most courts are reluctant to allow a payor to avoid child support by insisting the child maximize his or her contribution by student loans, since student loans are just cost deferrals. When the child is finished school, the loans must be paid." In ... *Lewi v. Lewi* (2006), 28 R.F.L. (6th) 250 (Ont. C.A.); additional reasons at (2006), 2006 CarswellOnt 3214 (C.A.), Juriansz J.A. observed that "children should suffer as little as possible as a consequence of their parents separating." *Lewi* was not about student debt, but rather was a case about the use of a trust fund to help pay for post-secondary education; ... the Court expected some use of the child's trust fund, but it did not require the use of all of those funds in order to eliminate all of the payor father's responsibility. The analysis of the Court in *Lewi* would suggest that the Court of Appeal may be sympathetic to the argument that the adult child should not be expected to assume a large debt to absolve a payor parent of the duty of support.

While parents have a responsibility to provide support to adult children undertaking studies, this must be balanced against the responsibility of young adults to contribute to their own education in a way that reflects self-reliance and diligence. Further, the duty of children to contribute to their education through loans and employment income is "gradually increased as they age and advance in their studies [especially] where the parents have limited income levels."

ZEDNER v. ZEDNER

(1989), 22 R.F.L. (3d) 207, 1989 CarswellOnt 287 (Ont. Prov. Ct.)

[Dana Zedner, aged 19, lived with her mother and her mother's husband, Mr. Jackson, in her grandmother's house following her mother's remarriage in 1986. The husband assumed total control over the family. Life in the home became tense and stressful, with constant fights. The husband interfered with Dana's relationship with her mother and sister, who moved out of the home. Further facts are revealed in the following excerpt from King Prov. J.'s reasons.]

This is an application [under the *FLA*] by 19-year-old Dana Zedner for support from her mother Susan Jackson. Susan Jackson disputes Dana's claim stating that, although Dana is enrolled in a full-time program of education, she has withdrawn from Mrs. Jackson's control. ...

Dana had terrible fights with Mr. Jackson. On one occasion, as she was going out with a friend, he called her a "tart" and physically kicked her out the door. She says her mother stood by and watched. More upsetting to her than Mr. Jackson's behaviour was her mother's passivity. She could not believe her mother would let Mr. Jackson do that to her, that her mother would never have stood for that sort of behaviour towards her before. Mr. Jackson often threatened to have the C.A.S. take Dana away. Eventually things in the household became so unbearable that Dana began preparing her own meals and eating them in her bedroom. She spent as much time as she could in her room or out of the house. She talked to neither Mr. nor Mrs. Jackson.

In November 1987 Mr. and Mrs. Jackson purchased a three-bedroom condominium and moved into it. Dana stayed on in her grandmother's home and has had no contact whatsoever with her mother. She says that she did not want to go with the Jacksons and that it was clear that they did not want her to.

Susan Jackson gave testimony and in it indicated that she had hoped Dana would move with the Jacksons into the condominium. She admits that the relationship between Dana and the Jacksons was extremely bad but that she hoped Dana would "come to her senses" and see what the real world was like. There was no evidence that she at any time actually asked Dana to join them in the condominium. ...

I have not reviewed the evidence in such detail in order to assign fault but rather to determine if the defence [based on s. 31(2) of the *FLA*] given by Mrs. Jackson has, in fact, been established. The predecessor to the *Family Law Act, 1986*, namely, the *Family Law Reform Act*, had a similar section (s. 16(2)). ... In the case of *Haskell v. Letourneau* (1980), 25 O.R. (2d) 139, 100 D.L.R. (3d) 329, 1 F.L.R.A.C. 306, Judge Clements of the County Court stated that in order for the "withdrawal" to be an established defence, it must be *voluntary*. The court stated at p. 151:

> ... It is his choice, freely made, to cut himself away from the family unit. Once this choice is freely made and the responsibility accepted by the child, the family unit has, in effect, been severed and the responsibility of the parents to support the child thus ceases.

> If the child is driven from parental control by the emotional or physical abuse in the home brought on due to the circumstances in the home, then surely he cannot be compelled to remain there. ... The choice of leaving was not voluntary but of necessity to ensure the physical and mental well-being of the child.

The court goes on to say at pp. 152-53:

> To force [the child] to return to that residence and endure the emotional and personal stress present there or as an alternative to deny him support would be unthinkable for his best interest. This is especially true by virtue of the fact that his present home surroundings are placid and supportive and provide him with the means to secure his legitimate aspirations.

In the case of *Dolabaille v. Carrington* (1981), 32 O.R. (2d) 442 at 445, 21 R.F.L. (2d) 207, Judge Weisman of the Ontario Provincial Court (Family Division) stated:

> In my view the Legislature intended that a very limited or narrow approach be taken to the defence contained in s. 16(2) of the Act. In my opinion it is only applicable in the clearest of cases of a free and voluntary withdrawal from reasonable parental control.

Judge Weisman gave a number of reasons for this interpretation, among others, that, "it recognizes that most normal, emancipated teenagers go through a period in which they become difficult for their parents to control, and excludes them from the operation of s. 16(2)".

Judge Ingram of the Ontario Provincial Court (Family Division) dealt with the new wording of the *Family Law Act, 1986*, as compared to the predecessor Act. In the case of *B. (S.) v. B. (R.)*, [1987] W.D.F.L. 2228, 18th September 1987 (unreported), he stated that the above interpretations still applied. I agree. The new Act has simply changed the parameters of parental obligation. Now a child must be enrolled in a full-time program of education, but a child who is 16 years of age or older must not have withdrawn from parental control.

I am satisfied that in this case Dana did not voluntarily withdraw from parental control. Circumstances simply made it impossible for her to continue to live with her mother. Although there was some faint evidence that Mrs. Jackson would indeed have Dana live with her, this is not a realistic proposal. Mrs. Jackson and Dana have not communicated for almost two years; there is no evidence that any professional help has been sought to improve this situation; there is no evidence that anything would be different should Dana move in with Mr. and Mrs. Jackson; Dana is doing well in her present setting.

Dana had net earnings of about $220 a month. In January 1989 she signed minutes of settlement with her father, Ralph Zedner, whereby he is to support her at the rate of $200 monthly. Since that time he has made one payment and Dana has taken the appropriate steps to have that order enforced. Even if that order is enforced, Dana still requires support from her mother. She has no money saved, no money for emergencies and requires ongoing money for food, clothing, accommodation, transit, school fees, books and entertainment. It is clear that Dana has the ability and the determination to go on to a higher level of education in order to eventually establish herself in the adult working world. Her expenses are reasonable and modest.

Mrs. Jackson has an income of approximately $27,000 and shares all expenses with Mr. Jackson whose income is "somewhat higher". I am satisfied that Mrs. Jackson has the means to support her daughter Dana. She has a secure monthly income, no debts other than a mortgage and no dependents other than Dana. I am satisfied that a reasonable figure for support would be the sum of $300 monthly. ...

WAHL v. WAHL

(2000), 2 R.F.L. (5th) 307, 2000 CarswellAlta 13 (Alta. Q.B.)

[On their divorce in 1990, the parents entered into minutes of settlement. They provided, *inter alia*, that the father would support the daughter, who lived with her mother, after she reached 18 if she continued her education. The mother moved to British Columbia in 1998, but the daughter stayed in Edmonton to complete secondary school. Both parents agreed to this arrangement and the father paid support directly to the daughter. In September 1998, the daughter and her father withdrew $12,600 from a registered education savings plan (RESP) set up for the daughter's education. The daughter then handed her father a strongly worded letter indicating that she did not wish to have any relationship with him, but that she would "take him to court" if he failed to pay support. The daughter used much of the RESP money to fund a trip to Egypt and the remainder was spent on living expenses and preparatory courses for a three-year Music Theatre-Performance Program at Sheridan College in Ontario.

The father stopped paying child support as soon as the daughter turned 18, in large part because he was upset by her letter. The daughter applied for support under the *Divorce Act* and the father was ordered to pay on an interim basis in August 1999 shortly before the daughter began her studies at Sheridan. The style of cause was subsequently amended to list the mother as the applicant, but the daughter and her lawyer actually conducted the litigation because of the mother's poor financial and emotional circumstances.

The financial information provided to the court indicated that the daughter's expenses for one academic year were approximately $19,000, consisting of about $4,600 in tuition and other fees, $165 for materials, and $14,350 for living costs. She had obtained a student loan for $7,100, but indicated that this amount would drop in the future if the father paid support. She also suggested that she could save about $2,000 from summer earnings and that she worked 20 hours weekly cleaning her building to defray rent. The father earned a little over $100,000 per year, but stated that he was taking early retirement effective in January 2000 and that his income would drop to about $63,000. The mother earned little.

Justice Johnstone began her analysis by confirming that a child, adult or minor, has no standing to claim support under the *Divorce Act*. The Justice then turned to the issues of whether the daughter was still a "child of the marriage" under s. 2 of the *Divorce Act* and, if so, the amount that the father should pay.]

JOHNSTONE J.: —

2. Child of the Marriage

29 The onus to prove that a child is a "child of the marriage" rests on the one seeking maintenance for a child who is over the age of 16 years (now the age of majority): *Whitton v. Whitton* (1989), 21 R.F.L. (3d) 261 at 263 (Ont. C.A.); *Elliott v. Elliott* (February 9, 1993), Doc. Prince George 15583 (B.C. S.C.), at para. 18; *Ciardullo v. Ciardullo* (1995), 15 R.F.L. (4th) 121 at p. 125 (B.C. S.C.).

30 In the case of *Pollard v. Pollard* (1999), 75 Alta. L.R. (3d) 350 (Alta. Q.B.), I conducted an extensive review of what the Court should consider when determining whether a child is a "child of the marriage". It is clearly a question of dependency, not age: *Ciardullo, supra*. It is unnecessary for me to repeat in detail the cases reviewed. However, once again I will rely

on the relevant circumstances enunciated by Master Joyce in the decision of *Farden v. Farden* (1993), 48 R.F.L. (3d) 60 (B.C. Master), at para 64:

> (1) whether the child is, in fact, enrolled in a course of studies and whether it is a full-time or part time [*sic*] course of studies;
>
> (2) whether or not the child has applied for, or is eligible for, student loans or other financial assistance;
>
> (3) the career plans of the child, i.e., whether the child has some reasonable and appropriate plan or is simply going to college because there is nothing better to do;
>
> (4) the ability of the child to contribute to his own support through part-time employment;
>
> (5) the age of the child;
>
> (6) the child's past academic performance, whether the child is demonstrating success in the chosen course of studies;
>
> (7) what plans the parents made for the education of their children, particularly where those plans were made during cohabitation; [and]
>
> (8) at least in the case of a mature child who has reached the age of majority, whether or not the child has unilaterally terminated a relationship from the parent from whom support is sought.

31 It is important to note that there does not have to be evidence on all of the factors to successfully show the child is a "child of the marriage": *Darlington v. Darlington* (1997), 32 R.F.L. (4th) 406 at p. 411 (B.C. C.A.); *Wesemann v. Wesemann* (1999), 49 R.F.L. (4th) 435 (B.C. S.C.), at para. 11. However, what is clear from a review of the extensive case law in this area, is that the Court's determination must be fact driven.

32 The fact that the child does not have a residence with one of the parents is not a prerequisite to being under the parent's charge: *Bates v. Bates* (1995), 165 A.R. 71 (Alta. C.A.) and *Pollard v. Pollard, supra*.

Discussion of the Farden Factors:

(1) Enrollment in post-secondary education

33 Courts have generally regarded a child over the age of majority who is in full-time attendance at an educational institution as a "child of the marriage" and therefore entitled to support. There has been a general acceptance of education pursuits as a "cause" that renders a child unable to withdraw from his or her parents' charge: *Fair v. Jones* (1999), 48 R.F.L. (4th) 279, Vertes, J. (N.W.T. S.C.)

34 As I found in *Sherlow v. Zubko* (1999), 50 R.F.L. (4th) 160 (Alta. Q.B.), at para. 20, education is considered an "other cause" which can limit an adult child's ability to provide for themselves the necessaries of life. This principle was also adopted in *Broumas v. Broumas* (1998), 233 A.R. 1 at p. 6 (Alta. Q.B.). This "presumption" does not entirely discharge the onus on the Applicant to prove that the child, by reason of attending school or college, is unable to withdraw from the charge of the parents or to obtain the necessaries of life: *Ciardullo, supra*; *Jackson v. Jackson* (1988), 69 Sask. R. 148 (Sask. Q.B.); *Duncan v. Duncan* (1989), 74 Sask. R. 100 (Sask. Q.B.). ...

36 As well, the payor parent's disapproval of the course of studies chosen by the child does not appear to relieve the payor parent from his or her support obligations: *Evans v. Evans*

(1998), 164 Sask. R. 101 (Sask. Q.B.). Yet, the Courts have often encouraged dialogue between the child and the parent as to the course choices and career plans of the child: *Ciardullo, supra*; *Whitton, supra*; *Duncan, supra*.

37 Furthermore, the Alberta Court of Appeal in *Degagne v. Sargeant* (1999), 47 R.F.L. (4th) 131 (Alta. C.A.) in *obiter* stated that the applicant would be required to make out a more compelling case for the child to go away to school before the Court would be inclined to require the payor to contribute to the additional expenses such as travel and housing in the future. However, the panel did not overturn the chamber justice's decision to require the payor father to pay extraordinary post-secondary expenses of the child when he could have taken the same course residing at home rather than going to Calgary because the course was only for one year.

38 Justice Quinn in *Welsh v. Welsh* (November 3, 1998), Doc. St. Catharines 35,110/95 (Ont. Gen. Div.) considered that there were three criteria that should be met if a child attending a post-secondary institution is to be considered a "child of the marriage":

(i) The adult child must have an aptitude that is reasonably likely to lead to academic success;

(ii) He or she must be pursuing the course of studies with diligence; and

(iii) There should be a reasonable likelihood that successful completion of the course of studies will lead to gainful and self-supporting employment.

39 Leah has satisfied these criteria. While the Respondent may have preferred her to attend a school in Edmonton or in Victoria, Leah has given evidence as to why she made the course selection she made. Additionally, as she has deposed, this choice of studies is not whimsical nor an attempt to put off studying a "real career" — she has always exhibited a desire and an intent to find employment in the entertainment business. Finally, given the academic coordinator's advice, there appears to be a reasonable likelihood of employability.

(2) Student Loans and Other Financial Assistance

40 In cases such as these, an adult child is expected to contribute towards her education to the fullest extent possible through bursaries, scholarships, student loans, or summer employment: *Bradley v. Zaba* (1996), 140 Sask. R. 297 (Sask. Q.B.); *Krueger v. Tunison* (1999), 183 Sask. R. 255 (Sask. Q.B.); *Janzen v. Janzen* (1980), 18 R.F.L. (2d) 152 (B.C. S.C.); *Louise v. Scheuer* (1995), 15 B.C.L.R. (3d) 270 (B.C. S.C.); *Sherlow v. Zubko, supra*. Leah has applied and secured a student loan for this school term and will be expected to do so for the balance of her educational program. However, if she is awarded child support it is doubtful that she will qualify for a significant level of student financing, or any for that matter.

(3) The Career Plans of the Child

41 The reasonableness of the child's course of studies in relation to their aptitude and past achievement is also considered: *Sherlow v. Zubko, supra*, at para. 51; *Ciardullo, supra*, at p. 127; *Newman v. Thompson* (1997), 118 Man. R. (2d) 177 at p. 181 (Man. C.A.).

42 As I indicated above, the course choice made by Leah appears a serious one and one in which she has the ability to succeed.

(4) Part-time Employment

43 It is very rare when a Court will not require a student to contribute, through his or her own earnings, to the cost of his or her maintenance. In *Louise v. Scheuer, supra*, part-time employment was not required because of health problems of the child and it was contrary to

her doctor's advice to work and attend school at the same time. Yet, she was encouraged to look for summer jobs. Also, in *Fair v. Jones, supra,* while the child stated she did not want to work during the school year so she could give all her attention to her studies, she was still required to seek out summer employment. Much more common is the case where the child is expected to work during the summer and during weekends of the school year: *Broumas, supra; Bradley v. Zaba, supra; Busko, supra; Evans, supra; Van de Pol, supra.*

44 Leah has deposed that Sheridan College forbids students in the Musical Theatre program from working during the school term but a letter from the College does not indicate such a prohibition. However, her course demands are high as are the expectations placed upon her by the College. Therefore, I do not find it unreasonable that Leah does not wish to work during the school term. She is desirous of channelling all of her energies into her school work. However, she will be expected to work during the four months of the summer.

(5) Age

45 As earlier discussed, the test is one of dependency not age. Yet the age of the child can be a factor to consider when determining dependency. As Madame Justice Trussler discussed in *Gamache v. Gamache* (1999), 49 R.F.L. (4th) 258 (Alta. Q.B.) at para. 9:

> A parent does not have an indefinite obligation to support a child who is attending school or is unemployed or underemployed. Instead, a parent has an obligation to assist the parent on whom the child is dependent through a reasonable transition period. What is a reasonable transition period is a question to be determined on the facts of each case. In all the cases, the emphasis is placed on the inability of the child to support him or herself.

46 Thus a 23 year old student pursuing his doctorate was considered to be a child of the marriage in *Newman v. Thompson, supra,* as was a 22 year old student in *Whitton, supra.* However, a 19 year old student in *Innes v. Innes* (1994), 154 A.R. 346 (Alta. Q.B.) who had chosen to live on her own was found not to be under the charge of either of her parents and thus not a child of the marriage, as was the case of an 18 year old girl in *Chaban (Brault) v. Chaban* (1985), 37 Man. R. (2d) 170 (Man. Q.B.).

47 Leah is currently 19 years of age. It is her reality and that of her peers that a good education is a necessity in today's society. Indeed sometimes economic viability will require even more than a bachelor degree. ... The circumstances of this case do not convince me that Leah has passed through the "transition period" to which Justice Trussler referred. She still requires the financial support of her parents. While she has in fact taken time away from her studies to travel, for those families who can afford this opportunity, it is a beneficial and educational experience in itself. It is not uncommon for students to take time off before beginning a post-secondary education. I am also alive to the fact that Leah did not spend the entire year travelling. She did take some courses and prepare for her audition at Sheridan College.

(6) Past Academic Performance — Success in the Chosen Course of Studies

48 As this is Leah's first semester at Sheridan College there is no official transcript of her academic performance for the Court to review. However, she must maintain certain grades ... and this factor will be taken into account in my determination.

(7) Parental Plans for the Child's Education

49 In cases where parents have made provision for their children's future education, the Courts have tended to enforce that obligation. For example, in *Ciardullo, supra,* the Court considered the past history of parental support and the parents' means as a factor in determining if it was reasonable for the child to continue to be supported even after the parents

had separated. In *Newman v. Thompson, supra,* the father's prior agreement to support his child for a maximum of 10 years at the post-secondary level was enforced although at a reduced amount. Also, in *Welsh, supra,* the child's reasonable expectation of support if the marriage had not broken down was also considered.

50 In this case, Leah's mother and father made provision for her post-secondary education in the Minutes of Settlement to their divorce, as discussed in the outline of the facts. Clearly Leah's parents intended that she should continue to be supported until she turned 21 if she was pursuing her education. The investment by the Respondent into an RESP account is further evidence of an intent to set aside money for the support of Leah's education.

(8) Supporting Parent's Relationship with the Adult Child

51 As this factor had great significance in my determination, I will deal with it as a separate issue.

3. Father/Daughter Relationship

52 With respect to the importance of the last *Farden* factor, Master Royce, at page 65 of that decision, made reference to the following passage from *Law v. Law* (1986), 2 R.F.L. (3d) 458 (Ont. H.C.) at 463:

> I am of the view that where, as here, a mature child unilaterally terminates a relationship with one of the parents without any apparent reason, that is a factor to be considered by the trial judge in determining whether it would be "fit and just" to provide maintenance for that child. A father-child relationship is more than simple economic dependency. The father is burdened with heavy financial responsibilities and the child has few duties in return. It seems reasonable to demand that a child who expects to receive support entertain some type of relationship with his or her father in the absence of any conduct by the father which might justify the child's neglect of his or her filial duties.

53 There is considerable case law supporting this premise. In *Farden, supra,* while the Court found that the mother had alienated the son from his father's affections as a boy, the adult son's refusal to attempt to reinstate the relationship, in the absence of any guilty conduct of the father, was an additional factor considered for dismissing the application for support.

54 In *Innes, supra,* the parents of a 19 year old girl had agreed that the father had full financial responsibility for the child and thus the girl was not under her mother's "charge". The child rejected an offer by the father to live with him while attending university. Thus, Justice Nash found that the father had no obligation to pay.

55 In *Whitton, supra,* at p. 264, the Ontario Court of Appeal considered this a serious factor and stated:

> ... the most troublesome issue is the attitude of the daughter to her father. At age 22 she should have the maturity to deal with her father directly to help him in discharging his legal and parental duties to assist in her education.

Thus, while the Court held that the daughter was still a "child of the marriage" as defined in her parents' Separation Agreement, the Court stated:

> [i]f she continues to refuse to engage in any sensible discussion with her father on the matter of her future education, the [father's] only recourse would be to ... have the quantum of her maintenance reviewed by the court.

56 In *Elliott, supra,* Justice Parrett recognized that a breakdown in a relationship is rarely the fault of one party but noted that the principles regarding filial responsibilities as discussed in *Law, supra,* have greater application as a child gets older.

57 In *Anderson v. Anderson* (1997), 27 R.F.L. (4th) 323 (B.C. S.C.), the Court found that the most significant factor in determining whether the daughter was no longer a "child of the

marriage" was the breakdown in communication between the child and her father. At p. 327:

> ... [i]n the absence of demonstrated need Ms. Anderson cannot expect indefinite and unqualified support without expending the effort to maintain the reciprocal bonds of respect and affection natural between father and daughter.

58 *Dalep v. Dalep* (1987), 11 R.F.L. (3d) 359 (B.C. S.C.) was a case of extreme parental abuse involving unprovoked physical assaults by the child on his mother and whether such conduct disentitled the child to support. Tyrwhitt-Drake, L.J.S.C. stated:

> His conduct towards his mother has been atrocious (and his conduct, unlike that of parties to a marriage, may be considered in maintenance matters). By his conduct, he has forfeited any right he may have had to be maintained by her as a "child of the marriage." By his own choice he is no longer such.

60 There have been contrary arguments expressed however. Madame Justice Veit discussed the importance of the parent/child relationship in *James v. Morris* (June 13, 1997), Doc. Fort McMurray 4813-00013 (Alta. Q.B.) at para. 20:

> If an adult child is a "child of the marriage" within the meaning of Parliament and the case law, the parents of that child must support the child whether or not the child has a good relationship with them. It is easy to demonstrate that the maintenance of a good relationship with a parent is not a feature of being a "child of the marriage": a child who was physically or sexually abused by a parent, and who therefore disliked that parent and did not wish to maintain a relationship with that parent, would be disentitled to financial support from that parent to undertake a university education; a child, denied a university education by a parent because she was a female child, and who therefore disliked the parent and did not wish to maintain a relationship with that parent would be disentitled to financial support from that parent to undertake a university education. Abusive and non-supporting parents would prevail. The result would be to undermine the very intention of Parliament in requiring parents to support their children.

61 This was the view taken in a number of other cases. In *Louise v. Scheuer, supra,* the "disharmony" between the father and daughter was found not to be a reason to refuse maintenance, even though the breakdown of the relationship was initiated by the child. In a case similar to the one at bar, the daughter had written a letter to her father but it was characterized by the Court as not whimsical but merely dramatic.

62 In *Fair v. Jones, supra,* at para. 9, the child's refusal to communicate with her father was viewed as a result of "a sincere inner conflict *vis-a-vis* her father and her refusal to communicate with him [was] not motivated by simple petulance, malice or vindictiveness". In *Welsh, supra,* at para. 22 the Court considered it important to determine who had caused the destruction of the relationship.

63 The Applicant submits that the Minutes of Settlement entered into between the parties say nothing about Leah's child support being predicated on the status of the relationship between father and daughter. The Minutes of Settlement merely state that support will be payable until Leah attains the age of 21, finishes her post-secondary education, gets married or becomes independent, whichever occurs first.

64 These decisions are interesting as they seem to imply that while a child of married parents would not be entitled to force the parents to support post-secondary education, a parent of a child of divorced parents can bring an application to require an unwilling parent to support the child. James McLeod discusses this paradox in an annotation of *Evans, supra,* at (1998), 35 R.F.L. (4th) 158 at 159:

> As a general rule, courts try to minimize the economic consequences of marriage breakdown on a child. If the family would have supported the child while it was intact, a court should not deny support after family breakdown. The converse is that a parent should not have a greater child-support obligation towards an adult child after family breakdown than if the family had remained intact. Surprisingly, there is little authority for this proposition.

65 In *Duncan, supra*, at 105, Justice Halvorson also considered this anomaly and stated:

> [i]n my view the submission [that the moral duty to provide support cannot be changed into a legal duty just because the parents are divorced] is not only intriguing but probably accurate. However in light of entrenched authority where jurisdiction was presumed and the fact that in the *Divorce Act*, 1985, the wording of s. 2(1) was not altered in face of that authority, this submission should be left to a higher court for sanction.

66 In the case at bar, Leah wrote a letter which announced she was ceasing all communication with her father and she wanted nothing to do with him. However, she still expected financial support from the Respondent. There is no question that Leah intended at the time of writing the letter to unilaterally renounce the relationship. She placed blame for her attitude on his prior actions and indicated that she felt angry. She felt that she took second place in priority to her father's money. She wrote the letter when she was 17 and gave it to him after her 18th birthday which would tend to show that there was some forethought given to sending the letter. However she was quite young at the time and has henceforth expressed regret. Notwithstanding, there appears to be no resumption of effective communication between Leah and her father, although she complied with my direction that she communicate with him by letter as to the ongoing status of her educational pursuits.

67 It is clear from these cases that the quality of the parent/child relationship rarely determines the matter. It is but one of the "failing" factors; that is, there must be others in addition to it, unless the circumstances are extremely grave. In fact, *Dalep, supra*, where the extreme case of physical parental abuse was found sufficient to deny support, the Court mentioned that the child had some type of employment to fall back on. ...

69 As a result of the foregoing, after considering all the relevant factors, I find that Leah still remains a "child of the marriage". However, the breakdown of the relationship with her father remains of utmost importance in the establishment of the conditions on which his ongoing support obligation is ordered.

4. RESP

70 As a result of my finding that Leah is a "child of the marriage" and therefore the obligation of support flows, there are further issues that I must address. An RESP account of $12,600.00 was paid out to Leah shortly after her 18th birthday. In the Affidavits there is some dispute as to the origin of the funds. Leah deposes it was a savings plan started by her grandmother, which her father merely managed. Conversely, the Respondent deposes that the money came solely from his resources. Nothing really turns on who made the deposits; the important point is that this was an asset available to Leah which has been expended. In *Bates, supra*, each of the children were given $16,000.00 by their grandparents for their education. The Court did not consider it significant that this money was put in trust by the grandparents, not by the parents. It was still considered an asset of the children that should be used to defray educational expenses. Furthermore, in *Achkewich v. Achkewich* (1998), 220 A.R. 385 (Alta. Q.B.) a trust fund, contributed to by the children's grandfather was partially depleted to finance the children's education, thereby decreasing their need for support. This was ordered even though the fund was allegedly a "nest egg" for *after* the children graduated from university. ...

74 There is no question that a child is expected to responsibly use money which has been saved on his or her behalf for the purposes of pursuing an education. A child cannot expect to unwisely spend what they have been given, and then be allowed to ask for more to replace it. Having said that, however, the Respondent did release the entire amount in the RESP before Leah was enrolled in any courses and in fact signed additional papers to effect a transfer even after receiving the "relationship destroying letter". As a result, I find that the

Respondent should bear some responsibility for acquiescing in the depletion of the majority of the funds for non-educational pursuits.

75 I accept that a portion of the RESP [totalling $1,145.00] was used in furtherance of Leah's studies. ... Leah must account for $11,455.00 over the three year period of her studies.

Section Section 7 Expenses

76 In circumstances where adult children are attending university or college away from home, the Courts normally do not establish child support based upon the Guideline amount but rather resort to the condition, means and needs consideration set forth in s. 3(2)(b) of the Guidelines: the rationale behind this is that the economics of scale are reflected in the table amounts of the Guidelines where the child is residing in the same household as the recipient parent. ... I find no need to deviate from that established approach in this case. Therefore, it is important to look carefully at the s. 7 expenses claimed by Leah in order to assess the appropriate quantum of child support.

[Justice Johnstone held that Leah would be required to work in the summer months and so her father would not be responsible for her expenses during that time. In addition, she was expected to save $250 each of those months and to contribute these savings to the cost of her education. The Justice continued.]

77 Calculation of Quantum

Annual Rent ($416.00 × 8 mos.)	$	3,328.00
Annual living expenses ($780.00 × 8 mos.)		6,240.00
Annual Sub Total:		9,568.00
Annual Tuition:		4,758.50
Annual Sub Total:	$	14,326.50
Factoring in the RESP, annualized ($ 11,455/3 yrs)	(	3,818.33)
Annual Sub Total:	$	10,508.17)
Less Summer Savings:	(	1,000.00)
	$	9,508.17
Monthly Equivalent ($9,508.17/8 mos.)	$	1,188.52

As a result, the Respondent is responsible for payment of child support in the amount of $1,188.52 per month commencing September 1, 1999. Pursuant to the interim Order of Justice Moreau which was continued by myself, the Respondent was paying $1,200.00 per month effective September 1, 1999. Therefore, excess payments have been made to Leah in the amount of $11.48 per month. Leah will account for this surplus over the next six months or the surplus can be deducted from subsequent payments, as the parties may agree.

78 I am fully aware that Leah had the benefit of a student loan in the amount of $7,100.00. I have chosen not to factor this into the quantum order given that if she had been receiving child support, she would likely not have qualified for this loan or at least a major portion of that student financing. She has the obligation to repay that loan upon graduation. Furthermore, I have required that Leah account for the majority of the proceeds of the RESP. If she would have used those funds for her educational expenditures, she would not have incurred the student loan obligation. However, the Respondent did agree that the RESP funds could be withdrawn and therefore that fact was taken into account in my treatment of the student

loan. I have also required that Leah seek summer employment and save a modest amount during that time.

79 The early retirement of the Respondent is academic to my determination given that I have chosen not to utilize the Guideline amounts and there has been no case of hardship argued by the Respondent.

5. Terms of the Child Support Order

80 It is common for the Court to order conditions in such circumstances: *Ciardullo*, *supra*, transcripts, expense reports and income sources were required; *Louise*, *supra*, summer work and student loans were conditions. In *Sherlow*, *supra*, if the children continued with their studies, support was ordered provided they secured employment and applied for student loans.

81 Also, more intrusive conditions have sometimes been ordered: *Ciardullo*, *supra*, required the father and child to meet and talk about the child's educational plan; *Hyde*, *supra*, though the father had not seen the child since she was eight, the Court granted access rights to the father, even though there was an expectation that the parties would thwart this condition; *Whitton*, *supra*, if the daughter continued to refuse to discuss the course of her education with her father, the father could apply to have the order reviewed. ...

83 The sum of $1,188.52 per month shall be paid by the Respondent to Leah commencing September 1, 1999 on the following conditions:

> 1. During the summer months of May through and including August, 1999 there will be no support obligation owed by the Respondent;

> 2. Leah is required to secure summer employment and apply for student loans, scholarships, and any bursaries or other funding for which she may be eligible. The Respondent is at liberty to reapply before me if the additional funding Leah receives is significant and would affect his obligation to pay, absent an agreement of the parties to a voluntary reduction;

> 3. Leah will provide all relevant information regarding her student loans including all applications that are made during the course of her studies, all correspondence received from the Student Finance Board, and any other sources of income she may receive;

> 4. That the child support order is subject to review if Leah does not achieve passing grades;

> 5. Child support will cease if Leah withdraws from full-time attendance at Sheridan College;

> 6. Leah will prepare a budget for each school term and provide it to the Respondent no later than September 30th of each year;

> 7. Leah will provide to the Respondent: her current address and all address changes, copies of all transcripts of her marks within one month of her receipt, and details of her courses and course activities, the latter on a quarterly basis.

As noted in Professor Bala's paper, in dealing with applications for child support for adults, the courts often turn to a four-step procedure suggested by Justice Martinson in *Wesemann v. Wesemann* (1999), 49 R.F.L. (4th) 435 (B.C. S.C.). The Justice elaborated on the four steps in paragraphs 8–26:

Step One — Child of the Marriage

8 The *Guidelines* consider quantum (the amount) of support only, not eligibility for support. The *Divorce Act* sets out when a child continues to be entitled to support. ...

9 Master Joyce, in a very helpful pre-*Guidelines* decision, considered factors to be taken into account in deciding when a child over the age of majority remains a child of the marriage for the purposes of the payment of maintenance: *Farden v. Farden* (1993), 48 R.F.L. (3d) 60 at 64-65 (B.C. Master). These factors were adopted by the British Columbia Court of Appeal in *Darlington v. Darlington* (1997), 32 R.F.L. (4th) 406 (B.C. C.A.) and have been followed in a number of post *Guidelines* cases. ... [These include *Wahl*, above.]

Step Two — The Guidelines Amount

12 If there is no challenge to the usual *Guidelines* approach the amount payable is determined under the *Guidelines* in the same way it is decided for a child under the age of majority. [This is usually the Table amount plus a proportionate amount for extraordinary expenses for post secondary education based on s. 7 of the CSG.]

Step Three — Is the usual Guidelines approach inappropriate?

13 The usual *Guidelines* approach applies unless the person claiming it is inappropriate proves that it is inappropriate. ...

16 The usual *Guidelines* approach is based on certain factors that normally apply to a child under the age of majority. That is, the child resides with one or both parents. The child is generally not earning an income and is dependent on his or her parents.

17 The usual *Guidelines* approach is, in most cases, based on the understanding that, though only the income of the person paying is used to calculate the amount payable, the other parent makes a significant contribution to the costs of that child's care because the child is residing with him or her.

18 The closer the circumstances of the child are to those upon which the usual *Guidelines* approach is based, the less likely it is that the usual *Guidelines* calculation will be inappropriate. The opposite is also true. Children over the age of majority may reside away from home and/or earn a significant income. If a child is not residing at home, the nature of the contribution towards the child's expenses may be quite different.

Step Four — What amount is appropriate if the under age amount is not?

19 If the usual *Guidelines* approach is inappropriate, a court must determine the amount that is considered appropriate, having regard to the condition, means, needs and other circumstances of the child and the financial ability of each spouse to contribute to the support of the child.

20 It is helpful to consider:

    1. the reasonable needs of the child,

    2. the ability and opportunity of the child to contribute to those needs, and

    3. the ability of the parents to contribute to those needs.

1. The reasonable needs of the child

21 This has two aspects to it. First, the child's needs for accommodation, food, clothing, and other miscellaneous expenses. Second, the child's actual post secondary expenses.

2. The ability of and opportunity for the child to contribute to his education

22 Post secondary education is a privilege, not a right. ... Children have an obligation to make a reasonable contribution to their education. However, just because a child is earning income, it does not follow that all of that income must be applied to the child's education. The desirability of allowing the child to experience some personal benefit from the fruits of his or her labours should also be considered. ...

24 It may well not be appropriate to require a child to work part-time during the school year in addition to summer employment as that might interfere with the child's studies and ability to pass. ...

25 Nor should the availability of student loan money automatically require the child to obtain the loan. To see a student loan as simply income available to a child is a fundamental misunderstanding of the nature, implications and financial obligations of a loan to that student. A student loan is not a

bursary, grant or scholarship fund, designed to defray a student's expenses. Rather, a student loan delays payment of certain expenses, rather than defraying them. ...

3. The ability of the parents to contribute to those needs

26 This involves a consideration of the ability to pay of both parents. The court may choose to apportion the amount payable on a proportionate basis. ...

The following case examines whether an adult can be considered a "child of the marriage" where she cannot find employment.

SMITH v. SMITH

(1987), 12 R.F.L. (3d) 50, 1987 CarswellBC 555 (B.C. S.C.)

OPPAL J.: — The petitioner husband seeks to vary a maintenance order by a declaration that his 20-year-old daughter is no longer a "child of the marriage" within the definition of the *Divorce Act*, R.S.C. 1970, c. D-8.

The issue in this application is as follows: ... whether the applicant's twenty year old daughter, who is unemployed and living at home is a "child of the marriage.

The background of this matter is as follows. The parties were divorced on 19th June 1978. They had two children including a daughter, Michele, who is the focal point of this application. Pursuant to the terms of the decree *nisi* the respondent husband was to pay maintenance of $100 per month per child for "as long as the aforementioned remained children of the marriage within the meaning of the *Divorce Act*". The respondent quickly fell into arrears on his maintenance payments. The arrears were cancelled by court order on 20th October 1980. The respondent is again in arrears and seeks an order pursuant to s. 11(2) of the Act to vary the order by declaring that his daughter, Michele, is no longer a "child of the marriage" within the definition of the Act and that her name should be deleted from the order, thus rescinding the requirement for payment for her maintenance.

Michele is 20 years of age. The respondent submits that she is in good health, has no mental or physical disabilities and is capable of working to provide herself with the necessaries of life. She is, however, a Grade X high school dropout who lives at home with the petitioner on whom she is financially dependent because she is unemployed. In the 2 1/2 years since leaving high school, she has only worked three months on a part-time basis. She has been unable to find full-time employment. There are two apparent reasons for her state of unemployment. Firstly, she has no particular qualifications or specialized training in any field. Secondly, it is deposed that she has been prevented from working on a full-time basis because of the somewhat depressed economy. She has applied for jobs at various women's sportswear stores, however, has had no success. It is the daughter's ambition to become a model. She wishes to enroll at a modelling agency.

... Generally, there are two lines of authority on whether s. 2(b) ought to be given a liberal or a restrictive interpretation. In *Bruehler v. Bruehler* (1985), 49 R.F.L. (2d) 44 at 46 (B.C. C.A.), Hutcheon J.A., in chambers, stated as follows:

> ... the words "other cause" may be sufficiently wide to include a state of depression in a province where young people of 18 or 19 years of age are unable to obtain employment to provide themselves with the necessaries of life.

In *Weir v. Weir* (1986), 1 R.F.L. (3d) 438 (B.C. S.C.), Errico L.J.S.C. held that the words "other cause" are extensive enough to encompass a state of depression in a province resulting in employment being difficult to obtain. In that case the parties had a son who was 20 years of age, who was unemployed and was receiving social assistance. He resided with the mother. He had left school in Grade IX and his prospects for employment were poor.

In *Gartner v. Gartner* (1978), 5 R.F.L. (2d) 270 at 274, 27 N.S.R. (2d) 482, 41 A.P.R. 482, the decision of the Nova Scotia Supreme Court, Trial Division, Cowan C.J.T.D. stated as follows:

> It seems to me that it was not the intention of the *Divorce Act* that parents should be required to support a child who is not ill or disabled, and who can withdraw himself from the parents' charge and can provide himself with the necessities of life, except that he cannot, in the present state of the labour market, find suitable work.

It may be instructive to examine the comments on *Weir* by Professor J.G. McLeod wherein he expresses concern that where support for adult children is dependent upon the inability to obtain employment and not merely on an unwillingness to work it may create a difficulty for a father who may be compelled to monitor both the job market and the efforts of his children to obtain employment. It is suggested that that may seem to place an unreasonable burden on the supporting spouse. The author suggests that perhaps the court should conduct a broad inquiry in order to determine whether the claimant should be required to seek retraining or further employment.

Whether an adult qualifies as a "child of the marriage" will depend upon the circumstances of each case. In the case at bar there is no evidence to suggest that the daughter has made no diligent efforts to obtain employment. Her financial dependence on her mother due to her unemployment and inability to find a job qualifies her as a "child of the marriage" within the meaning of the Act. This is a valid and legitimate "other cause". She clearly is in need of maintenance. The Act obviously contemplates circumstances where a child ... is over the age of 16 but is still in need of support for a valid reason. Hence the respondent's [obligations] to support her are to continue. However, they should not continue on an indefinite basis. The daughter must continue to make realistic efforts in order to obtain employment or retraining. It may be that her goals of becoming a model are unrealistic. Therefore, there ought to be a limit imposed upon the period of time during which the respondent's obligations are to continue. An appropriate period in the circumstances would be six months. By that time the daughter ought to have secured full-time employment. ...

NOTES AND QUESTIONS

1. For some other cases dealing with s. 31(2) of the *FLA*, see *Figuerido v. Figuerido* (1991), 33 R.F.L. (3d) 72 (Ont. Gen. Div.); *Fitzpatrick v. Karlein* (1994), 5 R.F.L. (4th) 290 (Ont. Prov. Div.); *Judd v. Judd* (1995), 16 R.F.L. (4th) 430 (Ont. Prov. Div.); *Lynch v. Lynch* (1999), 1 R.F.L. (5th) 309 (Ont. S.C.J.); and *Kincaid v. Arsenault* (2002), 27 R.F.L. (5th) 84 (Ont. S.C.J.). See also *Bennett (Guardian ad litem of) v. Bennett* (1993), 47 R.F.L. (3d) 61 (B.C. Prov. Ct.).

In *Fitzpatrick v. Karlein*, Nasmith Prov. J. reviewed the case law and concluded (at 294-295):

> I am persuaded that it is time to ask whether there is a valid basis for the "narrow" approach to the legislation now that the wording in s. 31 of the *Family Law Act* leaves open-ended the parental obligation to support a child after age 16 so long as the child remains a full-time student.

> The correct approach to the new legislation, in my opinion, once the defence under subs. 31(2) has been raised and it has been established that the child is past 16 years and outside of the control of the former custodial parent, is to assign to the child, as the applicant, the onus of demonstrating that the withdrawal was involuntary whether by reason of eviction or a living situation with the parent that is viewed as unbearable or impossible. ... It is not just a matter of showing that the choice to become independent was reasonable or understandable. Under s. 31 of the *Family Law Act*, for a youth past the age of 16, who has, ostensibly, withdrawn from parental control to succeed in obtaining court-ordered support, it must be demonstrated by her that the withdrawal was involuntary.

While I have sympathy for Carolyn and I understand her preference for living with the Bowens, she has not demonstrated that the living situation with her mother and Mr. Karlein was unbearable or impossible. She has shown that she was unhappy there; that she felt unloved; that she was feeling cut off from other members of the family. Her choice to move out made good sense to her. But it was a relatively free choice as it has been presented. Carolyn has not satisfied me that her withdrawal from her mother's control was involuntary.

Section 31(2) applies to all children over the age of 16, even those away at university. How does one determine if a university or college student has "withdrawn from parental control"? In *Figuerido*, FitzGerald J. stated (at 73):

For the child, this privilege is available on certain conditions, namely, that the child has not withdrawn from parental control and that the child is in need of support. The key word is "control". If the child wants to get support, the child must be prepared to submit to control by the paying parent. In my view, it is implicit in this section that the control sought to be exercised must be reasonable. What is reasonable will, of course, depend upon all of the surrounding circumstances and will vary with each individual case.

Foremost among the aspects of control to be considered is the requirement of the section that, if the applicant for support is over the age of 16, he or she must be enrolled in a full-time program of education. It is not sufficient that the student be merely enrolled. The stipulation that it be a full-time program implies that the student, if he or she is to receive support, must devote to that program, in priority to all other diversions, whatever effort within the capability of the student is required to achieve an acceptable level of performance. At a minimum, then, the degree of control to which the student must submit is that required to ensure that he or she attends the educational classes punctually and consistently, and devotes sufficient time and effort outside of school to keep up with all home study requirements.

How this control is exercised will vary with each individual situation. If the child is living at home, one would expect to find reasonable curfew rules on week nights, a control over spending, and reasonable consideration for the parent whose support is sought, particularly as the behaviour of the child may affect the well-being and employment of the parent. One would also expect to find reasonable consideration on the part of the parent for the well-being of the child. If the child, without justification, rejects such control or fails to pursue the course of education with reasonable diligence, that child, whether living at home or not, forfeits the right to parental support.

The legislation in some provinces does not have a provision comparable to s. 31(2) of the *FLA*. See, e.g., *The Family Maintenance Act, 1997*, S.S. 1997, c. F-6.2. As a result, a minor child in Saskatchewan has an "absolute" right to parental support: *Abell v. Abell* (2003), 43 R.F.L. (5th) 252 (Sask. Q.B.).

2. Under the *Divorce Act*, the term "child of the marriage" indicates that a person under the age of majority must not have "withdrawn from [the parents'] charge". In *Bast v. Dyck* (1997), 28 R.F.L. (4th) 131 (Sask. Q.B.), a depressed and suicidal sixteen-year-old girl moved out of her mother's house to live with her boyfriend and his parents. The mother accepted the move on the advice of a counselor and continued to support the girl financially. The court dismissed the father's application to vary an existing support order. Justice McIntyre reasoned (at 137):

I am not prepared to find at this time that Chandelle has voluntarily withdrawn from the charge of her parents. It is clear ... that she is a troubled child. There is no indication that the present arrangement has any degree of permanence to it. She is a full-time highschool student. She maintains a relationship with both parents. The evidence does not satisfy me that she has chosen to reject or withdraw from her parents and assume an independent lifestyle. Young people in their latter teens can go through personal and emotional difficulties. A parent cannot terminate their responsibility at the first sign of a bump in the road.

See also *James v. James* (1995), 18 R.F.L. (4th) 463 (B.C. S.C.) and *C. (J.J.D.) v. C. (S.L.)* (1996), 25 R.F.L. (4th) 288 (Ont. Gen. Div.).

In cases involving students living away from home, the courts have frequently simply equated being under their parents' "charge" with economic dependency. See, for example, *McKenster v. McKenster* (1996), 24 R.F.L. (4th) 325 (N.S. C.A.); *Arnold v. Washburn* (2000), 10 R.F.L. (5th) 1 (Ont. S.C.J.) (daughter with university degree who turned down $40,000 job in Ottawa to pursue graduate degree in England was still a "child of the marriage"); and *Molloy v. Molloy* (2001), 23 R.F.L. (5th) 307 (Y.T. S.C.) (19-year-old woman living with her boyfriend and his parents and working as a full-time waitress considered a "child of the marriage" because she wanted to return to school full-time). However, some cases such as *Chaban (Brault) v. Chaban* (1985), 49 R.F.L. (2d) 22 (Man. Q.B.);

Pritchard v. Pritchard (Zinck) (1991), 38 R.F.L. (3d) 45 (N.S. Fam. Ct.); and *Wieland v. Wieland* (1994), 3 R.F.L. (4th) 56 (Ont. Gen. Div.) have held that a child has withdrawn from parental charge where he or she has established an independent lifestyle and sets his or her own rules. In "Support for Adult Children" (1999), 17 C.F.L.Q. 39 at 45, Terry Hainsworth supports the former approach:

> The adoption of a strict economic test has many benefits. First, it avoids the necessity of having to make moral or value judgments within the context of a family setting. Second, it avoids the anomaly of having to assess conduct in a child support application when such assessment is irrelevant in applications between spouses. Third, in respect of "adult children" it does not undermine the role of parental authority because, by this stage, the normal emancipation process will be well advanced. Finally, it avoids the necessity of having to assign blame in situations where complex family dynamics may be involved.

Do you find this convincing? Is this approach possible under the *FLA* which refers specifically to "parental control"?

3. Until the 1990s, it was commonly thought that child support would terminate with the first college diploma or university degree. However, more recently courts have indicated that students seeking additional education may still qualify as "children of the marriage": *Martell v. Height* (1994), 3 R.F.L. (4th) 104 (N.S. C.A.); *Jamieson v. Jamieson* (1995), 14 R.F.L. (4th) 354 (N.B. C.A.); *Parsons v. Parsons* (1995), 17 R.F.L. (4th) 267 (Ont. Gen. Div.); *Newman, supra; Jonasson v. Jonasson* (1998), 37 R.F.L. (4th) 266 (B.C. S.C.); *Arnold v. Washburn* (2000), 10 R.F.L. (5th) 1 (Ont. S.C.J.); and *N. (W.P.) v. N. (B.J.)* (2005), 10 R.F.L. (6th) 440 (B.C. C.A.) (woman in medical school still qualified). The Nova Scotia Court of Appeal stated in *Martell v. Height*, at 106:

> There is no arbitrary cut-off point based either on age or scholastic attainment, although as these increase the onus of proving dependency grows heavier. As a general rule, parents of a *bona fide* student will remain responsible until the child has reached a level of education, commensurate with the abilities he or she has demonstrated, which fit the child for entry level employment in an appropriate field. In making this determination the trial judge cannot be blind to prevailing social and economic conditions: a bachelor's degree no longer assures self-sufficiency.

In *Ritchie v. Ritchie* (2003), 40 R.F.L. (5th) 352 (Sask. C.A.), the daughter was 26 years old. In the third year of a doctorate program, she was receiving about $13,000 per year as a teaching assistant. She had been living in a common law relationship for three years. The Saskatchewan Court of Appeal concluded (para. 6) that she "could hardly be said to be in the charge of either parent" and that she "certainly cannot be said to be unable to withdraw from their charge or unable to obtain the necessaries of life". The court suggested that the daughter might have to obtain a student loan.

4. An important emerging issue in the current economic climate is whether children who drop in and out of school can still remain "children of the marriage" under the *Divorce Act*. In *Haley v. Haley* (2008), 2008 CarswellOnt 369, 49 R.F.L. (6th) 190 (S.C.J.), Justice Pazaratz noted that if a child has a viable, cost-effective educational plan, the child may become "re-entitled" to child support after a reasonable time out of school (here, two years).

5. In their paper, "Support for Adult Children in Cases of Estrangement (The Parent as Wallet)", Law Society of Upper Canada Special Lectures, 2006, Philip Epstein and Ilana Zylberman suggest that adult children who unreasonably reject their parents should not be entitled to continued support. This is a controversial take on the *Farden* factors. Some commentators fear that this approach would reintroduce assessments of fault into family law. What do you think?

6. Children over the age of majority who have a disability do not qualify for support under the *FLA* unless they are in school. On the other hand, a child over the age of majority who has a disability may well still qualify as a "child of the marriage" under the *Divorce Act*. Is there any principled basis on which to explain this?

For a critical examination of the case law on the application of the definition of "child of the marriage" in the *Divorce Act* to adults with disabilities, see Dobby, "Whose Responsibility?: Disabled Adult 'Children of the Marriage' under the *Divorce Act* and the Canadian Social Welfare State" (2005), 20 W.R.L.S.I. 41.

7. Age limits in provincial child support legislation have survived challenges based on s. 15 of the *Canadian Charter of Rights and Freedoms* in *Penner v. Danbrook* (1992), 39 R.F.L. (3d) 286 (Sask. C.A.) and *Massingham-Pearce v. Konkolus* (1995), 13 R.F.L. (4th) 313 (Alta. Q.B.). These decisions, however, are limited in scope and application. There were other remedies available to children over the age of majority in each one, pursuant to the

relevant provincial legislation. In Ontario, a child of unmarried parents has no other remedy if he or she is over the age of majority and not in school full-time.

In Ontario, some courts have taken a very flexible approach to the provincial legislation. In *Sullivan v. Sullivan* (1999), 50 R.F.L. (4th) 326 (Ont. Div. Ct.), Court concluded that it had authority pursuant to the *FLA* to order support for a 23-year-old even though she was only in school part-time. The court concluded that this was a full-time program for this particular student who had a disability. The decision remains controversial and has not been consistently followed.

8. Entitlement to child support can vary from one province to another and the obligation under the *Divorce Act* sometimes differs from that set in the provincial legislation. In *Raciot v. Raciot* (2003), 47 R.F.L. (5th) 384 (Ont. S.C.J.), an 18-year-old daughter with a learning disability dropped out of school and had a baby. She and the baby lived with her mother. Justice Belch noted (para. 9) that the daughter was not entitled to support under the *FLA* because she was no longer a minor and was not enrolled in a full-time program of education. However, the Justice, emphasizing the daughter's learning disability, found that she was still a "child of the marriage" and entitled to support from her father under the *Divorce Act*. In *Michie v. Michie* (1997), 36 R.F.L. (4th) 90, the Saskatchewan Court of Queen's Bench noted that there was no obligation to support adult children under the provincial legislation in existence at that time, while there might be when the parents divorced. It held that this amounted to discrimination based on marital status, but concluded that there was no *Charter* violation because the discrimination was justifiable under s. 1. See also *Souliere v. Leclair* (1998), 38 R.F.L. (4th) 68 (Ont. Gen. Div.).

9. In *Crook v. Crook* (1992), 42 R.F.L. (3d) 297 (N.S. T.D.), Goodfellow J. stated (at 306) that there "have been occasions where [child support] orders were issued for children 50 years of age or more because of illness or disability". Is such an order possible under the *FLA*? How likely are such orders under the *Divorce Act*? Would not the presence of disability pensions or other forms of social security enable the individual to "obtain the necessaries of life"? Even if the person is still considered a "child of the marriage", will any amount of child support be considered appropriate under s. 3(2) of the *Guidelines*?

10. Determining the appropriate amount of support for children over the age of majority is often difficult. In *Wahl*, the daughter was away for 12 months of the year and the court applied s. 3(2)(b) of the CSG so that all her shelter and educational costs were apportioned between herself and her father. Because the mother earned little, her income was not a factor.

By contrast, where a student is living at home while attending university or college, the courts will often determine the appropriate quantum of support in accordance with s. 3(2)(a) of the CSG; that is, as if the student were under the age of majority. This involves determining the Table amount and then adding, under s. 7, a proportionate amount of the education costs such as tuition, book purchases, and transportation. Before apportionment of the education costs, the student's contribution is usually deducted in accordance with s. 7(2). However, in *Perfanick v. Panciera* (2001), 22 R.F.L. (5th) 178 (Man. C.A.), the Table amount was considered inappropriate because of the contribution that the daughter made to her own living expenses.

If a child lives away at school for most of the year, but returns to live with a parent for the summer months, the court may order the Table amount for the months while a child is living with one parent and then add a contribution to the child's tuition and other school costs. In *Lewi v. Lewi* (2006), 28 R.F.L. (6th) 250 (Ont. C.A.); additional reasons at (2006), 2006 CarswellOnt 3214 (C.A.), the court accepted that this was a permissible approach under s. 3(2)(b) of the CSG. See also *Park v. Thompson* (2005), 13 R.F.L. (6th) 415 (Ont. C.A.); additional reasons at (2005), 2005 CarswellOnt 2518 (C.A.) and *Coghill v. Coghill* (2006), 30 R.F.L. (6th) 398 (Ont. S.C.J.).

3. Determining the Amount

(1) Introduction

Canada undertook a massive rule-based reform of its child support system with the adoption of the *Federal Child Support Guidelines*, SOR/97-175, effective May 1, 1997. These are generally referred to as "the CSG" in this chapter. The *Uniform Federal and Provincial Child Support Guidelines Act, 1997*, S.O. 1997, c. 20, amended the *FLA* to provide for provincial *Guidelines* and the *Child Support Guidelines (Ontario)*, O.Reg. 391/97, which are virtually identical to their federal counterparts, came into effect on December 1, 1997. Ontario also adopted the federal Table amounts for computational purposes. To date, Ontario has not asked the Governor in Council to adopt the provincial *Guidelines* as applicable to divorce proceedings (see *Divorce Act*, s. 2(1) "applicable guidelines" and s. 2(5)). Accordingly, the Ontario *Guidelines* apply to proceedings under the *FLA* and the federal ones apply to *Divorce Act* proceedings, but this has little practical significance. Some other provinces have received designations for their own *Guidelines* and so these are applicable in divorce proceedings as well as proceedings under the provincial legislation.

Prior to the reforms, courts determined child support on a case-by-case basis in light of proven expenses associated with the child and the parents' ability to meet those expenses. This led to a lack of consistency from jurisdiction to jurisdiction. There was no consensus as to what children's "needs" were, and similarly no consensus as to how much the payor parent was expected to contribute to those needs. Evidence in child support applications frequently consisted of minute discussions of the expenditures in the recipient's household. The best approach prior to the passage of the *Guidelines* appeared in *Paras v. Paras* (1970), [1971] 1 O.R. 130, 2 R.F.L. 328 (C.A.), where the Ontario Court of Appeal required both parents to contribute to children's needs in proportion to their incomes. However, the *Paras* case did not establish any criteria for determining what expenses a payor parent should be contributing to. Child support applications therefore continued to present difficulty and often produced inconsistent results.

The enactment of the CSG represented a major change in how child support cases are decided. The household budget of the recipient parent became almost irrelevant. This eliminated protracted (and therefore expensive) evidence about what the recipient parent was spending the money on and whether these expenditures benefitted the child. Under the CSG, the starting point (and in many cases the ending point) in determining quantum is the Table amount. To establish this amount, one need know only (1) the relevant Table (there are different tables for different provinces to reflect differences in tax structure); (2) the number of children "to whom the order relates"; and (3) the annual income of the payor or non-custodial parent. Variations from this Table amount are permitted in limited circumstances set out in the CSG as mentioned earlier in this chapter. The incredible number of reported cases and the various methods of dealing with these limited circumstances should not mislead. Most commentators suggest that the CSG have succeeded in achieving at least the objectives of "certainty" and "consistency" in the vast majority of cases. See, e.g., Thompson, "Who Wants To Avoid the Guidelines? Contracting Out and Around" (2001–2003), 19 C.F.L.Q. 1. In *Children Come First*, the Department of Justice reported (Vol. 1 at 11) that 93% of all cases involving child support under the *Divorce Act* were "settled by consent". Joseph P. Hornick, Lorne D. Bertrand, Joanne Paetsch, and Nicholas M.C. Bala report in *The Survey of Child Support Awards: Analysis of Phase 2* (Minister of Justice, 2003) (available on the Department of Justice Canada Web site) that child support was contested in about 10% of the divorce cases between late 1998 and January 2002.

The first reading that follows is the Canadian government's explanation of the move towards child support guidelines. The CSG that were eventually adopted differ somewhat from those envisaged in this piece, but it does identify the rationale for and the basic features of the CSG. There then follows an overview of and some brief commentary on the CSG and a brief description of other aspects of the 1996 federal child support package.

For additional readings on the CSG, see *Federal Child Support Guidelines Reference Manual* (Ottawa: Dept. of Justice, looseleaf); Bala, "Ottawa's New Child Support Regime: A Guide to the Guidelines" (1996), 21 R.F.L. (4th) 301; Department of Justice Canada, *Formula for the Table of Amounts Contained in the Federal Child Support Guidelines: A Technical Report* (CSR-1997-1E) (Child Support team, December, 1997) (Available on the Department's Web site at <http://canada.justice.gc.ca>); Finnie, "The Government's Child Support Package" (1997-98), 15 C.F.L.Q. 79; Colman, "Child Support Guideline — New

Laws, New Challenges" (1997-98), 15 C.F.L.Q. 229; Aston, "An Update of Case Law under the Child Support Guidelines" (1998-99), 16 C.F.L.Q. 261; Maisonneuve, "Child Support under the Federal and Quebec Guidelines: A Step Forward or Behind?" (1999), 16 Can. J. Fam. L. 284; T.W. Hainsworth, *Child Support Guidelines Service* (Canada: Canada Law Book, looseleaf); Thompson, "The Second Family Conundrum in Child Support" (2001), 18 Can. J. Fam. L. 227; Thompson, "Who Wants to Avoid the Guidelines? Contracting Out and Around" (2001-2002), 19 C.F.L.Q. 1; Department of Justice Canada, *Children Come First: A Report to Parliament Reviewing the Provisions and Operations of the Federal Child Support Guidelines* (Ottawa, 2002); and Millar and Gauthier, "What Were They Thinking? The Development of Child Support Guidelines in Canada" (2002), 17 Can. J. Fam. L. 139.

THE NEW CHILD SUPPORT PACKAGE

(Ottawa: Government of Canada, March 6, 1996) 11–17 and 30-31

Federal Child Support Guidelines

The Family Law Committee found that the current method of determining child support awards is viewed as subjective, arbitrary and unfair. To help parents, lawyers and judges set fair and consistent child support awards, the government will introduce Child Support Guidelines ("the Guidelines") in the *Divorce Act*. The federal Guidelines will apply when a child support order is made in a divorce proceeding. Although they will not apply in cases of separation or when parents were not married — these situations are governed by provincial or territorial family law — the federal government is working closely with the provinces to encourage them to adopt guidelines in their own jurisdictions. By making the system more predictable and offering a simpler means to update awards, the introduction of guidelines can lower legal costs for parents, as well as legal aid and court costs for governments.

The Guidelines are designed to:

- establish a fair standard of support for children that ensures that children continue to benefit from the financial means of both parents after divorce;
- reduce conflict and tension by making the calculation of child support simpler and more objective;
- improve the efficiency of the legal process by giving courts and parties guidance in setting awards and encouraging settlement; and
- assure more consistent treatment of support-paying parents, while providing sufficient flexibility to ensure that awards are fair in individual family circumstances.

[These objectives are set out in slightly different words in s. 1 of the CSG.]

Presumptive Application of the Guidelines

Courts will be required to award the amount set out in the Child Support Payment Schedule, plus allowable special expenses, unless the court makes a written finding that the award causes undue hardship to either parent or to the child.

The Guidelines will not be mandatory for support awards that are negotiated out-of-court. However, they will provide guidance to parents as well as the courts — which are responsible for assessing whether reasonable arrangements have been made for the children's support.

Child Support Payment Schedules [The Tables]

The Child Support Payment Schedules show the basic amount that the support-paying parent should pay according to his or her income and the number of children. "Income" will be defined broadly in the Guidelines, but the income of a new partner or spouse will be relevant only if the court is asked to make a determination of undue hardship.

The Schedule amounts are fixed by a formula that calculates the appropriate amount of support in light of economic data on average expenditures on children across different income levels. The formula reserves a basic amount of income for the payer's self-support, and adjusts for the impact of federal and provincial income taxes. There are separate tables for each province to take differences in provincial income tax rates into account. ...

A New Approach to Setting Child Support

Guidelines which — like the Federal Child Support Guidelines — set support payments as a share of the support-paying parent's income are known as percentage-of-income guidelines. This style of guideline is used in many American states and in New Zealand. They are premised on a number of findings from economic research on the costs of raising children:

- spending on children is not fixed but changes as the income of either parent changes;
- the amount a family spends on their children is directly related to the means of both parents;
- spending on children increases as the number of children increases, but the incremental costs associated with each additional child are lower, as the family benefits from economies of scale;
- there is little regional variation in the proportion of family income devoted to children;
- because spending on children is not fixed, but varies with both parents' incomes, the contribution of the support-paying parent can be set independently of the income of the custodial parent. This allows the child to benefit from increases in the custodial parent's standard of living, and recognizes that the support-paying parent will not have a greater capacity to pay support if the custodial parent suffers a drop in income;
- the custodial parent will also contribute to the children in relation to his or her own means. The custodial parent is expected to contribute an amount similar to what a support-paying parent with a similar income would be required to pay.

This new approach to setting child support payments improves upon the existing system in three fundamental ways:

Awards Will be Based on Average Expenditures on Children

Because of the difficulties involved in calculating the *specific* costs of raising a child, the Guidelines are based on studies of *average* costs of raising children. Applying these Guidelines will result in more consistent child support awards across similar income levels and will ensure that more children will receive adequate amounts of child support.

Awards Will Recognize that Expenditures Vary With Income

The amounts set out in the Schedules are based on economic studies which show that spending on children is not fixed, but is directly related to the income level of both parents and to the number of children in the family. Families spend more on their children as family income increases, and spending on children changes with the income of either parent. As well, while overall spending on children increases with the number of children, incremental expenses for additional children are not as high because the family benefits from economies of scale.

Children Will Benefit From the Means of Both Parents

Under the Guidelines, the parents' financial obligations toward the child are treated independently. The support-paying parent's contribution is set according to his or her own income, without reference to the income of the custodial parent. The Schedule awards reflect the amount that a parent with a particular level of income is expected, on average, to spend on his or her children. The custodial parent is expected to contribute a similar share of his or her income to meet the costs of raising the child. In this way, the children will share in increases or decreases in either parent's income, just as they would if the two parents had continued to live together.

Adjustments to the Guideline Amount

Child support guidelines need to have a degree of flexibility, because not all children or families are alike. The federal Guidelines are designed to strike a balance between the need for more consistent and predictable awards, and the need to ensure that awards are equitable in individual situations. Support awards can be adjusted in two ways to recognize individual family circumstances.

Special Child-Related Expenses [See s. 7 of the CSG]

While the Child Support Payment Schedules reflect average expenditures on children, some kinds of expenses for children do not lend themselves to averages. To ensure that support awards are equitable when there are extraordinary expenses for a child, four categories of special child-related expenses can be added to the Schedule amount if they are reasonable and necessary in light of the needs of the children and the means of the parents:

- net child care expenses for children ...;
- medical and health-related expenses over [$100] per year per child that are not covered by provincial or territorial health insurance plans;
- educational expenses for primary, secondary or post-secondary education, or for an educational program that meets a child's particular needs; and
- extraordinary expenses for extracurricular activities that allow a child to pursue a special interest or talent, or attend a specialized program.

When appropriate, the support-paying parent's contribution to these special expenses will be added to the Schedule amount.

Undue Hardship [See s. 10 of the CSG]

A court will be able to award more or less than the Schedule amount plus allowable special expenses if this total amount causes "undue hardship" to either parent or to the child. The party pleading undue hardship will ... have to show that he or she has a lower standard of living than the other party. The situations which might justify a finding of undue hardship are not limited, but could include:

- an unusually high level of debt, reasonably incurred to support the family or earn a living;
- significant access expenses, such as travel or accommodation costs; and
- obligations for the support of other children, or spousal support obligations.

To help ensure consistency, the court will be required to give written reasons for ordering child support that is more or less than the amount set out in the Guidelines.

Adjustments for Special Custody Arrangements [See s. 8 and s. 9 of the CSG]

The Guidelines will provide a method for adjusting the support amount in cases of split custody (when each parent has custody of one or more children of the marriage) and shared custody (when parents share custody of the child fully and equally).

Application to Existing Child Support Orders

The new Child Support Guidelines will apply to new orders for child support made under the *Divorce Act*, and orders that change existing child support orders, made after the date that the Guidelines come into force.

This means that the new Guidelines and income tax rules for child support will not automatically affect the operation of existing child support orders. If neither parent seeks a change to their existing support order, then the order will not be affected by either the Guidelines or the tax change. However, either parent will be able to apply to a court to have their child support award varied to reflect the Guidelines and the new tax rules. ...

Four-Year Review of Guidelines

... The Guidelines will redefine the way child support awards are determined. To ensure that the Guidelines operate as fairly and effectively as possible, it is important to carefully review their impact. Justice Canada will monitor and evaluate their operation over the first four years after they come into force. All of those who will use the guidelines — parents, mediators, lawyers and judges — will be asked to provide input. Research will be conducted on the impact of the Guidelines. Experience with the Guidelines will provide guidance as to how to further refine them. ...

[One of the amendments to the *Divorce Act* in 1997 (see s. 28 of the Act) required the Minister of Justice to undertake a review and report to Parliament within five years. The Department's *Children Come First* constitutes that report.]

Although the notes preceding the Tables in Schedule I of the CSG state that "the tables are based on economic studies of average spending on children in families at different income levels in Canada", this is misleading. Indeed, the technical report explaining the development of the final tables acknowledges that they are based on "equivalence scales" rather than any empirical studies of average spending. See Department of Justice Canada, *Formula for the Table of Amounts Contained in the Federal Child Support Guidelines: A Technical Report* (CSR-1997-1E) (Child Support Team, December, 1997). Several assumptions underpin the "equivalence scales" or mathematical model used. First, the model uses a "Statistics Canada 40/30 scale" whereby the "adult equivalence unit" for a single parent with one child is 1.4 and an additional .3 for each additional child. In other words, a single parent with one child is assumed to need 40% more after tax income than an adult living alone to achieve the same standard of living. The second assumption underlying the tables is that both parents have the same income. Third, it is assumed that the non-custodial parent has the same costs or needs as a single person. In other words, any costs associated with exercising access such as providing a furnished bedroom, a bicycle, toys, and food are not considered. Finally, it is assumed that the parents do not form new relationships that might affect household income and needs. To the extent that these assumptions do not reflect the reality in any particular situation, they may result in inequities. Some of these are explored by Professors Millar and Gauthier in "What Were They Thinking? The Development of Child Support Guidelines in Canada" (2002), 17 Can. J. of Law & Society 139.

Canada's and Ontario's CSG are both based on a "percentage of income" model. This model assumes that the custodial parent is making contributions proportionate to his or her income in the same manner as would have occurred without separation or divorce. Quebec has adopted a version of the "income shares" model of child support guidelines, which is prevalent in the United States. Quebec's guidelines apply to all applications under the *Civil Code of Quebec* and to almost all divorce-related applications in Quebec. They determine the appropriate amount of child support in accordance with the income of both parents. See Fortin, "Quebec Guidelines for the Determination of Child Support" in *Federal Child Support Guidelines: Reference Manual* (Ottawa: Queen's Printer, 1997) J-1; Maisonneuve, "Child Support Under the Federal and Quebec Guidelines: A Step Forward or Behind?" (1999), 16 Can. J. Fam. L. 284; and Department of Justice Canada, *Children Come First: A Report to Parliament Reviewing the Provisions and Operation of the Federal Child Support Guidelines* (Ottawa, 2002) (Vol. 2 at 23–28).

The Table amounts in the CSG introduce some certainty and consistency to the determination of child support. To the extent that deviations are permitted to enhance the goal of fairness, the goals of certainty and consistency may suffer. Adjustments or deviations may also encourage litigation.

The rest of this chapter explores some of the sections in the CSG that allow adjustments and deviations from the Table amount. Under s. 7 of the CSG, a court may order an amount in addition to the Table amount to take into account certain special expenditures. See heading (3) **Special or Extraordinary Expenses**, below. In an attempt to ensure fairness in individual circumstances, some provisions in the CSG grant discretion to the courts to deviate from the Table amount. Two of these, namely, s. 3(2) (dealing with adult children) and s. 5 (dealing with a person standing in the place of a parent), have already been explored. In addition, s. 4 gives a court authority to determine the appropriate support amount where the paying parent's income is over $150,000. See heading (4) **High Income Earners**, below. Section 9 of the CSG allows a court to order child support that differs from the Table amount where a paying parent cares for the child for at least 40% of the time. See heading (5) **Split And Shared Custody**, below. Under s. 10 of the CSG, a court may adjust the amount of child support in certain situations of "undue hardship". See heading (6) **Undue Hardship**, below. Finally, the ability to deviate from the CSG by agreement is explored in Chapter 9 *DOMESTIC CONTRACTS*.

NOTES AND QUESTIONS

1. Where a court is determining applications for both child and spousal support, it must give priority to child support: s. 15.3 of the *Divorce Act* and s. 38.1 of the *FLA*. A court must, therefore, assess child support first and only order spousal support to the extent that there are sufficient funds remaining in the hands of the non-custodial parent after deducting child support.

In assessing the non-custodial parent's income for the purpose of determining the Table amount, any spousal support paid by this parent is not deducted. However, s. 3(1) of Schedule III of the CSG specifies that spousal support received by a parent is deducted from that parent's income for the purpose of determining the Table amount. Section 3(2) of Schedule III then goes on to stipulate that any spousal support paid by a parent to the other parent is deducted to calculate the first parent's income for the apportionment of "special or extraordinary expenses" under s. 7. The spousal support is then added to the recipient parent's income for the purpose of s. 7 of the CSG. This latter result occurs because s. 3(1) of Schedule III of the CSG only applies to the determination of income "for the purpose of determining an amount under an applicable table".

In *Schmid v. Smith* (1999), 1 R.F.L. (5th) 447 (Ont. S.C.J.), Justice Lack indicated (at 453) that the CSG create a conundrum in cases where there is a request for both spousal support and an order under s. 7 of the *Guidelines*. The statutory provisions noted above suggest that child support must be determined before spousal support. But the apportionment of special or extraordinary expenses, which is one component of child support, cannot take place until spousal support is assessed. A similar concern exists in determining whether undue hardship exists under s. 10 of the CSG if the court uses Schedule II to compare the living standards of the two households. Justice Lack dealt with these problems by considering the mother's claim for an amount of child support relating to extraordinary expenses and the father's claim for a reduction of child support on the basis of undue hardship at various potential levels of spousal support. He then determined the amount of spousal support that the husband could pay and used that figure in apportioning the extraordinary expenses and assessing the undue hardship claim.

The Department of Justice reports in *Children Come First* (Vol. 2 at 132) that courts generally decide if there are any qualifying special expenses, then determine spousal support and finally return to the apportionment of the special expenses, if any. At the latter stage, they deduct the spousal support just ordered from the paying parent and add it to the income of the recipient for the purposes of apportioning the special expenses. Computer software programs assist considerably in this exercise.

2. Since the passage of the CSG, lawyers and judges have increasingly relied on computer software to calculate the amount of child support. This is especially so in a variety of complex situations, including split and shared custody and situations in which the custodial parent has an obligation to pay spousal support to the non-custodial parent. It is not an overstatement to say that it is now impossible to practice family law effectively without access to this software. The software, however, makes certain assumptions that may not be apparent to a casual user. For example, in cases of shared custody, the software assumes that the amount of child support owing will be a "set-off" between the table amount payable by the higher income parent, and the table amount payable by the lower income parent. This result is not necessarily the result mandated by the Supreme Court of Canada in its consideration of s. 9 of the CSG in *Contino-Leonelli Contino*, [2005] 3 S.C.R. 217, reproduced in part later in this chapter. The convenience of the software, however, and the simplicity of the set-off, has resulted in many practitioners ignoring the *Contino* decision and applying the set-off when negotiating separation agreements or consent orders in which the children's time is shared approximately equally.

3. One of the reasons the software has become invaluable is because of the changed tax treatment of child support. Until May 1, 1997, the date the CSG became effective, child support was a deduction for the payor, and taxable income for the recipient. If both child and spousal support are payable, it is difficult to calculate the net disposable incomes of the parties without the help of the software. It is important to know the net disposable incomes of the two parental households so that the court can assess the fairness of the spousal support arrangement.

4. Under ss. 15.1(7) and (8) of the *Divorce Act* and ss. 33(14) and (15) of the *FLA* (similar provisions also apply to variation applications), a court may award an amount that is different from the amount that would have been determined in accordance with the CSG on the consent of both parents. However, the court must first be persuaded that "reasonable arrangements have been made for the support of the child to whom the order relates". There are very few reported cases under these provisions, although there are a number dealing with the similarly worded s. 11(1)(b) of the *Divorce Act* (discussed earlier in the materials in Chapter 3, *DIVORCE*). For general commentary, see Thompson, "Who Wants to Avoid the Guidelines? Contracting Out and Around" (2001-2002), 19 C.F.L.Q. 1 at 8–18, and Maur, "Child Support Below the Guidelines: Why a Bird in the Hand is Not Always Worth Two in the Bush" (2008) 27 C.F.L.Q. 201.

5. Because the Table amount is determined by the payor's income, a change in that income may be a reason for a variation of the amount specified in an order. Frequent variation is therefore likely to be the norm. Section 25 of the CSG provides that a parent who receives child support under an order can require the paying parent to provide new income information once a year. This information can then be used to request a variation.

Requesting a variation of a court order, however, requires a new proceeding to be commenced. This is expensive, and may work to the advantage of the payor because of the delay inherent in court proceedings generally. To avoid the necessity of variation applications, the parties may enter into agreements that contemplate recalculation or courts may order a procedure enabling parents to recalculate child support without returning to court. In *S. (D.B.) v. G. (S.R.)* (2005), 7 R.F.L. (6th) 373 (Alta. C.A.), (reversed (2006), 31 R.F.L. (6th) 1 (S.C.C.)) the Alberta Court of Appeal stated (at para. 94) that this was "a prudent approach which should be encouraged by bar and bench". In addition, the court made the following comments:

> ... In assessing fairness from the children's perspective, three factors weigh heavily in favour of a court's ordering recalculations of child support on a regular basis. First, while inflation in Canada remains at a very low rate, it nevertheless continues to trend in an upward direction. Second, more important, parents typically have their children at an age where they are still advancing in their careers and continue to do so while their children move towards adulthood. In other words, as children age, it can reasonably be expected that their parents' income will generally increase — and, if so, then the amount of child support being paid should increase accordingly. Third, the courts are well aware of the burdens — economic, psychological and otherwise — imposed on parents seeking to modify an outstanding court order. This applies equally whether the child support is to be increased or decreased. To the extent that these burdens can be minimized through court orders which address foreseeable contingencies, that is very much in the children's interests.

> 149 This being so, and having regard to the primary objective of the child-centred Guidelines — to ensure that children are properly cared for financially by both their parents — it is, in my view, incumbent on courts to ensure that child support orders provide for recalculations of child support on a regular basis. At a minimum, orders for payment of periodic child support should routinely include the following provisions, unless the court is otherwise satisfied that it is not appropriate to include these provisions. ...

> 150 First, the payor-parent should be required to provide, on an annual basis, income tax and other information as contemplated under s. 25 of the Guidelines to the recipient-parent and *vice versa* if the recipient parent's income is used to determine the amount of the child support order. This avoids all the practical problems associated with the issuance, and delivery, of repeated written requests for this information. Second, the court order should reflect that the amount of child support awarded under the order is subject to adjustment and that such amount shall be recalculated annually based on then current income or as agreed upon between the parties. Third, the court order should provide that if the parents are unable, within a specified period of time following the exchange of the relevant information or the date by which the information was to be exchanged, to agree on the amount of the child support payable or the date on which the adjusted amounts will commence, then either parent may apply to the court to settle these issues.

> 151 I appreciate that court orders framed in these terms still require the parties to agree in the first instance on both the amount of any increase or decrease and the date on which the adjusted payment is to take effect, failing which it will be necessary to bring a court application to settle these terms.

At the time of writing, Bill 133 has been passed but not yet proclaimed. It would add s. 39.1 to the *Family Law Act* to make variation of a court order for support much easier. It would allow the Family Responsibility Office (the support enforcement agency in Ontario) to recalculate the amount in accordance with anticipated regulations to "reflect updated income information". Subject to any review or appeal process, the recalculated amount would become the amount payable under the order 31 days after the parties are notified of the recalculation. Presumably, Ontario will also enter into agreement with the Government of Canada pursuant to s. 25.1 of the *Divorce Act* so that this procedure will apply to child support orders made under that Act.

(2) Determining Income

The most important step in most child support cases is the determination of the payor's income. Section 21 of the CSG imposes an obligation on the respondent served with an application for child support to disclose detailed information about his or her income. This includes income tax returns filed for the last three years, notices of assessment and reassessment, statements of earnings from employers, financial statements of a business or professional practice where the parent is self-employed, and financial statements of corporations controlled by a parent. An applicant has similar disclosure obligations only where that person's "income information is necessary to determine the amount of the order": s. 21(1). The income of the applicant is relevant only where 1) the child is over the age of majority (see s. 3(2) of the CSG); 2) the payor's income is over $150,000 (see s. 4); 3) there are special or extraordinary expenses (see s. 7); 4) there is split or shared custody (see ss. 8 and 9); or 5) there is claimed undue hardship (s. 10). By way of contrast, the province of Newfoundland and Labrador has adopted *Guidelines* requiring both parents to file financial information in all circumstances.

Section 15(1) of the CSG specifies that generally a parent's income is determined in accordance with ss. 16 to 20. Section 15(2) stipulates that the parties can agree in writing on the annual income of a parent, but the court retains authority not to accept this. Under s. 16, the starting point in arriving at a parent's income is Line 150, or the "Total Income" in the T1 General Form used for income tax purposes, as adjusted in accordance with Schedule III of the CSG. Pursuant to that Schedule, various listed items are deducted or added. For the most part, one is predicting income for the immediate future and past income is merely a guide: *Lee v. Lee* (1998), 43 R.F.L. (4th) 339 (Nfld. C.A.), at paras. 4–8. See also *L. (R.E.) v. L. (S.M.)* (2007), 40 R.F.L. (6th) 239 (Alta C.A.) where the court stressed that current, not past, income is crucial.

In situations where a parent's annual income, as determined under s. 16, does not provide the fairest determination of income for child support purposes, a court has discretion to determine income in accordance with ss. 17 to 19 of the CSG. Under s. 17(1), a court may select an amount of income that would be fairer than the amount suggested by the most recent income information. The court reviews the income over the past three years to make this assessment.

Pursuant to s. 18(1), if a parent is a shareholder, director, or officer of a corporation and the annual income shown on the T1 General Form does not fairly reflect all the money available to the parent for the purpose of child support, a court may add all or part of the pre-tax income of the corporation or an amount commensurate with the services provided to the corporation, up to the corporation's pre-tax income. For the purposes of s. 18(1), s. 18(2) stipulates that "all amounts paid by the corporation as salaries, wages or management fees, or other payments or benefits, to or on behalf of persons with whom the corporation does not deal at arm's length must be added to the pre-tax income, unless the [parent] establishes that the payments were reasonable in the circumstances".

Courts are granted the power to "impute" income in s. 19 of the CSG. The section covers numerous situations, including where the paying parent is exempt from paying income tax, lives in a country with significantly lower tax rates than Canada's, or fails to provide income information when under a legal obligation to do so. Imputing income most often occurs when a spouse is intentionally not working, or is underemployed; and when a self-employed spouse is able to deduct, under the *Income Tax Act*, certain expenses from income. A leading case dealing with the first situation is reproduced below. In the second situation, a court is not bound by the income of a payor for tax purposes and may add deductions back in where it considers them "unreasonable". See s. 19(1)(g) and s. 19(2). Deductions that may be added back into income for child support purposes include 1) "personal use" items such as deductions for cell phones, a home office and vehicles and 2) "excessive deductions" for items such as capital cost allowance on equipment that may not need replacement at the rate suggested by the *Income Tax Act*. See *Tether v. Tether* (2009), 2009 CarswellSask 8 (Q.B.), in which Sandomirsky, J. dealt with the issue of adding items back into income (paras. 18–20):

> Let me merely comment upon the fact that how a payor, who is self-employed, organizes his or her business and accounting affairs to reduce taxable income is one purpose. It is a very different purpose for imputing or recalculating a payor's income for child support. That distinction is always relevant. For the purpose of calculating a payor's income for child support purposes the proper lens with which

to view the income evidence is to gauge the true ability to pay child support. Therefore, a court often adds back any excessive claims for capital cost allowance if such claim was not realistic given the life expectancy of the income producing asset. Working assets wear out over time and varying percentages are used to depreciate such assets pegged to a reasonable life span of the asset and to provide for its eventual replacement. The tax payor may be more aggressive in claiming capital cost allowance in order to reduce business income in a particularly profitable year and conversely so in a slow year. However, viewed from the perspective of child support, a child is entitled to be sustained at a level or lifestyle commensurate with the payor's reasonable, but realistic, ability to pay child support — which may be quite different than what the payor may elect to do in any given tax year to maximize tax avoidance.

The reality in this case is that the respondent is obliged to pay interest accruing on commercially contracted debt regardless of the fact that such debt may represent the purchase price of a redundant or obsolete asset such as the gravel crushing equipment.

Meal deductions, of which the respondent claims the allowable 50% of cost is $7,318.00. The reality is that a long distance truck driver is on the road for excessive periods while working and must pay for meals in restaurants. This cost is greater than the economy of eating one's own cooking and groceries at home — hence, 50% is the amount allowed by Revenue Canada in recognition of that fact. I do not agree with the petitioner that this sum should be added back to the respondent's net income.

Determining the income of farmers and small business operators can present special problems. For a sample of the cases, see *Seidlikoski v. Hall* (1998), 40 R.F.L. (4th) 427 (Sask. Q.B.); *Tidball v. Tidball* (1999), 45 R.F.L. (4th) 437 (Ont. Gen. Div.); *Cornelius v. Andres* (1999), 45 R.F.L. (4th) 200 (Man. C.A.); reconsideration refused (1999), 1999 CarswellMan 273 (Man. C.A.); and *Rudachyck v. Rudachyck* (1999), 47 R.F.L. (4th) 363 (Sask. C.A.).

For descriptions of the rules governing income determination and the cases applying them, see Boutet and Kish, "Income Determination under the Child Support Guidelines: A Case Law Review" (2001-2002), C.F.L.Q. 283 and Department of Justice, *Children Come First* (Vol. 1 at 23–25 and Vol. 2 at 92–104).

DRYGALA v. PAULI

(2002), 29 R.F.L. (5th) 293, 2002 CarswellOnt 3228 (Ont. C.A.)

[In 1996, the father of one child earned about $33,000 as a certified tool and die maker, but he quit his job rather than work overtime. In April of the next year, the father separated from the child's mother. He made only two child support payments after the separation, although he did care for the child from February to September in 1998 while the mother worked. In January 1999, the father enrolled in university. He was initially on academic probation, but the university informed him on November 15, 1999, that he had satisfactorily demonstrated that he could take a regular program. He became a full-time student in January 2000 and thereafter took three courses per term, spending a total of nine hours in the classroom per week.

The mother commenced divorce proceedings on June 15, 1998, and applied for child support. The father testified at the trial in January 2001 that he did not enjoy his work as a tool and die maker and that he had never been very good at it. He indicated that he would graduate with a Bachelor of Arts after another year and a half or two years and that he hoped then to take a one-year program to become an elementary school teacher. His Financial Statement indicated that his expenses were over $48,000, all of which were paid with funds received from his mother or his step-father's company.

The trial judge concluded that the father had proved himself academically and that his goal of becoming a teacher was a realistic one. Nonetheless, using s. 19(1) of the CSG, he imputed income to the father for the purposes of child support. The judge reasoned that the father could be working part-time while at university and imputed an income of $30,000 per year. At that income level, the father was obligated to pay $266 per month. Although the judge noted that the father "did in a way contribute by providing childcare, definitely in 1998", he concluded that the appropriate start date for the payments was June 15th, 1998. The Ontario Court of Appeal allowed the father's appeal in part.]

GILLESE J.A.: —

Application of Section 19(1)(a) of the Guidelines

23 In my view, in applying this provision, the trial judge was required to consider the following three questions.

1. Is the spouse intentionally under-employed or unemployed?

2. If so, is the intentional under-employment or unemployment required by virtue of his reasonable educational needs?

3. If the answer to question #2 is negative, what income is appropriately imputed in the circumstances?

Intentional Under-Employment or Unemployment

24 The meaning of the word "intentionally" in s. 19(1)(a) has received inconsistent application in the courts. On the one hand, there are the so-called bad faith cases in which the word "intentionally" has been interpreted as meaning a deliberate course of conduct for the purpose of undermining or avoiding the parent's support obligation. These cases act on the explicit assumption that a court should not impute income in the absence of such a motive, as to do so results in an onerous financial obligation on a parent who chooses to make a career change. [See, e.g., *Woloshyn v. Woloshyn* (1996), 22 R.F.L. (4th) 129 (Man. Q.B.); aff'd (1997), 28 R.F.L. (4th) 70 (Man. C.A.).]

25 On the other hand, there are a number of conflicting cases in which the courts have held that there is no need to find a specific intent to evade child support obligations before income can be imputed. See, for example, *Montgomery v. Montgomery* (2000), 3 R.F.L. (5th) 126 (N.S. C.A.); and *Donovan v. Donovan* (2000), 190 D.L.R. (4th) 696 (Man. C.A.). ...

26 In my view, the latter approach is correct.

27 I begin by considering the words of s. 19(1)(a). The modern approach to statutory interpretation has been repeatedly stressed by the Supreme Court of Canada as one that is contextual and purposeful. Words in legislation are to be read in their entire context, giving them their grammatical and ordinary meaning in a way that is in harmony with the scheme, objects and intention of the legislation. (See, for example, *Francis v. Baker*, [1999] 3 S.C.R. 250 (S.C.C.).)

28 Read in context and given its ordinary meaning, "intentionally" means a voluntary act. The parent required to pay is intentionally under-employed if that parent chooses to earn less than he or she is capable of earning. That parent is intentionally unemployed when he or she chooses not to work when capable of earning an income. The word "intentionally" makes it clear that the section does not apply to situations in which, through no fault or act of their own, spouses are laid off, terminated or given reduced hours of work.

29 I note that there is no requirement of bad faith in the provision itself, nor is there language suggestive of such a requirement.

30 A consideration of the scheme of the legislation and its objects reinforces the conclusion that bad faith is not required. Section 26.1(2) of the *Divorce Act* ... says that the *Guidelines* "shall be based on the principle that spouses have a joint financial obligation to maintain the children of the marriage in accordance with their relative abilities to contribute to the performance of that obligation."

31 Section 1 of the *Guidelines* stipulates that one of its objectives is to establish a fair standard of support for children to ensure that they benefit from the financial means of both parents after separation.

32 Imputing income is one method by which the court gives effect to the joint and ongoing obligation of parents to support their children. In order to meet this legal obligation, a parent must earn what he or she is capable of earning.

33 The reason given in the cases that have required a bad faith finding relates to the needs of the spouse. It is said that to require spouses to support their children to the maximum of their earning capacity fails to recognize the fundamental importance of work to a person's life, including the pursuit of work which provides not only livelihood but also a sense of identity, self-worth and emotional well-being.

34 The contrary view stresses the paramountcy of parents' obligation to provide support for their children and notes that a focus on the detrimental effect that attribution of income may have for a parent obscures the detrimental consequences that may ensue when a parent fails to provide for the children to the best of his or her ability.

35 I am of the view that the debate is unwarranted. As will be seen in the following portions of these reasons, the legislation provides the necessary flexibility to respond to both sets of considerations. The need to ensure appropriate financial support for the children is dealt with by imputing income. The need to enable a parent to pursue meaningful work is to be addressed by the trial judge both when considering what the reasonable educational needs of the parent require and again when determining how much income is appropriately imputed.

36 A plain reading of s. 19(1)(a), done in a contextual and purposive fashion, leads me to conclude that the provision is unambiguous. There is no bad faith requirement.

37 The learned trial judge found that Mr. Pauli intentionally chose under-employment. While I would have characterized it as unemployment rather than under-employment, there is no doubt as to the correctness of his finding that Mr. Pauli acted "intentionally" within the meaning of s. 19(1)(a) when he chose to attend university rather than work. I see no error in the trial judge's determination to impute income to the appellant.

Reasonable Educational Needs

38 There is a duty to seek employment in a case where a parent is healthy. As a general rule, a parent cannot avoid child support obligations by a self-induced reduction of income. Thus, once it has been established that a spouse is intentionally unemployed or under-employed, the burden shifts to that spouse to establish what is required by virtue of his or her reasonable educational needs.

39 There are two aspects to this stage of inquiry. The trial judge must first determine whether the educational needs are reasonable. This involves a consideration of the course of study. A spouse is not to be excused from his or her child support obligations in furtherance of unrealistic or unproductive career aspirations.

40 But, s. 19(1)(a) speaks not only to the reasonableness of the spouse's educational needs. It also dictates that the trial judge determine what is required by virtue of those educational needs. The spouse has the burden of demonstrating that unemployment or under-employ-

ment is required by virtue of his or her reasonable educational needs. How many courses must be taken and when? How much time must be devoted in and out of the classroom to ensure continuation in the program? Are the academic demands such that the spouse is excused from pursuing part-time work? Could the program be completed over a longer period with the spouse taking fewer courses so that the spouse could obtain part-time employment? If the rigours of the program preclude part-time employment during the regular academic school year, is summer employment reasonably expected? Can the spouse take co-operative courses as part of the program and earn some income in that way? These are the types of considerations that go into determining what level of under-employment is required by the reasonable educational needs of a spouse.

41 The burden of proof is upon the spouse pursuing education as he or she is the person with access to the requisite information. The spouse is in the best position to know the particular requirements and demands of his or her educational program. He or she will have information about the hours of study necessary to fulfill such requirements, including the appropriate preparation time. He or she is in the best position to show whether part-time employment can be reasonably obtained in light of these educational requirements.

42 By implication, the trial judge found that Mr. Pauli's educational goals are reasonable. He appears also, in effect, to have determined that Mr. Pauli's intentional under-employment was required for that period in which he was on academic probation. This determination has implications for the period in which child support can be awarded, as will be seen later in these reasons in the context of retroactivity of child support.

Quantum of Income to be Imputed

43 The trial judge imputed an annual income of $30,000 based on s. 19(1)(a) of the *Guidelines*. No reasons are given for the choice of amount. All that is said is that it is not unreasonable to believe that lucrative part-time employment was available to Mr. Pauli.

44 Section 19 of the *Guidelines* is not an invitation to the court to arbitrarily select an amount as imputed income. There must be a rational basis underlying the selection of any such figure. The amount selected as an exercise of the court's discretion must be grounded in the evidence.

45 When imputing income based on intentional under-employment or unemployment, a court must consider what is reasonable in the circumstances. The factors to be considered have been stated in a number of cases as age, education, experience, skills and health of the parent. See, for example, *Hanson v. Hansen*, 1999 CarswellBC 2545 (B.C.S.C.) and *Cholodniuk v. Sears* (2001), 14 R.F.L. (5th) 9 (Sask. Q.B.). I accept those factors as appropriate and relevant considerations and would add such matters as the availability of job opportunities, the number of hours that could be worked in light of the parent's overall obligations including educational demands and the hourly rate that the parent could reasonably be expected to obtain.

46 When imputing income, the court must consider the amount that can be earned if a person is working to capacity while pursuing a reasonable educational objective. How is a court to decide that when, typically, there is little information provided on what the parent could earn by way of part-time or summer employment? If the parent does not provide the court with adequate information on the types of jobs available, the hourly rates for such jobs and the number of hours that could be worked, the court can consider the parent's previous earning history and impute an appropriate percentage thereof.

47 It was open to the trial judge to find that some or all of the amounts received by Mr. Pauli from his mother and from his stepfather's company should have been considered when de-

termining imputed income. The fact that he has chosen to rely upon his mother for his own support does not justify a failure to provide child support. Nor does it lessen Mr. Pauli's obligation to provide such support as is appropriate in the circumstances.

48 $30,000 is significantly less than Mr. Pauli's annual expenses, which exceed $48,000, and all of which are being paid without him incurring any debt. Mr. Pauli's financial statement shows that he has disposable and discretionary income, including $240 per month for cigarettes. Such information may have been relevant, as well, when determining an appropriate income figure.

49 The appellant has clearly failed to recognize his child support obligation. He has done well financially and despite that, he has paid almost nothing for child support. These, too, are relevant factors when determining the quantum of income to impute.

50 However, the trial judge imputed income on the basis of part-time employment, not Mr. Pauli's other sources of income. Having decided that the appropriate basis upon which to impute income was part-time employment, there was an obligation upon the trial judge to give some indication of how he arrived at the figure of $30,000. While significant deference must be given to trial judges in relation to support orders, a consideration of Mr. Pauli's prior earnings history demonstrates that the figure of $30,000 is unreasonable for part-time employment given that he seldom earned that much when working full time.

51 The trial judge had evidence of Mr. Pauli's age, education, experience, skills and health. He had, as well, various newspaper advertisements that Ms. Drygala presented at trial, indicating that local businesses were seeking tool and die makers.

52 It was entirely appropriate, on the record, to impute income to the appellant. The evidence shows that Mr. Pauli was taking 3 courses per term. He spends 3 hours of classroom time each week for each of the 3 courses for a total of 9 hours of classroom time. After making an appropriate allowance for study time outside of class, it is reasonable to assume that Mr. Pauli could work 50% of a normal work week. 1996 is the last year in which Mr. Pauli earned income from a job. He earned $33,000 in 1996. Child support shall be ordered based on an imputed income of $16,500.

[Regarding the date on which the order should commence, Justice Gillese concluded that the trial judge made no error in deciding to award retroactive support as the evidence demonstrated both the mother's financial need after the separation and the father's ability to pay. However, she held that the trial judge made two errors when making the order retroactive to June 15, 1998. First, having concluded that the father's care for the child from February to September of 1998 satisfied his child support obligation, the judge should not have awarded support for any portion of that period. Second, no income should have been imputed while the father was on academic probation because his educational goals were reasonable and he could not work during this period. Accordingly, the appellate court held that the appropriate commencement date for support was September 1, 1998, but that the order should be suspended for the probationary period of study.]

Where a payor truly has little or no income, the imputing power in s. 19 of the CSG will be no help. In the case below, the couple had one teenaged child. The payor father had a disability and earned little income, and his own father supported him fairly generously. The mother asked the trial court to impute income based on the gifts from the father's father. The trial judge declined to do so and the mother appealed.]

BAK v. DOBELL

(2007), 86 O.R. (3d) 196, 281 D.L.R. (4th) 494, 38 R.F.L. (6th) 7, 2007
CarswellOnt 2324 (C.A.)

S.E. LANG J.A., for the court: — ...

19 William Dobell testified that the monetary gifts he provided for his son, both by way of capital and as periodic support, were bestowed in an effort to promote the respondent's self-sufficiency and, pending that self-sufficiency, to keep the respondent from starving and "off the streets." Given his son's personality disorders, William Dobell testified that he was concerned about how the respondent would behave if he lived on the streets. William Dobell only supported his son for what he considered to be necessary for his day-to-day living. He saw no evidence of a "fancy" lifestyle on the respondent's part, or that of his current partner, and if he did see such evidence, he said he would reduce the amount of support. The trial judge accepted that William Dobell gave funds to his son out of a sense of obligation and to prevent the respondent from otherwise being a burden on the taxpayer.

The trial decision

21 After considering the relevant provisions of the *Guidelines*, including its definition of income and the potential for imputing income under s. 19(1), the trial judge declined to impute the gifts provided by William Dobell to Mark Dobell as *Guidelines* income. Furthermore, he held that the grandfather should not indirectly be required to pay support for an obligation that was not his responsibility.

22 In support of this conclusion, the trial judge found that William Dobell's generosity was purely voluntary, the respondent had no entitlement to the gifts, the gifts were intended only to encourage the respondent's self-sufficiency, the gifts did not provide the respondent with an extravagant lifestyle, and they were provided by William Dobell because he is a "person of substantial means that will not let his son depend on welfare."

23 Since the trial judge was not asked to impute any other income to the respondent, such as an amount equivalent to social assistance or a Canada Pension Plan disability pension, he dismissed the appellant's claim for child support and vacated the $117 consent order.

Analysis

24 In her factum on this appeal, the appellant argued that it is appropriate, in the circumstances of this case, to impute income to the respondent based on the respondent's lifestyle. In addition, the appellant submitted during oral argument that the gifts from the respondent's father should be imputed to the respondent as *Guidelines* income. As part of this second argument, the appellant submitted that the gift income was analogous to trust income.

25 Both arguments raise issues of statutory interpretation. Any question of statutory interpretation invokes the guiding principle of Elmer Driedger, frequently quoted with approval by this court and the Supreme Court of Canada: "Today there is only one principle or approach, namely, the words of an Act are to be read in their entire context, in their grammatical and ordinary sense harmoniously with the scheme of the Act, the object of the Act, and the intention of Parliament."

26 Before looking at the *Guidelines'* definition of income and its provisions for imputing income, it is helpful to consider the purpose of the legislation.

27 Prior to the *Guidelines*, child support was very much a matter of judicial discretion, a discretion that was generally broadly exercised to achieve a fair result in all the circumstances. This resulted in a correspondingly wide range of child support orders. Since family law lawyers were unable to predict a likely child support outcome with accuracy, the parties often chose to litigate, at significant emotional and financial expense to all.

28 The *Guidelines'* s. 1 objectives, which inform the meaning of the particular provisions at issue, are listed as follows:

> (a) to establish a fair standard of support for children that ensures that they benefit from the *financial means* of their parents and, in the case of divorce, from the financial means of both spouses after separation;
>
> (b) to reduce conflict and tension between parents or spouses by making the calculation of child support more objective;
>
> (c) to improve the efficiency of the legal process by giving courts, and parents and spouses, guidance in setting the levels of child support and encouraging settlement; and
>
> (d) to ensure consistent treatment of parents or spouses and their children who are in similar circumstances. [Emphasis added.]

29 With those objectives in mind, and except as otherwise specifically provided, Parliament decided that child support for minor children would be in "the amount set out in the applicable table" (Table support). Table support would be based on the number of children and on "the income of the parent or spouse against whom the order is sought" (*Guidelines*, s. 3(1)). In this way, Parliament sought to use fair and objective criteria to promote predictability and consistency so that parties would be able to resolve the issue of child support expeditiously, minimizing the financial and emotional costs of litigation.

30 To maximize predictability and consistency, Parliament provided a definition of income that is clear and unambiguous and that significantly narrowed the scope of judicial discretion. Section 2 restricts "income" to a person's "annual income determined under sections 15 to 20." Section 16, the one directly applicable to this case, provides that a "parent's or spouse's annual income is determined using the sources of income set out under the heading 'Total income' in the T1 General form issued by the Canada Revenue Agency". Thus, income for support purposes is presumptively the payor's income as it appears on line 150 of his or her income tax return. This restricts the definition of presumptive "income" to income that is subject to taxation. In this way, a payor's income can be easily ascertained by reference to the payor's income tax return.

31 It follows that gifts and lifestyle are not included in a payor's presumptive income because neither is subject to taxation.

32 However, there are provisions that can serve to adjust the presumptive amount of Table support. Of immediate application to this case is s. 19(1), which gives a court the discretion to impute income to a payor in enumerated circumstances. ...

33 Subsection 19(1) is clearly intended to capture cases that, in fairness, require an adjustment to the payor's presumptive income and, for this purpose, it provides a court with the discretion to impute income when it is "appropriate [to do so] in the circumstances".

34 The list of circumstances in s. 19(1) is not exhaustive: the legislature only provides that the list "include" items (a)–(i). Further, there is nothing in the provision that suggests other

appropriate circumstances must be analogous to those specifically enumerated, although similarity of circumstance to one listed in s. 19(1) would support the imputation of income, simply because such a circumstance would be consistent with legislative intention. The absence of analogy to a listed circumstance is simply a factor to be considered in interpreting the provision.

35 Some cases have held that there must be similarity between a new appropriate circumstance and the listed circumstances. However, *Riel v. Holland*, [2003] O.J. No. 3901 (C.A.) makes it clear that the listed circumstances are simply examples and it is open to find new circumstances in which to impute income, provided that the new ground is consistent with the purpose of s. 19(1) and the *Guidelines* generally. ...

36 If appropriate circumstances arise, particularly ones unforeseen by the legislature, a court has the discretion, to be exercised on a principled basis, to impute income to a payor parent. When considering whether a circumstance is an appropriate one in which to impute income, a court will bear in mind the objectives of the *Guidelines* to establish fair support based on the means of the parents in an objective manner that reduces conflict, ensures consistency and encourages resolution.

37 Thus, the open-ended wording of s. 19(1) does not mean that courts have an untrammelled discretion to add circumstances, particularly when a review of the legislation suggests a deliberate intention on the part of the legislature to exclude a particular circumstance.

38 Accordingly, I begin by asking whether any presumption of interpretation applies that would make it more or less likely to conclude that the legislature intended to either include or exclude gifts as *Guidelines* income, or whether the absence of reference to gifts in the *Guidelines* reflects a gap in the legislation.

39 Before turning to that question, I will first deal with the appellant's argument concerning lifestyle. I will then discuss separately gifts in their many forms, including in this case gifts in the nature of capital "given" to the respondent and those in the nature of monthly support.

Lifestyle

40 As I have said, under the *Guidelines*, child support is calculated on the payor's total income for income tax purposes. Lifestyle is clearly not a type of income, receipt or benefit included in total income. Canadians are not taxed on lifestyle.

41 Equally clearly, however, a payor's lifestyle often will be relevant to whether a court may impute income under s. 19(1) of the *Guidelines*. For example, it may be apparent from lifestyle that a payor is receiving undeclared income because he or she has historically worked, lives comfortably with the usual trappings, and yet declares minimal income for tax or child support purposes. In such a case, the recipient who calls evidence of the payor's lifestyle will ask the court to draw the reasonable inference that the payor must have a greater income than he or she has disclosed.

42 This occurred in *Davids v. Davids*, [1998] O.J. No. 2859 (Gen. Div.), where a chartered accountant was able to demonstrate from the husband's financial data that he was receiving income from a source he could or would not explain. Given the absence of any explanation, the court drew an inference that the husband's earnings were more than reported. Similarly, in *Biamonte v. Biamonte* (1998), 36 R.F.L. (4th) 349 (Ont. Gen. Div.), based on evidence of the parties' lifestyle, income was imputed to a husband who was shown to have a cash component to his restaurant business in addition to his declared income. While these cases demonstrate that a party's lifestyle can inform the question of whether the payor has diverted income, or underreported income, lifestyle is not a stand-alone ground for imputing income.

43 On this issue, I conclude that lifestyle is not income, but rather evidence from which an inference may be drawn that the payor has undisclosed income that may be imputed for the purpose of determining child support.

Imputed income

44 I turn to the appellant's second argument: whether the gifts from William Dobell should be imputed to the respondent as income, considering first, the capital amounts provided by William Dobell and second, the monthly support.

(i) Capital

45 The appellant argues that income should be imputed based on the lump sum amounts spent by William Dobell to provide education, shelter, a car, a motorcycle and medical and other benefits for the respondent.

46 This question is most easily approached by dividing the gifts into three categories: first, those funds advanced to finance the respondent's training and proposed business; second, the funds used to provide the respondent with a home and a car; and third, the funds provided to the respondent to cover professional fees, such as his medical and veterinary expenses.

47 First, William Dobell provided the respondent with large amounts of money to finance his training and to allow him to pursue his motorcycle business.

48 These funds were not used to finance the respondent's day-to-day expenses nor were they given to the respondent to spend in his discretion. Instead, they were akin to an investment by William Dobell in the respondent's future: an investment, as the trial judge noted, that may lead to the respondent generating income in his own right.

49 An example of this type of expenditure was the expensive scuba training, which included significant equipment costs as well as the expense of buying a vehicle adequate to transport equipment. Unfortunately, the respondent's potential for a scuba diving career ended when he suffered physical injuries, which continue to require treatment. The motorcycle business proposed at trial is similarly costly, both in terms of training and the cost to set up shop.

50 In my view, expenditures of this nature made, not by the respondent, but by his father for the specific cost of career advancement cannot be said to be income to the respondent under either the *Guidelines'* definition of presumptive income or as income that it is appropriate to impute to the respondent.

51 Second, in addition to supporting the respondent's training, William Dobell provided the respondent with a place to live, first in the condominium and later in the Stouffville property. As the trial judge found, the residences were bought to provide the respondent with a roof over his head so that he would not live on the street. The respondent was not at liberty to sell these properties and use the funds for other purposes. The evidence disclosed that the condominium was registered in the respondent's name for the sole purpose of trying to create a sense of pride of ownership so that the respondent would follow a "normal" lifestyle and become a functioning member of society. The evidence supports the conclusion that neither the condominium, nor its proceeds, were available to the respondent to expend as he wished. Furthermore, the respondent has no ownership interest or entitlement to the present Stouffville property, which is registered in his father's name. In these circumstances, the trial judge made no error in concluding that neither the capital value of the condominium, nor of the Stouffville property, should be imputed to the respondent as income.

52 This conclusion is consistent with a model of child support based on a payor's income, not on his or her capital. While income from investments is part of a payor's total income, his or her underlying investments are not. A payor is not expected to sell capital assets, such as a house and car, for the purpose of generating income from which to pay support, unless the "property is not reasonably utilized to generate income" (s. 19(1)(e)). Even assuming the applicability of this provision, on the facts of this case, the respondent did and does not have the option to sell capital assets to generate investment income, particularly in the circumstance that the particular acquisitions were made by William Dobell for the specific purpose of encouraging the respondent's conventional conduct, with the overall objective that he achieve financial independence. ...

58 Turning to the third category of medical, psychological, chiropractic, legal, and veterinary bills paid by the respondent's father, it was within the trial judge's discretion to refuse to impute these expenses to the respondent as income. The professional fees all came within a category of necessary medical or therapeutic expenses, or were truly in the nature of gifts to assist with unusual and non-recurring expenses. They were not given to the respondent to use for his day-to-day living, nor to be spent as he wished. For this reason, they should not be imputed to him for the purpose of calculating child support.

59 Thus, in my view, the trial judge made no error in refusing to impute income to the respondent on the basis of the gifts in the nature of capital.

(ii) Monthly support

60 I turn to consider the more difficult question of whether the periodic support received by the respondent from his father should be considered as the respondent's income for the purpose of calculating the respondent's child support obligation. I do this by returning first to the question of whether any presumptions of statutory interpretation assist with determining legislative intent on this issue. I look first at whether the government deliberately excluded gifts from the definition of income and from the circumstances included as appropriate ones in which to impute income. I then consider, if that is the case, whether gifts can ever be included in income for child support purposes.

61 When the *Guidelines* were enacted, the legislature is presumed to have been knowledgeable about the various sources of taxable and non-taxable income available to an individual, including the fact that neither gift nor trust income is taxable. It can be presumed from this knowledge that the legislature deliberately omitted both gifts and trust income from presumptive income.

62 The legislature, however, did list trust income as a s. 19(1) circumstance in which income could be imputed. It did not list gifts. Since the legislature did not include gifts within the ambit of imputed income, it can be presumed, *in the normal course*, that the legislature did not intend the receipt of gifts to be an "appropriate circumstance" in which to impute income. For this reason, usual gifts, such as those given to mark a special occasion, are not included as income.

63 If the legislature knowingly excluded gifts from presumptive and imputed income, can they ever be considered to be an appropriate circumstance in which to impute income under s. 19(1)? It is helpful to consider this question by comparing gifts to the "appropriate" circumstances listed by the legislature in s. 19(1). ... Income will be imputed where the respondent is intentionally unemployed or underemployed (s. 19(1)(a)); has special income tax circumstances or unreasonable deductions (s. 19(1)(b), (c), (g) or (h)); has diverted income (s. 19(1)(d)); has failed to reasonably utilize capital to generate income (s. 19(1)(e)); or has failed to make disclosure (s. 19(1)(f)).

64 These circumstances reflect two main themes: they either allow for the imputation of income to a spouse able to generate income who refuses to do so (or who does not provide proper disclosure of income information), or they adjust the payor's income to compensate for anomalous income tax treatment. Neither is relevant to the receipt of gifts generally and, clearly, the circumstances in this case bear no similarity to the examples listed in s. 19(1)(a)–(h).

65 The remaining listed circumstance is income or other benefits from a trust (s. 19(1)(i)). The trial judge in this case determined that the respondent is not the beneficiary of a trust; however, on appeal the appellant argues that the respondent's receipt of gifts is analogous to receipt of trust funds.

66 While the stream of income from William Dobell to the respondent bears some similarities to trust income, there are also important differences, most significantly that William Dobell remains in complete control of the funds, the amount of which are closely tied to the respondent's basic needs. The respondent has no entitlement to the stream of income, which could be reduced or terminated at any time by his father with no recourse to the respondent.

67 Nonetheless, it is important to consider s. 19(1) in light of the *Guidelines'* objectives of s. 1, which tell us that their purpose is to establish fair support for Jacqueline to ensure she benefits from the "financial means" of both her parents. ...

69 The appellant does cite cases that specifically consider parental gifts as income; however, those cases do so by agreement between the parties, without any discussion or analysis of the relevant provisions of the *Guidelines*. ...

74 Although it seems the legislature intentionally did not include the receipt of gifts given in the normal course in presumptive income, or as an example of an appropriate circumstance under s. 19(1), a court will consider whether the circumstances surrounding the particular gift are so unusual that they constitute an "appropriate circumstance" in which to impute income.

75 In considering whether it is appropriate to include the receipt of unusual gifts in income, a court will consider a number of factors. Those factors will include the regularity of the gifts; the duration of their receipt; whether the gifts were part of the family's income during cohabitation that entrenched a particular lifestyle; the circumstances of the gifts that earmark them as exceptional; whether the gifts do more than provide a basic standard of living; the income generated by the gifts in proportion to the payor's entire income; whether they are paid to support an adult child through a crisis or period of disability; whether the gifts are likely to continue; and the true purpose and nature of the gifts.

76 Clearly, on the facts of this case the amounts provided by William Dobell to the respondent are not gifts given "in the normal course" to mark a special occasion. This is apparent from the circumstances of the gifts, including the quantum, regularity, and duration of the periodic payments, as well as the fact that they provided the sole means of support for the respondent, and at least to some extent for his unemployed partner.

77 In exercising his discretion not to impute income to the respondent on the basis of the periodic support, the trial judge considered that the intended duration of the gifts was limited; that the gifts were intended only to encourage the respondent's self-sufficiency; that the gifts were made to a disabled child and were more in the nature of support for an adult child than in the nature of an allowance, and that the quantum of the gifts did no more than support a basic lifestyle. In my view, for these reasons, the trial judge was entitled to refuse to include these gifts in income.

78 Regarding the respondent's lifestyle, at trial, the appellant did not argue that the respondent had excess income from William Dobell's gifts that was available for the purposes of

child support. Indeed, the evidence established that the amount of the monthly support given by William Dobell met, but did not exceed, Mark Dobell's needs. ...

79 In any event, it is clear from the submissions made at trial, and a reading of the trial judge's reasons, that the essence of the appellant's argument was not that the respondent had the ability to provide child support, but that William Dobell had the ability. The appellant's trial counsel argued that a child support order would "not cost Mark Dobell a cent", because the expense would be assumed by William Dobell, who would not want his son found in contempt of a court order. The problem with this argument, as the trial judge noted, is that it is not William Dobell's obligation to pay child support and, in the circumstances of this case, any order of child support made against the respondent would "in fact be imposing that obligation on the respondent's father".

80 The respondent has a legal obligation to contribute to the support of his child; his father does not. The legislature neither provided William Dobell with any rights as a grandparent regarding his grandchild, nor imposed any obligations, such as the obligation to pay support.

81 Similarly, the income of a payor's new partner, and the payor's improved lifestyle resulting from cohabitation with a new partner, is not generally a relevant consideration in determining child support. If the income of the new spouse is not a relevant consideration, then neither should the gratuitous discretionary basic support provided by a parent to a disabled adult child be a relevant consideration.

82 There was ample evidence, which the trial judge accepted, to support a conclusion that the periodic support given by William Dobell to Mark Dobell was in the nature of support for a disabled adult child who was otherwise unable to support himself. In William Dobell's words, the support kept Mark off the streets and from being a burden on the taxpayer.

83 From a policy perspective, this type of support to an adult child is to be encouraged, not discouraged, particularly in the circumstances of this case where it may serve to provide a currently disabled parent with the means to become a self-sufficient member of society, and a parent capable of contributing to his child.

84 Despite Mark Dobell's statutory obligation to support his daughter, the evidence establishes that the respondent would be unable to support himself, absent the support provided by William Dobell. Unfortunately for Jacqueline, as for other children of disabled parents, her father was simply not able to contribute to her financial support.

85 Finally, I note that the appellant explicitly said she was not seeking an imputation of income to the respondent from sources such as social assistance or disability pensions. No evidence was called, for example, about whether the respondent is eligible for a Canada Pension Plan disability pension, which could include the separate child benefit payable directly to the custodial parent.

86 In summary, the trial judge had the best opportunity to weigh and consider the evidence as a whole and to determine whether it was appropriate to impute the gifts to the respondent as income. I see no basis to interfere with his exercise of that discretion. ...

NOTES AND QUESTIONS

1. As noted by Justice Gillese in *Drygala v. Pauli, supra*, some judges have held that a parent is "intentionally under-employed or unemployed" only where he or she intends to evade child support payments. The only recent appellate decision adopting that view is *Hunt v. Smolis-Hunt* (2001), 20 R.F.L. (5th) 409 (Alta. C.A.). The majority noted (para. 60) that an objective of the *Guidelines* was "to provide children with a *fair* standard of support, not the maximum standard of support which the parents are capable of contributing". It added (*ibid.*): "A fair standard of support does not require that a parent take on employment which provides the maximum income or to assume more

than one job in order to obtain greater income". The court also expressed concern for the unreasonable consequences that might follow for payors if they were forced to utilize their entire earning capacity (para. 64):

> ... [T]o require spouses to support their children to the maximum of their earning capacity also has the
> effect of dictating to divorced spouses that they may engage in a limited range of employment,
> namely, only those which pay the maximum they are capable of earning. This fails to recognize the
> fundamental importance of work to a person's life and fails to value the freedom to choose work
> which fulfills needs and interests extending beyond the receipt of income.

The view that a parent is underemployed or unemployed only where he or she is attempting to evade child
support obligations has been rejected, not only in *Drygala v. Pauli*, but also in *Montgomery v. Montgomery* (2000),
3 R.F.L. (5th) 126 (N.S. C.A.); *Donovan v. Donovan* (2000), 9 R.F.L. (5th) 306 (Man. C.A.); *Schindle v. Schindle*
(2001), 21 R.F.L. (5th) 188 (Man. C.A.); and *Steele v. Koppanyi* (2002), 29 R.F.L. (5th) 217 (Man. C.A.). However, the notion that an intention to evade support is relevant continues to appear inferentially in Ontario trial level
decisions. In *Rodrigues v. De Sousa*, [2008] O.J. No. 4541 (C.J.), the payor had made little effort to find appropriate
employment for the previous six years. Justice Sherr seemed to ground the finding of intentional underemployment
in the payor's clear animosity towards the recipient and his unwillingness to pay support.

Some judges will assume intentional underemployment if a payor does not make adequate financial disclosure:
Wilkins v. Wilkins (2008), 2008 CarswellOnt 139 (S.C.J.); additional reasons at (2008), 2008 CarswellOnt 1463
(S.C.J.), at para. 27. Of course, as acknowledged in that case, the dilemma is that a court cannot impute a specific
amount of income without some reasonable evidentiary foundation for doing so.

In *Grierson v. Brunton* (2004), 8 R.F.L. (6th) 146 (Ont. S.C.J.), Justice Mesbur states (para. 12) that the *Drygala* case establishes the following principle: "To be under-employed or unemployed, a parent must simply be
engaged in voluntary behaviour which is *unreasonable* given the obligation to support the children." Do you agree?
Did the court assess the reasonableness of the father's actions considered in *Drygala v. Pauli*? If so, at what stage of
the analysis?

Is a tax law professor "intentionally under-employed" when he can earn four times as much working for a Bay
Street law firm and there are no "reasonable educational or health needs" justifying this career choice? Does it
make any difference if the tax professor made this career choice long before the parents' relationship ended? If so,
how is this factor slotted into the analysis in *Drygala v. Pauli*?

On the issue of imputing income because of underemployment or unemployment, see Thompson, "Slackers,
Shirkers and Career Changers: Imputing Income for Under/Unemployment" (2007), C.F.L.Q. 135.

2. The *Montgomery* case, above, may be of particular interest to law students. When a husband and wife
divorced in 1997, the husband held a managerial position in a government department, earning about $60,000 per
year. The court issued a consent order requiring the husband to pay $1,864.33 monthly as combined spousal and
child support. In 1999, the husband received an LL.B. which he had been pursuing on a part-time basis since 1990.
He obtained an articling position for one year with the provincial government at a salary of approximately $20,000
and applied under s. 17 of the *Divorce Act* for a variation of the support order. The husband was willing to pay the
Table amount based on an income of $20,000. Acknowledging that it might take as long as ten years for a begin-
ning government lawyer to achieve a salary equivalent to that of his previous managerial position, the husband
suggested that he might pursue private sector employment after his call to the bar. He maintained that his career
change stemmed from a desire to secure more satisfying employment, which would, in the long run, result in an
increased level of income for himself and his dependants.

The Chambers Judge dismissed the application, holding that income should be imputed to the husband. In his
oral reasons, he also characterized the husband's argument that the career change would ultimately be financially
beneficial as "fanciful". The Nova Scotia Court of Appeal dismissed the husband's appeal, holding that the Chambers Judge made no error of law and that his conclusions were fully supported by the facts.

Should the court in *Montgomery* have considered whether the father could now return to his previous employment? Should it make any difference in a case such as *Montgomery* that the career change would have occurred
even if the family had stayed together?

Mr. Montgomery went into private practice and eventually earned $107,000 in 2005. He then applied to vary
the support order on the basis that his heart problems would not allow him to keep working long hours. Justice
Scanlan granted the application in *Montgomery v. Montgomery* (2006), 2006 CarswellNS 224 (N.S. S.C.), taking

into account (at para. 12) the fact that "Mr. Montgomery in the past was asked, and in fact ordered by this Court as confirmed by the Court of Appeal, to pay maintenance amounts that were totally out of line with his actual income". Child and spousal support payments had consumed most of Mr. Montgomery's income for years and he had survived only because his second wife was employed.

3. In *O'Neill v. O'Neill* (2004), 3 R.F.L. (6th) 449 (Ont. S.C.J.), the father was a farmer whose 250 acre farm was worth $750,000. However, his 2002 income was only $12,692. The mother argued that income should be imputed under ss. 19(1)(a) and (e) of the CSG because the father could sell the property, obtain $37,500 if the proceeds generated a 5% return, and earn additional income through employment. Even if he only leased out the land, he could get $15,000 a year. The court refused (para. 11) "to require Bernard to sell the farm and undertake menial employment", but did conclude (para. 12) that he should be "farming diligently and in a commercially reasonable manner". The father's child support payments were calculated on the basis that he earned $28,000 per year. It is unclear how the judge came up with this figure, but it was the amount that the mother earned from two jobs.

4. In *Bak v. Dobell*, above, the Ontario Court of Appeal noted that the money the father was receiving from his own father was in the nature of a disability pension. Disability pensions are often non-taxable. Section 19(1)(b) says that if the payor is exempt from paying income tax, income can be imputed to the payor, to increase his income for child support purposes. Should income have been imputed on the basis that the payor's money received was, in effect, a non-taxable pension? Could *Bak v. Dobell* encourage some families to arrange their affairs so that the payor continues to receive gifts from wealthy parents rather than benefits from a family trust? Might the result even discourage a payor from seeking employment?

5. For an analysis of the case law applying s. 19 of the CSG, see Davis and Kish, "Imputing Income: It's a Matter of Choice" (2003-2004), 21 C.F.L.Q. 217 and Department of Justice, *Children Come First* (Vol. 2 at 102-103). In the latter document, the Justice Department concluded (Vol. 2 at 103):

> No amendment to this section is recommended. Section 19 is one of the most litigated areas of the Federal Child Support Guidelines because these cases are contentious, not because of any deficiencies in the law. Courts consistently look at various fact patterns and determine whether income should be imputed. A change to section 19 would not reduce this type of litigation.

(3) Special or Extraordinary Expenses

Under the presumptive rule found in s. 3 of the CSG, the quantum of appropriate child support is the Table amount plus any amount determined under s. 7. Section 7(1) sets out an exhaustive list of "special or extraordinary expenses", the cost of which is to be shared in accordance with s. 7(2) by the parents in proportion to their incomes. Section 7 expenses can be onerous; their cost can sometimes approach or exceed the Table amount itself.

Section 7 creates two categories of expenses: "special expenses", which include child-care, health-related expenses and expenses for post-secondary education; and "extraordinary expenses" for extracurricular activities or for primary or secondary school education. To qualify as "extraordinary", the identified expenses must satisfy one of the two definitions in s. 7(1.1.) (added in 2006). The first definition indicates that "extraordinary expenses" are those that the parent requesting the amount cannot be expected to reasonably cover, considering his or her income and the child support that would otherwise be received. The second, alternative definition, encompasses expenses for extracurricular activities or for primary or secondary school education that the court considers extraordinary, taking into account the amount of the expenses in relation to the recipient parent's income, the nature and number of educational programs and/or activities, the special needs or talents of the child, the overall cost of the programs and activities, and any other similar factor. Whether an expense is "special" or "extraordinary", the court is to consider *both* the "necessity of the expense in relation to the child's best interests" and the "reasonableness of the expense in relation to the means of the spouses and those of the child and to the family's spending pattern prior to the separation" See *Park v. Thompson* (2005), 13 R.F.L. (6th) 415 (Ont. C.A.); additional reasons at (2005), 2005 CarswellOnt 2518 (C.A.).

On initial reading, s. 7 is difficult to parse. In practice, however, it is applied in a fairly straightforward manner. Most judges think that a plausible post-secondary education plan meets the test of necessity and reasonableness, and will require parents to contribute to it in proportion to their incomes (see *Coghill v. Coghill* (2006), 30 R.F.L. (6th) 398 (Ont. S.C.J.)). Similarly, a child will be permitted to participate in extracurricular activities if feasible, and the parents will very often be ordered to pay in proportion to income towards such costs (see *Bially v. Bially* (1997), 28 R.F.L. (4th) 418 (Sask. Q.B.)).

Prior to the May, 2006 amendments to the CSG, "extraordinary" was not defined in s. 7. This led to two different approaches to defining "extraordinary": a subjective approach, in which the expense was compared to the standard of living of the family before and after separation; and an objective approach, in which the parties' incomes and standard of living were considered irrelevant. The legislation now provides a more or less subjective definition of "extraordinary", which has reduced the need for litigation on this point.

Some litigation has proceeded regarding whether a parent who does not provide reasonable notice to the other spouse of s. 7 expenses can be reimbursed for them. Generally, Ontario courts have held that such notice is required. See *Luftspring v. Luftspring* (2004), 2004 CarswellOnt 1481 (C.A.) and *Park v. Thompson* (2005), 13 R.F.L. (6th) 415 (Ont. C.A.); additional reasons at (2005), 2005 CarswellOnt 2518 (C.A.). The rationale appears to be that s. 7 requires a balanced approach (Can the parties afford it? Is it necessary?) and the courts are encouraging parents to engage in this analysis together.

The case below provides a general discussion of the approach taken by Ontario courts to s. 7 expenses.

CELOTTI V. CELOTTI

(2007), 40 R.F.L. (6th) 411, 2007 CarswellOnt 4137 (Ont. S.C.J.)

OLAH, J.: ...

a. Child Support

43 The parties agree that the father's annual income be imputed at $221,000. Although there was some evidence that the father's current income is lower than that agreed, the parties agree that pursuant to the *Federal Child Support Guidelines*, the father shall pay to the mother monthly child support in the amount of $3,639 for the 3 biological children, commencing on the 1st of July, 2007 and every month thereafter so long as the children are dependants.

44 The evidence was that the children are engaged in special activities. Bianca and Vanessa attend at competitive dance, which costs approximately $10,000 per annum for both children. This includes such costs as the registration fees, competition fees, shoes, costumes and travel expenses, as they relate to competitions away from home. Matthew plays hockey and including his equipment costs approximately $2,000 per year. The parents also propose that the children attend swimming lessons to improve their swimming skills and no cost evidence was adduced as to this activity. While both parents actively participate in these activities, they disagree on whether they should be dealt with in addition to child support.

45 The mother submits that the cost of hockey and dance totals $12,000, and that these out of the ordinary expenses are not contemplated in the child support payments.

46 Section 7 of the *Federal Child Support Guidelines* provides a two-part test of necessity and reasonableness to determine whether a claimed expense is to be included in the child support amount. The expense must be necessary in relation to the child's best interests and

reasonable in relation to the means of the spouses and those of the child and the family's spending pattern before the separation. The weight of Ontario jurisprudence suggests that an extraordinary expense is one which, with the combined income of the parties, would not be incurred for their children as a matter of course.

47 In this case, both parties agreed that it was in the children's best interests to participate in extracurricular activities. Both until and after separation, all three children had participated in a slate of activities. It would appear that after separation, the wife increased the girls' participation in competitive dance with the attendant increase in costs. Nevertheless, there was no evidence to suggest that the family expended less than $12,000 per annum on the children's activities. Given the fact that the mother is not employed, she looks to the father to pay for the extraordinary expenses. The $12,000 expenditure represents a little over 5% of the father's total income of $221,000. The mother's current and taxable income is $108,000 per annum. As such, the extracurricular expenses represent a little over 12% of the mother's total annual income.

48 Despite the fact that the family is a family with an upper middle income, such expenses for extracurricular activities are extraordinary in relation to the family's income.

49 Accordingly, the father shall pay for the children's extraordinary activities the sum of $12,000 per annum by way of monthly payments of $1,000.00 in addition to his obligation to pay child support pursuant to the Child Support Guidelines.

NOTES AND QUESTIONS

1. The Department of Justice reported in *Children Come First* (Vol. 2, at 54) that almost one-third of all divorce cases dealing with child support included a s. 7 expense. Child care expenses were awarded or agreed to in 12.4% of all child support cases, while the percentages for medical or dental insurance, extra-curricular activities, health-related expenses, and post-secondary education costs were 10.8, 10.5, 10.0, and 6.6 respectively. The Department suggested (*ibid.*, at 56) that "courts seem willing to almost automatically order child care expenses under paragraph 7(1)(a)".

A study of child support awards in 1999 concluded (at 29) that "there was a consistent increase in the proportion of cases with special or extraordinary expenses awarded as income level increased." See Joseph P. Hornick, Lorne D. Bertrand, and Nicholas M.C. Bala, *The Survey of Child Support Awards: Final Analysis of Pilot Data and Recommendations for Continued Collection* (Ottawa: Minister of Justice, 1999). The authors reported (*ibid.*) that, at the lowest level of income, only 11.5% of the child support awards had special expenses and that this percentage increased to 59.6 at the highest level of income. This team, with the addition of Joanne Paetsch, found a similar trend in the second phase of this study, covering cases from 1998 to January 2002: *The Survey of Child Support Awards: Analysis of Phase 2* (Minister of Justice, 2003) (available on the Department of Justice Canada Web site). The most commonly awarded types of s. 7 expenses continued to be day care expenses, followed closely by medical-dental insurance premiums and extra-curricular activities.

2. Section 7(3) of the CSG indicates that it is the after-tax cost of an expense that is apportioned. Regarding the determination of the value of the personal deduction for daycare expenses, see *Kelly v. Kelly* (1998), 38 R.F.L. (4th) 444 (Alta. Q.B.).

3. In *Bland v. Bland* (1999), 48 R.F.L. (4th) 250 (Alta. Q.B.), a 15-year-old boy played AAA bantam hockey at a cost of $4,600 per year. The mother's income was $15,000 per year and the father's about $45,000. The parents accepted that the costs relating to the boy's hockey were extraordinary, but the father refused to contribute. The mother and her parents had paid for the expenses in the past and the mother indicated that the boy would play at this level whether or not the father contributed. Justice Burrows stated (at 255) that "a reasonable way to approach the question is to ask whether, assuming the participants in this conflict ... were living together as a family unit, with their existing financial situation, it would be reasonable for [the parents] to decide that despite the talents of their son and the opportunities his participation in elite hockey might create, their resources are insufficient to allow them to pay the significant cost". The Justice concluded that by this test the father's conclusion was reasonable and he was not required to contribute.

Compare *Lamarche c. Crevier* (2000), 4 R.F.L. (5th) 88 (Ont. S.C.J.); additional reasons at (2000), 2000 CarswellOnt 1142 (Ont. S.C.J.); varied (2001), 22 R.F.L. (5th) 354 (Ont. C.A.), where a child's step-father was ordered to pay about $2,500 per year for hockey registration fees, equipment and travel expenses. The biological father's child support was insufficient to pay the expenses and the court considered them reasonable and necessary because of the child's exceptional ability and the psychological dislocation suffered by the child in his relationships with the two fathers.

(4) High Income Earners

R. v. R.

(2002), 24 R.F.L. (5th) 96, 2002 CarswellOnt 902 (Ont. C.A.)

LASKIN J.A. (for the Court): —

1 Introduction

1 In 1997, the Federal Government established the Federal Child Support Guidelines (the "Guidelines"), which prescribe the amount of child support a parent must pay on separation or divorce. These Guidelines have achieved a highly desirable measure of fairness, objectivity and consistency in child support orders. With some very limited exceptions, a paying parent with an income of $150,000 or less pays a basic amount of child support equal to the table amount set out in the Schedule to the Guidelines. But, if a paying parent's income is over $150,000, the court has a wider discretion in making a child support award. For these high income earners, if the court concludes that the table amount is inappropriate, it has discretion under s. 4 of the Guidelines to substitute an amount that it considers appropriate. Cases of high income earners have on occasion caused difficulty for the courts. This is one of those cases.

[Justice Laskin's reasons reveal that the father and mother separated after eight years of marriage. They had four children and during the marriage the mother stayed home to care for them. In the two years immediately before separation, the father's income rose dramatically but the family continued to live modestly. The father's income doubled after separation to over $4.1 million annually. The parents agreed to a division of their property that left the mother with a net worth of about $1.3 million and the father with a net worth of almost $4 million.

In proceedings under the *Divorce Act*, the mother sought spousal support and child support. She prepared three budgets for the children: one in the year of separation when the father earned about two million dollars, another in the year after, and a final one when the father's annual income first rose to over four million dollars. In her last budget the mother proposed child expenditures of over $80,000 per month, compared to about $20,000 per month in the first two budgets.

At the father's income level, the Table amount of monthly child support for four children under the CSG was over $65,000. While s. 3 of the CSG established a presumptive rule in favour of the Table amount, s. 4 permitted a court to deviate from that amount where it considered the Table amount inappropriate and instead to award an amount it considered appropriate in light of: the condition, means, needs and other circumstances of the children and the financial ability of each spouse to contribute to the children's support.

The trial judge concluded that the Table amount of child support was inappropriately high. Relying on the family's accustomed lifestyle, he ordered that the father should pay

$12,000 monthly to cover the children's basic needs, $4,000 per month for discretionary expenses, and $4,000 per month for private schooling and extra-curricular activities as special expenses under s. 7 of the CSG. He also ordered the father to pay $5,000 per month in spousal support and to maintain one million dollars in life insurance to secure his support obligations.

The mother appealed. Her main contention was that the trial judge erred in not ordering the Table amount of child support or at least an amount closer to it.]

D. Discussion

1. Child Support

(a) Introduction

29 This is the fourth case in which this court has been called on to review a trial judge's discretion in ordering or declining to order a high income earner to pay the table amount of child support under the Guidelines. The three previous cases were *Francis v. Baker* (1998), 38 O.R. (3d) 481; aff'd on other grounds [1999] 3 S.C.R. 250 (S.C.C.), *Simon v. Simon* (1999), 46 O.R. (3d) 349 and *Tauber v. Tauber* (2000), 6 R.F.L. (5th) 442.

30 In *Francis v. Baker*, the parties had two children, aged 13 and 11 at the time of trial, and Mr. Baker's annual income was $945,538. The trial judge ordered the table amount of $10,034 per month. Her order was upheld in this court and in the Supreme Court of Canada. In *Simon v. Simon*, the parties had one child, who was nearly three years old at the time of trial. Mr. Simon, a professional hockey player with the Washington Capitals, had just signed a contract paying him $1 million U.S. per year. The table amount of child support was $9,215 monthly but the trial judge awarded only $5,000 monthly. This court, however, allowed Mrs. Simon's appeal and ordered the table amount. In *Tauber*, the parties had a one and one-half year old child and Mr. Tauber's annual income was $2.5 million. The trial judge ordered the table amount of $17,000 per month but said he would have reduced that amount had he the discretion to do so. He did not have the discretion to do so because of this court's decision in *Francis v. Baker*, which was then binding on him. By the time *Tauber* came to this court, the Supreme Court in *Francis v. Baker* had said a trial judge has discretion to reduce the table amount if that amount is inappropriate. This court in *Tauber* held that the table amount was inappropriate and ordered a new trial.

31 The numbers in those three previous cases may seem exceptionally high but even they pale in comparison to the numbers in this case. Mr. R.'s annual income for determining child support is over $4.1 million. For his four children, that annual income yields a table amount of support of $65,803 monthly or $16,451 per child. The trial judge considered the table amount to be inappropriate and exercised his discretion by ordering $16,000 monthly under s. 4. His order thus effectively reduced the table amount by 75%. The principal question on this appeal is whether he committed a reviewable error in the exercise of his discretion, either when he declined to order the table amount or when he ordered $16,000 monthly.

32 A trial judge's discretion in determining an appropriate child support order under s. 4 of the Guidelines is entitled to "significant deference" from an appellate court. An appellate court should intervene only if the trial judge has exercised his or her discretion unreasonably. As L'Heureux-Dubé J. wrote in *Hickey v. Hickey*, [1999] 2 S.C.R. 518, at para. 12, "though an appeal court must intervene when there is a material error, a serious misapprehension of the evidence, or an error in law, it is not entitled to overturn a support order simply because it would have made a different decision or balanced the factors differently".

33 Although I would not interfere with the trial judge's discretion in determining that the table amount was inappropriate, I would interfere with the order he did make. In my view, he committed two material and therefore reviewable errors in determining that an appropriate amount of support under s. 4 was $16,000 monthly. First, he based his order entirely on the parties' lifestyle and pattern of expenditure while they lived together. By doing so, the trial judge failed to adequately take into account the large increase in Mr. R.'s income after he and his wife separated. Second, the trial judge erred in failing to consider whether the options proposed by Mrs. R. in her April 2000 budget were reasonable in the light of the increase in Mr. R.'s income. Because of these two errors, I do not think that this order of $16,000 per month can stand.

(b) The Guidelines Regime

34 The starting point for determining the amount of child support payable by high income earners is the legislative regime, the Guidelines — especially ss. 1, 3(1) and 4 — and s. 26.1(2) of the *Divorce Act*. ...

39 Against that legislative regime, the Supreme Court's decision in *Francis v. Baker* provides further guidance in determining how much high income parents should pay in child support. *Francis v. Baker* established the following general principles:

1   Trial judges have discretion either to increase or decrease the table amount if they consider that amount inappropriate and instead to order an amount that they consider appropriate.

2   The table amount, however, is presumed to be the appropriate amount. A parent seeking an order different from the table amount bears the onus of rebutting the presumption in s. 3 of the Guidelines and must do so by "clear and compelling evidence". The sheer size of the table amount is not by itself an "articulable reason" for departing from it.

3   Although the considerations relevant to an appropriate child support order will differ from case to case, the courts must at least have regard to the objectives of the *Divorce Act* and the Guidelines, and to the factors expressly listed in s. 4(b)(ii) of the Guidelines. The legislative objectives are intended to ensure "that a divorce will affect the children as little as possible" and the factors in s. 4(b)(ii) further that intent by emphasizing "the centrality of the actual situation of the children".

4   Child support should meet a child's reasonable needs. For children of wealthy parents, reasonable needs include reasonable discretionary expenses. A paying parent who claims the table amount is inappropriate must, therefore, demonstrate that budgeted child expenses are so high that they "exceed the generous ambit within which reasonable disagreement is possible", in short that the budgeted expenses are unreasonable. Table amounts that so far exceed a child's reasonable needs that they become a transfer of wealth between the parents or spousal support under the guise of child support will be inappropriate.

(c) The Court's Discretion under s. 4 of the Guidelines

40 The legislative regime and the principles that emerge from *Francis v. Baker* provide the framework for determining child support under s. 4. But in any given case a number of specific considerations will be relevant to structuring the court's discretion. These considerations may well vary from case to case. In a case like the present one where the payer's

ability to pay is not in question, a trial judge should focus on the considerations relevant to determining the amount of support required to meet the children's reasonable needs.

41 Here, the trial judge decided that the governing considerations — indeed effectively the sole considerations — structuring his discretion under s. 4 were the family's accustomed lifestyle and pattern of expenditure. These considerations accounted for his decision to depart from the table amount and for $12,000 of his $16,000 child support award under s. 4. The remaining $4,000 reflects the trial judge's attempt to comply with this court's decision in *Tauber*, *supra*, which affirmed that the reasonable needs of children of wealthy parents include reasonable discretionary expenses.

42 Mrs. R. argues that the trial judge erred in the exercise of his discretion in three main ways. First, she submits that the trial judge erred in basing his order on the lifestyle and pattern of expenditure the family enjoyed while living together. Mrs. R. takes the position that those considerations are irrelevant in determining the appropriateness of support under s. 4. Second, she submits that the trial judge erred when he failed to take into account the substantial increase in Mr. R.'s income after separation. Third, she argues that the trial judge erred in failing to consider the reasonableness of Mrs. R.'s April 2000 budget, especially in the light of the increase in Mr. R.'s income. She contends that the trial judge should have ordered the table amount or at least an amount considerably higher than $16,000 monthly.

43 I do not agree that the family's lifestyle and pattern of expenditure were irrelevant. In my view, they were relevant and important considerations in determining appropriateness under s. 4. Indeed, I conclude that these considerations justified the trial judge's decision to depart from the table amount. But I do agree with Mrs. R. that in arriving at an amount of support under s. 4, the trial judge erred by not adequately taking into account the increase in Mr. R.'s income and by failing to consider the reasonableness of Mrs. R.'s April 2000 budget in light of that increase.

(d) The Family's Lifestyle and Pattern of Expenditure

. . . . .

45 Section 4 does not expressly refer to the family's spending pattern while living together. But in a case like this one, where the parties established over many years a lifestyle and spending pattern that met the children's reasonable needs, these considerations are surely relevant to the children's "condition, means, needs and other circumstances" under s. 4(b)(ii).

46 To say that they are irrelevant is to ignore the objectives of the Guidelines regime, the wording of s. 4(b)(ii) and the reasoning of Bastarache J. in *Francis v. Baker*. The *Divorce Act* states the principle underlying the Guidelines regime: parents have a joint responsibility to "maintain" their children. In *Francis v. Baker*, Bastarache J. observed that the overriding purpose of the Guidelines is to ensure "that a divorce will affect the children as little as possible". Therefore s. 4(b)(ii) of the Guidelines, which focuses on the children's needs, "emphasizes the centrality of the actual situation of the children".

47 Ordinarily, therefore, where the parties have established a family lifestyle and pattern of expenditure, these will be relevant considerations under s. 4. And, in my view, they will be relevant both in determining whether the table amount is inappropriate and, if so, what amount is appropriate having regard to the children's condition and needs. Their weight in individual cases will be for trial judges to determine in the exercise of their discretion.

48 In *Simon*, MacPherson J.A. concluded that the son's needs and Mr. Simon's income and ability to pay were the only considerations relevant under s. 4. As my colleague put it, "Mr. Simon's current lifestyle is irrelevant". But Simon was an unusual case and a very different

case from the one before us. The parties separated when Mrs. Simon was three months pregnant. They never established a family lifestyle or pattern of expenditure for the children. And my colleague properly rejected Mr. Simon's own post-separation lifestyle as a factor relevant to his child support obligations. *Simon* does not apply here. ...

53 Moreover, I do not think s. 1(d) of the Guidelines requires that the parties, or more likely the paying parent, lead evidence about the lifestyle and spending patterns of other families in similar circumstances to show that the table amount is inappropriate. To hold that a payor must lead this evidence to show inappropriateness would mean that either the table amount will always be appropriate or the court will always have to hear extensive, time consuming and perhaps unseemly evidence about how other wealthy families live. I do not think that was what was intended by the Guidelines. Instead, in many cases, the court can give effect to s. 1(d) by applying some common sense and by permitting reasonable, even generous, discretionary expenses as income rises. I now turn to the trial judge's findings in this case.

(e) The Table Amount was Inappropriate in this case

54 *Francis v. Baker* affirms that the considerations in s. 4(b)(ii) of the Guidelines are relevant both in determining whether the table amount is inappropriate, and if so, in determining what other amount is appropriate. These considerations include the children's needs and the payer's financial ability. Thus, the increase in Mr. R.'s income and the reasonableness of the additional discretionary expenses in Mrs. R.'s last budget — expenses designed to reflect Mr. R.'s increased income — were relevant in determining whether to depart from the table amount. The trial judge, however, did not consider them in concluding that the table amount was inappropriate. Although he did not do so, in my view, his conclusion on inappropriateness should stand.

55 The evidence before the trial judge showed two things. First, the evidence showed that the family's expenditures were relatively modest and that Mr. and Mrs. R. did not spend all of their disposable income when Mr. R.'s income was under $900,000, much less when it soared to over $2 million. Significantly, when Mr. R.'s income reached $2 million annually, the family's expenditures on the children were far less than the table amount of approximately $30,000 monthly. Second, the evidence showed that at Mr. R.'s level of income, the family's comparatively modest spending pattern met the children's reasonable needs while the family was together. This evidence of an established comfortable but not extravagant lifestyle was strong, and common sense tells us that the table amount of over $65,000 monthly would support a lifestyle grossly in excess of that established lifestyle. Although the trial judge should have considered Mr. R.'s post-separation increase in income and Mrs. R.'s proposed discretionary expenses, I am not persuaded that he erred when he concluded that the family lifestyle evidence alone constituted "clear and compelling evidence" of the inappropriateness of the table amount. His conclusion is entitled to deference from this court and I would not interfere with it.

(f) $16,000 Monthly Child Support was Inappropriate

56 But the trial judge could not ignore the increase in Mr. R.'s income when he came to fix an appropriate amount of support under s. 4. Thus, my disagreement with the trial judge's decision is not that he exercised his discretion to depart from the table amount but that in ordering $16,000 monthly as the appropriate amount of child support, he failed to adequately take into account the increase in Mr. R.'s income and then failed to consider the reasonableness of Mrs. R.'s proposed budget in the light of that increase in income. ...

57 This case is unusual because the paying parent's income increased substantially after separation. ... The children are entitled to benefit from that increase in income. That they are

entitled to do so is implicit in the words "continue to benefit from the financial means of both spouses after separation" in s. 1(a) of the Guidelines. ...

58 Moreover, s. 1(a) of the Guidelines prescribes a "fair standard of support". It is one thing for the family to live modestly and save money while together; it is quite another, and seemingly unfair, for the paying parent to hold his children to the family's pre-separation lifestyle while saving the increase in his post-separation income, but now for his benefit alone. The trial judge's failure to give any effect to the increase in Mr. R.'s income was a material error. Related to that error was his failure to consider the reasonableness of Mrs. R.'s proposed budget.

59 In *Tauber*, this court elaborated on what the Supreme Court said in *Francis v. Baker*: the reasonable needs of children of wealthy parents include both expenses for basic needs and reasonable discretionary expenses. Rosenberg J.A., who wrote for the court, said that where the payor's income is very high, child support should "include a large element of discretionary spending".

60 In April 2000, Mrs. R. prepared a budget [the third budget] that included a large element of discretionary spending, which she termed "options". These options were included to match her budget with the table amount under the Guidelines. The trial judge simply dismissed this budget because it included items never before contemplated by the parties. Instead, he added an arbitrary amount of $4,000 for discretionary expenses without any explanation of why that was a reasonable figure. In my view, he took the wrong approach.

61 Given the increase in Mr. R.'s income, I see nothing wrong with Mrs. R. having included in her proposed budget items not previously acquired or even contemplated by the parties. Instead of dismissing Mrs. R.'s April 2000 budget out of hand, the trial judge should have considered whether Mrs. R.'s options were reasonable having regard to the substantial increase in Mr. R.'s income. Only by determining the reasonableness of these discretionary items could he determine an appropriate amount of child support under s. 4(b)(ii) of the Guidelines.

(g) The Appropriate Remedy

62 Because of these two errors, which are related, I would set aside the order for child support. I am then left with deciding the appropriate remedy. The two choices are ordering a new trial and fixing an appropriate amount of support. The scant evidence on the discretionary items in Mrs. R.'s April 2000 budget and the absence of any findings on the reasonableness of these items or on the effect of the increase in Mr. R.'s income favour ordering a new trial. What favours fixing support is finality.

63 In this case I think it is better to fix support. Although either Mr. or Mrs. R. may seek to vary child support, fixing the amount of support now will at least end the current dispute between the parties. Thus, fixing support may avoid another costly, time consuming and no doubt emotionally draining trial for the parties. Moreover, the appropriate amount of support falls within a reasonably narrow range: considerably more than the amount required for the children's basic needs, found by the trial judge to be $12,000 monthly, and considerably less than the table amount of $65,000 monthly, found by the trial judge to be inappropriate.

64 Neither party seriously challenges the trial judge's figure of $12,000 monthly for the children's basic needs. The appropriate level of child support, however, depends on a reasonable amount for discretionary expenses, having regard to Mr. R.'s annual income of over $4.1 million.

65 In her April 2000 budget, Mrs. R. proposed an increase in vacation expenses from $1,200 to $6,000 monthly, an added $1,400 per month for the children's recreational and other

activities and the following list of optional monthly expenses: $10,000 for savings for the future, $10,800 for a cottage in Muskoka, $7,400 for a ski chalet in Ellicottville, New York, $740 for the Holi-Mont Ski Club, $2,100 for a sailboat and membership in the Hamilton Yacht Club, $1,200 for membership in the Hamilton Golf Club, $16,600 for a Florida residence and membership in a golf club, $1,250 for two horses and fees for a boarding stable, and $2,500 for world travel. Unfortunately, Mrs. R. gave no evidence about how she arrived at these figures and, more specifically, no evidence about whether she had investigated cottage prices in Muskoka, ski chalet prices in Ellicottville or condominium prices in Florida. This lack of evidence means that my figures will at best be general estimates of what appears reasonable.

66 Not all of the items in Mrs. R.'s April 2000 budget can be considered reasonable discretionary expenses. For example, I would not allow the proposed expense for a Florida residence and membership in a golf club, an expense that seems to me to be excessive. I would, however, include an amount for a cottage in Muskoka. The children have vacationed there frequently, and Mrs. R. testified that she and her husband had discussed buying a family cottage there. I would allow $6,000 monthly for this item. Skiing and golf expenses are reasonable for children of such a wealthy parent. The children have skied in the past and wish to take up golf. I would allow $3,000 monthly for these two activities. According to Mrs. R., the children are interested in travel and I think an additional $1,000 monthly for vacation and travel is justified. I would also allow $8,000 monthly for future savings for the children. I especially have in mind investing in their future education through a registered education savings plan or similar fund. Finally, I would allow $2,000 per month for miscellaneous expenses for the children including recreational and other activities.

67 Therefore, an appropriate amount of child support should include discretionary expenses of $20,000 monthly. The basic monthly expenses for the children are $12,000 monthly. I would therefore order child support of $32,000 per month under s. 4 of the Guidelines. The order of $4,000 per month under s. 7 stands. Thus, I would order total monthly child support of $36,000.

NOTES AND QUESTIONS

1. The strict application of the tables in cases involving high-income payors often results in very high awards of child support. Payors in such cases usually ask the court to exercise their discretion under s. 4 of the CSG to make an order for a lower amount. In *Francis v. Baker* (1999), 177 D.L.R. (4th) 1, 50 R.F.L. (4th) 228 (S.C.C.), Bastarache J. confirmed that the Table amount will be applied unless the payor can rebut the presumption that this amount is appropriate. There have been several cases since *Francis v. Baker*, and even subsequent to *R. v. R.*, in which the court has ordered the Table amount. See in particular *Desrochers v. Tait* (2008), 2008 CarswellOnt 8179 (S.C.J.), in which Greer J. held that the custodial parent is not required to justify the expenditure of the child support mandated by the application of the Tables (at para. 29). In the result, Justice Greer ordered the father to pay the Table amount of $35,000 a month as temporary support for a five-year-old child. In *This Week in Family Law*, Fam. L. Nws. 2009-08 (2009), Philip Epstein and Lene Madsen commented:

> It was the intention of those [members of the senior family law bar] advising on the Guidelines that the court would look at a reasonable means and needs test when determining appropriate child support in high-income cases. ...

> We suspect that this decision [*Desrochers v. Tait*] sets a new high-water mark in terms of child support, and is an indication that the courts have lost their way with respect to what is considered to be "appropriate." While we accept that Section 4 of the Guidelines makes the Guidelines presumptive, unless the amount is "inappropriate," surely the converse of that is that the amount awarded must be appropriate in all the circumstances. ...

> It is to be remembered that when family law legislation is passed, it is to take into account the vast majority of people who are being affected by it. Only two percent of Canadians earn more than

$150,000, per year. For the other 98 per cent the Guidelines work very well and do demonstrate efficiency, consistency and a means of establishing fair standard of support for children. ...

We are not sure, but we think, this is likely the largest child support order in Canada, for a five-year-old child who does not appear to have any special needs. To top it off, the Court ordered that the husband pay $724,580 in retroactive child support, less credit for what he had already paid.

... Section 4 of the Guidelines has been stripped of any meaning whatsoever, and *Francis v. Baker* cannot be read in such a way as to allow for that approach. The award in *Francis v. Baker* was, in all of the circumstances, particularly when one considers that the Section 7 expenses were included, not inappropriate or even unreasonable, particularly given the husband's very considerable net worth. Net worth will be a factor in the determination of overall support and lifestyle. ... The husband [in *Desrochers v. Tait*] argued, in vain, that this order was simply a wealth transfer, from him to his wife, but Justice Greer rejected that argument. We think the husband was right.

Respectfully, there is nothing fair in this award, and while, yes, it is true that the husband can afford the payments, surely they are nothing other than a disguised wealth transfer, in the circumstances. ...

Justice Greer quoted *Simon v. Simon*, 1 R.F.L. (5th) 119 (Ont. C.A.), to suggest there is no burden on the custodial parent to justify the child support "budget." We do not think that statement is correct either. We think that when Section 4 is engaged, there is an obligation on the custodial parent to justify the budget when the issue is raised by the payor. We agree that there is no onus initially on the recipient to justify a budget, but when the payor suggests that the amount is in excess of the reasonable needs of the child and the amount is inappropriate, the onus then shifts to the recipient to at least put forward an arguable case as to why the amount requested is justified.

All of this began to go wrong in *Simon v. Simon*. In that case the Court rejected the idea that Mr. Simon, then a successful hockey player, park some of the child support into a trust, so as to protect the child and provide reasonable support when his days as a hockey player were over. The Court unfortunately rejected that approach and that was probably very unwise. Mr. Simon's days as a successful hockey player are nearing a close and he is never going to earn the kind of income he earned as a successful hockey player. It is likely in the instant case that the husband will not maintain this significant earning (and we can't help but wonder what has happened to his earnings in light of the global recession). Awarding $35,000 a month without keeping an eye on the future, and without requiring some of the money be put aside for the future makes no sense whatsoever.

The Court needs to take a fresh look at high-income child support cases. They represent a very small fraction of reported cases, and most high-income cases are settled out of court. Nevertheless, when judgments result in manifestly unfair awards, something needs to be done. We either need a comprehensive appellate review, or to reword the legislation and perhaps increase the cap to something like $350,000 (as in the Spousal Support Advisory Guidelines), or even $500,000, and change the language so that *Francis v. Baker* is legislatively overruled.

That is not to say that children in high-income cases should not get significant support that includes discretionary amounts. No child, however, needs $35,000 per month, on a tax-free basis and legislation or court decisions that mandate that result simply create disrespect for the law.

2. In determining the appropriate amount of child support, Justice Laskin in *R. v. R.* examined the mother's proposed budget and concluded that it was reasonable to allow $6,000 per month for a cottage in Muskoka, $3,000 monthly for skiing and golfing, $1,000 per month for additional travel and recreation, and $8,000 a month for future savings for the children. Do you agree that child support should be used to fund the purchase of capital assets that the custodial parent will retain or to allow children to accumulate capital? Does this amount to wealth transfer to the custodial parent and the children rather than "child support"? What assurance is there that the amounts specified will be spent on the items listed? Is the custodial parent in a fiduciary relationship so as to allow for an accounting of some kind?

3. In *Bachorick v. Verdejo* (1999), 175 D.L.R. (4th) 633, the Saskatchewan Court of Appeal questioned, without deciding, the jurisdiction of the courts to make an order requiring the custodial parent to put some of the money received as child support into a trust fund. The Ontario Court of Appeal noted this issue in *Simon*, but "was content to proceed" on the parties' assumption that there was such jurisdiction.

Should the court only make such orders where the custodial parent is not "responsible" and "unselfish"? Would it be strategically wise in these "high earner" cases for a custodial parent to propose that a portion of the child support be set aside to secure the future needs of the children?

In *M. (O.) v. K. (A.)* (2000), 9 R.F.L. (5th) 111 (Que. S.C.), the judge ordered a very highly paid professional hockey player to pay $4,600 per month to the mother as child support for two children and in addition to contribute $5,400 per month to a trust that was to be set up for their benefit. The judge described (at para. 97) the mother as "hopelessly inept in handling financial matters". In *Debora v. Debora* (2006), 33 R.F.L. (6th) 252 (Ont. C.A.), the very wealthy payor father argued that the retroactive support owing to the mother, totaling almost $1 million, should be placed into a trust for the children. The court rejected the argument, indicating that "strong evidence" was required before it would impose a trust on a custodial parent so as to interfere with her discretion in spending or saving money on behalf of the children.

4. The Department of Justice reported in *Children Come First* (Vol. 2 at 43) that only 1.3% of almost 27,000 divorce cases involving children between 1998 and 2001 from across Canada (excluding Quebec and Nunavut) involved paying parents with incomes over $150,000. It also stated (*ibid.*) that there was no significant difference between the percentage (11%) of these cases that were contested and the percentage (12%) of cases that were contested when the paying parent earned less than $150,000. The Department indicated (at 45-46) that an amount greater than the Table amount was consented to or ordered in 30% of the cases where the payor's income was greater than $150,000, while an amount less than the Table amount was consented to or ordered in only 16% of those cases.

(5) Split and Shared Custody

Section 8 of the *Guidelines* deals with "split custody", a situation where one or more children reside with each parent. It mandates that the amount of child support in these situations is "the difference between the amount that each [parent] would otherwise pay if a child support order were sought against each of the [parents]". This method is commonly known as a "set off" because as each parent's obligation is set off against the child support obligation of the other. In "Child Support Under the Guidelines in Cases of Split and Shared Custody" (1998), 15 Can. J. Fam. L. 11, Professor Rogerson concludes (at 15):

> The cases involving split custody are relatively straight forward, and any complexity is the result of complexity built into the Guidelines calculations themselves. Because two support obligations are being calculated rather than one, that complexity is potentially doubled. In the simplest cases there is an offset of the two table amounts, subject of course to any issues regarding the determination of income. In other cases the calculation of the two child support obligations is complicated by additional factors such as s. 7 add-ons claimed by one or both parents; the fact that one or more of the children is over the age of majority allowing a departure from the table amount; the fact that one or more of the children for whom support is claimed are step-children to whom other persons also owe support obligations; or the combination of split and shared custody arrangements with respect to different children in the family.

The Survey of Child Support Awards: Analysis of Phase 2 (noted above) reported that 5% of divorce cases involving a child support order between 1998 to January 2002 dealt with a split custody situation.

In contrast to s. 8, s. 9 has spawned considerable litigation raising some complex issues. Section 9 deals with "shared custody". It provides the court with discretion to reduce the amount of child support payable if a parent exercises a right of access to, or has physical custody of, a child for at least 40% of the time over the course of a year. *The Survey of Child Support Awards: Analysis of Phase 2* (noted above) indicated that 6.2% of divorce cases involving a child support order between 1998 to January 2002 dealt with such a situation. The section goes on to say that the court "must" determine the amount by taking into account the applicable Table amount payable by each parent; the increased costs of shared custody arrangements; and the conditions, means, needs and other circumstances of each parent and the children. Accordingly, the court "must" take these factors into account, but the amount of support ordered is ultimately a matter of discretion.

The first issue to be resolved in applying s. 9 is determining whether the 40% threshold has been met. The outcome of this inquiry is critical. For example, the Ontario Table amount for three children where a payor parent earns $60,000 annually is $1,177 per month. This is a considerable sum of money, especially because it is paid in after-tax dollars. If the payor parent can establish that the children are with him or her for 40% or more of the time, a reduction in support may be called for. It may, therefore, be worth litigating the threshold issue. In some cases payors have argued that the time to be assessed should include only the time that the child is in the direct care of a parent. Once time at school or daycare is excluded, it is much easier for access parents to reach the 40% threshold. The courts have generally rejected this approach. See, for example, *Meloche v. Kales* (1997), 35 R.F.L. (4th) 297 (Ont. Gen. Div.), where the court assumed that the custodial parent started with responsibility for the child 100% of the time. The court held that it was insufficient for a payor to simply prove that he or she had the child 40% of the time that the child could spend with his or her parents. Rather, school and sleeping time was allocated between the parents according to who was responsible for the child during that time. The Department of Justice reports (*Children Come First*, Vol. 2 at 67) that there is an "emerging consistency in the case law" in favour of this approach. It also states (*ibid.*): "This is consistent with the intended application of the threshold, which was meant to measure the relative time that each parent is responsible for and cares for the children over the course of a year." The Ontario Court of Appeal endorsed this approach in *Froom v. Froom* (2005), 11 R.F.L. (6th) 254 (Ont. C.A.). It also noted that there is no universally accepted method of calculating the division of the children's time, and held that it is not a reviewable error to count days rather than hours. The majority noted (at para. 2): "That approach and that method were consistent with many trial decisions, which seek to avoid rigid calculations and, instead, look at whether physical custody of the children is truly shared."

There are some cases that refuse to apply a mathematical formula, preferring to consider the nature and quality of the time spent with the child. In *Dennett v. Dennett* (1998), 225 A.R. 50 (Q.B.), for example, Romaine J. suggested a more purposive approach "to take into account the quality of time spent by each parent with the children, both in determining whether the arrangement is in spirit a situation of shared custody and in determining whether in fact there are increased costs of care of the children for either or both parents that might make Regulation 9 appropriate to the circumstances." See also *Rosati v. Dellapenta* (1997), 35 R.F.L. (4th) 102 (Ont. Gen. Div.); *Ball v. Ball* (1998), 170 Sask. R. 192 (Sask. Q.B.); *Penner v. Penner* (1999), 44 R.F.L. (4th) 294 (Man. Q.B.); *Berry v. Hart* (2003), 48 R.F.L. (5th) 1 (B.C. C.A.); and *Franke v. Franke* (2008), 56 R.F.L. (6th) 276 (B.C. S.C.).

Some commentators have noted that s. 9 results in many applications for shared physical custody or increased access in an attempt to reduce child support: In "This Week in Family Law", Fam. L. News 2008-41, Philip Epstein and Lene Madsen commented on *Franke v. Franke*, above, as follows:

> The cases are literally all over the place and this is a section of the Guidelines that needs urgent review. There are far too many of these cases coming before the court, but even more importantly, the section of the statute creates conflict. Is the parent genuinely seeking more time with the child, or is the parent seeking more time in order to avoid child support obligations? Should it make a difference in support for either the payor or the recipient if the amount of time with the child is 38 per cent or 41 per cent? How does one calculate the 40 per cent in the first place? Do we count sleeping hours? Do we count hours at school? What happens when the child goes to a birthday party with friends or a sleepover?

Quebec's *Guidelines* provide for a reduction from the Table amount any time there is increased access above a minimum of 20%. Where access is between 20% and 40%, there is a "sliding scale" providing for a percentage decrease from the Table amount for every corresponding percentage increase in access. Over the 40% threshold, the situation is treated as one of shared custody and different rules apply. Regarding the possibility of making the fixed time threshold less arbitrary, the Department of Justice stated (*Children Come First*, Vol. 2 at 73):

> The test can only be made less arbitrary by introducing a two-step, multi-step, or sliding scale approach. While these methods are less arbitrary, each more closely links child contact with the amount of support than does the current test and may not reflect actual costs. This creates an even greater financial incentive for each parent to leverage time spent with the child. This has the likely effect of increasing litigation, contrary to the [Guidelines'] objectives. In addition, these approaches would complicate court processes and increase uncertainty, contrary to the [Guidelines'] objectives.

Once the threshold in s. 9 is crossed, a court must decide the amount of child support. In many cases prior to the Supreme Court of Canada decision in *Contino*, set out in part below, lawyers and judges took the same approach to s. 9 as they did to s. 8. They set off the two Table amounts that would otherwise be payable. However, this approach, while it has the benefit of simplicity, is not what the legislation dictates. While s. 9 requires the court to consider the two Table amounts, it does not mandate a set off.

Another approach used prior to *Contino* involved increasing the set-off of Table amounts by applying a "multiplier". The main idea behind the multiplier was that the shelter costs for the parent receiving support were fixed and so it was not equitable to simply set off the Table amounts. The Ontario Court of Appeal accepted the idea of a multiplier as reasonable, and as a way to ensure that the amount of support took into account the income differential between the two homes. As indicated below, the Supreme Court of Canada did not accept the idea of a multiplier, but stated that judges should carefully consider the detailed facts of each case to determine the appropriate amount of child support. It also suggested that this amount might well be higher than the basic set-off amount.

CONTINO v. LEONELLI-CONTINO

[2005] 3 S.C.R. 217, 19 R.F.L. (6th) 272

[A father and mother entered into a separation agreement in 1992 and divorced in 1993. The separation agreement provided that the parents had joint custody of their son who was to reside with the mother. The father was required to pay $500 per month child support with annual cost of living increases. No annual cost of living increases were ever made and in 1998 the mother brought an application to vary the amount of child support. By minutes of settlement, the father agreed to pay the monthly sum of $563 in accordance with the CSG. The quantum was to be adjusted annually in accordance with the Guidelines, but this never occurred.

In 2000, the mother purchased a new home because she thought a move to a different neighbourhood was in the child's best interests. To finance the purchase, the mother had to withdraw a significant amount from her RRSP and pay income tax on the amount.

After the child began to live with each parent 50 per cent of the time, the father, relying on s. 9, applied in 2001 for a reduction in support. The parents filed financial statements and tax returns for 1998, 1999, and 2000. The father's net worth was estimated at $255,750 and the mother's at $190,651. Each attributed 50 per cent of his or her fixed and variable living costs to the child. The mother's variable expenses relating to the child totalled just over $400 per month for such items as clothing, food, and school lunches and the father's amounted to $270 per month. The father and mother assigned $1814 and $1916.95 of their total expenses to the child respectively. The mother also contributed $153.84 per month to an RESP for the child.

The motion judge found that the father earned $87,315 annually and the mother $68,000. She required the father to pay the difference between the Table amounts at these income levels ($688 per month for the father and $560 per month for the mother), with an adjustment (a "multiplier") to reflect the shared custody arrangements and additional costs. As a result, the amount of monthly child support payable by the father was reduced to $100, retroactive to September 2000. On appeal, the Divisional Court overturned the motion judge's decision and ordered the father to pay the full Table amount of $688 monthly. It reasoned that the father had failed to establish that deviation from the Table amount was in his son's best interests.

The Ontario Court of Appeal allowed the father's appeal. It held that, once s. 9 applied, there was no longer a presumption that the father should pay the Table amount and that the section required an individualized, fact-specific approach. It concluded that there was sufficient evidence in the record from which to determine the appropriate amount of child support for 2001. It assumed that the parents would then be able to settle the amounts for 2002 and 2003. It used the set-off of each parent's Table amount as the starting point and then multiplied the resulting figure by 1.676 (the "multiplier") to reflect the mother's fixed costs. Finally, it apportioned all the variable costs in proportion to the parents' incomes. In the final result, the Ontario Court of Appeal concluded that the father should have paid $399.61 per month in 2001.

The mother appealed to the Supreme Court of Canada. The court, Fish J. dissenting, allowed the appeal and ordered the father to pay $500 per month. A portion of the majority's reasons, written by Justice Bastarache follow.]

1. Introduction

1 When the federal government decided to adopt in 1997 the *Federal Child Support Guidelines*, SOR/97-175 ("Guidelines"), its first decision was to choose between different formulae and design a system that would be adapted to the Canadian context. The formulae that were considered with greatest attention were the four in use in the United States: (1) the Income-Shares Model, where the child should receive the same amount of the parental income, in proportion to each parent's income, as before the separation; (2) the Delaware or Melson Model, where basic needs are met before determining how the child is to share the remaining parental income; (3) the Flat Percentage of Income Model, where it is assumed that each parent will spend the same percentage of his or her income on the child and the non-custodial parent's share is fixed by regulation; and (4) the Income Equalization Model which is designed to equalize the standards of living of custodial and non-custodial parents so that the child will experience the lowest reduction in standard of living possible (Federal/Provincial/Territorial Family Law Committee, *Child Support: Public Discussion Paper* (1991), at pp. 10-11).

2 The government decided to adopt a unique formula in the case of split custody; that is the situation where each spouse has custody of one or more children. It is best described as the revised fixed percentage. It is included in ss. 3 and 8 of the Guidelines (see Appendix) and has the features of the flat percentage formula, but uses a specific set of underlying principles to arrive at percentages that vary according to income level. The formula produces a schedule of payment amounts taking into consideration tax consequences. It provides for some add-ons with respect to special expenses (R. Finnie, C. Giliberti and D. Stripinis, *An Overview of the Research Program to Develop a Canadian Support Formula* (1995), at pp. 27-28).

3 When dealing with shared custody, however, the formula used in ss. 3 and 8 was not retained. New categories of custodial arrangements were created under s. 9. ... These shared custodial arrangements required the application of an entirely different formula, one that is not designed with the same guiding principles. Guidelines amounts applicable to the former non-custodial parent or to the highest income earner in the case of a first application cannot therefore be considered to be presumptively applicable. Shared custody arrangements are

not a simple variation of the general regime, they constitute by themselves a complete system.

4 The application of the factors under s. 9 of the Guidelines have [sic] proven to pose serious difficulties. The problems have been addressed in terms of fairness. As mentioned by Professor C. Rogerson in her 1998 article "Child Support Under the Guidelines in Cases of Split and Shared Custody" (1998), 15 *Can. J. Fam. L.* 11, at p. 20:

> Pushing in favour of some adjustment is a concern for fair and consistent treatment of payors who incur increased expenses during the time they spend with the child. There are two dimensions to the fairness claim. The first is fairness between the payor and the support recipient, who is arguably being relieved of some costs assumed by the payor. The second is fair and consistent treatment of the payor as compared to payors at the same income level who may not be spending any money directly on their children apart from the payment of child support.

But then adjustments are hard to evaluate. More time spent with a child may not involve increased spending or significant savings for the other parent. Where there is a significant disparity of incomes, a new formula can mean a drastic change in the amount of support for the lower-income parent, who was previously the custodial parent, and exacerbate the differences in standard of living in the two households. There is also a concern that shared custody can entail more cost in duplication of services and leave less money for support.

5 Against this backdrop, the role of the Court is to interpret the Guidelines as drafted by Parliament. Section 9 is labelled "Shared custody". Forty percent or more time spent with physical access to the child triggers the application of the three factors in s. 9. We are not concerned in this case with the difficulties sometimes encountered in determining whether the threshold has been met, but with the quantum of support to be awarded once it is. The Court is being asked to decide whether the s. 9 award can be greater than the Guidelines amount; whether the Guidelines amounts are presumptively applicable; whether all three factors in s. 9 are to be given equal weight; whether "increased costs" under s. 9 refers to increased costs of the previously non-custodial parent or increased costs resulting from the shared custodial arrangement; whether a multiplier can be used in the absence of evidence of increased costs; and how actual needs, conditions and means are taken into account in deciding on a deviation from the Guidelines amounts. These questions must be approached in the context of the particular facts of this case, to which I now turn.

[The Justice's overview of the facts and the decisions below are omitted.]

2. Analysis

2.1 Interpretation of Section 9 of the Guidelines

19 In order to determine the correct interpretation to be given to s. 9 of the Guidelines, it is necessary to examine the words of the provision in their entire context and in their grammatical and ordinary sense harmoniously with the scheme of the Guidelines, the object of the Guidelines, and the intention of Parliament. ...

20 Before turning to the heart of this case, it is important to point out what is in essence an issue of semantics. Parties and courts across the country have inconsistently referred to the parents under s. 9 as the "custodial" parent, "non-custodial" parent, "payor" parent and "recipient" parent. There is no perfect terminology. However, it is clear that in a shared physical custody arrangement, given the nature of child support, one cannot ignore that a transfer of money from one parent to the other will almost always occur. Thus, for sake of clarity, I will use the concepts of "payor" parent and "recipient" parent. ...

22 The mother submits that there is a presumption in favour of the Guidelines that applies to the exercise of all discretionary powers, including those found in s. 9. According to her, the

onus is on the party seeking a deviation to establish on "clear and compelling evidence" that the deviation is in the child's best interest. ... The same approach was taken by the Divisional Court. I cannot accept her argument.

23 In *Francis v. Baker*, I held that, under s. 4 of the Guidelines ..., which deals with the situation of high income earners (income over $150,000), there is a presumption in favour of the Guidelines amount. Guideline figures can only be increased or reduced if the party seeking such a deviation has rebutted the presumption of appropriateness. No right of deviation exists merely by pleading the discretionary provision. As earlier noted, s. 9 however expressly provides for a particular regime in cases of shared custody. This implies a departure from the payor/recipient model that comes under s. 3. In fact, s. 3 recognizes that the calculations under that provision will not apply where "otherwise provided under these Guidelines". ...

27 The three factors [in s. 9] structure the exercise of the discretion. These criteria are conjunctive: none of them should prevail. ... Consideration should be given to the overall situation of shared custody and the costs related to the arrangement while paying attention to the needs, resources and situation of parents and any child. This will allow sufficient flexibility to ensure that the economic reality and particular circumstances of each family are properly accounted for. It is meant to ensure a fair level of child support. ...

30 These comments may lead some parents to think that there should be an automatic reduction in the amount of child support in a case such as this one. In my opinion, there is only an automatic deviation *from the method used* under s. 3, but not necessarily *from the amount* of child support. As submitted by the mother, it is quite possible that after a careful review of all of the factors in s. 9, a trial judge will come to the conclusion that the Guidelines amount will remain the proper amount of child support (see, e.g., *Berry v. Hart* (2003), 233 D.L.R. (4th) 1, 2003 BCCA 659).

31 Thus, not only is there no presumption in favour of awarding at least the Guidelines amount under s. 3, there is no presumption in favour of reducing the parent's child support obligation downward from the Guidelines amount. ...

32 The underlining principle of the Guidelines is that "spouses have a joint financial obligation to maintain the children of the marriage in accordance with their relative abilities to contribute to the performance of that obligation" (*Divorce Act*, s. 26.1(2)) ... The Guidelines reflect this principle through these stated objectives (Guidelines, s. 1):

> (a) to establish a fair standard of support for children that ensures that they continue to benefit from the financial means of both spouses after separation;
>
> (b) to reduce conflict and tension between spouses by making the calculation of child support orders more objective;
>
> (c) to improve the efficiency of the legal process by giving courts and spouses guidance in setting the levels of child support orders and encouraging settlement; and
>
> (d) to ensure consistent treatment of spouses and children who are in similar circumstances.

33 These objectives create a palpable tension in the Guidelines. ... At para. 40 in *Francis v. Baker*, I wrote that the proper construction of a provision "requires that the objectives of predictability, consistency and efficiency on the one hand, be balanced with those of fairness, flexibility and recognition of the actual "condition[s], means, needs and other circumstances of the children" on the other". Like s. 4 in that case, s. 9 must here be interpreted with these objectives in mind. Parliament, in adopting s. 9, deliberately chose to emphasize the objectives of fairness, flexibility and recognition of the actual conditions, means, needs and other circumstances of each spouse and of any child for whom support is sought, even if to the detriment of predictability, consistency and efficiency to some degree. The legislator

recognized in s. 9 that there is a wide range of situations of shared custody depicting the reality of different families. ...

2.2 Factors Under Section 9

37 The framework of s. 9 requires a two-part determination: first, establishing that the 40 percent threshold has been met; and second, where it has been met, determining the appropriate amount of support.

38 With respect to the second part of the determination, the litigious issue in the case at bar, courts across the country have struggled to develop an interpretation of s. 9 that is consistent with the Guidelines' objectives. While the approaches vary widely, they can be divided in two categories. One approach, similar to the approach used by the motions judge, can be described as the "formulaic approach". The other approach, which may be described as the "discretionary approach", eschews the use of formulae.

39 The specific language of s. 9 warrants emphasis on flexibility and fairness. The discretion bestowed on courts to determine the child support amount in shared custody arrangement calls for the acknowledgment of the overall situation of the parents (conditions and means) and the needs of the children. The weight of each factor under s. 9 will vary according to the particular facts of each case. I will now consider each of the three s. 9 factors.

2.2.1 Section 9(a) — Amounts Set Out in the Applicable Tables for Each of the Spouses

40 The first factor requires that the court take into account the financial situations of both parents (instead of the sole income of the spouse against whom the order is sought, as in s. 3). It is important to highlight the fact that the final and fully considered version of s. 9 does not include a conclusive formula to determine how the Table amounts are to be considered or accounted for.

41 The Court of Appeal, while it agreed that the use of a formula is not explicitly required in the section, concluded that the set-off approach in s. 8 could be a useful starting point to bring consistency and objectivity to the determination, especially in cases where there is limited information and the incomes of the parties are not widely divergent. I agree, but would caution against deciding these issues without proper information. I would particularly caution against a rigid application of the set-off which can entail, in the case of a variation order, a drastic change in support, dubbed the "cliff effect" by commentators ..., that may not be warranted when a close examination of the financial situation of the parents and standard of living in both households is considered. The value of the set-off is in finding a starting point for a reasonable solution taking into account the separate financial contribution from each parent. A court will depart from the set-off amount or make adjustments to it if it is inappropriate in light of the factors considered under ss. 9(b) and 9(c). The set-off amount must therefore be followed by an examination of the continuing ability of the recipient parent to meet the needs of the child, especially in light of the fact that many costs are fixed. As mentioned by numerous commentators, this is a problem in many cases where there is a great discrepancy in the incomes of the parents. ... It is also a problem in cases where one parent actually incurs a higher share of the costs than the other (taking responsibility for clothing or activities for instance). I would also note that the 40 percent threshold itself should be irrelevant to this evaluation; the cliff effect is not merely a result of the threshold; it is a result of the different methodology. ...

43 The three main applications of the set-off formula adopted by the courts are:

> 1. Simple (or straight) set-off: The support payment is calculated by determining the Table amount for each of the parents as though each was seeking child support from the other. The amount payable is the difference between the two amounts ...

> 2. Pro-rated set-off: The Table amount for each of the parents is reduced by the percentage of time the child spends with each parent. The recipient parent's amount of time with the children is multiplied by the payor's Guidelines amount and the payor parent's amount of time with the children is multiplied by the recipient parent's Guidelines amount. These two pro-rated amounts are then set-off against one another ... A variation of this approach is the "straight pro-rate" which takes the percentage of time the recipient parent has custody of the children multiplied by the Guidelines amount for the payor parent.

> 3. Set-off plus multiplier: The set-off amount (simple set-off or pro-rated set-off) is increased by a multiplier (usually 1.5), based on the assumption that a portion of the recipient parent's costs are fixed, and therefore, unaffected by the increased time the child spends with the other parent.

44 I agree with the father and the Court of Appeal that the simple set-off is preferable to the pro-rated set-off as a starting point for the s. 9 analysis in view of the language used by the legislator in para. (a). The pro-rated set-off was criticized by a number of scholars and courts, including the Court of Appeal in the case at bar, who refused to apply it as it disproportionately impacts on the lower income spouse. ... Professor Rogerson, at pp. 74-75, explains the "cliff effect" created by this approach:

> The method of pro-rating the Table amounts to reflect custodial time that was adopted in *Hunter*, and which has been legislated as part of the shared custody formulas in some American jurisdictions, creates what commentators have called the "cliff" problem. A 1% increase in access, from 39% to 40%, can result in a 40% decrease in the Table amount of support to be paid. This is both a conceptual and a practical problem. On the conceptual level, in a sole custody situation, the full Table amount is paid even though the custodial parent may have the child only 61% of the time, and the access parent may have the child the remaining 39% of the time. It seems illogical that as a result of a 1% increase in access by the other parent, which allows him or her to reach the shared custody threshold, the custodial parent should be deprived of support for the full 40% of the time the child spends with the other parent. On a practical level, the "cliff" effect will make a custodial parent reluctant to allow an access parent even small amounts of extra time because they will carry such dramatic financial consequences.

45 I will address the problems related to the multiplier later in these reasons.

46 However, even the simple set-off is incomplete. ...

47 What is important is that the set-off does not take into account actual spending patterns as they relate to variable costs or the fact that fixed costs of the recipient parent are not reduced by the increased spending of the payor parent. ...

49 Hence, the simple set-off serves as the starting point, but it cannot be the end of the inquiry. It has no presumptive value. Its true value is in bringing the court to focus first on the fact that both parents must make a contribution and that fixed and variable costs of each of them have to be measured before making adjustments to take into account increased costs attributable to joint custody and further adjustments needed to ensure that the final outcome is fair in light of the conditions, means, needs and other circumstances of each spouse and child for whom support is sought. *Full consideration* must be given to these last two factors. ... The cliff effect is only resolved if the court covers and regards the other criteria set out in paras. (b) and (c) as equally important elements to determine the child support.

50 It should be noted here that the Table amounts are an estimate of the amount that is notionally being paid by the non-custodial parent; where both parents are making an effective contribution, it is therefore necessary to verify how their actual contribution compares to the Table amount that is provided for each of them when considered payor parents. This will provide the judge with better insight when deciding whether the adjustments to be made to the set-off amount are based on the actual sharing of child-related expenses.

51 This is where discretion comes into play. The court retains the discretion to modify the set-off amount where, considering the financial realities of the parents, it would lead to a significant variation in the standard of living experienced by the children as they move from one household to another, something which Parliament did not intend. As I said in *Francis v. Baker*, one of the overall objectives of the Guidelines is, to the extent possible, to avoid great disparities between households. It is also necessary to compare the situation of the parents while living under one roof with the situation that avails for each of them when the order pursuant to s. 9 is sought. As far as possible, the child should not suffer a noticeable decline in his or her standard of living. Still, it is not a discretion that is meant to set aside all rules and predictability. The court must not return to a time when there was no real method for determining child support. ...

2.2.2 Section 9(b) — Increased Costs of Shared Custody Arrangements

52 What should the courts examine under this heading? Section 9(b) does not refer merely to the expenses assumed by the payor parent as a result of the increase in access time from less than 40 percent to more than 40 percent, as argued in this Court. This cannot be for at least two reasons. First, it would be irreconcilable with the fact that some applications under s. 9 are not meant to obtain a variation of a support order, but constitute a first order. ... Second, as mentioned earlier, the Table amounts in the Guidelines do not assume that the payor parent pays for the housing, food, or any other expense for the child. The Tables are based on the amount needed to provide a reasonable standard of living for a single custodial parent (see *Formula for the Table of Amounts Contained in the Federal Child Support Guidelines: A Technical Report*, at p. 2). This Court cannot be blind to this reality and must simply conclude that s. 9(b) recognizes that the total cost of raising children in shared custody situations may be greater than in situations where there is sole custody. ... Consequently, *all* of the payor parent's costs should be considered under s. 9(b). This does not mean that the payor parent is in effect spending more money on the child than he or she was before shared custody was accomplished. As I discuss later in these reasons, it means that the court will generally be called upon to examine the budgets and actual expenditures of both parents in addressing the needs of the children and to determine whether shared custody has in effect resulted in increased costs globally. Increased costs would normally result from duplication resulting from the fact that the child is effectively being given two homes.

53 A change in the actual amount of time a payor parent spends with a child will therefore give rise under s. 9(b) to an inquiry in order to determine what are, in effect, the additional costs incurred by the payor as a result of the change in the custodial arrangement. I say this because not all increases in costs will result directly from the actual amount of time spent with the child. One parent can simply assume a larger share of responsibilities, for school supplies or sports activities for example. For these reasons, the court will be called upon to examine the budgets and actual child care expenses of each parent. These expenses will be apportioned between the parents in accordance with their respective incomes.

2.2.3 Section 9(c) — Conditions, Means, Needs and Other Circumstances

54 It is clear then that not every dollar spent by a parent in exercising access over the 40 percent threshold results in a dollar saved by the recipient parent. ... Professor Rogerson refers to this at pp. 20-21:

> On the other hand, allowing such an adjustment raises many concerns. Increased time spent with a child does not necessarily entail increased spending on the child. Furthermore, dollars spent by an access or secondary custodial parent do not necessarily translate into a dollar for dollar reduction in expenditures by the primary custodial parent, many of whose major child-related costs are fixed — such as housing and transportation; any savings will typically be only with respect to a small category of expenditures for food and entertainment. Particularly in cases where there is a significant disparity in income between the parents, reductions in the basic amount of child support may undermine a lower-income custodial parent's ability to make adequate provision for the child or children, and will certainly exacerbate the differences in standard of living between the two parental homes.

Indeed, irrespective of the residential arrangement, it is possible to presume, in the absence of evidence to the contrary, that the recipient parent's fixed costs have remained unchanged and that his or her variable costs have been reduced only modestly by the increased access. Thus, when no evidence is adduced, the court should recognize the *status quo* regarding the recipient parent.

55 The analysis should be contextual and remain focused on the particular facts of each case. For example, an application that represents a variation of a prior support arrangement, will usually raise different considerations from a s. 9 application where no prior order or agreement exists. In the former case, the recipient parent, when he or she first got custody, may have validly incurred expenses based on legitimate expectations about how much child support would be provided. These expenses should be taken into consideration and a court should have proper regard to the fixed costs of the recipient parent.

56 Moreover, ... it is important that the parties lead evidence relating to s. 9(b) and (c). This evidence has often been lacking, with the result that the courts have been forced either to make assumptions about increased costs (as was done by the Court of Appeal in the present case), or to dismiss the application under s. 9 for lack of an evidentiary foundation.

57 In my opinion, courts should demand information from the parties when it is deficient. Three main options have been discussed and applied by appellate courts:

(1) Rely on the parties' financial statements and child expense budgets which provide a fairly reliable source of information;

(2) Adjourn the motion to provide additional evidence ...;

(3) Make "common sense" assumptions about costs incurred by the payor parent and apply a multiplier to account for the fixed costs of the recipient parent.

The third option is not acceptable, as I will explain below.

58 In the present case, the Court of Appeal relied on "common sense" assumptions. The Court found that the father must have incurred additional variable costs for such items as food and entertainment. The Court of Appeal should have considered the total additional costs attributable to the situation of shared custody under s. 9(b), the evidence adduced permitting this, and should not have simply assumed what more additional costs would be.

59 The Court of Appeal also resorted to the multiplier. The assumption behind the multiplier is that 50 percent of the recipient parent's costs are fixed and, therefore, unaffected by the time the children spend with the payor parent. The multiplier operates to obviate the necessity of the parties calling evidence of the increased costs associated with children living for

substantial periods of time in two households. While this formula takes into consideration the increased costs of shared custody, it does so in a somewhat inflexible fashion. ...

60 In the opinion of the appellate court, the use of such a method recognizes the concerns raised by the commentators and the courts that dollars spent on increased access or shared custody do not necessarily lead to a reduction in expenditures for the recipient parent. The use of a multiplier also furthers two of the objectives of the Guidelines, predictability and consistency, in calculating support. According to the Court of Appeal, used with discretion, a multiplier can provide a mechanism for recognizing the relative inflexibility of some of the recipient parent's costs. In the absence of evidence concerning fixed costs of the recipient parent, the most common multiplier is 50 percent, which is applied to the set-off amount. The amount of the multiplier ought, however, according to the Court of Appeal, to be adjusted depending on the circumstances.

61 The father argues that, as currently drafted, the Guidelines do not support the use of a multiplier. He submits that while it may be correctly assumed that there are increased costs associated with a shared custody arrangement, it is not possible to simply assume the amount of that increase. I agree.

62 Multipliers are controversial in the jurisprudence and commentaries. They have been characterized as unfair and discriminatory. ... One cannot help observing that, in the case at bar, the Court of Appeal applied a multiplier to account for the fixed costs of the mother, but it required the father to prove his additional or increased costs of custody. There is no basis for such asymmetrical treatment of each parent's fixed and duplicated housing costs: D. A. R. Thompson, "Case Comment: *Contino v. Leonelli-Contino*" (2004), 42 R.F.L. (5th) 326, at p. 331. In fact, it seemingly ignores the fact that the initial set-off takes into account the fixed costs of both parents.

. . . . .

66 M. S. Melli in "Guideline Review: Child Support and Time Sharing by Parents" (1999), 22 *Fam. L.Q.* 219, at p. 232, observes that the multiplier is an instrument that may be difficult to use given its consequences:

> ... using a multiplier on the child support amount also has the effect of producing a lesser reduction in the payment by the nonresidential parent. When that parent is the lower income parent, the result may be as detrimental to the child as a decrease to the other parent. Furthermore, the principal costs of shared time, the duplication of facilities are borne by the nonresidential parent. Some of these costs are already factored into the child support formula as costs of visitation. To increase the child support award across the board to both parents makes the nonresidential parent pay twice for certain costs and seem structured to discourage time sharing by parents. For these reasons, guidelines reviewers should investigate carefully proposals to use a multiplier.

67 It is of primary importance to note that, so far, the research to support the multiplier of 1.5, or any other multiplier for that matter, has not been done in Canada. ... Even the Department of Justice in its *Children Come First Report*, at p. 74, does not recommend the use of a multiplier in the absence of available research in Canada to show how much shared custody increases cost. "Without empirical evidence on the relative proportion of fixed and "shiftable" costs, the Department of Justice cannot support the use of a multiplier as a presumption in shared custody cases": *Children Come First Report*, at p. 74.

68 Section 9(c) vests the court a broad discretion for conducting an analysis of the resources and needs of both the parents and the children. As mentioned earlier, this suggests that the Table amounts used in the simple set-off are not presumptively applicable and that the assumptions they hold must be verified against the facts, since all three factors must be applied. Here again, it will be important to keep in mind the objectives of the Guidelines mentioned earlier, requiring a fair standard of support for the child and fair contributions from both parents. The court will be especially concerned here with the standard of living of the

child in each household and the ability of each parent to absorb the costs required to maintain the appropriate standard of living in the circumstances.

69 The Court of Appeal enumerates a number of factors to be considered under this subsection:

> 1. Actual spending patterns of the parents;
>
> 2. Ability of each parent to bear the increased costs of shared custody (which entails consideration of assets, liabilities, income levels and income disparities); and
>
> 3. Standard of living for the children in each household.

70 The actual spending patterns of the parents have already been considered under s. 9(b). These factors are helpful, the last one being particularly useful for the exercise of discretion in a predictable manner. As I indicated above, financial statements and/or child expenses budgets are necessary for a proper evaluation of s. 9(c).

71 Moreover, given the broad discretion of the court conferred by s. 9(c), a claim by a parent for special or extraordinary expenses falling within s. 7 of the Guidelines ... can be examined directly in s. 9 with consideration of all the other factors. ... Section 9(c) is conspicuously broader than s. 7.

72 The Court of Appeal, when reversing the decision of the Divisional Court, posited that a reduction in support under s. 9 will sometimes result in undue hardship to the recipient parent and that in such cases the court will need to consider the provisions of s. 10(1) of the Guidelines. In my opinion, there is no need to resort to s. 10, either to increase or to reduce support, since the court has full discretion under s. 9(c) to consider "other circumstances" and order the payment of any amount, above or below the Table amounts. ... It is not that "other circumstances" of each spouse and "hardship" are equivalent terms, it is that the discretion of the court, properly exercised, should not result in hardship. It may be that s.10 would find application in an extraordinary situation, but that is certainly not the case here.

2.3 Application of Section 9 to the Facts

73 Now that the principles which regulate the appropriateness of child support awards under s. 9 of the Guidelines have been clarified, I will turn to the facts of this particular case.

74 In this case, the motions judge granted the motion and reduced the $563 in monthly child support that the father had been paying to $100. As the Court of Appeal stated, "[s]he applied a mathematical formula similar to the formula found in s. 8 of the Guidelines for split custody and essentially set-off the father's and mother's Table amounts. She then required the father to pay the difference, with a very minor adjustment" (para. 1).

75 It seems very clear from the reasons for judgment of Rogers J. that she did not exercise her discretion properly, having relied on a mathematical analysis which is at odds with the approach for determining child support under s. 9 of the Guidelines. ...

76 The motions judge's failure to provide adequate reasons for this conclusion is apparent from her order. For its part, the Divisional Court held that there was no right of deviation from the s. 3 presumptive amount merely upon passing the 40 percent threshold; this too, is an erroneous approach.

77 The Court of Appeal fell into error by assuming, rather than applying evidence of the additional costs attributable to the shared custody, and by using a multiplier. The simple set-offverified against the budgets submitted by the parties under factor 9(c) is however acceptable in the absence of other evidence, since it leads to an examination of the actual capacity

of each party to contribute to the expenses and consideration of the standard of living of both households. The Court of Appeal exercised its discretion to order the total variable expenses to be shared in proportion to respective incomes. In my analysis, I will confirm this but will give further attention to the actual ability of each parent to absorb increased costs.

78 The record before this Court contains sufficient evidence, i.e. affidavits and financial statements from both parents, in order to set the correct support payment without having to order a new trial. I nevertheless would caution against making awards without having taken steps to obtain a complete record. As determined by the motions judge, the Table amount for the father on an income of $87,315 is $688 per month; the Table amount for the mother on an income of $68,082 is $560. The set-off amount is $128. The father's child expense budget reveals monthly expenditures attributable to the child of $1,814 and the mother's child expense budget reveals monthly expenditures attributable to the child of $1,916.95. These budgets were accepted at trial and should not be questioned here. They establish that expenditures are not the same for both parents, and that there is in fact a large amount of duplication with regard to fixed costs. Both of these factors point to the need for significant adjustments to the set-off amounts. The second step in the analysis consists of looking at the ratio of income between the parties of 56:44 (in the interest of precision and exactitude, I have slightly modified the ratio used by the Court of Appeal); the father ought to be responsible for 56 percent of the total child related expenditures, $2,089.33, and the mother ought to be responsible for 44 percent of the total child-related expenditures, $1,641.62. Already contributing $1,814, the father would be required to pay the mother the sum of $275.33. In addition, attention must be given to the fact that the father's net worth is $255,750 and the mother's $190,651; this is consistent with the means and conditions test in s. 9(c) and will be dealt with later.

79 The set-off amount under s. 9(a) is $128, but, as I have just noted, other circumstances and the evidence presented under s. 9(c) requires that it be adjusted. Based only on the sharing of child-related expenditures apportioned against the income of the parents, the father would be required to pay the mother a sum of $275.33 per month. Furthermore, examining all the costs of both parents, I have found no evidence that the fixed or variable costs of the mother decreased in any way following the shared custody arrangement; on the other hand, there is no evidence that the extra time devoted by the father or, more generally, the change brought to the custodial arrangement, has resulted in any increase in the father's actual expenses. Because this s. 9 application represents a variation from a long-standing financial status quo upon which the mother incurred valid expenses on behalf of this child, these realities are important considerations. As mentioned earlier, the means and conditions test in s. 9(c) requires that I also consider the difference in net worth between the parents, which is $65,099, and the general ability of each parent to absorb increased costs.

80 This means that I must now consider the impact of a new support order on the standard of living of the child under s. 9(c). I cannot ignore the fact that, in this case, I am dealing with a variation order and not a first time order. Up until this litigation, by way of settlement, for a number of years, the mother was receiving over $500 from the father (an amount that was not adjusted in 1999 even though the father's income rose to $83,527.58). Finally, while the motions judge refused to consider this fact, it is clear from the record that the mother moved to a new house in 2000 because she believed it was in the child's best interest, in the reasonable expectation that she would continue to receive $563 a month or more from the father. This expense, which was not challenged as inappropriate by the father, has to be considered part of the contextual analysis which includes consideration of the financial conditions and means of the mother. The purchase of the new home created some financial difficulties for the mother since she had to collapse a significant amount of her RRSPs (and consequently pay income tax on what she cashed in). She was legitimately relying on the support payment

she was receiving from the father pursuant to the earlier arrangements made between them. He could not have ignored that. In light of these factors, I have come to the conclusion that: the child support must be set at $500 per month. ...

3. Conclusion

82 The determination of an equitable division of the costs of support for children in shared custody situations is a difficult matter; it is not amenable to simple solutions. Any attempt to apply strict formulae will fail to recognize the reality of various families. A contextual approach which takes into account all three factors enunciated by Parliament in s. 9 of the Guidelines must be applied.

83 The appeal is allowed and the amount of support to be paid by the father to the mother is set at $500 per month. ...

The following are the reasons delivered by

FISH J. (dissenting): —

I

84 Child support provides an economic safety net for its intended beneficiaries — the children, not the parents, of failed family relationships. It serves to "break the fall" by affording the children a reasonable standard of living commensurate with the combined resources of their parents.

85 And, in cases of shared custody, child support seeks to secure for the child, insofar as possible, a similar standard of living in the two households concerned. Children may prefer one household to the other, but that cannot be made to depend on the respective means or resources of their parents.

86 Where a child resides with one parent less than 40 percent of the time, that parent is deemed, by legislative fiction, to incur no child-related expenses at all. The appropriate level of child support is fixed with mathematical precision by the *Federal Child Support Guidelines*, SOR/97-175 (the "Guidelines") (or a corresponding provincial grid).

87 That sort of social policy decision is a matter for Parliament. And Parliament has spoken.

88 In cases of shared custody, where the parents each have access to or custody of the child at least 40 percent of the time, Parliament has spoken as well. There, instead of imposing a mathematical calculus or grid, Parliament has left to the courts the determination of child support in accordance with s. 9 of the Guidelines.

89 Section 9 sets out in general terms the factors that judges must take into account. But it does not assign them relative weight or indicate — even in general terms — how the factors bear on one another. Still less does s. 9 contemplate, with respect to the shared custody arrangements that are governed exclusively by its terms, a single "correct" award.

90 Rather, s. 9 requires the court in each instance to determine the amount of child support "by taking into account": (a) the Table amounts that would apply if it were a case of sole custody; (b) the increased costs of shared custody arrangements; and (c) "the conditions, means, needs and other circumstances of each spouse and of any child for whom support is sought". ...

92 In short, s. 9 support orders are discretionary by design, but constrained by principle and subject to the overriding requirement of fitness. Support orders in shared custody cases must fall within the boundaries drawn by Parliament in setting out the governing factors under s. 9 of the Guidelines. All of these factors must be considered by the courts in determining an

appropriate award. "Appropriate" does not mean mathematically or methodologically ascertainable with precision. It means *within an acceptable range* that is in each case determined by applying in a principled manner the factors set out in s. 9 to the proven facts and particular circumstances of the matter.

93 Of the widely divergent awards in the courts below, only the amount fixed in the Court of Appeal falls within that range. It appears to me reasonable on its face and consistent with the governing principles. I would therefore dismiss this appeal.

II

94 The predictability ensured with mathematical precision by the Guidelines for sole custody cases has in some quarters created an understandable but futile expectation of like certainty with respect to shared custody arrangements.

95 Predictability and precision in sole custody awards result from the mandatory application of Table amounts included in the Guidelines. These Table amounts are built on Statistics Canada's "40/30" Equivalence Scale (see: Canada, Department of Justice, *Formula for the Table of Amounts Contained in the Federal Child Support Guidelines: A Technical Report* (1997), at p. 3). The Equivalence Scale, in turn, is based on empirical research that showed a 40 percent increase in cost to a household upon adding a second member (child or adult), and 30 percent more for each additional member (both percentages being approximate). In this model, the additional members reside in the household 100 percent of the time.

96 In shared custody arrangements, the child joins *two* households, each for at least 40 percent of the time. Support orders are in those circumstances governed by s. 9 of the Guidelines. Section 9(a) requires that the Table amounts applicable to single custody be taken into account *as one of a series of factors*. There is no meaningful way to graft those Table amounts onto shared custody support orders. They are not meant to be either added to or substracted from the ratio of expenses incurred by either parent at the time the support order is made.

97 Likewise, s. 9(b) of the Guidelines assumes that two households are more expensive than one due to duplicated fixed costs and the loss of economies of scale. But this assumption adds nothing of concrete assistance in fixing an appropriate amount of support.

98 I understand very well that the Guidelines call for objectivity, predictability and efficiency. With respect to shared custody, however, Parliament has departed from the strict table-based model that leads to relative certainty. The focus of s. 9 is on fitness, not formulas. This approach relies on the wisdom and experience of trial judges — the responsibility is primarily theirs — to determine fair awards by applying to the facts as they find them the mandatory considerations set out in s. 9.

99 Parliament has thus favoured judicial discretion, exercised in a principled manner, over the relative certainty of mathematically driven determinations. This legislative choice leaves no statutory vacuum. It signifies Parliament's confidence that judges will exercise wisely and in accordance with the governing criteria the discretion vested in them by s. 9 of the Guidelines, ensuring a sufficiently reliable and reasonably predictable result.

100 In short, s. 9 requires judges to fix child support in shared custody arrangements without the benefits and constraints of a mandatory grid. This deliberate rejection by Parliament of a precise formula or methodology does not authorize the courts to conjure one up from the void. ...

V

114 Simple set-off of the Table amounts for sole custody may be a convenient way to begin the process of fixing an appropriate amount of support and, in this way, serve as a "starting point". It is not, however — and should not be thought of — as a preliminary amount to be increased or decreased, or to have added to it or subtracted from it, other amounts determined on examination of the factors set out in paras. (b) and (c) of s. 9.

115 I agree with Bastarache J. that the Court of Appeal erred in its apparent endorsement of "stock multipliers". The expression "stock multiplier" refers here to an abstract or predetermined figure that bears no relation to the specific facts of the case.

116 As I understand it, the Court of Appeal endorsed the use of a multiplier of 1.5 (sometimes called the "Colorado multiplier", in reference to the jurisdiction in which the figure apparently originated) where there is no evidentiary basis for taking into account, as required by s. 9(b), the increased costs of shared custody arrangements. In my view, stock multipliers of that sort should not be used at all. The better approach was suggested by the Court of Appeal itself: In the absence of evidence required to make a fact-based, case-specific determination, the trial court can reopen the hearing for that purpose.

117 I think it fair to emphasize, however, that the Court of Appeal did not in fact resort to a stock multiplier in this case. It applied instead a multiplicative factor based on the evidence in the record. To the extent that this factor may have been imperfectly established or applied, its impact on the result was limited and, in any event, offset by the countervailing effect of the other factors I shall examine below.

118 Section 9(a) requires the court to take the Table amounts into account in fixing child support for shared custody arrangements. For shared custody arrangements, simple set-off of the Table amounts credits each parent with what that parent would receive if he or she had sole custody. It may be thought, in that way, to adequately compensate both parents. But that compensation is more apparent than real, since it disregards the duplications and other incremental costs inherent in shared custody. The purpose of s. 9(b), in my view, is to ensure that these costs are properly reflected in every support order made under s. 9.

119 The phrase "increased costs of shared custody arrangements" in s. 9(b) must be viewed in this light and I do not find it particularly helpful to focus on either the starting point applied by the Court of Appeal or the starting point preferred by Bastarache J. With respect, I think it preferable to regard s. 9(b) as a binding reminder that setting-off the Table amounts is, like other "starting points", the beginning but not the end of the exercise.

120 Here, the ultimate burden of the exercise is to fashion a support order with the interests of the child foremost in mind. It must, however, be patterned on the facts and not made of whole cloth.

121 It may be useful to observe that the cliff effect can only arise on a modification of child support. A cliff exists where there is a large vertical change over a small horizontal change. On a first order, there is no risk that a small change in access or custody will cause a precipitous decline in support. There is simply a judicial determination in accordance with the applicable statutory provisions.

122 On the other hand, where there is a previous support order based on sole custody, it may create a kind of momentum that the change to shared custody will not be entirely capable of arresting. That is particularly so in this case, where concrete and irreversible financial decisions were made by the mother in reliance on the amount of child support then being paid to her by the father — such as collapsing her RRSP's and buying a new home. ...

124 This is one of the relevant factors under s. 9(c), all of which are well set out, indicatively and not exhaustively, by Bastarache J. And I agree with my colleague that commensu-

rate importance should be attached in this case to the respective resources of the parents and to the situation created *consensually* before they moved to shared custody. ...

VII

153 ... The Divisional Court substituted an award of $688. I agree with the Court of Appeal that the motions Judge and the Divisional Court both erred in their application of s. 9 of the Guidelines and both reached unacceptable results.

154 The Court of Appeal substituted a support order of $399.61. This award lies within the acceptable range that is in each case determined by applying to the facts, in a principled manner, all of the relevant factors set out by Parliament in s. 9 of the Guidelines. Except as indicated, I believe the Court of Appeal set out the basic principles correctly. Its unfortunate observation as to the permissible use in some circumstances of a "stock multiplier" of 1.5 had no bearing at all on its conclusion, and the limited effect of its resort to a multiplicative factor of 1.67 is adequately compensated by the other factors I have mentioned. ...

NOTES AND QUESTIONS

1. Section 9 does not apply where a child spends considerable periods of time (though slightly less than 40%) with the access parent who provides about half the meals, buys half the children's clothes and provides a suitable second home for the child during visits. Is this result fair? See the comments in *Hall v. Hall* (1997), 30 R.F.L. (4th) 333 (B.C. Master).

2. In his annotation in the Reports of Family Law to the Supreme Court decision in *Contino*, Professor Thompson summarizes the court's approach as follows:

Here's the step-by-step method for quantum laid out by Justice Bastarache:

(1) *Determine the Simple Set-Off Amount*. The starting point under s. 9(a) is the simple or straight set-off of each parent's table amount for the number of children involved in the shared custody arrangement. No pro-rating, no multiplier (paras. 40–51).

(2) *Review the Child Expense Budgets*. A court must look at the parents' actual spending patterns, based upon child expense budgets, and not just make assumptions about spending. Further, a court should look at *all* the expenses of *both* parents under s. 9(b): not just the additional expenses resulting from an increase in access, not just the variable or fixed expenses, not just the expenses of the recipient parent. Under s. 9(b), a court has two concerns: (i) the overall increased total costs of child-rearing for both parents, especially duplicated costs; and (ii) any disproportionate assumption of spending by one parent or the other (paras. 52-53). These expenses should be "apportioned between the parents in accordance with their respective incomes" (para. 53), to "verify" the set-off (para. 77) and to determine "the need for significant adjustments to the set-off amounts" (para. 78).

(3) *Consider the Ability of Each Parent to Bear the Increased Costs of Shared Custody and the Standard of Living for the Children in Each Household*. The consideration of these two factors lies at the heart of the s. 9(c) analysis, set out at paras. 54–72, especially paras. 69-70. In assessing each parent's ability to bear the increased costs of shared custody, a court should look at the income levels of each parent, the disparity in incomes, and the assets and liabilities of each. The child's standard of living in each household is "particularly useful for the exercise of discretion in a predictable manner" (para. 70). The children should not experience "a significant variation in the standard of living ... as they move from one household to another" (para. 51). As the term "household" is used, the incomes and resources of new partners in each household would presumably be relevant.

(4) *Distinguish Between Initial Orders or Agreements and Variations*. "An application that represents a variation of a prior support arrangement will usually raise different considerations from a s. 9 application where no prior order or agreement exists." (para. 55) A recipient parent "may have validly incurred expenses based on legitimate expectations about how much child support would be provided", especially for fixed costs (para. 55). This last step is a new and important contribution to the analysis. The "cliff effects" of section 9 are felt

more sharply in variation cases, where the recipient parent has been receiving the full table amount. By adding this helpful distinction, the Court retains greater flexibility in such cases to address some of the litigation and behavioural incentives around the 40 per cent threshold. The first three steps should then make it easier to resolve child support in initial shared custody arrangements.

Regarding the need for a factual basis on which to apply this analysis, Professor Thompson states:

The Supreme Court also repeats the frequent complaints of courts in section 9 cases, demanding more "information" and more "evidence" from the parties. The Court of Appeal is criticised for using "common sense" assumptions about parental spending in shared custody cases, even apart from its erroneous use of a multiplier. That's the problem with the exercise of "discretion", it requires a surfeit of facts, partly because we never know which facts will turn out to be important, which facts will move this decision-maker on this day in this case.

But these are family litigants, real parents, not cost accountants. Most have limited resources, more limited than the Continos. Many will not have lawyers or will have limited legal advice. And, even if they were cost accountants, some of this cost information remains essentially indeterminate: how much of the costs of housing or cable television or car should be allocated to the child's expense budget? would mom or dad have rented a smaller apartment or lived in a different neighbourhood without their child care responsibilities? did the power bill go up because that teenager has so many showers or was that because of something else? In the end, we will inevitably need to draw some "common sense" inferences about spending in shared custody situations, based upon what information we have. And we need to look more at net disposable income calculations in these cases, at the larger questions of living standards and resource sharing, rather than the specifics of expenses.

Finally, Professor Thompson makes the following comments about the actual result:

The real factual wild card here was the house purchase by the mother. It skewed the whole analysis. Apart from that one fact, the Court might have wound up somewhere between $128 and $275. ...

I'm not sure how much precedential value can be found in the factual result in *Contino*. At most, it points strongly toward adjusting support upwards from the set-off amount in variation cases, where there has been a long-standing financial status quo arising from primary care or a major fixed expenditure made in the expectation that child support will continue at the full table amount. *Contino* tells us little about the likely result for an initial order in a shared custody case.

... It doesn't seem like anyone did net income calculations in this case. A fast and dirty DIVORCE-mate calculation is instructive. At $500 per month, the mother has a noticeably higher monthly net disposable income, about $260 more than the father's $4,500 per month, leaving the mother with 51.4 per cent of the total NDI (all this assuming that the mother receives the Child Tax Benefit and claims the "equivalent to spouse" or "eligible dependent" credit). To equalise their net incomes, on these assumptions, the amount of child support would be $365, more than the $128 set-off amount. ...

In the end, despite the Court's stated concern for the child's standard of living, the Court overshot the mark here in ordering $500 per month, leaving the mother's household with a higher standard of living

3. The *Contino* decision has been widely criticized as not providing any real structure or guidance for lawyers or trial judges. Uncertainty encourages litigation and, in many cases involving s. 9 of the CSG, the cost of litigating often outstrips any gain. In *Martin v. Martin* (2007), 2007 CarswellMan 494, 46 R.F.L. (6th) 286 (Q.B.) Little J. commented:

80 I will conclude with something of a lament for the children whose parents engage in litigation over shared custody support issues. ...

81 If in the exercise of my judicial discretion under Section 9 I must give consideration to the "cliff effect", then parents who litigate this issue need to think long and hard about the "sinkhole effect", too. Justice, in many cases, may be priceless, but it is also pricey.

82 For those with counsel, the provision of a sufficient and complete evidentiary record necessary to undertake a proper Section 9 analysis, as contemplated by *Contino*, requires the investment of significant funds, often outstripping the gain to be realized through a child support award.

83 Self-represented litigants have little hope of being able to construct such an evidentiary record on their own. If they try there will inevitably be multiple appearances before the court before that record can be "made right". (But this is what *Contino* (para. 57) requires the court to do — see also *Cabot v. Mikkelson*, 2004 MBCA 107 (Man. C.A.), para. 43). Even then the evidentiary record will likely remain incomplete. In that event there will have been an inevitable cost in both time and resources to the system as a whole as litigants make multiple appearances to have matters adjudicated. In many cases the parties will face additional costs for the adjournments they require. ...

84 For either the represented litigant or the self-represented litigant, "fairness" may become an elusive commodity. ...

85 When does disproportionately complex litigation (having regard for the evidence required and the amount actually at stake) and the disproportionate frequency with which it can be advanced through variation proceedings year after year, need to give way to relative certainty? Predictability, particularly with respect to child support issues is exceedingly important. Family law after all is a place where sometimes people will spend $200 to gain $100 either because the "principle of the thing", or one's sense of having once been wronged, demands it — demands, in turn, often supercharged by other emotional, even irrational catalysts.

86 At some point, one must wonder whether it is appropriate to consider amendments to the shared custody provisions of Section 9 if only to create a presumption — if not one in favour of the table or the set-off amount, then one in favour of the mid-point. If the range of support between the table and set-off amounts is broad enough so that a mid-point is not a sensible compromise in a particular case, that party can then bear the onus to establish a different result is appropriate.

87 Until such time as something is done, I can only wonder how many parents may mortgage their own and their children's futures. In this case, it is reasonably apparent this child cannot afford much more.

4. While there continues to be no shortage of litigation on the issue of whether the 40% threshold has been met, litigation about the amount of support to be paid may be waning:

> [It is our] view that the set-off number is rarely the number chosen by the court; rather, it always seems to be the set-off number plus a reasonable amount to take the total below the table amount for a non-s. 9 case, accounting for and recognizing that the straight set off will frequently be inadequate. Why go to trial on these??? (Epstein & Madsen's "This Week in Family Law" Fam. L. News 2008 - 48)

5. One criticism of the *Contino* case is that it mandates detailed budgets in order to complete the analysis set out by the Supreme Court of Canada. In the *Contino* case itself, the parties arbitrarily attributed 50% of their respective fixed household costs to the child. Is this reasonable? Do you think it is possible to realistically attribute a percentage of shelter costs to children? Would your answer depend on the ages of the children?

(6) Special Provisions and Reasonable Arrangements

MAUR, "CHILD SUPPORT BELOW THE GUIDELINES: WHY A BIRD IN THE HAND ISN'T ALWAYS WORTH TWO IN THE BUSH

(2008) 27 C.F.L.Q. 201 (Footnotes omitted)

Family law practitioners are frequently asked by clients to write agreements that provide for less child support for their minor children than the *Child Support Guideline* tables, and s. 3 of the *Guidelines*, would mandate. Often, the parties have come to an agreement for less than table support that makes sense to them, but that may raise problems later, if circumstances (or feelings) change.

It is well settled law that private child support arrangements that call for less than table child support may not be binding, or may not be permanent, in subsequent court proceedings, and as practitioners, we approach any agreements of this kind with great caution. Federal and provincial legislation does provide, however, that agreements and consent orders can set out less than table support, with some restrictions. This paper describes the legislative provisions that allow for agreements and consent orders for less than table support, and to review the case law considering these provisions, to see what the essential ingredients are for an agreement or consent order that will hold up under judicial scrutiny.

(a) Legislative Provisions

Both the *Divorce Act* and the provincial legislation providing for child support across the country, provide that parties may make private agreements, or enter into consent orders, for less than table support, if certain conditions are met. The door is therefore open to some restricted private ordering of child support arrangements. The legislation begs the question "how far open is the door?"

The federal and provincial legislation in this area is essentially identical, and allows the parties to begin with agreements or court orders that provide for below table support with little or no judicial interference. Agreements can be drafted with no judicial supervision at all; and consent orders can be entered into with a minimum of judicial scrutiny. The difficulties, if there are going to be any, will arise when an agreement or consent order is looked at as part of an application *de novo* for child support, or when a party seeks to vary a consent order.

Special Provisions: These are financial provisions in *a previous order or agreement*. (See s. 15.1(5) and (6) of the *Divorce Act*). A common example is the transfer of equity in the matrimonial home (either by separation agreement, or in a previous court order) in exchange for the transferor paying reduced child support, or no child support. The transferee may later come to court asking that the agreement for less than *Guideline* child support be disregarded, and the transferor will defend by relying on the "special provisions" in the agreement or previous order. If the court agrees that there are special provisions sufficient enough that support should be reduced or eliminated, the court must give reasons.

Reasonable Arrangements: These are financial provisions in *a consent order* (see s. 15.1(7) and (8), and s. 11(1)(b) of the *Divorce Act*). The court must be "satisfied" that the financial arrangements are reasonable before the consent order is issued. The effect of the legislation is that, upon issuance of the order, the court has implicitly determined the arrangements to be reasonable, and there would be very little recourse against such an order later, except in a variation proceeding upon change in circumstance. The court is not required to give reasons supporting the presumed finding of reasonableness. The court is restrained from making a finding that the arrangements are not reasonable solely on the basis that the support is below table.

(b) Special Provisions — How "Special" is "Special"?

(i) Special Provisions must be "out of the ordinary"

The "special provisions" sections of the *Divorce Act* (DA) and the *Family Law Act* (FLA) will most commonly be triggered in cases in which the parties have entered into an agreement in which child support is reduced or relinquished, and the custodial parent later commences an application for full *Guideline* child support anyway.

The DA provides that the existence of an agreement is only one factor to be taken into account in the determination of the amount of child support (s. 15.1(5)). No change in circumstance is required for a party to commence an application if there is an agreement, as opposed to a court order. In the litigation, a party wishing to rely on an agreement providing for below table support will have the burden of proving: (a) that the provisions are "special";

(b) that the special provisions benefit at least one of the children; and (c) that the application of the tables would be inequitable.

The leading case in Ontario is *Wright v. Zaver* (2002), 2002 CarswellOnt 887, 24 R.F.L. (5th) 207 (C.A.). The facts are not unheard of, but certainly a little unusual. Ms. Wright and Mr. Zaver had a child (Michael). In 1985, Ms. Wright and Mr. Zaver signed Minutes of Settlement granting Ms. Wright sole custody. Mr. Zaver agreed to pay a lump sum of $4,000 in child support, and Mr. Zaver had virtually nothing to do with Michael. In 1990 Ms. Wright married Mr. Wright, and they had a child together. They separated in 1999. Mr. Wright paid child support for Michael and the second child. Following separation, Ms. Wright sued Mr. Zaver for support, in addition to the support being paid by Mr. Wright. The trial judge awarded child support in accordance with the tables. Mr. Zaver appealed.

The decision is densely-written, and deals with several difficult issues. The decision is also split 3:2, with detailed minority reasons. There was a direct conflict between the minority decision, written by Simmons, J.A., and the majority decision, written by Sharpe, J.A. Simmons, J.A. wrote that she saw no reason to limit "special provisions" to those that are "out of the ordinary". She thought that any arrangement that replaced the need for on-going periodic support, even in part, would satisfy the statutory requirement that the provision be "special":

> In my view, no principled reason emerges from the language or purpose of s. 37(2.3) [of the FLA] to limit special provisions to provisions that are "out of the ordinary or unusual". Rather, they refer simply to provisions that replace, in whole or in part, the need for support in accordance with the Ontario Guidelines.

Writing for the majority, Sharpe, J.A. went to some lengths to state that parties do not have unfettered power to create private deviations from the application of the child support tables, and that the provisions must be demonstrably "out of the ordinary", and must exceed the "common" expectation that table support will be paid:

> In my view, interpreting "special provisions" to include provisions that are not out of the ordinary or unusual would undermine the general rule that the child support guidelines provide the amount of a child support order. Under s. 3(1) of the Ontario Guidelines, the presumptive rule is the guideline amount of child support. Under s. 37(2.2) of the *Family Law Act*, a court that varies a child support order shall do so in accordance with the child support guidelines. The "special provisions" qualification in s. 37(2.3) is an exception to the presumptive rule. Its status as an exception suggests to me that its scope must be carefully delineated. If "special provisions" were not restricted to provisions that are out of the ordinary or unusual, the exception would, in my view, effectively displace the rule.

In other words, since the rule is that child support must be paid in accordance with the tables, to be "special", a provision obviating or reducing child support needs to go beyond the rule. This seems clear enough, yet Sharpe, J.A., like the minority, also seemed to indicate that an amount that fully, or even partially, replaced the child's need for support might be special:

> It follows that the only arrangements advanced by Mr. Zaver that are capable of falling within the "special provisions" exception are Mr. Zaver's $4,000 lump sum child support payment and Mr. Wright's ongoing child support of $879 per month.
>
> *In my view, Mr. Zaver's $4,000 lump sum child support payment does not constitute a "special provision" since it does not replace Michael's ongoing need for support. A lump sum payment may replace a child's ongoing need for support if the lump sum payment is sufficiently large.* It cannot be said that Mr. Zaver's one-time $4,000 lump sum payment was sufficiently large to replace Michael's ongoing need for support. On the contrary, as the applications judge found, this payment could not have met Michael's needs for more than a few years.
>
> *With respect to Mr. Wright's ongoing child support, this arguably constitutes a "special provision" by partially replacing Michael's ongoing need for child support.* The support also benefits Michael directly, thereby meeting the second part of the test under s. 37(2.3). However, I do not find it necessary to make a definitive determination of these issues, since, in any event, Mr. Wright's ongoing

> child support fails to meet the third part of the test in s. 37(2.3). Applying the child support guidelines in this case would not be inequitable. [emphasis added]

Sharpe, J.A. says, however, that he was not making any definitive finding about whether either the $4,000 lump, or the money paid by Mr. Wright was a special provision, since both provisions failed the inequitability test. Like the minority, he found that it would not be inequitable to apply the tables, even in view of both of these provisions. This leaves us with his remarks earlier in the judgment, in which he indicates that only provisions that exceed the table provisions are to be considered "special".

In summary, the minority decision by Simmons, J.A. held that the $4,000 lump, and the money paid by Mr. Wright, were both special provisions, because they replaced Michael's need for support in whole or in part, but that nonetheless, it would not be inequitable to apply the tables. The majority decision by Sharpe, J.A. held that the $4,000 lump was clearly not a special provision, because it was too small, and only replaced Michael's need for support for a short period of time. The money paid by Mr. Wright was possibly a special provision, but the court did not make a determinative finding on this point, and held that in either event, it would not be inequitable to apply the tables. ...

(c) "Reasonable Arrangements": Just how reasonable do they have to be?

As noted above, "reasonable arrangements" are not the same thing as "special provisions", and the Ontario Court of Appeal has specifically noted that the legislative provisions dealing with "reasonable arrangements" set out a less rigorous test than the sections regarding "special provisions".

Pursuant to s. 15.1(7) of the DA, and s. 37 (2.5) of the FLA, parents can enter into a consent order for below table support as long as the court is satisfied that "reasonable arrangements" have been made for the support of the children. Because these orders are on consent, and because the court is not required to give reasons, there is no case law directly on the issue of determining what is acceptable to put in such a consent order. The issue doesn't arise, given the way the orders are created. It doesn't arise on a variation application, either, because the original order is presumed to be correct, and the variation judge will not inquire as to whether the arrangements were reasonable in the first place. The variation judge will consider any arguments made by the payor that the terms of the consent order amount to "special provisions", and that the application of the *Guidelines* would be inequitable.

The term "reasonable arrangements", however, also appears in s. 11(1)(b) of the DA: it is the duty of the court to stay the granting of a divorce unless it is satisfied that "reasonable arrangements" have been made for the support of the children of the marriage, making the bar mandatory unless the condition precedent is satisfied. There is case law on this issue, and given that the same term is used in 15.1(7) as in 11(1)(b), the same general meaning should be ascribed to the term in both sections of the *Divorce Act*. Even here, however, the cases are scanty, and often inconsistent with one another.

In *Orellana v. Merino* (1998), 40 R.F.L. (4th) 129 (Ont. Gen. Div.), [portions of the reasons are reproduced in CHAPTER 3: *DIVORCE*], Mr. Justice Campbell stayed a divorce application on the basis that the petitioner mother had not done enough to enforce child support from a clearly recalcitrant payor. ... In this case, the mother had entered into a new relationship with a partner who was willing to help her support the children. In the court's view, the new relationship did not amount to "reasonable arrangements" sufficient to allow the divorce to proceed, and the court was fairly harsh with the petitioner mother, and her lack of effort to find the biological father and attempt to seek support payments against him.

This case raises a number of issues. It is not uncommon for a single mother to want to move forward, for many reasons unrelated to collecting child support. She may have found a partner who is willing to support the children. The biological father may be avoiding her for economic and social reasons, and the mother may be attempting to "buy peace" by not pursuing the biological father for support. If she has to chase him for the support in order to obtain a divorce, so she can move forward with a committed partner who is willing to parent the children, she may stir up old conflicts with the biological father, and find herself either unable to move forward with her new partner, and/or involved in support and access litigation with her old partner. The case still stands, however, as authority for the proposition a new partner does not create a "reasonable arrangement" for the support of the children that excuses the biological father from his support obligation. Single mothers in this position must make at least some reasonable effort to find biological fathers and seek child support against them in order to obtain a divorce.

In *MacKinnon v. MacKinnon* (1986), 78 N.S.R. (2d) 361 (T.D.), the Nova Scotia Supreme Court, Trial Division held that the fact that the petitioner mother was not asking for support did not render the arrangements "reasonable". On the other hand, in *Archibald v. Archibald* (1991), 38 R.F.L. (3d) 310 (Ont. Gen. Div.), the Ontario General Division held that the payor petitioner husband's offer to pay child support at a below-table rate would not be a bar to divorce, because the wife had not responded to the petition, or to his unreasonably low offer of child support. Presumably, the trial judge thought that some voluntarily paid support was better than no support at all. *Archibald* has not been considered in Ontario, or elsewhere.

In *Malcolm v. Malcolm* (1995), 1995 CarswellOnt 70 (Gen. Div.), Kurisko, J. indicated that a husband underpaying child support, in order to pay off family debt, did not constitute "reasonable arrangements", and stayed the divorce. *Malcolm* does not appear to have been cited in Ontario or elsewhere.

In *Evans v. Evans* (2003), 2003 CarswellOnt 3719 (S.C.J.), the husband petitioned for divorce. The wife responded with a claim for a stay of the divorce, pending "reasonable arrangements" being made for child support. In its reasons on all issues, the court sorted out the husband's income, and resolved the child support issue. The divorce was granted later in the judgment, after the issue of child support had been resolved. Presumably, the matter had to go all the way to trial before the divorce could be granted, so that the court could make arrangements regarding the child support, and was not severed and granted early, as is often the case. However, in *Marinovic v. Marinovic* (1989), 20 R.F.L. (3d) 404 (Ont. H.C.), Mr. Justice Salhany said that the divorce can be granted earlier, and the issue of child support reserved to later adjudication. In other words, the very reserving of the child support issue could constitute a "reasonable arrangement" removing the bar created by s. 11(1)(b).

---

(7) Undue Hardship

Under s. 10 of the CSG, a court may adjust the CSG amount where the parent asking for the adjustment establishes that 1) paying that amount would cause "undue hardship" and 2) that his or her household's standard of living is lower than that of the other parent. In comparing standards of living in the two households, the court may, as directed by s. 10(3), use Schedule II. Because the language of s. 10 is permissive, the court may refuse to adjust the amount even if the two conditions noted above exist: *Matthews v. Hancock* (1998), 42 R.F.L. (4th) 72 (Sask. Q.B.); *Crawley v. Tobin* (1998), 42 R.F.L. (4th) 327 (Nfld. U.F.C.); and *Van Gool v. Van Gool* (1998), 44 R.F.L. (4th) 314 at 327 (B.C. C.A.); additional reasons at (1999), 44 R.F.L. (4th) 331 (B.C. C.A.). Professor Thompson notes in "The Second Family Conundrum in Child Support" (2001), 18 Can. J. Fam. L. 227 at 231, that the exercise of discretion has turned out to be "a critical and unpredictable step in the hardship analysis".

Generally, successful s. 10 applications are rare. The following two cases illustrate the application of s. 10 in the context of a second family. The majority of undue hardship claims are based on this circumstance.

SWIFT v. SWIFT

(1998), 1998 CarswellOnt 402 (Gen. Div.)

1 ROBERTSON J.: — The husband earning $65,924 with a spouse earning an income of $29,600 seeks a reduction in the guideline support amount of $548.00 for one child on the basis of undue hardship. The recipient wife earns about $42,000. The husband paid the previous order of $350.00 per month (tax deductible) for years, in full and on time. He made his financial plans on the basis of his $350 per month obligation. This amount became low over time, despite an indexing clause.

2 The husband has two children of his second marriage and argues that the costs of raising his new children result in undue hardship for the court's consideration in applying the Federal Child Support Guidelines to the variation. The second family is not separated. He submits that the standard of living in his new household is less than that of his first wife after applying the Standard of living test, specifically, SOLMATE. In calculating step 2(a)(i) (d) [(s. 10(2)(d) of the CSG] of the standard of living test, he has presumed that the guideline amount of support that would be paid for his two new children if he separated should be deducted along with their daycare costs for a total deduction of $16,752 from his gross income. Using this reduced income, he compares the resources of the two households and submits it results in a lower standard of living for his new children than his child who is the subject of the variation motion.

3 The husband relies upon section 10(2)(d) of the Federal Child Support Guidelines, submitting that his legal obligation to support his two new children causes the undue hardship. The wife's lawyer argues that, in comparing the standard of living in the two households, no amount should be deducted from the husband's income for the support of his children of the second marriage because the standard of living test already considers the costs of second family unit members in its calculation.

4 The husband has the onus to satisfy the court that this is a case for undue hardship before the standard of living test is applied. The use of the word "may" in Para. 10(1) of the guidelines clearly shows that any digression from the guidelines even after a finding of undue hardship and a reduced standard of living is discretionary.

5 Undue hardship is a tough threshold to meet. Payment of child support is often seen as a financial hardship by the payor and the new family. It generally consumes a large portion of much needed cash or discretionary income. The payment of the guideline amount will rarely be a hardship that is undue in the legal sense.

6 Synonyms for undue include: excessive, extreme, improper, unreasonable, unjustified. It is more than awkward or inconvenient. The application of the guidelines may result in interference with existing financial planning strategy in many payor families.

7 A monthly family budget expense increasing from $350 (tax deductible) to $548 (after tax) plus some add-ons is a large change for this family to fund. There is nothing undue or extreme about the expenses for his new children as disclosed on his financial statement.

They are not ill or disabled. The comparison of household standards of living test in the Guidelines [See s. 10(4) of the CSG and Step 2 in Section 2 of Schedule II] ... states:

> Adjust the annual income of each person in each household by deducting the following amounts, calculated on an annual basis:
>
>> 1 any amount relied on by the court as a factor that resulted in a determination of undue hardship, except any amount attributable to the support of a member of the household that is not incurred due to a disability or serious illness of that member ...

8 This means that, when the standard of living is calculated, no allowance is deducted from the payor's income for the costs of raising the children of the second marriage (the other household) unless the expenses relate to disability or illness.

9 An allocation of expenses for household members is already considered in the calculation.

10 The guideline amount applies.

DEAN v. FRIESEN

(1999), 50 R.F.L. (4th) 363, 1999 CarswellSask 428 (Sask. Q.B.)

[A mother and father separated in 1982 after seven years of marriage during which they had two children. A separation agreement provided that the father would pay nominal child support, but stipulated that the mother could apply for an increase if circumstances changed. The father remarried in 1985 and had three more children. The father earned about $45,000 as a farmer, but he stated that he was so poor that there were times in the past winter when the family had no groceries. As a low-income family, they qualified for some dental and health-related benefits for the three children under the provincial Family Income Plan. The mother remarried, but this second marriage ended in the late 1980s. She raised cattle as a hobby farmer and earned about $28,000 as a bus driver. The parties' oldest child was no longer a child of the marriage as she had become independent.]

WILKINSON J.: — ... At this level of income, the existence of a second family with three children constitutes a ground for the determination of undue hardship under s. 10(2)(d) of the *Guidelines*, and the court has discretion to award an amount of child support that differs from the *Guideline* amount. ...

Under s. 10 of the *Guidelines*, even if a determination of undue hardship is made, the court must deny the application unless it is satisfied that the party suffering undue hardship has a standard of living lower than that of the other spouse. In this case, the comparison of household standards of living shows the respondent [the father] has the lower standard of living. The respondent's income, adjusted for average tax of $279.84 over the three year period, results in a net of $44,646.04. His spouse's net income after tax (averaged over three years) is $5,746 for a total household income of $50,392.04. At an income of $44,925, the *Guideline* amount for one child is $363 per month or $4,356 annually. Deducting $4,356 from the total household income results in total household adjusted income of $46,036.04. The low income measure for a household comprised of two adults and three children is $23,879. Accordingly, the respondent's household income ratio is $46,036 over $23,879 or 1.92.

The applicant's total household income is $24,406 after tax. Adding child support payments of $4,356 annually gives the applicant total household adjusted income of $28,762. The low income measure for a household consisting of one adult and one child is $14,535. The applicant's household income ratio is $28,762 over $14,535 or 1.97.

In this case, I consider an appropriate order for child support to be the sum of $236 per month, an amount which will make the parties' household income ratios relatively comparable. It also represents the *Guideline* amount the respondent would pay for four children at an annual income of $44,925, apportioned equally between all four children.

NOTES AND QUESTIONS

1. Section 10 provides a narrow exception and adjustments have been rare. Even if one of the circumstances listed in s. 10(2) exists and the parent seeking the adjustment resides in a household with a lesser standard of living, the courts may conclude that there is no undue hardship: *Hansvall v. Hansvall* (1997), 160 Sask. R. 201 (Q.B.); *Van Gool v. Van Gool* (1998), 44 R.F.L. (4th) 314 (B.C. C.A.); and *Chong v. Chong* (1999), 47 R.F.L. (4th) 301 (B.C. S.C.). In *Van Gool*, Prowse J.A. stated (at 328-329):

> Since the basic table amounts were designed to be a "floor" for the amount payable, rather than a ceiling, it is not surprising that the authorities have held that the threshold for a finding of undue hardship is high. Hardship is not sufficient; the hardship must be "undue", that is "exceptional", "excessive" or "disproportionate" in all the circumstances. The onus is on the party applying under s. 10 to establish undue hardship; it will not be presumed simply because the applicant has the legal responsibility for another child or children and/or because the standard of living of the applicant's household is lower than that of the other spouse. The applicant must lead cogent evidence to establish why the table amount would cause undue hardship.

Sometimes the courts will expressly conclude that there is hardship, but that it is not "undue". See, e.g., *Chong*, above; *Wislesky v. Wislesky* (1999), 47 R.F.L. (4th) 208 (Ont. Gen. Div.); and *St. Croix v. Maxwell* (1999), 3 R.F.L. (5th) 161 (Ont. S.C.J.).

2. *The Survey of Child Support Awards: Analysis of Phase 2* (noted above) reported that undue hardship was asserted in less than 1% of divorce cases involving a child support order between 1998 to January 2002. The vast majority of these cases involved applications by the payor and they were granted in a majority of the cases. In only one case was the payee's request for an increased amount successful.

3. Most of the reported cases in which someone has successfully invoked s. 10 involve payors with support obligations to second families. In addition to *Dean v. Friesen*, see *Reiter v. Reiter* (1997), 36 R.F.L. (4th) 102 (B.C. Master); *Aker v. Howard* (1998), 43 R.F.L. (4th) 159 (Ont. Gen. Div.); and *Hanmore v. Hanmore* (1999), 47 R.F.L. (4th) 157 (Alta. Q.B.). Claims on this basis failed in *Walkeden v. Zemlak* (1997), 33 R.F.L. (4th) 52 (Sask. Q.B.); *Nishnik v. Smith* (1998), 39 R.F.L. (4th) 105 (Sask. Q.B.); *Wislesky*, above; *Chong*, above; and *Van Gool*, above. In some of these cases, the claims failed even though the payor's new family had a lower standard of living than that of the payee's family.

In *Children Come First*, the Department of Justice suggested (Vol. 2 at 82-83) that the cases exhibit two approaches. Some judges believe that a parent's first family should be given priority and that a parent should be expected always to organize his or her affairs in light of this. Other judges are willing to give the second family a chance to succeed financially and are more likely to adjust child support obligations to the first family. The Department concluded (Vol. 2 at 83): "As a result of these two judicial approaches to the difficult issue of second families, the outcome of any given case is difficult to predict, thereby undermining the Guidelines objective of consistent treatment of parents."

For an extensive review of the cases up to 2001 and a survey of the approaches in other jurisdictions, see Thompson, "The Second Family Conundrum in Child Support" (2001), 18 Can. J. Fam. L. 227. Professor Thompson suggests that one can find support in the Canadian cases for five main policies: 1) "first family first"; 2) "let the second family succeed"; 3) "equal treatment of the payor's children"; 4) "equal treatment of all children"; and 5) case-by-case discretion. In the end, he favours "equal treatment of all children" which he argues (at 265) "means equalization of household living standards, at least when it comes to reducing support for payors with lower standards of living".

4. The *Guidelines* only allow access costs to be taken into account in lowering the amount of child support if the paying parent can satisfy the two hurdles in s. 10. First, he or she must establish that undue hardship arises out of "unusually high expenses in relation to exercising access to a child". Second, the court must conclude that the payor has a lower household standard of living. In general, access parents have not had much success in invoking s. 10. Often, this results from the mandatory comparison of household living standards test. But judges have also been

reluctant to find that the expenses are "unusually high". See, e.g., *Beeler v. Beeler* (1997), 32 R.F.L. (4th) 397 (Sask. Q.B.) and *Williams v. Williams* (1997), 32 R.F.L. (4th) 23 (N.W.T. S.C.).

In some cases such as *Ellis v. Ellis* (1999), 45 R.F.L. (4th) 234 (N.S. C.A.), the courts have required a moving custodial parent to help pay for the increased cost of exercising access either directly through reimbursement or indirectly through reduced child support. However, some cases have held that s. 10 of the *Guidelines* exhaustively covers the issue of access costs. See, e.g., *South v. South* (1998), [1998] B.C.J. No. 962, 1998 CarswellBC 933 (B.C. S.C.). Professor McLeod argued in several annotations in the Reports of Family Law that a court should be able to order a custodial parent to assume some of the costs of transportation relating to access simply as a condition of custody and independently of any child support issues. See, for example, his annotation to *Holtskog v. Holtskog* (1999), 47 R.F.L. (4th) 162 (Sask. C.A.). See also "Reforming the Child Support Guidelines" in *Federal Child Support Guidelines Reference Manual* (Ottawa: Dept. of Justice, looseleaf) where Professor Bala states (at K-75):

> The better view is articulated by the recent mobility cases where judges, in appropriate cases, exercise a discretion to require the custodial parent to pay all or part of the increased access costs. Technically, the judge is not reducing the Guidelines' child support order, which continues to be fully enforceable as child support, but rather is invoking subsection 16(6) of the *Divorce Act* to impose a "condition" on custody that permits the custodial parent to move, but requires that parent to pay all or part of the increased access costs, if and when access is exercised.

This is the approach that was adopted by Justice Quigley in *Morrone v. Morrone* (2007), 44 R.F.L. (6th) 289 (Ont. S.C.J.).

5. The circumstances listed in s. 10(2) of the *Guidelines* are not exhaustive. In *Petrocco v. von Michalofski* (1998), 36 R.F.L. (4th) 278 (Ont. Gen. Div.), the children lived with the father and his new wife. Their combined income was about $300,000 per year. The mother's annual income, including spousal support, was about $40,000. The court concluded that s. 10 applied and reduced the mother's child support obligation from $516 per month to $150 per month. It reasoned (at 285) that payment of child support at the *Guidelines* level would constitute undue hardship for the mother because her role as access parent would be "detrimentally affected by an inability to offer the children a reasonable level of activity and comforts relative to that enjoyed in their primary residence". See also *Scharf v. Scharf* (1998), 40 R.F.L. (4th) 422 (Ont. Gen. Div.), where a mother successfully argued that the amount of child support that would otherwise be ordered under s. 8 of the *Guidelines* should be increased in light of the difference in living standards between the two households and the fact that the father rarely exercised access to the child in the mother's care.

6. As the *Scharf* case illustrates, s. 10 has occasionally been used to increase the amount of child support. The case of *Scotcher v. Hampson* (1998), 41 R.F.L. (4th) 271 (Ont. Gen. Div.); additional reasons at (1998), 43 R.F.L. (4th) 132 (Ont. Gen. Div.) also suggests that a failure to exercise access can give rise to undue hardship where it increases the custodial parent's costs. Compare *Block v. Baltimore* (2000), 5 R.F.L. (5th) 18 (Man. Q.B.); additional reasons at (2000), 2000 CarswellMan 316 (Man. Q.B.).

The Department of Justice reports in *Children Come First* (Vol. 2 at 80): "Courts are especially cautious if the receiving parent wants to increase the table amount because other circumstances have caused undue hardship; very few cases have been successful." In "An Update of Case Law under the Child Support Guidelines" (1998-99), 16 C.F.L.Q. 261, Justice Aston suggests (at 292) that the "most likely scenario for increased child support, based on undue hardship, is the split custody or shared custody situation in which the court may consider maintaining a similar standard of living for siblings".

7. To compare household standards, s. 10(4) of the *Guidelines* indicates that the court may, but need not, use the formula set out in Schedule II. This formula appears complex and long, but this may be inevitable. Any comparison of household living standards has to determine the net income of the adult members and adjust for household size. Computer programs are available, and are now customarily used, to make the necessary calculations.

To use the formula, one needs the annual income of each household member. The case law holds that full disclosure of the income of household members should only be required where there appears to be a meritorious claim of undue hardship. In *Souliere v. Leclair* (1998), 38 R.F.L. (4th) 68 (Ont. Gen. Div.), Justice Boland rejected a *Charter* challenge to the requirement that each member of the household reveal his or her income.

(8) Retroactive Child Support

A NOTE ON RETROACTIVE CHILD SUPPORT

There are many reasons why a support applicant may not proceed quickly to court to ask for child support. Sometimes the applicant cannot afford to litigate and yet she may not qualify for legal aid. She may feel intimidated by the other parent and may be worried about the repercussions of applying for support. In other cases, time has simply passed, the custodial parent has managed (although perhaps not well) without the support and a *status quo* of no support has developed. In yet others, an appropriate amount of child support was either ordered or agreed to initially, but the payor's income has increased and a higher amount of child support is now warranted. The payor parent may be slow to reveal the income increase and the recipient may not be able to assess whether an upward variation is worth pursuing.

There are competing interests at stake if an application is brought well after the parties have separated, or if a variation proceeds a significant period of time after any income increase of the payor. On one hand, the recipient and her household were entitled to the support and have had to endure a reduced standard of living without it. On the other hand, the payor's household has developed a standard of living that does not include paying child support or an increased amount of child support. If a considerable period of time passes, the amount of child support that should already have been paid adds up and its payment, if ordered, can represent a large, and potentially insurmountable, burden for the payor.

Although this type of claim is commonly referred to as a claim for "retroactive" support, Justice Bastarache pointed out in *S. (D.B.) v. G. (S.R.)*, [2006] 2 S.C.R. 231, 270 D.L.R. (4th) 297, 31 R.F.L. (6th) 1 (hereinafter "*D.B.S.*"), that the word "retroactive" is misleading in a technical sense. The claim is for the amount that, in hindsight, should have been paid earlier.

An important, preliminary issue that arose in the *D.B.S.* case was whether a child had to be a "child of the marriage" at the time that a parent claims retroactive child support. The Alberta Court of Appeal had held that a parent could bring an application for retroactive support under the *Divorce Act* after a child had lost his or her status as a "child of the marriage" as defined in s. 2(1). The Supreme Court disagreed, holding that the term "material time" in the definition meant "the time of the making of the application" (see paragraphs 87–89).

The *D.B.S.* decision involved four different cases raising similar issues, all of which were heard and decided together. The Alberta Court of Appeal ((2005), [2005] A.J. No. 2, 7 R.F.L. (6th) 373 (C.A.)) had made the firm, and somewhat controversial, decision that entitlement to child support in accordance with the parent's income accrues from the time a child is born. The court reasoned further that this meant that retroactive child support simply accumulated whether or not the other parent demanded that it be paid. If the payor's income increased, the payor was deemed to know that he should be paying increased support. The Alberta court did not accept the argument that retroactive support could represent an unfair burden. The judgment is lengthy, but its essence appears in paragraph 117:

> One should expect to pay what one is obliged to pay. If there has been a change that would warrant a different child support order, it should be expected that the order will operate from the time of that change. Thus, if a person fails to disclose the change, it cannot be unexpected that he or she will be facing a retroactive claim for a significant amount when the facts come to light.

The majority of the Supreme Court disagreed with this approach. Justice Bastarache, writing for four members of the court, attempted to set out a framework that balanced the interests of certainty and predictability with the need for fairness and flexibility. In a sense, Justice Bastarache attributed the responsibility for ensuring that the correct amount of child support is paid to both parents. Support payors have a positive duty to disclose income and any increases in income and a positive duty to increase their support when their income increases. On the other hand, support recipients have a positive duty to actively explore and pursue the support increases to which the children may be entitled. Failure to do so may be a factor, depending on the circumstances, in determining the appropriateness of a retroactive award and may also affect the term covered by such an award.

Justice Bastarache's reasons are lengthy (covering over 50 pages in the D.L.R.s) and complex. At the risk of oversimplifying, the following is a brief description of the suggested three-stage approach:

> 1. Determine whether a retroactive award is appropriate. Here, the courts must consider the reason for the recipient parent's delay in seeking child support, the conduct of the payor parent, the past and present circumstances of the child, and any hardship imposed by a retroactive award.

> 2. Determine what period the award should cover. Having decided to make a retroactive award, a court must decide how far back it should go. It is presumed that the award should cover the period following the date on which the claimant parent gave "effective notice"; that is, when he or she signaled a desire for support or an increased amount of support. However, this is subject to a general maximum of a three-year period predating the date of "formal notice". In other words, it will usually be inappropriate to make a support award retroactive to a date more than three years before formal notice was given to respondent parent. However, this general three-year limit does not apply where the latter has engaged in blameworthy conduct that has interfered with the claimant parent's ability to pursue support or increased support. Examples of such conduct include a refusal to disclose increased income, a misrepresentation of income in response to a request for updated information, and intimidation of the claimant parent.

> 3. Adjust the commencement date if required. Having found that a retroactive award is appropriate and having determined the presumed commencement date, the court needs to determine the quantum. This is done in accordance with the applicable legislative scheme; for example, the CSG. After this, the court may adjust the total amount owing by altering the commencement date where this is needed to ensure overall fairness.

> (This description of this framework from the *D.B.S.* decision is based, in part, on D. Smith, "Retroactive Child Support — An Update" (2007), 26 C.F.L.Q. 209. This article also describes how the Ontario courts have applied the framework.)

Although the court was unanimous in its disposition of all four cases in the *D.B.S.* appeal, Justice Abella's concurring reasons (supported by two other Justices) differed in some significant ways from those of the majority. She stressed that parents have a free-standing joint obligation to support their children based on their ability to do so and that children have a corresponding right to be supported at that level. This fundamental principle led to three points of disagreement with Justice Batsarache's reasons. First, Justice Abella believed that retroactive support should not be tied to the date of the effective notice of an intention to enforce the child's right. So long as the change in the payor parent's income warranted different child support from what was being paid, the presumptive starting point for calculating the child's entitlement to increased support should be the date when the change occurred. Second, Justice Abella stated that blameworthy conduct was irrelevant in determining the date at which retroactive support should begin because the right to support belonged to the child regardless of how his or her parents behaved. The existence of the payor parent's increased obligation depended simply on his or her increased income. Third, and perhaps most significantly, Justice Abella disagreed with the presumptive limitation period of three years. She believed that, on an application for a variation, the increased support should generally be retroactive to the date on which a payor parent's income changed. However, she added that it was, nevertheless, up to the court in each case to decide whether this presumption had been rebutted, what the appropriate quantum should be, and how the retroactive support should be paid. Where calculating child support from the date of the change of circumstances would create undue hardship or where a fully informed recipient parent delayed seeking enforcement for an inordinate and unjustified period of time, a court might calculate entitlement from another date.

The Supreme Court established in the *D.B.S.* decision that an application for child support, whether prospective or retroactive, can only be made under the *Divorce Act* or provincial legislation while a child is still eligible for support. The possibility of adult children seeking damages or other compensation for lack of support was explored in *Louie v. Lastman* (2001), 18 R.F.L. (5th) 311 (Ont. S.C.J.); affirmed (2002), 29 R.F.L. (5th) 108 (Ont. C.A.). Two brothers, aged 38 and 42, brought an action against Lastman who, they learned in 1997, was likely their biological father. They asserted that they were conceived during a 14-year affair between their married mother and Lastman whom they knew only as a family friend during their childhood. Their mother and Lastman had entered into an agreement in 1974, after the mother and her husband separated and after the affair ended. The mother had received a total of $27,500 under this agreement and she had released all claims against Lastman and withdrew the allegation that he was the father of the children. In 2000, the brothers sought a declaration of paternity and damages flowing from Lastman's failure to provide adequate support during their dependency. Because they were independent adults, they could not bring a support application under the *FLA*. Their claims were based on breach of a fiduciary duty, unjust enrichment and the torts of intentional or negligent infliction of mental suffering and "intentional infliction of impoverishment". Lastman, a prominent businessman and mayor of Toronto at the time, successfully brought a motion asking the court to strike out all the claims prior to trial, except the request for a declaration of paternity, on the basis that they could not succeed at trial.

The brothers appealed, challenging only the motion judge's findings relating to the alleged breach of fiduciary duty. The Ontario Court of Appeal reasoned that no matter how the men attempted to frame their action, in the end it was nothing more than a claim for retroactive child support. As such, the appellate court held that the claim could not succeed because it amounted to an inappropriate attempt to bypass the statutory scheme governing child support. Justice Rosenberg added (para. 13):

> ... I would not foreclose the possibility of a fiduciary claim for child support outside the legislative scheme where the child is in need and there is a gap in the scheme. That, however, is not this case. The appellants conceded that had their mother made a claim for child support under the legislation in force when they were children, the court could have made an order for support. It is not open to the appellants to come forward and make a support claim decades after they are no longer dependent.

The Court of Appeal also held that, whatever fiduciary obligations might generally be imposed on a biological parent, it was plain and obvious that Lastman had no such obligations to the brothers. It noted (para. 29):

> ... The appellants' mother chose to raise them as part of the Louie family. In 1974, she released all claims against the respondent. He at no time acted as, or was called upon to act as, a parent to the appellants. Throughout, his role was that of a friend of the appellants' mother. The respondent did not assume any power or control over the lives of the appellants, nor did he dominate or influence their up-bringing. Because of the choices made by the appellants' mother, the respondent had no scope for the exercise of discretion or power over the day-to-day lives of the appellants.

The mother's action for rescission of the contract and for damages was also dismissed prior to trial as disclosing no reasonable cause of action. See *Louie v. Lastman* (2001), 18

R.F.L. (5th) 311 (Ont. S.C.J.); affirmed (2002), 29 R.F.L. (5th) 108 (Ont. C.A.). The mother asserted that the 1974 agreement resulted from Lastman's undue influence and coercion at a time when she was in poor health and in desperate financial straits. She asked for damages flowing from Lastman's failure to provide adequate support during her sons' dependency. Her claims were based on breach of a fiduciary duty, unjust enrichment and the torts of intentional or negligent infliction of mental suffering and "intentional infliction of impoverishment". In the Ontario Court of Appeal, she pursued only her equitable claims for rescission of the release and for compensation based on breach of a fiduciary duty and on unjust enrichment. The appellate court concluded that the woman's lengthy delay in pursuing rescission constituted acquiescence to Lastman's conduct as she long knew all the facts that might give rise to this remedy. Accordingly, it held that the equitable doctrine of *laches* applied. Since the release could not be rescinded, the woman's other equitable claims were also destined to fail.

The Ontario Court of Appeal added that the substance of the mother's other claims indicated that they would fail in any event. It suggested that the unjust enrichment claim, based on the fact that the man had retained money that he should have paid as child support, was nothing more than a request for retroactive child support and as such amounted to an attempt to enforce a statutory duty by means of an action rather than through the child support legislation.

NOTES AND QUESTIONS

1. *Tether v. Tether* (2009), 2009 CarswellSask 8 (Q.B.) is a recent decision dealing with the issue of "blameworthy conduct" in applying the *D.B.S.* framework. Many orders and agreements require a payor to produce his or her tax returns on a regular schedule in the future (usually once per year), so that the appropriateness of the amount of child support can be assessed. In *Tether*, Justice Sandomirsky held that the failure of a payor parent to follow the order or agreement requiring regular production of tax returns or income information is "blameworthy conduct".

2. Not disclosing a material change in circumstances such as a significant increase in income may, on its own, be blameworthy conduct. In *Baldwin v. Funston* (2007), 37 R.F.L. (6th) 309 (Ont. C.A.); additional reasons at (2007), 2007 CarswellOnt 5529 (C.A.) the father simply paid support in accordance with the parents' separation agreement even though his income increased dramatically. The court found that the father's failure to report the increase in his income was "blameworthy conduct given the magnitude of that increase" (para. 19), even though it agreed with the trial judge's conclusion that the agreement did not require the disclosure. Nevertheless, the appellate court went on to uphold the trial judge's refusal to order retroactive support. It noted (paras. 24 & 25) the following key findings of the trial judge: the father had complied with the agreement, the needs of the children had been met, the mother had known that the father's income had increased but did not ask for disclosure, an order for retroactive support as sought (in the $300,000 range) might impair that father's ability to meet his ongoing support obligations, and the mother had waited over five years before bringing an application for increased support. Do you think this result is consistent with *D.B.S.*?

The *Funston* case should be compared with *Debora v. Debora* (2006), 33 R.F.L. (6th) 252 (Ont. C.A.) where the court upheld an award of $950,000 in retroactive support. In that case, the wealthy father had concealed his income.

3. Bill 133 (passed but not yet proclaimed) will add a new s. 39.1 to the *Family Law Act*, providing that child support amounts payable under a court order or a domestic contract filed with the court can be recalculated by a child support service to reflect updated income information. The provision would also authorize the making of regulations to govern recalculation procedures. Presumably, the regulation will require payors to disclose their incomes on an annual basis. As a result, the issue of retroactive child support would occur much less frequently.

9

DOMESTIC CONTRACTS

1. Introduction

Part IV of the *Family Law Act* (*FLA*) specifically recognizes marriage contracts, separation agreements and cohabitation agreements as domestic contracts that can, to some extent, override or modify statutory rights. The general rule established in s. 2(10) is that a "domestic contract dealing with a matter that is also dealt with in this Act prevails unless this Act provides otherwise". Part IV also provides a framework for the making of all types of domestic contracts.

It is important to keep in mind that domestic contracts are, like all other contracts, governed by the general law of contract. The general principles of contract formation and breach of contract, as well as the conditions under which agreements may be rescinded, all apply to domestic contracts (see *Rosen v. Rosen* (1994), 3 R.F.L. (4th) 267 (Ont. C.A.); leave to appeal refused (1995), 10 R.F.L. (4th) 121 (note) (S.C.C.), excerpted in this chapter). In addition, as we shall see, the *FLA* contains special provisions regarding the formal validity of domestic agreements. That statute, in s. 56(4), also authorizes a court to set aside a domestic contract for lack of disclosure or where a party did not understand the nature or consequences of the contract. Finally, as we shall see, legislative provisions may allow courts to disregard or override certain provisions in a valid domestic contract. The special legislative treatment adds an extra dimension to the analysis of domestic contracts.

The next section of this chapter briefly examines the types of domestic contracts dealt with in Part IV of the *FLA*. The formal requirements and rules governing the capacity to contract as set out in the Act are the focus of the chapter's third section, while the fourth deals with the extent to which couples are free to govern their relationship by domestic contract. The chapter concludes with an examination of challenges to the validity of domestic contracts, sampling the grounds on which a court may ignore or set aside such a contract.

This chapter reveals a continuing tension between several conflicting policy objectives. While private settlement of disputes or potential disputes is almost always preferable to litigation, one party should not be allowed to unduly take advantage of the other and the interests of children or other matters of public interest must be protected. There is a continuing discussion about ensuring that this balance is properly addressed in the process of resolving disputes privately (see B. Landau, "Unpacking the Rational Alternative" (1990), 9 Can. J. Fam. Law 193). Thus, while the law permits considerable freedom of contract, it also imposes certain safeguards and controls. The following article provides both reasons why the legal system should permit, and indeed encourage, divorcing couples to work out their own arrangements and reasons for imposing some limits on private ordering.

MNOOKIN, "DIVORCE BARGAINING: THE LIMITS ON PRIVATE ORDERING"

Eekelar and Katz, eds., *The Resolution of Family Conflict: Comparative Legal Perspectives* (Toronto: Butterworths, 1984) 366–372 and 375–379 (Footnotes omitted)

The Advantages of Private Ordering

Let me begin with the arguments supporting the presumption in favor of private ordering. The core reason is rooted in notions of human liberty. Private ordering is supported by the liberal ideal that individuals have rights, and should largely be left free to make of their lives what they wish. In Charles Fried's words, a regime of law that "respects the dispositions individuals make of their rights, carries to its logical conclusion the liberal premise that individuals have rights." Professor Fried has elegantly defended on a non-utilitarian basis the principle that "persons may impose on themselves [through contracts] obligations where none existed before." He argues that "the capacity to form true and rational judgments and act on them is the heart of moral personality and the basis of a person's claim to respect as a moral being." Thus, as a general proposition, enforcement of agreements made at the time of divorce can be justified as giving expression to a "free man's rational decision about how to dispose of what is his, how to bind himself."

Private ordering can also be justified on grounds of efficiency. Ordinarily, the parties themselves are in the best position to evaluate the comparative advantages of alternative arrangements. Each spouse, in the words of John Stuart Mill, "is the person most interested in his own well-being: ... with respect to his own feelings and circumstances, the most ordinary man or woman has means of knowledge immeasurably surpassing those that can be possessed by anyone else." Through negotiations, there are opportunities for making *both* parents better off than either would be if a court or some third party simply imposed a result. A consensual solution is, by definition, more likely to be consistent with the preferences of each spouse than would a result imposed by a court. Parental preferences often vary with regard to money and child-rearing responsibilities. Through negotiations, it is possible that the divorcing spouses can divide money and child-raising responsibilities to reflect their own individual preferences.

Finally, there are obvious and substantial savings when a couple can resolve the distributional consequences of divorce without resort to formal adjudication. The financial cost of litigation, both private and public, is minimized. The pain of the formal adversarial proceedings is avoided. A negotiated settlement allows the parties to avoid the risks and uncertainties of litigation, which may involve all-or-nothing consequences. Given the substantial delays that often characterize contested judicial proceedings, agreement can often save time and allow each spouse to proceed with his or her life. In short, against a backdrop of fair standards in the shadow of which a couple bargains, divorcing couples should have very broad powers to make their own arrangements. Significant limitations are inconsistent with the premises of no-fault divorce. Parties should be encouraged to settle the distributional consequences of divorce for themselves, and the state should provide an efficient and fair mechanism for enforcing such agreements and for settling disputes when the parties are unable to agree.

Capacity

On an abstract level, I find the general defense of private ordering both appealing and persuasive. But it is premised on the notion that divorce bargaining involves rational, self-interested individuals — that the average adult has the intelligence and experience to make a well-informed judgment concerning the desirability of entering into a particular divorce settlement. Given the tasks facing an individual at the time of divorce, and the characteristics of the relationship between divorcing spouses, there are reasons to fear that this may not always be the case.

Informed bargaining requires a divorcing spouse to assess his or her own preferences concerning alternative arrangements. Radical changes in life circumstances complicate such assessments. Within a short period of time, separation and divorce often subject spouses to the stresses of many changes: "[S]pouses need to adjust to new living arrangements, new jobs, financial burdens, new patterns of parenting, and new conditions of social and sexual life." It may be particularly difficult for a parent to assess custodial alternatives. The past will be a very incomplete guide to the future. Preferences may be based on past experiences in which child-rearing tasks were performed in an ongoing two-parent family, and dissolution or divorce inevitably alters this division of responsibilities. Child-rearing may now have new advantages or disadvantages for the parents' own needs. A parent interested in dating may find the child an intrusion in a way that the child never was during marriage. Because children and parents both change, and changes may be unpredictable, projecting parental preferences for custody into the future is a formidable task. Nevertheless, most parents have some self-awareness, however imperfect, and no third party (such as a judge) is likely to have better information about a parent's tastes, present or future.

Separation often brings in its wake psychological turmoil and substantial emotional distress that can make deliberative and well-informed judgments unlikely. It can arouse "feelings about the former spouse, such as love, hate, bitterness, guilt, anger, envy, concern, and attachment; feelings about the marriage, such as regret, disappointment, bitterness, sadness, and failure; and more general feelings such as failure, depression, euphoria, relief, guilt, lowered self-esteem, and lowered self-confidence." Isolini Ricci has suggested that for many individuals "the emotions of ending a marriage" characteristically go through five stages during a two or three year period. For the first three stages, if Ricci's characterizations are correct, an otherwise competent person may at times have seriously impaired judgment. She suggests that the pre-separation stage is often marked by "anxiety, depression, hostility, and recurring illness." The separation stage can bring with it three dangerous side effects: "poor judgment; accident and illness-proneness, poor reflex action; and depression." The third stage, which follows the separation, arouses strong emotions that are "both natural and nasty". "Emotional roller-coasters are common at this stage, causing many people to feel permanent emotional instability." According to Ricci, "this is the worst possible time to make any permanent decisions — especially legal ones. Thinking and believing the worst about each other is one of the chief hazards of this stage, and such thoughts, exaggerated and extended, can lead to serious complications."

Such emotional turmoil may prevent for a time any negotiated settlement. Or it may lead to a settlement that a party later regrets. ...

Some might think that the stresses and emotional turmoil of separation and divorce undermine the essential premise of private ordering — the idea that individuals are capable of deliberate judgments. I disagree. After all, for most persons the emotional upheaval is transitory, and the stresses are an inevitable consequence of having to make a new life. Temporary incapacity does not justify state paternalism for an extended period of time. Nonetheless, safeguards are necessary, and the wooden application of the traditional contract defense of "incompetence" may not provide sufficient protection. More recent contract scholarship suggests a theory that respects the ideal of individual autonomy and the efficiency of private ordering, and avoids the unfairness of bargains that exploit a temporarily diminished capacity.

Professor Eisenberg recently suggested a concept of "transactional incapacity" to capture the notion that "an individual may be of average intelligence and yet may lack the aptitude, experience, or judgmental ability to make a deliberative and well-informed judgment concerning the desirability of entering into a given complex transaction." Eisenberg's concern was with situations where one party exploits the other party's incapacity to deal with a complex transaction, "by inducing ... a bargain that a person who had capacity to deal with the transaction probably would not make." In such circumstances, Eisenberg suggests that neither fairness nor efficiency support application of the principle that a bargain should be enforced to its full extent. It is unfair because it violates conventional moral standards "to make a bargain on unfair terms by exploiting ... incapacity." Moreover, "the maxim that a promisor is the best judge of his own utility can have little application: by hypothesis, the promisor is not able to make a well-informed judgment concerning the transaction."

An analogous concept could be applied to divorce bargaining within a system that encourages private ordering at the time of divorce. When one spouse knows or has reason to know of the diminished capacity, and exploits this incapacity, a court should reopen the agreement. Proof of exploitation is essential, however. For this, I would require a showing that the terms of the agreement considered as a whole fall outside the range of settlement. By providing a remedy only if a party exploited the other side's incapacity by securing an unusually one-sided bargain, this test will not create uncertainty in most cases. Many divorced spouses may in retrospect think they were unwise in accepting some provision, and some might be able to show a lack of deliberative judgment, but few will be able to show that the settlement as a whole would have been unacceptable to a competent person. Any additional uncertainty created for parties making "out of the ordinary" deals may not be a bad thing. Moreover, I would create a presumption against the application of this diminished capacity doctrine in any cases where the party making the claim was represented by counsel. Indeed, as Eisenberg suggests, "If a party who has been urged, fairly and in good faith, to seek advice, fails to do so, the doctrine of transactional incapacity would normally not apply, because the element of exploitation would be lacking" — at least where the party has sufficient capacity "to understand the importance of getting advice."

A second prophylactic to guard against transitory diminished capacity would involve a "cooling-off" period, during which either party would be free to rescind a settlement agreement. In a commercial context, this period is often very short — typically three days. In the divorce context, I would make it considerably longer — perhaps sixty or ninety days. Like any safeguard, this one has costs. Some agreements may come apart even though they involve no exploitation whatsoever, simply because of ambivalence or a change of heart. Moreover, this cooling-off period might be used strategically by a party — a tentative agreement may be reached, only to be later rescinded, in order to wear an opponent down. Nonetheless, it would seem appropriate to have a fixed, reasonable "boundary line" as a rough estimate of the time within which the "transitory state of acquiescence" induced by guilt or anxiety might be expected to lapse. In cases where both parties have assigned counsel, it might be possible to have a shorter period.

Unequal Bargaining Power

Let me now turn to a second possible justification for imposing limits on private ordering — the basic idea is simple; in negotiation between two competent adults, if there are great disparities in bargaining power, some bargains may be reached that are unconscionably one-sided.

The notion of bargaining power has intuitive appeal, but turns out to be very difficult to define. Without a complete theory of negotiations, it is hard to give precise substantive content to the notion of bargaining power, much less define precisely the idea of "relative bargaining power." Nonetheless, by briefly analyzing the five elements of the bargaining model I described in an earlier article, it is possible to suggest why some divorcing spouses may be seen as having unequal bargaining power.

First, there are the legal endowments. The legal rules governing marital property, alimony, child support, and custody give each spouse certain claims based on what each would get if the case goes to trial. In other words, the outcome the law will impose if no agreement is reached gives each parent certain bargaining chips — an endowment of sorts. These endowments themselves can create unequal bargaining power. For example, other things being equal, in a state where there is a tender years presumption in favor of maternal custody, a mother has considerably more bargaining power (at least if she wants custody) than the father. A new law creating a presumption against spousal support, on the other hand, would reduce the bargaining endowment of women as a class. To the extent that negotiated settlements simply reflect differences in bargaining power based on the legal rules themselves, this would not justify a claim of unfairness in an individual case. Instead, the legal endowments should be changed.

Second, a party's bargaining power is very much influenced by his or her preferences — i.e., how that party subjectively evaluates alternative outcomes. These preferences are not simply matters of taste — they can depend upon a party's economic resources and life circumstances. The parties' relative bargaining power depends on how they both subjectively evaluate the outcome a court would impose.

A third element that affects bargaining power has to do with uncertainty, and the parties' attitudes towards risk. Often the outcome in court is far from certain, and the parties are negotiating against a backdrop clouded by substantial uncertainty. Because the parties may have different risk preferences, this uncertainty can differentially affect the bargaining power of the two spouses. If there is substantial variance among the possible court-imposed outcomes, the relatively more risk averse party is comparatively disadvantaged.

A fourth element that can create differences in bargaining power relates to the differential ability to withstand the transaction costs — both emotional and economic — involved in negotiations. A party who is in no hurry, enjoys negotiations, and has plenty of resources to pay a lawyer, has an obvious advantage over an opponent who is impatient, hates negotiations, and cannot afford to wait.

A fifth element concerns the bargaining process itself, and strategic behaviour. In divorce bargaining, the spouses may not know each other's true preferences. Negotiations often involve the attempts by each side to discern the other side's true preferences, while making credible claims about their own, and what they intend to do if a particular proposal is not accepted. "Bargainers bluff, argue for their positions, attempt to deceive or manipulate each other, and make power plays to gain an advantage." Some people are more skilled negotiators than others. They are better at manipulating information and managing impressions. They have a more refined sense of tactical action. These differences can create inequalities in negotiations.

In short, the relative bargaining power of divorcing spouses depends upon how each evaluates the consequences of what will happen absent an agreement. This, in turn, depends not simply upon the legal endowments, but each party's subjective evaluation of the outcome absent a negotiated agreement, and the probable transaction costs of a court-imposed resolution. To the extent that a spouse sees himself as lacking alternatives, and is perceived as being dependent upon resources controlled by the other spouse, he lacks bargaining power. Bargaining power thus has both subjective and objective elements.

[Professor Mnookin examines two examples of negotiated outcomes that seem very one-sided. In the second, a wife, W, agrees to sell her half interest in a jointly-held home to her husband, H, for $40,000 even though the home is worth about $150,000. She does this because she is very short of funds and wishes to buy a condominium immediately and start over. Court action to realize her interest in the home would take about a year.]

In cases like this, the problem is not that W did not know what she was doing. To the contrary, her consent to this agreement is real. As Professor Dawson pointed out in his seminal article many years ago, "the more unpleasant the alternative, the more real the consent to a course which would avoid it." The underlying issue concerns in part the question of what pressures can legitimately be brought to bear in bargaining, and how and whether it is possible to regulate the manner in which such pressures are exercised. This would be an easy case if W had shown that she accepted $40,000 because of physical threats by H. The doctrine of "duress" has traditionally permitted a defense to enforcement of a contract brought about by threats of illegal conduct. In this case, however, H's conduct is not illegal, but it is nonetheless plain that H is taking advantage of W's desire to sell quickly. One's appraisal of the morality of H's conduct might well be influenced by an evaluation of whether he was somehow responsible for W's urgent need. ...

While I am reluctant to allow a court to evaluate the fairness of the price in divorce bargains, I am deeply troubled by this second case. It seems clear that various doctrines of contract law are sufficient to permit intervention in egregious cases where it is thought that inequality in bargaining power has brought about unjust enrichment. The underlying philosophical and jurisprudential issues are difficult ones, but they do not, in my view, undermine the general reasons to favor private ordering, any more than the doctrines of duress or unconscionability undermine all of contract law. There are a variety of legal mechanisms to change the results. The bargaining endowments can be changed, and *ex post* review can be permitted to prevent unjust enrichment brought about by conduct that is viewed as morally unacceptable.

Externalities — Third Party Effects

Third party effects provide the last set of reasons that justify limiting private ordering. A legal system that gives divorcing couples freedom to determine for themselves their post-dissolution rights and responsibilities may lead to settlements that reflect the spouses' interests. But negotiated agreements can also have important consequences for third parties, and affect social interests that are not adequately weighed in the private negotiations. The economists' idea of "externalities" — the notion that in some circumstances market prices that are affecting the behaviour of buyers and sellers will not adequately reflect the full range of social costs — has application here. In negotiating divorce settlements, the spouses may make decisions that have consequences for third parties, which, if taken into account, would suggest that some other settlement might be more socially desirable.

A divorce settlement may affect any number of interests not taken into account in the spouses negotiations. The state's fiscal interests can be affected, for example. The economic terms of the bargain between the two spouses may substantially affect the odds that a custodial parent will later require public transfer payments. The most important third party effects concern the children, although there can be externalities with respect to other family members as well. At a conceptual level, it is easy to see how a negotiated settlement may reflect parental preferences but not the child's desires or needs. From the perspective of spouses who are negotiating their own settlements, marital property, alimony, and child support issues are all basically problems of money, and the distinctions among them become very blurred. Each can be translated into present dollar values. Moreover, custodial arrangements can often be divided in a wide variety of ways. From a bargaining perspective, the money and custody issues are inextricably linked together. Negotiated settlements will certainly reflect parental preferences with regard to these money and custody issues. These preferences, of course, will not generally be determined solely by self-interested judgments. One hopes that parental preferences reflect a desire for their children's happiness and well-being, quite apart from any parental advantage. Nevertheless, it is also certainly possible that some parents may engage in divorce bargaining on the basis of preferences that narrowly reflect their selfish interests, and ignore the children's needs. A father may threaten a custody fight over the child, not because he wants custody, but because he wants to push his wife into accepting less support, even though this will have a detrimental effect on the child. A custodial parent, eager to escape an unhappy marriage, may offer to settle for a small amount in order to sever relations soon. A custodial parent may negotiate to largely eliminate the child's contact with the other parent, not because of the child's wants or needs, but because he despises his *ex*-spouse and wants to have nothing more to do with her.

Concerns about the effects of the divorce on the children underlie many of the formal limitations on private ordering — e.g., the requirement of court review of private agreements relating to custody and child support; the legal rules prohibiting parents from making non-modifiable and binding agreements concerning these elements. In addition, the potential conflict of interest between divorcing parents, on the one hand, and the children, on the other, have led many to advocate the appointment of counsel for children, so that the children's interests can be directly represented in the divorce proceedings. ...

I believe divorcing parents should be given considerable freedom to decide custody matters — subject only to the same minimum standards for protecting the child from neglect and abuse that the state imposes on *all* families. The actual determination of what is in fact in a child's best interests is ordinarily quite indeterminate. It requires predictions beyond the capacity of the behavioural sciences and involves imposition of values about which there is little consensus in our society. It is for this reason that I conclude that the basic question is who gets to decide on behalf of the child.

A negotiated resolution is desirable from the child's perspective for several reasons. First, a child's social and psychological relationships with both parents ordinarily continue after the divorce. A process that leads to agreement between the parents is preferable to one that necessarily has a winner and a loser. A child's future relationship with each of his parents is better ensured and his existing relationship less damaged by a negotiated settlement than by one imposed by a court after an adversary proceeding. Notions of child protection hardly justify general judicial suspicion of parental agreements; the state's interest in the child's well-being in fact implies a concomitant interest in facilitating parental agreement.

Second, the parents will know more about the child than will the judge, since they have better access to information about the child's circumstances and desires. Indeed, a custody decision privately negotiated by those who will be responsible for care after the divorce seems much more likely than a judicial decision to match the parents' capacities and desires with the child's needs.

If parents have the authority to decide custodial arrangements, there is no doubt that parents may make mistakes. But so may judges. More fundamentally, given the epistemological problems inherent in knowing what is best for a child, there is reason to doubt our capacity to know whether any given decision is a mistake. Therefore, the possibility that negotiated agreements may not be optimal for the child can hardly be a sufficient argument against a preference for private ordering. Moreover, because parents, not state officials, are primarily responsible for the day-to-day child-rearing decisions both before and after divorce, parents, not judges, should have primary authority to agree on custodial arrangements. This means that courts should not second-guess parental agreements unless judicial intervention is required by the narrow child-protection standard implicit in neglect laws. This is not to suggest that the state does not have an important responsibility to inform parents concerning the child's needs during and after the divorce; nor does it mean that the state does not have an important interest in facilitating parental agreement. Nevertheless, the law in action, which acknowledges substantial parental power, seems preferable to existing doctrine, which imposes substantial restrictions on the parents' power to decide for themselves. ...

NOTES AND QUESTIONS

1. The current interest in mediation of family disputes reflects a recognition that a primary function of family law is to provide a framework within which the couples themselves determine the rights and responsibilities arising out of their relationships. Note s. 9(2) of the *Divorce Act*; s. 3 of the *FLA*; and s. 31 of the *Children's Law Reform Act*. Regarding mediation generally, see Chapter 1, *INTRODUCTION*.

2. As Professor Mnookin observes, the preference for private ordering is based, in part, on the liberal ideals of individual autonomy and freedom of choice. See also Trebilcock and Keshvani, "The Role of Private Ordering in Family Law" (1991), 47 U.T.L.J. 533.

The premise that negotiations leading to domestic contracts involve two rational, self-interested individuals has been vigorously challenged. In "A Matter of Difference: Domestic Contracts and Gender Equality" (1990), 28 O.H.L.J. 303, Professor Cossman argues that the liberal model of contract is based on a male sense of self which is not shared by many females whose approach to negotiation may well be more altruistic. Also, she points out (at 318) that the private choice approach ignores the unequal bargaining positions of husbands and wives on marriage breakdown. Professor Neave asserts in "Resolving the Dilemma of Difference: A Critique of 'The Role of Private Ordering in Family Law'" (1994), 44 U.T.L.J. 97 at 99:

> [The] preference for private ordering takes insufficient account of the fact that men and women who are negotiating pre-martial and separation agreements are differently situated. Far from enhancing women's individuality and autonomy, such agreements may simply privatize unequal outcomes of divorce for men and women and exacerbate gender inequality.

The remedy suggested by many of these critics is a more liberal application in the family law context of the contract law doctrine of unconscionable bargain. This doctrine is examined in the last section of this chapter.

3. Craig Martin uses negotiation theory to argue in "Unequal Shadows: Negotiation Theory and Spousal Support Under Canadian Divorce Law" (1998), 56 U.T. Fac. L. Rev. 135 that the legal framework governing spousal support systematically disadvantages the spousal support claimant in negotiations. The claimant is likely to be less loss-averse, less concession-averse and more risk-averse relative to the respondent. These characteristics by themselves are disadvantages in negotiations. With the advent of the Child Support Guidelines and the Spousal Support Advisory Guidelines, however, a measure of certainty has been inserted into negotiations regarding support. Claimants now have a better idea of what might be ordered if the matter proceeds to litigation and, therefore, can maintain a stronger position in negotiations. See O'Hanlon and Saunders, "Can Lessons from Game Theory be Applied to Family Law Negotiations?" (2007), 26 C.F.L.Q. 1.

2. Types of Domestic Contracts

Section 51 of the *FLA* defines "marriage contract", "cohabitation agreement" and "separation agreement", and specifies that each is a domestic contract. Why is it necessary to distinguish between these contracts?

Marriage Contracts: A marriage contract may be made by two persons who are married to each other or who intend to marry: s. 52(1). Can you think of situations where it may be especially appropriate for a couple to enter into a pre-nuptial agreement? See Wolfson, "Love Ain't Easier the Second Time Around: Family Law Concerns of the Remarrying Client" (1998-99), 16 C.F.L.Q. 239. Why may a married couple want to make a marriage contract while cohabiting? A married couple who have separated may wish to enter into a contract as a precondition to the resumption of cohabitation. Would such a "reconciliation agreement" be a marriage contract or a separation agreement? If it is a marriage contract, what matters can they not deal with under the *FLA*?

In "Resolving the Dilemma of Difference: A Critique of 'The Role of Private Ordering in Family Law'" (1994), 44 U.T.L.J. 97, Professor Neave argues (at 120) that statutes such as the *FLA* inappropriately allow marriage contracts to override statutory rules dealing with the rights and obligations of spouses:

> Pre-nuptial agreements are negotiated at a time when couples are more likely to have unrealistic expectations of each other, may be reluctant to consider the possibility of future separation, and may have considerable difficulty in predicting the changes likely to occur in the future patterns of their lives. At this stage of their relationship couples may treat procedural safeguards simply as formalities to be overcome.

> ... Nor does independent legal advice or a cooling-off period address the difficulty of providing for contingencies which may not occur until many years later. Thus parties should be unable to contract out of family law rules by relying on pre-nuptial or nuptial agreements.

Do you agree?

In *Kaddoura v. Hammoud* (1998), 44 R.F.L. (4th) 228 (Ont. Gen. Div.), a couple, wishing to marry in accordance with the Muslim tradition, agreed orally before the marriage (an oral agreement being the Muslim tradition) that the husband would pay to the wife "Mahr", a gift or contribution for her exclusive property, totalling $35,000. The Muslim marriage certificate referred specifically to the payment of $5,000 immediately and $30,000 on demand by the wife, on divorce, or on the husband's death. When the marriage ended and a dispute over the payment of "Mahr" arose, the court found that the Mahr did not create a contract, and characterized the dispute as a non-justiciable religious matter to be resolved according to religious doctrine and principle. Could the court have taken this approach if the agreement had satisfied the formalities set out in the *FLA* for domestic contracts? The reasoning in the case is particularly suspect in light of *Marcovitz v. Bruker* (2007), 288 D.L.R. (4th) 257, 46 R.F.L. (6th) 1 (S.C.C.) where the majority held that a clause in a divorce settlement stipulating that the spouses would appear before the rabbinical authorities to obtain a traditional Jewish divorce or *ghet* was enforceable. The court upheld an award of damages to the wife.

In *Khan v. Khan* (2005), 15 R.F.L. (6th) 308 (Ont. C.J.), a written contract providing for a Mahr met the formal requirements of the *FLA*, but was set aside on the grounds set out in s. 56(4). The case of *Nasin v. Nasin* (2008), [2008] A.J. No. 390, 53 R.F.L. (6th) 446, 2008 CarswellAlta 468 (Alta. Q.B.) also involved the enforceability of a Mahr. The husband promised, orally, at the wedding ceremony, to pay $10,000 upon breakdown of the marriage. The court held that there was a valid contract, being an exchange of promises for consideration, but that it was not enforceable because it did not meet the formal requirements under Alberta's *Matrimonial Property Act* because it was not in writing.

Cohabitation Agreements: Section 53 of the *FLA* deals with cohabitation agreements. Why may a couple want to make a cohabitation agreement? What matter can a couple deal with in a cohabitation agreement that cannot be governed by a marriage contract? What happens to a cohabitation agreement if the couple subsequently gets married?

Separation Agreements: Section 54 specifies that two persons who cohabited and are living separate and apart can enter into a separation agreement. Why may two people who cohabited find such an agreement useful? Why may a husband and wife who already have a comprehensive marriage contract that makes provision for the rights and obligations of each party on separation nevertheless need a separation agreement? Consider ss. 52 and 54 of the *FLA*.

The statutory definitions of "marriage contract" and "separation agreement", when interpreted literally, suggest that married couples who wish to enter into agreements in anticipation of imminent separation can only make a marriage contract. What practical difficulties could this cause for separated couples? Is there any way to avoid this result?

3. Capacity and Formal Requirements

(1) Capacity

By virtue of s. 55(2) of the *FLA*, a minor has capacity to enter into a domestic contract subject to the approval of the court. Such approval may be given before or after the minor enters into the contract. Note also subsections (3) and (4) dealing with mentally incapable persons.

(2) Formal Requirements

WALDICK v. WALDICK

(2002), 22 R.F.L. (5th) 448, 2002 CarswellOnt 87 (Ont. S.C.J.)

HARRIS J.:

The 1976 Agreement

16 In 1976, after two years of marriage, the couple purchased their matrimonial home. Prior to the marriage the wife had received an inheritance of Proctor & Gamble shares valued at $14,000.00, which she cashed in to facilitate the home purchase.

17 At the time the husband signed an agreement (Ex. #15) which provided:

> In consideration of the sum of $14,000.00 being advanced by the [wife] for the [purchase of the house], the [husband] agrees that, in the event of the sale of the premises, the wife shall have a claim of $14,000.00 in priority to any claim by the husband, and that such sum from such sale shall be paid to the wife prior to any distribution of the proceeds of such sale.

18 The wife asserts a claim to those funds now on the basis that it is a contract and that it is binding on the husband in these proceedings. She claims this would result in a $14,000.00 benefit to her, which should come directly out of the proceeds of sale of the matrimonial home.

19 Alternatively the wife claims that the $14,000.00 is a deduction from her net family property calculations which would result in a $7,000.00 benefit to her after equalization.

Problems with Formal Validity

20 The "*agreement*" entered as Exhibit #15 in this case was signed only by the husband and it was witnessed by a lawyer. There was no provision for the wife's signature.

21 ... The "*contract*" in this case was not signed by the wife and on that ground would not be enforceable as a "*domestic contract*" [by virtue of s. 55(1) of the *FLA*.]

22 Having said that, the court did, in *Campbell v. Campbell* (1985), 47 R.F.L. (2d) 392 (Ont. H.C.), stretch that meaning. In that case both the husband and the wife's lawyer signed under the word "*accepted*" and it was not disputed that the parties had agreed to the terms in the agreement. The husband in that case attempted to vitiate the agreement on the grounds that there was no third party witness.

23 The court held that even though there was no third party witness, the section only required that the agreement be witnessed. The court concluded that the lawyer had witnessed the agreement and therefore the agreement was valid.

24 The facts in *Campbell* are similar but distinguishable in a material aspect to this case. In this case, the lawyer only witnessed the husband's signature but did not sign it on the wife's behalf. Nor did the wife sign it.

25 As such the wife has not signed the agreement and accordingly it does not meet the formal validity requirements of s. 55(1). ...

[The court also noted that the agreement did not "contain anything suggesting the parties turned their minds to the notion that the $14,000.00, or any interest in the matrimonial home would be exempt from any statutory property division regime". Accordingly, the agreement had no effect. However, the wife received credit for the value of the shares at marriage in the calculation of her net family property.]

NOTES AND QUESTIONS

1. The imposition of formal requirements for domestic contracts is a legislative recognition of the special nature of such contracts. By requiring that the contracts be in writing, the legislation seeks to avoid disputes over exactly what was settled by oral negotiation. See also s. 5(6)(g) and s. 24(3)(d) of the *FLA*. The formal requirements also serve to alert the parties to the fact that they are engaged in a serious matter that can have significant legal consequences. They are, therefore, less likely to enter the contract lightly. This "warning function" was explicitly noted by Mendes da Costa U.F.C.J. in *Grant-Hose v. Grant-Hose* (1991), 32 R.F.L. (3d) 26 at 45 (Ont. U.F.C.). Regarding the functions generally served by formal requirements relating to domestic contracts, see Law Reform Commission of British Columbia, *Report on Spousal Agreements* (Victoria: Queen's Printer, 1986) at 31-32.

2. The courts have held that settlements between counsel in pending litigation need not comply with s. 55(1) of the *FLA*. See *Geropoulos v. Geropoulos* (1982), 26 R.F.L. (2d) 225 (Ont. C.A.). However, there must be pending litigation at the time of the agreement. See *Tanaszczuk v. Tanaszczuk* (1988), 15 R.F.L. (3d) 441 (Ont. U.F.C.); *Davis v. Gregory* (1990), 29 R.F.L. (3d) 62 (Ont. Gen. Div.); *Tucker v. Tucker* (1993), 48 R.F.L. (3d) 5 (Nfld. C.A.); and *Hilton Estate v. Thompson* (2007), 2007 CarswellOnt 9242 (S.C.J.). The outcome in these cases is consistent with the general rule in civil litigation that counsel can bind their clients to settlements in correspondence or other writing. The *Ontario Family Law Rules* have attempted to address the potential for clients not understanding what their solicitors are offering. Rule 18 requires that offers to settle must be signed by both the parties and their solicitors.

3. Where a settlement is intended to be enforceable as a domestic contract and not simply the basis for consensual court orders in pending or ongoing litigation, the formalities prescribed by s. 55(1) should be met.

4. In *Campbell v. Campbell* (1985), 47 R.F.L. (2d) 392 (Ont. H.C.), Steele J. suggested that the principle in *Geropoulos* should apply whenever pending litigation is settled, whether or not the parties have legal representation. However, Langdon J. indicated in *Davis v. Gregory* (1990), 29 R.F.L. (3d) 62 at 67 (Ont. Gen. Div.) that the bar to enforcement imposed by s. 55(1) can only be ignored "in cases of settlement of pending litigation by counsel or ratified following the advice of counsel".

5. As noted in *Waldick*, Justice Steele also held in the *Campbell* case that the witnessing requirement in s. 5(1) of the *FLA* was met even though the parties' signature was not expressly witnessed. The *Campbell* case illustrates the general desire of the courts to hold parties to agreements and thus promote negotiated settlements. A similar approach is evident in *Hyldtoft v. Hyldtoft* (1991), 33 R.F.L. (3d) 99 (Ont. Gen. Div.). In that case, the wife, Mrs. Wilcox, signed the document some time before the husband signed it. The witness, Mr. McCormick, watched the husband sign and simply assumed that the wife had also signed it while he was in the room. Justice Haines concluded (at 107):

> Mrs. Wilcox raised no objection to the agreement in Mr. McCormick's presence, nor did she choose to absent herself from the room. In my view, she accepted Mr. McCormick as the witness for both signatures, thereby affirming her earlier execution of that document. I am, accordingly, satisfied that the formalities required by s. 55(1) of the *Family Law Act, 1986* were met.

See also *Lecot v. Lecot* (1995), 19 R.F.L. (4th) 14 (Ont. Gen. Div.) where the court held (at 23) that a "home-made" separation agreement that the parties signed in each other's presence without legal advice and without witnesses to their signatures was enforceable. However, in *Sagl v. Sagl* (1997), 31 R.F.L. (4th) 405 (Ont. Gen. Div.), the court held (at 418) that the cohabitation agreement "falls on a technicality as the law is clear that this witness [of the signatures] is to be someone other than the party". See also *Colafranceschi v. Colafranceschi* (2001), 15 R.F.L. (5th) 294 (Ont. S.C.J.), where Justice Heeney came to a similar conclusion.

6. It should be noted that s. 55(1) of the *FLA* specifies that a domestic contract that fails to comply with the formal requirements is "unenforceable". An unenforceable contract is a valid contract, unless set aside for some reason, and may have legal and practical effect. For example, the case law dealing with an analogous provision in the *Statute of Frauds* suggests that a court will not unwind a transaction simply because it was completed pursuant to an unenforceable contract. See, generally, Fridman, *The Law of Contract in Canada*, 3rd ed. (Toronto: Carswell, 1994) at 224–227. Unenforceable contracts may also influence the court's exercise of discretion in determining support or property applications. For example, such contracts, if written, might be considered under s. 24(3)(d) and s. 5(6)(g) of the *FLA*. See, generally, Hovius and Youdan, *The Law of Family Property* (Toronto: Carswell, 1991) at 650–652. See also *Corbeil v. Bebris* (1993), 105 D.L.R. (4th) 759 (Alta. C.A.) and *Hill v. Ilnicki* (2000), 13 R.F.L. (5th) 73 (Alta Q.B.); affirmed (2002), 31 R.F.L. (5th) 335 (Alta. C.A.); leave to appeal refused (2003), 317 N.R. 398 (note) (S.C.C.). In *Goudie v. Stapleford* (2004), 5 R.F.L. (6th) 55 (Ont. S.C.J.), Justice Pardu suggested, without deciding, (at para. 15) that an unwitnessed separation agreement that is unenforceable under the *FLA* might be given some weight in determining spousal support under the *Divorce Act*.

Any sections in the *FLA* providing for direct enforcement of a domestic contract, such as s. 35, are inapplicable to contracts that are unenforceable by virtue of s. 55(1). Such a contract should also not override the statutory provisions dealing with property and support. See *Davis v. Gregory* (1990), 29 R.F.L. (3d) 62 (Ont. Gen. Div.) and *Colafranceschi v. Colafranceschi* (2001), 15 R.F.L. (5th) 294 (Ont. S.C.J.) where the courts concluded that unenforceable domestic contracts did not bar applications for equalization of net family properties under the *FLA*.

7. Section 58 of the *FLA* specifies that the manner and formalities of making a domestic contract and its essential validity and effect are governed by the proper law of the contract. However, a contract, the proper law of which is a jurisdiction other than Ontario, is also valid and enforceable if entered into in accordance with Ontario's internal law. A contract that is valid according to its proper foreign law is nonetheless subject to ss. 33(4) and 56 of the Act: s. 58(b).

8. For further reading, see Thompson, "When is a Family Law Contract *Not* Invalid, Unenforceable, Overridden or Varied" (2001-2002), 19 C.F.L.Q. 399.

4. Effect of a Domestic Contract

(1) Property

Section 2(10) of the *FLA* stipulates that a domestic contract dealing with a matter that is also dealt with in the Act prevails unless the Act provides otherwise. This is the general rule that applies to all matters dealt with in the *FLA*.

There are no provisions limiting the ability of the spouses to contract out of Part I of the Act. Accordingly, spouses can preclude the equalization of net family properties under Part I of the Act by entering into a valid and enforceable domestic contract that deals comprehensively with their property rights. Appropriate release clauses can be used to indicate clearly that the contract is intended to prevail over the statutory right to equalization of net family properties. Alternatively, the contract can simply modify the general rule that net family properties are to be equalized on the happening of the triggering events listed in s. 5 of the *FLA*. For example, a husband and wife can agree in a marriage contract that the wife will be entitled to 60 per cent of the net family properties on separation. The parties can also stipulate that a specified property is not to be included in a spouse's net family property. In that event, Part I of the *FLA* would still apply but the value of this property would not form part of the spouse's net family property. Finally, s. 5(5) allows the spouses to stipulate in a domestic contract that they are entitled to apply to the court under s. 7 for a determination of any matter respecting their entitlement under s. 5 even though the net family properties have already been equalized pursuant to s. 5(3).

Any domestic contract entered into after the *FLA* came into force, at least where the parties have legal advice, will likely specifically address the relationship between the contract and Part I of the Act. Problems may arise, however, in relation to contracts that fail to take into account Part I of the Act specifically and clearly. Contracts validly made before the *FLA* came into effect and home-made agreements often fall into this category. By virtue of s. 60(1), contracts validly made before the Act came into effect are deemed to be domestic contracts for the purposes of the Act. Because the parties to most pre-existing contracts did not direct their minds to the rights later granted by the *FLA*, difficult issues of contractual interpretation may arise.

NURMI v. NURMI

(1988), 16 R.F.L. (3d) 201, 1988 CarswellOnt 283 (Ont. U.F.C.)

WALLACE U.F.C.J.: — ... The final issue in this matter requires a finding of whether there was an agreement between the parties that ought to interfere with the equalization of their net family properties.

Both parties testified that they discussed an agreement before marriage, although the applicant pleads some lack of understanding of that agreement and a lack of specificity; a document was signed, however, by the parties eleven days after marriage. ...

Counsel for the applicant submits that, because of the somewhat unusual form of the document executed by the parties and marked Ex. 6, it does not meet the definition of a domestic contract. I include it here in its entirety:

Jan. 11 1983

In the case of legal separation or divorse [sic], I *Pauline Nurmi (Wife of Paul Nurmi)* being of sound mind, do hereby release any claim I may have or hereafter have thereto to the said premises known as 49 Kingslea Dr. composed of the northerly four feet of lot # 340 and the whole of lot # 341 according to the plan of survey known as Huntington Park plan # 964 Hamilton Ont. Solely owned by Paul Nurmi. I also release all claims to Mr. Nurmi's R.R.S.P. and Likewise to $15,000.00 investment capital.

In witness and in the presence of

Nicki Klausmann	....
Herman Klausmann	....
J. Nurmi	....

I have not been referred to any contract case law which requires particular placement of signatures or form of wording in order to validate a contract and I find that Ex. 6 in its present form constitutes a domestic contract, although obviously its form is not a preferred one.

[Wallace U.F.C.J. rejected the argument that the applicant wife received no consideration because "the promise of marriage was consideration for the oral agreement; the oral agreement was subsequently confirmed in a written document."]

The applicant further submits that, even if the agreement is valid, it is unenforceable because of s. 52(2) ...

He refers the court to the case of *Sinnett v. Sinnett* (1980), 15 R.F.L. (2d) 115 (Ont. Co. Ct.), and submits that case stands for the proposition that the court cannot distinguish between possessory and title issues respecting the matrimonial home. With respect I must disagree; Pt. II of the *Family Law Act* clearly and specifically limits a spouse's powers respecting alienation and possession of a matrimonial home; that Part does not address a spouse's right to enter into a contract respecting ownership or degree of ownership of a matrimonial home. Section 52(2) renders a contract unenforceable only to the extent of Pt. II of the Act.

In that the contract between these parties did not address possession or alienation, the applicant's submissions on this point must fail.

The applicant goes on to claim that, although the applicant released her interest in specific assets, namely, the matrimonial home and the respondent's R.R.S.P.s, he submits that she released her interest in the property as it was valued at that time but not at its present value (which is significantly increased). Exhibit 6 clearly states that the applicant releases "any claim I may have or hereafter have" and so I must find that the present day value of the matrimonial home and the respondent's R.R.S.P.s are excluded from any net family property calculation; in addition, $15,000 of property owned on the date of marriage by the respondent is also excluded in accordance with the terms of the agreement. ...

In computing, then, the equalization of net family property of the parties, the property referred to in Ex. 6 will be "excluded property" within the meaning of s. 4(2)6 of the *Family Law Act* and will include the following:

(a) The present day value of the matrimonial home;

(b) The present day value of the respondent's R.R.S.P.; and

(c) $15,000, the respondent's pre-marriage holdings.

BOSCH v. BOSCH

(1991), 36 R.F.L. (3d) 302, 1991 CarswellOnt 336 (Ont. C.A.)

[The parties were married in The Netherlands in 1976. At that time the husband, who had lived in Ontario for some time, was the owner of a house located on a six-acre lot near Woodstock. Shortly before the marriage, at the husband's request, the parties entered into a marriage contract in The Netherlands in the presence of a notary. The wife acknowledged that the purpose of the contract was to ensure that the house remained the husband's. She understood that "it was to remain his exclusive property, and that she could have nothing to do with that property at any time". Soon after the marriage the wife joined her husband and they lived in the house until separation. The issue on appeal was whether the trial judge erred in including the value of the matrimonial home in the calculation of the husband's net family property. This was the main asset held by either spouse on separation.

The key clause in the contract provided:

PART A PROPERTY

1. That all property, money, and rights of every nature and kind held by the parties hereto, whether held at the time of the marriage or obtained afterwards, shall remain the property of the respective parties but each shall contribute equally to the upkeep and maintenance of the household (and children). If both parties contribute to the purchase of any property for purpose of the household it shall be deemed to be held jointly in equal shares, and not in proportion to their respective contributions.]

ARBOUR J.A. (CARTHY J.A. concurring): — ... [T]he question here is whether the parties have, by their marriage contract, "[dealt] with the matter that is also dealt with in this Act" in a manner such as to exclude the matrimonial home, which was owned by the husband before the marriage, from the calculation of his net family property for the purpose of equalization. They have not done so explicitly in the sense that they have not inserted a clause into their marriage contract to deal with their respective entitlement to equalization or to deal with the exclusion of some property from the calculation of their respective net family properties. This, of course, is hardly surprising since the *Family Law Act, 1986* had not been enacted at the time of the contract.

On the other hand, every effort must be made to give effect to the intention of the parties expressed in a domestic contract, and since a domestic contract validly made before the coming into force of the Act is deemed by s. 60 to have been made pursuant to the Act, its intent should not be defeated simply because its language did not accurately anticipate the Act.

... Under the *Family Law Act, 1986*, neither ownership nor any interest in the property of the title-holding spouse need be interfered with, as it is only the *value* of assets that is equalized. Therefore, provisions in a marriage contract dealing with ownership of property during marriage or even after its dissolution may not be sufficient to prevail over the equalization provisions of the *Family Law Act, 1986*. For instance, a provision which merely said that a particular spouse would continue to own the car after separation, while the other would continue to own the boat, does not address, and may not be adequate to displace, the provisions of the Act which contemplated a valuation of all things owned by each spouse on valuation date in order to equalize, by the payment of money, their economic posture as they come out of the marriage.

The entitlement of spouses in Ontario to equalization under the *Family Law Act, 1986* is a new substantive right, quite independent from any right of ownership, which can be ousted by a domestic contract, even one that pre-existed the Act. However, in order for a pre-existing contract to have that effect, it must deal, explicitly or by necessary implication, with "a matter" akin to the equalization provisions of the Act. An agreement as to ownership of property, without more, is insufficient. For the marriage contract to prevail over the equalization provisions of the Act, the contract must contain provisions which address, in their intent if not in their explicit language, the relative economic position of the parties upon the dissolution of the marriage, through the distribution of assets between them on the basis of ownership or otherwise. This can be done either through an agreement that a given property be excluded from a spouse's net family property, under s. 4(2)6 of the Act, or through an agreement in a domestic contract which deals with equalization-type rights so as to bring s. 2(10) into effect. ...

Ultimately, whether a domestic contract prevails over the equalization provisions of the *Family Law Act, 1986* will depend, in each individual case, on whether the parties turned their minds to the division of their assets, or to some other form of economic redress, upon the dissolution of their marriage. ...

The marriage contract of the parties here is silent not only as to their respective entitlements upon the dissolution of the marriage but also as to their matrimonial home. Parties are not precluded from agreeing to exempt the value of the matrimonial home from the equalization process or from agreeing that the spouse who owned the house prior to the marriage will deduct its pre-marital value in the equalization process. The marriage contract in this case cannot, in my view, be taken as doing either.

I am not persuaded by the argument that this marriage contract must be interpreted, as suggested by the husband, to avoid a redundancy. It does not follow, in my view, that since the law of Ontario in 1976, when the contract was entered into, provided for separation of property during marriage, the parties must have intended to do something more than recognize that fact in their marriage contract. The evidence clearly indicates that the parties entered into this marriage contract to ensure that the house owned by the husband prior to the marriage would continue to be owned by him afterwards. Beyond that, their intention in entering that contract is quite speculative. ... In any event, I find nothing in either the terms of the contract, or in the expressed or implied intention of the parties, that leads me to conclude that they intended to deprive the wife of any entitlement, present or future, to share in the financial worth of her husband, reflected in part by his ownership of the house that became the matrimonial home. Even if it could be construed as addressing the question of ownership of property after dissolution of the marriage, in my view, the marriage contract here would still fail to prevail over the equalization provisions of the *Family Law Act, 1986*, which deal with distribution of wealth between former marriage partners, on a basis other than in accordance with ownership.

For these reasons, I have concluded that the trial judge was correct in attributing the value of the matrimonial home to the husband in calculating his net family property. ...

FINLAYSON J.A. (dissenting): — ... The agreement is unlimited in duration. While it makes no provision for death, separation, or the breakup of the marriage, I can think of no reason why it should not be construed as establishing a separation of property for all purposes. The parties were separate as to property before the marriage, and this status did not change as a result of the marriage. Unlike other jurisdictions, there is no community of property arising from marriage in Ontario. The husband had legal title to the matrimonial home at the time of the marriage, and title remains with him to this date. The agreement, therefore, has no legal efficacy during the marriage because the parties were perfectly free, after the marriage, to make any arrangements between themselves as to how their money and property were to be utilized with or without a formal contract. Accordingly, what legal purpose could there be to such a document if it did not contemplate a breakup of the marriage from any cause? Clearly the parties, the husband in particular, intended that the property that each brought into the marriage was to remain the separate property of that spouse regardless of what might later transpire. ...

Accordingly, I am of the opinion that the domestic contract in question is sufficient to exclude the house and 6 acres of land owned by the husband from the husband's net family property by reason of s. 4(2)6 of the F.L.A.

NOTES AND QUESTIONS

1. As noted in *Bosch*, the *FLA* does not create an interest for either spouse in the property of the other. Rather, it creates the potential for an equalization debt owed by one spouse to the other. Is *Nurmi*, above, rightly decided? The contract made by the parties in *Nurmi* stated that the wife released claims to certain properties held by the husband. Would she have had a claim to them in any event? Is an application for equalization of net family properties a claim to a property interest? See also *Calvert (Litigation Guardian of) v. Calvert* (1998), 37 O.R. (2d) 221, 36 R.F.L. (4th) 169 (C.A.); leave to appeal refused (1998), 228 N.R. 98 (note) (S.C.C.).

2. Another difficult problem of interpretation that can be avoided by clear drafting concerns the effect of resumption of cohabitation on the rights and obligations created by a separation agreement. Courts often state that, as a general rule, the provisions of a separation agreement cease to have operative effect if the parties resume cohabitation. In each case, however, this issue must be determined in accordance with the intention of the parties. Where property has been transferred pursuant to the agreement, the court may be willing to infer that the parties intended an absolute and permanent transfer of ownership: see *Bebenek v. Bebenek* (1979), 11 R.F.L. (2d) 137 (Ont. C.A.). In some circumstances, such a transfer, coupled with a clause whereby the transferor releases any interest in the property, may preclude the inclusion of the value of the property in the transferee's net family property when the couple subsequently separates again: see *Avery v. Avery* (1991), 33 R.F.L. (3d) 288 (Ont. Gen. Div.). For other appellate court cases dealing with the effect of reconciliation, see *Bailey v. Bailey* (1982), 26 R.F.L. (2d) 209 (Ont. C.A.); *Smart v. Wiewior* (1990), 28 R.F.L. (3d) 225 (B.C. C.A.); *Hulleman v. Hulleman* (1999), 2 R.F.L. (5th) 406 (Alta. C.A.); *A. (E.S.J.) v. A. (J.D.)* (2003), 44 R.F.L. (5th) 237 (B.C. C.A.); and *Sydor v. Sydor* (2003), 44 R.F.L. (5th) 445 (Ont. C.A.).

In his annotation to the *A. (E.S.J.)* case in the RFLs, Professor McLeod suggests (at 238-239):

> Although courts commonly state that in the absence of a provision to the contrary in the agreement, reconciliation terminates a separation agreement, this is probably an over-statement. The better rule is that in the absence of an indication to the contrary in an agreement, any executory promises become inoperative, but executed transactions will not be rescinded.

3. Sections 52 and 53 of the *FLA* stipulate that the parties to a marriage contract or a cohabitation agreement may deal with ownership of property or division of property upon the death of one of the parties. While s. 54 does

not expressly provide that a separation agreement may cover the rights and obligations of the parties on death, such terms have also been given effect. See, for example, *Cairns v. Cairns* (1990), 25 R.F.L. (3d) 373 (Ont. H.C.) where it was held that the wife was barred from claiming an equalization of net family properties on the death of her husband. However, the wife was allowed to claim her preferential share in the husband's estate under the *Succession Law Reform Act*. Courts have generally required clear and cogent language to bar claims to a preferential share on an intestacy. See also *Re Saylor* (1983), 36 R.F.L. (2d) 288 (Ont. H.C.); *Cairns v. Cairns*, above; and *Brant v. Brant* (1997), 16 E.T.R. (2d) 134 (Ont. Gen. Div.). However, in *Phillips-Renwick v. Renwick Estate* (2003), 41 R.F.L. (5th) 337 (Ont. S.C.J.), Justice Mackinnon held that the release clause in a marriage contract did preclude the wife from claiming a preferential share in her husband's estate.

4. In a separation agreement, the spouses can agree that one of them has the exclusive right to possess the matrimonial home. By virtue of s. 2(10) of the *FLA*, such an agreement ousts the court's jurisdiction to make an exclusive possession order under Part II. Where the owning spouse is to have exclusive possession pursuant to a separation agreement, the other spouse can release all rights under Part II. The owner can then encumber or dispose of any interest in the home without the consent of the other spouse: s. 21(1)(b).

By contrast, s. 52(2) of the *FLA* states that a provision in a marriage contract purporting to limit a spouse's rights under Part II is unenforceable. Thus, a court has the power to make an order for exclusive possession in favour of either spouse notwithstanding any provision in a marriage contract. However, the contract, if written, is a factor that the court must consider: s. 24(3)(d).

5. Under ss. 55.1 and 55.2 of the *Canada Pension Plan*, R.S.C. 1985, c. C-8, couples cannot contract out of the statutory CPP credit splitting on separation or divorce unless this is expressly permitted under the provincial law that governs the agreement. While some provinces (e.g. British Columbia, Quebec and Saskatchewan) have specifically authorized the waiver of rights to a division of pensionable earnings under the Plan, other provinces, including Manitoba and Ontario, have not. See *Wiemer v. Canada (Minister of Employment & Immigration)* (1998), 42 R.F.L. (4th) 242 (Fed. C.A.) where a division occurred despite a Manitoba separation agreement intended to definitively settle all aspects of the couple's relationship.

6. Because the parties to a foreign domestic contract are unlikely to have contemplated Part I of the *FLA* when the contract was executed, difficult problems may arise in determining the extent to which they preclude equalization of net family properties. See *Sinnett v. Sinnett* (1980), 15 R.F.L. (2d) 115 (Ont. Co. Ct); *Kerr v. Kerr* (1981), 32 O.R. (2d) 146 (H.C.); affirmed (1983), 41 O.R. (2d) 704 (C.A.); *Roome v. Roome* (1984), 42 R.F.L. (2d) 337 (P.E.I. S.C.); and *Mittler v. Mittler* (1988), 17 R.F.L. (3d) 113 (Ont. H.C.). For an analysis of these cases, see Black, "Quebec Marriage Contracts in Common Law Courts: Room for Improvement" (1985), 45 R.F.L. (2d) 93.

Unlike Ontario, some provinces specifically empower courts to override the property provisions in a domestic contract in certain circumstances. See, e.g., *Matrimonial Property Act*, R.S.N.S. 1989, c. 275, s. 29 (if any term is "unconscionable, unduly harsh on one party or fraudulent"); *Family Property Act*, S.S. 1997, c. F-6.3, s. 24(2) (if the contract was unconscionable or grossly unfair at the time it was entered into); and *Marital Property Act*, S.N.B. 1980, c. M-1, s. 41 (if a spouse did not receive independent legal advice and application of the provision would be inequitable). The lowest threshold for judicial intervention appears in s. 65 of the *Family Relations Act*, R.S.B.C. 1996, c. 128. It permits a court to reapportion the division of property provided for in an agreement whenever the court considers the agreement "unfair". In 1996, the Law Reform Commission of British Columbia concluded in its *Report on Spousal Agreements* (Victoria: Queen's Printer, 1986) at 20:

> The law has proven to be uncertain. No person can predict the effect a separation agreement will have, nor what the courts will determine is an appropriate division of family property. The result has been an invitation to litigate.

Typically British Columbia courts readily overrode the property division in a contract until a majority of the Supreme Court of Canada suggested a different approach in *Hartshorne v.*

Hartshorne (2004), 47 R.F.L. (5th) 5 (S.C.C.). In that case, two lawyers, each of whom had been married before, began cohabiting in 1985. The man owned some valuable properties, while the woman had few assets and substantial debts. In June 1987, the woman stopped practising law and took maternity leave. She decided not to return to work after the birth of the child in July.

The man was adamant that he would not marry again without a marriage agreement that protected his property. In 1989, he consulted a lawyer who drafted a marriage contract. The woman's lawyer told her that the draft agreement was "grossly unfair" and that, in the event of a marriage breakdown, a court would redistribute the couple's property on a more equitable basis despite the agreement. Some minor changes were then made to the agreement and the couple signed it on March 11, 1989, the day they got married. The agreement specifically stated that the bride was signing it at the groom's insistence. Under the agreement, each party would remain "completely independent of the other as regard to their property". There was, however, a clause providing for the wife to acquire a three per cent interest in the family home for every year of cohabitation, up to a maximum of forty-nine per cent, and for a joint interest in household contents and any family car. Another clause, added at the wife's insistence, specifically stated that the agreement was not a bar to spousal or child support.

The couple's second child was born later in 1989. During the marriage, the wife did not work outside the home and was supported by the husband. The couple employed a nanny and a housekeeper and lived an affluent lifestyle. The husband's savings decreased from approximately $167,000 at marriage to about $25,000 in 1998 when the husband and wife separated. After the separation, the wife and children continued to live in the family home.

In divorce proceedings in 1999, the husband sought to rely on the marriage agreement to avoid the operation of the statutory property regime. Pursuant to the agreement, the wife was entitled to property valued at about $280,000 while the husband kept property worth about $1.2 million. The wife claimed that the couple's property should be divided without regard to the agreement because it was invalid or unenforceable according to the law of contract. In the alternative, she sought a reapportionment of property in accordance with s. 65 of the *Family Relations Act* (the "*FRA*"). While the *FRA* permitted spouses to enter into binding domestic contracts such as pre-nuptial agreements, s. 65(1) specified that, where a division of property under a marriage agreement was unfair having regard to a number of factors, a court could order that the property covered by the agreement be divided into shares fixed by the court. Section 65(2) provided that the court could then also order that any property not covered by the marriage agreement be vested in the non-owning spouse.

The trial judge concluded that the agreement was valid, finding that the wife had failed to establish that it was unconscionable or entered into under duress, coercion or undue influence. However, she held that the division of property was unfair in light of the duration of the relationship, the need of the wife to become economically independent, and the wife's indirect contribution to the husband's accumulation of property. She reapportioned the couple's property, giving the wife assets worth approximately $654,000 or about 46% of the total value of the family assets.

In 2002, the wife began work as an associate in a law firm at an annual salary of $52,000. The husband, who was earning about $267,000 a year, applied for a variation of the spousal support order. The application judge terminated spousal support as of the end of December 2002, but noted that the wife could bring a new application if the husband's appeal of the division of the couple's property succeeded.

The British Columbia Court of Appeal dismissed the husband's appeal, but the Supreme Court of Canada, Binnie, LeBel, and Deschamps JJ. dissenting in part, allowed his further appeal. The majority emphasized the importance of individual choice in entering a domestic contract and suggested that the courts should hesitate to conclude that a contractual division of property is unfair. A portion of Justice Bastarache's reasons follow:

HARTSHORNE v. HARTSHORNE

(2004), 47 R.F.L. (5th) 5 (S.C.C.)

I. Introduction

2 At issue in this appeal is whether a marriage agreement respecting the division of property, entered into after receiving independent legal advice, without duress, coercion or undue influence, can later be found to be unfair and set aside on the basis that it failed "to provide anything for the respondent's sacrifice in giving up her law practice and postponing her career development", notwithstanding that the parties' agreement preserved the right to spousal support. The parties in this appeal also raised the issues of whether an agreement entered into prior to or at the time of marriage should be subject to the same review on appeal as a separation agreement, and whether, where provisions for the division of property in a marriage agreement are found to be unfair at the time of distribution, the whole agreement should simply be ignored. ...

8 The primary policy objective guiding the courts' role in division of assets on marital breakdown in British Columbia is fairness; it is achieved by reviewing either the presumptive division provided for in the Act itself, or the parties' private agreement, in light of the factors set out in s. 65 of the *FRA*. To give effect to legislative intention, courts must encourage parties to enter into marriage agreements that are fair, and to respond to the changing circumstances of their marriage by reviewing and revising their own contracts for fairness when necessary.

9 The authorities generally agree that courts should respect private arrangements that spouses make for the division of their property on the breakdown of their relationship. This is particularly so where the agreement in question was negotiated with independent legal advice. The difficulty of course is in determining the proper approach to deciding, at the time of distribution, what is fair under the terms of s. 65 of the *FRA*. A domestic contract constituting a derogation from the statutory regime, it is obvious that its fairness cannot be determined simply on the basis of its consistency with the said regime. ... The appellant in these proceedings argues that the majority of the Court of Appeal effectively found the Agreement to be unfair on the basis that it derogated from the statutory regime. After reviewing the provisions of the *FRA* as well as the Agreement, it is my opinion that said Agreement operated fairly at the time of distribution. ...

25 The net effect was that the respondent received an interest in the family assets with a value of approximately $654,000, about 46 percent of the family assets valued at approximately $1,415,000. Under the Agreement, she would have received about 20 percent of the family assets with a value of about $280,000. ...

IV. Analysis

. . . . .

B. Marriage Agreements vs. Separation Agreements

38 Marital cases must reconcile respect for the parties' intent, on the one hand, and the assurance of an equitable result, on the other. The parties here adopted opposite views as to

the degree of deference to be afforded marriage agreements; the appellant submitted that more and the respondent submitted that less deference should be paid to marriage agreements than to separation agreements.

39 This Court has not established, and in my opinion should not establish, a "hard and fast" rule regarding the deference to be afforded to marriage agreements as compared to separation agreements. In some cases, marriage agreements ought to be accorded a greater degree of deference than separation agreements. Marriage agreements define the parties' expectations from the outset, usually before any rights are vested and before any entitlement arises. Often, perhaps most often, a desire to protect pre-acquired assets or an anticipated inheritance for children of a previous marriage will be the impetus for such an agreement. Separation agreements, by contrast, purport to deal with existing or vested rights and obligations, with the aggrieved party claiming he or she had given up something to which he or she was already entitled with an unfair result. In other cases, however, marriage agreements may be accorded less deference than separation agreements. The reason for this is that marriage agreements are anticipatory and may not fairly take into account the financial means, needs or other circumstances of the parties at the time of marriage breakdown. ...

C. Miglin v. Miglin and the Issue of Deference

40 In addressing the issue of deference, this Court may apply *Miglin v. Miglin*, [2003] 1 S.C.R. 303 (S.C.C.), for its general legal proposition that some weight should be given to marriage agreements. *Miglin*, raised the question of the proper weight to be given to a separation agreement that one of the parties subsequently wishes to have modified through an initial application in court for support. In that case, the agreement in issue was a separation agreement and the relevant provision was s. 15.2 of the *Divorce Act*. At paras. 45 and 46 of *Miglin*, in addressing the proper weight to be accorded to the agreement, Arbour J. and I stated:

> ... the answer to these questions does not lie in adopting a near-impermeable standard such that a court will endorse any agreement, regardless of the inequities it reveals. Neither, however, does the solution lie in unduly interfering with agreements freely entered into and on which the parties reasonably expected to rely. ...

> In exercising their discretion, trial judges must balance Parliament's objective of equitable sharing of the consequences of marriage and its breakdown with the parties' freedom to arrange their affairs as they see fit. Accordingly, *a court should be loathe to interfere with a pre-existing agreement unless it is convinced that the agreement does not comply substantially with the overall objectives of the Divorce Act.* (Emphasis added.)

At para. 67, we continue by stating:

> ... we are of the view that there is nevertheless a significant public interest in ensuring that the goal of negotiated settlements not be pursued, through judicial approbation of agreements, with such a vengeance that individual autonomy becomes a straitjacket. Therefore, assessment of the appropriate weight to be accorded a pre-existing agreement requires a balancing of the parties' interest in determining their own affairs with an appreciation of the peculiar aspects of separation agreements generally and spousal support in particular.

. . . . .

42 ... I agree that *Miglin* is helpful for its general propositions that "a court should be loathe to interfere with a pre-existing agreement unless it is convinced that the agreement does not comply substantially with the overall objectives" of the Act in question (para. 46), and that "[t]he court must not view spousal support arrangements in a vacuum ... it must look at the agreement or arrangement in its totality, bearing in mind that all aspects of the agreement are inextricably linked and that the parties have a large discretion in establishing priorities and goals for themselves" (para. 84). However, in my opinion, adopting *Miglin*, without

qualification would distort the analytical structure already provided in the British Columbia legislation.

44 Thus, the determination that a marriage agreement operates fairly or unfairly at the time of distribution cannot be made without regard to the parties' perspectives. A contract governing the distribution of property between spouses reflects what the parties believed to be fair at the time the contract was formed (presuming the absence of duress, coercion, and undue influence). The parties would usually not be expected to deal with their present situation without any consideration of how they expect their situation will evolve over time. If the parties' lives unfold in precisely the manner they had contemplated at the time of contract formation, then a finding that the contract operates unfairly at the time of distribution constitutes, in essence, a substitution of the parties' notion of fairness with the court's notion of fairness, providing that nothing else would suggest that the parties did not really consider the impact of their decision in a rational and comprehensive way. Thus, central to any analysis under s. 65(1) of the *FRA* is consideration of how accurately the parties predicted, at the time of contract formation, their actual circumstances at the time of distribution, whether they truly considered the impact of their decision and whether they adjusted their agreement during the marriage to meet the demands of a situation different from the one expected, either because the circumstances were different or simply because implications were inadequately addressed or proved to be unrealistic. ...

46 Where, as in the present case, the parties have anticipated with accuracy their personal and financial circumstances at the time of distribution, and where they have truly considered the impact of their choices, then, without more, a finding that their Agreement operates unfairly should not be made lightly. This does not mean that no attention should be given to the possible deficit in the assets and future income of the spouse who chose to stay at home and facilitate the professional development of the other spouse, compared to what they would realistically have been otherwise. Section 65 mandates as much. A fair distribution of assets must of course take into account sacrifices made and their impact, the situation of the parties at the time of distribution, their age, education and true capacity to reintegrate into the work force and achieve economic independence in particular. But this must be done in light of the personal choices made and of the overall situation considering all property rights under the marriage agreement and other entitlements. In the present case, the main feature of the Agreement was the desire that each spouse retain the assets earned before the marriage, sharing equitably assets acquired afterwards being the rule. This will be fair on dissolution of the marriage if Mrs. Hartshorne is not left without means and facing true hardship in reclaiming her professional status and income, in light also of her parental obligations. Consideration must be given to the actual situation as it unfolded. ...

47 The ultimate point then is this: in determining whether a marriage agreement operates unfairly, a court must first apply the agreement. In particular, the court must assess and award those financial entitlements provided to each spouse under the agreement, and other entitlements from all other sources, including spousal and child support. The court must then, in consideration of those factors listed in s. 65(1) of the *FRA*, make a determination as to whether the contract operates unfairly. At this second stage, consideration must be given to the parties' personal and financial circumstances, and in particular to the manner in which these circumstances evolved over time. Where the current circumstances were within the contemplation of the parties at the time the Agreement was formed, and where their Agreement and circumstances surrounding it reflect consideration and response to these circumstances, then the plaintiff's burden to establish unfairness is heavier. Thus, consideration of the factors listed in s. 65(1) of the *FRA*, taken together, would have to reveal that the economic consequences of the marriage breakdown were not shared equitably in all of the circumstances. This approach, in my view, accords with the underlying principle of the *FRA*,

striking an appropriate balance between deference to the parties' intentions, on the one hand, and assurance of an equitable result, on the other.

. . . . .

F. Independent Legal Advice

60 Independent legal advice at the time of negotiation is an important means of ensuring an informed decision to enter an agreement. In the case at bar, the respondent's lawyer prepared a written legal opinion for her. In that opinion letter, the lawyer: (1) confirmed that the respondent was in agreement with the principle that the appellant would retain ownership of the assets which he acquired prior to the relationship, but that she wished that any agreement be fair to both parties and to any children born of the marriage; (2) concluded that the Agreement proposed by the appellant was "grossly unfair"; (3) advised the respondent that, in the event that the marriage broke down, under the *FRA* she would have a *prima facie* right to an undivided one-half interest in all family assets, which would include any matrimonial home, furnishings, vehicles, savings and pensions; (4) informed the respondent that the Agreement was such that she would not "earn" even close to a one-half interest in the matrimonial home unless the marriage continued for approximately 20 years; (5) advised the respondent that "a Court would easily find such provision to be unfair and would intervene to redistribute the property on a more equitable basis"; (6) strongly recommended that the respondent not execute the Agreement "in its present form"; (7) recommended that in order to achieve a more fair result and yet still satisfy the desires of the appellant to retain the majority of his property separately, that the following assets remain the appellant's separate property — (a) bank deposits or securities, (b) the apartment at Osoyoos, (c) the Oroville lot, (d) interest in law firm and management company, (e) the 1969 Mercedes, (f) the boat, and (g) the motorcycle; and (8) strongly recommended that any agreement which the respondent executes makes it clear that there is nothing to bar any claim for maintenance or support for herself or for any children of the marriage.

61 It is clear from the detail in this opinion letter that the respondent was forewarned of the Agreement's "shortcomings". Indeed, the respondent made a few changes to the Agreement in response to her lawyer's advice, including the inclusion of the preservation of spousal support clause. The respondent was advised that the Agreement was "grossly unfair" and that a court would "easily find" the provision relating to interest in the matrimonial home to be unfair and would redistribute the property on a more equitable basis. Despite this advice, or because of it, as expressed by counsel for the respondent during the hearing before our Court, the respondent signed the Agreement. The respondent cannot now rely on her lawyer's opinion to support her allegation that because she thought the Agreement was unfair from its inception, for all intents and purposes, she never intended to live up to her end of the bargain. It is trite that a party could never be allowed to avoid his or her contractual obligations on the basis that he or she believed, from the moment of its formation, that the contract was void or unenforceable.

G. Application to this Appeal

62 The appellant brought into the marriage assets valuing approximately $1.6 million, including a home, two recreational properties, RRSPs and savings, and his law practice. At the time of separation, there had been no increase in these assets. Indeed, there had been, on the basis of the evidence before the Court, a depreciation in the values of the family home and the law practice. At the time of the Agreement, the appellant had estimated the value of the family home to be $800,000 and the law firm, $300,000. At the time of trial, after hearing

expert opinions, the trial judge held that the value of each had decreased to $755,000 and $255,000, respectively. Accordingly, I accept these estimates.

63 The respondent did not bring any assets into the marriage, but instead entered the relationship heavily in debt. As per the division of property in the Agreement, the appellant would come out of the marriage with $1.2 million and the respondent with $280,000. It has not been overlooked that the respondent gave up her own law practice to take primary care of their two children and postponed any further career development. However, these were decisions that the respondent herself made prior to the marriage. It is not realistic to assume that the consequences of such a choice were not understood and that the decision made should now be totally ignored. The implications of the Agreement were understood as well, the respondent having specifically reviewed its shortcomings with her lawyer. The appellant argues that the overall result is not unfair, pointing out that though the parties' "shares" under the Agreement are disproportionate, there is no indication that 12 years of practising law would have yielded the respondent more assets than those with which she is leaving this marriage. In my view, the disadvantage is not demonstrated.

64 What is more important, in my view, is that any economic disadvantage that the respondent suffered as a result of this decision can be compensated through spousal support. As mentioned earlier, this is significant with regard to the application of s. 65(1)(e) of the *FRA*, which deals with the need to become or remain economically independent.

65 Moreover, by signing the Agreement, the appellant and the respondent entered their marriage with certain expectations on which they were reasonably entitled to rely. If the respondent truly believed that the Agreement was unacceptable at that time, she should not have signed it. In this case, the intention of the parties, as expressed in the Agreement, was to leave with each party that which he or she had before the marriage. The question is not whether there is something fundamentally unfair about that, but whether the operation of the Agreement will prove to be unfair in the circumstances present at the time of distribution. In light of the provisions of the *FRA*, and after examining all of the provisions of the Agreement as well as the circumstances of the parties at the time of separation, it is my opinion that the Agreement was fair at the time of the triggering event. The trial judge erred in finding otherwise. The Agreement should be left intact.

. . . . .

V. Conclusion

67 Once an agreement has been reached, albeit a marriage agreement, the parties thereto are expected to fulfill the obligations that they have undertaken. A party cannot simply later state that he or she did not intend to live up to his or her end of the bargain. It is true that, in some cases, agreements that appear to be fair at the time of execution may become unfair at the time of the triggering event, depending on how the lives of the parties have unfolded. It is also clear that the *FRA* permits a court, upon application, to find that an agreement or the statutory regime is unfair and to reapportion the assets. However, in a framework within which private parties are permitted to take personal responsibility for their financial well-being upon the dissolution of marriage, courts should be reluctant to second-guess their initiative and arrangement, particularly where independent legal advice has been obtained. They should not conclude that unfairness is proven simply by demonstrating that the marriage agreement deviates from the statutory matrimonial property regime. Fairness must first take into account what was within the realistic contemplation of the parties, what attention they gave to changes in circumstances or unrealized implications, then what are their true circum-

stances, and whether the discrepancy is such, given the s. 65 factors, that a different apportionment should be made.

For a critical comment, see McLeod, "Annotation" (2004), 47 R.F.L. (5th) 10. For a case applying the *Hartshorne* approach, see *Frazer v. van Rootselaar* (2004), 2 R.F.L. (6th) 303 (B.C. S.C.); affirmed (2006), 25 R.F.L. (6th) 262 (B.C. C.A.).

(2) Spousal Support

(a) General

The *FLA* expressly indicates that the parties may agree on support obligations in a marriage contract, a cohabitation agreement, or a separation agreement. Part IV of the Act contains one explicit limitation on the freedom to contract regarding support. Section 56(2) stipulates that a provision in a domestic contract to take effect on separation whereby any right of a party is dependent upon remaining chaste is unenforceable. Accordingly, *dum casta* clauses that specify that support is to be paid during separation only so long as the recipient does not engage in sexual relations with a third party are ineffective. Section 56(2), however, expressly recognizes the validity of provisions in a domestic contract that terminate upon remarriage or cohabitation with another. Although s. 56(2) is not binding on a court exercising jurisdiction under the *Divorce Act*, it represents public policy for federal as well as provincial purposes: *Sleigh v. Sleigh* (1979), 23 O.R. (2d) 336 (H.C.).

To encourage parties to enter into domestic contracts, the *FLA* establishes a special mechanism for judicial enforcement of contractual support obligations. It applies notwithstanding an agreement to the contrary: s. 35(4). Under s. 35(1), a party to a domestic contract may file the contract with the court together with an affidavit stating that the contract or agreement is in effect and has not been set aside or varied by a court or agreement. Once the contract is filed in this manner, any provision for support may be enforced as if it were an order of the court where it is filed: s. 35(2).

A provision for support in a domestic contract that is filed with the court may also be varied as if it were an order of the court where it is filed: s. 35(2)(b). However, the parties can preclude the exercise of this judicial power by agreement: *Wark v. Wark* (1988), 14 R.F.L. (3d) 137 (Ont. Fam. Ct.); affirmed (1989), 18 R.F.L. (3d) 75 (Ont. Dist. Ct.); affirmed (1990), 28 R.F.L. (3d) 410 (Ont. Div. Ct.) and *O'Connor v. O'Connor* (1990), 28 R.F.L. (3d) 99 (Ont. Fam. Ct.).

(b) Judicial Controls

(i) Under the Divorce Act — Applications in the Face of Valid Agreements Eliminating or Restricting Spousal Support

It is clearly established that parties cannot write a domestic agreement so as to oust the jurisdiction of the court to grant spousal support under the *Divorce Act*. The real question is: when should this jurisdiction be exercised in the face of a valid and enforceable contract?

It is important to keep the procedural issues straight when thinking about promises to limit or end spousal support. The promise can appear in two different forms: in a separation agreement or in a consent court order. Thus, both consent court orders and agreements begin with a private agreement between the parties. However, in the case of an agreement, the parties' private agreement has not received the approval of the court, and is therefore subject to review as to its appropriateness. The recipient can proceed to court and ask for spousal support under s. 15.2 of the *Divorce Act* without having to prove a "change in circumstance", and regardless of the promise not to seek spousal support in the agreement. The court has jurisdiction to consider all of the facts of the marriage, and all of the facts that occurred post-separation. Pursuant to the *Divorce Act*, the existence of the agreement is just one more factor, albeit a very important one as we shall see, to consider (s. 15.2(4)(c)).

By contrast, if the provision regarding spousal support appears in a consent order, a court has technically (although not necessarily substantively) already approved the arrangement. It is therefore not subject to any further review — but only to variation upon proof of a change in circumstance. See s. 17(4.1) of the *Divorce Act*. The variation proceeding cannot go ahead without the existence of such a change. If a change in circumstance is established, the court will start from the presumption that the initial order was correct (see *Willick v. Willick*, [1994] 3 S.C.R. 670, 6 R.F.L. (4th) 161), and will not allow the parties to re-litigate the original order.

In *Miglin v. Miglin*, excerpted immediately below, the parties had entered into a separation agreement in which they had mutually agreed never to make a claim for spousal support. The court was therefore considering an application for support pursuant to s. 15.2 of the *Divorce Act*. It had to consider whether to uphold the parties' private contract or to award spousal support at variance with the agreement. The Supreme Court of Canada had last tackled this issue in the *Pelech* trilogy (*Pelech v. Pelech* (1987), 7 R.F.L. (3d) 225 (S.C.C.); *Caron v. Caron* (1987), 7 R.F.L. (3d) 274 (S.C.C.); and *Richardson v. Richardson* (1987), 7 R.F.L. (3d) 304 (S.C.C.)). In these cases, the court came down firmly in favour of a restrictive approach and held that a court should order spousal support at variance with a separation agreement that settled support in a final way only where there had been a radical and unforeseen change in circumstances that was causally related to the marriage. In *Miglin*, the court concluded that this test should no longer apply.

MIGLIN v. MIGLIN

(2003), 34 R.F.L. (5th) 255, 2003 CarswellOnt 1374, 2003 CarswellOnt 1375 (S.C.C.)

[Following their marriage in 1979, a husband and wife purchased a lodge. The husband managed the business, while the wife was responsible for its day-to-day operations. The wife was also the primary caregiver for the couple's four children, born in 1985, 1988, 1989 and 1991. After their separation in 1993, the husband and wife each retained a lawyer and eventually reached a settlement in 1994. The settlement consisted of three agreements that were intended to govern all of the financial and non-financial matters arising out of the marriage and its breakdown. The separation agreement stipulated that the wife would receive her husband's interest in the matrimonial home in exchange for giving up her interest in the lodge. At the time, these assets each had net values of approximately $500,000. Under the agreement, the husband was to make all the mortgage payments on the home. Each of the parties specifically abandoned all possible claims for spousal support. Under the parenting agreement, the husband and wife were to share responsibility for bringing up their children who would reside primarily with the wife. The husband was to provide $60,000 per year in child support. Finally, a consulting agreement between the wife and the lodge provided for payments of $15,000 per year to the wife. The agreement covered five years, but was renewable by mutual consent. Both the child support and consulting payments were subject to annual cost of living increases.

The couple divorced in 1997 and the divorce judgment was silent with respect to spousal support, child support, and custody and access. Soon after the divorce, the couple's relationship turned acrimonious. Just before the consulting agreement was to expire, the wife brought proceedings pursuant to the *Divorce Act* for sole custody, child support in accordance with the *Federal Child Support Guidelines* and spousal support. Later that year, the husband caused the lodge not to renew the consulting agreement. By the time the proceedings were heard, the oldest child had gone to live with the husband. The parents eventually agreed to joint custody, but disputed how much time the children should spend in each home.

At trial, the judge awarded the wife monthly child support of $3,000 for the three children residing with her and monthly spousal support of $4,400 for five years. Regarding spousal support, the trial judge reasoned that the standard for interference with a contractual provision set out in the *Pelech* trilogy did not apply to the 1985 *Divorce Act*. He held that he could override the negotiated provision simply on the basis that it was unfair in the sense that it failed to meet the objectives for spousal support set out in s. 15(7) of the *Divorce Act*.

The husband appealed. The wife cross-appealed, asking that the time limit on spousal support be removed. In the course of the appeal, the wife conceded that the husband's annual income was about $14,000 a year lower than the amount assessed by the trial judge and that there should accordingly be a reduction in the monthly amount of child support for the three children from $3,000 to $2,767.

The Ontario Court of Appeal allowed the appeal in part and allowed the cross-appeal. It adjusted the quantum of monthly child support in accordance with the wife's concession. However, it ruled that the trial judge's determination of the custody and access issues should stand. In dealing with spousal support, the appellate court concluded that the *Pelech* trilogy no longer applied. Instead, it suggested a two-stage inquiry. The first and threshold stage simply involved the determination of a material change in circumstances since the agreement. At the second stage, a court was to determine what amount of support, if any, was appropriate in light of the statutory principles as refined in the leading Supreme Court of Canada cases. Applying this analysis, the appellate court determined that the trial judge had correctly ordered support in the amount that he did, but removed the five-year term.

The Supreme Court of Canada, LeBel and Deschamps JJ. dissenting, allowed the husband's appeal and set aside the spousal support award. Portions of the majority's reasons, written jointly by Justices Bastarache and Arbour, follow.]

I. Introduction

1 This appeal concerns the proper approach to determining an application for spousal support pursuant to s. 15.2(1) of the *Divorce Act*, R.S.C. 1985, c. 3 (2nd Supp.) (the "1985 Act"), where the spouses have executed a final agreement that addresses all matters respecting their separation, including a release of any future claim for spousal support. Accordingly, this appeal presents the Court with an opportunity to address directly the question of the continued application of the *Pelech* trilogy ... in light of the significant legislative and jurisprudential changes that have taken place since its facts arose and since its release.

2 In broader terms, the appeal raises the question of the proper weight to be given to any type of spousal support agreement that one of the parties subsequently wishes to have modified through an initial application in court for such support. In that sense, the matter is not restricted to spousal support agreements that contain a time-limited support arrangement or to agreements which contain a full and final release from support obligations by one or both parties.

3 The parties to this appeal, now divorced, entered into a final agreement that sought to settle all of their financial and personal affairs surrounding the breakdown of their marriage. In addition to property equalization, custody, access and support of their children, and a commercial contract between the respondent and the appellant's company, the parties agreed

to release one another from any claims to spousal support. This Court must determine the proper weight to be accorded that agreement where one party subsequently makes an application for spousal support under the *Divorce Act*.

4 As we explain below, we believe that a fairly negotiated agreement that represents the intentions and expectations of the parties and that complies substantially with the objectives of the *Divorce Act* as a whole should receive considerable weight. In an originating application for spousal support, where the parties have executed a pre-existing agreement, the court should look first to the circumstances of negotiation and execution to determine whether the applicant has established a reason to discount the agreement. The court would inquire whether one party was vulnerable and the other party took advantage of that vulnerability. The court also examines whether the substance of the agreement, at formation, complied substantially with the general objectives of the Act. As we elaborate later, these general objectives include not only an equitable sharing of the consequences of the marriage breakdown under s. 15.2, but also certainty, finality and autonomy. Second, the court would ask whether, viewed from the time the application is made, the applicant has established that the agreement no longer reflects the original intention of the parties and whether the agreement is still in substantial compliance with the objectives of the Act. In contrast, the trial judge's and the Court of Appeal's approaches failed to value a determination by the parties as to what is mutually acceptable to them. We would thus allow this appeal. ...

V. Analysis

B. Spousal Support

28 As mentioned earlier in these reasons, this appeal is concerned with the continued application of the *Pelech* trilogy. The three cases making up this trilogy were decided immediately after the promulgation of the 1985 Act, but dealt with situations governed by the 1968 Act. Those cases establish a change-based test under which a court is permitted to override a final agreement on spousal support only where there has been a significant change in circumstances since the making of the agreement. The test establishes a threshold that is defined as a radical and unforeseen change that is causally connected to the marriage. It does not deal with the fairness of the agreement or its attention to the objectives of the *Divorce Act*. It is designed to promote certainty and to facilitate a clean break in the relationship of the parties, focussing on individual autonomy and respect for contracts. Since the release of the trilogy, the law of spousal support has evolved. A compensatory approach was adopted in *Moge v. Moge*, [1992] 3 S.C.R. 813. A more nuanced approach was developed in *Bracklow v. Bracklow*, [1999] 1 S.C.R. 420. Self-sufficiency, autonomy and finality remain relevant factors in our case law, but many question whether the emphasis put on them by the trilogy remains. The question posed is whether agreements concluded with the intent that they be final can, under the 1985 Act, be overridden on grounds other than those defined in the trilogy.

1. Does the Pelech Trilogy Still Apply?

29 The issues in the present appeal resemble those facing this Court in the *Pelech* trilogy. Despite significant changes in the intervening years, the basic question remains: What role should a pre-existing agreement play in determining an application for spousal support? Writing for the majority of this Court in *Pelech*, Wilson J. described the issue the following way, at p. 382:

> While it is generally accepted that the existence of an antecedent settlement agreement made by the parties is an important fact, there is a wide range of views as to how this affects the legal principles governing the exercise of the discretion conferred in s. 11 [of the 1968 Act].

30 Except for the statutory reference, these words could easily have been written by us today. The statutory and jurisprudential context, however, is of utmost importance. As counsel for both parties recognized, the resolution of this appeal rests primarily on an exercise in statutory interpretation. The revision of the *Divorce Act* in 1985 and changing judicial and societal understandings of the function of spousal support make it appropriate for this Court to revisit Parliament's intention regarding agreements relating to spousal support.

31 The facts and reasoning of the three cases constituting the trilogy have attracted substantial scholarly and judicial commentary. We do not propose to review those decisions in detail again here. Suffice it to say that the *Pelech* trilogy has come to stand for the proposition that a court will not interfere with a pre-existing agreement that attempts fully and finally to settle the matter of spousal support as between the parties unless the applicant can establish that there has been a radical and unforeseen change in circumstances that is causally connected to the marriage. The trilogy represents an approach to spousal support that has been described as a "clean break," emphasising finality and the severing of ties between former spouses. As Wilson J. put it in *Pelech*, at p. 851:

> [I]t seems to me that parties who have declared their relationship at an end should be taken at their word. They made the decision to marry and they made the decision to terminate their marriage. Their decisions should be respected. They should thereafter be free to make new lives for themselves without an ongoing contingent liability for future misfortunes which may befall the other.

32 With the coming into force of the 1985 Act and the release of the trilogy the following year, confusion ensued as to whether the trilogy had any continued application. ...

34 In addition to generating some confusion, the trilogy received no small degree of criticism, from both legal scholars and family law practitioners. The main thrust of the criticism levied at the trilogy was summarized by McLachlin J. (as she then was) in a speech delivered to the National Family Law Program over a decade ago. McLachlin J. suggested that the "joint venture model" of marriage, which viewed married persons as autonomous individuals entering into equal partnerships who should and do take responsibility for themselves, informed the economic self-sufficiency or "clean break" theory of spousal support endorsed by this Court in *Pelech*. Although McLachlin J. fully endorsed the model of equality on which the trilogy was based, she cautioned that that model did not necessarily conform to everyone's reality. This disjuncture, in her view, explained much of the criticism to which the trilogy has been subjected (The Honourable Madame Justice B. McLachlin, "Spousal Support: Is it Fair to Apply New-Style Rules to Old-Style Marriages?" (1990), 9 *Can. J. Fam. L.* 131).

35 Since the trilogy, decisions from this Court have recognized a shift in the normative standards informing spousal support orders. In *Moge, supra*, at p. 849 L'Heureux-Dubé J. held for the majority that the underlying theme of the 1985 Act is the "fair and equitable distribution of resources to alleviate the economic consequences of marriage or marriage breakdown". In making an order for support, she noted that the court must have regard to *all four* of the objectives of spousal support, none of which is paramount. Self-sufficiency is only one of those objectives and an attenuated one at that (to be promoted "insofar as practicable" (p. 852)). L'Heureux-Dubé J. concluded that Parliament appears to have adopted a compensatory model of support, one which attempts to ensure the equitable sharing of the economic consequences of marriage and its breakdown. ...

39 Whereas the 1968 Act refers only to the "conduct of the parties and the condition, means, and other circumstances of each of them" (s. 11(1)), the 1985 Act abandons the reference to the conduct of the parties and makes explicit both the objectives of spousal support and the factors to be considered in making an order. That these objectives can and do often conflict and compete suggests an intention on the part of Parliament to vest in trial judges a significant discretion to assess the weight to be given each objective against the very particular

backdrop of the parties' circumstances. Moreover, we agree that the importance given to self-sufficiency and a "clean break" in the jurisprudence relying on the trilogy is not only incompatible with the new Act, but too often fails to accord with the realities faced by many divorcing couples. Indeed, in *Bracklow, supra*, this Court recognized how these different realities also mirror competing normative standards justifying entitlement to spousal support. ...

40 In light of these developments in the understanding of spousal support, the question "Does the trilogy apply or not?" is perhaps too mechanical, and the answer does not turn solely on the existence of a new Act. Parliament's recognition of competing objectives of spousal support renders the trilogy's privileging of "clean break" principles inappropriate, but this is not to suggest that the policy concerns that drove the trilogy are wholly irrelevant to the new legislative context. On the contrary, the objectives of autonomy and finality, as well as the recognition that the parties may go on to undertake new family obligations, continue to inform the current *Divorce Act* and remain significant today. What has changed is the singular emphasis on self-sufficiency as a policy goal to the virtual exclusion of other objectives that may or may not be equally pressing according to the specific circumstances of the parties. Such an emphasis on self-sufficiency is inconsistent with both the compensatory model of support developed in *Moge*, and the non-compensatory model of support developed in *Bracklow*. It is also inconsistent with the interpretive point made in both cases that no single objective in s. 15.2(6) is paramount: *Bracklow*, at para. 35; *Moge*, at p. 852. Nevertheless, promoting self-sufficiency remains an explicit legislative objective.

41 In addition to these competing policy goals, we also note that the current statutory language does not support direct incorporation of the trilogy test. ...

42 The current statutory context, however, is quite different in that Parliament has explicitly directed the court to consider a change in circumstances only where the application is for variation to an existing spousal support order. ...

43 Section 15.2 provides no such similar direction. [The reference here is to the requirement in s. 17.4 of the *Divorce Act* that there must be a material change in circumstances before a court has authority to vary an existing order made under the Act.] Rather, the court is explicitly directed to take into account certain non-exhaustive factors, and instructed that a support order should advance certain specified objectives. On a plain reading of the statute, then, there is simply no basis for importing a change threshold, radical, material or otherwise, into the provision. Indeed, on an initial application for support, the very concept of "change of circumstances" has no relevance, except to the limited extent that there might have been a pre-existing order or agreement that needs to be considered.

44 How, then, should trial judges exercise the discretion vested in them by virtue of the Act where a party who makes an initial application for support has previously entered into an agreement that purports to have settled all matters between the spouses? How should trial judges assess the appropriate weight to be given such an agreement where s. 15.2 of the 1985 Act appears to accord it no greater priority than other factors?

45 It is helpful initially to identify several inappropriate approaches. In our view, the answer to these questions does not lie in adopting a near-impermeable standard such that a court will endorse any agreement, regardless of the inequities it reveals. Neither, however, does the solution lie in unduly interfering with agreements freely entered into and on which the parties reasonably expected to rely. It is also not helpful to read between the lines in s. 15.2 so as to identify a single implicit overriding legislative objective overshadowing the factors specifically set out. The fact that judicial and societal understandings of spousal support have changed since the release of *Pelech* and the adoption of admittedly competing factors in s. 15.2(6) does not lead to an unfettered discretion on the part of trial judges to substitute

their own view of what is required for what the parties considered mutually acceptable. In this respect, we agree in principle with Wilson J.'s comments in *Pelech, supra*, at p. 853:

> Where parties, instead of resorting to litigation, have acted in a mature and responsible fashion to settle their financial affairs in a final way and their settlement is not vulnerable to attack on any other basis, it should not, in my view, be undermined by courts concluding with the benefit of hindsight that they should have done it differently.

46 Nevertheless, the language and purpose of the 1985 Act militate in favour of a contextual assessment of all the circumstances. This includes the content of the agreement, in order to determine the proper weight it should be accorded in a s. 15.2 application. In exercising their discretion, trial judges must balance Parliament's objective of equitable sharing of the consequences of marriage and its breakdown with the parties' freedom to arrange their affairs as they see fit. Accordingly, a court should be loathe to interfere with a pre-existing agreement unless it is convinced that the agreement does not comply substantially with the overall objectives of the *Divorce Act*. This is particularly so when the pre-existing spousal support agreement is part of a comprehensive settlement of all issues related to the termination of the marriage. Since the issues, as well as their settlement, are likely interrelated, the support part of the agreement would at times be difficult to modify without putting into question the entire arrangement.

47 Having determined that the narrow test enunciated in the *Pelech* trilogy for interfering with a pre-existing agreement is not appropriate in the current statutory context, we now consider the approaches taken by the courts below in this appeal. ... [The analysis of the trial judge's and Court of Appeal's approaches is omitted.]

4. The Proper Approach to Applications Under Section 15.2

64 An initial application for spousal support inconsistent with a pre-existing agreement requires an investigation into all the circumstances surrounding that agreement, first, at the time of its formation, and second, at the time of the application. In our view, this two-stage analysis provides the court with a principled way of balancing the competing objectives underlying the *Divorce Act* and of locating the potentially problematic aspects of spousal support arrangements in their appropriate temporal context. Before doing so, however, it is necessary to discuss some of the interpretive difficulties affecting spousal support.

65 As a starting point, we endorse the reasoning of this Court in *Moge, supra*, where L'Heureux-Dubé J. held that the spousal support objectives of the *Divorce Act* are designed to achieve an equitable sharing of the economic consequences of marriage and marriage breakdown. By explicitly directing the court to consider the objectives listed in s. 15.2(6), the 1985 Act departs significantly from the exclusive "means and needs" approach of the former statute. We note, however, that there is a potential tension between recognizing any economic advantages or disadvantages to the spouses arising from the marriage or its breakdown and promoting, even if only to the extent practicable, the economic self-sufficiency of each spouse (ss. 15.2(6)(a), and (d)). The way to reconcile these competing objectives is to recognize that the meaning of the term "equitable sharing" is not fixed in the Act and will, rather, vary according to the facts of a particular marriage. Parliament, aware of the many ways in which parties structure a marriage and particularly its economic aspects, drafted legislation broad enough that one cannot say that the spousal support provisions have a narrow fixed content. Contrasted with the former Act, then, these objectives expressly direct the court to consider different criteria on which to base entitlement to spousal support, while retaining the objective of fostering the parties' ability to get on with their lives.

66 The role that these objectives was intended to play, however, must be understood in the proper statutory context. Whether by way of an initial application or an application to vary,

the criteria listed in s. 15.2(6) and s. 17(7) pertain to spousal support orders imposed by the court. Nowhere in the *Divorce Act* is it expressed that parties *must* adhere strictly, or at all, to these objectives in reaching a mutually acceptable agreement. Rather, the listed objectives relate only to orders for spousal support, that is, to circumstances where the parties have been unable to reach an agreement. Moreover, the positive obligation that the Act places on counsel to advise their clients of alternatives to litigation, noted above, indicates Parliament's clear conception of the new divorce regime as one that places a high premium on private settlement. Parliament's preference appears to be that parties settle their dispute, without asking a court to apply s. 15.2(6) to make an order. This is not to suggest that the objectives are irrelevant in the context of a negotiated agreement. The parties, or at least their counsel, will be conscious of the likely outcome of litigation in the event that negotiation fails. Consideration of the statutory entitlements will undoubtedly influence negotiations. But the mutually acceptable agreement negotiated by the parties will not necessarily mirror the spousal support that a judge would have awarded. Holding that any agreement that deviates from the objectives listed in s. 15.2(6) be given little or no weight would seriously undermine the significant policy goal of negotiated settlement. It would also undermine the parties' autonomy and freedom to structure their post-divorce lives in a manner that reflects their own objectives and concerns. Such a position would leave little room to recognize the terms that the parties determined were mutually acceptable to them and in substantial compliance with the objectives of the *Divorce Act.*

67 Having said this, we are of the view that there is nevertheless a significant public interest in ensuring that the goal of negotiated settlements not be pursued, through judicial approbation of agreements, with such a vengeance that individual autonomy becomes a straightjacket. Therefore, assessment of the appropriate weight to be accorded a pre-existing agreement requires a balancing of the parties' interest in determining their own affairs with an appreciation of the peculiar aspects of separation agreements generally and spousal support in particular. ...

[Having rejected the approaches taken by the trial judge and by Justice Abella in the Ontario Court of Appeal, the majority of the Supreme Court also rejected the models suggested by the two parties. In particular, it rejected the husband's suggestion that the court should adopt the same approach as set out in s. 33(4)(a) of Ontario's *Family Law Act*, whereby a court can override a contractual provision where it results in "unconscionable circumstances". The majority noted (at para. 73) that its approach "takes greater account of the parties' subjective sense of equitable sharing than the objective 'unconscionable circumstances' standard". Before presenting its own two-stage approach, the majority noted the context in which separation agreements are negotiated.]

74 Negotiations in the family law context of separation or divorce are conducted in a unique environment. Both academics and practitioners have acknowledged that this is a time of intense personal and emotional turmoil, in which one or both of the parties may be particularly vulnerable. Unlike emotionally neutral economic actors negotiating in the commercial context, divorcing couples inevitably bring to the table a host of emotions and concerns that do not obviously accord with the making of rational economic decisions. ...

75 Add to this mix the intimate nature of the marital relationship that makes it difficult to overcome potential power imbalances and modes of influence. ...

76 We also note that, depending on the circumstances of the parties, a wide array of interrelated elements may make up a global separation agreement. Such a separation agreement may comprise division or equalization of marital property, provision for custody and support of any children, as well as provisions for spousal support, be it in the form of lump sum, periodic payment, time-limited payment or a waiver and release. These matters, with the

exception of the property division, are primarily prospective in nature, although compensatory spousal support is retrospective. ...

77 In our view, Parliament's recognition of the potential complications in the process of contracting spousal support is reflected in the *Divorce Act* itself. We see this in the direction to the court to consider an agreement as only one factor among others, rather than to treat it as binding, subject merely to remedies in contract law. Accordingly, contract law principles are not only better suited to the commercial context, but it is implicit in s. 15 of the 1985 Act that they were not intended to govern the applicability of private contractual arrangements for spousal support.

78 Therefore, in searching for a proper balance between consensus and finality on the one hand, and sensitivity to the unique concerns that arise in the post-divorce context on the other, a court should be guided by the objectives of spousal support listed in the Act. In doing so, however, the court should treat the parties' reasonable best efforts to meet those objectives as presumptively dispositive of the spousal support issue. The court should set aside the wishes of the parties as expressed in a pre-existing agreement only where the applicant shows that the agreement fails to be in substantial compliance with the overall objectives of the Act. These include not only those apparent in s. 15.2 but also, as noted above, certainty, finality and autonomy.

79 With these broad concerns in mind, we now turn to the specifics of the two-stage approach to the exercise of the court's discretion.

(a) Stage One

80 In an originating application for spousal support, where the parties have executed a pre-existing agreement, the court should first look to the circumstances in which the agreement was negotiated and executed to determine whether there is any reason to discount it.

(i) The Circumstances of Execution

81 It is difficult to provide a definitive list of factors to consider in assessing the circumstances of negotiation and execution of an agreement. We simply state that the court should be alive to the conditions of the parties, including whether there were any circumstances of oppression, pressure, or other vulnerabilities, taking into account all of the circumstances, including those set out in s. 15.2(4)(a) and (b) and the conditions under which the negotiations were held, such as their duration and whether there was professional assistance.

82 We pause here to note three important points. First, we are not suggesting that courts must necessarily look for "unconscionability" as it is understood in the common law of contract. There is a danger in borrowing terminology rooted in other branches of the law and transposing it into what all agree is a unique legal context. There may be persuasive evidence brought before the court that one party took advantage of the vulnerability of the other party in separation or divorce negotiations that would fall short of evidence of the power imbalance necessary to demonstrate unconscionability in a commercial context between, say, a consumer and a large financial institution. Next, the court should not presume an imbalance of power in the relationship or a vulnerability on the part of one party, nor should it presume that the apparently stronger party took advantage of any vulnerability on the part of the other. Rather, there must be evidence to warrant the court's finding that the agreement should not stand on the basis of a fundamental flaw in the negotiation process. Recognition of the emotional stress of separation or divorce should not be taken as giving rise to a presumption that parties in such circumstances are incapable of assenting to a binding agreement. If separating or divorcing parties were generally incapable of making agreements it

would be fair to enforce, it would be difficult to see why Parliament included "agreement or arrangement" in s. 15.2(4)(c). Finally, we stress that the mere presence of vulnerabilities will not, in and of itself, justify the court's intervention. The degree of professional assistance received by the parties will often overcome any systemic imbalances between the parties.

83 Where vulnerabilities are not present, or are effectively compensated by the presence of counsel or other professionals or both, or have not been taken advantage of, the court should consider the agreement as a genuine mutual desire to finalize the terms of the parties' separation and as indicative of their substantive intentions. Accordingly, the court should be loathe to interfere. In contrast, where the power imbalance did vitiate the bargaining process, the agreement should not be read as expressing the parties' notion of equitable sharing in their circumstances and the agreement will merit little weight.

(ii) The Substance of the Agreement

84 Where the court is satisfied that the conditions under which the agreement was negotiated are satisfactory, it must then turn its attention to the substance of the agreement. The court must determine the extent to which the agreement takes into account the factors and objectives listed in the Act, thereby reflecting an equitable sharing of the economic consequences of marriage and its breakdown. Only a significant departure from the general objectives of the Act will warrant the court's intervention on the basis that there is not substantial compliance with the Act. The court must not view spousal support arrangements in a vacuum; however, it must look at the agreement or arrangement in its totality, bearing in mind that all aspects of the agreement are inextricably linked and that the parties have a large discretion in establishing priorities and goals for themselves.

85 When examining the substance of the agreement, the court should ask itself whether the agreement is in substantial compliance with the *Divorce Act*. As just noted, this "substantial compliance" should be determined by considering whether the agreement represents a significant departure from the general objectives of the Act, which necessarily include, as well as the spousal support considerations in s. 15.2, finality, certainty, and the invitation in the Act for parties to determine their own affairs. The greater the vulnerabilities present at the time of formation, the more searching the court's review at this stage.

86 Two comments are necessary here. First, assessment of an agreement's substantial compliance with the entire Act will necessarily permit a broader gamut of arrangements than would be the case if testing agreements narrowly against the support order objectives in s. 15.2(6). Second, a determination that an agreement fails to comply substantially with the Act does not necessarily mean that the entire agreement must be set aside and ignored. Provided that demonstrated vulnerability and exploitation did not vitiate negotiation, even a negotiated agreement that it would be wrong to enforce in its totality may nevertheless indicate the parties' understanding of their marriage and, at least in a general sense, their intentions for the future. Consideration of such an agreement would continue to be mandatory under s. 15.2(4). For example, if it appeared inappropriate to enforce a time limit in a support agreement, the quantum of support agreed upon might still be appropriate, and the agreement might then simply be extended, indefinitely or for a different fixed term.

(b) Stage Two

87 Where negotiation of the agreement is not impugned on the basis set out above and the agreement was in substantial compliance with the general objectives of the Act at its time of creation, the court should defer to the wishes of the parties and afford the agreement great weight. Nevertheless, the vicissitudes of life mean that, in some circumstances, parties may find themselves down the road of their post-divorce life in circumstances not contemplated.

Accordingly, on the bringing of an application under s. 15.2, the court should assess the extent to which enforcement of the agreement still reflects the original intention of the parties and the extent to which it is still in substantial compliance with the objectives of the Act.

88 The parties' intentions, as reflected by the agreement, are the backdrop against which the court must consider whether the situation of the parties at the time of the application makes it no longer appropriate to accord the agreement conclusive weight. We note that it is unlikely that the court will be persuaded to disregard the agreement in its entirety but for a significant change in the parties' circumstances from what could reasonably be anticipated at the time of negotiation. Although the change need not be "radically unforeseen," and the applicant need not demonstrate a causal connection to the marriage, the applicant must nevertheless clearly show that, in light of the new circumstances, the terms of the agreement no longer reflect the parties' intentions at the time of execution and the objectives of the Act. Accordingly, it will be necessary to show that these new circumstances were not reasonably anticipated by the parties, and have led to a situation that cannot be condoned.

89 We stress that a certain degree of change is foreseeable most of the time. The prospective nature of these agreements cannot be lost on the parties and they must be presumed to be aware that the future is, to a greater or lesser extent, uncertain. It will be unconvincing, for example, to tell a judge that an agreement never contemplated that the job market might change, or that parenting responsibilities under an agreement might be somewhat more onerous than imagined, or that a transition into the workforce might be challenging. Negotiating parties should know that each person's health cannot be guaranteed as a constant. An agreement must also contemplate, for example, that the relative values of assets in a property division will not necessarily remain the same. Housing prices may rise or fall. A business may take a downturn or become more profitable. Moreover, some changes may be caused or provoked by the parties themselves. A party may remarry or decide not to work. Where the parties have demonstrated their intention to release one another from all claims to spousal support, changes of this nature are unlikely to be considered sufficient to justify dispensing with that declared intention. That said, we repeat that a judge is not bound by the strict *Pelech* standard to intervene only once a change is shown to be "radical". Likewise, it is unnecessary for the party seeking court-ordered support to demonstrate that the circumstances rendering enforcement of the agreement inappropriate are causally connected to the marriage or its breakdown. The test here is not strict foreseeability; a thorough review of case law leaves virtually no change entirely unforeseeable. The question, rather, is the extent to which the unimpeachably negotiated agreement can be said to have contemplated the situation before the court at the time of the application.

90 The court's focus should be on the agreement's continued correspondence to the parties' original intentions as to their relative positions and the overall objectives of the Act, not on whether a change occurred *per se*. That is to say, we do not consider "change" of any particular nature to be a threshold requirement which, once established, entitles the court to jettison the agreement entirely. Rather, the court should be persuaded that both the intervention and the degree of intervention are warranted. That is, at this stage, even if unbending enforcement of the agreement is inappropriate, that agreement may still indicate to a trial judge the parties' understanding of their relationship and their intentions. Even an agreement that is not determinative as a result of the parties' circumstances at the time of the application warrants compulsory consideration under s. 15.2(4).

91 Although we recognize the unique nature of separation agreements and their differences from commercial contracts, they are contracts nonetheless. Parties must take responsibility for the contract they execute as well as for their own lives. It is only where the current circumstances represent a significant departure from the range of reasonable outcomes anticipated by the parties, in a manner that puts them at odds with the objectives of the Act, that

the court may be persuaded to give the agreement little weight. As we noted above, it would be inconsistent if a different test applied to change an agreement in the form of an initial order under s. 15.2 and to variation of an agreement incorporated into an order under s. 17. In our view, the Act does not create such inconsistency. We do not agree with the Ontario Court of Appeal when it suggests at para. 71, that once a material change has been found, a court has "a wide discretion" to determine what amount of support, if any, should be ordered, based solely on the factors set out in s. 17(7). As La Forest J. said in his dissent in *Richardson, supra*, at p. 881, an order made under the Act has already been judicially determined to be fit and just. The objectives of finality and certainty noted above caution against too broad a discretion in varying an order that the parties have been relying on in arranging their affairs. Consideration of the overall objectives of the Act is consistent with the non-exhaustive direction in s. 17(7) that a variation order "should" consider the four objectives listed there. More generally, a contextual approach to interpretation, reading the entire Act, would indicate that the court would apply those objectives in light of the entire statute. Where the order at issue incorporated the mutually acceptable agreement of the parties, that order reflected the parties' understanding of what constituted an equitable sharing of the economic consequences of the marriage. In our view, whether acting under s. 15.2 or under s. 17, the Court should take that into consideration.

C. Application to the Facts of this Case

92 In the circumstances of this appeal, we are of the view that the global Separation Agreement should be accorded significant and determinative weight. Looking to the Separation Agreement at the time of its formation, we find nothing to indicate that circumstances surrounding the negotiation and execution of the agreement were fraught with vulnerabilities. On the contrary, the record reveals that these parties underwent extensive negotiation over a substantial time period and engaged the services of several professionals, including experienced and expert counsel. Negotiation of the Separation Agreement lasted some 15 months. Ms. Miglin, in addition to legal advice, received detailed financial advice, both in terms of tax planning and income projections, throughout the negotiation process.

93 At the trial, Ms. Miglin suggested that she was not content with the Separation Agreement and felt pressured by her husband to agree to the spousal support release. As she phrased it, it was a confusing and emotional time for her. We do not doubt that marital separation is almost inevitably a time of emotional upheaval and confusion. Regardless, in this case there is ample evidence to conclude that any vulnerability experienced by Ms. Miglin was more than adequately compensated by the independent and competent legal counsel representing her interests over a prolonged period, not to mention the services provided to her by other professionals. It is unnecessary, therefore, for us to determine whether Ms. Miglin's evidence relating to her personal feelings would have been sufficient to demonstrate a vulnerability in this case and, if so, whether that vulnerability was exploited. The extent of Ms. Miglin's professional assistance obviously comes at the upper end of the range, and we would not wish to suggest that hers was the minimum required to assure fair negotiation.

94 Turning to the substance of the Separation Agreement, we also find nothing to demonstrate a significant departure from the overall objectives of the *Divorce Act*. At the time of separation both the Lodge and the matrimonial home had net values of approximately $500,000. The Separation Agreement provided for Ms. Miglin to transfer to Mr. Miglin her one-half interest in the Lodge in exchange for the transfer to her of his one-half interest in the matrimonial home. Mr. Miglin agreed to assume sole responsibility for the mortgage on the house. We cannot agree with the trial judge's characterization of this arrangement as "not an equal split." He made this assessment on the basis that the business was income-

producing and the house was not. Valuation of an asset necessarily takes into account its characteristics, including its potential income, capital appreciation and risks. In the same way that a single asset should not be counted twice (*Boston v. Boston*, [2001] 2 S.C.R. 413, 2001 SCC 43 (S.C.C.)), the factors that went into an asset's valuation should not be considered a second time. Presumably, viewed subjectively, in light of Mr. Miglin's and Ms. Miglin's respective abilities, interests and needs, the business was of greater interest to him and the matrimonial home more attractive to her. That is why they divided the assets as they did. There was no basis for the trial judge to conclude that one asset was worth more than another of identical value. In our view, the division in the Separation Agreement reflects the parties' needs and wishes and fairly distributed the assets acquired and created by them over the course of their marriage.

95 The Separation Agreement also provided that Ms. Miglin would receive child support in the amount of $1,250 per month, per child, for an annual total of approximately $60,000, taxable in her hands and tax-deductible to Mr. Miglin. The child support arrangement was subject to both an annual cost of living increase and the caveat that it would be revisited, if necessary, once reasons for judgment were released from this Court in *Thibaudeau* ... [*Thibaudeau v. R.* (1995), 12 R.F.L. (4th) 1 (S.C.C.)], or Parliament enacted legislation that altered the child support tax scheme. The record reveals that the quantum of child support was arrived at in full contemplation of Ms. Miglin's spousal support release. We also note that correspondence between counsel suggests that it was Ms. Miglin's preference to release Mr. Miglin from spousal support on condition that her economic needs were addressed through child support.

96 The Consulting Agreement, executed between the Lodge and Ms. Miglin, was for a term of five years, with an option to renew on the consent of both parties. Both the trial judge and the Court of Appeal found this arrangement to be "thinly veiled spousal support." If it was, there should be no pejorative sense to the term. If the commercial contract is construed as a form of spousal support, it simply means that the agreement contains a time-limited spousal support agreement with a renewal option, rather than a total waiver of spousal support. Either way, neither is intrinsically unfair nor contrary to the objectives of the Act. There is nothing inherently sinister about a release or a waiver any more than there is about a time-limited arrangement. Any support clause has to be assessed in the full context of the broader agreement, the overall circumstances of the parties, and the degree of compliance with the objectives of the Act. In our view, the Consulting Agreement reflects the parties' intentions to provide Ms. Miglin with a source of employment income for a limited time. That the parties chose such a method to provide the income to Ms. Miglin does not detract from the commercial nature of the contract. Moreover, the vehicle chosen is appropriate to the manner in which the parties structured their economic lives during the marriage.

97 It is true that Ms. Miglin stopped receiving her salary of $80,500 from the Lodge. The obvious reason, though, is that she had also stopped working more or less full-time for the Lodge. During the marriage she had hired babysitters to permit her to work at the Lodge. After the separation she could hire babysitters so she could work for a new employer. Or, as in fact she chose, she was free not to seek other employment and to support herself and her children, during the five years of the Consulting Agreement, on the combined income of roughly $75,000 consisting of $60,000 in child support and $15,000 from the Consulting Agreement. Her own financial analyst's tables indicated her choice not to work. Recall too that, since Mr. Miglin had assumed sole responsibility for the mortgage on the matrimonial home, Ms. Miglin's expenses included no rent or mortgage payments.

98 It is in the context of these arrangements that the final release and waiver of spousal support must be assessed. Overall, the Separation Agreement provided for a certain level of revenue to the wife, in the form of ongoing child support and the consulting fees for a five-

year period, with a possibility of renewal. In this way, the Agreement sought to redress any disadvantages arising from the marriage and its breakup in part through the vehicle of the business which was, as it had been throughout the marriage, the parties' major source of income. At the same time, the Separation Agreement sought to facilitate the disentanglement of the parties' economic lives and promote their self-sufficiency. The Separation Agreement advances the 1985 Act's goals of finality and autonomy. During the marriage, Ms. Miglin continued her education (obtaining her B.A.), earned a salary and obtained work experience; a case was therefore not made out for compensatory support. It is unnecessary, therefore, to determine whether the Separation Agreement would still have complied substantially with the objectives of the Act on facts closer, say, to those in *Moge*.

99 Accordingly, we find the Separation Agreement at the time of its formation to have been in substantial compliance with the *Divorce Act*.

100 The Court of Appeal found that, at the time of the support application, the non-renewal of the Consulting Agreement and changes in the child-care arrangements constituted a material change sufficient to justify overriding the spousal support release. As we noted earlier, we do not accept the Court of Appeal's "material change" test as the appropriate basis for dispensing with an otherwise enforceable agreement. Still, with respect to the findings, we believe them to be in error.

101 With respect to the Consulting Agreement, we note that Ms. Miglin brought her application for corollary relief in June of 1998 — prior to the expiry of the five-year term of the contract. Moreover, the parties agree that Ms. Miglin performed the terms of her contract for a period but performed no work for the Lodge, contrary to the Consulting Agreement, for the last two years of the contract. She did, however, continue to receive payment under that contract until its expiry in December 1998. Needless to say, Mr. Miglin opted not to renew the Consulting Agreement at the end of its term. We fail to see how, at the time of application, the ongoing receipt of payment for services not being performed can constitute a change of any kind.

102 Regarding the purported changes to the child-care arrangements, the *ad hoc* parenting arrangements that developed during the period of amicable relations between the parties no doubt reflected the changing needs of the growing children. These changes are an ordinary fact of life. We note too that by the time of the trial, the eldest child was residing primarily with Mr. Miglin.

103 Moreover, even if we accept that the expiry of the Consulting Agreement can be construed as occurring at the time of Ms. Miglin's application, we do not consider its non-renewal to be sufficient to render continued reliance on the original agreement inappropriate. First, the contract stipulated that renewal required the consent of both parties. Second, the income projections and tax planning advice provided by Ms. Miglin's accountant at the time of negotiation carried that assumption and thus made her fully aware that she would be without that income in five years. Third, there is no evidence of any damaging long-term impact of the marriage on Ms. Miglin's employability or that at the time of negotiation she underestimated how long it would take to become self-sufficient. Ms. Miglin is an educated woman with employable skills who worked in the business throughout the marriage. Although she is no doubt responsible for the day-to-day care of the three children residing with her, she has previously demonstrated her willingness to engage child-care services. The parties dispute whether Ms. Miglin attempted to pursue any employment. What is clear from the correspondence between counsel during negotiation of the agreement, however, is that Ms. Miglin had no intention of working.

104 The only real changes we see are the variation of the child support award in accordance with the Guidelines and the fact that the eldest child is now residing primarily with Mr.

Miglin. The quantum of child support established in the Agreement provided Ms. Miglin with a minimum amount of income in contemplation of her not working. Her lawyer, in a letter to Mr. Miglin's counsel, states: "She is clearly not going to be working. Taking care of the children is a full time job at this time. It does not change the nature of the spousal support release anyway. ..." Furthermore, the correspondence makes it clear that Ms. Miglin contemplated a reduction in income when the Consulting Agreement ended and was advised by her accountant to plan ahead for this drop in income. In our view, the change to the obligations regarding child care did not take Ms. Miglin's current position outside the reasonable range of circumstances that the parties contemplated in making the Separation Agreement.

105 At the Court of Appeal, counsel for Ms. Miglin suggested that her financial position deteriorated after the breakdown of the marriage. The record demonstrates (and she concedes), however, that her net worth in fact increased by at least 20 percent. At the time of her support application, a financial statement dated June 2, 1998, filed as part of the record, valued her net worth at $750,000 with essentially no debt. The statement shows that she held $246,000 in RRSPs, $83,000 in cash, and an unencumbered five-bedroom home valued at $395,000. The only debt listed on the statement was an unsubstantial debt for a credit card. By the time of trial, one year later, she valued her home at $400,000. There was no evidence that the terms of the agreement resulted in conditions under which Ms. Miglin could not assure her family's livelihood and had to deplete her assets, thus bringing her outside the range of circumstances in which she pictured herself at the time of executing the Separation Agreement.

106 The respondent's evidence and argument regarding her circumstances at the time of her support application fail to demonstrate that the agreement fairly negotiated and substantially compliant with the objectives of the 1985 Act at its formation should not continue to govern the parties' post-divorce obligations towards each other.

[JUSTICE LeBEL wrote a dissenting opinion with which Deschamps J. concurred. He accepted the majority's view that the *Pelech* trilogy's high threshold for an original spousal support order at variance with a separation agreement was no longer appropriate in light of the 1985 *Divorce Act* and the more contextual approach to spousal support in the Supreme Court of Canada's recent jurisprudence.

The dissenters suggested that the appropriate threshold for overriding an agreed-upon spousal support provision was whether the agreement was objectively fair at the time of the application for corollary relief. In their view, this test was based on the language of the statute and was also grounded in sound policy reasons that reflected the context in which these agreements were made and the complex circumstances that evolved after a marriage break-up. This threshold allowed a court to intervene whether the unfairness at the time of the application stemmed from the initial unfairness of the agreement, the failure of the spouses to predict accurately how the economic consequences of the marriage or its break-down would play out, or changes in the spouses' circumstances. By testing whether an agreement had in fact brought about an equitable distribution of the economic consequences of the marriage and its breakdown, this approach determined whether the agreement had achieved the ultimate goal of spousal support embodied in the *Divorce Act* and affirmed by the Supreme Court of Canada's recent jurisprudence.

Justice LeBel noted that the process of determining whether an agreement was fair would necessarily be fact specific. The issue in each case would be whether, in light of all the parties' circumstances at the time of the application, the agreement adequately met the spousal support objectives of s. 15.2(6) of the *Divorce Act*. This would require judges to make case-by-case determinations based on the parties' respective functions during the marriage, their allocation of capital and income upon breakup, their childcare responsibilities, their employment prospects, and a range of other factors. While he stated that the parties' own attempts to achieve the objectives codified in s. 15.2(6) should not be lightly disregarded, he stressed that an agreement only merited respect in an application for spousal support where it genuinely attempted to apportion the economic consequences of the marriage and its breakdown equitably. Even then, he believed that the court had a duty to intervene if, at the time of the application, the agreement fell outside the parameters of the generous ambit within which reasonable disagreement was possible in terms of realizing the objectives of s. 15.2(6).

Responding to the main criticism of a low threshold for judicial intervention, Justice LeBel argued that the requirement that an agreement be objectively fair would not discourage negotiated settlements. Rather, in his view, it would motivate spouses to reach an equitable distribution of the economic consequences of their marriage and its breakdown.

Turning to the specific case under appeal, Justice LeBel concluded that it was not appropriate to give effect to the waiver of spousal support. He found that the negotiated financial arrangements fell outside the generous ambit of reasonable attempts to meet the objectives of s. 15.2(6) of the *Divorce Act*, both at the time that they were negotiated and when the wife applied for corollary relief.

In the result, Justice LeBel would have upheld the decision of the Ontario Court of Appeal. He agreed specifically with the appellate court's removal of the five-year term on spousal support. Given the ages of the children and the wife's responsibilities towards them, he suggested that it had been pure speculation to assume that the wife would be self-sufficient in five years.]

COOPER v. COOPER

(2007), 2007 CarswellNS 345 (S.C.)

[The following case illustrates how courts now interpret and apply *Miglin*. The case is interesting because the husband gave up significant property in exchange for a reduced term of spousal support payments. Absent the generous property settlement, the husband could have expected to pay spousal support for a much longer time in light of the length of marriage, and the relative financial situations of the parties. When spousal support was no longer payable under the agreement, the wife asked a court to make a support order under the *Divorce Act*.

Note the court alludes (in para. 3) to the fact that the spousal support terms of the separation agreement were not included in the divorce judgment. Accordingly, the wife's application for spousal support was an initial application, just as in *Miglin*.]

WARNER J.:

A. Issue and Introduction

1 On application of the *Miglin* analysis, should a Separation Agreement which provides fixed term spousal support following a long-term traditional marriage in exchange for a significant unequal division of assets be upheld or overridden? What constitutes a reasonable level of self-sufficiency?

2 The parties separated in February 1998 after a long-term "traditional" marriage. After extended negotiations with experienced counsel a Separation Agreement was executed in October 2000. The agreement: split equally Mr. Cooper's military pension ($212,000 to Ms.

Cooper); gave Ms. Cooper more matrimonial assets than their net value (assets of $300,000, debts of $200,000); left Mr. Cooper with a deficit (assets of $3,000, debts of $40,000); and directed payment of spouse support of $2500.00 per month (40% of Mr. Cooper's employment income) for six years (in addition to the two and a half years between separation and the agreement).

3 Mr. Cooper petitioned for and obtained a Divorce Judgment in Ontario in May 2001. A Corollary Relief Judgment was not applied for or issued at that time. Spousal support ended in November 2006. In February 2007 Ms. Cooper applied in Nova Scotia for a Corollary Relief Judgment seeking continuation of indefinite spousal support. Mr. Cooper asks that the terms of the Separation Agreement be upheld. The jurisdiction of this court to determine the issue, and the applicability of the Miglin analysis, are not disputed.

B. Factual Background

4 The Coopers were married in 1972. Mr. Cooper was a twenty-one-year-old private in the Air Force with a Grade 10 education. Ms. Cooper was a twenty-five-year-old single parent of a six month old child on social assistance, with a Grade 12 education. They had two children together. Mr. Cooper raised Ms. Cooper's first child as his own. The children are now independent. By agreement the marriage was a "traditional" one. Ms. Cooper was a stay-at-home parent and Mr. Cooper the breadwinner. ...

6 As is typical of military families, the Coopers moved eight times between 1972 and 1995 when Mr. Cooper took early retirement. I find no reliable evidence that Ms. Cooper expressed a desire to pursue higher education or career opportunities outside the home until 1995 when she expressed the desire to purchase a farm in rural Nova Scotia and commence llama farming, in which pursuit she received Mr. Cooper's full support.

7 On retirement, Mr. Cooper initially obtained employment with the nearby Michelin Tire plant. The Coopers' income totalled $68,000.00 (Mr. Cooper's employment income and pension) less farm losses. In August 1997 Mr. Cooper accepted a position in Ontario as a professional engineer. Ms. Cooper remained on the farm. In February 1998 Mr. Cooper informed Ms. Cooper that the marriage was over.

Post-separation

8 At the time of separation and the Separation Agreement, Mr. Cooper's annual income consisted of $74,984.00 employment income from ADGA Group and an unindexed military pension of $28,224.00.

9 After separation Ms. Cooper continued to operate the llama farm at East Dalhousie, Nova Scotia. When started, the parties had agreed to try to establish it as a going concern for a period of five years. The five years were up in 2000. Post-separation the farm continued to incur an annual deficit and consumed a significant portion of Mr. Cooper's income, the family savings, and caused further debt. The financial records before the Court show that, since the Separation Agreement, the llama farm has continued to incur annual deficits; it has never generated a net profit or income. ...

13 Attached to Mr. Cooper's Affidavit as exhibit 5B and 5H are 172 pages of correspondence and emails between the parties and their lawyers related to the negotiation and execution of the Separation Agreement. From not later than September 1998, Ms. Cooper was represented by Lynn Reierson, one of the preeminent lawyers practising family law. Exhibit 5B and 5H confirm that all the relevant legal and factual issues were thoroughly canvassed. It is clear Ms. Reierson advised Ms. Cooper and told Mr. Cooper on many occasions that

courts do not generally support fixed term spousal support orders for long-term traditional marriages.

14 As a result of the Separation Agreement:

(a) Mr. Cooper's military pension was divided equally, with Ms. Cooper receiving $212,192.00 in January 2001;

(b) Ms. Cooper received the farm, llamas, RSPs, one vehicle and most of the household effects with a value of approximately $300,000.00, and she assumed the mortgage and her VISA bill in the amount of approximately $97,000.00 for net assets in excess of $200,000.00;

(c) Mr. Cooper ended up with one vehicle and a few household effects, worth $3,000.00, and the remaining debts of approximately $41,000.00; that is, net debt of $37,000.00;

(e) Mr. Cooper's pension income was reduced by $1,006.00 per month ($12,000.00 per year) or from $28,000.00 to $16,000.00 per year (to be further reduced at age sixty-five);

(f) Ms. Cooper invested all or most of her share of the pension in a manner that nets her approximately $800.00 per month;

(g) In addition to $120,000.00 paid by Mr. Cooper for two and a half years before the Agreement, he paid spousal support of $2,500.00 per month — approximately 40% of his employment income at that time for six more years.

15 The Separation Agreement included [a term indicating that it was intended to be a "full and final settlement between the parties" and "a complete defence to any action brought by either party to assert a claim in respect of any matter dealt with". There were also a number of release clauses, including one specifically dealing with spousal support. The latter included the statements that the parties "realize that there may be future changes in their financial circumstances by reason of their health, the cost of living, their employment, financial management, financial reversals, inheritance or otherwise" and that "no change whatsoever, even if it be material, profound, catastrophic or otherwise, will give either the right to claim or obtain support".]

C. Parties' Submissions

Applicant's Argument

16 The Applicant acknowledges that the *Miglin* analysis is the applicable test. She acknowledges that the negotiation of the agreement itself (stage 1 step 1) was unimpeachable. She argues, with respect to the stage 1 step 2 analysis, that the agreement did not meet the objectives of the *Divorce Act* when negotiated because self-sufficiency was not an attainable goal within the time allowed. She cites *Camp v. Camp*, 2006 BCSC 608 (B.C. S.C.) as support for this submission.

17 Given her age (51 at separation), education (High School) and work experience (sporadic minimum-wage jobs during a long-term marriage), and despite her optimism at the time of the agreement, self-sufficiency through employment was not an attainable goal. Self-sufficiency was dependent upon investment income, supplemented by the Canada Pension and some minimum-wage employment. The maximum attainable investment income (assuming liquidation of all assets) was $20,400.00 per year, Canada Pension was $323.00 per month or $3,876.00 per year, and minimum wage employment would earn her a maximum of

$1,300.00 per month or $15,600.00 per year. She argues that this level of income would not suffice to attain a reasonable economic self-sufficiency. Although not expressly argued in her memorandum, I assume that Ms. Cooper's budget (Exhibit 2), which lists expenses of $4,200.00 per month or $50,000.00 per year exclusive of income tax, constitutes her representation of reasonable economic self-sufficiency in her circumstances.

18 With respect to the stage 2 analysis, the Applicant argues that if the agreement did pass the stage 1 step 2 test, the agreement does not meet the objectives of the *Divorce Act* today, since the unequal division of assets (the value of which assets is less today than at the time of the agreement), has not generated sufficient income for reasonable self-sufficiency.

19 The Applicant acknowledges that the Respondent's circumstances have also changed:

> a) He remarried; his new wife had a remunerative career, but by reason of a serious illness has been hospitalized and is unable to contribute to the family income except minimally; in addition, her condition has contributed to higher living expenses in their household.

> b) In 2003, in anticipation of the termination of spousal support, the Respondent and his wife (then age 46 and without a child) adopted a one-year-old child from China at a significant cost; that child is now starting school.

> c) The Respondent suffered a financial setback from the sale of a property for less than the expected value; this, added to other debts, with a significantly higher debt load than at the time of the agreement ($190,000.00 now versus $41,000.00 then); his ability to borrow money has been maxed out.

> d) He intended to retire within two years — to stay home to raise their child and do woodworking while his wife continued her career. The Applicant submits (correctly in my view) that this plan is unreasonable in light of the inability of his wife to work more than minimally, his substantial debts, and the cost of raising a young child, even if Mr. Cooper is correct in concluding that he is burnt out from stressful employment since the age of seventeen.

20 Despite the Respondent's setbacks, the Applicant argues that the Respondent has employment income of about $90,000.00 per year plus his share of the military pension ($18,000.00 per year) and can afford to pay some spousal support.

Respondent's Argument

21 Regarding the stage 1 step 2 analysis, the Respondent argues that the *Camp* decision is distinguishable from this case for several reasons:

> a) Mr. Camp never made full financial disclosure (para. 32). From the disclosed information, the court concluded that Ms. Camp's one-half share of the matrimonial assets would have totalled $590,000.00 (versus the $750,000.00 capital sum invested for her under the agreement) but this $590,000.00 excluded many items. It appears that he concluded that Mr. Camp did not prove an uneven division of assets in favour of Ms. Camp.

> b) Mr. Camp breached his guarantee that Ms. Camp's capital fund would generate at least 8% return for fifteen years.

> c) Despite Ms, Camp's reasonable efforts to seek and maintain employment during the marriage, she had a serious heart-related health issue that prevented her from obtaining employment income after separation.

22 With respect to the stage 2 analysis, the Respondent argues that the Applicant was and is a healthy and productive person who is able to contribute to her own support through employment income. He argues that since she agreed to exchange indefinite or open spousal support for a substantially unequal division of matrimonial assets in her favour, she has made choices that were unreasonable. These choices included continuing to pursue her passion for llama farming when it clearly was not economic and when it consumed the spousal support paid and the assets acquired since separation. The Respondent argues that this choice was made with knowledge of the consequences. He submits that the Applicant's position that these consequences were not foreseeable or were beyond her control, did not hold up on cross-examination. ...

D. Law

24 The leading case is still *Miglin v. Miglin*, 2003 SCC 24 (S.C.C.). *Annual Review of Family Law 2006*, by the late James G. McLeod and Alfred A. Mamo (2006: Carswell, Toronto), c. 5, contains a useful enumeration of factors relevant to the application of the *Miglin* test to this case. McLeod and Mamo divide their analysis into the four inter-related issues of validity, enforcement, overriding the agreement and interpretation of the agreement.

25 They write that courts encourage spouses to settle their disputes, and if they do, generally respect their settlements. This does not mean courts will uphold unfair but valid agreements, or agreements which become unfair as a result of changed circumstances outside the spouses' reasonable contemplation; however, the onus is on the person challenging the agreement to establish that it is either not valid or should be overridden.

E. Analysis

26 Stage 1 step 1 of the *Miglin* analysis requires the Court to look at the circumstances of the negotiation and execution of the agreement. The Applicant does not argue that the circumstances surrounding the negotiation and execution of the agreement make the agreement invalid. A review of the affidavits, and the cross-examination of the parties on their affidavits, and in particular a review of Exhibit 5B and 5H, the emails and correspondence between the parties over the two years of their negotiations, gives a clear picture of the process that led to the agreement. It shows that:

> a) Both spouses were directly involved in the protracted negotiations and were at all times aware of the circumstances and the position of each other.

> b) Both spouses were represented by legal counsel throughout. Ms. Cooper was represented by Lynn Reierson, one of the preeminent lawyers in the area of family law. She advised the Applicant and advocated to the Respondent in an aggressive and capable manner throughout the negotiation and execution process. The Applicant's present case is based on the proposition that spousal support should have been indefinite. Exhibit 5B shows many occasions when Ms. Reierson advised the Applicant and advocated to the Respondent the attitude of courts on this issue. ...

27 The emails and correspondence in Exhibit 5B further demonstrate the Applicant's and Respondent's views with regards to the contribution that llama farming could make towards her efforts to attain self-sufficiency. The exchanges include:

> a) A July 23, 1999 email from the Applicant to the Respondent, "I was shocked at your suggestion of outside employment ... we have discussed a five-year plan where

we expected to build a reputation and a good line of breeding stock. When you originally moved to Ottawa no mention was made to change the plan. I am far ahead of this plan on my own in less than four years and have sold more llamas than anyone in Atlantic Canada ... if one looks at the books and sees only the red at the infancy of this business, it does not measure the success so far."

b) In an October 25, 1999 email to the Applicant the Respondent wrote, "When we got into the llama business we agreed that we would give it five years to make money, which to my way of thinking meant that if it was not making a profit by year five then it would be time to get out of the business. I supported the business for four years investing most of my retirement money, my spare time working on the barn, house and fields ... I do not want to fight over this separation, but I also do not want to be taken advantage of just because you want to keep a business that you yourself said was ahead of the five year plan after only four years, yet has not come even close to making a profit. If you insist on keeping the farm and animals then you must be prepared to subsidize the business yourself. ... You are an intelligent and resourceful woman and I know that you would have little difficulty getting a job and eventually becoming self-sufficient. The five years that I have offered to pay this spousal support would allow you time to get settled and possibly allow you to save some money for retirement.". ...

28 The affidavits and cross-examination confirm that the Applicant was informed of and understood the effect and implication of her decision to negotiate for retention of the farm and llama business in exchange for time-limited spousal support, and that she was prepared to accept the consequences of that choice.

29 In this case it is not contested that the Respondent provided full financial disclosure. The agreement itself is detailed and explicit and without ambiguities of any kind.

30 In some cases, both before and since *Miglin*, courts have set aside agreements where duress, compulsion or "practical compulsion" is shown to exist. Some courts have relaxed the concept of duress in divorce circumstances, but it is clear that the concept of practical compulsion does not arise solely from the parties being under stress associated with the marriage breakdown. In the case at bar, the Applicant was under no particular financial pressure. Her expenses were being paid by the Respondent together with spousal support on an unofficial basis. The Respondent's retirement allowance and some RSPs had been cashed in to support the farm and llama business. There was no particular urgency to resolve the issue, even though both spouses expressed frustration with respect to the position of the other.

31 There was no evidence of undue influence based on any control or power that the Respondent had over the Applicant. There was no evidence of imbalance arising from the dynamics of the relationship of the spouses to each other from which the Court might imply that the Respondent took advantage of the Applicant to obtain an unfair bargain. On the contrary, the advocacy of the Applicant in her communications to the Respondent and in her lawyer's communications to the Respondent were clear, effective and aggressive.

32 No mistake of law or fact was claimed or shown to exist during the negotiations or in respect of the execution of the agreement.

33 No misrepresentation or misstatement of any material fact by the Respondent was alleged or shown to exist.

34 The fact that the Applicant was represented by eminent legal counsel speaks to the validity of the agreement and to the unambiguous clarity with which it sets out the intentions of the parties at the time of its execution. ...

35 I agree that the Applicant is intelligent and resourceful and during the eight and a half years that she received spousal support had time and the ability to embark upon a career, or undertake retraining, to eventually pay some of her living expenses. Instead she became a hobby farmer and pursued a passion which she knew, or should have known, would not contribute to her financial well-being. It drained the capital from which she could eventually receive investment income. The division of assets was entirely in the Applicant's favour. Including the division of the military pension, the Applicant received over two-thirds of their assets. She made the choice to accept the farm and llama "business" in exchange for time-limited spousal support in order to maintain a lifestyle that she chose. At the time of the Agreement, financial independence — to the standard that prevailed during the marriage — was a realistic and attainable goal with the combination of investment income and employment income. Based on my assessment of her obvious intelligence, if she had pursued further training or education, she could have attained a standard of living greater than that which appears to have prevailed during most of the marriage. ...

43 I conclude that prudent investment of the Applicant's share of the military pension, together with reasonable steps to supplement that income with pursuit of employment opportunities during the eight plus years since the separation (including retraining if necessary), even without the Canada Pension that she now receives, could have provided her with a level of self-sufficiency based on the lifestyle of the parties that prevailed during most of their marriage.

44 At paragraph 46 in *Miglin*, the Supreme Court confirms that trial courts must balance Parliament's objective of equitable sharing of the consequences of marriage and its breakdown, with the parties *freed to arrange their affairs as they see fit*. ...

46 A summary of my analysis of the four objectives in s. 15.1(6) of the *Divorce Act* as they apply to this case are as follows:

a) First Objective

The Applicant's circumstances at the time she entered the marriage were not made worse, but rather improved, by the marriage, and there was no offsetting financial advantage to the Respondent. During the marriage the Applicant did not appear to intend to pursue a career outside the home; however, she did adopt a role in the marriage that caused her not to focus on financial self-sufficiency in the future. This circumstance creates some entitlement. This circumstance is balanced against the sharing of the financial benefits accrued through the Respondent's employment, that is, the lifestyle during the marriage and the division of the assets (including military pension) at separation.

b) Second Objective

The children were independent as of the separation Agreement. The Respondent supported the youngest child after the separation.

c) Third Objective

While the Applicant has not identified any specific advantage to the Respondent, or disadvantage to her, by reason of their marriage, she clearly would, but for the division of assets and provision of spousal support, have suffered economic hardship by reason of the breakdown of the marriage. Despite the division of their assets, unequally in her favour, she had not focussed during the marriage on financial independence in the event of its breakdown. In my view, this third objective is the primary basis upon which the Applicant has an entitlement to spousal support.

d) Fourth Objective

The practicality of the Applicant attaining economic self-sufficiency within the eight and half years after separation has been the battleground of this application. The Applicant's age and lack of post-secondary education constitute the limitations on her ability to attain self-sufficiency through employment alone. This limitation has been cushioned by the division of the military pension and by the fact that the Applicant received all of the family's assets, leaving the Respondent with net debt.

47 It appears that the Applicant acted as if she were entitled to continue to operate the llama farm at a substantial annual loss long after it became apparent, or should have become apparent, that it was not a viable source of income. She had and has intelligence and energy. She has the capacity to retrain and to otherwise establish herself in the workforce. The combination of her age and lack of post-secondary education, that made it unlikely that she could attain a reasonable financial independence through employment alone, does not release her from the obligation to use her obvious intelligence to pursue employment, or retraining, that would supplement her investment income. The evidence, and in particular the cross-examination of the Applicant, left no doubt that the Applicant did not act on her obligation to promote her own self-sufficiency until the spousal support contained in the Separation Agreement ended.

F. Conclusion

48 Self-sufficiency, based on investment income and employment income, combined with the family home, effects, and other assets she retained, was a reasonably attainable goal at the time of the negotiation and entering into of the agreement.

49 The Respondent too has suffered many reverses since the Separation Agreement. Some of these reverses were unforeseen. The serious illness of his wife that has taken her out of the workforce and the reverses in respect of a property transaction in Ontario were unforeseen. These circumstances would likely not have been sufficient, in light of the clear and unambiguous terms of the Separation Agreement, to entitle the Respondent to relief from the terms of the agreement. The Respondent's undertaking, late in life, to adopt a child (now five years of age) was reasonable conduct with the expectation that his support obligation would end in 2006. These circumstances are relevant factors in the stage 2 analysis. They affect the Respondent's ability to pay at this time, and mitigate against overriding the agreement. The stage 2 *Miglin* analysis deals with unfairness to the parties, not just unfairness to the Applicant.

50 The Separation Agreement was a fair settlement of the financial consequences of the breakdown of the marriage when it was negotiated and executed. There have been changes in circumstances since the Separation Agreement; however, none of those changes makes the agreement as originally executed unfair. I measure unfairness in the context of the objectives described in s. 15.2(6) of the *Divorce Act*.

51 I grant the Corollary Relief Judgment incorporating the terms of the Separation Agreement.

NOTES AND QUESTIONS

1. Professor Rogerson states in "*Miglin v. Miglin* 2003 SCC 24: They are Agreements Nonetheless" (2003), 20 Can. J. Fam. L. 197 (at paras. 8, 9, and 44):

> The Court's judgment in *Miglin* is, to put it simply, a disappointing one. The majority reasons ... ostensibly overrule the *Pelech* trilogy, finding its privileging of values of clean break inappropriate in the current legislative and jurisprudential context. But the majority reasons also emphasize the continued relevance of the policy reasons that underlie the trilogy — certainty, finality, and autonomy. Seeking what is portrayed as a more "balanced" approach, the majority replaces the trilogy with a complex, multi-part, fact-driven test. At best, the new test will create considerable confusion in the law as to its meaning, thus failing to resolve the uncertainty that has plagued this area of law for at least a decade. At worst, the new test reintroduces the stringency of the trilogy test in a new guise.
>
> The majority reasons speak in two voices: one emphasizing fairness concerns and the unique context in which spousal support agreements are negotiated, the other emphasizing the continued relevance of values of certainty, finality, and autonomy. In the end, the latter voice speaks louder and conveys the dominant language of the judgment. ...
>
> Continuing the pattern established in cases like *Bracklow* and *Gordon v. Goertz*, the Supreme Court of Canada continues to abdicate its responsibility to establish clear principles to guide the resolution of family law disputes, preferring to delegate to trial judges an unfettered discretion to balance numerous factors and objectives in the rendering of fine-tuned, individualized justice. The result, however, is most often uncertainty and unpredictability in the application of the law, with outcomes shaped by the subjective values of judges and lawyers. *Miglin* continues a pattern of the Court avoiding hard policy choices in family law, under the guise that the correct answer will emerge simply from a sensitive reading of the facts of particular cases and/ or of the legislation.

Professor Rogerson also predicts (at para. 48): "In practice, the *Miglin* test will likely operate as an 'unconsionable circumstances' test: the test proposed by Mr. Miglin's counsel and ostensibly rejected by the majority."

2. In *Dolson v. Dolson* (2004), 7 R.F.L. (6th) 25 (Ont. S.C.J.), Justice Heeney struggled to apply the *Miglin* test to an application under the *Divorce Act* to vary a limited term support order that incorporated a provision from the parties' Minutes of Settlement. He noted (at para. 4): "*Miglin* raises as many questions as it answers, at least with respect to the fact situation before this court." However, he suggested (para. 75): "The recurring theme that is woven throughout the majority decision in *Miglin* is that written agreements between spouses should generally be upheld."

In his annotation to the case in the RFLs, Professor McLeod notes that case law prior to the *Miglin* case held that a court hearing a variation application had to accept that a prior order was fair and reasonable at the time that it was made even if it merely incorporated the parties' agreement. He then states (at 29):

> This seems to suggest that once a support agreement is converted into a court order, the order is *res judicata* of the first step in the *Miglin* analysis. ...
>
> If this is correct, on an application to vary a support order that incorporates a support agreement, a court must assume that the prior order and *a fortiori* the underlying agreement was reasonable and decide whether to change support if: (a) there has been a material change that would justify varying the order in the absence of an agreement and (b) the change also meets the second stage of the *Miglin* analysis. The former gives the court the statutory authority to vary and the latter provides special discretion-structuring factors to assist the court in deciding whether to exercise that power in the circumstances of the case.

However, Professor McLeod acknowledges (at 30) that the difficulty with this approach is that courts, in Ontario at least, "routinely 'rubber stamp' consensual spousal support arrangements" without assessing the circumstances surrounding the negotiation of the agreement or its content. He suggests (*ibid*) that, when courts are asked to convert a contractual provision into a consensual court order, they should determine whether it is appropriate to do so in light of the *Miglin* test.

3. In *Marinangeli v. Marinangeli* (2003), 38 R.F.L. (5th) 307 (Ont. C.A.), the husband and wife signed minutes of settlement in which the husband agreed to pay $6,000 monthly as spousal support. The minutes specified that the support provisions could be varied in the event of a material change in circumstances. Justice Weiler, for the court, reviewed the agreement and concluded that the parties intended the term "material change in circumstances" to

include foreseeable events such as an increase or decrease in income. Accordingly, she stated (para. 46) that the *Miglin* test did not apply. The appellate court upheld the substantial increase in spousal support ordered by the trial judge.

Based partly on cases such as *Marinangeli*, it is sometimes suggested that the *Miglin* case is irrelevant where an agreement or consent order contemplates variation. This is probably an over-statement. The approach in *Miglin* suggests that the parties should be held to their agreement, including the terms of the variation clause, unless the two-stage *Miglin* test is met. This may be very significant where a variation clause is quite limited or specifically sets out the changes that will allow variation. See McLeod, "Annotation" (2004), 4 R.F.L. (5th) 26 at 26.

4. Whether a court should order interim spousal support at variance with a domestic contract in proceedings where the applicant is challenging the validity of the contract or asking the court to override its terms on the basis of *Miglin* is a difficult issue. If the applicant ultimately fails at trial, the contract should have governed throughout the proceedings. However, at the interim stage a court is unlikely to be in a good position to assess the likelihood of success at trial. For post-*Miglin* cases dealing with the matter, see *Palmer v. Palmer* (2003), 45 R.F.L. (5th) 447 (Sask. Q.B.) (refusal to order interim support in the absence of exceptional circumstances); *Cherneski v. Cherneski* (2003), 49 R.F.L. (5th) 299 (Ont. S.C.J.) (refusal to order interim support); and *Salzmann v. Salzmann* (2004), 50 R.F.L. (5th) 181 (Ont. S.C.J.) (interim support ordered where the motions judge believed that the wife had a strong case).

5. There is some overlap between the circumstances that might lead to a successful challenge to the validity of a domestic contract and the first stage of the *Miglin* test. This has caused some judges to confuse setting aside a domestic contract with overriding a contractual provision dealing with spousal support. See, e.g., *Rogerson v. Rogerson* (2004), 5 R.F.L. (6th) 151 (N.S. S.C.).

The distinction between setting aside an agreement because of a flaw in the formation of the contract and overriding a contractual support provision is important. In the first situation, the agreement no longer exists and cannot bar any statutory claim, whether it relates to property, spousal support or any other matter. In the second situation, a court is using its statutory power to order support at variance with a term in a valid, enforceable contract. The other contractual terms continue to govern.

(ii) Under the Family Law Act — Applications in the Face of Valid Agreements Eliminating or Restricting Spousal Support

Section 33(4) of the *FLA* gives a court jurisdiction, in three circumstances, to set aside a contractual provision for support or a waiver of the right to support and then to determine and order support under the Act. This authority exists even though the contract is valid and enforceable and notwithstanding an express provision in the contract purporting to exclude the application of the subsection.

SCHEEL v. HENKELMAN

(2001), 11 R.F.L. (5th) 376, 2001 CarswellOnt 28 (Ont. C.A.)

BORINS J.A.: —

1 This appeal by Jacoba Scheel from the judgment of Cosgrove J. presents a single issue. It is whether the trial judge correctly interpreted and applied s. 33(4)(a) of the *Family Law Act*, R.S.O. 1990, c. F.3 (the "FLA") in rejecting Ms. Scheel's claim for support from Henry Henkelman with whom she had entered into a domestic contract by which they had each waived their right to support.

Background

2 Ms. Scheel, who is now about 65 years of age, and Mr. Henkelman, who is now about 69 years of age, have known each other for many years. In 1978 Mr. Henkelman employed Ms. Scheel as his assistant. At that time he was engaged in substantial real estate and business

activities. In 1986 the parties decided to live together in a house that was owned by one of Mr. Henkelman's companies. Each was married, but separated.

3 On July 4, 1986, the appellant and the respondent signed a cohabitation agreement. It is common ground that it is a cohabitation agreement within the meaning of s. 53(1) of the FLA and a domestic contract with the meaning of s. 33(4) of the FLA. The agreement contained the following provision:

> The parties each agree to be responsible at all times, subject this agreement, for his or her own support and not to any degree for the support of the other. They acknowledge that this is a fair and equitable arrangement at the present and for the future.

The agreement also contained a detailed, comprehensive and far-reaching mutual release of virtually every claim which either party might have in the present or in the future against the property of the other, including rights to interim or permanent support.

4 In addition, the agreement addressed living arrangements for Ms. Scheel in the event the parties ceased cohabitation. In essence, the parties agreed to resolve the mechanism by which she was to vacate the matrimonial home "in a non contentious fashion".

5 The relationship of employer and employee continued until 1996 when Mr. Henkelman retired from his business activities. Until then, Ms. Scheel had worked full time for Mr. Henkelman for 18 years. Although she received a termination payment of $52,500.00, she continued to work on a part time basis for several months. Given her age, it is not surprising that when this work came to an end, Ms. Scheel was unable to find employment.

6 After several disagreements, the parties separated in 1997. The cause of the separation was Mr. Henkelman's chronic alcohol abuse. He locked Ms. Scheel out of their residence on June 25, 1997. Early in 1998 Ms. Scheel commenced proceedings against Mr. Henkelman for relief pursuant to the FLA. She sought an order "setting aside" the cohabitation agreement, and for spousal support of $5,000 a month, a constructive trust on Mr. Henkelman's shares in his companies, severance pay in the amount of $100,000, "back wages" of $30,000 for work done subsequent to Mr. Henkelman's retirement, and damages for battery.

7 The master awarded Ms. Scheel interim support of $2,500 a month commencing December 1, 1998. An appeal from this order was dismissed by Panet J. Cosgrove J. dismissed the majority of Ms. Scheel's claims. However, he awarded her damages of $15,000 on the ground that the respondent had breached the provision of the cohabitation agreement dealing with her living arrangements, and damages of $3,200 for back wages.

8 Ms. Scheel has appealed from the dismissal of her claims for an order setting aside the cohabitation agreement and spousal support. ...

[In addition to the facts described above, the trial judge found the following: the couple entered into the agreement before they began their cohabitation; each party had independent legal advice; Henkelman had assets worth approximately $2.5 million before the couple began to cohabit; and Scheel had assets worth about $187,000 when they separated.]

12 The trial judge dismissed the appellant's claims for the following reasons:

> When the parties separated in 1997, the plaintiff's net worth was approximately $187,000. She had managed these savings by the sale of property and by saving her salary while employed by the defendant. In addition, she received a payment of $52,500 from the defendant when some of his holdings were sold. The plaintiff had demonstrated her resourcefulness in the responsibilities she undertook for the defendant in his business operations including property management, bookkeeping and even manual labour in re-painting some of the property. In my view, she today continues with the potential to offer these skills and experiences in the work place. In addition, she has the potential in managing her real estate to achieve rental income to offset carrying charges which to date she has not attempted.

> Because I find that the plaintiff was fully aware of the implications inherent in signing the Cohabitation Agreement, that she gained valuable work experience and was able to save for her future while

cohabiting with the defendant since 1986, and that she impressed in her evidence that she was capable of promoting her skills in the areas of remunerable experience gained during cohabitation. I make no finding of "unconscionability", notwithstanding the evidence of her apparent support and nurture of the defendant during his cohabitation.

13 The trial judge made no reference to the appellant's age, which was 64 at the time of the trial, to the fact that she was unemployable and that her only income was a monthly Canada Pension Plan pension of $407.00, to the fact that the respondent had apparent assets worth over $3,000,000, or to the fact that the appellant, largely due to her employment by the respondent, was financially independent when the parties signed the cohabitation agreement as a result of the salary she received from the respondent which had come to an end in February, 1996. It should be noted that a portion of the appellant's net worth of $187,000 consists of a home that she purchased for $129,000 following her separation from the respondent, which is mortgaged for $82,000.

Analysis

15 It is well established that s. 33(4) empowers the court to set aside a waiver of support contained in a domestic contract only when an application for support has been commenced, as in this appeal, under s. 33(1): *Mealey v. Broadbent* (1984), 47 O.R. (2d) 161 (Ont. Div. Ct.); aff'd. (1987), 5 R.F.L. (3d) 214 (Ont. C.A.). ... The use of the phrase "results in" in s. 33(4)(a) means that the subsection is not directed to unconscionable agreements, but to unconscionable results of a provision waiving support. An agreement which was fair and reasonable when it was signed, may, through circumstances that occur in the future, result in unconscionable circumstances at the time of a support application: *Mance v. Mance* (1981), 22 R.F.L. (2d) 445 (Ont. Co. Ct.); aff'd. (December 18, 1981), Cory, Jessup, Wilson JJ.A. (Ont. C.A.); *Newby v. Newby* (1986), 56 O.R. (2d) 483 (H.C.). As for an unconscionable agreement, it may be set aside under s. 56(4) of the FLA which is a codification of the general law of contract applicable to unconscionable agreements. It differs from s. 33(4), which operates in respect of valid and subsisting domestic contracts and enables the court to set aside a support provision, or a waiver of a right to support, in the contract where such provision "results in unconscionable circumstances". In other words, s. 33(4) concerns unconscionable circumstances and not unconscionable agreements.

16 As the appellant's claim under s. 33(4) to set aside the waiver of support was brought concurrently with a claim for support under s. 33(1), the claim was properly before the court. However, in my view the trial judge made several errors in his resolution of the claim.

17 In referring to ... the proposition that the courts are reluctant to set aside a domestic contract, the trial judge overlooked the fact that the appellant did not seek to set aside a domestic contract. She sought to have the waiver of the right to support contained in the domestic contract set aside on the ground that unconscionable circumstances had arisen from the waiver. She was entitled to seek this relief under s. 33(4) of the FLA. The appellant was not required to meet the more stringent test arising from the case law under the *Divorce Act*, R.S.C. 1985, c. D-3.4, where a party seeks to override support provisions in the parties' own agreement. [The case was decided prior to the Supreme Court of Canada's decision in *Miglin v. Miglin*, *supra*, and so this may be a reference to the *Pelech* trilogy.]

18 The issue before Cosgrove J. was straight forward and was whether the appellant had demonstrated that the waiver of her right to support had resulted in unconscionable circumstances, within the meaning of s. 33(4), at the time she commenced her application. Unfortunately, the trial judge failed to address this issue properly, and decided it on the basis of the substantial hurdle which a party must overcome when seeking to set aside an entire domestic contract. Moreover, he did not consider the authorities which have interpreted "unconscionablity" within the meaning of s. 33(4).

19 Although it does not appear that s. 33(4) has been considered by this court, there are a number of trial court decisions which have done so, the most helpful being *Newby*. At p. 486, Bolan L.J.S.C. considered the meaning of "unconscionable":

> The word "unconscionable" is defined in the Canadian Law Dictionary as "that which is contrary to the conscience of the Court". It is defined in the Webster's New Collegiate Dictionary as shockingly unfair or unjust. Whether "unconscionable" is used in a legal or non-legal sense, it can best be described as "something which is shocking, oppressive, not in keeping with a caring society".

20 He then stated that there are a number of factors to be considered in determining whether unconscionable circumstances have resulted, which he discussed at pp. 486 — 487, and which I would summarize as follows:

> (a) the circumstances surrounding the execution of the agreement, including the fact that each party was represented by competent counsel, the absence of any undue influence, the good faith and the expectations of the parties;
>
> (b) the results of the support provisions of the agreement, including any hardship visited upon a party, and
>
> (c) the parties' circumstances at the time of the hearing including their health, employability and ability to maintain their life-style.

21 The discussion in MacDonald and Wilton, *The 2000 Annotated Ontario Family Law Act*, 1999 at 259, on the meaning of "unconscionable" is also helpful:

> The use of the world "unconscionable" is important as well. The Legislature did not use phrases such as "harsh or unjust" or "improvident or unfortunate". It is submitted that the use of "unconscionable" creates a test that is more grave and weighty than mere harshness or injustice. Some assistance as to the meaning of unconscionable may be provided by various dictionary definitions. *Black's Law Dictionary* defines an unconscionable contract as "one which no man in his senses, not under delusion, would make on the one hand, and which no fair and honest man would expect on the other". The definition of unconscionable contract is one which is "monstrously harsh and shocking to the conscience". However, the standard dictionary definition of the term as found in the *Oxford English Dictionary* when applied to actions is defined as "showing no regard for conscience; not in accordance with what is right or reasonable". The *Random House Dictionary of the English Language*, which gives the definition in terms of American usage, defines the word as "not guided by conscience: unscrupulous; not in accordance with what is just or reasonable; excessive, extortionate".

22 In my view, the trial judge erred in placing too much emphasis on antecedent factors and failing to consider all of the parties' circumstances at the time of the appellant's application. Moreover, the evidence did not support his finding that the appellant was capable of supporting herself. In paragraph 13, I have outlined the factors which the trial judge failed to consider, the most significant of which were the appellant's age, that she was unemployable, her only income was a monthly pension of $407.00, that the respondent had removed the appellant as a beneficiary of his will and that the respondent had assets of $2,500,000 to $3,000,000. At the time of the trial, it was clear that the appellant was enduring significant economic hardship. It was equally clear that the respondent was capable of supporting the appellant.

23 I am satisfied that in failing to apply the proper test to the evidence the trial judge erred in failing to find that the support waiver provision in the domestic contract had resulted in unconscionable circumstances within the meaning of s. 33(4) of the FLA. Given the relative circumstances of the parties, it would be shocking to the conscience to require the appellant to live on her modest pension. The trial judge should have set aside the support waiver provision in the domestic contract and replaced it with a support order.

Conclusion

24 Rather than ordering a new trial to determine the appropriate amount of support, I am satisfied that there is sufficient evidence before this court to enable it to do so under s. 134(1) of the *Courts of Justice Act*, R.S.O. 1990, c. C.43. The master's award of interim support of $2,500 a month was upheld on appeal by Panet J. The respondent has substantial assets, which the appellant does not. She is in need. In my view, the appellant is entitled to support of $3,500 a month commencing from December 14, 1999, being the date on which her claim was dismissed.

NOTES AND QUESTIONS

1. Could Scheel have obtained spousal support under the *Divorce Act* if the couple had married? In other words, could she have met the *Miglin* test?

2. For cases applying *Scheel v. Henkelman*, see *Griffore v. Adsett* (2001), 18 R.F.L. (5th) 63 (Ont. S.C.J.); additional reasons at (2001), 2001 CarswellOnt 2523 (Ont. S.C.J.) *Camilleri v. Camilleri* (2001), 19 R.F.L. (5th) 15 (Ont. Div. Ct.); and *Mongillo v. Mongillo* (2007), 2007 CarswellOnt 2731 (S.C.J.).

3. The threshold set by s. 33(4)(b) of the *FLA* for a court to set aside a contractual waiver for support is crossed as soon as the applicant qualifies for "support out of public money". However, this only empowers a court to exercise its discretionary power to order spousal support. Should this power be exercised where a substantial period of time has elapsed since the separation and the dependant's need for public assistance cannot in some way be linked to the relationship?

4. Section 33(4) of the *FLA* sets a threshold for the setting aside of a contractual term dealing with spousal support that differs from the *Miglin* test. Should courts, nonetheless, be guided by the *Miglin* test in deciding whether to exercise their discretionary power under s. 33(4)? Consider that the setting of a lower threshold under provincial legislation may tempt a married payor to commence divorce proceedings and request a determination of the support issue under the *Divorce Act*. The federal law should then apply to the issue of support pursuant to the constitutional doctrine of paramountcy.

5. Where a court has incorporated the provisions of a separation agreement or other domestic contract into a support order under the *FLA*, it is not necessary to resort to s. 33(4) to obtain a variation. In that situation, either party can apply for a variation of the court order under s. 37. See *Ott v. Ott* (1982), 30 R.F.L. (2d) 370 (Ont. C.A.) and *Forder v. Forder* (1984), 40 R.F.L. (2d) 159 (Ont. Co. Ct.). While the court has jurisdiction to vary such an order whenever there has been a material change of circumstances, the policy considerations enunciated in *Miglin* may dictate deference in the exercise of this discretionary power.

6. The power to override the support provisions of a domestic contract granted by s. 33(4) of the *FLA* should be contrasted with the power to vary those provisions where the contract is filed with a court pursuant to s. 35(1). A provision for support in a contract that is filed with the court may be varied as if it were an order of the court where it is filed: s. 35(2)(b). There are several significant differences between the power to override support provisions under s. 33(4) and the power to vary them under s. 35(2). First, s. 33(4) only applies where a claim for support is made and so only the dependant can invoke the court's jurisdiction. On the other hand, either spouse can bring an application for variation if the contract is filed. Second, the power to vary only applies where the filed contract provides for support. Unlike s. 33(4), therefore, it has no application where there is a waiver of the right to support. Third, the parties can stipulate in a domestic contract that the support provisions are not subject to the court's power to vary them. On the other hand, the parties cannot oust the court's jurisdiction under s. 33(4). For cases applying s. 35(2), see *Wark v. Wark* (1989), 18 R.F.L. (3d) 75 (Ont. Dist. Ct.); *O'Connor v. O'Connor* (1990), 28 R.F.L. (3d) 99 (Ont. Fam. Ct.); and *Zegil v. Zegil* (1993), 50 R.F.L. (3d) 317 (Ont. Gen. Div.).

(3) Children

Section 56(1) of the *FLA* gives the court the authority to disregard any provision of a domestic contract pertaining to the education, moral training, or custody of or access to a child if it is in the best interest of the child to do so. Courts acting under the *Divorce Act* have been guided by the same general principle, overriding provisions of a separation agreement that deal with custody, access or child support if this is perceived to be in the child's interest. Does the rest of the contract remain operative where a court overrides the provisions dealing with a child? See *McKenzie v. McKenzie* (2001), 15 R.F.L. (5th) 135 (Alta. Q.B.).

Recall that the parties may not deal with the custody of or access to their children in either marriage contracts or cohabitation agreements: s. 52(1)(c) and s. 53(1)(c) of the *FLA*. What is the purpose of this limitation?

The custody and access provisions in a separation agreement may establish a *status quo* arrangement that the court will be reluctant to alter in the absence of clear evidence that it is not in the child's best interests. See, e.g, *Hartling v. Williams* (2003), 41 R.F.L. (5th) 275 (N.S. S.C.). The fact that the parents agreed to a particular arrangement is also a factor to be considered, as it indicates their perceptions of the child's best interests at the time of the agreement: *Liang v. Liang* (1978), 5 R.F.L. (2d) 103 (Ont. H.C.) and *Sabbagh v. Sabbagh* (1994), 2 R.F.L. (4th) 44 (Man. C.A.). In *M. (T.J.) v. M. (P.G.)* (2002), 25 R.F.L. (5th) 78 (Ont. S.C.J.), Justice Aston suggested (at para. 23) that a court should defer to the custody arrangements agreed to by the parents "unless they are demonstrably no longer in the best interest of the child or the person relying on the agreement has breached it in a fundamental way". Agreements are particularly important on interim custody applications. See, e.g., *Colter v. Colter* (1982), 38 O.R. (2d) 221 (Master) and *Cabott v. Binns* (1987), 9 R.F.L. (3d) 296 (B.C. S.C.); affirmed (1987), 9 R.F.L. (3d) 390 (B.C. C.A.).

Courts will not hesitate to order child support at variance with an agreement between the parents where the agreement prejudicially affects the welfare of a child. Child support is a child's right and a parent cannot barter away that right: *Richardson v. Richardson*, [1987] 1 S.C.R. 857 at 869-870 and *Willick v. Willick*, [1994] 3 S.C.R. 670, at paras. 15–19.

With the adoption of the *Federal Child Support Guidelines*, the Parliament of Canada amended the *Divorce Act* in 1997 to include specific provisions dealing with consent orders and the effect of provisions dealing with child support in domestic contracts. See ss. 15.1(5), (6), (7), and (8) and ss. 17(6.2), (6.3), (6.4), and (6.5). The comparable provisions in the *FLA* are ss. 33(12), (13), (14), and (15) and ss. 37(2.3), (2.4), (2.5), and (2.6). See also s. 56(1.1) of the *FLA* confirming that a court can disregard any provision in a domestic contract dealing with child support where "the provision is unreasonable having regard to the child support guidelines".

Sections 15.1(7) and 17(6.4) of the *Divorce Act* allow a court to order support "that is different from the amount that would be determined in accordance with the applicable guidelines" where the spouses consent and the court "is satisfied that reasonable arrangements have been made for the support of the child". In determining whether such reasonable arrangements have been made, the court is directed by s. 15.1(8) to have regard to the applicable *Guidelines*. See also s. 33(14) of the *FLA*, which adds that "where support for the child is payable out of public money", consent orders deviating from the *Guidelines* must "not provide for an amount less than the amount that would be determined in accordance with the child support guidelines". Professor McLeod suggests in "Annotation" (1998), 33 R.F.L. (4th) 453 at 454:

> ... [I]n reviewing an agreement, a court should consider the extent of the deviation and why the parties have agreed not to comply with the Guidelines. Practically, unless the parties can show offsetting benefits, it is difficult to see how a court can approve any agreement that does not comply with the Guidelines. After a brief period of adjustment, most judges will probably accept a consent with minimal explanation; otherwise, the system will slowly grind to a halt.

Of course, the parents can simply agree to informal arrangements or child support provisions in a domestic contract without securing a court order of any kind. As long as they are both content and neither needs a divorce, the matter is unlikely to reach a court even if the support differs from that suggested by the *Guidelines*. Recall, however, that once one or both of them seek a divorce, s. 11(1)(b) of the *Divorce Act* directs the court "to satisfy itself that reasonable arrangements have been made for the support of any children of the marriage, having regard to the applicable guidelines, and, if such arrangements have not been made, to stay the granting of the divorce until such arrangements are made". See Chapter 3, *DIVORCE*, for a review of the case law dealing with this provision. See also Thompson, "Who Wants to Avoid the Guidelines? Contracting Out and Around" (2001-2002), 19 C.F.L.Q. 1.

Sections 15.1(5) and 17(6.2) of the *Divorce Act* permit a court to order child support that is different from the *Guidelines* amount if (a) "special provisions in an order, a judgment or a written agreement respecting the financial obligations of the spouses, or the division or transfer of their property, directly or indirectly benefit a child" or "special provisions have otherwise been made for the benefit of a child"; and (b) "the application of the applicable guidelines would result in an amount of child support that is inequitable given those special provisions". See ss. 33(12) and 37(2.3) for the equivalent provisions in the *FLA*. This "special provisions" exception to the *Guidelines* applies where one party is now asking the court to override the prior agreement. The party seeking to uphold the agreement and avoid the standard *Guidelines* calculation bears the burden of proof under this exception.

The following case deals with an application under the *FLA* for a variation of a child support order that incorporated the parents' minutes of settlement. The same reasoning should apply to the "special provisions" exception in the context of original applications for child support under the *FLA* and in the context of original applications and applications for variation under the *Divorce Act*.

WRIGHT v. ZAVER

(2002), 24 R.F.L. (5th) 207, 2002 CarswellOnt 887 (Ont. C.A.)

[Shortly after she gave birth, an unmarried mother denied the father and his family any contact with the child. A 1985 court order, incorporating the couple's minutes of settlement, awarded custody to the mother, required the father to pay lump sum child support of $4,000, and provided that the father would have no access. Less than a year later, the father sought access and indicated a willingness to revisit the issue of child support. The mother opposed his application for access vigorously, asserting that she hoped to marry and that it would not be good for the child to have the father involved in his life. The father withdrew his application and did not see the child again.

The mother married another man who treated the child as his own and the couple then had one additional child. In 1999, the mother and step-father agreed to a consent order in divorce proceedings requiring the stepfather to pay child support of $879 per month for two children based on the *Guidelines*. Meanwhile the mother commenced a proceeding under the *FLA*, seeking support from the biological father. She claimed that she still faced a monthly deficit of $120.

The applications judge found that there had been two material changes in circumstances warranting a variation of the 1985 order. First, the lump sum had proved inadequate and, second, the *Guidelines* had come into force. The applications judge also found that the court was not bound by the child support provisions of a settlement, even when incorporated into a court order, where those provisions were inadequate. He ordered the father to pay $509 per month, that being the Table amount under the Ontario *Guidelines*.

The appellate court unanimously dismissed the appeal. In so doing, it concluded that the coming into force of the Ontario *Guidelines* was a change in circumstances automatically entitling the mother to a variation in accordance with the new child support regime. It also rejected the argument that a court retained a residual discretion to refuse to vary the order. Rather, it held that the applications judge correctly concluded that he was required to reconsider the original order under the parameters of the new child support regime and to determine the appropriate amount of support. In so doing, the Ontario Court of Appeal specifically overruled its earlier decision in *Sherman v. Sherman* (1999), 45 R.F.L. (4th) 424 (Ont. C.A.).

In the course of his appeal, the father raised, for the first time, the applicability of s. 37(2.3) of the *FLA*. The appellate court allowed this issue to be argued to provide some finality to the proceeding. Only portions of the court's reasons regarding this issue are reproduced here.]

SIMMONS J.A. (FELDMAN J.A. concurring): — ...

iv) Did The Applications Judge Err By Failing To Give Effect To S. 37(2.3) Of The *Family Law Act* And By Failing To Find That Special Provisions were Made For The Child In This Case Such That Application Of The Ontario Guidelines Would Be Inequitable?

84 I accept Mr. Zaver's submission that arrangements capable of constituting special provisions were made for Michael's benefit. I am not however satisfied that application of the *Ontario Guidelines* would result in an amount of support that is inequitable given those provisions. I would not, accordingly, give effect to this ground of appeal. ...

86 Section 37(2.3) sets out a three-part test for departing from the application of the *Ontario Guidelines*. First, the court must find "special provisions". Second, the court must determine that the special provisions benefit the child in the specified way. Third, the court must find that applying the *Ontario Guidelines* would result in an amount of support that is "inequitable" given the special provisions. Only if each part of this test is satisfied can a court depart from the application of the *Ontario Guidelines* under s. 37(2.3).

[Justice Simmons concluded that, in this case, there were "special provisions" for the purposes of s. 37(2.3). She noted that the lump sum was intended to replace, in part at least, the need for ongoing child support and that the mother entered into the 1985 agreement expecting to be able to provide for the child's needs either through her own resources or with the assistance of a new partner. The Justice concluded that that expectation formed part of the arrangements that the parents made, as did the father's release of any claim to access. Finally, in Justice Simmons' view, the support being paid by the step-father also qualified as part of the arrangements constituting "special provisions".

Justice Simmons next found that these "special provisions" met the second requirement of s. 37(2.3). She noted that the 1985 agreement, including the denial of access for the father, was made for the child's benefit and the step-father's support payments were of direct benefit to the child.

However, in the end, Justice Simmons held that it would not be inequitable in all the circumstances to require the father to pay the Table amount set by the Ontario Guidelines. The most important factor was that the mother was no longer able to meet all of the child's financial needs independently of the father, even with the additional support provided by the stepfather. Accordingly, the 1985 agreement did not relieve the father of the continuing obligation to ensure that the child's needs were properly met. Justice Simmons also noted that, while the father had not had the opportunity of establishing a personal relationship with his son, he had had a holiday from support for many years and there was no indication that paying support at the Table amount would be a financial burden. Finally, the amount was not so large as to leave the mother with a surplus that might unfairly increase her standard of living.]

SHARPE J.A. (CARTHY AND CHARRON JJ.A. concurring): — ...

109 I have had the benefit of reading the reasons of Simmons J.A. and I too would dismiss this appeal. I agree, for the reasons given by my colleague, that the enactment of the *Child Support Guidelines* creates a right to a variation of pre-existing orders for child support. While I agree with the result she reaches, I respectfully disagree with Simmons J.A.'s analysis and interpretation of the "special provisions" exception contained in s. 37(2.3) of the *Family Law Act*.

110 I agree with the structure of the three-part test with respect to the "special provisions" exception set out at paragraph 86 of Simmons J.A.'s reasons. However, I disagree with the proposition that "special provisions" need not be out of the ordinary or unusual. Nor do I accept the contention that the subjective goals and expectations of the parties are relevant in determining whether a pre-*Guidelines* arrangement qualifies as a special provision within the meaning of s. 37(2.3).

111 For the reasons that follow, I conclude that the "special provisions" exception does not apply to the circumstances of this case. While Mr. Wright's ongoing child support arguably does qualify as a special provision, that arrangement fails to meet the test in s. 37(2.3), since applying the child support guidelines would not be inequitable.

112 Courts have held that "special provisions" must be out of the ordinary or unusual. ...

113 I agree with the approach in these cases. Under s. 37(2.3), a court may only depart from the amount under the child support guidelines if there are "special provisions". In my view, the very use of the word "special" suggests that the provisions in question must be out of the ordinary or unusual. If provisions that were not out of the ordinary or unusual could qualify as "special provisions", the word "special" in s. 37(2.3) would have no meaning.

114 In my view, interpreting "special provisions" to include provisions that are not out of the ordinary or unusual would undermine the general rule that the child support guidelines provide the amount of a child support order. Under s. 3(1) of the *Ontario Guidelines*, the presumptive rule is the guideline amount of child support. Under s. 37(2.2) of the *Family Law Act*, a court that varies a child support order shall do so in accordance with the child support guidelines. The "special provisions" qualification in s. 37(2.3) is an exception to the presumptive rule. Its status as an exception suggests to me that its scope must be carefully delineated. If "special provisions" were not restricted to provisions that are out of the ordinary or unusual, the exception would, in my view, effectively displace the rule. ...

116 I do not accept the submission that the parties' goals and expectations when entering into the prior arrangement are relevant in determining whether that arrangement qualifies under the "special provisions" exception. Examining the goals and expectations of the parties would import into s. 37(2.3) an uncertainty that is, in my view, both unnecessary and inappropriate. The uncertainty is unnecessary because the question under s. 37(2.3) is not whether the parties *subjectively* intended to make special provisions in favour of the child. Rather, the question is whether the parties actually *objectively* made those provisions, which *objectively* replace the child's ongoing need for support. The uncertainty is inappropriate, because the objectives of the *Ontario Guidelines* are to enhance fairness, objectivity, efficiency, and consistency. Far from enhancing these objectives, the examination of subjective goals and expectations would undermine them by re-importing the uncertainty that characterized the former child support regime.

117 For the same reasons, I would hold that the goals and expectations of the parties in entering into an agreement are equally irrelevant in determining whether special provisions

benefit the child. The question is not whether the parties *subjectively* intended to benefit the child, but whether the special provisions actually *objectively* benefit the child.

118 I turn to the application of s. 37(2.3) to the circumstances of the present case. Mr. Zaver advanced several arrangements as being capable of constituting "special provisions" under s. 37(2.3): the goals and expectations of Ms. Wright and Mr. Zaver in entering into the 1985 agreement; the agreement itself, including Mr. Zaver's $4,000 lump sum child support payment; the court order resulting from the agreement; and Mr. Wright's ongoing child support of $879.00 per month.

119 For the reasons stated above, I do not accept the argument that the goals and expectations of Ms. Wright and Mr. Zaver in entering into the 1985 agreement are relevant in determining whether there are "special provisions". It is therefore irrelevant whether or not Ms. Wright's goal in entering the agreement was to remarry and effect a *de facto* adoption for Michael and whether or not Ms. Wright expected to be able to provide for Michael's needs. What is relevant is whether, viewed objectively, the arrangement between Ms. Wright and Mr. Zaver amounted to a special provision for the financial benefit of their child.

120 The mere existence of an agreement or a court order cannot constitute a "special provision". As I have already stated, the presumptive rule under s. 37(2.2) is that a court that varies a child support order shall do so in accordance with the child support guidelines. To read "special provisions" as embracing all agreements or orders providing for child support, or even all those agreements or orders that provide for adequate child support, would be to nullify the presumption and make the exception the rule. In and of itself, it is irrelevant whether there was an agreement or whether the agreement was incorporated into a court order. What are relevant are the actual provisions for the child's benefit contained in the agreement or court order, since it is those provisions that must qualify as "special provisions" under s. 37(2.3).

121 It follows that the only arrangements advanced by Mr. Zaver that are capable of falling within the "special provisions" exception are Mr. Zaver's $4,000 lump sum child support payment and Mr. Wright's ongoing child support of $879.00 per month.

122 In my view, Mr. Zaver's $4,000 lump sum child support payment does not constitute a "special provision" since it does not replace Michael's ongoing need for support. A lump sum payment may replace a child's ongoing need for support if the lump sum payment is sufficiently large. It cannot be said that Mr. Zaver's one-time $4,000 lump sum payment was sufficiently large to replace Michael's ongoing need for support. On the contrary, as the applications judge found, this payment could not have met Michael's needs for more than a few years.

123 With respect to Mr. Wright's ongoing child support, this arguably constitutes a "special provision" by partially replacing Michael's ongoing need for child support. The support also benefits Michael directly, thereby meeting the second part of the test under s. 37(2.3). However, I do not find it necessary to make a definitive determination of these issues, since, in any event, Mr. Wright's ongoing child support fails to meet the third part of the test in s. 37(2.3). Applying the child support guidelines in this case would not be inequitable. At first glance, it might seem inequitable for both Mr. Zaver and Mr. Wright to pay child support for Michael, since this support may increase Ms. Wright's personal standard of living along with that of her son. But further examination indicates that this is not actually inequitable for two reasons.

124 First, any increase in Ms. Wright's personal standard of living from Mr. Wright's ongoing child support for Michael is insignificant. Based on the guideline amount of child support for two children, Mr. Wright is currently paying $879 per month. If Mr. Wright were not paying child support for Michael, his monthly payment would be $543. This means that

Mr. Wright's child support for Michael amounts to only an additional $336 per month, or only $4032 per year.

125 Second, any increase in Ms. Wright's personal standard of living from Mr. Wright's ongoing child support for Michael is irrelevant. Child support is awarded for the child and not for the custodial parent; it is therefore the child's interests that must govern. Further, Mr. Zaver could not have relied on s. 37(2.3) to relieve him of the obligation to pay the guideline amount of child support if Mr. Wright and Ms. Wright had remained together. The result should be no different simply because Mr. Wright and Ms. Wright are separated and Mr. Wright is making direct monthly payments of child support. ...

NOTES AND QUESTIONS

1. As explained earlier, there is authority for the view that, even after the adoption of the *Child Support Guidelines* ("CSG") and the resultant legislative changes, a court still has discretion to determine whether to make a child support order at all. See *Wang v. Wang* (1998), 39 R.F.L. (4th) 426 (B.C. C.A.); *Fung-Sunter v. Fabian* (1999), 48 R.F.L. (4th) 95 (B.C. C.A.); *Parent c. Pelletier* (1999), 1 R.F.L. (5th) 66 (N.B. C.A.); and *Laird v. Laird* (2000), 3 R.F.L. (5th) 241 (Alta. C.A.); additional reasons at (2000), 10 R.F.L. (5th) 86 (Alta. C.A.). This controversial reasoning is significant in the context of domestic contracts because it suggests that a court can refuse to make an order in the face of a contract even if the conditions of s. 15.1(5) or s. 17(6.2) of the *Divorce Act* (or the equivalent provisions in the provincial legislation) are not met. The Ontario Court of Appeal rejected this approach in the *Wright* case, as did the courts in *Dergousoff v. Dergousoff* (1999), 48 R.F.L. (4th) 1 (Sask. C.A.) and *MacKay v. Bucher* (2001), 21 R.F.L. (5th) 336 (N.S. C.A.).

2. In an annotation to *Anderson-Devine v. Anderson* (2002), 33 R.F.L. (5th) 29 (Man. C.A.), Professor McLeod suggests (at 33) that the majority in the Ontario Court of Appeal in *Wright v. Zaver* "imposed an artificial requirement that there must be something extraordinary in the agreement" to trigger the "special provision" exception. Professor McLeod here identified the very disagreement between the majority and minority decisions in *Wright v. Zaver*. Did the majority, in essence, hold that a provision was "special" only where it improved upon what would be ordered under the *Guidelines*?

3. In "When is a Family Law Contract *Not* Invalid, Unenforceable, Overridden or Varied?" (2001-2002), 19 C.F.L.Q. 399, Professor Thompson concludes (at 433) that the contracts that survive scrutiny as containing "special provisions" are those that (i) provide for child support higher than the *Guidelines* amount; (ii) reduce child support as part of an unusual parenting arrangement such as shared or split custody; or (iii) transfer the equity in the matrimonial home in exchange for reduced or no child support. Professor Thompson also examines which contracts survive and which do not in "Who Wants to Avoid the Guidelines? Contracting Out and Around" (2001-2002), 19 C.F.L.Q. 1. He concludes (at 39) that the clear message from the cases is that the agreement should spell out the necessary link between the contractual provisions and the benefit to a child or children.

4. The problem not tackled by *Wright v. Zaver*, or by any of the subsequent cases dealing with child support and agreements, is the interrelationship between the various sections in the *FLA* providing that an agreement can be overruled, set aside, or disregarded:

Section 56(1.1) — Agreements for child support can be "disregarded" where the child support provision is "unreasonable" having regard to the *CSG*;

Section 33(4) — Agreements that include a provision for support, or a waiver of either spousal or child support may be "set aside" if the waiver results in "unconscionable circumstances", if the waiver is by or on behalf of an applicant who qualifies for an allowance out of "public money" (most often, someone who qualifies for Ontario Works payments), or if there is a default in the payment of support that is provided under the contract;

Sections 33(12) and (15) — Courts are empowered to award amounts of child support different from the *CSG*'s amount where there are "special provisions" in an order or written agreement or where the parties consent and there are "reasonable arrangements" for child support.

These sections are not rationalized with one another, and may even work against each other. See Maur, "Child Support Below the Guidelines: Why a Bird in the Hand Isn't Always Worth Two in the Bush", 27 C.F.L.Q. 201:

> Section 56(1.1) of the *Family Law Act* says that a court may "disregard" any agreement that is "unreasonable", having regard to the *Child Support Guidelines*. If an agreement is "disregarded", presumably a court is free to substitute its own decision as to the child support that should be paid.
>
> This section is difficult to reconcile with 33(12) and (14) of the *Family Law Act* and with 15.2(5) and (7) of the *Divorce Act*. One might ask whether the two sets of provisions are even meant to be reconciled, or to be consistent with one another. One problem resides in the word "may" in s. 56(1.1). ...
>
> The section gives the court the power to decide, in a discretionary way, whether to disregard a provision in a domestic agreement regarding child support. It does not say, however, what the consequences are of "disregarding" the provisions in an agreement. Presumably, a court is then free to substitute its own decision on child support. Given the mandatory nature of the tables, as provided in s. 33(11), one would presume further that upon disregarding the provisions as unreasonable, the court would be bound to apply the tables. The section therefore raises obvious questions as to how courts have used their discretion under this section, and maybe more importantly, why they might use it.
>
> It is important to keep in mind that s. 56(1.1) comes into play as an application to "disregard" the agreement, and presumably, to substitute regular table support for whatever is in the agreement (although, as noted, the section does not state what the consequences are of disregarding an agreement). It may be pleaded as alternative relief, as part of a regular application for support where there is a preexisting agreement. The parent looking for support would ask for the support *simpliciter*, and would also ask to have the provisions of the agreement disregarded. This makes it necessary to sort out the relationship between s. 56(1.1) and the "special provisions" sections.
>
> The word "unreasonable" in the section also creates an issue. Is the word "unreasonable" in this section meant to be the antonym of "reasonable" in the "reasonable arrangements" sections? Or does "unreasonable" have its own particular legal meaning in the context of this section? Are we to make anything of the fact that the word "reasonable" only appears in ss. 33(14) and 37(2.5), which talks about *consent orders*, and not in s. 33(12), or 37(2.3) which deals with *agreements*, and creates "special provisions"? In other words, was there any coherence meant to exist between s. 56(1.1) and ss. 33(12) and (14) and 37(2.3) and (2.5)? The above issues are not well-resolved in the case law to date.

5. Setting Aside a Domestic Contract

The *FLA* contains four distinct provisions for the setting aside of domestic contracts or parts of domestic contracts. As discussed above in the particular context of support, s. 33(4) of the *FLA* provides that a provision for support, or the waiver of the right to support, in a domestic contract may be set aside if it results in unconscionable circumstances, and s. 56(1.1) allows a court to set aside an unreasonable child support provision. Section 56(5) of the *FLA* specifies that a court may set aside all or part of a separation agreement or settlement if "removal by one spouse of barriers that would prevent the other spouse's remarriage within that spouse's faith was a consideration in the making of the agreement or settlement". This subsection was inserted into the Act because the legislative committee considering an earlier draft became aware of situations where husbands refused to grant a *gett* — a divorce recognized by the Jewish law — unless their wives agreed to the terms of a separation agreement. See generally, "Solution Sought to Problems of Jewish Divorce", *Globe and Mail* (June 17, 1985); "Ontario Measure Should Remove Simmering Jewish Divorce Issue", *Globe and Mail* (December 14, 1985); and Syrtash, "Removing Barriers to Religious Remarriage in Ontario: Rights and Remedies" (1986-1987), 1 C.F.L.Q. 309. Of course, the subsection as written applies to all religions.

The rest of the chapter is devoted to the setting aside of domestic agreements pursuant to s. 56(4) of the *FLA*. That section provides that any domestic agreement, or any provision in it, may be set aside if (a) a party failed to disclose to the other significant assets, or significant debts or other liabilities; (b) a party did not understand the nature or consequences of the domestic contract; or (c) otherwise in accordance with the law of contract. Note that the section is discretionary (a court "may" set the agreement aside).

As set out in the *LeVan* case below, "complete, fair and frank disclosure" of assets, liabilities, and their values, is necessary if the agreement is to be upheld, particularly where it is a marriage agreement.

A failure to understand the nature or consequences of a domestic contract can arise in several situations. It can result from an inability to understand the language of the contract in cases where literacy in the language of the contract is an issue. Or, it can arise where a party has been misled as to the purpose of the instrument (*non est factum*). Finally, a failure to disclose significant assets or debts may cause the other party not to understand the consequences of an agreement. This situation is, of course, already covered by s. 56(4)(a).

Pursuant to s. 56(4)(c), domestic contracts or provisions in them may also be set aside "otherwise in accordance with the law of contract". The law of contract focuses mainly on problems in the formation of an agreement, but also relates to the agreement's substance. A contract may be, or may become, invalid for various reasons related to its formation. Sometimes the parties' attempt to enter into a valid, operative contract is unsuccessful because the agreed terms are uncertain. The contract may also be rendered a nullity by the presence of certain kinds of mistakes. In these situations the contract is void *ab initio* and of no legal effect according to the law of contract. Void domestic contracts cannot prevail over legislation relating to the rights of the parties even if they are never set aside. They should readily be set aside if an application is made under s. 56(4).

On other occasions the contract may be voidable rather than void. Where one party has been guilty of fraud, material misrepresentation, duress, undue influence or some other form of unconscionable conduct, the other is given the privilege of avoiding the contract. If the party permitted to avoid the contract does not do so, the contract remains valid and fully effective. According to contract law, such a contract also continues to be effective where a court refuses to set it aside because a bar to rescission exists. A bar may arise by virtue of undue delay or other conduct on the part of the party seeking rescission or because the parties cannot be substantially restored to their original positions. Because s. 56(4)(c) only authorizes the court to set aside a domestic contract in accordance with the law of contract, the established bars to rescission should apply when the court is asked to set aside a voidable contract under that paragraph. See, however, *B. (J.F.) v. B. (M.A.)* (1999), 1 R.F.L. (5th) 339 (Ont. S.C.J.), where the court set aside a separation agreement even though restoration of the status quo was impossible. The court concluded that "practical justice" could still be done through a monetary adjustment. As Professor McLeod asserts in his annotation to the case, it is unclear from the reasons whether the court is suggesting that the usual bars to rescission do not apply to applications under s. 56(4) or that no bar to rescission arose on the facts.

The principles of contract law allow the courts to focus on the particular circumstances of each case. As will be seen in the cases that follow, the courts, therefore, can and do take into account the special nature of the spousal relationship and the unique circumstances in which domestic contracts are made.

Because s. 56(4)(c) already permits a court to set aside a contract "in accordance with the law of contract", paragraphs (a) and (b) are intended to grant the courts the power to act in some circumstances where the contract is valid according to the law of contract. If the contract is to be disregarded in those circumstances, an application should be made under s. 56 of the *FLA*.

The first case in this section (*LeVan*) explores the consequences of non-disclosure and the second discusses what is meant by a "failure to understand" the agreement (*Grant-Hose*). The third and fourth (*Rosen* and *Rick*) focus on the concept of unconscionable bargain in the context of domestic contracts.

(1) Inadequate Disclosure

LeVAN v. LeVAN

(2008), 51 R.F.L. (6th) 237, 2008 CarswellOnt 2738 (C.A.); leave to appeal
refused (2008), 2008 CarswellOnt 6207 (S.C.C.)

[The primary purpose of marriage agreements is usually to avoid or modify the statutory scheme that would otherwise apply in the event of marriage breakdown. It is therefore essential that the parties know what each is bringing into the marriage. Without this information, neither can know for certain what will be gained or lost in executing the agreement.

Section 56(4) of the *FLA* provides that a court "may" set aside a domestic contract if a party "failed to disclose to the other significant assets, or significant debts or other liabilities, existing when the domestic contract was made." The *LeVan* case, in large part, involved whether the court should exercise this discretionary power once it was established that the husband had breached his duty to disclose his significant assets.]

S. BORINS J.A.: —

I

1 Richard Bruce LeVan (the "husband") appeals from the judgment of Backhouse J., which set aside a marriage contract that he entered into with the respondent, Erika Margaret LeVan (the "wife") prior to their marriage for failure to comply with s. 56(4) of the *Family Law Act*, R.S.O. 1990, c. F.3 ("*FLA*"). The husband was ordered to pay the wife an equalization payment of $5.3 million as well as retroactive spousal support of $163,340. The trial judge ordered that post-judgment interest shall accrue on the entire equalization payment and the lump sum spousal support from the date of the judgment. In addition, the trial judge awarded monthly spousal support of $6,640 based on the husband's yearly income of $370,000 commencing June 1, 2006, to be reduced pursuant to a formula in accordance with receipt of the equalization payment and to be credited against post-judgment interest. The husband was also ordered to pay child support for two children in the amount of $4,544 monthly, and retroactive child support of $43,792. Costs of $646,602.20 were awarded to the wife.

2 The appellant contends that the trial judge erred as follows:

> 1 In setting aside the marriage contract in accordance with s. 56(4) of the *FLA*.
>
> 2 In importing the word and concept of "value" into s. 56(4)(a) of the *FLA*. ...

IV

6 The parties lived together in Listowel, Ontario from June 1995 until their marriage on June 22, 1996. There are two young children of the marriage. The parties separated on October 27, 2003. The issues involved in this dispute revolve around a marriage contract that was signed by the parties on June 20, 1996, two days prior to the marriage.

7 At the time the marriage contract was signed, the husband was a very wealthy man. The husband and his family own the majority of shares of Wescast Industries Inc. ("Wescast"), the world's largest manufacturer of exhaust manifolds, and a publicly traded company. Mr.

LeVan Sr., together with his wife, created a complex corporate structure that included a number of different companies and a family trust (the "LeVan Family Trust").

8 In 1996, the husband and his three siblings each held 25 per cent of the common shares of three companies within the corporate structure: RyVan Inc. ("RyVan"), Grannyco Investments Ltd. ("Grannyco") and RWL Investments Ltd. ("RWL"). In addition, all four siblings were the sole beneficiaries of the LeVan Family Trust, in which there were significant assets. It was the opinion of Linda Brent, the wife's valuator, that at the date of marriage, the midpoint value of the husband's business assets was over $14 million, after applying significant discounts and deducting contingent taxes. Ms. Brent's evidence was uncontradicted, as the husband did not provide the court with a valuation of his net worth at the dates of marriage, separation or trial. This would have assisted the court in assessing the impact of the equalization payment on his net worth.

9 It was always the desire of Mr. LeVan, Sr. to protect the shares of the family company. Thus, any child contemplating marriage was instructed to enter into a pre-nuptial agreement, or marriage contract, in which it was provided that the proposed spouse release all claims to Wescast shares. In this way, Mr. LeVan, Sr. intended to keep the shares of the family company within the family.

10 Mr. LeVan, Sr. retained the services of George Wilson at Gowling LaFleur Henderson ("Gowlings") as his corporate legal adviser. With Mr. Wilson's assistance, the LeVan family members entered into a Voting Trust Agreement and a Unanimous Shareholders Agreement, to which were attached model marriage contracts. Each agreement provided that any family member, who was to be married and who wished to continue to hold shares in Wescast, had to enter into a marriage contract based on the model contract. As it was frequently the subject of conversation around the dinner table at family gatherings, the husband, his siblings, and their prospective partners knew of the desire to maintain control of Wescast shares within the family.

11 The model marriage contract contained provisions to protect the LeVan family's control of Wescast. However, it did not require the prospective spouse to agree to exclude assets from equalization or to limit support rights. Rather, the agreements restricted the actions that could be taken directly against the LeVan family companies and stipulated the method of valuation of the LeVan company shares for the purposes of a property or support claim.

12 The husband was the first of the four siblings to enter into a marriage contract. Before their engagement in December 1995, the wife was aware that if she and Mr. LeVan were to marry, they would have to enter into a marriage contract as Mr. LeVan, Sr. wanted to make sure that the Wescast shares stayed within the family. A month or so after the engagement, and shortly after the wedding venue was booked for June 22, 1996, the wife broached the subject of the marriage contract with the husband as she thought it would have to be dealt with before the wedding. The husband told her not to worry because there was a lot of time until the wedding. He said that his lawyers were working on it. He reassured the wife, telling her that the marriage contract was only to ensure that if they split up, there would be no possibility of an outsider taking over Wescast.

13 However, the husband did nothing about the marriage contract until May 8, 1996, six weeks before the wedding date. On that occasion, for the first time, he met with Karen Bales, a family law lawyer at Gowlings, the corporate lawyers for the LeVan companies. The husband testified that he had nothing to do with the property provisions of the marriage contract which were created and mandated by his father and Mr. Wilson. As confirmed by Ms. Bales, the husband was only interested in support provisions and the provision regarding the matrimonial home. He did not wish to pay the wife support in the event of a marriage breakdown. Mr. LeVan, Sr. died in April, 2003. Mr. Wilson was not called as a witness.

V

14 Ms. Bales' first draft of the contract, which she sent to the husband, provided that the LeVan companies were to be treated as excluded property, including any property into which they could be traced. However, there was no restriction on the wife's right to support and she was entitled to a joint interest in the matrimonial home. Subsequent changes to the first draft made the marriage contract more favourable to the husband and less favourable to the wife. Subsequent drafts maintained this inequity. A significant change in the final draft was the insertion of paragraph 8(c), which severely restricted the wife's right to claim support if there was a marriage breakdown. That clause limited the wife's support to the income and assets that were not excluded in the contract. These changes extended far beyond the model marriage contract attached to the Voting Trust Agreement and the Unanimous Shareholders Agreement.

15 On May 16, 1996, Ms. Bales sent the draft marriage contract to Mr. Wilson. Her accompanying memo informed Mr. Wilson that under the *FLA* the husband was required to disclose to the wife all of his significant assets and liabilities. She told him that she would like to provide enough detail to satisfy the other side, without providing more information than was necessary. She directed Mr. Wilson's attention to Schedule A to the contract, which constituted the husband's disclosure. She also directed his attention to a footnote in that Schedule, which stated that the interests of the LeVan family members in the LeVan Family Companies were frozen through an estate freeze in January 1996 at a freeze value per share of $9.75 (U.S.). Mr. Wilson did not reply to Ms. Bales' memo.

16 Schedule A was the only financial disclosure provided by the husband. It indicated that the husband had no debts. His net worth was disclosed as "$80,000 + LeVan Family Companies interest". It disclosed that the $80,000 was held in RRSPs, bank accounts and the original house deposit. It disclosed that the husband owned 100 common shares in RyVan Inc. This Schedule was accompanied by a declaration that each party had fully and completely disclosed to the other the nature and extent of all of his or her significant assets.

17 However, there was a great deal of information that was not included in the Schedule A disclosure. The Schedule provided no disclosure of the husband's income. No values were inserted for his interest in the LeVan Companies or for his contingent beneficial interest in the LeVan Family Trust. The absence of this information proved to be significant, as the wife's valuator valued the mid-point range of the husband's business assets at the date of marriage at $14,664,500. In addition, the husband did not disclose that he owned one common share in each of Grannyco and RWL. Ms. Brent valued the midpoint range of these two shares at the date of marriage as $1.9 million and $7.250 million respectively.

18 In addition, the footnote included in the Schedule was later found to have been inaccurate, since not all the interest in the LeVan Family companies were frozen. The footnote also failed to disclose how many shares were frozen or how many shares the husband held. It was of no help in providing disclosure of the husband's assets. Indeed, as Ms. Bales acknowledged, the footnote was meaningless as it disclosed insufficient information.

19 In late May, the wife was provided with a copy of the final draft of the marriage contract. The husband advised her to get her own lawyer to review the contract. She had never had any dealings with a lawyer. Based on her parents' recommendation, she retained Paul Ross, a general practitioner in Goderich, Ontario, who had experience in family law.

20 On May 28, 1996, Ms. Bales sent Mr. Ross the draft marriage contract with a covering letter that gave him some background. She described this as a "first go-round" in the expectation that Mr. Ross would ask for more information. Mr. Ross did request additional information. He asked for the values of the husband's interest in the LeVan companies and for

the holdings in the Family Trust. Although she acknowledged in her testimony that it was essential that the wife know the husband's income and her worth, Ms. Bales did not give Mr. Ross any information other than Schedule A. She testified that she sent Mr. Ross the information that had been provided to her. However, as the trial judge observed, Ms. Bales had access to much more significant information about the husband's income and net worth through Gowlings and the corporate accountants of the LeVan Family Companies.

21 Mr. Ross first met with the wife on June 3, 1996. At that time, she informed him that her understanding was that the purpose of the contract was to protect the shares in the LeVan Family Companies and to ensure that the Wescast shares did not go outside the family. She also told him that her husband had said that there would be no marriage unless she signed the contract. Mr. Ross informed her that the agreement went much further than merely protecting the family's shares in Wescast and that, in his opinion, it did not treat her fairly.

22 In written correspondence to Ms. Bales, Mr. Ross expressed the view that the contract was unfair and overreaching and continued to request disclosure of the value of the holdings in the Family Trust. He even proposed drafting his own contract. In subsequent correspondence, Ms. Bales provided some more detailed information concerning the husband's share holdings, however, she did not provide values.

23 The further disclosure provided by Ms. Bales was seriously misleading and littered with informational gaps. Ms. Bales failed to disclose that that husband and his three siblings had always been treated equally under the LeVan Family Trust, and that it was his parents' intention to continue to treat the children equally. She misrepresented that the husband's contingent interest in the Trust had a "very minimal value" at the date of marriage, whereas Ms. Brent valued the holdings of the Trust at $30 million. She responded to Mr. Ross' request for values for the husband's business interests as a request for full valuations and refused to provide such on the basis of cost and time.

24 In addition, at the request of Mr. Ross, she sent him copies of the Voting Trust Agreement and the Unanimous Shareholders Agreement, and directed his attention to the Schedules to those agreements which set out the minimum terms of the model marriage contract. This simply served to enhance Mr. Ross' confusion since the marriage contract prepared by Ms. Bales did not contemplate equalization of net family property and was substantially and materially different from the model contracts in the two agreements.

25 As the wedding approached and without a contract signed, the husband began to undermine the wife's relationship with, and confidence in, Mr. Ross. On June 18, 1996, Mr. Ross received a message from Ms. Bales' secretary informing him of the husband's instructions that Ms. Bales have no further communications with him. Mr. Ross wrote to the wife advising her that the contract was "unconscionable" and expressing his concern that undue pressure was being put on her to sign the contract. It would appear that the wife disregarded this advice.

26 With Mr. Ross out of the picture and the wedding a few days away, Ms. Bales decided to ask Susan Heakes, a family law specialist with Blake, Cassels and Graydon, if she would provide independent legal advice to the wife. On Tuesday, June 18, 1996, Ms. Bales left a voicemail for Ms. Heakes requesting that she act for a wife on a marriage contract. She explained that the wedding was on Saturday and that the wife wanted to see her on Thursday to have the contract explained. Ms. Heakes agreed to act for the wife notwithstanding that the wedding was imminent because she was comfortable with Ms. Bales being on the other side and with the wife having had a previous lawyer. Ms. Heakes had acted for Ms. Bales in her recent divorce. This was not disclosed to the wife. The wife testified that she was told by the husband that his lawyer had found another lawyer in Toronto willing to let her sign the contract.

27 Ms. Heakes met alone with the wife for approximately one hour two days before the wedding. During this meeting the wife's disclosure statement was prepared and a change was made to the contract to reflect that the house deal had fallen through. As such, the trial judge found that it was unlikely that the contract was reviewed in detail. Ms. Heakes relied entirely on documents provided by Ms. Bales, which consisted of the same documents provided to Mr. Ross, as well as correspondence between counsel. These documents contained the misrepresentations about the husband's financial position. She did not ask Ms. Bales to insert values for the husband's assets into Schedule A. Ms. Heakes did not appreciate that [t]he model marriage contracts did not require the exclusion of business assets from equalization of net family property. She testified that she did not remember if she reviewed with the wife the model marriage contracts contained in the Voting Trust Agreement and the Unanimous Shareholders Agreement.

28 The marriage contract was signed on the day the wife met with Ms. Heakes. The husband testified that up to the day the contract was signed, he was continuing to tell the wife that if the contract was not signed, there would be no marriage. As the trial judge found, in the contract that was signed, the wife's ability to claim spousal support, contrary to the model marriage contracts, was significantly compromised. She gave up her right to share in the increase in value of virtually all of the husband's assets without knowing the husband's income from all sources, and without having any idea of his net worth. Moreover, Ms. Heakes also did not possess this information at the time she provided legal advice to the wife for the purpose of signing the marriage contract. Even though she testified that she would not advise a client without financial disclosure, she failed to request financial disclosure from Ms. Bales. Consequently, Ms. Heakes was in no position to advise the wife in a meaningful way about the marriage contract. ...

VII

32 The trial judge['s] principal finding of fact was that husband had breached his statutory obligation to provide financial disclosure to the wife. She found that he didn't make the required disclosure for two reasons. First, he did not want his wife to know his income or the value of his assets because he wanted to control their lifestyle during marriage. Second, he was afraid that full disclosure might lead to more aggressive demands and a less favourable contract. Thus, the trial judge concluded that the husband had deliberately breached s. 56(4)(a) of the *FLA* by choosing not to make complete financial disclosure to the wife of his income and his assets when entering into the contract.

33 It is now well established that a finding that a party has violated a provision of s. 56(4) of the *FLA* does not automatically render the contract a nullity. Rather, a trial judge must determine whether it is appropriate, in the circumstances, to order that the contract be set aside. This is a discretionary exercise. See *Dochuk v. Dochuk* (1999), 44 R.F.L. (4th) 97 (Ont. Gen. Div.). Here, the trial judge determined that it was appropriate to set aside the marriage contract. She recognized that it was appropriate to exercise that discretion not simply because of the failure to disclose, but also because of other factors relevant to s. 56(4), such as the wife's failure to understand the nature and consequences of the contract in accordance with s. 56(4)(b).

34 The trial judge relied upon the following findings to set aside the marriage contract apart from the husband's failure to disclose the value of his significant assets:

    1 The husband failed to disclose his income tax returns.

    2 The husband failed to disclose shares that he held in Grannyco and RWL.

3 The footnote to Schedule A was inaccurate and did not contain sufficient information to be meaningful.

4 The disclosure provided was misleading. For example, the husband's lawyer stated that his interest in the Family Trust had a very "minimal value".

5 The husband's lawyer failed to disclose that he had three siblings, and that the four LeVan children had always been treated equally under the Family Trust.

6 The financial statements for RWL, Grannyco and the Family Trust were not provided.

7 The husband's lawyer failed to disclose that, in addition to being a capital beneficiary of the Trust, the husband was also an income beneficiary.

35 The trial judge recognized each of these factors in support of her determination that the husband had failed to comply with his disclosure obligation under s. 56(4)(a) of the *FLA*. In exercising her discretion to set aside the marriage contract, the trial judge further identified the following factors:

1 The wife did not receive effective independent legal advice and some advice provided was wrong.

2 The wife did not understand the nature and consequence of the marriage contract.

3 The husband misrepresented the nature and terms of the marriage contract to the wife.

4 The husband's failure to disclose his entire assets to his wife was deliberate.

5 The husband interfered with the wife's receipt of legal assistance from her first lawyer, Mr. Ross.

36 Virtually all of the trial judge's findings that I have outlined, in one way of another, were material to the wife's decision to sign the marriage contract.

37 In exercising discretion to set aside the marriage contract, the trial judge rejected the husband's position that even though he failed to disclose his assets, the wife would have signed the contract in any event because she was intent on marrying him. At paragraph 226, the trial judge commented:

> It is submitted on behalf of the husband that regardless of what his net worth and income were and regardless of whether there were misrepresentations about his finances, they were not material as the wife would have signed the contract anyway. It is clear that the wife wanted to get married and that the husband was insisting that the contract be signed before getting married. The wife stated on cross-examination that no matter what number was in the husband's Schedule A, that she was going to sign the contract because she wanted to get married and "because she was signing this contract to protect Bruce's interest in Wescast." I find that the wife was acknowledging that she understood that there would be no marriage without a marriage contract. I do not agree that she was acknowledging that she would sign any contract regardless of its terms and regardless of the extent of her future husband's income and assets. She was prepared to "protect Bruce's interest in Wescast." I find that she understood that the contract did this because of her future husband's misrepresentations. Had the husband disclosed the value of his assets and his income, this would have given the wife's lawyers an opportunity to negotiate provisions less onerous to the wife. I find that had he fully disclosed as required, it is likely that the marriage contract would have been more favourable to the wife, or that the wife, recognizing how unfair it was, would have refused to sign it.

. . . . .

X

50 Section 56(4) of the *FLA* was designed to address and codify prior concerns maintained by courts that both parties fully understood their rights under the law when contracting with their spouses. It has been characterized as the "judicial oversight" provision of marriage agreements: *Hartshorne v. Hartshorne*, [2004] 1 S.C.R. 550, ¶14. The provision is of such significance that, in accordance with s. 56(7), it cannot be waived by the parties.

51 The analysis undertaken under s. 56(4) is essentially comprised of a two-part process: *Demchuk v. Demchuk* (1986), 1 R.F.L. (3d) 176 (Ont. H.C.J.). First, the court must consider whether the party seeking to set aside the agreement can demonstrate that one or more of the circumstances set out within the provision have been engaged. Once that hurdle has been overcome, the court must then consider whether it is appropriate to exercise discretion in favour of setting aside the agreement. This approach was adopted and applied by the trial judge in this case.

52 As discussed, the issue of focus at trial was whether the husband had complied with his financial disclosure obligation under s. 56(4)(a). ...

54 In this case, the disclosure provided by the husband was insufficient to enable the wife to have a clear understanding of exactly what rights she was giving up by entering into the contract. The husband failed to disclose that he held shares in Grannyco and RWL, which were found to be of significant value. He failed to provide any financial statements for Grannyco, RWL or the Family Trust. No income tax returns were provided for the husband and there was no disclosure whatsoever of his income. Overall, the information provided by the husband made it impossible to calculate or determine his net worth.

55 While he disclosed his interest in "significant assets" such as the LeVan Companies and the LeVan Family Trust, he failed to disclose values for these interests. At trial, the husband's interest in the Family Trust was valued at $3.4 million at the date of marriage. The trial judge found that the husband's disclosure obligation required him to disclose the value of these significant assets.

56 On appeal, the husband argued that the trial judge erred in importing the word "value" into section 56(4)(a), contrary to the plain wording of the section. He noted that the term "value" is used extensively throughout other parts of the statute. Thus, the legislature is presumed to have expressly excluded "value" from s. 56(4). In addition, the husband submitted that it would be onerous and expensive to require valuations for marriage contracts and would often result in parties making estimates of values, thereby creating a risk of misrepresentation, which in itself could be a basis to set aside the agreement.

57 The trial judge relied on the decision in *Demchuk v. Demchuk* (1986), 1 R.F.L. (3d) 176 (Ont. H.C.J.) in support of her conclusion that the disclosure obligation under s. 56(4)(a) encompasses an obligation to disclose the *value* of the assets. There is no case law that supports the husband's position that the positive obligation required by s. 56(4)(a) can be met by providing only a list of significant assets without some indication of value being attributed to them. Having said this, I note that the trial judge did not engage in a detailed statutory interpretation of the absence of the term "value" from the provision. As such, I see no reason to engage in such an analysis here. Moreover, the trial judge's findings of fact which I have outlined in paras. 34 and 35 fully support her decision to set aside the marriage contract, essentially on the basis of the husband's reprehensible conduct leading to the signing of the marriage contract.

58 In the circumstances of this case, it is my view that the husband's failure to disclose value for his interests in the LeVan Companies and the Family Trust is not critical to the

disclosure analysis. As the trial judge indicated in her findings, there is an abundance of evidence indicating that the husband had failed to comply with his disclosure obligation apart from his failure to disclose value for these assets. As discussed, this failure was compounded by the serious misrepresentations respecting the extent and value of certain of the assets disclosed.

59 In addition, the marriage contract itself was misleading. Ms. Bales incorporated the terms of the model marriage contract under the Voting Trust Agreement which stipulated the method of valuation of the LeVan company shares for the purpose of a property or support claim. As admitted by Ms. Bales, someone reading this agreement might believe that it contemplated a valuation of the shares in the LeVan family companies. These facts coupled with the wife's misunderstanding about the effect of the contract meant that the wife had no chance whatsoever of understanding what she was giving up when she signed the contract.

60 Based upon the trial judge's twelve findings of fact that I have outlined, she properly exercised her discretion to set aside the contract for failure to comply with s. 56(4)(a). In deciding how to exercise discretion, the trial judge considered the "fairness" of the contract. The appellant emphasizes that unfairness in a contract is not a proper basis for setting aside marriage contracts in Ontario. Although there is nothing in the governing legislation that suggests that fairness is a consideration in deciding whether or not to set aside a marriage contract, I do not see why fairness is not an appropriate consideration in the exercise of the court's discretion in the second stage of the s. 56(4)(a) analysis. In my view, once a judge has found one of [the] statutory preconditions to exist, he or she should be entitled to consider the fairness of the contract together with other factors in the exercise of his or her discretion. It seems to me that a judge would be more inclined to set aside a clearly unfair contract than one that treated the parties fairly.

61 However, this was not the only reason the trial judge articulated in support of her decision to set aside the contract. As I have stated, in exercising her discretion, the trial judge also made the following findings: (i) the husband had interfered [with] the wife's lawyer of choice; (ii) the wife's lawyers were unable to appreciate the consequences of the contract and impart them to the wife due to lack of financial disclosure and misrepresentations; (iii) the wife had not received effective independent legal advice and some advice provided was wrong; and (iv) the wife did not understand the nature or consequences of the contract she signed.

62 These findings are reasonably supported by the evidence presented at trial. I therefore see no reason to interfere with them in this case. In essence, the trial judge found that the husband failed to make full disclosure of his significant assets, that his disclosure was incomplete and inadequate and that his failure to make full disclosure was a deliberate attempt to mislead his wife. As such, the trial judge's decision to set aside the contract should be upheld.

NOTES AND QUESTIONS

1. The *LeVan* case raises serious issues in practice. Many family law practitioners will refuse to represent a client in the execution of a marriage agreement just before the wedding is to take place. Adequate disclosure is unlikely in such a short time and there may be undue pressure for one party to execute an unfavourable agreement if the wedding is only a short time away. Counsel for the successful wife in *LeVan* was Philip Epstein. Of the appeal decision, he writes (TWIFL, Fam. L.News 2009 - 05): "*LeVan* is also an important lesson to counsel to do marriage contracts only at a leisurely and sensible pace, and is also a reminder that it is poor practice to just send off a draft contract to the other side rather than having a meeting with the parties and both counsel to discuss the purpose and intent of the contract."

Some practitioners have reacted to the *LeVan* decision by refusing to assist clients in negotiating and drafting a marriage contract unless there is a complete and detailed valuation of each party's assets. Such a valuation may well be expensive and time-consuming and require the involvement of several expert valuators. Is this an over-reaction? Is a "reasonable estimate" of the value of significant assets insufficient?

2. It can often be very difficult to obtain proper financial disclosure in any family law case. There may be many reasons why one party does not want to make disclosure. Without it, however, the other party is at a clear disadvantage, and it may therefore be impossible for him or her to make reasonable decisions. The Supreme Court of Canada endorsed the trial justice's view in *Leskun v. Leskun*, [2006] 1 S.C.R. 920, 34 R.F.L. (6th) 1 that non-disclosure is the "cancer of family law". This may be particularly true when marriage agreements are being negotiated.

3. The reasoning in *LeVan* was applied in *Lambert v. Lambert* (2008), 52 R.F.L. (6th) 363 (Ont. S.C.J.), in which Plantana J. dismissed the husband's application for enforcement of the marriage agreement in circumstances similar to those in *LeVan*. The wife in *Lambert* did not have independent legal advice, and the husband had not disclosed the value of his assets as of the date of marriage.

4. In *Rick v. Brandsema* (2009), 2009 CarswellBC 342 (S.C.C.), the Supreme Court of Canada recently stated that a duty to make full disclosure in negotiations leading to separation agreements exists even where there is no special statutory rule. Justice Abella, for the Court, stated:

> 47 In my view, it flows from the observations and principles set out in *Miglin* that a duty to make full and honest disclosure of all relevant financial information is required to protect the integrity of the result of negotiations undertaken in these uniquely vulnerable circumstances. The deliberate failure to make such disclosure may render the agreement vulnerable to judicial intervention where the result is a negotiated settlement that is substantially at variance from the objectives of the governing legislation.

> 48 Such a duty in matrimonial negotiations anchors the ability of separating spouses to genuinely decide for themselves what constitutes an acceptable bargain. It also helps protect the possibility of finality in agreements. An agreement based on full and honest disclosure is an agreement that, *prima facie*, is based on the informed consent of both parties. It is, as a result, an agreement that courts are more likely to respect. Where, on the other hand, an agreement is based on misinformation, it cannot be said to be a true bargain which is entitled to judicial deference.

(2) Failure to Understand

GRANT-HOSE v. GRANT-HOSE

(1991), 32 R.F.L. (3d) 26, 1991 CarswellOnt 251 (Ont. U.F.C.)

[The parties were married in 1977 and separated in 1987. In 1988 they signed a separation agreement which provided, *inter alia*, that the husband would pay $1,200 child support per month for the two children in the wife's custody; that he would pay her $200 a month spousal support for 12 months; and that the wife would have exclusive possession of the matrimonial home until the earliest of certain specified events, at which time it would be sold and the proceeds divided equally. When the agreement was negotiated, the husband believed that he was seeing a lawyer, but, in reality, he was being advised by a law clerk. She advised him that the court would not order partition and sale of the matrimonial home in any event and that $600 per month was the "going rate" for child support. The divorce judgment in 1989 contained no corollary relief. In 1990 the husband applied to set aside the separation agreement and to reduce child support. He alleged that he had not read or understood the agreement.]

MENDES DA COSTA U.F.C.J.: — ... Section 56(4) is designed to provide a check to the overriding effect afforded a domestic contract by s. 2(10) and embodies the curative philosophy of the Act. The balance between these two provisions seems discernible in the Preamble of the Act, which propounds the necessity of providing in law for the "orderly and equitable settlement of the affairs of the spouses upon the breakdown of the partnership." In proceedings to impugn a domestic contract, the burden of proof lies upon the applicant.

(i) Nature or Consequences

Section 56(4)(b) speaks in language reminiscent of the common law doctrine of non est factum. However, the subsection enables a court to grant relief where a party did not understand the nature "or" consequences of a domestic contract, that is, relief would appear to be available where a party understood the nature of the document but did not understand its consequences. Moreover, by empowering the court to set aside a "domestic contract" or "a provision in it", the legislation seems to draw no distinction between a lack of understanding as to the very nature or character of the document as a whole and a lack of understanding of its individual contents ... The word "nature" relates to the fundamental character of the document, its class or type. The word "consequences" would seem to reach the effect or impact of the document upon the spouses' affairs. The words "a provision" would seem broad enough to cover any such provision, whether it be one relating to support or property.

Did the applicant understand the "nature" or "consequences" of the agreement? The position of the applicant is that he thought he was dealing with Linda Carey, a lawyer, whereas, as he later discovered, the lady he saw was Elaine Smith, a law clerk. The applicant asserted that he did not receive proper legal advice as to the substantive law relating to the equalization of the spouses' net family properties and to the matrimonial home. The applicant took the position, also, that when he attended at the Hughson Law Centre to sign the separation agreement, he did not read the document, and that, in relation to the matrimonial home, the document did not correspond to his instructions.

The applicant knew that the document he signed was a separation agreement. He had been given an early draft by Mr. Williams, the respondent's counsel, during the second meeting after matters relating to the spouses' separation, exclusive possession of the matrimonial home, and support had been discussed. He was then advised to obtain independent legal advice. The applicant contacted the Hughson Law Centre. He was introduced to Elaine Smith and saw her on three or four occasions, the first meeting lasting about 1 hour. He telephoned the Hughson Law Centre and spoke to Elaine Smith several times. The separation agreement contains 20 amendments, each initialled by the applicant. He signed the document, and his signature was witnessed by "Elaine F. Smith". She, likewise, witnessed his signature to schedule "B" of the agreement. The account of the Hughson Law Centre, Exhibit 3, was signed by Elaine F. Smith, as I have reviewed earlier in these reasons. From this account, it appears that the applicant's contact with the Hughson Law Centre commenced on February 11, 1988, and continued until the separation agreement was signed on May 20, 1988. During his cross-examination by Mr. Greenhow, the applicant stated that he did not sign cheques, letters, house leases, or mortgages without reading them. He acknowledged that he knew that the separation agreement governed his obligation to provide support for the respondent and the children. When asked whether he knew that it governed his rights to the matrimonial home, the applicant replied that his lawyer told him that everything was okay ... [T]he applicant was not a credible witness, and I do not believe that I can rely upon his evidence as to the separation agreement. In my opinion, the applicant knew what he was doing when he signed the document, and I find, as stated in para 22(1)(c), that the applicant understood the nature and consequences of the agreement. He has not persuaded me that the separation agreement should be set aside under s. 56(4)(b) of the Act.

Even, however, had I accepted the applicant's testimony, my conclusion would have been no different. In *Marvco Color Research Ltd v. Harris*, [1982] 2 S.C.R. 774, the Supreme Court of Canada considered, anew, the issue whether a party who has signed a document might be precluded by carelessness from raising the defence of non est factum. The judgment of the Court was delivered by Estey J. Referring to the Court's prior decision of *Prudential Trust Co. v. Cugnet*, [1956] S.C.R. 915, 5 D.L.R. (2d) 1, Estey J., at [pp. 585-586, 141 D.L.R.; pp. 785-786, [1982] 2 S.C.R.; pp. 59-60, 26 R.P.R.; pp. 155-156, 20 B.L.R.], stated:

> In my view, with all due respect to those who have expressed views to the contrary, the dissenting view of Cartwright J. (as he then was) in *Prudential, supra,* correctly enunciated the principles of the law of non est factum. In the result the defendants-respondents are barred by reason of their carelessness from pleading that their minds did not follow their hands when executing the mortgage so as to be able to plead that the mortgage is not binding upon them. ...

> The defendants, in executing the security without the simple precaution of ascertaining its nature in fact and in law, have nonetheless taken an intended and deliberate step in signing the document and have caused it to be legally binding upon themselves. In the words of *Foster v. Mackinnon* this negligence, even though it may have sprung from good intentions, precludes the defendants in this circumstance from disowning the document, that is to say, from pleading that their minds did not follow their respective hands when signing the document and hence that no document in law was executed by them.

... In my opinion, the Legislature did not contemplate or intend that s. 56(4)(b) should be interpreted in a manner inconsistent with the principle enunciated by the Supreme Court of Canada. I know of no reason why a domestic contract should be set aside, on this ground alone, in circumstances where an agreement of another kind would be upheld.

Each case must, of course, depend upon its own circumstances. The court should consider all relevant facts, including the magnitude and extent of the carelessness alleged, and the context in which the carelessness occurred. In the case before me, the applicant, in executing the separation agreement, took an intended and deliberate step. The separation agreement complied with the formalities required by the Act. In this way, the applicant was exposed to the "warning" function of s. 55(1). The respondent negotiated the separation agreement through the office of Mr. Williams, her solicitor. From her evidence, which I accept, it appears that the first time she heard that the applicant felt that the agreement should be set aside was in July 1989. Her evidence was that, up until that time, as far as she could tell, the applicant abided by the terms of the agreement and made no objection to any of its terms. In my opinion, even had I accepted the applicant's testimony, I would have found that the separation agreement was legally binding upon him, and that he would have been unable to assert that, in signing the document, his mind did not follow his hand. To hold otherwise, I believe, would be wholly inconsonant with the necessity, expressed in the Preamble, of providing in law for the "orderly and equitable settlement of the affairs" of the parties.

Nor do I believe that the applicant could have disowned the separation agreement on the basis that he did not receive proper legal advice. The respondent's solicitor, Mr. Williams, suggested to the applicant that he obtain independent legal advice, and the applicant attended at the Hughson Law Centre. It is clear that the applicant retained the Hughson Law Centre and that the separation agreement emerged as a result of negotiations between the Hughson Law Centre and Mr. Williams's office. The authority of a solicitor arises from his retainer. In *Scherer v. Paletta*, [1966] 2 O.R. 524, 57 D.L.R. (2d) 532, the Ontario Court of Appeal considered the law generally applicable to the settlement of litigation by counsel. The judgment of the Court was delivered by Evans J.A. In the course of his judgment, at [pp. 534-535 D.L.R., pp. 526-527 O.R.], Evans J.A. enunciated this principle:

> A client, having retained a solicitor in a particular matter, holds that solicitor out as his agent to conduct the matter in which the solicitor is retained. In general, the solicitor is the client's authorized agent in all matters that may reasonably be expected to arise for decision in the particular proceedings for which he has been retained. Where a principal gives an agent general authority to conduct any

business on his behalf, he is bound as regards third persons by every act done by the agent which is incidental to the ordinary course of such business or which falls within the apparent scope of the agent's authority. As between principal and agent, the authority may be limited by agreement or special instructions but as regards third parties the authority which the agent has is that which he is reasonably believed to have, having regard to all the circumstances, and which is reasonably to be gathered from the nature of his employment and duties.

In my opinion, this principle applies to the situation before me. The applicant held out the Hughson Law Centre as his agent to negotiate the separation agreement. The respondent, it seems to me, was entitled to rely upon the fact that the Hughson Law Centre was the applicant's authorized agent "in all matters that may reasonably be expected to arise for decision" in the negotiation process. It was not the responsibility of the respondent to inquire into the knowledge or qualifications of the individual who advised the applicant, or to probe the quality of advice given. To interpret s. 56(4)(b) in this fashion would have far-reaching and, I believe, destructive effects on the relationship of solicitor and client, and on the negotiation, between solicitors, of domestic contracts. Such a construction would attribute to the statutory words a meaning that they do not reasonably embrace.

[Although Mendes da Costa U.F.C.J. concluded that there was no basis to set aside or override the agreement, child support was significantly reduced. Pursuant to the agreement, the provisions for child support could be varied if there was a "material change in circumstances." This test was met because of a considerable drop in the husband's income.]

NOTES AND QUESTIONS

1. Do the comments of Mendes da Costa U.F.C.J. in *Grant-Hose* on the authority of solicitors mean that a person can never rely on s. 56(4)(b) where the domestic contract is the result of negotiations between lawyers?

2. Section 56(4)(b) of the *FLA* appears to be closely related to the common law doctrine of *non est factum* whereby a court will not hold a party to a contract where he or she so misunderstood its true nature and intent as to negate apparent consent. To succeed at common law, the party must prove that the document signed was fundamentally different from that which he or she believed it to be. Where a party failed to understand the precise meaning and content of the document but did have a good idea as to its general nature and purpose, the plea of *non est factum* will not succeed. Moreover, it will fail unless the party can demonstrate an absence of carelessness in the circumstances. To what extent are the circumstances covered by s. 56(4)(b) broader than those encompassed by the concept of *non est factum*?

How does s. 56(4)(b) re-enforce the desirability of independent legal advice for both parties who desire a legally effective domestic contract?

If one party is informed of the desirability of independent legal advice but chooses not to seek it prior to signing a domestic contract, should the court still use s. 56(4)(b) to set aside the contract later? See *Ablaka v. Ablaka* (1991), 32 R.F.L. (3d) 369 (Ont. U.F.C.); affirmed (1994), 4 R.F.L. (4th) 167 (Ont. C.A.).

(3) Law of Contract

ROSEN v. ROSEN

(1994), 3 R.F.L. (4th) 267, 1994 CarswellOnt 390 (Ont. C.A.); leave to appeal
refused (1995), 10 R.F.L. (4th) 121 (note) (S.C.C.)

GRANGE J.A.: —

This appeal is brought by the husband from a judgment setting aside the separation agreement between the parties and imposing an equalization payment upon the husband considerably in excess of the benefits provided in the agreement [unreported (December 4, 1992), Doc. 70447/ 91Q, [1993] W.D.F.L. 105, Conant J. (Ont. Gen. Div.),]. There were many other issues in the litigation but all except the agreement and the equalization payment were resolved before or at trial and were not the subject of dispute before us.

2 The parties were married in November of 1981. There was a twenty-two-year-age differential, the wife being then thirty-two, and the husband, fifty-four. There was an even more pronounced financial difference, the husband having assets worth more than one million dollars and the wife having virtually none. The husband had four adult children by a previous marriage; the wife had not been married before. There were twin daughters of the marriage, born in 1983. The parties lived in a house owned by the husband for many years prior to marriage, apparently without serious incident until 1988, when marital problems arose, culminating in the wife's decision to separate. After a spate of unsuccessful counselling, there was a physical separation on February 1, 1989, and the separation agreement in dispute was signed.

3 By the agreement the wife has custody of the daughters, with liberal access to the husband; the husband would pay to the wife for her support $1,700 per month from May 1, 1988, to April 1, 1991, and $500 for each child until the child reached twenty-one, subject to cost of living adjustment, together with income tax suffered by the wife for such payments. The wife transferred to the husband all interest in the matrimonial home but the husband essentially paid for another home purchased by the wife, partly by paying the down payment and partly by assuming payment obligations on a mortgage. He further paid her $30,000 for furniture in her new home. The wife agreed to execute a will leaving the new home to the husband should she predecease him.

4 In September of 1990, the wife expressed an intention to move to Novi, Michigan, where her fiancé resided, which would have the effect of limiting or depriving the husband of his right to access. The husband then commenced an application for joint custody. He also stopped making mortgage payments on the wife's new home. The wife thereupon counterclaimed to set aside the separation agreement. The mortgage problem was eventually solved by the husband paying off the remaining principal in June of 1992. The custody problem was resolved by consent and incorporated in a very detailed order of Walsh J. dated April 22, 1992. The issue of the wife's counterclaim to set aside the separation agreement went on to trial.

5 Subsections 56(4)(a), (b), and (c) of the *Family Law Act*, R.S.O. 1990, c. F.3, govern the case. ...

6 At trial the wife argued all three subsections applied:

(a) particularly because of a settlement made by the husband upon his six children,

(b) because the wife allegedly did not know that the signing of the separation agreement would preclude an equalization payment, and

(c) because the wife lacked independent legal advice and was owed a fiduciary duty by the husband and because the agreement was unconscionable.

7 The trial judge found against the wife on (a) and (b) and the first two grounds of (c) but found in her favour on the unconscionability ground of (c). He declared the agreement unconscionable, set it aside, and ordered an equalization payment of $406,477. In so doing, he stated as follows [at pp. 9-10 unreported]:

> The test applied in determining whether an agreement is unconscionable is the following: where the parties are unequal and the agreement is improvident, the party seeking to uphold the contract bears the onus of proving that he or she was scrupulously considerate of the other's interest or that the contract was just, fair and reasonable. ...

> ... I find that the parties were unequal at the time they executed the agreement. The husband was an experienced business person whose occupation involved negotiating contracts. The wife, on the other hand, left all financial matters to her husband who admitted in his testimony that she would sign whatever documents he put before her. When the husband urged that they amicably settle their affairs without resort to lawyers, the wife was put at a distinct disadvantage. Furthermore, after the negotiations but before the agreement was committed to paper, the wife put an offer in on what is now her home. The husband warned her that this step was premature because the agreement requiring him to pay for that home had not yet been drafted. When the agreement was drafted, a clause not previously discussed was added which I find exhibited an awareness of the wife's precarious position and drove an even harder bargain. The new clause required the wife to leave her home to her husband should she predecease him. In addition, the husband added a clause enabling him to fund the purchase of the home by way of mortgage rather than purchasing it outright.

8 The trial judge then went on to find (not without some doubt) that the agreement was, from the wife's viewpoint, improvident and the husband did not satisfy the onus of being scrupulously considerate of the wife's interest. It was the finding that the parties were unequal that has given me concern.

9 I consider the matter with two general principles in mind.

10 The first is the approach the court should take towards the validity of separation agreements. Zuber J.A. in *Farquar v. Farquar* (1983), 43 O.R. (2d) 423 (C.A.), at p. 430, had this to say on the subject:

> I start with the proposition that it is desirable that the parties should settle their own affairs if possible. I think that they are more likely to accept their own solution to their problem than one imposed upon them. A more pedestrian reason for encouraging parties to settle their own affairs is that the courts may simply be incapable of dealing with the ever-increasing mass of matrimonial disputes.

> It is, I think, obvious that the settlement of matrimonial disputes can only be encouraged if the parties can expect that the terms of such settlement will be binding and will be recognized by the courts. ...

I agreed with his comments then and I agree with them now. They do not, of course, purport to apply to unconscionable agreements.

11 On the proper test for unconscionability I refer to the words of Schroeder J.A. in *Mundinger v. Mundinger* (1968), [1969] 1 O.R. 606 (C.A.), at pp. 609-610:

> The governing principle applicable here was laid down by this Court in the oft-cited case of *Vanzant v. Coates* (1917), 40 O.L.R. 556, 39 D.L.R. 485. It was there held that the equitable rule is that if the donor is in a situation in which he is not a free agent and is not equal to protecting himself, a Court of Equity will protect him, not against his own folly or carelessness, but against his being taken advantage of by those in a position to do so because of their position. In that case the circumstances were the advanced age of the donor, her infirmity, her dependence on the donee; the position of influence occupied by the donee, her acts in procuring the drawing and execution of the deed; and the consequent complete change of a well-understood and defined purpose in reference to the disposition of the donor's property. It was held that in those circumstances the onus was on the plaintiff to prove by

satisfactory evidence that the gift was a voluntary and deliberate act by a person mentally competent to know, and who did know, the nature and effect of the deed, and that it was not the result of undue influence. That onus had not been discharged; and it was therefore held to be unnecessary for the defendant to prove affirmatively that the influence possessed by the plaintiff had been unduly exercised.

The principle enunciated in *Vanzant v. Coates, supra*, has been consistently followed and applied by the Courts of this Province and the other common law Provinces of Canada. The effect of the relevant decisions was neatly stated by Professor Bradley E. Crawford in a commentary written by him and appearing in 44 Can. Bar Rev. 142 (1966) at p. 143, from which I quote the following extract:

> If the bargain is fair the fact that the parties were not equally vigilant of their interest is immaterial. Likewise, if one was not preyed upon by the other, an improvident or even grossly inadequate consideration is no ground upon which to set aside a contract freely entered into. It is the combination of inequality and improvidence which alone may invoke this jurisdiction. Then the onus is placed upon the party seeking to uphold the contract to show that his conduct throughout was scrupulously considerate of the other's interests.

12 This is slightly different from the test set forth by the trial judge in the case at bar. It is, however, the basis of our modern law of unconscionability and I would unhesitatingly follow it. The question therefore becomes, was there an inequality between the parties, a preying of one upon the other which, combined with improvidence, cast the onus upon the husband of acting with scrupulous care for the welfare and interests of the wife? I think not.

13 We must always remember that it is not the ability of one party to make a better bargain that counts. Seldom are contracting parties equal. It is the taking advantage of that ability to prey upon the other party that produces the unconscionability. I can find nothing in the reasons for judgment quoted above to denote that advantage was taken.

14 The wife was not without business experience. She had once managed a bar and had bookkeeping experience. She was trained as an addiction counsellor. There was no evidence of abuse or intimidation, or of learning or other disability, of anxiety or stress, or a nervous breakdown or indulgence in drugs or alcohol (as in *Mundinger*). At one time she was concerned about alcohol and joined Alcoholics Anonymous but it appears not to have been a serious continuing problem.

15 The wife consulted at least three lawyers in the course of the negotiations and at a critical point the wife sought out a "top of the line" lawyer and was referred to a family law practitioner of high reputation. She was able to give him a reasonably accurate account of her husband's assets and, although he was reluctant to give specific advice without more information, he did give her a rough outline of the equalization entitlement. She then became concerned over the cost of continuing with a lawyer and, in discussion with her husband, it was decided that they would negotiate their own agreement. He continued to seek advice from lawyers and a consultant, but she must have been aware of this both from the name of the lawyer on the draft agreement and from negotiations of terms having tax implications. When the final agreement was drawn the husband told her to see a lawyer and she took it to a stranger, insisting that he merely witness her signature. She was foolish and penny wise, but knowledgable and acting with free will. The husband did nothing to deny her proper advice.

16 I must concede that had she consulted a reasonably competent lawyer for advice at the time of signing, he or she would have advised against signing, not because of oppression by the husband but because it was not a good bargain for the wife. As I have said, however, this

is not the test for unconscionability. As Professor Crawford put it, "even grossly inadequate consideration is no ground upon which to set aside a contract freely entered into."

Appeal allowed.

RICK v. BRANDSEMA

(2009), 62 R.F.L. (6th) 239, 2009 CarswellBC 342 (S.C.C.)

[A husband and wife separated in 2000, after almost 27 years of married life. They had five children, two of whom were still under 19 years of age. The spouses were equal shareholders in a corporation that owned and operated a dairy farm. They also held some other family assets such as RRSPs, vehicles and real property. After the separation, the corporation provided almost $200,000 to the wife so that she could purchase a home for herself.

In 2000, the wife retained a lawyer who commenced divorce proceedings. She terminated his services and those of a business valuator shortly thereafter. In 2001, the spouses retained a mediator and reached a memorandum of understanding (the "MOU") after the husband provided estimates of the family assets' values. The key provision of the MOU was that the wife would retain her home and would receive $750,000 as a settlement of her property and support claims. The $750,000 figure had been proposed by the wife. The wife then returned to her lawyer who told her that he could not comment on the fairness of the MOU without further financial information. He later obtained additional information about the values of the family assets. The wife again terminated the services of the lawyer.

The wife next arranged for a new mediator. She told this mediator that she intended to sign a separation agreement to obtain about $1 million and then to sue the husband to obtain "justice". After a period of negotiation through the mediator, the MOU was revised to include an additional payment to the wife of $100,000 for child support. The second mediator referred the wife to a new lawyer. This lawyer told her that she might be able to obtain more property through litigation and that she should not waive her claim to spousal support. He also arranged for the wife to see an accountant who advised her on a tax plan that would eliminate personal taxes on the transfer of the corporate shares pursuant to the MOU.

In 2001, the spouses signed a separation agreement and a share transfer agreement to implement the revised MOU. The spouses were divorced and a consent order was entered in January 2001 whereby the wife's claims against the husband were dismissed.

In 2003, the wife commenced a legal action asking that the separation agreement and the related share-transfer agreement be set aside based on the husband's misrepresentation and the doctrine of unconscionability. In the alternative, she asked that the court reapportion the family assets under s. 65 or s. 68 of the *Family Law Act*, R.S.B.C. 1996, c. 128. Section 65(1) specified that, where a division of property under a marriage agreement was unfair having regard to a number of factors, a court could order that the property covered by the agreement be divided into shares fixed by the court.

The trial judge concluded that the date for assessing the separation agreement and for the valuation of any relief to which the wife might be entitled was October 2000, the date of valuation set out in the MOU. He found that, under the separation agreement, the wife had received $344,752 less than half of the October 2000 value of the family assets. Characterizing the wife as mentally unstable and vulnerable, he suggested that the husband had seized the opportunity to accept the wife's proposal for an unequal sharing of the family assets. He therefore held that the separation agreement was unconscionable. However, he declined to rescind the agreement because the wife could not make restitution. Instead, he ordered the husband to make a compensatory payment of $461,252 pursuant to the *Family Law Act* or, if that Act did not authorize this payment, damages in the same amount. This sum included

$116,000 as the wife's one-half share of assets that the husband had failed to disclose and $344,752 to ensure an equal sharing of all the family assets.

The husband appealed. He accepted that he should pay his wife the $116,000, but quarreled with the award of an additional $344,752. In a cross-appeal, the wife contended that the trial judge should have set aside the agreement as a result of the husband's failure to disclose assets and that he erred in his selection of October 2000 as the date on which to value the family assets. The British Columbia Court of Appeal allowed the husband's appeal and dismissed the cross-appeal. It held that the trial judge erred in finding that the agreement was unconscionable because, in effect, he concluded that the husband had an obligation not to accept a proposal from the wife that was advantageous to him. It also questioned whether there was a power imbalance between the husband and wife, noting that the wife had consulted lawyers and accountants and she had arranged for two mediations. In sum, the appellate court saw her as a troubled woman who clearly knew what she was doing.

The Supreme Court of Canada unanimously allowed the wife's appeal. For the Court, Justice Abella stressed the deference that appellate courts owed to the findings of a trial judge. As noted earlier, she also emphasized the husband's lack of full and honest disclosure. Finally, she made the following comments on the trial judge's conclusion that the agreement was unconscionable.]

58 Moreover, it is worth remembering that in addition to the husband's failure to provide his wife with the information she needed to decide what bargain would best reflect their mutual intention to divide their assets equally, the trial judge also based his finding of unconscionability on the fact that the husband deliberately exploited his wife's known mental fragility.

59 The Court of Appeal overturned these findings about exploitative conduct. It relied on *Miglin v. Miglin* in concluding that the wife's access in this case to professional advice and assistance cured her vulnerabilities.

60 It may well be that in a particular case, professional assistance will effectively compensate for vulnerabilities. But the Court of Appeal appears to have assumed that the mere presence of professional assistance automatically neutralized vulnerabilities in this case. This interpretation does not, with respect, accord with a plain reading of para. 83 of *Miglin*, which states: "Where vulnerabilities are not present, or are effectively compensated by the presence of counsel or other professionals or both, or have not been taken advantage of, the court should consider the agreement as a genuine mutual desire to finalize the terms of the parties' separation and as indicative of their substantive intentions."

61 This passage indicates that when vulnerabilities have been compensated for by the presence of professionals, the agreement should be respected. This is an important observation. Given that vulnerabilities are almost always present in these negotiations, the parties' genuine wish to finalize their arrangements should, absent psychological exploitation or misinformation, be respected. One way to help attenuate the possibility of such negotiating abuses is undoubtedly through professional assistance. But exploitation is not rendered anodyne merely because a spouse has access to professional advice. It is a question of fact in each case.

62 In this case, the trial judge found that the wife's vulnerabilities were *not* compensated for. On the contrary, he concluded that her emotional and mental condition left her unable to make use of the professional assistance available to her. Moreover, and significantly, he found that her mental instability was well known to her husband.

63 The combination in this case, therefore, of misleading informational deficits and psychologically exploitative conduct, led the trial judge to conclude that the resulting, significant

deviation from the wife's statutory entitlement rendered the agreement unconscionable and therefore unenforceable. This conclusion is amply supported by the evidence. ...

65 The trial judge's remedy for unconscionability was to order the husband to pay the wife an amount representing the difference between the negotiated "equalization payment" and the wife's entitlement under the *Family Relations Act*.

66 Historically, rescission was the remedy when a contract was found to be unenforceable because of unconscionability. Increasingly, however, when rescission is unavailable because restitution, as a practical matter, cannot be made, damages in the form of "equitable compensation" are imposed to provide relief to the wronged party. ...

NOTES AND QUESTIONS

1. Although the doctrines of undue influence, duress and unconscionability are conceptually distinct, they overlap to a considerable extent and the courts have sometimes subsumed them under the general rubric of unconscionability. The resultant confusion was noted in *Williams v. Downey-Waterbury* (1994), 11 R.F.L. (4th) 106 (Man. C.A.).

2. A lack of independent legal advice is often treated as one of the hallmarks of an unconscionable agreement. A lack of independent legal advice, however, will not lead inexorably to a finding of unconscionability (see *Loy v. Loy* (2007), 45 R.F.L. (6th) 296 (Ont. S.C.J.)). Unconscionability arises out of an "overwhelming imbalance in the power relationship between the parties" (*Norberg v. Wynrib*, [1992] 2 S.C.R. 226; additional reasons at (1992), 1992 CarswellBC 338 (S.C.C.), at para. 30.) Similarly, as *Rick v. Brandsema* indicates, the presence of independent legal advice does not necessarily prevent a characterization of an agreement as an unconscionable bargain. Nor does it necessarily avoid a finding of fraud, material misrepresentation, duress, or undue influence.

Professor Majury argues in "Unconscionability in an Equality Context" (1990-1991), 7 C.F.L.Q. 123 at 144–149, that the presence of independent legal advice has often been given too much significance. She states (at 144) that "the advice provides little or no protection but makes it difficult to challenge a domestic contract on the ground of unconscionability".

3. For a review of the law relating to duress, see *P. (M.L.) v. P. (G.W.)* (2000), 12 R.F.L. (5th) 434 (Ont. S.C.J.).

4. Because the relationship of husband and wife does not give rise to a presumption of undue influence, the party attacking a domestic contract must prove actual undue influence. This entails establishing "the ability of one person to dominate the will of another, whether through manipulation, coercion or outright but subtle abuse of power" (*per* Justice Wilson in *Goodman Estate v. Geffen* (1991), 81 D.L.R. (4th) 211 (S.C.C.)). Given the difficulty of establishing this, most successful challenges focus on unconscionability. Undue influence, as well as unconscionability, was established in *Bennett v. Bennett* (1997), 34 R.F.L. (4th) 290 (Ont. Gen. Div.); affirmed (1999), 1999 CarswellOnt 2139 (Ont. C.A.); leave to appeal refused (1999), 251 N.R. 400 (note) (S.C.C.) and *Bradley v. Bradley* (2000), 7 R.F.L. (5th) 270 (Ont. S.C.J.). As Professor Thompson indicates in "When is a Family Law Contract *Not* Invalid, Unenforceable, Overridden or Varied?" (2001-2002), 19 C.F.L.Q. 399 at 413, the latter case is "really a classic case of unconscionability".

5. For cases examining the concepts of unilateral mistake and mutual mistake and their application in the context of domestic contracts, see *Wilde v. Wilde* (2000), 9 R.F.L. (5th) 442 (Ont. S.C.J.); additional reasons at (2000), 2000 CarswellOnt 3563 (Ont. S.C.J.); *Bogue v. Bogue* (1999), 1 R.F.L. (5th) 213 (Ont. C.A.); *Works v. Works* (2002), 29 R.F.L. (5th) 459 (N.S. S.C.); and *Williamson v. Williamson* (2004), 50 R.F.L. (5th) 459 (Sask. C.A.).

6. In *Marinangeli v. Marinangeli* (2003), 38 R.F.L. (5th) 307 (Ont. C.A.), a settlement agreement required the husband to pay indexed spousal and child support and it stipulated that the amounts could be varied in the event of a material change in circumstances. The trial judge ordered retroactive support, partially on the basis that the husband had failed to meet his implied contractual duty to tell his wife about material increases in his income. The

Ontario Court of Appeal held that it was open to the trial judge to imply this term. Justice Weiler reasoned (at para. 64):

> The lengthy protracted negotiations over four years, the [husband's] representation as to his financial situation, the disclosure respecting the [stock] options combined with the very short time frame after signing the Minutes within which the options were exercised, the fact that the [husband] controlled the timing of the realization of his income from the options that had vested, and the fact that the [wife] had no means of accessing this information, are all factors supporting the trial judge's conclusion that the [husband] had an implicit obligation to disclose his change in circumstances in order to give business efficacy to the agreement.

Although language of this type usually suggests that a decision is very much factually driven, Professor McLeod speculated in "Case Comment: *Marinangeli v. Marinangeli*" (2003), 38 R.F.L. (5th) 340 at 340, that the decision "may be one of the court's more far-reaching family law decisions in recent years" and suggested (at 349) that the practical effect of the decision is that courts will imply a duty to disclose material changes into contracts that provide for variation of support obligations. Professor McLeod's prediction is supported by *Pearce v. Murphy* (2004), 47 R.F.L. (5th) 192 (Ont. S.C.J.); additional reasons at (2004), 47 R.F.L. (5th) 237 (Ont. S.C.J.); additional reasons at (2004), 3 R.F.L. (6th) 173 (Ont. S.C.J.) where Justice E. MacDonald held that the father had an implied contractual duty to disclose material changes in income. However, compare *Baldwin v. Funston* (2007), 37 R.F.L. (6th) 309 (Ont. C.A.); additional reasons at (2007), 2007 CarswellOnt 5529 (C.A.), where the court distinguished *Marinangeli v. Marinangeli*.

10

CHILD IN NEED OF PROTECTION

1. Introduction

(1) General

BALA, "CHILD WELFARE LAW IN CANADA: AN INTRODUCTION"

Bala, Zapf, Williams, Vogl, and Hornick, eds., *Canadian Child Welfare Law: Children, Families and the State*, 2d ed. (Toronto: Thompson Educational Publishing, Inc., 2004) (Footnotes omitted) (Reprinted with the permission of the author and publisher.)

The Role of the State in the Raising of Children

There is much controversy in Canada over the "best" way to raise children. Parental practices concerning such matters as children's nutrition, discipline, toilet training, day care, schooling, sports, sex education, dating and recreation are all the subject of heated debate among experts and social commentators. However, parents are largely left to make their own decisions about the best way to care for their children, according to their own values, beliefs and experience. This includes the parental right to determine the extent to which their children will be involved in making decisions about their own lives, though inevitably as children grow older they begin to exercise more autonomy.

Parents are human and none are "perfect"; some parents are far from perfect. Many parents may lack the education, understanding, and resources to do what is "best" for their children. Even if parents think they know what is "best" for their children, they may be unwilling or unable to do it. Nevertheless, it is a fundamental premise of our society that coercive government interference in family life should be kept to a minimum. ...

There are, however, some situations in which the care parents provide is considered so inadequate that direct interference by the state is justified to protect children from their parents. These are situations where parental care has fallen below the minimum standards that our society will tolerate. State interference in the family and removal of a child from parental care is not legally justified merely because the child might have greater opportunities elsewhere.

Rather, state interference through removal of a child from parental care will only be justified if it is proven that there is a significant risk to the child. ...

The History of Child Protection in Canada

... Children's Aid Societies were established in various Canadian municipalities in the last decade of the nineteenth century, with the objective of helping orphaned, abandoned and neglected children. In 1893, reformers persuaded the Ontario legislature to enact *The Children's Protection Act*, which gave these privately controlled societies broad legal powers, including the right to remove neglected or abused children from their homes and become legal guardians for such children.

Child welfare agencies were established throughout Canada by the early years of the twentieth century, and child welfare legislation was enacted in each province. However, the enormous growth and the legalization of the field has only occurred in the last 40 years.

Until the early 1960s, child welfare agencies dealt largely with the most obvious cases of abuse and neglect, and with situations of adolescent unmanageability. Agencies also had responsibility for the placement and adoption of some illegitimate children (i.e., those born out of wedlock) and had considerable responsibility for dealing with delinquent youth as well. While the courts exercised a supervisory function over the removal of children from their homes and over the adoption process, in practice the system tended to operate informally. Historically, most of the judges who sat in the Family Courts and dealt with this type of case lacked legal training, and lawyers rarely appeared in these proceedings. Parents who were involved in the protection process were often poor and poorly educated individuals who lacked the sophistication and resources to challenge the actions of the agencies. Many of the parents whose children were removed from their care were Aboriginal, or members of religious minority groups like the Doukhobors in British Columbia, who were socially marginalized. There was no thought given to notions of children's rights and children were not overtly involved in the child welfare proceedings where courts made decisions profoundly affecting their futures.

In the last 40 years, enormous changes have occurred in the child welfare field in Canada. An important development was the identification of the battered child syndrome in the early 1960s. Until that time, doctors and social workers tended to suspect physical abuse only in cases where there was a witness to the abuse, or a child stated that an assault had occurred. But in the 1960s there was a growing recognition that parents often lie about abusing their children, describing injuries they inflicted as the result of "accidents," and that children are often too frightened or too young to disclose the truth to investigators during a single interview. Increased understanding of the problem led to changes in legislation to require professionals and members of the public to report suspected cases of child abuse. Child Abuse Registers were established in many North American jurisdictions in the mid-1960s to help keep track of abusers and abused children, and to facilitate research. Changes in reporting laws and growing professional awareness led to significant increases in the number of reports of physical abuse.

The late 1970s and early 1980s were marked by a "discovery" of child sexual abuse, similar to the earlier uncovering of physical abuse. Researchers learned that children were often too intimidated, [guilt-ridden] or ill-informed to report sexual abuse, and that parents and professionals often ignored reports or symptoms of sexual abuse. Changes in public and professional awareness resulted in enormous increases in the number of reported cases of child sexual abuse in the 1980s, with both children and adult survivors of abuse from previous decades coming forward to disclose what had happened to them in childhood. There were also fundamental changes in how child witnesses are treated in the Canadian criminal justice system, resulting in many more prosecutions of abusers.

While child welfare agencies were dealing with more reports of sexual abuse in the 1980s and 1990s than in previous decades, agency involvement in other areas declined. Illegitimacy no longer bore a great stigma. Single mothers received more social and financial support than in the past. The concept of "family" broadened (and continues to evolve). Although single mothers face real challenges in raising their children alone, many more single mothers are keeping their children, resulting in a major decline in the adoption work of child welfare agencies. When the *Juvenile Delinquents Act* was replaced by the *Young Offenders Act* in 1984, Canadian child protection agencies also ceased to have direct responsibility for delinquent youth. The *Young Offenders Act* was in turn replaced by the *Youth Criminal Justice Act* in 2003, and there has continued to be a formal separation of the child welfare and youth justice systems, though it is not uncommon for adolescents in the care of child welfare agencies to be charged with offences, and there continues to be concerns that some agency wards with behavioural problems are being "dumped" into the youth justice and corrections systems.

The Legal Revolution

Related to some of the fundamental changes in the child protection field has been a veritable revolution in the role of law and the courts in Canadian society. ... Law has become an important social policy tool, affecting virtually every aspect of Canadian public policy. ...

Both reflecting and reinforcing the importance of law in defining society was the enactment of the *Canadian Charter of Rights and Freedoms* in 1982. The *Charter* has had a profound effect on Canadian society. While in the first few years that the *Charter* was in effect it had only limited impact on child welfare law, in its 1999 decision in *New Brunswick (Minister of Health) v. G.(J.)*, [1999] 3 S.C.R. 46, 50 R.F.L. (4th) 63, the Supreme Court of Canada sent a strong message that parents have a vital interest in their relationship with their children, an interest that is entitled to protection under s. 7 of the *Charter* as an aspect of "security of the person." The Court concluded that, pursuant to s. 7 of the *Charter*, a single mother on social assistance whose children had been apprehended by a child welfare agency had the constitutional right to be represented by counsel paid by the government. The provision of counsel is intended to ensure that the temporary wardship proceedings are conducted "in accordance with the principles of fundamental justice." In *G.(J.)* the Supreme Court invoked the constitutional rights of a parent, but was clearly also influenced by a concern for the promotion of the welfare of children. ...

It is now clear that when faced with a concrete situation in which parents or children are being subjected to treatment in a child protection proceeding that does not accord with the "principles of fundamental justice," the courts will respond. The *Charter* has also been used by the courts to eliminate unjustified discrimination and has, for example, been invoked to give biological fathers greater rights in the adoption process [*MacVicar v. British Columbia Superintendent of Family and Child Services* (1986), 34 D.L.R. (4th) 488 (B.C. S.C.)], and by same-sex partners seeking the right to adopt children [*Re K.* (1995), 15 R.F.L. (4th) 129 (Ont. Prov. Ct.)]. However, ... the rights that it guarantees are not absolute, but rather are subject (under s. 1) to "such reasonable limits ... as can be demonstrably justified in a free and democratic society." The courts are continually struggling to balance concerns about the protection of the constitutional rights of parents and children within the family, with the desire to promote the welfare of children, or at least ensure that children are not endangered by the recognition of their legal rights.

In 2004 the Supreme Court of Canada decided *Canadian Foundation for Children, Youth and the Law v. Canada* [(2004), 46 R.F.L. (5th) 1 (S.C.C.)], a case that required the Court to carefully balance the rights of children and the rights of parents in deciding on the constitutional validity of s. 43 of the *Criminal Code*, a provision that allows a parent to use force to "correct" a child, provided that the force does not exceed what is "reasonable" under the circumstances. The Court narrowed the scope of this provision by overruling earlier cases that had, for example, held that parents could use a belt or paddle to correct a child. While the Court recognized that children are vulnerable and entitled to special protections, it also recognized that they are not just small adults who should always be given the same rights as adults, but rather generally be viewed in the context of their families. Parents are entitled to a significant degree of authority to raise their children as they see fit, without undue state interference. Chief Justice MacLachlin wrote [para. 58]:

> Children need to be protected from abusive treatment. They are vulnerable members of Canadian society and Parliament [must] ... shield children from psychological and physical harm. In so acting, the government responds to the critical need of all children for a safe environment. Yet this is not the only need of children. Children also depend on parents ... for guidance and discipline, to protect them

from harm and to promote their healthy development within society. A stable and secure family ... is essential to this growth process.

The Supreme Court ruled that it was not appropriate to criminalize parents who spank their children, though emphasizing that any parental conduct that injures or degrades child is a crime. While the Court did not advocate the use of corporal punishment, it recognized that the criminal law is a "blunt instrument" for educating parents about appropriate parenting.

The increased emphasis on individual rights has had a strong impact on child protection proceedings in Canada. Over the past quarter century the child protection process has become much more legally oriented. There is a greater recognition of the rights of parents and children; there are greater controls placed on the power of the state to intervene in the family. The child protection system is now premised on the notion that children may only be removed from parental care in accordance with "due process" of law. This reflects fundamental values in our society, as well as ensuring that decisions about state intervention are based on careful consideration of the issues by an impartial arbiter.

Due process is not without costs, monetary and other, however. With the legalization of the child protection system has come an expanded legal aid system to ensure representation for indigent parents and, in some Canadian jurisdictions, legal representation for children. Child protection proceedings have become more complex and hence more costly, not only for legal aid plans, but for child protection agencies and for the court system. More serious than the financial costs of due process are the human costs. Due process takes time. Delays due to the court process can be very stressful for children and families, though sometimes parents can take advantage of delays to improve their parenting skills and relationships with their children.

While due process may ensure fairness and considered decision making, it can make the job of social workers and other child welfare professionals more difficult and complex. The child protection system now has a more sharply adversarial nature than it had in the past, and professionals in that system may have their opinions and decisions challenged in the sometimes hostile environment of the courtroom, by lawyers who may seem insensitive to constraints placed on those who work in the child protection system. It must be recognized that parents and children separated from one another by the child welfare system have always felt a level of hostility towards agency workers. However, it is only with the rise of due process that parents and children have had a forum to effectively challenge decisions that profoundly affect their lives.

Although a key component of Canada's legal system is the adversarial trial, there is a growing recognition that having a trial is an emotionally and financially expensive process that will inevitably strain relations between agency workers and parents. Accordingly, in recent years there has been an emphasis on trying to use mediation, settlement conferences and other methods to try to resolve child welfare cases without a trial. ...

Balancing Parental Rights and Protection Concerns

One of most significant developments in the child welfare field in Canada in the late 1990s was a growing focus on protecting children from abusive or neglectful home situations, and providing them with permanent, safe homes. There was a concern that there may have been too much effort in the 1980s and early 1990s directed to "family preservation," and not enough attention to the protection of children. These concerns were heightened by some highly publicized, tragic cases where children died in the care of parents, even though child welfare workers were aware of some problems in the home but had not removed the children from parental care. There was also a growing awareness in the 1990s of the potentially devastating effects to a child's well-being from emotional neglect, and abuse, that might, for example, result from poor attachment to parent figures in a child's early years or from witnessing parents engaging in spousal abuse.

The perception that agencies were not doing enough to protect children resulted in investigations and inquiries in British Columbia, Quebec, Ontario, Manitoba and New Brunswick in the late 1990s. ...

In Ontario, after a series of coroners' inquests, a special committee was appointed by the Ontario government to study the child welfare system and recommend legislative reforms. This committee, ... chaired by Family Court Judge Mary Jane Hatton, did not hold public hearings, and had a limited budget and little time to produce a report. The Ontario *Report of the Panel of Experts on Child Protection: Protecting Vulnerable Children* was released in 1998, and resulted in significant new amendments to the *Child and Family Services Act*, which came into effect in 2000. [For further analysis, see Bala, "Reforming Ontario's *Child and Family Services Act*: Is the Pendulum Swinging Too Far?" (2000), 17 C.F.L.Q. 117.] This legislation both facilitated earlier intervention in cases of physical abuse or neglect, and broadened the grounds for intervention in cases of emotional abuse or neglect.

In addition to the legislative changes that occurred in some Canadian provinces, most jurisdictions have developed more standardized approaches to the assessment of risk of abuse or neglect. ... These tools are intended to promote a consistent, structured approach to the investigation of cases, and to the making of critical decisions about a case, such as whether to apprehend and remove a child from parental care. While these tools are useful there is inevitably also a degree of professional judgement involved in the risk and safety assessment process. ...

While there were important differences in the approaches to child welfare reform in different North American jurisdictions in the late 1990s, there were common themes of developing more effective measures to remove children from the care of parents who were perceived to be inadequate, and to having "permanent decisions" about children's futures made more quickly once they were in agency care. These changes were intended to increase the protections available to children, but they also reflected the more conservative political attitudes of that period and related efforts to reduce government spending. ... In the child welfare field, if parental care was not considered acceptable, parents were more likely to face the prospect of earlier termination of parental rights than under the previous legislative regimes. As a result, there has been less spent on trying to help parents gain the capacity to effectively care for their children. In addition, in the late 1990s there were cuts to many government-funded social programs that had previously been available to assist parents in the community.

In the late 1990s and in the early years of the new century there were very substantial increases in the number of children taken into the care of child welfare agencies in many jurisdictions in North America. While there were many causes for these increases, the changes in the law, which were intended to reduce the risk of abuse of children, clearly played a significant role.

Legal Contexts and the Protection of Children

There are a number of different legal contexts in which issues related to the protection of children from abuse, neglect or ill treatment can arise. While the factual issues may be similar, the legal outcome that is being sought varies with the legal context, and there are important procedural differences between these different types of legal proceedings.

Historically, the criminal law was the only legal tool employed to protect children. It still has an important role. It is a criminal offence to sexually abuse or physically assault a child. However, with regard to the use of physical force, caretakers can raise the defence of "using force by way of correction ... if the force used does not exceed what is reasonable under the circumstances" [*Criminal Code*, s. 43]. It is also an offence for a parent or guardian to fail to provide a child with "necessaries of life" or to abandon a child under the age of 10 [*Criminal Code*, ss. 215, 218]. While the *Criminal Code* can be used to prosecute those who harm children, it is a blunt tool that is often difficult to employ.

Persons charged with criminal offences are guaranteed a broad set of rights. ... Abuse cases can be especially difficult to prove because it is often necessary to rely heavily on the evidence of the child who was the victim of abuse. The traditional rules of evidence and procedure governing criminal cases made it difficult for children to testify, and the courts discounted their evidence. While beginning in the late 1980s legal reforms in Canada and changes in the administration of justice made it easier for children to testify, and resulted in a significant increase in the number of child abuse prosecutions, especially for sexual abuse, it can still be difficult to prove in a criminal proceeding that a particular person has been guilty of abuse and should be punished by the state, for example, by being sent to jail.

... There have been efforts to improve liaison and co-ordination between child protection agencies and those responsible for criminal prosecutions, and it is now common for local police and child welfare agencies to have a "protocol" or joint policy to guide joint investigations. This improved co-ordination has resulted in more support for children in the prosecution of cases in the criminal justice system. Even now, however, criminal prosecutions for physical abuse are relatively rare, except in cases involving serious physical injury or death, and overall only a relatively small portion of abuse and neglect cases that child protection agencies are involved with result in criminal prosecutions.

It is generally easier to prove abuse or neglect in a civil child protection proceeding than in a criminal proceeding, even if exactly the same conduct is at issue in both cases. The rules about what types of evidence a court may consider are less restrictive in a civil trial, and the standard of proof is lower, requiring only proof "on the balance of probabilities." While the *Charter of Rights* is applicable to child protection proceedings, the type of rights granted to those alleged to have abused or neglected their children in these civil proceedings is much narrower than the rights afforded to those accused of the same acts in the criminal justice process.

Allegations of parental abuse and neglect are most commonly dealt with as a child protection issue rather than as one requiring criminal prosecution. The child protection case is a civil proceeding in which the state-mandated child protection agency seeks to intervene in the family, either by making the child the subject of court-ordered supervision, or by having the child removed from parental care, on either a temporary or permanent basis.

Sometimes abuse or neglect issues are raised in a civil case involving separated parents who are in a dispute over custody or access to their children. With growing awareness of the problem of child abuse, the number of cases involving this type of allegation has increased.

It is also possible for a child who has been the victim of abuse, or a guardian acting on behalf of the child, to bring a civil suit for monetary damages. However, abusers frequently lack the financial resources to satisfy a judgement and such suits have been rare. Further, children are often reluctant to sue their parents, even after they reach adulthood. However, victims may feel a sense of psychological vindication from recovering an award, and such civil suits are becoming more common. It is also becoming more common for victims of abuse to seek monetary awards from their provincial Criminal Injuries Compensation Board. It is not necessary for there actually to be a criminal conviction for compensation to be granted, though there must be proof that abuse occurred. In theory, the Board may seek reimbursement from an abuser for compensation paid, but in practice the Boards do not pursue abusers if they are without assets or reasonable income. ...

The Role of the Child Welfare Agency

In every Canadian jurisdiction there is an agency that has the legal responsibility for investigating reports that a child may be in need of protection and taking appropriate steps to protect children from ill-treatment. The agency may provide services to the child and parents in their home, or may remove the child from the home on a temporary or permanent wardship basis. The child welfare agency may provide services on either a voluntary or an involuntary basis, making use of the legal system to require children and parents to receive services. Child welfare agencies also are responsible for arranging some adoptions, though in most jurisdictions private adoption agencies or licensees are involved in this type of work as well. In some localities child welfare agencies assume other responsibilities related to their principal mandates, such as organizing programs for the prevention of child abuse.

Child welfare agencies are given very significant powers under legislation to search for children who may be in need of protection and, if necessary, to force parents to surrender custody. These agencies receive all or most of their funding from the state. From a conceptual perspective, child welfare agencies are agents of the state, in some cases exercising the coercive power of the state.

In most Canadian jurisdictions, child welfare services are provided by provincial employees serving out of local offices, typically of the Ministry of Social Services. In Manitoba, Nova Scotia and Ontario there are local child welfare agencies, called Children's Aid Societies or Child and Family Service Agencies. These non-profit agencies serve a particular geographical area. In Ontario, a few Children's Aid Societies are denominational, serving only Catholic or Jewish families and children in a particular region. Recently in some provinces child welfare agencies have been established to serve native children exclusively. Even in provinces with these local semi-autonomous child welfare agencies, ultimate statutory and financial responsibility for the agencies rests with the provincial government, and their employees should be viewed in many respects as agents of the state.

While the structure of each child welfare agency or local office is unique, the agencies share certain common features. Agencies have two basic functions: child protection (or family services) and child care. In some agencies workers have both child protection and child care responsibilities. In other agencies, however, workers have a more specialized role.

Child protection workers are responsible for investigating suspected cases of abuse or neglect, and working with children and parents in their homes. Some agencies have intake departments, with a special mandate to deal with initial investigations and crisis situations; in such agencies, if ongoing service is required, the cases are usually transferred to a family service worker after the initial investigation is completed by the intake worker.

Child care workers have responsibility for children who have been taken into care on either a temporary or permanent basis. Typically, children are actually cared for in foster or group homes, and child care workers have a liaison function with foster parents and group home staff. In some agencies, adoption work is done as part of child care while in others it is the responsibility of a separate department.

In some agencies there are specialized workers who are responsible for dealing with specific types of cases such as adolescents living on the streets or child sexual abuse; in others, workers have a more generalized protection caseload. In some localities, particularly in smaller agencies, staff members are responsible for both child protection and child care work. ...

Child welfare agencies are involved with the court system and must have access to adequate legal services. In some localities, especially larger centres, there are staff lawyers who work exclusively in representing agencies in child protection cases. In some locales, Department of Justice lawyers represent agencies. In other places, child welfare agencies hire lawyers in private practice to provide representation in individual cases, typically establishing a relationship with a specific law firm. Use may also be made of court workers; these are employees of child welfare agencies who are not lawyers, but who are familiar with the court system. These workers handle certain cases in court, typically those which are less contentious, leaving the more complex cases to lawyers who are on staff or retained from private practice.

Child welfare agencies provide services in conjunction with other agencies and professionals in private practice. For example, initial reports of suspected abuse or neglect may come from doctors in hospital emergency departments, public health nurses or teachers. When determining how a case should be handled, a child welfare agency, may refer a case to a psychologist, psychiatrist or mental health clinic for an assessment, sometimes as part of the court process. If a child is taken into the care of an agency, it may be necessary for agency staff to work with therapists or educators. While some agencies have facilities where their own employees care for children, it is common for agencies to have foster parents or group home operators who are not agency employees provide care for children.

If there is a criminal prosecution, child protection workers will have to maintain contact with the police and Crown prosecutor's office. To be effective, child welfare agencies must have good working relationships with others in the community.

Working for a child welfare agency can be a difficult, stressful job. There tends to be high staff turnover in these agencies. While most workers in this field are quite well educated, having a college diploma or university degree, often in social work, they are relatively young and inexperienced. Young social workers not infrequently start their careers in child welfare agencies and, after gaining experience, move to less stressful work elsewhere in the helping professions.

The stress in the child protection field relates to both the nature of the cases and the nature of the work. There is an inevitable degree of tension, as the role of child protection workers has both supportive and investigative functions. Child protection workers usually try to be supportive to parents and to provide services on an informal, voluntary basis. Indeed, most families that a worker comes into contact with do not end up in court, and in these cases the role of the protection worker can be regarded as similar to that of a therapist or counsellor, or of an educator in parenting skills. However, the role of a child protection worker can also in some ways be viewed as similar to that of a police officer. Protection workers have legal responsibility for investigating allegations of abuse or neglect. Even if their involvement with a family is at one time voluntary, in the event of later difficulties, anything a parent or child has told a worker may be relevant and admissible in a subsequent protection hearing.

Through education and disposition, most child protection workers want to have a therapeutic role, helping children and parents. Large caseloads mitigate against such a role, reducing the time the social worker has for each case. Understandably, however, workers may be viewed with hostility and distrust by parents, who may focus on the investigative role of child protection work. This often makes the job frustrating and contributes to the high turnover rate.

Some would argue that legal constraints make child protection work even more demanding. The law sometimes can make it difficult for child protection staff to take effective measures to protect a child. It is not enough for a worker to feel or believe that a child is at risk and should be removed from parental care. Involuntary removal of a child from parental care can only occur if legal requirements are satisfied and the need for this is documented in court. However, if a child is inappropriately left in parental care and suffers further abuse, the worker will inevitably feel a sense of guilt and moral responsibility.

Further, there is the threat of personal legal liability for taking inappropriate actions. While the likelihood of a social worker facing personal legal responsibility for being either too aggressive in removing a child, or insufficiently protective and leaving a child with a family that subsequently injures the child is low, even the threat of personal liability can make workers apprehensive. ...

The Law and the Child Protection Process

Child welfare agencies are charged with the legal and moral obligation of protecting children from abuse and neglect, and thereby promoting their welfare. Provincial legislation gives these agencies the legal authority to intervene in the lives of parents and children in order to provide protection. While the legislation varies from one jurisdiction to another, and different judges have conflicting views about how to interpret and apply the legislation, the law clearly presumes that parents are capable of raising their children without state interference. The law places a burden on child welfare agencies to clearly establish the need for intervention.

The nature of this burden was discussed by Judge Stortini in *Re Brown* [(1975), 9 O.R. 185 at 189 (Co. Ct.).]:

> In attempting to establish what is best for the children, I must accept the realities and accidents of life and refrain from judging the needs of the children and the parents' ability to satisfy them on an unfair or unrealistic basis. ...
>
> In other words, the community ought not to interfere merely because our institutions may be able to offer a greater opportunity to the children to achieve their potential. Society's interference in the natural family is only justified when the level of care of the children falls below that which no child in this country should be subjected to.

An onus is placed on the agency to establish its case based on the recognition that in some cases, the child protection workers involved will be mistaken in concluding that a child has been a victim of parental abuse or neglect and would benefit from removal from parental care. At least part of the rationale for placing an onus on child welfare agencies to justify their intervention is based on fundamental values of our society. Parents are viewed as having the moral right to raise their children in the manner they see fit; state-imposed restrictions on individual freedom, including the right to bear and raise children, require justification by the state. In *Re Chrysler* (1978), 5 R.F.L. (2d) 50 at 58 (Ont. Prov. Ct.), Judge Karswick frankly recognized the potential risk of placing the burden on the Children's Aid Society (C.A.S.) to prove its case:

> It seems to me that ... the potential for real and immediate abuse must be clear before the state should be permitted to intervene by removing the child from her parents. If it were otherwise, it would allow a C.A.S. to be the final arbitrator in a so-called child abuse case and would leave the parents and the child with no real recourse to a really independent and impartial court. In adopting this principle, I realize that there is always the danger that some real and even irreparable harm may be inflicted upon the child if the parents are really potential child abusers, but the C.A.S. has not been able to prove that fact because of the unavailability of witnesses who can testify to the alleged abuse and therefore has not been able to meet the standard of proof required by the court.
>
> I think that this risk must still give way to the greater risk of the irreparable harm that can be inflicted upon a child and the danger to society of the serious undermining of the parents and the family if a C.A.S. is permitted to act in an arbitrary way, even though its intentions are motivated by the highest ideals and concerns.

While placing an onus on child welfare agencies to prove their case creates the risk that in some cases the courts may fail to take appropriate steps to protect children, inappropriate intervention also creates risks for children. Removal of children from their homes by child welfare agencies inevitably involves some risks for the child. At least in the short term, removal of children from their homes is always disruptive and often emotionally traumatic for children, even if the parents are neglectful or abusive. Assessing what will be best for a child is often very difficult: it may be impossible to make an accurate prediction about a child's long-term psychological development in different settings simply by observing child-rearing practices in the home. Determining what will best promote a child's welfare is often an inherently speculative exercise.

Children who are placed in agency care often experience emotionally damaging moves from one placement to another. Placements that are intended to be temporary and short-term often turn out to be long-term, sometimes extending over several years. Parental contact during foster care placements frequently is limited or even non-existent. It has also been found that the longer children remain in care and the less contact they have with their parents, the more likely that they will never return home.

Child Welfare Legislation in Canada

Every Canadian jurisdiction has child welfare legislation in place to regulate the child protection process. While there are variations in philosophy and approach, all of the legislative regimes deal with the same fundamental issues, and have similar basic features.

Declaration of Principle and the "Best Interests of the Child"

Almost all child welfare statutes in Canada have a statement of principles that, is intended to guide the courts and child welfare agencies in the implementation of the law, and a definition of "best interests" that requires consideration of a number of listed factors when making a decision about a child. ...

The central themes that appear in these declarations of principles and definitions of the best interests of the child are:

- *Respect for family autonomy and support of families*: Most of these statements recognize the importance of respecting the family and the parents' primary responsibility in child rearing. For example, Ontario's *Child and Family Services Act* states that "... while parents often need help in caring for their children, that help should give support to the autonomy and integrity of the family. ..." [*Child and Family Services Act*, R.S.O. 1990, c. C.11, s. 1(2)] Manitoba's *Act* states that: "The family is the basic source of care, nurture and acculturation of children and parents have the primary responsibility to ensure the well- being of their children". [*The Child and Family Services Act*, R.S.M. 1987, c. C80, Declaration of Principles]

- *Continuity of care*: Most of these statements explicitly recognize the importance of continuity and stability for the child. For example, Manitoba's *The Child and Family Services Act* states that: "Children have a right to a continuous family environment in which they can flourish" [Declaration of Principles]. Quebec's *Youth Protection Act* provides: "Every decision made under this Act must contemplate the child's remaining with his family. If in the interest of the child, his remaining with [his family] ... is impossible, the decision must contemplate his being provided with continuous care and stable conditions of life ... as nearly similar to those of a normal family environment as possible."

These principles emphasize the importance of permanence for children, a preference for children continuing to remain with their own family and, if removal is necessary, the need for a stable foster or adoptive family.

- *Consideration of views of children*: All child welfare statutes in Canada specify that decision makers are to take into consideration the views and wishes of children when making decisions, but it is clear that the preferences of children are not determinative of how child protection cases are to be resolved.

- *Respect for cultural heritage, especially for Aboriginal children*: All of the statutes have statements that recognize the desirability of respecting a child's cultural and religiousheritage, and most have a statement that gives particular emphasis on the unique significance in Canada of Aboriginal cultural heritage.

- *The paramountcy of the protection of children from harm*: In some provinces, like Ontario and British Columbia, where there was a concern that too much of an emphasis may have been given to preservation of families or parental rights and as a result children were left in abusive or neglectful home situations where they were died, statements of principle were added to the legislation in the late 1990s that the protection of children from abuse, neglect, and harm is to be "a paramount objective". [See s. 1(1) of the *Child and Family Services Act*, R.S.O. 1990, c. C.11.]

These statements of principles and definitions may be of some assistance to judges and social workers in making decisions under the legislation, especially when these decision makers are applying the legislation to a particular case and the relevant, specific section does not provide sufficient guidance. Most of these declarations and definitions, however, do not clearly prioritize how different considerations are weighed in individual cases, and hence tend to confer significant discretion on individual decision makers. In practice, child protection workers are more likely to be influenced by professional ethics and government and agency policies, while courts receive more direction from specific provisions of the legislation and from leading judicial precedents than from generalized statements of principles. Tension can develop between agency and legislative policies. ...

The "Child in Need of Protection"

Each child welfare statute has a definition of a "child in need of protection" (or an "endangered child"). This is a key legal concept, as only children within this definition are subject to involuntary state intervention under the legislation. While there is some variation in how the concept of the "child in need of protection" is defined, there is a common core of situations of physical and sexual abuse, parental neglect (including failure to provide needed medical treatment) and abandonment that are within the definition in every jurisdiction. Further, in all jurisdictions, a child may be brought into agency care with the consent of the parents. In all jurisdictions there is also provision for finding a child in need of protection in cases of emotional maltreatment or if the child is an adolescent whose parents are having serious difficulties in caring for the child, though there are variations in the statutory definitions for these types of situations. For example, in some jurisdictions like New Brunswick, the fact that a child resides in a home where spousal abuse has occurred is in itself a basis for finding a child in need of protection; in other provinces, such as Ontario, spousal abuse is not a specific ground for establishing that a child is in need of protection, but this could be a contributing factor in determining that a child is at risk of suffering "emotional harm" or physical injury.

The last national survey of child welfare agency files reported that there were an estimated 21.5 child protection investigations per 1,000 children in Canada. About 45% of these investigations were regarded as "substantiated" by the child protection workers involved, 33% were considered unsubstantiated after investigation, and 22% remained suspected but not substantiated within three months of opening the file. These child maltreatment investigations were classified into four categories: physical abuse was the primary subject of 31% of all investigations; sexual abuse was the primary issue in 10% of investigations; neglect was the primary concern in 40% of investigations, and emotional maltreatment was the primary concern in 19% of investigations.

One significant variation between provinces is in the age of children who may be found to be in need of protection. In most Canadian jurisdictions, the maximum age for an initial finding that a child is in need of protection is a child's eighteenth birthday, while in British Columbia and New Brunswick it is the nineteenth birthday, and in Saskatchewan, Ontario, Nova Scotia and Newfoundland it is the sixteenth birthday. There are provisions in all jurisdictions for providing financial and other support for children taken into care at a younger age until they reach the age of 20 or 21. But even in jurisdictions like British Columbia that have a high maximum age for an initial finding that a child is need of protection, there are significant practical problems in providing involuntary care or assistance for older adolescents and young adults, who may be resistant to agency involvement in their lives. ...

Voluntary Involvement

While the main focus of legislation is on involuntary intervention in the lives of children and parents, in most cases a child protection agency is involved with a family with the consent of the parents, and in some cases at the request of the parents. In some cases, the parents may only be "consenting" to agency involvement because the agency is threatening to commence child protection proceedings and the parents may regard "voluntary involvement" as preferable to the involuntary agency involvement that would be the likely result of any court action. In some cases, the parents may lack the financial or emotional resources to litigate, and feel that they have no choice but to "consent" to agency involvement in their lives. In other cases, however, the parents may genuinely appreciate the help and support that the agency and its staff can provide, and they will be truly agreeing to have agency involvement.

In several provinces, including Ontario, there are legislative provisions that govern cases where a parent voluntarily agrees to place a child in care for a temporary period. In all jurisdictions there are statutory provisions that allow for a child to be permanently taken into care with the consent of the parents, as might occur, for example, if a single unmarried mother wants a child welfare agency to take the child and have the child placed for adoption.

Reporting, Apprehension, and Interim Care

Child welfare legislation governs the reporting of child abuse, and every Canadian jurisdiction except the Yukon imposes an obligation on individuals who become aware of possible situations of abuse or neglect to report to their local child welfare agency or the police so that an investigation can be carried out. If a child protection worker has reasonable grounds to believe that a child may be at risk, legislation in all Canadian jurisdictions allows the worker to "apprehend" the child, that is, to immediately take the child into the care of the agency. There must be a court hearing within days to decide whether the child will remain in agency care pending a full hearing. ...

The Child Protection Hearing

When a child protection proceeding has been commenced, either by the apprehension of a child by the agency or by the agency's filing of court documents, it will usually take several weeks or more typically months before a trial can be held. During this period arrangements will be made for the parents, and in some provinces the children, to have access to a lawyer. Many parents who are involved in the child protection process will be unable to afford a lawyer, but will be eligible for legal aid. In preparation for a trial, counsel for parents will have the opportunity to have "disclosure" of documents and records that the agency has acquired during the course of its investigation. The lawyers and agency staff may also be contacting third parties, like a family doctor or relatives, to prepare for the trial, and often to develop a possible "plan of care" that may be put before the court. Outside experts may also be retained to assess the child or the "parenting capacity" of the parents of the child, and ultimately to provide testimony in court.

A child protection trial is held in private, though legislation generally allows for the publication of non-identifying information about child protection proceedings in the relatively rare cases that attract media attention. The judges who decide child protection cases generally have a special expertise in family and children's law. These cases never involve a jury.

At a child protection hearing, the court may determine that a child is not in need of protection, and dismiss the agency application. Most commonly, however, when the agency begins a child protection application, there is some legitimate cause for agency concern, and the court will find that the child is in need of protection. If a child is found to be in need of protection, the court will make a decision that accords with the "best interests" of the child. There are three basic types of orders that can be made: supervision, temporary wardship, or permanent wardship. In some provinces, like Ontario, there may be a formal "bifurcation" or division of the child protection hearing into two stages, the first dealing with the issue of whether the child is in need of protection, and the second stage dealing with the type of order to be made, with somewhat different rules of evidence and procedure at each stage. In most provinces there is usually a single hearing to deal with both issues.

Under a supervision order the child remains at home under parental care, but the agency staff will conduct supervisory visits at the child's home, and the parents may be subject to other conditions, such as a requirement that they attend a parenting effectiveness course. Temporary wards are placed in the care of the protection agency, usually in a foster or group home. Reunification with parents is generally contemplated when a child is made a temporary ward, and parents typically have the right to visit children who are temporary wards. Children made permanent (or Crown) wards are generally expected to be wards of the protection agency until they reach adulthood. Parental access to a child who is a permanent ward may be terminated, especially if the child is young, and the child may be placed for adoption by the agency. If the child is older when made a permanent ward, it is likely that the child will remain in a foster home or group home, and the parents are more likely to be given a continuing right to see their child, though in practice it can be difficult to keep parents involved in the lives of children who are made permanent wards.

Child protection legislation in each jurisdiction provides for court review of prior orders, and may result in the termination, extension or alteration of a prior order. If a permanent ward is placed for adoption, the parents generally lose the right to seek a review.

It is increasingly common when children are made agency wards for the parents to be expected to contribute to the cost of their support, though a significant portion of parents involved in these cases are without the means to make any contribution. ...

Evidentiary Issues in Child Protection Cases

While the strict laws of evidence that govern criminal cases do not apply in child protection cases, there are rules of evidence that may result in the exclusion of certain types of evidence in child protection cases or may restrict what witnesses can say when testifying. There are, for example, rules about the necessary level of "expertise" that a witness must be able to demonstrate before being permitted to give "expert" or "opinion" testimony in a child protection case. In each province and territory there are also special legislative provisions that deal with some of the evidentiary issues that arise in child protection cases. ...

The Child in Care

If a child is made a temporary or permanent ward of a child welfare agency, the agency will have legal guardianship of the child, and subject to any order of the court concerning the child's access to parents or siblings, may determine where the child will reside. Children in state care were historically a very vulnerable population, and were not infrequently subject to exploitation or abuse in foster homes or child welfare institutions. Legislation and programs are now in place in many Canadian jurisdictions to protect the rights of children in agencies and to give them access to advocates.

An important set of issues relate to the situations in which the agency is obliged to plan for and support efforts of the child to be returned to his or her family. There are also cases in which a court will require that a child is to have contact with siblings who may also be in care. ...

Adoption

In some jurisdictions, such as Ontario, adoption is governed by the same statute as child protection proceedings, as part of a comprehensive child welfare scheme. In other jurisdictions, such as Saskatchewan, adoption is dealt with in a separate statute — though even in these jurisdictions, child welfare agencies are involved in some, though not all, adoptions. ...

The Role of the Trial Judge

While trial judges dealing with child protection cases are governed by a statute and bound by appeal court decisions, they also have considerable discretion. Judges have a range of views and attitudes about the child protection process. Some judges tend to emphasize the adversarial nature of the process, and may place relatively high expectations on the state agency that is challenging the integrity of the family unit to justify its position. Other judges may tend to focus a little more on the protection of children, and may interpret the statute and procedural rules somewhat more flexibly. The attitude of the presiding judge can have a significant impact on the manner in which child protection legislation is interpreted and applied. ...

Who Speaks for the Child?

A fundamental question in the child welfare field is: "Who speaks for the child?" It is a question that defies an easy answer. Some would argue that the child welfare agency, with its statutory mandate to protect children, is speaking on behalf of the child. Others would point out that child welfare agencies often have financial, institutional and professional constraints that prevent them from truly advocating what is best for the child. There may also be disagreements between the agency and foster parents or within the agency about how a particular case should be handled. While the agency will have an administrative mechanism for establishing how such disagreements will be resolved, there may still be controversy over what is truly best for the child.

In British Columbia, Alberta, Saskatchewan, Manitoba, Ontario, Quebec and Newfoundland the government has established offices of child advocacy, separate from child welfare agencies, with responsibility to act as advocates for children involved in the protection process or in the legal care of a protection agency. These offices are not intended to provide legal representation for children in court, but rather to act as advocates for them within the context of the child protection system. The establishment of these offices reflects a concern that the bureaucratic nature of child welfare agencies may result in situations where the agencies are not acting in the best interests of children.

Since it is difficult to understand a child separate from his or her community, there can also be situations where the community or its representatives purport to speak for the child; this most commonly occurs with Aboriginal children.

Parents involved in protection cases typically believe that they know and care for their children more than any of the professionals. Parents may thus claim that they speak for their children.

The children who are the subject of a protection case may also have their own views about what they want to have happen. Some children are too young to express their views, and older children are sometimes reluctant or ambivalent about expressing their views. However, many children involved in the protection process have definite ideas about their futures. In most jurisdictions, legislation specifies that courts should consider the "child's views and wishes, if they can be reasonably ascertained." In some jurisdictions, children involved in child protection proceedings can have lawyers who represent them and claim to speak on their behalf. In some cases a psychologist or other mental health professional will interview or assess the child and report the child's views to the court, and in other situations the child may come to court and testify.

In some sense, the judges who decide child protection cases also have a role in acting on behalf of children. Although judges have a responsibility for balancing the rights of the litigants and acting in accordance with the legislation, judges may be regarded as having ultimate responsibility for the protection of children and the promotion of their welfare. ...

Child Welfare in a Social Context

Child abuse and neglect are endemic to all parts of our society, and are not restricted to a particular region, economic or cultural group or race. One of the most infamous cases of physical abuse in North America in the last years of the twentieth century involved a prominent, wealthy New York City lawyer, who was convicted of murdering his foster daughter. The Canadian public has learned that even trusted and respected community members like doctors, teachers and priests can be guilty of sexual abuse.

Despite the widespread nature of child abuse and neglect, child welfare agencies are more likely to be involved with families from disadvantaged, economic, social and cultural groups. While child protection workers are typically white, well-educated and from middle-class backgrounds, their clients are generally socially marginalized. The clients of child welfare agencies are often poorly educated, living in or near poverty, and not infrequently members of a racial minority group and living in a family led by a single parent, usually the mother. Many of the clients of child welfare agencies are living on social assistance.

The National Council of Welfare observed that the clients of the child welfare system are "overwhelmingly drawn from the ranks of Canada's poor." In some cases, the personal or emotional problems that result in a life of poverty also may make it difficult to parent adequately. The Council also explained:

> There are two major reasons why poor families are more likely than those with higher incomes to use children's social services. First, low-income parents run a greater risk of encountering problems that reduce their capacity to provide adequate care for their children. Second, poor families are largely dependent upon a single, overburdened source of help — the child welfare system — in coping with their problems, whereas more affluent families enjoy access to a broader and superior range of supportive resources.

The Council further observed:

> ... [T]he state can only intervene when it judges parents unable or unwilling to care properly for their children. What is often forgotten, however, is that the term "unable or unwilling to provide care" is nothing more than a convenient administrative label lumping together a wide variety of family problems, many of which stem from inadequate income, unemployment and other factors that cannot fairly be blamed on their victims.

Most judges dealing with child protection cases are aware of the need to be sensitive to the realities of poverty in Canada. In *Re Warren* (1973), 13 R.F.L. 51 at 52 (Ont. Co. Ct.), the judge wrote:

> In a hearing such as this there is danger in over-reliance upon any group of witnesses self-conscious respecting their professionalization. I resolved not to fall victim to this specific bias of the profession, the group psychology of the social workers. ...
>
> It was manifest from the opening that this was a contest between the right of a subsocio-economic family to subsist together and the right of the public, represented by the Children's Aid Society, to insist upon higher standards of parental care than the couple in question were capable of offering. Many witnesses called for the Society were persons of superior education with post-graduate degrees in social work or some other related specialty. One could not listen to their testimony with all the somber implications of this application without resolving that this Court must not be persuaded to impose unrealistic or unfair middle-class standards of child care upon a poor family of extremely limited potential.

Those who work in the child welfare system must be sensitive to problems of poverty. They must also be sensitive to cultural and racial differences between themselves and their clients.

A number of racial minorities and immigrant groups are over-represented in Canada's child welfare system, but probably the most pervasive problems are with Aboriginal children. Aboriginal children are apprehended and taken into care at more than three times the rate of other Canadian children. In some western provinces, more than half the children in care are Aboriginal. Compounding conditions of poverty, chronic underemployment, inadequate housing and poor nutrition, are a history of racial discrimination and insensitivity to different child-rearing values. For many of those Aboriginal people who come to live in cities, culture shock adds another source of stress and instability.

NOTES AND QUESTIONS

1. Part I of Ontario's *Child and Family Services Act* (the *CFSA*) governs the operations of the Children's Aid Societies in Ontario. While they continue to have considerable administrative autonomy, the agencies have become increasingly subject to controls by the government. Note the revocation and takeover powers in ss. 22–24; the system of review procedures set out in ss. 66 and 68; the possibility of review by a Residential Placement Advisory Committee under ss. 34–36; and the powers of the Director set out in ss. 20.1 and 77. The *CFSA* also includes provisions that permit the Minister to provide services directly or purchase them for children and their families, allowing a more direct provincial government role in child care: ss. 7–10 and 30(2).

2. There were significant amendments to the *CFSA* in 2006 that will be noted from time to time in this chapter. One of these (s. 20.2) created the requirement that a Children's Aid Society consider whether "a prescribed method of alternative dispute resolution could assist in resolving any issue relating to the child or a plan for the child's care". Similarly, s. 51.1 now authorizes a court, with the consent of the parties, to adjourn a proceeding "to permit the parties to attempt through a prescribed method of alternative dispute resolution to resolve any dispute between them with respect to any matter that is relevant to the proceeding". In a similar vein, s. 145.2(7) provides for the possibility of alternative dispute resolution where an application has been made to a court for a variation or a termination of an "openness order" in relation to a Crown ward. These orders will be explained later.

The relevant regulation, *Methods and Procedures Regarding Alternative Dispute Resolution*, O. Reg. 496/06, indicates that the prescribed method of alternative dispute resolution is mediation and not arbitration. It also sets out requirements of confidentiality during the process.

On the use of mediation in the child protection context, see Crush, "The State of Child Protection Mediation in Canada" (2005), 24 C.F.L.Q. 191.

3. For further analysis of child welfare laws in Canada, see Bernstein *et al.*, *Child Protection Law in Canada* (Toronto: Carswell) (looseleaf) and Human Resources Development Canada, *Child Welfare in Canada — 2000* (Ottawa: 2002).

4. For an analysis of the application of criminal law to child abuse and neglect, see Hallett and Bala, "Criminal Prosecutions for Abuse and Neglect", in Bala, Zapf, Williams, Vogl, and Hornick, ed. *Canadian Child Welfare Law: Children, Families and the State*, 2d ed. (Toronto: Thompson Educational Publishing, Inc., 2004).

5. Survivors of childhood abuse sometimes initiate civil suits for monetary damages. Section 81 of the *CFSA* authorizes the Children's Lawyer to begin an action on behalf of the child where he or she has suffered abuse. In *Queen (Litigation Guardian of) v. Hodgins* (1991), 36 R.F.L. (3d) 159 (Ont. Gen. Div.), a 9-year-old child (through her guardian) and her parents received a $25,000 judgment against a family friend who had sexually abused the child.

More commonly, the cases involve adults bringing actions for abuse suffered during childhood, often at the hands of family members. For a case where damages were awarded to adult children because of parental abuse, see *Cho v. Cho* (2003), 36 R.F.L. (5th) 79 (Ont. S.C.J.). Regarding limitation periods on such claims in Ontario, see the *Limitations Act, 2002*, S.O. 2002, c. 24, Sch. B, ss. 4–7 and s. 16(1)(h).

The Supreme Court of Canada dealt with a damage claim by former foster children against the Crown in *B. (K.L.) v. British Columbia* (2003), 44 R.F.L. (5th) 245. It concluded that the Crown would have been directly liable for the negligence of governmental social workers in selecting the foster parents and failing to adequately monitor their care but for the fact that the statutory limitation period had passed. It also found that the Crown was not liable vicariously for the intentional torts that the foster parents committed because the parents were independent of government in their day-to-day actions.

6. In *J. (L.A.) v. J. (H.)* (1993), 13 O.R. (3d) 306 (Gen. Div.), a mother was held liable in tort and for breach of a fiduciary duty for failing to take reasonable steps to protect her daughter from sexual abuse by her common law husband. Justice Rutherford stated (at 315): "In the circumstances of this case, recognizing that the defendant mother was of limited means and education, it was still well within her ability ... to take her daughter away from the abusive situation which she was well aware of or report the situation to the authorities with the probable result of the abuser being removed from the situation." He also found that the mother had turned a blind eye and once had deflected an inquiry by the Children's Aid Society. For a critical commentary on this case, see Grace and Vella, "Vesting Mothers with Power They Do Not Have: The Non-Offending Parent in Civil Sexual Assault Cases" (1994), 7 Can. J. Women & L. 184.

In *T. (L.) v. T. (R.W.)* (1997), 36 C.C.L.T. (2d) 207 (B.C. S.C.), an adult woman recovered damages from her father for sexual assault during her childhood. However, the court dismissed the woman's claim against her mother. The judge observed that the mother had "limited education and imagination" and concluded (at 222):

> ... [I]t is not at all clear that [the mother] had the ability, awareness or means to take effective action in the circumstances. She did not act out of a wish to preserve the relationship with the plaintiff's father. She certainly did not encourage or enable the abuse. She simply could not come to grips with the situation which was, in fact, a confusing one for her. ... In the result, I cannot find that [the mother] was in breach of her duty to protect her daughter from her father's abuse.

See also *M. (M.) v. F. (R.)* (1997), 52 B.C.L.R. (3d) 127 (C.A.); additional reasons at (1998), 48 B.C.L.R. (3d) 360 (C.A.), where the court dismissed a claim against a woman involving abuse perpetrated by her son on the plaintiff, her former foster daughter. The court took account of the woman's lack of sophistication about sex in concluding that she was not negligent in failing to spot the abuse. The court considered that "there is good reason to be cautious [in imposing liability] because there is a grave potential for injustice to bystander parents if the court commits itself to broad ... definitions of the duty resting on such parents." Compare *D. (C.) v. Newfoundland (Minister of Social Services)* (1996), 137 Nfld. & P.E.I.R. 206 (Nfld. T.D.), where foster parents were held liable, along with the Director of Child Welfare, for their negligence when the mother's brother sexually assaulted a child in their care.

Can a child be in need of protection from the non-offending parent who ignores recurring incidents of abuse by the other parent? See *Re H. (A.)* (1994), 6 R.F.L. (4th) 33 (B.C. Prov. Ct.). For a comment on a similar American case, see "Comment: Revictimized Battered Women: Termination of Parental Rights for Failure to Protect Children from Child Abuse" (1992), 38 Wayne State Law Rev. 1549. See also *Re G. (T.L.M.)* (1996), 26 R.F.L. (4th) 192 (Alta. Prov. Ct.), where the mother was unable to protect her daughter from the sexual assaults of the girl's brother. For further reading, see B. Carter, *Who's to Blame: Child Sexual Abuse and Non-offending Mothers* (Toronto: University of Toronto Press, 1999).

(2) Aboriginal Children and the Child Welfare System

SINCLAIR, BALA, LILLES AND BLACKSTOCK, "ABORIGINAL CHILD WELFARE"

Bala, Zapf, Williams, Vogl, and Hornick, eds., *Canadian Child Welfare Law: Children, Families and the State*, 2d ed. (Toronto: Thompson Educational Publishing, Inc., 2004) (Footnotes omitted) (Reprinted with the permission of the authors and the publisher.)

For well over one hundred years, the policies of Canadian governments towards Aboriginal children were a major factor in the deterioration of Aboriginal cultures in Canada, and often resulted in the suffering and abuse of Aboriginal children. Aboriginal people have a justified concern about the deterioration of their families, communities, values and customs as a result of the policies that were adopted by Canadian governments, first in the residential schools and later in the child welfare system. Recently there has been significant recognition of the harm caused by previous policies and practices. Laws and policies have been introduced that are more sensitive to the needs of Aboriginal children, families and communities, and Aboriginal child welfare agencies have been established in many places in Canada. Past government policies, however, continue to have intergenerational effects, and many Aboriginal parents and communities now face great challenges in caring adequately for their children.

An obvious and important indicator of the deterioration in Aboriginal cultures and communities is that Aboriginal children are taken into the child welfare system in disproportionately large numbers — at least five times greater than the rate of non-Aboriginal children. In some jurisdictions and in all of the territories, the majority of child apprehensions involve Aboriginal children. The problem for Aboriginal communities is magnified by the fact that children make up over half of the current Aboriginal population and that the Aboriginal population continues to increase at a much faster rate than the non-Aboriginal population of Canada.

Aboriginal children who become involved with the child welfare system at an early age often spend time in multiple foster placements, and later in young offender institutions, and then in the adult correctional system. Although this "life path" is often followed by non-Aboriginal children, the adverse consequences of child welfare involvement are exacerbated when children are moved from their community and culture to a distant location as a result of child welfare involvement, as often happens with Aboriginal children. Aboriginal groups have expressed deep concerns that the pattern of apprehensions inhibits the development of these children as future contributing members of Aboriginal communities; it also has negative implications for Canadian society in general. One Aboriginal group asks: "Is the system conditioning our young for lives in institutions and not in society?" ...

In recent years, provincial child welfare legislation has given greater recognition to the special needs and status of Aboriginal children. In some places, child welfare agencies have been established that are controlled by Aboriginal peoples, albeit generally operating within the framework of provincial child welfare statutes. In other places, Aboriginal voluntary agencies are working with provincially mandated child welfare agencies to provide services to Aboriginal children and families. Although many Aboriginal communities have made significant strides in gaining more control over the future of their children and communities, they have yet to obtain full control free from federal and provincial government involvement. Further, there remain many Aboriginal children who receive child welfare services that are provided without any direct involvement of Aboriginal agencies.

There is no doubt that the history of racist and insensitive government policies towards Aboriginal children and families has played an important role in contributing to the overrepresentation of Aboriginal children in Canada's child welfare system. But it must also be recognized that many Aboriginal communities now suffer from a range of social and economic problems that are linked to high rates of child neglect and abuse, such as high rates of family violence, poverty, alcoholism and drug use. While increasing the degree of control and involvement of Aboriginal communities in the provision of child welfare services is having positive effects, the transfer of responsibility is a complex and contentious process, and will not be a panacea for the problems of Aboriginal child welfare. ...

Historical Background

Assimilation

Since the earliest contact between Canada's Aboriginal people and European colonists, there have been conflicting values about many fundamental issues, including family relationships and child-rearing. Initially, however, there was little social interaction between the colonists and Aboriginal peoples, and these differences in values and behaviours had little impact on the lives of Aboriginal peoples. However, as the number of settlers increased and the colonists began to exert their military and political power over Aboriginal peoples, the European colonists began to attempt to impose their values, beliefs, and practices on the original inhabitants of North America.

When European powers began to colonize North America, they formed trade and military alliances with Aboriginal peoples, and religious proselytizing of the "savages" began. The religious missionaries were the first to attempt to fundamentally change Canada's Aboriginal population, seeking to convert them to Christianity. ...

The commitment to assimilation was reflected in the policies initiated in the nineteenth century by Canadian governments to "educate" Aboriginal children in the ways of the "white man." Many of the treaty negotiations that occurred after Confederation contain references by the government treaty commissioners to promote this objective. The residential school system ..., established in the late nineteenth century, was premised on the belief of governments and the dominant Canadian society that assimilation through education of young Aboriginal children was necessary and was to be achieved by removing the children from the influence of their parents and their communities.

In many parts of Canada, especially in the North and West, Aboriginal children were required pursuant to the *Indian Act* to attend these residential schools, often located far from their homes, removing them from the influences of their traditional culture and way of life, as well as from the emotional and social support of their parents and communities. The federal government funded these schools, but almost all of the schools were operated by religious groups affiliated with various Christian churches. In residential schools the children were forbidden to speak their own languages or practice any of their customs which were considered to be "uncivilized." ...

Many Aboriginal parents appeared to co-operate with the placing of their children in residential schools, believing that it was beneficial to have their children educated in non-Aboriginal schools. Indeed, available evidence suggests that with some of the treaties, the "schoolhouse" clauses were requested by the Indians and not simply imposed by the government negotiators. While Aboriginal parents were saddened at the absence of their children, at least some of them believed that the benefits of obtaining a "white man's" education justified this separation. ...

While by the middle of the twentieth century health conditions at residential schools had improved, it is now clear that the removal of children from their families and communities was a highly destructive emotional experience for Aboriginal children. As well, the devaluation of the children's culture and heritage that occurred in these institutions had very damaging effects on their self-esteem.

Further, at many residential schools there were devastating patterns of physical and sexual abuse. While it is clear that the government was receiving reports of abuse and neglect, little was done to prevent the abuse of Aboriginal children in these schools. The extent of abuse in these schools was not publicly known at the time that it was occurring, with the assumption being that the religious groups that operated the schools were providing appropriate care. It is now clear, however, that many abusive adults took jobs as teachers in these schools and were able to exploit and abuse a very vulnerable population of children. ...

The federal government began to phase out residential schools in the 1950s, although the last of these schools was only closed in the 1990s. Day schools have been established on or near most reserves. Children from reserves began to be integrated into the public school system, although some Aboriginal children from remote communities still have to board with other families while attending school, especially high school. While there are no longer any residential schools, the intergenerational legacy of these institutions is still present. Due to an absence of parenting role models, children who grew up in residential schools often have great difficulty in effectively parenting their own children. As is common with survivors of childhood abuse, drug and alcohol addiction, depression and patterns of family violence are endemic among those who attended residential schools. Further, the experience of many Aboriginal parents in residential schools has meant that some do little to encourage their own children to attend school, contributing to very high drop out rates among Aboriginal students, and hence to the poverty and unemployment of a new generation of Aboriginal peoples.

Also during the 1950s, there was an increase in the number of Aboriginal families moving from reserves to urban centres in order to find employment and pursue educational opportunities. These families were faced with the stresses of entering a foreign, urban culture as well as a loss of community support. Many Aboriginal children in urban settings were, and still are, considered by child welfare authorities to be neglected.

> Life for a child on a Reserve or in a native community is described as one of safety, love, adventure, and freedom. A child feels, and is welcome in any home and may join any family for a meal. A mother is not concerned if a child does not return home for a meal or even to sleep. The mother knows that some family is willingly providing for the child. This pattern is one that causes native parents grief when they move into urban centers because the reality is that urban life is different and dangerous. A mother who does not immediately report her child as missing is viewed as neglectful by the urban agencies.

More than half of all Aboriginal people now live off reserve, many in urban settings, and the child welfare concerns of this population raise especially challenging social and jurisdictional issues.

The "60s Scoop"

Since the establishment of Canada in 1867, under the *Constitution Act, 1867*, legislation regarding Aboriginal people has been the responsibility of the federal Parliament, while child welfare matters have fallen under provincial jurisdiction. Prior to the 1950s, it was rare for provincial child welfare services to be offered on Indian reserves. Children considered to be in need of protection were apprehended by Indian Agents and either placed with another family on the reserve or sent to residential schools.

While s. 91(24) of the *Constitution Act, 1867* gives the federal government legislative authority over "Indians and lands reserved for Indians," the federal government is not obligated to provide services under s. 91(24) of the *Constitution Act, 1867* or the *Indian Act*. Although Parliament has the jurisdiction to enact legislation in regard to Aboriginal child welfare, it has chosen not to do so.

In 1951, the federal government amended the *Indian Act* to include a provision clarifying the extent to which provincial legislation applies to Aboriginal people. Section 88 states:

"Subject to the terms of any treaty and any other Act of the Parliament of Canada, all laws of general application ... in force in any province are applicable to ... Indians in that province, except to the extent that such laws are inconsistent with this Act and except to the extent that such laws make provision for any matter for which provision is made ... under this Act."

Because the *Indian Act* contains no reference to child welfare, this section implicitly requires that provincial child protection laws and services extend to Aboriginal children, both on- and off-reserve. However, in the 1950s and 1960s, there was little federal effort to provide financial assistance to the provinces to pay for Aboriginal child welfare services, and provincial governments were reluctant to extend provincial services to Indian reserves, primarily for financial reasons.

The result of this prolonged jurisdictional dispute was that the quantity and quality of child welfare services provided to Aboriginal children on reserves across Canada varied considerably. In several provinces, especially in western Canada, child welfare services were provided to Aboriginal children living on reserves only in "life-or-death" situations. The result was that many Aboriginal families in need of family support services were not provided with even basic services, and difficult situations worsened until they became life-threatening and children had to be removed from parental care.

In the 1960s and early 1970s, as residential schools began to close and child welfare agencies were growing and starting to take responsibility for Aboriginal children, there were massive increases in the number of Aboriginal children taken into agency care. ...

The Aboriginal children who were removed from parental care in the 1960s and 1970s were usually placed in non-Aboriginal foster or group homes, or were adopted by Caucasian families. Some of them were placed for adoption in the United States or Europe. Aboriginal parents rarely had access to lawyers and these apprehensions and adoptions were invariably rushed through the courts without any type of meaningful judicial review. On some reserves, as many as one third of all children were taken into care and permanently removed by child welfare agencies. This is an event that is now known as the "60s scoop." While child welfare laws and policies have changed since then, this massive intervention created an atmosphere of mistrust and resentment of child welfare authorities that exists to this day.

The result of the "60s scoop" was that even though the residential school system started to fade away in the 1960s, Aboriginal people continued to be dominated by the push towards assimilation. In fact, many Aboriginal people came to view the child welfare system as a vehicle for "cultural genocide," since it typically gave "little weight to the values, lifestyle and laws" of the Aboriginal people in Canada, and because it has imposed on them the "standards, cultural values, laws and systems" of the dominant society.

Cultural Issues

Philosophy of Life

Many Aboriginal people are working to gain control of the child welfare programs that affect their lives. This struggle is more than just a legal or jurisdictional dispute. Aboriginal child welfare is grounded in an understanding of the world that is very different from the dominant European perspective. To understand the movement towards Aboriginal child welfare and the complexity of the cultural issues involved, one must consider elements of the world view common to many Aboriginal cultures. Fundamental to this world view is the interrelationship of all living things (including the physical environment as a living conscious entity). Children are gifts from the Creator and are nurtured within flexible and extensive extended family systems. Aboriginal healers work with concepts of balance, holism, harmony, and relationships to promote growth and connectedness. Models for this work are often expressed using a circle or Medicine Wheel framework.

Aboriginal peoples also place great emphasis on the well-being and survival of the community, with a focus on individual identity within the context of a community rather than individual rights. Notions of private property ownership are not part of Aboriginal traditions, and even today land on reserves is not privately owned. Individuals are expected to share their good fortune with their extended family and their community. When disputes arise in an Aboriginal community, the focus is on finding a consensual resolution that restores harmony in the community, not on punishment of the offender or on vindication of individual rights. ...

In many Canadian jurisdictions, over half of the Aboriginal population live off reserves, many in large cities where there may be better employment and education prospects. Many Aboriginal people, especially those who are younger and live in cities, no longer speak their Aboriginal language; their culture and heritage, however, remain integral to their self-identity. The courts and child welfare agencies generally now recognize that Aboriginal heritage is an important factor, even in cases where families are living in urban areas and do not speak an Aboriginal language. This was, for example, recognized in *Winnipeg (Child and Family Services) v. M.S.N.*, [2002] M.J. 154 (Man Q.B. Fam. Div.) where the child welfare agency was seeking permanent wardship of a three-and-a-half year old Aboriginal child, who had been living with Caucasian foster parents for two years as a result of the poor care provided by his mother. The grandparents, who lived in Winnipeg, were seeking custody. The grandparents were practicing Christians, spoke English and admitted that they only occasionally attended Aboriginal cultural events. In awarding custody to the grandparents, McCawley J. placed significant emphasis on the importance of maintaining the child's cultural heritage and noted that if the child remained an agency ward, the agency's plan for the child was adoption, and it was probable that this would not be in an Aboriginal home. The judge remarked (para. 35–40):

> Both R.M.F. and A.J.F. [the grandparents] candidly admitted that they do not attend a lot of Aboriginal cultural events. Although ... they ... attend pow wows once or twice a year ... they are not members of any cultural organizations and do not otherwise participate. R.M.F. said they did not have a lot of time because of their work and family commitments.
>
> I do not accept this as an indication that the F's do not value their Aboriginal culture. It is apparent that they place considerable importance on their race and Aboriginal heritage and have a strong desire to see their grandson raised within their immediate and extended Aboriginal family. I found their evidence on this point to be refreshingly honest and practical. ...
>
> In assessing the merits of the two plans proposed for the future care and well-being of K.B.N., I am persuaded that his best interests are served by allowing him to live with his paternal grandparents. They, in my view, are capable of providing him with a loving parent-child relationship and will be able to meet his mental, emotional, physical and educational needs adequately within their immediate and extended family. In addition, they are his blood, his race and Aboriginal heritage and, although they have assimilated many aspects of white urban culture into their lives, they will, as they said several times in this trial, teach K.B.N. "who he is."

This judgment illustrates that Aboriginal cultural heritage is a factor in making decisions in child welfare cases even for children and families who are living in urban settings.

Child-Rearing

While there are many different Aboriginal peoples in Canada, each with a distinctive language and culture, there are striking similarities, including similar philosophies and practices regarding children. The Aboriginal philosophy that humans are a part of, and must sustain, the delicate balance with nature is different from the dominant Euro-Canadian view that humans are superior to all other forms of life. The fundamentally different world views of Aboriginal and non-Aboriginal peoples have resulted in cultural conflict. These differing philosophies are, for example, reflected in fundamental differences between Aboriginal and Euro-Canadian child-rearing practices.

There are critical differences between the traditional child-rearing practices of Aboriginal peoples and those who are of European background. One difference is that, generally, Aboriginal parents respect their child's individuality and allow the child greater freedom to develop naturally, whereas non-Aboriginal parents tend to direct and control their children. Another is that Aboriginal children are socialized in a different way than non-Aboriginal children, learning through example to display feelings only at appropriate times and in private, for the public display of emotion is considered to be a source of discomfort to the viewer. This emotional self-control is often mistaken for indifference by non-Aboriginal people.

An Aboriginal child may be cared for by several households of an extended family with the natural parents' understanding that the child is receiving the same love and care that they would provide while in the care of relatives. This contrasts with the non-Aboriginal emphasis on the nuclear family as the basic unit of child care provision.

An important difference in discipline is the use of humour and teasing in many tribal groups to shame and humour a child into good behaviour. This may be interpreted as emotional abuse by those unfamiliar with Aboriginal ways. Also, since Aboriginal children are considered by their Elders to be at one with nature, they are allowed great freedom to search for their enlightenment. The directive approach of non-Aboriginal schools conflicts with this non-directive approach, and many Aboriginal children have difficulty achieving goals set in the formal Canadian classroom, causing them to become discouraged with school. Children caught between Aboriginal and non-Aboriginal customs and expectations such as these are often confused and find it extremely difficult to conform to either.

When viewed by social workers not knowledgeable of and sensitive to the child rearing practices of Aboriginal people, Aboriginal approaches to child care could be construed as neglectful, or even emotionally abusive, and as reasons for intervention.

The Importance of Cultural Heritage to Aboriginal Children

Historically, the implicit objective of many government policies was to destroy Aboriginal culture; this was most obvious in the residential schools policy, which was intended to change the language and culture of Aboriginal children. The child welfare policies of the 1960s may not have been intended to attack Aboriginal families and communities, but they clearly had this effect. It is now recognized that an attack on a child's cultural heritage is a violation of the rights of the child and of the Aboriginal community, and it can have highly destructive psychological effects on the child.

Child welfare laws and policies in Canada now give a preference to placement of Aboriginal children within their own community and culture. This is, in part, based on the recognition that all children have the right to maintain their cultural heritage, as recognized in Article 20 of the *United Nations Convention on the Rights of the Child*, which provides that "due regard shall be paid to the desirability of continuity in a child's upbringing and to the child's ethnic, religious, cultural and linguistic background." This right is especially important in Canada, where Aboriginal peoples have a unique constitutional status, and where individual Aboriginal persons may have special legal rights and status.

The claim for a preference for placements of Aboriginal children within Aboriginal communities is also made by First Nation communities, as they recognize that their children are their future, and that the transmission of their culture and heritage to future generations is central to their survival as distinct communities. Aboriginal advocates have charged that the high rates of apprehension by child welfare agencies and placement of Aboriginal children in non-Aboriginal homes has constituted "cultural genocide."

In addition to these essentially political and rights-based arguments about the importance of cultural heritage, there is a growing recognition that the placement of Aboriginal children in non-Aboriginal homes has often been emotionally damaging to these children. The confusion and identity crises that are often experienced by Aboriginal children and adolescents who were apprehended by child welfare agencies and placed in non-Aboriginal foster homes and adoption placements is now widely documented. ...

Aboriginal Customary Adoption

Until recently, the legal system failed to recognize the importance of Aboriginal customary law and traditions. Of particular importance is the idea that the child is a member of a total community, not just a member of a single nuclear family. A number of Aboriginal customs, such as extended family parenting, stem from this. Many Aboriginal people think that the courts still do not give enough recognition to specific customs and laws such as these.

Aboriginal customary adoption was one of the first Aboriginal practices to receive recognition by Canadian courts. For such civil law purposes as inheritance or pursing monetary claims for fatal injuries, since the 1960s the courts have accepted that the legal relationship of parent and child can be established by Aboriginal persons who were not so related biologically, if they have followed the customary practices of their tribe to establish the parent-child relationship. [See *Re Katie's Adoption Petition* (1962), 38 W.W.R. 100 (N.W.T. Terr. Ct.); *Re Beaulieu's Petition* (1969), W.W.R. 669 (N.W.T.); and *Re M.R.B.*, [2002] 2 C.N.L.R. 169 (Que. Ct.). See also Lomax, "Hluwit'y, Hluuxw'y — My Family, My Child: The Survival of Customary Adoption in British Columbia" (1997), 14 C.J.F.L. 197.] ...

For many Aboriginal people, customary Aboriginal adoption is preferable to statutory adoption schemes as it permits the natural parents to know where their child has been placed, and it emphasizes and recognizes the importance of maintaining the child's cultural ties. ...

Standard of Care

It has been argued that Aboriginal people should decide what constitutes neglect and inadequate parenting within their own community and that the evaluation of Aboriginal parenting by non-Aboriginal professionals and judges usually does not take into account the different value systems, customs and community characteristics. A disproportionately large number of Aboriginal child welfare cases are based on allegations of neglect as opposed to other forms of child maltreatment such as physical or sexual abuse. A finding of neglect by a child welfare worker or a court may implicitly suggest that the parents have the capacity to meet their children's needs. However, there has been insufficient study of how to redress the systemic risk factors, such as poverty and lack of community support services, that may lie outside the caregivers' sphere of influence. Many Aboriginal peoples express concern that there has been inadequate research and dialogue on the interrelationship between poverty and the disproportionate reported incidence of neglect in Aboriginal families. Allegations of neglect by a non-Aboriginal child protection worker may reflect a worker's middle-class world view of both the standard of living and Aboriginal parenting style rather than constituting a pattern of behaviour that presents a real harm to the child.

Though the concept of neglect has not yet been defined by Aboriginal people for Aboriginal people, a number of more sensitive court decisions in Canada have ruled that different standards of care may be applied to parents in poor Aboriginal communities than those that are applied to non-Aboriginal middle-class communities.

In *Re E.C.D.M.* (1980), 17 R.F.L. (2d) 274 (Sask. Prov. Ct.), the court held that it should apply "different" expectations and "standards of parenting" for parents of Aboriginal ancestry living in remote, impoverished communities than it had for middle-class parents living in urban areas. In this case, a 24-year-old single mother residing in a rural Cree community in northern Saskatchewan opposed a permanent wardship application for her 2-year-old child. Judge Moxley outlined some community differences to be taken into account. These included cultural differences such as an extended family concept and non-intervention in child-rearing, acquired community habits such as widespread drinking, and conditions forced on the community such as a high level of unemployment and dependence upon government assistance, and a lack of social support services. These differences formed the basis of a "different" standard which the court applied to the case, though ultimately concluding that the children should be made permanent wards since even by the standards of her community, the mother lacked the ability to care adequately for her child and the grandmother was not willing to take them in. [See also *Mooswa et al. v. Minister of Social Services for the Province of Saskatchewan* (1976), 30 R.F.L. 101 (Sask. Q.B.).] ...

The issue of the community standard of care was also considered in *Director of Child Welfare of Manitoba v. B.B.* (1988), 14 R.F.L. (3d) 113 (Man. C.A.) where the trial judge, in considering whether two Aboriginal siblings were in need of protection, took account of the standards of care and resources available in the children's Aboriginal community. The trial judge held the 18-month-old twins were no longer in need of protection and were to be returned to their mother. The mother had never had custody of these children. She was living in a four-room house with another 5-year-old child, her 65-year-old mother, her sister, and her sister's two young children. The three adults received social assistance, and all were Non-Status Indians living on the outskirts of a reserve community. Alcohol abuse was evident in the home. In deciding the twins were not in need of protection, Judge Martin stated [quoted by the Manitoba Court of Appeal at 115]:

> I have carefully reviewed the evidence and while I find the ... condition[s], and I refer to the extended family at Easterville, deplorable by standards which I take to be the norm for middle class white society, I cannot find proof, on balance, of the kind required that would allow me to say that B.B. should be denied the return of her children.

> I find that none of the incidents referred to or the living conditions reported are so far out of the ordinary, for Easterville, that I can say that the children would probably be at risk if returned to the mother.

The trial decision was appealed by the protection agency, and overturned by the Manitoba Court of Appeal, with Justice Monnin stating [at 114]:

> That there is poverty in the area is not denied but poverty and the customs of the inhabitants of Easterville are not the issue. The sole issue is what is in the best interests of the twins.

> I do not accept as sound the principle enunciated by the trial judge that there are certain standards or norms which are acceptable for Easterville but unacceptable for the rest of the province. Economic conditions may differ but there is only one standard of care to be considered and applied whether the infants reside or whether the household is situated in Easterville, The Pas, Churchill, Brandon, Crescentwood, Tuxedo, West Kildonan or the Core area. In my opinion, the type of household in the case before us cannot provide the simple and essential elements of life since all three adults have shown themselves to be irresponsible where the other children are concerned and regularly overindulge in alcohol.

The decision of the Manitoba Court of Appeal was appealed to the Supreme Court of Canada. The Supreme Court [[1989] 2 S.C.R. 291] rejected the approach of the Court of Appeal to the issue of the appropriate standard of care and ordered a new trial. Justice Sopinka in the Supreme Court wrote a very brief decision, stating:

> Although we do not agree with the test applied by the majority of the Court of Appeal, we agree with their conclusion that the children are in need of protection. We are of the opinion, however, that the Court of Appeal failed to adequately consider the alternatives in s. 38 of the Act, and in addition, we have been told of evidence that indicates a change of circumstances have occurred. Accordingly, we

would refer the matter back to the trial judge to consider what order is now appropriate under s. 38 [supervision, temporary wardship or permanent wardship].

This case is a good example of the child welfare dilemma faced by Aboriginal people. It is encouraging that the Supreme Court of Canada appears to recognize the inappropriateness of automatically applying the standards of the dominant society to Aboriginal peoples. Increasingly, Aboriginal communities are demanding that their own values and standards be applied when decisions are made concerning their children. ...

Contemporary Aboriginal Child Welfare

. . . . .

Aboriginal Child Welfare in Canada

Although there is considerable variation across Canada in how governments and First Nations are responding to child welfare issues for Aboriginal children, there are a number of related developments that have substantially changed the laws and institutional structures over the past two decades. The major developments are:

- establishment of Aboriginal child welfare agencies, operating within the framework of provincial and territorial law; some of these agencies have a full legal mandate, while others are voluntary agencies;

- notification and involvement of bands in child welfare proceedings;

- development of community-based dispute resolution models for child welfare cases involving Aboriginal children;

- recognition of the importance of culture and heritage as factors in determining the best interests of the child; and

- introduction of laws and policies giving preference to placement of Aboriginal children in Aboriginal families and communities.

These developments are discussed separately here, though there are interrelationships between them.

Aboriginal Child Welfare Agencies

Perhaps the most significant development in Aboriginal child welfare in Canada in the past two decades has been the gradual establishment of a large number of agencies that are operated under the direction of Aboriginal peoples to provide services to Aboriginal children and families. At present in Canada many, but far from all, Aboriginal children and families are receiving at least some child welfare services from agencies which are controlled to a significant degree by Aboriginal communities. These agencies do not exist everywhere in Canada, and there is great variation in the role, structure and functioning of these agencies.

The most common model of Aboriginal child welfare agency in Canada is what is termed the "delegated model," where First Nations or other Aboriginal communities receive authority from the provincial or territorial child welfare statute to provide either a full range of child protection services (full delegation), or family support and guardianship services (partial delegation). There is also a group of agencies, primarily located in Ontario, which provide a range of child welfare support services outside of the child welfare statute, but under licence to the province — these are known as "pre-mandated agencies." The federal government provides funding only for child welfare for on-reserve residents pursuant to a national funding formula known as Directive 20-1. Provincial (and territorial) governments fund child welfare services to Aboriginal peoples living off reserves.

Most importantly, with one notable exception — the Spallumcheen Band in British Columbia — ... these Aboriginal child welfare agencies operate within the framework of provincial child welfare legislation and are subject to a degree of provincial supervision.

There are essentially two types of Aboriginal-controlled agencies that provide child welfare services:

- agencies delegated by provincial governments that carry out statutory duties in regard to child protection and adoption; and

- agencies that are not delegated to carry out statutory child welfare functions, and provide services that supplement the statutory child welfare agency.

Generally the delegated agencies operate on reserves, and the voluntary agencies operate to serve off-reserve populations, especially in cities.

Delegated Aboriginal Child Welfare Agencies: Directive 20-1

. . . . .

... In 1991, the federal government established a framework policy, known as Directive 20-1 for the provision of child welfare services to Aboriginal communities. This policy is intended to support "the creation of Indian designed, controlled and managed services" and provides federal funding for the provision of child welfare services to Aboriginal communities. A key part of the policy is that any child welfare agencies that are established are to operate within provincial (or territorial) child welfare statutes, and that legal proceedings are to be dealt with in the established provincial court systems.

Tripartite agreements have become the common method of addressing jurisdictional disputes over the provision of Indian child welfare services. These tripartite agreements between the Indian, provincial and federal governments are established under existing provincial child welfare legislation. Under these agreements the province delegates authority for child welfare for a specific population of Aboriginal children to a First Nations Child and Family Service Agency. In many cases provinces and territories will also spell out terms and conditions for the exercise of the delegated authority (i.e. requirement to follow provincial standards). The federal government provides full or partial financial assistance for these agencies pursuant to the Directive, or in Ontario, pursuant to a separate funding agreement. Under a tripartite agreement, the provincial laws governing child welfare services are followed both on and off the reserves. Aboriginal people may be given authority to administer the laws, but this is generally restricted to on-reserve geographic locations. Under the delegated model, Aboriginal peoples do not have the jurisdiction to enforce their own laws or customs, and the adoption of this model by First Nations is generally viewed by them as an interim capacity building measure pending recognition of self-government. Until tribal laws are recognized, the delegated model does afford Aboriginal communities an opportunity to put their own interpretation on the provincial laws, thereby incorporating some Aboriginal values, beliefs and customs in the provision of child welfare services to Aboriginal children.

Since the implementation of Directive 20-1, over one hundred First Nations Child and Family Services have been established that provide services to more than two-thirds of Canada's reserves, as well as providing some services to off-reserve Status Indians. Some of these agencies are very small, with as few as three employees and serve only one reserve, while others are quite large with over one hundred employees and responsibility for provision of services over a large geographical area that covers several reserves. ...

When the first Aboriginal child welfare agencies were established in the 1980s, some of them aggressively pursued policies of "repatriation," taking Aboriginal children who had been in long-term foster care in non-Aboriginal settings and returning them to their reserves and to a native culture that was alien to them. This was sometimes done in a way that disregarded the rights and wishes of these children, and sometimes caused them harm.

A particularly tragic example of "repatriation" was *Doe v. Awasis Agency of Northern Manitoba*, [1990] M.J. 402 (Q.B.), a case that eventually received national media attention. When she was about a year old, in 1973, this status Indian girl needed medical treatment that was not available in her remote community and was removed from her isolated reserve in northern Manitoba and sent to a hospital in a northern mining community. After her release from hospital she was placed with a non-Aboriginal foster family, who later moved with her to Alberta, where they eventually adopted her. By the time that she was 14 years old, an Aboriginal child welfare agency had been established to serve her reserve. The agency located the girl, and had the adoption order set aside because the biological parents had not been notified of the adoption proceedings. While the girl had clearly come to view the foster parents as her psychological parents, her prior removal from her native family had violated fundamental rights.

Against her wishes, the girl was taken from her father's family in Alberta by the Aboriginal agency and returned to her reserve and family of origin. The girl did not speak the Dene language that was spoken on the reserve, and most people on the reserve, including her parents, did not speak much English, so communication was difficult. Life on the reserve was very foreign to the girl, and she was treated as an outcast. She was repeatedly, forcibly confined and raped by male residents of the community, and contracted venereal disease as a result of the sexual assaults. She wrote in despair to her foster parents, who contacted the agency about the situation, but nothing was done. Eventually the girl was flown out of the reserve by a doctor, and she was hospitalized suffering from depression. The agency wanted her to return to her community, but a court ordered that she was to return to her foster parents in Alberta. She suffered enormous trauma from her experiences and twice attempted suicide while again living with her foster family. The girl received counselling and support and launched a court action against the Aboriginal agency for its negligence. The action was settled without trial for $75,000. The judge, who had to approve the settlement as the girl was still a minor, considered the settlement low, but accepted it as she was still too vulnerable to withstand the stress of a trial.

Since the early cases of repatriation, there has been more support for children who are being repatriated, development of Aboriginal repatriation programs that reflect past learnings and closer supervision from provincial governments, but these cases continue to cause controversy and pose difficult questions of balancing concerns about a child's emotional attachment against cultural heritage and Aboriginal community interests. Non-Aboriginal foster parents continue to seek hearings in the courts before Aboriginal children in their long-term care are removed and returned to their communities of origin, arguing ... that this is contrary to [the] wishes, rights and needs of these children, who have become closely attached to their foster parents. There are no easy solutions to these cases, but it must be appreciated that *preventing removal* of Aboriginal children from their communities by having suitable Aboriginal placements is quite different from *forcing their return* after long periods in care. In the Canadian legal system, the courts focus on the needs and interests of the child, not the interests or rights of the community.

... While Aboriginal agencies (like traditional agencies) give priority to placement of children who have been apprehended with members of their extended family, and failing that in foster homes in their community, frequently it is not possible to arrange an Aboriginal placement. It is difficult to recruit foster parents from reserves who meet provincial standards as, for example, many families on reserves live in substandard homes or may have a member who has a criminal record. Further, with the poverty and housing shortages on many reserves, some families simply do not have the resources to care for another child. As a result, some Aboriginal child welfare agencies make quite extensive use of non-Aboriginal foster and group homes, though efforts are made to keep children in these placements in contact with their culture. Some placements made by Aboriginal agencies, however, may be quite far from the child's home on a reserve, and these children may experience significant culture shock, especially if taken from a relatively remote reserve and placed in southern Canada.

The establishment of Aboriginal child welfare agencies has resulted in the provision of services to Aboriginal children in a more sensitive and culturally appropriate fashion, but there remain very significant challenges in the transition to new institutions and service delivery arrangements. The establishment of these agencies has not ended the substantial over-representation of Aboriginal children in care. Since the mid-1990s, well over half of the Aboriginal children in the care of child welfare agencies in Canada have been in the care of Aboriginal agencies. ...

Voluntary Aboriginal Organizations

The majority of reserves now have an Aboriginal controlled child welfare agency, and the number of these agencies is gradually increasing. However, there remain many reserves that do not have such services. In some cases the Aboriginal community may lack the financial and human resources or the political will to seek to establish such a service, while in other cases the Aboriginal community has been unable to reach an agreement with the federal and provincial (or territorial) governments about the service. Further, pursuant to Directive 20-1, First Nations with less than 251 Status Indian children resident on reserve are ineligible for child and family service funding.

For off-reserve Aboriginal peoples, provincial governments have been more reluctant to mandate Aboriginal agencies, and the provincial and federal governments have been less willing to provide funding support, so that off-reserve children and families generally receive statutory child welfare services from non-Aboriginal agencies. Manitoba has gone the farthest in establishing Aboriginal child welfare agencies' with jurisdiction over off-reserve families and children.

Increasingly, however, where the statutory child welfare agency is not controlled by the Aboriginal community, there are various other social service agencies that are operated by the Aboriginal community that may be able to voluntarily provide culturally appropriate services to the parents and children. These voluntary Aboriginal agencies include Friendship Centers and other social service agencies. They may get funding from the federal, provincial or municipal governments, or may get support from the United Way. These non-mandated agencies may, for example, provide counselling or support to parents or children, or operate group homes that can provide care for Aboriginal children who are child welfare agency wards on a contract basis. A number of these non-mandated agencies operate in medium sized and large cities.

It is important for mandated child welfare agencies to be receptive to working with non-mandated Aboriginal agencies. It is now common for mandated agencies to work with non-mandated agencies, for example, to arrange for a culturally appropriate foster care or group home placement for an Aboriginal child who has been made a ward. It is also common for a non-Aboriginal child welfare agency that apprehends a child, for example, in an urban area where the child was living with a parent, to arrange for a voluntary transfer of the case to the mandated Aboriginal agency that provides service to the parent's band. ...

Band Involvement in Child Welfare Proceedings

Aboriginal children are not only considered to be members of their families but also members of their First Nations. Accordingly, if a child's parents are unable to provide suitable care, the band of which the child is a member may have an interest in finding them suitable care in their communities. Legislation in several provinces, including Alberta, Manitoba and Ontario, requires that a child welfare agency that is commencing child protection or adoption proceedings concerning an Aboriginal child give notice to the band. Notification will allow the band to participate in the proceedings and, if appropriate, to put forward a plan for the care of the child by members of their community. In Nova Scotia, notice of the proceedings anywhere in the province involving an Aboriginal child must be given to Mi 'kmaq Family and Children's Services, which will usually notify the child's band of the proceedings. In jurisdictions where there is no statutory provision giving a band the right to notification of the proceedings and standing to participate, the courts have held that they have the jurisdiction to allow a child's band to intervene in child welfare proceedings.

While some Aboriginal parents welcome the involvement, and in some cases the support, of their band in their litigation against a child welfare agency, other parents may resent the intrusion into their lives and privacy that occurs from band involvement. Regardless of parental feelings, if a child is living on reserve at the time of apprehension, members of the band will know the child, and may be in a position to put forward a plan that will allow the child to remain in his or her Aboriginal community and continue to receive care from members of that community.

More difficult issues may arise when a child with Aboriginal status who has been living off-reserve is apprehended; in some of these cases one of the parents may be non-Aboriginal, and one or both of the parents may object to the involvement of the band in their litigation. In some of these cases the children were born and lived off-reserve, and there will usually be real questions as to whether the band has the resources to put forward a plan of care that will meet the best interests of the child. The general tendency of the courts in these cases is to allow the band to participate in the proceedings, even if not required by legislation, and to give consideration to the child's heritage when assessing the child's best interests. However, when dealing with the future of a child, a judge may well prefer placement with a parent or relative off-reserve, even if that person is not Aboriginal, though there may be an expectation that the parent or relative will make efforts to maintain contact with the child's Aboriginal community. ...

Alternative Dispute Resolution in Aboriginal Communities

... Alternate dispute resolution [which has been increasingly used in child welfare cases generally] may be especially valuable in Aboriginal communities where there are long traditions of consensus-based dispute resolution that are intended to preserve relationships within the community and develop harmonious outcomes to disputes. The growing use of circle sentencing and community justice projects to deal with the sentencing of adult and youth Aboriginal offenders is another type of alternative dispute resolution that attempts to involve the community in developing appropriate plans to deal with the causes of offending.

In Aboriginal communities, respected Elders may have an important role in attempting to mediate or resolve a dispute about the care of children. In Re J.D., [2003] S.J. 453 (Sask. Q.B.), ... the parties and judge decided to make use of an Opikinawasowin (a Cree term for a council of Elders) to attempt to resolve a dispute between two estranged parents and the child welfare agency about the care of their five children. ...

Aboriginal Heritage as a Best Interests Factor

Legislatures, courts and child welfare agencies now recognize that cultural heritage is an important factor in determining what is in a child's best interests, and in particular that Aboriginal heritage is an important factor in making placement decisions for Aboriginal children. There is now widespread agreement that if the parents of an Aboriginal child cannot adequately care for the child, there should be a preference for placing the child with members of the child's extended family or with other members of the child's community. When decisions are being made about individual children and in formulating policies, however, there are still contentious questions about how much weight to place on a child's Aboriginal heritage when determining what is in the best interests of a child. ...

Ontario's *Child and Family Services Act* has the most explicit provincial legislative provisions for the recognition of Aboriginal heritage in making decisions about children. The Declaration of Principles of Ontario's *Child and Family Services Act* states [s. 1(2)] "so long as [measures taken] ... are consistent with the best interests, protection and well being of children," it is the intent of the *Act* "to recognize that Indian and native people should be entitled to provide, wherever possible, their own child and family services, and that all services to Indian and native children and families should be provided in a manner that recognizes their culture, heritage and traditions and the concept of the extended family."

There are also specific provisions [ss. 37(3)3 and 136(2)3] that require that a child welfare agency or court making a determination about the "best interests" of any child in a protection or adoption proceeding take into consideration the importance of preserving the child's heritage and cultural identity. If a protection or adoption application involves an Aboriginal child, the decision maker "shall take into consideration the importance, in recognition of the uniqueness of Indian and native culture, heritage and culture, of preserving the child's cultural identity" [ss. 37(4) and 136(3)].

To help operationalize these general statements, there are also provisions in the Ontario statute for notification and involvement of the band of an Indian child in protection proceedings [see s. 39(1)4]. If a child welfare agency is planning to place an Aboriginal child for adoption, the agency must give prior notification to the child's band or native community [see s. 141.2]. This is to allow Aboriginal communities to have input in the decision-making about the adoption of their children, and make representations about culturally appropriate placements.

When an Ontario court is considering what type of order to make in regard to a child who has been found to be in need of protection, unless there is a "substantial reason for placing the child elsewhere," under s. 57(5) of the *Child and Family Services Act* the judge is required to consider placements for the child in the following order: (a) with a member of the child's extended family; (b) with a member of the child's band or native community; or (c) with another Indian or native family.

With the enactment of this type of legislation, the courts are starting to give more weight to Aboriginal heritage when making decisions about Aboriginal children, as illustrated by a 1992 Ontario case, *Weechi-it-te-win Child and Family Services v. A.M.*, [1993] 1 C.N.L.R. 169 (Ont. Prov. Div.). The two young children, one just five weeks old and the other three years of age, were taken into care because of their mother's inability to care for them due to alcohol and solvent abuse, and her violence towards others, and placed by the agency in the care of non-Aboriginal foster parents. After a year, the case had been transferred to a newly established Aboriginal child welfare agency, which wanted the children returned to their reserve to live with a woman on the reserve under agency supervision. The Children's Lawyer supported the plan of the foster parents to continue to care for the children, to whom they had become closely attached. The judge noted:

> Weechi-it-te-win Family Services and the people of [the] Wabaseemoong [First Nation] are struggling with important childcare issues. There is a political desire not to lose children from their re-

> serve. At the same time, decisions in cases such as this must be made having regard to the individual circumstances and plans proposed for the specific children before the court. There also appears to be a shortage of competent homes which are available to provide alternate care for children. ...

The judge recognized that the foster parents would provide a "good home" and that they had a "sincere regard for the children" and a close psychological tie. The judge, however, was concerned that the children would lose contact with their native language and culture from such a placement, and decided that the children should be returned to a home on their reserve: "I am satisfied that this disposition is in the best interests of the children because it is more likely that they will ultimately then be placed in a home which will safeguard their cultural and language roots." ...

In the past few years, the courts have made statements in child protection cases recognizing the importance of Aboriginal heritage. However, if Aboriginal parents are not able to care adequately for their children and cannot deal with problems such as alcohol abuse within the period for temporary wardship (set by legislation, in Ontario at one year for children under the age of 6), the courts are prepared to uphold agency requests for termination of access to young children to allow for adoption by non-Aboriginal persons. [See, e.g., *Kenora-Patricia Child & Family Services v. O. (D.)*, [2001] 4 C.N.L.R. 103 (Ont. C. J.).]

Although there is now more judicial recognition of the importance of Aboriginal children's cultural identity, many Aboriginal commentators believe this factor has not been weighed heavily enough by the courts when Aboriginal parents or communities are seeking custody of their children from child welfare agencies, or seeking to prevent the adoption of their children by non-Aboriginal persons.

It is clear from the case law that judges are still prepared to accept claims by child welfare agencies that the best interests of an Aboriginal child requires adoption and severance of the tie to Aboriginal parents and their community. Increasingly, however, child welfare agencies, both Aboriginal and traditional, are putting forward plans of care that involve long-term foster care by a non-Aboriginal foster parent, but allow for continuing visits with parents or other relatives and contact with members of their community. While the courts have generally accepted these plans, in a Manitoba case, the failure of the agency to seek adoption was the subject of adverse comment by the judge.

In *Winnipeg Child and Family Services v. M.A.* (2002), 216 D.L.R. (4th) 500 (Man. Q.B.) the court was dealing with a case where a child was apprehended at two months of age from the care of his 15-year-old mother and his grandmother. The mother and grandmother both had serious alcohol abuse problems, and the mother was associating with gang members. The child was in foster care for two years but had to be moved as the foster parents were unable to continue to care for the child. Agency workers concluded that adoption would be best for the child, as it would give the child an assurance of permanency, but the agency could not find an Aboriginal adoptive home and had a policy of not placing Aboriginal children for adoption in non-Aboriginal homes. The mother and grandmother were still not able to care for the child, and because the maximum two-year period for temporary wardship had expired, the agency was seeking permanent wardship. The judge granted the permanent wardship order, but expressed "frustration" that she did not have the power to direct that the child should be adopted by a non-Aboriginal family if a suitable Aboriginal family could not be found. Justice Beard commented [paras. 1-2]:

> This is a case about an Aboriginal child who is being denied her right to a permanent, secure family because the ... agency ... vetoed any such placement. The reason for the veto arises from a desire to stop the removal of Aboriginal children from their cultural heritage. While a laudable goal, its dogmatic application is counterproductive and unfair. The tragedy in this case is that the best plan for the child, which would see her placed with a permanent family, has been rejected for historical and political reasons that have nothing to do with her case. While non-Aboriginal children are offered a permanent adoptive family, Aboriginal children continue to be offered the lesser option of a foster family, which lacks the permanence and security that would come with an adoption.

> It is important to point out that this is not a case about the non-Aboriginal child welfare system preferring a non-Aboriginal family over an Aboriginal family, because ... [an] Aboriginal placement is not an option, in any form, so the child is left to be raised by one or more non-Aboriginal foster families, which is clearly not the best available option for her. The end result is that the child is being held hostage by a child welfare system that has put its own political interests and expediencies ahead of her best interests. Surely this is unfair to her.

The judge noted that Manitoba has gone further than most provinces in making statutory provision for "open adoption" that would allow the band and birth parents to have a role in the selection of a suitable non-Aboriginal adoptive family and to sign an agreement with them that would allow for some contact. This would, in the judge's view, permit the child to have the "security of being a permanent member of an adoptive family and also ensure that she maintained her contact with her culture and birth family." ...

Conclusion

The dominant non-Aboriginal society in Canada has not responded adequately to the problems of Aboriginal children and communities. Assimilationist and culturally insensitive policies have often harmed these children and their communities. While child welfare laws, institutions and policies have become more sensitive to the needs of Aboriginal children and communities, Canada's Aboriginal peoples now face enormous problems with their children and families. Poverty, alcoholism, spousal violence, fetal alcohol syndrome, neglect of children and child sexual abuse are very serious problems in many Aboriginal families and communities, and must be addressed by the communities themselves. Addressing these problems requires a significant investment in education, health and social services over an extended period of time. Many Aboriginal adults were themselves brought up in residential schools or child welfare institutions and may lack appropriate role models for being nurturing parents. Some of these survivors are now functioning effectively as parents and community leaders despite histories of substance abuse, domestic violence or other criminal behaviours. Many survivors of residential school are fragile and vulnerable to relapse. As a result there are many parenting challenges in these communities.

The problems of providing appropriate child welfare services for Aboriginal children will defy a single, quick solution. Different First Nations have different strengths and problems. The challenges facing isolated northern communities, where Aboriginal languages are still spoken, are different from those faced by Aboriginal people who have moved to large urban areas in southern Canada.

An important step is for non-Aboriginal professionals who work with Aboriginal children and families to be better-trained and more sensitive to the culture, heritage and values of Canada's Aboriginal people, and to recognize their unique strengths and challenges. The professionals involved include social workers, childcare workers, teachers, doctors, nurses, psychologists, police officers, lawyers and judges. As much as possible, the education should be provided by Aboriginal people to others about the problems faced by Aboriginal families and children and the resources in Aboriginal communities.

Another important measure will be the increased recruitment and training of Aboriginal people to work with their communities and help them solve their problems. ...

There must also be changes in our policies and laws, and in the manner in which services are provided to Aboriginal communities. Such changes have been occurring and Aboriginal people are slowly gaining control over services provided to their communities, though it is apparent that some communities are more willing and able to do so than others. ...

Many Aboriginal people, however, feel that these measures are not adequate. They feel that it is not sufficient that the federal and provincial governments should be delegating responsibilities to Aboriginal communities, but rather believe that they should have responsibility for their own children and should enact their own child welfare codes. The federal

Parliament clearly has the constitutional authority to permit Indian bands to enact their own child welfare laws, but it has thus far failed to act. Some Aboriginal groups are advocating such action or asserting that responsibility for the provision of child welfare services should be granted to Aboriginal communities as part of broader moves towards recognition of Aboriginal self-government and sovereignty.

The reform of laws and changes in institutional structures to better meet the needs of Aboriginal children and communities is a process that will go on for many years. In the interim, it is essential that non-Aboriginal agencies and professionals are educated and sensitized to Aboriginal child welfare issues, and that larger numbers of Aboriginal professionals are educated, recruited and retained in the child welfare field. ...

NOTES AND QUESTIONS

1. The 2006 amendments to the *CFSA* continued the trend, noted in the above article, to ensure that the child protection system and the Children's Aid Societies in particular take into account the cultural heritage and traditions of Aboriginal children:

- Section 213.1 now stipulates that a "society or agency that proposes to provide prescribed services to a child who is an Indian or native person or to exercise a prescribed power under this Act in relation to such a child shall consult with a representative chosen by the child's band or native community in accordance with the regulations". The regulations define "prescribed services" to include 1) the completion of a child protection investigation if the society concludes that the child is in need of protection and that the case needs a "plan of ongoing protection services"; 2) the apprehension of a child by a child protection worker under ss. 40, 41 or 43 of the Act; and 3) the placement of a child, by a society, in a children's residence or in a foster home. See s. 123 of Regulation 70, R.R.O. 1990. Section 124 of that regulation sets out the consultative procedure.

- Before making certain orders listed in s. 56, a court is required by that section to consider the society's plan of care for the child. That plan now must include "a description of the arrangements made or being made to recognize the importance of the child's culture and to preserve the child's heritage, traditions and cultural identity".

- Section 3(1) defines "extended family" to include, in the case of a child who is an Indian or native person, "any member of the child's band or native community". This is significant, *inter alia*, in temporary and long-term placement decisions under the *CFSA*. See ss. 37(5), 51(3.1), 51(4) and 51(5).

- In considering whether a method of alternative dispute resolution could assist in resolving any issue relating to a child who is an Indian or native person, the society must consult with the child's band or native community. See s. 20.2(2).

- Section 144 gives a band or native community a special status in relation to reviews of a society's refusal of a particular person's application to adopt a child or of a society's decision to remove a child who has been placed for adoption where the child is an Indian or native person.

- Where a child is made a Crown ward, one of the options available to the society is a "plan for customary care" under Part X of the *CFSA*. See s. 63.1.

- Section 141.2(1) now requires a society that intends to begin planning for the adoption of a child who is an Indian or native person to give "written notice of its intention to a representative chosen by the child's band or native community". Under s. 141.2(2), the band or native community then has 90 days within which to prepare its own plan and submit it to the society. The society, by virtue of s. 141.2(3), must consider this plan before placing the child for adoption.

- In "open adoptions", an "openness agreement" can be made between the prospective adoptive parent or the adoptive parent and, where the child is an Indian or native person, "a member of the child's band or native community who may not have had a significant relationship or emotional tie with the child in the past but may help the child recognize the importance of his or her Indian or native culture and preserve his heritage, traditions and cultural identity". See s. 153.6(1).

- An "openness order" can be made under s. 145.1 of the *CFSA* in respect of a Crown ward who is being placed for adoption. Where the child is an Indian or native person, an "openness order" can be made to facilitate communication between the child and "a member of the child's band or native community who may not have had a significant relationship or emotional tie with the child in the past but may help the child recognize the importance of his or her Indian or native culture and preserve his heritage, traditions and cultural identity". See s. 136(1). The purpose of such an order is to provide a link with his or her traditions and heritage. See *Native Child & Family Services of Toronto v. W. (K.)* (2007), 2007 Carswell-Ont 2534 (Ont. C.J.).

2. For more detailed descriptions of the residential school system, see A.C. Hamilton and S.M. Sinclair, *The Justice System and Aboriginal Peoples: Report of the Aboriginal Justice Inquiry in Manitoba* (1996), Vol. 1, 509–520 and J. Molloy, *The National Crime: The Canadian Government and the Residential School System 1879 to 1986* (Winnipeg: University of Manitoba Press, 1999).

3. In *T. (R.), Re* (2004), 248 D.L.R. (4th) 303 (Sask. Q.B.), Justice Ryan-Froslie held that the policy of the Saskatchewan Department of Community Resources and Employment, whereby no aboriginal child was placed for adoption without the consent of the child's First Nation, violated the child's *Charter* rights. This ruling arose in the following context. In a child protection hearing, a court had to determine the appropriate placement orders regarding five children who were members of the Sturgeon Lake First Nation and who had previously been found to be in need of protection. There was no evidence to indicate that any of the five children had ever lived on the First Nation's reserve or that they had ever had any contact with it. The two oldest children, Dan and Jane, had experienced at least 13 foster placements each and wished to remain with their current foster mother. The third oldest, Maggie, had been in 20 different foster homes even though she was only eight years old. She suffered from Reactive Attachment Disorder because of the numerous placements, but was doing well in her current foster home. The fourth child, John, was four and had spent all but fifteen months of his life in foster care. The fifth child, Sally, was 23 months old and had spent her entire life in her current foster home. Her foster parents were prepared to consider any option, including adoption. A social worker testified that no extended family members or Sturgeon Lake First Nation's families could take the children. She described the children as "adoptable", but stated that, as a result of the Department's policy, they would not be placed for adoption even if a permanent or Crown wardship order were made. She stated that the Sturgeon Lake First Nation never consented to the placement for adoption of an aboriginal child in a non-aboriginal home.

The Justice found that an open adoption that permitted Maggie and John to maintain contact with the aboriginal community and their culture would be in their best interests. Similarly, Sally's best interests would be served through adoption by her foster parents, provided that she could maintain contact with her biological mother and siblings as well as her aboriginal community and culture. The Justice concluded that the policy precluded these results and doomed the children to remain in long-term foster care. It, therefore, affected their security of the person for the purposes of s. 7 of the *Charter*. It did not accord with the principles of fundamental justice because it undercut the hearing process and the court's determination of the children's best interests. The Justice also held that the policy constituted unjustified discrimination on the basis of race contrary to the *Charter*.

In "Reparations for Historical Injustice: Can Cultural Appropriation as a Result of Residential Schools Provide Justification for Aboriginal Cultural Rights?" (2007), 70 Sask. L. Rev. 425, Celeste Hutchinson describes (at 454) this case as a "recent example of failure to recognize or protect an Aboriginal cultural custom". She adds (at 454): "This case is somewhat analogous to the situation of residential schools in that the children were forcefully removed from their communities and their culture." Do you agree?

4. Justice Mesbur held in *Algonquins of Pikwakanagan First Nation v. Children's Aid Society of Toronto* (2004), 5 R.F.L. (6th) 9 (Ont. S.C.J.) that the Canadian Constitution did not preclude the placement of aboriginal children in non-aboriginal homes. In that case, the CAS apprehended three children whose mother was of Chinese origin and whose father was a member of the Algonquins of Pikwakanagan First Nation. The CAS began proceedings for an order for Crown wardship with no parental access so that the children could be placed for adoption. It served the First Nation with notice as required by the *CFSA*. The First Nation did not file an answer or otherwise participate in the proceedings and, with the consent of the parents, the Crown wardship orders followed. Ultimately, the CAS selected the father's aunt and two non-aboriginal couples as prospective adoptive parents for each of the three children. The First Nation initially advised that it was not opposed to the placements. However, the children's father was concerned that two of the children were placed with non-native families and urged the First Nation to get involved. The First Nation then notified the CAS of the father's concerns, but advised that it had no available homes for the children. The next day, however, the First Nation informed the CAS that a Metis family had come forward to look after the children. By that time, the children had been in care for about eighteen months and the CAS was not prepared to alter its adoption plans.

The First Nation then applied for declarations that the CAS had violated the rights of the children under s. 7 of the *Canadian Charter of Rights and Freedoms* and the Band's rights under s. 35 of the *Constitution Act, 1982*. The First Nation also sought an injunction to enjoin the CAS from finalizing the adoptions, either on a permanent or interlocutory basis. In the alternative, it asked the court to exercise its *parens patriae* jurisdiction to transfer the children to the Metis family.

Justice Mesbur held that neither the legislation nor the actions of the CAS affected the children's rights to liberty or security of the person as guaranteed by s. 7 of the *Charter*. She stated that the children did not have a constitutional right to be raised by a native family. Such a right, in her view, would mean that only native families or bands could adopt native children and the lack of native adoptive homes would leave many children in limbo, contrary to their best interests. She noted that adoption by non-aboriginal families would not deprive the children of their status as Indians under the *Indian Act* or of their membership in the Band.

The Justice also held that the First Nation was not entitled to a declaration that the *CFSA* infringed either the *Charter* or s. 35 of the *Constitution Act, 1982*. She suggested that, in general, the provisions of the Act dealing with aboriginal children responded appropriately and sensitively to the special interests of the aboriginal community. Finally, the Justice held that there was no basis for exercising the court's *parens patriae* jurisdiction because the children's best interests dictated that they remain where they were.

(3) The Legislative Framework

The following case illustrates various elements of the *CFSA*, as well as the role of the Children's Aid Society in protecting children. Many of the specific issues raised will be examined again in the materials that follow.

CHILDREN'S AID SOCIETY OF TORONTO v. L. (E.L.)

(1999), 2 R.F.L. (5th) 78, 1999 CarswellOnt 2647 (Ont. C.J.)

JONES J.: —

1: Introduction

This is an original protection application brought by the Children's Aid Society of Toronto (hereinafter referred to as the "society") for a finding that the child B.L.L., born on 8 August 1997 is a child in need of protection pursuant to clause 37(2)(b) of the *Child and Family Services Act*, R.S.O. 1990, c. C-11 (hereinafter referred to as the "Act") and further, for an order that he be made a Crown ward without access for the purposes of adoption.

The mother, Ms. E.L.L. consents to a finding that B.L.L. is a child in need of protection pursuant to clause 37(2)(b). Further, she is prepared to consent to a Crown wardship order provided she is granted access to B.L.L.

The father, Mr. Ew.L., contests that B.L.L. is a child in need of protection. He seeks B.L.L.'s immediate return. He indicates that he is prepared to co-operate with the society on a voluntary basis, but is opposed to a supervisory order being made.

2: Narrative History and Findings of Fact

Both parents have intellectual limitations, but are residing independently in the community. They married shortly before B.L.L. was born and were intending to parent B.L.L. jointly. B.L.L. is Mr. Ew.L.'s first child. B.L.L. is Ms. E.L.L.'s second child; her first child was voluntarily placed for adoption approximately nine years ago.

B.L.L. has never been cared for by his parents; he was apprehended from the hospital on 11 August 1997. The decision to apprehend B.L.L. was made by the society after a meeting at the hospital attended by representatives from the various social agencies that had been involved with the family prior to B.L.L.'s birth. ... The decision to apprehend B.L.L. at birth was based not only on concerns arising from the intellectual limitations of the parents, but also on concerns arising from the parents' lifestyle, and living conditions as described to the society by persons who had actually met with the couple and visited their home.

2.1: Description of Mr. Ew.L. and Ms. E.L.L.'s Life Skills

Serious concerns around personal hygiene, nutrition, financial management, life style and housing were raised at the time of the apprehension. These same concerns have, more or less, continued unabated to date. This is true, notwithstanding the considerable efforts made by various agencies to assist this couple in addressing these concerns.

On the issue of life skills, I heard evidence in a number of areas. Mr. Ew.L. and Ms. E.L.L. continue to experience problems with housing. Although I was advised that they generally manage to pay their rent, they are only able to do so by sharing their accommodations with roommates who have been described as untrustworthy or abusive. The condition of their residence has been variously described as dirty, cockroach-infested and, on one occasion, as having rotting food in the refrigerator. Although the housekeeping standards have shown some improvements at various times, Mr. Ew.L. and Ms. E.L.L. have been unable to maintain these improvements. Budgeting continues to be an on-going problem for this family. For example, I was advised that periodically the phone has been disconnected and the family is frequently without money for food. Notwithstanding their limited finances, Mr. Ew.L. has managed to purchase a Sega machine with video games and has maintained his cable television subscription.

Ms. E.L.L. has experienced significant difficulty caring for herself. I heard that she required counselling on hygiene and has to be reminded to shower and to wash her hair on a regular basis. She appears to eat poorly and presents as pale and thin. In this regard, I was advised that, even when she was three months pregnant, she weighed ninety pounds. She does not eat at regular times and I was advised that she frequently comes to visits hungry. She and her husband use food banks on a regular basis and frequently access community based meal programs.

Mr. Ew.L. confirmed in his evidence that he habitually stays up to 4 a.m. or later playing video games or watching television. He indicated that he would not change this behaviour even if B.L.L. were returned as it was his belief that he would be able to stay up all day and supervise B.L.L. without any change in his habits. Mr. Ew.L. appeared to live without any routines and, although he indicated he wished to obtain regular employment, it appeared that he has not been regularly employed for many years.

2.2: Description of Mr. Ew.L. and Ms. E.L.L.'s Parenting Skills

All efforts to teach Mr. Ew.L. and Ms. E.L.L. the skills necessary to parent B.L.L. successfully have failed. With respect to Ms. E.L.L., I am satisfied that her lack of success has occurred because of her inherent intellectual limitations and was not related to her desire to learn such skills or her willingness to co-operate with her teachers. All the witnesses have described her as gentle and co-operative.

The reason for Mr. Ew.L.'s lack of success in acquiring the necessary parenting skills appears to be more complicated. Mr. Ew.L.'s intellectual limitations are not as marked as Ms. E.L.L.'s and it is possible that he might have learned these skills if his oppositional nature had not interfered with his ability to form therapeutic alliances. He appeared unable to modify his behaviour if he felt his independence or his sense of control was being challenged.

This stubbornness I see as seriously compromising his plan to care for his son. A good example of this refusal to modify his behaviour or accept new ideas arose in the context of the Thistletown parenting assessment. Mr. Ew.L. and Ms. E.L.L. spent a number of days in the intensive family therapy unit. I was advised that one of the therapists had corrected Mr. Ew.L. when he placed an opened jar of mayonnaise in the cupboard rather than in the refrigerator. After a lengthy, often heated exchange and after receiving a detailed explanation of the health risks associated with leaving an opened mayonnaise jar unrefrigerated, Mr. Ew.L. placed the jar in the refrigerator, all the time muttering loudly to himself that he would place it back into the cupboard as soon as the worker left.

Mary Rella from Thistletown Regional Centre testified that Mr. Ew.L. had great difficulty accepting suggestions from workers and often expressed anger when challenged. His low frustration level and his resistance to authority, coupled with his intellectual limitations have translated into a lack of progress in acquiring needed parenting skills.

The Thistletown Regional Centre prepared a report after Mr. Ew.L., Ms. E.L.L. and B.L.L. were assessed in the Intensive Family Therapy Unit. On separate occasions, each parent was assessed on his or her ability to be the primary care-taker for B.L.L.

Ms. E.L.L. was observed to become easily frustrated with B.L.L. She was observed to become angry with him if he did not do what she thought he should do or if she was unable to understand what the child wanted. The report noted that, at such times, she would rock him roughly and yell at him. Even when Mr. Ew.L. was present, he did not come to his wife's assistance. When asked why he did not do so, he is quoted as saying that "[Ms. E.L.L.] should try it on her own." Quickly, the assessment team concluded that Ms. E.L.L. was not capable of being the child's primary care-taker and, in fact, should not be left alone with B.L.L. Further, the team observed that Mr. Ew.L. was not a good source of support to Ms. E.L.L. in caring for B.L.L. It was noted that Ms. E.L.L. was unable to solve problems and that, unless she received hands-on assistance with B.L.L., her frustration would quickly escalate to a level of panic.

When Mr. Ew.L. was assessed on his ability to act as the primary care-taker for B.L.L., it was noted that, with some assistance and with prompting from the team to follow through with routines, he appeared able to meet the child's instrumental needs. The child was reported to respond positively to his father and Mr. Ew.L. was able to soothe B.L.L. when he was distressed. However, the assessment noted serious concerns about the general level of the father's parenting skills, his difficulty in accepting advice and in problem solving. The report concluded that B.L.L. would be at risk in Mr. Ew.L.'s care, not only because of his lack of parenting skills but, most importantly, because he did not recognise that leaving B.L.L. alone with Ms. E.L.L. posed the greatest risk to his son's safety and well-being. I was advised that, notwithstanding lengthy discussions with Mr. Ew.L. about Ms. E.L.L.'s lack of knowledge around safety issues and her behaviour with B.L.L., which placed the child at risk, he refused to acknowledge that B.L.L. should not be left alone with Ms. E.L.L. He continued to maintain that Ms. E.L.L. just needed to "try harder".

The parents have regularly attended supervised access visits. I noted that the observations made by the access supervisors as to the quality of the interaction between B.L.L. and his parents generally accorded with the opinions expressed by the assessment team at Thistletown Regional Centre.

3: Finding in Need of Protection

The society is seeking a finding under clause 37(2)(b) of the Act, which reads as follows:

> 37. (2) A child is in need of protection where, ...
>
> (b) there is a substantial risk that the child will suffer physical harm inflicted or caused as described in clause (a).

Clause (a) reads as follows:

> (a) the child has suffered physical harm inflicted by the person having charge of the child or caused
> by that person's failure to care and provide for or supervise and protect the child adequately.

On the facts I have found, there is more than sufficient evidence on which to find that there is a substantial risk that B.L.L. would suffer physical harm if placed in the care of his parents. Their lifestyle, living environment and intellectual limitations all lead to this inevitable conclusion. Accordingly, I make a finding that B.L.L. is a child in need of protection pursuant to clause 37(2)(b) of the Act.

4: Order of Disposition Request for Crown Wardship Order

The society seeks a Crown wardship order with no access for the purposes of adoption. The mother is prepared to consent to a Crown wardship order, provided she is afforded on-going access. She is opposed [to] the society's request that B.L.L. be placed for adoption, even if the foster mother is the one seeking the adoption order. She expressed the wish that B.L.L. remain in long-term foster care at the home of his current foster parents as she feels that they are taking very good care of her son.

Mr. Ew.L. seeks immediate return of B.L.L. In his plan of care presented verbally, he indicated that he plans to continue to live with Ms. E.L.L., but he would be B.L.L.'s primary caretaker. He did express the wish to obtain employment and, in that event, he indicated that he would place B.L.L. in day care. He promised not to leave B.L.L. alone with his mother. When asked how he intended to ensure that B.L.L. was not left along with his mother, he went so far as to say that, if he felt the need to go to the washroom when he was alone in the apartment with B.L.L. and Ms. E.L.L., he would control the urge until someone came to visit them. However, in cross-examination, he expressed his intention to continue to teach Ms. E.L.L. more about how to care for B.L.L. and help her to understand more about his needs. When questioned further, he reversed his position and stated that he did not feel that constant supervision of B.L.L. with Ms. E.L.L. was necessary as she was the mother and, as such, she had the right to be with the baby. His frustration with social workers coming into his home was evident when he testified that he felt that he and Ms. E.L.L. were doing a pretty good job taking care of themselves and it was not the social worker's job to talk about his habits. He said, "She's not my mother. It's rude and it's embarrassing to have a worker coming into my home."

The father's plan of care is patently unrealistic and unworkable and it is not in B.L.L.'s best interests. It is obvious to me that his parents would be unable to meet the needs of a child given the significant difficulties they are experiencing meeting their own needs. I do not see any possibility that their personal circumstances will change in the future so as to allow them to parent B.L.L.

I see no alternative but to grant the society's request for a Crown wardship order.

5: The Access Issue

5.1: Statutory Provisions

With respect to the making of an access order, a clear demarcation is made between all dispositions short of a Crown wardship order and a Crown wardship order. The Act creates a presumption against court-ordered access if an order of Crown wardship is made, no doubt to facilitate permanency planning by way of adoption as only children who are Crown wards without access orders are eligible for adoption.

Subsection 59(2) deals with the relationship between Crown wardship orders and subsequent access orders. [See now s. 59(2.1)]. ...

Subsection 58(1) of the Act mandates that all access orders be made in a child's best interests. ...

5.2: Parents Position on Access

Mr. Ew.L. and Ms. E.L.L. are vehemently opposed to adoption for B.L.L. as they wish to maintain contact with him. As I understand the argument in favour of access it rests on two grounds, namely,

> 1. In the circumstances of this case, long-term foster care with access does not limit in any way a permanent placement in a family setting as it is the society's plan to leave B.L.L. with his current foster family either as a long-term ward with access or as a candidate for adoption.
>
> 2. The recommendation of the Thistletown Regional Centre, which advocates long-term access to the parents, ... justifies the making of an order for access. ...

Counsel referred to the Thistletown Regional Centre's recommendations, which read as follows:

> 1. In the best interests of [B.L.L.], the CAS should begin to make long-term plans in seeking adoptive parents for [B.L.L.].
>
> 2. Given [E.L.'s] and [E.L.L.'s] ability to connect with supports and their motivation to follow through with recommendations of the IFTU team during this assessment period, and their stated desire to parent [B.L.L.], an ideal arrangement in addressing the needs of these parents is to co-ordinate a parenting plan between [E.L.] and [E.L.L.] and [B.L.L.'s] foster and/ or adoptive parents. This plan would require a great deal of support from all helping systems involved as well as commitment from [E.L.] and [E.L.L.] to work co-operatively with such systems and parents. This plan could include [E.L.'s] and [E.L.L.'s] having supervised access visits with [B.L.L.] as he develops.

5.3: Permanency Planning Long-Term Foster Care versus Adoption

Counsel for the mother argued that the making of an access order would not affect permanency planning in a family setting as B.L.L. would continue in the same foster home as a long-term Crown ward with access. It was noted that the foster mother had agreed to continue to care for him on a long-term foster care basis but she had expressed a desire to adopt and terminate access. Counsel argued that permanent placement in a family setting does not always refer to adoption and, in this case, long-term foster care would be as permanent as adoption. Further, he argued that there was no evidence before me that long-term foster care does, in fact, result in placements that are less permanent than adoptive homes.

At the request of counsel, I adjourned the matter to permit further evidence and submissions to be made on this point. When the trial recommenced, the society called Mr. Richard Partridge as an expert witness to give evidence on the issue of permanency planning for Crown wards. Mr. Partridge is an employee of the Ministry of Community and Social Services. Between 1993–1998, he held the position of Co-ordinator of the Crown Ward Review and the Private/ International adoption department.

Mr. Partridge brought to court a memorandum dated 25 March 1999 prepared by the Ministry from the data collected under the mandatory section 66 annual review of Crown wards that compared the Children's Aid Society of Metropolitan Toronto with the provincial average in a number of areas, including placement length, placement change, worker change, access ordered or exercised, and adoption breakdown or disruption. ...

The statistics, although not complete, are informative. In Ontario, a Crown ward can expect to change caretakers every 2.3 years. Further, he or she can expect to be assigned a new social worker every two years. These statistics would suggest that, the younger a child is at the time he or she becomes a Crown ward, the more likely he or she is to experience multiple placements and several primary workers.

From his experience as co-ordinator of the Crown ward review department and previously, from his role as Children's Services Co-ordinator, Mr. Partridge outlined some of the reasons why placement changes in foster care might occur. He prefaced his remarks by saying that foster parents are generally a very dedicated, hard-working group. However, he noted that foster parenting is a job, and as in other occupations, people retire, transfer out of the area, leave for health reasons or quit to take up other employment opportunities. He observed that fostering is a difficult job emotionally and some people simply suffer burn out. In the case of foster parents, he indicated that marital separation and divorce might impact on fostering. Other times, Crown wards are moved to other settings in order better to meet their special needs or because the foster parents are unable to manage the ward's disruptive behaviour.

He compared foster parenting to parenthood. He noted that, unlike fostering, parenting is a life-long commitment. People and families make provision for their children regardless of life's changes. He noted that, in his experience as Co-ordinator of Private/ International Adoptions, there are few adoption breakdowns when children are placed at an early age. Adoption breakdowns, in his experience, occur more frequently when older or "special needs" children are involved in an adoption.

No contradictory evidence was called by the parents. On the evidence, I am satisfied that an adoption is most likely to result in a permanent placement in a family setting for an infant or young child.

5.4: Special Circumstances Justifying Access

[At the time of this decision, s. 59(2) stipulated that a court could only make an access order relating to a Crown ward if one of four paragraphs applied. One of these, paragraph (d), provided for an access order where "some other special circumstance justifies making an order of access".]

It was argued that the Thistletown assessment report and its recommendation for access with or without adoption constitutes some other special circumstances justifying an access order within the meaning of clause 59(2)(d). As I am persuaded that any access order I make must be in B.L.L.'s best interest in accordance with subsection 58(1) of the Act, I have assessed the proposed access not from the parents' perspective but from the child's perspective. The recommendation by Thistletown for continued access is not particularly helpful to me as I am persuaded that this recommendation for access focuses on the best interests of Mr. Ew.L. and Ms. E.L.L.; the very wording of the recommendation makes no mention of the effect that such access might have on B.L.L. or on his caretakers, but rather speaks to the parents wishes, the parents' efforts and the parents' needs to parent B.L.L.

In evaluating the effect that continued access to his parents might have on B.L.L. and his best interests, I have identified the following questions as relevant to such a determination.

1. What is the society's long-range plan for this Crown ward?
2. Does this plan satisfy the need for permanency planning in light of the child's age?
3. What effect has the current access regime had on the child?
4. What effect would a termination of access have on the child?
5. Would continued access to the biological parents support or undermine the child's placement?

After reviewing the evidence, I have answered the questions in the following way:

1. The long-term plan proffered by the society contemplates that B.L.L. will be adopted by his current foster parents. An access order would preclude the foster family from adopting B.L.L. B.L.L. has been with this family since he was four days old and, by all accounts, sees this family as his psychological family. The foster parents have been described as experienced, competent parents who are prepared to make a life-long commitment to B.L.L., notwithstanding the fact that B.L.L. may be a "special needs" child who is already showing signs of language delay.

2. An adoption will afford B.L.L. his best chance of being raised to his majority in one home with one set of parents.

3. Although B.L.L.'s biological parents love him and he enjoys visits, B.L.L.'s primary attachment is to his foster family.

4. B.L.L. is young enough that, if his access to his biological parents is terminated, he will not remember them. ...

6. I do not believe that Mr. Ew.L. would be able to accept a secondary role in parenting and I am concerned that, over time, he would undermine the relationship between B.L.L. and his current foster family, which might well lead to a breakdown in place-ment. B.L.L.'s foster mother has indicated her desire to have access terminated be-cause she feared access might prove too disruptive to B.L.L. and to her family.

From this analysis, the answer is clear; continuing contact with his parents is not in B.L.L.'s best interests.

6: Conclusion

In all the circumstances, I find that the least intrusive order I can make consistent with the best interests of B.L.L. is an order for Crown wardship no access for the purpose of adoption, and I so order.

---

(4) Protection Issues and Unborn Children

The *L. (E.L.)* case involved an apprehension of a child at birth. However, child protec-tion agencies and others are sometimes concerned about the effect that a mother's conduct during pregnancy has on the health of her unborn child. Consumption of alcohol or other drugs is especially disconcerting as it can have serious consequences for the health of a child. In a number of cases, child protection agencies have attempted to control the mother's behaviour. The legal question that then arises is whether an unborn child can ever be consid-ered a "child in need of protection" under the relevant legislation or whether the court can authorize the agencies' intervention on some other basis.

This issue was canvassed in *Children's Aid Society of Kenora (District) v. L. (J.)* (1981), 134 D.L.R. (3d) 249 (Ont. Prov. Ct.) where a child was born suffering from fetal-alcohol syndrome and was apprehended four days after birth. The doctor who had diagnosed the pregnancy at about 19 weeks contacted the local Children's Aid Society at that stage expres-sing concerns about the health of the fetus. However, the society refused to act, believing it lacked jurisdiction until after the birth of the child. Judge Bradley suggested in *obiter dicta* that the child had been in need of protection prior to birth. In *Children's Aid Society of*

Belleville (City) v. T. (L.) (No. 2) (1987), 7 R.F.L. (3d) 191 (Ont. Fam. Ct.), Kirkland Prov. J. too held that an unborn child could be a child in need of protection. However, the courts in *Re Baby R.* (1988), 15 R.F.L. (3d) 225 (B.C. S.C.) and *Re A.* (1990), 28 R.F.L. (3d) 288 (Ont. U.F.C.) held that they had no jurisdiction under the relevant child protection legislation to require mothers to obtain proper prenatal care and proper medical care on delivery.

Although not dealing directly with the statutory definition of "child in need of protection", the Supreme Court of Canada's decision in *Winnipeg Child & Family Services (Northwest Area) v. G. (D.F.)* (1997), 31 R.F.L. (4th) 165 appears to settle the issue in the absence of specific legislation authorizing action prior to birth. The Winnipeg Child and Family Services applied for an order requiring a pregnant woman to stay in a place of safety and refrain from the use of intoxicants during her pregnancy. Two of the woman's three previous children had been severely harmed before they were born due to their mother's glue sniffing. All three were made permanent wards of the state as a result of her chronic addiction. Initially, the order sought by the agency regarding the unborn child was granted, but it was stayed two days later and reversed by the Manitoba Court of Appeal. Notwithstanding the staying of the order, the mother remained voluntarily in hospital for treatment. The agency appealed further. In the meantime, the mother delivered a healthy child.

Although the case was now moot, the Supreme Court of Canada decided (at 173) to continue with the appeal because "[w]hile the problem that gave rise to these proceedings has been resolved, the legal issues it raised have not". In delivering the majority judgment, McLachlin J. identified two legal issues (at 201):

> (1) Does tort law, as it exists or may properly be extended by the Court, permit an order detaining a pregnant woman against her will in order to protect her unborn child from conduct that may harm the child?
>
> (2) Alternatively, does the power of a court to make orders for the protection of children (its *parens patriae* jurisdiction), as it exists or may properly be extended by the Court, permit an order detaining a pregnant woman against her will in order to protect her unborn child from conduct that may harm the child?

The majority held that neither tort law nor the inherent *parens patriae* jurisdiction permitted an order detaining the woman for treatment against her wishes. While she recognized that a child born alive could bring a tort action for injuries sustained while *in utero*, Justice McLachlin ruled that the common law did not recognize the unborn child as a legal or juridical person. Similarly, the majority declined to extend the courts' *parens patriae* jurisdiction to the protection of the unborn. To do so would "require a major change to the law of *parens patriae*. The ramifications of the change would be significant and complex [and involve] conflicts of fundamental rights and interests and different policy issues" (at 187). In particular, "to make orders protecting foetuses would radically impinge on the fundamental liberties of the pregnant woman, both as to lifestyle choices and how and as to where she chooses to live and be" (at 190). Justice McLachlin concluded (at 190): "If anything is to be done, the legislature is in a much better position to weigh the competing interests and arrive at a solution that is principled and minimally intrusive to pregnant women."

In his dissent, Justice Major (Sopinka J. concurring) emphasized the risk to the unborn child if its mother was not compelled to refrain from continuing her addictive habits. He characterized (at 198-99) the *parens patriae* jurisdiction as one of "undefined and undefinable breadth ... [that] resides in the provincial superior courts to act on behalf of those who cannot act to protect themselves." He concluded (at 199-200):

> [A] superior court, on a proper motion should be able to exercise its *parens patriae* jurisdiction to restrain a mother's conduct when there is a reasonable probability of that conduct causing serious and irreparable harm to the foetus within her. While the granting of this type of remedy may interfere with the mother's liberty interests, in my view, those interests must bend when faced with a situation where devastating harm and a life of suffering can so easily be prevented. In any event, this interference is always subject to the mother's right to end it by deciding to have an abortion. ...

Once the mother decides to bear the child, the state has an interest in trying to ensure the child's health. What circumstances permit state intervention? The 'slippery slope' was raised. ... Questions were raised about women who smoked, who lived with a smoker, who ate unhealthy diets, etc. In response to the query of where a reasonable line can be drawn it is submitted that the pen should not even be lifted. This approach would entail the state to stand idly by while a reckless and/ or addicted mother inflicts serious and permanent harm on a child she had decided to bring into the world.

There can be no general formula and each case must be decided on its own facts. However, as a minimum to justify intervention the following thresholds have to be met:

(1)   The woman must have decided to carry the child to term.

(2)   Proof must be presented to a civil standard that the abusive activity will cause serious and irreparable harm to the foetus.

(3)   The remedy must be the least intrusive option.

(4)   The process must be procedurally fair.

Only the New Brunswick child protection legislation specifically refers to the "unborn child" in its definition of "child" for protection purposes. See *Family Services Act*, S.N.B. 1980, c. F-2.2, s. 1 "child" (a). However, there are no specific provisions that indicate how the child protection law is to apply to the unborn. In *New Brunswick (Minister of Health & Community Services) v. Hickey* (1996), [1996] N.B.J. No. 660, (sub nom. *New Brunswick (Minister of Health & Community Services) v. N.H.)* 224 N.B.R. (2d) 80, the New Brunswick Court of Queen's Bench held that this legislative scheme could not be invoked to make a "supervision order" to protect an unborn child because it violated the constitutional rights of pregnant women. The case involved a 22-year-old woman who was pregnant with her third child. She had consumed drugs and alcohol during her first two pregnancies and both of these children had been permanently removed from her care. The child protection agency, with the support of the "potential father" and some professionals who had been working with the woman, sought a supervision order to require the woman to have mental health care and to follow the directives of the medical staff in regard to the delivery. The court recognized that there was some risk for the child in the situation. However, it held that, in the absence of specific legislative provisions authorizing such an order and stipulating how the rights of a pregnant woman were to be balanced along with the concerns relating to the unborn child, the New Brunswick legislation conflicted with s. 7 of the *Canadian Charter of Rights and Freedoms*.

NOTES AND QUESTIONS

1. In Canada, there is currently no legal obstacle to access to an abortion. Does a pregnant woman's right to abort her fetus necessarily carry with it a right to intentionally or recklessly inflict harm upon it? Would recognition of any degree of legal personality of the unborn necessarily and logically circumscribe the legal right to an abortion? Was the majority in the *Winnipeg Child and Family Services (Northwest Area)* case influenced by this concern? How did Major J. handle this point? Is his answer logical and convincing?

2. While the Yukon's *Children's Act*, R.S.Y. 2002, c. 31, does not expressly include the unborn child within the definition of child in need of protection, s. 135 does authorize the Director of Child Welfare to apply for a supervision order where a pregnant woman uses addictive or intoxicating substances that might endanger her fetus. The Yukon Territory Supreme Court suggested in *Joe v. Yukon (Director of Family & Children's Services)* (1986), 5 B.C.L.R. (2d) 267, that this provision violated s. 7 of the *Canadian Charter of Rights and Freedoms*. However, the comments were *obiter dicta* as the mother's appeal was dismissed for mootness since she had completed her obligations under the appealed order.

3. In *The Fatality Inquiries Act Report by Provincial Judge on Inquest Respecting the Death of Patrick Norman Redhead*, released on January 16, 2003 (available online at <www.manitobacourts.mb.ca> under the heading "Notices of Inquest Reports"), Judge Giesbrecht recommended that the Government of Manitoba consider "appro-

priate, constitutional legislation to protect fetuses from the effects of substance abuse". She was conducting an inquest into the suicide of a 15-year-old boy. The report contains much information about fetal alcohol syndrome and fetal alcohol effects. See also Driver, "Judge recommends legislation to protect fetuses from effects of mother's substance abuse" *The Lawyers Weekly*, Vol. 22, No. 40, February 28, 2003.

4. If the law does not authorize intervention prior to birth, what other action might child protection agencies or health care professionals take if they are concerned about the conduct of a pregnant woman?

5. The Supreme Court of Canada has consistently denied any legal personality to the unborn child. In addition to the *Winnipeg Child and Family Services* case, see *R. v. Morgentaler*, [1988] 1 S.C.R. 30 (striking down *Criminal Code* restrictions on abortion); *Borowski v. Canada (Attorney General)*, [1989] 1 S.C.R. 342 (declining to determine whether unborn child had a right to life under s. 7 of *Charter*); *Tremblay v. Daigle*, [1989] 2 S.C.R. 530 (ruling that unborn child was not a "human being" for purpose of right to life under the Quebec *Charter of human rights and freedoms* and holding that courts had no jurisdiction under that *Charter*, the *Civil Code of Quebec*, or the common law to issue injunctions to prevent abortions in individual cases); *R. v. Sullivan*, [1991] 1 S.C.R. 489 (baby boy killed during birthing process not a "person" for the *Criminal Code* offence of causing death by criminal negligence); and *Dobson (Litigation Guardian of) v. Dobson* (1999), 174 D.L.R. (4th) 1 (S.C.C.) (born-alive child could not bring civil suit for pre-natal injuries caused by mother's negligent driving). For commentary, see McCourt, "Foetus Status After *R. v. Sullivan and Lemay*" (1991), 29 Alta. L. Rev. 916 and McCourt, "Fetus Status and Supreme Injustice: *Dobson v. Dobson*" (1999-2000), 17 C.F.L.Q. 175.

6. For commentary on the Supreme Court of Canada's decision in *Winnipeg Child & Family Services (Northwest Area) v. G. (D.F.)*, see Martin, "Case Comment: *Winnipeg Child and Family Services (Northwest Area) v. G.(D.F.)*" (1998), 32 R.F.L. (4th) 381; Bartlett, "A Comment on *Winnipeg Child and Family Services (Northwest Area) v. G. (D.F.)*" (1997), 31 U.B.C. Law Rev. 179; Rodgers, "*Winnipeg Child and Family Services v. D.G.F.*: Juridical Interference with Pregnant Women in the Alleged Interest of the Fetus" (1998), 36 Alta Law Rev. 711; DeCoste, "*Winnipeg Child and Family Services (Northwest Area) v. D.F.G.*" (1998), 36 Alta. L. Rev. 725; Shanner, "Pregnancy Intervention and Models of Maternal-Fetal Relationship: Philosophical Reflections on the *Winnipeg CFS* Dissent" (1998), 39 Alta. L. Rev. 751; Elman and Mason, "The Failure of Dialogue: *Winnipeg Child and Family Services (Northwest Area) v. G. (D.F.)*" (1998), 36 Alta. L. Rev. 768; and McCormack, "Fetal Syndromes and the Charter: The Winnipeg Glue Sniffing Case" (1999), 14 Can. J. Law & Society 77.

2. Child Welfare Agency's Initial Involvement

WINNIPEG CHILD & FAMILY SERVICES (CENTRAL AREA)
v. W. (K.L.)

(2000), 10 R.F.L. (5th) 122, 2000 CarswellMan 469, 2000 CarswellMan 470 (S.C.C.)

[A mother was unable to care properly for her two children, primarily due to her alcoholism. She voluntarily became a client of a child protection agency. Although there was no evidence that she or her various partners ever physically assaulted the children, the agency apprehended the children on several occasions. Early in 1996, the agency began proceedings for an order for permanent guardianship of the children. In July of that year, the mother informed the agency that she was expecting a third child. The agency made arrangements for the mother to move into a residential facility designed to assist pregnant women and young mothers with parenting, life-skills and personal problems. The mother refused to move, fearing the loss of her apartment.

Approximately two weeks before the expected date of delivery, the mother changed her mind and agreed to enter the facility. However, the child was born the next day, Thursday, October 24. The agency apprehended the child on Friday, October 25, by instructing the hospital not to discharge the mother with the child. The mother and child remained in the hospital for the weekend. On the following Monday, October 28, the agency concluded that the mother could not stay safely at the residential facility. It had learned of the mother's continuing relationship with the baby's father who had been convicted of assaulting her. The child was discharged from the hospital and placed in a foster home.

The agency's action was taken pursuant to s. 21(1) in Part III of *The Child and Family Services Act*, S.M. 1985-86, c. 8, which authorized a representative of a child protection agency to apprehend a child without a warrant if he or she believed on reasonable and probable grounds that the child was in need of protection. By way of contrast, a prior warrant obtained under s. 21(3) of the Act was generally required for forced entry into a building to apprehend a child believed to be in need of protection. However, such entry could occur without a warrant under s. 21(2) where the agency's representative believed on reasonable and probable grounds that the child was in immediate danger or that a vulnerable child had been left without a responsible caregiver.

Also on October 28, the mother began collateral proceedings seeking the return of the child, a declaration that Part III of the Act was unconstitutional, and damages under s. 24(1) of the *Canadian Charter of Rights and Freedoms* for an infringement of her rights under s. 7. The mother's interlocutory claims for return of the child failed and her lawsuit was eventually consolidated with the agency's child protection proceedings with respect to the three children.

The child protection hearing began on April 21, 1997. The trial judge dismissed the mother's constitutional challenge and ordered that the agency be appointed permanent guardian of the three children. The Manitoba Court of Appeal dismissed the mother's appeal of both decisions. The mother then exercised her right under the statute to apply to the Manitoba Court of Queen's Bench for an order terminating the previous orders of permanent guardianship. In April 1999, this court found that the mother had made significant improvements to her life and ordered that the youngest child be returned to her. The agency continued as permanent guardian of the two older children.

The Supreme Court of Canada granted the mother leave to appeal the Manitoba Court of Appeal's ruling on the constitutional validity of the legislation. The mother argued that a child protection agency's apprehension of a child triggered the application of s. 7 of the *Charter* because it affected a parent's liberty and security of the person and that the principles of fundamental justice dictated that such an apprehension without a warrant could only occur in emergencies.

The Supreme Court of Canada, Arbour J. and McLachlin C.J.C. dissenting, dismissed her appeal. Justice L'Heureux-Dubé, for the majority, concluded that s. 21(1) of the Act affected security of the person. While apprehension was an interim measure, the Justice reasoned that the removal of a child from parental care was one of the most disruptive forms of intervention undertaken to protect children. It could lead to a relatively lengthy separation of parents and children where the child was in a child protection agency's care pending the disposition of the child protection hearing and the hearing was delayed for any reason. Justice L'Heureux-Dubé concluded that any forced separation of parent and child affected a parent's security of the person as it could give rise to great emotional and psychological distress and constituted a serious intrusion into the family sphere. Accordingly, this impairment of a parent's right to security of the person had to accord with the principles of fundamental justice. Justice L'Heureux-Dubé concluded that the Manitoba legislation met this requirement. She reasoned as follows:]

C. Prior Judicial Authorization of Apprehension and the Principles of Fundamental Justice

88 ... I now turn to the question squarely raised in this appeal: do the principles of fundamental justice applicable in the child protection context require prior judicial authorization of apprehensions in "non-emergency" situations?

89 The appellant [mother] concedes that in "emergency" situations, the principles of fundamental justice dictate that a hearing occur subsequent to the child's removal. This concession is clearly based on the recognition that in cases of imminent danger, the child's right to life and health, and the state's duty to intervene to protect that right, are so compelling as to justify *post facto* assessment of state action. ... For this reason, no provincial or territorial child protection legislation requires any form of notice or prior judicial authorization of apprehension in "emergency" situations.

90 Accordingly, we are dealing in this appeal only with what the appellant has termed "nonemergency" child protection situations. The appellant submits that there must be notice to the parents and an *inter partes* hearing prior to a "non-emergency" apprehension. In the alternative, she submits that prior *ex parte* authorization is required with respect to "nonemergency" apprehensions. The respondent agency and provincial interveners submit, for their part, that a prompt post-apprehension protection hearing may conform to the principles of fundamental justice in a broader range of child protection situations than emergencies alone. ...

93 It remains, therefore, for this Court to determine what the principles of fundamental justice require with respect to the threshold for apprehension without prior judicial authorization. In doing so, it is necessary to balance the following factors: (1) the seriousness of the interests at stake; (2) the difficulties associated with distinguishing emergency from nonemergency child protection situations; and (3) an assessment of the risks to children associated with adopting an "emergency" threshold, as opposed to the benefits of prior judicial authorization.

(1) Interests at Stake

94 ... [T]he interests at stake in cases of apprehension are of the highest order, given the impact that state action involving the separation of parents and children may have on all of their lives, and particularly on their psychological and emotional well-being. From the child's perspective, state action in the form of apprehension seeks to ensure the protection, and indeed the very survival, of another interest of fundamental importance: the child's life and health. Given that children are highly vulnerable members of our society, and given society's interest in protecting them from harm, fair process in the child protection context must reflect the fact that children's lives and health may need to be given priority where the protection of these interests diverges from the protection of parents' rights to freedom from state intervention. ...

98 To summarize, the interests at stake in the child protection context dictate a somewhat different balancing analysis from that undertaken with respect to the accused's s. 7 and s. 8 rights in the criminal context. Moreover, the state's protective purpose in apprehending a child is clearly distinguishable from the state's punitive purpose in the criminal context, namely that of seeing that justice is done with respect to a criminal act. These distinctions should make courts reluctant to import procedural protections developed in the criminal context into the child protection context. ...

(2) Emergency vs. Non-Emergency Distinction in the Child Protection Context

99 There are a number of factors specific to the child protection context that must be considered in determining the appropriate threshold for apprehension without prior judicial authorization. These factors include: the evidentiary difficulties and time pressures associated with child protection situations; and the need for preventive as well as protective state intervention with respect to children. The factors point to several difficulties associated with establishing an "emergency" threshold for the apprehension of a child. I emphasize that these

difficulties are related primarily to the effective protection of children's lives and health, rather than to considerations of administrative convenience.

100 The evidentiary difficulties particular to the child protection context arise out of the fact that child protection authorities are almost always concerned with situations taking place within the intimacy of private homes. ...

... [C]hild protection workers are inevitably called upon to make highly time-sensitive decisions in situations in which it is often difficult, if not impossible, to determine whether a child is at risk of imminent harm, or at risk of non-imminent but serious harm, while the child remains in the parents' care. ...

101 My colleague Madam Justice Arbour writes at para. 38 that:

> even if we only focus on the four or five days of intense decision-making around the time of the infant's birth, there was ample time for the respondent to seek a prior judicial authorization of the apprehension, with no risk to the infant, who during this time was in hospital where he and his mother were under medical supervision.

I disagree with this characterization. In my view, this case illustrates very well how time-sensitive apprehension decisions can be. Far from having four or five days to decide, the agency had to act on Friday October 25, 1996 after the baby's birth the night before. If the apprehension had not been accomplished immediately, the mother would have been free to leave the hospital with the baby. The reason the social worker needed to intervene so quickly was because the appellant "had a history of drug and alcohol abuse. We weren't sure exactly how long it had been since she had been sober". In preparing for the apprehension, the agency could not have anticipated that the child would be born two weeks ahead of its due date. The agency's attempt to place the appellant into a residential facility immediately upon her October 23, 1996 request, two months after her refusal to go, shows that the agency used apprehension as a last resort. Only after the birth of her child and the resulting impossibility of the appellant's staying safely at the residential facility — because of minimal supervision and the threat posed by her abusive partner — did the agency finally decide to apprehend. At this stage immediate action was imperative since the appellant's discharge from the hospital could have taken place at any moment, subject only to her own volition. Even if counsel's estimate at oral argument that it would take 20 hours to prepare affidavits for an *ex parte* warrant application is high, the time pressures of that Friday would have caused the type of *ex parte* proceeding proposed by Madam Justice Arbour to impose a risk of serious harm on the baby.

102 Aside from evidentiary difficulties and time pressures, it is also important to recognize that the state must be able to take preventive action to protect children. ... This means that the state should not always be required to wait until a child has been seriously harmed before being allowed to intervene. Requiring prior judicial authorization in "non-emergency" situations, assuming that they can be distinguished, may impede pro-active intervention by placing the burden on the state to justify intervention in situations of arguably "non-imminent", yet serious, danger to the child.

103 Some of the difficulties associated with the emergency standard are illustrated by s. 17(2)(a) of the Manitoba *Child and Family Services Act*, which defines "child in need of protection" to include situations in which a child is "without adequate care, supervision or control". While this term is broad, it contemplates situations of serious risk of harm to children, including, for example, those in which they are found alone in the street without anyone to care for them, or in which they are with adults who are unable to provide adequate care because they are intoxicated. Given the state's duty to protect a child at risk of serious harm, as well as the child's compelling interest in being so protected, immediate apprehen-

sion may be appropriate in such circumstances, even though there might be some dispute as to whether the danger of harm is "imminent".

104 All of these factors point to serious harm or risk of serious harm as an appropriate threshold for apprehension without prior judicial authorization. I recognize that with respect to prior *ex parte* authorization, several child protection statutes in Canada distinguish between situations of "imminent danger", sometimes also expressed in terms of situations in which "substantial risk" would be posed to the child if prior judicial authorization were sought, and other child protection situations: see, e.g., Alberta *Child Welfare Act*, S.A. 1984, c. C-8.1, s. 17(9); Ontario *Child and Family Services Act*, R.S.O. 1990, c. C.11, s. 40(7). The Manitoba Act itself makes a similar distinction in s. 21(2), with respect to entry into premises to search for a child in situations of "immediate danger". Section 21(2) goes on to include situations in which "a child who is unable to look after and care for himself or herself has been left without any responsible person to care for him or her". No statute defines the term "emergency", however, and many statutes qualify the notion of immediate danger by adding words to the effect that "no other less disruptive measure that is available is adequate to protect the child": see *Child, Family and Community Service Act*, R.S.B.C. 1996, c. 46, s. 30; *Children and Family Services Act*, S.N.S. 1990, c. 5, s. 33; *The Child and Family Services Act*, S.S. 1989-90, c. C-7.2, s. 17.

105 In addition to these considerations, a recent report by a panel of experts in Ontario acknowledges that practices among Ontario agencies and courts diverge significantly as to when a warrant is sought and granted prior to apprehension. According to the panel, "[t]he process required to obtain a warrant in some jurisdictions can lead to unnecessary delay in early decisive intervention." [Ontario Panel of Experts on Child Protection, *Protecting Vulnerable Children* (1998) at p. 40.] Consequently, the panel recommended "that the requirement to obtain a warrant to apprehend a child be eliminated": Ontario Panel Report, *supra*, at p. 41. ...

106 The legislative practice in other provinces and territories is neither consistent nor determinative. In my view, however, it tends to confirm the conclusion that adopting an "emergency" threshold as the constitutional minimum for apprehension without prior judicial authorization risks allowing significant danger to children's lives and health. ...

(3) Assessment of the Risks and Benefits of an "Emergency" Threshold

107 My conclusion regarding the inappropriateness of an "emergency" threshold for apprehension without prior judicial authorization is further supported by an assessment of the risks to children associated with adopting an "emergency" threshold, as opposed to the benefits of prior judicial authorization. Section 7 requires this balancing in the child protection context, given that the protection of the child as a vulnerable human being is a basic tenet of our legal system that must be weighed against the requirements of procedural fairness. ...

108 Child protection authorities may err, of course, in their assessment of whether a child is in need of protection through apprehension, and they may intervene unnecessarily. If court supervision occurs post-apprehension, this risk of a wrongful infringement of rights lies with both parents and children. They may be subjected to the trauma of separation and unjustified state interference in their family lives. This may have a significant impact on both the parents' and the child's emotional well-being. It also affects their underlying dignity and privacy interests.

109 In contrast, if this Court were to find that prior judicial authorization of apprehension is required in so-called "non-emergency" situations, the risk inherent in the process of obtaining such authorization would fall primarily on the child. This risk can result from delays related to the need to gather proof of reasonable and probable grounds that the child is in

need of protection, whether in the form of an affidavit or of testimony and documentary evidence. While the delays associated with prior *ex parte* authorization are not as significant as those associated with a prior hearing, they would still leave children at risk of serious, or even life-threatening, harm for at least a number of hours, or even days. A child should never be placed in such jeopardy.

110 Moreover, a requirement to obtain prior judicial authorization in such situations will tend to divert the resources of the child protection authorities away from their duty to protect children at risk of serious harm, toward the process of obtaining prior judicial determinations of whether a child is in need of protection or not: see Manitoba, *Report of the Child and Family Services Act Review Committee on the Community Consultation Process* (1997), at p. 15.

111 It is also clear that a wrongful apprehension does not give rise to the same risk of serious, and potentially even fatal, harm to a child, as would an inability on the part of the state to intervene promptly when a child is at risk of serious harm.

112 These risks must be weighed against the benefits associated with prior judicial authorization of apprehension in terms of procedural fairness. Prior notice and a hearing would provide parents and children with significant protection against wrongful apprehensions, as they would be able to present their arguments and evidence to the court as to why a child is not in need of protection. In my view, however, even in situations of non-imminent danger, the risks posed to the child's life and health by the delays associated with a prior hearing, compounded by the evidentiary difficulties outlined above, more than outweigh the benefits of a hearing. The risks render prior notice and a hearing unfeasible with respect to apprehension in the child protection context.

113 In *ex parte* proceedings, the court relies on affidavit evidence prepared by a child protection worker in determining whether a child should be apprehended. While a review of this information by the court will provide some protection against unjustified apprehensions, courts will tend to defer to the agency's assessment of the situation given the highly particularized nature of child protection proceedings and the highly compelling purpose for state action in this context. This deference will be all the more warranted when the child protection worker's assessment has already been subject to an internal review process within the agency. Thus, an *ex parte* authorization requirement provides only a limited enhancement of the fairness of the apprehension process. Neither the parents nor the child have any input into the decision. The appellant herself concedes this point to some extent, since her principal argument is that the principles of fundamental justice require notice and a hearing prior to apprehension, rather than an *ex parte* authorization.

114 Madam Justice Arbour believes that s. 7 does require an *ex parte* warrant procedure in this type of case. She writes at para. 24 that "any concerns that the judge may have about the appropriateness of the initiative may result in *further information being requested*" (emphasis added). This comment points to the acute risk of delay that requiring a prior *ex parte* warrant would occasion. To meet the evidentiary threshold for a warrant, agency workers would have to assume a third role in addition to the two identified by Madam Justice Arbour (para. 23). They would not only have to make the difficult, *but only interim*, decisions of "whether a child is in need of protection" and "whether or not the need for protection has risen to the level where the child must be removed from his or her parent's care", but they would also have to weigh time pressures against the need to provide enough information to the judge to avoid judicial delays. The full 79 paragraphs of the appellant's case history submitted by the respondent agency to this Court may not all be needed for a judge to grant an *ex parte* warrant. Yet agency workers could not, in good conscience, save precious time by submitting only a small fraction of this information to the judge and thereby inadver-

tently put a child at risk of serious harm through judicial delay. Requiring an *ex parte* proceeding creates a double bind: the more time the agency spends on its affidavits, the greater the risk to the child. The less time the agency spends on them, the greater the risk that the judge will require "further information". Again, the child unacceptably bears the increased risk.

115 Madam Justice Arbour adds at para. 41 that: "An *ex parte* application to an independent and impartial judicial officer would provide *some assurance* to families experiencing a dramatic disruption to their lives at the hands of the state, that this disruption is being conducted in a manner that is procedurally fair and constitutionally sound" (emphasis added). Although Madam Justice Arbour argues at para. 17 on behalf of the *nemo debet esse judex in propria causa* principle (no one ought to be a judge in his or her own cause), she does not consider how minimal the assurance would be for families denied the opportunity to be heard in the *ex parte* proceeding. In the *ex parte* procedure, another fundamental principle, *audi alteram partem* (hear the other side), cannot, by definition, be respected. ...

116 I acknowledge that there may be valid policy justifications for requiring prior *ex parte* authorization for apprehensions in so-called "non-emergency" child protection situations. I find for the purposes of the s. 7 constitutional analysis, however, that the procedural protections against state interference provided by prior *ex parte* authorization do not enhance the fairness of the apprehension process sufficiently to outweigh the countervailing interests of, and potential risks to, a child who may be in need of the state's protection. Rather, the balancing of risks and benefits suggests that while the trauma of an unjustified separation of parent and child cannot be fully redressed by a post-apprehension hearing, the infringement will be adequately reduced when the hearing is both prompt and fair. Pending the hearing, the child will be in a safe environment, thereby minimizing the risk of harm. At the hearing, the court will determine, based on a more complete record and in an adversarial forum, whether the child is in need of protection and in need of some form of state supervision or guardianship, or whether the child should be returned to the parents' care.

(4) Conclusions on Prior Judicial Authorization and Application to the Impugned Provisions

117 Apprehension should be used only as a measure of last resort where no less disruptive means are available. For the reasons set out above, I find that the appropriate minimum s. 7 threshold for apprehension without prior judicial authorization is not the "emergency" threshold. Rather the constitutional standard may be expressed as follows: where a statute provides that apprehension may occur without prior judicial authorization in situations of serious harm or risk of serious harm to the child, the statute will not necessarily offend the principles of fundamental justice. Determining whether a specific statute establishes such a minimum threshold will require an examination of the relevant provisions in their legislative context. ...

118 I come now to the impugned s. 21(1) of the Act, which establishes (as it established at the time of the apprehension of the appellant's child, John) that apprehension must be based on "reasonable and probable grounds" for believing "that a child is in need of protection". ...

119 The definition of "child in need of protection" found in s. 17 clearly encompasses situations that do not involve imminent danger to the child, including those in which the child is "without adequate care, supervision or control". I do not find, however, that the statutory definition is vague or overbroad. The definition of "child in need of protection" uses clear terms, and is limited to situations involving a risk of harm to a child's life, health or emotional well-being. ...

121 When read as a whole, ... the Act provides for apprehension as a measure of last resort in cases where child protection authorities have reasonable and probable grounds to believe that the child is at risk of serious harm. Given the above conclusions, the fact that the impugned s. 21(1) does not establish an "emergency" threshold for apprehension without prior judicial authorization does not offend the principles of fundamental justice, subject to the conclusions below regarding the need for a fair and prompt post-apprehension hearing.

D. Post-Apprehension Hearing and the Principles of Fundamental Justice

122 While the infringement of a parent's right to security of the person caused by the interim removal of his or her child through apprehension in situations of harm or risk of serious harm to the child does not require prior judicial authorization for the reasons outlined above, the seriousness of the interests at stake demands that the resulting disruption of the parent-child relationship be minimized as much as possible by a fair and prompt post-apprehension hearing.

123 In order to be fair, the hearing must involve reasonable notice with particulars to the parents, as well as an opportunity for them to participate meaningfully in the proceedings

124 The child's need for continuity in relationships provides the most compelling basis for requiring a prompt post-apprehension hearing. ...

125 While a two-week delay between the removal of a child and, at a minimum, an interim child protection hearing, would seem to lie at the outside limit of what is constitutionally acceptable, it does not seem advisable in this case to state a precise constitutional standard for delays in the child protection context. ...

E. Conclusions on the Constitutional Validity of the Act

131 The apprehension of children constitutes a significant state intrusion into the family. Less disruptive means of dealing with parenting issues are to be preferred as a matter of policy whenever possible. As set out above, however, provided that the threshold for apprehension is, at a minimum, that of a risk of serious harm to the child, the need for swift and preventive state action to protect a child's life or health in such situations dictates that a fair and prompt post-apprehension hearing is the minimum procedural protection mandated by the principles of fundamental justice in the child protection context.

[Justice L'Heureux-Dubé concluded that the Manitoba statute did provide for a fair and prompt post-apprehension hearing. She also found that the mother was not entitled to an individual remedy against the agency.

In dissent, Justice Arbour, McLachlin C. J. concurring, found that the apprehension of the mother's child without a warrant infringed her right to security of the person and was not carried out in accordance with the principles of fundamental justice. She believed that s. 7 of the *Charter* mandated prior judicial authorization for non-emergency apprehensions of children to protect both parents and children from unreasonable state interference. In her view, it was possible to distinguish between emergencies and non-emergencies in the child protection context and to provide for measures that would obviate the risks to children associated with obtaining prior judicial authorization in non-exigent circumstances. She noted that the Manitoba legislation already employed such a distinction in relation to forced entry into a building. She also noted that the legislation in many provinces, including Ontario, required a warrant, most often available on an *ex parte* basis, to apprehend a child in non-emergency situations.

Justice Arbour stated that requiring a child protection agency to obtain a judicial warrant before it could apprehend a child in non-emergencies provided an important procedural safeguard, even if the warrant were available on an *ex parte* basis. It ensured that child protection agencies acted on reasonable and probable grounds that they could articulate and that apprehension remained a measure of last resort.]

NOTES AND QUESTIONS

1. For a critical assessment of the Supreme Court of Canada's decision, see Thompson, "Case Comment: *Winnipeg Child & Family Services (Central Area) v. W. (K.L.)*" (2001), 10 R.F.L. (5th) 221.

2. An agency may provide support services in the home on a voluntary basis. Most protection workers will have some cases where the family has either voluntarily approached the agency for help or agreed to co-operate after the agency began an investigation. In "Initial Involvement: Reporting Abuse and Protecting Children" in Bala, Zapf, Williams, Vogl, and Hornick, eds. *Canadian Child Welfare Law: Children, Families and the State*, 2d ed. (Toronto: Thompson Educational Publishing, Inc., 2004), Robin Vogl and Nicholas Bala indicate (at 43-44):

> The distinction between voluntary and involuntary involvement is often quite subtle, and frequently there are situations where a family will reluctantly agree to work "voluntarily" with the agency. Given the authority of the child protection agency to remove children if necessary, it is not surprising that families may not realize their right to decline the "voluntary offer" of services of the child protection agency. As a practical matter, in many cases the "right" to decline services may be somewhat illusory, given the society's mandate to ensure the protection of children through the court process.

3. Where support services on a voluntary basis are not feasible or have not worked, the *CFSA* indicates that the child protection worker should consider the least disruptive measure available to protect the child in the following progression. First, the society could simply apply under s. 40(1) of the *CFSA* for a hearing to determine whether the child is in need of protection. This approach could be used where the society believes that the child can safely be left in his or her home pending the hearing. Second, the child protection worker may be able to obtain a warrant under s. 40(2) to apprehend the child. This alternative is available where the child's need for protection dictates removal from the home and there is enough time to obtain a warrant. In order to obtain a warrant to apprehend a child the worker must swear an information before a justice of the peace setting out reasonable and probable grounds to believe that the child is in need of protection and that a less restrictive course of action is either not available or will not protect the child adequately. The most drastic step that a child protection worker could take is to apprehend the child without a warrant under s. 40(7). This procedure may be adopted only if the worker believes, on reasonable and probable grounds, that the child is in need of protection and that there would be a "substantial risk to the child's health or safety" during the time necessary to obtain a warrant.

4. For an example of an apprehension without a warrant that attracted considerable media attention, see *Family & Children's Services of St. Thomas & Elgin v. F. (W.)* (2003), 36 R.F.L. (5th) 310 (Ont. C.J.); affirmed (March 7, 2005), Doc. C170/ 01 (Ont. S.C.J.). The social worker solicited the help of the local police in apprehending seven children in Aylmer over the objections of the parents and congregants of the Church of God. Justice Schnall concluded that the social worker acted lawfully.

In contrast, Justice Quinn found (para. 52) in *Children's Aid Society of Niagara Region v. P. (T.)* (2003), 35 R.F.L. (5th) 290 (Ont. S.C.J.) that a social worker's apprehension of a four-year-old girl without a warrant in the circumstances of that case was "heavy handed" and had to "be condemned in the strongest terms". Nevertheless, the Justice found that the child was in need of protection, based in part on the angry reaction of the mother's boyfriend to the society's unlawful action.

5. Apprehension at birth without a warrant occurred in *Children's Aid Society of Toronto v. R. (A.)* (2003), 36 R.F.L. (5th) 51 (Ont. C.J.) and in *Children's Aid Society of Kingston (City) & Frontenac (County) v. S. (J.M.)* (2004), 1 R.F.L. (6th) 56 (Ont. S.C.J.). In both cases, the babies were ultimately made Crown wards without access by the parents. The legality of the warrantless apprehension was not discussed in the first case. In the second, Justice Robertson did not expressly apply s. 40(7) of the *CFSA* to the facts, but merely stated (para. 5) that the social worker made the "correct choice". The Justice was, however, critical of the society's failure to explain to the mother why it had decided to reverse its original decision to help her care for the baby.

6. In *Children's Aid Society of London & Middlesex v. S. (E.V.F.)* (2004), 1 R.F.L. (6th) 68 (Ont. S.C.J.), Justice Vogelsang criticized a society's apprehension of three children with a warrant (para. 42):

> The Society position is "quite bereft of merit". The conduct of [the social worker] represents a shocking departure from reasonable standards of both fair play and honest reporting. Her investigation into this family was prejudicial and desultory. Not only was she indiscriminate in her acceptance of the contents of the Society file [from previous reports regarding the children], she changed the facts of the previous investigations to suit her purposes in supporting her own conclusion of misconduct. ... She used those exaggerated and altered "facts" as a basis for obtaining a warrant from a judicial officer to carry the apprehension into effect. What she did completely disregards the seriousness of the apprehension of children from their parents. ...

7. Section 40(6) of the *CFSA* permits a protection worker acting under a warrant to enter premises specified in the warrant, by force if necessary, to search for and remove the child. Section 40(11) authorizes similar action where the worker is lawfully apprehending a child without a warrant.

8. To facilitate a child protection agency's investigation of suspected abuse or neglect, ss. 74, 74.1, and 74.2 of the *CFSA* allow an agency to apply for a court order requiring a third party to release information contained in a record.

In *Family & Children's Services of St. Thomas & Elgin v. F. (W.)* (noted above), Justice Schnall concluded (para. 408) that 1) where allegations of abuse had been made, the society was empowered to ask questions of the parents; 2) the parents were not obligated to answer the questions, but the society could reasonably draw a negative inference when they refused to do so; and 3) the society did not need parental consent to speak to the children in the course of the investigation.

9. If a child is apprehended with or without a warrant in Ontario, he or she must be brought before the court within five days unless the child is returned to the home or a temporary care agreement is executed (s. 46(1) of the *CFSA*). In the interim, the child must be taken to a "place of safety" defined in s. 37(1) and s. 37(5). Note that s. 37(5) stipulates that the home of a relative or a member of the child's extended family may be a place of safety if the society has carried out a prescribed assessment.

10. Section 46 of the *CFSA* provides that, where a child is apprehended, one of three options must be selected by the protection agency as soon as is practicable and, in any event, within five days of detention. What remedy is available to the parent where none of these options is exercised within five days? In *Kenora-Patricia Child & Family Services v. G. (J.)* (2001), 21 R.F.L. (5th) 80 (Ont. C.J.), the court concluded that jurisdiction was lost where six days elapsed before the child was brought before it. Might this not simply lead to a new apprehension?

In dealing with other time limits for procedural steps in child protection cases, the courts generally favour a more flexible approach and allow extensions if they are in the child's best interests. See, in particular, *Children's Aid Society & Family Services of Colchester (County) v. W. (H.)* (1996), 25 R.F.L. (4th) 82 (N.S. C.A.); *L. (R.) v. Children's Aid Society of Niagara Region* (2002), 34 R.F.L. (5th) 44 (Ont. C.A.); additional reasons at (2003), 34 R.F.L. (5th) 62 (Ont. C.A.); *Nova Scotia (Minister of Community Services) v. B. (J.)* (2003), 50 R.F.L. (5th) 379 (N.S. S.C.); and *Children's Aid Society of Windsor-Essex v. B. (B.)* (2008), 2008 CarswellOnt 2298 (Ont. C.J.).

11. Where a child is apprehended, none of the parties will be prepared at the first appearance in court to proceed with a formal hearing to determine whether the child is in need of protection. Indeed, all parties may agree to an adjournment of even the interim care hearing necessary to deal with the temporary care and custody of the child pending the trial. Sections 51 to 53 of the *CFSA* govern adjournments and interim care arrangements. In "The Ontario *Child and Family Services Act, 1984*: Maintaining the Balance Between Competing Rights" (1992), 8 C.F.L.Q. 129, W.J. Sammon comments (at 176):

> Because any adjournment of this interim hearing will result, in most cases, in the child remaining in care, it is extremely important for counsel not to adjourn for a long period of time, only long enough to meet with the worker, review the Children's Aid Society's file, speak with important witnesses and prepare affidavit material to be used in the care and custody hearing. Although the Act provides for a hearing within 5 days, it is not unusual for this preliminary hearing to be adjourned for at least [a] 2- to-3 week period during which time the apprehended child will remain in care. This is a serious infringement on both parental and the child's right but it is the price that one has to pay to keep the legal and adversarial model for determining child welfare cases.

Regarding the interim care or temporary custody hearing and the difficulty that judges have in assessing evidence that is often conflicting and untested through cross-examination, see Vogl and Bala, "Initial Involvement: Reporting Abuse and Protecting Children" in Bala, Zapf, Williams, Vogl, and Hornick, eds. *Canadian Child Welfare Law: Children, Families and the State*, 2d ed. (Toronto: Thompson Educational Publishing, Inc., 2004).

12. Before the amendments that came into effect in 2000, s. 51(3) of the *CFSA* (governing temporary custody or interim care during adjournments) directed the court to return the child to the care of the person who had charge of the child immediately before the society's intervention unless "the court is satisfied that there are reasonable and probable grounds to believe that there is a substantial risk to the child's health or safety". The 2000 amendments changed this standard to "reasonable grounds ... that there is a risk that the child is likely to suffer harm". In *Children's Aid Society of Ottawa-Carleton v. T.* (2000), [2000] O.J. No. 2273, 2000 CarswellOnt 2156 (Ont. S.C.J.), Blishen J. wrote (para. 10) that this required the child protection agency to:

> ... establish, on credible and trustworthy evidence, reasonable grounds to believe that there is a real possibility that if the child is returned to his parents, it is more probable than not that he will suffer harm. Further, the Society must establish that the child cannot be adequately protected by terms and conditions of an interim supervision order to the parents.

For some other cases applying the new standard, see *Children's Aid Society of Toronto v. M. (A.)* (2002), 26 R.F.L. (5th) 265 (Ont. C.J.) and *R. (S.M.) v. Children's Aid Society of Oxford County* (2003), 41 R.F.L. (5th) 168 (Ont. S.C.J.). See also *S. (B.) v. British Columbia (Director of Child, Family & Community Service)* (1998), 38 R.F.L. (4th) 138 (B.C. C.A.) where the legislation required the agency to show that a child "is likely to be physically harmed by the child's parent".

13. In *C.C.A.S. of Metro. Toronto v. D. (A.)* (1994), 1 R.F.L. (4th) 268 (Ont. Gen. Div.), the court dealt with s. 51(7) of the *CFSA* which permits the court in temporary protection applications to "admit and act on evidence that the court considers credible and trustworthy". Justice Wilson noted that most of the evidence in a motion for a temporary protection order will necessarily be in affidavit form and accepted (at 278) that the court may act on evidence "which is such that there is about it some apparent real sense of believability and reliability arising from the subject matter of the evidence, the proximity of the witness or author of the document to that subject matter, the nature of the relationship between the witness or author of the document and the person whose statements are recorded or repeated in evidence and the degree to which the evidence is material to the paramount issues in the case." See also *Children's Aid Society of Toronto v. M. (A.)* (2002), 26 R.F.L. (5th) 265 (Ont. C.J.) where Katarynych J. was quite critical of the evidence that the agency filed with the court at the interim care hearing.

14. Delay in child protection proceedings is a major concern and usually impacts negatively on the parents' position. Section 52 of the *CFSA* and Rule 33 of the *Family Law Rules*, O. Reg. 114/99, attempt to address this concern. However, Professor McLeod stated in an annotation to *Children's Aid Society of Hamilton-Wentworth v. R. (C.)* (2002), 27 R.F.L. (5th) 293 (Ont. S.C.J.): "As any lawyer who practices in the area knows, the time lines established in the Rules [for protection hearings] are unrealistic and are usually honoured in the breach". More recently, Justice Bondy noted (at para. 20) in *Children's Aid Society of Windsor-Essex v. B. (B.)* (2008), 2008 CarswellOnt 2298 (Ont. C.J.): "The record reflects that the child protection timetable for this case has been well exceeded time and time again." Delays may result from such factors as difficulties in finding and serving parents, problems finding and serving a child's band or native community, scarcity of lawyers willing and able to act for family members, the limited number of appropriate assessors, and crowded court dockets.

15. There are a number of methods employed to avoid an adversarial confrontation in court and as a result, only some child protection cases are resolved through litigation. After an initial investigation the child welfare agency may conclude that the child can remain in the home and the agency can work with the family on a voluntary basis. Some parents genuinely welcome the support provided by an agency in dealing with a difficult child. Some observers argue, however, that many parents "agree" to the involvement of a protection agency out of fear that a refusal may result in court action. There is another problem with the agency's role in this situation. After a period of consensual involvement the child protection agency may decide that a child protection hearing is required. Then all of the evidence discovered during the period of consensual involvement can be used in the hearing.

Where a temporary or even permanent alternative to parental care is required, individuals such as grandparents, aunts, uncles or family friends can often provide the short-term or long-term care needed by the child. A parent may voluntarily agree that the child should live with a known and trusted person for a period of time.

A Children's Aid Society may also enter into a formal written agreement with the parents and, in some cases, the child. Section 29 of the *CFSA* governs temporary care agreements while s. 30 deals with special needs agreements. Section 4 of the *CFSA* attempts to ensure that these agreements are entered into voluntarily and with full knowledge of their implications. Note also that s. 29(4) specifies that a society shall not enter into a temporary care agreement unless the society "is satisfied that no less disruptive course of action, such as care in the child's own home, is appropriate for the child in the circumstances". Finally, there are provisions in s. 29 to ensure that the child does not simply "drift into care" on a permanent basis without judicial scrutiny. In particular, see subsections (5), (6), (6.1), and (6.2).

Recall that s. 20.2 of the *CFSA* now requires a Children's Aid Society to consider whether mediation could resolve any issue. Similarly, s. 51.1 now authorizes a court, with the consent of the parties, to adjourn a proceeding to permit the parties to attempt to resolve a dispute by mediation.

16. If a child is inappropriately left in parental care by the child protection worker and suffers further abuse, the child protection worker will inevitably feel a sense of guilt and moral responsibility and may even face civil or criminal liability for the failure to protect the child. On the other hand, if the worker is overly aggressive in protecting a child, parents may bring actions for damages.

Despite s. 15(6) and s. 40(14) of the *CFSA*, civil liability may be imposed in Ontario in extreme cases. See, e.g., *B. (D.) v. Children's Aid Society of Durham (Region)* (1996), 136 D.L.R. (4th) 297 (Ont. C.A.). For further reading, see Bernstein, Regehr, and Kanani, "Liability for Child Welfare Workers: Weighing the Risks" in Bala, Zapf, Williams, Vogl, and Hornick, eds. *Canadian Child Welfare Law: Children, Families and the State*, 2d ed. (Toronto: Thompson Educational Publishing, Inc., 2004).

A child protection agency often becomes involved with a family through a third party's report of suspected child abuse or neglect. To encourage reporting, legislation requires those who are aware that a child may be in need of protection to inform the appropriate authorities. In general, prosecutions under reporting laws are rare.

BALA, "REFORMING ONTARIO'S *CHILD AND FAMILY SERVICES ACT*: IS THE PENDULUM SWINGING BACK TOO FAR?"

(1999) 17 C.F.L.Q. 121 at 165-166 (Footnotes omitted)

(i) Reporting Child Abuse and Neglect: Section 72 [of CFSA]

A number of the recent child abuse deaths in Ontario raised concerns about professionals and community members being slow or unwilling to report suspected abuse to Children's Aid Societies. Bill 6 [amendments to the *CFSA* enacted in 1999 and most sections proclaimed on March 31, 2000] attempts to address these concerns by increasing reporting requirements. [See ss. 72 and 72.1 of the *CFSA*.] However, the major problems related to under-reporting do not arise out of the legislation. Rather, such problems as poor communication and mistrust between the C.A.S. and other agencies and professionals in their communities, and lack of training and support for community professionals need to be addressed. Bill 6 consolidates the reporting provisions with the relevant definitions of child in need of protection. This is useful for the purposes of public and professional education. However, when the widened reporting provisions are combined with the expanded definitions of child in need of protection, there is the prospect for a substantial increase in the number of cases reported to the C.A.S. Already only about one quarter of cases of abuse and neglect that are reported to the C.A.S. in Ontario are substantiated by the agencies, with another third being suspected, and about 40 per cent of the reports being regarded as unfounded. The prospect is that only a small portion of any increase in reporting will be high-risk cases.

At present, it is only an offence for professionals to fail to report reasonable suspicions of "abuse." Bill 6 extends the mandatory reporting to require professionals to report in any situation where they have "reasonable grounds to suspect" any situation where a child may be in need of protection.

The new section [see s. 72(2)] will require a person who has reported abuse to again report if the person later discovers a new basis to suspect abuse or neglect.

The new section [see s. 72(3)] provides that a person who has a duty to report shall report directly to the C.A.S. and shall not delegate this duty. While this amendment was presumably made to ensure that the agencies receive the fullest possible information, it may make busy professionals, who often work in teams, feel less inclined to report or delay reporting.

The *Panel of Experts Report* recommended abrogation of solicitor-client privilege, imposing a requirement on lawyers to report based on communication with clients, other than in the context of child protection proceedings. This recommendation would have been very controversial, especially with criminal lawyers who represent those charged with abuse, and is not included in Bill 6. [The solicitor-client privilege is recognized in s. 72(8).]

One of the issues not addressed by Bill 6 is the extent to which the C.A.S. may share information with other agencies and professionals in the community. Some of the under-reporting from community professionals may reflect a sense that information tends to "flow in only one direction," undermining the establishment of co-operative relationships with professionals that might encourage reporting.

NOTES AND QUESTIONS

1. Can a doctor who fails to report abuse be held civilly liable to a child who suffers as a result? See *Landerose v. Flood*, 551 P. 2d 389 (Cal., June 30, 1976); *O'Keefe v. Osorio* (1984), 27 American Trial Lawyers Assoc. L.R. 392 (Illinois); and *Brown (Next Friend of) v. University of Alberta Hospital* (1997), 145 D.L.R. (4th) 63 (Alta. Q.B.). See also Brown and Truitt, "Civil Liability in Child Abuse Cases" (1979), 54 Chi.-Kent L.R. 753 and Bala "Tort Remedies & the Family Law Practitioner" (1998-99), 16 C.F.L.Q. 423.

2. Can a person who mistakenly reports child abuse to the child welfare authorities be held civilly liable to the parent? See s. 72(7) of the *CFSA*. See also the article by Professor Bala listed in the previous note.

3. The reporting obligations under the *CFSA* apply to everyone. However, only the professionals covered by s. 72(5) who learn the relevant information in the course of their professional or official duties commit an offence by failing to report: s. 72(4). There have been few cases in which persons have been charged with failure to report and most of these have led to acquittals. The cases and other aspects of reporting legislation are reviewed in Bessner, "The Duty to Report Child Abuse" (1999-2000), 17 C.F.L.Q. 277.

4. Section 72(7) and (8) of the *CFSA* differentiate between the solicitor-client relationship and relationships involving other professionals. Is this justifiable?

In "The Duty of Confidentiality and the Child Beating Client: An Ethical Conundrum" (1995), 13 C.F.L.Q. 49, Ken Armstrong argues (at 56) that, although a lawyer may not have a legal obligation to disclose privileged communications under the child protection legislation, "the lawyer has an ethical obligation to disclose any confidential information, privileged or not, that indicates a child might be beaten in the future. Considering the nature of child abuse, a confession of past abuse should qualify". However, Marvin Bernstein suggests in "Towards a New Approach to Child Representation: How Less is More in Child Welfare Proceedings" (1994), 10 C.F.L.Q. 187 at 222-223, that the Ontario Rules of Professional Conduct permit but do not obligate a lawyer to disclose privileged information to prevent a crime. See Rule 2.03 of the Law Society of Upper Canada's *Rules of Professional Conduct*.

The Supreme Court of Canada confirmed that the solicitor-client privilege is not absolute in *Smith v. Jones* (1999), 169 D.L.R. (4th) 385. Justice Cory stated that in some situations, the importance of public safety might allow a lawyer to disclose information received during the solicitor-client relationship. Three questions must be considered: (i) Is there a clear risk to an identifiable person or group of persons? (ii) Is there a risk of serious bodily harm or death? and (iii) Is the danger imminent? (at 408)

5. Section 40(4) of the *CFSA* provides that a person who reports the suspected child abuse or neglect to the society may apply to the court in an attempt to initiate a child protection hearing where the society refuses to apprehend the child or to initiate the hearing itself. What is the purpose of this provision?

6. A number of Canadian provinces have formal child abuse registers. In these jurisdictions, child protection agencies are required to report cases of abuse to the centralized register. In theory, these registers may serve a number of functions:

(i) Detection and Identification. Parents who abuse their children may attempt to avoid detection by taking children to different hospitals or different doctors for treatment each time the abuse results in the need for medical attention. A check of the centralized register may confirm a suspicion of abuse.

(ii) Research. A register may be a valuable research tool, both for academic research into the nature, causes and treatment of abuse and for authorities monitoring child abuse and programs in a particular jurisdiction.

(iii) Case Management. Information gleaned from the register may cause an agency to emphasize a particular type of case because more serious abuse in the future may be predicted.

(iv) Screening. A register might be used to screen foster and adoptive parents, employees with responsibility for children, and those who require a licence to operate a facility such as a day-care centre.

The Ontario Child Abuse Register (see ss. 75 and 76 of the *CFSA*) establishes a low threshold for placing names on the registry and, accordingly, is not used as a screening device for employees or volunteers who are seeking to work with children. Indeed, a thorough review of the register by an interdisciplinary study group headed by Professor Bala concluded (*Review of the Ontario Child Abuse Register* (Toronto: Ontario Ministry of Community and Social Services, 1988, at VIII):

> The Register has very limited utility for identification and its deterrent effect is questionable. It is not effectively used for research or case management. There is substantial variability in the application of criteria for registration and the entire process raises very serious civil liberties concerns. The current Register has insufficient safeguards to be used for screening. *The Register system, in its present form, should be discontinued.*

> Disbandonment of any form of register may be considered a viable option by some, but a significantly restructured register can play an important role in combating child abuse without compromising the rights of individuals identified as abusers.

Section 27 of the *Child and Family Services Amendment Act (Child Welfare Reform), 1999* repealed the provisions setting up the Ontario Child Abuse Registry, but it has not yet been proclaimed into effect. In the meantime, the Ontario government developed a "fast track" computerized information system to enable child protection agencies to access information concerning any families and children who have been investigated by other agencies in Ontario.

3. The Protection Hearing

(1) Notice

Those affected by the court proceeding must be properly notified of the time, place and nature of the proceedings. Examine s. 39 of the *CFSA* to determine who is entitled to participate in and receive notice of the hearing. Note that where a child is an Indian or native person, a representative chosen by the child's band or native community is a party to the proceeding.

The wording and legislative history of the definition of "parent" in the Ontario child protection legislation indicates that the Legislature clearly believed it was inappropriate to require notice to be given to all fathers. A similar definition appears in Part VII of the Act in relation to parental consent to adoption. An obvious question is whether this differential treatment of fathers and mothers violates s. 15 of the *Charter*. In *S. (C.E.) v. Children's Aid Society of Metropolitan Toronto (Municipality)* (1988), 49 D.L.R. (4th) 469 (Ont. Div. Ct.) the court rejected a s. 15 challenge to the Ontario adoption consent provisions. The court noted that s. 131(1) of the *CFSA* (now s. 137(1), which provides a definition of "parent" similar to that in s. 37(1)) cast a fairly wide net for consent purposes and that only a "casual fornicator" who impregnated a woman and demonstrated no sense of responsibility for the natural consequences was excluded. The case suggests that serious legislative attempts to address the unmarried father's position may receive deferential treatment by the courts. Professor Thompson comments in "A Family Law Hitchhiker's Guide to the Charter Galaxy" (1988), 3 C.F.L.Q. 315 at 343-344: "Much as the Divisional Court may have been correct in their result, that does not excuse a judgment that reads like a guest editorial in the Toronto Sun, typified by the Court's labelling of the excluded fathers as 'casual fornicators'."

More recently, Justice Wolder dealt with the failure to notify a biological father of adoption proceedings. The father's identity was known, but he did not fit within the statutory definition of parent in s. 137 of the *CFSA*. The Justice initially concluded in *C. (D.G.) v. Y. (R.H.G.)* (2003), 41 R.F.L. (5th) 245 (Ont. C.J.), at para. 12 that "the failure to notify the biological father of this proceeding and the failure to give him an opportunity to respond to the motion to dispense with his consent, on the basis that he is statutorily excluded ... violates his rights under subsection 15(1) of the Charter ... [and] is not saved by s. 1 ... ." However, in *C. (D.) v. A. (W.)* (2003), 48 R.F.L. (5th) 21 (Ont. C.J.), Justice Wolder, after hearing further submissions, "corrected" this earlier ruling. The Justice was especially influenced by s. 137(1)(f) of the *CFSA*. This provision allowed a biological father to bring himself within the definition of parent by filing a statutory declaration with the Registrar General affirming that he was the father of the child under s. 12 of the *Children's Law Reform Act*, R.S.O. 1990, c. C.12.

Regarding the method of giving notice and what constitutes reasonable attempts to serve notice of a protection hearing, see *Re Pearson*, 10 R.F.L. 234, [1973] 4 W.W.R. 274 (B.C. S.C.). See also *Re P. (N.)* (2001), 15 R.F.L. (5th) 151 (Ont. S.C.J.).

In *N. (B.) v. Alberta (Director of Child Welfare)* (2004), 4 R.F.L. (6th) 380 (Alta. C.A.), the Alberta Court of Appeal dealt with the proper approach to take where the parents fail to appear at the hearing. The appellate court held that the importance and near finality of permanent guardianship orders required a judge to take special measures to ensure that parents had an optimal opportunity to participate in a child welfare proceeding where such orders were sought. In particular, the court concluded that it was not enough simply to ensure that notice was given. Rather, it stipulated that a judge should consider a) the nature and date of the notice and its adequacy; b) the circumstances of the parent's residence and the parent's ability to receive messages or correspondence; c) the parent's pattern of past attendances at scheduled trials or hearings; d) the number of adjournments and length of delay leading up to the hearing; e) the extent of the parent's involvement with the child or children prior to the hearing; f) the possibility of some reasonable explanation for the parent's absence; and g) the likelihood of success if further attempts to secure the parent's attendance were attempted. It stated that, in the end, a court had to determine whether to proceed in a parent's absence by balancing the parent's procedural rights and the need to avoid unreasonable delay, remembering that the child's best interests remained paramount.

Where the court is satisfied that the time required to provide notice might endanger the child's health or safety, it may dispense with notice to a person: s. 39(7) of the *CFSA*. If such a dispensation is granted, the court cannot make a Crown wardship order or a temporary wardship order exceeding 30 days: s. 57(7).

In medical emergencies, especially where a parent refuses to consent to particular treatment, the hearing may take place with extremely short notice. However, some effort must be made to hold a hearing and to permit the parents to attend and participate in whatever hearing is held. See *Forsyth v. Children's Aid Society of Kingston (City)* (1962), [1963] 1 O.R. 49, 35 D.L.R. (2d) 690 (H.C.) and *M. (J.) v. Alberta (Director of Child Welfare)* (2004), 4 R.F.L. (6th) 362 (Alta. Q.B.). Indeed, the *CFSA* indicates that the protecting agency can only authorize medical treatment after a hearing and court order. Although a child protection worker may authorize a medical examination of the child upon apprehension (s. 40(9)), s. 62 grants power to the child protection agency to consent to and authorize medical treatment for the child only after a court has found the child to be in need of protection and has made a wardship order. In *Re L. (C.P.)* (1988), 70 Nfld. & P.E.I.R. 287 (Nfld. U.F.C.); affirmed (1993), 112 Nfld. & P.E.I.R. 148 (Nfld. C.A.); leave to appeal refused (1995), 186 N.R. 78 (note) (S.C.C.), the court held that legislation that permitted a child protection agency to authorize medical treatment without a court order as soon as the child was apprehended violated s. 7 of the *Charter*. The procedures provided by the *CFSA* for dealing with a medical emergency withstood a *Charter* challenge in *B. (R.) v. Children's Aid Society of Metropolitan Toronto* (1995), 9 R.F.L. (4th) 157 (S.C.C.) (reproduced later in this chapter). Justice La Forest summarized the procedural rights of the parents as follows (at 214): "In sum, the appellants were entitled to such notice, access to information, and rights of representation as may be fair and reasonable having regard to the nature of the proceedings and the urgency with which they must be carried out." This test was applied in *M. (J.) v. Alberta (Director of Child Welfare)*, *supra*.

(2) Nature of the Hearing

In a child protection hearing there are essentially two basic issues. First, the court must determine whether the child is in need of protection as defined in s. 37(2) of the *CFSA* and whether a court order is necessary to protect the child in the future (see s. 57(1)). In this "protection finding" or "adjudication" stage, the court is essentially required to decide if any state intrusion into the life of the child and family is warranted. Second, where the court concludes that a court order is necessary, the court must choose which of the orders under s. 57 would be in the child's best interests. These two issues are conceptually distinct.

In Ontario, unlike most other provinces, there is a "bifurcation" or division of the hearing into two stages corresponding to these two issues. Indeed, s. 50(2) of the Act provides that "evidence relating only to the disposition of the matter shall not be admitted before the court has determined that the child is in need of protection". It is only in the second or "disposition" stage that the statute specifically mandates the use of the best interests of the child test. Section 37(3) provides a non-exhaustive list of factors that the court may consider at this stage (see also s. 37(4)).

In *D. v. Children's Aid Society of Kent (County)* (1980), 18 R.F.L. (2d) 223, 1980 CarswellOnt 282 (Ont. Co. Ct.), County Court Judge Clements stressed the need to preserve the distinction between the two issues raised in a child protection hearing, even if the agency is seeking an order that would transfer custody from one parent to the other subject to the supervision of the society. The judge stated:

> The power given to the children's aid society under the Act is to impose an agency of the government on behalf of the society into the home when necessary. The contest, it must be remembered, is between the society and the natural parents in most instances. This is not a custody dispute between the parents, although the child's welfare is every bit as important as it always is in dealing with children, but rather an issue as to whether the conditions, in the home with the parent or the person in whose charge the children were, are such as to warrant the intervention of the state for the protection of the child.

For other cases in which the courts emphasized the need to maintain a clear distinction between the "protection finding" and "disposition" phases of the child protection hearing, see *Prince Edward Island (Director of Child Welfare) v. W. (N.)* (1994), 10 R.F.L. (4th) 203 (P.E.I. C.A.); additional reasons at (1994), 10 R.F.L. (4th) 203 at 206 (P.E.I. C.A.); *Winnipeg Child & Family Services (East Area) v. D. (K.A.)* (1995), 13 R.F.L. (4th) 357 (Man. C.A.); and *Children's Aid Society of Niagara Region v. P. (T.)* (2003), 35 R.F.L. (5th) 290 (Ont. S.C.J.).

One of the more significant changes to the *CFSA* in 2006 was the addition of s. 57.1. It allows a court, where it finds that an order under this section instead of an order under s. 57(1) would be in the child's best interests, to grant custody of the child to one or more persons. Unlike the orders sought in cases such as *D. v. Children's Aid Society of Kent (County)* and *Children's Aid Society of Niagara Region v. P. (T.)*, these orders do not require that the Society supervise the exercise of that custody. The chief impetus for the adoption of this section was the rather common occurrence of a relative (aunt or grandparent, for example) responding to a child protection proceeding by launching a separate custody application under the *Children's Law Reform Act*. The custody and protection proceedings might then both go forward. The Society would often seek to end its involvement with the child once the third person received custody and its protection concerns were no longer engaged. Where the protection hearing had not yet ended, it would seek to withdraw its application. Where that hearing had resulted in a wardship order or a supervision order, it might seek to terminate that order. The parallel proceedings often created confusion and multiple court appearances. They also caused problems for Legal Aid which often was asked to fund both proceedings simultaneously.

Although this point could have been addressed more directly, it appears that s. 57.1 contemplates a finding that a child is in need of protection before a court can make a custody order. In *Children's Aid Society of Toronto v. K. (C.)* (2008), CarswellOnt 790 (Ont. C.J.), Justice S.B. Sherr stated (at para. 8):

> The important elements of this section are as follows:
>
> (a) The custody order in s. 57.1 can only be made once there has been a finding that a child is in need of protection.
>
> (b) Once the finding has been made, the test is whether it is in a child's best interests to make this type of order as opposed to an order under s. 57(1) of the Act. Criteria for a child's best interests are set out in s. 37(3) of the Act.
>
> (c) The society or any other party can apply for a party or other persons to have custody of the child. These "other persons" are not required to be parties to the action, but they must consent to the custody order (as does any party).
>
> (d) Section 57.1 custody orders and any access orders made at the same time as these custody orders are deemed to be orders made under section 28 of the *Children's Law Reform Act*. ... Any subsequent variations of this order are brought under the *Children's Law Reform Act* and the society would not be a party.

Justice S.B. Sherr also spelled out (paras. 9 and 10) the significant implications of the custody order for the aunt and the evidence needed to establish that she had given a fully informed consent.

The possibility that a protection hearing may result in a custody order in favour of a family member may make it more difficult to preserve the distinction between the "protection finding" or "adjudication" stage and the disposition stage. In other words, the court may, at least subconsciously, begin to consider the child's best interests while determining whether the Society has established that he or she is in need of protection. The following case suggests that, under the Nova Scotia legislation at least, the best interests of the child are to be considered at every stage of the protection hearing. Is this desirable? Is there any danger in this approach? Is it perhaps inevitable? The case also raises issues relating to the meaning of the statutory term "in need of protection", which is the focus of the next section of this chapter.

NOVA SCOTIA (MINISTER OF COMMUNITY SERVICES) v. M. (B.)

(1998), 42 R.F.L. (4th) 208, 1998 CarswellNS 178 (N.S. C.A.)

PUGSLEY, J.A. (for the court): — The Minister of Community Services (the Agency) appeals from a decision and order of Judge Robert White of the Family Court, dismissing the Agency's application for a finding that the six children of the respondents, BM and LM, were children in need of protective services as defined by s. 22(2)(a) and (b) of the *Children and Family Services Act*. ...

The grounds of appeal may be summarized as follows: Judge White failed to properly determine, and apply, the burden imposed on the Agency under the *Act*, and made a palpable and overriding error in his assessment of the facts disregarding material evidence.

Background

The children, EM (male, DOB January 8, 1986), SM (female, DOB May 15, 1988), JM (male, DOB January 1, 1990), RM (female, DOB December 31, 1992), GM (female, DOB October 16, 1994), and YM (female, DOB May 22, 1996) are the biological children of the respondents.

The respondents and their six children live in rural Nova Scotia and occupy a mobile home (64' by 14') located on a large tract of land. BM is apparently in his late 30's and his wife, LM, was 34 at the time of the hearing in December, 1997.

In mid-September, 1997, a confidential informant contacted the RCMP alleging that the respondent BM:

- Dominated his wife, and children, and had openly stated that he did not believe the law in regard to discipline of children and that he would discipline his children as he saw fit.; and

- Had been witnessed by the confidential informant spanking his children and hitting them with a stick, leaving observable bruises.

It was further alleged that SM disclosed that her father had given her the bruise observed. Finally, concerns were raised that the children were schooled at home, did not socialize with other children, and that their only outing "would be to church".

Acting upon the referral, protection workers employed by the Agency attended at the mobile home on September 16, 1997. As the respondents would not permit the children to be interviewed by the protection workers, an *ex parte* application was made on behalf of the Agency for an investigative order pursuant to s. 26(2) of the *Act*.

The order was granted on September 18 authorizing the Agency, among other things, to enter the respondents' mobile home, conduct a physical examination of the children, remove the children for a medical examination if one was deemed reasonably necessary, and further to remove the children and attend with them at the offices of the Agency, or the RCMP in Antigonish to interview them with respect to the allegations made against their parents. The order further provided for the interview to be video taped.

The children were accordingly taken to the RCMP detachment in Antigonish and the three oldest, EM (eleven years, nine months), SM (nine and a half), and JM (six years, nine months), all provided individual video-taped statements, collectively lasting approximately two hours.

As a result of the interviews, the Agency sought, and subsequently obtained, certain assurances from the respondents, who by then had obtained legal advice, that they would not use corporal punishment while the Agency brought the matter before the Court.

The Agency initiated an application on September 25 for an order that the children were in need of protection. The interim hearing was resolved by a "without prejudice" consent order entered into by counsel for both parties.

During the course of the protection hearing heard in mid-December, 1997, the video-taped interviews of EM, SM and JM were introduced as exhibits. *Viva voce* evidence, in addition, was called on behalf of the Agency and the respondents. SM was the only child who gave *viva voce* evidence at trial. Judge White reserved decision after submissions were advanced on December 15, and subsequently released a written decision on December 23 dismissing the Agency's application. He declined to award costs, noting that there was no *mala fides* exhibited in the conduct of the Agency, and further concluded that none of the agents of the Agency acted in an excessive, or officious, manner.

Scope of Inquiry at the Protection Hearing

The *Act* provides a three-stage process — a process that may involve an interim hearing, a protection hearing, and finally, a disposition hearing.

The first stage requires the Agency, within five days of an application being made to determine whether a child is in need of protective services, to bring the matter before the Court for an interim hearing (s. 39(1)).

At the end of the interim hearing, the Court is given a wide discretion to take steps for the protection of the child if the child is found to be in need of protection. The Court is obliged to dismiss the Agency's application, however, if it finds that there are no reasonable and probable grounds to believe the child is in need of protective services (s. 39(2)).

In this case, the only evidence tendered before Judge White at the interim hearing was by way of affidavit deposed by Cathy Cashen, a protection worker employed by the Agency. No *viva voce* evidence was called. A "without prejudice" order, consented to by counsel for the parties, was issued declaring that there were reasonable and probable grounds to believe the children were in need of protective services. The children were permitted to remain in the care and custody of the respondents, subject to the supervision of the Agency.

The *Act* then provides for a second hearing, the protection hearing, which must be held not later than 90 days after the date of the application. If, as was determined in this case, the Court finds after the protection hearing that a child is not in need of protective services, the Court is obliged to dismiss the application brought by the Agency (s. 40(5)).

If the Court determines at the conclusion of the protection hearing that the child is in need of protective services, the Court must convene a disposition hearing within 90 days. At the conclusion of the disposition hearing the Court has a number of options under s. 42, including the option to "dismiss the matter".

All of the options available under s. 42 are to be made, however, in "a child's best interests". This phrase does not appear in the sections of the *Act* relating to the interim hearing, or the protection hearing.

A preliminary question is whether the Court, at a protection hearing, should consider the best interests of the children or whether the inquiry should be limited to the narrow question of whether the Agency has established that the children were in need of protective services pursuant to s. 22.

Section 76 of the former *Children's Services Act*, c. 8, S.N.S. (1976), provided that: "In an action under this Act, the court shall apply the principle that the welfare of the child is the paramount consideration."

Commenting on this provision, Jones, J.A., on behalf of this Court, in *Children's Aid Society of Halifax (City) v. Lake* (1981), 45 N.S.R. (2d) 361 (N.S. C.A.) stated at 375:

> An order cannot be made under the *Children's Services Act* on the sole ground that it is in the best interests of the child to do so without making a determination that the child is in need of protection. If a judge cannot make a finding that the child is in need of protection, he must dismiss the case.

In place of s. 76 of the former *Children's Services Act*, s.2(2) of the *Act* provides: "In all proceedings and matters pursuant to this Act, the paramount consideration is the best interests of the child."

The change of the wording ensures that the best interests of the child is an issue to be considered at every proceeding, and matter, including the protection hearing.

While some of Judge White's observations arguably related to this issue, unfortunately he failed to review the evidence or make any findings, as required by the *Act*, respecting the critical issue before him — namely, whether the Agency established that the children were in need of protective services pursuant to s. 22.

The Respondents' Disciplinary Beliefs

The respondents were married in June of 1984. The respondent BM is a manufacturer's representative, as well as a self-employed woodsman. The respondent LM, in addition to caring for and looking after the education of all of the children, sells her own crafts and baking products. She teaches the children with texts approved by the local Board of Education. She believes the public schools: "... teach a lot of humanism and come from an atheist situation, an evolutionist and I would rather teach them from a theistic point of view and I prefer a creationist point of view ...".

Both respondents accept the Bible as literal truth "inspired by God". The respondents are not members of any church, but have found fellowship in the Southeastern Mennonite Conference.

The respondents testified that their disciplinary methods respecting the children are determined from their understanding of the Bible. It is therefore relevant to consider these beliefs. ...

[BM] acknowledges that there are many methods of discipline, but if a child is wilfully disobedient to his parents, then it is appropriate for that child to be chastised.

He explained chastisement as: "... where you would use ... ah ... the rod on the child, you would basically take the rod in your hand ... it's a stick and you would ... strike the child with the rod on the, ah, basically on the buttock area."

The purpose of chastisement, BM explained, is: "... for the moral moulding the character of the child and also to relieve the child of the guilt that he would have developed by disobeying you."

The respondent BM testified that his method of chastisement was "fairly constant. I don't vary it ... it's a very relaxed thing"; that his objective was to use the rod "maybe three times" as there was "no reason to hit them more". BM employed two "rods" (i.e. birch sticks) for discipline — the larger for the older children was about 18 inches long, tapering in width from three-eighths of an inch to one-half inch. The smaller, approximately 12 inches long, three-eighths inches wide, was made of "much lighter wood" and was usually used for the younger children.

The evidence discloses that the rod was used only on a child who was clothed, and on the child's buttocks. In the case of an infant, the rod was applied to the diaper.

The respondent BM was responsible for approximately 90 per cent of the chastisement in the home; discipline carried out by the respondent LM occurred only when BM was absent.

While the respondent BM acknowledged that a child being chastised would cry because "it would hurt ... there shouldn't be any physical harm to the child".

The initial pain would last "maybe a minute or two minutes ... I can't imagine there being much more pain beyond that". He stressed he did not want to hurt the child and was "very conscious ... of how much pain I'd be causing".

The respondent LM stressed that chastisement was only a "very minor area of the discipline in our home".

The respondent BM admitted using the rod to hit YM when she was approximately 15 months old. He testified that he gave her "maybe two very, very light swats on the diaper ... possibly for biting".

Chastisement was carried out usually in private to preserve "the child's dignity".

Findings of the Trial Judge

Section 22(2) of the *Act* provides:

> A child is in need of protective services where
>
> > (a) the child has suffered physical harm, inflicted by a parent or guardian of the child or caused by the failure of a parent or guardian to supervise and protect the child adequately;
> >
> > (b) there is a substantial risk that the child will suffer physical harm inflicted or caused as described in clause (a);

The trial judge made some specific findings: ...

> ... it does appear that the frequency with which punishment is administered, the reasons for such punishment for trivial incidents such as some sibling rivalry and some sibling squabbling, seems excessive when other methods to command obedience would be equally as practical and finally, the age of some of the children being disciplined appears to offend common sense as to their ability to appreciate the reason for the corporal punishment.
>
> Having said this, on the one hand, I share the concerns of the child protection authorities over not only the issues related to the corporal punishment, but also on issues related to the emotional or psychological and social development of the children. *Notwithstanding these concerns, based upon the balance of probabilities. I am not persuaded that there is sufficient evidence before the court to make an order directing protective services.* (emphasis added)

... Unfortunately, the trial judge did not analyze the evidence in light of the issue raised in s. 22, nor did he make any specific findings respecting that evidence. This failure constituted a failure to exercise jurisdiction amounting to an error of law (*Lowe v. Tramble* (1980), 42 N.S.R. (2d) 481 (T.D.)).

It is necessary, therefore, to review the evidence to determine whether the Agency, at the protection hearing, met the burden of proof imposed on it, namely to establish on the balance of probabilities that the children, or one or more of them, were in need of protective services.

It is helpful in conducting this review, to consider the evidence arising out of s. 22(2)(a) separately from that relevant to s. 22(2)(b).

Section 22(2)(a)

The term "physical harm" as it appears in the section is not defined in the *Act*.

Both counsel direct our attention, however, to Professor E. A. Rollie Thompson's comments (see *The Annotated Children and Family Services Act*, August, 1991), at p.41:

> (1) *Degree of harm* Clause (a) does not on its face distinguish between degrees of physical harm. It does not require "serious" or "substantial and observable" harm. Does this mean that any physical

harm, however slight, can give rise to intervention? Faced with the potential scope of such a wide definition, some courts have drawn back and introduced some threshold notion of degree of harm. ...

It is submitted that some guidance may be drawn from a definition of "bodily harm" found in s. 267 of the *Criminal Code* which covers "any hurt or injury to the complainant that interferes with the health or comfort of the complainant and that is more than merely transient or trifling in nature". A test of this kind would serve to ensure the screening-out of trivial cases, *while maintaining a low enough threshold to capture cases where the child has experienced observable bruising.* (emphasis added)

The Agency submits that there are three specific examples disclosed in the evidence where the children of the respondents experienced "observable bruising" amounting to physical harm from the actions of their father — a bruise on SM's buttocks, a bruise on JM's lower back, and a bruise suffered by RM. [The court concluded that the agency failed to establish that the first two bruises were caused by "chastisement". The father acknowledged that RM had suffered a bruise as a result of a spanking in the winter of 1997, but that it had not affected her and had disappeared in two days.]

... I conclude that in these circumstances, one observable bruise on a child who is particularly susceptible to bruising, is not sufficient to satisfy the burden imposed under s. 22(2)(a) that the child has suffered physical harm.

I would not disturb the conclusion of the trial judge that there was not sufficient evidence before the Court to make an order directing protective services under s. 22(2)(a).

Section 22(2)(b)

The term "substantial risk" that appears in this section is defined in s. 22(1) as meaning:

... a real chance of danger that is apparent on the evidence.

The Agency submits that Judge White imposed a heavier burden on the Agency than that imposed under the *Act*, when he stated:

As well, I am cognizant of the current status of the law with respect to the rights of parents to raise their children in accordance with their religious beliefs. This is subject however, to the obligation of the state to intervene when there is a *pressing and substantial risk* to the child or children. More especially in the case law related to the charges under s. 43 of the *Criminal Code* of Canada, courts have to be aware as to whether there is *real risk of danger* to the child, that the age and sex of the child should be considered, that the effects flowing from the punishment, and the force does not exceed what is reasonable in the circumstances. It does appear that there are cases which state that the child must be capable of appreciating the reason for the correction. The fact that there is some bruising which is not extensive is not a ground for a criminal conviction. (emphasis added)

Section 22(2)(b) of the *Act* does not require the Agency to establish a "*pressing and substantial risk*" that a child will suffer physical harm. Rather, the burden is to establish that there is a "substantial risk". I conclude that the trial judge erred in imposing on the Agency a burden of adducing evidence greater than that imposed under s. 22(2)(b).

I do not agree with the Agency's submission that there is a significant difference between the term "a real risk of danger" as used by the trial judge, and a "real chance of danger" as used in s. 22(1) of the *Act*.

I further conclude, however, that the trial judge erred to the extent that he considered s. 43 of the *Criminal Code*, and cases decided thereunder, to be relevant to the issues in this case. ... The "reasonable force" exception in s. 43 does not appear in the *Act*. A parent may not be criminally responsible for using force against a child, yet the child nevertheless may be in need of protective services under s. 22. ...

I do not consider that the failure of the Agency to establish that the children, or one or more of them, have suffered physical harm under s. 22(2)(a) of the *Act* is determinative of the issue raised under s. 22(2)(b). ...

In view of the failure of the trial judge to make any specific findings, or analysis, of the evidence on this issue, the questions for this Court are whether the trial judge has erred, and if so, whether the Agency has met the burden to establish that there is a real chance of danger that the children, or one or more of them, will suffer physical harm inflicted by the respondents.

I consider the evidence on the following issues to be of particular significance in this case:

- the reasons for chastisement;
- the frequency of chastisement;
- the number of strokes employed by the respondents;
- the age of the children when chastisement commenced;
- the granting of authority to SM to discipline her younger siblings;
- the respondents' belief that incidental bruising should not be a concern.

... The evidence of the disciplinary methods exacted by the respondents is extremely disturbing. Children, at an increasingly younger age, and at more frequent intervals, are disciplined with a rod for minor misconduct which the respondents characterize as disobedience. Although both respondents testified that they take care to ensure the children are not harmed, incidental bruising, in the words of the respondent, BM, "should not be a concern" when the purpose is to bring a child under control to relieve him or her of a "guilty conscience of disobedience".

The use of the rod for discipline purposes seems to be all pervasive. It occurred frequently, both in and outside the house, when the children were taken to visit relatives, and also occurred both in, and outside, the van used for transportation.

The respondents were not prepared, at least at the time of the protection hearing in December, 1997, to moderate their disciplinary methods as they believe that they are carrying out God's will as revealed to them in the Bible.

I am mindful that the Agency employees testified the children: "... seemed comfortable at home and happy ... engaged in conversation very naturally ... very forthcoming, pleasant ... didn't seem fearful ... seemed happy and content and interacted freely with their parents."

I have also noted the evidence of Dr. Sadler who examined the children approximately three times a year for their physical needs. She testified that they always were lively, and bright children, who interacted normally with their parents as well as herself. ...

Notwithstanding these favourable observations, the weight of the evidence convinces me that there is good reason to be troubled about the frequency of the use of the rod, the force with which it is applied, the young age at which it is introduced and the delegation to SM of the authority to use it.

While the parents are recognized as having the responsibility and the right to discipline their children in a manner they deem appropriate, which could include reasonable use of a rod, that right is restricted by the duty to ensure that no action they take will result in a substantial risk the children will suffer physical harm.

The rod was used on children who could not possibly understand the use of force, and was being used on children at decreasing age thresholds. ...

While the evidence falls short of demonstrating that the children have suffered "physical harm" within the meaning of s. 22(2)(a), I conclude that the Agency has established, on a balance of probabilities, there is a substantial risk that the children will suffer physical harm as a consequence of the actions of the respondents. ...

I would order that the children are in need of protective services as defined by s. 22(2)(b). I would further direct that a disposition hearing be held within 90 days from the date of the order of the Court. At that hearing the Court will have the freedom to consider the options available under s. 42 that should be exercised in the best interests of the children.

NOTES AND QUESTIONS

1. Note s. 49 of the *CFSA*. Does it suggest that the courts should generally adopt an inquisitorial or investigatory approach in child protection hearings?

2. Section 50(1)(a) of the *CFSA* expressly authorizes a court to admit evidence about a person's past conduct towards any child at any stage of a protection hearing, including determining if the child is in need of protection. Note also s. 50(1)(b). In "Reforming Ontario's *Child and Family Services Act*: Is the Pendulum Swinging Back Too Far?" (1999), 17 C.F.L.Q. 121, Professor Bala argues (at 161) that the new s. 50(1)(b) "is intended only to deal with evidence of past conduct towards children, and to make clear that any evidence of this type of conduct '*is* admissible', including prior reasons for a decision in a civil or criminal proceeding". However, he acknowledges (at 162) that the provision may be interpreted more broadly and suggests (at 162) that the "unfortunate wording and punctuation of section 50(1)(b) ... illustrates the dangers of enacting legislation without public hearings".

In *Children's Aid Society of Sudbury & Manitoulin (Districts) v. M. (P.)* (2002), 2002 CarswellOnt 965 (Ont. C.J.), Justice Renaud preferred the "cautious" or "limited" interpretation of s. 50(1)(b) and held that it applied only to such hearsay evidence relating to "past conduct towards children as the court may consider ... relevant". The Justice also noted that "concerns about reliability and fairness" should also be taken into account. See also *Catholic Children's Aid Society of Toronto v. L. (J.)* (2003), 39 R.F.L. (5th) 54 (Ont. C.J.).

3. Courts in child protection proceedings have often admitted reports of out-of-court statements by a child victim of abuse even though this is hearsay evidence. However, there are two distinct approaches in the cases even though each may often produce the same result. In *Winnipeg Child & Family Services v. L. (L.)* (1994), 4 R.F.L. (4th) 10, the Manitoba Court of Appeal concluded that out-of-court statements by children should readily be admitted and their hearsay nature should only affect the weight accorded to them. In particular, the court held that there was no need to establish that it was necessary to admit the evidence as it would be in criminal proceedings. See also *Children's Aid Society of London & Middlesex v. H. (R.)* (1999), 1999 CarswellOnt 4380 (Ont. S.C.J.).

For the most part, this approach has been rejected. The Newfoundland Court of Appeal stated in *Re B. (J.)* (1998), 40 R.F.L. (4th) 165 at 200–202; leave to appeal refused (1999), 236 N.R. 396 (note) (S.C.C.):

> Since the decisions ... in *R. v. Khan*, [1990] 2 S.C.R. 531 and *R. v. Smith*, [1992] 2 S.C.R. 915, the approach to hearsay evidence has changed from a search to determine whether the circumstances fall within one of the exceptions that had been judicially developed over the years, to a determination, on a principled basis, of whether the reception of the evidence, notwithstanding the dangers of its use without an opportunity to cross-examine and to have had the information stated on oath, can be justified on the basis of necessity and reliability.

> ... [W]e see no reason why the principled approach to admission of hearsay evidence enunciated in *Khan* and *Smith* ought not to be applicable in child protection cases. ... The *Khan-Smith* approach provides both the justification for the reception of the evidence (necessity and reliability) and, by imposing an admissibility threshold, accords to the party against whom the evidence will be used, protection against being prejudiced by the reception of untrustworthy information.

> To adopt the seductively simple approach of allowing all hearsay evidence to be received without any threshold test of admissibility, and relegating it merely to a consideration of the weight to be accorded to it, is in effect to abandon any pretext at deciding evidentiary issues according to appropriate principle and to expose those who may be adversely affected by the reception and use of the evidence (parents facing the loss of their children as a result of allegations they are in need of protection) to considerable risk of having their interests determined or at least influenced by potentially untrustworthy evidence which they may find difficult to rebut.

> Furthermore, such an approach would, in the vast majority of cases, insulate the decision to receive and act on the evidence from the possibility of appellate review.

See also *Children's Aid Society of London & Middlesex v. B. (B.)* (2000), 4 R.F.L. (5th) 183 (Ont. S.C.J.); *Children's Aid Society of Ottawa-Carleton v. L. (L.)* (2001), 22 R.F.L. (5th) 24 (Ont. S.C.J.); and *Children's Aid Society of Ottawa-Carleton v. B.* (2002), 2002 CarswellOnt 1280 (Ont. S.C.J.).

4. The evidence of experts is commonly relied on in child protection hearings. In *Re Warren* (1973), 13 R.F.L. 51 (Ont. Co. Ct.), Matheson Co. Ct. J. cautioned (at 52-53):

> In a hearing such as this there is danger in over-reliance upon any group of witnesses selfconscious respecting their professionalization. I resolved not to fall victim to this specific bias of the profession.
>
> ...
>
> It was manifest from the opening that this was a contest between the right of a subsocio-economic family to subsist together and the right of the public, represented by the Children's Aid Society, to insist upon higher standards of parental care than the couple in question were capable of offering. Many witnesses called for the Society were persons of superior education with post-graduate degrees in social work or some other related specialty. One could not listen to their testimony with all the sombre implications of this application without resolving that this Court must not be persuaded to impose unrealistic or unfair middle class standards of child care upon a poor family of extremely limited potential.

Most provincial child welfare legislation provides for court-ordered assessments of the child and parents. Until the 2006 amendments, the *CFSA* only authorized a court to order an assessment of the child and parents after the child was found in need of protection. Now, a parenting capacity assessment can be ordered earlier. See s. 54 and *Court Ordered Assessments*, O. Reg. 25/07. Section 3 of the regulation states that a court can order an assessment at any time with the consent of the parties. Otherwise, the section stipulates that an assessment should not occur until the court "has received evidence, held a temporary care and custody hearing and made an order pursuant to subsection 51 (2) of the Act" or "has made a finding that a child is in need of protection pursuant to subsection 37 (2) of the Act".

In *Children's Aid Society of Halton Region v. A. (K.)* (2008), 54 R.F.L. (6th) 432 (Ont. C.J.), Justice Zisman refused to accept a father's consent to a court ordered assessment until he had received legal advice. When the father then opposed the Children's Aid Society's request for such an assessment, the Justice stated (at para. 20): "Despite the change in the legislation, it is my view that, before a finding of protection is made, the court should carefully scrutinize any request by a society to make such a significant intrusion into the life of a person whose parenting capacity is being assessed — especially if that person is opposing the assessment." Ultimately, the Justice denied the Society's request.

On the nature and use of expert evidence in child protection hearings, see Bala, "Mental Health Professionals in Child-Related Proceedings: Understanding the Ambivalence of the Judiciary" (1996), 13 C.F.L.Q. 260; Daley, "Parenting Capacity Assessments" (1999-2000), 17 C.F.L.Q. 101; Bala and Saunders, "Understanding the Family Context: Why the Law of Expert Evidence is Different in Family Law Cases" (2002-2003), 20 C.F.L.Q. 277; Thompson, "Rules of Evidence and Preparing for Court" in Bala, Zapf, Williams, Vogl, and Hornick, eds., *Canadian Child Welfare Law: Children, Families and the State*, 2d ed. (Toronto: Thompson Educational Publishing, Inc., 2004); Bala and Leschied, "Court-ordered Assessments in Ontario Child Welfare Cases: Review and Recommendations for Reform" (2008), Can. J. Fam. L. 11; and Curtis, "Limits of Parenting Capacity Assessments in Child Protection Cases" (2009), 28 C.F.L.Q. 1.

5. For discussion of the principal issues relating to the law of evidence that arise in child protection proceedings and the different general approaches taken in the cases, see the following articles by Professor Thompson: "Taking Children and Facts Seriously: Evidence Law in Child Protection Proceedings — Part I" (1988), 7 Can. J. Fam. L. 11; "Taking Children and Facts Seriously: Evidence Law in Child Protection Proceedings — Part II" (1989), 7 Can. J. Fam. L. 223; "Are There *Any* Rules of Evidence in Family Law?" (2003-2004), 21 C.F.L.Q. 245; "The Cheshire Cat, or Just his Smile? Evidence in Child Protection" (2003-2004), 21 C.F.L.Q. 319; and "Rules of Evidence and Preparing for Court" in Bala, Zapf, Williams, Vogl, and Hornick, eds. *Canadian Child Welfare Law: Children, Families and the State*, 2d ed. (Toronto: Thompson Educational Publishing, Inc., 2004).

6. In *New Brunswick (Minister of Health and Community Services) v. G. (J.)* (1999), 177 D.L.R. (4th) 124, the Supreme Court of Canada held that the provincial government was under a constitutional obligation to provide an indigent mother with legal representation where a child welfare agency was threatening to remove her child from her custody. The court recognized that removing a child from parental custody had a "serious and profound effect on a [parent's] psychological integrity" and hence was a restraint on a parent's "security of the person" under section 7 of the *Charter*. The court concluded that, given the nature of child protection proceedings and their "profound effect on the lives of both parents and children", the "principles of fundamental justice" generally required that the government to fund counsel for indigent parents.

(3) Finding a Child In Need of Protection

One of the more significant changes to the *CFSA* made by the *Child and Family Services Amendment Act (Child Welfare Reform), 1999* dealt with the definition of "child in need of protection". The following excerpt discusses these changes.

BALA, "REFORMING ONTARIO'S *CHILD AND FAMILY SERVICES ACT*: IS THE PENDULUM SWINGING BACK TOO FAR?

(1999-2000), 17 C.F.L.Q. 121 (Footnotes omitted)

(c) The Definition of Child in Need of Protection: Section 37(2)

A central theme of criticism of the 1984 C.F.S.A. has been that children have been endangered because the definition of "child in need of protection" is too narrow, and that the definition required agencies to leave children with parents who abused or even killed them. However, all of the child abuse deaths arose in cases that were within the present definitions of "substantial risk of physical harm." The problems arose because of difficulties that agency workers had with evidence gathering or (at least with hindsight) from the failure to exercise proper judgement. No definition of child in need of protection will eliminate the need for professional judgement and sometimes very difficult individualized decision making.

Neglect added: Bill 6 adds section 37(2)(a)(ii) so that a child who suffers "physical harm" as result of a parental "*pattern of neglect* in caring for, providing for, supervising or protecting the child" is a "child in need of protection." (Emphasis added.) Since section 37(2)(a) of the 1984 C.F.S.A. already included a child who suffers physical harm as a result of a parental failure to "care and provide or supervise and protect the child adequately," there would not appear to be significant change by adding neglect. There may be controversy over the meaning of the term "*pattern*" of neglect, which suggests that there must be several incidents.

To the extent that the new words simply clarify the old definition, it is useful for educative purposes for child protection workers and potential child abuse reporters, making clear to them that neglect is included in the concept of "harm".

Emotional abuse and neglect widened: Because of the vagueness of the concept of "emotional abuse", the definition in the present section 37(2)(f) is intentionally narrow. The 1984 C.F.S.A emotional abuse provision is not frequently invoked. It requires the agency to prove "*severe* (i) anxiety, (ii) depression, (iii) withdrawal, or (iv) self-destructive or aggressive behaviour", (emphasis added) *and* that the parent is unable or unwilling to provide services or treatment that would alleviate that condition. Bill 6 amends this definition by providing that:

> 1. the condition only needs to [be] "*serious*" not "*severe*" and by adding "delayed development" to the list; and

> 2. adding to parental unwillingness or inability to provide services [section 37(2)(f.1)], cases where "there are *reasonable grounds*" (emphasis added) to believe a child's emotional condition "results from [parental] actions, failure to act, or pattern of neglect" [section 37(2)(f)].

I submit that under the new provision judges should require expert evidence from qualified mental health professionals to establish that the child has one of the conditions listed.

It is often difficult to be certain why a child or adolescent (or an adult) suffers from a particular emotional, psychological or behavioural condition. There may be a number of genetic, environmental, life history and parenting factors that have contributed. Section 37(2)(f) will require the agency to establish at least "reasonable grounds" (i.e. less than proof on the balance of probabilities) that the condition "*results* from" parental conduct or neglect. Even at this lower standard of proof, the *causal link* may be difficult to establish. The statute does not make clear how the courts should deal with interacting factors; the wording ("results from") would appear to suggest that the parental action or neglect must at least be the dominant factor in the child's condition.

As many as one fifth of the child and adolescent population in Ontario at some point has emotional or psychological problems that might fit within the listed conditions. If a broad interpretation of the new provisions were to be adopted, very large numbers of children might be considered to be in "need of protection," rather that merely being in need of mental health services. However, it is submitted that the courts should not take an expansive interpretative approach, as Bill 6 requires that the conditions must be "*serious*" (though not necessarily "*severe*").

Further, the definitions also require that there must be parental failure to consent to treatment, or responsibility for the condition. One of the biggest problems that Ontario children and adolescents with emotional and behavioural conditions face is not parental unwillingness to seek help, but the lack of access to mental health professionals. While those who are financially well off may seek private treatment, for families and children who have to rely on the public education and health systems to diagnose and treat emotional, psychological and behavioural problems, there are very long waiting lists for mental health services. Frequently in low income families mental health problems cannot be properly addressed due to a lack of resources. Judges should not penalize families because of their inability to access mental health services.

"Substantial risk" that a child will suffer harm replaced by "risk of likely harm": Bill 6 will change the verbal formula for establishing that a child is in need of protection in situations where there is a concern about future risk as opposed to past harm. While this change is intended to provide for greater consistency in approach by agencies and judges, it is not clear that this change is intended to alter the approach taken by the leading precedents to this issue.

Under the 1984 C.F.S.A. future risk of physical, sexual or emotional harm is a ground for intervention if there is a "substantial risk" that a child will suffer harm. The concept of "substantial risk" appears at different places in the 1984 C.F.S.A., including the risk of future harm and in the test for keeping a child in interim care under s. 51. The *Panel of Experts Report* noted that there have been differing interpretations of the term "substantial risk" by protection workers and judges. The *Panel* recommended that there should be a "clearer" and "less onerous" test.

There were some decisions which interpreted the term "substantial risk" as placing a burden on agencies that is "almost massive ... in that the risk must be substantial ... risks which are significant [are] not [necessarily] substantial." Most decisions, however, interpreted the term "substantial risk" as indicating that the agency must establish, on the balance of probabilities, that there is an "actual, real and not illusory risk" or that the agency faces an evidentiary burden that is "more than a mere suspicion."

Bill 6 is intended to provide a clearer test for risk of future harm, though whether it is less onerous depends on the interpretation one took of the old "substantial risk" test. The words of Bill 6 are less ambiguous, though there is still a lack of clarity in the new words.

For the risk of future harm, the new test uses the phrase: "risk that the child is likely to be harmed." While the term "risk" is unmodified, it is grammatically linked to "likely." This new test is not unproblematic. The term "risk" on its own might suggest that a *low* probability of future harm would suffice to allow intervention. But the word "likely" connotes more probable than not, and some dictionary definitions suggest an even higher standard, including as synonyms for "likely" such as "probable" or "to be expected" and even "apparently destined."

The 1998 decision of the British Columbia Court of Appeal in *S. (B.) v. British Columbia Director of Child and Family Services* (1998), 38 R.F.L. (4th) 138 may be helpful for the interpretation of the new future risk provision. The Court in that case was applying a definition that requires the agency to show that a child "is likely to be physically harmed by the child's parent." Justice Lambert concluded that in the context of a child protection proceeding, that the word "'likely' was to be used in the sense of a 'real possibility, a possibility that cannot sensibly be ignored having regard to the nature and gravity of the feared harm.'" The judge also went on to emphasize the need for a balancing of concerns, and the need to consider both the nature and the likelihood of harm. He warned of the dangers of over-intervention:

> I remain concerned that interpreting the word "harm" too broadly may result in casting the protection net too widely, thus leading to the removal of children from the care of their parents in circumstances in which the appropriate course of action would be to offer the family support services.

> I cannot conceive that the Legislature intended ... to authorize the removal of children from their parents' care on the basis of any harm to those children, no matter how trifling or transitory the harm might be. I am of the view, therefore, that s. 13 must be interpreted as justifying a finding that a child is in need of protection only if the harm established is significant harm. By "significant", I mean harm that is more than trifling or transitory in nature; that is substantial enough to warrant government intervention, rather than government assistance through the provision of support services. Inadequate diet or hygiene, for example, would not meet this threshold; the type of life-threatening harm found in this case, would.

While it will ultimately be for judges to interpret the definitions in Bill 6, the definitional words (inevitably) still give decision-makers significant interpretative discretion. The new definition of future risk is somewhat clearer, and reminds decision-makers that there does *not* need to be certainty of future harm. However, the new definition ("risk of likely harm") may not be less onerous for agencies than the commonly used approach to the old test ("substantial risk").

In *Children's Aid Society of Ottawa-Carleton v. T.* (2000), 2000 CarswellOnt 2156 (Ont. S.C.J.), Justice Blishen interpreted the new language in s. 51(3) of the *CFSA* which refers to "a risk that the child is likely to suffer harm". She stated (at paras. 7 and 10):

> In my view, the word "likely" suggests at least more probable than not. The *Concise Oxford Dictionary* (10th edition) ... defines "likely" as "such as well might happen or be true". Therefore, the harm must be more than possible. It must be more probable than not.

> ... Therefore, the test in my view is as follows: The Children's Aid Society must establish ... that there is a real possibility that if the child is returned to his parents, it is more probable than not that he will suffer harm.

Cases dealing with s. 37 of the *CFSA* frequently cite and apply this passage. See, e.g., *Re S. (D.)* (2001), 14 R.F.L. (5th) 414 (Ont. S.C.J.); additional reasons at (2001), 2001 CarswellOnt 1243 (Ont. S.C.J.); affirmed (2002), 2002 CarswellOnt 4897 (Ont. Div. Ct.); additional reasons at (2003), 39 R.F.L. (5th) 209 (Ont. Div. Ct.) and *Children's Aid Society of Niagara Region v. P. (T)* (2003), 35 R.F.L. (5th) 290 (Ont. S.C.J.). In the latter case, Justice Quinn concluded (at para. 64) that the child protection agency had to establish that there was a real possibility that the child would suffer physical harm in his parents' care.

Child welfare agencies sometimes become involved in parental alienation cases because the alienating parent complains that the other parent has abused the child. When the resulting investigation establishes that the complaints are unfounded, an agency may decide that the alienating parent is exposing the child to a risk of emotional harm. See *Children's Aid Society of Waterloo (Regional Municipality) v. A. (B.)* (2004), 2004 CarswellOnt 2595 (S.C.J.) and *Catholic Children's Aid Society of Toronto v. H. (L.)* (2008), 2008 CarswellOnt 5655 (Div. Ct.).

Two cases reproduced earlier, *Children's Aid Society of Toronto v. L. (E.L.)* and *Nova Scotia (Minister of Community & Social Services) v. M. (B.)*, examined whether children were in need of protection. In the first case, the concern was the parents' lack of parenting ability and in the second, the parents' disciplinary techniques resulted in a protection hearing. In the case that follows, the state wished to override the parents' decision regarding appropriate medical care for their child.

B. (R.) v. CHILDREN'S AID SOCIETY OF METROPOLITAN TORONTO

(1995), 9 R.F.L. (4th) 157, 1995 CarswellOnt 105, 1995 CarswellOnt 515 (S.C.C.)

LA FOREST J. (GONTHIER and McLACHLIN JJ. concurring): — This appeal raises the constitutionality of state interference with child-rearing decisions. The appellants are parents who argue that the Ontario *Child Welfare Act*, R.S.O. 1980, c. 66, infringes their right to choose medical treatment for their infant in accordance with the tenets of their faith. They claim that this right is protected under both ss. 7 and 2(a) of the *Canadian Charter of Rights and Freedoms*.

Facts

S.B. was born four weeks prematurely, on June 25, 1983. Soon after, she was transferred to the Hospital for Sick Children in Toronto because of her physical condition. Within the first few weeks of her life she exhibited many physical ailments and received a number of medical treatments. Her parents, the appellants, consented to all the treatments provided during those initial weeks. At their request, the attending physicians avoided the use of a blood transfusion in the treatment of S. because, as Jehovah's Witnesses, the appellants objected to it for religious reasons; they also claimed it was unnecessary.

On July 30, the child's hemoglobin level had dropped to such an extent that the attending physicians believed her life was in danger and that she might require a blood transfusion to treat potentially life-threatening congestive heart failure. On July 31, following a hearing on short notice to the appellants, Judge Main of the Ontario Provincial Court (Family Division) granted the respondent Children's Aid Society a 72-hour wardship, on the basis of the evidence of Dr. Perlman that a transfusion might be necessary and that it would not be for experimental purposes. A status review was held on August 3, but was adjourned; it resumed on August 18 and 19. Dr. Pape and Dr. Swyer both testified that although the child's condition had improved, it was still marginal, and they wished to maintain the ability to transfuse in case of an emergency. Dr. Morin, head of ophthalmology at the Hospital for Sick Children, testified that he suspected S. had infantile glaucoma and needed to undergo exploratory surgery within the following week to confirm the diagnosis. This procedure had to be performed under general anesthetic, and Dr. Swyer testified that a blood transfusion would be necessary. Main Prov. J. extended the wardship order for a period of 21 days: *Re B. (S.)* (1983), 36 R.F.L. (2d) 70. On August 23, S. received a blood transfusion as part of the examination and operation for the suspected glaucoma.

A second Provincial Court order terminated the respondent's wardship on September 15, and the child was returned to her parents. ...

[Ultimately, the parents challenged the legislation on the basis that it infringed their rights under ss. 2(a) and 7 of the *Canadian Charter of Rights and Freedoms*. The District Court ruled against them, but awarded costs against the Attorney General of Ontario who had intervened in the case. The Ontario Court of Appeal dismissed both the parents' appeal and the Attorney General's cross-appeal of the costs order. The parents appealed to the Supreme Court of Canada and the Attorney General again cross-appealed.]

Section 7 of the Charter and Parental Liberty

Although I am of the view that the principles of fundamental justice have been complied with in the present case, I nonetheless propose to comment on the scope of the protection afforded by the *Charter* as it relates to the right of parents to choose medical treatment for their infant. ... I also note that while this case can be disposed of solely on the issue of the right of parents to choose medical treatment for their infant, it is not without consequence for child protection as a whole. Intervention may well be compelling here, but this appeal raises the more general question of the right of parents to rear their children without undue interference by the state.

The appellants claim that parents have the right to choose medical treatment for their infant, relying for this contention on s. 7 of the *Charter*, and, more precisely, on the liberty interest. They assert that the right enures in the family as an entity, basing this argument on statements made by American courts in the definition of liberty under their Constitution. While, as I will indicate, American experience may be useful in defining the scope of the liberty interest protected under our Constitution, I agree that s. 7 of the *Charter* does not afford protection to the integrity of the family unit as such. The Canadian *Charter*, and s. 7 in particular, protects individuals. It is the individual's right to liberty under the *Charter* with which we are here concerned. ...

... [L]iberty does not mean mere freedom from physical restraint. In a free and democratic society, the individual must be left room for personal autonomy to live his or her own life and to make decisions that are of fundamental personal importance.

... On this point, the American experience can give us valuable guidance as to the proper meaning and limits of liberty. The United States Supreme Court has given a liberal interpretation to the concept of liberty, as it relates to family matters. It has elevated both the notion of the integrity of the family unit and that of parental rights to the status of constitutional values, through its interpretation of the Fifth and Fourteenth Amendments. *Meyer v. Nebraska*, 262 U.S. 390 (S. Ct. 1923), and *Pierce v. Society of Sisters*, 268 U.S. 510 (S. Ct. 1925), are the two landmark cases most often cited. In the former, the Supreme Court invalidated a statute that purported to limit the teaching of foreign languages. Its decision was grounded, in part at least, on a finding that the statute interfered with the right of the parents to control the education of their children. In *Pierce v. Society of Sisters*, the Supreme Court declared unconstitutional a statute that required that children attend public schools. ...

... I would have thought it plain that the right to nurture a child, to care for its development, and to make decisions for it in fundamental matters, such as medical care, are part of the liberty interest of a parent. As observed by Dickson J. in *R. v. Big M Drug Mart Ltd.*, [1985] 1 S.C.R. 295, the *Charter* was not enacted in a vacuum or absent an historical context. The common law has long recognized that parents are in the best position to take care of their children and make all the decisions necessary to ensure their well-being. ... Although the philosophy underlying state intervention has changed over time, most contemporary statutes dealing with child protection matters, and in particular the Ontario Act, while focusing on the best interests of the child, favour minimal intervention. In recent years, courts have expressed some reluctance to interfere with parental rights, and state intervention has been tolerated only when necessity was demonstrated. This only serves to confirm that the parental interest in bringing up, nurturing, and caring for a child, including medical care and moral upbringing, is an individual interest of fundamental importance to our society.

The respondents have argued that the "parental liberty" asserted by the appellants is an obligation owed to the child which does not fall within the scope of s. 7 of the *Charter*. ...

While acknowledging that parents bear responsibilities towards their children, it seems to me that they must enjoy correlative rights to exercise them. The contrary view would not recognize the fundamental importance of choice and personal autonomy in our society. As already stated, the common law has always, in the absence of demonstrated neglect or unsuitability, presumed that parents should make all significant choices affecting their children, and has afforded them a general liberty to do as they choose. This liberty interest is not a parental right tantamount to a right of property in children. (Fortunately, we have distanced ourselves from the ancient juridical conception of children as chattels of their parents.) The state is now actively involved in a number of areas traditionally conceived of as properly belonging to the private sphere. Nonetheless, our society is far from having repudiated the privileged role parents exercise in the upbringing of their children. This role translates into a protected sphere of parental decision making which is rooted in the presumption that parents should make important decisions affecting their children both because parents are more likely to appreciate the best interests of their children and because the state is ill-equipped to make such decisions itself. Moreover, individuals have a deep personal interest as parents in fostering the growth of their own children. This is not to say that the state cannot intervene when it considers it necessary to safeguard the child's autonomy or health. But such intervention must be justified. In other words, parental decision making must receive the protection of the *Charter* in order for state interference to be properly monitored by the courts, and be permitted only when it conforms to the values underlying the *Charter*.

The respondents also argued that the infant's rights were paramount to those of the appellants and, on that basis alone, state intervention was justified. ... Children undeniably benefit from the *Charter*, most notably in its protection of their rights to life and to the security of their person. As children are unable to assert these, our society presumes that parents will exercise their freedom of choice in a manner that does not offend the rights of their children. If one considers the multitude of decisions parents make daily, it is clear that in practice, state interference in order to balance the rights of parents and children will arise only in exceptional cases. In fact, we must accept that parents can, at times, make decisions contrary to their children's wishes — and rights — as long as they do not exceed the threshold dictated by public policy, in its broad conception. For instance, it would be difficult to deny that a parent can dictate to his or her child the place where he or she will live, or which school he or she will attend. However, the state can properly intervene in situations where parental conduct falls below the socially acceptable threshold. But in doing so, the state is limiting the constitutional rights of parents rather then vindicating the constitutional rights of children. ...

Once it is decided that the parents have a liberty interest, further balancing of parents' and children's rights should be done in the course of determining whether state interference conforms to the principles of fundamental justice, rather than when defining the scope of the liberty interest. Even assuming that the rights of children can qualify the liberty interest of their parents, that interest exists nonetheless. In the case at bar, the application of the Act deprived the appellants of their right to decide which medical treatment should be administered to their infant. In so doing, the Act has infringed upon the parental "liberty" protected in s. 7 of the *Charter*. I now propose to determine whether this deprivation was made in accordance with the principles of fundamental justice.

Principles of Fundamental Justice

This court has on different occasions stated that the principles of fundamental justice are to be found in the basic tenets and principles of our judicial system, as well as in the other components of our legal system. ... The state's interest in legislating in matters affecting children has a long-standing history. ... The protection of a child's right to life and to health, when it becomes necessary to do so, is a basic tenet of our legal system, and legislation to that end accords with the principles of fundamental justice, so long, of course, as it also meets the requirements of fair procedure. Section 19 of the Act [the *Child Welfare Act* which was later replaced by the *CFSA*] is but one of the numerous legislative expressions of the *parens patriae* power. It contemplates different situations where state intervention is mandated in order to ensure the protection of children. Only one of those is of interest here. It appears in s. 19(1)(b)(ix), which reads:

> 19. (1) In this Part and Part IV,
>
> > (b)
> >
> > "child in need of protection" means,
> >
> > > (ix) a child where the person in whose charge the child is neglects or refuses to provide or obtain proper medical, surgical or other recognized remedial care or treatment *necessary* for the child's health or well-being, or refuses to permit such care or treatment to be supplied to the child when it is recommended by a legally qualified practitioner, or otherwise fails to protect the child adequately. (Emphasis added.)

I note at the outset that this section is not limited to situations where the life of the child may be in jeopardy. It encompasses situations where treatments might be warranted to ensure his or her health or well-being. Although broad in scope, the section is compatible with a modern conception of life that embodies the notion of quality of life. ...

The appellants attack the general procedure under the *Child Welfare Act*, and, in particular, the specific way in which it was carried out in the present case. As for the constitutionality of the procedure under the Act, there is no need to discuss it at length, since I am of the opinion that the scheme designed by the legislature accords with the principles of fundamental justice. The parents must receive reasonable notice of the hearing in which their rights might be affected. "Reasonable" is a flexible criterion that permits adjustments to different situations. While it is possible to hold a wardship hearing without notice in situations of emergency, s. 28(11) of the Act provides that the wardship order cannot, in the absence of another hearing with notice, exceed 30 days. In *Re B.C.G.E.U.*, (sub nom. *B.C.G.E.U. v. British Columbia (Attorney General))* [1988] 2 S.C.R. 214, this court held that an injunction granted ex parte did not violate s. 7 of the *Charter*. That case differs from the present one, but its underlying proposition holds true: the procedural requirements of the principles of fundamental justice can be attenuated when urgent and unusual circumstances require expedited court action.

Further, the wardship order depriving the parents of the right to refuse medical treatment for their infant is granted by a judge following an adversarial process where conflicting evidence may be presented. The parents can act through counsel, present arguments, cross-examine witnesses, and so on. The onus of proof is on the Children's Aid Society, and it has been recognized by the courts, and by Main Prov. J. in this case, that the Children's Aid Society must present a strong case.

Finally, the initial order granting wardship to the Children's Aid Society must be reviewed before its expiry. ...

[Following a detailed examination of the application of the Act in the particular case, Justice La Forest continued:]

An examination of the application of the impugned provisions to the facts of this case amply demonstrates that the legislative scheme, which deprives parents of their right to choose medical treatment for their infant under certain circumstances, is in accordance with the principles of fundamental justice. Section 7 requires that a deprivation of liberty be in conformity with the principles of fundamental justice, but it does not guarantee the most equitable process of all; it dictates a threshold below which state intervention will not be tolerated. ... Section 19(1)(b)(ix) of the Act applies to treatments which are deemed necessary. The hearing is adversarial so that a debate on the medical questions can be presented. The Act requires that the Children's Aid Society notify the parents of a hearing that might affect their rights. The epithet "reasonable" ensures that the process will be adaptable to a myriad of situations. The wardship order is circumscribed and must be reviewed before its expiry.

In sum, the appellants were entitled to such notice, access to information, and rights of representation as may be fair and reasonable having regard to the nature of the proceedings and the urgency with which they must be carried out. Tarnopolsky J.A. [in the Ontario Court of Appeal] carefully examined these issues and concluded, and I agree with him, that the procedure, having regard to all the circumstances, did not violate the principles of fundamental justice.

Section 2(a) of the Charter

Turning now to s. 2(a) of the *Charter*, the appellants argued that the Act, which deprives them of the right to refuse medical treatment for their infant on religious grounds, violates their freedom of religion guaranteed by s. 2(a) of the *Charter*. ... I note at the outset that it is the freedom of religion of the appellants — S.'s parents — that is at stake in this appeal, not that of the child herself. While it may be conceivable to ground a claim on a child's own freedom of religion, the child must be old enough to entertain some religious beliefs in order to do so. S. was only a few weeks old at the time of the transfusion.

... In *Droit de la famille* — 1150, (sub nom. *P. (D.) v. S. (C.)*, [1993] 4 S.C.R. 141, a case involving a custody dispute in which one of the parents was a Jehovah's Witness, L'Heureux-Dubé J. stated that custody rights included the right to decide the child's religious education. It seems to me that the right of parents to rear their children according to their religious beliefs, including that of choosing medical and other treatments, is an equally fundamental aspect of freedom of religion.

It is evident that the purpose of the Act is not directed at limiting the freedom of Jehovah's Witnesses to choose medical treatment for their children, including the freedom to refuse a blood transfusion on religious grounds. It was not until 1945 that the Jehovah's Witnesses adhered to that precept, while the Act originates from a law first adopted in 1927, *The Children's Protection Act*, R.S.O. 1927, c. 279. I do not rely solely on this historical fact, however. It seems to me that a simple reading of the Act makes it clear that its purpose is nothing more or less than the protection of children. But if the purpose of the Act does not infringe on the freedom of religion of the appellants, the same cannot be said of its effects. The legislative scheme implemented by the Act, which culminates in a wardship order depriving the parents of the custody of their child, has denied them the right to choose medical treatment for their infant according to their religious beliefs.

However, as the Court of Appeal noted, freedom of religion is not absolute. While it is difficult to conceive of any limitations on religious beliefs, the same cannot be said of religious practices, notably when they impact on the fundamental rights and freedoms of others.

...

A more difficult issue is whether the freedom of religion of the appellants is intrinsically limited by the very reasons underlying the state's intervention, namely, the protection of the health and well-being of S., or whether further analysis should be carried out under s. 1 of the *Charter*. ...

In my view, it appears sounder to leave to the state the burden of justifying the restrictions it has chosen. Any ambiguity or hesitation should be resolved in favour of individual rights. Not only is this consistent with the broad and liberal interpretation of rights favoured by this court, but s. 1 is a much more flexible tool with which to balance competing rights than s. 2(a). ...

As I am of the view that the Act seriously infringed on the appellants' freedom to choose medical treatment for their child in accordance with the tenets of their faith, it remains to be determined whether this infringement was justified under s. 1 of the *Charter*.

Section 1 of the Charter

Turning now to s. 1 of the *Charter*, the appellants have argued that the state has not demonstrated, on a balance of probabilities, that S. was in need of protection within the meaning of the Act when she was apprehended by the Children's Aid Society. This argument fails to distinguish between the demonstration of the necessity of the treatment, as contemplated in the Act, and the demonstration of the reasonable nature of the legislative scheme, under s. 1 of the *Charter*. For the reasons already stated, one must take for granted the necessity of the medical treatment and, thus, the need for protection under the Act.

The appellants have conceded that the state interest in protecting children at risk is a pressing and substantial objective. The Act allows the state to assume parental rights when a judge has determined that a child is in need of treatment that his parents will not consent to. As already stated, when discussing the conformity of state intervention with the principles of fundamental justice, the process contemplated by the Act is carefully crafted, adaptable to a myriad of different situations, and far from arbitrary. The Act makes provision for notice to be given, for evidence to be called, for time limits to be imposed upon Crown wardship and other orders, as well as for procedural protections to be afforded to parents. The restrictions the Act imposes on parental rights are, in my view, amply justified.

Addendum

Since writing the foregoing, I have read the reasons of my colleagues Justices Iacobucci and Major. I must confess to being somewhat mystified by the purport they attribute to my reasons. I agree, of course, that parents may not, in the exercise of their right to nurture their children, refuse them medical treatment that is necessary and for which there is no reasonable alternative. That, I thought, was the conclusion I came to. That conclusion is, of course, clearly contemplated by s. 1 of the *Charter*, which is the provision that "guarantees the rights and freedoms set out in it," but it does so "subject only to such reasonable limits prescribed by law as can be demonstrably justified in a free and democratic society" and, as far as s. 7 is concerned, by the requirements of fundamental justice.

If my colleagues are concerned with my mode of approach — the approach, I may say, traditionally employed by this court from the earliest stages of *Charter* adjudication — I have concerns with their method of limiting one constitutional right against another without relevance to context. Thus, some of their remarks may be understood as supporting a parent's rights being overturned simply because a professional thinks it is necessary to do so. I would be very much concerned if a medical professional were able to override the parent's views without demonstrating that necessity. On my approach to the issues so far as s. 7 is concerned, it would be necessary to show that such action would not be contrary to the principles of fundamental justice. More generally, s. 1 requires an interference with the right to be demonstrably justified. That, I think, is perfectly right. In a case like the present, where there is no immediate urgency, a procedure meeting the demands of fundamental justice, which I was at pains to note the Act fully provides for, would be required.

In an emergency, the demands of fundamental justice are more easily met. ...

My colleagues express concern that my reasons would create a situation in which a child's right to life or security is reduced to a limitation of the parent's constitutionally protected right. I should observe that my approach is dictated by the nature of the case presented to us. The sole issue before us was that raised by the parents, i.e., that *their* constitutional rights were infringed in the circumstances in which medical treatment was given to the child. In such a case, the parent's rights must, under s. 1, be balanced against the interests of others in a free and democratic society — in this particular case, the right of their child. In that situation, I, not surprisingly, found the parent's rights were clearly overridden. If a situation arose where it was alleged that the child's right was violated, other rights might be raised as reasonable limits, but if the right alleged was the security of the child, as in the present case, then the child's right would again prevail over a parent's rights. In short, the issue raised governs the form, but not the substance, of the analysis. ...

I add, incidentally, that I do not (as my colleagues Iacobucci and Major JJ. appear to suggest) think that liberty is all-encompassing. I have been at pains to underline that it is limited to those essentially personal rights that are inherent to the individual, which, in my view, include (and on this I believe we agree) the right of parents to nurture their children. Even as so defined, an interference with liberty may be justified as being in conformity with the principles of "fundamental justice." ...

[L'Heureux-Dubé J. concurred with Justice La Forest's reasons with respect to the appeal, but disagreed with his treatment of the cross-appeal. Unlike the other members of the court, she would not have upheld the award of costs against the Attorney General of Ontario.

Lamer C.J., concurring in the result, agreed with the joint reasons of Iacobucci and Major JJ. regarding freedom of religion. With respect to the analysis under s. 7 of the *Charter*, he concluded that the liberty interest had not been infringed because it included neither the right of parents to choose (or refuse) medical treatment for their children nor, more generally, the right to bring up or educate their children without undue interference by the state. More generally, he stated that the word "liberty" in s. 7 encompassed only physical liberty.

Justice Sopinka also concurred with the result. He stated that it was unnecessary to determine if the parents' liberty interest had been affected because "the threshold requirement of a breach of the principles of fundamental justice was not met".]

IACOBUCCI AND MAJOR JJ. (CORY J. concurring): — We have read the reasons of Mr. Justice La Forest, and we agree with the result that there has been no unconstitutional violation of the appellants' rights. ... However, we respectfully disagree with La Forest J.'s reliance on s. 1 of the *Charter* and the principles of fundamental justice in s. 7 in order to establish the constitutionality of the repealed *Child Welfare Act*, R.S.O. 1980, c. 66. Instead, we conclude that the class of parents caught by s. 19(1)(b)(ix) of the Act simply cannot benefit from the protection of the liberty interest in s. 7 or freedom of religion encapsulated in s. 2(a) of the *Charter*. We therefore find the appellants incapable of crossing the first threshold of *Charter* analysis. There is thus no initial constitutional infringement and, consequently, no need to uphold any such infringement either through its consonance with fundamental justice or its status as a reasonable limit in a free and democratic society. ...

It is important to bear in mind that the impugned provisions of the *Child Welfare Act* are geared to the promotion of the health, safety, and personal integrity of the child. To this end, although this appeal raises issues related to the right of parents to rear their children without undue influence by the state, it also touches on the s. 7 right of the child to life and security of the person. It is this perspective that we find absent from the reasons of La Forest J. As such, we are concerned by the fact that our colleague's decision creates a situation in which the child's right to life or security of the person is reduced to a limitation on the parents' constitutionally protected ability to deny that child the necessities of life owing to parental liberty and freedom of religion.

1. Section 7

We find that the right to liberty embedded in s. 7 does not include a parent's right to deny a child medical treatment that has been adjudged necessary by a medical professional.
...

This is clearly a case where S.'s right to liberty, security of the person, and potentially even to life is deprived. It is important to note that the abridgment of S.'s s. 7 rights operates independently from the question whether the parents honestly believe that their refusal to consent to the transfusion is in the best interests of the child, since such a refusal shall, according to the appellants, prevent her from being "defiled in the eyes of God." Whether or not her parents' motivations are well-intentioned, the physical effects upon S. of the refusal to transfuse blood are equally deleterious.

We note that La Forest J. holds that "liberty" encompasses the right of parents to have input into the education of their child. In fact, "liberty" may very well permit parents to choose among *equally effective* types of medical treatment for their children, but we do not find it necessary to determine this question in the instant case. We say this because, assuming without deciding that "liberty" has such a reach, it certainly does not extend to protect the appellants in the case at bar. There is simply no room within s. 7 for parents to override the child's right to life and security of the person. ...

Our colleague's reasons open the door to the possibility that a violation of a guardian's s. 7 rights will be found should the state deny a guardian his or her right to refuse a child in his or her charge medical treatment *and* should that denial fail to conform with fundamental justice. In the case at bar, S.'s condition, although believed to be serious, was not sufficiently urgent to prevent the Children's Aid Society from seeking a court ordered wardship, thereby complying with procedural fundamental justice. But what if S. were injured in a car accident and required an immediate blood transfusion to save her life? Even if her parents would have been in agreement that the transfusion was necessary and urgently required, their personal convictions would still likely have compelled them to refuse their daughter the treatment. To this end, this exercise of parental liberty can engender the death of an infant.

We find it counter-intuitive that "parental liberty" would permit a parent to deny a child medical treatment felt to be necessary until some element of procedural fundamental justice is complied with. Although an individual may refuse any medical procedures upon her own person, it is quite another matter to speak for another separate individual, especially when that individual cannot speak for herself and, in S.'s case, has never spoken for herself. The rights enumerated in the *Charter* are individual rights to which children are clearly entitled in their relationships with the state and all persons — regardless of their status as strangers, friends, relatives, guardians, or parents.

The suggestion that parents have the ability to refuse their children medical procedures, such as blood transfusions, in situations where such a transfusion is necessary to sustain that child's health is consistent with the view, now long gone, that parents have some sort of "property interest" in their children. Indeed, in recent years, this court has emphasized that parental duties are to be discharged according to the "best interests" of the child: *Young v. Young*, [1993] 4 S.C.R. 3; *Droit de la famille — 1150*, (sub nom. *P. (D.) v. S. (C.)*) [1993] 4 S.C.R. 141. ...

The exercise of parental beliefs that grossly invades the "best interests" of the child is not activity protected by the right to "liberty" in s. 7. To hold otherwise would be to risk undermining the ability of the state to exercise its legitimate *parens patriae* jurisdiction and jeopardize the *Charter's* goal of protecting the most vulnerable members of society. As society becomes increasingly cognizant of the fact that the family is often a very dangerous place for children, the *parens patriae* jurisdiction assumes greater importance. Although there are times when the family should be shielded from the intrusions of the state, S.'s situation is one in which the state should be readily able to intervene not only to protect the public interest, but also to preserve the security of infants who cannot yet speak for themselves. ...

In sum, since we find the parental decision to withhold medical care to be outside the scope of "liberty" it does not qualify for *Charter* protection in the first place. ...

2. Section 2(a)

The parents of S. are constitutionally entitled to manifest their beliefs and practise their religion, as is their daughter. That constitutional freedom includes the right to educate and rear their child in the tenets of their faith. In effect, until the child reaches an age where she can make an independent decision regarding her own religious beliefs, her parents may decide on her religion for her and raise her in accordance with that religion.

However, the freedom of religion is not absolute. Although La Forest J. considered that limitations on this right are best considered under a s. 1 analysis, we are of the view that the right itself must have a definition, and even if a broad and flexible definition is appropriate, there must be an outer boundary. Conduct which lies outside that boundary is not protected by the *Charter*. That boundary is reached in the circumstances of this case.

We are of the view that the constitutional question should be: To what extent can an infant's right to life and health be subordinated to conduct emanating from a parent's religious convictions? With this perspective as a starting point, we find that the appellants do not benefit from the protection of s. 2(a) of the *Charter* since a parent's freedom of religion does not include the imposition upon the child of religious practices which threaten the safety, health, or life of the child. ...

NOTES AND QUESTIONS

1. In "Case Comment: *B. (R.) v. Children's Aid Society of Metropolitan Toronto*" (1995), 9 R.F.L. (4th) 345, Professor Thompson describes Justice La Forest's reasons in the case as "seminal" and a "landmark" for the application of the *Charter* to child protection issues because the "clear message ... is that the parent-child relationship is one of 'fundamental importance' and that it deserves serious constitutional analysis and protection". Professor Thompson suggests that Justice La Forest's reasons attracted "a five-judge majority on s. 2(a) and a four-and-three-eighths majority on s. 7". He supports the latter claim as follows:

> It is important to appreciate that La Forest J. attracts the support of four other judges on s. 2(a), with Sopinka J. joining in. On s. 7 Sopinka J. avoids defining "liberty" by concluding that "the threshold requirement of a breach of the principles of fundamental justice was not met" (at p. 248). As suggested earlier, that determination amounts to a three-eighths concurrence, for two reasons. First, Sopinka J. did *not* join in with the minority (Iacobucci and Major JJ. (Cory J. concurring)) and its truncation of s. 7 rights. Second, through his s. 2(a) concurrence he accepts the same parental rights under a different heading, one where the state bears the s. 1 burden of justifying intervention.

2. In two later cases, the Supreme Court of Canada again applied s. 7 in the child protection context. It held in *New Brunswick (Minister of Health & Community Services) v. G. (J.)* (1999), 177 D.L.R. (4th) 124 (S.C.C.), that the provincial government was obliged by s. 7 of the *Charter* to provide an indigent mother with legal representation where a child welfare agency was threatening to remove her child from her custody. The court unanimously recognized that removing a child from parental custody had a serious and profound effect on a parent's psychologi-

cal integrity and hence affected security of the person. The court also concluded unanimously that the principles of fundamental justice required a fair hearing and that the mother would not have such a hearing without a lawyer. A minority concluded that the mother's liberty interest was also engaged because the proceeding might deprive her of the right to make decisions on behalf of her child. The majority decided not to address the mother's right to liberty since it was possible to dispose of the case by focusing on the mother's security of the person and since "there have been differing views expressed about the scope of the right to liberty in the Court's previous judgments" (para. 56).

Recall that the Supreme Court of Canada unanimously held in *Winnipeg Child & Family Services (Central Area) v. W. (K.L.)* (2000), 10 R.F.L. (5th) 122, 2000 CarswellMan 469, 2000 CarswellMan 470, that the apprehension of a child from parental care constituted an infringement of a parent's right to security of the person that could only be carried out in accordance with the principles of fundamental justice. Justice L'Heureux-Dubé, for the majority, concluded that the Manitoba legislation did accord with these principles.

3. Where a patient is not capable of giving or refusing consent, both the common law and legislation such as the *Health Care Consent Act, 1996* recognize that others may validly make the decision. For example, s. 20(1) of the *Health Care Consent Act, 1996* specifies that the following may provide or withhold the necessary consent for a person who lacks capacity to consent:

> [paragraph] 5. A ... parent of the incapable person, or a children's aid society or other person who is lawfully entitled to give or refuse consent to the treatment in the place of the parent. This paragraph does not include a parent who has only a right of access. If a children's aid society or other person is lawfully entitled to give or refuse consent to the treatment in the place of the parent, this paragraph does not include the parent.

> [paragraph] 6. A parent of the incapable person who has only a right of access.

Subsections (3) and (4) go on to stipulate that the access parent may give consent only if (1) the custodial parent is unavailable, incapable, or is unwilling to assume the responsibility; or (2) the access parent believes that the custodial parent would not object.

As *B. (R.) v. Children's Aid Society of Metropolitan Toronto* illustrates, parental refusal to consent may lead to a child protection proceeding. In emergency situations, these may be hurriedly convened and conducted. See, e.g., *Catholic Children's Aid Society of Metropolitan Toronto v. F. (R.)* (1988), 66 O.R. (2d) 528 (Prov. Ct.).

Section 27 of Ontario's *Health Care Consent Act, 1996* specifies that a health practitioner may treat a child who is incapable of consenting and whose parents refuse to consent where the health practitioner believes that: (1) there is an emergency (defined as a situation where the child "is apparently experiencing severe suffering or is at risk, if the treatment is not administered promptly, of sustaining serious bodily harm"); and (2) the parents are not properly acting in the best interests of the child. Section 25 deals with emergency treatment where consent cannot be obtained promptly and "the delay required to obtain a consent or refusal on the [child's] behalf will prolong the suffering that the [child] is apparently experiencing or will put the [child] at risk of sustaining serious bodily harm". Section 29(4) then specifies that a health practitioner who, in good faith, administers treatment in accordance with s. 25 or s. 27 is not liable for administering treatment without consent. Can these provisions withstand a *Charter* challenge in light of *B. (R.) v. C.A.S. of Metropolitan Toronto*?

(4) Dispositional Stage

CHILDREN'S AID SOCIETY OF TORONTO v. U. (L.)

(2007), 2007 CarswellOnt 9492 (Ont. C.J.); affirmed (2008), 56 R.F.L. (6th) 186, 2008 CarswellOnt 3192 (Ont. S.C.J.) (Footnotes omitted)

1 MURRAY J.: This is an application by the Children's Aid Society of Toronto ("the Society") for an order that the child, John U., born June 30, 2006, be made a Crown Ward without access for the purpose of adoption. John's mother, L. U., opposes the application and asks that John be returned to her under an order of supervision. John's Father, G. S., has been noted in default.

2 John was found to be a child in need of protection pursuant to section 37(2)(b) of the Act on July 16, 2007 on the basis of a statement of agreed facts in which the parties acknowledged that John was "likely to suffer physical harm, inflicted by the person having charge of the child or caused by that person's failure to care and provide for or to supervise and protect the child adequately".

3 John has been in care since November 15, 2006, when he was apprehended from his mother's care.

4 Ms. U. has another child, Joanna, born December 12, 2003. Joanna was apprehended on April 21, 2005 and found to be a child in need of protection pursuant to section 37(2)(1) of the Act on July 11, 2005. Protection proceedings were terminated after an order was made on February 15, 2007 pursuant to section 57.1 of the Act placing Joanna in her paternal grandmother's custody with access to the parents in the discretion of the paternal grandmother and supervised at her discretion. Because the paternal grandmother has moved from the Toronto area, Ms. U. sees Joanna only occasionally when grandmother visits Toronto.

5 The Society's concerns with respect to Ms. U. as a parent set out in its initial protection application of November 2006 were "domestic violence (Father against Mother), drug use by the parents, ability to parent and the mother's transience". At trial the Society acknowledged that Mother had dealt successfully with her problem with drug abuse, but submitted that she is still unable or unwilling to meet John's needs in a timely fashion at least in part because of the continued instability in her personal circumstances — instability in the areas of housing, finances, and in personal relationships. The Society submits that it has made considerable efforts to assist Mother in her parenting, through its Therapeutic Access program and through the Thistletown ATTENDS Program, but that Mother is still unable to parent safely in a consistent manner.

6 Mother submits that her success in dealing with past drug abuse shows that she is capable of positive change. She submits that her personal circumstances are more stable than the Society credits; for the past six months she has maintained both a stable residence and a stable and positive relationship with her boyfriend, M. A. She strongly asserts that she is both willing and able to care for John.

7 John has been in care for over twelve months. The Society presented evidence that John is adoptable, and this evidence was not seriously challenged by Mother. There is no family plan being presented for John.

Statutory Framework: Options on Disposition

8 If a child is found to be in need of protection and the Court is satisfied that a court order is necessary to protect the child in the future, the Court shall make one of the following orders pursuant to section 57(1) of the Act in the child's best interests: [supervision order, Society wardship, Crown wardship, and consecutive orders of Society wardship and supervision].

9 The Society has a duty to help parents who need assistance in caring for children, always keeping in mind that the paramount objective of the Act is to promote the best interests, protection and well being of children. A court is required before making an order of disposition to consider what efforts the Society has made to assist the parent before making an order that would remove a child from that parent's care: s. 57(2) *CFSA*. In some cases, a Society's failure to assist a parent and offer her a fair chance to parent has been decisive in determining that a Crown Wardship request will be refused. (See for example, *Children's Aid Society of Timiskaming (District) v. C. (J.)*, [2002] O.J. No. 1646 (Ont. C.J.). Failure by a Society to offer adequate assistance to a parent does not, however, invariably mean that a

wardship request will be refused; all factors must be considered in determining the child's best interests.

10 Before an order is made removing a child from a person who is caring for her immediately before Society intervention, a court is also required to consider whether less disruptive alternatives will serve the child's best interests and whether it is possible to place the child with a relative or a member of the child's community or extended family. See s. 57(3) *CFSA*. The Society made inquiries from both Father's and Mother's families, and no one came forward presenting an alternate plan for John.

Section 70 Time Limit

11 Section 70 of the Act is statutory recognition that permanency planning is of paramount importance for children. Section 70 (1) provides as follows:

> 70. (1) Subject to subsections (3) and (4), the court shall not make an order for society wardship under this Part that results in a child being a society ward for a period exceeding,
>
>> (a) 12 months, if the child is less than 6 years of age on the day the court makes an order for society wardship; or
>>
>> (b) 24 months, if the child is 6 years of age or older on the day the court makes an order for society wardship.

Section 70(4) provides that this period may be extended by a period "not to exceed six months if it is in the child's best interests to do so".

12 There has been debate about the extent of a court's powers under this section to extend a child's period of Society wardship. Some courts have held that the section allows a court to extend Society wardship for a child under six years of age only up to the point where the child will have spent a total of eighteen months in Society care. Other courts have held that this section gives the court discretion to extend the 12-month limit by six months from the date of trial by individual and separate periods of up to six-months. In my view, the latter interpretation is most consistent with the overall purposes of the Act. If the Legislature had intended greater restriction on the court's ability to extend the time limit in appropriate circumstances, it could have drafted the section accordingly.

13 In calculating the allowable period for a child to be a Society ward, the Act provides that any time a child has spent in care under a temporary order shall be counted. John has been in the Society's care since November 15, 2006, and thus has already exceeded the statutory limit. Mother conceded that if John is placed in her care that a further court order providing for Society supervision should be made.

14 Thus, the options open to the Court are limited to returning John to his mother under a supervision order or making John a Crown Ward, unless a case for an extension of a period of Society wardship could be made out. Neither the Society nor Mother requested such an extension. If an extension is granted, it must be because the extension is in the child's (and not just the parent's) best interests, as seen from the child's perspective. Best interests must be determined in reference to the factors set out in s. 37(3) of the Act.

Best Interests

15 The decision as to disposition must be based on what is in a child's best interests. [See s. 37(3) of the *CFSA* for the factors that a court must consider.]

Access

16 If a court makes an order that a child be made a Crown ward, any previous order for access which existed under the Act is terminated: s. 59(2). Section 59 (2.1) provides that the court shall not make a new order with respect to access unless a two-pronged test is satisfied. ...

17 It is important to note that the terms of the Act dealing with adoption provide that there may not be an outstanding access order between a child and parent at the time an adoption order is made. While the Act does allow for "openness" orders, such orders are different from access orders and are only available on the application of a Society and on the consent of all parties, including the adoptive parents.

The Evidence

18 Mother is 21 years old. Mother and Father came to the attention of the Society soon after the birth of their first child, Joanna, when it was reported that Father assaulted Mother.

19 The Society provided a number of support services and arranged for Mother to move with the baby to Massey Centre, which provided a supportive semi-supervised environment. Mother returned to live with Father. Hair tests confirmed that Mother and Father were using amphetamines and methamphetamines. Visiting Society workers found the home in a deplorable and unsafe condition.

20 In April 2005 Mother separated from Father and went to a shelter. (They apparently did not cohabit again, although Mr. S. is the father of John.) The baby Joanna's condition was deteriorating and on April 21, 2005, she was apprehended and quickly hospitalized, suffering from dehydration.

21 After Joanna's apprehension, Mother was transient for a number of months and lost her subsidized housing due to non-payment of rent. Mother testified that this non-payment was the result of a mix up between Social Services, which was supposed to pay her rent, and the housing agency. It was during this period of transience that Mother became pregnant with John.

22 In April 2006, Mother moved into Robertson House, a shelter in the city of Toronto, where she lived until November 2006.

23 At Robertson house a number of supports were available to Mother. ...

25 Mother did not complete the parenting program offered by Robertson House, but did complete another parenting course, "Nobody's Perfect" in May 2006. She also completed a substance abuse program offered by the Jean Tweed Center in early November 2006.

26 When John was born both he and Mother were tested for the presence of drugs which had been a concern in the past; the tests were negative. There is no evidence that Mother has abused substances since before John's birth. ...

27 After John was born on June 30, 2006, he returned with Mother to live at Robertson House. Within a month, Robertson House staff contacted the Society with concerns that Mother appeared "overwhelmed" in caring for the child. Robertson House staff reported that Mother was not feeding the child regularly, that he was left alone to cry by himself for long periods of time, and that she was not attending to his hygiene, despite constant reminders.

28 Over three months the Society staff, Robertson House staff, and the high-risk infant nurse monitored Mother and John. In November John began to lose weight; he was apprehended on November 13, 2006. Soon after John came into care he began gaining weight.

29 Shortly after John's apprehension, Mother was asked to leave Robertson House because of disruptive behaviour. Mother acknowledged that she was quite upset because of the apprehension, and blamed some of the Robertson House staff because of what she viewed as inaccurate reports of her care giving.

30 Mother has moved six times since leaving Robertson House a year ago. ... In late June 2007, Mother moved to her current accommodation ... This is a basement room in which other facilities are shared. A Society worker testified that the room is well-kept. Mother testified that she considered this accommodation "temporary" and that if John was placed in her care that she would rent an apartment. She testified that she had recently looked at a two-bedroom apartment which was affordable.

31 With respect to personal relationships, Mother's evidence was that she has been in three intimate relationships over the last two years, two of them for very brief periods. ...

32 Society worker Susan Hansford testified that Ms. U. advised her that she was going to be living with Mr. A. at the end of June 2007. By September 2007, Mother advised the Society that she was no longer living with Mr. A. In her evidence at trial, Mother said that, in fact, she has been living with Mr. A. since early July 2007. Mr. A. confirmed this in his evidence. Mother explained the variance with what she told Ms. Hansford by saying that she wanted to make sure that her intimate relationship was stable and met the Society's expectations — the implication being that she did not think it wise to advise the Society that she was living with Mr. A. until she was sure of him.

33 Mr. A. will be twenty years old this month. He works full time at a grocery store. He has known Mother for ten years through their church. Both he and Mother testified that they planned to marry, and wanted to parent John together. Mr. A. has introduced Mother to his own mother. Mr. A. has attended several visits with John. Mr. A. has no children of his own, and testified that he has no prior experience in raising children.

34 Mr. A. was not assessed by the Society as part of Mother's plan because she did not advise them that he was part of her plan.

35 With respect to Mother's employment, she worked at McDonald's until May 2007, when she lost that job because she was taking too much time off (according to Mother, because of appointments related to John). The Society's evidence is that Mother has given them vague and sometimes conflicting information about her employment/educational endeavors since May 2007. At trial, Ms. U. testified that after her employment at McDonald's, she began working for an agency that sends her to different factories; she continues to do this work. She also collects social assistance payments. In addition to working, Mother is attending two high school courses with the goal of obtaining her secondary school diploma. Mother testified that she expected to be able to arrange work hours consistent with John's daycare schedule if he is returned to her.

36 In the past Mother has had difficulty managing her finances responsibly. ...

37 Mother appears to have little family support. She reported to one social worker that her parents were abusive and that she was separated from them at three years of age. She was raised by her grandmother, whom she described as nurturing. Her grandmother died in August 2007. Mother had not had contact with her for several months prior to her death. Although Mother testified at trial that she had the support of an aunt, the aunt did not give evidence. Society workers contacted the aunt in February of 2007. She was not co-operative in giving them information and although she stated she would "get back" to the Society, she has not done so. Although Mother referred in passing to her church, I heard no evidence about any support available to her from that source.

38 The Society has made concerted efforts to work with Mother to improve what they perceive to be deficiencies in her parenting. After apprehension until July 2007 Mother visited with John at the Society's Therapeutic Access program two days a week for six hours; at the program staff worked with Mother modeling appropriate behaviour. In December 2006, the Society referred Mother to the Interface Program at Thistletown Regional Centre, a children's mental health centre. Over a six month period, Thistletown provided intensive services for Mother which were geared to meet her identified parenting deficits. After initial meetings with Mother, there were six weekly instructional visits of two hours. Thistletown staff coordinated with staff at the Therapeutic Access centre to provide consistent teaching about providing instrumental and emotional care. The objective was not only to teach Mother how to provide consistent instrumental care for John, but to improve their parent-child relationship. Thistletown staff aimed in particular to teach Mother to "recognize and respond to John's cues so that she can best meet his developmental and emotional needs". It was arranged that John's foster parents would prepare a communication book that would give Mother information about John's daily routines, and in which she could send back information about John at visits.

39 Part of the learning that Mother engaged in during the first phase of the Thistletown program involved discussions about how stability or instability in her own life affected her ability to care for John. This included discussion about how Mother might select an appropriate partner, one who was not abusive and who was child-positive. Staff thought that Mother understood this message.

40 For three days in March 2007, Mother and John lived at the Intensive Family and Community Resource (IFCR) Assessment Unit. Staff there observed Mother and John and worked with Mother. At the IFCR Assessment unit, Mother was expected to care for John on a continuous basis, while carrying out other household functions. Adult food was provided, but it was up to Mother to bring most necessary items for the child, such as formula, bottles, bibs and clothes and toys. It was up to Mother to prepare meals, to play with the child, to feed and bathe him, to get him to sleep, and to care for herself and the household during this time. IFCR staff observed and intervened when they thought when direction was necessary.

41 The assessment report, prepared immediately after completion of three-day observation, was positive. Thistletown staff were of the opinion that Mother understood the importance of routine and structure for the child, was learning to read his cues, and was able to consistently care for him.

42 Mother's ability to feed John consistently had been a major concern to the Society prior to the assessment. The assessment reported that she demonstrated an ability to read the child's cues and to attend to all areas of instrumental care, including feeding. Staff speculated that prior difficulties in feeding had been rooted in relationship difficulties between Mother and John, which they felt were on their way to repair. Mother learned how to make a chart noting the times and amount of food for John. She was well prepared for bath time. She engaged in creative play with the child and implemented appropriate routines for nap and bedtime.

43 Thistletown staff identified that the next hurdle for Mother was to demonstrate that she could apply what she had learned outside the supported environment of the IFCR house, in the real world where there were external risk factors — the problems around the instability of relationships, housing, poor financial choices, and substance abuse.

44 After the IFCR assessment, Mother continued to see John two times a week at the Therapeutic Access program, and she also saw John at Thistletown's follow-up program, "ATTEND" (Attachment, Therapy, Teaching, Enhancing Newborn Development) for nine

weeks. In this follow-up phase, both Thistletown and Society staff observed a significant regression in her parenting behaviour. Mother again demonstrated problems in consistently feeding the child appropriately, recognizing when to check and change his diapers, supervising him when he was in her care, and playing with him. Staff tried to go back to the beginning and reinforce her in delivering appropriate instrumental care. They observed that there appeared to be some important external stressors — break -up with a boyfriend and loss of housing — which claimed her attention.

45 Thistletown staff noted in this last phase of their work with Mother that she was angry at them and the Society for not supporting a return of John to her now. Mother admitted that because of anger she sometimes did not focus on John, and for example, during visits would not feed him on time or change his diaper.

46 The Thistletown team recommended in its report of July 10, 2007 that John not be returned to Mother. I heard evidence from a member of that team, Tara Noble, whom I qualified as an expert in the assessment of parenting capacity.

47 Shortly after this, Thistletown terminated its involvement, with an offer to assist Mother again if her parenting behaviour improved. The Society decreased visits to two hours twice a week and amended its application to seek Crown wardship without access for the purpose of adoption.

48 The Society's witnesses concede that Mother was regular in her attendance at visits for the past year. They recognize that she can care for John well on some visits and that the child, when engaged, is affectionate with his mother. They testified that Mother "does better" on shorter as opposed to longer visits.

49 The Society's and Thistletown's concerns about Mother's post-assessment behaviour focus on Mother's her ability to read John's cues and lack of consistent attention to the child. They were particularly concerned about what they saw as her inability to consistently feed him appropriately. John is a small child, and everyone acknowledges that he is a fussy eater, who must be fed carefully. ...

50 Mother testified that she tried her best, but that she was getting conflicting advice about caring for John from different sources offered by the Society. For example, Mother said that the foster parents in the communication book reported that they found it helpful when trying to get John to eat to permit him to roam about the room, and follow him with the food. Society workers admonished her that the child must be kept in a high chair.

51 There are particular concerns about John's hygiene. John suffers from eczema and it is important that he stay clean and have regular diaper changes. Society workers testified that Mother still must be reminded regularly to change John's diaper. ...

53 Society workers had other complaints about Mother, which were offered in support of the proposition that she does not prioritize the child's needs:

- During a visit when John naps, Mother will sometimes nap.
- Mother sometimes conducts a phone conversation during the visit, and is not fully focused on John.
- Mother does not always select appropriate toys.
- On one occasion, John's finger was caught in a door during a visit. Staff were concerned that Mother was not paying close enough attention. ...

55 It was difficult for me to ascertain from Mother's evidence whether she accepted that there was ever a significant problem (other than her history of substance abuse) in her fitness

to care for John. At one point, Mother seemed to indicate that in her opinion she had always cared for the child well. Later, in discussing the Thistletown program, Mother testified that she had learned a lot in the program. ...

Analysis

56 If John can have his physical, mental and emotional needs met in his mother's care, his return to Mother is the preferable alternative.

57 Mother has tried hard since John's apprehension to meet the Society's concerns, even though she may not fully agree with those concerns. ...

- Mother completed a substance abuse program, and has remained drug-free.
- Mother completed a parenting program.
- Mother has regularly attended visits.
- Mother has worked cooperatively with the therapists at the Thistletown program, completing a six-month program there.
- After great instability in her residence and her partners for the first seven months after John's apprehension, Mother appears to be moving towards more stability. She has been in her current accommodation for six months. According to her evidence and that of Mr. A. they have been in a relationship for seven months. There is no evidence that domestic violence is a problem in this relationship, as it was with Mr. S. The evidence suggests that Mother's relationship with Mr. A. is a positive factor for her stability. (I note, however, that the Society has not had an opportunity to assess Mr. A. as a part of Mother's plan.)
- Mother may be moving towards more financial stability. Discounting the money which she apparently receives from social assistance fraudulently, she appears to be making realistic plans about the type of accommodation that she and Mr. A. can afford. Although the Society appeared to be critical of Mother that she had not yet rented an apartment appropriate for the care of a child, I am not. She does not know if John will be returned to her. She and Mr. A. are low-income, and cannot afford to spend money unnecessarily.

I note that Mother has made this move towards greater stability despite the death of her most important parent figure, her grandmother, in August 2007.

58 I note that the negative observations made by the Thistletown staff about Mother's care occurred during a period (April-June 2007) of what appears to have been exceptional stress for Mother. She lost her job. She had to move twice. Her relationship with the boyfriend who preceded Mr. A. ruptured. Ms. Noble testified that part of good parenting is learning how to manage when stressed. I accept that, but I do not think that means that an individual's parenting ability should be judged solely based on her actions during what may have been one of the most stressful times of her life. Part of good parenting is about making choices that lead to fewer stressors in life, and Mother appears to be heading in that direction.

59 I am still left with significant concerns about Mother's ability to care for John safely on a consistent basis, and about the viability of a supervision order if he is returned to her now. After June 2007 — when Mother appears to have begun a period of greater stability-Society staff continued to observe the concerning behaviour on visits set out above. Society staff may be focusing too strongly on the negatives in these visits. Some of the behaviours which they find "concerning" I do not, such as Mother napping when John naps. That does not

seem to be an unsafe practice. Mother may be correct that some of the behaviours that the Society workers found "concerning" were in fact behaviours suggested by John's foster parents.

60 I have no reason to believe, however, that Society workers were not telling the truth in their observations. Despite the reservations that I may have about Society evidence, that evidence establishes for me that John should not be returned home now.

61 Although the Society has made commendable efforts to instruct Mother in parenting practices, there are two areas in which it appears that more could be done to assist her. First, as noted in the Society records, Mother may have a learning disability. She needs to be assessed for this. If she does have a learning disability, that fact will affect how services should be delivered to her.

62 Second, efforts should be made to organize what family and community potential sources of support exist for Mother. I acknowledge that workers have contacted Ms. U.'s aunt to canvas alternate placements, without much response. But further efforts can be made to identify and mobilize what support exists for Mother and John. An agency other than the Children's Aid Society may be better placed to undertake this role. An effective family/group conference can identify all the sources of support for this family and how they will interact — for example, from Ms. U's family, Mr. A's family, and from their church.

63 I have concerns about Mother's attitude towards working with the Society and other professionals who might assist her. If she feels unfairly treated by Society workers, she cannot let resentment blind her to her child's real needs. *Mother must be absolutely open and clear with Society workers*. If she is not, they (and the court) cannot trust her. They cannot fairly assess her plan. And they will, not be able to adequately supervise.

64 In my view, a further brief period of Society wardship — for six months — is in John's best interests. That is the period of time that is required to establish whether he can be placed safely in the care of his mother. In my view, this delay in permanency planning for John is justified in view of the progress which his mother has made in the past year and in view of the benefit to him of being raised by his mother if placement with her is possible. The negative for John is that if Mother is unable within this six months to continue her progress towards greater stability and to demonstrate that she can consistently deliver an acceptable level of care, then permanency planning for him is delayed, probably by at least nine months if a further trial is required.

65 During the six month period of further Society wardship, the following can be accomplished:

1. The Society can assess Mr. A. and form an opinion of whether he brings greater stability to Mother's plan.

2. The Society shall arrange for Mother to be assessed for learning disabilities.

3. The Society shall contact the George Hull Family/Group Conferencing program forthwith to begin the process for a family/group conference that will identify and mobilize sources of support for this family. Mother shall cooperate in this process. It may be that Mother is better able to receive and apply parenting advice and assistance from members of her family or religious community than from child care professionals.

4. Mother will have a further opportunity to attempt to demonstrate that she can focus and deliver consistently adequate care to John. The expectation is that Mother must be not a perfect parent, but an adequate one. The Society may want to coordinate with John's foster parents so that Mother gets a consistent message about recommended parenting strategies.

5. Mother shall have unsupervised, in addition to supervised, access. The duration shall be in the discretion of the Society. Obviously if Mother and Mr. A. move ahead to obtain accommodation suitable for a child, the Society will be able to consider more extensive access.

6. The Society may want to enlist the help of the Thistletown program to assist Mother further.

7. An updated parenting capacity assessment, either from Thistletown or another source, should be prepared for the end of this six month period.

My order will provide that the parties attend for a settlement/trial management conference with the case management judge in May 2008. Hopefully, Mother will have made sufficient progress that a resolution will be agreed upon, but if not, the matter should proceed to trial as soon as possible.

NOTES AND QUESTIONS

1. As noted earlier, the 2006 addition of s. 57.1 to the *CFSA* allows a court, where it finds that an order under this section instead of an order under s. 57(1) would be in the child's best interests, to grant custody of the child to one or more persons. In *Children's Aid Society of Toronto v. K. (C.)* (2008), 2008 CarswellOnt 790 (Ont. C.J.), Justice S.B. Sherr stated (at para. 8):

The important elements of this section are as follows:

(a) The custody order in s. 57.1 can only be made once there has been a finding that a child is in need of protection.

(b) Once the finding has been made, the test is whether it is in a child's best interests to make this type of order as opposed to an order under s. 57(1) of the Act. Criteria for a child's best interests are set out in s. 37(3) of the Act.

(c) The society or any other party can apply for a party or other persons to have custody of the child. These "other persons" are not required to be parties to the action, but they must consent to the custody order (as does any party).

(d) Section 57.1 custody orders and any access orders made at the same time as these custody orders are deemed to be orders made under section 28 of the *Children's Law Reform Act* ... Any subsequent variations of this order are brought under the *Children's Law Reform Act* and the society would not be a party.

Note that, where a custody order under s. 57.1 results in the removal of a child from the person who had charge of the child immediately before the Society's intervention, s. 59(1.1) requires the court to make an access order "unless the court is satisfied that continued contact will not be in the child's best interests". See also s. 59(1.2) which deals with access orders where the custody order is made on a status review.

2. The conditions attached to a supervision order usually allow the child protection agency to monitor the child's well-being through visits to the home and the receipt of information. They may also require the parents to obtain specific services such as counselling for themselves and perhaps the child. In keeping with the philosophy that the least disruptive alternative is to be favoured, s. 57(3) directs the court to keep the child in its home if possible. If the child cannot be left there, even subject to the agency's supervision, s. 57(4) requires the court to consider placing the child with a relative, neighbour or other member of the child's community or extended family subject to supervision by the society.

3. Under a temporary wardship or society wardship order, the agency has "the rights and responsibilities of a parent for the purpose of the child's care, custody and control" (see s. 63(2) of the *CFSA*). The order removes the child from the care of his or her parents for a fixed period of time with the hope that, at its expiration, the situation will have changed sufficiently to permit a return home. If that hope is not realized, more permanent planning for the child's care outside the home will be undertaken. In the meantime, the child may be placed with foster parents or in

a group home. An agency may seek out suitable relatives to provide "kinship foster care". During a society ward-ship order, the parents retain any right that they may have under the *Marriage Act* to give or refuse consent to the child's marriage (s. 62(4) of the *CFSA*). In some circumstances, the court may also order that the parent retain the right to give consent to the medical treatment of the child (see s. 62(1)–(3)). In Ontario, no single society wardship order can be for a period longer than 12 months (s. 57(1) para. 2) and a child must not be a society ward for a continuous period exceeding 12 months if the child is less than six years old or 24 months if the child is six or over (s. 70(1)). See also subsections (2), (2.1), (3), and (4) of s. 70. For an analysis of these time periods, shortened by the 2000 amendments, see Bala, "Reforming Ontario's *Child and Family Services Act*: Is the Pendulum Swinging Back Too Far?" (1999) 17 C.F.L.Q. 121 at 152–158.

Why did the court in the *U. (L.)* case, above, extend the period of society wardship for another six months? Do you agree with the result?

4. Where a permanent or Crown wardship order is made, the child is removed from the home and the legal tie between parent and child is seriously threatened. By s. 63(1) of the *CFSA*, the Crown, represented by the local child protection agency, has all "the rights and responsibilities of a parent for the purpose of the child's care, custody and control". It must be remembered also that Crown wardship can lead to adoption and the severance of the legal parent-child tie. Section 63.1 stipulates that a society must make all reasonable efforts to assist a Crown ward "to develop a positive, secure and enduring relationship within a family" through an adoption or a custody award under s. 65.2(1) on a status review. Where the ward is an Indian or native person, the Society can also consider achieving the overall goal through a plan for customary care as defined in Part X of the *CFSA*.

Once a Crown ward has been placed for adoption, the child may be adopted without notice to the parents and without their consent (ss. 151(4)(c) and 137(2)). Because the underlying objective of a Crown wardship order is frequently to permit the eventual adoption of the child, the courts will consider the likelihood of adoption of a particular child before deciding to make such an order: *Child & Family Services Agency of Winnipeg South v. S. (D.D.)* (1990), 24 R.F.L. (3d) 290 (Man. Q.B.) and *Catholic Children's Aid Society v. W. (V.)* (2002), 27 R.F.L. (5th) 9 (Ont. C.A.); leave to appeal refused (2002), 302 N.R. 395 (note) (S.C.C.).

5. A court dealing with a child under Part III of the *CFSA* may make an access order under s. 58. Note that s. 59(1) creates a presumption in favour of access where the court makes a society wardship order, while s. 59(2.1) indicates that an access order is exceptional where a child is made a Crown ward. Where a child is made a Crown ward, any existing access order made under Part III of the *CFSA* is terminated: s. 59(2). Nor can an access order be made after a Crown ward has been placed for adoption and while the child continues to reside in the home of the prospective adopting parents: s. 58(7). Once an adoption order is made, a court cannot make an order for access under the *CFSA*: s. 160(1).

See generally, McCarty, "Crown Wardship and Access: The Impact of Amendments to the *Child and Family Services Act* in Ontario" (2008), 27 C.F.L.Q. 129.

6. In the past, Ontario courts have sometimes expressed frustration with the inability to provide both the per-manency of adoption and the opportunity for ongoing court-ordered contact or communication with the birth fam-ily. Justice Blishen stated in *Children's Aid Society of Ottawa v. K. (D.)* (2002), [2002] O.J. No. 2483, 2002 Cars-wellOnt 2095 (Ont. S.C.J.) (at para. 54):

> It is necessary to ask whether the risks of emotional and behavioural difficulties inherent in terminat-ing Ross' access to his family members outweigh the benefits of placement in a permanent stable, secure adoptive home. The *Child and Family Services Act* does not permit orders of access to con-tinue after adoption. This is indeed unfortunate for children such as Ross, who at seven and a half years of age knows and is attached to his family. He will never forget them. It, therefore, becomes a matter of weighing and balancing the benefits and risks, as already noted. In this particular case, the Society recognizes the need to maintain Ross' family attachments and has agreed to continue access to his mother, paternal grandparents and sister while searching for an appropriate adoptive home to meet his needs. In addition, Ms. Reece [a child protection worker with the society] testified that the Society will seek out an adoptive family that would permit some form of ongoing contact with the paternal grandparents, although there are no guarantees. According to Ms. Murray [a social worker with special expertise in adoption planning and placement], the Society will require a prospective adoptive family for Ross to accept that he has two families. He will always have a birth family and an adoptive family. Ms. Murray made it clear that the Society recognizes and respects the fact that Ross' birth family is indeed important to him. However, Ms. Murray emphasized that the need to have the structure and permanency of a family placement is also important. Although there are no open adop-

tions in Ontario, Ms. Murray testified that decisions are made on a case by case basis as to whether or not contact with birth families may be beneficial post adoption. As previously indicated, Ms. Reece testified that the Society would search for a home that would permit contact to continue with the paternal grandparents.

Following the 2006 amendments to the *CFSA*, a Society, as the child's parent, may allow contact between a child and a parent after a Crown wardship order has been made even where there is no access order. See s. 59(4) of the *CFSA*. The Society may also apply for an "openness order" in respect of a Crown ward at any time before the child is adopted. See s. 145.1. Such an order allows the person named in the order to communicate with or have a relationship with the child in accordance with the terms of the order. Note that the person with whom the society has placed or plans to place the child for adoption must consent: s. 145.1(3)(c). Regarding the variation or termination of openness orders, see s. 153.1. The 2006 amendments also introduced "openness agreements" relating to a child who is placed for adoption or who is adopted. See s. 153.6. The contact provision in s. 59(4) takes on significant importance because neither an openness order nor an openness agreement can come into existence until an adoptive home has been identified and the prospective adoptive parents have consented. Without the authority now specifically granted by s. 59(4), the Society would have to suspend contact in the interim. "Openness orders" and "openness agreements" are discussed further in the next chapter.

7. If a child is committed to the care of a child protection authority, the state incurs considerable expense in caring for the child. Section 60 of the *CFSA* authorizes the court to order the parents to make support payments for the child in this situation. For an example where this power was used, see *Children's Aid Society of Haldimand-Norfolk v. A. (L.M.)* (2002), 33 R.F.L. (5th) 54 (Ont. C.J.). Why are such orders quite rare?

8. Part V of the *CFSA* sets out a number of rights of a child in the care of the child protection agency. Section 61 also restricts the agency's exercise of discretion in providing for the care and custody of a child who is a society or Crown ward. For a description of the child care system provided for children in need of protection, see MacLauren and Bala, "Children in Care" in Bala, Zapf, Williams, Vogl, and Hornick, eds., *Canadian Child Welfare Law: Children, Families and the State*, 2d ed. (Toronto: Thompson Educational Publishing, Inc., 2004).

9. Regarding subsequent judicial review of orders made under s. 57 of the *CFSA*, see ss. 64, 65, 65.1, and 65.2. In *Catholic Children's Aid Society of Metropolitan Toronto v. M. (C.)* (1994), 2 R.F.L. (4th) 313 (S.C.C.), the court struggled with the appropriate approach to a status review. The litigants presented two clear alternative views. The appellant mother argued that the threshold issue was whether there was a continuing need for a court order pursuant to s. 57 and that a court could consider the best interests of the child only after it had made this determination. The respondent society argued that the court did not have to make a new determination that the child was in need of protection and that the sole issue was to assess what disposition was in the best interests of the child. Justice L'Heureux-Dubé, for the court, attempted to adopt a middle position. Although recognizing (at 342) that the society had to justify continuing intervention in the family by establishing the continued need for protection by way of a court order, she ultimately adopted (at 343) a "flexible approach" which "seeks to balance the best interests of children with the need to prevent indeterminate State intervention, while at the same time recognizing that the best interests of the child must always prevail". In particular, she held that state intervention might be justified even if the parent could now reasonably care for the child. "The determination of whether the child continues to be in need of protection cannot solely focus on the parent's parenting ability, ... but must have a child-centred focus and must examine whether the child, in light of the interceding events, continues to require State protection" (at 346). The child involved in this case had bonded with her foster parents and the court held that a protection order could be based on the need to protect her from the emotional harm that would result if she were to be removed from their home and returned to her mother's care.

For commentary on *C.C.A.S. of Metropolitan Toronto v. M. (C.)*, see Freedman, "Parents' Rights and Best Interests of Children Under the *Child and Family Services Act*" (1994), 11 C.F.L.Q. 216 and Thompson, "Case Comment: *C.C.A.S. of Metropolitan Toronto v. M. (C.)*" (1994-95), 12 C.F.L.Q. 45.

Note that a court can, as a result of the 2006 amendments, make a custody order as a result of a review: ss. 65(1)(d) and 65.2(1).

Section 65.1(9) precludes a status review where a Crown ward has been placed for adoption and continues to reside in the prospective adopting parents' home. A *Charter* challenge to the equivalent provision in Nova Scotia legislation failed in *C. (D.) v. Family & Children's Services of Cumberland (County)* (1988), 16 R.F.L. (3d) 222 (N.S. C.A.); leave to appeal refused (1989), 89 N.S.R. (2d) 270 (note) (S.C.C.).

10. Section 66 of the *CFSA* provides for an annual administrative review of the care of each Crown ward.

11. In *D. (B.) v. Children's Aid Society of Halton (Region)* (2007), 39 R.F.L. (6th) 245 (S.C.C.), various family members attempted to sue a Society, a treatment centre and a social worker. They alleged that the defendants' negligence in the treatment of an adolescent, who eventually became a Crown ward, had caused her to be completely alienated from her family. The statement of claim was struck out as disclosing no cause of action. The Supreme Court held that the defendants did not owe a duty of care to the family members, only to the girl.

(5) Representation of the Child

Section 38 of the *CFSA* specifically recognizes that a child may be represented by counsel. It also requires the court, whenever a child does not have legal representation, to determine whether legal representation is desirable to protect the child's interests and to direct that legal representation be provided for the child if at any stage of the proceedings such representation is considered desirable. Where a parent, a child protection agency, or a child, usually through a social worker, asks the court to appoint a lawyer, the court will usually do so. It is then mandatory for the Office of the Children's Lawyer to act as the child's counsel. The Office of the Children's Lawyer has staff counsel and also administers a specially trained panel of private practitioners. The Ministry of the Attorney General provides the funding and there is no charge to the child or the parents.

There are at least three possible roles that a child's lawyer might adopt: *amicus curiae*, *guardian ad litem*, and advocate. In the first role, the lawyer acts as a "friend of the court" who takes a neutral stance and ensures that the court receives all the relevant evidence, including the child's views and preferences. In the second, the lawyer attempts to achieve the result that accords with the child's best interests. In the third, the child's lawyer is an advocate for the child and tries to achieve the result that the child desires.

In 1981, the Law Society of Upper Canada adopted the recommendations made in the *Report of the Law Society of Upper Canada Subcommittee on Representation of Children*. The main thrust of the report was that lawyers representing children should be guided by the principles governing solicitor-client relations generally. However, it also acknowledged that these might have to be adjusted in some circumstances.

> When the child does not have the capacity to fully understand the consequences of the proceedings he is involved in then the relationship with his or her lawyer is not the normal solicitor/ client relationship. ... If the child is mature and responsible enough to accept the consequences of his or her acts and decisions and understands fully the nature of the proceedings and can express a preference as to its resolution, the Committee tends to favour the traditional solicitor/ client approach rather than the guardian-type of representation. Decisions as to the capacity of the child to properly instruct counsel must be determined by the individual lawyer in the particular circumstances. One of the factors that the lawyer would take into account in making this decision would be the ability of the child to accept rationally the advice he or she is receiving. If the child stubbornly, without reason, refuses to accept the advice of the counsel, it may be that the child lacks the maturity to properly instruct counsel. ...

> The Sub-Committee especially rejects the suggestions that there is a duty on the solicitor to make any disclosure to the court, or to anyone, with respect to the information in his possession acquired in the course of the solicitor and client relationship, even when, in the opinion of the solicitor, it is in the best interests of the child to act contrary to the child's instructions. The solicitor is not the judge of the best interests of the child, and is not, under any circumstances, to be excused for a breach of the solicitor and client relationship. If the solicitor does not believe he can accept the instructions of the child, then he should withdraw from the matter. He should, in all events, conduct himself as if he was acting for an adult.

> The Sub-Committee rejects the suggestions that the solicitor has a duty to the court to advise the court, or to help or assist the court in coming to its deliberation, if such advice or assistance constitutes a disclosure of information which is otherwise privileged, or if it is to act contrary to the instructions of the client. No such duty exists upon a solicitor in law, and there are no special circumstances made out in the case of infants. ...

The sub-committee noted that *The Rules of Professional Conduct of the Law Society of Upper Canada* modified the solicitor-client privilege by specifying: "Disclosure of information [concerning a client acquired in the course of the professional relationship] necessary to prevent a crime will be justified if the lawyer has reasonable grounds for believing that a crime is likely to be committed." See now Rule 2.03 of the Law Society of Upper Canada's *Rules of Professional Conduct* which allows, but does not compel, counsel to breach the solicitor-client privilege where there is "imminent risk to an identifiable person or group of death or serious bodily harm, including serious psychological harm that substantially interferes with health or well-being".

The Office of the Children's Lawyer's *Policy Statement, Role of Child's Counsel* (1995, revised 2001 and 2004) accepts that, where a child is competent to instruct a lawyer, the role of the child's lawyer is that of "legal representative" of the child and not "litigation guardian" or "amicus curiae". It also states that the relationship between the child's counsel and the child is a "solicitor-client" relationship, in which the lawyer should generally advance the position consistent with the child's wishes and preferences. However, the *Policy Statement* adds that, "in taking a position on behalf of the child" and in "ascertaining the wishes and preferences of a child", the lawyer is to consider (a) the independency, strength and consistency of the child's views and preferences; (b) the circumstances surrounding those views and preferences; and (c) "all other relevant evidence about the child's interests". Finally, the *Policy Statement* goes on to indicate that, in a contested hearing, the lawyer should "advocate a position on behalf of the child and ensure that evidence of (a) the child's views and preferences, (b) the circumstances surrounding those views and preferences, and (c) all other relevant information about the child's interest is before the court." In the final result, where the child's lawyer concludes that a child's preferences and views were not independently formed, he or she may advocate a position that advances the interests of the child even if that position is inconsistent with the child's wishes. However, even then, the child's lawyer must still ensure that the child's wishes and preferences are before the court.

In *Boukema v. Boukema* (1997), 31 R.F.L. (4th) 329 (Ont. Gen. Div.); additional reasons at (1997), 1997 CarswellOnt 5151 (Ont. Gen. Div.), in the context of a custody dispute, the 11-year-old girl's lawyer indicated that the mother had pressured the girl into expressing a wish to live with the mother. He also cautioned the judge about placing too much emphasis on her wishes. The judge severely discounted the girl's preference.

NOTES AND QUESTIONS

1. When, if ever, should a court appoint a lawyer for an infant? See Benstein. "Towards a New Approach to Child Representation: How Less is More in Child Welfare Proceedings" (1994), 10 C.F.L.Q. 187. What guidance does s. 38 of the *CFSA* give?

Dealing with the issue of whether a child's counsel should be acting as *amicus curiae* or guardian in the case of non-instructing children, Bernstein concludes (at 240): "In my view, the *amicus curiae* option may be an attractive option, as it allows the lawyer to use his or her legal training and investigative abilities, while eliminating the temptations to be a second social worker or judge, as the case may be." See also *Re F. (T.L.)* (2001), 19 R.F.L. (5th) 265 (Sask. Q.B.)

2. Although a child is not a party in the protection proceeding, the child's counsel effectively has most of the rights and responsibilities of a party's lawyer. See generally, *R. (C.) v. Children's Aid Society of Hamilton* (2004), 50 R.F.L. (5th) 394 (Ont. S.C.J.) and Professor McLeod's annotation to the case in the RFLs.

3. Sometimes the Office of the Children's Lawyer's aggressive stance to promote what it considers to be the best interests of children results in conflict with the affected Children's Aid Society. See, e.g., *R. (C.) v. Children's Aid Society of Hamilton* (2004), 4 R.F.L. (6th) 98 (Ont. S.C.J.), where the Squamish Nation of British Columbia, supported by the Children's Aid Society of Hamilton, unsuccessfully sought the removal of the Office of the Chil-

dren's Lawyer as counsel for two aboriginal children. The case contains an extensive review of the case law dealing with motions to remove a child's counsel as well as a discussion of the role of the child's lawyer where the child is not capable of instructing counsel. Professor McLeod's annotation to the case also explores the role of the Office of the Children's Lawyer in child protection cases.

4. Recall that the Ontario Court of Appeal stressed in *Strobridge v. Strobridge* (1994), 4 R.F.L. (4th) 169 that a lawyer appointed as child's counsel in a custody and access dispute could not simply advise the court of the child's views and preferences unless the parties consented. In other words, the child's wishes constitute evidence that must be proved in the normal way.

5. For further reading regarding legal representation of the child in child protection hearings and other proceedings, see Ward, Translator, "The Legal Representation of Children: A Consultation Paper Prepared by the Quebec Bar Committee" (1996), 13 Can. J. Fam. L. 49 and Goldberg, "The Lawyer's Role: Representing Children" in Bala, Zapf, Williams, Vogl, and Hornick, eds., *Canadian Child Welfare Law: Children, Families and the State*, 2d ed. (Toronto: Thompson Educational Publishing, Inc., 2004).

6. In *Re C.* (1980), 14 R.F.L. (2d) 21 (Ont. Fam. Ct.), Karswick Prov. J. suggested (at 29) that counsel for the parents in child protection hearings also has a duty to "ensure that all relevant evidence is adduced, that no such evidence is suppressed and, further, to be prepared to give an honest and professional statement of what they feel is in the best interest of the child and the reason for that position". How is this position to be reconciled with the traditional doctrine of solicitor-client privilege? Would this move away from a strictly adversarial process be desirable? See the critical commentary in Professor McLeod's annotation in the RFLs.

For a general discussion of the ethical and professional challenges faced by the parents' counsel in a child protection proceeding, see Hutton, Bala, and Curtis, "The Lawyer's Role: Representing Parents" in Bala, Zapf, Williams, Vogl, and Hornick, eds., *Canadian Child Welfare Law: Children, Families and the State*, 2d ed. (Toronto: Thompson Educational Publishing, Inc., 2004).

7. In "The Lawyer's Role: Representing the Agency" in Bala, Zapf, Williams, Vogl, and Hornick, eds., *Canadian Child Welfare Law: Children, Families and the State*, 2d ed. (Toronto: Thompson Educational Publishing, Inc., 2004), Gordon Kelly suggests that the role of the protection agency's lawyer is somewhat like that of a prosecutor in a criminal proceeding in that the lawyer has a public duty as well as a duty to advocate the agency's position. Therefore, the agency's lawyer should ensure that all the relevant evidence is before the court and that the proceeding is fair.

11

THE LEGAL CONCEPT OF PARENT: GENETIC PARENTAGE, SOCIAL PARENTAGE, AND ADOPTION

1. Introduction

The assumption underpinning the traditional approach to determining who should be considered a "parent" was that a child is conceived through sexual intercourse. The child's biological father and mother, it was also assumed, would register the birth and raise the child or the mother alone would do so. Where this did not occur, a child might be adopted and its legal parentage and birth certificate altered accordingly. In addition, as we have seen, the law might consider a non-biological parent to be a parent for a specific purpose such as child support.

The development of artificial reproductive technology (ART) has tested these assumptions in the last few decades, particularly when it is used by same-sex couples. New conception technologies are now very common, if not commonplace. If money is not a concern, children can be conceived in several ways.

There is federal legislation, the *Assisted Human Reproduction Act*, S.C. 2004, c. 2, governing the procedural aspects of ART. It is primarily concerned with the ways in which conception technologies may be used. Particularly, it prohibits payment for participation in ART to prevent "trade in the reproductive capabilities of women and men". However, this legislation is largely a skeletal framework and most of the anticipated regulations have not been created. Also, it does not deal with issues of parentage because these fall within provincial authority. As it is, the Quebec Court of Appeal has declared that significant portions of the Act are outside Parliament's constitutional power: *Québec v. Canada* (2008), 2008 CarswellQue 9848. A Supreme Court of Canada decision is awaited.

The two main medical interventions available to cause a pregnancy are intrauterine insemination (IUI) and in vitro fertilization (IVF). IUI involves the insertion of sperm from the intended father or a third party donor (known or anonymous) into a woman's uterus. In IVF, ova are fertilized in a lab and one or more of the fertilized ova are then transferred into either the intended mother or a gestational carrier. The result of ART is that the birth of a child may involve multiple participants: genetic parents, a birth mother, and intended or social parents.

For example, in *D. (M.) v. L. (L.)* (2008), 52 R.F.L. (6th) 122 (Ont. S.C.J.) (discussed below), a husband and wife wished to have a child, but the wife was unable to carry a pregnancy to term. Using IVF, the wife's ovum was fertilized with the husband's sperm. A female friend then acted as a surrogate mother and eventually gave birth. This scenario arguably created three potential parents for the child and, as we shall see, a court was asked to declare that only the two genetic and social parents should be recognized in law as the child's parents.

Another situation in which a child arguably has three parents is where a lesbian couple decides that one of them should bear a child through IUI, using sperm donated by a friend.

Here, the child has two genetic parents, one of whom is also the birth mother, and a social parent (the same-sex partner who did not provide any biological material). In *A. (A.) v. B. (B.)* (2007), 35 R.F.L. (6th) 1 (Ont. C.A.) (reproduced below), this scenario was complicated by the fact that all three adults wished to have an active role in raising the child.

There are yet other situations in which two genetic parents donate sperm and an ovum so that a second woman and her partner can have a child. This scenario can create four possible parents: two genetic parents and two social or intended parents, one of whom is also the birth mother. If a surrogate mother is introduced into this picture, there are five persons who might be described as "parents".

A traditional adoption (explored in the third section of this chapter) may be one way in which to sort out who should be legally recognized as a child's parent or parents in these situations. For example, in *D. (M.) v. L. (L.)*, above, the married couple could have adopted the child. However, no more than two persons can adopt a child and the consequence is that only the adoptive parents are legally recognized as the parents. This route, therefore, is problematic in cases such as *A. (A.) v. B. (B.)*, above, where the hope is that all three adults will be parents and actively raise the child.

The concepts of custody and access can also be brought into play in these situations. The intended parents in a surrogacy arrangement, for example, can be granted custody even though they may not be genetically related to the child. Such an order would allow the child to reside with them and they would have legal authority to make decisions about how the child should be raised. Depending on the context, the birth mother (and others) could be granted access.

As we shall see, courts have increasingly been asked to make declarations of parentage and even declarations of non-parentage in an attempt to sort out the legal relationships between a number of adults and a child. The courts have generally responded sympathetically and creatively where the various parties are in agreement. Greater difficulty and complexity is encountered where the parties are not in agreement and some want to "freeze out" one of the potential parents.

In short, in Ontario and other Canadian jurisdictions, courts are being asked to fill in large public policy gaps in what is now outdated legislation covering birth registration, presumptions of parentage, recognition of parentage, and so on. A working group of the Uniform Law Commission of Canada is currently developing recommendations for uniform provincial legislation to deal with the determination of parentage. Legislation of this type, however, is almost certain to be controversial, even though ART is already in use. It is, therefore, not likely to be a high priority for any government, especially if it appears that the courts are resolving the issues as they arise.

In the next section of this chapter, we examine birth registration, statutory presumptions of parentage, and declarations of parentage. However, there are a number of additional issues raised by ART. These include:

- Should those who donate genetic material, but have no intention of raising the resulting child, have the right to information about their biological children? What about contact?

- Should surrogate mothers have any claim to on-going contact with the children they bore?

- What about the costs of surrogacy? Is a claim for pregnancy costs enforceable?

- Can a surrogate mother change her mind? Are agreements to carry a child for another person or a couple enforceable?

There is little guidance, legislative or judicial, for the resolution of such issues. The only Canadian case to date dealing with a dispute between a surrogate mother and the intended parents is *W. (H.L.) v. T. (J.C.)* (2005), 2005 CarswellBC 2898 (B.C. Master). The parties had consented to a surrogacy arrangement in which HLW would act as surrogate mother for a married couple, JCT and JT. The surrogate mother was impregnated through IUI using JCT's sperm. The arrangement was not in writing and the parties eventually began to quarrel. HLW did relinquish the child soon after his birth, following a "good-bye party" attended by herself, her husband, and their four children. However, HLW then indicated that she would not consent to the child's adoption and she and her husband began custody proceedings. The Master was asked to grant interim access to the birth mother and her husband. He refused to grant access, largely on the basis that there should not be a disturbance in the child's life until the trial judge had had an opportunity to more fully assess all the factors and the evidence. The Master was also influenced by the fact that the original intention was that the birth mother would have only limited contact, through photos and some correspondence, with the child. How could a judge decide, even after a trial, what contact with the birth mother would be in the young baby's best interest?

Access issues arose in a different setting in *H. (D.W.) v. R. (D.J.)* (2007), 280 D.L.R. (4th) 90 (Alta. C.A.). Here, a same-sex male couple and a same-sex female couple became good friends. The couples decided that one of the women would birth two children, one for each couple, using assisted conception with sperm donated from one of the men. The couples agreed that the first child would be raised primarily in the men's home. The plan was put into operation and a girl was born in May 2003. After staying in her mother's house for a few months, the girl lived in the men's home as part of their family. In 2006, the men separated and the biological father and mother refused to allow the father's former partner to have any contact with the child. The former partner's application for access was denied by a chambers judge, but granted at the appellate level. The Alberta Court of Appeal reasoned that the former partner stood in the place of a parent to the child and that this created a presumption that continued contact between the former partner and the child was in her best interests.

Access was, however, denied in rather unique circumstances in *S. (G.E.) v. C. (D.L.)* (2006), 29 R.F.L. (6th) 74 (Sask. C.A.); leave to appeal refused (2006), 2006 CarswellSask 790 (S.C.C.). Here, a single woman became pregnant through *in vitro* fertilization and gave birth to twins in 2000. The mother had a close male friend who was not the biological father of the twins and did not live with her. However, the friend was supportive during the pregnancy and the birth. For the first two weeks after the twins came home, the friend stayed overnight to help to care for them. Later, he frequently visited and looked after them. The relationship deteriorated and the mother and the twins moved to another city at the end of 2002. The friend saw the twins in February 2003 and again in August of that year. The interaction between the mother and the friend on these occasions was strained. The mother refused to facilitate additional access and did not cash the cheques that the friend sent for child support. The friend then applied for access under *The Children's Law Act*, 1997, S.S. 1997, c. C-8.2. Section 6(1) of the Act stated that a court could make an access order "on the application of a parent, or other person having, in the opinion of the court, a sufficient interest". Section 9(1) stated that a court, in making an access order, should have regard only for the best interests of the child. The evidence before the trial judge indicated that the twins were happy and healthy and that the mother was an excellent parent. The judge concluded that the friend had "a sufficient interest" and that an access order was in the twins' best interests because they had a significant relationship with him and that there was an emotional benefit in maintaining that relationship.

The Saskatchewan Court of Appeal allowed the mother's appeal. In its view, the record was capable of sustaining the conclusion that the friend had a sufficient interest to bring the application on the basis of his involvement with the pregnancy and the birth and his care of the twins on numerous occasions. However, it further ruled that, because the friend was not a parent, step-parent, or blood relative, the judge should have required him to demonstrate clearly and convincingly that access was in the twins' best interests. In light of the weight that should be accorded to the mother's views and the potential for continued conflict, the father had not been able to satisfy this burden.

NOTES AND QUESTIONS

1. Should persons have a right to know their genetic origins? This question is usually asked in the context of adoption (see below), but it may also arise where a child is conceived through artificial insemination or ova donation. In British Columbia, the courts are currently considering a class action filed by Olivia Pratton as the representative plaintiff on behalf of all persons conceived in that province by "gamete donation". See also Schneller, "The Rights of Donor Inseminated Children to Know Their Genetic Origins in Australia" (2005), 24 C.F.L.Q. 191.

2. For further reading, see Kelly, "Nuclear Norms or Fluid Families? Incorporating Lesbian and Gay Parents and Their Children into Canadian Family Law" (2004), 21 Can. J. Fam. L. 133; Boyd, "Gendering Legal Parenthood: Bio-Genetic Ties, Intentionality and Responsibility" (2007), Windsor Y.B. Access Justice 63; Cameron, "Regulating the Queer Family: The Assisted Human Reproduction Act" (2008), 24 Can. J. Fam. L. 101; and Jordan, "ART Class: Assisted Reproductive Technology Class — Six Questions Answered" (2009), 28 C.F.L.Q. 191.

2. Legal Concept of Parentage: Birth Registration, Presumptions and Declarations

(1) Birth Registration

All the provinces have legislation providing for birth registration. In Ontario, s. 8 of the *Vital Statistics Act* ("*VSA*") and s. 1 of *General Regulation*, R.R.O. 1990, O. Reg. 1094, provide that all medical practitioners who attend at a birth must give notice in the prescribed form to the Registrar of Vital Statistics. Such notice contains information about the child such as gender, birth weight, and place of birth. Section 9 of the *VSA* requires the "mother and father, or either of them, in such circumstances as may be prescribed" to certify the birth as well, again in a prescribed form. This Statement of Live Birth includes additional information such as the child's name, mother's name, and sometimes father's name. Section 2(2) of the *General Regulation* states that, generally, both the father and mother have to send this document. However, s. 2(3) goes on to specify that this duty does not fall on the child's father where he is "unacknowledged by or unknown to the mother".

The *VSA* also deals with the naming of a child on the birth registration. See s. 10. Where the mother certifies the child's birth and the father is unknown or "unacknowledged", she may give the child her surname or former surname: s. 10(3). The father may react emotionally and, as illustrated in the following cases, commence litigation when a mother simply certifies that the father is "unacknowledged" even though she knows who he is.

KREKLEWETZ v. SCOPEL

(2002), 60 O.R. (3d) 187, 29 R.F.L. (5th) 367, 2002 CarswellOnt 1981 (C.A.);
leave to appeal refused (2003), 2003 CarswellOnt 266 (S.C.C.)

FELDMAN J.A.:

1 The parties to this appeal are the parents of William Joseph Kreklewetz Scopel. The issue is the proper interpretation of the provisions of the *Vital Statistics Act*, R.S.O. 1990 c. V. 4 with respect to the registration of the name of a child, and under what circumstances the mother is entitled to register the child's name with her surname, without the consent or participation of the father.

Facts

2 The parties had an "on again, off again" relationship beginning in January, 1995, and finally ending shortly after William's birth on January 25, 1998. Their last period of cohabitation terminated in November, 1997. Both parties agree that the appellant is the father of William. After William's birth the appellant paid for some expenses for William, and eventually began to pay child support in accordance with the *Child Support Guidelines*, O. Reg. 126/00. There is no formal custody order, but the respondent has full *de facto* custody, and full responsibility for William. The appellant exercises access rights. The appellant has since married. ...

[The mother had certified the child's birth unilaterally, describing the father as "unacknowledged". She had given the child her surname, but the father wanted him to have a hyphenated one.]

Analysis

Issue 1: Interpretation of "unacknowledged by" in the *Vital Statistics Act*

History of the Legislation

16 In 1986, the *Vital Statistics Act* was amended following recommendations arising from the *Ontario Law Reform Commission Report* of 1976, and from the redrafted *Uniform Law Conference Vital Statistics Act*, which was recommended for adoption by the Conference in 1986, replacing the 1949 version. On the issue of names, much of the discussion and impetus for reform was based on equality rights of women and the s. 15 equality guarantee of the *Charter*. Interestingly, neither the Law Reform Commission Report not the Report of the Uniform Law Conference specifically discusses the situation where a mother does not acknowledge the father.

17 The current Act remains in the form of the 1986 amendments. With respect to the naming of a child at birth, s. 10 of the Act provides a scheme which allows the parents of a child to effectively agree to give the child either of their surnames, or any combination of their surnames. It provides a method of determining the surname of the child if the parents cannot agree on a surname, or if one or both is incapable. If the mother does not know or acknowledge the father, it provides that the child shall have the mother's surname. ...

Current Provisions of the Vital Statistics Act

20 Section 9 obligates the mother and father of a child to make and certify a statement respecting the child's birth. However, that obligation does not apply to a mother who is incapable, as defined, or to a father who is incapable, or who is either unknown to or unacknowledged by the mother, in which case the obligation falls solely on the other parent. The term "incapable" is defined as "unable, because of illness or death, to make a statement." A statutory declaration is required to be filed by the certifying parent that the other is incapable. However, no such statutory declaration is required where the mother states that the father is unknown to her or unacknowledged by her. The statement always contains the particulars of the mother, but only contains the particulars of the father when he makes the statement. Nor can a father apply unilaterally to amend the registered statement of birth that was made by the mother, unless she is incapable. However, if the father obtains a declaration of paternity under the *Children's Law Reform Act*, he can provide a certified copy to the Registrar General of the *Vital Statistics Act*, who will then amend the particulars of the child's parents in the registration. There is no provision, however, for amending the surname of the child in those circumstances.

21 Section 10 provides a protocol for the naming of children born in Ontario. It is linked to whether one or both parents (or another person if both were incapable or the mother was incapable and the father was unknown to or unacknowledged by the mother) made and certified the statement of birth of the child. There are four circumstances within the protocol where the child can be given the mother's surname: (i) where both parents have certified the birth and agreed to give the child the mother's surname; (ii) where the mother has certified the child's birth and the father is unknown to or unacknowledged by her; (iii) where the mother has certified the birth and the father is incapable; (iv) where another person has certified the birth and only the mother is known. Also, the protocol can be avoided with the approval of the Registrar, if the person who certifies the birth wishes to give the child a surname that is in accordance with the child's cultural, ethnic or religious heritage.

24 The disagreement is whether the term "unacknowledged by" the mother, refers to a position she takes only for the purposes of the certification of the birth of the child under the Act, or refers to the mother's conduct generally in admitting, for any purpose, the identity of the father of the child. ...

29 The legislative purpose of the registration and naming provisions of the Act is to provide a system which ensures that children born in Ontario will have their births registered with a central registry, in a timely manner, and with the accurate particulars the legislature has determined are needed. It is the intention of the Act that children born in Ontario will receive at least one forename, and a surname which conforms with a standard protocol. Essentially, a child will have either the family surname, or if the mother's and father's names are different, then either the mother's surname, the father's surname, or a hyphenated or combined name including both. In the exceptional case, the surname will be a name that reflects the child's cultural, ethnic or religious heritage.

30 In the context of the legislative purpose of the provisions, it is important to note that, unlike the former Acts, the scheme no longer turns on the marital status of the parents of the child. The scheme is the same whether the parents are married, in an ongoing relationship, or not in a relationship at all. It turns on the wishes of both parents if they are capable, or the wishes of only the mother if the father is unknown to or unacknowledged by her.

31 Sections 9 and 10 both use the term "unknown to or unacknowledged by" the mother. Where a statute uses two different terms in the alternative, they are not to be treated as redundant but as having two different meanings. ... Therefore, although a mother knows the identity of the father, the Act contemplates that she may still not acknowledge him as the

father. Because acknowledgment involves a volitional act of admitting knowledge of a fact, it is possible for a person to acknowledge something to be true in one context, but to decline to do so in another context.

32 That is the interpretation given to the provisions by the City of Toronto Clerk, a division registrar under the Act. In the document entitled "Important Information" sent to the respondent with the Statement of Live Birth Form, para. 20 provides that "Signatures of BOTH parents are required unless the mother does *not know or wish to acknowledge* the Father." [Italics added] ...

36 In my view, in structuring the provisions as it did, the legislature made a policy decision to allow the mother to have the ultimate ability to determine the surname of the child in recognition of the fact that there will be circumstances where a mother will have the ongoing responsibility for the child, and should not be forced to have the child linked by name with the biological father. Counsel for the appellant acknowledged that, for example, in the case of rape, a mother should not be forced to have the child bear the surname of the father. Yet there is no provision in the Act for specific exceptions. It is the ability of the mother to treat the father as "unacknowledged by" her which accomplishes that legitimate legislative goal. ...

GALLANT v. LEWIS

(2008), 57 R.F.L. (6th) 345, 2008 CarswellOnt 4384 (Ont. S.C.J.) (Footnotes omitted)

QUINN J.: —

Introduction

1 The applicant, Douglas Edward Gallant ("father"), and the respondent, Suzanne Randelle Lewis ("mother"), are the parents of a child whose birth was registered by the mother (without the knowledge or consent of the father) using her surname. The father asks for an order changing the child's surname to the hyphenated last names of the parties.

2 The application is not brought pursuant to any specific legislative authority. It was heard and decided under the expansive *parens patriae* jurisdiction of the Superior Court of Justice. At issue is the right of the mother, under the *Vital Statistics Act* ... to arbitrarily exclude the father from the birth registration process and, more particularly, to arbitrarily use her last name as the surname for the child.

Background

3 The parties began seeing each other socially in April 2006, commenced a common law relationship in October 2006 and separated in December 2006. The mother gave birth to their child, a daughter, on July 1, 2007.

4 The parties are now both 21 years of age and the child is a few days short of being one. Neither party is married nor has children from any other relationship.

5 The father enjoys access to the child "almost every day" and there is no suggestion that he is an unfit parent.

6 It is undisputed that the father did not have a say in naming the child. The mother admits that she did not inform him when she went to the hospital to give birth. She did so deliber-

ately, explaining that she "did not want him there." The father testified that it was his wish to be present.

7 Subsequently, the mother completed a Statement of Live Birth (Form 2) under the *Vital Statistics Act* filling out Section A ("child's information"), Section B ("mother's information"), Section D ("birth information") and Section E ("certification of informant"). Section C ("father's information"), was left blank.

8 Section A is accompanied by Instruction #2 and includes the following, which I set out in part (emphasis added):

> If both parents' information is included on this form, the child's surname may be either parent's surname or ... both parents' surnames ... hyphenated or combined. *If only the mother's information is included on the form, the child's surname may be the mother's surname. ...*

9 The mother completed Section A by giving the child her surname and Section F was certified accordingly. She testified that she did not fill out Section C, the father's information, "because he would have to sign."

10 The mother justifies the exclusion of the father from the birth registration process by saying that she is the primary caregiver and the child "is living with me." The father testified that he "would like the world to know" that this is his child and, understandably, he feels slighted.

11 The father moved swiftly, commencing this application nine days after the child's birth. It is not suggested that the father is anything but genuine and well-intentioned in his desire to change the surname of the child.

12 To their credit, the parties have signed minutes of settlement dealing with custody (to the mother), access (generous) and child support.

Discussion

. . . . .

16 With Section C of the Statement of Live Birth form being uncompleted, this triggered the statutory right of the mother to give her surname to the child.

17 Mr. Newell, counsel for the mother, relies heavily upon *Kreklewetz v. Scopel* (2002), 60 O.R. (3d) 187 (C.A.) in support of his argument that the mother was entitled to register the child's birth using her surname and to do so without consulting, or obtaining the consent of, the father. ...

20 At para. 42, Feldman J.A. referred to, and agreed with, the decision of the British Columbia Court of Appeal in *Trociuk v. British Columbia (Attorney General)* (2001), 200 D.L.R. (4th) 685 which, dealing with similar legislation, held that the statute allows a mother to know the identity of the father while not acknowledging him for the purposes of registering the birth of their child.

21 The decision in *Trociuk* has since been overturned by the Supreme Court of Canada.

22 In *Trociuk v. British Columbia (Attorney General)*, [2003] 1 S.C.R. 835, the Supreme Court found that sections 3(1)(b) and 3(6)(b) of the *Vital Statistics Act*, R.S.B.C. 1996, c. 479, were unconstitutional as they constitute discrimination on the basis of sex and are not saved under s. 1 of the *Canadian Charter of Rights and Freedoms*. ... The *Vital Statistics Acts* of Ontario and British Columbia are very similar. ...

23 Deschamps J., writing for the Supreme Court in *Trociuk*, concluded that: (1) "A birth registration is not only an instrument of prompt recording. It evidences the biological ties between parent and child, and including one's particulars on the registration is a means of affirming these ties". (see para. 16); (2) "Contribution to the process of determining a child's

surname is [a] significant mode of participation in the life of a child. For many in our society, the act of naming a child holds great significance". (see para. 17); (3) "A father who is arbitrarily excluded from [naming a child] would reasonably perceive that a significant interest has been affected". (see para. 18); (4) "... the reasonable claimant in the father's position, apprised of all relevant circumstances, would observe that the impugned provisions impose a disadvantage on him that they do not impose on a mother. It would be reasonable for him to perceive that the legislature is sending a message that a father's relationship with his children is less worthy of respect than that between a mother and her children ... [and] would perceive the message to be a negative judgment of his worth as a human being". (see para. 21).

Conclusion

24 In my opinion, it would bring the administration of justice into disrepute, be manifestly unfair to the father and not be in the best interests of the child, if I were to enforce the child-naming provisions of Ontario's *Vital Statistics Act* where British Columbia's virtually identical statute has been ruled unconstitutional as amounting to discrimination on the basis of sex.

25 The right of a mother to arbitrarily exclude the father in the naming of their child is a breathtaking example of sexual discrimination, leaving the father without recourse (short of the application launched) and rendering him a second-class parent. It is not in the best interests of a child to have his or her parents differentiated in this fashion. There will be obvious instances where it will be entirely appropriate for a father to be unacknowledged and for a child to be given only the surname of the mother — but this is not one of them.

Result

26 Accordingly, despite the able arguments of Mr. Newell, I allow the application. As I have already mentioned, there being no statutory authority for the relief sought by the father, I grant it under the *parens patriae* jurisdiction of the court and for the benefit of the child.

27 I order that the Registrar General amend the registration of the child's birth to include the hyphenated surnames of the parties (in alphabetical order) such that the name of the child shall be changed from Kiera Mary-Lynn Lewis to Kiera Mary-Lynn Gallant-Lewis. The Registrar General shall also provide the father with a copy of the child's amended birth certificate. ...

NOTES AND QUESTIONS

1. The *Gallant v. Lewis* and *Kreklewetz v. Scopel* decisions are arguably at odds with one another regarding the right of a mother to make a unilateral decision about a child's name in Ontario. Justice Quinn, in a footnote in *Gallant*, made the following remark about the possibility of any further judicial consideration of this issue in Ontario:

> And, to be blunt about it, in the circumstances, I think that it would be an unwise use of court resources to give notice to the Attorney General to argue the constitutionality of Ontario's *Vital Statistics Act* when that trail has already been blazed in British Columbia.

Recall that there was no constitutional challenge to the Ontario legislation in *Gallant*. From what source did Justice Quinn get authority to refuse to follow the legislative scheme?

2. In *Gallant*, Justice Quinn alluded (para. 25) to situations where a father may justifiably be excluded from the birth registration and naming process. In a footnote he elaborated: "For example, where the father does not play, or is not likely to play, a meaningful role in the life of the child and certainly where the birth is the result of rape or

incest." He added: "However, when it comes to children's surnames, the *Vital Statistics Act* does not have a mechanism to distinguish the valid from the arbitrary." Should the legislation be amended to deal with this issue?

The Supreme Court in *Trociuk* noted that applications by biological fathers to challenge the naming of their children could have very public and negative effects in some cases. It endorsed a private procedure, in chambers, as the best method of ensuring the mother's and child's privacy to determine whether a father has been justifiably excluded from the birth record. Is this again an issue that should be addressed by legislation?

3. In light of *Gallant*, does a mother have a duty to disclose a child's birth to the father? Does the Registrar of Vital Statistics have an obligation to notify a father, if known, that the mother has not acknowledged him in the birth registration?

4. In *British Columbia Birth Registration No. 06-014023, Re* (2007), 42 R.F.L. (6th) 388 (B.C. S.C.), the British Columbia Supreme Court considered an appeal from a Master's decision that the adoption applicants were required to serve the biological father with notice of the application where the birth mother had not acknowledged him on the birth registration. The court noted that, in the wake of the *Trociuk* decision, British Columbia had amended its *Vital Statistics Act* to include a provision specifying that fathers have the right to have their information appended to the birth registration where mothers have refused to acknowledge them. However, it pointed out that the revised legislation still allowed mothers to refuse to acknowledge the fathers. In the case at bar, the father had not registered his information as an appendix to the birth registry. The court held that the adoption applicants were not required to notify the birth father of the proposed adoption and that his consent was not required.

The development of ART tested the assumptions underpinning traditional birth registration rules. This has led to several court cases and some limited legislative reform.

RUTHERFORD v. ONTARIO (DEPUTY REGISTRAR GENERAL)

(2006), 30 R.F.L. (6th) 25, 2006 CarswellOnt 3463 (Ont. S.C.J.)

[In this case, several birth mothers wished to include the particulars of their same-sex partners (the "co-mothers") on the Statement of Live Birth relating to each of their children for inclusion in the birth registry established under the *VSA*. In each case, the co-mother had supported the birth mother's decision to conceive a child through artificial insemination and the couple intended to raise the child together. The Deputy Registrar General for the Province of Ontario took the view that the *VSA* did not permit the co-mothers to be listed on the Statements of Live Birth. Section 9(2) of the *VSA* stipulated that "the mother and father" of a child had to provide a statement of birth in the prescribed form within 30 days of a child's birth. The form indicated that the particulars of one mother and one father were to be provided. There were exceptions in s. 9(3) to 9(4) of the *VSA* for situations where a mother or father was unable to make a statement or the father was unacknowledged by or unknown to the mother.

The couples applied for an order requiring the Deputy Registrar General to accept their Statements of Live Birth and similar ones in the future. They argued that the term "father" in the *VSA* should be read as a gender-neutral term, capable of encompassing the co-mothers. In the alternative, they asked the court to exercise its *parens patriae* jurisdiction to make the requested order to protect the best interests of children born into lesbian families. In the further alternative, they submitted that the *VSA*'s provisions dealing with birth registration conflicted with ss. 7 and 15(1) of the Charter.

Two expert witnesses who testified on behalf of the couples stated that it was their understanding that heterosexual couples using anonymous donor semen simply listed the mother's spouse or male partner as the child's father on the Statement of Live Birth. They also stated that they were unaware of any non-biological fathers who had had difficulties in so registering.

The couples also sought declarations of parentage under the *Children's Law Reform Act* (the *CLRA*) whereby each of the co-mothers would be recognized as a parent. During an emergency case conference, a justice of the Ontario Superior Court of Justice issued such a declaration for one of the couples with the consent of the Deputy Registrar General. The Deputy Registrar General then consented to the issuance of such declarations for the remaining couples and the court granted them during the course of the hearing. These declarations permitted the issuance of birth certificates for each child listing the birth mother and the co-mother as parents. The Deputy Registrar General then argued that obtaining a court declaration of parentage rather than inclusion in the birth registry was the appropriate means by which the co-mothers could receive legal recognition of their status as parents.]

RIVARD J.:

Vital Statistics Act

Short Summary of the Parties' Positions

28 The Applicants argue that the term "father" in the VSA should be read as a plural and gender neutral term in order to include lesbian co-mothers. The interpretation of "father", they argue, is consistent with the purpose of the statute, which is recording social parentage. "Mother", "father" and "parent" are broad legal concepts that are not simply concerned with biology. There are a number of other Ontario statutes, including the CLRA, that recognize social parentage. ... They argue for consistency between statutes when dealing with the same subject manner. They request a declaration (previously a *mandamus* order) that same-sex parents may register under the VSA. The Respondent has undertaken to comply with a declaration.

29 The Respondent, on the other hand, argues that the term "father" refers strictly to the biological father. The birth registry does not define social families. Rather, its purpose is to accurately register the biological parents at the moment of birth. They [sic] argue that a declaration under the CLRA or an adoption order is the proper forum for determining whether the relationship of social parent is established.

30 The government also identifies secondary purposes that include: (i) the provision of birth certificates, which are primary identity documents for persons born in Ontario, and (ii) the collection of statistical information for medical, sociological and familial research and for public policy decision-making.

Conclusion

31 Part of the difficulty with this analysis is that the legislation is clearly outdated. Due to the advent of reproductive technology, even the Ministry of the Attorney General interprets the VSA and CLRA in a liberal, flexible manner that seems to stretch the meaning of the text. For instance, genetic mothers (as compared to gestational mothers) have been registered on the Statement of Live Birth under the rubric of [mother]. The Ministry also suggests that the proper approach to achieve legal parental status is via a declaration under the CLRA; however, this avenue is still fragile. ...

32 The purpose of the VSA is to record the child's birth and to create a record of parentage. A record of parentage is important to affirm the parent-child relationship. Often the biological parents are the same as the social parents. However, there is nothing in the text or context of the VSA to suggest that parentage is restricted to biological/genetic parentage. The

VSA should be interpreted in "such fair, large and liberal a construction and interpretation as will best ensure the attainment of the object of the Act according to its true intent, meaning and spirit." (s. 10 *Interpretation Act*). The notion of parentage should be interpreted broadly, to include not only biological parents, but also social parents.

33 Despite the broad purpose of the VSA, there can only be two parents according to the textual analysis: one mother and one father. This is because the terms mother and father are preceded throughout the VSA by "the", so that they read "the mother" and "the father". ... Therefore, in a situation of anonymous donor insemination, a father who is not the biological father, meaning one who has no genetic relationship to the child, can still register on the Statement of Live Birth. However, in a lesbian relationship, the co-mother cannot be included, because including her would mean that there would be two mothers on the Statement of Live Birth: the birth mother and the co-mother.

34 Even if the article "the" were interpreted to mean a group of mothers or fathers, it is implausible to interpret "father" as including women. To alter the meaning of "father" to include non-biological lesbian co-mothers is stretching the plausible use of the expression.

35 Therefore, although the purpose of the VSA includes recording social parentage when it furthers important social values, a textual analysis reveals that parents are restricted to one mother and one father: a maximum of two parents per child. As a result, statutory interpretation is not the proper tool for granting the co-mother Applicants status as "mothers". An examination of *parens patriae* is therefore necessary.

Purposive Analysis

37 The VSA works as follows. According to s. 9(2) "within thirty days of a child's birth in Ontario, the mother and father shall make and certify a statement in the prescribed form respecting the child's birth" and mail it to the Deputy Registrar's Office. As stated in paras. 20 and 21 of the Respondent's factum:

> The Province of Ontario has kept records of vital events under statutory authority since 1869. The VSA governs the registration of vital life events in Ontario, including births, deaths, marriages, adoptions and changes of name. The Act requires the Registrar General (Minister of Government Services) to direct a uniform system of registration of these events, and provides that the Registrar General is charged with the enforcement of the provisions of the Act. ...

38 The Statement of Live Birth, the form in which the particulars of the parents are recorded, is the foundational document of the Birth Certificate. Once the birth has been registered, persons named as parents on the Statement of Live Birth (or persons with legal custody of the child) can apply for a birth certificate. A birth certificate, according to s. 46 of the VSA, is proof of parentage in the absence of evidence to the contrary. As put by the Applicants:

> Birth registration provides an important means for parents to participate in their child's life. The inclusion of a parent's particulars on a child's birth registration document ensures that consent is required for an application for the child's adoption and that the parent is entitled to participate in determining the child's surname. It allows the named parent(s) to obtain a birth certificate, an OHIP card, a social insurance number, register the child in school, obtain airline tickets and passports for the child, and to assert his or her rights under various laws. It facilitates cross-border travel by the named parent(s) with the child. It is a marker of the parent-child relationship and the composition of the child's family. (Applicants factum at Para. 102).

39 In examining the registration and naming provisions ..., the Ontario Court of Appeal outlined the legislative purpose as providing: "a system which ensures that children born in Ontario will have their births registered with a central registry, in a timely manner, and with the accurate particulars the legislature has determined are needed ...". *Kreklewetz v. Scopel* (2002), 60 O.R. (3d) 187 (Ont. C.A.) at paras. 29 and 30. ...

40 The language of *Kreklewetz* articulates a broad purpose to the VSA, which does not specifically state that social parentage is registered, but also does not speak to the issue of biology, suggesting that it is not relevant, or has little import in understanding the purpose. That said, this case was primarily focused on the naming provisions of the VSA and appears to have focused on those provisions, and birth registration as it relates to naming, rather than on the system of birth registration overall. Naming is only one aspect of VSA, and not necessarily linked to registration of parents, given the possibility under the current scheme to use the surname of a lesbian co-parent under the cultural reasons exception.

41 The VSA, however, does more than simply record; it also creates a presumption of parentage based on the particulars in the Statement of Live Birth. This secondary purpose of the VSA was highlighted by the Ontario Law Reform Commission in their Report on Human Artificial Reproduction and Related Matters (Ministry of the Attorney General, Volume 1, 1985) at 65 [OLRC Report]: "In addition to functioning as a record of the circumstances of birth, the system of birth registration has a second purpose; along with the CLRA, it is a means by which the parentage of children is established ... the relationship of a parent and child is presumptively established by the administrative act of registering the birth."

42 If the VSA creates a presumption of parentage, then what kinds of parentage is it recognizing? Is the purpose of the VSA to record social or simply biological parentage?

43 The ambiguity in the concept of parentage was referred to in the OLRC Report back in 1985: "various reproductive technologies in current and foreseeable use may allow children to be produced by numerous combinations of participants. Depending on how the term "parent" is to be defined, several individuals involved in the creation of a single infant may justifiably claim that status by reason of some form of connection to the child." (OLR Report at 70).

44 In *Trociuk*, the Supreme Court of Canada asserted as a secondary purpose of the British Columbia VSA the establishment of biological ties between parent and child. Deschamps J. for the court said:

> A birth registration is not only an instrument of prompt recording. It evidences the biological ties between parent and child, and including one's particulars on the registration is a means of affirming these ties. *Such ties do not exhaustively define the parent-child relationship.* (emphasis added) (*Trociuk* para. 16).

It is clear that the Supreme Court thought that included in purpose of the VSA was recording biological ties. ...

47 The significance of *Trociuk* and *Kreklewetz* when read in conjunction is that the purpose of birth registration is accurate and prompt recording of births, as I believe all parties would agree. However, one aspect of this purpose is to "evidence biological ties between parent and child". That does not, however, mean that this is the only purpose of the VSA. The VSA has always balanced the registration of biological parentage with social parentage due to the need to promote other important purposes, the most clear purpose in the past being to ensure the legitimacy of children.

48 The government recognized that the importance of identifying biological parentage was tempered by the need historically to promote legitimacy. Part of that social goal was to protect children in a society that differentiated between legitimate and illegitimate children. In the pre-1986 legislation, social parentage trumped registration of biological parentage where a child was born to married parents. At the time, a married woman was required to register her husband's information on the Statement of Live Birth regardless of whether he was the actual father of the child. The only exception was if the mother filed a statutory declaration asserting that at the time of conception she was living apart from her husband.

49 The irony is that under the pre-1986 version of the VSA where wedlock determined parental status, married couples who used assisted reproductive technology were registered on the Statement of Live Birth regardless of biological connection. Presumably, lesbian co-mothers married to birth mothers could have availed themselves of a similar provision (minus the requirement that they be a father).

50 The current VSA, introduced in 1986, abandons the focus on legitimacy. Marital status is no longer determinative of the particulars to be entered on the Statement of Live Birth. ...

51 Since the 1986 amendment where the mother's husband was no longer required to be registered, there were no amendments to either the forms or the instructions to signal any change in approach. ... The legislative history of this provision reveals that the birth registration scheme has tracked the particulars of parentage differently depending on the government's and society's views in any given historical period. ...

55 Some social purposes are important enough to justify a departure from the collection of purely genetic material. Identifying biological parentage remains a key purpose of the act, but the VSA reflects other overarching concerns of the day including the inclusion of marginalized groups within Canadian institutions.

56 Including non-biological parents in situations where they clearly intend to parent the child would fall under a purpose of the VSA. Where the genetic father is unknown, for example an unknown sperm donor, there is no reason for him to think that he is doing anything wrong; it is common sense to view the non-biological father in such a situation as "the father" of the child. Being a parent is not only about being genetically related to the child, as other family Acts illustrate. Moreover, there are no procedures or mechanisms in place to indicate to a social father that he should not be listed on the Statement of Live Birth. ...

Textual and Contextual Analysis

58 The terms "mother", "father", and "parent" are not defined in the VSA. These are broad terms that at first blush can refer to either biological parents or social parents. In our cultural lexicon both understandings of the term are common. Furthermore the *Divorce Act*, the *Family Law Act*, and the *Children's Law Reform Act* recognize social parentage (s. 1(1) FLA "Parent: includes a person who has demonstrated a settled intention to treat a child as a child of his or her family ...", *Divorce Act* s. 2(2). ...

59 In the VSA there are no adjectives to elucidate the meaning of terms such as the "relationship of mother" or "natural father". The only textual aid in breaking down the meaning of the terms is the inclusion of the term "mother" in the definition of birth in s. 1 of the VSA: "the complete expulsion or extraction from its *mother* of a fetus ..." [emphasis added]. This reference to "mother" does not actually define what is meant by mother. The definition provides an exhaustive definition of birth. Clearly, the person giving birth is a mother. ...

60 The Applicants argue that the terms "mother" and "father" should be interpreted in light of s. 28(j) of the *Interpretation Act*. This section provides that "Unless the contrary intention appears ... the words importing the singular number or the masculine gender only include more persons, parties or things of the same kind than one ..." However, in the context of s. 9(2) of the VSA, a plural interpretation does not make sense. Section 9(2) refers to "the mother and father" in contrast to "mothers", "a mother" or "parents". ...

69 There was no evidence in this case, of a lesbian co-mother calling herself father — rather, it indicated that she sought to change the term father to co-parent etc, and only used the term father when seeking to pass under the radar. ...

Conclusion

72 Although a purpose of the VSA includes social parentage, only one woman and one man shall be listed. Biological particulars are one piece of information that are gathered, although not exclusively. This purpose is balanced with the need to promote other important social values, including the equality of all children in Ontario and privacy of families. ...

[Justice Rivard therefore concluded that the birth registration provisions in the *VSA* did not permit two women to register as "parents" on the Statement of Live Birth. He also held that the court's *parens patriae* jurisdiction did not permit it to grant the relief sought because the fact that the co-mothers could not appear as parents in the birth registry did not result from a gap in the legislative scheme, but from a legislative decision. It was the legislature's choice that the primary source of recognition of the co-mothers as parents should be through adoption or possibly a declaration of parentage under the *CLRA*.

However, Justice Rivard concluded that s. 9 of the *VSA* unjustifiably violated s. 15 of the *Charter*. To reach this conclusion, he compared the treatment of lesbian co-mothers whose partners used assistive reproductive technology and heterosexual, non-biological fathers in a similar situation. The Justice found that, while s. 9 did not permit the registration of two mothers, it did not preclude the registration of a birth mother and her male spouse even if he were not the biological father. On its face, therefore, the legislation contained the potential for differential impact. Moreover, while there was no direct evidence that non-biological fathers were registering as "fathers" under the *VSA*, it was reasonable to infer that they were doing so. Neither the *VSA* nor the prescribed form specified that only biological parents could register. Furthermore, the Deputy Registrar did not attempt to ensure that those who registered as mother and father were biologically related to the child. Essentially, the Ontario birth registry system was self-reporting without any real checks. On this basis, Justice Rivard concluded that the effect of the *VSA* and its enforcement was to exclude lesbian co-mothers from the birth registry without excluding non-biological fathers in heterosexual relationships.

Next, the Justice found that this differential treatment resulted in the denial of a benefit. The co-mothers were denied access to the birth registry as of right. Even if they might be able to obtain a declaration of parentage under the *CLRA*, they were denied the benefit of the presumption of parentage flowing from being listed as a parent on the Statement of Live Birth. Applying for a declaration of parentage under the *CLRA* was also time-consuming and expensive and required the disclosure of private information. Moreover, the co-mothers were not merely seeking accommodation through a separate system of parental recognition. They were challenging the social institution of parentage and wished to alter it so that it reflected their needs and experiences. In Justice Rivard's view, the failure to register the co-mothers as of right symbolized a societal failure to recognize their family units as legitimate and normal.

The differential treatment, Justice Rivard concluded, was based on both sex and sexual orientation. Sex was a ground listed in s. 15(1) of the *Charter*, while sexual orientation was an analogous ground.

Finally, Justice Rivard held that the differential treatment was substantively discriminatory because it demeaned the dignity of the co-mothers and their children. The Justice believed that exclusion of lesbian mothers from the benefits of the registry system implied that they were not "real" parents.

Turning to s. 1 of the *Charter*, Justice Rivard held that the discrimination against lesbian mothers and their children caused by s. 9 of the *VSA* and its enforcement could not be justified. He accepted that one of the purposes of the system of birth registration was to record the biological parentage of children born in Ontario. However, by allowing the registration of some non-biological fathers, it did so in a way that recognized other important social values such as privacy and the equality of all children. Given his conclusion that the birth registry system as it operated in Ontario served in part to recognize social parentage as well as biological parentage, Justice Rivard held that the exclusion of the co-mothers was not rationally related to that purpose. He also suggested that there were alternatives to the current system of birth registration that still achieved the goal of collecting the biological particulars of a child's parentage while simultaneously recognizing all social parents.

Justice Rivard declared s. 9 of the *VSA* to be of no force or effect, but suspended the declaration for 12 months. He noted that it was ultimately up to the legislature rather than the courts to determine who should qualify as a parent under the *VSA* as long as the legislature recognized the equality rights of lesbian mothers and their children.]

The Government of Ontario responded to this decision by amending the regulation and the form dealing with the registration of births. Under the amended *General Regulation*, there are now three possible scenarios: a mother and father of a child are registered as parents, a mother is registered as the only parent, and a mother and "other parent" are registered as parents. Although "mother" and "father" are not defined in the *VSA* or the *General Regulation*, the context clearly indicates that the woman who gave birth to the child is the child's mother and the man whose sperm led to the conception is the child's father. This is certainly the Government's view as indicated in the instructions accompanying Form 2, the Statement of Live Birth. They state that the "mother on the form must be the woman who gave birth to the child" and that a "'Father', for the purposes of this form, must be the biological father of the child and consent to be acknowledged as the father". The registration of the mother and "other parent" can only occur where the child was conceived by "assisted conception", the mother acknowledges this person as the other parent, this person wishes to be recognized as the "other parent", and the "father is unknown". Essentially, this possibility exists only where the child was conceived by artificial insemination and the biological father is an anonymous sperm donor. In that situation, a mother's spouse or partner, whether of the same or opposite sex, can be listed as "other parent".

Given the range of reproductive and birth technologies available today, the new approach to birth registration may still be problematic. A child conceived by ART can have two genetic parents and two social parents, as well as a birth mother if a surrogate is used. Which of these should be considered parents for the purposes of birth registration? Should only two of them be registered? As illustrated in *D. (M.) v. L. (L.)* (2008), 52 R.F.L. (6th) 122 (Ont. S.C.J.) (described in detail in the NOTES AND QUESTIONS following the *A. (A.) v. B. (B.)* (2007), 35 R.F.L. (6th) 1 (Ont. C.A.)), the Deputy General has suggested that these issues be resolved through applications for declarations of parentage and declarations of non-parentage.

The *A. (A.) v. B. (B.)* case, set out in part below, canvassed the issue of how many legally recognized parents a child can have. The case began with an application under s. 4 of the *CLRA* for a declaration that a person was a parent of a child. Note that s. 9(7) of the *VSA* requires the Registrar General to "amend the particulars of the child's parents shown on the registration" upon the receipt of a certified copy of an order under ss. 4–6 of the *CLRA*. Bill 133, passed but not proclaimed, proposes the addition of s. 6.1 to that Act which will allow a court to change a child's name where it declares that a person is "the mother or father of a child". The proposed section would allow the court to change the child's surname to any name that the child could have been given at birth under the *VSA* (the mother's surname, the father's surname, or a hyphenated combination of the two), but the court's discretion to do so would be subject to the best interests of the child. Bill 133 would also alter s. 9 of the *VSA* in a limited way by adding a subsection (8) that would require the Registrar General to amend the particulars of the birth registration where a court orders a name change under the new s. 6.1 of the *Children's Law Reform Act*.

(2) Presumptions and Declarations of Parentage

Part II of the *CLRA* deals generally with establishing the parentage of children. Section 8 provides that a male person will be presumed to be the father of a child in certain specified circumstances. The main use to which s. 8 has traditionally been put is to allow a court to make a finding of paternity so that child support obligations can be imposed on biological fathers who refuse to acknowledge paternity. It has also been used, however, to secure parental rights on behalf of fathers whose paternity is not acknowledged by the child's mother. The development of DNA testing has provided a conclusive, scientific means of resolving situations where biological paternity is asserted or denied.

Section 4 of the *CLRA* allows "any person having an interest" to apply for a declaration that a "male person" is the father of a child or that a "female person" is the mother of a child. Similarly, s. 5 allows a person to apply in some circumstances for a declaration that a man is his or her father. The wording of these sections, as well as the rest of the Part, does not easily accommodate families in which a child has been produced using artificial reproductive technology or a surrogate mother. This is particularly so where same-sex couples are involved.

Section 12 of the *CLRA* permits anyone to file a statutory declaration with the Registrar General, stating that he or she is the "mother" or "father" of a child. Any two people can file a joint statutory declaration that they are the "father" and "mother" of a child. There is no provision, however, for more than two people to file a declaration, and there is no provision that same-sex partners can file a declaration that they are both the parents of a child.

In the case that follows, two women who had cohabited for about nine years agreed that one of them (B.B.) should bear a child (D.D.) fathered by a mutual friend (C.C.). After the birth, both women cared for the child and he referred to each as "mom". The boy's father also continued to play an active role in his upbringing. The biological mother's partner (A.A.), with the support of the biological parents, applied under the *CLRA* for a declaration that she was a mother of the child. Justice Aston, the application judge, dismissed the application because the *CLRA* did not allow a court to declare that more than two persons were the parents of a child. He pointed out that s. 4 used the definite article "the" in both subsections (1) and (3) and that, in the particular context, this word connoted a singular person or relationship. He also held that he could not use the superior court's *parens patriae* authority to grant the application because there was no legislative gap or oversight.

On her appeal, A.A. argued that the application judge erred in concluding that he did not have the authority under the *CLRA* or the court's *parens patriae* jurisdiction to issue the requested declaration. She also raised, for the first time, constitutional issues alleging violation of her rights under the Charter. The Ontario Court of Appeal did not consider the merits of the Charter arguments, noting that there might not be a sufficient evidentiary record to resolve the issue. Furthermore, it concluded that no miscarriage of justice would result from the refusal to deal with these issues because the court's *parens patriae* jurisdiction was available to grant the requested remedy

A. (A.) v. B. (B.)

(2007), 35 R.F.L. (6th) 1, 2007 CarswellOnt 2 (Ont. C.A.)

ROSENBERG J.A.: ...

7 For the following reasons, I would allow the appeal. While I agree with the application judge that the *CLRA* does not permit the making of the order sought, I am satisfied that the order can be made by exercising this court's *parens patriae* jurisdiction.

The Importance of a Declaration of Parentage

13 A.A. seeks a declaration that she is a mother of D.D. She and C.C. have not applied for an adoption order because, if they did so, B.B. would lose his status as D.D.'s parent by reason of s. 158(2) of the *Child and Family Services Act*. ...

14 A.A., B.B. and C.C. seek to have A.A.'s motherhood recognized to give her all the rights and obligations of a custodial parent. Legal recognition of her relationship with her son would also determine other kindred relationships. In their very helpful factums, the *M.D.R.* Intervenors and the Children's Lawyer summarize the importance of a declaration of parentage from the point of view of the parent and the child:

- the declaration of parentage is a lifelong immutable declaration of status;
- it allows the parent to fully participate in the child's life;
- the declared parent has to consent to any future adoption;
- the declaration determines lineage;
- the declaration ensures that the child will inherit on intestacy;
- the declared parent may obtain an OHIP card, a social insurance number, airline tickets and passports for the child;
- the child of a Canadian citizen is a Canadian citizen, even if born outside of Canada. ...
- the declared parent may register the child in school; and,
- the declared parent may assert her rights under various laws such as the *Health Care Consent Act, 1996*, S.O. 1996, c. 2, Sched. A., s. 20(1)5.

15 Perhaps one of the greatest fears faced by lesbian mothers is the death of the birth mother. Without a declaration of parentage or some other order, the surviving partner would be unable to make decisions for their minor child, such as critical decisions about health care. ... As the *M.D.R.* Intervenors [the applicants in the *Rutherford* case, reproduced in part in the previous section] say: "A declaration of parentage provides practical and symbolic recognition of the parent-child relationship." An excerpt from the *M.D.R.* record dramatically demonstrates the importance of the declaration from the child's point of view. I resort to this part of the *M.D.R.* record because D.D. is too young to provide this kind of information. The twelve-year old child of one of the applicants said this in her affidavit:

> I just want both my moms recognized as my moms. Most of my friends have not had to think about things like this — they take for granted that their parents are legally recognized as their parents. I

would like my family recognized the same way as any other family, not treated differently because both my parents are women. ...

It would help if the government and the law recognized that I have two moms. It would help more people to understand. It would make my life easier. I want my family to be accepted and included, just like everybody else's family.

16 In *M.D.R.* at paras. 227 and 228, Rivard J. referred to some of the submissions discussed in the Victorian Law Reform Commission's position paper entitled *Assisted Reproductive Technology & Adoption: Position Paper Two: Parentage* at pp. 15 and 17:

These submissions reported that the non-birth mother often encounters obstacles and ignorance, and at times hostility, in her dealings with government agencies and service providers where legal status is a relevant factor. Because the non-birth mother cannot be named as a parent on the child's birth certificate, she is unable to produce evidence of her relationship to the child unless she has taken steps to obtain a Family Court parenting order or some form of written authority from the birth mother.

[W]e [Lesbian Parents Project Group] feel that legal recognition of our role as parents to our children is essential for their safety and social well being. It is critical to children that they have reflected back to them the value and integrity of their lives, including the legitimacy of their families ... Equal familial status sends a powerfully positive message to all social institutions that have an influence on our children's lives. It obliges them to acknowledge and respect the families our children live in.

The *Children's Law Reform Act*

17 The appellant applied for an order that she is the mother of D.D. under s. 4. ...

18 The application judge accepted that the relationship of mother and child need not be biological or genetic, but after a careful consideration of the legislative scheme and the applicable rules of interpretation, he held that Part II of the *CLRA* contemplates only one mother of a child. He relied principally on the use of the words "the father" and "the mother" in s. 4(1), which connote a single father and a single mother. ... I agree with his analysis of the statute. I would, however, elaborate on three points. ...

Legislative History and Intention of the Legislature

20 The *CLRA* was intended to remove disabilities suffered by children born outside of marriage. As the Ontario Law Reform Commission observed in its 1973 Report on Family Law at p. 1: "These disabilities arise at the moment of birth and may remain with the child throughout his lifetime." The Commission therefore "accorded high priority to finding a means by which the child born outside marriage may be allowed to enjoy the same rights and privileges as other children in our society". The Commission's central recommendation was that Ontario should abolish the concepts of legitimacy and illegitimacy and declare positively that all children have equal status in law. The Commission's recommendations were enacted into legislation in the form of Parts I and II of the *CLRA*. ...

21 The *CLRA* was progressive legislation, but it was a product of its time. It was intended to deal with the specific problem of the incidents of illegitimacy — the need to "remove, as far as the law is capable of doing so, a stigma which has been cast on children who in the nature of things cannot be said to bear responsibility for it" (p. 11). The possibility of legally and socially recognized same-sex unions and the implications of advances in reproductive technology were not on the radar scheme. The Act does not deal with, nor contemplate, the disadvantages that a child born into a relationship of two mothers, two fathers or as in this case two mothers and one father might suffer. This is not surprising given that nothing in the Commission's report suggests that it contemplated that such relationships might even exist.

Scheme of the Act

22 When the scheme of the *CLRA* is considered, especially the relationship between the various provisions in Parts I and II, it is apparent that the Act contemplates only one mother and one father. The application judge drew attention to many of these provisions. He referred in particular to s. 8, which deals with the presumption of paternity. He was of the view that this section contemplated only one father. This view of the legislation is also consistent with the adoption provisions in the Act whereby no more than two persons can apply for an adoption order and the order extinguishes other parental status. I agree with that interpretation of the legislation.

23 Further, in my view, an interpretation of the Act that allows for a declaration of a single father and a single mother is fortified by s. 12(2) of the Act, which provides that: "*Two persons* may file in the office of the Registrar General a statutory declaration, in the form prescribed by the regulations, *jointly affirming that they are the father and mother of a child.*" [Emphasis added]

24 I agree with the application judge that the *CLRA*, and in particular s. 4(1), is unambiguous. The court has jurisdiction to make a declaration in favour of one male person as the father and one female person as the mother. Since D.D. already had one mother, the application judge had no jurisdiction under s. 4(1) to make an order in favour of A.A. that she too was the mother of D.D.

Use of the *Charter* as an Interpretative Aid

25 A.A. and certain intervenors submit that the *CLRA* should be interpreted in a manner consistent with the *Charter*, and in particular the equality rights guaranteed in s. 15. However, the *Charter* may be used as an interpretive guide only in circumstances of genuine ambiguity. ...

26 Since I have found that there is no ambiguity, it is not open to this court to use *Charter* values to interpret the provision.

Parens Patriae Jurisdiction

27 The court's inherent *parens patriae* jurisdiction may be applied to rescue a child in danger or to bridge a legislative gap. This is not a case about a child being in danger. If the *parens patriae* authority were to be exercised it would have to be on the basis of a legislative gap.

28 The application judge held that the court's *parens patriae* authority was not available to make the declaration in favour of A.A., although he appeared to accept that such an order would be in the best interests of the child. In his view, any gap was deliberate and the court was effectively being asked to legislate because of a perception that the legislation was under-inclusive. The application judge was also concerned about the potential impact on other children if other persons, such as stepparents or members of a child's extended family, came forward seeking declarations of parenthood.

29 I take a different view of the exercise of the *parens patriae* jurisdiction. The Supreme Court of Canada has considered this jurisdiction on several occasions, in particular in *Beson v. Director of Child Welfare for Newfoundland*, [1982] 2 S.C.R. 716 and *E.(Mrs) v. Eve.*, [1986] 2 S.C.R. 388. La Forest J. reviewed the history of the *parens patriae* jurisdiction at length in *Eve*. He concluded at p. 426 with the following statement:

> As Lord MacDermott put it in *J. v. C.*, [1970] A.C. 668, at p. 703, the authorities are not consistent and there are many twists and turns, *but they have inexorably "moved towards a broader discretion, under the impact of changing social conditions and the weight of opinion. ..."* In other words, the

categories under which the jurisdiction can be exercised are never closed. Thus I agree with Latey J. in *Re X, supra*, [1975] 1 All E.R. 697 at p. 699, that the *jurisdiction is of a very broad nature*, and that it can be invoked in such matters as custody, protection of property, health problems, religious upbringing and protection against harmful associations. This list, as he notes, is not exhaustive [Emphasis added].

30 The comments of La Forest J. about the broad nature of the *parens patriae* jurisdiction and the broader discretion under the impact of changing social conditions are particularly apt in this case. However, *Eve* concerned the court's jurisdiction to authorize a medical procedure. It was not principally concerned with the court's jurisdiction to fill a legislative gap. A case somewhat closer to the problem at hand is the Supreme Court's decision in *Beson*. In that case, the Director of Child Welfare for Newfoundland removed a child from an adoptive home shortly before the expiration of the probationary residence period required for an adoption. The legislation did not give the potential adoptive parents any right of appeal from the Director's action taken during the probationary period. Speaking for the court, Wilson J. found that there was accordingly a legislative gap that could be filled by the exercise of the *parens patriae* jurisdiction. ...

31 The determination of whether a legislative gap exists in this case requires a consideration of whether the *CLRA* was intended to be a complete code and, in particular, whether it was intended to confine declarations of parentage to biological or genetic relationships. If the *CLRA* was intended to be confined to declarations of parentage based on biology or genetics, it would be difficult to find that there is a legislative gap, at least as concerns persons with no genetic or biological link to the child.

32 As discussed above, the application judge was of the view that the jurisdiction to make parentage declarations is not confined to biological or genetic relationships. The Alliance for Marriage and Family challenges that proposition. The Alliance points out that s. 1(1) of the *CLRA* refers to a person being the child of his or her "natural parents". I agree that the Act favours biological parents. For example, s. 10 gives a court power to order blood tests or DNA tests where it is called upon to determine a child's parentage. However, the Act does not define parentage solely on the basis of biology. For example, s. 1(2) treats adopting parents as natural parents. Often one or both of the adopting parents will not be the biological parents of the child. Similarly, s. 8 enacts presumptions of paternity that do not all turn upon biology; the obvious example is the presumption of paternity flowing simply from the fact that the father was married to the child's mother at the time of birth. Further, as Ferrier J. pointed out in *T.D.L. v. L.R.L.*, [1994] O.J. No. 896 (S.C.J.) at para. 18, the declaration made under s. 4(1) is not that the applicant is a child's natural parent, but that he or she is recognized in law to be the father or mother of the child.

33 Further, even if the *CLRA* was intended to limit declarations of paternity and maternity to biological parents, that would not answer the question of whether there is a gap. Advances in reproductive technology require re-examination of the most basic questions of who is a biological mother. For example, consider the facts of *M.D.R. v. Ontario (Deputy Registrar General)*. *M.D.R.* involved a case where one lesbian partner was the gestational or birth mother and the other partner was the biological mother, having been the donor of the egg.

34 I return to the earlier discussion of the intention of the *CLRA*. The legislation was not about the status of natural parents but the status of children. The purpose of the legislation was to declare that all children should have equal status. At the time, equality of status meant recognizing the equality of children born inside and outside of marriage. The Legislature had in mind traditional unions between one mother and one father. It did not legislate in relation to other types of relationships because those relationships and the advent of reproductive technology were beyond the vision of the Law Reform Commission and the Legislature of the day. ...

35 Present social conditions and attitudes have changed. Advances in our appreciation of the value of other types of relationships and in the science of reproductive technology have created gaps in the *CLRA*'s legislative scheme. Because of these changes the parents of a child can be two women or two men. They are as much the child's parents as adopting parents or "natural" parents. The *CLRA*, however, does not recognize these forms of parenting and thus the children of these relationships are deprived of the equality of status that declarations of parentage provide.

36 In my view, this is as much a gap as the gap found in *Beson*, where adopting parents were deprived of a right of appeal. ...

37 It is contrary to D.D.'s best interests that he is deprived of the legal recognition of the parentage of one of his mothers. There is no other way to fill this deficiency except through the exercise of the *parens patriae* jurisdiction. As indicated, A.A. and C.C. cannot apply for an adoption order without depriving D.D. of the parentage of B.B., which would not be in D.D.'s best interests.

38 I disagree with the application judge that the legislative gap in this case is deliberate. There is no doubt that the Legislature did not foresee for the possibility of declarations of parentage for two women, but that is a product of the social conditions and medical knowledge at the time. The Legislature did not turn its mind to that possibility, so that over thirty years later the gap in the legislation has been revealed. In the result, the statute does not provide for the best interests of D.D. Moreover, a finding that the legislative gap is deliberate requires assigning to the Legislature a discriminatory intent in a statute designed to treat all children equally. I am not prepared to do so. See the comments of Rivard J. in *M.D.R.* at paras. 93–103. There is nothing in the legislative history of the *CLRA* to suggest that the Legislature made a deliberate policy choice to exclude the children of lesbian mothers from the advantages of equality of status accorded to other children under the Act.

39 This holding would, it seems, be consistent with the position of the government. As stated earlier, the Crown in Right of Ontario did not intervene in this case, but its position on this issue is known. In *M.D.R.*, the Crown took the position that the *CLRA* in fact could be interpreted to allow for a declaration that two women were the mothers of a child. Since I have found otherwise, it does no violence to the government's position to make the declaration sought by the appellant in this case through exercise of the *parens patriae* jurisdiction.

Disposition

41 Accordingly, I would allow the appeal and issue a declaration that A.A. is a mother of D.D. ...

NOTES AND QUESTIONS

1. The Ontario Court of Appeal in *A. (A.) v. B. (B.)* held that it had *parens patriae* jurisdiction to "bridge the legislative gap" created because the *CLRA* had been eclipsed by modern notions of family and by newer birth technologies. Did the court, in effect, assert authority to "update" legislation as social or technological conditions change? Absent a constitutional challenge to the legislation, was the court's action appropriate? Should the court have waited for either legislative action or a constitutional challenge to the legislation?

The applications judge, Justice Aston, is a senior and very experienced Family Court Justice. Recall that he held that it was an improper use of the court's *parens patriae* jurisdiction to re-write legislation in a major way. In *Family & Children's Services of Lennox & Addington v. S. (T.)* (2000), 6 R.F.L. (5th) 331 (Ont. S.C.J.), Madam

Justice C.J. Robertson, also a senior and experienced Family Court Justice, suggested similar limits on a court's *parens patriae* authority (para. 20):

> The court is unable to repair any legislative shortcoming through parens patriae. As a court of superior jurisdiction, parens patriae authorizes the court through its inherent jurisdiction to intervene and rescue a child in danger. It can sometimes be used to bridge a legislative gap. It does not confer supplemental jurisdiction so as to rewrite legislation and procedure.

Should the Ontario legislature amend the *CLRA* to take into account the *A.A. v. B.B.* decision? Why may politicians be content to let the courts deal with these "gaps" in the legislation on a case-by-case basis?

2. In *D. (M.) v. L. (L.)* (2008), 52 R.F.L. (6th) 122 (Ont. S.C.J.), M.D. and J.D., a married couple, applied for declarations that they were the mother and father of a child and that the respondent couple, L.L. and I.L., were *not*. M.D. was unable to carry a pregnancy to term and L.L. agreed to act as a surrogate, using embryo transfer. M.D. provided the ova and J.D. provided the sperm, making them the genetic parents. Because L.L. was the birth mother, she was required, pursuant to the *VSA* to name herself as the mother on the birth registration. The Registrar General suggested that the Ds pursue an application for the declarations and provided them with a "sample order" that would allow him to register them as the child's parents. The application proceeded with the consent of L.L. and I.L.

The court had little difficulty concluding that it had jurisdiction under s. 4 of the *CLRA* to declare that M.D. and J.D. were parents of the child and that such a declaration should issue. It also directed the Deputy Registrar "to amend the registration of the birth of the child in such a fashion as to show the applicant, M.D., as the mother of the child and the applicant, J.D., as the father of the child". It also concluded that there was no real difficulty with the declaration that I.L. was not the child's father.

However, Justice Nelsen found the application for a declaration that L.L. (the surrogate mother) was not the child's mother to be very problematic. The basic problem was that the *VSA* indicated that the term "mother" of a child referred to the woman who gave birth. Indeed, this was why L.L. had to register the child's birth and certify that she was the mother. In an amazing paragraph, Justice Nelsen stated (para. 54):

> The issue as restated is, therefore, whether this court can declare a person *not* to be the mother of a child when she is, in fact, the mother of that child pursuant to a statute. For the following reasons, I answer that question in the affirmative.

Justice Nelsen explained that the authority for the requested declaration was the court's *parens patriae* jurisdiction:

> 61 In my opinion there is a gap in the current *VSA* legislation that does not operate in the best interests of the child, insofar as the inferential definition of "mother" under that statute impedes the court's jurisdiction to declare a person *not* to be the mother of a child. ...

> 63 As can be seen, this definition [in the 1948 *VSA*] is in essence the same definition of birth that we have today, exactly 60 years later. In 1948, the notion that ova could be fertilized in a laboratory, and then implanted into a surrogate mother to gestate, would have been the stuff of science fiction. The current *VSA* has not changed with respect to its definition of "birth", and the consequent inference that the "mother" is the person who gave birth to the child. There is no recognition in the *VSA* that there can be two mothers: the birth mother and the genetic mother.

> 64 Clearly, regulatory reasons could exist as to why the government would require the birth mother to record her name on the Statement of Live Birth. In fact, the instructions on the current Statement of Live Birth form state: "The mother on the form must be the woman who gave birth to the child."

> 65 The legislative gap that arises in this case is thus distinct from the type of gap that was before the Court of Appeal in *A. (A.)*. In *A. (A.)* there was a direct legislative gap, in that the gap arose out of the statute from which the order was sought. In this case, the order [declaring non-parentage] is sought pursuant to the *CJA* [the *Courts of Justice Act*]. There is no gap that arises out of the *CJA*; rather, the gap stems from the effect of the *VSA* upon the ability of this court to issue a declaration of non-maternity. Therefore, the gap is indirect in nature. That said, it is no less of a gap, and I can think of no principled reason why the court's remedial *parens patriae* jurisdiction should not be available to rectify the situation by clarifying the legal status and rights of the parties.

> 66 This ruling does not affect in any way the legitimacy of the statutory and regulatory scheme of birth registration. This ruling simply pertains to the issue of whether the inferred definition of "mother" under the *VSA* prevents a declaration that the woman who gave birth to a child is *not* the mother of that same child after that child's birth has been registered in accordance with the law.

67 It is in the best interests of the child that this court issue a declaration that the child's surrogate mother, who is without genetic link to the child, is not that child's mother. ... In my opinion, there is no doubt that it is additionally in the best interests of the child to remove any ambiguity about who the child's mother is, where the circumstances of the child's birth and the operation of a statute combine to produce such ambiguity.

The orders issued in this case included one directing the Deputy Registrar to amend the registration of the birth to show M.D. as the mother and J.D. as the father. Kelly Jordan reports in "ART Class: Assisted Reproductive Technology Class — Six Questions Answered" (2009), 28 C.F.L.Q. 71, at 82, that such declarations and directions will not result in the removal of the birth mother's name from the birth registry if she has filed a Statement of Live Birth. Rather, her name will be struck out.

Should Justice Nelsen have considered the fact that the Ds could have adopted the child with the birth mother's consent? See the next section of the chapter.

3. Other cases dealing with declarations of parentage where ART technology and/or surrogate mothers were involved include *L. (T.D.) v. L. (L.R.)* (1994), 4 R.F.L. (4th) 103 (Ont. Gen. Div.) (non-biological father, husband of the mother, declared to be child's father where anonymous sperm donor used); *Z. (M.J.) v. Z. (A.M.)* (1997), 10 R.F.L. (4th) 384 (Ont. Gen. Div.); varied (1997), 31 R.F.L. (4th) 446 (Ont. C.A.) (non-biological father, husband of the mother, declared to be child's father where anonymous sperm donor used); *R. (J.) v. H. (L.)* (2002), 2002 CarswellOnt 3445 (Ont. S.C.J.) (genetic parents declared to be the mother and father of the child and surrogate mother, with her consent, declared to be a non-parent); *Rypkema v. British Columbia* (2003), 47 R.F.L. (5th) 398 (B.C. S.C.) (genetic parents declared to be the mother and father of the child and surrogate mother, with her consent, declared to be a non-parent); and *N. (B.A.) v. H. (J.)* (2008), 294 D.L.R. (4th) 564 (B.C. S.C.) (husband who provided sperm and his wife declared to be mother and father of twins while egg donor and surrogate mother, with their consent, declared to be non-parents).

4. Recall that Bill 133, passed but not yet proclaimed, proposes the addition of s. 6.1 to the *CLRA* to allow a court to change a child's name where it declares that a person is "the mother or father of a child". It would also alter s. 9 of the *VSA* in a limited way by adding a subsection (8) to require the Registrar General to amend the particulars of the birth registration where a court orders a name change.

5. In *A.A. v. B.B.* and *D. (M.) v. L. (L.)*, all the parties were in agreement about what the court should do. Would the cases have been decided differently if there had not been this consensus? In *N. (B.A.) v. H. (J.)*, above, Justice Metzger specifically noted (para. 25):

I wish to make it clear that I granted the declarations sought on the basis that there is universal consent amongst the intended parents, the egg donor, the surrogate mother, and the VSA [the Registrar]. If any of those parties did not consent ... the result may have been different. ... In the absence of legislation dealing specifically with this situation, courts will be cautious about granting a declaration without confirmation that the VSA's policy regarding birth registrations flowing from surrogacy, which may change over time, has been complied with.

6. Does the *A.A. v. B.B.* decision allow a step-parent to apply for a declaration of parentage? For a comment on the case, see Bouchard, "The Three-Parent Decision: A Case Commentary on *AA v. BB*" (2007), 70 Sask. L. Rev. 459.

3. Adoption

(1) Introduction

(a) General

GIESBRECHT, "ADOPTION"

Bala, Zapf, Williams, Vogl, and Hornick, eds., *Canadian Child Welfare Law: Children, Families and the State*, 2d ed. (Toronto: Thompson Educational Publishing, Inc., 2004) (Footnotes omitted) (Reprinted with the permission of the author and publisher.)

The Social and Historical Context of Adoption

Adoption is the process by which the law creates a child-parent relationship and, by extension, brings the child into the kinship lines of the adoptive family, while at the same time terminating the child's legal relationships with the birth parents and family. The adoption process in Canada also results in the amendment of birth records, so that it appears that the adoptive parents gave birth to the child. Adoption has profound social and psychological effects on adoptees, birth parents and adoptive parents. Adoption also results in a profound change in a child's legal status. Adoption is closely regulated by law in Canada, and is based on principles that place the child's best interests as paramount, but that also recognize the rights of biological parents. ...

Adoption is a matter of provincial jurisdiction under s. 92 of the *Constitution Act, 1867*, and the first adoption legislation that was enacted in Canada was in New Brunswick in 1873. In most provinces adoption laws were only enacted in the period during and after World War I, when a great increase in "illegitimacy" (children born to single mothers) gave rise to the need to find families to provide care for these children. At the same time, the growing middle class and the emergence of the "housewife" as an occupation meant that married women who were unable to biologically bear children wanted to adopt children to have "as their own." Adoption was shrouded in secrecy; for the unwed mother there was the shame of having had an illegitimate child, and for the adoptive parents there was the stigma of illegitimacy. Children were often not told that they were adopted until well into life, and sometimes did not find out until after the deaths of their adoptive parents.

Until well past the middle of the twentieth century, there were more healthy newborn infants available for adoption in Canada than there were adoptive parents. Abortion was illegal; women who became pregnant out of wedlock faced social stigma, had very poor economic prospects, and would usually place their children for adoption. In the last decades of the twentieth century there were dramatic changes in the adoption field. Improved birth control and access to abortion meant that fewer children were being born to single mothers; social attitudes and supports for single mothers improved and more of these women chose to parent their children. At the same time, as more women postponed pregnancy, there was an increase in infertility. As a result, there is now a much greater demand in Canada for infants to adopt than there are children available. This has led to changes in adoption, such as more interest in international and inter-racial adoption, more adoptions of older children, and increased efforts to ensure that biological parents are involved in selecting adoptive parents.

Historically in Canada, custom adoption was practised among the Aboriginal people. Custom adoption provided caregivers for children in situations where biological parents were dead, or had too many children to care for, and usually involved caregiving by biological relatives of the child. Under Aboriginal custom adoption, children are aware that their adoptive parents are not their biological parents and continue to have contact with biological relatives. Custom adoption recognizes the strength of extended families and does not only focus on the biological family but rather the community as a whole. Today custom adoption is recognized by statute in the Northwest Territories, Nunavut, and British Columbia, and has recognition at common law elsewhere. Interestingly, Aboriginal custom adoption is in some ways serving as a model for a new, more open approach that is being developed in the broader Canadian society.

The Legal Framework for Adoption

Today there is legislation in every province and territory in Canada that regulates all aspects of domestic adoption within the jurisdictions, and in some cases provides guidance in relation to interprovincial adoptions. In Canada, children who are adopted from foreign countries are subject to the rules set out in the 1993 *Hague Convention on Intercountry Adoption*, which has been implemented in all provinces and territories in Canada.

While there is some variation within Canada in the details of adoption statutes, the legislative schemes share the same fundamental features, namely to:

- regulate adoption service providers, such as government child welfare agencies (like Ontario's Children's Aid Societies) and private adoption licensees;

- establish how children qualify for adoption, either by voluntary placement by their birth parents or by involuntary placement through state intervention in cases where children are neglected or in need or protection;

- define who qualifies as a legal "parent" of the child for the purposes of identifying those persons whose consent to adoption is required, or alter- natively, whose consent must be dispensed with before an adoption order can be made;

- specify rules surrounding the giving of consent to adoption;

- set out the requirements for prospective adoptive parents;

- provide authority for a judge to make an adoption order and provide the basis for making such an order;

- provide for the changing of the name and birth registration particulars of the child;

- emphasize the need to help Aboriginal children preserve their cultural identity;

- provide rules relating to the maintenance of confidential records;

- implement proper procedures for disclosure of identifying information for adoptees and birth parents who wish to reunite;

- define offences and provide penalties for those who breach the legislation; and

- list exceptions to the regular adoption process in cases of step-parent or relative adoptions.

. . . . .

During the last decade, adoption practices have evolved towards more openness among the parties involved, including a call by adoptees and birth parents for more and earlier disclosure of identifying information and the opening of original birth registration records.

Best Interests of the Child

The most basic principle of adoption is that this institution is intended to promote the best interests of the child. While the interests of the biological and adoptive parents are subordinate to the interests of the child, in some contexts the law gives priority to the rights of birth parents and to maintaining a relationship between biological relatives and a child, but this is done with the objective of promoting the best interests of the child. Section 136(2) of Ontario's *Child and Family Services Act* is representative of the considerations in making decisions about adoption that are set out in legislation in other jurisdictions in Canada. ...

In addition to the above-noted criteria, most jurisdictions, including Ontario, have provisions that direct decision makers in the adoption process to consider the importance of preserving a child's cultural identity where that child is Aboriginal.

Many cases dealing with determining the best interests of a child in relation to adoption focus on balancing the benefits of placing a child in a stable two parent family against the loss of breaking ties with the child's biological family. The balancing task becomes increasingly more difficult with the passage of time as the child is generally forming ever-strengthening psychological attachments with his or her caregivers, and to break this attachment would cause serious emotional trauma. Therefore, it is always preferable that decisions regarding the long-term placement of children be dealt with at the earliest opportunity. ...

In most jurisdictions, in cases of involuntary relinquishment of children, children who are to be placed for adoption by a child welfare agency must be permanent wards without access to their biological parents. The traditional view has been that to sever the child's ties to the biological family is in the best interests of the child for many reasons, including the freedom of the adoptive parents to raise the child without intervention or contact from the child's birth family.

Recently the idea of the automatic severance of all links between the biological parents and an adopted child has been challenged. Although in most adoptions this severance will continue to occur, in some cases it may be in the best interests of the child to have both the permanency of adoption and a continued tie to biological parents. For example, in the 2002 Yukon case *of Re R.A.*, [2002] Y.J. No. 48 (Terr. Ct.) Chief Judge Stuart held that s. 7 of the *Charter of Rights* requires that courts must, in appropriate cases, have the flexibility to allow adoption with continued access to the biological parents, if this is in the best interests of the child before the court. Even though this is not permitted by legislation, Stuart C.J. concluded that the child's *Charter*-based right to be treated "in accordance with the principles of fundamental justice" requires that courts have the flexibility to allow such continued contact. The judge concluded that it was in the best interests of this particular special needs child to be a permanent ward with a view to adoption, but to have continued visits from her Aboriginal mother. The mother loved the child and had continued to have visits with the child, who clearly benefited from them, but she was unable to care for the child as she suffered from fetal alcohol effect. The prospective adoptive parents welcomed the continued visits with the biological mother. It is interesting that in this case, involving an Aboriginal child, the judge used the *Charter of Rights* to develop a legal response that is in some ways similar to the traditional Aboriginal custom adoption.

Across Canada, there are developments intended to make adoption a more flexible and diverse institution. These developments, based on a concern about promoting the best interests of the child, are resulting in an evolution of adoption that includes:

- more openness in relationships between adoptees, their biological families and their adoptive 'lfamilies;

- confirmation of the link between adoptees and their biological parents by acknowledging the original birth record details and making them available to adoptees; and

- the preservation of Aboriginal culture in cases where the child has Aboriginal ancestry.

Types of Adoption

There are two basic types of adoption in Canada:

- familial adoptions where the adoptive parents are related to the child by blood or marriage and arrange the adoption privately; and

- adoptions where there is no prior relationship between the adoptive parents and the child, and the adoption is arranged with the involvement of an intermediary.

In the category of adoptions where the parties are not biologically related or connected to the child through marriage, adoptions involve either voluntary or involuntary placements. *Voluntary placements* occur when birth parents plan for the adoption of their children, consent to the adoption, and engage a government child welfare agency or a private adoption licensee to facilitate the adoption. *Involuntary adoption placements* occur when a child is removed by court order from the care of the birth parents because the child has been neglected, abused or abandoned, and the child is made a permanent ward, usually without the parents having access rights, thereby putting the agency in the position of being able to place the child for adoption without the consent of the biological parents.

Familial adoptions, where the parties are related to each other or are connected through marriage, are either relative adoptions or step-parent adoptions. Familial adoptions are subject to less onerous regulations as the parties are known to each other and can assist in addressing the child's best interests. Often in familial adoptions the children involved are already living with the adoptive parents, and the adoption is intended to make permanent the legal tie between children and parents.

Involuntary Adoption Placements

. . . . .

If a court has determined that a child is to be a permanent ward, the child welfare agency has a duty to make a plan for the permanent care of the child. Indeed, an initial tentative plan will usually be developed before the agency comes to court seeking permanent wardship and will be presented to the court as part of the case for permanent wardship. If parental access rights are terminated under the child protection statute (and in some jurisdictions even if the parents have access rights), the agency's plans for permanent care are likely to include an adoption plan. Adoption is often considered the best option for a child, as it offers the prospect of the permanent benefit of belonging to a family and enjoying a stable, positive child-parent relationship.

Child welfare agencies recruit and screen potential adoptive parents, and are likely to have on file many prospective adoptive families who have been investigated and approved after an agency home study process. Government child welfare agencies have the mandate to match a child in accordance with the child's physical, mental, and emotional needs; the child's cultural, racial, and ethnic background; the child's religious faith; and, where ascertainable, the birth parents' wishes. Racial, cultural, ethnic, and religious congruence between the child and the prospective adoptive family, and placement of a child with previously placed siblings, are factors that will normally be heavily weighted when the agency is considering a potential match, though none is determinative. While there is now a preference in child welfare agencies in Canada for intra-racial adoption, the reality in Canada is that there are relatively few non-Caucasian prospective adoptive parents and a relatively large number of visible minority and Aboriginal children who are permanent wards, and interracial adoption is not uncommon.

There are today in Canada many more couples who want to adopt healthy infants than there are such children available for adoption, and with these children the agency will usually not have difficulty making a match. Often, however, the children who become available for adoption through involuntary placements are older, and may have experienced abuse or neglect at the hands of their parents. Some of these children may have special needs and may, for example, be suffering from the effects of maternal alcohol or drug abuse during pregnancy. Local agencies sometimes have to contact other agencies to find suitable adoptive parents for children with special needs. Agencies may be more willing to consider single persons and gay or lesbian partners for these "hard-to-place" children, as many "traditional adoptive parents" (heterosexual married couples) are unwilling to consider this type of child.

In involuntary placements, it is not uncommon for a child to be in foster care for an extended period of time before a permanent wardship order is made. If the foster family is among the pool of prospective adoptive families under consideration, weight is usually given to the degree of attachment that has developed between the child and the foster family. Typically, the longer the child has been in the care of the foster family the greater the degree of attachment, and therefore, the greater the risk of emotional harm if the child is removed from the foster home and the greater the likely value of adoption. Indeed, the fact that a child has been in the care of a foster family for a significant period and wants to be adopted by the foster parents may be a reason for terminating the right of access of the biological parents, especially if they lack in parenting abilities and are unlikely to ever resume care of the child. In most jurisdictions in Canada there are also programs to allow subsidies to be paid to adoptive parents who undertake the care of special needs children; the payment of subsidy may also make a long-term foster parent more willing to adopt a special needs child, as otherwise adoption may result in a significant loss of income.

The child welfare agency is solely responsible for selecting prospective adoptive parents for children who have been made permanent wards. Foster parents who take in children and want to adopt have "at risk" pre-adoptive placements, and adoption will only occur if the child is made a permanent ward and parents lose their rights to the child. Further, once a child is made a permanent ward without the parents having access, the child welfare agency is the legal guardian of the child and has the responsibility to find an adoptive placement that best meets the needs of the child. While in practice foster parents who want to adopt a child whom they have cared for will usually be given priority, the agency is not obliged to allow them to adopt and will have the right to place the child with another family for adoption.

Voluntary Adoption Placements

Birth parents, for varying reasons, may decide to place their children for adoption. Such voluntary adoption placements almost always involve newborns or very young infants, usually born to parents who are not married or cohabiting with one another. The decision to place a child for adoption is often wrenching and emotional. The decision may involve consideration of the life plans of the parents, and their ability and interest in caring for children. Birth parents, in deciding to place their child for adoption, usually want to ensure the best possible future for their child. As discussed further below, those who arrange adoptions have an obligation to counsel biological parents before they consent to adoption and their children are placed for adoption. The adoption process is regulated to attempt to ensure that any decision that a parent makes is carefully considered and voluntary. No payment may be made to a biological parent in exchange for the consent to an adoption; the decision to place a child must be voluntary and it is an offence for a parent to receive any compensation for agreeing to the adoption of their child.

In all provinces and territories, child welfare agencies are authorized to undertake voluntary adoption placements, which typically involve the newborn children of unwed mothers who contact the agency, usually before the child is born. In some cases when an unwed mother contacts a child welfare agency and indicates that she wants to place her child for adoption, the agency will decide to apply to the court to have the child made a permanent ward without access, with the plan being adoption. The mother will be notified of the application and may consent to it, which will make the hearing a formality. This process is in many practical ways similar to a voluntary placement adoption with a child welfare agency, but may give the agency more flexibility about changing the plans for the child after the initial involvement of the mother is over.

Many of the mothers who voluntarily place their children for adoption were (or are) themselves wards of child welfare agencies, and prefer not to deal with that agency for the adoption of their child. Most Canadian jurisdictions also permit private adoption agencies and professionals to act as adoption licensees to provide adoption services, providing birth parents and adoptive parents with an alternative to the public adoption system. While public agencies charge no fees to adoptive parents, a private domestic adoption can cost $6,000 to $10,000 or more, but adoptive parents who are able to pay these fees may have an adoption arranged in a shorter period than through a public agency as licensees typically have shorter "waiting lists," and may have more children available for placement than public agencies.

The voluntary placement process also differs from the involuntary placement process in that the consent of the birth parents is required before an adoption order can be made. The subject of parental consent is discussed in detail below.

In a voluntary placement, the sharing of the social and medical history of the child's birth family is usually more complete than with an involuntary adoption because birth parents who voluntarily place their children for adoption are more likely to be willing to provide detailed information. Further, it is a common practice with private adoptions in Canada today for the birth parents to be involved in selecting the prospective adoptive parents. This is done by the agency or licensee providing the birth parents with non-identifying written and pictorial profiles of prospective adoptive parents and allowing them to select the parents whom they prefer. It is also becoming more common to share identifying information once a match is made since birth and adoptive parents often wish to develop an open adoption plan, which may provide for the regular exchange of letters, pictures, and visits. In voluntary placements, an open adoption may be available as an option for consideration by the birth and adoptive parents, if they all feel comfortable with this type of arrangement.

The steps for finalizing a voluntary placement adoption are similar to those in an involuntary placement, in that an application is made to the court for a final adoption order. In a voluntary placement, however, the child's "parents" must consent to the adoption, though as further discussed below some biological fathers may not be legally regarded as "parents" and hence their consent will not be required, or a court may dispense with the consent of a biological parent to an adoption.

Familial Adoptions

Most adoption legislative schemes in Canada provide for a substantial relaxation of the statutory requirements for children who will be adopted by family members, as all of the adults involved know each other before the adoption occurs. The difference in approach is intended to facilitate this type of adoption, on the premise that when biological parents cannot care for their children, familial adoption is likely to promote the child's interests by allowing the child to remain in the care of blood relatives and maintain his or her cultural heritage.

Outside of the context of adoption of a child by a close relative, biological parents cannot place their children for adoption; only a child welfare agency or a licensee can make such placements, as these intermediaries are trained and supervised to promote the best interests of the child. However, when biological parents, usually single mothers, decide to place a child with close relatives, they can do so without the involvement of a child welfare agency, adoption agency or licensee. There is no need for a home study, criminal records check or medical reports before a familial placement occurs, because birth parents are presumed to be able to satisfy themselves as to the prospective adoptive parents' suitability. Further, there is no requirement for a probationary period prior to obtaining an adoption order. Adoptive applicants will, however, be required to obtain the consents of the child's birth mother and any other legal "parent" of the child. The child's consent will also be required if the child has attained the statutory age threshold. ...

In a relative adoption, an adoption order re-orders the relationship of the child to its birth and adoptive relatives. For example, if the birth mother's mother adopts the child, the biological grandmother of the child becomes the adoptive mother, and the biological mother becomes the adoptive sister of the child.

Step-Parent Adoptions

Just as in relative adoptions, and for similar reasons, the various statutes regulating adoptions relax the requirements for the adoption of children by the spouse of their custodial parent. While the consent of every legal "parent" (discussed below) is required for a step-parent adoption, there are no requirements for home studies, probationary periods, or involvement of child welfare agencies or licensees.

Most step-parent adoptions arise in situations where the biological father has little or no relationship with his child and the child has developed a close relationship with the stepfather. In such cases the step-father must apply to the court for an adoption order, usually on the strength of his affidavit evidence establishing that he is a suitable parent and the filing of the consents of the child's birth parents or any other legal parent and the child, if the child is old enough. As is discussed more fully below, in cases where the birth father will not consent, an application can be brought to dispense with his consent.

Once the issues of consent are resolved, if the judge is satisfied that the step-father is a suitable parent and that the adoption would be in the best interests of the child, an adoption order will be made. For legal purposes, the child joins the adoptive father's kinship line and is no longer part of the birth father's family. The child's relationship with the birth mother and her family remains intact. At the time of the order the child's name is usually changed and birth registration particulars are re-registered naming the adoptive father as the biological father of record.

Generally, in Canada, the definition of "spouse" for adoption purposes means a married or common law partner. This definition causes problems when a birth parent dies and the step-parent wants to adopt the child; the step-parent was a "spouse" prior to the death, but at the time of the adoption application is not a "spouse" and, therefore, does not qualify for the less onerous step-parent adoption process. Even though the child may have lived with the step-parent for many years, or even since birth, the adoption must be under the more stringent procedure that governs adoption by persons who are not relatives. ...

Until recently, the definition of "spouse" also made it difficult for the same-sex partners of biological parents to adopt. In many same-sex adoption cases, the children are conceived by artificial insemination and live their entire lives with the biological parent and the same-sex step-parent. In the 1995 Ontario case of *K., Re* (1995), 15 R.F.L. (4th) 129 (Ont. Prov. Div.), Justice Nevins dealt with a constitutional challenge by a number of same-sex partners of biological parents who wanted to have step-parent adoptions. Interestingly, this case was decided before any of the major cases in which Canadian courts granted same-sex partners "spousal" status or the right to marry. In ruling on the exclusion of same-sex partners from the step-parent adoption provisions of Ontario's *Child and Family Services Act*, the judge considered that this was both discrimination on the basis of sexual orientation and contrary to the best interests of the children involved. [See now the definition of "spouse" in s. 136(1) of the *CFSA*.]

Regulation of Adoption Service Providers

In all jurisdictions in Canada, government child welfare agencies are authorized to carry out adoptions, and in most provinces private adoption licensees may also place children for adoption. It is an offence for any other individual or agency to process adoptions. The purpose of restricting involvement in adoption is to ensure that the best possible placements are made for children, and that all of those involved in the adoption process receive appropriate services and support. The legislation provides avenues to hold service providers accountable. This type of regulation reduces the risk of unscrupulous persons wishing to profit from the marketing of children or from persons trying to effect adoptions through the bypassing of legislative requirements.

The ultimate authority to regulate adoption rests with each provincial and territorial government, as domestic adoption is not within federal jurisdiction. In each jurisdiction, adoption is regulated by the ministry charged with child welfare responsibilities. That ministry appoints an officer, sometimes referred to as a "director," who oversees the provision of adoption services by authorized government child welfare agencies, private adoption agencies and licensed individuals.

All aspects of the activities of public child welfare agencies, including their adoption work, are subject to direct government control, and governments are responsible for the policies and work of these agencies.

In the case of private adoption agencies or licensed individuals, the ministry uses a licensing process to regulate entry into the adoption field. A licence will only be provided to an applicant if the ministry is satisfied that the agency or individual has sufficient skill, knowledge, and access to counsellors and medical services, to properly effect an adoption. In Ontario, once a private agency or individual is licensed, the licence remains in effect for one year. Annually, the licensee must report to the ministry and request a renewal of the licence.

Some of the private adoptive agencies are non-profit, religion-based agencies, and most of the professionals (usually social workers or lawyers) who act as private licensees are competent, reputable professionals. There are, however, concerns that with private adoptions there is the potential for the profit motive or personal prejudices to affect decisions, and private adoptions are subject to more legal controls than adoptions arranged by public child welfare agencies. This regulation is intended to ensure accountability and to maintain a focus on the needs of children. ...

In most jurisdictions, all financial transactions between the licensee and the prospective adoptive parents must be recorded by the licensee, held in a trust account, and be reported to the licensing ministry on an annual basis. The ministry must renew licences on an annual basis, and will only do so after reviewing the financial transactions and information regarding the files processed by the licensee in the preceding year.

(b) Inter-Country Adoptions

The number of adoptions of children from foreign countries by Canadian families has increased dramatically in the last few decades. Between 1995 and 2003, approximately 2,000 foreign children per year were adopted by Canadians. See Adoption Canada, *Interna-*

tional Adoptions Up 2,181 in 2003 (June 28, 2004) online at <www.adoption.ca>. Foreign adoption is now the most utilized means of adopting an infant by Canadians. This reflects the "supply" of homeless or needy children in the developing countries and the "demand" for adoptable children in Canada. There has been a marked decrease in the number of healthy children available for adoption within Canada as a result of the availability of contraception and abortion, elimination of some of the stigma associated with single parenthood, and extended social benefits for single parents. Cross-border adoption most commonly involves the completion of the adoption in the country where the child is originally resident. This usually involves the adoptive parents traveling to the foreign country, locating a child, pursuing the adoption application there, and then bringing the child to Canada. The process, therefore, is quite expensive, with total costs reaching $25,000 in some cases. See Giesbrecht, "Adoption" in Bala, Zapf, Williams, Vogl, and Hornick, eds., *Canadian Child Welfare Law: Children, Families and the State*, 2d ed. (Toronto: Thompson Educational Publishing, Inc., 2004) at 194.

Canada's liberal rules governing the recognition of foreign adoptions generally ensure that such adoptions are recognized. Some have suggested that adoptions completed abroad be redone in the country to which the child is brought to avoid any recognition problems. However, Justice Wolder held in *Re P. (A.)* (2002), 30 R.F.L. (5th) 377 (Ont. C.J.) that an Ontario court had no jurisdiction to continue with an adoption application where the adoptive parents had already adopted the child in Thailand and were recognized as the child's lawful parents in Ontario. Compare *Re R. (A.)* (1982), 30 R.F.L. (2d) 73 (Ont. Prov. Ct.).

Professor Black explores the legal and social problems associated with transnational adoptions in "GATT for Kids: New Rules for Intercountry Adoption of Children" (1994), 11 C.F.L.Q. 253. The article also describes the *Hague Convention on Protection of Children and Co-operation in Respect of Intercountry Adoption* which Canada signed on April 12, 1994. This Convention, implemented in Ontario by the *Intercountry Adoption Act, 1998*, S.O. 1998, c. 29, provides for a mandatory regime for intercountry adoptions involving ratifying states. The Convention establishes a system to co-ordinate efforts between the various jurisdictions and to ensure that the authorities in each jurisdiction properly supervise the adoption process. In Ontario, the Ministry of Community and Social Services is the Central Authority and it is required to ensure that 1) the agencies that arrange these adoptions are licensed and have qualified staff; 2) the prospective adoptive parents are screened appropriately; and 3) the Canadian government will allow the child to enter and reside permanently in Canada. The last point emphasizes that an international adoption involves both adoption and immigration into Canada. Since 2007, it has been possible for Canadian citizens to apply for a grant of Canadian citizenship for their foreign adoptee without the child first becoming a permanent resident. An alternative is the immigration process through which the parents sponsor the adoptee. See generally, the Citizenship and Immigration Canada website: *www.cic.gc.ca*.

Under the Convention, the authorities in the country of origin are required to establish that the child is adoptable, that the appropriate consents have been given, and that the adoption is in the child's best interest. Only after the authorities of both states have agreed that the adoption may take place and that the child will be free to reside permanently in the receiving state may the child be physically transferred to the adoptive parents. The Convention does not stipulate where or when the adoption must take place. It can happen before or after the child is physically entrusted to the adoptive parents. It can occur either in the state of origin or the receiving state, although states of origin can provide that the adoption must take place there.

It should be noted that Ontario's *Intercountry Adoption Act, 1998* applies to any "intercountry adoption". This expression is defined to include any adoption by an Ontario resident of a child who is habitually resident outside Canada where the adoption is finalized in the child's country of origin even if that country has not ratified the Convention. Accordingly, the screening process outlined in the Act applies to all such adoptions.

(c) Aboriginal Customary Adoption

As noted earlier by Theodore Giesbrecht, Canadian courts have increasingly recognized aboriginal custom adoption. In particular, since the 1960s the courts have accepted that the legal relationship of parent and child can be established for purposes such as inheritance by aboriginal persons who have followed customary practices: *Re K's Adoption Petition* (1961), (sub nom. *Re Katie*) 32 D.L.R. (2d) 686 (N.W.T. Terr. Ct.); *Re Beaulieu* (1969), 3 D.L.R. (3d) 479 (N.W.T. Terr. Ct.); *Re Deborah E4-789* (1972), 6 R.F.L. 299 (N.W.T. S.C.); affirmed (1972), 8 R.F.L. 202 (N.W.T. C.A.); *Re Tagornak* (1983), 50 A.R. 237 (N.W.T. S.C.); *Michell v. Dennis* (1983), [1984] 2 W.W.R. 449 (B.C. S.C.); and *Casimel v. Insurance Corp. of British Columbia* (1993), 106 D.L.R. (4th) 720 (B.C. C.A.). In *Casimel*, the British Columbia Court of Appeal concluded (at 731): "[T]here is a well-established body of authority in Canada for the proposition that the status conferred by aboriginal customary adoption will be recognized by the courts for the purposes of the application of the principles of the common law and the provisions of statute law to the persons whose status is established by the customary adoption."

In *K. (S.K.) v. S. (J.)* (1999), 1999 CarswellNWT 95 (N.W.T. S.C.), a grandmother sought child support, both interim and final, from the child's father. The parties agreed and the court accepted that the grandmother and her deceased husband had adopted the child as an infant at the request of his mother in accordance with Inuit tradition. The biological father argued that in accordance with s. 37 of the *Adoption Act*, S.N.W.T. 1998, c. 9, he was no longer considered a parent of the child and so did not have any obligation to support him. Section 37 stipulated that, for all purposes, the parent-child relationship was ended by an adoption order. Justice Schuler held that this section did not apply to an aboriginal custom adoption and that the effect of such an adoption was governed by the relevant aboriginal customary law. There being no evidence about that law, Justice Schuler declined to award interim support. The Justice noted that evidence about the effect of the adoption could be presented at trial.

In the Northwest Territories, the *Aboriginal Custom Adoption Recognition Act*, S.N.W.T. 1994, c. 26, establishes statutory rules for recognition of custom adoption. By virtue of the *Nunavut Act*, S.C. 1993, c. 28, this statute also applies in Nunavut. The *Aboriginal Custom Adoption Recognition Act* allows a person who has adopted a child in accordance with aboriginal customary law to apply to a "custom adoption commissioner" for a certificate recognizing the adoption. The commissioner must then file the certificate with the Supreme Court. Once filed, it is deemed to be an order of that court. In *K. (S.K.) v. S. (J.)* (1999), 1999 CarswellNWT 95 (N.W.T. S.C.), Justice Schuler stated that the filing of the certificate did not mean that there was a deemed adoption order. Rather, the filing operated only as a legal recognition of the custom adoption. In Justice Schuler's view, the relevant aboriginal customary law still determined the effects of such an adoption. If this is correct, the situation may be different in British Columbia because of the wording of s. 46(1) of the *Adoption Act*, R.S.B.C. 1996, c. 5, likely as a response to the *Casimel* case, above. That section authorizes a court to "recognize that an adoption of a person effected by the custom of an Indian band or aboriginal community has the effect of an adoption under this Act". Section 46(2) goes on to stipulate that the previous subsection "does not affect any aboriginal rights a person has". For a case where a court used s. 46 to recognize an adoption, see *Re B.C. Birth Registration No. 1994-09-040399* (1998), 45 R.F.L. (4th) 458 (B.C. S.C.).

Further Reading

For additional information about customary adoption, see Baldassi, "The Legal Status of Aboriginal Customary Adoption Across Canada: Comparisons, Contrasts, and Convergences" (2006), 39 U.B.C.L. Rev. 63.

(2) Eligibility

(a) Who May Be Adopted?

Section 146(5) of the *CFSA* specifies that the person being adopted must be a resident of Ontario. This requirement was the subject of the following case decided under the *Child Welfare Act*.

RE RAI

(1980), 27 O.R. (2d) 425, 1980 CarswellOnt 1305 (C.A.)

WEATHERSTON J.A.: — The appellants, Roy Chandan Persaud and Satyavatee Persaud came to Canada in 1968 and have been Canadian citizens since 1975. They have applied to adopt Chandra Muni Rai (the child). Their application was dismissed without hearing from the appellants or the child, by His Honour Judge Webb, who found on the authority of *Re Khan* (1978), 21 O.R. (2d) 748, 92 D.L.R. (3d) 287, that the child was not resident in Ontario. It is that finding that is the sole issue now. ...

The child is the niece of the male appellant. She was born in Guyana on December 7, 1962, and came to Canada on February 27, 1977. She was admitted as a non-immigrant, a visitor. By the Regulations under the *Immigration Act* ... she was deemed to have been granted entry for a limited period of not more than three months. Within that period of time she reported to an immigration officer. The report that he made out contains the following remarks: "pending adoption". She has been allowed to stay pending the examination that is required to be made by an immigration officer. That examination has not been concluded but awaits the outcome of this adoption application. The child has lived with the appellants since her arrival in Canada and is a student in a junior high school. The immigration authorities consider her to be a person seeking admission to Canada as an immigrant and have agreed that if the adoption order is made before the child's 18th birthday, they will recommend that the necessary Regulations be passed to regularize her admission to Canada as a permanent resident. ...

Re Kahn, *supra*, was an application by a 28-year-old man and his wife to adopt the 18-year-old brother of the male applicant. In that case, at pp. 748-9 O.R., p. 288 D.L.R., this Court expressed three concerns:

> (1) If an adoption order is granted in order to regularize the child's presence in this country and to satisfy the requirements of the immigration laws, it appears to us that such an order does not fall within the intent and the purpose of the provincial adoption legislation. (2) Section 71 of the *Child Welfare Act*, R.S.O. 1970, c. 64, requires the child to be "resident" in this Province for the purposes of an adoption order. We do not think that someone here on a visitor's permit fulfils that requirement of residence. (3) Finally, the adoption of one brother by another with a 10-year age difference (as pointed out by the Director of Child Welfare in this case), appears to us to be inconsistent with the intent ... of the *Child Welfare Act*. It has the appearance of an accommodation adoption to get around the stringencies or requirements of the *Immigration Act* ... and the Court and the provincial legislation should not be used as a means to achieve that end.

In the present case, it has been acknowledged by all concerned that the application is *bona fide* and was not made merely to enable the child to regularize her presence here. It is not an "accommodation adoption". The Director of Child Welfare has recommended that an order for the adoption of the child be made. The only question is whether she complies with the condition in s. 71 of the Act that she be "resident in Ontario".

Legal adoptions in Ontario are wholly statutory and the Legislature has used the residence of the child and of the adopting parents as the basis for the exercise of jurisdiction. We are not concerned in the present case whether the proposed adoption order would be given foreign recognition. ... Whether or not an adoption order would be recognized by a foreign jurisdiction might be a factor when considering the best interests of the child — for instance, if the natural parents, domiciled elsewhere, opposed the adoption, or if property or inheritance rights would be affected. That is not the case here.

The status of a child under the immigration laws does not affect the jurisdiction of the Court. It is undoubtedly a factor to be considered before an adoption order is made, for adoption would not be in the best interests of a child if that child were likely to be deported immediately afterwards. It is also relevant when considering whether the applicants really intend to create a new relationship of parent and child, or whether the statute is being used for a collateral purpose.

... Residence is not established by mere presence in the Province on a casual visit, or while passing through. Indeed, in such a case, our Courts would decline jurisdiction to change the status of a person belonging to another civilized country because of the respect we have for the laws of that country. But, apart from exceptional cases, the purpose of the statutory requirement of residence will have been met if there is a reasonable connection between the child and Ontario, and if the child has lived here for sufficient time to enable an effective investigation to be made into the suitability of the adopting parents and whether the proposed adoption order would be in the best interests of the child.

In the present case, the child is no longer a mere visitor, whatever may be her technical status under the *Immigration Act*. She has lived in Ontario with permanent residents since her arrival on February 27, 1977, in the hope of adoption, and she attends school as a regular student. I think she has met the jurisdictional requirement that she reside in Ontario and that the application for adoption ought to have been dealt with on its merits. ...

NOTES AND QUESTIONS

1. In *B. (J.) v. S. (C.W.)* (1996), 19 R.F.L. (4th) 49 (Ont. Gen. Div.), the child was an eight-year-old American citizen who had been placed by a Maryland court in the custody of two persons residing in Ontario. The child was in Canada on a temporary ministerial permit. Justice Steinberg found that the child resided in Ontario and granted the adoption order.

2. The Manitoba Court of Appeal held in *L. (T.I.) v. F. (J.L.)* (2001), 16 R.F.L. (5th) 173, that a baby born in North Dakota and brought to Manitoba so that a Manitoba couple could adopt him was resident in Manitoba. The court held that there were only two simple questions that needed to be addressed: Did the prospective adoptive parents reside in Manitoba? Did the child reside with them? It answered both questions in the affirmative and also concluded that Manitoba was the *forum conveniens* to hear the application.

Note that s. 141(2) of the *CFSA* prohibits anyone other than a "society or a licensee" from bringing a child who is not a resident of Ontario into Ontario to be placed for adoption. Section 141(8) then creates an exception for family adoptions. Would this prohibition in s. 141(2) apply to a situation comparable to that in *L. (T.I.) v. F. (J.L.)*?

3. Prior to 1979, the *Child Welfare Act* expressly provided that an adult could only be adopted where the applicant had raised the proposed adoptee during infancy under a *de facto* adoption. In June 1979, a revised *Child Welfare Act* permitted the adoption of persons who were 18 years of age or older or who had been married in "special circumstances". What is the position under the *CFSA*? See ss. 146(3) and 152(4). Note that s. 137(6) stipulates that no order for adoption of a person who is seven years of age or more can be made without that person's consent.

4. Where the proposed adoptee is at least 18 years of age, certain provisions of the *CFSA* do not apply. For example, no parental consents are required. See s. 137(2) and definition of "child" in s. 3(1).

(b) Who May Adopt?

Most provinces require the adoptive parents to be at least 18 years of age and resident in the province. See, e.g., ss. 146(5) and 147 of the *CFSA*. Note, however, that an Ontario adoption order can be made on the application of a person who is less than 18 years of age if the "court is satisfied that special circumstances justify making the order" (s. 147).

Can an unmarried person adopt a child in Ontario? See s. 146(4) of the *CFSA*. Can two unmarried cohabitees jointly adopt a child in Ontario? See ss. 146(4) and 136(1) of the *CFSA*. Section 136(1) incorporates by reference the definition of "spouse" contained in s. 10(1) of the *Human Rights Code*, R.S.O. 1990, c. H.19. This definition was amended in February 2005 by the *Spousal Relationships Statute Law Amendment Act, 2005* and the phrase "a person of the opposite sex" was replaced by "a person".

Prior to 1999, the *CFSA* precluded a joint adoption application by two persons who were not married or in an opposite-sex conjugal relationship. This definition was successfully challenged on the basis of the *Canadian Charter of Rights and Freedoms* in *K., Re* (1995), 15 R.F.L. (4th) 129 (Ont. Prov. Ct.) by four lesbian couples who had been living together for a long time. All of the children involved had been conceived through artificial insemination and had been born to one of the partners during the relationship. For a similar case in Nova Scotia, see *M. (S.C.), Re* (2001), 202 D.L.R. (4th) 172 (N.S. S.C.).

NOTES AND QUESTIONS

1. When an application to adopt is brought by a person who is a spouse as defined in s. 136(1) of the *CFSA*, the applicant's spouse can either join in the application as a co-adopter (s. 146(4)(b)) or give written consent to the adoption (s. 137(10)). How do the legal consequences of these two acts differ? Can one spouse ever adopt a child without at least the consent of the other? See ss. 137(10) and 138.

2. In what circumstances should a single person be permitted to adopt? Is it generally in a child's best interests to be adopted by a couple? See *M. (S.K.A.) v. A. (C.)* (1995), 11 R.F.L. (4th) 25 (Alta. C.A.) where the court granted an adoption order to a 42-year-old widow even though the four-year-old's mother refused to consent.

3. Non-aboriginals may adopt an aboriginal child in accordance with the relevant provincial legislation. By virtue of s. 88 of the *Indian Act*, R.S.C. 1985, c. I-5, laws of general application that are in force in a province apply to Indians except where they are inconsistent with the *Indian Act* or a treaty between a first nation and the Crown. Pursuant to this provision, the courts have concluded that provincial adoption legislation applies to Indian children, but that an Indian child adopted by non-Indians does not lose his or her Indian status. Sometimes the provincial adoption legislation spells this out.

4. The child's cultural and social background may, of course, be a factor in the original placement of the child for the purpose of adoption (see below) and in determining whether an adoption order would be in the best interests of the child (see ss. 61(2), 136(2), and 136(3) of the *CFSA*).

(3) Placement for Adoption

(a) Introduction

The term "placement" is often used to refer simply to the actual physical placing of a child in the home of the prospective adopting parents. However, it can also be used to describe the entire process of selecting adopting parents, placing the child in their home, and monitoring the situation until the court order for adoption is made. It is the broader concept of placement that is the subject of this section.

Section 141(1) of the *CFSA* stipulates that only a children's aid society or the holder of a licence issued under Part IX may place a child with another person for adoption. This basic rule is subject to the exception created by s. 141(8), which permits anyone to place a child with the child's relative (as defined in s. 3(1)), the child's parent or a spouse of the child's parent. Where a child is placed for adoption by a person other than a society or licensee, s. 146(1) indicates that an adoption order should not be made until the child has resided with the prospective adoptee for at least two years. Any person who unlawfully places a child for adoption is guilty of an offence punishable by a fine of not more than $2,000 or by imprisonment for a term of not more than two years or both: s. 176(1).

A children's aid society is not required to obtain a licence before placing children for adoption: s. 193(2). No Crown ward is to be placed for adoption until any outstanding order of access made under s. 58(1) has been terminated and any appeal from the Crown wardship order or from any decision reviewing it has been disposed of or abandoned or the time for commencing such an appeal has expired: s. 141.1.

In 2004, Ontario's Minister of Children and Youth Services pledged to increase the number of adoptions involving Crown wards and suggested that it might be necessary to change the *CFSA* to allow placement for adoption and, indeed, adoption of Crown wards even where parents had an access order under the *CFSA*. When the *CFSA* was amended in 2006, however, the prohibition described in the previous paragraph remained. The amendments did introduce "openness orders" (ss. 145.1 and 145.2 and ss. 153.1 to 153.5) and "openness agreements" (s. 153.6). Such orders or agreements can provide for a continuing relationship between a birth parent and the child through exchange of information or actual visits. A Society can now place a Crown ward with prospective adoptive parents subject to an openness order or openness agreement. Note that, in either case, the prospective parents must consent. As a result, neither an openness order nor an openness agreement is available until an adoptive home has been identified and the prospective adoptive parents have consented. However, until that time, a Society may allow contact between a Crown ward and a parent even where there is no access order. See s. 59(4) of the *CFSA*. For more on openness orders and agreements, see (5) EFFECT OF ADOPTION, *(b) Access, "Openness Orders" and "Openness Agreements"*, below.

A society may also be involved in the placement of non-wards for adoption. Here, however, the society does not have a monopoly. An individual or non-profit agency may obtain a licence under Part IX for the purpose of placing a child for adoption. Lawyers, doctors and other private intermediaries generally become involved in adoption placements when they come into contact with unwed mothers who want their children adopted but who do not want to be involved with the child welfare agency. Licensees can only receive payment, generally from the adopting parents, for "prescribed expenses" and "proper legal fees and disbursements": s. 175 of the *CFSA*.

Under the *CFSA*, a "homestudy" will usually be conducted to determine if the prospective adoptive parents are suitable before the physical placement of a child in the home. Where the child is being placed by a licensee, the licensee is generally required to notify the Director of the proposed placement and to submit a homestudy: ss. 141 and 142. In these circumstances, the Director must approve the placement: s. 142(2). If the children's aid society is placing the child, the society itself will often conduct a homestudy before the placement of the child.

Generally, a child placed by a children's aid society or licensee must reside in the home of the prospective adopting parents for a period of six months before an adoption order is made: s. 149(1). At the end of this period, the local children's aid society or "a person approved by the Director or local director" prepares a report on the adjustment of the child in the home: s. 149(5). On the basis of this report, the Director determines whether or not to recommend the proposed adoption and files a statement to this effect with the court: s.

149(1). If the child has been placed for adoption by a children's aid society, the local director may make this determination and file the statement with the court: s. 149(2). Where the Director determines that it is in the best interests of the child that the six-month probationary period be dispensed with, the Director may so recommend after obtaining a report on the adjustment of the child: s. 149(1).

As noted earlier, many of the statutory and regulatory provisions governing the placement of children do not apply when a child's relative or step-parent seeks to adopt. See s. 141(8) and s. 149(6) of the *CFSA*. In these situations, the only control imposed by the state in most cases is the requirement of a judicial proceeding before the adoption order is made.

(b) Choosing Prospective Adoptive Parents

There are many more people who wish to adopt young children than there are young children available for adoption. As a result, the way in which prospective adoptive parents are screened and ranked is very important. For a general examination of the selection criteria used in public and private adoptions, see Daly and Sobol, *Adoption in Canada: Final Report* (Guelph: University of Guelph, 1993) at 55–57.

Views on interracial placements and adoption have undergone considerable change in the last 50 years. In the following article, Professor Davies reviews the literature on interracial adoption. She also examines the views of the child welfare authorities and racial or cultural groups in this issue.

DAVIES "RACIAL AND CULTURAL MATTERS IN CUSTODY DISPUTES"

(1993), 10 C.F.L.Q. 1 (Footnotes edited)

- *Premise #2: Children run the risk of harm if raised outside their own race and culture*

The reasons given for this premise are primarily twofold. It is said that cultural identity is essential to develop one's feeling of self worth. As one writer put it, "pride in one's cultural heritage is essential to reducing the crisis of adolescent identity and resolving role conflict."

Secondly, in the United States, the placing of Black children in white foster or adoptive homes has been opposed by many in the Black community on the basis that it prevents a child from developing "survival skills" necessary to live in contemporary American society. In one writer's opinion:

> My basic premise, in opposing placement of black children in white homes, is that being black in the United States is a special state of being. At a time of intense racial polarity, recognition of this fact is crucial to survival. I question the ability of white parents — no matter how deeply imbued with good will — to grasp the totality of the problem of being black in this society. I question their ability to create what I believe is crucial in these youngsters — a black identity.

The need for a black child to develop survival skills is a sad commentary on North American society. ...

Let us turn to the other reasons given for preferring racial congruity in child placement: the need for racial identity and the importance of self-esteem. These two facets are usually seen as interlinked: racial identity is *necessary* for the development of self-esteem. Is it true that the two *are* interlinked, *i.e.*, that one cannot have a healthy self-esteem without positive racial identity? Is it true that a positive racial identity and healthy self-esteem can only result from being brought up by someone of one's own race and culture?

First, then, the linkage between self-esteem and racial identity. Some recent studies indicate that self-esteem and racial self-perception may operate independently in children of one race adopted by parents of another. A team from the University of Texas in Austin carried out a study involving 30 Black families who had adopted Black children and 30 white families who had adopted Black children.[29] They found that the children of both sets of families had almost identical levels of self-esteem. Furthermore, the level of self-esteem of the adoptees was as high as that reported among individuals in the general population. However, there appeared to be a difference between the transracial and in racial adoptees in their sense of racial identity. Some of the Black children adopted by white families seemed to have a problem with racial identity (*i.e.*, some devalued or did not acknowledge a Black identity). Whether the Black children adopted by whites had a positive racial identity depended on whether the adoptive family nurtured the Black child's identity, gave the child access to Black role models and peers in the community and in school, paid attention to the child's Black heritage, etc. Thus, the study seems to show that self-esteem may be generated as effectively among Black children in white adoptive homes as in Black adoptive homes. Positive racial identity may also be generated in white adoptive homes, but the white adoptive parents must make efforts to foster this. ...

There have been several studies conducted with respect to the success of interracial adoptions. These studies have been consistent in their findings that by far the majority of transracial adoptions are successful. As one team of researchers put it, "There is no evidence that any of the serious problems of adjustment suggested by the critics of transracial adoption are present in any meaningful proportion for non-white children who have been adopted by white parents." Initially, researchers expressed caution that, whilst showing good adaptation as young children, the transracial adoptees might show themselves as less well-adapted in adolescence. However, subsequent studies have shown these fears to have been groundless and most of the adoptees were well-integrated into their families, experiencing no more than typical adolescent problems. This research contrasts markedly with the views expressed by some courts with respect to the danger of transracial adoption, particularly in the adolescent years.[33] As one writer has commented, "The puberty argument has instilled in it a life of its own."

It would be simplistic to suggest that transracial adoption is without its problems. The researchers all agree that it is important for the adoptive parents to make an effort to foster the child's sense of racial identity by affirming her racial heritage and by giving the child appropriate racially congruent role models and peers. However, the empirical research does not support the view that transracial adoption is in itself harmful to the child. Many of the problems transracially-reared children display in adolescence may be attributed to factors other than adoption, factors such as institutional or foster care and discrimination that might well have occurred regardless of the adoption. ...

The Child Welfare Authorities

... A child welfare authority at any given time will generally have in effect a policy with respect to placement. The authority will make placement decisions on the basis of that policy. This policy will generally have been developed in light of prevailing political as well as

---

[29] R. McRoy, L. Zurcher, M. Lauderdale & R. Anderson, "Self-Esteem and Racial Identity in Transracial and Inracial Adoptees" (1982) Social Work 522.

[33] See *N. (K.) v. M. (K.M.)* (1989), 97 A.R. 38 (Q.B.); varied (1989), 71 Alta. L.R. (2d) 42 (C.A.); leave to appeal to S.C.C. refused (1989), 102 A.R. 239 (note) (S.C.C.); *P. (L.) v. H. (D.J.)* (1986), 69 A.R. 327 (Q.B.); rev'd in part (1987), 55 Alta. L.R. (2d) 227 (C.A.). Compare *Winnipeg Child & Family Services v. B. (B.A.)* (1992), 99 D.L.R. (4th) 504 (Man. Q.B.).

child-related considerations. The implementation of this policy may or may not be in the interests of an individual child who becomes subject to it.

To give some examples, in the United States, the policy followed by child welfare workers with respect to the adoption of Black children by white parents has changed significantly over the past number of years. In 1958, the Standards for Adoption Services of the Child Welfare League of America (C.W.L.A.) stated that, "Children placed in adoptive families with similar racial characteristics such as colour, can become more easily integrated into the family group and community." It also stated that, "Physical resemblances should not be a determining factor in the selection of a home, *with the possible exception of such racial characteristics as colour*." By 1968, the C.W.L.A. had changed its position. The Standards provided:

> It should not be assumed by the agency or staff members that difficulties will necessarily arise if adoptive parents and children are of different racial origin. ... In most communities there are families who have the capacity to adopt a child whose racial background is different from their own. Such couples should be encouraged to consider such a child.

Further, the Standards stated that "physical resemblances of the adoptive parents, the child or his natural parents, should not be a determining factor in the selection of a home." The proviso emphasized above was now removed.

In 1972, the National Association of Black Social Workers condemned transracial adoption. In direct response to this, the C.W.L.A. standards changed again so that in 1972, the Standards provided:

> While we specifically affirm transracial adoptions as one means of achieving needed permanence for some children, we recognize that other things being equal in today's social climate, it is preferable to place a child in a family of his own racial background.

In the Canadian context, we see a similar fluctuating policy applied with respect to the placement of Native children.

For many years Native Indian children were placed, both for purposes of foster care and for purposes of adoption, with white families. In Manitoba, Native children were placed as a regular, ongoing practice out of province. By the mid-1980s, the approach to the placement of Native children had changed dramatically. Not only were they being placed with Native foster and adoptive parents more frequently, and wherever possible kept within their communities, the child welfare departments of some provinces pursued a policy of "repatriation." Thus, Native children who had settled into white homes were uprooted and relocated to Native communities.

The shifting policies of the child welfare authorities both in the United States and Canada may, in part, be attributed to growing sensitivity to the needs of Black and Native children. It is, perhaps, not overly cynical to suggest that the shifting policy is also a product of political awareness of the claims of the Black and Native population of the two countries. Whatever the motivation of the policy in question, it may or may not be in the interests of a particular child that he be subject to it. It is important that we be aware that beneath the platitude "best interests of the child," policies are at work. These policies may not *in fact* reflect the interests of this particular child. ...

Racial or Cultural Groups

... We have seen that in the United States there have been shifts in attitude with respect to the placement of Black children in white homes. One particularly violent shift was led by the National Association of Black Social Workers in 1972. This Association condemned bi-racial adoptions in such strong terms that such adoptions fell by 39 per cent in a single year.

A position paper of the National Association of Black Social Workers, dated April 1972, states:

> [W]e have taken the position that Black children should be placed only with Black families whether in foster care or for adoption. Black children belong, physically, psychologically and culturally in Black families in order that they receive the total sense of themselves and develop a sound projection of their future. Human beings are products of their environment and develop their sense of values, attitudes and self concept within their family structures. Black children in white homes are cut off from the healthy development of themselves as Black people.
>
> Our position is based on:
>
> > 1. the necessity of self-determination from birth to death, of all Black people;
> >
> > 2. the need of our young ones to begin at birth to identify with all Black people in a Black community; and
> >
> > 3. the philosophy that we need our own to build a strong nation.
>
> The socialization process for every child begins at birth. Included in the socialization process is the child's cultural heritage which is an important segment of the total process. This must begin at the earliest moment. Otherwise our children will not have the background and knowledge which is necessary to survive in a racist society. This is impossible if the child is placed with white parents in a white environment. ...
>
> We the participants of the workshop have committed ourselves to go back to our communities and work to end this particular form of genocide.

We can see that the view of this group that Black children should be placed in Black homes is based on factors some of which stem from a perception of the Black child's interest, but some of which do not. The statement that, "we need our own to build a strong nation," and the reference to placement in white homes being "a particular form of genocide," clearly relate to the interests of the Black community as a whole rather than to the interests of an individual child.

The idea that interracial placement constitutes a form of genocide has particular relevance in the context of Canada's Native people. It is trite knowledge that a people's heritage is its children. If the community does not rear its own children, then the values and culture of the community are lost. For many years a disproportionate number of Native children have been reared by non-Natives. There were the missionaries with their misguided zeal to teach Indian children the white man's ways. There were the residential schools to which Native children were sent in an attempt to "wash out" their Indianness. There were the white social workers with no understanding of Native customs and parenting practices who took Native children into care and placed them with white families. There was the appalling poverty on reserves that left Native parents few resources with which to help their children. ...

Since the mid-1970s, changes have been made. The residential schools are no more. There is greater sensitivity among social workers to cultural differences, and attempts are made to place Native children in care within their communities. The Native communities themselves are more involved with the child welfare system as it relates to Native children. By virtue of a number of agreements between the federal and provincial governments and Indian bands, bands are involved in the provision of child welfare services and take administrative responsibility with respect to Native children. The level of responsibility and control of an Indian band will depend on the type of agreement it has with the provincial and/ or federal government. ...

Are the changes that have been made since the mid-1970s sufficient to satisfy the Native community? The answer seems generally to be "No." Albeit Native people have greater control over the operation of the child welfare system as it relates to their children, the laws generally applied to them are the provincial child welfare statutes and the courts making decisions are the provincial courts. Canadian Natives point across the border to the Federal *Indian Child Welfare Act* and the tribal courts.

In the United States, the Federal *Indian Child Welfare Act*[66] provides that a tribal court has exclusive jurisdiction over "child custody proceeding" (broadly defined to include pre-adoptive and adoptive placement) if a child is domiciled or resident within the reservation of the tribe. If the child is not so domiciled or resident, a state court shall transfer any proceeding to the tribal court in the absence of good cause to the contrary and absent objection by either parent. The tribe has the right to intervene in any state court proceedings regarding the child's custody. In either court, the following rule applies: In any adoptive placement of an Indian child under State law, a preference shall be given, in the absence of good cause to the contrary, to a placement with (1) a member of the child's extended family; (2) other members of the Indian child's tribe; or (3) other Indian families.

The rationale of the Act has been said to be,

> 1. To promote the stability and security of Indian tribes. The large number of Indian children adopted by non-Indians threatened the continued existence and integrity of Indian tribes.
>
> 2. To avoid the damaging social and psychological impact on individual Indian children which is brought about by placements outside their culture.[67]

Thus, the American statute does not pretend that it caters only to the best interests of the child. It caters equally to the interests of the Native community.

NOTES AND QUESTIONS

1. The literature on interracial adoption is assessed and summarized in Bagley, *International and Transracial Adoptions* (Aldershot, Eng.: Avenbury, 1993); Triseliotis, "Intercountry Adoption: In Whose Best Interest?" in Humphrey and Humphrey, eds., *Inter-Country Adoption: Practical Experiences* (London: Tavistock, 1993) and Simon *et al.*, *The Case for Transracial Adoption* (Washington, D.C.: American University Press, 1994). Generally, these authors support the conclusion that interracial adoption poses no great risk to the mental or developmental health of the children involved.

However, there is some evidence that the adoption of aboriginal children by white families has not furthered the best interests of some adoptees. See Black "GATT for Kids: New Rules for Intercountry Adoption of Children" (1994), 11 C.F.L.Q. 253 at 290 and Adams, *Our Son, a Stranger: Adoption Breakdown and Its Effects on Parents* (Montreal and Kingston: McGill-Queen's University Press, 2002).

2. Absolute legal bars to interracial adoptions have been held unconstitutional in the United States: *Drummond v. Fulton County Dep't of Family & Children's Services* (1977), 563 F.2d 1200 (5th Cir.); cert. denied 437 U.S. 910 (1978). However, Professor Black notes in "GATT for Kids: New Rules for Intercountry Adoption of Children" (1994), 11 C.F.L.Q. 253, fn. 83, that "practical bars to such adoptions may be imposed by social workers and adoption agencies".

3. The *CFSA* indicates that the child's racial, cultural and social background may be a factor in the original placement of the child for the purpose of adoption and in determining whether an adoption order would be in the best interests of the child: ss. 61(2) and s. 136(2) of the *CFSA*.

---

[66] 25 U.S.C. 1901–1963. Discussed in *S. (S.M.) v. A. (J.P.)* (1990), 65 D.L.R. (4th) 222 (B.C.S.C.); rev'd (1992), 38 R.F.L. (3d) 113, 89 D.L.R. (4th) 204 (B.C.C.A.).

[67] See *Mississippi Board of Choctaw Indians v. Holyfield*, 104 L.Ed. 29 (S.C. 1989). See also *S. (S.M.) v. A. (J.P.)*, above, note 66.

Theodore Giesbrecht reports in "Adoption" in Bala, Zapf, Williams, Vogl, and Hornick, eds., *Canadian Child Welfare Law: Children, Families and the State*, 2d ed. (Toronto: Thompson Educational Publishing, Inc., 2004) (at 162): "While there is now a preference in child welfare agencies in Canada for intra-racial adoption, the reality in Canada is that there are relatively few non-Caucasian prospective adoptive parents and a relatively large number of visible minority and Aboriginal children who are permanent wards, and interracial adoption is not uncommon."

4. As noted earlier, the *CFSA* contains many special provisions that apply when a child is an Indian or native person as defined in s. 3(1). Regarding adoption, see particularly ss. 136(3), 141.2, 144(6), and 153.6(1).

Recall the decisions in *Algonquins of Pikwakanagan First Nation v. Children's Aid Society of Toronto* (2004), 5 R.F.L. (6th) 9 (Ont. S.C.J.) and *Re T. (R.)*, 2004 SKQB 503 (Sask. Q.B.), discussed in Chapter 10, *CHILD IN NEED OF PROTECTION*. In the first case, Justice Mesbur held that the Canadian Constitution did not preclude the placement of aboriginal children in non-aboriginal homes. In the second case, the court found that open adoptions by non-aboriginal families would be in the best interests of three aboriginal children. The court went on to find that a Saskatchewan policy that precluded this result (by granting a veto to a First Nation) violated the children's *Charter* rights.

5. In *R. (A.N.) v. W. (L.J.)*, 36 R.F.L. (2d) 1, [1983] 2 S.C.R. 173, the Supreme Court of Canada reinstated an adoption order allowing a Caucasian couple to adopt an Indian child despite the mother's refusal to consent. The court was heavily influenced by the fact that the child had developed a bond with the couple in whose home she had lived for a number of years and had not had contact with her mother for four years. Acknowledging that the child's aboriginal background was a factor to consider in determining the child's best interests, Madam Justice Wilson, in delivering judgment for the court, observed (at 14):

> Much was made in this case of the inter-racial aspect of the adoption. I believe that inter-racial adoption, like inter-racial marriage, is now an accepted phenomenon in our pluralist society. The implications of it may have been overly dramatized by the respondent in this case.

For criticisms of this case, see Carasco, "Canadian Native Children: Have Child Welfare Laws Broken the Circle?" (1986), 5 Can. J. Fam. L. 111 at 124; Bull, "The Special Case of the Native Child" (1989), 47 Advocate 523 at 526; and Monture, "A Vicious Circle: Child Welfare and First Nations" (1989), 3 C.J.W.L. 1 at 14. Professor Davies supports the result in "Native Children and the Child Welfare System in Canada" (1992), 30 Alta. Law Rev. 1200 at 1214. For a similar result, see *Sawan v. Tearoe* (1993), 48 R.F.L. (3d) 392 (B.C. C.A.).

In *C. (J.M.N.) v. Winnipeg Child & Family Services (Central)* (1997), 33 R.F.L. (4th) 175 (Man. Q.B.), Goodman J. noted (at 185) that the adoption in *R. (A.N.) v. W. (L.J.)* broke down. Despite this, Goodman J. determined that the child's best interests in this case lay in staying with his Caucasian foster parents rather than having guardianship transferred to the Awasis Agency of Northern Manitoba, a native organization.

6. In *H. (R.) v. B. (T.)* (1991), 36 R.F.L. (3d) 208 (Ont. Prov. Div.), the mother and father separated shortly after the mother became pregnant. The mother wished to have the child adopted by strangers or, if this were impossible, to retain custody herself. The father wanted the child adopted by his sister and brother-in-law. All of this was known to the adoption licensee two months before the child was born. The licensee took no steps to investigate the father's plan, but placed the child with prospective adoptive parents shortly after its birth. The extensive litigation which followed was eventually settled by a consent order placing the child with the father's relatives. The court allowed a claim for costs by the father and his relatives against the licensee. In the course of his reasons, Nevins Prov. J. reviewed the proper role of a licensee under the *CFSA*. He stated (at 217) that the Act indicated that an adoption by relatives should generally be given priority. He pointed to sections 1 and 130 [now 136]. Do you agree with this interpretation of the Act?

7. In "Adoption" in Hornick, Bala and Vogl, eds., *Canadian Child Welfare Law: Children, Families and the State* (Toronto: Thompson Educational Publishing Inc., 1991), Ms. Katarynych reported (at 153) that some child protection agencies and adoption licensees in Canada had begun to give birth parents a role in selecting among suitable applicants, without providing identifying information. She also indicated (at 152) that some agencies in the early 1990s permitted meetings between the two sets of parents once the selection had been made, provided the adoptive parents were willing and no identifying information was disclosed.

A decade or so later, Theodore Giebrecht noted in "Adoption" in Bala, Zapf, Williams, Vogl, and Hornick, eds., *Canadian Child Welfare Law: Children, Families and the State*, 2d ed. (Toronto: Thompson Educational Publishing, Inc., 2004) (at 164) that in a voluntary placement adoption:

> It is also becoming more common to share identifying information once a match is made since birth and adoptive parents often wish to develop an open adoption plan, which may provide for the regular exchange of letters, pictures, and visits. In voluntary placements, an open adoption may be available as an option for consideration by the birth and adoptive parents, if they feel comfortable with this type of arrangement.

See also (5) EFFECT OF ADOPTION later in this chapter.

(c) Removal of the Child from the Prospective Adopting Parents' Home

Decisions by a child protection agency to remove a child from the home of prospective adoptive parents can have grave consequences for all concerned, as is illustrated in the following case.

BESON v. NEWFOUNDLAND (DIRECTOR OF CHILD WELFARE)

(sub nom. *B. (D.) v. Newfoundland (Director of Child Welfare))* 30 R.F.L. (2d) 438, [1982] 2 S.C.R. 716, 1982 CarswellNfld 29, 1982 CarswellNfld 38

WILSON J.: — The issue on this appeal is not one which normally confronts us. It arises out of a rather sad saga which discloses how one small boy can be caught in a legislative and administrative net and have to come to the highest court in the land to extricate himself. The chronological history of the matter is a procedural nightmare.

The child C. was born on 21st May 1977 and immediately following his birth became a ward of the Director of Child Welfare in Newfoundland. In January 1979 the appellants, Mr. and Mrs. B., applied to adopt a child, and in July 1980 C. was placed by the director in their custody with a view to adoption. A social worker was assigned to monitor the adoption in the normal manner and his reports, made to the director on 21st August 1980 and 23rd October 1980, were very favourable. However, on 8th January 1981 Mrs. B. was advised that allegations of child abuse by her husband had come to the attention of the director. Mrs. B., naturally greatly upset at this, denied any such abuse as did also her husband. Mr. B. was asked to return the child, which he did under protest on 9th January 1981. Neither Mr. nor Mrs. B. were able to elicit from the director or his staff the source of the allegations. Nor were they given any opportunity to respond. In seven days following the removal of C. from the B. home the six-month period of residence required for an adoption would have been completed. C. was returned to the foster home in which he had resided prior to his placement with the B.'s.

Immediately after the return of C. the B.'s advised the director that they wished to appeal his decision to the Adoption Appeal Board. He told them that in his opinion there was no right of appeal in a case where a child was removed from a prospective adoptive home prior to the expiry of the six-month period. The B.'s filed an appeal nonetheless but the appeal board apparently shared the view of the director and refused to entertain the appeal. The B.'s thereupon commenced habeas corpus proceedings in the Supreme Court of Newfoundland to try to get the child back. At the hearing of this application on 28th May 1981 the allegations of abuse against Mr. B. were fully canvassed and Noel J. held that they were unfounded. However, he dismissed the habeas corpus application on the basis that the director had a discretion under the *Adoption of Children Act, 1972* (Nfld.), No. 36, as amended, and that he should not substitute his views for the views of the director. He did, however, state that: "It would be in this child's interest for the director to sit down with the [B.'s] and come to an agreement, subject to supervision, to give this boy a chance to have this fine home". The director indicated to the B.'s that he would not follow this advice and they thereupon appealed the decision of Noel J. to the Newfoundland Court of Appeal.

The Court of Appeal dismissed the appeal on the ground that the *Adoption of Children Act* is a complete code with respect to adoption and that habeas corpus does not lie. It held, moreover, that the *parens patriae* jurisdiction of the court, which had been put forward in argument by counsel for the B.'s, could be resorted to only where the legislation afforded no remedy. In the court's view the legislation in this case did afford a remedy. The director's decision was appealable to the Adoption Appeal Board and a mandamus would have lain to compel the board to hear the appeal. Although the B.'s had been treated unfairly by the director and the manner in which he made his decision was "to say the least most unfortunate", there was nothing the court could do.

The B.'s applied for leave to appeal to this court and, during the hearing of the application on 22nd June 1982, the court asked counsel for the director where and with whom C. was currently residing. It was then disclosed that, unknown to the B.'s, and indeed to the Newfoundland Court of Appeal at the time it heard the B.s' appeal on the habeas corpus application, C. had been in a new adoptive home since January 1982. This information was subsequently corrected by counsel for the director and the court advised that C. had been placed with Mr. and Mrs. J. for adoption in November 1981.

The court gave leave to appeal, granted the subsequent application of Mr. and Mrs. J. to intervene in the appeal and appointed separate counsel to represent the child C. All counsel agreed that there should be the fullest evidence before the court on the hearing of the appeal so that the matter could be brought to a finality and that it would be appropriate to have it taken on commission in Newfoundland. It was agreed also that it was in the child's best interests that the appeal be heard as soon as possible. An order to expedite was accordingly made.

[Justice Wilson reviewed the case law regarding a superior court's *parens patriae* jurisdiction to act in the best interest of a child. She concluded that a court could use its *parens patriae* jurisdiction if there were "gaps" in the legislation. She found that there was a "gap" in the legislation because there was no right of appeal from the Director's decision. Furthermore, she suggested that an application for judicial review might well have been successful on the ground that the Director had failed to act fairly. The allegations of abuse had come from a completely unreliable source and no effort had been made by the Director to substantiate them. On either basis, the trial judge could have acted in this case.]

The available relief

What recourse then is open to this court to settle the rights not only of the B.'s but also of Mr. and Mrs. J., the intervenors, who through no fault of their own are now caught up in what must be a most traumatic and painful experience? Mr. and Mrs. J. had apparently no knowledge of the claim of the B.'s to the child who had been so enthusiastically welcomed into their family until the bombshell was dropped on them by the registrar of this court.

We have now had the benefit of very complete evidence taken on commission in Newfoundland before Goodridge J. This includes the evidence of a pediatrician, two psychologists, a child psychiatrist, two social workers, the Director of Child Welfare and Mr. and Mrs. B. We have also had the benefit of thorough argument from counsel for the appellants and for the intervenors, from counsel for the director and from Mr. Day, counsel appointed by the court to represent C. Having been advised by Dr. Boddie, the child psychiatrist retained by him that C. was neither capable of instructing counsel nor "of expressing his wishes as to his future custodians", Mr. Day assessed his role as being to advance his client's best interests as he saw them to the court. In order to satisfy himself as to where C.'s best interests lay, Mr. Day conducted a very thorough investigation of C.'s social, medical and legal antecedents and of his present circumstances. In the course of this investigation he reviewed the director's files on C. and interviewed all the people who had had C. under care including the appellants and the intervenors, former foster parents, child welfare workers, health care persons and his teacher. He also spent time with C. at his present residence.

Mr. Day's submissions to the court, based on his investigations and the assistance he received from the professionals he retained on C.'s behalf, are that C.'s best interests were being served when he was a member of the appellants' family and would likely have continued to be served by his being left there. However, given that he was removed from their care by the director, the court must decide whether his best interests would now be served by leaving him where he is, i.e., with the intervenors, or by returning him to the appellants. This in turn would depend, counsel submitted, on whether the quality of care he would receive from the appellants would outweigh any prejudice to him arising from yet another move.

As to the quality of care available to C. in the appellants' home, Mr. Day stated that "the quality of care which can be afforded by the appellants is superior to a significant degree to that which can be afforded by the intervenors". He hastened to point out that this was not to say that C. was not currently being materially and emotionally well cared for to the best of their ability by the intervenors. He simply needs a great deal of care and attention and requires, according to counsel, "the time, patience, vigilance and sensitivity of supportive and stimulating custodians". The appellants are more able to spend time with C. and have been and continue to be motivated to do so. They clearly love him very much as witness their pursuit of this matter through all the various levels of the court. They want him back as their son despite the fact that they now have a baby girl of their own.

Mrs. B. is at home all day and Mr. B. is a businessman with considerable latitude in his working hours. Their elder son, L., is devoted to C. Mrs. J., on the other hand, has a job and both she and her husband function on fairly stringent work schedules. C. has to be looked after by a neighbour until they return from work. They are simply not able to give the child the time and attention he needs. They have two children, a boy of 9 and a girl of 7. In the context of the longer term interests of C. the appellants are more able to handle financial family contingencies and to save for their children's post-secondary education and training, which is a high priority with them. While financial security is not by any means a determining factor, it is a relevant one. It is not surprising, counsel submitted, that on the basis of the evidence Noel J. was concerned that C. have the opportunity of this fine home.

Nevertheless, Mr. Day submitted, the court must be concerned about the effect of another move on a boy who has lived up to this time what he described as "a nomadic existence". The advice he had received from the child psychiatrist was encouraging in this respect. The child was extremely resilient (doubtless as a result of his background to date) and Dr. Boddie was of the opinion that he would adjust to the return of his former home since "proper care and love can prevent permanent impairment due to separation". The pediatrician and psychologists who assessed C. were less sanguine on this count.

Having reviewed all of the evidence and considered the submissions of counsel, and being particularly impressed by the totally impartial and objective submissions of C.'s counsel, I am of the view that it is in C.'s best interests that he now be returned to the appellants. In so saying I am certainly not unmindful of the upset this will unquestionably involve for the child and that the courts have cautioned against the disturbance of the status quo. I am also aware that it will cause anguish for the intervenors. Indeed, hurt all round is the tragic feature of this sorry situation.

What kind of relief then is it open to this court to grant? As I understand it, the exercise of the court's *parens patriae* jurisdiction has traditionally resulted in an order for custody, the jurisdiction being of ancient origin and pre-dating the concept of adoption. It would, however, in my view serve C. ill if the court made an order for custody in favour of the appellants. Counsel for the director advised that if this were done it would amount in his view to a new placement and, since Mr. and Mrs. J. have already had C. in excess of the six-month period, a certificate could be issued by the director in their favour at any time. It is quite clear that further litigation would ensue if this court made an order for custody only, and this could hardly be in C.'s best interests. Moreover, an order for custody only would deprive C. of the status of being the appellants' "child" in the fullest sense of the term. If ever a child needed the security of that status, this one does. Accordingly, having found that the Newfoundland Court of Appeal was in error in considering itself powerless to safeguard the interests of this child, I would allow the appeal and make the order which that court ought to have made, namely, an order under s. 12 of the *Adoption of Children Act*, for the adoption of C. by the appellants.

NOTES AND QUESTIONS

1. The Supreme Court decision in *B. (D.)* is remarkable for a number of reasons. It is highly unusual for the Supreme Court of Canada to receive new evidence taken on commission. The child's lawyer seems also to have presented much evidence to the court, almost as if he were an expert witness. Finally, the court appeared to grant relief, the adoption order, that was not requested by the appellants. For commentary on the case, see Day, "Counsel for Christopher: Representing an Infant's Best Interests in the Supreme Court of Canada" (1982), 33 R.F.L. (2d) 16 and Bissett-Johnson, "Case Comment" (1983), 35 R.F.L. (2d) 27.

2. What remedies are available under the *CFSA* where a society or licensee removes a child from the home of the prospective adopting parents? See ss. 144 and 145.

3. Who has legal custody of a child after it is placed in the home of the prospective adopting parents but before an adoption occurs: (a) where the child is a Crown ward? (b) where the placement is made by a licensee?, and (c) where the child is placed in the home of a relative by a natural parent? See ss. 63(1) and 137(5) of the *CFSA*.

(4) Consents to Adoption

(a) Consent of the Adoptee

The number of consents required before an adoption order can be made varies considerably depending on the circumstances and the type of adoption involved (see s. 137 of the *CFSA*). Under s. 137(6) an order for the adoption of a person who is seven years of age or more is not to be made without the person's consent. Before such consent is given the person is to be accorded "an opportunity to obtain counselling and independent legal advice with respect to the consent": s. 137(7). Someone appointed by the Office of the Children's Lawyer usually witnesses the child's consent to ensure that it is informed and voluntary. Section 137(8) stipulates that the consent can be withdrawn within a 21-day period.

Section 69(6) of Ontario's repealed *Child Welfare Act* also required the consent of a child seven years or older, but it authorized the court to dispense with this requirement if this was in the best interests of the child. A similar provision was considered in *Re R.*, 7 R.F.L. (2d) 344, [1979] 1 W.W.R. 496 (B.C. S.C.) where the court dispensed with the consent of a 16-year-old boy in a step-parent adoption. The boy was not aware of his true parentage and it was felt that disclosure at that particular time would be upsetting to the entire family. In *Re A.* (1980), 3 F.L.R.R. 47 (Ont. Prov. Ct.), Nasmith Prov. J. used s. 69(6) to dispense with the need for the consent of a 13-year-old boy. He expressed "serious reservations about this entire exercise" but decided that the judicial discretion should be exercised where the mother and step-father believed the boy would be devastated if he learned that the step-father was not his biological father. See also *Re H. (V.)* (1984), 47 O.R. (2d) 272 (Fam. Ct.) where the court dispensed with the requirement of consent of a seven-year-old girl because of concern over the confusion that would be caused by seeking her consent to an adoption that merely formalized an existing arrangement.

Note that under s. 137(9) of the *CFSA* the court may now only dispense with the requirement that a child of seven or over consent where it is satisfied that obtaining the consent would cause the child emotional harm or the child is not able to consent because of a developmental disability. Would the results reached in the cases outlined above have been different under s. 137(9)?

Section 152(2) of the *CFSA* requires the court to be satisfied that any consent given by a child was given with the understanding of the nature and effect of an adoption order. Note also s. 152(3) and (4).

(b) Parental Consent

(i) Who is a "Parent"?

In all Canadian jurisdictions there are legislative provisions generally requiring the consent of parents to the adoption of their minor children (see s. 137 of the *CFSA*). A consent is not required if a child is already a Crown ward: s. 137(2). There is also legislative provision for dispensing with the consent of a parent to an adoption (see s. 138). This possibility is the subject of a later section of this chapter.

The British Columbia Supreme Court held in *M. (N.) v. British Columbia (Superintendent of Family & Child Services)* (1986), [1987] 3 W.W.R. 176, 10 B.C.L.R. (2d) 234, that s. 8(1)(b) of British Columbia's *Adoption Act* was unconstitutional because it unjustifiably discriminated on the basis of sex and marital status. The legislation provided that parental consent was generally required before the court could make an adoption order, but that where the child had been born out of wedlock only the mother needed to consent. The court was not persuaded by the argument that the legislation was justified because it permitted timely adoption of unwanted children where the natural father was unknown or could not be found. The court noted that in some cases it might be as difficult to locate a natural father or natural mother whose marriage had been terminated by divorce and that the Act already provided mechanisms for dealing with situations where the biological father could not be located.

Ontario's definition of "parent" in s. 137(1) of the *CFSA* is clearly broader than the one considered in the British Columbia case. However, not all biological fathers qualify. In the following case, the court dismissed a *Charter* challenge to the Ontario definition.

S. (C.E.) v. CAS OF METROPOLITAN TORONTO

(1988), 49 D.L.R. (4th) 469, 1988 CarswellOnt 218 (Ont. Div. Ct.)

BY THE COURT: — Adoption is a very important matter. It is clear that in establishing the legal framework for it the legislature has given careful study to the complex issues involved in it. It has obviously considered that the best interests of the child are the paramount concern and that all so-called rights of the biological parents are subsidiary to what is best for the child. Debate could go on forever as to whether or not the legislative scheme that is embodied in the law of Ontario is the best one that can be devised by human beings. But the legislature considered all of the competing positions and decided the issue as it saw it in the best interests of the child. The legislation before the court has been carefully thought out after experiments with other legislative schemes had been tried and found by the legislature not to be in the child's best interests.

When a legislature has weighed a complex social issue and has determined what to it is the best solution, the courts should be cautious indeed before using provisions of the Charter to frustrate the solution.

... [O]ur reading of the sections as a whole lead us to the view that the only natural father who is not by definition a "parent" whose consent is required by s. 131(1) [now s. 137(1)] of the Act, is a male person who by an act of casual sexual intercourse impregnates a woman and demonstrates no sense of responsibility for the natural consequences of the act of sexual intercourse. It is a man who shows no sense of responsibility to the woman he has made pregnant nor to the life that he has helped to procreate. ...

We think it is an erroneous oversimplification to say that the mother and a father who does not fall within the statutory definition of parent are similarly situated. The mother because of physical necessity has shown responsibility to the child. She carried and gave birth to it. The casual fornicator who has not demonstrated any interest in whether he did cause a pregnancy or demonstrate even the minimum responsibility to the child required by s. 131 cannot be said to be similarly situated to the mother. The statute recognizes as a parent, a father who demonstrates the minimum interest in the consequences of his sexual activity. Most fathers are defined as parents. Only those who do not demonstrate some responsibility to the child are not. It is thus apparent to us that the different statutory treatment of the two persons is based upon their respective demonstrated responsibility to the child, not upon their different sexes.

We do not think that a statutory difference in treatment between a natural parent who is responsible to her child and one who has not shown even minimal interest in whether a child exists because of his sexual activity can be said to be irrational, insidious or unfair.

We are thus of the opinion that the provisions of s. 131 of the Act does [*sic*] not violate s. 15 of the Charter.

Even if it could be said in some way which we are unable to accept that there is a violation of s. 15 we are satisfied that the provisions of s. 131 of the Act are saved by s. 1 of the Charter. ...

It is our opinion that the obvious objective of this legislation is to ensure that children whose parents are unwilling or unable to care for them receive early placement in a permanent home where they will have the opportunity to be reared as members of a family. There was ample evidence before the legislature, and there is ample evidence before this court, that such placement should be made as early in the child's life as possible, and that there should be a maximum feeling of certainty on the part of the adoptive parents and the child that the placement is permanent.

The evidence in this case is overwhelming that delay in placement or in finalizing the adoption incur[s] serious risks of long-term behavioural, emotional or psychological harm for the child. Delay in finalization of an adoption can cause intolerable strains on the prospective adoptive parents. The legislature has on reasonable grounds concluded that it is in the best interests of the child and the families by whom he or she is to be adopted that the process be as quick and certain as is reasonably possible.

The objective of providing for the well-being of children such as A.H. can surely be categorized as one of the highest priorities of government in a civilized society. The legislative measure by which the consent of the irresponsible casual fornicator is dispensed with is obviously fair and cannot be said to be arbitrary.

This particular legislative scheme can also be looked at in the light of a previous one that the legislature found to be unsatisfactory. For sometime before the enactment of this Act there was a legislative scheme in place in which all natural fathers were within a definition of "parent". Those professionals who were involved in the adoption process found, and the legislature was convinced, that the delays which were often encountered in determining who the father was and then getting his consent, or having it dispensed with, led to serious frustration of the legislative object of expeditious adoptions to the prejudice of the best interests of children and adoptive families.

This legislation does not impair in the least the right of natural fathers who have demonstrated their responsibility to the child they have fathered to participate in the adoption process. If there is little realistic possibility that the right of the casual fornicator would be accepted and exercised by him, a court should be cautious indeed before letting the protection of that right obstruct the fulfillment of an important governmental objective. We are of the opinion that the remote chance that a casual fornicator might wish to acknowledge and assume responsibility for the child he casually fathered bears no realistic proportion at all to the important government objective of providing for an expeditious and final adoption.

While it is not conclusive to the validity of the impugned legislation, it is worth noting what has been very properly said in para. 60 of the factum filed on behalf of the Attorney-General. That paragraph reads as follows:

> Provincial Legislatures throughout Canada have recognized the priority of the best interests of the child in establishing adoption procedures. In accordance with this priority, almost no provincial legislation gives status in adoption proceedings to those natural fathers who have not acknowledged parentage nor taken any steps beyond the time of conception to indicate their interest in the child.

We think it significant that the legislation enacted by the Legislature of Ontario in respect of adoptions is in substantial conformity with the legislative views taken in most of the other provinces.

NOTES AND QUESTIONS

1. Regarding the *S. (C.E.)* case, Professor Thompson commented in "A Family Law Hitchhiker's Guide to the Charter Galaxy" (1988), 3 C.F.L.Q. 315 at 343-344: "Much as the Divisional Court may have been correct in their result, that does not excuse a judgment that reads like a guest editorial in the Toronto Sun, typified by the Court's labelling of the excluded fathers as 'casual fornicators'."

2. In *C. (D.G.) v. Y. (R.H.G.)* (2003), 41 R.F.L. (5th) 245 (Ont. C.J.), Justice Wolder revisited the failure to notify a biological father of adoption proceedings. The father's identity was known, but he did not fit within the statutory definition of parent in s. 137 of the *CFSA*. The Justice concluded (at para. 12) that "the failure to notify the biological father of this proceeding and the failure to give him an opportunity to respond to the motion to dispense with his consent, on the basis that he is statutorily excluded ... violates his rights under subsection 15(1) of the Charter ... [and] is not saved by s. 1." In so doing, Justice Wolder relied on the Supreme Court of Canada's decision in *Trociuk v. British Columbia (Attorney General)* (2003), 226 D.L.R. (4th) 1, where the court determined that a portion of the British Columbia *Vital Statistics Act* was unconstitutional. That statute allowed a mother to designate a father as "unacknowledged" on a child's birth certificate whenever she wished. In that situation, the mother had sole authority to choose the child's surname. The Supreme Court of Canada found that this differential treatment of fathers and mothers discriminated on the basis of sex because it sent the message that a father's relationship with his children was less worthy than that between a mother and her children. The court went on to hold that the differential treatment could not be justified under s. 1 of the *Charter*. While accepting that there might be situations where a mother should not be forced to disclose the identity of a child's father, it concluded that the British Columbia legislation did not impair the rights of fathers as little as reasonably possible. It declared portions of the legislation invalid, but suspended the declaration for 12 months to permit the legislature to remedy the constitutional defect without compromising the interests of mothers.

However, Justice Wolder, after hearing further submissions in *C. (D.) v. A. (W.)* (2003), 48 R.F.L. (5th) 21 (Ont. C.J.), "corrected" the earlier ruling that the failure to notify a known biological father of pending adoption proceedings violated his equality rights. The Justice was especially influenced by s. 137(1)(f) of the *CFSA*. This provision allowed a biological father to bring himself within the definition of parent by filing a statutory declaration with the Registrar General affirming that he was the father of the child under s. 12 of the *Children's Law Reform Act*, R.S.O. 1990, c. C.12.

See also *Re T. (D.)* (1992), (sub nom. *T. (D.) v. Children's Aid Society & Family Services of Colchester County)* 92 D.L.R. (4th) 289 (N.S. C.A.) where the court found (at 293) "no merit" in a father's argument that his exclusion from the definition of parent violated s. 15 of the *Charter*.

Theodore Giesbrecht notes in "Adoption" in Bala, Zapf, Williams, Vogl, and Hornick, eds., *Canadian Child Welfare Law: Children, Families and the State*, 2d ed. (Toronto: Thompson Educational Publishing, Inc., 2004) (at 178) that Ontario has one of the broader definitions of "parent" for the purposes of adoption.

(ii) Granting Consent and Revoking Consent

Certain provisions in the *CFSA* attempt to ensure that the parent's consent has been given knowingly and voluntarily (see ss. 137(4), 137(11), 137(12) and 152(2)). As s. 175 makes clear, the consent may not be given in return for money or other consideration. The following case deals with the nature of the required parental consent and the possibility of revoking that consent.

SAWAN v. TEAROE

(1993), 48 R.F.L. (3d) 392, 1993 CarswellBC 280 (B.C. C.A.); leave to appeal refused (1994), 3 R.F.L. (4th) 196 (note) (S.C.C.)

PROUDFOOT J.A.: — This is an appeal from a judgment pronounced June 19th, 1993, dismissing the petition of James and Faye Tearoe for the adoption of a child, then eighteen months old, and ordering the child returned to the respondent mother, Cecilia Sawan. ...

The appellants contend that the learned trial judge erred in concluding that it was in the best interest of the child to revoke the respondent's consent to adoption, when the evidence established that the child had become strongly bonded to them.

Background to Proceedings

The facts, which are substantially not in dispute, are these: the child, the centre of the dispute, was born to Cecilia Sawan on December 3rd, 1991, in the province of Alberta. The mother was 18 years of age and unmarried. The father of the child was not involved in these proceedings. After the birth, the child remained in the hospital until December 13th, 1991, and then was released into the care of the mother. The child remained with the mother until January 6th, 1992. At that time, the mother approached the Alberta Family and Social Services and signed a one-month custody agreement with the department. The department placed the child in a foster home.

The child remained in the care of the foster home until January 30, 1992. During that period, the evidence is that the mother visited the child from two to four times. Near the end of this period, about January 28th to 30th, 1992, the respondent, Cecilia Sawan, first contacted the appellants, James and Faye Tearoe, concerning their adoption of the child.

It is not clear what happened next but the child was moved from the foster home and returned to his mother on February 1st, 1992. The child was again placed in the foster home on February 4th. On February 4th, 1992, Ms Sawan contacted the Tearoes again and asked them to come to Alberta and pick up the child. The Tearoes live in Victoria, British Columbia.

On February 6th, 1992, the Tearoes arrived in Fairview, Alberta, and took the child into their care. On the same day, the mother signed two forms: (i) a "Consent by Guardian to Adoption"; and (ii) a "Notice by Relinquishing Parent of Direct Adoption Placement" pursuant to the requirements of the *Child Welfare Act*, S.A. 1984, c. C-8.1, of Alberta.

On February 12, 1992, the respondent called the Ministry of Family and Social Services in Peace River, Alberta, and asked for her child to be returned, that is, she verbally revoked her consent. The evidence is that the respondent was told that her revocation had to be in writing.

On February 13th, 1992, the mother called the department again. She was reminded abut the necessity of written notice of revocation being sent to the department within ten days of the consent she had given on February 6th, 1992. On this date an official of the department advised the Tearoes by telephone that the mother was attempting to revoke her consent to adoption. They were told not to return the child as a written revocation had not yet been received.

On February 14th, the mother called the Tearoes and asked that the child be returned to her. Relying on the advice they had received from the Ministry of Family and Social Services in Alberta, their response was non-committal.

On February 19th, 1992, Ms Sawan made another call to the department to ascertain if the letter of revocation, which she stated she had sent, had been received. Although other correspondence had been received by the department from Ms Sawan, the letter in question did not arrive. It appears from the evidence that no written notice was ever received by the department.

Next, on February 24th, 1992, the department wrote to the respondent to clarify the situation. The letter concluded by asking the respondent, "do you wish to proceed with the placement or will you be seeking legal advice?" There was no response to the department's letter of February 24th, but on April 22nd, 1992, the respondent was again in touch with the department asking for the return of her child. At that time she stated she had not received the department's letter of February 24th, and a copy was mailed to her.

On May 21st, 1992, she wrote to the Tearoes asking them to return the child to her care. A copy of this letter was not forwarded to the department.

On May 29th, 1992, the Tearoes, wishing to complete the adoption, had their solicitor forward to Ms Sawan documents to be executed by her to complete the adoption. These were never completed and returned to the solicitor.

No further action appears to have been taken by the mother until October 1992, when she sought assistance to obtain legal advice through the education co-ordinator at the Woodland Cree Indian Band.

On December 8th, 1992, a solicitor in High Prairie, Alberta, wrote to the Tearoes' solicitor advising him that the mother had revoked her consent to the adoption of her child.

A petition for adoption was filed by the Tearoes on December 22nd, 1992. On April 23rd, Ms Sawan filed a petition in which she sought habeas corpus directing the return of her child. Alternatively, she sought sole custody or a declaration that her consent had been revoked.

An expedited trial date was obtained and the proceedings came on for hearing on June 14th, 1993. Judgment was given orally on June 19th, 1993.

The Parties to the Proceedings

The appellants, James and Faye Tearoe, are 49 and 47 years of age respectively. They are married and have one adopted child, Heidi, approximately 8 years of age. She has been with the appellants since birth. James Tearoe is employed as a forester with the Ministry of Forests for British Columbia. Mrs. Tearoe is a homemaker. She cares for Heidi and, at times, provides day care for another child.

The trial judge stated the following when commenting on the Tearoes [at pp. 19-20 unreported]:

> Mr. and Mrs. Tearoe are competent, caring, loving proposed adoptive parents. I have been impressed by them. They have testified to a very caring and close relationship where a bonding having been developed with between [sic] them, or between the four members of their family and I say four because Mr. Tearoe and Mrs. Tearoe, their daughter, Heidi, an adopted daughter, and of course the child in question. I have no doubt as [to] their suitability as adopting parents and I note the report of

the Superintendent of British Columbia, that is the Superintendent of Family and Child Services, to the same effect.

. . . . .

Cecilia Sawan, now 20 years of age, is unmarried and is attending school. There is evidence that she has had some problems in her life, including alcohol abuse. There is also evidence that she has sought help for this problem.

Ms Sawan's mother is native; her father, non-native. Ms Sawan stated that she wishes to raise her son in her native culture. Recently, she has gained status as a member of the Woodland Cree Indian Band. She has not lived on the reserve for approximately six years. There is evidence that she has an extended family living on the reserve and off the reserve. There is little, if any, evidence of any contact by her with members of her family. Ms Sawan testified that she planned to return to the band but was uncertain as to when. The Woodland Band members speak Cree. She concedes she would have difficulties living on the reserve because she does not know the language. However, her evidence is that there are facilities to assist her in learning Cree.

Ms Sawan's future plans are not settled. She wants to complete her education. At present, she is financially supported by social assistance and the band. Ms Sawan testified that she has a fiancé, who is not a native Indian, and that they plan to marry in July 1994. Ms Sawan anticipates that her fiancé, who works in the oil fields in Northern Alberta, will live on the reserve with her and her child. Ms Sawan's fiancé was not called as a witness.

The trial judge said the following with respect to Ms Sawan: ...

Insofar as Miss Sawan is concerned, her background, naivety, her lack of sophistication, despite all of those, I am impressed with her evidence and impressed with her attitude toward her child.

The Child

At the time of the trial the child was eighteen months old. It can be readily concluded from all the evidence presented that he is a healthy, happy, well-cared for child. He is one quarter native Indian. As just noted, his mother has placed his name on the list to become a member of the Woodland Cree Native Indian Band.

From the time of the child's birth to February 6th, 1992, the child had been in his mother's care, in total, for twenty-two days. The child has been with the appellants continuously since February 6th, 1992.

[The trial judge found that the mother's consent was signed freely and voluntarily, and that Ms Sawan understood all of the ramifications of the consent, both legally and emotionally. He also found that the mother was aware that a revocation of consent had to be made in writing and within ten days. The judge concluded that, nevertheless, he could allow the mother to revoke her consent on the basis of s. 8(7) of the *Adoption Act*, R.S.B.C. 1979, c. 4. That section stated: "No person who has given his consent to adoption, other than the child to be adopted, may revoke his consent unless it is shown to the court's satisfaction that the revocation is in the best interests of the child."]

Discussion

This test of the best interest of the child is most clearly enunciated in the often-cited passage from the case of *King v. Low*, [1985] 1 S.C.R. 87, 44 R.F.L. (2d) 113 ... Mr. Justice McIntyre ... said ... (at p. 126 [R.F.L.]):

The matter will not be determined solely on the basis of the physical comfort and material advantages that may be available in the home of one contender or the other. The welfare of the child must be decided on a consideration of these and all other relevant factors, including the general psychological, spiritual and emotional welfare of the child. *It must be the aim of the court, when resolving disputes between rival claimants for the custody of a child, to choose the course which will best provide for the healthy growth, development and education of the child so that he will be equipped to face the problems of life as a mature adult. Parental claims must not be lightly set aside, and they are entitled to serious consideration in reaching any conclusion. Where it is clear that the welfare of the child requires it, however, they must be set aside.* (my emphasis)

Earlier, Madam Justice Wilson, in *R. (A.N.) v. W. (L.J.)*, [1983] 2 S.C.R. 173, discussed the best interest test when dealing with an adoption which involved interracial considerations. After commenting that the child should not become "a battleground" she stated (at pp. 187-188):

In my view, when the test to be met is the best interests of the child, the significance of cultural background and heritage as opposed to bonding abates over time. The closer the bond that develops with the prospective adoptive parents the less important the racial element becomes.

When dealing with the best interests, the trial judge discussed a number of factors, the most critical of which were his comments in the following passages [at pp. 27–29 unreported]:

Bonding; that is the bonding that Mr. and Mrs. Tearoe have described and others have described in their relationship with the child. Compared of course to the mother's short interval with the child, nevertheless this is not a child that was taken from the delivery room and delivered to the Tearoes. She had the child in her care and custody for a considerable period of time. That issue of bonding also must take into consideration the time interval between February 6 and today. ...

In my opinion, the connection between the mother and the child has not been irretrievably broken as in [*R. (A.N.) v. W. (L.J.)*]. ... She has sought, albeit ineffectively, to seek the return of her child and she did within a relatively short period of time after she executed the consent.

This child was with his mother, in total, for twenty-two days. The child had been with the Tearoes for over 16 months when this matter went to trial. On the evidence, the trial judge's conclusion that the child was with his mother for a "considerable period of time" is plainly in error.

The trial judge's conclusion that "the connection between the mother and the child has not been irretrievably broken" is not supported by the evidence. There is no evidence from which to conclude either that a bond between the mother and the child had ever been established in the period during which the child was with her, or that if any such bond had been established it was likely still remaining at the time of trial. Indeed, the evidence establishes beyond doubt that the only mother and father this child knows are Faye and James Tearoe.

The welfare of the child is the paramount concern. This child presently lives in a loving, stable, comfortable environment, with a family that has looked after all his needs for virtually all his life. By all accounts the child is thriving. To end that relationship would destroy the family bonds that have been established between the child and the adoptive parents.

Although she offered no specific plans for the future, it is quite possible that Ms Sawan could also provide a loving environment in which the child could thrive if he were returned to her. But in the absence of any evidence from which it could reasonably be inferred that there ever was or now remains any bond between natural mother and child, or that such a bond could now successfully be established, it is impossible to conclude that the best interests of the child require the consent to adoption to be set aside.

Furthermore, common sense dictates that to disrupt the child from his present environment, and to put him through the uncertainty associated with an attempt to establish a bond with his natural mother, would cause him considerable trauma. In the absence of evidence from which it could reasonably be inferred that such trauma would be both minimal and fleeting in nature, it is impossible to conclude that the best interests of the child would now be met by setting aside the consent to adoption.

The trial judge stated the Tearoes are "competent, caring, loving, proposed adoptive parents" and that a close relationship had developed. To return this child, as requested by the respondent, is to place him in an uncertain future that would take away from him the continuity and stability which he now has. As in the *R. (A.N.)* case, the cultural background and heritage must give way in the circumstances of this case. A difficult choice must be made. The child's best interests must come first. The respondent has not discharged the onus which s. 8(7) places on her. It is not in the best interests of this child to revoke Ms Sawan's consent to adoption.

The child will remain with James and Faye Tearoe. The appeal is allowed and the orders of the trial judge set aside. The petition for adoption will be granted. The child will assume the name David James Tearoe.

NOTES AND QUESTIONS

1. For cases in which it was alleged that the parental consent was invalid, see *McKeever v. Children's Aid Society of Metropolitan Toronto* (1975), 22 R.F.L. 346 (Ont. Co. Ct.); *Re J.* (1979), 9 R.F.L. (2d) 281 (Ont. H.C.); *R. (A.M.) v. Children's Aid Society of Winnipeg* (1983), 35 R.F.L. (2d) 113 (Man. C.A.); *T. (N.P.) v. Superintendent of Family & Child Service* (1987), 8 R.F.L. (3d) 405 (B.C. S.C.); and *B. (S.L.) v. C. (J.M.)* (1987), 10 R.F.L. (3d) 96 (Alta. Q.B.).

2. There is a possibility that prospective adoptive parents can retain custody of the child even if the natural parent establishes that his or her consent to the adoption of the child was not valid. In *B. (S.L.) v. C. (J.M.)* (1987), 10 R.F.L. (3d) 96 (Alta. Q.B.), the mother decided to place the child for private adoption with C. (J.M.) and C. (B.S.). She signed a consent to adoption in their favour and they were granted guardianship by court order in November 1985. The Cs separated in 1986 before the adoption process was complete and they agreed that C. (J.M.) should have custody of the child. After a divorce in 1987, C. (J.M.) married C. (P.J.). The biological mother applied for custody. The court concluded that the mother's consent to the adoption had no legal effect since it was conditional upon the child being adopted by the persons described in the consent, C. (J.M.) and C. (B.S.). Nevertheless, it also found that the child's best interests dictated that he remain with C. (J.M.), whom he regarded as his father. Although the court was not asked to make an adoption order, it indicated that it would have been prepared to dispense with the mother's consent to the adoption of the child by C. (J.M.) and C. (P.J.)

3. Section 137(8) of the *CFSA* gives a parent 21 days to revoke a consent to adoption. It appears that the revocation can occur even if the child has been placed for adoption. Note that the section specifies that where the person who revokes the consent had custody of the child immediately before the consent, the child shall be returned to him or her as soon as the consent is withdrawn.

A court may permit a parent to revoke the consent after the 21-day period if it is in the child's best interest: s. 139(1). Note that in contrast to the British Columbia legislation that applied in *Tearoe*, s. 139(1) does not apply where the child has been placed with a person for adoption and remains in that person's care: s. 139(2). However, a birth parent can still seek to convince the court that an adoption order under s. 146(1) of the *CFSA* is not in the child's best interests. In *C. (B.L.) v. W. (B.J.)* (1997), 29 R.F.L. (4th) 175 (Alta. Q.B.), the mother of the child consented to the adoption of the child by the petitioners. The petitioners were subsequently charged with a property-related criminal offence. As a result, the mother changed her mind and appeared in court to oppose the petition for adoption. The court nonetheless granted the adoption order. It held that the presumption of innocence forbade the consideration of the criminal charge.

4. At one time, it was often possible for natural parents to regain custody of their children prior to an adoption order even if they had been placed for adoption. See, for example, *Martin v. Duffell*, [1950] S.C.R. 737 and *Re Mugford*, [1970] 1 O.R. 601 (C.A.); affirmed (sub nom. *Children's Aid Society of Ottawa v. Mugford*) [1970] S.C.R. 261, [1970] 1 O.R. 610n. This situation has now changed. In part, this is due to legislative provisions such as ss. 137(8) and 139(2) of the *CFSA*. However, as *Sawan v. Tearoe* and the cases discussed in it illustrate, the courts have also moved away from parental rights towards the best interests of the child test. More significantly, in applying this rather open-ended test, the courts in these cases have downplayed the importance of the blood tie and have been heavily influenced by the "psychological parent theory". This theory stresses the child's need for continuity and stability. It postulates that there is a risk of harm if a bond between a psychological parent and the child is broken. For analysis of the "psychological parent theory", an explanation of its influence, and a review of the literature criticizing it, see Davies, "Racial and Cultural Issues in Custody Matters" (1993), 10 C.F.L.Q. 1.

For commentary on *Sawan v. Tearoe*, see Mosikatsana, "Case Comment: *Sawan v. Tearoe*" (1994), 11 C.F.L.Q. 89 and Westad, *The God-Sent Child: The Bitter Adoption of Baby David* (Toronto: Penguin Books, 1994).

6. In *Re British Columbia Birth Registration No. 99-00733* (2000), 182 D.L.R. (4th) 280 (B.C. C.A.), an unmarried mother consented, within a few weeks of her daughter's birth, to the girl's adoption by a couple whom she helped to select. The couple agreed to facilitate continuing contact between the mother and child. When the father learned of the placement of the child about four months later, he sought custody. The father planned to have the child live with him, his parents and his brother. The couple with whom the girl was living responded with a petition for adoption, asking that the court dispense with the father's consent. The girl's birth mother then indicated that she had changed her mind and supported the father's position. She asked the court to grant her joint custody or, at least, access.

The girl was thriving in the prospective adoptive couple's care. A clinical psychologist's report stated that the couple offered an ideal parenting, social and economic environment. It also concluded that the biological father had significant support from his family, was thoughtful in his concerns about the girl, and had a family background espousing positive child-rearing attitudes and values. However, it noted that the father had fewer economic and social resources and that, partly because of his relative youth, his future was less certain than the couple's. The psychologist testified at trial that the child had bonded to the adoptive couple. He indicated that there was limited empirical evidence relating to a change of primary caregivers for a child of this age, but suggested that there were unlikely to be long-term negative effects. The trial judge awarded custody to the father, but the British Columbia Court of Appeal overturned the decision, dispensed with the father's consent, and granted an adoption order.

7. Where someone's consent is required for an adoption, that person is generally entitled to notice of the proposed adoption. See s. 138 of the *CFSA*. However, note s. 151(4).

In some provinces the courts have ruled that the absence of a specific statutory provision similar to s. 151(4) of the *CFSA*, directing that notice need not be given, means that it must be given to parents who previously consented to the adoption or whose consent is not required because the child is a permanent ward of a child protection agency. The cases are reviewed in *Re H.* (1992), 40 R.F.L. (3d) 13 (Alta. C.A.) where the court concluded that such notice should be provided only where a biological parent maintains a relationship or contact with the child after the wardship order. See also *B. (B.) v. New Brunswick (Minister of Health and Community Services)* (1995), 13 R.F.L. (4th) 350 (N.B. C.A.).

8. In *M. (R.) v. M. (S.)* (1994), 20 O.R. (3d) 621 (C.A.), the grandparents of a child who had been placed for adoption by a licensed agency with the consent of his mother and father applied for custody under the *Children's Law Reform Act*. The court held that Part VII of the *CFSA* provided a comprehensive code for adoptions and that the adoption process had to be allowed to proceed to its conclusion. Accordingly, the grandparents could not apply for custody. This case was applied in *Family, Youth and Child Services of Muskoka v. R. (L.)* (1998), 37 R.F.L. (4th) 167 (Ont. Gen. Div.), where the parents of the child initially consented to the adoption, but the mother later supported her parents' attempt to derail the process after the society placed the child for adoption. The grandparents brought an action to set aside the consents and for custody of the child. The court concluded that it could not grant interim access to either the mother or the grandparents. It ruled that it could deal with a custody or access claim only if the placement were invalid because of a defect in the required consents.

The case of *M. (R.) v. M. (S.)* was distinguished in *L. (C.) v. F. (A.)* (1998), 43 R.F.L. (4th) 332 (Ont. Gen. Div.), where a mother and father, without the assistance of a society or a licensee, placed their child in the home of close friends one day after its birth. Within days, they met with a lawyer and signed adoption consents. The child's maternal grandmother commenced an application for custody. The prospective adoptive parents responded by asking the court to dismiss her application on the basis that the child had been placed for adoption. The court held that the grandmother's application should go forward as, in contrast to the situation in *M. (R.) v. M. (S.)*, there had been no placement in accordance with the provisions of the *CFSA*.

9. Does a biological parent have any remedy if he or she discovers, after the child has been adopted, that the consent to the adoption was not valid? Does a biological parent have any remedy if he or she was unaware of the adoption proceeding because the required notice was not given? Examine ss. 156 and 157 of the *CFSA*. See also *Children's Aid Society of Metropolitan Toronto (Municipality) v. Lyttle* (1973), 10 R.F.L. 131 (S.C.C.); *C. (F.E.) v. T. (D.)* (1984), 38 R.F.L. (2d) 304 (Man. Co. Ct.); *S. v. Saskatchewan (Minister of Social Services)*, [1983] 3 W.W.R. 373 (Sask. C.A.); *R. (J.) v. New Brunswick (Minister of Health & Community Services)* (1990), 26 R.F.L. (3d) 62 (N.B. C.A.); *K. (L.) v. Saskatchewan (Minister of Social Services)* (1996), 23 R.F.L. (4th) 423 (Sask. C.A.); and *M. (R.K.) v. K. (L.D.)* (1996), 25 R.F.L. (4th) 285 (Alta. C.A.). In the last case, the mother retained custody of the child after separation. The father paid support and exercised regular access. The mother eventually remarried and her new husband adopted the child. However, notice had not been given to the biological father. The appellate

court upheld a lower court decision that set aside the adoption order. Could the same result occur in Ontario in light of s. 157 of the *CFSA*?

(iii) Dispensing with the Requirement of Parental Consent

Some of the cases referred to in the Notes and Questions in the previous section involved orders dispensing with parental consent. For another case dispensing with a father's consent to adoption of his infant daughter by strangers, see *M. (J.F.) v. P. (V.)* (2004), 3 R.F.L. (6th) 426 (Alta. Q.B.). However, most of the contested applications for adoption involve step-parent adoptions.

STOODLEY v. BLUNDEN

(1980), 17 R.F.L. (2d) 280, 1980 CarswellNS 44 (N.S. C.A.)

PACE J.A.: — ... This is an appeal from the decision of O'Hearn Co. Ct. J. wherein he dispensed with the consent of the divorced natural father of a nine-year-old boy and permitted the child's adoption by the natural mother and her present husband. ...

The female respondent married the appellant in March 1971 and the child whom the respondents seek to adopt was born on 3rd December 1971. This was the only child of the marriage. The natural parents separated in 1974 and subsequently divorced on 21st January 1976.

At the time of this application, the natural father was 29 years old and the natural mother was 27. Both parents have now remarried and the child is presently in the custody of his natural mother.

The child knows his father and enjoys his contact with him. As well, the child has a good relationship with his paternal grandmother and cousins. It would appear that the contact between the natural father and the child is not frequent, however, and this is somewhat understandable as the father is a fisherman and spends lengthy periods at sea.

The male respondent is 25 years old and has known the child since the child was three years of age. He is very fond of the child and appears to have supplanted the natural father with no ill effects upon the child. ...

In my opinion, the test and the only test to be applied in determining the issue before us is whether there would be a positive contribution to the welfare of the child by dispensing with the consent of the natural father to the adoption. Application of this test requires a review of the past, present, and future circumstances which have or may affect the welfare of the child and to then determine whether the child will benefit by permanently cutting the parental tie.

In rendering his decision, O'Hearn Co. Ct. J. stated:

> In the instant case, I am strongly of the opinion that the child will on balance gain a great deal by granting the dispensation and allowing the adoption to take place. His rights on intestacy, of course, as well as under the *Testators' Family Maintenance Act*, R.S.N.S. 1967, c. 303, will, as far as we can now tell, be in all likelihood much more substantial where Mr. Blunden is the parent rather than Mr. Stoodley. More important, he will become a lawful member of the family, which is, in fact, his family, and be entitled to a fully recognized legal and social status as such with respect to other children in the family and his peers in general. He will not lose the association with his grandmother and cousins, nor need he necessarily lose the existing association with his natural father. The court cannot, of course, command that access be given to the natural father and it would be perhaps unwise to order it if the court could do so in this particular case, but he will certainly retain most of the benefits mentioned by Zalev Co. Ct. J. in *Re Kennette and Munro*, [1973] 3 O.R. 156, 11 R.F.L. 21, (sub nom. *Re Munro*) 36 D.L.R. (3d) 180, i.e., whatever love, understanding and guidance the natural father can provide in the relationship, the intimacy of the relationship will depend upon the friendship between

natural father and child to a large extent. If the association is not a normal one, that is the unfortunate outcome of the divorce rather than of the adoption. ...

The male applicant, it should be noted, while quite a young man, is the manager of a local building firm. His own family has a similar business and he expects to become part of that in due course. He and his wife belong to the same religious denomination and this family attends church together. He testified that the child has benefited from the marriage and from the new relationship with him, and I accept this testimony. While Mr. Blunden stressed the material advantages that adoption would provide for the child, he felt that even more important would be the child's own feeling that this step would bring him closer to his mother and stepfather. The child, while very young, is of an age to appreciate the symbolic effect of this and some of its social effect.

It appears that the child is and has been a normal, healthy child who enjoys the contact with his natural father and his paternal relatives. He has adapted well to his present home with the respondents and I think that there can be no doubt that mutual love and affection flows from this relationship. The mother has legal custody of the child and thus a secure home environment prevails under the present circumstances. In weighing all the factors which must be taken into account is the very difficult duty of looking to the future which cannot, by its very nature, be foreseen with certainty. The question immediately arises in making this determination: what positive advantage will the child receive in future which could not be obtained by preserving the non-consenting natural parent status? I cannot see with any degree of certainty that any advantages could be obtained by the child which could not be obtained by alternative legal means.

The male respondent can provide for the economic security of the child, either by will or other means, without the necessity of depriving the child of his inheritance from his natural father. The love and affection between the respondents and the child should not in any way be affected and, in fact, if the present relationship continues, the bonds should become more enduring as time progresses.

In my opinion, and after weighing all the factors, I am not satisfied that this is a case where the consent of the parent to the adoption should be dispensed with. ...

I am not unmindful of the fact that in a case such as this we should not disturb the decision of the County Court Judge unless he erred by applying wrong principles of law or by ignoring or misinterpreting or misconstruing material evidence of fact. With deference to the judge, it is my opinion that he applied the evidence to matters chiefly concerned with custody and not to that of whether the consent of the appellant to the adoption should be dispensed with and thus he fell into reversible error.

R. (N.J.) v. M. (R.J.)

(1994), 5 R.F.L. (4th) 375, 1994 CarswellOnt 422 (Ont. Prov. Div.)

[The mother and father were divorced in the United States in 1986 and the mother and three children moved to Canada. The mother remarried in 1989. In 1990, the parents agreed to share custody of their oldest son and he began to reside with his father. At the same time the father consented to the adoption of the youngest child, a son, by the mother and her new husband. The husband also wished to adopt the daughter, aged 10. The child consented, but the father opposed the adoption. The father had little contact with the daughter, although he paid support. The mother and her husband applied for an order to dispense with the father's consent.]

HARDMAN PROV. J.: — ... In considering an application under section 138, it is clear that the statutory test is one of best interests. ...

Application of the Law

While it is clear the test is a strict one, with the onus squarely on the applicant, it is the application of this test to the facts that often leads to different outcomes. The benefits to the child in this application from the adoption are those commonly raised:

1. similar family name,

2. security at home in family unit,

3. benefit of stability in inheritance situation or upon the death of a biological parent,

4. confirmation of the reality of who is doing the parenting, and

5. reaffirmation of sibling relationships.

Many cases ... make it clear that the advantages must be weighed against the disadvantages. In this case, the father has had little contact with the child as the result of perhaps some resistance by the mother but more so as the direct result of the distance between the parties.

It is clear from the original "stipulation and agreement" that both parents had anticipated being very involved in the decisions affecting the lives of the children. Although there has been no abandonment or misbehaviour to disentitle the father, it is the reality that little, if any, bond exists between the child and the father, although clearly the father wishes to strengthen any existing bond and be a part of the child's life in the future. ... [T]his court sees little loss to the child by a permanent separation given the lack of contact in the past few years.

However, it is this court's opinion that the emphasis should be on what is to be gained. ...

There are circumstances before the court that are relevant:

1. The child has lived most of her life in Canada with her mother.

2. Since 1987, she has known the co-applicant as a fully involved parent.

3. One of her brothers, only 21 months younger, has been adopted by the co-applicant.

4. The child has executed a consent, being almost ten years of age at the time, and there has been no indication of any change in that position despite the child now being eleven years of age.

5. It is the wish of the child, expressed through the mother as well, that she be adopted by the co-applicant.

6. The mother has indicated that the child may continue to visit the biological father if she so desires.

Many cases state that matters such as name change, inheritance, and so on can and should be dealt with through less intrusive types of orders. Also, there is academic opinion ... that suggests caution in using the vehicle of adoption, originally designed to place unwanted children, to "shore-up" step relationship families. Given the fluidity of family relationships, a cautious approach is an appropriate one. The matter before the court must therefore be approached cautiously but determined on the particular situation before the court. ... In this case, the court did not hear from the child *viva voce* but only has indirect information and an executed consent concerning that issue. Nevertheless, the child's opinion is properly before the court. ...

There is ample reason before the court for the child to choose adoption: the co-applicant is her parent in her experience and her brother has affirmed his status already with that co-applicant. ... The gain from her perspective no doubt is the solidifying of that family unit and also from her perspective she has nothing to lose in terms of her very slight relationship with her biological father. While it is this court's hope that she may decide to maintain a relationship with her biological father, and hence enhance her relationship with her older brother, nevertheless this application should be allowed. Based on the factors before this court and the application of the law to the facts, this court is prepared to find on a best interests basis that the consent of the respondent father should be dispensed with in the adoption of the child. ...

NOTES AND QUESTIONS

1. List reasons that may motivate a parent and step-parent to adopt the parent's child from a previous marriage. Which of these can be achieved within the existing legal framework without adoption? In "The Misuse of Adoption by the Custodial Parent" (1979), 2 Can. J. Fam. L. 141, Weiss argued that step-parent adoptions were often motivated by a desire to end the biological father's access rights and, indeed, sever all ties between the father and his child. He also suggested that problems caused by the child's name, the child's need to feel part of the new family, and securing the child's right to inherit from the step-father did not warrant the legal changes involved in an adoption. Rather, in his view, these issues could be dealt with by other means and were often mere rationalisations on the part of the custodial parent and step-parent.

2. As noted by Weiss, the traditional view is that adoption of a child by one birth parent and a step-parent generally terminates the access rights of the other parent. However, legislation in some provinces specifically provides for the possibility of access by a biological parent in a step-parent adoption. For example, s. 15(3) of the *Adoption Act, 1998*, S.S. 1998, c. A-5.2, stipulates that, in step-parent adoptions, any existing access right of the biological parent continues unless the court orders otherwise. Also, s. 23(8) authorizes the court, in a step-parent adoption, to order access for a birth parent. It also now appears that courts in all jurisdictions including Ontario can order post-adoption access, either under the general legislation dealing with access or the courts' inherent *parens patriae* jurisdiction. See the next section of this chapter. How might the possibility of access for the biological parent affect applications to dispense with a parent's consent to a step-parent adoption?

3. Should there be an alternative means of formalizing step-parent and child relationships, giving the relationship a clear legal identity and psychological stability? Should courts, for example, grant joint custody orders to the parent and step-parent? This gives legal recognition to the relationship without cutting off all legal ties between the child and his or her other biological parent.

C. (M.A.) v. K. (M.)

(2009), 63 R.F.L. (6th) 438, 2009 CarswellOnt 428 (C.J.) (Footnotes omitted)

COHEN J:

1 This is a ruling on a motion for an order dispensing with the consent of a parent to an adoption. The applicants Ms. M.A.C. and Ms. C.A.D. are a lesbian couple who have cohabited for a lengthy period of time. They are the custodial parents and primary caregivers of the child B. (born on 11 September 2002). Ms. M.A.C. is B.'s biological mother, and Ms. C.A.D. is her non-biological mother. The respondent Mr. M.K. is a gay man. He is B.'s biological father and access parent. Although B. was conceived by Mr. M.K.'s sperm dona-

tion, Mr. M.K. is not merely B.'s genetic or biological parent. He is a known and involved father.

2 Ms. M.A.C. and Ms. C.A.D. have commenced a joint application for the adoption of B. Their intention is to secure for Ms. C.A.D. the same legal status that Ms. M.A.C. and Mr. M.K. enjoy as B.'s biological parents. Under the current adoption law in Ontario, in order for Ms. C.A.D. to acquire this status, Mr. M.K. must cease to be her legal parent. Mr. M.K. is unwilling to lose this status and refuses his consent to the adoption.

3 The applicants distinguish their family structure from what they call the "heterosexual norm". They argue that their particular social position as lesbian parents renders their need to have Ms. C.A.D. pronounced a legal parent more urgent than it would be for a heterosexual couple. They assert that Ms. C.A.D. is "treated like a second class citizen", that she is "invisible", a "legal stranger" to B., and that "titles matter". The applicants submit that Mr. M.K.'s consent to the adoption should be dispensed with to solidify Ms. C.A.D.'s position as an equal legal parent to B.

4 The applicants also seek to adopt B. as a way of resolving the conflict that has developed between them and Mr. M.K. Although relations between the applicants and the respondent were amicable at one time, they have deteriorated. The respondent has persistently sought to increase his access to B. The respondent has exercised access to B. on Thursday evenings and one weekend per month since she was two years of age. He wishes to spend additional time with her on a regular basis. The applicants have been equally persistent in refusing any expansion of the access. The applicants argue that an order for adoption is the only way to resolve this ongoing conflict.

5 The applicants experience the respondent's claims to increased access as a threat to the security of their family. They state that they are "parenting out of a place of deep fear, insecurity and alienation", and they believe an adoption would "create some peace". They believe that an adoption would produce security, structure, boundaries and clarity for their family. After an adoption, B. would have "one family to be in charge of her interests". In my view, the applicants seek an adoption order not only because they wish to change Ms. C.A.D.'s legal status, but also because they wish to change Mr. M.K.'s.

6 For this very reason, among others, Mr. M.K. opposes the motion to dispense with his consent. He argues that an adoption would extinguish his role as B.'s parent, not only legally, but also for many practical purposes. He denies that an adoption would reduce tensions between the parties. Although the applicants perceive his position as overly powerful because of his biological parenthood, the respondent views it as vulnerable. He believes an adoption order in favour of the applicants would enable them to marginalize his role in B.'s life — that he would become "little more than a friendly uncle". ...

7 In an application to dispense with consent to an adoption, the court must decide whether making the order is in the child's best interests. All three parties argue that the issues they have raised bear directly on B.'s best interests. As will be evident, I have decided that an order dispensing with consent is contrary to B.'s best interests. ...

33 Notwithstanding the absence of any legal action [for a custody order or a declaration of parentage] taken by the parties to strengthen Ms. C.A.D.'s position, it appears that she has in fact been recognized as B.'s parent for all practical purposes, that is, by B.'s schools, doctors, and in recreational activities, *etc.* A custody order or a declaration would confirm a situation that already exists. Marriage might also assist, a path the applicants apparently are considering. The fact that the applicants have chosen to pursue the end game of adoption with this application, rather than pursuing any of the avenues available to them, leads me to question whether the situation is as urgent as they claim, and whether the applicants are

motivated more by animus towards the respondent, than by concern for Ms. C.A.D.'s status.
...

66 ... Adoption is inescapably about biology, because adoption severs a child's biological link to a parent. Even in a society that has placed affectional ties at the centre of a child's best interests, the child's biological connections remain a fundamental value. Indeed the applicants seek the adoption order precisely so the respondent's biological connection to B. can be severed and so that Ms. C.A.D., the child's non-biological mother, and one of her primary caregivers, can assume the position that biology conferred on the respondent. However, in this case, the applicants also propose that the respondent will "continue to be a father" and continue to exercise access. Since the child's relationship by blood is only one of the factors in the "best interests" test, what weight should be attributed to the blood tie in these circumstances? ...

68 Paragraph 6 of s. 136(2) of the Act, which defines "best interests" in adoption proceedings, was not amended [in 2005]. It continues to provide that "the child's relationships by blood or through an adoption order" shall be taken into account, where relevant, when a court is directed to make an order in the best interests of a child.

69 The amending legislation also introduced the concept of "openness agreements" and "openness orders", which are agreements and orders made, *inter alia*, for the purposes of "facilitating communication or maintaining a relationship" between the child and a birth parent, birth sibling or birth relative of the child. The introduction of openness provisions suggests that a child's best interests may lie in knowing and maintaining a connection to a biological parent. That the legislature chose to retain the test of blood ties in Part VII of the Act and to permit a role for birth parents after an adoption is an indication of the importance that society continues to place on the biological relationship between parent and child. At the same time, it is well established that affectional relationships, i.e, "the parental tie as a meaningful and positive force in the life of the child", fundamentally govern the interpretation of a child's best interests. Considering blood ties in this context, I conclude that the biological connection is of enhanced significance where, as in this case, the child has an important relationship with a parent.

70 The *Child and Family Services Act* provides that an order of adoption is final and irrevocable. ... For all purposes of law, as of the date of the making of an adoption order, the adopted child becomes the child of the adoptive parent, the adopted child ceases to be the child of the person who was his or her parent before the adoption order was made, and ceases to be the relative of the former parent's relatives. For this reason, adoption has been characterized in many cases as "the statutory guillotine of the biological relationship." Adoption results in the final and irrevocable severance of the biological bond between parent and child.

71 In most reported cases where consent was dispensed with, the court found that the child had no knowledge of or relationship with the parent, or the parent posed a risk to the child. Although parental misconduct is not required to support a motion to dispense, the courts generally rely on such circumstances to balance what the child would lose against what he or she would gain by permitting the adoption to proceed. As I have indicated, in the case before me there is no abuse or abandonment by the respondent. There is no risk of harm to the child. There is no evidence the respondent lacks parenting skills. There is no evidence the respondent is a bad moral influence. There is no improper motive on the respondent's part relating to his own interests rather than the child's. ...

73 The respondent has acted as a responsible parent. He has involved himself to the extent he was permitted in B.'s education and recreation. Whenever he was given the opportunity to care for B. by the applicants, he accepted the responsibility. The respondent's "parental

rights" and his parental relationship with B. have arisen not only because he is her biological father, but because he has been actively and wholeheartedly involved with her as a father. It is relevant in this proceeding that the respondent's relationship with B. also developed because the applicants invited him to be a parent, initially agreed to, and encouraged, his relationship with B., and, whether willingly or not, allowed that relationship to grow.

74 The applicants in this case are intelligent, thoughtful and politically conscious of their positions as lesbians in a predominantly heterosexual society. Everything about who they are went into their decision to have this child. When they decided to have a child, they fully understood that, although engaging a sperm donor was a biological necessity, engaging a known sperm donor was not. Thus, when they decided, even before they had chosen the respondent, that they wanted their child to have a known and involved father, they knew that, if they chose well, their child would develop a relationship with a parent who was not part of their immediate family. They knew that a parent-and-child relationship gives rise to rights and responsibilities. They anticipated that a third parent would be involved with their family and had to have anticipated that this parent might disagree with, or challenge, their parenting choices, just as they must do with one another. It is likely that they also knew, since Ms. M.A.C. is a lawyer and fraternizes with family lawyers, that some day, if their relations went badly with the biological father, a mediator or an arbitrator or a judge might interpret their child's best interests to include preserving her connection with that father. Now they want to turn back the clock and make a different choice. If this was ever possible, it is not possible after six years. Time and experience have proven that the respondent is not a "mere sperm donor" and B. is no longer a theoretical proposition, nor is her relationship with her father.

75 I want to make two observations in closing. The first is that, despite the fact that this case involved gay and lesbian parties, many of the issues are common to those experienced by any couple who do not have complete control over the biological process of conception and by newly reconstituted families who must contend with a child's other parent. This case is not about protecting nuclear families to reduce their anxieties. The same imperative that compels us to reconsider our definition of parent in the modern context has equally compelled us to reconsider the concept of the nuclear family. In this case, I am considering the legal situation of a self-constructed, non-traditional family — the three-parent family created by these parties. However, even in this new context, this case is governed by the law of adoption and, having considered that law, I have concluded that the applicants are not entitled to an order dispensing with Mr. M.K.'s consent to their adoption of B. My second observation is that I appreciate how the applicants, as lesbians, might fear the loss of control over their own reproduction occasioned by the necessary involvement of a sperm donor in the creation of their family. I would remind them, using Ms. M.A.C.'s words, that the options for gay men "are in some ways much more bleaker than even ... ours." For the sake of B., and in their own best interests, these parties will have to learn to live with their choices.

NOTES AND QUESTIONS

1. In para. 30 of the reasons, Justice Cohen noted in *C. (M.A.)* v. *K. (M.)* that the parties had prepared the pleadings for an application for a declaration that B. had two legal mothers and a father, but that the two women no longer wished to pursue this option. Why might they have favoured adoption?

(5) Effect of Adoption

(a) Introduction

As a general rule, adoption places an adopted child in the same position as he or she would have been if born to the adopted parents and it terminates all of the legal ties between the child and the biological parents (see s. 158 of the *CFSA*). However, there is an exception to the severance of ties with the birth family for the purpose of laws relating to incest and the prohibited degrees of marriage: s. 158(6) of the *CFSA*. There is another qualification to the general rule that an adopted child is in the same position as he or she would have been if born to the adopted parents. An adoption under provincial law cannot affect a child's status as an "Indian" under the *Indian Act*, R.S.C. 1985, c. I-5. See *Re Birth Registration No. 67-09-022272* (1975), 21 R.F.L. 267 (S.C.C.). In some provinces, the preservation of a child's aboriginal status and rights is spelled out in legislation.

The traditional or closed model of adoption is perceived as a total transfer of parenthood. Under this model, the birth parents' relationship with the child ends. Indeed, the adoptive parents are substituted for the birth parents on the child's birth certificate and the adoption records are sealed, to be opened in limited circumstances only. The model also provides certain guarantees for the birth parents (strict confidentiality), the adoptive parents (birth parents will not interfere in the upbringing of the child), and the child (personal history starts with a new birth certificate). To complete the break between the child and the birth parents, this adoption model provides that placement for adoption terminates outstanding access orders and prohibits a court from granting access to a birth parent at the time of the adoption or thereafter.

In the last few decades, there has been a movement towards a more open adoption process. Although the term "open adoption" is difficult to define, it may encompass any arrangement whereby there is a continuing role in the child's life for the birth parents. In "The Changing Face of Adoption: The Challenge of Open and Custom Adoption" (1996), 13 C.F.L.Q. 333, Jeannie House stated (at 342): "The main features of an open adoption include access by the natural/ birth family, information about the child's history (medical and social), involvement of the child's birthparent/ s in the adoption process (particularly in the choice of adoptive home), involvement of the older child in his or her own adoption." She reported (at 349) that the following "openness procedures" have been used in Canada, particularly by private adoption agencies: "birth mothers choosing from pre-selected, non-identifying family profiles (54 per cent); regular exchange of letters and information through adoption agency (34 per cent); pre-placement meeting of birth and adoptive parents without identifying information (18 per cent); and exchange of names (13 per cent)". For further reading, see Senoff, "Open Adoptions in Ontario and the Need for Legislative Reform" (1998), 15 Can. J. Fam. L. 183.

The remainder of this chapter focuses on the possibility of the maintenance or re-establishment of links between the adopted child and the biological parents by examining "openness orders" and "openness agreements" under the recently amended *CFSA*, the possibility of access by birth parents to their adopted child and the confidentiality of adoption records.

NOTES AND QUESTIONS

1. In *Mernickle v. Westaway*, 1 B.C.L.R. (2d) 267, [1986] 3 W.W.R. 665 (C.A.) the court held that an adopted child could not take on the intestacy of a natural parent. The British Columbia legislative provisions were similar to s. 158 of the *CFSA*. See also *Co-operative Trust Co. of Canada v. Saskatchewan (Administrator of Estates)* (1983), 36 R.F.L. (2d) 391, (sub nom. *Re Kowbel*) 27 Sask. R. 65 (Q.B.); *Clayton v. Markolefas* (2002), 31 R.F.L. (5th) 64 (B.C. C.A.); and *Marshall Estate, Re* (2009), 2009 CarswellNS 128 (N.S. C.A.). In the latter case, the court rejected a Charter challenge to the legislation that prevented the adoptee from taking on an intestacy of her birth aunt.

2. In *Zien v. Woida* (2003), 43 R.F.L. (5th) 241 (B.C. S.C.), the court held that a university student, who had been adopted by his step-father, could not apply for support from his biological father. See also *R. (K.M.) v. R. (D.E.)* (2001), 14 R.F.L. (5th) 168 (Sask. Q.B.), where a step-father who had adopted his wife's two children from a previous relationship tried unsuccessfully to have the children's biological father added as a third party to a child support application under the *Divorce Act*. The court noted that the adoption ended the biological father's legal status as a parent and, therefore, the support obligation under the *Divorce Act*. The court also refused to find that the biological father stood in the place of a parent based on his behaviour after the adoption. He had continued to see the two children approximately every six weeks and on special occasions, sometimes bringing gifts.

(b) Access, "Openness Orders", and "Openness Agreements"

A number of complex issues arise when considering a birth parent's access after adoption. A preliminary issue is whether existing orders granting access are terminated by the adoption. One view is that any right of access, including one under an access order, is terminated by an adoption order. Cases such as *Z. (G.M.) v. B. (T.F.S.)*, 18 R.F.L. (2d) 47, [1981] 1 W.W.R. 152 (Man. C.A.); *W. v. H.*, 25 R.F.L. (2d) 337, [1982] 1 W.W.R. 397 (Alta. C.A.); and *Kunkel v. Kunkel* (1994), 2 R.F.L. (4th) 1 (Alta. C.A.) suggest that adoption ends a right of access or a duty of support, even if set out in an order under the federal *Divorce Act*. Some provinces have specific legislation stipulating that adoption ends any order for access unless the court specifies otherwise: s. 85(2)(a) of the *Family Services Act*, S.N.B. 1980, c. F-2.2 and s. 38 of the *Adoption Act*, R.S.B.C 1996, c. 5.

In Ontario, s. 143(1) of the *CSFA* provides that any outstanding access order with respect to a child, other than an order made under Part III (Child Protection) of the Act, is terminated as soon as the child is placed for adoption by a children's aid society or licensee. Similarly, s. 141.1 specifies that an access order made under Part III itself must be terminated before a Crown ward can be placed for adoption. Finally, s. 160 stipulates that no court shall make an order under Part VII for access to the adopted child by a birth parent or a member of the birth parent's family. These provisions would suggest that the Ontario legislature did not anticipate continued access by a birth parent following the child's adoption, at least where the adoption involves a Crown ward or a child placed by a licensee. Support for this view was provided by the case of *Catholic Children's Aid Society of Metropolitan Toronto v. S. (T.)* (1989), 20 R.F.L. (3d) 337, where the Ontario Court of Appeal concluded that Namith Prov. J. had no jurisdiction, on making a Crown wardship order, to stipulate that access by the birth parents would continue beyond the anticipated adoption by the foster parents. The court went on to hold that the statutory provisions requiring termination of access upon placement of a Crown ward for adoption did not contravene the *Charter*. In "Annotation" (1989), 20 R.F.L. (3d) 337, Professor Thompson interpreted the case as follows (at 337):

> The Court of Appeal has now spoken: there is not room under the Ontario legislation, either the old *Child Welfare Act* or the new *Child and Family Services Act*, for legal access by natural parents to survive adoption. Prior to this decision, there had been some debate amongst lower courts, largely inspired by the trial decision here and other decisions of Nasmith Prov. J. ...

However, the situation is not so clear cut, especially where the adoption involves the child's relatives or step-parent. Walsmley A.C. Prov. J. stated in *R. (S.) v. R. (M.)* (1995), 14 R.F.L. (4th) 180 (Ont. Prov. Div.) at 194 that "access orders made before a *relative* adoption survive the adoption order" [emphasis added]. This statement received apparent approval from the Ontario Court of Appeal in later proceedings involving the same child: *R. (S.) v. R. (M.)* (1998), 43 R.F.L. (4th) 116 (Ont. C.A.) (reproduced below). See also *M. (R.) v. K. (M.J.)* (2003), 1 R.F.L. (6th) 255 (Ont. C.J.) and *C. (R.) v. K. (I.D.)* (2006), 2006 Carswell-Ont 3440 (C.J. [In Chambers]). In the last case, the court concluded that a court order granting a birth mother access would survive an adoption by the child's paternal grandparents.

As alluded to above, a separate issue is whether a court has jurisdiction to grant an access order to the birth parent, either at the time of the adoption or subsequently. In *W. (C.G.) v. J. (M.)* (1981), 24 R.F.L. (2d) 342 (Ont. C.A.), a majority of the Ontario Court of Appeal held that the birth mother could not apply for an access order under the *Family Law Reform Act* after her child had been adopted as a Crown ward. It stressed that the adoption legislation intended to "ensure a safe and secure environment for the child, the stability and continuation of which should be immediately threatened by access granted to the natural parents". It suggested, in *obiter dicta*, that an access application might be possible where a relationship developed between a birth mother and a child following the child's adoption.

The following case indicated that the Ontario Court of Appeal, despite its earlier pronouncements, was moving towards an acceptance of access orders in "exceptional cases".

R. (S.) v. R. (M.)

(1998), 43 R.F.L. (4th) 116, 1998 CarswellOnt 4763 (Ont. C.A.)

[A.R. was born on October 28, 1992. His mother, S.R., was 31 years old when A.R. was born. About four months before the child's birth, S.R. moved to Guelph to live with her 50-year-old sister, M.R., and her sister's 56-year-old husband, P.J. It was then agreed that the child would be raised by M.R. and her husband. In February 1993, the mother changed her mind and asked for the child's return. M.R. and her husband refused this request. After attempted negotiations failed, S.R. applied for custody of A.R. in June 1993. Her sister and brother-in-law cross-applied in July. In September 1993, an interim order was made giving custody to M.R. and her husband, with access to S.R. for three hours every other weekend. In July 1994, M.R. and her husband applied to adopt A.R. and to dispense with S.R.'s consent to the adoption. The custody and adoption proceedings were consolidated in November 1994. The trial did not take place until March 1995 at which time the child had bonded with his aunt and uncle. He regarded their home as his and was unaware that he was related to S.R.]

ABELLA J.A. (for the court): —
... Based on the evidence before him, including a court-ordered assessment by Samuel R. Luker, and a report by Dr. Nitza Perlman who was retained by the adoptive parents, Judge Walmsley concluded that it was in the best interests of the child to remain with his aunt and uncle. But he was also firmly of the view that notwithstanding the pending adoption of A. by M. and her husband, there should be access by S.R. He recited four reasons for giving her access:

(a) The mother has a healthy and comfortable relationship with the child and this relationship poses no threat to A.'s development and well-being;

(b) Mr. Luker was in favour of *continuing* and *broadening* access to the mother as set out in his recommendation #4. He found that the custody parents were not opposed to access provided it was supervised, as they had a concern that the mother might abscond with the child;

(c) Dr. Perlman found that the custody parents were strongly in favour of [A.] knowing his birth mother but worried that if she had *free* access it might interfere with [A.]'s sense of a secure environment;

(d) Finally, it must be borne in mind that this is a "relative" adoption. The adoption order may make [M.R.] and [P.J.] the legal parents of [A.]. But it will also make [S.R.] his aunt and they will all still be part of the same extended family. Further, the evidence showed that were it not for the extended family concept and a cultural tradition of informal adoption within the family, [S.R.] would not have felt able to turn to [M.] and her husband for the support and commitment involved in raising a child. Clearly, access in the context of a

> "relative" adoption is a very different matter from access in the context of a stranger adoption. My conclusion is that [A.] should continue to enjoy an access relationship with his soon-to-be aunt. (Emphasis in the original.)

In making an order for access, Associate Chief Judge Walmsley was making an order he knew would survive the adoption order. It was an order he considered not only jurisprudentially available, but in fact desirable in the context of these three adults being related to one another. In his words: "I conclude that access orders made before a relative adoption survive the adoption order, and that there exists in Ontario no jurisprudence to the contrary." He referred to a number of authorities in support of his conclusion that access and guardianship need not be inconsistent. ...

If there remained any doubt about whether an access order could survive an order for adoption, *Nouveau-Brunswick (Ministre de la santé & des services communautaires) c. L. (M.)*, a judgment of the Supreme Court of Canada, delivered October 1, 1998 [reported at 41 R.F.L. (4th) 339], definitively articulates the possibility that in exceptional circumstances, access and adoption orders can co-exist.

Judge Walmsley's decision was appealed both by S.R. and by the adoptive parents. Efforts at access arrangements were unsuccessful and a long period of time elapsed between visits for S.R. Eventually, however, in an effort to settle the appeal, S. agreed to abandon her appeal on the following bases: (1) S.R. would have access to A.; (2) M.R. and P.J. would adopt him. In addition, the parties agreed to mediation in order to assist access arrangements. Minutes of Settlement giving effect to these terms were signed on December 3, 1996.

The adoption order was made on January 21, 1997.

Although the access arrangements initially appeared to be adequate, problems emerged by the spring of 1997. Efforts at mediation were unsuccessful and an application was brought by S. seeking unsupervised access, police intervention to enforce access, and mediation. M. and her husband sought to have access terminated. The matter was heard by O'Connor J.

The expert evidence before Justice O'Connor persuaded him that access to A. by S.R. was in the child's best interests. The expert evidence available to this panel confirms this conclusion. [Later the court referred to a report from Dr. James Deutsch, who reviewed all the documents but did not have access to any of the parties directly.] There is no doubt that the child has a good relationship with S.R. and that it would be in his interest to continue a relationship with her. He ordered overnight access every three weekends, plus an additional day every second weekend, in accordance with the terms of an outstanding interim access order. He also ordered mediation and police intervention to assist in the enforcement of access. ...

We agree, therefore, with Justice O'Connor's decision that a positive relationship exists between A. and his biological mother and that he should continue to enjoy access to her.

Justice O'Connor found M.R. and P.J. largely responsible for the frustration of access rights. ...

There was ample evidence to support this conclusion. ...

There is no doubt that S.R. agreed to the Minutes of Settlement permitting the adoption of A. only on the condition that she be given access. Notwithstanding this settlement, difficulties with access quickly emerged and it was clear that the adopting parents had every intention of attempting to deprive S.R. of access. This intention cannot be given legal effect. There is overwhelming evidence that access to S. is in the child's best interests. What is clearly not in A.'s best interests is to have his adoptive parents continue their preoccupation with thwarting this access.

We do not, however, see any basis for an order of mediation. Mediation cannot be effective unless both sides are genuinely open to the process. In the past five years, M.R. and P.J.

have given every indication that they are not prepared to cooperate with mediators. Accordingly, we think an imposed process of mediation would impose an undue burden on S.R. with no likelihood of constructive results.

As to the assistance of the police, this can be a traumatic intervention for a 6 year-old child. It was requested by S. because of the consistent intransigence of M.R. and P.J. in frustrating rather than facilitating access. We expect at this stage that it is clear to them that their obstructive conduct will not be judicially tolerated. To continue to behave in a way which would leave S. no alternative but to invoke outside intervention, would reflect an unwillingness on their part to act in the child's best interests, a reflection that would certainly be relevant in any subsequent proceedings.

The amount of access should be once every four weekends from Friday at 6:00 p.m. until Sunday at 6:00 p.m. The respondent indicated her willingness to pick up and return the child.

Accordingly, the order of O'Connor J. is to be varied by an order directing that access take place once every four weekends. The order for mediation and police intervention are set aside. The appeal is otherwise dismissed with costs.

McLEOD, "ANNOTATION"

(1999), 32 R.F.L. (4th) 98

The Ontario Court of Appeal's reasons for judgment in *R. (S.) v. R. (M.)* signal the court's willingness to extend access to first-family members that survives a child's adoption. The court's reasons also suggest that a birth parent may be granted access to an adopted child in a broader range of cases than had previously been believed.

Standing to claim access varies from province to province under local custody and adoption legislation. In Ontario, a court may not make an order for access under the *Child and Family Services Act* ... once an adoption order is made: s. 160(1). ... Accordingly, any application for access following adoption must be made under the *Children's Law Reform Act*. ... A parent or other interested person may claim custody or access under the *Children's Law Reform Act*. A birth parent is no longer a parent once an adoption order is made: s. 158(2), *Child and Family Services Act*. The adoption order severs the parent-child relationship. However, a birth parent should be able to claim access or custody to an adopted child under the *Children's Law Reform Act* in the same way as any other non-parent.

Historically, judges were divided as to whether to allow a birth parent to claim access after adoption. While most judges accepted the view that any interested person could apply for access to a child, some judges insisted that a biological parent could not rely on a pre-adoption relationship with the child to support an access claim: contrast the views in *W. (C.G.) v. J. (M.)* (1981), 24 R.F.L. (2d) 342, 34 O.R. (2d) 44, 130 D.L.R. (3d) 418 (C.A.). Post-adoption access had to be based on a post-adoption relationship between the person and the child. Those judges who allowed a birth parent to apply for access usually took the view that access should be granted only in an exceptional case. Most judges were reluctant to grant access to a birth parent after adoption because of the fear that maintaining a first-family relationship might undermine the stability of the child's new family. ...

Some courts, primarily in Western Canada, suggested that judges should apply a more relaxed rule to determine whether to grant access to a birth-family member following a step-parent adoption where the child knew the reality of its situation and had an established relationship with various members of its former family. Although Society adoptions usually are preceded by parental abandonment or misconduct, a step-parent adoption may be motivated only by a desire to formalize the child's second-family living arrangements. ...

Section 143(1) of the *Child and Family Services Act*, which provides that access orders terminate when a child is placed for adoption, does not apply to family adoptions since a child is not "placed" in a family adoption: see, as to family adoption, s. 146(1), (2) of the Act. There is nothing in the *Child and Family Services Act* that provides that an access order ends upon a family adoption. However, some judges suggested that the extinguishment of the parent-child relationship necessarily extinguished a pre-adoption access order because the order was based on a status that no longer existed. The Ontario Court of Appeal rejected this argument in *R. (S.) v. R. (M.)* by approving the trial judge's statement that an access order made before a family adoption survives the adoption order. As indicated, the *Child and Family Services Act* mandates a different result in the case of non-family adoptions. Although the Ontario Court of Appeal's brief reasons suggest that the trial judge's conclusion and comments are commonly held, in fact the law on point was unclear prior to *R. (S.) v. R. (M.)*: Hovius, *Family Law* (4th ed.), pp. 1049–1064.

Since the court does not think that there is anything inherently inconsistent between granting an adoption order and maintaining a first-family member's right to access, a birth parent or member of a first family should be able to seek access following adoption. The issue in such cases is whether access should be granted on the merits, according to the best interests of the child, on a case-by-case basis. Prior authorities should be approached with caution, to the extent that they suggest otherwise.

The court did not have to decide whether a birth parent or first-family member may apply for custody or access after a Society adoption or adoption arising by placement. However, the tenor of the court's analysis is that such people have standing to claim custody or access as "other persons" [under the *Children's Law Reform Act*]. The issue is whether custody/ access is in the best interests of the child in the circumstances, not whether a first-family member has standing to seek the relief.

It is surprising that the court was so willing to accept the view that it was in the child's best interests to have continued contact with the mother. It is unlikely that the tension between the mother and the adoptive parents will decrease over time. Most courts are reluctant to extend access to a non-parent if the custodial parent objects and if continued contact may threaten the custodial parent's relationship with the child. The possibility that the mother will tell the child the truth — that his friend is really his mother and his parents are his aunt and uncle — could upset the child and his relationship with the adoptive parents. The real reason for continuing access appears to be that the adoptive parents obtained the mother's consent to adoption by agreeing to access and the court was not willing to let them circumvent their agreement. Although the birth mother is not a parent, neither is she simply a stranger.

The court also relied on "expert evidence" to support the conclusion to continue access. The report in question was prepared by a doctor who did not see or interview any of the participants. Instead, his opinion was based solely on reviewing the material prepared and filed by others. With respect, courts should be cautious about relying on an expert witness's opinion of what is in a particular child's best interests if the witness never interviewed the child or any of the adults involved in the child's life. ...

The court's decision that a biological parent has standing to claim or enforce access rights after adoption is correct in Ontario but may not be so elsewhere. Standing to claim custody/ access depends on the local legislation. As long as a person has an interest in the child's well-being, he or she should be allowed to maintain custody and access proceedings. The question of whether to continue contact should be decided on the merits of the case, not on jurisdictional grounds. However, it is surprising that the Ontario Court of Appeal considered the issue so settled that it did not even address any cases that suggested a contrary result. It is also surprising that the court was so willing to accept the trial judge's conclusion that continued contact is in the child's best interests, given the conflict between the birth mother and adoptive parents and the potential confusion when the child learns the truth and is forced to realign his relationship with the significant adults in his life.

NOTES AND QUESTIONS

1. The Ontario Court of Appeal's reliance on the decision in *Nouveau-Brunswick (Ministre de la santé & des services communautaires) c. L. (M.)* (1998), 41 R.F.L. (4th) 339 (S.C.C.), as authority for the principle that "access and adoption orders can co-exist" in Ontario was something of a stretch. The Supreme Court of Canada's very limited comments in the *L. (M.)* case about the possibility of combining an adoption order with access were made in the context of a legislative provision that specifically indicated that the court making the adoption order could preserve an existing right of access. There is no comparable legislation in Ontario.

2. In *G. (C.) v. H. (J.)* (1989), 23 R.F.L. (3d) 300 (Ont. C.A.), the foster parents had been the child's *de facto* parents since his infancy. Their application to adopt was opposed by the child's grandparents who also wished to adopt the child. The trial judge dismissed the application but the appeal judge reversed this decision because she felt adoption by the foster parents would provide better stability for the child and provide him with a more secure and certain future than an order granting the foster parents custody with access to the grandparents. In doing so, she relied on the foster parents' assurance of access to the grandparents. The Ontario Court of Appeal dismissed a further appeal by the grandparents. It noted (at 301) that if the adoptive order was affirmed "no order for access can be incorporated". It also expressed agreement (at 301) with the finding that "access in the present circumstances is desirable". The endorsement on the appeal record indicated that Tarnopolsky J.A. agreed with the result and the reasons "except as to this court expressing its opinion whether it is desirable that the foster parents should grant access to the biological grandparents".

Some four years later, Nevins Prov. J. dealt with an application by the grandparents and the birth parent for an access order to this child in *H. (J.) v. G. (B.)*, unreported, March 9, 1993, Doc. Toronto D1711/ 86; affirmed May 31, 1993, unreported (Ont. Div. Ct.). The applicants alleged that the adoptive parents had immediately reneged on their promise to permit access following the adoption. Provincial Judge Nevins held that he had jurisdiction to deal with the access application. He reasoned that the Ontario Court of Appeal's earlier decisions had left open the possibility for such applications by birth relatives after adoption in exceptional circumstances. These were exceptional circumstances because (at 17) the applicants were "no strangers to the child and adoptive parents" and the adoptive parents gave "clear and unequivocal assurances" that there would be continued contact.

3. Some provinces have enacted legislation to specifically empower a judge to grant access to a parent where a child is adopted by the other parent and his or her spouse. See, e.g., *Adoption Act*, C.C.S.M., c. A2, s. 92(1) and *The Adoption Act, 1998*, S.S. 1998, c. A-5.2, s. 23. Do you favour such legislation? Is a step-parent adoption ever in the best interests of a child if it is also in the best interests of the child to maintain contact with the non-custodial biological parent? See *D. (R.) v. S. (W.B.)* (1991), 33 R.F.L. (3d) 1 (B.C. C.A.); leave to appeal refused (1992), 38 R.F.L. (3d) 255 (note) (S.C.C.).

Would it be preferable to have legislation stipulating that the court can grant access in any adoption, if this is in the child's best interest? Following the Ontario Court of Appeal's decision in *R. (S.) v. R. (M.)*, is this now the law in Ontario in any event?

In "Adoption with Access or 'Open Adoption'" (1991-1992), 8 C.F.L.Q. 283, the Adoption with Access Sub-Committee of the Canadian Bar Association — Ontario concluded that 1) an increasing tendency to order Crown wardship with access combined with a prohibition on adoption placement of a Crown ward while such an order was in place had resulted in more children remaining in foster care (at 288); 2) there had been increasing use of informal arrangements whereby a birth parent had some degree of contact with the child after adoption (at 289); and 3) there were some situations such as adoptions of older Crown wards and step-parent adoptions where continued contact between the adoptee and a birth relative might be in the best interest of the child (at 289). The committee recommended amendments to the *CFSA* to permit court-ordered birth parent contact with adopted Crown wards and suggested that the *Children's Law Reform Act* should be amended to "provide a restricted right to a birth parent to apply for access after a family adoption" (at 296).

These recommendations were never adopted; but, as noted earlier, the 2006 amendments to the *CFSA* did introduce "openness orders" (ss. 145.1 and 145.2 and ss. 153.1 to 153.5) and "openness agreements" (s. 153.6). Openness orders are available only on the application of a Society in relation to a Crown ward. Openness agreements are possible in all adoptions, including step-parent and relative adoptions. They can be made before or after the adoption. Note that the consent of the prospective or actual adoptive parents is required for either an order or agreement. Section 153.6, dealing with "openness agreements" was put to creative use in the following case.

M. (S.), RE

(2007), 45 R.F.L. (6th) 345, 2007 CarswellOnt 6943 (Ont. C.J.) (Footnotes omitted)

SPENCE J.:

1. Introduction

1 The applicants in this case are two women, Ms. Susan Y. and Ms. Yelena M., who have been in a loving and committed relationship with each other for more than four years. Ms. Susan Y. is the mother of one child from a prior relationship. A few years ago, Ms. Susan Y. and Yelena M. decided that they wished to become parents of their own child. Not wanting to have an anonymous donor, they approached their friend, Mr. Stephen M., who agreed to become their sperm donor. As a result, Ms. Yelena M. became pregnant and, on 10 February 2005, Stas M. was born. Everyone was thrilled. Shortly afterwards, Ms. Susan Y. and Ms. Yelena M. launched their joint application for adoption, as spouses of each [other], fully hoping and expecting the adoption to be granted quickly. But sometimes, the wheels of justice grind slowly. ...

2. Factual Background

[The women wanted the child to know his genetic father and to have an opportunity to have a relationship with him. The biological mother registered him as the father. The women then did some research and found a model sperm donor agreement from California. That sample agreement ultimately led to a complex 16-page agreement which both women and Stephen M. signed in 2006 with the benefit of independent legal advice. The agreement provided that M. was to be acknowledged as the child's father, that M. and the child would be encouraged to develop a relationship with each other and spend time with each other, that M. would have the right to receive information about the child and that, in the event of both women's deaths during the child's minority, M. would assume custody.

The women applied to adopt Stas and the father signed a consent form. The matter came before Spence J. as a "paper application" and he was troubled by it. In particular, he was not sure that, in light of the tri-partite agreement, the father was aware of the implications of the adoption and that he really consented to becoming a "non-parent". Accordingly, the judge directed a trial that was eventually held in 2007.]

4. Evidence at Trial

16 In the more than two and one-half years since Stas M.'s birth, it appears that the routine in the household is what one might expect in any busy household where there are two work-

ing parents with two young children. Ms. Susan Y.'s daughter and Stas M. are described as "very much siblings", two children who have a "special relationship". Stas M. refers to Ms. Susan Y. as "mummy" and Ms. Yelena M. as "mamma". He calls Mr. Stephen M. "daddy". Ms. Susan Y.'s daughter considers herself to have two moms and a dad. Both Ms. Susan Y. and Ms. Yelena M. want the same for Stas M., namely, to have two moms — themselves — and one dad — Mr. Stephen M. In short, I have no reason to believe that Stas M. is anything other than well cared-for, anything other than being raised in a loving household with two mothers who are committed to Stas M.'s needs and his best interests. ...

5. When an Adoption May be Granted

18 The factors that a court must consider in determining the best interests of the child are set out at subsection 136(2) of the Act. I need not recite those factors in these reasons. Suffice it to state that the evidence in this case points in one direction only, namely, that Stas M.'s best interests are amply addressed in Ms. Susan Y.'s and Ms. Yelena M.'s family constellation.

19 However, that is not the end of the inquiry. There are at least two other issues to be addressed. The first issue concerns the necessity of obtaining the consent of a "parent" to the proposed adoption. Subsection 137(2) of the Act requires the child's "parent" to consent to the adoption for a child under the age of 16 years. In this case, as I noted earlier, "parent" would include Mr. Stephen M. Section 138 of the Act does permit a court to dispense with that parent's consent, where "it is in the child's best interests to do so".

20 The second issue raised on the facts of this case is what to do about the rights purportedly conferred on Mr. Stephen M. under the agreement, including not only the rights to access but, as well, the residual custody rights upon the death of Ms. Susan Y. and Ms. Yelena M. Although the issue of informed consent and the issue of the purported rights in the agreement are inextricably tied to one another, I will attempt to deal with them separately, addressing first the issue of informed consent.

6. Has Mr. Stephen M. Given Informed Consent to the Proposed Adoption?

21 Mr. Stephen M. visits with Stas M. on a regular basis. His visits are always in the presence of Ms. Susan Y. and Ms. Yelena M. Although he acknowledges that he is Stas M.'s biological father, he testified at trial that he considers Ms. Susan Y. and Ms. Yelena M. only to be Stas M.'s parents. He says that his intention is not to have any legal rights in respect of Stas M. Instead, the purpose of the agreement was to set out the basis for creating a relationship between himself and Stas M. He claims to be clear that "any and all [of his] rights terminate" upon the granting of an adoption. He also says he understands that the agreement, and its provisions, are not legally enforceable.

22 How is the court to reconcile the contents of the agreement with Mr. Stephen M.'s oral testimony? As I noted earlier, when I read the agreement in chambers in October 2006, the contents seemed to me to be inconsistent with a person who was purporting to relinquish all parental rights. And yet, this is exactly what Mr. Stephen M., in his oral testimony says he is intending to do. On the one hand, he states that he executed the agreement knowing full well that it would be unenforceable and that the sole purpose of entering into the agreement was to reduce to writing the results of the parties' earlier discussions. On the other hand, assuming this to be the case, I was puzzled why the parties would pay what surely amounted to considerable legal fees, to three different lawyers, to draft a 16-page agreement that, according to Mr. Stephen M.'s testimony at trial, no one expected would have any legal effect.

23 Whatever Mr. Stephen M. in fact believed prior to trial, I am prepared to accept his testimony that he now understands Stas M. will have only two parents, namely Ms. Susan Y.

and Ms. Yelena M. I also accept his testimony that he now understands his parental rights would terminate upon the granting of an adoption order. I am not certain, however, that he understood these things at the time that he executed the agreement more than a year ago. Specifically, it will be recalled to what Ms. Yelena M. testified, namely, that the agreement was prepared and entered into "mostly for [Mr. Stephen M.'s] comfort". In my opinion, that comment, together with the contents of the agreement itself, reveal much as to Mr. Stephen M.'s expectations at the time he signed the agreement.

24 Nevertheless, it is open for the court to conclude from all of the evidence that, even if Mr. Stephen M. was not fully informed of his legal rights and obligations at the time he signed the Form 34F [the adoption consent form], he is now so fully informed, as revealed by his testimony in court. In fact, on the basis of the totality of the evidence, I am prepared to reach that conclusion.

7: Was The Agreement Necessary?

25 I now turn to the second issue, namely, what to do about the rights purportedly conferred on Mr. Stephen M. in the agreement. If the primary purpose of the agreement was to provide for an ongoing relationship between Mr. Stephen M. and Stas M., the parties have gone about this in an unnecessarily complicated, expensive and time-consuming manner. I do not intend my following comments to be critical of any party or any lawyer involved in these proceedings. Instead, my intent is to indicate how the primary purpose of the agreement — the access provisions — could have been achieved in a far less complex and legally more straightforward manner. Immediately following Stas M.'s birth, Ms. Susan Y. and Ms. Yelena M. ought to have applied for a joint custody order, under Part III of the *Childrens Law Reform Act, with access* to Mr. Stephen M. By minutes of settlement, the parties would have obtained this order on consent. They could have done this quickly and likely without the necessity of any court appearance whatsoever.

26 Following this, Ms. Susan Y. and Ms. Yelena M. would have initiated their adoption application, with Mr. Stephen M. simply consenting. Because Stas M. was not being "placed for adoption by a society or licensee", Mr. Stephen M.'s access order obtained under the *Children's Law Reform Act* would automatically survive the granting of the adoption. See for example, *R. (S.) v. R. (M.)* (1995), 14 R.F.L. (4th) 180, [1995] O.J. No. 1201, 1995 CarswellOnt 430 (Ont. Prov. Div.), *per* Associate Chief Judge Robert J.K. Walmsley, effectively affirmed at *R. (S.) v. R. (M.)* (1998), 116 O.A.C. 150, 43 R.F.L. (4th) 116 (Ont. C.A.) and also *M. (R.) v. K. (M.J.)*, 1 R.F.L. (6th) 255, [2003] O.J. No. 5142, 2003 CarswellOnt 5168 (Ont. C.J.), *per* Justice John Kukurin. ...

28 Nevertheless, the parties did not proceed in the foregoing manner. They did negotiate this agreement and they have presented it to the court for whatever it is worth. Accordingly, I will attempt to sort this out without putting the parties to the additional time and expense of initiating a *Children's Law Reform Act* application, drafting minutes of settlement and obtaining a consent order under that Act.

8: How to Characterize The Agreement

29 Paragraph 3 of the agreement is headed "Domestic Contract". ...

30 Section 51 of the *Family Law Act* ... defines a "domestic contract" as a "marriage contract, separation agreement or cohabitation agreement." In substance, the agreement is none of these and, accordingly, cannot be "construed as a domestic contract". ...

31 However, notwithstanding that the agreement is not a domestic contract it is, nonetheless, a contract into which the parties entered, wherein they intended to set out the rights, respon-

sibilities and obligations of one another, as regards Stas M. and, more specifically, the basis for an ongoing relationship between Mr. Stephen M. and Stas M.

32 Mr. Finlayson, on behalf of Ms. Susan Y. and Ms. Yelena M., urged me to find that, if the agreement could not be construed as a domestic contract, it ought to be construed as an openness agreement under the *[Child and Family Services] Act*. Section 153.6 of the Act states (in part), as follows (my emphasis):

> 153.6 *Who may enter into openness agreement.* — (1) For the purposes of facilitating communication or maintaining relationships, an openness agreement may be made by an *adoptive parent* of a child or by a person with whom a society or licensee has placed or plans to place a child for adoption and any of the following persons:
>
> 1. *A birth parent*, birth relative or birth sibling of the child. ...
>
> (2) *When agreement may be made.* — An openness agreement may be made *at any time* before or after an adoption order is made. ...

33 On its face, subsection 153.6(1) is satisfied in that, at least arguably, the primary purpose of the agreement is to facilitate communication and to foster a relationship. Further, the agreement itself was "made by an adoptive parent" (Ms. Susan Y. and Ms. Yelena M.) and a "birth parent" (Mr. Stephen M.).

34 However, the agreement was entered into by the parties between May 2006 and August 2006. Section 153.6 of the Act was not proclaimed in force until 30 November 2006. ... Accordingly, the agreement could not have been an openness agreement when it was made, as no such provision yet existed in the Act. Furthermore, neither paragraph 3 of the agreement (the paragraph which is headed "Domestic Contract") nor any other part of the agreement makes any reference whatsoever to openness agreements.

35 Therefore, the question to be answered is whether it is nonetheless open to the court to construe the agreement as an openness agreement, even though the legislation creating openness agreements had not yet come into existence when the agreement was last-signed in August 2006. ...

39 ... Implicit in the enactment of section 153.6 is the legislature's recognition that there are circumstances where it is in the best interests of a child to have access to his or her birth parent. Clearly, it will not be the case that, in all adoptions, there ought to be a relationship between the birth parent and the child. However, in those cases where the adoptive parents and the birth parent all believe that such a relationship would benefit the child and would be in the best interests of the child, section 153.6 of the Act permits those parties to reduce their beliefs to writing in the form of an openness agreement. Accordingly, in my view section 153.6 must be regarded as remedial in nature. As such, the presumption that it is not to be given retroactive or retrospective interpretation does not apply. Rather, I have concluded that the only way to give effect to the recognition that the best interests of children sometimes requires the making of an openness agreement, is to accord section 153.6 with retroactive or retrospective application.

40 In my view, what Ms. Susan Y., Ms. Yelena M. and Mr. Stephen M. were attempting to do when they crafted the agreement, is the very kind of thing that is contemplated by section 153.6, namely to create, in substance, an openness agreement. Of course, they were unable to call it that because openness agreements did not yet have statutory life.

41 In as much as I have attempted to save at least a portion of the agreement by characterizing it as an openness agreement, I am unable to save the entire agreement. Although open-

ness agreements may provide for the fostering of relationships between a birth parent and a child, they do not provide for, or permit, the granting of residual custody rights to the birth parent — something which this agreement expressly purports to do. Accordingly, a word of caution is necessary. Although Mr. Stephen M. may understand that he is giving up his parental rights upon the granting of an adoption order, he also must understand — as must both Ms. Susan Y. and Ms. Yelena M. — that the residual custody rights to which the parties have agreed upon the death of Ms. Susan Y. and Ms. Yelena M. are entirely unenforceable and not binding upon any court. Without intending to give legal advice to the parties, it would be far more preferable to provide for such residual rights by way of a testamentary guardianship clause. Section 61 of the *Children's Law Reform Act* permits a party to make such a guardianship appointment and provides that any such appointment continues for 90 days "after the appointment becomes effective".

9. Conclusion

42 By way of summarizing, I conclude the following:

1. Stas M.'s best interests are being met by the care he receives from the applicants, Ms. Susan Y. and Ms. Yelena M.

2. Although Mr. Stephen M. initially may not have understood the nature and consequences of his so-called consent in Form 34F, he has subsequently become fully informed of what that consent means. I find that he is giving his consent freely and voluntarily and, accordingly, it is not necessary to make an order dispensing with his consent.

3. Because section 153.6 of the Act is directed to the best interests of children, it is remedial in nature. As such, it is to be accorded retroactive or retrospective application.

4. To the extent that the agreement provides for a fostering of the relationship between Mr. Stephen M. and Stas M., at least that portion of the agreement properly fits within what is intended by section 153.6 of the Act and, as such, may be construed as an openness agreement.

43 In view of the foregoing, all of the preconditions set out in Part VII of the Act have been met, and I make the adoption order requested by the applicants, Ms. Susan Y. and Ms. Yelena M. ...

NOTES AND QUESTIONS

1. Openness orders or agreements can provide for a continuing relationship between a birth parent and the child along a broad continuum. For example, an openness agreement may simply provide that the adoptive parents will provide an annual report about the child or that there will an exchange of Christmas cards. At the other end of the spectrum, an agreement such as that described in *Re M. (S.)*, above, may envision that the birth parent will play an active role in the child's life.

2. Note that a Children's Aid Society can now place a Crown ward with prospective adoptive parents subject to an openness order or openness agreement. In either case, the prospective parents must consent.

3. Where a birth parent consents to an adoption in exchange for an openness agreement, what legal recourse does this parent have if the adoptive parents later lose their enthusiasm for maintaining any communication or relationship between the child and the birth parent? Note that s. 153.6(3) specifically states that an openness agreement may include a process to resolve any disputes.

(c) Adoption Records and Disclosure

There are two kinds of information relating to an adoption: identifying and non-identifying. Identifying information is anything that would allow the identification of a person involved in the adoption process. Non-identifying information provides background information about the participants. The birth parents, for example, might wish to know such non-identifying information as the ages and religion of the adoptive parents or reports on the child's progress in school and sports. The adult adoptee might want to know the reasons for the adoption and obtain a medical history of the biological parents. Generally, the laws governing disclosure of identifying information are stricter than those dealing with non-identifying information. The general trend in most jurisdictions has been towards increased disclosure of information, both identifying and non-identifying.

In 1978, Ontario created a voluntary disclosure registry for adult adoptees and birth parents. In *Ferguson v. Ontario (Director of Child Welfare)* (1983), 40 O.R. (2d) 294 (Co. Ct.); affirmed (1983), 36 R.F.L. (2d) 405 (Ont. C.A.), Killeen Co. Ct. J. described the mechanisms of the registry as follows (at 310 [O.R.]):

> The adoption disclosure registry is maintained in Ministry facilities at Toronto. An adopted child who is 18 or more years of age and a birth parent of the child may apply to a local Children's Aid Society to be registered in the registry at Toronto. If the Director ascertains that both the adopted child and birth parent are registered, he must then contact any living adoptive parent and obtain a written consent to the disclosure of the identifying information. If the adoptive parent refuses, the Director can do nothing further. If the adoptive parent consents, the Director must then obtain a written confirmation of both the adoptee and the birth parent. At this point, a "matching" occurs which permits the Director to divulge identifying information from the documents used on the court adoption application, ... and the forms filed by adoptee and birth parent in the registry.

The voluntary register, involving consents from all three members of the adoption triangle, resulted in few matches. It was of no help to someone like Mrs. Ferguson whose birth parents did not register. However, it had been possible for some time to obtain a court order opening adoption records. Mrs. Ferguson applied for such an order under s. 80(1) of the *Child Welfare Act*. She was unsuccessful. The trial judge concluded that, in light of the statute's emphasis on secrecy in the adoption process, an order should be granted only in compelling or exceptional circumstances. As an example of such circumstances, the court referred to situations where the applicant's mental or physical health required disclosure. Accordingly, the order was refused where Mrs. Ferguson's application was based solely on a desire to know more about herself and her roots. The Ontario Court of Appeal affirmed the trial judgment. The court held (at 407) that "sufficient cause [for the purpose of s. 80(1)] must be a cause of such gravity and importance to displace the statutory rights of the other parties as well as the interests of the province in maintaining the integrity of the adoption system". It also concluded (at 408) that ss. 2(b), 2(d) and 7 of the *Charter* did not have "any bearing whatever on s. 80(1) of the *Child Welfare Act*." The Court of Appeal noted (at 408): "The real basis of Mr. Wilson's argument in this court was an attack on the wisdom of the secrecy provisions of the *Child Welfare Act* dealing with adoption. This is a kind of argument that may be addressed appropriately to the legislature but which has little place in this courtroom."

Eventually, the Minister of Community and Social Services appointed a Special Commissioner, Ralph Garber, to report on access to non-identifying and identifying information. *The Report of the Special Commissioner: Disclosure of Adoption Information* (Toronto: Ministry of Community and Social Services, 1985) favoured much greater disclosure of non-identifying and identifying information. In particular, it suggested that adoptive parents, birth parents, minor adoptees with the consent of adoptive parents, emancipated adoptees over the age of 16 (without the consent of adoptive parents), adult adoptees (without the consent of adoptive parents), adult birth siblings of adoptees, birth grandparents of adoptees, and the physician of the minor adoptee should all have access to non-identifying informa-tion. It also recommended that adult adoptees should have access to their original birth cer-tificate and to other identifying information in their adoption file. No consents from either the adoptive or birth parents would be required. However, where the adult adoptee sought contact or reunion with a birth parent, the latter had to indicate consent through registration.

In 1987, in response to this report, the Ontario legislature amended the *CFSA* to enact new provisions dealing with disclosure of adoption information. These reflected the recom-mendations of the Special Commissioner regarding non-identifying information, but they were more restrictive in allowing access to identifying information. While the consent of the adoptive parents was no longer required for the disclosure of identifying information where the adult adoptee and the birth family member were both registered in the Adoption Disclo-sure Register, disclosure still did not generally occur unless both an adult adoptee and a birth parent (or a birth grandparent or sibling) registered and consented in writing to the disclo-sure. Where there was no "match", the Registrar could be asked to conduct a "discreet and reasonable search" to determine if the non-registered person wished to be named in the Reg-ister. The statutory requirement that counselling be provided to the person receiving the information, whether identifying or non-identifying, put a strain on the process. Lack of resources resulted in waiting lists and long delays. The Registrar had discretion to permit disclosure of identifying information without the consents noted above where the disclosure was required for the health, safety or welfare of any individual. Policy guidelines indicated that the Registrar used this discretion only in "true emergency" situations and "not to cir-cumvent the normal disclosure process and consent requirement".

In 2005, the Ontario legislature passed the *Adoption Information Disclosure Act, 2005*. This Act repealed the disclosure provisions in the *CFSA*, including the counselling require-ments, and amended the *Vital Statistics Act*, R.S.O. 1990, c.V.4, to provide the most liberal disclosure rules in Canada. An *adopted person* who was at least 18 years old could obtain from the Registrar General an uncertified copy of the original registration, if any, of his or her birth and of any adoption order registered under the Act. A *birth parent* could obtain from the Registrar General all of the information contained in specified registered docu-ments concerning the adopted person (with the exception of information about persons other than the birth parent and the adopted person), once the adopted person was at least 19 years old.

Under the 2005 amendments, adult adoptees or birth parents who did not wish to be contacted could register a *non-contact notice* to that effect. Where such a notice was filed, the searching birth parent or adoptee had to agree in writing not to contact the person who had registered the notice before they could obtain a copy of the birth registration or adoption order. Anyone who violated this undertaking could be prosecuted and fined up to $50,000. Similarly, it was an offence for another person to contact someone on behalf of the adopted person or birth parent contrary to the undertaking.

Finally, the 2005 amendments allowed birth parents and adult adoptees who did not wish their identifying information disclosed to apply to the Child and Family Services Review Board for a "non-disclosure order". Such an order had to be made where "appropriate to prevent sexual harm or significant physical or emotional harm".

The 2005 disclosure law was proclaimed in force in September 2007. Within two weeks, it was successfully challenged on the basis of the *Charter* by three adult adoptees and a birth parent in the following case.

CHESKES v. ONTARIO (ATTORNEY GENERAL)

(2007), 42 R.F.L. (6th) 53, 2007 CarswellOnt 5849 (Ont. S.C.J.) (Footnotes omitted)

BELOBABA J.:

(3) Section 7 of the Charter

25 Section 7 of the *Charter* provides that everyone has the right to life, liberty and security of the person and the right not to be deprived thereof except in accordance with the principles of fundamental justice.

26 The analysis under s. 7 involves a two-step process: the applicants must show first, that there has been a deprivation of their right to life, liberty or security of the person, and second, that this deprivation was not in accordance with the principles of fundamental justice. If a breach of s. 7 has been established by the applicants, the burden then shifts to the government respondent to show, under s. 1, that the breach of s. 7 is nonetheless a reasonable limit on the s. 7 right and can be demonstrably justified in a free and democratic society. ...

III. The Parties' Position

(1) The applicants' position

27 The applicants do not oppose the new law on a going-forward basis. They do not argue that the registrations and records of future adoptions must be sealed. Rather they object to the retroactive application of the legislation — that the new law now allows searching birth parents and adoptees to access identifying information that up to now has been sealed or otherwise inaccessible. ...

(2) The respondent's position

53 Ontario's position is also relatively straightforward. The Attorney General submits that any system for the disclosure of information relating to adoption must make difficult choices between the competing and often irreconcilable demands of those who seek access to information and those who seek protection of privacy. Among the members of the adoption triad — adopted persons, adoptive parents, and birth parents — there is a broad divergence of views on how the balance between these competing demands should be struck. Ontario's new adoption disclosure legislation, says the Attorney General, balances the legitimate needs of all parties by permitting the disclosure of adoption records within a framework that protects the privacy and well-being of the triad members. The approach in the new law is supported by expert opinion that favours openness in adoption records and by the positive experience of other jurisdictions that have opened their adoption records. Ontario says the new law is carefully balanced and does not infringe the applicants' right to liberty or security of the person. ...

54 Even if the applicants can establish this infringement, argues Ontario, they cannot show that this infringement is contrary to any accepted principle of fundamental justice. On the contrary, says the Attorney General, the new law is carefully tailored to protect the privacy of adopted adults and birth parents as much as is reasonably possible, while providing individuals with information that is of significant personal importance to their self-identity and self-esteem. Section 7 of the *Charter* has not been breached. And, even if it has, the breach can be justified under s. 1.

(3) The intervener's position

55 The Coalition for Open Adoption Records ("COAR") represents "searching" adopted adults and birth parents that favour open adoption records and retroactive access. It does not speak for "non-searching" adoptees or birth parents, such as the applicants, who oppose the retroactive aspect of the new law.

56 COAR believes that adopted adults and their birth parents have a right to know each other. COAR argues that when Ontario started to seal adoption records in 1927, social attitudes were very different from what they are today. It was considered shameful to have a baby outside of marriage. Sealing adoption records was considered necessary as a protection from the embarrassment of "bastardy." But the times have changed, says COAR. The new law reflects society's current view, which no longer deems illegitimacy or infertility to be shameful and which is based on the premise that adopted adults should have the same access to their medical and personal history that non-adopted people have. ...

IV. Some additional background points

58 The written submissions of the parties were extensive. I have reviewed a wide array of relevant evidence, including the filed affidavits and cross-examinations of the parties and their experts, the history of adoption legislation in Ontario, the legislative debates leading to the enactment of the new law, and the legislative approaches that have been taken in other jurisdictions.

59 From this small mountain of paper, I have distilled a number of key points. ...

60 One, the movement for open adoption records is prompted in large part by the fact that social attitudes have changed. The Garber Report reviewed the assumptions underlying the need for secrecy in adoption information, including the stigma of illegitimacy, the shame of the birth mother, and the shame of infertility for the adoptive parents. The Report found that these assumptions, which prevailed in 1927 when adoption records were sealed, are no longer supported by modern practice or by the public's changing attitudes of morality. According to the Garber Report, these changes in social attitudes "have combined to create increasing public pressure for more openness in adoption".

61 Two, the birth and adoption information that is at issue in this lawsuit is intensely private information and may well be, as the federal Privacy Commissioner has noted, "some of the most sensitive information in our society." ...

62 Three, the protection of privacy is a fundamental value in modern democracies. ...

63 Four, the opening of government adoption records is not the only way that identifying information can be obtained, but it is the most efficient and most reliable route. Other methods are also available. Since 1958, for example, an adoptive parent has been entitled to obtain the original adoption order relating to his or her adopted child. There is no legal reason why the adoptive parent cannot share this information with his or her adopted child or with anyone else. Searchers can also register with Internet search sites and self-help search agencies. They can check city directories, court records, historical town documents, church baptismal and marriage records, gravestones, school year-books and newspaper files. Some searchers have interviewed neighbours, teachers, doctors, clergy and pharmacists who they believe may know the identity of the person being sought. Ads can be placed in newspapers. Accessing information from government adoption records, however, is the preferred and most efficient method. ...

64 Five, the demand for more openness in the disclosure of adoption information is based on experiences and arguments that are compelling and heart-felt. The adoption literature is replete with studies that show that many adopted adults and biological parents experience an

extraordinary level of grief, anxiety, and stress because they lack personal and family infor-mation. The efforts of these "searching" adoptees and birth parents, and of organizations lobbying on their behalf, are rooted in feelings and beliefs that are genuine and completely understandable. The primary motivating factor for each group, according to the literature, is the desire to reconcile personal uncertainties created by adoption. Whether an adopted adult lacks biological background information or a biological parent is denied details on a birth child's life circumstances, each party considers access to this knowledge as a way to reclaim hidden parts of his or herself. ...

65 Six, the feelings and the fears of the "non-searching" adoptees and birth parents who do not want to be found are no less legitimate and no less compelling. The impact on their lives and those of their families is just as significant. The difference here is that there are few, if any, clinical studies documenting this impact because the non-searching population prefers anonymity and is hence unorganized. ...

66 Seven, because there has been little to no study of the non-searching population, the social science evidence can only be described as inconclusive in terms of appropriate legis-lative design. ...

68 Eight, the applicants are very much in the minority in the debate about open adoption records. Most adoptees want to know something about their birth parents and even make contact with them, and most birth parents want to know something about the whereabouts and well-being of the child that was adopted. The applicants, however, are part of a small minority of "non-searching" adult adoptees and birth parents who would not consent to the release of their identifying information. The data indicates that the size of this non-searching and non-consenting minority is very small in percentage terms. Only about 3 to 5% of adoptees and birth parents would not consent to the disclosure of their identifying informa-tion and would exercise a disclosure veto if it were available.

69 Nine, the applicants have established a reasonable expectation of privacy — a reasonable expectation that their adoption or birth registration information, absent health or safety rea-sons, would remain private and would not be disclosed without their permission. I make this finding on several grounds. Since 1927, the statutory framework in Ontario has been predi-cated on confidentiality. Over the years, as is plain from the evidence, birth and adoptive parents have been reassured by private adoption practitioners, children's aid societies, social workers, lawyers and sometimes government officials that the adoption records would be sealed and no identifying information would be released without consent. ...

70 The tenth and final background fact is this: Ontario is the only jurisdiction in Canada, indeed in North America, that gives a retroactive, unqualified right to obtain confidential identifying information of an adopted person or birth parent without the consent and even over the objections of the individual whose personal information is being disclosed. No other Canadian province allows the disclosure of personal identifying information, absent issues of health or safety, without the consent of the person being identified. The provinces that have amended their legislation to improve access to adoption records have ensured that individuals who choose to maintain absolute privacy over their identifying information may do so through the use of a disclosure veto. ...

VI. Analysis

(3) Has there been a breach of the applicants' right to liberty?

78 This case, in essence, is about the applicants' right to privacy. The basic issue is whether the applicants have a *Charter*-protected right to privacy in circumstances such as these where confidential, personal information is about to be released by the government, retroac-

tively and without their permission, to the persons whom they would least want to have it. The issue is not whether the applicants' privacy has in fact been infringed by the impugned provisions — clearly it has — but whether this infringement constitutes a breach of their rights under the *Charter* and is therefore unconstitutional. ...

83 In this case, ... the disclosure of the birth and adoption records under the new law, in circumstances where a reasonable expectation of privacy has been created (recall the finding of fact above) constitutes an invasion of the dignity and self-worth of each of the individual applicants, and their right to privacy as an essential aspect of their right to liberty in a free and democratic society has been violated.

84 Neither the no-contact provision nor the non-disclosure procedure tempers this breach of the applicants' liberty interest. The no-contact provision does not prevent the release of the information. As for the non-disclosure procedure, as I have already noted, the Board will grant a non-disclosure order only in exceptional circumstances and only to prevent sexual harm or "significant" physical or emotional harm. The non-disclosure order will not granted simply to protect one's privacy.

85 I therefore have no difficulty concluding on the evidence before me that the applicants' right to liberty as set out in s. 7 ... has been infringed. ...

(4) Has there been a violation of a principle of fundamental justice?

97 The second stage of the s. 7 analysis, on the facts of this case, is to ask if the infringement of the applicants' right to liberty is in violation of a principle of fundamental justice. The applicants say that two separate principles of fundamental justice have been contravened — the right to be protected against laws that are "grossly disproportional" and the right to privacy, or at least a formulation of the right to privacy as it applies in the circumstances of this case. ...

107 In my view, the principle being suggested by the applicants can be stated more directly as follows: where a reasonable expectation of privacy has been established in the collection and storage of one's personal and confidential information, one should have the ability to control the dissemination of this information. Or, to put it even more plainly: Where an individual has a reasonable expectation of privacy in personal and confidential information, that information may not be disclosed to third parties without his or her consent ("the Suggested Principle."). ...

113 Counsel for the Attorney General raised some concerns about the need to balance interests in the process of formulating a principle of fundamental justice. ...

114 The balancing of individual and societal interests within s. 7 is only relevant when elucidating a particular principle of fundamental justice — and here the relevant interests were balanced by using language such as "reasonable expectation of privacy." Once the principle of fundamental justice has been elucidated, however, it is not within the ambit of s. 7 to bring into account any further societal interests, such as the rights of the searching adoptee or birth parent or the implications for government record-keeping etc. These considerations will be looked at, if at all, under s. 1. ...

115 The respondent's argument that the rights of the searching adoptee or birth parent should figure in the formulation of the applicable principle of fundamental justice is misguided. It is correct to say that in certain circumstances the court is obliged to balance competing rights. As the Supreme Court has noted, "when the *protected* rights of two individuals come into conflict ... *Charter* principles require a balance to be achieved that fully respects the importance of both sets of rights." But this is not a case where we have competing *Charter*-protected rights. The applicants' right to liberty under s. 7 has been breached. The

rights of the searching adoptees or birth parents to the disclosure of confidential adoption information, although important and heart-felt, are not protected by s. 7 or any other provision of the *Charter*.

116 The searching adoptee's or birth parents' right to access identifying information — "the right to know one's past" — is not a constitutionally protected right under Canadian law. Claims by adoptees seeking unqualified access to adoption records have been repeatedly refused by Canadian courts and quasi-judicial bodies such [as] the Information and Privacy Commissioners. The right to access information has always been subordinated to the right to maintain personal privacy. ...

119 To return to the issue at hand, this is not a case where the court has to balance competing *Charter*-protected rights because the right to access confidential information as claimed by searching adoptees and birth parents is not a *Charter*-protected right. ...

132 The suggested principle ... is, in my view, a principle of fundamental justice that has been contravened on the facts of this case. The applicants have established a reasonable expectation of privacy in the government's collection and storage of their confidential birth and adoption records. The impugned provisions (ss. 48.1, 48.2 and 48.11) will permit the release of this information to third parties without their consent. The applicants are thus being denied the ability to control the dissemination of this personal and confidential information. Neither the no-contact provision nor the non-disclosure order responds to this essential point. The deprivation of the applicants' liberty interest under s. 7 is therefore not in accordance with the principles of fundamental justice.

133 Having found that the Suggested Principle is a principle of fundamental justice that has been contravened, it is not necessary for me to consider the principle of "gross disproportionality" which the applicants say has also been contravened. I should say, however, that if I were to consider this argument I would not accept it. ...

(7) Can the breach of section 7 be saved under section 1?

(a) Is section 1 available?

137 Can the denial of a liberty right in violation of a principle of fundamental justice be justified as a reasonable limit in a free and democratic society? The Supreme Court has made clear that justifying s. 7 violations under s. 1 is a difficult task for two reasons: (1) the rights protected are very significant and cannot ordinarily be overruled by competing social interests; and (2) contraventions of principles of fundamental justice will rarely be upheld. Indeed in the *B.C. Reference*, Lamer J. (as he then was), speaking for the majority, noted that s. 1 can save a s. 7 violation but "only in cases arising out of exceptional conditions, such as natural disasters, the outbreak of war, epidemics and the like." In *Charkaoui* the Supreme Court restated this proposition by noting that it would be possible to justify a s. 7 violation under s. 1 only "in extraordinary circumstances where concerns are grave and the challenges complex."

138 If these Supreme Court pronouncements are to be taken seriously, and I assume that they are, then s. 1 is not available in the circumstances of this case to justify the violation of the applicants' rights under s. 7. This is not a case involving a natural disaster or the outbreak of a war or an epidemic; nor is it a case where the circumstances can be described as extraordinary, the concerns as grave and the challenges as complex. Legislation opening adoption records on a retroactive basis is no doubt extremely important for many, but the new law cannot be said to fall within any of the extraordinary or emergency categories listed above.

139 In my view, recourse to s. 1 is not available on the facts of this case. There is therefore no need for me to engage in a s. 1 analysis. However, if I am wrong in this regard and for the sake of completeness, I will undertake the s. 1 analysis.

(b) The section 1 analysis

140 Section 1 of the *Charter* provides that the rights and freedoms set out in the *Charter* are guaranteed "subject only to such reasonable limits prescribed by law as can be demonstrably justified in a free and democratic society." A limitation to a constitutional guarantee will be justified and sustained if two conditions are met. First, the objective of the legislation must be pressing and substantial. Second, the means chosen to attain this legislative objective must be reasonable and demonstrably justified in a free and democratic society. In order to satisfy the second requirement, three criteria have to be satisfied: (1) the rights violation must be rationally connected to the *Charter* guarantee; (2) the impugned provision must minimally impair the *Charter* guarantee; and (3) there must be a proportionality between the effect of the measure and its objective so that the attainment of the legislative goal is not outweighed by the abridgement of the *Charter* right. In all s. 1 cases, the burden of proof is on the government to show on a balance of probability that the violation is justifiable.

(i) Pressing and substantial objective

141 I agree with counsel for the Attorney General that the objective of the new law is pressing and substantial and that the first hurdle in the s. 1 analysis is cleared. The stated purpose of the AIDA, according to the Minister of Community and Social Services who introduced the new law and whose ministry is responsible for its implementation, is to provide both birth parents and adult adoptees information about their past. ...

142 The applicants also agree that improving access to adoption records for the purposes just stated may well be a pressing and substantial objective, but only to the extent that the legislation is not retroactive and does not, as they say, trample on the rights of other citizens to their own sense of identity, personal history and family.

(ii) Rational connection

143 I also agree with counsel for the Attorney General that the "rational connection" hurdle has also been cleared. The rational connection component in the proportionality test requires that the measures abridging the right or freedom in question be rationally connected to the legislative objectives. As long as the challenged provision can be said to further in a general way an important government aim it cannot be seen as irrational. ...

(iii) Minimal impairment

144 Here is where I part company with the Attorney General and the intervener. The question under the "minimal impairment" prong is whether the Legislature had a reasonable basis for concluding that the impugned limit interferes as little as possible with the guaranteed right given the Legislature's objectives. ...

145 Counsel for the Attorney General says that the adoption disclosure provisions in the new law are "carefully tailored" and do not unreasonably overshoot their purposes. Other free and democratic societies that share Canadian legal and constitutional values, argues Ontario, such as the United Kingdom, the United States, and Australia, employ analogous legislative mechanisms to provide access to adoption information within a framework of respecting the rights and needs of all parties to adoption.

146 With respect, I do not agree with this characterization of the evidence.

147 As I have already noted, no other province that has reformed its adoption disclosure law on a retroactive basis has done so without providing non-searching adoptees and birth parents with a disclosure veto. Ontario is the only province in Canada, indeed, the only jurisdiction in North America that gives a retroactive, unqualified right to obtain confidential identifying information of an adopted person or birth parent without, and even directly contrary to, the consent of the individual whose personal information is disclosed.

148 Four provinces continue to maintain the system that prevailed in Ontario under the old law and that requires mutual consent before identifying information can be released: Quebec, Nova Scotia, New Brunswick and P.E.I. In the four provinces that have recently reformed their adoption information disclosure to provide access to identifying information on a retroactive basis, non-searching adoptees and birth parents are provided a disclosure veto: B.C., Alberta, Manitoba and Newfoundland. In Saskatchewan, the adoption disclosure law combines both approaches: for adoptions that took place after the 1996 law took effect, the records are made available subject to a disclosure veto; for adoptions that took place prior to 1996 mutual consent is still required. ...

149 In the U.S., the handful of states that have opened their adoption records on a retroactive basis have limited the access to identifying information to adoptees only, not birth parents. ...

151 The situation in the U.K. is similar to that in the seven American states noted above, with one minor difference that relates to birth parents. In Scotland, an adult adopted person has the right to access his or her adoption and original birth records. In England and Wales, adopted persons over the age of eighteen have the right to obtain their original birth certificates. ...

152 The only jurisdiction that has opened its adoption records to both adoptees and birth parents is New South Wales, Australia. ...

153 The admonition of the Supreme Court in *Oakes* is that a *Charter* right should be interfered with as little as possible. If a *Charter* right is to be breached by a legislative provision, the impairment of that right should be minimal. Here, the new law jettisons completely the historical requirement for mutual consent. Identifying information will now be released to searching adoptees and birth parents without regard to the fact that the non-searching party has not consented to the release of this personal information and may even be objecting to its disclosure. Unlike the law in several of the other provinces, there is no disclosure veto. This is not a minimal impairment of a *Charter*-protected right but its total obliteration. ...

155 ... [N]either the no-contact provision nor the possibility of being granted a non-disclosure order from the Board can transform a clear breach of s. 7 into a reasonable and justifiable infringement. ...

156 *The no-contact provision.* As the affidavit evidence before me makes clear, the harm is not contact, but disclosure. The applicants object to the fact that their identities will be disclosed to persons that they would least want to have this information. Whether or not contact actually takes place in breach of the no-contact provision is a secondary concern. ...

160 *The non-disclosure order.* ...

161 The jurisdiction of the Board to issue a non-disclosure order is extremely limited — only in "exceptional circumstances" and only "to prevent sexual harm or significant physical or emotional harm." It is evident that the new law limits the jurisdiction of the Board to grant non-disclosure orders, basically, in situations involving personal safety. ...

165 The problem with the Board is, at root, the idea of having to go before a government board to plead for a right to privacy and a right to have some degree of control over the disclosure of intensely personal information.

166 In my view, the total eradication of the applicants' s. 7 right to privacy and their right to control the dissemination of their private information is not saved by the no-contact provision or by the provision that offers the possibility of a non-disclosure order but restricts it to situations relating to personal safety and involves, as the applicants see it, a humiliating and adversarial application procedure. For the reasons already stated, this is not minimal impairment.

(iv) Overall proportionality

167 The final step in the proportionality analysis under s. 1 of the *Charter* requires the court to weigh the benefits and the costs of the challenged law. ...

169 I have already found that the reasonable expectation of privacy, in the context of this case because it involves the disclosure of adoption information, is at a high level. It is also apparent from the uncontradicted evidence of the applicants that the impact of uncontrolled disclosure on their lives and families could be devastating. In light of these facts, how compelling is the state objective? And, more importantly, how compelling are the "salutary effects" as compared to the harm that would be caused to the applicants?

170 Recall my earlier finding that only a small minority, about 3% of adoptees and birth parents, would use a disclosure veto to prevent the release of their identifying information. That is, in about 97% of the cases, searching adoptees or birth parents would be able to obtain the identifying information that they seek even in jurisdictions that have a disclosure veto. Where, then, is the overall proportionality between the costs and the benefits? Is it reasonably proportional to breach the *Charter* rights of a minority so that an additional 3% of searching adoptees and birth parents will be successful in accessing the information that they seek? Do these additional three percentage points justify the total denial of a minority's rights under s. 7 of the *Charter*? In my view, they do not. ...

171 In sum, the government has failed to show that the breach of the applicants' rights under s. 7 of the *Charter* is demonstrably justified in a free and democratic society. More specifically, the government has failed to show that the impairment of this *Charter* right was as minimal as possible and that there is an overall and reasonable proportionality between the benefits of the new law and the costs or the harm that would result.

172 It is not the obligation of the applicants and certainly not that of the court to suggest ways how the new law could comply with [the] *Charter*. In this case, however, the answer seems obvious. In her submission to the standing committee that was considering the new law, the Information and Privacy Commissioner of Ontario, Ann Cavoukian, argued that a disclosure veto would not only protect the privacy rights of the minority but would in fact allow the vast majority to get the information they were seeking. Not to adopt a disclosure veto for past adoptions, said Ms. Cavoukian, "would be to ignore the wishes of an entire segment of society: birth parents and adopted persons who were once promised privacy, who still want it and who have governed their entire lives according to that assurance.". ...

VIII. Disposition

179 Sections 48.1, 48.2 and 48.11 of the *Vital Statistics Act*, R.S.O. 1990, c.V.4 are declared invalid and of no force or effect pursuant to s. 52(1) of the *Constitution Act [1982]*.

NOTES AND QUESTIONS

1. The Ontario legislature responded to the *Cheskes* decision by repealing and replacing (effective June 1, 2009) the sections of the *Vital Statistics Act* that had been declared of no force. Adult adoptees and birth parents of adult adoptees can still apply for identifying information. However, regarding adoptions that were completed prior to September 1, 2008, adult adoptees and birth parents can file a disclosure veto to preclude the release of such information. Such vetoes are not available for adoptions completed after that date. Non-contact vetoes remain available regarding all adoptions. It is also possible for adult adoptees and birth parents to file a Notice of Contact Preference Form to provide contact information and to specify the preferred means of contact. See ss. 48.1–48.7 of the *Vital Statistics Act* and *Disclosure of Adoption Information*, O. Reg. 272/08.

2. In Ontario, disclosure of non-identifying information regarding adoptions is governed by ss. 162.1–162.4 of the *CFSA* and, in particular, by *Adoption Information Disclosure*, O. Reg. 464/07. Section 11 of the regulation allows, among others, an adult adoptee (or an adoptee who has the written consent of an adoptive parent), an adoptive parent, and a birth parent to request non-identifying information relating to an adoption. The regulation also deals with searches and disclosure where, among others, an adopted person or a birth parent suffers from a "severe mental or physical illness" and "either the person requesting the search will derive a direct medical benefit should the search result in the location of the person being sought or there is reason to believe that the person being sought will derive a direct medical benefit".

3. Did the court in the *Cheskes* case give enough weight to an adoptee's interest in knowing his or her biological origins? Is "security of the person" in s. 7 of the Charter sufficiently broad to encompass this interest? Article 7 of the *Convention on the Rights of the Child* states that a "child shall ... have ..., as far as possible, the right to know and be cared for by his or her parents". Is this article relevant to the debate over disclosure of an adoptee's birth parents?

4. For further reading, see Blair, "The Impact of Family Paradigms, Domestic Constitutions and International Conventions on Disclosure of an Adopted Person's Identities and Heritage: A Comparative Examination" (2001), 22 Mich. J. Int'l Law 587 and Baldassi, "The Quest to Access Closed Adoption Files in Canada: Understanding Social Context and Legal Resistance to Change" (2005), 21 Can. J. Fam. L. 211.